1994 Working Press of the Nation™

Volume 4

Feature Writers, Photograpers & Professional Speakers Directory

44th Edition

Published by National Register Publishing,
A Reed Reference Publishing Company

International Standard Book Number (set): 0-8352-3426-6
International Standard Book Number (Volume 4): 0-8352-3430-4
International Standard Serial Number: 0084-1323
Library of Congress Catalog Card Number: 46-7041

Printed and bound in the United States of America.

1994 Working Press of the Nation™

Volume 4
Feature Writers, Photographers &
Professional Speakers Directory

44th Edition

Working Press of the Nation™ Feature Writers, Photographers & Professional Speakers Directory is compiled by

NATIONAL REGISTER PUBLISHING
A Reed Reference Publishing Company
121 Chanlon Road
New Providence, New Jersey 07974

Bernie Isaacson . . . . Vice President, Publisher
Edward R. Blank . . . . Director of Sales
Allyn Gilhooley . . . . Telemarketing Sales Manager
Brian Newman . . . . Sales Administrator
Michael Meyer . . . . Marketing Coordinator

Dean Hollister . . . . Vice President, Production-Directories
Edgar Adcock . . . . Editorial Director
Darrell Buono . . . . Managing Editor
Alvin Crooks . . . . Associate Editor

Peter Simon, Senior Vice President, Database Publishing

1994
WORKING PRESS OF THE NATION™

VOLUME 1 - NEWSPAPER DIRECTORY

This volume contains listings of Newspapers, Feature Syndicates, News and Photo Services. Complete information is given, including circulation, frequency, wire services, material requirements, deadlines, etc. Here in one volume is the direct route to over 8,000 management and editorial personnel of daily and weekly newspapers in the United States. There are also numerous indexes, such as an index of editorial personnel by subject, an index of newspapers by Area of Dominant Influence and an index of newspapers with Sunday supplements and TV supplements.

VOLUME 2 - MAGAZINES & INTERNAL PUBLICATIONS DIRECTORY

This volume lists more than 5,500 magazines, including consumer, farm and agricultural, service, trade, profession, and industrial publications. Listings are grouped by subject area so similar publications are easily referenced. There is also an alphabetical index of publications. Combined in Volume 2 for the first time is internal publication. This section provides detailed information about internal and external publications of more than 2,500 companies, government agencies, clubs and other groups located in the United States.

VOLUME 3 - TV & RADIO DIRECTORY

This volume lists more than 10,500 TV and radio stations plus more than 26,000 local programs by subject. Detailed information includes station name, address, ownership, area population, power, network affiliation, wire services utilized, air time, and management and programming personnel and publicity materials accepted.

VOLUME 4 - FEATURE WRITERS, PHOTOGRAPHERS & PROFESSIONAL SPEAKERS

This volume lists more than 3,000 feature writers, photographers and professional speakers with their complete address, telephone and fax numbers, subject areas of interest, and publications accepting their work (if applicable.) All categories are indexed by subject specialties. A new feature consists of a business card display advertising section, located between each subject listing and the biographical data listing.

> Each publication individually is an excellent source of information on a specific media. As a convenience to our customers, volumes 1 & 2 are now available as a special print media set or included in a complete set of all four volumes.

> Also available are mailing labels, customized for your use, with various selects including, type of media, personnel, state selection, etc. Call our list department at 800-521-8110 for details.

TABLE OF CONTENTS

Volume 4
Feature Writers, Photographers, &
Professional Speakers Directory
1994 Working Press of the Nation™

Preface

Welcome to the 44th edition of *WORKING PRESS OF THE NATION*, and the first published by National Register Publishing (NRP). NRP is a Reed Reference Publishing Company, one of the most respected publishers of information for libraries and industry.

Through the editorial resources available to NRP, we have been able to improve *WORKING PRESS OF THE NATION* significantly. Responding to long-time customers of *WORKING PRESS OF THE NATION*, we have reformatted the directories to make it more user-friendly by increasing type size, using brighter paper, and adding column lines to make it easier to read. Other changes include, but are not limited to:

> • **Volume 1 - Newspaper Directory** identifies more categories of this print media, including dailies and weeklies and local & national newspapers.

> • **Volume 2 - Magazines & Internal Publications Directory** has added virtually hundreds of additional categories and titles to make it the most comprehensive edition ever. We have also combine Internal Publications, which prior to this year has been a separate volume.

> • **Volume 3 - TV & Radio Directory** has more than 4,000 additional listings of radio and television stations than prior editions. You will be able to locate the most up-to-date data on the broadcast media.

> • **Volume 4 - Feature Writers, Photographers & Professional Speakers** has under gone a dramatic change. As noted by the title, we have added professional speakers to round out this important publication. Now all executives, including meeting planners at corporations and associations, who are responsible for hiring freelance professionals will be able to find these elusive individuals in one resource.

Since all information in *WORKING PRESS OF THE NATION* is computerized, we can now offer customized mailing lists and database programs as a complement to the printed directories.

In an ongoing effort to improve our products, we encourage you to contact any of our staff with recommendations or criticism that you may have. For your convenience, we have included in a postage-paid survey post card for your comments. If the card is missing or you wish to contact our us at a later time, our address is: *WORKING PRESS OF THE NATION*, 121 Chanlon Road, New Providence, NJ 07974, Fax: 908-665-3560.

We trust you will find the *1994 WORKING PRESS OF THE NATION* to be a valuable, well-organized and easy to use resource.

Bernie Isaacson
Publisher

INTRODUCTION

The 1994 Feature Writers, Photographers & Professional Speakers Directory is Volume 4 of Working Press of the Nation™, a four-volume set segmented by specialized professional occupations. The Feature Writers, Photographers & Professional Speakers Directory is designed for those who need information for freelance professionals.

Complete feature writer listings are found beginning in Section 1, followed by photographers in section 4 and professional speakers in stection 7.

The main sections allow you to locate these professionals by subject matter and are followed by a new section of business card display ads and then complete biographical information.

A detailed profile of the information presented in each section follows.

HOW TO USE

ORGANIZATION

Feature Writers, Photographers & Professional Speakers is divided into three parts, one covering each of type of professional listed in the directory. Each part is comprised of three sections: Index by Subject; Professional Services; Individual Listings.

Professional Speakers are included in the *1994 Working Press of the Nation* for the first time. Also new to this edition are paid advertising sections in which the business cards of entrants are reproduced. These sections (numbers 2, 5 and 8) are placed between the subject index and the main listing sections for each type of professionals listed in this volume. Entrants who wish to advertise in future editions should contact Michael Meyer at (908) 665-3595.

Section 1   **Index of Feature Writers by Subject** – This 2 part section lists various the subject specialties and indicates the page on which they are located. It is then organized alphabetically by subject specialty listing the appropriate feature writers.

Section 2   **Professional Services Feature Writers** – is a paid advertising section where business cards of participating feature writers are reproduced for easy identification.

Section 3   **Feature Writers** – is organized alphabetically by feature writers' name. Listings contain details about each writer including - complete address, telephone and fax numbers; subject specialties; trade memberships; and publications where their work has appeared.

Section 4	Index of Photographers by Subject – This 2 part section lists various the subject specialties and indicates the page on which they appear. It is then organized alphabetical by subject specialty listing the appropriate photographers.
Section 5	Professional Services Photographers – is a paid advertising section where business cards of participating photographers are reproduced for easy identification.
Section 6	Photographers – are organized alphabetically by photographers' name. Listings contain details about each photographer including - complete address, telephone and fax numbers; subject specialties; trade memberships; and publications where their work has appeared.
Section 7	Index of Professional Speakers by Subject – This 2 part section lists the various subject specialties and indicates the page on which they appear. It is then organized alphabetical by subject specialty listing the appropriate professional speakers.
Section 8	Professional Services Professional Speakers – is a paid advertising section where business cards of participating professional speakers are reproduced for easy identification.
Section 9	Professional Speakers – are organized alphabetically by professional speakers' name. Listing contain details about each speaker including - complete address, telephone and fax numbers; topic specialties; trade memberships and certification; typical audience; and speaker bureau representation.

HOW TO FIND INDIVIDUALS BY SUBJECT SPECIALTY

If you are seeking a professional who specializes in a given subject, check the alphabetical listing on the first page of the subject index: Feature Writers - Section 1; Photographers - Section 3; and Professional Speakers - Section 7. This index will refer you the page where the list of professionals for that specific subject appears. You will then be able to locate specific details on those individuals you select from the alphabetical section of prossionals.

HOW TO FIND AN INDIVIDUAL BY NAME

If you are seeking detailed information about a particular individual, look in the main listing section for that person's profession. For Feature Writers - Section 3; Photographers - Section 6; and Professional Speakers - Section 9. These sections are alphabetized by surname of the entrants.

BASIC COMPONENTS OF A LISTING

The basic structure of listings in each section is the same. The professional's name appears first, followed by address and telecommunications information. Associations and other affiliations appear in the center of the entry, which is completed by the subjects of specialty, and publications list (or typical audience).

SAMPLE FEATURE WRITERS, PHOTOGRAPHERS & PROFESSIONAL SPEAKERS ENTRY

MILLER, Judy S. CSP	Name of Entrant, Certification*
MMT Corp.	Corporate Affiliation*
90 Fountain of Youth Dr.	Address
Clearwater, FL 34615	
Telephone: 813-555-5852	Telephone
Fax: 813-555-5853	Fax
ASSOCIATION MEMBERSHIP:	
Natl. Speakers Assn	Trade Memberships
REPRESENTED BY:	
Speakers Resource Group	Representation (speakers only)*
Miami, FL	
PRINCIPAL TOPICS:	
Family	Subjects
Humor	
Senior Citizens	
TYPICAL AUDIENCE:	
Association	Audience (speakers)*
Fraternal	Publications (writers, photographers)
SEE AD IN SECTION 8	Reference to Professional Services advertising section

* Certification, Corporate Affiliation, Representation and Audience are listed for professional speakers only. Entries for writers and photographers, indicate those publications where their work has appeared.

ABBREVIATIONS

The following abbreviations are used within the listings:

AARWBA . . . . American Auto Racing Writers & Broadcasters

AG . . . . Authors Guild

AMWA . . . . American Medical Writers Association

ANWC . . . . American News Women's Club

APA . . . . Advertising Photographers of America

API . . . . Association Photographers International

ASJA . . . . American Society of Journalists and Authors

ASMP . . . . American Society of Media Photographers

ASP . . . . American Society of Photographers

ABBREVATIONS con't

ATCA . . . . American Theatre Critics Association

AWSM . . . . Association for Women in Sports Media

AWA . . . . Aviation/Space Writers Association

BWAA . . . . Baseball Writers Association of America

BPA . . . . Biological Photographers Association

BWI . . . . Boating Writers International

CPAE . . . . Council of Peer Award for Excellence

CSP . . . . . . Certified Speaking Professional

CWA . . . . Construction Writers Association

DG . . . . Dramatists' Guild

DJA . . . . Disabled Journalists of America

DWAA . . . . .Dog Writers Association of America

EFA . . . . Editorial Freelancers of America

EWA . . . . . . Education Writers Association

FPA . . . . Foreign Press Association

GCW . . . . Gridiron Club of Washington

IABC . . . . International Association of Business Communicators

IFPA . . . . International Fire Photographers Association

IFSEA . . . . International Federation of Scientific Editors Association

IFTWA . . . . International Food, Wine and Travel Writers Association

IRE . . . . Investigative Reporters and Editors

IWWG . . . . . International Women's Writing Guild

MWA . . . . Mystery Writers of America

NAAJ . . . . National Association of Agricultural Journalists

NABJ . . . . National Association of Black Journalists

NAHJ . . . . National Association of Hispanic Journalists

NASW . . . . National Association of Science Writers

NCBWA . . . . National Collegiate Baseball Writers Association

NCNY . . . Newswomen's Club of New York

NFPA . . . . National Freelance Photographers Association

NPC . . . . National Press Club

NPPA . . . . . . National Press Photographers of America

NSSA . . . . National Sportscasters and Sportswriters Association

NYFWA . . . . New York Financial Writers Association

NWU . . . . National Writers Union

OWAA . . . . Outdoor Writers Association of America

OPC . . . . Overseas Press Club

OW . . . . Overseas Writers

PAA . . . . Photographic Association of America

PBWAA . . . . Professional Basketball Writers' Association of America

PHA . . . . Professional Hockey Writers' Association

PPA . . . . Professional Photographers of America

PWP . . . . Professional Women Photographers

PRSA . . . . Public Relations Society of America

ABBREVATIONS con't

SABEW .... Society of American Business
Editors and Writers

SATW .... Society of American Travel
Writers

SPJ .... Society of Professional
Journalists

TCA .... Television Critics Association

TJC .... Travel Journalists Guild

UPS ..... Underwater Photographic Society

USBWA .... United States Basketball
Writers Association

WHNPA .... White House News
Photographers Association

WPC .... Washington Press Club

WICI .... Women in Communication

WTWA .... World Trade Writers
Association

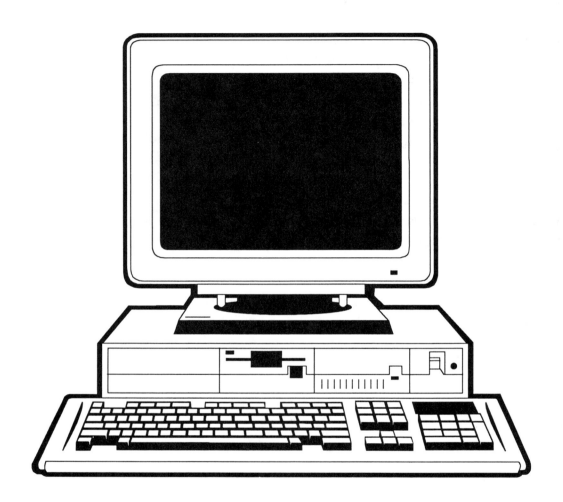

Section 1
INDEX OF FEATURE WRITERS BY SUBJECT

ADVERTISING

BARONE, JEANINE
BARSKY, MARTIN
BAYSURA, STEVEN A.
BERMAN, BRIAN J.
BLY, ROBERT W.
BOONE, GENE
BRODY, PEG
CALABRO, MARIAN
CANNON, DORIS
CASSELL, DANA
CATALANO, JULIE
CHANDLER, JO
CHELEKIS, GEORGE
CHRISTIAN, ALLGAIER
  DONNA
COREY, JOHN R.
CORWEN, LEONARD
CRANDELL, CHERYL
DALEY, LAVERNE
DEMAN, ELAINE
DIAMOND, LEN
DOWNEY, CHARLES E.
FINGER, ANNE L.
FNA NEWS
FOX, BARRY
FRIESE, RICK
FULLMAN, LYNN GRISARD
GALLO, DIANE
GLASSER, SELMA
GREENBERG, JAN
HAGGITH, DAVID
HELM, SYLVIA
HONE, HARRY
HOROWITZ, SHEL ALAN
HOWARD, ELIZABETH M.
JOHNSTON, MELANIE LEE
KARLIN, ELYSE ZORN
KELLY, KATE
KIMMERLY, MAUREEN C.
LARBERG, ANN
MARGOLIS, LYNNE
MESSNER, FRED R.
MOATES, MARIANNE
  MERRILL
POPHAL, LIN GRENSING-
REYNOLDS, WILLIAM J.
SAKELY, THOMAS
SEIDEN, OTHNIEL J.
SILBEY, PAULA J.

SILVA, KATE
SPRINGER, P. GREGORY
STICKLER, JOHN C.
WELCH, RANDY
WESTHEIMER, MARY
WUCHERER, RUTH
YARMON, MORTON
ZWICKER, DENISE ALLEN

AGRICULTURE

BARKSDALE, WILLIAM E
BATTERSBY, MARK E.
BEAN, ALICE PEARSE
BECK, LAUREL
BERG, MARGARET C.
BOYKIN, JOHN E.
CHANDLER, JO
CHIN, RUTH
CLIFFORD, WILLIAM
DAMEROW, GAIL J.
DEFOREST, SHERWOOD S.
FEIT, EDWARD
FNA NEWS
FREEDMAN, ERIC
GRANHOLM, JACKSON W.
GRANT, NANCY S.
HARDER, PAUL B.
HOLCOMB, GEORGE B.
HOYT, ERICH
KEEN, MARJORIE
KLINE, LLOYD W.
KNIGHT, DOUG
LEERBURGER, BENEDICT
MAXWELL, KATIE
MCMAHON, KAREN
MCPHEE, MARNIE
MESSINEO, JOHN
MOON, BEN L.
MUMMERT, ROGER
MURPHY, WENDY B.
OGDEN, SHEPHERD
RUDOLPH, JOHN K.
SHEPARD, SUSAN J.
SOLOMON, GOODY L.
WAGNER, BILL
WILCOX, CHARLOTTE
WOMACK, ROCKY

AMUSEMENTS

AUERBACK, PHD., STEVANNE
AUSTIN, JOHN
BASCH, BUDDY
BATTERSBY, MARK E.
BERRY, S.L.
BISHER, FURMAN
BOONE, GENE
BORTSTEIN, LARRY
CAPOTOSTO, JOHN
CLIFFORD, WILLIAM
DALY, MAUREEN
DODGE, ELLIN
FNA NEWS
GALLO, DIANE
GROENE, GORDON &
  GROENE, JANET
HAMALIAN, LEO
HAUSER, HILLARY
HEMMING, ROY
HINTZ, MARTIN
HOROWITZ, SHEL ALAN
HYYPIA, JORMA
INGE, ARLINE
IRA, ALLEN
KONNER, LINDA
KOONTZ, KATY
LANDT, DENNIS
LEVINE, FAYE
LEVY, RICHARD C.
LOSCHIAVO, LINDA ANN
MACDONALD, SANDY
MARGOLIS, LYNNE
MASTROLIA, LILYAN S.
MCNEES, PAT
NEELY, BONNIE BURGESS
REISS, ALVIN H.
ROESSING, WALTER
ROSENDO, JOSEPH
SCHWALBERG, CAROL
SILBEY, PAULA J.
SLATE, LIBBY
SLATTERY, WILLIAM J.
SMITH, LIZ
SOHN, DAVID A.
TROMBETTI, STEVEN E.
WALTER, EUGENE
WOODARD, BERT
ZATZ, ARLINE

ANIMALS

ACKERMAN, DR., LOWELL
ALPERSTEIN, ELLEN
ARMSTRONG III, MARTIN F.
BARNES, DUNCAN
BARTEL, PAULINE C.
BAUER, ERWIN A.
BENDINER, ROBERT
BLIZZARD, WILLIAM C.
BODGER, CAROLE
BOONE, GENE
BOREA, PHYLLIS GILBERT
BRESLAV, MARC
CALABRO, MARIAN
CARRENO, RICHARD D.
CATALANO, JULIE
CLEDE, BILL
COOPER, JILL A.
COX, VIC
DAVIDSON, MARK
DICTOR-LEBLANC, RENA
DUNHAM, ROBERT
ENGMAN, RONDA
FEHL, MARTHA R.
FNA NEWS
FOSTER, NANCY
FROME, MICHAEL
GRANT, NANCY S.
HALLADAY, GENEVA
HAY, PHD., VICTORIA
HAZEN, BARBARA SHOOK
HEILMAN, JOAN RATTNER
HIBBEN, DR. FRANK C.
HOYT, ERICH
KNIGHT, DOUG
LAMPE, DAVID
LEBLANC, RENA DICTOR
LEERBURGER, BENEDICT
MALLETTE, MAL
MARGOLIS, LYNNE
MASTROLIA, LILYAN S.
MATTHEWS, DOWNS
MESSINEO, JOHN
NEMIROW-NELSON, JILL
PARADISE, PAUL RICHARD
PARK, ED
PAUST, GIL
RANDOLPH, ELIZABETH
REARDEN, JIM
ROGAK, LISA

SABIN, FRANCENE
SCHLICK, JACK
SCHLOSS, MURIEL
SCHNECK, MARCUS H.
SEAMANS, ANDY
SHAW, EVA
SMITH, CARIN A., DVM
SPIOTTA-DIMARE, LOREN
STOCKER, JOSEPH
TAJER, JOSIE
TERRES, JOHN K.
THOMSON, PEGGY
WILKINSON, PAMELA L.
WOLKOMIR, RICHARD AND
  JOYCE ROGERS
  WOLKOMIR
WUCHERER, RUTH
ZATZ, ARLINE
ZEILLER, WARREN
ZURCHER, MARVIN

ARCHITECTURE

BYRNE-DODGE, TERESA
CLIFFORD, WILLIAM
COHEN, DANIEL
DAVIDSON, MARK
FUSCO, MARY ANN
  CASTRONOVO
GAMAGE, DOUGLAS C.
GLASS, JUDITH E.
GOODING, JUDSON
GOODMAN, JACK
GRANHOLM, JACKSON W.
HAIT, PAM
HARRIS, ELEANOR
HUFF, DARRELL
LAMPE, DAVID
LANDT, DENNIS
MACDONALD, SANDY
MAYER, BARBARA
MEOLA, PATRICIA E.
MIX, SHELDON A.
MOLDAFSKY, ANNIE
MORRILL, STEPHEN
NASON, STEPHEN
PERRY, ERMA
PETROWSKI, ELAINE MARTIN
POMADA, ELIZABETH
ROBERTS, JANET M.
STAR, JACK
STICKLER, JOHN C.
WOOD, SHARON M.

AUTOMOTIVE

ANDERSON, ERIC G.
BERGER, IVAN
BRAMS, STANLEY H.
BRIGHTMAN, ROBERT
BROWN, TERRY T.

CANDLER, JULIE
CANDLER, JULIE
CONNOR, J. ROBERT
DARK, HARRIS EDWARD
DUNHAM, ROBERT
EISENSTEIN, PAUL A.
FEHL, MARTHA R.
FEIT, EDWARD
FNA NEWS
GROENE, GORDON &
  GROENE, JANET
GROENE, JANET
GYSI, CHUCK
HARRIS, JUDITH
HARWOOD, JAMES
  QUITTNER
JACKSON, WILLIAM S.
JANICKI, EDWARD
KEMPER, SU
KOCIVAR, BEN
KRANISH, ARTHUR
LAMPE, DAVID
LANGWORTH, RICHARD M.
LANKARD, TOM
LEERBURGER, BENEDICT
LEIF, ROBERT
MCDONALD, MAUREEN
MESSINEO, JOHN
NELSON, ED
NICKLAS, NICK
O'REILLY, DON
SCAGNETTI, JACK
SCHLICK, JACK
SCHULTZ, MORTON J.

AVIATION

ALBANESE, DAVID J.
ANDERSON, ERIC G.
CLARKE, PHILIP C.
DALEY, LAVERNE
DEMAN, ELAINE
DIAMOND, LEN
DOWNEY, CHARLES E.
FEIT, EDWARD
FNA NEWS
GEBHART, FRED
GLINES, CARROLL V.
GOODSELL, JAMES NELSON
GROENE, GORDON &
  GROENE, JANET
GROENE, JANET
HAMMEL, ERIC
HARVEY, FRANK
HOWE, RUSSELL WARREN
HUNT, DIANA
HYYPIA, ERIK J.
KOCIVAR, BEN
KRANISH, ARTHUR
LAMPE, DAVID
LEERBURGER, BENEDICT

LEIF, ROBERT
MACKOWSKI, MAURA J.
MILLNER, CORK
MOON, BEN L.
OLNEY, ROSS R.
PAANANEN, ELOISE
POLKING, MISS KIRK
REARDEN, JIM
SAMBROT, WILLIAM
SKLAREWITZ, NORMAN
SMITH, RICHARD AUSTIN
STAR, JACK
SZUPROWICZ, BOHDAN O.
WALTER, CLAIRE
WATSON, DELMAR
YOUNG, WARREN R.

BOOK REVIEWS

ABBOTT, R. TUCKER
ACKERMAN, DR., LOWELL
ALPER, PHILIP
ARMSTRONG III, MARTIN F.
ASNER, MARIE A.
ASTON, ATHINA LEKA
AUSTIN, JOHN
BAKER, CHRISTOPHER PAUL
BANDLER, MICHAEL J.
BARBATO, JOSEPH
BEHRENS, JOHN
BENFORD, MARILYN
BENFORD, TIMOTHY B.
BOONE, GENE
BOUCHIER, DAVID
BYRNE-DODGE, TERESA
CARRENO, RICHARD D.
CARUBA, ALAN
CASSELL, DANA
CHELEKIS, GEORGE
CLIFFORD, WILLIAM
COHEN, DANIEL
COLBERT, JUDY
COLEMAN, A.D.
CORWEN, LEONARD
COX, VIC
DALY, MAUREEN
DAMEROW, GAIL J.
DARDICK, GEETA
DARLINGTON, JOY
DEBARTOLO, ANTHONY
DEMAN, ELAINE
DEVINE, GEORGE
DICKERSON, NANCY
DRAGONWAGON, CRESCENT
DYKEMAN, WILMA
EVANS, GLEN
FAREWELL, SUSAN
FEHL, MARTHA R.
FELD, KAREN
FELDMAN, ELANE
FERGUSON, JOSEPH

FINKE, BLYTHE FOOTE
FRUMKES, LEWIS BURKE
FULLMAN, LYNN GRISARD
FUSCO, MARY ANN
  CASTRONOVO
GELTNER, SHARON
GIBBONS, BARBARA
GILES, MARJORIE GORDON-
GLASSER, SELMA
GLINES, CARROLL V.
GOODING, JUDSON
GOODMAN, JACK
GOODSELL, JAMES NELSON
GROENE, GORDON &
  GROENE, JANET
GROENE, JANET
HAAPOJA, MARGARET A.
HACKETT, BLANCHE
HALPERN, FRANCES
HAMILTON, PHD., ELEANOR
HANLE, ZACK
HAY, PHD., VICTORIA
HAY, VICTORIA
HEATH, JARRETT A.
HEMMING, ROY
HOCHMAN, GLORIA
HOFFMAN, NANCY YANES
HOLCOMB, GEORGE B.
HONE, HARRY
HORNER, SHIRLEY
HOWE, RUSSELL WARREN
HOYT, ERICH
IRA, ALLEN
JOHNSTON, MELANIE LEE
KAHN, ADA PASKIND
KANIGEL, ROBERT
KARPEL, CRAIG S.
KAUFMAN, WALLACE
KNIGHT, DOUG
KRANISH, ARTHUR
KREIG, ANDREW, ESQ.
LANGER, CASSANDRA
LARBERG, ANN
LEERBURGER, BENEDICT
LEVINE, FAYE
LIEBERMAN, ROBERT H.
LONDON, BILL
LORENZ-FIFE, IRIS
LOSCHIAVO, LINDA ANN
LYHNE, BOB
MACDONALD, SANDY
MALLETTE, MAL
MARGOLIS, LYNNE
MASTROLIA, LILYAN S.
MCKENZIE, J. NORMAN
MCPHEE, MARNIE
MEOLA, PATRICIA E.
MESSINEO, JOHN
MILNE, ROBERT SCOTT
MIX, SHELDON A.
NEMIRO, BEVERLY

ANDERSON
NEMSER, CINDY
OGDEN, SHEPHERD
OPPENHEIM M.D., MICHAEL
ORTH, JOAN
PARK, ED
PAUST, GIL
PERRY, ERMA
PERRY, SUSAN K.
PODOLSKY, M. LAWRENCE
POLAND, NANCY
POMADA, ELIZABETH
ROBERTS, JANET M.
ROES, NICHOLAS A.
ROGERS, BARBARA
  RADCLIFFE
ROSENDO, JOSEPH
RUBIN, NANCY
SCHULTZ, DODI
SEAMAN, BARBARA
SHAPIRO, CECILE
SKLAR, DUSTY
SMITH, RUTH BAYARD
SOMAN, SHIRLEY CAMPER
SOTER, TOM
SPRINGER, P. GREGORY
STAR, JACK
STICKLER, JOHN C.
TEGELER, DOROTHY
TURECAMO, DORRINE
URROWS, HENRY AND
  ELIZABETH
VALENTI, DAN
VAN DILLEN, LAILEE
VIORST, MILTON
WALKER, DR. MORTON
WESTON, CAROL
WHALIN, W. TERRY
WUCHERER, RUTH
YARMON, MORTON
ZATZ, ARLINE
ZURCHER, MARVIN

BUSINESS & INDUSTRY

AGUILAR, NONA
ALBERTSON, MILA
ALLEN, LOUIS A.
ALPERN, LYNNE S.
ALTER, JOANNE
ANDERSON, BARRY C.
ARKIN, JOSEPH
ASTON, ATHINA LEKA
AUERBACH, SYLVIA
BABSON, O. BONNI
BAKAL, CARL
BAKER, SAMM SINCLAIR
BARRY, DON
BARTEL, PAULINE C.
BATTERSBY, MARK E.
BAYERS, RAPP LEA

BEEBE, F. LISA
BEHRENS, JOHN
BELL, SALLY
BERG, MARGARET C.
BERGER, IVAN
BERMAN, BRIAN J.
BERMAN, CLAIRE
BERRY, S.L.
BIGELOW, ROBERT
BIRNBAUM, NATALIE
BITETTI, MARGE
BLASK, ANN SABATINI
BLISHAK, SYLVIA ANN
BLODGETT, RICHARD
BLOOM, MURRAY TEIGH
BOEHM, GEORGE A. W.
BOONE, GENE
BOROSON, WARREN
BOYKIN, JOHN E.
BRAMS, STANLEY H.
BRICKMAN, NANCI
BROOKS, LESTER
BROWN, GAIL
BROY, ANTHONY
BYAM, LINDA G.
CALABRO, MARIAN
CAMPBELL, CANDACE
CARUBA, ALAN
CASS, MAXINE
CASSELL, DANA
CHANDLER, JO
CHARLES, JOANNA
CHELEKIS, GEORGE
CHIN, RUTH
CHRISTIAN, ALLGAIER
  DONNA
CLARKE, PHILIP C.
CLAXTON, COLETTE
CLINE, ANDY
COHEN, DANIEL
CONKLIN, WILLIAM B.
CONNIFF, JAMES C. G.
CONSIDINE, SHERIDAN
COOPER, ANDREA
COOPER, DR. JOHN C.
COREY, JOHN R.
CORWEN, LEONARD
CROSS, WILBUR
CUPPER, DAN
DAILY, LAURA
DALEY, LAVERNE
DANIELS, LEE
DARDICK, GEETA
DAVID, LESTER
DAVIS, BEATRICE G.
DAVIS, ELISE MILLER
DEFOREST, SHERWOOD S.
DEMPEWOLFF, RICHARD F.
DETZ, JOAN
DIAMOND, LEN
DICKINSON, PETER A.

DIENSTAG, ELEANOR
DITZEL, PAUL
DOOLEY, BRIAN J.
DOWNEY, CHARLES E.
DREYFACK, RAYMOND
DUNAIEF, LEAH S.
DUNAWAY, JAMES O.
EDSON, ANDREW S.
EDSON, LEE
EISCHEN, CHARLES N.
EISENSTEIN, PAUL A.
ELWOOD, MRS. EDITH
  MUESING
ENGLISH, JOHN W.
FAILLA, KATHLEEN SALUK
FARIS, CHARLENE
FEIT, EDWARD
FERRIS, PAUL
FINGER, ANNE L.
FLUENT, MIKE
FNA NEWS
FORTNEY, DAVID L.
FORTSON, LOWRANCE
  SANNA
FOX, BARRY
FRANCISCUS, ALEXANDRA
FRASER, BRUCE W.
FRAZER, LANCE
FRIZZI, VIRGINIA
FUSCO, MARY ANN
  CASTRONOVO
GAGE, DIANE
GALLESE, LIZ ROMAN
GALLO, DIANE
GALUB, JACK
GAMAGE, DOUGLAS C.
GANNON, ROBERT
GEBHART, FRED
GELTNER, SHARON
GEM PUBLISHING GROUP
GEORGE, KATHRYN E.
GERSON, VICKI
GEYER, SHERREE
GIBBS, RAFE
GLASS, JUDITH E.
GLINES, CARROLL V.
GOLDSTEIN, GREG
GOODING, JUDSON
GOODMAN, GERSON W.
GOODRICH, DONNA CLARK
GOODWIN, DAVE
GRAF, RUDOLF F.
GRAPES, JOAN A.
GRECO, GAIL
GREENE, FREDA
GREENGARD, SAMUEL
GRIFFIN, C. W.
GRIFFIN, KELLY L.
HAAS, ALAN D.
HACKETT, BLANCHE
HADDOCK, PATRICIA

HAMMER, ROGER A.
HARDER, PAUL B.
HARMAN, HARRY & JEANNE
HARSHAM, PHILIP
HARVEY, FRANK
HASTINGS, ROBERT A.
HAY, VICTORIA
HEDDEN, JAY W.
HEITZIG, JAMES L.
HELM, SYLVIA
HILL, NORMAN
HINTZ, MARTIN
HOCH, DR. DEAN E.
HOCH, NANCY M.
HODGE, ADELE
HOFFMAN, NANCY YANES
HOLDER, DENNIS
HOLTJE, HERBERT F.
HONE, HARRY
HOROWITZ, SHEL ALAN
HOUSE, DARLENE
HOWDEN, D. MURIEL
HOWES, CONNIE B.
HUNT, JAMES E.
HYYPIA, JORMA
IRA, ALLEN
JACKSON, LESLIE
JACOKES, DIANE
JAMISON, WARREN
JANICKI, EDWARD
JOHNSTON, MELANIE LEE
K-TURKEL, JUDI
KANIGEL, ROBERT
KARPEL, CRAIG S.
KARTEN, HOWARD A.
KASS, BENNY L.
KAUFMAN, WALLACE
KELLY, KATE
KLINE, LLOYD W.
KNICELY, FAY
KNIGHT, DOUG
KRANISH, ARTHUR
KREMEN, BENNETT
LACEY, DIANE G.
LAGAN, CONSTANCE
  HALLINAN
LAMONT, DOUGLAS
LAMPE, DAVID
LANGHAM, BARBARA
LEDERER, MURIEL
LEE, SHIRLEY
LEERBURGER, BENEDICT
LEVITSKY, DR. SERGE L.
LEVY, ERIC
LEVY, RICHARD C.
LEWIS, JACK
LONDON, BILL
LOOMIS, JAMIE
LORENZ-FIFE, IRIS
LOSCHIAVO, LINDA ANN
LYNCH, PAT

MACKOWSKI, MAURA J.
MAPPES, DR. CARL R.
MARGOLIUS, ESTHER
MARQUARDT, DEBORAH
MASTROLIA, LILYAN S.
MATHEWS, BEVERLY
MATTHEWS, DOWNS
MATURI, RICHARDS J.
MCCARTNEY, LUCINDA L.
MCDERMOTT, MICHAEL J.
MCDONALD, MAUREEN
MCKENZIE, J. NORMAN
MCKEON, KEVIN
MCNEES, PAT
MENKUS, BELDEN
MICHAEL, JOYCE EMMETT
MILLER, BRUCE
MILLER, DOROTHY G.
MILLMAN, SANDY K.
MINKOW, ROSALIE
MIX, SHELDON A.
MONROE, KEITH
MOON, BEN L.
MORGAN, ARJAY
MORGAN, JOHN S.
MORRIS, HAL
MOST, BRUCE W.
MOYLAN, TOM
MURPHY, RAYMOND J.
MURPHY, WENDY B.
NADLER, BOB
NASON, STEPHEN
NEW, AMY ROFFMANN
NEWCOMB, DUANE G.
NICKLAS, NICK
NOSSAMAN, MICHAEL
NOVITZ, CHARLES R.
OGDEN, SHEPHERD
OLECK, HOWARD L.
OPPENHEIMER, ERNEST J.
ORTH, JOAN
OWEN, JENNIFER BRYON
PAAJANEN, ANNETTE LAABS
PARADISE, PAUL RICHARD
PERLOFF, SUSAN
PETERS, JANE S.
PETERSON, FRANKLYNN
PITTMAN, RUTH
PODOLSKY, M. LAWRENCE
POPHAL, LIN GRENSING-
PUGH JR., JAMES E.
RADCLIFFE, DONALD
RAKSTIS, TED J.
REICHEK, MORTON
REISS, ALVIN H.
RICKEY, GAIL
RIVOIRE, JOHN
ROBINSON, TED
ROCK, MAXINE
ROES, NICHOLAS A.
ROESSING, WALTER

ROGAK, LISA
ROSEN, M. DANIEL
ROSS, MARILYN HEIMBERG
ROTHMAN, HOWARD
RUDOLPH, JOHN K.
RUSSELL, BARBARA
SAKELY, THOMAS
SAMBROT, WILLIAM
SAUNDERS, LUCY
SAYLOR DOPPENBERG,
  JEAN
SCAGNETTI, JACK
SCHARFENBERGER, JOHN
SCHERMERHORN, DERICK D.
SCHNECK, MARCUS H.
SCHREIBER, NORMAN
SCHWARZ, TED
SCOTT, GINI GRAHAM
SEITEL, FRASER PAUL
SHEFFE, EDWARD D.
SHELDON, GEORGE
SHERMAN, SIGNE L.
SHERWOOD, HUGH C.
SILBAR, HOWARD J.
SILBEY, PAULA J.
SKLAREWITZ, NORMAN
SLATTERY, WILLIAM J.
SLEAR, TOM
SLOME, JESSE R.
SMITH, CARIN A., DVM
SMITH, RICHARD AUSTIN
SPANO SR., JOHN J.
ST. JOHN, TERRY
STACK, ROBERT
STEIN, M. L.
STEINER, SHARI
STICKLER, JOHN C.
STICKLER, JOHN C.
STODDARD, BROOKE C.
STRUGATCH, WARREN
SZUPROWICZ, BOHDAN O.
TAYLOR, GARY
THOMPSON, JACQUELINE
TOWLE, LISA H.
TRASOBARES, CAESAR M.
TUPPER, MARGO
TURECAMO, DORRINE
URROWS, HENRY AND
  ELIZABETH
WAGNER, BILL
WALKER, GLADYS H.
WALTER, CLAIRE
WARREN, CAMERON A.
WARREN, DAVID
WEINSTEIN, GRACE W.
WEISBERG, JACOB
WEISS, FRED E.
WELCH, RANDY
WESTGATE, ROBERT D.
WESTHEIMER, MARY
WHALEY, PEGGY

WHITFORD, JAMES
WISE, CHRISTY
WOMACK, ROCKY
WOODSON, R. DODGE
WOOG, DAN
WORKMAN, BARBARA L.
WRIGHT JR., ED
WRIGHT, SYLVIA HOEHNS
WUCHERER, RUTH
YAGER, JAN
YARMON, MORTON
ZWEIG, PHILLIP L.
ZWICKER, DENISE ALLEN

COMPUTER TECHNOLOGY

ANDERSON, ERIC G.
BARNES-SVARNEY,
  PATRICIA L.
BATTERSBY, MARK E.
BEHRENS, JOHN
BERG, MARGARET C.
BERGER, IVAN
BIGELOW, ROBERT
BLY, ROBERT W.
BREECHER, M.P.H.,
  MAURY M.
CALABRO, MARIAN
CHELEKIS, GEORGE
CLEDE, BILL
COHEN, DANIEL
DOOLEY, BRIAN J.
EDSON, LEE
EISENSTEIN, PAUL A.
FANTEL, HAS
FENTEN, D. X.
GEBHART, FRED
GOLDSTEIN, GREG
GOLIN, MILTON
GRAF, RUDOLF F.
GRANHOLM, JACKSON W.
GREENGARD, SAMUEL
GYSI, CHUCK
HARWOOD, JAMES
  QUITTNER
HELM, SYLVIA
HOLTON, FELICIA
  ANTONELLI
HOROWITZ, SHEL ALAN
HUFF, DARRELL
HUNT, JAMES E.
HURWOOD, BERNHARDT J.
HYYPIA, ERIK J.
IRA, ALLEN
JACOKES, DIANE
JOHNSON, SABEEHA H.
JOHNSTON, MELANIE LEE
K-TURKEL, JUDI
KARTEN, HOWARD A.
KOCIVAR, BEN
KOWAL, JOHN PAUL

KRANISH, ARTHUR
LEERBURGER, BENEDICT
LESLIE, JACQUES
LEWIS, HOWARD R.
LOCKWOOD, GEORGENE
  MULLER
MACKOWSKI, MAURA J.
MASTROLIA, LILYAN S.
MCCOMB, GORDON
MENKUS, BELDEN
MORGAN, ARJAY
NADLER, BOB
NEW, AMY ROFFMANN
OGDEN, SHEPHERD
OLSEN, J.W.
PETERS, JANE S.
PETERSON, FRANKLYNN
PINKWAS, STAN
PLANT, JANET
POSTER, CAROL
REYNOLDS, WILLIAM J.
ROESSING, WALTER
ROHAN, REBECCA
ROSEN, M. DANIEL
SCHERMERHORN, DERICK D.
SCHOTT-JONES, ELAINE
SCHULTZ, MORTON J.
SHEFFE, EDWARD D.
SHELDON, GEORGE
SINBERG, STAN
STAR, JACK
STEINER, SHARI
STODDARD, BROOKE C.
SWANN, CHRISTOPHER
SZUPROWICZ, BOHDAN O.
TRUSSO, JOSEPH
URROWS, HENRY AND
  ELIZABETH
VAN COLLIE, SHIMON-CRAIG
WHALIN, W. TERRY
WOLFE, DARRELL K.
YARMON, MORTON

ECOLOGY

ABBOTT, R. TUCKER
ANDERSON, KENNETH N.
ARNETTE, JOSEPH
BAKER, ROLINDA B.
BARBATO, JOSEPH
BARNES, DUNCAN
BARTEL, PAULINE C.
BASSETT, ELIZABETH
BAUER, ERWIN A.
BEHRENS, JOHN
BENDINER, ROBERT
BERMAN, BRIAN J.
BOEHM, GEORGE A. W.
BRESLAV, MARC
BRUNING, NANCY
CADIEUX, CHARLES L.

CAREW, RUTH M. HARMER
CELLIERS, PETER J.
CLINE, ANDY
CONNIFF, JAMES C. G.
COX, VIC
DANIELS, LEE
DARDICK, GEETA
DARLINGTON, JOY
DEMAN, ELAINE
DUNAWAY, JAMES O.
DYKEMAN, WILMA
ENGH, JERI
FEHL, MARTHA R.
FINKE, BLYTHE FOOTE
FNA NEWS
FRIEDMAN, KENNETH A.
GANNON, ROBERT
GEBHART, FRED
GEORGE, KATHRYN E.
GLASS, JUDITH E.
GORDON, BERNARD LUDWIG
GOULD, LARK ELLEN
GRESHAM, GRITS
GRIFFIN, C. W.
HAAPOJA, MARGARET A.
HAIT, PAM
HANCOCK, M. A.
HASTINGS, ROBERT A.
HAY, PHD., VICTORIA
HAY, VICTORIA
HAZEN, BARBARA SHOOK
HEMBREE, DIANA
HIBBEN, DR. FRANK C.
HINTZ, MARTIN
HOYT, ERICH
IRA, ALLEN
JAMES JR., JESSE A.
KAUFMAN, WALLACE
KAVALER, LUCY
KAY, JANE HOLTZ
KAYE, EVELYN
KEATING, BERN
KEEN, MARJORIE
KNIGHT, DOUG
KNIGHT, MRS. RICHARD
  ALDEN
KOONTZ, KATY
KRANISH, ARTHUR
LAMPE, DAVID
LANGER, CASSANDRA
LEE, SHIRLEY
LEERBURGER, BENEDICT
LEONARD, GEORGE
LYHNE, BOB
MANNERS, DAVID X.
MARGOLIS, LYNNE
MARSH, SUSAN
MCCARTNEY, LUCINDA L.
MCPHEE, MARNIE
MESSINEO, JOHN
MILNE, DR. MARGERY

MILNE, ROBERT SCOTT
MORRILL, STEPHEN
NORTON, PHILLIP
OGDEN, SHEPHERD
PARK, ED
PAUST, GIL
PEEPLES, EDWIN A.
POSTER, CAROL
REARDEN, JIM
REISS, ALVIN H.
RICHARD, JEROME
RIEGER, TED
ROBERTS, JANET M.
ROSENBERG, SHIRLEY
  SIROTA
RUDOLPH, JOHN K.
SABIN, FRANCENE
SCHERMERHORN, DERICK D.
SCHNECK, MARCUS H.
SCHWANZ, MICHAEL L.
SOLOMON, GOODY L.
SOSIN, MARK
STAUB, MOLLY AROST
TANNER, OGDEN
TERRES, JOHN K.
TRUSSO, JOSEPH
WALKER, DR. MORTON
WEISS, FRED E.
WESLEY, MARX
WOLKOMIR, RICHARD AND
  JOYCE ROGERS
  WOLKOMIR
YARMON, MORTON
YOUNG, DONALD
ZIMMERMAN, DAVID R.

EDITORIAL

ACKERMAN, DR., LOWELL
ALBANESE, DAVID J.
ANDERSON, ERIC G.
ASNER, MARIE A.
ASTON, ATHINA LEKA
BARRY, DON
BARSKY, MARTIN
BARTEL, PAULINE C.
BELL, JOSEPH N.
BERGER, IVAN
BLIZZARD, WILLIAM C.
BLY, ROBERT W.
BOECKMAN, CHARLES
BOORSTIN, DANIEL J.
BOSE, MICHAEL ALAN
BRASSELL, SEARLES
  LUCINDA
CLARK, LARRY
CLARKE, PHILIP C.
COAN, PETER M.
CORWEN, LEONARD
CRANDELL, CHERYL
CROSS, WILBUR

DAMEROW, GAIL J.
DAVIS, ELISE MILLER
DEFOREST, SHERWOOD S.
DEGNAN, JAMES P.
DEVINE, GEORGE
ELLIOTT, JOY
EVANS, GLEN
FAREWELL, SUSAN
FEIN, ELAINE
FENSCH, THOMAS C.
FNA NEWS
FOX, BARRY
FRIESE, RICK
FUSCO, MARY ANN
  CASTRONOVO
GLASS, JUDITH E.
GOODING, JUDSON
GOODRICH, DONNA CLARK
GOODSELL, JAMES NELSON
GORDON, SUSAN J.
HASTINGS, ROBERT A.
HAY, PHD., VICTORIA
HENLEY, ARTHUR
HODGE, ADELE
HOFFMAN, NANCY YANES
HONE, HARRY
HOROWITZ, SHEL ALAN
HOWE, RUSSELL WARREN
IACONETTI, JOAN
INGE, ARLINE
KAHN, ADA PASKIND
KAUFMAN, WALLACE
KEMPER, SU
KLINE, LLOYD W.
KOONTZ, KATY
LEVIN, AARON
LEVINE, FAYE
LOSCHIAVO, LINDA ANN
LYONS, CHRISTINE
MACDONALD, SANDY
MALLETTE, MAL
MARGOLIS, LYNNE
MAZIE, DAVID
MCCORMICK, MICHELE
MEOLA, PATRICIA E.
MIX, SHELDON A.
NELSON, ED
NEMSER, CINDY
PITTMAN, RUTH
POLAND, NANCY
ROBERTS, JANET M.
ROSENDO, JOSEPH
RUBIN, NANCY
SCHERMERHORN, DERICK D.
SHEFFE, EDWARD D.
SPANO, SUSAN
SPRINGER, P. GREGORY
TUTHILL JR., OLIVER W.
VAN COLLIE, SHIMON-CRAIG
VIORST, MILTON
WHITLEY, SHARON

WILSON, ROBERT L.
WOLFE, DARRELL K.
WOMACK, ROCKY
WOODARD, BERT
WUCHERER, RUTH

EDUCATION

ALLEN, ROBERT A.
ASTON, ATHINA LEKA
AUERBACK, PHD., STEVANNE
BALDWIN, JOYCE
BARTEL, PAULINE C.
BAYERS, RAPP LEA
BEHRENS, JOHN
BENDINER, ROBERT
BERG, MARGARET C.
BERMAN, BRIAN J.
BERMAN, CLAIRE
BERRY, S.L.
BIRNBAUM, NATALIE
BODGER, CAROLE
BOUCHIER, DAVID
BRASSELL, SEARLES
  LUCINDA
BRINLEY, MARYANN
  BUCKNUM
BRODSKY, RUTHAN
CALLAHAN, FLORENCE
CAREW, RUTH M. HARMER
CARUANA, CLAUDIA M.
CHEASEBRO, MARGARET
CIERVO, ARTHUR
CLARKE, PHILIP C.
COLTON, HELEN
DALEY, LAVERNE
DALY, MAUREEN
DAVIDSON, MARK
DAVIS, BEATRICE G.
DEBARTOLO, ANTHONY
DEGNAN, JAMES P.
DEVINE, GEORGE
DOWNEY, CHARLES E.
DRISCOLL, CYNTHIA
DYKEMAN, WILMA
EDELSTEIN, SCOTT
FEHL, MARTHA R.
FELDMAN, RUTH DUSKIN
FORTNEY, DAVID L.
FOSTER, NANCY
FRUMKES, LEWIS BURKE
GATTO, JOHN TAYLOR
GILBERT, SARA D.
GILINSKY, RHODA M.
GLASS, JUDITH E.
GLASSER, SELMA
GOODING, JUDSON
GROSS, RONALD
HAAPOJA, MARGARET A.
HAAS, ALAN D.
HALL, JAMES B.

HAMILTON, PHD., ELEANOR
HARRIS, JUDITH
HASKIN, PHD., JOHN A.
HECHLER, DAVID
HELM, SYLVIA
HOCH, DR. DEAN E.
HOCH, NANCY M.
HOFFMAN, NANCY YANES
HOLCOMB, GEORGE B.
HOLTON, FELICIA
  ANTONELLI
HONE, HARRY
HOWARD, ELIZABETH M.
HUNT, JAMES E.
IRA, ALLEN
JAMES, LAURIE
JOHNSON, JAN
K-TURKEL, JUDI
KANIGEL, ROBERT
KELLY, KATE
KLINE, LLOYD W.
KNIGHT, DOUG
KOERNER, THOMAS F.
LANGHAM, BARBARA
LARBERG, ANN
LEERBURGER, BENEDICT
LEERBURGER, BENEDICT
LEONARD, GEORGE
LEVIN, AARON
LEVINE, FAYE
LONDON, BILL
LORE, DIANE C.
MACDONALD, SANDY
MARKS, EDITH
MAZIE, DAVID
MCNAIR, MARCIA L.
MCNEES, PAT
MEOLA, PATRICIA E.
MIRVIS, KENNETH W.
MOATES, MARIANNE
  MERRILL
MOWRY, SERENA BLODGETT
MURPHY, RAYMOND J.
NOVITZ, CHARLES R.
PAAJANEN, ANNETTE LAABS
PERRY, ERMA
PERRY, SUSAN K.
PINES, MAYA
ROES, NICHOLAS A.
RUBIN, NANCY
SABIN, FRANCENE
SCHILLER, ANDREW
SCOTT, GINI GRAHAM
SEAMANS, ANDY
SIEGEL, DOROTHY
SILBERMAN, ARLENE
SMITH, RUTH BAYARD
SOHN, DAVID A.
SOMAN, SHIRLEY CAMPER
SZUPROWICZ, BOHDAN O.
TEGELER, DOROTHY

TEMKO, FLORENCE
TOWLE, LISA H.
TRUSSO, JOSEPH
TURECAMO, DORRINE
URROWS, HENRY AND
  ELIZABETH
VALENTI, DAN
VAN DILLEN, LAILEE
WEHRWEIN, AUSTIN C.
WHITLEY, SHARON
WILLIAMS, RUSSELL J.
WOLKOMIR, RICHARD AND
  JOYCE ROGERS
  WOLKOMIR
WOMACK, ROCKY
WOOD, SHARON M.
WOOG, DAN
ZATZ, ARLINE

ELECTRONICS

BARNES-SVARNEY,
  PATRICIA L.
BARSKY, MARTIN
BERGER, IVAN
BLY, ROBERT W.
CLEDE, BILL
DAVIDSON, MARK
DIAMOND, LEN
DITZEL, PAUL
FANTEL, HAS
FEIT, EDWARD
FNA NEWS
GOLIN, MILTON
GRAF, RUDOLF F.
GRANHOLM, JACKSON W.
GYSI, CHUCK
HECHT, JEFF
HELLMAN, HAL
IRA, ALLEN
JOHNSTON, MELANIE LEE
KRANISH, ARTHUR
LANDER, KATHLEEN
LEVY, RICHARD C.
LORENZ-FIFE, IRIS
PINKWAS, STAN
ROSENBLUM, DEBBIE
SCHOTT-JONES, ELAINE
URROWS, HENRY AND
  ELIZABETH

ENTERTAINMENT

ALLEN, ROBERT A.
ARCELLA, LISA
ARDMORE, JANE KESNER
ASNER, MARIE A.
ASTON, ATHINA LEKA
BARTEL, PAULINE C.
BASCH, BUDDY
BELL, JOSEPH N.

BERGER, AMY H.
BERGER, IVAN
BERRY, S.L.
BITETTI, MARGE
BOONE, GENE
BOSCO, ANTOINETTE
BROWN, TERRY T.
CALABRO, MARIAN
CARUBA, ALAN
CATALANO, JULIE
COAN, PETER M.
CONNIFF, JAMES C. G.
COX, VIC
DALY, MAUREEN
DAVID, LESTER
DAVIDSON, MARK
DAVIS, ELISE MILLER
DEBARTOLO, ANTHONY
DOWNEY, CHARLES E.
FELD, KAREN
FNA NEWS
FREY, RICHARD L.
GILES, MARJORIE GORDON-
GLASSER, SELMA
GOLDSTEIN, GREG
GOULD, LARK ELLEN
GRANT, NANCY S.
GREENBERG, JAN
HARRIS, ELEANOR
HEMMING, ROY
HINTZ, MARTIN
HODGE, ADELE
HORNBAKER, ALICE J.
HOROWITZ, SHEL ALAN
HOWARD, ELIZABETH M.
HURWOOD, BERNHARDT J.
IRA, ALLEN
JOHNSON, SABEEHA H.
JOHNSTON, MELANIE LEE
KONNER, LINDA
LANGER, CASSANDRA
LEBLANC, RENA DICTOR
LEE, SHIRLEY
LEVINE, FAYE
LOSCHIAVO, LINDA ANN
MACDONALD, SANDY
MARGOLIS, LYNNE
MASARACCHIA, SUSAN
MASTROLIA, LILYAN S.
MCMORROW, TOM
MEOLA, PATRICIA E.
MICHAEL, JOYCE EMMETT
MILLER, BRUCE
MILLNER, CORK
MONROE, KEITH
MONSON, NANCY P.
NANESS, BARBARA
NEELY, BONNIE BURGESS
OLNEY, ROSS R.
PEEPLES, EDWIN A.
PEPE, BARBARA

PFEIFER, LUANNE
PINKWAS, STAN
REISS, ALVIN H.
ROSENBAUM, HELEN
ROSENDO, JOSEPH
SCAGNETTI, JACK
SCHREIBER, NORMAN
SCOTT, GINI GRAHAM
SEAMANS, ANDY
SHEMANSKI, FRANCES
SILBEY, PAULA J.
SLATE, LIBBY
SMALL, SYLVIA ADAMSON
SMITH, LIZ
SOTER, TOM
SPRINGER, P. GREGORY
STACK, ROBERT
STICH, SALLY
STREHLOW, LORETTA
TROMBETTI, STEVEN E.
TUTHILL JR., OLIVER W.
VALENTI, DAN
VAN COLLIE, SHIMON-CRAIG
VOTANO, PAUL A.
WATSON, DELMAR
WILKINSON, PAMELA L.
WILLISTEIN, PAUL
WOLLMAN, JANE
WORTH, HELEN

FAMILY

ADLER, LINDA J.
AGUILAR, NONA
ANDERSON, JOAN WESTER
ARKIN, JOSEPH
ARRIGO, MARY
AUERBACK, PHD., STEVANNE
BARTOCCI, BARBARA
BELL, SALLY
BERGER, AMY H.
BERMAN, CLAIRE
BERRY, S.L.
BLACK, DEAN
BLISHAK, SYLVIA ANN
BLOCK, JEAN LIBMAN
BOONE, GENE
BOREA, PHYLLIS GILBERT
BOTTEL, HELEN
BOTWIN, CAROL
BRINLEY, MARYANN
  BUCKNUM
CASSILL, KAY
COLTON, HELEN
CONNIFF, JAMES C. G.
COYLE, ELIZABETH
DALRYMPLE, BYRON W.
DALY, MAUREEN
DARDICK, GEETA
DARK, HARRIS EDWARD
DARLINGTON, JOY

DAVID, LESTER
DAVIS, BEATRICE G.
DE CRISTOFORO, R. J.
DEANE, BARBARA
DENNY, ALMA
DEVINE, GEORGE
DONELSON, IRENE
DOWNEY, CHARLES E.
DREYFACK, RAYMOND
ELLIS, ALBERT
ELWOOD, MRS. EDITH
  MUESING
EVANS, GLEN
FADER, SHIRLEY SLOAN
FAUX, MARIAN
FEHL, MARTHA R.
FEIN, ELAINE
FELDMAN, RUTH DUSKIN
FINGER, ANNE L.
FINLEY, MITCH
FLEMING, ALICE
FORTNEY, DAVID L.
FUSCO, MARY ANN
  CASTRONOVO
GATTO, JOHN TAYLOR
GILINSKY, RHODA M.
GLASSER, SELMA
GOLDFEIN, DONNA
GORDON, SUSAN J.
GROENE, GORDON &
  GROENE, JANET
GROENE, JANET
GROSSMAN, ELLIE
HAAPOJA, MARGARET A.
HAIT, PAM
HALLADAY, GENEVA
HALLADAY, GENEVA
HAMILTON, PHD., ELEANOR
HARMON, MARY
HINTZ, MARTIN
HOCH, DR. DEAN E.
HOCH, NANCY M.
HOCHMAN, GLORIA
HORNBAKER, ALICE J.
HOROWITZ, SHEL ALAN
HOWARD, ELIZABETH M.
IACONETTI, JOAN
IRA, ALLEN
ISAACS, FLORENCE
JACKSON, LESLIE
JOHNSON, JAN
JOURNEY, ALFRED E. 'BUD'
KAHN, ADA PASKIND
KARAS, NICHOLAS
KARLIN, ELYSE ZORN
KAYE, EVELYN
KELLY, KATE
KIMMERLY, MAUREEN C.
KLAVAN, ELLEN
KLINE, LLOYD W.
KOCH, JOANNE & LEWIS

KOONTZ, KATY
LAGAN, CONSTANCE
  HALLINAN
LAMPE, DAVID
LARBERG, ANN
LAYNE, MARIE
LEW, IRVINA
LICHTENBERG, MARGARET
  KLEE
LINDSAY, RAE
LIPPERT, JOAN
LORENZ-FIFE, IRIS
LOSCHIAVO, LINDA ANN
LYONS, CHRISTINE
MACDONALD, SANDY
MALLETTE, MAL
MARKS, JANE
MARSH, SUSAN
MARTIN, MILDRED CROWL
MASTROLIA, LILYAN S.
MATHEWS, BEVERLY
MAYER, BARBARA
MAZIE, DAVID
MCNEES, PAT
MCVAY, ROSANNE
MEEKER, EUNICE JUCKETT
MEOLA, PATRICIA E.
MEYERS, CAROLE
  TERWILLIGER
MILLER, CATHERINE
  LANHAM
MOATES, MARIANNE
  MERRILL
MOLDAFSKY, ANNIE
MONSON, NANCY P.
MOORE, DIANNE
MORRIS, GLEN
MOSLEY, JEAN BELL
MUMMERT, ROGER
NEELY, BONNIE BURGESS
NELSON, ED
O'CONNOR, KAREN
OLDS, SALLY WENDKOS
PARADISE, PAUL RICHARD
PERRY, ERMA
PERRY, SUSAN K.
PITTMAN, RUTH
PODOLSKY, M. LAWRENCE
POGREBIN, LETTY COTTIN
REIMER, KATHLEEN
ROBERTS, JANET M.
ROESCH, ROBERTA
ROESSING, WALTER
ROGAK, LISA
ROOD, RONALD
ROTHMAN, HOWARD
ROWLES, GENEVIEVE
RUBIN, NANCY
SABIN, FRANCENE
SCHLOSS, MURIEL
SCHMITH, CINDY

SEAMAN, BARBARA
SEAMANS, ANDY
SECUNDA, VICTORIA
SERVINO, CAROL
SHAPIRO, PATRICIA
  GOTTLIEB
SHIMBERG, ELAINE FANTLE
SIEGEL, DOROTHY
SIEGEL, MARY ELLEN
SIEGEL, PAULA M.
SILBAR, HOWARD J.
SILBERMAN, ARLENE
SILBEY, PAULA J.
SKLAR, DUSTY
SOLOMON, GOODY L.
SOMAN, SHIRLEY CAMPER
STICH, SALLY
TEGELER, DOROTHY
TESSINA, PHD., TINA B.
TUPPER, MARGO
TURECAMO, DORRINE
VOLLMAR, ALICE M.
WALKER, GLADYS H.
WARREN, DAVID
WATLINGTON, JERILYNN
WESTEN, ROBIN
WESTGATE, ROBERT D.
WESTON, CAROL
WHALIN, W. TERRY
WHITLEY, SHARON
WOOG, DAN
YARMON, MORTON
ZATZ, ARLINE
ZOBEL, LOUISE PURWIN

FASHION

ARCELLA, LISA
BLOCK, JEAN LIBMAN
CANNON, DORIS
CANNON, DORIS
CARRENO, RICHARD D.
CIRONE, BETTINA
DAVIS, ELISE MILLER
FELDMAN, ELANE
FNA NEWS
FUSCO, MARY ANN
  CASTRONOVO
GEIS, DARLENE S.
GELTNER, SHARON
HAIT, PAM
HARMAN, HARRY & JEANNE
HOUSTON, RUTH
IRA, ALLEN
JOHNSON, SABEEHA H.
KATZ, RUTH J.
KAVALER, LUCY
KREDENSER, PETER
LACEY, DIANE G.
LANDT, DENNIS
LOSCHIAVO, LINDA ANN

MATURI, RICHARDS J.
MCVAY, ROSANNE
MEEKER, EUNICE JUCKETT
MILLER, BRUCE
MILLNER, CORK
NASON, STEPHEN
NEMIROW-NELSON, JILL
PFEIFER, LUANNE
ROSENBAUM, HELEN
SILBEY, PAULA J.
SMITH, LEE A.
STEINBERG, JANET
THOMPSON, JACQUELINE
ULRICH, ELISE VONS

FOREIGN

ANDERSON, ERIC G.
BAKER, CHRISTOPHER PAUL
BANDLER, MICHAEL J.
BARRY, DON
BASSETT, ELIZABETH
BATTERSBY, MARK E.
BOSE, MICHAEL ALAN
BRASSELL, SEARLES
  LUCINDA
CAREW, RUTH M. HARMER
CASS, MAXINE
CELLIERS, PETER J.
CLARKE, PHILIP C.
ELLIOTT, JOY
FEHL, MARTHA R.
FINKE, BLYTHE FOOTE
FORTNEY, DAVID L.
FRANCISCUS, ALEXANDRA
FUSCO, MARY ANN
  CASTRONOVO
GEBHART, FRED
GOODING, JUDSON
GOODSELL, JAMES NELSON
GRAND, CARMEN T.
GREENE, FREDA
HARSHAM, PHILIP
HEMBREE, DIANA
HEMMING, ROY
HIBBEN, DR. FRANK C.
HINTZ, MARTIN
HOLCOMB, GEORGE B.
HONE, HARRY
HOWE, RUSSELL WARREN
HOYT, ERICH
HUBBELL, JOHN G.
KAUFMAN, WALLACE
KNIGHT, DOUG
KOONTZ, KATY
KUSTANOWITZ, SHULAMIT E.
LEERBURGER, BENEDICT
LESLIE, JACQUES
LEVIN, AARON
LEVINE, FAYE
LEW, IRVINA

LORENZ-FIFE, IRIS
LOSCHIAVO, LINDA ANN
LYONS, CHRISTINE
MARZECKI, LONGIN W.
MAZIE, DAVID
MCDOWELL-LYNCH, JUNE
MEEKER, EUNICE JUCKETT
MILLER AND MARK ELLIS
  MILLER, JUDITH BRAFFMAN
MILNE, ROBERT SCOTT
MOLDAFSKY, ANNIE
NOSSAMAN, MICHAEL
PAUST, GIL
PFEIFER, LUANNE
POLAND, NANCY
REICHEK, MORTON
ROESSING, WALTER
ROSENDO, JOSEPH
RUDOLPH, JOHN K.
SCHWALBERG, CAROL
SEIDEN, OTHNIEL J.
SILBEY, PAULA J.
SISCO, PAUL C.
SZUPROWICZ, BOHDAN O.
URROWS, HENRY AND
  ELIZABETH
VIORST, MILTON

GENERAL INTEREST

ADLER, LINDA J.
AGUILAR, NONA
ALLEN, ROBERT A.
ALPER, PHILIP
ALPERSTEIN, ELLEN
ALTER, JOANNE
ANDERSON, BARRY C.
ANDERSON, ERIC G.
ASTON, ATHINA LEKA
BABSON, O. BONNI
BAKAL, CARL
BAKER, CHRISTOPHER PAUL
BARNES, DUNCAN
BARRY, DON
BARTEL, PAULINE C.
BATTERSBY, MARK E.
BAYERS, RAPP LEA
BEAUGE, JOHN Q.
BEHRENS, JOHN
BELL, JOSEPH N.
BELL, SALLY
BENFORD, MARILYN
BENFORD, TIMOTHY B.
BERG, MARGARET C.
BERKO, ROBERT L.
BERMAN, CLAIRE
BERRY, S.L.
BLIVEN JR., BRUCE
BLIZZARD, WILLIAM C.
BLOOM, MURRAY TEIGH
BLY, ROBERT W.

BODGER, CAROLE
BOTTEL, HELEN
BOTWIN, CAROL
BRESCOLL, JAMES
BRESLAUER, IRWIN J.
BRESNICK, JAN
BROOKS, PATRICIA
BROWN, TERRY T.
BROY, ANTHONY
BURTON, MARDA
CANDLER, JULIE
CANNON, DORIS
CANNON, DORIS
CARUBA, ALAN
CHAGALL, DAVID
CHANDLER, JO
CHEASEBRO, MARGARET
CHIN, RUTH
CHRISTIAN, ALLGAIER
  DONNA
CIRONE, BETTINA
CLARK, LARRY
CLINE, ANDY
COLBERT, JUDY
COLEBERD, FRANCES
COLTON, HELEN
CONNOR, J. ROBERT
CORBETT, GERALDINE
CORWEN, LEONARD
COYLE, ELIZABETH
CRANDELL, CHERYL
CROSS, WILBUR
CROTEAU, MAUREEN E.
CUMMINGS, SANDRA OTTO
CURRAN, BOB
DAILY, LAURA
DALEY, LAVERNE
DAMEROW, GAIL J.
DARK, HARRIS EDWARD
DARLINGTON, JOY
DAY, BETH
DE CRISTOFORO, R. J.
DEANE, BARBARA
DEBARTOLO, ANTHONY
DEKTAR, JOAN A.
DEMPEWOLFF, RICHARD F.
DENNY, ALMA
DICKINSON, PETER A.
DITZEL, PAUL
DODGE, ELLIN
DONELSON, IRENE
DRAGONWAGON, CRESCENT
DREYFACK, RAYMOND
DUNHAM, ROBERT
EDMONDS, PATRICIA
ELIOT, JANE WINSLOW
ENGLEBARDT, STANLEY L.
EVANS, GLEN
FALES, EDWARD
FAREWELL, SUSAN
FEHL, MARTHA R.

FELD, KAREN
FINGER, ANNE L.
FINKE, BLYTHE FOOTE
FISH, BYRON
FLUENT, MIKE
FORTNEY, DAVID L.
FOSTER, NANCY
FRIED, EUNICE
FRIESE, RICK
FRUMKES, LEWIS BURKE
FULLMAN, LYNN GRISARD
FUSCO, MARY ANN
  CASTRONOVO
GALUB, JACK
GAMAGE, DOUGLAS C.
GANNON, ROBERT
GEBHART, FRED
GEIS, DARLENE S.
GELTNER, SHARON
GLASS, JUDITH E.
GLASSER, SELMA
GOLDFEIN, DONNA
GOODHEART, BARBARA
GOODING, JUDSON
GORDON, BERNARD LUDWIG
GRAF, RUDOLF F.
GRAPES, JOAN A.
GREENGARD, SAMUEL
GRESHAM, GRITS
GRIMM, TOM
GROENE, GORDON &
  GROENE, JANET
GROENE, JANET
GROSSINGER, TANIA
GROSSMAN, ELLIE
GYSI, CHUCK
HAAPOJA, MARGARET A.
HACKETT, BLANCHE
HALL, JAMES B.
HALPERN, FRANCES
HAMMER, ROGER A.
HANCOCK, M. A.
HARMAN, HARRY & JEANNE
HARRIS, ELEANOR
HARSHAM, PHILIP
HARVEY, FRANK
HAY, PHD., VICTORIA
HAY, VICTORIA
HAZEN, BARBARA SHOOK
HEATH, JARRETT A.
HEDDEN, JAY W.
HELLMAN, HAL
HIBBEN, DR. FRANK C.
HIGDON, HAL
HINTZ, MARTIN
HOCH, DR. DEAN E.
HOCH, NANCY M.
HOCHMAN, GLORIA
HODGE, ADELE
HOFFMAN, NANCY YANES
HONE, HARRY

HORNBAKER, ALICE J.
HORNER, SHIRLEY
HOROWITZ, SHEL ALAN
HOTCHKISS, JUDY
HOUSTON, RUTH
HOWARD, ELIZABETH M.
HOWE, RUSSELL WARREN
HOWES, CONNIE B.
HUBBELL, JOHN G.
HUFF, DARRELL
HYYPIA, JORMA
IRA, ALLEN
JOHNSON, SABEEHA H.
KANIGEL, ROBERT
KAVALER, LUCY
KLAUS, BARBARA
KLAVAN, ELLEN
KLINE, LLOYD W.
KNICELY, FAY
KNIGHT, DOUG
KOEHLER, MARGARET
  HUDSON
KOLUS, HOWARD
KOONTZ, KATY
KOWAL, JOHN PAUL
KRANISH, ARTHUR
KREMEN, BENNETT
KUHN, IRENE CORBALLY
LAMPE, DAVID
LANDT, DENNIS
LARBERG, ANN
LAYNE, MARIE
LEE, SHIRLEY
LEERBURGER, BENEDICT
LEIF, ROBERT
LEMKOWITZ, FLORENCE
LEONARD, JOHN EDWARD
LESLIE, JACQUES
LEVINE, FAYE
LEVY, RICHARD C.
LEWIS, JACK
LINDSAY, RAE
LORENZ-FIFE, IRIS
LOSCHIAVO, LINDA ANN
MALLETTE, MAL
MANDELL, PATRICIA
MAPPES, DR. CARL R.
MARGOLIUS, ESTHER
MARKS, EDITH
MARQUARDT, DEBORAH
MARSH, SUSAN
MARTIN, MILDRED CROWL
MARZECKI, LONGIN W.
MASARACCHIA, SUSAN
MASON, LEE FRANZ
MASSEY, R. L.
MASSOW, ROSALIND
MASTROLIA, LILYAN S.
MATHEWS, BEVERLY
MATURI, RICHARDS J.
MATUSIK, JO ELLEN

MCCORMICK, MICHELE
MCDERMOTT, MICHAEL J.
MCKENZIE, J. NORMAN
MCKEON, KEVIN
MENKUS, BELDEN
MEOLA, PATRICIA E.
MILLER AND MARK ELLIS
MILLER, JUDITH BRAFFMAN
MILNE, ROBERT SCOTT
MIRVIS, KENNETH W.
MIX, SHELDON A.
MONROE, KEITH
MONSON, NANCY P.
MOORE, DIANNE
MORGAN, JOHN S.
MORGAN, NEIL
MORRILL, STEPHEN
MORRIS, HAL
MOSLEY, JEAN BELL
NADLER, BOB
NASON, STEPHEN
NEELY, BONNIE BURGESS
NELSON, ED
NEWCOMB, DUANE G.
NICKLAS, NICK
OATIS, JONATHAN W.
OLECK, HOWARD L.
PARADISE, PAUL RICHARD
PAUST, GIL
PAYNE, PEGGY
PEAKE, JACQUELYN
PERRY, ERMA
PICKENS, THOMAS M.
PITTMAN, RUTH
POLVAY, MARINA
RADCLIFFE, DONALD
RAND, ABBY
REIMER, KATHLEEN
REISS, ALVIN H.
RILLY, CHERYL
ROBINSON, TED
ROESCH, ROBERTA
ROSEN, M. DANIEL
ROSENBAUM, HELEN
ROSS, MARILYN HEIMBERG
RUBIN, NANCY
SAMBROT, WILLIAM
SANDEL, SUSAN L.
SCHILLER, ANDREW
SCHLOSS, MURIEL
SCHREIBER, NORMAN
SCHWALBERG, CAROL
SCOTT, GINI GRAHAM
SEAMANS, ANDY
SEITEL, FRASER PAUL
SHELDON, GEORGE
SHIMBERG, ELAINE FANTLE
SHIPLER, GUY
SHUBIN, SEYMOUR
SIEGEL, DOROTHY
SILBAR, HOWARD J.

SILBERMAN, ARLENE
SILBEY, PAULA J.
SISCO, PAUL C.
SKLAR, DUSTY
SLATTERY, WILLIAM J.
SMITH, LIZ
SMITH, RUTH BAYARD
SOHN, DAVID A.
SOMAN, SHIRLEY CAMPER
SOTER, TOM
SPANO SR., JOHN J.
STAR, JACK
STEIN, M. L.
STICH, SALLY
STITT, ABBY
STREHLOW, LORETTA
STRESHINSKY, SHIRLEY G.
TAMIS, VALERIE B.
TAYLOR, GARY
TEGELER, DOROTHY
TERRES, JOHN K.
THOMPSON, JACQUELINE
TOWLE, LISA H.
TUPPER, MARGO
VOLLMAR, ALICE M.
VOTANO, PAUL A.
WALTERS GROUP
WARREN, CAMERON A.
WATSON, DELMAR
WELCH, RANDY
WESLEY, MARX
WESSEL, MORRIS A.
WESTEN, ROBIN
WESTHEIMER, MARY
WHITE, BARBARA
WHITLEY, SHARON
WILKINSON, PAMELA L.
WILSON, ROBERT L.
WOLFE, DARRELL K.
WOLKOMIR, RICHARD AND
  JOYCE ROGERS
WOLKOMIR
WOMACK, ROCKY
WOOD, SHARON M.
WOODSON, R. DODGE
WOOG, DAN
WRIGHT JR., ED
WUCHERER, RUTH
YARMON, MORTON
YOUNG, WARREN R.
ZATZ, ARLINE
ZOBEL, LOUISE PURWIN
ZURCHER, MARVIN
ZWEIG, PHILLIP L.
ZWICKER, DENISE ALLEN

GEOGRAPHY

BAKER, CHRISTOPHER PAUL
FEHL, MARTHA R.
GILES, DAVID N.

GOODSELL, JAMES NELSON
GREENGARD, SAMUEL
HINTZ, MARTIN
HOYT, ERICH
KAYE, EVELYN
KOONTZ, KATY
SEAMANS, ANDY
STAR, JACK

GOVERNMENT

ALBANESE, DAVID J.
ARKIN, JOSEPH
BAKAL, CARL
BARON, HARRY
BARRY, DON
BARRY, DON
BATTERSBY, MARK E.
BATTERSBY, MARK E.
BELL, JOSEPH N.
BENDINER, ROBERT
BERMAN, BRIAN J.
BLOOM, MURRAY TEIGH
BLUM, MICHELLE E.
BRESCOLL, JAMES
CHAGALL, DAVID
CHELEKIS, GEORGE
CLARKE, PHILIP C.
CONNIFF, JAMES C. G.
COYLE, ELIZABETH
DAVIDSON, MARK
DAY, BETH
DEGREGORIO, WILLIAM A.
DICKERSON, NANCY
DUSKY, LORRAINE
ELWOOD, MRS. EDITH
  MUESING
ENGLE, PAANANEN ELOISE
FEHL, MARTHA R.
FELD, KAREN
FERMAN, IRVING
FINGER, ANNE L.
FNA NEWS
FREEDMAN, ERIC
GATTO, JOHN TAYLOR
GELTNER, SHARON
GLASS, JUDITH E.
GOODING, JUDSON
GOODSELL, JAMES NELSON
GOULD, LARK ELLEN
GREENGARD, SAMUEL
GRIFFIN, C. W.
GROSS, RONALD
HAMMITT, HARRY
HARVEY, FRANK
HASTINGS, ROBERT A.
HONE, HARRY
HORNER, SHIRLEY
HORNSTEIN, HAROLD
HOROWITZ, SHEL ALAN
HOWE, RUSSELL WARREN

HUBBELL, JOHN G.
JAMES JR., JESSE A.
KEITH, ALLAN
KEMPTON-SMITH, DEBBI
KRANISH, ARTHUR
KREIG, ANDREW, ESQ.
KUHN, IRENE CORBALLY
LANGHAM, BARBARA
LEERBURGER, BENEDICT
LEONARD, GEORGE
LEONARD, JOHN EDWARD
LESLIE, JACQUES
LEVINE, FAYE
LEVITSKY, DR. SERGE L.
LIEBERMAN, ROBERT H.
LORE, DIANE C.
MARTIN, MILDRED CROWL
MARZECKI, LONGIN W.
MAZIE, DAVID
MCCLENDON, SARAH
MCKENZIE, J. NORMAN
MCKEON, KEVIN
MEOLA, PATRICIA E.
MILLER AND MARK ELLIS
MILLER, JUDITH BRAFFMAN
MONTGOMERY, ED
MOSKIN, J. ROBERT
MOWRY, SERENA BLODGETT
NELSON, ED
NEUMEYER, KATHLEEN
NICKLAS, NICK
NOSSAMAN, MICHAEL
OLECK, HOWARD L.
OPPENHEIMER, ERNEST J.
OSTROW, RONALD J.
OWEN, JENNIFER BRYON
POGUE, FORREST C.
POLAND, NANCY
RODDIN, MIKE
ROSEN, M. DANIEL
RUDOLPH, JOHN K.
SCHLEIN, ALAN M.
SCOTT, GINI GRAHAM
SEAMANS, ANDY
SHEPARD, SUSAN J.
SHIPLER, GUY
SMITH, RICHARD AUSTIN
SOMAN, SHIRLEY CAMPER
SPANO SR., JOHN J.
STOCKER, JOSEPH
STRUGATCH, WARREN
TAYLOR, GARY
TAYLOR, THEODORE
TRILLING, DIANA
TRUSSO, JOSEPH
TUTHILL JR., OLIVER W.
URROWS, HENRY AND
  ELIZABETH
VIORST, MILTON
WEHRWEIN, AUSTIN C.
WELCH, RANDY

WESLEY, MARX
WESTGATE, ROBERT D.
WILLIAMS, RUSSELL J.
WRIGHT JR., ED
YOUNG, DONALD

HEALTH

ACKERMAN, DR., LOWELL
AGUILAR, NONA
ALPERSTEIN, ELLEN
ALTER, JOANNE
ANDERSON, ERIC G.
ANDERSON, KENNETH N.
ARCELLA, LISA
ARRIGO, MARY
BAHR, ROBERT A.
BAHR, ROBERT A.
BAILEY, JANET
BAKAL, CARL
BAKER, ROLINDA B.
BAKER, SAMM SINCLAIR
BALDWIN, JOYCE
BARBATO, JOSEPH
BARNES-SVARNEY,
  PATRICIA L.
BARON, HARRY
BARONE, JEANINE
BARTEL, PAULINE C.
BASCH, BUDDY
BAYERS, RAPP LEA
BAYUS, LENORE
BELL, SALLY
BENZAIA, DIANA
BERLAND, THEODORE
BERMAN, BRIAN J.
BERMAN, CLAIRE
BERRY, S.L.
BLACK, DEAN
BLAKE, PATRICIA
BLOCK, BARRY
BLOCK, JEAN LIBMAN
BOBROW, JUDITH
BODGER, CAROLE
BOECKMAN, CHARLES
BOEHM, GEORGE A. W.
BOROSON, WARREN
BOSCO, ANTOINETTE
BOTTEL, HELEN
BOTWIN, CAROL
BRAMS, STANLEY H.
BRASSELL, SEARLES
  LUCINDA
BRAUN, VICKI
BREECHER, M.P.H.,
  MAURY M.
BRESNICK, JAN
BRINLEY, MARYANN
  BUCKNUM
BRODSKY, RUTHAN
BROOKS, PATRICIA

BROY, ANTHONY
BRUNING, NANCY
BUCHMAN, DIAN DINCIN
BUONOCORE, JULIA
CAMPBELL, CANDACE
CAREW, RUTH M. HARMER
CARUANA, CLAUDIA M.
CASS, MAXINE
CASSILL, KAY
CATALANO, JULIE
CHANDLER, JO
CHARLES, JOANNA
CIERVO, ARTHUR
CLAXTON, COLETTE
CLIFFORD, WILLIAM
CLINE, ANDY
CONNIFF, JAMES C. G.
COOPER, PAULETTE
CORWEN, LEONARD
COX, VIC
DANOWSKI, JENNY
DARDICK, GEETA
DARK, HARRIS EDWARD
DARLINGTON, JOY
DAVID, LESTER
DAVIDSON, MARK
DAVIS, BEATRICE G.
DAVIS, FLORA M.
DEANE, BARBARA
DICKINSON, PETER A.
DICTOR-LEBLANC, RENA
DONELSON, IRENE
DOWNEY, CHARLES E.
DRAGONWAGON, CRESCENT
DUNAIEF, LEAH S.
DUNHAM, ROBERT
ELLIS, ALBERT
ENGH, JERI
ENGLE, PAANANEN ELOISE
ENGLEBARDT, STANLEY L.
EVANS, GLEN
FAREWELL, SUSAN
FARIS, CHARLENE
FEIN, ELAINE
FELD, KAREN
FERTIG, JUDITH
FINGER, ANNE L.
FNA NEWS
FORTNEY, DAVID L.
FOSTER, NANCY
FOX, BARRY
FRIEDMAN, KENNETH A.
FRUMKES, LEWIS BURKE
FUERST, MARK L.
FUSCO, MARY ANN
  CASTRONOVO
GAGE, DIANE
GALUB, JACK
GANNON, ROBERT
GEBHART, FRED
GERSON, VICKI

GEYER, SHERREE
GILINSKY, RHODA M.
GLASS, JUDITH E.
GLASSER, SELMA
GOLIN, MILTON
GOODHEART, BARBARA
GOODING, JUDSON
GREENBERG, JAN
GREENGARD, SAMUEL
GREGG, JAMES R.
GRICE, MARY A.
GRIFFIN, KELLY L.
GROSSMAN, ELLIE
HAIT, PAM
HAMILTON, PHD., ELEANOR
HANLE, ZACK
HARRIS, JUDITH
HASKIN, PHD., JOHN A.
HASTINGS, ROBERT A.
HEATH, JARRETT A.
HEILMAN, JOAN RATTNER
HELLER, MARION
HELMLINGER, TRUDY
HENLEY, ARTHUR
HIGDON, HAL
HOCHMAN, GLORIA
HOFFMAN, NANCY YANES
HOLCOMB, GEORGE B.
HORNSTEIN, HAROLD
HOWARD, ELIZABETH M.
HUBBELL, JOHN G.
HUFF, DARRELL
HUFF, FRANCES N.
HUNT, JAMES E.
HURWOOD, BERNHARDT J.
IRA, ALLEN
ISAACS, FLORENCE
JACOBSON, BEVERLY
JAMISON, WARREN
JOHNSON, JAN
JOHNSON, SABEEHA H.
JOSEPH, LOU
JUDSON, KAREN
KAHN, ADA PASKIND
KANIGEL, ROBERT
KAVALER, LUCY
KIEL, STUART
KITAY, WILLIAM
KLINE, LLOYD W.
KNIGHT, DOUG
KONNER, LINDA
KOONTZ, KATY
KRANISH, ARTHUR
KRYMOW, VINCENZINA
LACEY, DIANE G.
LANGER, CASSANDRA
LANGHAM, BARBARA
LARBERG, ANN
LAYNE, MARIE
LEERBURGER, BENEDICT
LEONARD, GEORGE

LESLIE, JACQUES
LEVIN, AARON
LEVINSON, ROBIN
LEVY, ERIC
LEW, IRVINA
LEWIS, HOWARD R.
LINDSAY, RAE
LIPPERT, JOAN
LOCKETT-JOHN, SUE
LOEBL, SUZANNE
LORENZ-FIFE, IRIS
LOSCHIAVO, LINDA ANN
LYONS, CHRISTINE
MALLETTE, MAL
MARGOLIUS, ESTHER
MARKS, EDITH
MARKS, JANE
MARTIN, MILDRED CROWL
MASARACCHIA, SUSAN
MASSEY, R. L.
MASSOW, ROSALIND
MASTROLIA, LILYAN S.
MCCORMICK, MICHELE
MCDOWELL, LEONARD O.
MCGRADY JR., PATRICK M.
MCPHEE, MARNIE
MCVAY, ROSANNE
MERWIN, PHILIP DEAN
MILLER AND MARK ELLIS
  MILLER, JUDITH BRAFFMAN
MILLMAN, SANDY K.
MIX, SHELDON A.
MOATES, MARIANNE
  MERRILL
MOATES, MARIANNE
  MERRILL
MOFFAT, SHANNON
MOLDAFSKY, ANNIE
MONSON, NANCY P.
MOORE, DIANNE
MORRIS, MRS. TERRY
MOSKIN, J. ROBERT
MUMMERT, ROGER
MURPHY, WENDY B.
NADEL PH.D., LAURIE
NELSON, ED
NELSON, JANET
NEMIROW-NELSON, JILL
NEUMEYER, KATHLEEN
NEW, AMY ROFFMANN
NUWER, HANK
OLDS, SALLY WENDKOS
OPPENHEIM M.D., MICHAEL
PITTMAN, RUTH
PLANT, JANET
RADCLIFFE, DONALD
RANDOLPH, ELIZABETH
RILLY, CHERYL
ROBERTS, D.P.M.,
  ELIZABETH H.
ROCK, MAXINE

RODDIN, MIKE
ROES, NICHOLAS A.
ROES, NICHOLAS A.
ROESCH, ROBERTA
ROGAK, LISA
ROSEN, M. DANIEL
ROSENBERG, SHIRLEY
  SIROTA
ROSENDO, JOSEPH
ROTHMAN, HOWARD
RUSSELL, BARBARA
SABIN, FRANCENE
SAFRAN, CLAIRE
SAMBROT, WILLIAM
SANDEL, SUSAN L.
SCAGNETTI, JACK
SCHELL, NORMAN B.
SCHERMERHORN, DERICK D.
SCHLEIN, ALAN M.
SCHOTT-JONES, ELAINE
SCHULTZ, DODI
SCHWANZ, MICHAEL L.
SEAMAN, BARBARA
SEIDEN, OTHNIEL J.
SERVINO, CAROL
SHAKESPEARE, MARGARET
SHAPIRO, PATRICIA
  GOTTLIEB
SHAW, EVA
SHIMBERG, ELAINE FANTLE
SHUBIN, SEYMOUR
SIEGEL, DOROTHY
SIEGEL, MARY ELLEN
SIEGEL, PAULA M.
SILBEY, PAULA J.
SKLAR, DUSTY
SMITH, BEVERLY BUSH
SMITH, RUTH BAYARD
SOLOMON, GOODY L.
SOMAN, SHIRLEY CAMPER
SOTER, TOM
STAR, JACK
STEPHEN, RAE
STITT, ABBY
STUART, ANNE ELIZABETH
TANNE, JANICE HOPKINS
TAUB, HARALD J.
TEGELER, DOROTHY
TONNESSEN, DIANA
TOWLE, LISA H.
TRUBO, RICHARD
TURECAMO, DORRINE
ULRICH, ELISE VONS
URROWS, HENRY AND
  ELIZABETH
WALKER, DR. MORTON
WALKER, GLADYS H.
WALTERS GROUP
WATLINGTON, JERILYNN
WEISBERG, JACOB
WESSEL, MORRIS A.

WESTGATE, ROBERT D.
WESTHEIMER, MARY
WHITFORD, JAMES
WHITLEY, SHARON
WINTER, RUTH
WOLFE, DARRELL K.
WOLKOMIR, RICHARD AND
  JOYCE ROGERS
  WOLKOMIR
WOLLMAN, JANE
WOLLMAN, PHYLLIS
WOMACK, ROCKY
YARMON, MORTON
YOUNG, WARREN R.
ZATZ, ARLINE
ZIMMERMAN, DAVID R.

HISTORY

ALBANESE, DAVID J.
ALLEN, ROBERT A.
ANDERSON, KENNETH N.
ASTON, ATHINA LEKA
BARTEL, PAULINE C.
BAYUS, LENORE
BEEBE, F. LISA
BEHRENS, JOHN
BELL, JOSEPH N.
BENFORD, TIMOTHY B.
BLIVEN JR., BRUCE
BOORSTIN, DANIEL J.
BOSE, MICHAEL ALAN
BREECHER, M.P.H.,
  MAURY M.
BRESLAV, MARC
BROOKS, LESTER
BUDROW, NANCY
CELLIERS, PETER J.
CHAGALL, DAVID
CIERVO, ARTHUR
COHEN, DANIEL
CORBETT, GERALDINE
COX, VIC
CROSS, WILBUR
CUPPER, DAN
DARK, HARRIS EDWARD
DAVIS, FLORA M.
DEBARTOLO, ANTHONY
DEGREGORIO, WILLIAM A.
DEMAN, ELAINE
DIENSTAG, ELEANOR
DOWNEY, CHARLES E.
DYKEMAN, WILMA
ENGLE, PAANANEN ELOISE
FEHL, MARTHA R.
FEUER, A.B.
FNA NEWS
FONTAINE, ANDRE
FREEDMAN, ERIC
FRIZZI, VIRGINIA
GATTO, JOHN TAYLOR

GILES, DAVID N.
GILES, MARJORIE GORDON-
GILFERT, SHIRLEY
GLINES, CARROLL V.
GOODING, JUDSON
GOODSELL, JAMES NELSON
GORDON, BERNARD LUDWIG
GRANHOLM, JACKSON W.
GROENE, JANET
HACKETT, BLANCHE
HAMMEL, ERIC
HANCOCK, M. A.
HARRIS, ELEANOR
HAY, PHD., VICTORIA
HAY, VICTORIA
HEMMING, ROY
HIBBEN, DR. FRANK C.
HINTZ, MARTIN
HOLCOMB, GEORGE B.
HORNER, SHIRLEY
HORNSTEIN, HAROLD
HURWOOD, BERNHARDT J.
JAMES, LAURIE
KANIGEL, ROBERT
KAVALER, LUCY
KEATING, BERN
KELLY, KATE
KIMMERLY, MAUREEN C.
KNICELY, FAY
KOEHLER, MARGARET
  HUDSON
LAMANGA, JOSEPH
LANDT, DENNIS
LANGWORTH, RICHARD M.
LARBERG, ANN
LASHUA, MARGERY F.
LEVIN, AARON
LEVINE, FAYE
LEVITSKY, DR. SERGE L.
LEWIS, JACK
LOCKWOOD, GEORGENE
  MULLER
MAPPES, DR. CARL R.
MARZECKI, LONGIN W.
MATUSIK, JO ELLEN
MAYNARD, MARY
MEEKER, EUNICE JUCKETT
MEROWITZ, MORTON J.
MILLMAN, SANDY K.
MIX, SHELDON A.
MIX, SHELDON A.
MOLDAFSKY, ANNIE
MORGAN, MURRAY
MORLAND, ALVIN
MORRILL, STEPHEN
MOSKIN, J. ROBERT
NANESS, BARBARA
O'REILLY, DON
OLECK, HOWARD L.
OLNEY, ROSS R.
OXFORD, EDWARD

PAANANEN, ELOISE
PALMQUIST, RON
PAUST, GIL
PITTMAN, RUTH
PODOLSKY, M. LAWRENCE
POGUE, FORREST C.
POLKING, MISS KIRK
POWER, CHARLOTTE A.
REIMER, KATHLEEN
RIEGER, TED
RILLY, CHERYL
ROGAK, LISA
ROOD, RONALD
ROWLES, GENEVIEVE
RUBIN, NANCY
SCHERMERHORN, DERICK D.
SCOTT, GINI GRAHAM
SEAMAN, BARBARA
SEAMANS, ANDY
SEIDEN, OTHNIEL J.
SILBAR, HOWARD J.
SMITH, RUTH BAYARD
SOMAN, SHIRLEY CAMPER
STEWART-LALE, CISSY
STOCKER, JOSEPH
STRICKLER, CAROLYN J.
SULLIVAN, GEORGE
THOMSON, PEGGY
VIORST, MILTON
WALTON, CHELLE KOSTER
WARREN, DAVID
WHITLEY, SHARON
WILKINSON, PAMELA L.
WOLFE, DARRELL K.
WOOD, SHARON M.
WUCHERER, RUTH
YOUNG, DONALD

HOBBIES

ARMSTRONG III, MARTIN F.
BALDWIN, JOYCE
BARNES, DUNCAN
BATTERSBY, MARK E.
BERGER, IVAN
BLIZZARD, WILLIAM C.
BOYKIN, JOHN E.
BUONOCORE, JULIA
BURCH, MONTE
COCHRAN, ADA
CONNOR, J. ROBERT
DAVIS, O. K.
DE CRISTOFORO, R. J.
FEHL, MARTHA R.
FREEDMAN, ERIC
FREY, RICHARD L.
GLASSER, SELMA
GRAF, RUDOLF F.
GROENE, JANET
GYSI, CHUCK
HAAPOJA, MARGARET A.

HALLADAY, GENEVA
HEDDEN, JAY W.
HUFF, DARRELL
HYYPIA, JORMA
JOHNSON, SABEEHA H.
JUDSON, KAREN
KNIGHT, DOUG
LAGAN, CONSTANCE
  HALLINAN
LAMANGA, JOSEPH
LASSEN, JEFF
LEE, SHIRLEY
LEWIS, JACK
LORENZ-FIFE, IRIS
LOSCHIAVO, LINDA ANN
MASSEY, R. L.
MASTROLIA, LILYAN S.
MEEKER, EUNICE JUCKETT
MEOLA, PATRICIA E.
MILLER, BRUCE
MIX, SHELDON A.
MONSON, NANCY P.
NADLER, BOB
NEELY, BONNIE BURGESS
PAUGH, TOM
PAUST, GIL
ROBERTS, JANET M.
SHAW, EVA
SHELDON, GEORGE
SLOME, JESSE R.
SOSIN, MARK
SULLIVAN, GEORGE
TEMKO, FLORENCE
WHALIN, W. TERRY
WHITE, BARBARA
WHITLEY, SHARON
WOODSON, R. DODGE
WULFF, JOAN SALVATO
ZOLLMAN, JOSEPH
ZURCHER, MARVIN

HOME & GARDEN

ASTON, ATHINA LEKA
BAKER, SAMM SINCLAIR
BEAN, ALICE PEARSE
BERRY, S.L.
BOONE, GENE
BRICKMAN, NANCI
BRIGHTMAN, ROBERT
BURTON, MARDA
BYRNE-DODGE, TERESA
CHRISTIAN, ALLGAIER
  DONNA
COCHRAN, ADA
DAMEROW, GAIL J.
DARDICK, GEETA
DARK, HARRIS EDWARD
DARLINGTON, JOY
DE CRISTOFORO, R. J.
DEKTAR, JOAN A.

DICKINSON, PETER A.
DRAGONWAGON, CRESCENT
DRISCOLL, CYNTHIA
ENGMAN, RONDA
FAREWELL, SUSAN
FEHL, MARTHA R.
FENTEN, D. X.
FERTIG, JUDITH
FORTSON, LOWRANCE
  SANNA
FUSCO, MARY ANN
  CASTRONOVO
GLASSER, SELMA
GRAF, RUDOLF F.
GRECO, GAIL
GREENGARD, SAMUEL
GROENE, GORDON &
  GROENE, JANET
HAAPOJA, MARGARET A.
HACKETT, BLANCHE
HAMILTON, KATIE
HANCOCK, M. A.
HEDDEN, JAY W.
HICKS, JUNE L.
HINTZ, MARTIN
HOTCHKISS, JUDY
HUFF, DARRELL
HUFF, FRANCES N.
HYYPIA, JORMA
JOHNSON, SABEEHA H.
JOLLIFFE, LEE
KATZ, RUTH J.
KNIGHT, DOUG
KOFRANEK, ANTON M.
KOONTZ, KATY
LACEY, DIANE G.
LADACH, PAULETTE
LAMPE, DAVID
LEE, SHIRLEY
LORENZ-FIFE, IRIS
LOSCHIAVO, LINDA ANN
MACDONALD, SANDY
MANNERS, DAVID X.
MASSEY, R. L.
MAYER, BARBARA
MCCARTNEY, LUCINDA L.
MCKENZIE, J. NORMAN
MEOLA, PATRICIA E.
MILLER, BRUCE
MORRILL, STEPHEN
MURPHY, WENDY B.
NEELY, BONNIE BURGESS
NEWCOMB, DUANE G.
NIELSEN, DOLLY
OGDEN, SHEPHERD
PEEPLES, EDWIN A.
PERRY, ERMA
PETROWSKI, ELAINE MARTIN
PODOLSKY, M. LAWRENCE
POMADA, ELIZABETH
REIMER, KATHLEEN

RILLY, CHERYL
ROBERTS, JANET M.
ROES, NICHOLAS A.
ROGAK, LISA
ROGERS, BARBARA
  RADCLIFFE
ROSENBAUM, HELEN
RUBIN, NANCY
SCHULTZ, MORTON J.
SHAPIRO, CECILE
SIEGEL, DOROTHY
SMALL, SYLVIA ADAMSON
SPATTER, SAM
STICH, SALLY
TANNER, OGDEN
TEEVAN, CATHERINE J.
TROMBETTI, STEVEN E.
TUPPER, MARGO
WALTER, EUGENE
WARREN, DAVID
WHALEY, PEGGY
WHITLEY, SHARON
WILKES, RALPH S.
WOODSON, R. DODGE
ZATZ, ARLINE
ZOBEL, LOUISE PURWIN

HUMAN INTEREST

ALPER, PHILIP
ALPERN, DAVID M.
ARDMORE, JANE KESNER
AUERBACK, PHD., STEVANNE
BARTEL, PAULINE C.
BARTOCCI, BARBARA
BASCH, BUDDY
BAYERS, RAPP LEA
BEHRENS, JOHN
BELL, JOSEPH N.
BELL, SALLY
BERGER, AMY H.
BERRY, S.L.
BLACK, DEAN
BLIZZARD, WILLIAM C.
BLOOM, MURRAY TEIGH
BODGER, CAROLE
BOECKMAN, CHARLES
BOTWIN, CAROL
BRAUN, VICKI
BREECHER, M.P.H.,
  MAURY M.
BROWN, GAIL
BUDROW, NANCY
CAHILL, CARL
CHANDLER, JO
CHRISTIAN, ALLGAIER
  DONNA
CIERVO, ARTHUR
CLARK, LARRY
COCHRAN, ADA
COLBERT, JUDY

CRANDELL, CHERYL
DARDICK, GEETA
DAVIS, ELISE MILLER
DAVIS, O. K.
DEANE, BARBARA
DENNY, ALMA
DICKERSON, NANCY
DITZEL, PAUL
DOWNEY, CHARLES E.
ENGLISH, JOHN W.
EVANS, GLEN
FEHL, MARTHA R.
FEIN, ELAINE
FELD, KAREN
FELDMAN, RUTH DUSKIN
FENSCH, THOMAS C.
FINKE, BLYTHE FOOTE
FNA NEWS
FORTNEY, DAVID L.
FOSTER, NANCY
FOX, BARRY
FREEDMAN, ERIC
FRIED, EUNICE
FRIZZI, VIRGINIA
FULLMAN, LYNN GRISARD
GILINSKY, RHODA M.
GLASS, JUDITH E.
GLASSER, SELMA
GLOECKL, ROBYN
GOLDSTEIN, GREG
GOODWIN, DAVE
GORDON, BERNARD LUDWIG
GOULD, LARK ELLEN
GREENGARD, SAMUEL
GROENE, JANET
HAAPOJA, MARGARET A.
HAIT, PAM
HAMILTON, PHD., ELEANOR
HAMMER, ROGER A.
HINTZ, MARTIN
HOCHMAN, GLORIA
HODGE, ADELE
HOFFMAN, NANCY YANES
HOROWITZ, SHEL ALAN
HOWARD, ELIZABETH M.
INGE, ARLINE
IRA, ALLEN
JENSEN, CHERYL
JOHNSON, JAN
JOHNSTON, MELANIE LEE
KAHN, ADA PASKIND
KAVALER, LUCY
KIEL, STUART
KLAVAN, ELLEN
KLINE, LLOYD W.
KNIGHT, DOUG
KOCH, JOANNE & LEWIS
KUSTANOWITZ, SHULAMIT E.
LAGAN, CONSTANCE
  HALLINAN
LAMPE, DAVID

LEBLANC, RENA DICTOR
LEE, SHIRLEY
LEONARD, JOHN EDWARD
LEVINE, FAYE
LEVINSON, ROBIN
LEVY, ERIC
LEVY, RICHARD C.
LEW, IRVINA
LEWIS, PARNELLS
LONDON, BILL
LORE, DIANE C.
LOSCHIAVO, LINDA ANN
LYHNE, BOB
MARGOLIS, LYNNE
MASARACCHIA, SUSAN
MASSOW, ROSALIND
MASTROLIA, LILYAN S.
MATHEWS, BEVERLY
MATURI, RICHARDS J.
MAZIE, DAVID
MCCLENDON, SARAH
MCNAIR, MARCIA L.
MCNEES, PAT
MEOLA, PATRICIA E.
MILLER AND MARK ELLIS
  MILLER, JUDITH BRAFFMAN
MILLER, CATHERINE
  LANHAM
MIX, SHELDON A.
MORRILL, STEPHEN
MORRIS, GLEN
NANESS, BARBARA
NOVITZ, CHARLES R.
OLDS, SALLY WENDKOS
PITTMAN, RUTH
PIZER, VERNON
POLAND, NANCY
ROBERTS, JANET M.
RODNEY, JAMES C.
ROESCH, ROBERTA
ROOD, RONALD
ROSENDO, JOSEPH
ROSS, MARILYN HEIMBERG
SABIN, FRANCENE
SCHLOSS, MURIEL
SCHWANZ, MICHAEL L.
SCOBEY, JOAN
SHAPIRO, PATRICIA
  GOTTLIEB
SHAW, EVA
SHEVIS, JIM
SILBEY, PAULA J.
SLATE, LIBBY
SMITH, BEVERLY BUSH
SMITH, RUTH BAYARD
SOLOMON, GOODY L.
SOMAN, SHIRLEY CAMPER
SOTER, TOM
STICH, SALLY
STUART, ANNE ELIZABETH
TAMIS, VALERIE B.

TUPPER, MARGO
TUTHILL JR., OLIVER W.
WALKER, GLADYS H.
WELCH, RANDY
WHALIN, W. TERRY
WHITLEY, SHARON
WILKINSON, PAMELA L.
WINTER, RUTH
WOLKOMIR, RICHARD AND
  JOYCE ROGERS
  WOLKOMIR
WOODARD, BERT
WORKMAN, BARBARA L.
YOUNG, WARREN R.
ZATZ, ARLINE

HUMAN RELATIONS

ALLEN, LOUIS A.
ANDERSON, ERIC G.
AUERBACK, PHD., STEVANNE
BAHR, ROBERT A.
BAILEY, JANET
BAKER, SAMM SINCLAIR
BAKER, SAMM SINCLAIR
BARONE, JEANINE
BARTOCCI, BARBARA
BERGER, AMY H.
BERMAN, CLAIRE
BOTTEL, HELEN
BOTWIN, CAROL
BOUCHIER, DAVID
BRESCOLL, JAMES
CASSILL, KAY
COCHRAN, ADA
COLTON, HELEN
CORWEN, LEONARD
COX, VIC
COYLE, ELIZABETH
DALY, MAUREEN
DAVIS, BEATRICE G.
DEANE, BARBARA
DEBARTOLO, ANTHONY
DENNY, ALMA
DRAGONWAGON, CRESCENT
DREYFACK, RAYMOND
DYKEMAN, WILMA
ELLIS, ALBERT
ELWOOD, MRS. EDITH
  MUESING
ENGH, JERI
FEIN, ELAINE
FELDMAN, RUTH DUSKIN
FELDMAN, RUTH DUSKIN
FINGER, ANNE L.
FOSTER, NANCY
FOX, BARRY
GAGE, DIANE
GALLO, DIANE
GAMAGE, DOUGLAS C.
GARFIELD, JOHANNA

GILBERT, SARA D.
GILES, MARJORIE GORDON-
GILINSKY, RHODA M.
GLASSER, SELMA
GORDON, SUSAN J.
GREENGARD, SAMUEL
GRIFFIN, KELLY L.
GROSSMAN, ELLIE
HAIT, PAM
HAZEN, BARBARA SHOOK
HECHLER, DAVID
HEILMAN, JOAN RATTNER
HENLEY, ARTHUR
HIBBEN, DR. FRANK C.
HOCHMAN, GLORIA
HOFFMAN, NANCY YANES
HONE, HARRY
HOWARD, ELIZABETH M.
IACONETTI, JOAN
IRA, ALLEN
ISAACS, FLORENCE
JACOBS, DORRI
JOHNSON, JAN
KAHN, ADA PASKIND
KLAVAN, ELLEN
KLINE, LLOYD W.
KOCH, JOANNE & LEWIS
KOCIVAR, BEN
KONNER, LINDA
LANGHAM, BARBARA
LICHTENBERG, MARGARET
  KLEE
LILES, BRENDA
LORENZ-FIFE, IRIS
LYONS, CHRISTINE
MARTIN, MILDRED CROWL
MASARACCHIA, SUSAN
MASTROLIA, LILYAN S.
MCDOWELL, LEONARD O.
MEEKER, EUNICE JUCKETT
MOATES, MARIANNE
  MERRILL
MONSON, NANCY P.
MOORE, DIANNE
MORRIS, GLEN
MORRIS, MRS. TERRY
MURPHY, RAYMOND J.
NEELY, BONNIE BURGESS
NELSON, ED
NEMIRO, BEVERLY
  ANDERSON
OWEN, JENNIFER BRYON
PALMQUIST, RON
PITTMAN, RUTH
POLAND, NANCY
RUBIN, NANCY
SABIN, FRANCENE
SCHERMERHORN, DERICK D.
SCHLICK, JACK
SCHLOSS, MURIEL
SEAMAN, BARBARA

SECUNDA, VICTORIA
SIEGEL, MARY ELLEN
SIEGEL, PAULA M.
SILBERMAN, ARLENE
SMALL, SYLVIA
  ADAMSON
SMITH, RUTH BAYARD
SOMAN, SHIRLEY CAMPER
SPRINGER, P. GREGORY
STEIN, HERBERT G.
STEWART-LALE, CISSY
TESSINA, PHD.,
  TINA B.
TUPPER, MARGO
TUTHILL JR.,
  OLIVER W.
WALTERS GROUP
WEINSTEIN, GRACE W.
WEISBERG, JACOB
WESTEN, ROBIN
WOOG, DAN
YAGER, JAN
YARMON, MORTON
ZOBEL, LOUISE
  PURWIN

HUMOR

ALPERN, LYNNE S.
ANDERSON, JOAN WESTER
ARMSTRONG III, MARTIN F.
ASNER, MARIE A.
BARRY, DON
BARTEL, PAULINE C.
BEAN, ALICE PEARSE
BELL, JOSEPH N.
BELL, JOSEPH N.
BENDINER, ROBERT
BLIZZARD, WILLIAM C.
BLUE, MARIAN
BOONE, GENE
BOTTEL, HELEN
BOUCHIER, DAVID
BROOKS, PATRICIA
CAHILL, CARL
COCHRAN, ADA
CONKLIN, WILLIAM B.
CORBETT, GERALDINE
DAVIS, ELISE MILLER
DE CRISTOFORO, R. J.
DEBARTOLO, ANTHONY
DEGNAN, JAMES P.
DENNY, ALMA
DOWNEY, CHARLES E.
DRAGONWAGON, CRESCENT
DUNHAM, ROBERT
EGERTON, JOHN
EVANS, GLEN
FEHL, MARTHA R.
FELDMAN, ELANE
FERRIS, PAUL

FINGER, ANNE L.
FISH, BYRON
FNA NEWS
FRUMKES, LEWIS BURKE
FULLMAN, LYNN GRISARD
GALLO, DIANE
GLASSER, SELMA
GORDON, SUSAN J.
HAGGITH, DAVID
HAIT, PAM
HENLEY, ARTHUR
HOCH, DR. DEAN E.
HOCH, NANCY M.
HORNBAKER, ALICE J.
HUBBELL, JOHN G.
JACOBS, FRANK
JOHNSON, JAN
KAHN, ADA PASKIND
KEMPTON-SMITH, DEBBI
KIEL, STUART
KLAUS, BARBARA
KONNER, LINDA
KOONTZ, KATY
LEAS, MARLIN
LEMKOWITZ, FLORENCE
LESLIE, JACQUES
LEVINE, FAYE
LORENZ-FIFE, IRIS
MAPPES, DR. CARL R.
MARGOLIS, LYNNE
MASTROLIA, LILYAN S.
MCCORMICK, MICHELE
MEOLA, PATRICIA E.
MONTGOMERY, ED
MORRILL, STEPHEN
NANESS, BARBARA
NEELY, BONNIE BURGESS
NEMIROW-NELSON, JILL
NEMSER, CINDY
PAUST, GIL
PEEPLES, EDWIN A.
PERLOFF, SUSAN
PETROWSKI, ELAINE MARTIN
POWER, CHARLOTTE A.
REISS, ALVIN H.
RILLY, CHERYL
ROBINSON, TED
ROSENDO, JOSEPH
RUSSELL, FRED
SCHWALBERG, CAROL
SCOBEY, JOAN
SEITEL, FRASER PAUL
SHAW, EVA
SHUBIN, SEYMOUR
SINBERG, STAN
SKLAR, DUSTY
SLATTERY, WILLIAM J.
STICH, SALLY
STUART, KIEL
TAJER, JOSIE
TURECAMO, DORRINE

WESTHEIMER, MARY
WHITLEY, SHARON
WOLKOMIR, RICHARD AND
 JOYCE ROGERS
 WOLKOMIR

JOURNALISM

ALLEN, ROBERT A.
ALPER, PHILIP
BASCH, BUDDY
BATTERSBY, MARK E.
BAYSURA, STEVEN A.
BEHRENS, JOHN
BELL, SALLY
BENDINER, ROBERT
BERGER, IVAN
BERRY, S.L.
BIRNBAUM, NATALIE
BISHER, FURMAN
BLIZZARD, WILLIAM C.
BREECHER, M.P.H.,
 MAURY M.
BRODY, PEG
BURGETT, GORDON
CARRENO, RICHARD D.
CLARK, LARRY
CLARKE, PHILIP C.
COREY, JOHN R.
CORWEN, LEONARD
COURIC, EMILY
COX, VIC
CROTEAU, MAUREEN E.
DALEY, LAVERNE
DE CRISTOFORO, R. J.
DENNY, ALMA
DICKERSON, NANCY
DOWNEY, CHARLES E.
EDELSTEIN, SCOTT
FAREWELL, SUSAN
FEHL, MARTHA R.
FEIN, ELAINE
FENSCH, THOMAS C.
FNA NEWS
FORTNEY, DAVID L.
FREEDMAN, ERIC
FREEMAN, LUCY
GATTO, JOHN TAYLOR
GEBHART, FRED
GELTNER, SHARON
GILES, MARJORIE GORDON-
GLASS, JUDITH E.
GOLIN, MILTON
GOODING, JUDSON
GOODSELL, JAMES NELSON
GREENE, FREDA
HABIBI, MOE
HACKETT, BLANCHE
HALPERN, FRANCES
HAMMER, ROGER A.
HANSEN, ELIZABETH

HAUSMANN, WERNER K.
HAY, PHD., VICTORIA
HAY, VICTORIA
HECHLER, DAVID
HELM, SYLVIA
HOROWITZ, SHEL ALAN
JOHNSON, JAN
JOHNSTON, MELANIE LEE
KLINE, LLOYD W.
KOLUS, HOWARD
KONNER, LINDA
KREIG, ANDREW, ESQ.
LEONARD, JOHN EDWARD
LESLIE, JACQUES
LEVIN, AARON
LEVINE, FAYE
LOOMIS, JAMIE
LOSCHIAVO, LINDA ANN
LYNCH, PAT
MALLETTE, MAL
MARGOLIS, LYNNE
MAYNARD, JOANNA
MEOLA, PATRICIA E.
MILNE, ROBERT SCOTT
MORRILL, STEPHEN
NASON, STEPHEN
NOVITZ, CHARLES R.
PALMQUIST, RON
PARADISE, PAUL RICHARD
PARK, ED
PAUST, GIL
PERLOFF, SUSAN
ROSENBERG, SHIRLEY
 SIROTA
ROSS, MARILYN HEIMBERG
RUDOLPH, JOHN K.
SHELDON, GEORGE
SIEGEL, DOROTHY
SILBEY, PAULA J.
SMITH, RUTH BAYARD
STEIN, HERBERT G.
TEMKO, FLORENCE
TUTHILL JR., OLIVER W.
WALTER, EUGENE
WALTERS GROUP
WATLINGTON, JERILYNN
WELCH, RANDY
WHALIN, W. TERRY
WHITLEY, SHARON
WOOD, SHARON M.
WOODARD, BERT

MANAGEMENT

ALLEN, LOUIS A.
ARKIN, JOSEPH
BABSON, O. BONNI
BAER, ORA JUDITH
BARSKY, MARTIN
BATTERSBY, MARK E.
BEHRENS, JOHN

BIGELOW, ROBERT
BLISHAK, SYLVIA ANN
BLOOM, MURRAY TEIGH
BROY, ANTHONY
CALABRO, MARIAN
CARUBA, ALAN
CASSELL, DANA
CONNOR, J. ROBERT
CORWEN, LEONARD
CROSS, WILBUR
DANOWSKI, JENNY
DONELSON, IRENE
DREYFACK, RAYMOND
FNA NEWS
FOX, BARRY
FUSCO, MARY ANN
 CASTRONOVO
GOODWIN, DAVE
GREENGARD, SAMUEL
GRIFFIN, KELLY L.
HADDOCK, PATRICIA
HARDER, PAUL B.
HINTZ, MARTIN
HOCH, DR. DEAN E.
HOCH, NANCY M.
HOFFMAN, NANCY YANES
IACONETTI, JOAN
IRA, ALLEN
JACOBS, DORRI
K-TURKEL, JUDI
KANIGEL, ROBERT
KIMMERLY, MAUREEN C.
KLINE, LLOYD W.
KOERNER, THOMAS F.
LAGAN, CONSTANCE
 HALLINAN
LAMONT, DOUGLAS
LEDERER, MURIEL
LEERBURGER, BENEDICT
LOSCHIAVO, LINDA ANN
MATURI, RICHARDS J.
MCCARTNEY, LUCINDA L.
MCCORMICK, MICHELE
MENKUS, BELDEN
MILLER, BRUCE
MIX, SHELDON A.
MOLDAFSKY, ANNIE
MORGAN, JOHN S.
NASON, STEPHEN
NEWCOMB, DUANE G.
NICKLAS, NICK
NOSSAMAN, MICHAEL
NOVITZ, CHARLES R.
OGDEN, SHEPHERD
PALMQUIST, RON
PETERSON, FRANKLYNN
PITTMAN, RUTH
POPHAL, LIN GRENSING-
RAKSTIS, TED J.
ROESSING, WALTER
ROTHMAN, HOWARD

SCHERMERHORN, DERICK D.
SCHOTT-JONES, ELAINE
SCOTT, GINI GRAHAM
SEITEL, FRASER PAUL
SHAPIRO, PATRICIA
  GOTTLIEB
SHERWOOD, HUGH C.
SMITH, BEVERLY BUSH
STICKLER, JOHN C.
TURECAMO, DORRINE
WARREN, DAVID
WEISBERG, JACOB
WELCH, RANDY
WHITFORD, JAMES
WOODSON, R. DODGE
WRIGHT, SYLVIA HOEHNS

MARINE

BEHRENS, JOHN
BRESLAV, MARC
CANDLER, JULIE
CANDLER, JULIE
COX, VIC
DEMAN, ELAINE
DUNHAM, ROBERT
FEIT, EDWARD
FNA NEWS
FRIESE, RICK
GANNON, ROBERT
GEBHART, FRED
GORDON, BERNARD LUDWIG
GROENE, JANET
HARKNESS, CHRIS
HAUSER, HILLARY
HOYT, ERICH
MCCARTNEY, LUCINDA L.
MCKEOWN, WM. TAYLOR
MCPHEE, MARNIE
MILNE, ROBERT SCOTT
MORGAN, ARJAY
MORGAN, MURRAY
MORRILL, STEPHEN
POLKING, MISS KIRK
ROESSING, WALTER
SWANN, CHRISTOPHER
WALKER, DR. MORTON

MARKETING

ASTON, ATHINA LEKA
BARONE, JEANINE
BARSKY, MARTIN
BARTEL, PAULINE C.
BLY, ROBERT W.
BUDROW, NANCY
BYAM, LINDA G.
CARUBA, ALAN
CASSELL, DANA
CHRISTIAN, ALLGAIER
  DONNA

CRANDELL, CHERYL
CROSS, WILBUR
CROSS, WILBUR
DALEY, LAVERNE
DAVIS, BEATRICE G.
DETZ, JOAN
DIAMOND, LEN
FOX, BARRY
GEBHART, FRED
GLASSER, SELMA
GREENBERG, JAN
HADDOCK, PATRICIA
HAIT, PAM
HOROWITZ, SHEL ALAN
IRA, ALLEN
JAMISON, WARREN
JOHNSTON, MELANIE LEE
KLINE, LLOYD W.
LAMONT, DOUGLAS
LEDERER, MURIEL
LEERBURGER, BENEDICT
LEVY, RICHARD C.
LOSCHIAVO, LINDA ANN
MARGOLIS, LYNNE
MASARACCHIA, SUSAN
MATURI, RICHARDS J.
MCCORMICK, MICHELE
MESSNER, FRED R.
MOLDAFSKY, ANNIE
MUMMERT, ROGER
NELSON, ED
NOSSAMAN, MICHAEL
OGDEN, SHEPHERD
PAUST, GIL
RAKSTIS, TED J.
REISS, ALVIN H.
ROGERS, KRISTA
SAKELY, THOMAS
SEITEL, FRASER PAUL
SHELDON, GEORGE
SILBEY, PAULA J.
STICKLER, JOHN C.
TUTHILL JR., OLIVER W.
WESTHEIMER, MARY
WOODSON, R. DODGE

MEDIA

AUSTIN, JOHN
BARTEL, PAULINE C.
BEHRENS, JOHN
BERMAN, BRIAN J.
BOUCHIER, DAVID
BROOKS, PATRICIA
CARRENO, RICHARD D.
CARUBA, ALAN
CASSELL, DANA
CATALANO, JULIE
CHAGALL, DAVID
CLARKE, PHILIP C.
CLARKE, PHILIP C.

COAN, PETER M.
COLEMAN, A.D.
COREY, JOHN R.
DAVIDSON, MARK
DEBARTOLO, ANTHONY
DUSKY, LORRAINE
ENGLISH, JOHN W.
FENSCH, THOMAS C.
FNA NEWS
GALLAGHER, RACHEL
GEBHART, FRED
GLASS, JUDITH E.
GOODSELL, JAMES NELSON
GREENBERG, JAN
HEMMING, ROY
HENNESSEE, JUDITH ADLER
HILL, NORMAN
HODGE, ADELE
HOLDER, DENNIS
HOWE, RUSSELL WARREN
IRA, ALLEN
JOHNSTON, MELANIE LEE
JOLLIFFE, LEE
LESLIE, JACQUES
MACDONALD, SANDY
MALLETTE, MAL
MARGOLIS, LYNNE
MASARACCHIA, SUSAN
MASTROLIA, LILYAN S.
MCCOMB, GORDON
MEOLA, PATRICIA E.
MESSNER, FRED R.
MILLER, BRUCE
MILNE, ROBERT SCOTT
NASON, STEPHEN
NEMIROW-NELSON, JILL
NOVITZ, CHARLES R.
PALMQUIST, RON
PINKWAS, STAN
POPHAL, LIN GRENSING-
RODNEY, JAMES C.
SECUNDA, VICTORIA
SMITH, RUTH BAYARD
SOHN, DAVID A.
SOTER, TOM
STAR, JACK
STEIN, M. L.
STUART, ANNE ELIZABETH
SZUPROWICZ, BOHDAN O.
URROWS, HENRY AND
  ELIZABETH
VALENTI, DAN
VAN DILLEN, LAILEE
WHITNALL, JACK
YARMON, MORTON
ZIMMERMAN, DAVID R.

MEDICAL

ACKERMAN, DR., LOWELL
ALPER, PHILIP

ALPERSTEIN, ELLEN
ANDERSON, ERIC G.
ANDERSON, KENNETH N.
ANDERSON, KENNETH N.
ARRIGO, MARY
BAER, ORA JUDITH
BAHR, ROBERT A.
BARNES-SVARNEY,
  PATRICIA L.
BARONE, JEANINE
BARTEL, PAULINE C.
BASCH, BUDDY
BELL, SALLY
BENSON, VIRGINIA PERKINS
BENZAIA, DIANA
BERRY, S.L.
BIRNBAUM, NATALIE
BLY, ROBERT W.
BODGER, CAROLE
BOTWIN, CAROL
BRAUN, VICKI
BREECHER, M.P.H.,
  MAURY M.
BRINLEY, MARYANN
  BUCKNUM
BRODSKY, RUTHAN
CAREW, RUTH M. HARMER
CARUANA, CLAUDIA M.
CASANO, KATE
CATALANO, JULIE
CLAXTON, COLETTE
COHEN, DANIEL
COX, VIC
CUMMINGS, SANDRA OTTO
DEANE, BARBARA
DICTOR-LEBLANC, RENA
DONELSON, IRENE
DOWNEY, CHARLES E.
DUNAIEF, LEAH S.
EDSON, LEE
EGERTON, JOHN
ENGH, JERI
EVANS, GLEN
FARIS, CHARLENE
FELD, KAREN
FINGER, ANNE L.
FINLEY, MITCH
FNA NEWS
FOX, BARRY
FUERST, MARK L.
GALUB, JACK
GEBHART, FRED
GERSON, VICKI
GEYER, SHERREE
GLASS, JUDITH E.
GLASSER, SELMA
GOLIN, MILTON
GOODHEART, BARBARA
GOODING, JUDSON
GREENBERG, JAN
GREENGARD, SAMUEL

HAIT, PAM
HAMMER, ROGER A.
HEATH, JARRETT A.
HEILMAN, JOAN RATTNER
HEITZIG, JAMES L.
HELLMAN, HAL
HELM, SYLVIA
HENLEY, ARTHUR
HOCHMAN, GLORIA
HOFFMAN, NANCY YANES
HORNBAKER, ALICE J.
HUBBELL, JOHN G.
HURWOOD, BERNHARDT J.
IRA, ALLEN
ISAACS, FLORENCE
JACOKES, DIANE
JAMISON, WARREN
JENSEN, CHERYL
JOSEPH, LOU
KAHN, ADA PASKIND
KANIGEL, ROBERT
KAVALER, LUCY
KITAY, WILLIAM
KLINE, LLOYD W.
KOONTZ, KATY
KRANISH, ARTHUR
LAMPE, DAVID
LARBERG, ANN
LEBLANC, RENA DICTOR
LEERBURGER, BENEDICT
LEVIN, AARON
LEVINE, FAYE
LEVINSON, ROBIN
LEVY, ERIC
LEWIS, HOWARD R.
LICHTENBERG, MARGARET
  KLEE
LIPPERT, JOAN
LOOMIS, JAMIE
LORENZ-FIFE, IRIS
LOSCHIAVO, LINDA ANN
LYONS, CHRISTINE
MALLETTE, MAL
MARQUARDT, DEBORAH
MASARACCHIA, SUSAN
MASSOW, ROSALIND
MASTROLIA, LILYAN S.
MERWIN, PHILIP DEAN
MILLER, DOROTHY G.
MILLMAN, SANDY K.
MONSON, NANCY P.
MORRIS, MRS. TERRY
MURPHY, WENDY B.
OPPENHEIM M.D., MICHAEL
PERLOFF, SUSAN
PIZER, VERNON
PLUMEZ, DR. JACQUELINE
  HORNER
PODOLSKY, M. LAWRENCE
POWER, CHARLOTTE A.
ROBERTS, D.P.M.,

ELIZABETH H.
ROCK, MAXINE
RODDIN, MIKE
ROTHMAN, HOWARD
SABIN, FRANCENE
SCHULTZ, DODI
SCHWARZ, TED
SEAMAN, BARBARA
SEIDEN, OTHNIEL J.
SHAPIRO, PATRICIA
  GOTTLIEB
SHIMBERG, ELAINE FANTLE
SIEGEL, DOROTHY
SIEGEL, PAULA M.
SMITH, CARIN A., DVM
SOMAN, SHIRLEY CAMPER
STUART, ANNE ELIZABETH
TANNE, JANICE HOPKINS
TAYLOR, GARY
TEGELER, DOROTHY
TONNESSEN, DIANA
URROWS, HENRY AND
  ELIZABETH
VAN COLLIE, SHIMON-CRAIG
WALKER, DR. MORTON
WALKER, GLADYS H.
WALTERS GROUP
WESSEL, MORRIS A.
WHITLEY, SHARON
WOLKOMIR, RICHARD AND
  JOYCE ROGERS
WOLKOMIR
ZATZ, ARLINE
ZIMMERMAN, DAVID R.
ZWICKER, DENISE ALLEN

MEDICAL ECONOMICS

EGERTON, JOHN

MEN'S INTEREST

BAHR, ROBERT A.
BARONE, JEANINE
BARRY, DON
BERGER, IVAN
BLIZZARD, WILLIAM C.
BOSE, MICHAEL ALAN
BOYKIN, JOHN E.
BRIGHTMAN, ROBERT
CLINE, ANDY
CONNOR, J. ROBERT
DALRYMPLE, BYRON W.
DEVANEY, JOHN
DOWNEY, CHARLES E.
DUNHAM, ROBERT
ELLIOTT, CHARLES
FEHL, MARTHA R.
FORTNEY, DAVID L.
GEBHART, FRED
GREENGARD, SAMUEL

IRA, ALLEN
JANICKI, EDWARD
JOURNEY, ALFRED E. 'BUD'
KARAS, NICHOLAS
KNIGHT, DOUG
KNIGHT, MRS. RICHARD
  ALDEN
LEIF, ROBERT
MATURI, RICHARDS J.
MEOLA, PATRICIA E.
MOLDAFSKY, ANNIE
NEELY, WILLIAM
OLNEY, ROSS R.
ROESSING, WALTER
ROGAK, LISA
ROSENDO, JOSEPH
SCAGNETTI, JACK
SPRINGER, P. GREGORY
TANNE, JANICE HOPKINS
TROMBETTI, STEVEN E.
ULRICH, ELISE VONS
ZURCHER, MARVIN

MILITARY

ALBANESE, DAVID J.
ANDERSON, ERIC G.
CLARKE, PHILIP C.
CORBETT, GERALDINE
FEIT, EDWARD
FEUER, A.B.
FNA NEWS
GLINES, CARROLL V.
HAMMEL, ERIC
HOWE, RUSSELL WARREN
JACKSON, WILLIAM S.
KNIGHT, DOUG
LAMPE, DAVID
MCCLENDON, SARAH
MCCORMICK, MICHELE
MORLAND, ALVIN
NELSON, ED
NOSSAMAN, MICHAEL
PAANANEN, ELOISE
REARDEN, JIM
ROSENBERG, SHIRLEY
  SIROTA
SLEAR, TOM
SULLIVAN, GEORGE

MOTIVATION

BARSKY, MARTIN
BEHRENS, JOHN
BREECHER, M.P.H.,
  MAURY M.
DAVIS, BEATRICE G.
DODGE, ELLIN
FEHL, MARTHA R.
FOX, BARRY
HADDOCK, PATRICIA

HEATH, JARRETT A.
HOFFMAN, NANCY YANES
IACONETTI, JOAN
IRA, ALLEN
KONNER, LINDA
LORENZ-FIFE, IRIS
LOSCHIAVO, LINDA ANN
NADEL PH.D., LAURIE
NELSON, ED
NOVITZ, CHARLES R.
RAKSTIS, TED J.
ROES, NICHOLAS A.
SHEIN, ARN
WRIGHT, SYLVIA HOEHNS
YUDKIN, MARCIA

MOVIE REVIEWS

DARLINGTON, JOY
DEVINE, GEORGE
FNA NEWS
GATTO, JOHN TAYLOR
GLASSER, SELMA
HALPERN, FRANCES
HEMMING, ROY
KNIGHT, DOUG
LANGER, CASSANDRA
LOSCHIAVO, LINDA ANN
MARGOLIS, LYNNE
MASTROLIA, LILYAN S.
ROBERTS, JANET M.
SOTER, TOM
SPRINGER, P. GREGORY
TUTHILL JR., OLIVER W.
WUCHERER, RUTH

NATURE

ABBOTT, R. TUCKER
ALPERSTEIN, ELLEN
ANDERSON, KENNETH N.
ARNETTE, JOSEPH
AUERBACK, PHD., STEVANNE
BARNES, JILL
BARNES-SVARNEY,
  PATRICIA L.
BARRY, DON
BASSETT, ELIZABETH
BAUER, ERWIN A.
BERMAN, BRIAN J.
BLUE, MARIAN
BOONE, GENE
BRESLAV, MARC
BUDROW, NANCY
BURCH, MONTE
CALABRO, MARIAN
CELLIERS, PETER J.
CLEDE, BILL
CLINE, ANDY
COAN, PETER M.
COCHRAN, ADA

COX, VIC
DALY, MAUREEN
DAVENPORT, ARTHUR
DAVIDSON, MARK
DEGNAN, JAMES P.
DRISCOLL, CYNTHIA
ENGMAN, RONDA
FEHL, MARTHA R.
FORTSON, LOWRANCE
  SANNA
FRAZER, LANCE
FROME, MICHAEL
GANNON, ROBERT
GEBHART, FRED
GLASS, JUDITH E.
GLASSER, SELMA
GORDON, BERNARD LUDWIG
GRANT, NANCY S.
GRESHAM, GRITS
HAAPOJA, MARGARET A.
HAY, PHD., VICTORIA
HAY, VICTORIA
HECHT, JEFF
HELLMAN, HAL
HIBBEN, DR. FRANK C.
HICKS, JUNE L.
HOYT, ERICH
IRA, ALLEN
JOHNSON, SABEEHA H.
JOURNEY, ALFRED E. 'BUD'
KAUFMAN, WALLACE
KAVALER, LUCY
KAYE, EVELYN
KEIL, BILL
KINGDOM, GERRY
KNIGHT, DOUG
KOONTZ, KATY
KRANISH, ARTHUR
LAMANGA, JOSEPH
LAMPE, DAVID
LANGER, CASSANDRA
LEE, SHIRLEY
LEERBURGER, BENEDICT
LOOMIS, JAMIE
MARGOLIS, LYNNE
MASON, LEE FRANZ
MATTHEWS, DOWNS
MCCARTNEY, LUCINDA L.
MCKEOWN, WM. TAYLOR
MCPHEE, MARNIE
MESSINEO, JOHN
MIRVIS, KENNETH W.
MIX, SHELDON A.
MORRILL, STEPHEN
NEELY, BONNIE BURGESS
NORTON, PHILLIP
OGDEN, SHEPHERD
PARK, ED
PAUST, GIL
PERRY, ERMA
PLANT, JANET

PODOLSKY, M. LAWRENCE
POSTER, CAROL
RANDOLPH, ELIZABETH
REARDEN, JIM
REIMER, KATHLEEN
RICCIUTI, EDWARD R.
RIEGER, TED
ROBERTS, JANET M.
RODNEY, JAMES C.
ROGERS, BARBARA
  RADCLIFFE
SABIN, FRANCENE
SOLOMON, GOODY L.
TANNER, OGDEN
TERRES, JOHN K.
THOMSON, PEGGY
WALKER, DR. MORTON
WALTON, CHELLE KOSTER
WESLEY, MARX
WILCOX, CHARLOTTE
WILLIAMS, RUSSELL J.
YOUNG, DONALD
ZATZ, ARLINE
ZURCHER, MARVIN

NEWS

ALPER, PHILIP
ALPERN, DAVID M.
BEAUGE, JOHN Q.
BELL, SALLY
BERMAN, BRIAN J.
BROWN, GAIL
CANNON, DORIS
CASS, MAXINE
CHIN, RUTH
CLARKE, PHILIP C.
COYLE, ELIZABETH
CROTEAU, MAUREEN E.
CUMMINGS, SANDRA OTTO
DALY, MAUREEN
DALY, MAUREEN
DAVIDSON, MARK
DEGREGORIO, WILLIAM A.
DOWNEY, CHARLES E.
DUNAWAY, JAMES O.
FEHL, MARTHA R.
FELD, KAREN
FENSCH, THOMAS C.
FINKE, BLYTHE FOOTE
FNA NEWS
FORTNEY, DAVID L.
FREEDMAN, ERIC
GEBHART, FRED
GELTNER, SHARON
GLASS, JUDITH E.
GOODMAN, JACK
HACKETT, BLANCHE
HAMMEL, ERIC
HAMMER, ROGER A.
HEATH, JARRETT A.

HECHLER, DAVID
HELM, SYLVIA
HINTZ, MARTIN
HOCHMAN, GLORIA
HOLCOMB, GEORGE B.
HONE, HARRY
HOROWITZ, SHEL ALAN
IRA, ALLEN
JOURNEY, ALFRED E. 'BUD'
KLAUS, BARBARA
KLINE, LLOYD W.
KNICELY, FAY
KRANISH, ARTHUR
KRASNER, MICHAEL F.
LARBERG, ANN
LEVINE, FAYE
LEVY, ERIC
LEVY, RICHARD C.
LEWIS, PARNELLS
LORE, DIANE C.
LOSCHIAVO, LINDA ANN
LYONS, CHRISTINE
MAPPES, DR. CARL R.
MEOLA, PATRICIA E.
MICHAEL, JOYCE EMMETT
MICHAEL, JOYCE EMMETT
MILLER AND MARK ELLIS
MILLER, JUDITH BRAFFMAN
MORGAN, ARJAY
MORRILL, STEPHEN
NASON, STEPHEN
NELSON, ED
NOVITZ, CHARLES R.
OATIS, JONATHAN W.
POGREBIN, LETTY COTTIN
POLAND, NANCY
RUDOLPH, JOHN K.
SHEVIS, JIM
SILBEY, PAULA J.
SISCO, PAUL C.
SMALL, SYLVIA ADAMSON
SOTER, TOM
TUTHILL JR., OLIVER W.
VIORST, MILTON
WELCH, RANDY
WILCOX, CHARLOTTE
WOODARD, BERT
ZURCHER, MARVIN

PERSONAL FINANCE

AUERBACH, SYLVIA
BEHRENS, JOHN
BLOCK, JULIAN
BLODGETT, RICHARD
BLOOM, MURRAY TEIGH
CHELEKIS, GEORGE
CLINE, ANDY
CONNIFF, JAMES C. G.
DIDDLEBOCK, BOB
DOWNEY, CHARLES E.

DUNNAN, NANCY
EDSON, ANDREW S.
EISENSTEIN, PAUL A.
FAUX, MARIAN
FEHL, MARTHA R.
FNA NEWS
FRASER, BRUCE W.
GEBHART, FRED
GEM PUBLISHING GROUP
GEORGE, KATHRYN E.
GERMAN-GRAPES, JOAN
GREENGARD, SAMUEL
GROENE, GORDON &
GROENE, JANET
HELM, SYLVIA
HONE, HARRY
IRA, ALLEN
JOHNSTON, MELANIE LEE
K-TURKEL, JUDI
KAUFMAN, WALLACE
KELLY, KATE
LINDSAY, RAE
LORENZ-FIFE, IRIS
MALOTT, GENE
MARGOLIUS, ESTHER
MASTROLIA, LILYAN S.
MATURI, RICHARDS J.
MCCARTNEY, LUCINDA L.
MINKOW, ROSALIE
MOLDAFSKY, ANNIE
MOST, BRUCE W.
NASON, STEPHEN
NEMIRO, BEVERLY
  ANDERSON
NOVITZ, CHARLES R.
PAAJANEN, ANNETTE LAABS
PODOLSKY, M. LAWRENCE
ROES, NICHOLAS A.
ROESSING, WALTER
SHERWOOD, HUGH C.
SLEAR, TOM
SLOME, JESSE R.
STAR, JACK
STEINER, SHARI
STODDARD, BROOKE C.
TAJER, JOSIE
TAYLOR, GARY
THOMPSON, JACQUELINE
WEINSTEIN, GRACE W.
WHITFORD, JAMES
WHITLEY, SHARON
WOODSON, R. DODGE
YARMON, MORTON
ZWEIG, PHILLIP L.

PERSONALITIES

ARCELLA, LISA
ARDMORE, JANE KESNER
BANDLER, MICHAEL J.
BAYERS, RAPP LEA

BEEBE, F. LISA
BEHRENS, JOHN
BELL, JOSEPH N.
BERG, MARGARET C.
BERGER, AMY H.
BERRY, S.L.
BISHER, FURMAN
BITETTI, MARGE
BLIZZARD, WILLIAM C.
BLOCK, JEAN LIBMAN
BLUE, MARIAN
BOSCO, ANTOINETTE
BRESCOLL, JAMES
BROOKS, PATRICIA
BUCHMAN, DIAN DINCIN
BURTON, MARDA
CARUBA, ALAN
CASS, MAXINE
CASSILL, KAY
CATALANO, JULIE
CHARLES, JOANNA
CHIN, RUTH
CIRONE, BETTINA
CLARK, LARRY
COAN, PETER M.
COLBERT, JUDY
CONNIFF, JAMES C. G.
CORBETT, GERALDINE
COX, VIC
COYLE, ELIZABETH
CURRAN, BOB
DAILY, LAURA
DALY, MAUREEN
DAVID, LESTER
DAVIS, ELISE MILLER
DAVIS, O. K.
DEANE, BARBARA
DEGNAN, JAMES P.
DEGREGORIO, WILLIAM A.
DENNY, ALMA
DICTOR-LEBLANC, RENA
DODGE, ELLIN
DOWNEY, CHARLES E.
DRAGONWAGON, CRESCENT
DUNAWAY, JAMES O.
DYKEMAN, WILMA
EDSON, LEE
ENGLE, PAANANEN ELOISE
EVANS, GLEN
FELD, KAREN
FONTAINE, ANDRE
FORTNEY, DAVID L.
FOSTER, NANCY
FOX, BARRY
FRAZER, LANCE
FRIED, EUNICE
FRIED, EUNICE
FUSCO, MARY ANN
  CASTRONOVO
GALLO, DIANE
GIBBS, RAFE

GLASS, JUDITH E.
GOLDSTEIN, GREG
GOULD, LARK ELLEN
GRANT, NANCY S.
GROSSMAN, ELLIE
GUNST, KATHY
HAAPOJA, MARGARET A.
HAAS, ALAN D.
HAIT, PAM
HEILMAN, JOAN RATTNER
HELM, SYLVIA
HINTZ, MARTIN
HOCHMAN, GLORIA
HODGE, ADELE
HOLDER, DENNIS
HONE, HARRY
HORNBAKER, ALICE J.
HORNER, SHIRLEY
HORNSTEIN, HAROLD
HOUSTON, RUTH
HOWARD, ELIZABETH M.
HUBBELL, JOHN G.
HURWOOD, BERNHARDT J.
INGE, ARLINE
IRA, ALLEN
JACOKES, DIANE
JOHNSON, SABEEHA H.
JOHNSTON, MELANIE LEE
KONNER, LINDA
KREDENSER, PETER
KUHN, IRENE CORBALLY
LAMPE, DAVID
LANDT, DENNIS
LANGWORTH, RICHARD M.
LEBLANC, RENA DICTOR
LEE, SHIRLEY
LEMKOWITZ, FLORENCE
LEVINE, FAYE
LEVINSON, ROBIN
LEVITSKY, DR. SERGE L.
LICHTENBERG, MARGARET
  KLEE
LOOMIS, JAMIE
LORENZ-FIFE, IRIS
LOSCHIAVO, LINDA ANN
LYONS, CHRISTINE
MALLETTE, MAL
MARGOLIS, LYNNE
MARTIN, MILDRED CROWL
MASARACCHIA, SUSAN
MASTROLIA, LILYAN S.
MATUSIK, JO ELLEN
MCDOWELL, LEONARD O.
MCPHEE, MARNIE
MEOLA, PATRICIA E.
MERWIN, PHILIP DEAN
MICHAEL, JOYCE EMMETT
MILLNER, CORK
MOLDAFSKY, ANNIE
MONTGOMERY, ED
MORRIS, HAL

MOSKIN, J. ROBERT
NEELY, BONNIE BURGESS
NUWER, HANK
O'REILLY, DON
OLNEY, ROSS R.
PERRY, ERMA
PFEIFER, LUANNE
PICKENS, THOMAS M.
PINES, MAYA
PITTMAN, RUTH
POGUE, FORREST C.
POLAND, NANCY
POWER, CHARLOTTE A.
REYNOLDS, WILLIAM J.
ROSEN, M. DANIEL
RUSSELL, FRED
SABIN, FRANCENE
SAFRAN, CLAIRE
SCHREIBER, NORMAN
SEAMAN, BARBARA
SERVINO, CAROL
SHAKESPEARE, MARGARET
SHAW, EVA
SHEIN, ARN
SHELDON, GEORGE
SHUBIN, SEYMOUR
SIEGEL, DOROTHY
SILBEY, PAULA J.
SKLAR, DUSTY
SLATE, LIBBY
SMALL, SYLVIA ADAMSON
SMITH, LEE A.
SMITH, RICHARD AUSTIN
SOMAN, SHIRLEY CAMPER
STACK, ROBERT
STAUB, MOLLY AROST
STEINBERG, JANET
THOMSON, PEGGY
URROWS, HENRY AND
  ELIZABETH
VAN DILLEN, LAILEE
VOTANO, PAUL A.
WALTER, CLAIRE
WALTER, EUGENE
WATSON, DELMAR
WHALIN, W. TERRY
WHITLEY, SHARON
WOODARD, BERT
WRIGHT JR., ED
ZATZ, ARLINE

PHILOSOPHY

BAHR, ROBERT A.
BEEBE, F. LISA
BELL, JOSEPH N.
BOEHM, GEORGE A. W.
BRESCOLL, JAMES
COLTON, HELEN
DENNY, ALMA
DEVINE, GEORGE

EDSON, LEE
ELWOOD, MRS. EDITH
  MUESING
ENGH, JERI
FERMAN, IRVING
FONTAINE, ANDRE
FRUMKES, LEWIS BURKE
GORDON, BERNARD LUDWIG
GRICE, MARY A.
HAMALIAN, LEO
HOCHMAN, GLORIA
HONE, HARRY
HUFF, DARRELL
JOHNSON, JAN
LAYNE, MARIE
LEONARD, GEORGE
MOSLEY, JEAN BELL
MURPHY, RAYMOND J.
SKLAR, DUSTY
SMITH, LIZ
SOHN, DAVID A.
STOCKER, JOSEPH
TRILLING, DIANA
TUTHILL JR., OLIVER W.

PHOTOGRAPHY

ANDERSON, ERIC G.
BARNES-SVARNEY,
  PATRICIA L.
BARRINGTON, CAROL
  BISBEE
BERG, MARGARET C.
BERGER, IVAN
BERGER, IVAN
BERMAN, BRIAN J.
BOREA, PHYLLIS GILBERT
BRIGHTMAN, ROBERT
BUDROW, NANCY
BURTON, MARDA
CAMPER, FRED
CASS, MAXINE
COHEN, DANIEL
COLEMAN, A.D.
DE CRISTOFORO, R. J.
DEMAN, ELAINE
DOWNEY, CHARLES E.
ENGH, JERI
FEHL, MARTHA R.
FENSCH, THOMAS C.
FNA NEWS
FRIESE, RICK
GAMAGE, DOUGLAS C.
GEBHART, FRED
GRAF, RUDOLF F.
GREENGARD, SAMUEL
GREWELL, BOB
GRIMM, TOM
GROENE, GORDON &
  GROENE, JANET
HANSEN, ELIZABETH

HARKNESS, CHRIS
HARRIS, ELEANOR
HYYPIA, JORMA
JOURNEY, ALFRED E. 'BUD'
KOONTZ, KATY
LARBERG, ANN
LEVIN, AARON
MARGOLIS, LYNNE
MARTIN, NORMA MILNER
MASARACCHIA, SUSAN
MASON, LEE FRANZ
MCCOMB, GORDON
MESSINEO, JOHN
NADLER, BOB
NELSON, JANET
OGDEN, SHEPHERD
PAAJANEN, ANNETTE LAABS
PARK, ED
PAUGH, TOM
PODOLSKY, M. LAWRENCE
ROBERTS, JANET M.
ROWLES, GENEVIEVE
SABIN, FRANCENE
SCHOTT-JONES, ELAINE
SCHREIBER, NORMAN
SCHWARZ, TED
SCOTT, GINI GRAHAM
SHELDON, GEORGE
SHERMAN, SIGNE L.
SMALL, SYLVIA ADAMSON
STEINER, SHARI
TUTHILL JR., OLIVER W.
VOLLMAR, ALICE M.
WATSON, DELMAR
WHITLEY, SHARON
WHITNALL, JACK
WOODSON, R. DODGE
YARBROUGH, CAROLYN J.
ZATZ, ARLINE
ZURCHER, MARVIN

PHYSICAL FITNESS

ALPERSTEIN, ELLEN
ANDERSON, KENNETH N.
BAHR, ROBERT A.
BARONE, JEANINE
BERRY, S.L.
BRAUN, VICKI
BREECHER, M.P.H.,
  MAURY M.
BRODSKY, RUTHAN
CATALANO, JULIE
DAILY, LAURA
DEANE, BARBARA
DOWNEY, CHARLES E.
FEHL, MARTHA R.
FNA NEWS
GEBHART, FRED
IRA, ALLEN
JAMISON, WARREN

KONNER, LINDA
KOONTZ, KATY
LEE, SHIRLEY
LEW, IRVINA
LIPPERT, JOAN
LORENZ-FIFE, IRIS
LOSCHIAVO, LINDA ANN
MALLETTE, MAL
MONSON, NANCY P.
NADEL PH.D., LAURIE
NEELY, BONNIE BURGESS
NEMIRO, BEVERLY
  ANDERSON
NEMIROW-NELSON, JILL
PFEIFER, LUANNE
ROBERTS, D.P.M.,
  ELIZABETH H.
ROCK, MAXINE
ROGAK, LISA
ROTHMAN, HOWARD
SHAW, EVA
SIEGEL, MARY ELLEN
SIEGEL, PAULA M.
SLEAR, TOM
STUART, KIEL
TANNE, JANICE HOPKINS
THOMPSON, JACQUELINE
TONNESSEN, DIANA
ULRICH, ELISE VONS
WALKER, DR. MORTON
WATLINGTON, JERILYNN
ZATZ, ARLINE

PSYCHOLOGY

ARRIGO, MARY
AUERBACK, PHD., STEVANNE
BAHR, ROBERT A.
BAILEY, JANET
BALDWIN, JOYCE
BARONE, JEANINE
BARTEL, PAULINE C.
BARTOCCI, BARBARA
BOTWIN, CAROL
BRAUN, VICKI
BREECHER, M.P.H.,
  MAURY M.
BRESNICK, JAN
BRINLEY, MARYANN
  BUCKNUM
BRODSKY, RUTHAN
CARUBA, ALAN
COLTON, HELEN
DARDICK, GEETA
DAVIDSON, MARK
DEANE, BARBARA
DENNY, ALMA
DOWNEY, CHARLES E.
ELLIS, ALBERT
FADER, SHIRLEY SLOAN
FEHL, MARTHA R.

FELDMAN, RUTH DUSKIN
FERTIG, JUDITH
FINGER, ANNE L.
FREEMAN, LUCY
FRUMKES, LEWIS BURKE
GALLO, DIANE
GLASSER, SELMA
GREENGARD, SAMUEL
GROSSMAN, ELLIE
HAMILTON, PHD., ELEANOR
HASKIN, PHD., JOHN A.
HEATH, JARRETT A.
HECHLER, DAVID
HELMLINGER, TRUDY
HENLEY, ARTHUR
HOCHMAN, GLORIA
HOFFMAN, NANCY YANES
HONE, HARRY
HOWARD, ELIZABETH M.
IRA, ALLEN
JOHNSON, JAN
KAHN, ADA PASKIND
KANIGEL, ROBERT
KEMPTON-SMITH, DEBBI
KOONTZ, KATY
LARBERG, ANN
LEBLANC, RENA DICTOR
LORENZ-FIFE, IRIS
LOSCHIAVO, LINDA ANN
MASTROLIA, LILYAN S.
MAXWELL, KATIE
MCNEES, PAT
MONSON, NANCY P.
NADEL PH.D., LAURIE
NEELY, BONNIE BURGESS
NELSON, ED
O'CONNOR, KAREN
PAAJANEN, ANNETTE LAABS
PERRY, SUSAN K.
PLUMEZ, DR. JACQUELINE
  HORNER
RAKSTIS, TED J.
ROESCH, ROBERTA
SECUNDA, VICTORIA
SHAPIRO, PATRICIA
  GOTTLIEB
SIEGEL, PAULA M.
SOMAN, SHIRLEY CAMPER
STICH, SALLY
TANNE, JANICE HOPKINS
TEGELER, DOROTHY
TESSINA, PHD., TINA B.
TUTHILL JR., OLIVER W.
WALKER, DR. MORTON
WATLINGTON, JERILYNN
WESTEN, ROBIN
WHITLEY, SHARON
WOLKOMIR, RICHARD AND
  JOYCE ROGERS
WOLKOMIR
YUDKIN, MARCIA

RELIGION

ANDERSON, JOAN WESTER
BAKER, SAMM SINCLAIR
BARTOCCI, BARBARA
BAYUS, LENORE
BENSON, VIRGINIA PERKINS
BERMAN, BRIAN J.
BITETTI, MARGE
BOSCO, ANTOINETTE
CAHILL, CARL
CHAGALL, DAVID
CLARK, LARRY
COCHRAN, ADA
COOPER, DR. JOHN C.
DEANE, BARBARA
DEVINE, GEORGE
FEHL, MARTHA R.
FELDMAN, RUTH DUSKIN
FINLEY, MITCH
FNA NEWS
GATTO, JOHN TAYLOR
GOODRICH, DONNA CLARK
GRICE, MARY A.
HAGGITH, DAVID
HALLADAY, GENEVA
HEATH, JARRETT A.
HINTZ, MARTIN
HONE, HARRY
JOHNSON, JAN
KRYMOW, VINCENZINA
KUSTANOWITZ, SHULAMIT E.
LARBERG, ANN
LAYNE, MARIE
LEVINE, FAYE
MARTIN, MILDRED CROWL
MCDOWELL, LEONARD O.
MENKUS, BELDEN
MEROWITZ, MORTON J.
MORRIS, GLEN
MOSLEY, JEAN BELL
NEELY, BONNIE BURGESS
O'CONNOR, KAREN
OWEN, JENNIFER BRYON
POGREBIN, LETTY COTTIN
REICHEK, MORTON
RICKS, JACKIE D.
SCHARFENBERGER, JOHN
SCHMITH, CINDY
SCHNEIDER-AKER,
  KATHERINE
SCOTT, GINI GRAHAM
SEAMANS, ANDY
SMITH, BEVERLY BUSH
STEPHEN, RAE
TOWLE, LISA H.
TURECAMO, DORRINE
VALENTI, DAN
VANDERTUIN, VICTORIA E.
WELCH, RANDY
WHALIN, W. TERRY

WHITLEY, SHARON
WILCOX, CHARLOTTE
WOLFE, DARRELL K.

SALES

BARSKY, MARTIN
BLISHAK, SYLVIA ANN
BLY, ROBERT W.
BOONE, GENE
CASSELL, DANA
CHELEKIS, GEORGE
FEHL, MARTHA R.
FOX, BARRY
HONE, HARRY
IRA, ALLEN
JAMISON, WARREN
KLINE, LLOYD W.
NELSON, ED
NOSSAMAN, MICHAEL
RAKSTIS, TED J.
SEAMANS, ANDY
SILBEY, PAULA J.
TUTHILL JR., OLIVER W.

SCIENCE

ALLEN, ROBERT A.
ALPER, PHILIP
ALPERSTEIN, ELLEN
ANDERSON, KENNETH N.
BAKAL, CARL
BAKER, CHRISTOPHER PAUL
BAKER, ROLINDA B.
BARNES-SVARNEY,
  PATRICIA L.
BARON, HARRY
BARONE, JEANINE
BARRY, DON
BARTEL, PAULINE C.
BELL, SALLY
BOEHM, GEORGE A. W.
BRESLAV, MARC
BRIGHTMAN, ROBERT
BROY, ANTHONY
CARUANA, CLAUDIA M.
CARUBA, ALAN
CASS, MAXINE
CHARLES, JOANNA
CLIFFORD, WILLIAM
CONNIFF, JAMES C. G.
CONNOR, J. ROBERT
COX, VIC
CROSS, WILBUR
DAVIDSON, MARK
DEMPEWOLFF, RICHARD F.
DIAMOND, LEN
DICTOR-LEBLANC, RENA
DUNAIEF, LEAH S.
EDSON, LEE
ENGLE, PAANANEN ELOISE

ENGLEBARDT, STANLEY L.
FALES, EDWARD
FANTEL, HAS
FEHL, MARTHA R.
FENTEN, D. X.
FNA NEWS
FRAZER, LANCE
FRIEDMAN, KENNETH A.
FRUMKES, LEWIS BURKE
GANNON, ROBERT
GEBHART, FRED
GIBBS, RAFE
GILES, DAVID N.
GOLIN, MILTON
GORDON, BERNARD LUDWIG
GRAF, RUDOLF F.
GRANHOLM, JACKSON W.
GREENGARD, SAMUEL
GREGG, JAMES R.
GRIFFIN, C. W.
HAMMER, ROGER A.
HECHT, JEFF
HEITZIG, JAMES L.
HELLMAN, HAL
HIBBEN, DR. FRANK C.
HOFFMAN, NANCY YANES
HOLCOMB, GEORGE B.
HOLTON, FELICIA
  ANTONELLI
HOYT, ERICH
HYYPIA, JORMA
IRA, ALLEN
IRA, ALLEN
JACOKES, DIANE
JOLLIFFE, LEE
JOSEPH, LOU
K-TURKEL, JUDI
KAHN, ADA PASKIND
KANIGEL, ROBERT
KAUFMAN, WALLACE
KAVALER, LUCY
KNIGHT, DOUG
KOWAL, JOHN PAUL
KRANISH, ARTHUR
LARBERG, ANN
LEBLANC, RENA DICTOR
LEERBURGER, BENEDICT
LEIF, ROBERT
LEVIN, AARON
LEVINE, FAYE
LEVINSON, ROBIN
LOSCHIAVO, LINDA ANN
LYON, DAVID
MACKOWSKI, MAURA J.
MAPPES, DR. CARL R.
MARTIN, NORMA MILNER
MASTROLIA, LILYAN S.
MATTHEWS, DOWNS
MICHAEL, JOYCE EMMETT
MILLER AND MARK ELLIS
  MILLER, JUDITH BRAFFMAN

MILNE, DR. MARGERY
MIRVIS, KENNETH W.
MOFFAT, SHANNON
MOST, BRUCE W.
MOYLAN, TOM
NADLER, BOB
NELSON, ED
NEWCOMB, DUANE G.
OPPENHEIM M.D., MICHAEL
OPPENHEIMER, ERNEST J.
PINES, MAYA
PIZER, VERNON
PODOLSKY, M. LAWRENCE
POLKING, MISS KIRK
PUGH JR., JAMES E.
RADCLIFFE, DONALD
REYNOLDS, WILLIAM J.
RICCIUTI, EDWARD R.
RIEGER, TED
RILLY, CHERYL
RIVOIRE, JOHN
RODNEY, JAMES C.
ROESSING, WALTER
ROGERS, KRISTA
SABIN, FRANCENE
SAMBROT, WILLIAM
SCHLOSS, MURIEL
SHERMAN, SIGNE L.
SMITH, CARIN A., DVM
SOMAN, SHIRLEY CAMPER
SPANO SR., JOHN J.
STITT, ABBY
SWANN, CHRISTOPHER
TANNE, JANICE HOPKINS
TRUBO, RICHARD
URROWS, HENRY AND
  ELIZABETH
WHITNALL, JACK
WINTER, RUTH
WOLKOMIR, RICHARD AND
  JOYCE ROGERS
  WOLKOMIR
WOLLMAN, JANE
WOLLMAN, PHYLLIS
WOOD, SHARON M.
ZIMMERMAN, DAVID R.

SENIOR CITIZENS

ALPERSTEIN, ELLEN
ANDERSON, ERIC G.
ANDERSON, KENNETH N.
AUERBACH, SYLVIA
BERMAN, BRIAN J.
BLASK, ANN SABATINI
BLIZZARD, WILLIAM C.
BOECKMAN, CHARLES
BOTTEL, HELEN
BRAUN, VICKI
BRINLEY, MARYANN
  BUCKNUM

BRODSKY, RUTHAN
CELLIERS, PETER J.
CHANDLER, JO
CIERVO, ARTHUR
CLAXTON, COLETTE
COCHRAN, ADA
COLTON, HELEN
CORBETT, GERALDINE
CORWEN, LEONARD
CROSS, WILBUR
CUMMINGS, SANDRA OTTO
DEANE, BARBARA
DONELSON, IRENE
DOWNEY, CHARLES E.
DUNHAM, ROBERT
FEHL, MARTHA R.
FINKE, BLYTHE FOOTE
GEBHART, FRED
GEM PUBLISHING GROUP
GILINSKY, RHODA M.
GLASSER, SELMA
GROENE, GORDON &
  GROENE, JANET
GROSSMAN, ELLIE
HAAPOJA, MARGARET A.
HAMILTON, PHD., ELEANOR
HARRIS, ELEANOR
HAY, VICTORIA
HEATH, JARRETT A.
HEILMAN, JOAN RATTNER
HENLEY, ARTHUR
HOFFMAN, NANCY YANES
HOLCOMB, GEORGE B.
HONE, HARRY
HORNBAKER, ALICE J.
HOWARD, ELIZABETH M.
JAMISON, WARREN
JENSEN, CHERYL
JOHNSTON, MELANIE LEE
KAHN, ADA PASKIND
KLINE, LLOYD W.
KRYMOW, VINCENZINA
LEBLANC, RENA DICTOR
LEERBURGER, BENEDICT
LEW, IRVINA
LICHTENBERG,
  MARGARET KLEE
MALLETTE, MAL
MALOTT, GENE
MARSH, SUSAN
MASSOW, ROSALIND
MASTROLIA, LILYAN S.
MATHEWS, BEVERLY
MAZIE, DAVID
MCCORMICK, MICHELE
MCVAY, ROSANNE
MOLDAFSKY, ANNIE
NEMIRO, BEVERLY
  ANDERSON
PARK, ED
PRYOR, HUBERT

ROBERTS, D.P.M.,
  ELIZABETH H.
ROCK, MAXINE
ROESCH, ROBERTA
ROESSING, WALTER
ROSENBAUM, HELEN
ROSS, BETTY
SANDEL, SUSAN L.
SHAW, EVA
SIEGEL, MARY ELLEN
SILBEY, PAULA J.
SOMAN, SHIRLEY CAMPER
TESSINA, PHD., TINA B.
TUPPER, MARGO
UCHITELLE, ROBERT
URROWS, HENRY AND
  ELIZABETH
WALKER, DR. MORTON
WEINSTEIN, GRACE W.
WESTGATE, ROBERT D.
WHITLEY, SHARON
WUCHERER, RUTH
ZATZ, ARLINE

SOCIAL TRENDS

ALPER, PHILIP
ANDERSON, ERIC G.
BAHR, ROBERT A.
BAKER, SAMM SINCLAIR
BASSETT, ELIZABETH
BELL, JOSEPH N.
BELL, SALLY
BERMAN, CLAIRE
BERRY, S.L.
BOTTEL, HELEN
BOTWIN, CAROL
BOUCHIER, DAVID
BYRNE-DODGE, TERESA
CAREW, RUTH M. HARMER
CARUBA, ALAN
CATALANO, JULIE
CHRISTENSEN, KAREN
CLARKE, PHILIP C.
COHEN, DANIEL
COLTON, HELEN
CONSIDINE, SHERIDAN
DALY, MAUREEN
DARLINGTON, JOY
DAVIDSON, MARK
DEANE, BARBARA
DEBARTOLO, ANTHONY
DENNY, ALMA
DRAGONWAGON, CRESCENT
ELWOOD, MRS. EDITH
  MUESING
EVANS, GLEN
FAUX, MARIAN
FEHL, MARTHA R.
FINGER, ANNE L.
FNA NEWS

FUSCO, MARY ANN
  CASTRONOVO
GALLAGHER, RACHEL
GEBHART, FRED
GILINSKY, RHODA M.
GOODING, JUDSON
GREENGARD, SAMUEL
GROSS, RONALD
GROSSINGER, TANIA
HAMILTON, PHD., ELEANOR
HARMON, MARY
HENNESSEE, JUDITH ADLER
HOCHMAN, GLORIA
HOROWITZ, SHEL ALAN
HOUSTON, RUTH
HOWARD, ELIZABETH M.
IRA, ALLEN
JOHNSON, JAN
JOHNSTON, MELANIE LEE
KAHN, ADA PASKIND
LAMPE, DAVID
LASHUA, MARGERY F.
LESLIE, JACQUES
LEVINE, FAYE
LEVY, RICHARD C.
LINDSAY, RAE
LONDON, BILL
LORENZ-FIFE, IRIS
LOSCHIAVO, LINDA ANN
MARGOLIS, LYNNE
MASARACCHIA, SUSAN
MASTROLIA, LILYAN S.
MAYER, BARBARA
MAZIE, DAVID
MCKEON, KEVIN
MCNEES, PAT
MILLER AND MARK ELLIS
  MILLER, JUDITH BRAFFMAN
MOATES, MARIANNE
  MERRILL
MOLDAFSKY, ANNIE
MOST, BRUCE W.
NEMIRO, BEVERLY
  ANDERSON
OGDEN, SHEPHERD
OLDS, SALLY WENDKOS
PAUST, GIL
PIZER, VERNON
PODOLSKY, M. LAWRENCE
POGREBIN, LETTY COTTIN
POLAND, NANCY
PURDY, SUSAN
RAKSTIS, TED J.
RAKSTIS, TED J.
REICHEK, MORTON
REISS, ALVIN H.
ROESSING, WALTER
RUDOLPH, JOHN K.
SAFRAN, CLAIRE
SCOBEY, JOAN
SCOTT, GINI GRAHAM

SEAMAN, BARBARA
SMITH, RUTH BAYARD
SOMAN, SHIRLEY CAMPER
STICKLER, JOHN C.
STITT, ABBY
TRILLING, DIANA
TURECAMO, DORRINE
URROWS, HENRY AND
  ELIZABETH
WALKER, GLADYS H.
WATLINGTON, JERILYNN
WESTHEIMER, MARY
WHITLEY, SHARON
WOLKOMIR, RICHARD AND
  JOYCE ROGERS
  WOLKOMIR
WOOG, DAN
YAGER, JAN
YARMON, MORTON
YUDKIN, MARCIA

SPORTS

ALPERSTEIN, ELLEN
ANDERSON, KENNETH N.
ARMSTRONG III, MARTIN F.
BARNES, JILL
BARONE, JEANINE
BAUER, ERWIN A.
BEAUGE, JOHN Q.
BERRY, S.L.
BISHER, FURMAN
BLUE, MARIAN
BOEHM, GEORGE A. W.
BORTSTEIN, LARRY
BOYKIN, JOHN E.
BRASSELL, SEARLES
  LUCINDA
BRODSKY, RUTHAN
BUDROW, NANCY
BURCH, MONTE
CADIEUX, CHARLES L.
CAHILL, CARL
CHARLES, JOANNA
CLARK, LARRY
CLINE, ANDY
COAN, PETER M.
COPE, MYRON
CUMMINGS, SANDRA OTTO
CURRAN, BOB
DALRYMPLE, BYRON W.
DAVENPORT, ARTHUR
DAVIS, O. K.
DEVANEY, JOHN
DEVINE, GEORGE
DIDDLEBOCK, BOB
DODGE, ELLIN
DUNAWAY, JAMES O.
DUNHAM, ROBERT
EBERLY, PHILIP K.
EDSON, ANDREW S.

ELLIOTT, CHARLES
ENGH, JERI
FEHL, MARTHA R.
FENSCH, THOMAS C.
FNA NEWS
FREEMAN, LUCY
FUSCO, MARY ANN
  CASTRONOVO
GAMAGE, DOUGLAS C.
GIBBS, RAFE
GOLDSTEIN, GREG
GORDON, BERNARD LUDWIG
GREENGARD, SAMUEL
GREGG, JAMES R.
GRIFFIN, C. W.
GROENE, GORDON &
  GROENE, JANET
HAAS, ALAN D.
HAMMER, ROGER A.
HARMAN, HARRY & JEANNE
HARRIS, ELEANOR
HIBBEN, DR. FRANK C.
HIGDON, HAL
HINTZ, MARTIN
HORNSTEIN, HAROLD
HOWES, CONNIE B.
HUFF, DARRELL
HUNT, DIANA
HYYPIA, ERIK J.
HYYPIA, JORMA
JAMES JR., JESSE A.
JOURNEY, ALFRED E. 'BUD'
KARAS, NICHOLAS
KEIL, BILL
KINGDOM, GERRY
KNIGHT, DOUG
KNIGHT, MRS. RICHARD
  ALDEN
KOCIVAR, BEN
LEIF, ROBERT
LEONARD, GEORGE
LEWIS, PARNELLS
LOCKWOOD, GEORGENE
  MULLER
LOSCHIAVO, LINDA ANN
MALLETTE, MAL
MARSH, SUSAN
MCKENZIE, J. NORMAN
MCMORROW, TOM
MILLMAN, SANDY K.
MIX, SHELDON A.
MONROE, KEITH
MONTGOMERY, ED
NEELY, WILLIAM
NELSON, JANET
NORTON, PHILLIP
NUWER, HANK
O'REILLY, DON
OLLOVE, STEVE
PARK, ED
PAUGH, TOM

PEPE, BARBARA
PFEIFER, LUANNE
PICKENS, THOMAS M.
POSTER, CAROL
RAND, ABBY
RIEGER, TED
ROBINSON, TED
RODDIN, MIKE
ROESSING, WALTER
ROSENBAUM, HELEN
RUSSELL, FRED
SABIN, FRANCENE
SCAGNETTI, JACK
SCHNECK, MARCUS H.
SCHWANZ, MICHAEL L.
SCHWARZ, TED
SEITEL, FRASER PAUL
SHEIN, ARN
SLATE, LIBBY
SLEAR, TOM
SOSIN, MARK
ST. JOHN, TERRY
STACK, ROBERT
SULLIVAN, GEORGE
TAJER, JOSIE
TAYLOR, GARY
TAYLOR, THEODORE
TUTHILL JR., OLIVER W.
VALENTI, DAN
VAN COLLIE, SHIMON-CRAIG
VOTANO, PAUL A.
WALTER, CLAIRE
WARREN, CAMERON A.
WATSON, DELMAR
WESLEY, MARX
WOOG, DAN
WULFF, JOAN SALVATO
ZATZ, ARLINE
ZURCHER, MARVIN
ZWEIG, PHILLIP L.

THE ARTS

ALLEN, LOUIS A.
ARDMORE, JANE KESNER
AUSTIN, JOHN
BAILEY, JANET
BAKAL, CARL
BAKER, SAMM SINCLAIR
BANDLER, MICHAEL J.
BARBATO, JOSEPH
BARTEL, PAULINE C.
BEEBE, F. LISA
BELL, JOSEPH N.
BENSON, VIRGINIA PERKINS
BERMAN, BRIAN J.
BERRY, S.L.
BLODGETT, RICHARD
BOECKMAN, CHARLES
BOORSTIN, DANIEL J.
BOREA, PHYLLIS GILBERT

BORTSTEIN, LARRY
BRASSELL, SEARLES
   LUCINDA
BROOKS, PATRICIA
BYRNE-DODGE, TERESA
CALABRO, MARIAN
CAMPER, FRED
CASSILL, KAY
CASSILL, R. V.
CATALANO, JULIE
CHEASEBRO, MARGARET
CHEASEBRO, MARGARET
CHIN, RUTH
CLIFFORD, WILLIAM
COHEN, DANIEL
COLBERT, JUDY
COLEMAN, A.D.
CONKLIN, WILLIAM B.
COOPER, ANDREA
DAILY, LAURA
DALY, MAUREEN
DEGNAN, JAMES P.
DEVINE, GEORGE
DRISCOLL, CYNTHIA
DYKEMAN, WILMA
EBERLY, PHILIP K.
EDELSTEIN, SCOTT
ELWOOD, MRS. EDITH
   MUESING
ENGLISH, JOHN W.
FALES, EDWARD
FANTEL, HAS
FEHL, MARTHA R.
FEIT, EDWARD
FELD, KAREN
FELDMAN, RUTH DUSKIN
FOX, BARRY
FRANCISCUS, ALEXANDRA
FRIED, EUNICE
GALLO, DIANE
GATTO, JOHN TAYLOR
GEIS, DARLENE S.
GILES, MARJORIE GORDON-
GILINSKY, RHODA M.
GLASSER, SELMA
GOODMAN, JACK
GORDON, BERNARD LUDWIG
GRICE, MARY A.
HAAS, ALAN D.
HACKETT, BLANCHE
HAGGITH, DAVID
HAIT, PAM
HAMALIAN, LEO
HARRIS, ELEANOR
HARRIS, PATRICIA
HAY, PHD., VICTORIA
HEMMING, ROY
HIGDON, HAL
HILL, NORMAN
HINTZ, MARTIN
HODGE, ADELE

HORNSTEIN, HAROLD
HOROWITZ, SHEL ALAN
HOWARD, ELIZABETH M.
INGE, ARLINE
IRA, ALLEN
JACOBS, DORRI
JACOBS, FRANK
JAMES JR., JESSE A.
KONNER, LINDA
KRANISH, ARTHUR
KREMEN, BENNETT
LACEY, DIANE G.
LAMPE, DAVID
LANGER, CASSANDRA
LANGHAM, BARBARA
LEE, SHIRLEY
LEVIN, AARON
LEVINE, FAYE
LEW, IRVINA
LONDON, BILL
LORENZ-FIFE, IRIS
MACDONALD, SANDY
MARGOLIS, LYNNE
MARSH, SUSAN
MASTROLIA, LILYAN S.
MAYER, BARBARA
MESSNER, FRED R.
MILLER, BRUCE
MILNE, ROBERT SCOTT
MOLDAFSKY, ANNIE
MONSON, NANCY P.
NEMSER, CINDY
NEWCOMB, DUANE G.
PAAJANEN, ANNETTE LAABS
PAYNE, PEGGY
PEPE, BARBARA
PERRY, ERMA
POLAND, NANCY
POMADA, ELIZABETH
PONZO, MARIE
POSTER, CAROL
REISS, ALVIN H.
ROBERTS, JANET M.
ROESSING, WALTER
ROSENDO, JOSEPH
ROSS, BETTY
SANDEL, SUSAN L.
SCHREIBER, NORMAN
SEAMANS, ANDY
SHAKESPEARE, MARGARET
SHAPIRO, CECILE
SHELDON, GEORGE
SHEMANSKI, FRANCES
SILBEY, PAULA J.
SKLAR, DUSTY
SLATE, LIBBY
SMITH, LEE A.
SOHN, DAVID A.
SOLOMON, GOODY L.
SOMAN, SHIRLEY CAMPER
SOTER, TOM

SPANO, SUSAN
SPRINGER, P. GREGORY
STREHLOW, LORETTA
STRUGATCH, WARREN
STUART, ANNE ELIZABETH
TEMKO, FLORENCE
THOMSON, PEGGY
TRASOBARES, CAESAR M.
TRILLING, DIANA
TURECAMO, DORRINE
URROWS, HENRY AND
   ELIZABETH
WALTER, EUGENE
WALTON, CHELLE KOSTER
WATLINGTON, JERILYNN
WESTHEIMER, MARY
WILLIAMS, RUSSELL J.
WILLISTEIN, PAUL
WUCHERER, RUTH
YARMON, MORTON

TRAVEL

AFRICANO, LILLIAN
ALLEN, ROBERT A.
ALPER, PHILIP
ALPERN, DAVID M.
ALPERSTEIN, ELLEN
ANDERSON, BARRY C.
ANDERSON, ERIC G.
ANDERSON, KENNETH N.
ARCELLA, LISA
ASTON, ATHINA LEKA
AUSTIN, JOHN
BAGG, ALAN R.
BAILEY, JANET
BAKAL, CARL
BAKER, CHRISTOPHER PAUL
BARNES, JILL
BARNES-SVARNEY,
   PATRICIA L.
BARON, HARRY
BARONE, JEANINE
BARRINGTON, CAROL
   BISBEE
BASCH, BUDDY
BAUER, ERWIN A.
BAYERS, RAPP LEA
BEEBE, F. LISA
BEHRENS, JOHN
BELL, SALLY
BENDINER, ROBERT
BENFORD, MARILYN
BENFORD, TIMOTHY B.
BERG, MARGARET C.
BERRY, S.L.
BISHER, FURMAN
BLASK, ANN SABATINI
BLISHAK, SYLVIA ANN
BLOCK, VICTOR
BOECKMAN, CHARLES

BOTTEL, HELEN
BOYKIN, JOHN E.
BRAMS, STANLEY H.
BRESLAUER, IRWIN J.
BRESNICK, JAN
BROOKS, LESTER
BROOKS, PATRICIA
BUDROW, NANCY
BUDROW, NANCY
BURGETT, GORDON
BURTON, MARDA
BYRNE-DODGE, TERESA
CADIEUX, CHARLES L.
CAHILL, CARL
CALABRO, MARIAN
CAMPBELL, CANDACE
CANDLER, JULIE
CANDLER, JULIE
CARUANA, CLAUDIA M.
CASS, MAXINE
CATALANO, JULIE
CELLIERS, PETER J.
CELLIERS, PETER J.
CHARLES, JOANNA
CHIN, RUTH
CHRISTENSEN, KAREN
CIRONE, BETTINA
CLIFFORD, WILLIAM
CLINE, ANDY
COAN, PETER M.
COLBERT, JUDY
COLEBERD, FRANCES
COLEMAN, A.D.
CONKLIN, WILLIAM B.
COOPER, PAULETTE
CORBETT, GERALDINE
COX, VIC
CUPPER, DAN
DAILY, LAURA
DALRYMPLE, BYRON W.
DALY, MAUREEN
DARDICK, GEETA
DARK, HARRIS EDWARD
DARLINGTON, JOY
DAVENPORT, ARTHUR
DAVENPORT, ARTHUR
DAVIDSON, MARK
DEANE, BARBARA
DEBARTOLO, ANTHONY
DEGNAN, JAMES P.
DEMAN, ELAINE
DEVANEY, JOHN
DICTOR-LEBLANC, RENA
DIDDLEBOCK, BOB
DRAGONWAGON, CRESCENT
DRISCOLL, CYNTHIA
DUNAWAY, JAMES O.
DUNHAM, ROBERT
DUNNAN, NANCY
DUSKY, LORRAINE
DYKEMAN, WILMA

EDSON, ANDREW S.
EGERTON, JOHN
ELIOT, JANE WINSLOW
ELLIOTT, JOY
ENGH, JERI
ENGLE, PAANANEN ELOISE
ENGLISH, JOHN W.
ENSRUD, BARBARA
FADER, SHIRLEY SLOAN
FALES, EDWARD
FAREWELL, SUSAN
FARIS, CHARLENE
FEHL, MARTHA R.
FELD, KAREN
FELDMAN, ELANE
FELDMAN, RUTH DUSKIN
FINKE, BLYTHE FOOTE
FNA NEWS
FORTNEY, DAVID L.
FOSTER, NANCY
FRAZER, LANCE
FREEDMAN, ERIC
FRIED, EUNICE
FRIED, EUNICE
FRIESE, RICK
FRIZZI, VIRGINIA
FRUMKES, LEWIS BURKE
FULLMAN, LYNN GRISARD
FURLONG, ISABEL M.
FUSCO, MARY ANN
  CASTRONOVO
GALLO, DIANE
GARFIELD, JOHANNA
GARRARD, ALICE
GEBHART, FRED
GEIS, DARLENE S.
GELTNER, SHARON
GEM PUBLISHING GROUP
GIBBONS, BARBARA
GIBBS, RAFE
GIBBS, RAFE
GILES, MARJORIE GORDON-
GILFERT, SHIRLEY
GILINSKY, RHODA M.
GLEASNER, DIANA C.
GOLDFEIN, DONNA
GOLIN, MILTON
GOODING, JUDSON
GOODMAN, JACK
GOODWIN, DAVE
GORDON, SUSAN J.
GOULD, LARK ELLEN
GRECO, GAIL
GREENE, FREDA
GREGG, JAMES R.
GRESHAM, GRITS
GRIMM, TOM
GROENE, GORDON &
  GROENE, JANET
GROENE, JANET
GROSSINGER, TANIA

GUNST, KATHY
GYSI, CHUCK
HAAPOJA, MARGARET A.
HACKETT, BLANCHE
HAIT, PAM
HALL, JAMES B.
HAMALIAN, LEO
HANLE, ZACK
HANSEN, ELIZABETH
HARKNESS, CHRIS
HARMAN, HARRY & JEANNE
HARRIS, ELEANOR
HARRIS, PATRICIA
HARSHAM, PHILIP
HARTLEY, JEAN AYRES
HASTINGS, ROBERT A.
HAUSER, HILLARY
HAY, PHD., VICTORIA
HEILMAN, JOAN RATTNER
HELLER, MARION
HEMMING, ROY
HEMMING, ROY
HENLEY, ARTHUR
HINTZ, MARTIN
HOCH, DR. DEAN E.
HOCH, NANCY M.
HOFFMAN, NANCY YANES
HOLDER, DENNIS
HONE, HARRY
HORN, YVONNE MICHIE
HORNBAKER, ALICE J.
HORNIK-BEER, EDITH LYNN
HORNSTEIN, HAROLD
HOROWITZ, SHEL ALAN
HOUSTON, RUTH
HOWES, CONNIE B.
HOYT, ERICH
HUFF, DARRELL
HUFF, FRANCES N.
HUNT, DIANA
HURWOOD, BERNHARDT J.
HYYPIA, ERIK J.
IACONETTI, JOAN
INGE, ARLINE
IRA, ALLEN
JACKSON, LESLIE
JACOBS, FRANK
JOHNSON, SABEEHA H.
JOHNSTON, MELANIE LEE
KARAS, NICHOLAS
KARPEL, CRAIG S.
KAUFMAN, WALLACE
KAYE, EVELYN
KEATING, BERN
KEEN, MARJORIE
KEIL, BILL
KEMPER, SU
KEMPTON-SMITH, DEBBI
KINGDOM, GERRY
KLAUS, BARBARA
KNIGHT, DOUG

KOCIVAR, BEN
KOEHLER, MARGARET
  HUDSON
KONNER, LINDA
KOONTZ, KATY
KOWAL, JOHN PAUL
KRANISH, ARTHUR
KUHN, IRENE CORBALLY
KUSTANOWITZ, SHULAMIT E.
LAMPE, DAVID
LANDT, DENNIS
LANDWEHR, SHELDON
LARBERG, ANN
LARBERG, ANN
LASSEN, JEFF
LAYNE, MARIE
LEBLANC, RENA DICTOR
LEE, SHIRLEY
LEERBURGER, BENEDICT
LEMKOWITZ, FLORENCE
LEVIN, AARON
LEVINE, FAYE
LEVY, RICHARD C.
LEW, IRVINA
LIEBERMAN, ROBERT H.
LINDSAY, RAE
LONDON, BILL
LOOMIS, JAMIE
LORENZ-FIFE, IRIS
LOSCHIAVO, LINDA ANN
LYNCH, PAT
LYON, DAVID
LYONS, CHRISTINE
MACDONALD, SANDY
MALLETTE, MAL
MALOTT, GENE
MANDELL, PATRICIA
MANNERS, DAVID X.
MAPPES, DR. CARL R.
MARGOLIS, LYNNE
MARKS, JASON
MARSH, SUSAN
MARTIN, NORMA MILNER
MARZECKI, LONGIN W.
MASARACCHIA, SUSAN
MASON, LEE FRANZ
MASSEY, R. L.
MASSOW, ROSALIND
MASTROLIA, LILYAN S.
MASTROLIA, LILYAN S.
MATHEWS, BEVERLY
MATUSIK, JO ELLEN
MAXWELL, KATIE
MAYNARD, MARY
MAZIE, DAVID
MCKENZIE, J. NORMAN
MCKEOWN, WM. TAYLOR
MCKINNEY, SALLY BROWN
MCNEES, PAT
MCPHEE, MARNIE
MEEKER, EUNICE JUCKETT

MEOLA, PATRICIA E.
MESSINEO, JOHN
MEYERS, CAROLE
 TERWILLIGER
MILLER, BRUCE
MILLER, CATHERINE
 LANHAM
MILLMAN, SANDY K.
MILLNER, CORK
MILNE, DR. MARGERY
MILNE, ROBERT SCOTT
MIX, SHELDON A.
MOLDAFSKY, ANNIE
MONSON, NANCY P.
MORGAN, ARJAY
MORGAN, NEIL
MORLAND, ALVIN
MORRIS, HAL
MUMMERT, ROGER
MURPHY, RAYMOND J.
NADEL PH.D., LAURIE
NEELY, BONNIE BURGESS
NEELY, WILLIAM
NELSON, ED
NELSON, JANET
NELSON, KAY SHAW
NEMIRO, BEVERLY
 ANDERSON
NICKLAS, NICK
NIELSEN, DOLLY
NORTON, PHILLIP
OCKERSHAUSEN, JANE
OGDEN, SHEPHERD
ORTH, JOAN
OXFORD, EDWARD
PAANANEN, ELOISE
PALMQUIST, RON
PARK, ED
PAYNE, PEGGY
PEAKE, JACQUELYN
PEPE, BARBARA
PERRY, ERMA
PETROWSKI, ELAINE MARTIN
PFEIFER, LUANNE
PICKENS, THOMAS M.
PIZER, VERNON
PLUMEZ, DR. JACQUELINE
 HORNER
PODOLSKY, M. LAWRENCE
POLAND, NANCY
POLVAY, MARINA
POMADA, ELIZABETH
PONZO, MARIE
POSTER, CAROL
PURDY, SUSAN
RAND, ABBY
REIMER, KATHLEEN
REISS, ALVIN H.
RICHARD, JEROME
RICKEY, GAIL
RIEGER, TED

ROBERTS, JANET M.
ROESSING, WALTER
ROGAK, LISA
ROGERS, BARBARA
 RADCLIFFE
ROOD, RONALD
ROSEN, M. DANIEL
ROSENBAUM, HELEN
ROSENDO, JOSEPH
ROSS, BETTY
ROTHMAN, HOWARD
ROWLES, GENEVIEVE
RUDOLPH, JOHN K.
RUDOLPH, JOHN K.
SABIN, FRANCENE
SAYLOR DOPPENBERG,
 JEAN
SCHLICK, JACK
SCHLOSS, MURIEL
SCHREIBER, NORMAN
SCHWALBERG, CAROL
SCHWANZ, MICHAEL L.
SCOBEY, JOAN
SEAMANS, ANDY
SEITEL, FRASER PAUL
SHAKESPEARE, MARGARET
SHEFFE, EDWARD D.
SHELDON, GEORGE
SHEMANSKI, FRANCES
SIEGEL, DOROTHY
SILBAR, HOWARD J.
SILBEY, PAULA J.
SILVA, KATE
SKLAREWITZ, NORMAN
SLOME, JESSE R.
SMITH, BEVERLY BUSH
SOMAN, SHIRLEY CAMPER
SOSIN, MARK
SPANO, SUSAN
SPRING, BOB & NORMA
STAR, JACK
STAUB, MOLLY AROST
STEIN, M. L.
STEINBERG, JANET
STEINER, SHARI
STEPHEN, RAE
STICKLER, JOHN C.
STOCKER, JOSEPH
STREHLOW, LORETTA
STRESHINSKY, SHIRLEY G.
STRICKLER, CAROLYN J.
STRUGATCH, WARREN
TAMIS, VALERIE B.
TEGELER, DOROTHY
TROMBETTI, STEVEN E.
TUPPER, MARGO
ULRICH, ELISE VONS
URROWS, HENRY AND
 ELIZABETH
VALENTI, DAN
VOLLMAR, ALICE M.

WALKER, DR. MORTON
WALTER, CLAIRE
WALTER, EUGENE
WALTON, CHELLE KOSTER
WELCH, RANDY
WESTGATE, ROBERT D.
WESTHEIMER, MARY
WHITLEY, SHARON
WILKINSON, PAMELA L.
WILLIAMS, RUSSELL J.
WISE, CHRISTY
WOLKOMIR, RICHARD AND
 JOYCE ROGERS
WOLKOMIR
WOOG, DAN
WUCHERER, RUTH
YAGER, JAN
YARBROUGH, CAROLYN J.
YOUNG, DONALD
ZATZ, ARLINE
ZOBEL, LOUISE PURWIN

URBAN AFFAIRS

BERMAN, BRIAN J.
BOECKMAN, CHARLES
DEBARTOLO, ANTHONY
DEGNAN, JAMES P.
DUNNAN, NANCY
EISCHEN, CHARLES N.
FNA NEWS
GOODING, JUDSON
GREENGARD, SAMUEL
HAIT, PAM
IRA, ALLEN
KANIGEL, ROBERT
KAY, JANE HOLTZ
LEONARD, JOHN EDWARD
LEVINE, FAYE
MAZIE, DAVID
MILLER AND MARK ELLIS
MILLER, JUDITH BRAFFMAN
NELSON, ED
NOSSAMAN, MICHAEL
REISS, ALVIN H.
SOMAN, SHIRLEY CAMPER
TANNE, JANICE HOPKINS
TANNER, OGDEN
URROWS, HENRY AND
 ELIZABETH

VIDEO

AUSTIN, JOHN
BAYSURA, STEVEN A.
BERGER, IVAN
BOONE, GENE
BRODY, PEG
FANTEL, HAS
FERGUSON, JOSEPH
FNA NEWS

GALLO, DIANE
GRAF, RUDOLF F.
HALPERN, FRANCES
HEMMING, ROY
HODGE, ADELE
KONNER, LINDA
LEIF, ROBERT
MACDONALD, SANDY
MARGOLIS, LYNNE
MASTROLIA, LILYAN S.
MCCOMB, GORDON
MILLER, BRUCE
NEELY, BONNIE BURGESS
NOVITZ, CHARLES R.
ORTH, JOAN
OWEN, JENNIFER BRYON
PETERS, JANE S.
PINKWAS, STAN
ROSENBLUM, DEBBIE
SEIDEN, OTHNIEL J.
SOLOMON, GOODY L.
SOTER, TOM
WHITFORD, JAMES

WOMEN'S INTEREST

ADLER, LINDA J.
AFRICANO, LILLIAN
AGUILAR, NONA
ALTER, JOANNE
ANDERSON, JOAN WESTER
ARRIGO, MARY
BAKER, ROLINDA B.
BALDWIN, JOYCE
BARNES-SVARNEY,
 PATRICIA L.
BARONE, JEANINE
BARTEL, PAULINE C.
BARTOCCI, BARBARA
BASSETT, ELIZABETH
BERGER, AMY H.
BOTTEL, HELEN
BOTWIN, CAROL
BRASSELL, SEARLES
 LUCINDA
BRINLEY, MARYANN
 BUCKNUM
BROOKS, PATRICIA
BUONOCORE, JULIA
BYRNE-DODGE, TERESA
CATALANO, JULIE
CHANDLER, JO
COAN, PETER M.
COCHRAN, ADA
COLTON, HELEN
COOPER, ANDREA
DALY, MAUREEN
DARDICK, GEETA
DAVIS, FLORA M.
DEANE, BARBARA
DEMAN, ELAINE

DOWNEY, CHARLES E.
DRAGONWAGON, CRESCENT
DRISCOLL, CYNTHIA
DUSKY, LORRAINE
DYKEMAN, WILMA
ENGLE, PAANANEN ELOISE
FADER, SHIRLEY SLOAN
FAREWELL, SUSAN
FAUX, MARIAN
FEHL, MARTHA R.
FELDMAN, ELANE
FINGER, ANNE L.
FINKE, BLYTHE FOOTE
FLEMING, ALICE
FNA NEWS
FURLONG, ISABEL M.
FUSCO, MARY ANN
  CASTRONOVO
GALLAGHER, RACHEL
GALLESE, LIZ ROMAN
GALLO, DIANE
GIBBONS, BARBARA
GILINSKY, RHODA M.
GLASS, JUDITH E.
GLASSER, SELMA
GORDON, SUSAN J.
GRIFFIN, KELLY L.
GROSSMAN, ELLIE
HAAPOJA, MARGARET A.
HACKETT, BLANCHE
HAIT, PAM
HALLADAY, GENEVA
HAMILTON, PHD., ELEANOR
HANSEN, ELIZABETH
HARRIS, ELEANOR
HAY, PHD., VICTORIA
HELM, SYLVIA
HEMBREE, DIANA
HOCHMAN, GLORIA
HODGE, ADELE
HOFFMAN, NANCY YANES
HONE, HARRY
HORNBAKER, ALICE J.
HOWARD, ELIZABETH M.
HOWES, CONNIE B.
IACONETTI, JOAN
INGE, ARLINE
JACKSON, LESLIE
JACOBSON, BEVERLY
JAMES, LAURIE
JOHNSON, SABEEHA H.
KAHN, ADA PASKIND
KAVALER, LUCY
KAYE, EVELYN
KELLY, KATE
KLAVAN, ELLEN
KONNER, LINDA
KOONTZ, KATY
LAGAN, CONSTANCE
  HALLINAN
LEBLANC, RENA DICTOR

LEE, SHIRLEY
LEVINE, FAYE
LEW, IRVINA
LICHTENBERG, MARGARET
  KLEE
LOCKWOOD, GEORGENE
  MULLER
LORENZ-FIFE, IRIS
LOSCHIAVO, LINDA ANN
MARGOLIS, LYNNE
MARKS, JASON
MASARACCHIA, SUSAN
MASSOW, ROSALIND
MATHEWS, BEVERLY
MAYER, BARBARA
MAYNARD, MARY
MCCLENDON, SARAH
MCPHEE, MARNIE
MEEKER, EUNICE JUCKETT
MEOLA, PATRICIA E.
MILLER AND MARK ELLIS
  MILLER, JUDITH BRAFFMAN
MILLER, CATHERINE
  LANHAM
MOATES, MARIANNE
  MERRILL
MOLDAFSKY, ANNIE
MONSON, NANCY P.
MOORE, DIANNE
NEELY, BONNIE BURGESS
NELSON, KAY SHAW
NEMIRO, BEVERLY
  ANDERSON
NEMIROW-NELSON, JILL
NEMSER, CINDY
O'CONNOR, KAREN
OLDS, SALLY WENDKOS
PEPE, BARBARA
PERRY, SUSAN K.
PETROWSKI, ELAINE MARTIN
PITTMAN, RUTH
PLUMEZ, DR. JACQUELINE
  HORNER
POGREBIN, LETTY COTTIN
POLVAY, MARINA
PURDY, SUSAN
ROBERTS, JANET M.
ROESCH, ROBERTA
ROESSING, WALTER
ROGAK, LISA
ROSENBAUM, HELEN
ROSS, BETTY
RUBIN, NANCY
SABIN, FRANCENE
SCHNEIDER-AKER,
  KATHERINE
SEAMAN, BARBARA
SECUNDA, VICTORIA
SHAPIRO, PATRICIA
  GOTTLIEB
SHAW, EVA

SHIMBERG, ELAINE FANTLE
SIEGEL, PAULA M.
SILBEY, PAULA J.
SLATE, LIBBY
SMITH, CARIN A., DVM
SMITH, RUTH BAYARD
SOLOMON, GOODY L.
SOMAN, SHIRLEY CAMPER
SPANO, SUSAN
STEINBERG, JANET
STEINER, SHARI
STITT, ABBY
TAMIS, VALERIE B.
TANNE, JANICE HOPKINS
TESSINA, PHD., TINA B.
TONNESSEN, DIANA
ULRICH, ELISE VONS
WALKER, GLADYS H.
WESTEN, ROBIN
WESTHEIMER, MARY
WHITLEY, SHARON
WINTER, RUTH
WORKMAN, BARBARA L.
WUCHERER, RUTH
YUDKIN, MARCIA
ZURCHER, MARVIN

WORLD AFFAIRS

ALBANESE, DAVID J.
ANDERSON, KENNETH N.
BAKER, CHRISTOPHER PAUL
BANDLER, MICHAEL J.
BARONE, JEANINE
BASSETT, ELIZABETH
BENFORD, MARILYN
CLARKE, PHILIP C.
CONNIFF, JAMES C. G.
COX, VIC
DARLINGTON, JOY
DICKERSON, NANCY
DOOLEY, BRIAN J.
ELLIOTT, JOY
FEHL, MARTHA R.
FINKE, BLYTHE FOOTE
FNA NEWS
GELTNER, SHARON
GOODSELL, JAMES NELSON
GOULD, LARK ELLEN
HAMALIAN, LEO
HARVEY, FRANK
HINTZ, MARTIN
HOLCOMB, GEORGE B.
HONE, HARRY
HOWE, RUSSELL WARREN
KAPLAN, DAVID
KAYE, EVELYN
KEATING, BERN
KNIGHT, DOUG
KUHN, IRENE CORBALLY
LAMONT, DOUGLAS

LARBERG, ANN
LEVITSKY, DR. SERGE L.
LORENZ-FIFE, IRIS
MAZIE, DAVID
MILLER AND MARK ELLIS
  MILLER, JUDITH BRAFFMAN
MORGAN, NEIL
MOSKIN, J. ROBERT
MURPHY, RAYMOND J.
OLECK, HOWARD L.
OLSEN, J.W.
PICKENS, THOMAS M.
POLAND, NANCY
ROSEN, M. DANIEL
ROSENBERG, SHIRLEY
  SIROTA
SOMAN, SHIRLEY CAMPER
TUTHILL JR., OLIVER W.
URROWS, HENRY AND
  ELIZABETH
VIORST, MILTON
WESTGATE, ROBERT D.
WISE, CHRISTY
YOUNG, DONALD

YOUTH

ARRIGO, MARY
AUERBACK, PHD., STEVANNE
BAHR, ROBERT A.
BERMAN, BRIAN J.
BERRY, S.L.
BOECKMAN, CHARLES
BOONE, GENE
BOTWIN, CAROL
BRASSELL, SEARLES
  LUCINDA
BRINLEY, MARYANN
BUCKNUM
CHEASEBRO, MARGARET
CIRONE, BETTINA
CLARK, LARRY
COX, VIC
DAILY, LAURA
DALY, MAUREEN
DANOWSKI, JENNY
DAVIS, BEATRICE G.
DOWNEY, CHARLES E.
FEHL, MARTHA R.
FORTSON, LOWRANCE
  SANNA
GEIS, DARLENE S.
GILBERT, SARA D.
GILINSKY, RHODA M.
GLASSER, SELMA
GORDON, BERNARD LUDWIG
GORDON, SUSAN J.
GRAND, CARMEN T.
GRANT, NANCY S.
GUNST, KATHY
HAMILTON, PHD., ELEANOR

HAZEN, BARBARA SHOOK
HOWARD, ELIZABETH M.
IRA, ALLEN
KOCH, JOANNE & LEWIS
KRANISH, ARTHUR
LANGHAM, BARBARA
LARBERG, ANN
LAYNE, MARIE
LEE, SHIRLEY
LINDSAY, RAE
LOCKETT-JOHN, SUE
MALLETTE, MAL
MARKS, JANE
MASARACCHIA, SUSAN
MAZIE, DAVID
MCPHEE, MARNIE
MEOLA, PATRICIA E.
MESSINEO, JOHN
MILLER, CATHERINE
  LANHAM
MOLDAFSKY, ANNIE
NEELY, BONNIE BURGESS
NELSON, ED
NEMIROW-NELSON, JILL
NUWER, HANK
O'CONNOR, KAREN
OLDS, SALLY WENDKOS
PERRY, SUSAN K.
RICKS, JACKIE D.
ROES, NICHOLAS A.
ROESSING, WALTER
ROOD, RONALD
ROSENBAUM, HELEN
SERVINO, CAROL
SHIMBERG, ELAINE FANTLE
SIEGEL, DOROTHY
SILBERMAN, ARLENE
SKLAR, DUSTY
SOMAN, SHIRLEY CAMPER
STITT, ABBY
TAYLOR, THEODORE
TURECAMO, DORRINE
WESSEL, MORRIS A.
WESTON, CAROL
WILCOX, CHARLOTTE
WILSON, KATHY
WOOG, DAN

Professional Services

FEATURE WRITERS

LEE EDSON

203-322-8791

36 IRON GATE ROAD
STAMFORD, CT 06903

Freelance Writer

MORTON J. MEROWITZ

71 N. Maplemere Road
Buffalo, NY 14221-3121

GORDON L. BURGETT

Communication Unlimited
(Write to Sell)

P.O. Box 6405
Santa Maria, CA 93456
(805) 937-8711

Lynn Grisard Fullman
2446 MONTE VISTA DRIVE
BIRMINGHAM, ALABAMA 35216
205-822-1402

FREE-LANCE WRITER/EDITOR

MEMBER:
- AMERICAN SOCIETY OF JOURNALISTS AND AUTHORS
- NORTH AMERICAN TRAVEL JOURNALISTS ASSOCIATION
- INTERNATIONAL FOOD, WINE & TRAVEL WRITERS ASSOCIATION

Journalist
Author

NANCY RUBIN

(914) 834-6841
8 Avon Road
Larchmont, NY 10538

Food Arts, The Paris Review, The Pepper Mill, etc.

Eugene Walter
Critic, Reviewer, Commentator,
Air and Print

161 Grand Boulevard,
Mobile, AL 36607-3012
(201) 479-9828

Soon to be released:
- *Adam's Housecat (novel)*
- *The Ginger Fiend's Cookbook*
- *The Calico Crowd*

TELEPHONE
(203) 329-8738

JAN YAGER, PH.D

Business Protocol, (Wiley, '91)
PARADE, NEWSDAY, REDBOOK, etc.

*international
food, wine & travel
writers
assn.*

6350 Dorchester Court
Carmichael, CA 95608
(916) 944-3185

Grace Ertel

American Medical Writers
American Society of Journalists of Authors

Lectures   Seminars   Articles

Sally Wiener Grotta & Daniel Grotta
609 East Philadelphia Avenue
Boyertown, PA 19512 USA
(215) 367-9496
(215) 367-7130 (fax)
MCI: DGrotta

The people who wrote the book on
Digital Imaging

SHARON WHITLEY
Writer/Editor

5666 Meredith Avenue
San Diego, California 92120
(619) 583-7346

Section 3
FEATURE WRITERS

ABBOTT, R. TUCKER
2208 S. Colonial Dr.
Melbourne, FL 32901
Telephone: 407-725-2260
Fax: 407-725-2260
MAILING ADDRESS:
American Malacologists, Inc.
P.O. Box 2255
Melbourne, FL 32901
AFFILIATIONS:
ASJA
PRINCIPAL SUBJECTS:
Nature
Book Reviews
Ecology
PUBLICATIONS:
American Malacologists
Natural History
Science Digest
Palm Beach Life
Sojourn
Mariner's Guide to
   Oceanography
Nautilus
Golden Years
Science Counselor

ACKERMAN, DR., LOWELL
HC3 Box 672N
Payson, AZ 85541
Telephone: 602-474-8538
Fax: 602-474-8538
AFFILIATIONS:
ASJA, DWAA, AVMA
PRINCIPAL SUBJECTS:
Animals
Book Reviews
Editorial
Health
Medical
PUBLICATIONS:
JAVMA
JAAHA
Veterinary Medicine
MVP
AKC Gazette
Pet Focus
Compendium

ADLER, LINDA J.
10500 Rockville Pike, Ste. 602
Rockville, MD 20852
Telephone: 301-564-9508
AFFILIATIONS:
NPC, WIW, SPJ
PRINCIPAL SUBJECTS:
Women's Interest
General Interest
Family
PUBLICATIONS:
Christian Science Monitor, The
Robb Report, The
Savvy
Working Woman
The Washington Post

AFRICANO, LILLIAN
1 Roseld Ave.
Deal, NJ 07723
Telephone: 908-531-5399
AFFILIATIONS:
ASJA, NPC, IFW, AG
PRINCIPAL SUBJECTS:
Travel
Women's Interest
PUBLICATIONS:
Harper's Bazaar
New York Daily News
New York Times
Woman's Day
Bridal Guide
New York Magazine
Readers' Digest
Woman's World
The Nation
Chicago Sun-Times
Executive Magazine
New York Times Syndicate
Ranch & Coast Magazine
Brides Today
Asbury Park Press
LA West

AGUILAR, NONA
29 W. 26th St.
New York, NY 10010
Telephone: 212-532-5303
Fax: 212-532-5129
AFFILIATIONS:
ASJA

PRINCIPAL SUBJECTS:
Business & Industry
Family
General Interest
Health
Women's Interest
PUBLICATIONS:
Family Circle
Free Enterprise
The Business Owner
World Money Digest
Women & Co.
Cosmopolitan
Ladies Home Journal
National Catholic Register
Cathoiic Twin Circle
North American Growth
   Report

ALBANESE, DAVID J.
126 LaSalle Ave.
Kenmore, NY 14217
Telephone: 716-884-8524
MAILING ADDRESS:
Unicon Systems, Ltd.
2316 Delaware Ave, #150
Buffalo, NY 14216
AFFILIATIONS:
AAPS
PRINCIPAL SUBJECTS:
Government
History
Aviation
Editorial
Military
World Affairs
PUBLICATIONS:
West Side Times
Buffalo News, The
Spectrum, The
Generation
AM - POL Eagle
Midnight Oil
Up - Tight Citizen, The
Uni - Speak
Army Times
Air Force Magazine
Military Magazine
Senior Beacon
The Sentinal
Buffalo Business First

Today
Observer, The
Deuce
Regional Roundup, The

ALBERTSON, MILA
4501 Arlington Blvd., #300
Arlington, VA 22203
Telephone: 703-527-3120
AFFILIATIONS:
SPJ, AWRT, WIC
PRINCIPAL SUBJECTS:
Business & Industry
PUBLICATIONS:
WWPR News
Standby
AWRT News & Views

ALLEN, LOUIS A.
370 Distel Circle, #D
Los Altos, CA 94022
Telephone: 415-940-1222
MAILING ADDRESS:
Louis A. Allen
Los Altos, CA 94002
AFFILIATIONS:
AM
PRINCIPAL SUBJECTS:
Management
Business & Industry
Human Relations
The Arts
PUBLICATIONS:
Business Horizons
Dun's Review
Nation's Business
Sales Management
World Executive's Digest
Journal of Biological
   Psychology
Management Review
Management Record
International Management
Sinapore Management Review
Pairbola

ALLEN, ROBERT A.
359 Hazelhurst Ave.
Garden City, NY 11530
Telephone: 516-222-7250
Fax: 516-222-7497

AFFILIATIONS:
Long Island Press Club
PRINCIPAL SUBJECTS:
Education
History
Science
Travel
General Interest
Journalism
Entertainment
PUBLICATIONS:
Dallas (Texas) Morning News
Newsday
The New York Times
Shreveport (La.) Journal
Economic Times of Long
  Island
The Women's Record

ALPER, PHILIP
1838 El Camino Real #102
Burlingame, CA 94010
Telephone: 415-697-0361
Fax: 415-697-8752
AFFILIATIONS:
ASJA
PRINCIPAL SUBJECTS:
Book Reviews
General Interest
Human Interest
Journalism
Medical
News
Science
Social Trends
Travel
PUBLICATIONS:
Wall Street Journal
Medical Economics
HealthWire
Vogue
California Living
San Francisco Examiner

ALPERN, DAVID M.
Newsweek - 444 Madison Ave.
New York, NY 10022
Telephone: 212-350-4432
AFFILIATIONS:
SPJ
PRINCIPAL SUBJECTS:
News
Human Interest
Travel
PUBLICATIONS:
Newsweek
New York Times - Sunday
  Travel, The
Philadelphia Inquirer - Sunday
  Travel, The

Diversion Magazine
Travel Holiday Magazine
Cosmopolitan Magazine

ALPERN, LYNNE S.
650 Idlewood Dr., N.W.
Atlanta, GA 30327
Telephone: 404-255-5924
AFFILIATIONS:
ASJA
PRINCIPAL SUBJECTS:
Humor
Business & Industry
PUBLICATIONS:
Business Atlanta
Kiwanis
Good Housekeeping
Writer's Digest
Executive Review
St. Petersburg Times
Oh, Lord, I Sound Just Like
  Mama
Smile Cnnctn The/How to Use
  Humor in Dlng w/People
Inlaws, Outlaws & Other
  Theories of Relativity
Mama's Cooking
Celebrities
Remember Mama's Best
  Recipe
Oh, Lord, It's Monday Again
I Remember When...
Humor At Work: Promoting the
  Pleasure of Your Co.

ALPERSTEIN, ELLEN
2730 Second Street
Santa Monica, CA 90405
Telephone: 310-396-4092
AFFILIATIONS:
ASJA
PRINCIPAL SUBJECTS:
Animals
General Interest
Health
Medical
Nature
Physical Fitness
Science
Senior Citizens
Sports
Travel
PUBLICATIONS:
Islands
TravelAge
Los Angeles Times
Los Angeles Magazine
Relax

ALTER, JOANNE
4 Devon Rd.
Great Neck, NY 11023
Telephone: 516-487-2735
Fax: 516-482-4465
AFFILIATIONS:
WICI, AG
PRINCIPAL SUBJECTS:
Business & Industry
Health
Women's Interest
General Interest
PUBLICATIONS:
Self
Sunday Magazine N.Y. Daily
  News

ANDERSON, BARRY C.
25832 S.E. 152nd St.
Issaquah, WA 98027
Telephone: 206-392-5865
Fax: 206-557-0924
AFFILIATIONS:
SATW
PRINCIPAL SUBJECTS:
Travel
General Interest
Business & Industry
PUBLICATIONS:
Successful Meetings
U.S. Travel & Tourism
  Administration
Avis Traveler
Friendly Exchange
Berlitz Travel Guides
ENDLESS VACATION
Coast to Coast Magazine
LA Times
Seattle Post-Intelligences
Portland Oregonian
Chicago Sun Times
Denver Post
Fodor's Modern Guides
United Airlines Fly-Drive Guides
Gulf & Montgomery Ward
  Travel Guides
Rand McNally
Fisher's Travel Guides
Insight Guides

ANDERSON, ERIC G.
10205 Rue Touraine
San Diego, CA 92131
Telephone: 619-693-6073
Fax: 619-693-6073
AFFILIATIONS:
ASJA, SATW, MOTOR PRESS
  GUILD
PRINCIPAL SUBJECTS:
Automotive
Aviation

Computer Technology
Editorial
Foreign
General Interest
Health
Human Relations
Medical
Military
Photography
Senior Citizens
Social Trends
Travel
PUBLICATIONS:
Boston Globe
Geriatrics
Physician's Management
Modern Maturity
Readers Digest

ANDERSON, JOAN WESTER
811 N. Hickory
Arlington Hts, IL 60004
Telephone: 708-394-9598
Fax: 708-394-1077
AFFILIATIONS:
ASJA
PRINCIPAL SUBJECTS:
Family
Humor
Religion
Women's Interest
PUBLICATIONS:
Family
Parenting
Woman's Day
Ladies Home Journal
Modern Bride
Catholic Digest

ANDERSON, KENNETH N.
Rt. 5 Box 222
Mountain Home, AR 72653
Telephone: 501-424-4236
Fax: 501-424-4237
MAILING ADDRESS:
Kenneth Anderson
Mountain Home, AR 72653
Telephone: 914-232-5246
AFFILIATIONS:
AAAS, AMWA, ASJA,
  APHA, NASW,AG
PRINCIPAL SUBJECTS:
Medical
Health
Medical
Sports
Travel
Ecology
History
Nature
Physical Fitness

Science
Senior Citizens
World Affairs
PUBLICATIONS:
Field and Stream
Popular Mechanics
Reader's Digest
Science Digest
Popular Science
Health Scenes
Energy Horizons

ARCELLA, LISA
19 Pascack Ave.
Harrington Pk, NJ 07640
Telephone: 201-784-0883
MAILING ADDRESS:
Lisa Arcella
Harrington Pk, NJ 07640
AFFILIATIONS:
WIC
PRINCIPAL SUBJECTS:
Entertainment
Travel
Personalities
Health
Fashion
PUBLICATIONS:
Celebrity Focus Magazine
Playgirl
New York Daily News
First For Women
Rock Magazine
Bridal Guide Magazine
Weekend Magazine (U.K.)
Soap Opera Update Magazine
Hello (Britain)
First Magazine
Cosmopolitan
Star Magazine

ARDMORE, JANE KESNER
10469 Dunleer Dr.
Los Angeles, CA 90064
Telephone: 310-838-7927
AFFILIATIONS:
HWPC, WC
PRINCIPAL SUBJECTS:
Entertainment
Human Interest
Personalities
The Arts
PUBLICATIONS:
Good Housekeeping
Ladies' Home Journal
McCall's
Cosmopolitan
Family Circle
Redbook
Readers Digest

ARKIN, JOSEPH
300 Bayview Dr., #A-8
North Miami Bch, FL 33160
Telephone: 305-949-9573
Fax: 305-949-7824
MAILING ADDRESS:
Arkin, Joseph
500 Bayview Dr., Unit 1126
North Miami Bch, FL 33160
Telephone: 310-838-7929
AFFILIATIONS:
ABWA, BBA
PRINCIPAL SUBJECTS:
Business & Industry
Family
Government
Management
PUBLICATIONS:
Family Circle
Chevron USA

ARMSTRONG III, MARTIN F.
2612 North Ave, B - 11
Bridgeport, CT 06604
Telephone: 203-334-2508
AFFILIATIONS:
OWAA
PRINCIPAL SUBJECTS:
Sports
Humor
Hobbies
Book Reviews
Animals
PUBLICATIONS:
Stamford Advocate
Providence Sunday Journal
Boston Globe
Greenwich Times
Petersons Fishing

ARNETTE, JOSEPH
P.O. Box 616A
Kennebunkport, ME 04046
Telephone: 207-967-5360
AFFILIATIONS:
OWAA, NPPA, DWA, AAAS
PRINCIPAL SUBJECTS:
Nature
Ecology
PUBLICATIONS:
Audubon
Wing & Shot
Gun Dog
Wildfowl
Sporting Clays
Turkey
Turkey Hunting
Maine Sportsman
Quail Unlimited

ARRIGO, MARY
51 Nimitz Street
Huntington, NY 11743
Telephone: 516-427-8671
AFFILIATIONS:
ASJA
PRINCIPAL SUBJECTS:
Family
Health
Medical
Psychology
Women's Interest
Youth
PUBLICATIONS:
Parenting
American Baby
Newsday
Country Accents
Working Mother
Cosmopolitan

ASNER, MARIE A.
9000 W. 82nd Pl.
Shawnee Msn, KS 66204
Telephone: 913-341-9439
AFFILIATIONS:
PWI
PRINCIPAL SUBJECTS:
Book Reviews
Humor
Editorial
Entertainment
PUBLICATIONS:
Shawnee Journal - Herald
Omaha World - Herald (Poetry)
American Music Teacher
 Magazine
Christian Music Bulletin
Encore Poetry Magazine
Byline Writers Magazine
American Organist Magazine
Sunflower Petals Magazine
 (KS. State Poetry Soc.)
CSS Publications, Des Moines,
 Iowa
Kansas Music Review
 Magazine
Clavier Magazine
Passages North
Potpourri Poetry Journal
Poets and Writers, Inc.
Poets of Now
Metis
Broadcast Credits
Prairie Woman Magazine
Poet Magazine

ASTON, ATHINA LEKA
86-15 Ava Place
Jamaica, NY 11432
Telephone: 718-291-7777

AFFILIATIONS:
ASJA
PRINCIPAL SUBJECTS:
Education
History
Business & Industry
Travel
Book Reviews
Editorial
Entertainment
General Interest
Home & Garden
Marketing
PUBLICATIONS:
Parent Guide Magazine
American Feasts & Festivals

AUERBACH, SYLVIA
Cedarbrook Hill,
 8460 Limekiln Pike
Wyncote, PA 19095
AFFILIATIONS:
AG, WY, ASJA
PRINCIPAL SUBJECTS:
Personal Finance
Business & Industry
Senior Citizens
PUBLICATIONS:
Cosmopolitan
New Woman
Sylvia Porter's Personal
 Finance Magazine
Fact
Financial Planner, The
Physicians Financial News
Rx Being Well

AUERBACK, PHD., STEVANNE
220 Montgomery Street #2811
San Francisco, CA 94104
Telephone: 415-864-1169
Fax: 510-540-0171
AFFILIATIONS:
ASJA, NWU, CPW
PRINCIPAL SUBJECTS:
Amusements
Education
Family
Human Interest
Human Relations
Nature
Psychology
Youth
PUBLICATIONS:
San Francisco Independent
Parenting
San Francisco Chronicle
Detroit Free Press
Early Childhood News
San Francisco Examiner
Family Circle

AUSTIN, JOHN
P.O. Box 49957
Los Angeles, CA 90049
Telephone: 909-678-6237
Fax: 909-678-6237
MAILING ADDRESS:
John Austin
Los Angeles, CA 90049
PRINCIPAL SUBJECTS:
Amusements
Book Reviews
Media
Travel
The Arts
Video
PUBLICATIONS:
Photoplay, (United Kingdom)
Truth, (New Zealand)
San Fran Chronicle
Screen International, (London)
The Hollywood Reporter
  Syndicate
Sunday People London
Sun Tribune, Riverside, CA
New York Times
Springer News Service,
  (Germany)
International Hollywood Image
Palm Beacher, (Florida)
Journal - Gazette, (Largo, FL)
Oakland Tribune
Independent, (Corona, CA)
Toronto Sun (Sunday)
Miami Herald
Philadelphia Inquirer

BABSON, O. BONNI
66 Old Chester Rd.
Essex Fells, NJ 07021
Telephone: 201-226-1953
PRINCIPAL SUBJECTS:
Business & Industry
General Interest
Management
PUBLICATIONS:
Design News
Wire Journal International
Montclair Times
Courier - News
  (Bridgewater, NJ)

BAER, ORA JUDITH
80 - 21 Grenfell St.
Kew Gardens, NY 11415
Telephone: 718-805-1859
AFFILIATIONS:
EFA, WICI, AMWA, MWA
PRINCIPAL SUBJECTS:
Medical
Management

PUBLICATIONS:
New York Times Health
  Supplement, The
Boston Globe Magazine, The
Norfolk Compass
Virginian Pilot, The
AMIT Woman
COPE Magazine
Cancer Investigation
Physician's Weekly
Nursing Life
Healthcare Financial News
Health Matters
Medstar Communications, Inc.
UJF Virginia News, The
Tidewater Virginian
Cancer News
Extra (Magazine)
Nursing Pulse of New England
Jewish Advocate
  of Boston, The
Old Dominion University
  Courier, The
Jewish Press, The
Long Island Jewish World, The
Forum
(Mass.) Citizen Advocate, The
Brookline Chronicle
  Citizen, The
Winchester Star, The
Woburn Times, The
Boston Phoenix, The
Success with Youth Report
Oncology Times
Stethoscope
NYU (New York University)
  Physician, The
Criminal Justice Newsletter
Healthwatch
Adult's Health Adviser
Medical Tribune

BAGG, ALAN R.
417 6th St.
Racine, WI 53403
Telephone: 414-633-7772
Fax: 414-633-5310
AFFILIATIONS:
SMEI, MBNA
PRINCIPAL SUBJECTS:
Travel
PUBLICATIONS:
Outdoor Life
Venture
Midwest Outdoors
Milwaukee Journal
Grit

BAHR, ROBERT A.
1070 Zurich St.
Mobile, AL 36608

Telephone: 205-344-4488
AFFILIATIONS:
ASJA, WG, SPJ
PRINCIPAL SUBJECTS:
Health
Social Trends
Medical
Health
Human Relations
Men's Interest
Physical Fitness
Psychology
Philosophy
Youth
PUBLICATIONS:
Parade
Playboy
Popular Mechanics
Reader's Digest Books
Smithsonian
T V Guide
Glamour
Boy's Life
Kiwanis
Sports Illustrated
New Age

BAILEY, JANET
80 Cranberry St., 11h
Brooklyn, NY 11201
Telephone: 718-855-3317
AFFILIATIONS:
ASJA
PRINCIPAL SUBJECTS:
Travel
Health
Psychology
Human Relations
The Arts
PUBLICATIONS:
Travel & Leisure
Harper's Bazaar
Glamour
Health
McCall's
Woman's Day
Modern Maturity
New Woman
Redbook
Self
Cosmopolitan
Physicians' Travel &
  Meeting Guide
Arts & Entertainment Program
  Guide

BAKAL, CARL
225 W. 86th St.
New York, NY 10024
Telephone: 212-362-0550

AFFILIATIONS:
PEN, ASJA, AG
PRINCIPAL SUBJECTS:
The Arts
Business & Industry
Government
Health
General Interest
Science
Travel
PUBLICATIONS:
Harper's
McCall's
Reader's Digest
Redbook
Esquire
Parade
Town & Country
Good Housekeeping
Playboy
Wall Street Journal

BAKER, CHRISTOPHER PAUL
484 Lake Park, #67
Oakland, CA 94610
Telephone: 510-839-9874
Fax: 510-452-4601
AFFILIATIONS:
PATAGA, SATW
PRINCIPAL SUBJECTS:
Travel
Science
General Interest
Geography
Foreign
World Affairs
Book Reviews
PUBLICATIONS:
Writer's Digest
Westways
ASU Travel Guide
ASTA Travel News
Los Angeles Times
Far East Traveler
Newsday
Baltimore Sun
Chicago Tribune
Detroit News
Boston Globe
San Francisco Examiner
Travelage West
Newsweek
New York Post
Tours & Resorts
MD Magazine
Relax
Globehopper
Travel Today
National Wildlife
National Parks
Discovery

Preferred Traveler
Caribbean Travel & Life
GEO
World Magazine
Regent
Bicycling
Travellife
San Francisco Focus
The Peak
Fitness Plus
Asia Pacific Travel
Thomas Cook Traveler
Silver Kris
Sabena Review
Air Alaska in Flight
Pacific Art & Travel
Christian Science Monitor
Upper Class Magazine
U.S. Air Magazine
Delta Sky
Mercedes
Sojourn
Morning Calm
Country Inns

BAKER, ROLINDA B.
35 Park Lane Dr.
Orinda, CA 94563
Telephone: 510-254-3438
AFFILIATIONS:
NASW
PRINCIPAL SUBJECTS:
Health
Science
Women's Interest
Ecology
PUBLICATIONS:
Bride Magazine
Ob-Gyn News
Family Practice News
Bicycling
Medical Tribune
California County
American Medical News
Nursing Care
Pacific News Service
American Surgeon
Gastrointestinal Endoscopy
Annals Of Surgery
Journal Of Immunological
   Methods

BAKER, SAMM SINCLAIR
1027 Constable Dr., S.
Mamaroneck, NY 10543
Telephone: 914-698-5535
AFFILIATIONS:
AG, GWAA
PRINCIPAL SUBJECTS:
The Arts
Business & Industry

Health
Home & Garden
Human Relations
Social Trends
Human Relations
Religion
PUBLICATIONS:
Family Circle
Good Housekeeping
Ladies' Home Journal
McCall's
Reader's Digest
Saturday Review
Woman's Day
The Writer
Redbook

BALDWIN, JOYCE
2601 Hendrickson Ave.
Oceanside, NY 11572
AFFILIATIONS:
ASJA
PRINCIPAL SUBJECTS:
Education
Health
Hobbies
Psychology
Women's Interest
PUBLICATIONS:
New York Times
Newsday
American Medical News

BANDLER, MICHAEL J.
1101 N. Belgrade Rd.
Silver Spring, MD 20902
Telephone: 301-649-2460
AFFILIATIONS:
NBCC, ASJA, WIW
PRINCIPAL SUBJECTS:
The Arts
Personalities
World Affairs
Book Reviews
Foreign
PUBLICATIONS:
Parade
Redbook
Ladies' Home Journal
Chicago Tribune
Atlanta Constitution
New York Newsday
McCall's
Theater Week
Fort Worth Star-Telegram
Parents Magazine
Cable Guide, The
Child Magazine
US Magazine
Travel/Holiday
USA Today Baseball Weekly

BARBATO, JOSEPH
5361 Taney Ave.
Alexandria, VA 22304
Telephone: 703-370-0663
AFFILIATIONS:
SPJ, AG
PRINCIPAL SUBJECTS:
Book Reviews
Ecology
Health
The Arts
PUBLICATIONS:
Smithsonian
Village Voice
N.J. Monthly
World Press Review
Progressive
Network in Flight Magazines
Publishers Weekly
N.Y. Times
Christian Science Monitor
New Age Journal

BARKSDALE, WILLIAM E
P.O. Box 17726
Memphis, TN 38187
Telephone: 901-767-9540
AFFILIATIONS:
NAMA, AAEA
PRINCIPAL SUBJECTS:
Agriculture
PUBLICATIONS:
Casel/IH Farm Forum
Progressive Farmer
Cotton Farming
Successful Farming
Agri-Finance
Crop Protection Management

BARNES, DUNCAN
125 Witch Ln.
Norwalk, CT 06853
Telephone: 203-838-5837
PRINCIPAL SUBJECTS:
Animals
Ecology
General Interest
Hobbies
PUBLICATIONS:
Sports Afield
Sports Illustrated
Gray's Sporting Journal
Field & Stream
New York Daily News
Field & Stream

BARNES, JILL
26 - 11 Kipp St.
Fair Lawn, NJ 07410
Telephone: 201-796-5650
Fax: 201-796-7744

AFFILIATIONS:
NJOW, OWAA, NYSOW, OWC
PRINCIPAL SUBJECTS:
Sports
Travel
Nature
PUBLICATIONS:
Outdoor Life
Vista
Bassing
Fur - Fish - Game
Nation's Business
Trailer Life
Bassmaster
Newsweek (Japan)

BARNES-SVARNEY,
   PATRICIA L.
840 Hooper Road, Suite 305
Endwell, NY 137600
Telephone: 607-748-0892
Fax: 607-748-0892
AFFILIATIONS:
ASJA, NASW, AGU
PRINCIPAL SUBJECTS:
Computer Technology
Electronics
Health
Medical
Nature
Photography
Science
Travel
Women's Interest
PUBLICATIONS:
Omni
Popular Science
Air & Space/Smithsonian
USAir
Endlesss Vacation
Sky Magazine
Longevity
Computer Graphics World

BARON, HARRY
150 W. 87th St.
New York, NY 10024
Telephone: 212-787-6260
PRINCIPAL SUBJECTS:
Health
Science
Travel
Government
PUBLICATIONS:
Reader's Digest
Esquire
Golf
New York Times, The
TV Guide
Boy's Life

BARONE, JEANINE
P.O. Box 444, Grand Central
  Station
New York, NY 10163
Telephone: 212-229-8363
AFFILIATIONS:
ASJA, AMWA, IFWTWA
PRINCIPAL SUBJECTS:
Advertising
Health
Human Relations
Marketing
Medical
Men's Interest
Physical Fitness
Psychology
Science
Sports
Travel
Women's Interest
World Affairs
PUBLICATIONS:
Cooking Light
Food & Wine
Men's Journal
American Health
Outside
Walking
Bicycling

**BARRINGTON, CAROL
  BISBEE**
5323 Lookout Mountain Dr.
Houston, TX 77069
Telephone: 713-444-6598
AFFILIATIONS:
SATW, ASMP, ASJA, SPJ,
  Houston Press Club
PRINCIPAL SUBJECTS:
Travel
Photography
PUBLICATIONS:
Vacations
Travel 50 & Beyond
Texas Highways
Sunset
Houston Chronicle
Chicago Tribune
Dallas Morning News
Orange County Register
San Diego Union
San Francisco Examiner
Miami Herald
New York Daily News
Kansas City Star
Oregonian
San Antonio Express News

BARRY, DON
17 Eugene St.
Tonawanda, NY 14150

Telephone: 716-694-7433
Fax: 716-694-7433
AFFILIATIONS:
SPJ
PRINCIPAL SUBJECTS:
Business & Industry
Nature
Humor
Editorial
Foreign
General Interest
Government
Government
Men's Interest
Science

BARSKY, MARTIN
14962 Prospector Court
Victorville, CA 92392
Telephone: 619-241-2514
AFFILIATIONS:
SPJ
PRINCIPAL SUBJECTS:
Advertising
Editorial
Electronics
Management
Marketing
Motivation
Sales
PUBLICATIONS:
Retailing News
Rental Dealer News
Video Software Dealer

BARTEL, PAULINE C.
12-1/2 Division St.
Waterford, NY 12188
Telephone: 518-237-1353
Fax: 518-237-1353
AFFILIATIONS:
ASJA
PRINCIPAL SUBJECTS:
Animals
Business & Industry
Ecology
Editorial
Education
Entertainment
General Interest
Health
History
Human Interest
Humor
Marketing
Media
Medical
Psychology
Science
The Arts
Women's Interest

PUBLICATIONS:
Woman's Day
Mademoiselle
USAir
Delta Sky
The Saturday Evening Post
Seventeen
Boy's Life
Writer's Digest

BARTOCCI, BARBARA
P.O. Box 520, 36 Lazy Glen
Snowmass, CO 81654
Telephone: 303-927-3605
Fax: 303-927-3605
AFFILIATIONS:
NSA, ASJA
PRINCIPAL SUBJECTS:
Family
Human Interest
Human Relations
Psychology
Religion
Women's Interest
PUBLICATIONS:
Reader's Digest
Good Housekeeping
Glamour
Womans Day

BASCH, BUDDY
771 West End Ave.
New York, NY 10025
Telephone: 212-666-2300
PRINCIPAL SUBJECTS:
Amusements
Entertainment
Travel
Human Interest
Journalism
Medical
Health
PUBLICATIONS:
Argosy
Christian Science Monitor
National Enquirer
Travel - Holiday
True
A. P.
Kaleidoscope
Frontier Magazine
Grit
Gannett Westchester-Rockland
  Newspapers
Bergen (N.J.) Record
N.A.N.A. (No. American
  Newspaper Alliance)
W.N.S. (Women's News
  Service)
N.Y. Times Syndication Sales
Today Magazine

Globe
Catholic Golden Age Magazine
United Features Syndicate
New York Post
Ampersand
Readers Digest
Inflight Magazine, (Colorado)
Deseret News (Salt Lake City)
Detroit Free Press
California Canadian
TV Guide
New York Post
(Mesa, AZ) Tribune
NY Daily News

BASSETT, ELIZABETH
521 E. 14th St., #4F
New York, NY 10009
Telephone: 212-533-3082
Fax: 212-533-3082
AFFILIATIONS:
SDCSPJ, SEJ, ISWA
PRINCIPAL SUBJECTS:
World Affairs
Women's Interest
Ecology
Nature
Foreign
Social Trends
PUBLICATIONS:
New Age
Science World
The IDRC Reports
UNEP North America News
Newsweek
WorldWIDE News
World Environment Report
Interdependent, The
Near East Business
Modern Africa
Mideast Markets
Environment Magazine
Shared Vision
Update
Earth Care
  News/Environmental Sabbath
  Newsletter
Newsday
A.P.

BATTERSBY, MARK E.
63 W. Lancaster Ave.
Ardmore, PA 19003
Telephone: 215-789-2480
MAILING ADDRESS:
Mark E. Battersby
P.O. Box 527
Ardmore, PA 19003
AFFILIATIONS:
IBW NSPA IPA

PRINCIPAL SUBJECTS:
Agriculture
Business & Industry
Government
General Interest
Amusements
Computer Technology
Foreign
Government
Hobbies
Journalism
Management
PUBLICATIONS:
Area Development Magazine
Canine Chronicle
CEE
Farm Store Merchandising
Floral & Nursery Times
Greyhound Review
Horseman
Micro Marketworld
Modern Recording
Printing Impressions
Resource Recycling
Spray Dust

BAUER, ERWIN A.
P.O. Box 987, E. River Rd.
Livingston, MT 59047
Telephone: 406-222-7100
Fax: 406-222-8216
AFFILIATIONS:
SATW ASMP OWAA
PRINCIPAL SUBJECTS:
Animals
Ecology
Sports
Travel
Nature
PUBLICATIONS:
Audubon
Wildlife Conservation
Outdoor Life
Travel
National Wildlife
National Geographic
Discovery
Chevron Odyssey, USA
International Wildlife
Relax
Travel & Leisure

BAYERS, RAPP LEA
82 Marsh Ave.
Sayreville, NJ 08872
Telephone: 908-238-9373
AFFILIATIONS:
SPJ, NFP, North Jersey PC,
  NJPW
PRINCIPAL SUBJECTS:
Business & Industry

Education
Personalities
General Interest
Human Interest
Travel
Health
PUBLICATIONS:
USA Today
NY Times
Business Journal of N.J.
In Business Magazine
Christian Science Monitor
Technical Photography
  Magazine
Playbill Magazine
NY Daily News
NY Post
Japan Times - Column
The Star-Ledger
Complete Woman Magazine
New Woman Magazine
Real Estate Forum
Asbury Park Press
New Jersey Monthly

BAYSURA, STEVEN A.
1750 Locust Rd.
Sewickley, PA 15143
Telephone: 412-741-7601
AFFILIATIONS:
SPJ
PRINCIPAL SUBJECTS:
Advertising
Journalism
Video
PUBLICATIONS:
Pittsburgh Press

BAYUS, LENORE
203 Shackelford Drive
Monroeville, PA 15146
Telephone: 412-372-3600
PRINCIPAL SUBJECTS:
Health
History
Religion
PUBLICATIONS:
Allegheny Business News
Pittsburgh Magazine
Alive Magazine
Pittsburgh Post-Gazette

BEAN, ALICE PEARSE
Belmont Rd. P.O. Box 15
Mica, WA 99023
Telephone: 509-926-5182
MAILING ADDRESS:
Bean, Alice
RR1, #15
Mica, WA 99023

PRINCIPAL SUBJECTS:
Agriculture
Home & Garden
Humor
PUBLICATIONS:
Reader's Digest
Washington Farmer
Calgary Herald

BEAUGE, JOHN Q.
2230 Reed St.
Williamsport, PA 17701
Telephone: 717-323-2460
AFFILIATIONS:
SPJ, SDX
PRINCIPAL SUBJECTS:
News
Sports
General Interest
PUBLICATIONS:
Harrisburg Patriot - News
Associated Press
United Press International
Pennsylvania Magazine
Northeast Business Journal

BECK, LAUREL
1184 Bradford Rd., NE
Massillon, OH 44646
Telephone: 216-833-8518
PRINCIPAL SUBJECTS:
Agriculture

BEDELL, THOMAS
HCR 63 Box 6
Williamsville, VT 05362
Telephone: 802-348-7992

BEEBE, F. LISA
407 Park Ave., S., Apt. 17E
New York, NY 10016
Telephone: 212-447-5920
AFFILIATIONS:
ASJA, TJG
PRINCIPAL SUBJECTS:
Travel
The Arts
History
Business & Industry
Personalities
Philosophy
PUBLICATIONS:
APA Insight Guide
  (Continental Europe)
Chicago Tribune
Miami Herald, The
Mabuhay (Philippine Airlines'
  Inflight Magazine)
Baltimore Sun
American Way
Pan Am Clipper

APA Insight Guide Spain
Washington Post
Los Angeles Times
Toronto Globe & Mail
Palm Beach Life
Birnbaum's
  Spain/Portugal 1990
Endless Vacation
Frommer's Barcelona Plus
  Majorca, Ibiza, & Minorca
New York Post
European Travel & Life
Frommer's Guides
The Washington Post

BEHRENS, JOHN
57 Stebbins Dr.
Clinton, NY 13323
Telephone: 315-853-6424
Fax: 315-853-6424
AFFILIATIONS:
ASJA, AG, SPJ
PRINCIPAL SUBJECTS:
Business & Industry
Ecology
History
Personalities
Media
Travel
Book Reviews
Human Interest
Education
Computer Technology
General Interest
Personal Finance
Motivation
Marine
Management
Journalism
PUBLICATIONS:
The Elks
Writer's Digest
Financial Weekly
College Press Review
American Forests
Mankind
Vocational Biographies
Nieman Reports
Commerce Commentary
American Printer
Career World
The Typographer
The Quill
College Management
Friends
True
North American Newspaper
  Alliance
Literacy Advance
Minorities in Business
Nursing

Freelancer's Newsletter
U.S. Oil Week
Leisure Living
Business Journal of New York
National Observer
Physician's Financial News
Omnigraphics
Editor & Publisher
Publisher's Auxiliary

BELL, JOSEPH N.
2382 Azure Ave.
Santa Ana, CA 92707
Telephone: 714-852-9569
Fax: 714-852-9569
MAILING ADDRESS:
Joseph N. Bell
Santa Ana, CA 92707
AFFILIATIONS:
SDC, ASJA
PRINCIPAL SUBJECTS:
Entertainment
Government
Personalities
Social Trends
Editorial
General Interest
History
Human Interest
Humor
Humor
Philosophy
The Arts
PUBLICATIONS:
Christian Science Monitor
Good Housekeeping
Harper's
McCall's
New York Times
National Observer
Los Angeles Times
Family Circle
Reader's Digest
Saturday Evening Post
Saturday Review

BELL, SALLY
6702 Sunnyland
Dallas, TX 75214
Telephone: 214-823-8448
Fax: 214-823-8448
PRINCIPAL SUBJECTS:
Business & Industry
Medical
Family
General Interest
Health
Human Interest
Journalism
News
Science

Social Trends
Travel
PUBLICATIONS:
Paris Herald Tribune
Sunday Times of London

BENDINER, ROBERT
45 Central Pkwy.
Huntington, NY 11743
Telephone: 516-421-5631
AFFILIATIONS:
NPC
PRINCIPAL SUBJECTS:
Ecology
Government
Travel
Humor
Animals
Journalism
Education
PUBLICATIONS:
Atlantic Monthly
New York Times
New York Times Magazine
World Press Review
Newsday
American Heritage
New Statesman

BENFORD, MARILYN
1464 Whippoorwill Way
Mountainside, NJ 07092
Telephone: 908-232-6701
Fax: 908-233-0485
AFFILIATIONS:
WPANJ, NATJA, FIJET
PRINCIPAL SUBJECTS:
Travel
World Affairs
Book Reviews
General Interest
PUBLICATIONS:
Columbia
Asbury Park Press
Daily Journal
Suburban News, The
Todays Seniors
New York Post
Denver Post
Hartford Courant

BENFORD, TIMOTHY B.
1464 Whippoorwill Way
Mountainside, NJ 07092
Telephone: 908-232-6701
Fax: 908-233-0485
AFFILIATIONS:
WPANJ, NATJA, FIJET
PRINCIPAL SUBJECTS:
Travel
History

Book Reviews
General Interest
PUBLICATIONS:
Columbia
Travel & Leisure
Star, The
Canadian Coin News - Coins
   (Columnist)
Suburban News, The
Numismatist, The
New York Post
Denver Post
Hartford Courant
Trenton Times
Asbury Park Press
Courier - News
Toronto Sun
Ft. Lauderdale News
N.Y. Times Syndication
Delaware Valley Mag. - Travel
   (Columnist)
Military History Mag.
Numismatic News
Coins Monthly, U.K. - Coins
   (Columnist)
Coins Mag. (U.S.)
Daily Journal, The
Today's Seniors
Coinage Magazine
Asta Congress Daily
Travel Weekly
Travel Agent Mag.
Travel Trade
Jersey Journal
Associated Press

BENSON, VIRGINIA PERKINS
1210 Locust St.
Saint Louis, MO 63103
Telephone: 314-231-1220
Fax: 314-231-3373
PRINCIPAL SUBJECTS:
The Arts
Medical
Religion

BENZAIA, DIANA
215 West 92nd Street
New York, NY 10025
Telephone: 212-580-8433
AFFILIATIONS:
NASW, ASJA
PRINCIPAL SUBJECTS:
Health
Medical
PUBLICATIONS:
Family Circle
McCall's
Self
Consumer's Digest
American Health

Glamour
Saturday Evening Post
Harper's Bazaar

BERG, MARGARET C.
199 N. El Camino Real, F-143
Encinitas, CA 92024
Telephone: 619-753-0787
Fax: 619-753-0787
AFFILIATIONS:
NPPA,ASPP,NWC
PRINCIPAL SUBJECTS:
Business & Industry
General Interest
Personalities
Travel
Photography
Computer Technology
Agriculture
Education
PUBLICATIONS:
Career Briefs - Chronicle
   Guidance

BERGER, AMY H.
1 Scheid Dr.
Parlin, NJ 08859
Telephone: 908-727-4670
Fax: 908-727-8677
AFFILIATIONS:
ASJA, NAP, NJP
PRINCIPAL SUBJECTS:
Entertainment
Family
Human Interest
Human Relations
Personalities
Women's Interest
PUBLICATIONS:
New York Times
Good Housekeeping
Seventeen
Working Mother

BERGER, IVAN
459 La Grande Ave.
Fanwood, NJ 07023
Telephone: 908-889-5818
Fax: 908-889-5528
AFFILIATIONS:
AES, ASJA, CPA
PRINCIPAL SUBJECTS:
Automotive
Computer Technology
Photography
Video
Entertainment
Business & Industry
Editorial
Electronics
Hobbies

Journalism
Men's Interest
Photography
PUBLICATIONS:
New York Times
Audio Magazine
Video Magazine
Road & Track
San Jose Mercury News
Audio
Home
Newsday
Popular Science
New York Times
Washington Post
Popular Photography
Esquire
GQ
Boys' Life
Home Mechanix

BERKO, ROBERT L.
439 Clark St.
South Orange, NJ 07079
Telephone: 201-762-6714
PRINCIPAL SUBJECTS:
General Interest
PUBLICATIONS:
Los Angeles Times
NY Times
San Diego Union
Changing Times
Womans World
Kiplinger
Chicago Defender
Today's Woman
Cosmopolitan

BERLAND, THEODORE
P.O. Box 597602
Chicago, IL 60659
Telephone: 312-274-0981
Fax: 312-274-2792
AFFILIATIONS:
NASW,AMWA,SDX,SMA
PRINCIPAL SUBJECTS:
Health
PUBLICATIONS:
Parade
Reader's Digest
Consumer Guide
Field News Wire
Better Homes & Gardens
N.E.A. Features
Time
American Health

BERMAN, BRIAN J.
P.O. Box 398
Allenhurst, NJ 07711
Telephone: 908-531-6834

Fax: 413-253-6490
PRINCIPAL SUBJECTS:
Government
Religion
Senior Citizens
News
Advertising
Photography
The Arts
Ecology
Youth
Urban Affairs
Business & Industry
Nature
Media
Health
Education
PUBLICATIONS:
New York Times
New York Daily News
Emergency
Time Off
Glamor
EC Rocker
People
N.J. Focus
Asbury Park Press
Bazaar
USA Weekend
Associated Press

BERMAN, CLAIRE
52 Riverside Dr.
New York, NY 10024
Telephone: 212-874-7633
AFFILIATIONS:
ASJA, AUTHORS GUILD
PRINCIPAL SUBJECTS:
Business & Industry
Family
General Interest
Health
Human Relations
Education
Social Trends
PUBLICATIONS:
New York Times-(Newspaper &
  Magazine)
Reader's Digest
New York Magazine
Working Woman
McCall's
Family Circle
Parents
Redbook
Family Circle
American Health
Working Mother
Video Digest
Comopolitain
Self

BERNTHAL, RON
Sunday Record
Middletown, NY 10940
Telephone: 914-343-2180
MAILING ADDRESS:
P.O. Box D
Hurleyville, NY 12747
Telephone: 914-434-1529
AFFILIATIONS:
SATW SEJ NSNC
PUBLICATIONS:
Middletown Sunday Record
Boston Herald
Buffalo News
Raleigh News & Observer
Fort Myers Press
America (German)
Toronto Globe & Mail
Newsday

BERRY, S.L.
439 East 49th Street
Indianapolis, IN 46205
Telephone: 317-925-3404
AFFILIATIONS:
Skip, ASJA, AG
PRINCIPAL SUBJECTS:
Amusements
Business & Industry
Education
Entertainment
Family
General Interest
Health
Home & Garden
Human Interest
Journalism
Medical
Personalities
Physical Fitness
Social Trends
Sports
The Arts
Travel
Youth
PUBLICATIONS:
New York Times
Travel & Leisure
Home
USAir Magazine
Nation's Business
Sport
U.S. Art
Endless Vacation

BIGELOW, ROBERT
10 Converse Pl.
Winchester, MA 01890
Telephone: 617-729-2334
Fax: 617-729-2336

AFFILIATIONS:
ABA
PRINCIPAL SUBJECTS:
Management
Business & Industry
Computer Technology
PUBLICATIONS:
Computer Law & Tax report
  (Editor 1974 - 1984)
Law Office Economics & Mgt.
  (Editor 1969 - 1978)
Computer Decisions
Infosystems
Law Practice Management
  (Editorial Staff 1976-1993
Computerdata (American
  Correspondent)
Computer Security Journal
  (Editor 1981)
Datamation
Computerworld
Harvard Business Review
Computer Law Service
Computer Law Newsletter
  (Editor 1979 - 1987)
American Bar Assn. Journal
Jurimetrics Journal (Editor
  1974 - 1977)
Bullentin of Law Science
  Technology (Ed 1977-1980)
Hard Copy
Computer Negotiations Report
Mini Micro Systems (Formerly
  Modern Data)
Legal Times
Lawyers Weekly
Lawyers Alert
Emory Law Journal
Hastings Law Journal
Computing Reviews
Abacus
ICP Insiders' Letter
Encyclopedia of Computer
  Science & Engineering
Legal Times of Washington
Executive Perspectives
Information Privacy
Washington University Law
  Quarterly
Criminal Law Review
Computers & Public Policy
Practical Lawyer, The
Informatica e Diritto
Information Systems
  Handbook
Massachusetts Law Quarterly
Facts & Figures
Rutgers Journal of Computers
  & the Law
EDP Industry Report
Law & Computer Technology

Boston Bar Journal
Western New England Law
  Review
Florida Bar Journal
Transnational Data &
  Communications Report
Corporate Counsellor
Computer Law & Practice
Canadian Computer Law
  Reporter
Computer Law & Security
  Report
Computer Lawyer
Washington State Bar News
Rutgers Computer &
  Technology L. Journal
EDP Auditor Journal
128 News
Bulletin of The Computer Law
  Association

BIRNBAUM, NATALIE
3166 Twin Lakes Trace
Marietta, GA 30062
Telephone: 404-977-3492
PRINCIPAL SUBJECTS:
Medical
Business & Industry
Journalism
Education
PUBLICATIONS:
Arthritis Foundation Medical
  Imformation Series
Joint Movement - Arthritis
  Newsletter
Soc. of Technical
  Communicators Atlanta
  Newsletter

BISHER, FURMAN
431 Lester Rd.
Fayetteville, GA 30214
Telephone: 404-487-6202
AFFILIATIONS:
GWAP, NJSA, FWAR, TWA,
  BBWA
PRINCIPAL SUBJECTS:
Amusements
Journalism
Personalities
Sports
Travel
PUBLICATIONS:
Atlanta Journal/Constitution
Golf Digest
Southern Living
The Sporting News
Sky Magazine
Saturday Evening Post
Collier's
Saturday Evening Post

True
Sport
Look
PGA
Atlanta Magazine
N.Y. Times Magazine
Gentlemen's Quarterly
Mercedes Benz World
  Magazine
Progressive Farmer
Golf Magazine
Sports Illustrated
Wall Street Journal
Golf
Southern Links Magazine
Business Week

BITETTI, MARGE
P.O. Box 7694
Huntington Bch., CA 92615
Telephone: 714-965-3682
Fax: 714-965-3683
MAILING ADDRESS:
Bitetti & Associates
Huntington Bch., CA 92615
Telephone: 714-965-3683
AFFILIATIONS:
Toastmaster, NBWE, PASS
PRINCIPAL SUBJECTS:
Entertainment
Business & Industry
Personalities
Religion
PUBLICATIONS:
Boston Globe
Orange Coast Magazine
Daily Pilot Newspaper
National Catholic Register
The Tidings
Liberty Street Chronicle
Los Angeles

BITETTI, TONY
P.O. Box 7694
Huntington Bch., CA 92615
Telephone: 714-965-3683
MAILING ADDRESS:
Bitetti & Associates
Huntington Bch., CA 92615
Telephone: 714-965-3682
PUBLICATIONS:
The Daily Pilot
The Barnstormer
Doggie Bazaar
The Bakersfield Californian

BLACK, DEAN
371 North 900 East
Springville, UT 84663
Telephone: 801-489-9432
Fax: 801-489-9850

MAILING ADDRESS:
Dean Black, Ph.D.
P.O. Box 653
Springville, UT 84663
PRINCIPAL SUBJECTS:
Health
Family
Human Interest

BLAKE, PATRICIA
2800 N. Hamline Ave., 326
Saint Paul, MN 55113
Telephone: 612-633-8092
PRINCIPAL SUBJECTS:
Health

BLASK, ANN SABATINI
18 Harvard Pl.
Orchard Park, NY 14127
Telephone: 716-662-1742
Fax: 716-662-1385
AFFILIATIONS:
ASJA
PRINCIPAL SUBJECTS:
Travel
Business & Industry
Senior Citizens
PUBLICATIONS:
Travel & Leisure
Business New York
Travel Age
Frequent Flyer

BLISHAK, SYLVIA ANN
14333 Hill Road
Klamath Falls, OR 97603
Telephone: 503-885-7333
Fax: 503-885-2180
AFFILIATIONS:
ASJA, NWC
PRINCIPAL SUBJECTS:
Business & Industry
Family
Management
Sales
Travel
PUBLICATIONS:
Amtrak Express
International Living
Interval Int. Traveler
Passenger Train Journal
Office Systems
Rotarian
Travel Agent
Entrepreneur

BLIVEN JR., BRUCE
C/O The New Yorker
New York, NY 10036
Telephone: 212-840-3800

AFFILIATIONS:
AG, PEN
PRINCIPAL SUBJECTS:
General Interest
History
PUBLICATIONS:
New York Times
New Yorker
Atlantic
Harper's
Readers Digest
Life
Look
Ladies Home Journal
McCall's
Redbook
Saturday Review
Intellectual Digest
Esquire
Ford Times
Woman's Home Companion
Manchester Guardian
New York Post

BLIZZARD, WILLIAM C.
11 Riverside Glen
Winfield, WV 25213
Telephone: 304-755-0094
AFFILIATIONS:
NWU
PRINCIPAL SUBJECTS:
Animals
Editorial
General Interest
Hobbies
Human Interest
Humor
Journalism
Men's Interest
Personalities
Senior Citizens

BLOCK, BARRY
P.O. Box 50
New York, NY 10044
Telephone: 212-355-5216
PRINCIPAL SUBJECTS:
Health
PUBLICATIONS:
Foot Health
Law & Medicine
Practice Management
Footwear

BLOCK, JEAN LIBMAN
529 W. 42nd St., #4P
New York, NY 10036
Telephone: 212-736-0135
AFFILIATIONS:
ASJA

PRINCIPAL SUBJECTS:
Family
Fashion
Health
Personalities
PUBLICATIONS:
Good Housekeeping
Reader's Digest
Woman's Day

BLOCK, JULIAN
3 Washington Sq., Apt. 1-G
Larchmont, NY 10538
Telephone: 914-834-3227
AFFILIATIONS:
ASJA, NYSBA
PRINCIPAL SUBJECTS:
Personal Finance
PUBLICATIONS:
Argosy
Family Health
Family Weekly
Farm Journal
Good Housekeeping
House Beautiful
McCalls
Mechanix Illustrated
Medical Economics
Playboy
Popular Mechanics
Successful Farming
Vogue
Writer's Digest
TWA Ambassador
Business Week
American Bookseller
Money Magazine
American Way
Electrical Contractor
Bookstore Journal
Physicians Management
Viva
Various
Easy Living
Industry Week
Life and Health
Prime Times
Southern Motor Cargo
Success
U. S. Air Magazine
Woman's Day
Fence Industry
Home Video
New Woman
Better Homes And Gardens
In Business
Single Parent
Working Woman
Dental Mangement
Campground Management
Dynamic Years

Sylvia Porter's Personal
  Finance Magazine
Consumers Digest
Consumer Reports
Medical World News
New Choices
Baltimore Sun
Inc. Magazine
National Business Employment
  Weekly
San Antonio Light
Veterinary Economics
Self - Employed America
Bergen Record
New York Daily News
Player, The
Orlando Sentinel
Chicago Tribune
Sacramento Bee
St. Louis Post Dispatch
IB Independent Business
Winning
Women's News
Spotlight Magazine
Newark Star Ledger
Tax Savings Report
Washington Times

BLOCK, VICTOR
5415 Connecticut Ave., N.W.
Washington, DC 20015
Telephone: 202-364-0705
AFFILIATIONS:
SATW,OWAA,TJG
PRINCIPAL SUBJECTS:
Travel
PUBLICATIONS:
Green Bay Press Gazette, The
Washington Times, The
New York Post, The
New Hampshire Sunday
  News, The
Senior Digest, The
Travel Agent Magazine

BLODGETT, RICHARD
9 Charlton St.
New York, NY 10014
Telephone: 212-620-0928
AFFILIATIONS:
AG, ASJA
PRINCIPAL SUBJECTS:
The Arts
Business & Industry
Personal Finance
PUBLICATIONS:
McCall's
New York Times
Games

Reader's Digest
New York
Working Mother

BLOOM, MURRAY TEIGH
40 Hemlock Dr.
Great Neck, NY 11024
Telephone: 516-487-8528
AFFILIATIONS:
ASJA
PRINCIPAL SUBJECTS:
Government
Management
Personal Finance
Business & Industry
Human Interest
General Interest
PUBLICATIONS:
McCall's
N.Y. Times Magazine
Reader's Digest
Redbook
New Republic
Harper's

BLUE, MARIAN
527 Delaware Ave.
Norfolk, VA 23508
Telephone: 804-640-1262
MAILING ADDRESS:
Marian Blue
Norfolk, VA 23508
PRINCIPAL SUBJECTS:
Humor
Nature
Personalities
Sports
PUBLICATIONS:
Coastal Cruising
Chesapeake Bay Magazine
Christian Science Monitor
Virginia Business
La Republica Dominicana
Soundings
Sail Magazine
Northwest Magazine

BLUM, MICHELLE E.
2239 Eoff St.
Wheeling, WV 26003
Telephone: 304-233-5622
Fax: 304-233-0100
AFFILIATIONS:
SIGMA, DELTA CHI
PRINCIPAL SUBJECTS:
Government
PUBLICATIONS:
Youngstown Business Journal
Poland Clarion
Wheeling News - Register
Wheeling Hospital Magazine

BLUMENFELD, ESTHER
1231 Lenox Circle, NE
Atlanta, GA 30306
Telephone: 404-872-1026

BLY, ROBERT W.
22 E. Quakenbush Ave.
Dumont, NJ 07628
Telephone: 201-385-1220
AFFILIATIONS:
BPAA, AICHE
PRINCIPAL SUBJECTS:
Electronics
Advertising
Computer Technology
Editorial
General Interest
Medical
Marketing
Sales
PUBLICATIONS:
Amtrak Express
Cosmopolitan
Computer Decisions
Writer's Digest
Business Marketing
Direct Marketing
Money Paper, The
Audio - Visual Directions
New Jersey Monthly

BOBROW, JUDITH
13361 Victoria
Huntington Wood, MI 48070
Telephone: 313-543-7342
AFFILIATIONS:
WICI
PRINCIPAL SUBJECTS:
Health

BODGER, CAROLE
931 Lyons Rd.
Coconut Creek, FL 33063
Telephone: 305-977-6607
PRINCIPAL SUBJECTS:
Health
General Interest
Human Interest
Animals
Medical
Education
PUBLICATIONS:
New York Times
Glamour
McCall's
Working Woman
50 Plus

Westsider/Chelsea - Clinton
  News, The
New York Torch, The
Report, The
Fitness Magazine

BOECKMAN, CHARLES
322 Del Mar Blvd.
Corpus Christi, TX 78404
Telephone: 512-884-7079
Fax: 512-884-6010
AFFILIATIONS:
ASJA, MWA, RWA
PRINCIPAL SUBJECTS:
Editorial
Health
Human Interest
Senior Citizens
The Arts
Travel
Urban Affairs
Youth

BOEHM, GEORGE A. W.
330 East 79th St.
New York, NY 10021
Telephone: 212-737-6422
AFFILIATIONS:
NASW, AMS
PRINCIPAL SUBJECTS:
Business & Industry
Ecology
Health
Philosophy
Science
Sports
PUBLICATIONS:
Reader's Digest
Technology Review
Focus
Fortune
Harvard Business Review
N.Y. Times Magazine

BOND, ALMA H., PHD
606 Truman Avenue, #1
Key West, FL 33040
Telephone: 305-292-9173
Fax: 305-292-9173

BOONE, GENE
Rt. 2, Box 194
Society Hill, SC 29593
Telephone: 803-378-4556
MAILING ADDRESS:
Gene Boone
Box 394
Society Hill, SC 29593
PRINCIPAL SUBJECTS:
Business & Industry
Advertising

Amusements
Animals
Book Reviews
Entertainment
Family
Home & Garden
Humor
Nature
Sales
Youth
Video
PUBLICATIONS:
Fate Magazine
Women's Circle
Byline Magazine
Poet's Market/Writers Digest
Writer's Lifeline
Writers Exchange
Standard
Romantic Times

BOORSTIN, DANIEL J.
3541 Ordway St., N.W.
Washington, DC 20016
Telephone: 202-966-1853
MAILING ADDRESS:
Daniel J. Boorstin
Washington, DC 20016
AFFILIATIONS:
AHA OAH
PRINCIPAL SUBJECTS:
Editorial
History
The Arts
PUBLICATIONS:
Esquire
Fortune
N.Y. Times
Newsweek
Reader's Digest
TV Guide
Yale Review
U.S. News and World Report

BOREA, PHYLLIS GILBERT
245 W. 104th St., #15D
New York, NY 10025
Telephone: 212-880-2748
AFFILIATIONS:
ASPP
PRINCIPAL SUBJECTS:
Animals
Photography
The Arts
Family
PUBLICATIONS:
Lady's Circle
Popular Photography
Art Business News
Today's Art & Graphics

BOROSON, WARREN
47 Ridge Rd.
Glen Rock, NJ 07452
Telephone: 201-444-3583
AFFILIATIONS:
AG NASW, AMWA
PRINCIPAL SUBJECTS:
Business & Industry
Health
PUBLICATIONS:
Family Circle
New York News
N.Y. Times Magazine
Next Magazine
Better Homes & Gardens
Reader's Digest
TV Guide
Woman's Day

BORTSTEIN, LARRY
765 W. Colorado Blvd.
Monrovia, CA 91016
Telephone: 818-359-6536
AFFILIATIONS:
FWAA, NTWA
PRINCIPAL SUBJECTS:
Amusements
The Arts
Sports
PUBLICATIONS:
Christian Science Monitor
Sport
The Sporting News
TWA Ambassador
US Magazine
Oui
Newsday
Empire
Thoroughbred of California
New Orleans Times-Picayune
The Olympian
New York Times

BOSCO, ANTOINETTE
23 Stony Hill Rd.
Brookfield, CT 06804
Telephone: 203-775-2612
AFFILIATIONS:
ASJA
PRINCIPAL SUBJECTS:
Entertainment
Health
Religion
Personalities
PUBLICATIONS:
Litchfield County Times, The
Catholic News Service

BOSE, MICHAEL ALAN
1195 Virginia Ave.
York, PA 17403

Telephone: 717-848-2043
PRINCIPAL SUBJECTS:
Editorial
Foreign
History
Men's Interest
PUBLICATIONS:
York Daily Record
Travel/Food Newsletter

BOTTEL, HELEN
2060 56TH Ave.
Sacramento, CA 95822
Telephone: 916-421-5832
AFFILIATIONS:
CWC, CRCPC, ASJA
PRINCIPAL SUBJECTS:
Family
General Interest
Women's Interest
Humor
Health
Travel
Social Trends
Senior Citizens
Human Relations
PUBLICATIONS:
Family Circle
Good Housekeeping
McCall's
Motor Boating & Sailing
Pageant
Reader's Digest
Retirement Living
Writer's Digest
American Education
Runners' World
Real World
Sunday Woman
Sacramento Bee
Yomiuri Shimbun,
  Tokyo(Regular Column)
Playboy
Sacramento Sports Magazine
Sacramento Union (Regular
  Column)
Sacramento Magazine
Los Angeles Times

BOTWIN, CAROL
200 E. 63rd St.
New York, NY 10021
Telephone: 212-935-1611
AFFILIATIONS:
ASJA
PRINCIPAL SUBJECTS:
Family
General Interest
Health
Medical
Youth

Social Trends
Human Relations
Human Interest
Psychology
Women's Interest
PUBLICATIONS:
Woman's Day
Family Weekly
Glamour
New York Times Magazine
Redbook
Reader's Digest
Cosmopolitan
Ladies Home Journal
New Woman
Woman

BOUCHIER, DAVID
P.O. Box 468
Wading River, NY 11792
Telephone: 516-929-6215
Fax: 516-929-6215
AFFILIATIONS:
ASJA, EFA, ASA
PRINCIPAL SUBJECTS:
Book Reviews
Education
Human Relations
Humor
Media
Social Trends
PUBLICATIONS:
New York Times
Newsday
Atlanta Journal/Constitution
Chronicle Higher Education
New Statesman & Society (UK)

BOYKIN, JOHN E.
Rt. 1, Box 174C
Buffalo, TX 75831
Telephone: 214-536-7675
AFFILIATIONS:
SPE
PRINCIPAL SUBJECTS:
Agriculture
Hobbies
Business & Industry
Men's Interest
Sports
Travel
PUBLICATIONS:
Argosy
Ford Times
Modern Cycle
Popular Mechanics
AC LAND HANDLER
Treasure & Treasure Search

Farmer-Stockman
Visions
Case Mark
Sunset

BRAMS, STANLEY H.
24500 Southfield Rd.
Southfield, MI 48075
Telephone: 313-569-3537
Fax: 313-585-1926
AFFILIATIONS:
IMPA, DAWG, SAE
PRINCIPAL SUBJECTS:
Automotive
Travel
Business & Industry
Health
PUBLICATIONS:
Michigan Living
Family Week
New Yorker
New York Times Mag.
Passages
Parents Magazine
American Legion Magazine

BRASSELL, SEARLES
  LUCINDA
16 Rue Deauville
Newport Beach, CA 92660
Telephone: 714-640-8044
Fax: 714-460-8044
AFFILIATIONS:
Women in Broadcasting
PRINCIPAL SUBJECTS:
Editorial
Education
Foreign
Health
Sports
The Arts
Women's Interest
Youth
PUBLICATIONS:
Los Angeles Times
Scholastic

BRAUN, VICKI
128 Oak Knoll Drive
Dayton, OH 45419
Telephone: 513-299-7935
Fax: 513-299-7935
AFFILIATIONS:
WIC
PRINCIPAL SUBJECTS:
Health
Human Interest
Medical
Physical Fitness
Psychology
Senior Citizens

PUBLICATIONS:
Dayton Daily News
Sport Pulse
Growing Together

BREECHER, M.P.H.,
  MAURY M.
33 Bellwood
Northport, AL 35476
Telephone: 205-752-3705
AFFILIATIONS:
NASW, ASJA, SPJ,
  AJHA, AEJMC
PRINCIPAL SUBJECTS:
Computer Technology
Health
History
Human Interest
Journalism
Medical
Motivation
Physical Fitness
Psychology
PUBLICATIONS:
Reader's Digest
Ladies' Home Journal
Medical World News
LA Times
News America/Times of
  London
New York Times

BRESCOLL, JAMES
1315 W. Roosevelt Rd.
Wheaton, IL 60187
Telephone: 708-665-1115
PRINCIPAL SUBJECTS:
General Interest
Government
Human Relations
Personalities
Philosophy

BRESLAUER, IRWIN J.
545 West End Ave.
New York, NY 10024
Telephone: 212-580-8559
MAILING ADDRESS:
Scripps Howard News Service
New York, NY 10024
Telephone: 212-769-4384
PRINCIPAL SUBJECTS:
Travel
General Interest
PUBLICATIONS:
Scripps Howard News Service

BRESLAV, MARC
11 Peekskill Rd.
Cold Spring, NY 10516
Telephone: 914-265-2624

AFFILIATIONS:
AAM, ACI, NAI, NRC, SEJ
PRINCIPAL SUBJECTS:
Animals
Ecology
History
Marine
Nature
Science
PUBLICATIONS:
Garden
Living Bird Quarterly
Natural History
Outdoor Communicator
American Biology Teacher
Balance Wheel
Resource Recycling
Community Greening Review
Backpacker

BRESNICK, JAN
17 Witherspoon
Morristown, NJ 07960
Telephone: 201-605-1440
PRINCIPAL SUBJECTS:
Health
Psychology
Travel
General Interest
PUBLICATIONS:
Cosmopolitan
Savvy
Adweek
Madison Ave.
Quick & Healthy Cooking
Good Toys
Men's Health
New Jersey Monthly

BRICKMAN, NANCI
153 Lincoln Ave.
Hastings-on-Hud, NY 10706
Telephone: 914-478-5536
Fax: 914-478-5680
AFFILIATIONS:
WICI
PRINCIPAL SUBJECTS:
Home & Garden
Business & Industry

BRIGHTMAN, ROBERT
5 Sussex Rd.
Great Neck, NY 11020
Telephone: 516-482-2074
AFFILIATIONS:
NAHWW
PRINCIPAL SUBJECTS:
Automotive
Men's Interest
Home & Garden
Photography

Science
PUBLICATIONS:
Better Homes & Gardens
Popular Mechanics
Reader's Digest
N.Y. Times
How-To Magazine
Woodworking
Scribners
Scholastic Magazines
McCalls

BRINLEY, MARYANN
　BUCKNUM
167 Cooper Avenue
Upper Montclair, NJ 07043
Telephone: 201-746-1608
AFFILIATIONS:
ASJA
PRINCIPAL SUBJECTS:
Education
Family
Health
Medical
Psychology
Senior Citizens
Women's Interest
Youth
PUBLICATIONS:
Good Housekeeping
Family Circle
Woman's Day
McCall's
Health
New Choices

BRODSKY, RUTHAN
722 Parkman
Bloomfield, MI 48304
Telephone: 313-644-0233
Fax: 313-855-3207
PRINCIPAL SUBJECTS:
Education
Physical Fitness
Psychology
Sports
Health
Medical
Senior Citizens

BRODY, PEG
1516 Hillcrest Road
Lancaster, PA 17603
Telephone: 717-299-4795
Fax: 717-299-4971
PRINCIPAL SUBJECTS:
Video
Journalism
Advertising

BROOKS, LESTER
43 Marshall Ridge Rd.
New Canaan, CT 06840
Telephone: 203-966-0610
AFFILIATIONS:
AL NABE SATW TJ
PRINCIPAL SUBJECTS:
Business & Industry
History
Travel
PUBLICATIONS:
Eyewitness Guide to New York
Fisher's World Spain &
　Portugal, 1988
Crown Insiders' Guide to
　Britain
Crown Insiders' Guide to
　New York

BROOKS, PATRICIA
43 Marshall Ridge Rd.
New Canaan, CT 06840
Telephone: 203-966-0610
AFFILIATIONS:
SATW NYTW
PRINCIPAL SUBJECTS:
The Arts
General Interest
Health
Humor
Personalities
Travel
Women's Interest
Media
PUBLICATIONS:
Family Circle
House & Garden
Modern Bride
New York Times
Saturday Review
Travel & Leisure
IBM's Think Magazine
Bon Appetit
Vogue
Modern Bride

BROWN, GAIL
20 Crocker Pond Rd.
Wrentham, MA 02093
Telephone: 508-384-3369
AFFILIATIONS:
SPJ
PRINCIPAL SUBJECTS:
Human Interest
Business & Industry
News

BROWN, TERRY T.
25885 York Rd.
Royal Oak, MI 48067
Telephone: 313-545-5039

Fax: 313-545-4761
AFFILIATIONS:
SAE
PRINCIPAL SUBJECTS:
Automotive
Entertainment
General Interest
PUBLICATIONS:
Daily Tribune, (Royal Oak, Mi)

BROY, ANTHONY
85 - 17 57TH Rd.
Flushing, NY 11373
Telephone: 718-779-2259
AFFILIATIONS:
ASJA, NSW
PRINCIPAL SUBJECTS:
Business & Industry
General Interest
Management
Science
Health
PUBLICATIONS:
Dun's Review
Flightime
New York Times
Financial World
Stock Market Magazine
Market Chronicle
New York News
INC Magazine
Sydney Morning Herald
　(Australia)
Australian Financial Review
Nation, The
Magazine of Wall Street
Managing Your Money

BRUNING, NANCY
980 Bush St. #503
San Francisco, CA 94109
Telephone: 415-928-6811
Fax: 415-928-6849
AFFILIATIONS:
AG
PRINCIPAL SUBJECTS:
Health
Ecology
PUBLICATIONS:
Travel & Leisure
Longevity
Garbage
Buzzworm

BUCHMAN, DIAN DINCIN
640 West End Ave.
New York, NY 10024
Telephone: 212-362-3525
Fax: 212-362-3630
AFFILIATIONS:
NASW, ASJA

PRINCIPAL SUBJECTS:
Health
Personalities
PUBLICATIONS:
Harper's Bazaar
New York Magazine
Show
Health Quarterly
Cosmopolitan

BUDROW, NANCY
5755 S.W. Jean Rd., #204-A
Lake Oswego, OR 97035
Telephone: 503-635-2411
Fax: 503-635-2312
AFFILIATIONS:
NWI, ASMP, NASJA, OREGON
　PRESS WOMEN
PRINCIPAL SUBJECTS:
Travel
Nature
History
Human Interest
Marketing
Photography
Sports
Travel
PUBLICATIONS:
Christian Science Monitor
Cross Country Skier Magazine
Nordic West
Northwest Magazine
Northern Adventures
Las Vegas City Magazine
Balloon Life
Quintescence
Ski Oregon
Northwest Sports Report
The Oregonian
Northwest Runner
Oregon Sports and Recreation

BUONOCORE, JULIA
140 E 56 St.
New York, NY 10022
Telephone: 212-421-5196
AFFILIATIONS:
ASJA, NWU
PRINCIPAL SUBJECTS:
Health
Women's Interest
Hobbies
PUBLICATIONS:
New Baby
Walking Magazine
N.Y. Newsday
Knife & Fork
Cosmopolitan
YM
Brides Today

BURCH, MONTE
Rt. 1, P.O. Box 278
Humansville, MO 65674
Telephone: 417-754-8379
AFFILIATIONS:
OWAA, AGLOW, SCOPA,
  NHWAA
PRINCIPAL SUBJECTS:
Nature
Hobbies
Sports
PUBLICATIONS:
Field & Stream
Organic Gardening
Outdoor Life
Popular Mechanics
Popular Science
Sports Afield
Work Bench
Bassmaster
Petersen's Hunting
How-To
Guns & Ammo
Family Handyman
Mechanic Illustrated
USA Outdoors
Agua - Field
Harris Publications

BURGETT, GORDON
3863 Cherry Hill Rd.
Santa Maria, CA 93455
Telephone: 805-937-8711
Fax: 805-937-3035
MAILING ADDRESS:
Gordon Burgett
P.O. Box 6405
Santa Maria, CA 93456
AFFILIATIONS:
ASJA, NSA, PMA
PRINCIPAL SUBJECTS:
Journalism
Travel
PUBLICATIONS:
Better Homes and Gardens
Travel
Dynamic Years
The Runner
Washington Post
Chicago Sun-Times
Miami Herald
Highlights For Children
House Beautiful
Modern Maturity

BURTON, MARDA
431 Royal #2
New Orleans, LA 70130
Telephone: 504-561-0420
Fax: 504-561-0420

AFFILIATIONS:
ASJA, TJG, SATW
PRINCIPAL SUBJECTS:
General Interest
Home & Garden
Personalities
Photography
Travel
PUBLICATIONS:
Veranda
Recommend
Saturday Evening Post
Lear's
Physician's Travel &
  Meeting Guide
Cosmopolitan
Travel & Leisure
Travel-Holiday

BYAM, LINDA G.
P.O. Box 1273
Troy, MI 48099
Telephone: 313-244-8458
Fax: 313-244-8491
AFFILIATIONS:
WICI
PRINCIPAL SUBJECTS:
Marketing
Business & Industry

BYRNE-DODGE, TERESA
15 Carolane Trail
Houston, TX 77024
Telephone: 713-468-5528
Fax: 713-468-0651
AFFILIATIONS:
ASJA
PRINCIPAL SUBJECTS:
Architecture
Book Reviews
Home & Garden
Social Trends
The Arts
Travel
Women's Interest
PUBLICATIONS:
New York Times
Southern Accents
Houston Metropolitan
Texas Monthly
Town & Country
Food & Wine
Houston Post

CADIEUX, CHARLES L.
8209 Harwood NE
Albuquerque, NM 87110
Telephone: 505-299-3483
Fax: 505-271-4884
AFFILIATIONS:
OWAA, ASJA

PRINCIPAL SUBJECTS:
Ecology
Sports
Travel
PUBLICATIONS:
Outdoor Life
Field and Stream
Salt Water Sportsman
Field & Stream
Yachting

CAHILL, CARL
244 Old Dr.
Chesapeake, VA 23320
Telephone: 804-547-8622
AFFILIATIONS:
ASJA
PRINCIPAL SUBJECTS:
Sports
Travel
Religion
Human Interest
Humor
PUBLICATIONS:
New York Journal Of
  Commerce
Religious News Service
Richmond Times - Dispatch
Air Conditioning And
  Heating News
Grocers' Spotlight
Nations Restaurant News
Los Angeles Times
New York Times
Christian Science Monitor
Nation, The
Recreation News
Camping Today
Norfolk Ledger - Star
Bike Report
Baltimore Sun
Washington Times
Washington Post
Jacksonville Today
Senior Voice Newspaper
New York Daily News
Richmond Times - Dispatch
Miami Herald
Collector's News

CALABRO, MARIAN
327 Cleveland Ave.
Hasbrouck Hts., NJ 07604
Telephone: 201-288-2036
Fax: 201-288-0567
AFFILIATIONS:
ASJA, IABC
PRINCIPAL SUBJECTS:
Advertising
Animals
Business & Industry

Computer Technology
Entertainment
Management
Nature
The Arts
Travel
PUBLICATIONS:
Bank Technology Report
Bank Security Report

CALLAHAN, FLORENCE
506 Marion Ave.
New Milford, NJ 07646
Telephone: 201-265-1094
MAILING ADDRESS:
Florence Callahan
New Milford, NJ 07646
AFFILIATIONS:
SPJ
PRINCIPAL SUBJECTS:
Education
PUBLICATIONS:
Bergen Record, N.J.
New York Post

CAMPBELL, CANDACE
459 Walker Rd.
Great Falls, VA 22066
Telephone: 703-759-5126
Fax: 703-759-6711
PRINCIPAL SUBJECTS:
Business & Industry
Travel
Health
PUBLICATIONS:
New York Times
Self Magazine
Advertising Age Magazine
Washingtonian Magazine
House Beautiful
Runner's World

CAMPER, FRED
P.O. Box A 3866
Chicago, IL 60690
Telephone: 312-561-9368
PRINCIPAL SUBJECTS:
The Arts
Photography
PUBLICATIONS:
Chicago Reader
Film Culture

CANDLER, JULIE
19400 W. Ten Mile #217
Southfield, MI 48075-2433
Telephone: 313-354-5265
Fax: 313-354-0517
AFFILIATIONS:
SPJ, ASJA, WIC

PRINCIPAL SUBJECTS:
Automotive
Marine
Travel
PUBLICATIONS:
Nation's Business
Woman's Day
McCall's
Redbook
Advertising Age
Michigan Living
Ford Times

CANDLER, JULIE
19400 W. Ten Mile #217
Southfield, MI 48075
Telephone: 313-354-5265
Fax: 313-354-0517
AFFILIATIONS:
ASJA WICI SPJ
PRINCIPAL SUBJECTS:
Automotive
Travel
Marine
General Interest
PUBLICATIONS:
Nations Business
Red Book
McCalls
Woman's Day
Style

CANNON, DORIS
2914 Orlando St.
Knoxville, TN 37917
Telephone: 615-524-0029
AFFILIATIONS:
TWA
PRINCIPAL SUBJECTS:
Advertising
Fashion
Fashion
News
General Interest
General Interest

CAPOTOSTO, JOHN
10 S. Hollow Rd.
Huntingtn Sta, NY 11746
Telephone: 516-643-8326
AFFILIATIONS:
NAHWW
PRINCIPAL SUBJECTS:
Amusements
    Hobbies

CAREW, RUTH M. HARMER
437 Crane Blvd.
Los Angeles, CA 90065
Telephone: 213-225-4839

AFFILIATIONS:
WPC, PEN, AG, NWLI
PRINCIPAL SUBJECTS:
Health
Education
Foreign
Ecology
Medical
Social Trends
PUBLICATIONS:
Atlanta Monthly
Modern Maturity
Reader's Digest
Progressive
Los Angeles Times

CARRENO, RICHARD D.
P.O. Box 607
Quinebaug, CT 06262
Telephone: 203-923-9925
Fax: 202-619-5478
AFFILIATIONS:
SPJ
PRINCIPAL SUBJECTS:
Fashion
Book Reviews
Animals
Journalism
Media
PUBLICATIONS:
Boston Globe
Horseplay
Hartford Courant
N.Y. Times
Worcester Magazine
Cineaste
American Journalism Review

CARUANA, CLAUDIA M.
P.O. Box 20077 Dag
    Hammarskjold Sta.
New York, NY 10017
Telephone: 516-488-5815
PRINCIPAL SUBJECTS:
Travel
Health
Medical
Science
Education
PUBLICATIONS:
American Baby
Chicago Tribune
Christian Science Monitor
Consumers Digest
Weight Watchers
New York Magazine
Parents
Travel Age
New York Times
Working Mother
Seventeen

Brides
McCall's
Lears
Galapagos
Italy

CARUBA, ALAN
9 Brookside Rd.
Maplewood, NJ 07040
Telephone: 201-763-6392
Fax: 201-763-4287
MAILING ADDRESS:
Alan Caruba
Maplewood, NJ 07040
AFFILIATIONS:
NSWA, ASJA, SPJ
PRINCIPAL SUBJECTS:
Business & Industry
Management
Media
Science
Book Reviews
Entertainment
General Interest
Marketing
Personalities
Psychology
Social Trends
PUBLICATIONS:
New York Times
Travel Holiday
Advertising Age
Progressive Farmer
Food Executive
Public Relations Journal
Medical Marketing & Media
Progressive Grocer
Club Management
Executive Housekeeping
    Today
Communication World
Nursing Homes
Communication World
Homeowner
Folio

CASANO, KATE
158 Cotton St.
Philadelphia, PA 19127
Telephone: 215-483-1454
Fax: 215-483-7045
AFFILIATIONS:
AMWA
PRINCIPAL SUBJECTS:
Medical
PUBLICATIONS:
ACP Observer (American
    College of Physicians)
Research Resources Reporter
Physician's News Digest

Oncology News International
Drug Topics
Convention Reporter

CASS, MAXINE
2346 25th Avenue
San Francisco, CA 94116
Telephone: 415-681-3018
Fax: 415-681-0350
AFFILIATIONS:
ASJA, PPA, PP of SF, MA
PRINCIPAL SUBJECTS:
Business & Industry
Foreign
Health
News
Personalities
Photography
Science
Travel
PUBLICATIONS:
Travel Agent
Holidaymaker (Canada)
Westways
Genetic Engineering News
Travelage West
San Francisco Examiner
AAA Today
American Fitness
Boston Herald
Pacific Northwest Magazine

CASSELL, DANA
Maple Ridge Rd.
North Sandwich, NH 03259
Telephone: 603-284-6367
Fax: 603-284-6648
AFFILIATIONS:
TAG ASJA ABW ABA
    American Management
    Assoc.
PRINCIPAL SUBJECTS:
Advertising
Media
Book Reviews
Business & Industry
Management
Marketing
Sales
PUBLICATIONS:
Working Woman
Modern Bride
Dun's Business Month
Income Opportunities
Guest Informant
Farm Journal
American Legion Magazine
Barron's
Mechanix Illustrated

CASSILL, KAY
22 Boylston Ave.
Providence, RI 02906
Telephone: 401-751-4949
Fax: 401-353-9223
AFFILIATIONS:
ASJA, AG, AWP
PRINCIPAL SUBJECTS:
The Arts
Family
Health
Human Relations
Personalities
PUBLICATIONS:
Better Homes & Gardens
Christian Science Monitor
Cosmopolitan
Discovery
Kiwanis
McCall's
People
Smithsonian
Marathon World

CASSILL, R. V.
22 Boylston Ave.
Providence, RI 02906
Telephone: 401-751-4949
AFFILIATIONS:
AG, ASJA, AWP,
PRINCIPAL SUBJECTS:
The Arts
PUBLICATIONS:
Atlantic Monthly
Esquire
Holiday
Saturday Evening Post
Horizon

CATALANO, JULIE
6900 North Vandiver, #204-G
San Antonio, TX 78209
Telephone: 210-822-6181
AFFILIATIONS:
ASJA, AWL
PRINCIPAL SUBJECTS:
Advertising
Animals
Entertainment
Health
Media
Medical
Personalities
Physical Fitness
Social Trends
The Arts
Travel
Women's Interest
PUBLICATIONS:
Vista
AdWeek

AAA World
Country Home
Modern Bride
Beauty

CELLIERS, PETER J.
240 Garth Rd.
Scarsdale, NY 10583
Telephone: 914-472-7516
Fax: 914-472-7516
AFFILIATIONS:
SATW, NYTWA, ASJA
PRINCIPAL SUBJECTS:
Ecology
Travel
Foreign
History
Nature
Senior Citizens
Travel
PUBLICATIONS:
Playboy
Farm Journal
True Story
Good Housekeeping
Science Digest

CHAGALL, DAVID
28232 Foothill Dr.
Agoura Hills, CA 91301
Telephone: 818-889-3711
Fax: 818-889-3711
MAILING ADDRESS:
David Chagall
P.O. Box 85
Agoura Hills, CA 91376
AFFILIATIONS:
AG
PRINCIPAL SUBJECTS:
Government
Religion
General Interest
Media
History
PUBLICATIONS:
Time/Life
T.V. Guide
New York Times Syndicate
Los Angeles Magazine
Los Angeles Times Syndicate
Family Weekly
New West
Panorama Emmy
California Business
Valley Magazine

CHANDLER, JO
3004 Tango Street
Sacramento, CA 95826
Telephone: 916-361-2370
Fax: 916-361-2370

PRINCIPAL SUBJECTS:
Advertising
Agriculture
Business & Industry
General Interest
Health
Human Interest
Senior Citizens
Women's Interest
PUBLICATIONS:
The Sacramento Bee
Comstock's Business
The Business Journal
California Farm Bureau
  Federation
Senior
Neighbor's Newspaper
The Sacramento Union

CHARLES, JOANNA
P.O. Box 36593
Grosse Point, MI 48236
Telephone: 313-884-4483
PRINCIPAL SUBJECTS:
Business & Industry
Personalities
Sports
Health
Travel
Science
PUBLICATIONS:
Detroit Free Press
Michigan Runner
Professional Communicator

CHEASEBRO, MARGARET
246 Rd., #2900
Aztec, NM 87410
Telephone: 505-334-2869
AFFILIATIONS:
SCWA
PRINCIPAL SUBJECTS:
Education
The Arts
General Interest
Youth
The Arts
PUBLICATIONS:
Farmington Daily Times
Aztec Independent Review
Albuquerque Journal
Empire Magazine
San Juan Geographic
American Education
Industrial Education
Instructor
Frontier
New Mexico Magazine
World Vision
Sunshine
Good Reading

Lion, The
Good Housekeeping
Guideposts
Power for Living
Native Times
His People
Mother Earth News
Desert
Insight
Country Woman
Columbia
On the Line
Mature Living
High Adventure
Augsburn Publishing House
Broadman Press
Grit
Youth Illustrated
Lillenas
Contemporary Drama Service
Teen Quest
Church Recreation Magazine
Hosanna
Freeway
Hi - Call
R - A - D - A - R
Cross Currents
Purpose
This People
Standard Publishing
Christian Standard
Mesa Connection
Air Destinations
Life Glow
Family Day Caring
New Mexico Business Journal
New Mexico Wildlife
Upper Room
Warner Press

CHELEKIS, GEORGE
P.O. Box 2401
Clearwater, FL 34617
Telephone: 813-441-3548
Fax: 813-441-4034
AFFILIATIONS:
ASJA
PRINCIPAL SUBJECTS:
Advertising
Book Reviews
Business & Industry
Computer Technology
Government
Personal Finance
Sales
PUBLICATIONS:
Nation's Business
Entrepreneur
Sarasota Business
Sky

Bull & Bear
Income Opportunities
Monetary Digest

CHIN, RUTH
1007 N. Tillotson Ave.
Muncie, IN 47304
Telephone: 317-284-4582
Fax: 317-284-4582
MAILING ADDRESS:
Ruth Chin
Muncie, IN 47304
AFFILIATIONS:
IPC,NFPW,MTWA
PRINCIPAL SUBJECTS:
The Arts
Business & Industry
General Interest
Personalities
Travel
Agriculture
News
PUBLICATIONS:
Modern Maturity
Readers Digest
Trailer Life
Travel
Muncie Star Columnist
RV Dealer
Horizons
Farm Futures
News & Views
Online Today
Service Employees

CHRISTENSEN, KAREN
P.O. Box 177
Great Barington, MA 01230
Telephone: 413-528-0206
PRINCIPAL SUBJECTS:
Travel
Social Trends
PUBLICATIONS:
Telegraph Magazine, The
Daily Express, The
New Age Journal
Upriver/Downriver
Resurgence
Woman's Realm
Mrs. Beetons Traditional
  Housekeeping
Bloomsbury Review, The

CHRISTIAN, ALLGAIER
 DONNA
154 Fairview
Kalamazoo, MI 49001
Telephone: 616-342-1260
Fax: 616-342-8988
AFFILIATIONS:
WICI

PRINCIPAL SUBJECTS:
Human Interest
Business & Industry
Advertising
General Interest
Home & Garden
Marketing
PUBLICATIONS:
Kalamazoo Gazette
Detroit Free Press
Michiana Magazine
Grand Rapids Press
West Michigan Magazine
Spinnoff Magazine
Better Homes & Garden's
  Country Home
Grand Rapids Magazine
Michigan Woman
Country Magazine

CIERVO, ARTHUR
31 Hillside Dr.
Carlisle, PA 17013
Telephone: 717-243-8464
AFFILIATIONS:
ASJA
PRINCIPAL SUBJECTS:
History
Health
Education
Human Interest
Senior Citizens
PUBLICATIONS:
Parents
Washingtonian
Catholic Digest
Marriage
American Baby

CIRONE, BETTINA
211 W. 56th St., #14K
New York, NY 10019
Telephone: 212-262-3062
PRINCIPAL SUBJECTS:
General Interest
Fashion
Travel
Youth
Personalities
PUBLICATIONS:
Dynamite
Manhattan, Inc.
New York Times
New York Daily News
New York Post
New York Magazine
People
US
The Star
Enquirer
Ladies Home Journal

Photo Methods
Travel Agent
Oggi & Anabella (Italy)
Manchete (Brazil)
Bunte (German)
Epoca (Italy)
Nat'l Geographic World
Junior Scholastic
American Photographer
Vogue
Quick (German)
Playboy
Cosmopolitan
Travel/Holiday
Gente
Vanidades
Revista Geografica
Mundo
Blick (Switzerland)
Scope (South Africa)
Italian Playboy
Hola
Panorama (Italy)
Traveller
Panorama
7 Days
L'Europeo (Italy)
Vanity Fair
Grazia (Italy)
Hello (England)
Gong Publications (Germany)
SPY
Anabella (Italy)
Freitzeit Revue
NY Newsday

CLARK, LARRY
2222 S. Maddock St.
Santa Ana, CA 92704
Telephone: 714-549-3440
Fax: 714-969-4661
PRINCIPAL SUBJECTS:
Editorial
General Interest
Human Interest
Journalism
Personalities
Religion
Sports
Youth
PUBLICATIONS:
Christian Herald
Family Life Today
Decision
Eternity
His
Commission, The
Sharing the Victory
Power for Living
Moody Magazine

CLARKE, PHILIP C.
3738 Greene's Crossing
Greensboro, NC 27410
Telephone: 919-282-4860
MAILING ADDRESS:
Philip C. Clarke
Greensboro, NC 27410
AFFILIATIONS:
OPC
PRINCIPAL SUBJECTS:
Journalism
Government
World Affairs
Aviation
News
Business & Industry
Editorial
Education
Foreign
Media
Media
Military
Social Trends
PUBLICATIONS:
Reader's Digest
American Legion Magazine
Newsweek
New York Times

CLAXTON, COLETTE
8703 NW 49 Dr.
Pompano Beach, FL 33067
Telephone: 305-752-6872
Fax: 305-752-6872
AFFILIATIONS:
WICI
PRINCIPAL SUBJECTS:
Medical
Business & Industry
Senior Citizens
Health

CLEDE, BILL
272 Ridge Rd.
Wethersfield, CT 06109
Telephone: 203-563-9555
AFFILIATIONS:
SPJ, OWAA
PRINCIPAL SUBJECTS:
Computer Technology
Animals
Nature
Electronics
PUBLICATIONS:
Law & Order - Tech. Ed.
Washington Crime News
  Service - Correspondent
Field & Stream
Guns Australia
Diana Armi (IT.)
Offshore

Bristol Press (CT) Outdoor
  Columnist
Salt Water Sportsman
Dog World
Outdoor Life
Game & Fish
Armas (Spain)
Crime Beat
Modern Maturity

CLIFFORD, WILLIAM
35 West St.
Morris, CT 06763
Telephone: 203-567-5336
AFFILIATIONS:
AIM
PRINCIPAL SUBJECTS:
Health
Travel
Agriculture
Amusements
Architecture
Book Reviews
Science
The Arts

CLINE, ANDY
2521 S. Whitney
Independence, MO 64057
Telephone: 816-478-3309
AFFILIATIONS:
ASJA
PRINCIPAL SUBJECTS:
Business & Industry
Ecology
General Interest
Health
Men's Interest
Nature
Personal Finance
Sports
Travel
PUBLICATIONS:
Field & Stream
Meeting & Conventions
Ingram's
Kansas City Business Journal
Outdoor America
Bassmaster
Kansas City Health Care Times
Trilogy

COAN, PETER M.
68 - 64 Yellowstone Bld.
Forest Hills, NY 11375
Telephone: 718-897-7967
AFFILIATIONS:
AGA, TWA, WGA
PRINCIPAL SUBJECTS:
Editorial
Personalities

Entertainment
Media
Nature
Sports
Travel
Women's Interest
PUBLICATIONS:
Time Magazine
NY Times
World Tennis Magazine
Boating Industry Magazine
Newsday
New York Magazine
Endless Vacation
Travel & Leisure
Madomoiselle
Fitness Magazine
Women's Sports & Fitness
  Magazine

COCHRAN, ADA
225 Ralston
Converse, TX 78109
Telephone: 210-659-5062
MAILING ADDRESS:
Ada Cochran
Converse, TX 78109
AFFILIATIONS:
PWW
PRINCIPAL SUBJECTS:
Home & Garden
Hobbies
Human Interest
Human Relations
Humor
Nature
Religion
Senior Citizens
Women's Interest
PUBLICATIONS:
Jackson Times
Maryland Daily
L & C Magazine
Fate
Catholic's Singles
Dreams & Visions
Jess's Poets
Songwriter's Expo
Editor's Desk
Singles Magazine
Modern Romances
True Love
True Experience
Yes, Press
Swanee
Mayland Ind
Phoenix Press
Showcase
Quill, The
Final Draft
Pschyce

Channels
Sundipitx
RFD
Writers World
Scary Stuff
Spine Tingler
Free Lance Report
Sport Stay Review
Culli's Tales

COHEN, DANIEL
235 Hudson St. #910
Hoboken, NJ 07030
Telephone: 201-659-0952
AFFILIATIONS:
ASJA, ASMP
PRINCIPAL SUBJECTS:
Architecture
Book Reviews
Business & Industry
Computer Technology
History
Medical
Photography
Social Trends
The Arts
PUBLICATIONS:
Smithsonian
The Atlantic
New York Times
Business Week
House Beautiful
Washington Post
Historic Preservation
Connoisseur

COLBERT, JUDY
12411 Sexton Lane
Bowie, MD 20715
Telephone: 301-262-0177
MAILING ADDRESS:
Judy Colbert
P.O. Box 3308
Crofton, MD 21114
AFFILIATIONS:
ACTA
PRINCIPAL SUBJECTS:
Travel
The Arts
General Interest
Personalities
Human Interest
Book Reviews
PUBLICATIONS:
Arizona Daily Star
Baltimore Sun
Dallas Morning News
Destinations
Diversion
Washington Post
Chronicle Express

McCall's
Frequent Flyer
Meetings & Conventions
Pace
AAA World
Mid - Atlantic Country
Photo District News
Richmond Times - Dispatch
Public Relations Journal
Recommend Florida
Recommend Worldwide
Review, The
Presidential Airways
St. Paul Pioneer Press &
  Dispatch
Successful American
  Entrepreneurs
Caribbean Travel & Life
Quarante
Akron Beacon Journal
Home & Away
Vocational Biographies
Odyssey
Outdoors in Maryland
Tours & Resorts
Recommend
Washingtonian
Beauty Digest
Women's Sports and Fitness
Spa Vacations
Self
American Health
Recreation News
Baltimore Magazine
Relax
QuickTrips Travel Letter
Events USA
Baltimore Business Journal
Recreation News

COLEBERD, FRANCES
1273 Mills St., Ste. 3
Menlo Park, CA 94025
Telephone: 415-325-4731
AFFILIATIONS:
WIC
PRINCIPAL SUBJECTS:
General Interest
Travel
PUBLICATIONS:
Christian Science Monitor
Lane Magazine And Book Co
  (Sunset Magazine)
Chevron USA
San Francisco Chronicle
  Books
San Francisco Examiner
  (California Living)
Time Magazine
Motorland Magazine
GEO (German Geo)

COLEMAN, A.D.
465 Van Duzer Street
Staten Island, NY 10304
Telephone: 718-447-3280
Fax: 718-447-3091
AFFILIATIONS:
PEN, AG, NWU, ASJA
PRINCIPAL SUBJECTS:
Book Reviews
Media
Photography
The Arts
Travel
PUBLICATIONS:
New York Times
Village Voice
New York Observer
New York Magazine
Art in America
Camera & Darkroom
The World & I
Popular Photography

COLTON, HELEN
1539 N. Courtney Ave.
Los Angeles, CA 90046
Telephone: 213-876-1410
AFFILIATIONS:
ASJA, ITAA,SS
PRINCIPAL SUBJECTS:
Family
General Interest
Education
Human Relations
Philosophy
Psychology
Senior Citizens
Social Trends
Women's Interest
PUBLICATIONS:
Forum
The Humanist Magazine
Osteopathic Physician
  Magazine
Reader's Digest
McCall's
Redbook
N. Y. Times
Family Circle
Coronet
Cosmopolitan

CONKLIN, WILLIAM B.
Washington Sq.
Walpole, NH 03608
Telephone: 603-756-4275
MAILING ADDRESS:
William B. Conklin
P.O. Box 232
Walpole, NH 03608
Telephone: 603-756-3135

AFFILIATIONS:
AG
PRINCIPAL SUBJECTS:
The Arts
Business & Industry
Humor
Travel
PUBLICATIONS:
Reader's Digest
Saturday Evening Post
Yankee Magazine

CONNIFF, JAMES C. G.
P.O. Box 812
Upper Montclair, NJ 07043
Telephone: 201-746-2317
MAILING ADDRESS:
Upper Montclair, NJ 07043
AFFILIATIONS:
AG, ASJA
PRINCIPAL SUBJECTS:
Business & Industry
Ecology
Entertainment
Family
Government
Health
Personalities
Science
World Affairs
Personal Finance
PUBLICATIONS:
Family Circle
Ladies' Home Journal
McCall's
New York Times Magazine
Reader's Digest
Today's Health
Popular Science Monthly
The Runner
Good Housekeeping
Family Weekly
Sports Illustrated

CONNOR, J. ROBERT
8 Woodvale Lane
Huntington, NY 11743
Telephone: 516-271-5537
AFFILIATIONS:
ASMC IMPA
PRINCIPAL SUBJECTS:
General Interest
Hobbies
Management
Men's Interest
Science
Automotive
PUBLICATIONS:
Family Weekly

Mechanix Illustrated
Motor
The National Job-Finding
  Guide

CONSIDINE, SHERIDAN
191 Motsinger Rd.
Winston Salem, NC 27107
Telephone: 919-784-8583
AFFILIATIONS:
Press Women
PRINCIPAL SUBJECTS:
Business & Industry
Social Trends
PUBLICATIONS:
Charlotte Observer
Winston - Salem Magazine
Reader's Digest
Winston-Salem Chronicle
The Hospitals Magazine
Minorities & Women in
  Business
NC Homes & Garden

COOPER, ANDREA
315 E. Worthington Avenue
Charlotte, NC 28203
Telephone: 704-343-2543
Fax: 704-343-0701
AFFILIATIONS:
WICI PRSA NCWN
PRINCIPAL SUBJECTS:
Business & Industry
Women's Interest
The Arts
PUBLICATIONS:
North Carolina Magazine
Business North Carolina
New York Times

COOPER, DR. JOHN C.
2241 Bohan Rd.
Harrodsburg, KY 40330
Telephone: 606-734-5731
MAILING ADDRESS:
John C. Cooper
Cooper, Dr. John C.
Harrodsburg, KY 40330
PRINCIPAL SUBJECTS:
Religion
Business & Industry
PUBLICATIONS:
Christianity Today
Christian Century
Marathon World
Clergy Journal, The
Journal of Ecumenical Studies
Lutheran, The

COOPER, JILL A.
4220 Bodenheiner
Boise, ID 83703
Telephone: 208-345-4855
MAILING ADDRESS:
Jill A. Cooper
P.O. Box 3232
Boise, ID 83703
Telephone: 208-342-6647
PRINCIPAL SUBJECTS:
Animals
PUBLICATIONS:
Boise Cascade Corp.
  Magazine "Insight"
Weight Watchers Magazine
Cat Fancy
Gun Dog
Bureau of Business Practice
  Bulletins
ID Systems
Executive Excellence

COOPER, PAULETTE
401 E. 74 St.
New York, NY 10021
Telephone: 212-744-4623
Fax: 212-744-4623
AFFILIATIONS:
ASJA, TJG
PRINCIPAL SUBJECTS:
Health
Travel
PUBLICATIONS:
New York Times
Parade
Cosmopolitan
Working Woman
The Washington Post

COPE, MYRON
513 Harrogate Rd.
Pittsburgh, PA 15241
Telephone: 412-731-1250
MAILING ADDRESS:
WTAE Radio - TV
P.O. Box 1250
Pittsburgh, PA 15230
Telephone: 412-835-7096
AFFILIATIONS:
AFTRA
PRINCIPAL SUBJECTS:
Sports
PUBLICATIONS:
Sports Illustrated
TV Guide

CORBETT, GERALDINE
9951 Ne Lake Washington
  Blvd., 305
Bellevue, WA 98004
Telephone: 206-454-4465

AFFILIATIONS:
SATW, ASJA
PRINCIPAL SUBJECTS:
Travel
Humor
Personalities
History
Military
Senior Citizens
General Interest
PUBLICATIONS:
Northwest Travel
Worcester Telegram

COREY, JOHN R.
937 Bridgewater Dr.
Pittsburgh, PA 15216
Telephone: 412-531-3344
Fax: 412-831-5184
MAILING ADDRESS:
John R. Corey
Metromountain Assoc,
  Box 14500
Pittsburgh, PA 15234
Telephone: 412-531-0570
AFFILIATIONS:
PRSA, SDX
PRINCIPAL SUBJECTS:
Advertising
Journalism
Business & Industry
Media

CORWEN, LEONARD
2632 W. Second St.
Brooklyn, NY 11223
Telephone: 718-646-7581
Fax: 718-934-8392
AFFILIATIONS:
ASJA, ABPE
PRINCIPAL SUBJECTS:
Advertising
Book Reviews
Business & Industry
Editorial
General Interest
Health
Human Relations
Journalism
Management
Senior Citizens

COURIC, EMILY
714 Rugby Rd.
Charlottesvle, VA 22903
Telephone: 804-296-3962
Fax: 804-296-5949
AFFILIATIONS:
AG, ASJA, NFPW
PRINCIPAL SUBJECTS:
Journalism

PUBLICATIONS:
The Washington Post
Legal Times
ABA Journal
Time

**COURTSAL, FRANCES
  CHASE**
1208 Woodland Rd.
Pittsburgh, PA 15237
Telephone: 412-364-1398

COX, VIC
82 Warwick Place
Goleta, CA 93117
Telephone: 805-968-1109
AFFILIATIONS:
NASW, ASJA, AG
PRINCIPAL SUBJECTS:
Animals
Book Reviews
Ecology
Entertainment
Health
History
Human Relations
Journalism
Marine
Medical
Nature
Personalities
Science
Travel
World Affairs
Youth
PUBLICATIONS:
Sea Frontiers
National Wildlife
American Film
Popular Science
Westways
Final Frontier
The Nation
US

COYLE, ELIZABETH
8125 Donnawood Way
Orangevale, CA 95662
Telephone: 916-726-0591
AFFILIATIONS:
AFTRA, MWA, SIC
PRINCIPAL SUBJECTS:
Family
General Interest
Government
Human Relations
Personalities
News
PUBLICATIONS:
Catholic Digest
Lady's Circle

McCall's
Modern Maturity
National Enquirer
American Education
National Star
Reader's Digest

CRANDELL, CHERYL
P.O. Box 432095
Pontiac, MI 48343
Telephone: 313-335-5896
AFFILIATIONS:
WICI
PRINCIPAL SUBJECTS:
Advertising
Editorial
General Interest
Human Interest
Marketing
PUBLICATIONS:
Detroit News
Oakland Press
Midwest Living

CROSS, WILBUR
27 Royal Crest Dr., Pt. Royal
Hilton Head, SC 29928
Telephone: 803-689-2450
AFFILIATIONS:
ASJA, AG
PRINCIPAL SUBJECTS:
Business & Industry
History
Management
Editorial
General Interest
Marketing
Marketing
Science
Senior Citizens
PUBLICATIONS:
Science Digest
American Heritage
Readers Digest, The
Life

CROTEAU, MAUREEN E.
University of Connecticut
Storrs, CT 06269
Telephone: 203-486-4221
Fax: 203-486-3294
AFFILIATIONS:
CFOG, SPJ, IRU
PRINCIPAL SUBJECTS:
News
General Interest
Journalism
PUBLICATIONS:
Providence Journal
Hartford Courant
Washington Post

New London Day
New Physician (Magazine)
London (Ontario) Free Press
Essential Researcher

CUMMINGS, SANDRA OTTO
Patten Point
Long Branch, NJ 07740
Telephone: 908-229-0618
Fax: 908-615-0108
MAILING ADDRESS:
Asbury Park Press
3601 Rt. 66, Box 1550
Neptune, NJ 07753
AFFILIATIONS:
AMWA, SPJ, NJPW
PRINCIPAL SUBJECTS:
Medical
General Interest
Sports
News
Senior Citizens
PUBLICATIONS:
N.Y. Times
Asbury Park (N.J.) Press
Nordic Skiing
Ski Magazine
Cross Country Skier

CUPPER, DAN
4741 Spring Creek Rd.
Harrisburg, PA 17111
Telephone: 717-564-3366
PRINCIPAL SUBJECTS:
Business & Industry
History
Travel
PUBLICATIONS:
Philadelphia Inquirer
Boston Globe
Mass Transit Magazine
Trains Magazine
Passenger Train Journal
  Magazine
Amtrak Express Magazine
Central Pennsylvania Business
  Journal
American Heritage Magazine
Pittsburgh Post-Gazette

CURRAN, BOB
1 News Plaza
Buffalo, NY 14240
Telephone: 716-849-4521
Fax: 716-856-5150
AFFILIATIONS:
ASJA
PRINCIPAL SUBJECTS:
General Interest
Personalities
Sports

PUBLICATIONS:
Family Weekly
Reader's Digest
Sport
Sports Illustrated
TV Guide

DAILY, LAURA
P.O. Box 5658
Snowmas Village, CO 81615
Telephone: 303-923-4657
Fax: 303-923-6839
AFFILIATIONS:
SATW
PRINCIPAL SUBJECTS:
Travel
Business & Industry
General Interest
The Arts
Physical Fitness
Youth
Personalities
PUBLICATIONS:
Copley News Service
Arthritis Today
Boys Life
Physicians Lifestyle
Hemispheres

DALEY, LAVERNE
615 Vaughn Road
Memphis, TN 38122
Telephone: 901-323-6983
Fax: 901-323-9689
AFFILIATIONS:
SPJ WICI
PRINCIPAL SUBJECTS:
Business & Industry
Advertising
Aviation
Education
General Interest
Journalism
Marketing
PUBLICATIONS:
Adweek
Memphis Business Journal
Photo District News

DALRYMPLE, BYRON W.
P.O. Box 709
Kerrville, TX 78029
Telephone: 512-895-1991
PRINCIPAL SUBJECTS:
Family
Men's Interest
Sports
Travel
PUBLICATIONS:
Field and Stream
Holiday

Mechanics Illustrated
Outdoor Life
Southern Living
Sports Afield
Trailer Life
American Hunter
Bassmaster
Southern Outdoors
Texas Sportsman
Southwest Farm Press
Texas Fish and Game
Wing & Shot
Wildfowl Magazine

DALY, MAUREEN
73-305 Ironwood Dr.
Palm Desert, CA 92260
Telephone: 619-346-7077
Fax: 619-341-6201
MAILING ADDRESS:
Daly, Maureen
P.O. Box 3875
Palm Desert, CA 92260
Telephone: 714-346-7077
PRINCIPAL SUBJECTS:
Amusements
Family
Personalities
Travel
Women's Interest
Youth
Entertainment
Nature
Book Reviews
Education
Human Relations
News
News
Social Trends
The Arts
PUBLICATIONS:
Cosmopolitan
Esquire
Harper's
Ladies' Home Journal
Vogue
Chicago Tribune
New West
Los Angeles Magazine
New York Times Magazine
Philadelphia Inquirer
Mademoiselle
National Wildlife Federation
   Publications
Gannett Newspapers, The
Desert Sun, columnist

DAMEROW, GAIL J.
281 Dean Ridge Lane
Gainesboro, TN 38562
Telephone: 615-268-0655

PRINCIPAL SUBJECTS:
Agriculture
General Interest
Home & Garden
Book Reviews
Editorial
PUBLICATIONS:
Americana
Country Journal
Dairy Goat Journal (Columnist)
Farm Family America
Herb Companion, The
Writer, The
Rural Heritage
Back Home

DANIELS, LEE
670 Conklin St.
Farmingdale, NY 11735
Telephone: 516-293-4325
MAILING ADDRESS:
Daniels Mailing Services, Inc.
Farmingdale, NY 11735
PRINCIPAL SUBJECTS:
Ecology
Business & Industry
PUBLICATIONS:
The Realtor, Long Island
The Village Report, Inc., Village
   of Farmingdale
The Farmingdale Market Place

DANOWSKI, JENNY
2004 235th Place, NE
Redmond, WA 98053
Telephone: 206-868-3483
PRINCIPAL SUBJECTS:
Management
Health
Youth
PUBLICATIONS:
Washington CEO Magazine
Executive Strategies Newsletter
Working Smart Newsletter
Total Quality Newsletter
McCalls
Woman's Day

DARDICK, GEETA
Geeta Dardick Writing and
   Photography
P.O. Box 294
N. San Juan, CA 95960
Telephone: 916-292-3059
Fax: 916-272-7793
AFFILIATIONS:
ASJA, CAMFT
PRINCIPAL SUBJECTS:
Health
Business & Industry
Travel

Family
Psychology
Ecology
Book Reviews
Home & Garden
Human Interest
Women's Interest
PUBLICATIONS:
The Christian Science Monitor
Reader's Digest
Family Circle
Arthritis Today
Utne Reader
The Lion
Amtrak Express
Motorland

DARK, HARRIS EDWARD
401 Forest Trail Dr.
Bandera, TX 78003
Telephone: 210-796-8416
AFFILIATIONS:
SATW, CPC, CHC
PRINCIPAL SUBJECTS:
Family
General Interest
Health
Home & Garden
Travel
History
Automotive
PUBLICATIONS:
Changing Times
Modern Maturity
Odyssey
Vista USA (Exxon)
Adventure Road
Chicago Tribune
Rand McNally
   Campground Guide
Rand McNally Travel Guide
Midwest Motorist
Dallas Morning News
Discovery

DARLINGTON, JOY
310 W. 56th St.
New York, NY 10019
Telephone: 212-246-6811
AFFILIATIONS:
PWA, AG
PRINCIPAL SUBJECTS:
Health
Family
Home & Garden
Social Trends
Book Reviews
Ecology
Movie Reviews
General Interest
World Affairs

Travel
PUBLICATIONS:
New York Post, The
New York Woman
Manhatten, Inc.
New York Times
Good Housekeeping
New York Daily News

DAVENPORT, ARTHUR
403 East St.
Belchertown, MA 01007
Telephone: 413-323-6727
MAILING ADDRESS:
Arthur Davenport
P.O. Box 489
Belchertown, MA 01007
AFFILIATIONS:
NYSOWA, NCOWA, OWAA
PRINCIPAL SUBJECTS:
Travel
Sports
Travel
Nature
PUBLICATIONS:
Field & Stream
Local Newspapers
Ford Times
New York Times
Yankee Mag.
Hampshire Life,
  (Northampton, Ma.)
Turkey Magazine
Fisherman, The

DAVID, LESTER
946 Carol Ave.
Woodmere, NY 11598
Telephone: 516-374-4467
AFFILIATIONS:
AG, ASJA
PRINCIPAL SUBJECTS:
Business & Industry
Family
Health
Personalities
Entertainment
PUBLICATIONS:
Family Circle
Good Housekeeping
Ladies' Home Journal
American Legion
New York Times
Sunday Express (London)
McCall's Magazine
Los Angeles Times Syndicate
Sunday People (London)
Sunday Mirror Magazine
  (London_
Die Bunte (W. Germany)
Readers Digest

DAVIDSON, MARK
195 Malcolm Dr.
Pasadena, CA 91105
Telephone: 310-516-3881
AFFILIATIONS:
ASJA, AMWA, NSWA,
  AL, WGAW
PRINCIPAL SUBJECTS:
Science
Health
Social Trends
Education
Travel
Psychology
News
Media
Nature
Animals
Architecture
Electronics
Entertainment
Government
PUBLICATIONS:
Family Circle
Good Housekeeping
Popular Science
Science Digest
California Living
Architectural Digest
Argosy
Los Angeles Magazine
Los Angeles Times
Travel & Leisure
Westways
U S A Today
T.V. Guide

DAVIS, BEATRICE G.
105 Ludwig Ln.
East Williston, NY 11596
Telephone: 516-742-2583
AFFILIATIONS:
NNC AJW IRA
PRINCIPAL SUBJECTS:
Education
Human Relations
Family
Business & Industry
Health
Marketing
Motivation
Youth
PUBLICATIONS:
Learning Links - Study Guides
Friendly Exchange
Published!
Writer's Guidelines
Freelancer's Report
Women's Record, The
L I Parent
Psychological Corporation

The Chronicle-Westport MA
Today's Parent
The Single Parent
Just Grand
LA Parent

DAVIS, ELISE MILLER
7838 Caruth Court
Dallas, TX 75225
AFFILIATIONS:
ASJA
PRINCIPAL SUBJECTS:
Fashion
Editorial
Business & Industry
Personalities
Humor
Entertainment
Human Interest
PUBLICATIONS:
Reader's Digest
Woman's Day
Nation's Business

DAVIS, FLORA M.
62 Erdman Ave.
Princeton, NJ 08540
Telephone: 609-924-9174
Fax: 609-924-6081
AFFILIATIONS:
ASJA, AL
PRINCIPAL SUBJECTS:
Health
History
Women's Interest
PUBLICATIONS:
Ladies Home Journal
Woman's Day
The New York Times Magazine
Mademoiselle
Working Woman
Glamour
Readers Digest

DAVIS, O. K.
1000 Spring Ave.
Ruston, LA 71270
Telephone: 318-255-3990
Fax: 318-255-4006
MAILING ADDRESS:
O. K. Davis
P.O. Box 520
Ruston, LA 71270
AFFILIATIONS:
UBA FWAA HTSC BWOA LSA
  TFWA NASS
PRINCIPAL SUBJECTS:
Human Interest
Sports
Hobbies
Personalities

PUBLICATIONS:
Sports Illustrated
USA Today
Sporting News, The
Basketball Digest
Football Digest
Grit
Baseball Digest

DAY, BETH
35 E. 38th
New York, NY 10016
Telephone: 212-986-4785
AFFILIATIONS:
ASJA, AL, AG
PRINCIPAL SUBJECTS:
General Interest
Government
PUBLICATIONS:
Reader's Digest
Woman's Day
Saturday Review
Ladies Home Journal

DE CRISTOFORO, R. J.
27861 Natoma Rd.
Los Altos, CA 94022
Telephone: 415-948-0540
AFFILIATIONS:
PPSCV, PPC, NWA
PRINCIPAL SUBJECTS:
General Interest
Hobbies
Photography
Humor
Journalism
Family
Home & Garden
PUBLICATIONS:
Mechanix Illustrated
Popular Mechanics
Popular Science
Workbench
Sunset Magaine
Better Homes & Gardens
How-To Magazine
Family Circle
Hardware Age
Science & Mechanics
Writer's Digest

DEANE, BARBARA
4937 Red Oak Dr.
Gainesville, GA 30506
Telephone: 404-534-8365
AFFILIATIONS:
ASJA
PRINCIPAL SUBJECTS:
Family
General Interest
Health

Human Interest
Human Relations
Medical
Personalities
Physical Fitness
Psychology
Religion
Senior Citizens
Social Trends
Travel
Women's Interest
PUBLICATIONS:
Reader's Digest
Woman's Day
Family Circle
New Woman
Ladies' Home Journal
Virtue
Discipleship Journal

DEBARTOLO, ANTHONY
1314 Howard St., Ste. 2
Chicago, IL 60626
Telephone: 312-274-3337
AFFILIATIONS:
CHC
PRINCIPAL SUBJECTS:
Education
Media
Humor
Urban Affairs
Social Trends
Human Relations
History
General Interest
Entertainment
Book Reviews
Travel
PUBLICATIONS:
The Chicago Tribune
USA Today
Milwaukee Journal
Minneapolis Star & Tribune
State (Columbia, S.C.) The
Chicago Times Magazine
St. Louis Post Dispatch
Sacramento Bee
Detroit News
Orange County Register
Ft. Lauderdale News/Sun
  Sentinel
San Francisco Chronicle
Baltimore Sun
Toronto Star
Metro Magazine/Exeter
  Magazine
Chicago Magazine

DEFOREST, SHERWOOD S.
106 Fitzrandolph Rd.
Coraopolis, PA 15108

Telephone: 412-269-0939
PRINCIPAL SUBJECTS:
Agriculture
Editorial
Business & Industry
PUBLICATIONS:
Agricultural Engineering
  magazine
Successful Farming magazine
1960 USDA Yearbook, Power
  to Produce

DEGNAN, JAMES P.
4151 Porter Gulch Rd. Box 906
Aptos, CA 95003
Telephone: 408-475-4888
MAILING ADDRESS:
P.O. Box 906
Aptos, CA 95003
AFFILIATIONS:
ASJA
PRINCIPAL SUBJECTS:
The Arts
Nature
Humor
Urban Affairs
Travel
Education
Editorial
Personalities
PUBLICATIONS:
Atlantic
Esquire
The Nation
Hudson Review
The Critic
Harper's
The New Yorker
American West
Change
Sewanee Review
New West
Wilderness Magazine

DEGREGORIO, WILLIAM A.
129 Denham Cir. N.E.
N. Canton, OH 44721
Telephone: 216-499-6271
PRINCIPAL SUBJECTS:
Government
History
News
Personalities
PUBLICATIONS:
Good Housekeeping
Cleveland Plain Dealer
Columbus Dispatch
Cincinnati Enquirer
American History Illustrated

DEKTAR, JOAN A.
5047 Bellaire Ave.
N Hollywood, CA 91607
Telephone: 818-762-7705
PRINCIPAL SUBJECTS:
General Interest
Home & Garden
PUBLICATIONS:
Better Homes & Gardens
Family Circle
Good Housekeeping

DEMAN, ELAINE
P.O. Box 2878
Alameda, CA 94501
Telephone: 510-769-9768
AFFILIATIONS:
ASJA
PRINCIPAL SUBJECTS:
Aviation
Travel
Ecology
Advertising
Book Reviews
History
Marine
Photography
Women's Interest
PUBLICATIONS:
Omni
Food & Wine
American Way
Air & Space

DEMPEWOLFF, RICHARD F.
R.D. 1, Box 29E
Henryville, PA 18332
Telephone: 717-629-1223
AFFILIATIONS:
OPC NASW NPC
PRINCIPAL SUBJECTS:
General Interest
Business & Industry
Science
PUBLICATIONS:
International Wildlife
National Wildlife
Popular Mechanics
Reader's Digest
Science Digest
Omni

DENNY, ALMA
353 W. 56th St. (3B)
New York, NY 10019
Telephone: 212-757-4648
AFFILIATIONS:
ASJA
PRINCIPAL SUBJECTS:
Family
General Interest

Human Interest
Human Relations
Humor
Journalism
Personalities
Philosophy
Psychology
Social Trends
PUBLICATIONS:
New York Times
Wall St. Journal
Good Housekeeping
Christian Science Monitor
The Rotarian
Light
Saturday Evening Post
Ladies Home Journal

DETZ, JOAN
73 Harvey Avenue
Doylestown, PA 18901
Telephone: 215-340-9752
PRINCIPAL SUBJECTS:
Business & Industry
Marketing

DEVANEY, JOHN
520 LaGuardia Pl.
New York, NY 10012
Telephone: 212-228-6405
AFFILIATIONS:
PEN, FW
PRINCIPAL SUBJECTS:
Men's Interest
Sports
Travel
PUBLICATIONS:
Sport
Readers Digest
Modern Maturity
Graduating Engineer
Harris Golf
Memories Magazine

DEVINE, GEORGE
1960 10TH Ave.
San Francisco, CA 94116
Telephone: 415-661-4853
Fax: 415-666-2502
AFFILIATIONS:
ASJA
PRINCIPAL SUBJECTS:
Book Reviews
Editorial
Sports
Religion
Education
Family
Movie Reviews
Philosophy
The Arts

PUBLICATIONS:
New York Times
National Observer
The National Catholic Reporter
Commonweal
Cross Currents
U.S. Catholic and Jubilee
San Francisco Giants Journal
California Living
San Francisco Progress

DIAMOND, LEN
5061 Kingscross Rd.
Westminster, CA 92683
Telephone: 714-892-7249
AFFILIATIONS:
STC, IWSC, GLAPC
PRINCIPAL SUBJECTS:
Advertising
Aviation
Business & Industry
Electronics
Marketing
Science
PUBLICATIONS:
Aviation Convention News
Southland High Tech
GrowerTalks
Private Label
Expert Reports
Bizjet
Runways
Hospitals
Air Conditioning News
Decorative Products World
Selling Space
Optometric Management

DICKERSON, NANCY
16 Sutton Square
New York, NY 10022
Telephone: 212-371-1645
Fax: 212-751-3505
AFFILIATIONS:
NPC
PRINCIPAL SUBJECTS:
Journalism
Human Interest
Government
Book Reviews
World Affairs
PUBLICATIONS:
Ladies Home Journal

DICKINSON, PETER A.
44 Wildwood Dr.
Prescott, AZ 86301
Telephone: 602-776-8849
Fax: 602-776-8849
AFFILIATIONS:
ASJA, GS

PRINCIPAL SUBJECTS:
Business & Industry
General Interest
Health
Home & Garden
PUBLICATIONS:
Better Homes & Gardens
Modern Maturity
Consumer Digest
Consumer Guide

DICTOR-LEBLANC, RENA
P.O. Box 68
Woodland Hls, CA 91365
Telephone: 818-887-6053
Fax: 818-884-9795
AFFILIATIONS:
ASJA PEN
PRINCIPAL SUBJECTS:
Personalities
Travel
Medical
Science
Health
Animals
PUBLICATIONS:
McCalls
Redbook
Good Housekeeping
Ladies Home Journal
Womens World
LA Times Syndicate
Reader's Digest
Nevada Magazine

DIDDLEBOCK, BOB
1951 S. Milwaukee St.
Denver, CO 80210
Telephone: 303-759-1314
PRINCIPAL SUBJECTS:
Travel
Sports
Personal Finance

DIENSTAG, ELEANOR
435 East 79 St.
New York, NY 10021
Telephone: 212-879-1542
Fax: 212-879-1676
PRINCIPAL SUBJECTS:
History
Business & Industry
PUBLICATIONS:
NY Times
NY Observer
Working Women
McCalls

DITZEL, PAUL
23401 Aetna St.
Woodland Hls, CA 91367

Telephone: 818-992-5081
PRINCIPAL SUBJECTS:
Electronics
Business & Industry
General Interest
Human Interest
PUBLICATIONS:
Money
Reader's Digest
Forbes
Time Life
Firehouse
Westways
Fire Engineering

DODGE, ELLIN
10614 N. 11th Street
Phoenix, AZ 85020
Telephone: 602-944-6443
Fax: 602-944-0006
AFFILIATIONS:
ASJA, AG, PEN
PRINCIPAL SUBJECTS:
Amusements
General Interest
Motivation
Personalities
Sports
PUBLICATIONS:
New York Times
MTA Express
LI Mariner
National Enquirer

DONELSON, IRENE
708-10th St. Suite 150
Sacramento, CA 95814
Telephone: 916-448-9355
AFFILIATIONS:
AG
PRINCIPAL SUBJECTS:
Family
Health
Management
Medical
Senior Citizens
General Interest
PUBLICATIONS:
Dynamic Years
Medical Economics
Modern Maturity
Reader's Digest
Signature
50 Plus
Retirement Living

DOOLEY, BRIAN J.
2106 Nevarra Ave.
Vero Beach, FL 32960
Telephone: 609-397-5742

AFFILIATIONS:
SOC-TEC COMM
PRINCIPAL SUBJECTS:
Computer Technology
World Affairs
Business & Industry
PUBLICATIONS:
Today's Office
Printing Impressions
Graphic Arts Monthly
Computer Dealer
Communications Week
Datapro Management of
    Microcomputer Systems
Datapro Management of
    Application Software
Faulkners Technical Reports
Datapro Reports on Data
    Communications
Society for Technical
    Communications Journal

DOWNEY, CHARLES E.
P.O. Box 406
Fawnskin, CA 92333
Telephone: 909-866-6566
Fax: 909-866-6566
AFFILIATIONS:
ASJA, NPC
PRINCIPAL SUBJECTS:
Advertising
Aviation
Business & Industry
Education
Entertainment
Family
Health
History
Human Interest
Humor
Journalism
Medical
Men's Interest
News
Personal Finance
Personalities
Photography
Physical Fitness
Psychology
Senior Citizens
Women's Interest
Youth
PUBLICATIONS:
Money
Playboy
Mechanix
Better Home & Gardens
Men's Fitness
Modern Maturity
Boys' Life

DRAGONWAGON, CRESCENT
Rt. 4, Box 1
Eureka Spgs, AR 72632
Telephone: 501-253-7444
MAILING ADDRESS:
Dragonwagon Crescent
Eureka Spgs, AR 72632
AFFILIATIONS:
AG, P&W, WORDS
PRINCIPAL SUBJECTS:
General Interest
Women's Interest
Home & Garden
Social Trends
Humor
Human Relations
Travel
Health
Personalities
Book Reviews
PUBLICATIONS:
Cosmopolitan
Ms.
New Woman
Organic Gardening & Farming
Arkansan
Arkansas Gazette
McCall's
Atlanta
Arkansas Times
The Writer
Ladies Home Journal
New Age
Los Angeles
New York Times Review of
 Books
Travel Holiday
Lear's

DREYFACK, RAYMOND
3502 Bimini Lane
Coconut Creek, FL 33066
Telephone: 305-979-1536
AFFILIATIONS:
ASJA
PRINCIPAL SUBJECTS:
Business & Industry
Family
General Interest
Human Relations
Management

DRISCOLL, CYNTHIA
1221 Fourth Street SW
Grand Rapids, MN 55744
Telephone: 218-327-1045
AFFILIATIONS:
ASJA
PRINCIPAL SUBJECTS:
Travel
Women's Interest

The Arts
Education
Home & Garden
Nature
PUBLICATIONS:
MD
Minnesota Monthly
Organic Gardening
Harrowsmith
Flower and Garden
Family Circle
Vegetarian Times

DUNAIEF, LEAH S.
The Village Times, Box 707
East Setauket, NY 11733
Telephone: 516-751-7744
PRINCIPAL SUBJECTS:
Medical
Science
Business & Industry
Health
PUBLICATIONS:
New York Times, The
Time - Life Books
Life Magazine
Daily News, The
Village Times, The
Village Beacon, The
Newsday
St. James Time (England)

DUNAWAY, JAMES O.
24 Standish Ct.
Tenafly, NJ 07670
Telephone: 201-569-5441
Fax: 201-871-7308
MAILING ADDRESS:
Dunoway Ink
P.O. Box 126
Tenafly, NJ 07670
AFFILIATIONS:
TAFWA
PRINCIPAL SUBJECTS:
Business & Industry
Ecology
Personalities
Sports
News
Travel
PUBLICATIONS:
Esquire
Madison Avenue
MS.
New York Times
Signature
Sports Illustrated
Presstime

Track & Field News
Runner's World
1984,1988,1992 Official
 Olympic Viewer's Guide

DUNHAM, ROBERT
5584 Shadowlawn Dr.
Sarasota, FL 34242
Telephone: 813-349-7737
MAILING ADDRESS:
Robt. Dunham
5584 Shadowland Dr.
Sarasota, FL 34242
Telephone: 813-921-4692
AFFILIATIONS:
ASJA, IMPA, FADAA
PRINCIPAL SUBJECTS:
Automotive
General Interest
Health
Humor
Men's Interest
Sports
Travel
Senior Citizens
Animals
Marine
PUBLICATIONS:
Saturday Review
Swank
Adam
Beyond Reality
Pillow Talk
Stag
Variations
Motorsports Weekly
Oceans
Insight
Autocar
Knave
Motor
Modern Motor
Fling
Cat Fancy
Let's Live
Saturday Evening Post
Driver
Fate
Probe
Dude
Gent
Nugget
Cavalier
Canadian Connection
Velvet Touch
Independent Living
Accent on Living
Yankee Magazine
Transformation Times
Senior Magazine
Action Digest

UFO Review
Pleasure Boating
National Examiner
Police Times
Far East Traveler
Supervision
Massage Magazine
Positive Living
Recovery Today
Sober Times
The Phoenix
Alcoholism Review
Alive
50-Plus
American Psychic
Modern Office
UFO Magazine
Modern Maturity
Treasure
Dog Fancy
Cats Magazine
Greyhound Review
Suncoast Times
The Pelican
Sarasota Times

DUNNAN, NANCY
36 Gramercy Park
New York, NY 10003
Telephone: 212-228-4769
AFFILIATIONS:
ASJA, NAC
PRINCIPAL SUBJECTS:
Travel
Personal Finance
Urban Affairs
PUBLICATIONS:
Dunn & Bradstreet Guide to
 Your Investment
Travel Smart
Your Money

DUSKY, LORRAINE
Box 968
Sag Harbor, NY 11963
Telephone: 516-725-4174
AFFILIATIONS:
ASJA
PRINCIPAL SUBJECTS:
Government
Media
Travel
Women's Interest
PUBLICATIONS:
New York Times Magazine
Newsweek
Working Woman
McCall's
Glamour
Mademoiselle
Sears

DYKEMAN, WILMA
282 Clifton Heights
Newport, TN 37821
Telephone: 615-623-7394
AFFILIATIONS:
PEN, AG, SDC
PRINCIPAL SUBJECTS:
Ecology
Human Relations
History
Travel
Women's Interest
Book Reviews
Personalities
Education
The Arts
PUBLICATIONS:
New York Times
Historical Magazines
Knoxville Tenn.
  News-Sentinel-Weekly
  Editorial
Reader's Digest
Harper's
Diversion
Ebony
New Republic
Nation

EBERLY, PHILIP K.
6228 Lincoln Hwy.
Wrightsville, PA 17368
Telephone: 717-252-1361
PRINCIPAL SUBJECTS:
The Arts
Sports
PUBLICATIONS:
Baltimore Sun
Philadelphia Bulletin
Television/Radio Age
New York Times
Philadelphia Inquirer
Tobacco Observer, The
Broadcasting
Washington Post
Variety
Advertising Age
Apprise Magazine

EDELSTEIN, SCOTT
3319 Emerson Ave., S.
Minneapolis, MN 55408
Telephone: 612-823-5838
PRINCIPAL SUBJECTS:
Education
Journalism
The Arts
PUBLICATIONS:
Glamour
Essence
Writers Digest

Artists Magazine, The
Campus Life
Writer's Yearbook
Artlines
Single Parent

EDMONDS, PATRICIA
1000 Wilson Blvd.
Arlington, VA 22229
Telephone: 703-276-5979
PRINCIPAL SUBJECTS:
General Interest
PUBLICATIONS:
Miami Herald
Philadelphia Inquirer
Detroit Free Press
San Jose Mercury
Charlotte Observer
Akron Beacon Journal
USA Today

EDSON, ANDREW S.
89 Bounty Ln.
Jericho, NY 11753
Telephone: 212-752-8338
MAILING ADDRESS:
Andrew S. Edson
950 Third Ave., Ste. 1600
New York, NY 10022
Telephone: 516-931-0873
AFFILIATIONS:
PRSA, WG
PRINCIPAL SUBJECTS:
Business & Industry
Sports
Travel
Personal Finance
PUBLICATIONS:
AD East
Management Review
The Scene
North Liner
Public Relations Journal
Public Relations Review
Private Banking

EDSON, LEE
36 Iron Gate Rd.
Stamford, CT 06903
Telephone: 203-322-8791
Fax: 203-329-2103
AFFILIATIONS:
NASW, ASJA, AG
PRINCIPAL SUBJECTS:
Business & Industry
Personalities
Philosophy
Science
Computer Technology
Medical

PUBLICATIONS:
New York Times
Reader's Digest
Time/Life
Family Circle
Think Magazine
Across The Board
The Lamp
Mosaic
New York
Science Year

EGERTON, JOHN
807 South Friendswood Drive
Friendswood, TX 77546
Telephone: 713-482-4003
Fax: 713-482-4301
PRINCIPAL SUBJECTS:
Medical
Travel
Medical Economics
Humor
PUBLICATIONS:
Newsweek
Houston Chronicle

EISCHEN, CHARLES N.
3040 Idaho Ave., N.W.
Washington, DC 20016
Telephone: 202-966-6287
AFFILIATIONS:
NPC, SIGMA DELTA CHI
PRINCIPAL SUBJECTS:
Business & Industry
Urban Affairs
PUBLICATIONS:
Christian Science Monitor
Editor & Publisher Magazine
North America Newspaper
  Alliance

EISENSTEIN, PAUL A.
22 Cambridge Blvd.
Pleasant Rdg, MI 48069
Telephone: 313-544-8700
AFFILIATIONS:
DPC, DAPA
PRINCIPAL SUBJECTS:
Automotive
Personal Finance
Business & Industry
Computer Technology
PUBLICATIONS:
Invester's Business Daily
Christian Science
Metropolitan Detroit
The Detroit News
The Washington Time
Manufacturing Week
US Banker
Michigan Business

Videography
Computer Decisions Magazine
Detroit Monthly
The Chicago Tribune
Solutions
Auto Motor & Sport (German)
Auto Bild (German)
Journal of Commerce
Family Circle
CBS
Economist
Nikkon Jidosha Shimbun
  Sha/Japan
Global Business
The Engineer (British)
American Machinist
Off-Duty
Automotive Executive
Automotive Industries

ELIOT, JANE WINSLOW
105 Paloma Ave.
Venice, CA 90291
Telephone: 310-392-2048
AFFILIATIONS:
ASJA, AG
PRINCIPAL SUBJECTS:
General Interest
Travel
PUBLICATIONS:
Atlantic Monthly
Travel & Leisure
Horticulture
Los Angeles Reader

ELLIOTT, CHARLES
7283 Flat Rock Trail
Covington, GA 30209
Telephone: 404-786-5090
MAILING ADDRESS:
Charles Elliott
P.O. Box 1217
Covington, GA 30209
AFFILIATIONS:
OWAA, SEOPA, GOWA
PRINCIPAL SUBJECTS:
Men's Interest
Sports
PUBLICATIONS:
Outdoor Life
Georgia Sportsman
Atlanta Constitution
Harris Hunting & Fishing
  Annuals

ELLIOTT, JOY
220 E. 63rd St., #125
New York, NY 10021
Telephone: 212-838-1550
Fax: 212-223-2878

AFFILIATIONS:
Womens Media Group
PRINCIPAL SUBJECTS:
World Affairs
Foreign
Travel
Editorial

ELLIS, ALBERT
45 East 65th St.
New York, NY 10021
Telephone: 212-535-0822
Fax: 212-249-3582
PRINCIPAL SUBJECTS:
Family
Health
Human Relations
Psychology
PUBLICATIONS:
Cosmopolitan
Penthouse
Playboy
Psychology Today
Penthouse Forum
The Humanist

ELWOOD, MRS. EDITH
  MUESING
229 B Pond Way
Staten Island, NY 10303
Telephone: 718-761-8170
AFFILIATIONS:
NWU NWC
PRINCIPAL SUBJECTS:
Social Trends
Government
Philosophy
Business & Industry
Family
The Arts
Human Relations
PUBLICATIONS:
Minnesota Ink
Black Mountain Review
Piedmont Literary Review
Wind Chimes
Dragonfly: East/West Haiku
  Quarterly
Inkstone
Plover, The
Parent to Parent Newsletter
Working at Home
Brussels Sprout
The Red Pagoda
Cappers
Advocate
ICA-Update
Today's Family

ENGH, JERI
1910 35th Rd., Pine Lake Farm
Osceola, WI 54020
Telephone: 715-248-7392
Fax: 715-248-7394
AFFILIATIONS:
ASJA SATW
PRINCIPAL SUBJECTS:
Ecology
Health
Human Relations
Philosophy
Sports
Travel
Medical
Photography
PUBLICATIONS:
Parents' Magazine
Reader's Digest
Redbook
Saturday Review
Today's Health
Saturday Evening Post
Chicago Tribune

ENGLE, PAANANEN ELOISE
6348 Cross Woods Dr.
Falls Church, VA 22044
Telephone: 703-256-6077
MAILING ADDRESS:
Eloise Engle Paananen
Falls Church, VA 22044
AFFILIATIONS:
ASJA, SWG, AG
PRINCIPAL SUBJECTS:
Science
Government
History
Personalities
Health
Travel
Women's Interest
PUBLICATIONS:
Yankee
Washington Post Travel
National Forum
Ladycom
Career World
Exxon Air World
Marine Corps Gazette
Medical World News
VFW
Woman's World
World and I
Washington Times
Life in The Times
Washington International

ENGLEBARDT, STANLEY L.
258 Bayberry Ln.
Westport, CT 06880

Telephone: 203-227-1914
PRINCIPAL SUBJECTS:
General Interest
Health
Science
PUBLICATIONS:
Reader's Digest

ENGLISH, JOHN W.
565 Prince Ave.
Athens, GA 30601
Telephone: 706-353-1832
Fax: 706-542-4785
MAILING ADDRESS:
College of Journalism
The University of Georgia
Athens, GA 30602
Telephone: 404-353-1832
AFFILIATIONS:
ASJA, SPJ
PRINCIPAL SUBJECTS:
Media
The Arts
Business & Industry
Human Interest
Travel
PUBLICATIONS:
New York Times
Atlanta
Fodor's Travel Guides
Southern Exposure
Atlanta Weekly Magazine
American Film

ENGMAN, RONDA
571 S. Danby Rd.
Spencer, NY 14883
Telephone: 607-589-4031
AFFILIATIONS:
GWAA AEJMC
PRINCIPAL SUBJECTS:
Nature
Home & Garden
Animals
PUBLICATIONS:
N.Y. Times
Connoisseur
Womens Day
Amercian Way

ENSRUD, BARBARA
404 Cherokee Dr.
Oxford, MA 38655
Telephone: 601-236-7998
PRINCIPAL SUBJECTS:
Travel
PUBLICATIONS:
Wine With Foods
American Vineyards
Best Wine Buys
Pocket Guide to Cheese

EVANOFF, VLAD
P.O. Box 770036
Pompano Beach, FL 33077
Telephone: 305-974-7076
AFFILIATIONS:
OWAA
PUBLICATIONS:
Field and Stream
Outdoor Life
Salt Water Sportsman
Sports Afield
Pleasure Boating
Motor Boating
The Florida Fisherman
American Legion
Eastern Outdoors
Eastern - Southeastern Boating

EVANS, GLEN
122 Cedar Heights Rd.
Stamford, CT 06905
Telephone: 203-329-3216
AFFILIATIONS:
ASJA, AUTHORS GUILD, SPJ,
  NWC
PRINCIPAL SUBJECTS:
Book Reviews
Editorial
Family
General Interest
Health
Human Interest
Humor
Medical
Personalities
Social Trends
PUBLICATIONS:
Family Circle
Good Housekeeping
Brides
Travel & Leisure
Seventeen
Playboy
Essence
Parade

EWING, DAVID W.
195 Cambridge St.
Wichester, MA 01890
Telephone: 617-729-6196
PUBLICATIONS:
Fortune
Harper's
Psychology Today
Saturday Review
Harvard Business Review
Civil Liberties Review
New York Times
New York Bar Journal

FADER, SHIRLEY SLOAN
377 McKinley Blvd.
Paramus, NJ 07652
Telephone: 201-261-8751
AFFILIATIONS:
ASJA, AUTHORS GUILD
PRINCIPAL SUBJECTS:
Family
Travel
Psychology
Women's Interest
PUBLICATIONS:
Glamour
House Beautiful
McCall's
Trailer Life
Family Circle
New York Times
Ladies Home Journal (Column)
Working Woman Magazine
Self Magazine
Cosmopolitan
Seventeen
Harper's Bazaar
Los Angeles Times Travel
Houston Chronicle Travel
  Section
San Francisco Chronicle

FAILLA, KATHLEEN SALUK
21 Samuelson Rd.
Weston, CT 06883
Telephone: 203-544-1048
AFFILIATIONS:
SPJ WICI
PRINCIPAL SUBJECTS:
Business & Industry
PUBLICATIONS:
New York Times

FALES, EDWARD
54 Lime Rock Sta. Rd.
Falls Village, CT 06031
Telephone: 203-824-7850
MAILING ADDRESS:
Edward Fales Studio
Falls Village, CT 06031
PRINCIPAL SUBJECTS:
General Interest
Science
Travel
The Arts
PUBLICATIONS:
Popular Mechanics
Reader's Digest
50 Plus
Parade
McCall's
Motor Boating & Sailing
Popular Science
Better Homes & Gardens

Yachting
Associated Press Member
  Newspapers
Litchfield County Times

FANTEL, HAS
187 E. Broadway
New York, NY 10002
Telephone: 212-777-7588
PRINCIPAL SUBJECTS:
Electronics
Science
The Arts
Video
Computer Technology
PUBLICATIONS:
N.Y. Times
Opera News
Popular Mechanics
Popular Science
Reader's Digest
House & Garden
Connoisseur

FAREWELL, SUSAN
9 Hoyt Street
South Salem, NY 10590
Telephone: 914-763-9344
Fax: 914-763-9344
AFFILIATIONS:
ASJA, SATW, NYTW
PRINCIPAL SUBJECTS:
Book Reviews
Editorial
General Interest
Health
Home & Garden
Journalism
Travel
Women's Interest
PUBLICATIONS:
Travel & Leisure
Metropolitan Home
Vogue Espana
Child
Brides
New York Post
Travel Holiday
Caribbean Travel & Life

FARIS, CHARLENE
9524 Guilford Dr., #A
Indianapolis, IN 46240
Telephone: 317-848-2634
MAILING ADDRESS:
Charlene Faris
9524 Guilford Dr., A
Indianapolis, IN 46240
AFFILIATIONS:
IWOSC, NLAPW

PRINCIPAL SUBJECTS:
Health
Medical
Business & Industry
Travel
PUBLICATIONS:
Saturday Evening Post, The
Reader's Digest
Runner's World
Sales Motivation & Assn. &
  Society Mgr.
Successful Meetings
Indiana Business Magazine
Indianapolis Monthly Magazine
Christian Science Monitor
Grit
Southwest Airlines Spirit
Meeting News
American Fitness
Golden Rule Insurance Co.
Taco Bell Corporation
Guideposts

FAUX, MARIAN
300 Riverside Dr., #7H
New York, NY 10025
Telephone: 212-678-0183
AFFILIATIONS:
ASJA
PRINCIPAL SUBJECTS:
Family
Personal Finance
Social Trends
Women's Interest
PUBLICATIONS:
Glamour
Mademoiselle
Savvy
Working Women
Chatelaine
Worth
Family Weeky
Memories

FEHL, MARTHA R.
8125 Smith Rd.
Brookville, IN 47012
Telephone: 317-647-5823
AFFILIATIONS:
NWC, SCBW
PRINCIPAL SUBJECTS:
Animals
Automotive
Book Reviews
Ecology
Education
Family
Foreign
General Interest
Geography
Government

History
Hobbies
Home & Garden
Human Interest
Humor
Journalism
Men's Interest
Motivation
Nature
News
Personal Finance
Photography
Physical Fitness
Psychology
Religion
Sales
Science
Senior Citizens
Social Trends
Sports
The Arts
Travel
Women's Interest
World Affairs
Youth
PUBLICATIONS:
Family Circle
Lake Superior Magazine
The Cincinnati Enquirer
On The Line - Pacific Press
Seattle's Child
Lollipop Magazine -
  Contributing Editor
Highlights for Children
Pennsylvania Magazine
Camping Today
Country Magazine
Senior Life Magazine
Creative Years
Capper's
Virginia State Trooper
  Magazine
Illinois Magazine
National Research Bureau, Inc.
Radar Magazine
Reminisce Magazine
Country Extra
Outdoor Indiana
Happiness Magazine
Tuff Stuff Magazine
Midwest Living
Atlantic Monthly
West Texas Sun
Single Parent
Lady's Circle
McCall's
Atlanta Weekly
Indiana Game & Fish
Lady's Circle

FEIN, ELAINE
80 Garden Road
Scarsdale, NY 10583
Telephone: 914-723-7996
Fax: 914-723-6210
AFFILIATIONS:
ASJA, OPC, NASW
PRINCIPAL SUBJECTS:
Editorial
Family
Health
Human Interest
Human Relations
Journalism

FEIT, EDWARD
9 Eaton Ct.
Amherst, MA 01002
Telephone: 413-253-5415
PRINCIPAL SUBJECTS:
Agriculture
Automotive
Aviation
Business & Industry
Electronics
Marine
Military
The Arts
PUBLICATIONS:
Advanced Imaging
Boating Product News
Commuter Air
Healthcare Systems
Insulation Outlook
Intech
M & C
Roofer
Chemical Engineering
Food Technology
Quality

FELD, KAREN
1698 32nd St., N.W.
Washington, DC 20007
Telephone: 202-337-2044
Fax: 202-338-4750
AFFILIATIONS:
ASJA, SPJ, NFPW, CPW, NPC,
   USSPG, SDC, AFTRA, ANC
PRINCIPAL SUBJECTS:
Personalities
General Interest
Human Interest
Health
Book Reviews
Entertainment
Government
Medical
News
The Arts
Travel

PUBLICATIONS:
Toronto Sun
Parade
People
Los Angeles Times
Family Circle
Vogue
Philadelphia Inquirer
Nashville Tennesean
Prodigy
Time
Money

FELDMAN, ELANE
101 - A Clark St., #17B
Brooklyn, NY 11201
Telephone: 718-875-3383
Fax: 718-875-3384
PRINCIPAL SUBJECTS:
Travel
Fashion
Humor
Women's Interest
Book Reviews
PUBLICATIONS:
New York Magazine
New York Daily News
Readers Digest
American Home
American Bookseller
Cosmopolitan
Publishers Weekly
Antioch Review

FELDMAN, RUTH DUSKIN
935 Fairview Rd.
Highland Park, IL 60035
Telephone: 708-433-2632
Fax: 708-433-2634
AFFILIATIONS:
ASJA, AG, SMA, IWC, NWU
PRINCIPAL SUBJECTS:
Education
Family
Human Relations
Travel
The Arts
Human Interest
Human Relations
Religion
Psychology
PUBLICATIONS:
Better Homes & Gardens
Dynamic Years
Discovery
Travel & Leisure
New York Daily News
Chicago Sun - Times
Chicago Parent
Delta Sky
Mature Outlook

North Shore
Sunshine (Ft. Lauderdale
   News/Sun - Sentinel)
USAir
Woman's Day
Vista/USA
Relax (Regular Contributor)
Chicago Tribune Magazine
New Choices for
   The Best Years
Boston Herald
Toronto Star

FENSCH, THOMAS C.
Sam Houston State University,
   Box 2072
Huntsville, TX 77341
Telephone: 409-294-1522
Fax: 402-294-1598
AFFILIATIONS:
ASJA
PRINCIPAL SUBJECTS:
Editorial
Human Interest
Journalism
Media
News
Photography
Sports
PUBLICATIONS:
Presstime
Chicago Sun Times
Dallas Morning News
Houston Chronicle
The Steinbeck Quarterly
Journalism Educator

FENTEN, D. X.
27 Bowdon Rd.
Greenlawn, NY 11740
Telephone: 516-271-3199
Fax: 516-271-3177
PRINCIPAL SUBJECTS:
Home & Garden
Science
Computer Technology
PUBLICATIONS:
"Computer Bits"
"The Weekend Gardener"
Newsday
Family Circle

FERGUSON, JOSEPH
26 Bank Street
Cold Springs, NY 10516
Telephone: 914-265-4630
PRINCIPAL SUBJECTS:
Book Reviews
Video

PUBLICATIONS:
American Bookk Review
The Times Herald Record
Hudson Valley Magazine
Quality Living

FERMAN, IRVING
3818 Huntington St., NW
Washington, DC 20015
Telephone: 202-363-7093
MAILING ADDRESS:
Irving Ferman
3818 Huntington St., N.W.
Washington, DC 20015
AFFILIATIONS:
ABA DCBA
PRINCIPAL SUBJECTS:
Government
Philosophy
PUBLICATIONS:
Reader's Digest
Law Reviews

FERRIS, PAUL
13808 Ranch Lake Dr.
Pound, WI 54161
Telephone: 715-854-2484
AFFILIATIONS:
NWC, WRWA
PRINCIPAL SUBJECTS:
Humor
Business & Industry
PUBLICATIONS:
American Salesman
Grit
Growing Child/Parent
Byline
Green Bay Press-Gazette
Lutheran Digest
Christian Writer, The
Selling Direct
Milwaukee Journal

FERTIG, JUDITH
9451 Connell
Shawnee Msn, KS 66212
Telephone: 913-492-3313
PRINCIPAL SUBJECTS:
Health
Home & Garden
Psychology

FEUER, A.B.
2318 Aveham Ave. SW
Roanoke, VA 24014
Telephone: 703-342-3222
AFFILIATIONS:
SPJ, PEN, ASJA
PRINCIPAL SUBJECTS:
History
Military

PUBLICATIONS:
Military History
World War II
Sea Classics
Civil War Quarterly
America's Civil War

FINGER, ANNE L.
711 Penn Avenue
Teaneck, NJ 07666
Telephone: 201-836-9549
AFFILIATIONS:
ASJA
PRINCIPAL SUBJECTS:
Advertising
Business & Industry
Family
General Interest
Government
Health
Human Relations
Humor
Medical
Psychology
Social Trends
Women's Interest
PUBLICATIONS:
New York Times
LA Times
Parents
Health
New Body
Medical Tribune
New Directions for Women
The Record

FINKE, BLYTHE FOOTE
45 Kyleswood Place
Inverness, CA 94937
Telephone: 415-663-9459
AFFILIATIONS:
NPC, OPCA, ASJA, CWO, TJG
PRINCIPAL SUBJECTS:
Book Reviews
Ecology
Foreign
General Interest
Human Interest
News
Senior Citizens
Travel
Women's Interest
World Affairs
PUBLICATIONS:
New York Times
Los Angeles Times
Christian Science Monitor
Milwaukee Journal
Baltimore Sun
Chicago Tribune
Going Places

International Living
Maturity News Service
Womens' News Service
United Nations Observer and
   International Report

FINLEY, MITCH
East 1657 Gordon Avenue
Spokane, WA 99207
Telephone: 509-484-4668
Fax: 509-484-4668
PRINCIPAL SUBJECTS:
Religion
Family
Medical

FISH, BYRON
801 S.W. 168th St.
Seattle, WA 98166
Telephone: 206-242-5785
AFFILIATIONS:
SATW, SPJ, SFL, PSG
PRINCIPAL SUBJECTS:
General Interest
Humor
PUBLICATIONS:
Seattle Times
Alaska Northwest
   Publishing Co.
Family Circle
Reader's Digest
At Home
Ford Times

FISHMAN, KATHARINE DAVIS
64 Eighth Avenue
Brooklyn, NY 11217
Telephone: 718-622-0027

FLEMING, ALICE
315 E. 72nd St.
New York, NY 10021
Telephone: 212-988-9160
AFFILIATIONS:
AG, PEN
PRINCIPAL SUBJECTS:
Family
Women's Interest
PUBLICATIONS:
Cosmopolitan
Reader's Digest
Redbook
Woman's Day

FLUENT, MIKE
217 Ripplewood
Mesquite, TX 75150
Telephone: 214-285-7009
PRINCIPAL SUBJECTS:
General Interest
Business & Industry

PUBLICATIONS:
American History Illustrated
Publishers Weekly
Quality Champlin Oil

FNA NEWS
P.O. Box 11999
Salt Lake Cty, UT 84147
Telephone: 801-355-1901
MAILING ADDRESS:
FNA News
Salt Lake City, UT 84117
AFFILIATIONS:
SDC
PRINCIPAL SUBJECTS:
Advertising
Agriculture
Amusements
Animals
Automotive
Aviation
Business & Industry
Ecology
Editorial
Electronics
Entertainment
Fashion
Government
Health
History
Human Interest
Humor
Journalism
Management
Marine
Media
Medical
Military
Movie Reviews
News
Personal Finance
Photography
Physical Fitness
Religion
Science
Social Trends
Sports
Travel
Urban Affairs
Video
Women's Interest
World Affairs
PUBLICATIONS:
Deseret News
Associated Press
United Press International
Time
Wall Street Journal
Ogden Standard
Utah Holiday Magazine
Utah Press Assoc., Syndicate

Newsweek
Salt Lake Tribune
Agency French Press (AFP)

FONTAINE, ANDRE
124 Remington Ave.
Syracuse, NY 13210
Telephone: 315-472-1476
PRINCIPAL SUBJECTS:
History
Personalities
Philosophy
PUBLICATIONS:
Good Housekeeping
McCall's
Reader's Digest
Redbook
Yachting

FORTNEY, DAVID L.
516 S. Bradford
Kirksville, MO 63501
Telephone: 816-665-0814
AFFILIATIONS:
ASJA, SPJ, IRE
PRINCIPAL SUBJECTS:
General Interest
Personalities
Health
Travel
Business & Industry
Education
Family
Foreign
Human Interest
Journalism
Men's Interest
News
PUBLICATIONS:
Good Housekeeping
Guideposts
Kiwanis
National Enquirer
Reader's Digest
US Magazine
American Way
Success
Rotarian
Today's Health

FORTSON, LOWRANCE
   SANNA
108 S. 20th Ave.
Hattiesburg, MS 39401
Telephone: 601-584-1049
PRINCIPAL SUBJECTS:
Business & Industry
Home & Garden
Nature
Youth

PUBLICATIONS:
Memphis Business Journal
Learning '88
Home Lighting and
  Accessories
LP Gas
Law & Order
Police Times
Pest Control Magazine
Glass Digest
Small Town Development
  (Newspaper Column)
MIssissippi Business Journal
Office World News
Food People
Snack Food
Fuel Oil News
National Fisherman
Police Product News
Today's Fireman
Tennessee Retailing
Ward's Auto World
Amicus Journal
Woodall's Trailer Travel
Entrepreneur
Woman Magazine
Mississippi State Alumnus
Your Home
National Gardening News
Fate
CB Times
Grit
Metropolitan Review
Jackson Daily News
United Press International
American Junior Red
  Cross News
Clubhouse
Mississippi Outdoors
Soundings
Income Opportunities
Mississippi Magazine
Delta Scene
Gurney's Gardening News
ECM Newsletters
Beyond Reality
Southern CB Times
Zygote
Farm Woman News (Photo)
Gulf Coast Horizon
American Youth
Touch
BNA Energy Users Report
Clinton Times, The
Berryville Star - Progress
Yacht, The
Hattiesburg American
Aquaculture News
Treasure Search
Black Family
Business Today

Equal Opportunity
Home Mechanix
Home Magazine
Your Home, Work - at -
  Home Report

FOSTER, NANCY
342 Asilomar Blvd.
Pacific Grove, CA 93950
Telephone: 408-655-3689
PRINCIPAL SUBJECTS:
Travel
Personalities
Human Interest
General Interest
Human Relations
Animals
Health
Education
PUBLICATIONS:
Boston Globe
Boston Phoenix
Yankee Magazine
New England Coastal Journal
South End News
Elko Lion
Pacific Monthly

FOX, BARRY
462 N. Linden Dr., #440
Beverly Hills, CA 90212
Telephone: 310-278-5671
Fax: 310-271-6019
AFFILIATIONS:
ASJA, SMWA, IWSC,
  PRSA, IABC
PRINCIPAL SUBJECTS:
Advertising
Business & Industry
Editorial
Health
Human Interest
Human Relations
Management
Marketing
Motivation
Personalities
Sales
The Arts
Medical
PUBLICATIONS:
Let's Live
Business Report
Total Health
Inside Vitamins

FRANCISCUS, ALEXANDRA
9 Willow St., #32
Boston, MA 02108
Telephone: 617-723-5732

PRINCIPAL SUBJECTS:
Business & Industry
The Arts
Foreign

FRASER, BRUCE W.
229 E. 28th St., #1 - B
New York, NY 10016
Telephone: 212-779-3219
Fax: 212-779-3175
AFFILIATIONS:
EFA, IABC, NYBPE
PRINCIPAL SUBJECTS:
Business & Industry
Personal Finance
PUBLICATIONS:
Journal of Commerce
The Christian Science Monitor
Nation's Business
Financial World
New York Times, The
US Air
The Rotarian
American Banker
Adweek

FRAZER, LANCE
209 Gareffa Way
Santa Rosa, CA 95401
Telephone: 707-546-7406
AFFILIATIONS:
NWC, SPJ, ASJA, IAWW
PRINCIPAL SUBJECTS:
Business & Industry
Science
Nature
Travel
Personalities
PUBLICATIONS:
Ad Astra
Arizona Highways
Barrister
Diversion
Hemisheres
Men's Fitness
Prime Times
The New Physician
The Scientist
U.S. Air

FREEDMAN, ERIC
2698 Linden Dr.
East Lansing, MI 48823
Telephone: 517-337-0269
Fax: 517-371-4153
AFFILIATIONS:
IRE, NAAJ
PRINCIPAL SUBJECTS:
Government
Travel
Agriculture

History
Hobbies
Human Interest
Journalism
News
PUBLICATIONS:
The Knickerbocker News
The New York Law Journal
PC Magazine
American Banker
Des Moines Register
Empire State Report Magazine
Detroit News
National Law Journal
Los Angeles Times
PC Week
American Medical News
Chicago Sun - Times
Great Lakes Quarterly
Dance Teacher Now
Milwaukee Sentinel
Toronto Globe & Mail
Boston Globe
USA Today
Produce News

FREEMAN, LUCY
210 Central Park S.
New York, NY 10019
Telephone: 212-586-7452
AFFILIATIONS:
MWA, SMW
PRINCIPAL SUBJECTS:
Psychology
Journalism
Sports
PUBLICATIONS:
Cosmopolitan
N. Y. Times Magazine

FREY, RICHARD L.
235 E. 87 St., Apt. 5C
New York, NY 10128
Telephone: 212-427-0198
AFFILIATIONS:
ASJA
PRINCIPAL SUBJECTS:
Entertainment
Hobbies
PUBLICATIONS:
Good Housekeeping
Reader's Digest
Sports Illustrated
Woman's Day
Diversion
Bridge World
Cosmopolitan
Popular Bridge
Mc Call's

FRIED, EUNICE
85 Fourth Ave., #2KK
New York, NY 10003
Telephone: 212-674-1609
AFFILIATIONS:
WWC
PRINCIPAL SUBJECTS:
Travel
Personalities
General Interest
Human Interest
Personalities
The Arts
Travel
PUBLICATIONS:
Connoisseur
House Beautiful
Elle
New York Times
Black Enterprise
Almanac
Wine & Spirits
Fine Wine Folio
Harper's Bazaar

FRIEDMAN, KENNETH A.
3061 Powder Mill Cir.
Bethlehem, PA 18017
Telephone: 215-694-3239
PRINCIPAL SUBJECTS:
Science
Ecology
Health

FRIESE, RICK
P.O. Box 31658
Palm Bch Garden, FL 33420
Telephone: 407-627-8989
Fax: 407-624-3961
AFFILIATIONS:
ASMP
PRINCIPAL SUBJECTS:
Marine
Advertising
General Interest
Editorial
Photography
Travel
PUBLICATIONS:
Architectural Digest
Boating
Cruising World
Power & Motor Yacht
Sail
McCall's
Nautical Quarterly
Yachting

FRIZZI, VIRGINIA
1715 Chislett St.
Pittsburgh, PA 15206

Telephone: 412-361-6028
Fax: 412-391-1980
MAILING ADDRESS:
Virginia Frizzi
Pittsburgh, PA 15206
AFFILIATIONS:
ASMP SPJ
PRINCIPAL SUBJECTS:
Travel
History
Human Interest
Business & Industry
PUBLICATIONS:
Pittsburgh Press, The
Seventeen
Christian Science Monitor, The
Pittsburgh
Pennsylvania Illustrated
Capper's Weekly
Mid - Atlantic Country
Majestry
Allegheny Business News

FROME, MICHAEL
Huxley College, Western
  Washington University
Bellingham, WA 98225
Telephone: 206-650-3978
Fax: 206-650-7284
MAILING ADDRESS:
Michael Frome
Huxley College,
  W. Wash. Univ.
Bellingham, WA 98225
PRINCIPAL SUBJECTS:
Animals
Nature

FRUMKES, LEWIS BURKE
Marymount Manhattan College,
  221 E. 71st St.
New York, NY 10021
Telephone: 000-000-0000
AFFILIATIONS:
AJSA, PEN, SPW
PRINCIPAL SUBJECTS:
Book Reviews
Education
General Interest
Health
Humor
Philosophy
Psychology
Science
Travel
PUBLICATIONS:
New York Times
Reader's Digest
Harper's Bazaar
Town & Country
McCall's

FUERST, MARK L.
30 Butler Street, #1
Brooklyn, NY 11231
Telephone: 718-852-2782
AFFILIATIONS:
ASJA, NASW
PRINCIPAL SUBJECTS:
Health
Medical
PUBLICATIONS:
American Health
Good Housekeeping
Cooking Light
Medical Tribune
Medical World News

FULLMAN, LYNN GRISARD
2446 Monte Vista Dr.
Birmingham, AL 35216
Telephone: 205-822-1402
AFFILIATIONS:
ASJA, NATJA, IFWTWA,
  WBOC, AMP
PRINCIPAL SUBJECTS:
Advertising
Book Reviews
General Interest
Human Interest
Humor
Travel
PUBLICATIONS:
Golfweek
Guideposts
The Birmingham News
Baby Talk
Military History
Over the Mtn Journal

FURLONG, ISABEL M.
3140 Klingle Rd., N.W.
Washington, DC 20008
Telephone: 202-333-3345
AFFILIATIONS:
WWC
PRINCIPAL SUBJECTS:
Travel
Women's Interest
PUBLICATIONS:
Good Housekeeping
Holiday
Chicago Tribune

**FUSCO, MARY ANN
  CASTRONOVO**
212 Ft. Lee Rd.
Leonia, NJ 07605
Telephone: 201-461-4036
AFFILIATIONS:
ASJA, ASME, WICI
PRINCIPAL SUBJECTS:
Architecture

Book Reviews
Business & Industry
Editorial
Fashion
Foreign
General Interest
Health
Home & Garden
Management
Personalities
Family
Social Trends
Sports
Travel
Women's Interest
PUBLICATIONS:
Business Week
Redbook
New York Times
Child
McCall's
House & Garden
New York Daily News
Bridal Guide
NJ Monthly
Travel & Leisure
Home

GAGE, DIANE
4204 Explorer Court
La Mesa, CA 91941
Telephone: 619-670-9942
Fax: 619-670-8614
AFFILIATIONS:
ASJA
PRINCIPAL SUBJECTS:
Business & Industry
Human Relations
Health
PUBLICATIONS:
Good Housekeeping
Woman's Day
American Health
McCalls

GALLAGHER, RACHEL
65 Bank St.
New York, NY 10014
Telephone: 212-708-9600
Fax: 212-708-9531
AFFILIATIONS:
NWU, AG
PRINCIPAL SUBJECTS:
Women's Interest
Media
Social Trends
PUBLICATIONS:
New York Times

New York Magazine
Esquire
Self
Mademoiselle

GALLESE, LIZ ROMAN
25 Caroline St.
Wellesley Hills, MA 02181
Telephone: 617-235-1855
Fax: 617-235-5175
AFFILIATIONS:
ASJA
PRINCIPAL SUBJECTS:
Business & Industry
Women's Interest
PUBLICATIONS:
Wall St. Journal
Forbes
Fortune
Across the Board
Working Woman
The New York Times
Boston Business
World Monitor

GALLO, DIANE
Box 231, Oxford Rd.
Mount Upton, NY 13809
Telephone: 607-764-8139
AFFILIATIONS:
PWI, PWN, IWWG
PRINCIPAL SUBJECTS:
Business & Industry
Human Relations
Personalities
Travel
Women's Interest
Advertising
Amusements
Humor
Psychology
The Arts
Video
PUBLICATIONS:
New York Daily News
Better Homes & Garden
Norwich Evening Sun
Small World
New York Alive
Women's World
Southern Tier IMAGES
Fodor's Travel
New York State Travel Guide
Travel Holiday
MD Magazine
Business New York
IBM Heritage
Binghamton Press

Capital Magazine
Time Peace, Inspirational
  Calendar Publ. By
Keith Clark Inc.

GALUB, JACK
27 West 96th St.
New York, NY 10025
Telephone: 212-865-7886
AFFILIATIONS:
AMWA, OPC
PRINCIPAL SUBJECTS:
Business & Industry
General Interest
Health
Medical
PUBLICATIONS:
Family Circle
Glamour
Mechanix Illustrated
Parents
Popular Mechanics
Sports Afield
Woman's Day
Scanorama
Good Housekeeping
Financial Markets Reporter
The Jmarket Chronicle

GAMAGE, DOUGLAS C.
26 Glen St.
Riverside, RI 02915
Telephone: 401-433-4475
AFFILIATIONS:
RINPA, IABC, RI
PRINCIPAL SUBJECTS:
General Interest
Human Relations
Business & Industry
Sports
Architecture
Photography
PUBLICATIONS:
Prov. Sunday Journal
East Prov. Post
Life
Barrington Times
Life Magazine
American Banker

GANNON, ROBERT
334 E. Howard St.,
  Gatehouse, The
Bellefonte, PA 16823
Telephone: 814-355-4800
AFFILIATIONS:
ASJA, AG, NASW
PRINCIPAL SUBJECTS:
Ecology
General Interest
Health

Business & Industry
Science
Nature
Marine
PUBLICATIONS:
Popular Science
Reader's Digest
Science Digest
Saturday Evening Post
Glamour
TV Guide
Technology Illustrated
Some 20 Others

GARFIELD, JOHANNA
200 E. 94 (1517)
New York, NY 10128
Telephone: 212-966-2568
AFFILIATIONS:
ASJA, AG, WU, PWI
PRINCIPAL SUBJECTS:
Human Relations
Travel
PUBLICATIONS:
New York Times
Christian Science Monitor
New York Newsday
Ladies Home Journal
Reader's Digest
Ms.
Seventeen

GARRARD, ALICE
264 Elizabeth St., #2
New York, NY 10012
Telephone: 212-966-2328
Fax: 212-966-2328
AFFILIATIONS:
ASJA, SATW
PRINCIPAL SUBJECTS:
Travel
PUBLICATIONS:
Travel & Leisure
Frequent Flyer
Ms.
Modern Bride
Good Housekeeping
Better Homes & Gardens
Working Mother
The Boston Globe
Miami Herald
Atlanta Journal Constitution

GATTO, JOHN TAYLOR
235 W. 76th St.
New York, NY 10023
Telephone: 212-874-3631
Fax: 212-529-3555
AFFILIATIONS:
CS, AMS, SH

PRINCIPAL SUBJECTS:
Religion
Education
History
Government
Journalism
The Arts
Family
Movie Reviews
PUBLICATIONS:
ZPB's Simon & Schuster
NY Times, NY News, New
  York Post, Newsday
Westside Teenage News
Media & Methods
Trailer Life
ASCAP Listed Songwriter
Whole Earth Review
Intellectual Quarterly
Norwich Sun
Provincetown Advocate
Village Voice
Steel City Bugle, The
Monongahela Quarterly
New Yorker
New York Review of Books
Atlantic Monthly
Teacher
Common Weal
Christian Science Monitor
San Jose Mercury News
Miami Herald
UTNE Reader
The Sun
The New Age Journal
San Francisco Chronicle
Growing Without Schooling
Oxford: The Village Press
The Star
The Maine Scholar
New Society Publishers
The Wall Street Journal

GEBHART, FRED
2346 25th Ave.
San Francisco, CA 94116
Telephone: 415-681-3018
Fax: 415-681-0350
AFFILIATIONS:
ASJA, SATW
PRINCIPAL SUBJECTS:
Business & Industry
Travel
Health
Computer Technology
Science
Aviation
Ecology
Foreign
General Interest
Journalism

Marine
Marketing
Media
Medical
Men's Interest
Nature
News
Personal Finance
Photography
Physical Fitness
Senior Citizens
Social Trends
PUBLICATIONS:
Discovery
McCalls
Drug Topics
Travel Holiday
Travel News Asia
Travel & Leisure
Consumers Digest
Genetic Engineering News
Readers Digest
Travel Courier

GEIS, DARLENE S.
1385 York Ave., Apt. 31-F
New York, NY 10021
Telephone: 212-988-2509
PRINCIPAL SUBJECTS:
The Arts
Fashion
General Interest
Travel
Youth

GELTNER, SHARON
9982-B Watermill Circle
Boynton Beach, FL 33437
Telephone: 407-364-9661
MAILING ADDRESS:
Sharon Geltner
33 S.E. Third St.
Boca Raton, FL 33432
AFFILIATIONS:
ASNE, NWA
PRINCIPAL SUBJECTS:
Journalism
News
Business & Industry
General Interest
Travel
World Affairs
Book Reviews
Fashion
Government
PUBLICATIONS:
Saturday Evening Post
Los Angeles Times
Changing Times
Sylvia Porter's Personal
    Finance

USA Today
Quill
Working Women
Chicago Tribune
Boca Raton (FL) News
San Jose Mercury News
Miami Herald
Atlanta Constitution
Arizona Republic
Nation's Business
Philadelphia Inquirer
Detroit Free Press
Washington Journalism Review
Media Business Journal

GEM PUBLISHING GROUP
250 E. Riverview Cir.
Reno, NV 89509
Telephone: 702-786-7419
MAILING ADDRESS:
Mature Traveler, The
P.O. Box 50820
Reno, NV 89513
AFFILIATIONS:
SATW, NFPW
PRINCIPAL SUBJECTS:
Travel
Business & Industry
Personal Finance
Senior Citizens
PUBLICATIONS:
Friendly Exchange
AAA World
TWA Ambassador
U.S. Air
Nevada Magazine
Better Homes & Gardens
Midwest Living
Mature Traveler, The
USA Weekend
Home & Away
Outposts
Camper World

GEORGE, KATHRYN E.
16625 Alden Ave.
Gaithersburg, MD 20877
Telephone: 301-869-4948
AFFILIATIONS:
SPJ
PRINCIPAL SUBJECTS:
Business & Industry
Ecology
Personal Finance
PUBLICATIONS:
Modern Power Systems
    (Surrey England);

Securities Traders' Monthly
    Magazine (New York);
Southern Motor Cargo
Rutgers University Cook
    College Extension Bulletin

GERMAN-GRAPES, JOAN
1008 West Mountain Road
Cheshire, MA 01225
Telephone: 413-743-2036
AFFILIATIONS:
ASJA, AG, BAC
PRINCIPAL SUBJECTS:
Personal Finance
PUBLICATIONS:
Bankers
Consumer Digest
Easy Living
Modern Maturity
Woman's Day
National Enquirer

GERSON, VICKI
2978 Acorn Lane
Northbrook, IL 60062
Telephone: 708-480-9087
Fax: 708-205-9644
AFFILIATIONS:
WC
PRINCIPAL SUBJECTS:
Business & Industry
Health
Medical
PUBLICATIONS:
Dairy Field
Refrigerated & Frozen Foods
Accent
Medical Device & Diagnostic
    Industry
Media & Methods
Illinois Medicine
Chicago Tribune
Chicago Sun-Times
Curriculum Product News

GEYER, SHERREE
7306 N. Greenview
Chicago, IL 60626
Telephone: 312-761-8697
AFFILIATIONS:
WICI
PRINCIPAL SUBJECTS:
Medical
Business & Industry
Health
PUBLICATIONS:
Safety & Health Magazine
Family Safety & Health

GIBBONS, BARBARA
4346 Cochran Chapel Circle
Dallas, TX 75209
Telephone: 214-358-4655
Fax: 214-358-0770
MAILING ADDRESS:
Gibbons, Barbara
Dallas, TX 75209
AFFILIATIONS:
AL, AG, IJG
PRINCIPAL SUBJECTS:
Book Reviews
Travel
Women's Interest
PUBLICATIONS:
Family Circle
United Feature Syndicate
Consumer Guide
Modern Maturity
Mademoiselle
Womans World
Bon Appetit
Author of 16 Books
Modern Maturity
Cooking Light
In - Flight Magazines

GIBBS, RAFE
4260 Village Dr., #202
Kissimmee, FL 34746
Telephone: 407-783-4057
Fax: 407-870-2566
PRINCIPAL SUBJECTS:
Travel
Business & Industry
Personalities
Science
Sports
Travel
PUBLICATIONS:
Saturday Evening Post, The
Esquire
Ford Times
Popular Mechanics
Sports Afield
Better Homes And Gardens

GILBERT, SARA D.
100 Bleecker St.
New York, NY 10012
Telephone: 212-420-0415
Fax: 212-995-3656
AFFILIATIONS:
ASJA, PRSA, AG
PRINCIPAL SUBJECTS:
Youth
Education
Human Relations
PUBLICATIONS:
Good Housekeeping

N.Y. Times Supplements
Ms.
McGraw Hill, MacMillan,
  Morrow, Scholastic Publ.

GILES, DAVID N.
P.O. Box 178
Dobbins, CA 95935
Telephone: 916-692-1581
AFFILIATIONS:
CWC
PRINCIPAL SUBJECTS:
Geography
History
Science
PUBLICATIONS:
Wildcat, CSU
Valley Herald
Independent Herald
Sierra Heritage
Pelican Post
Changes in Harmony
Single Woman Homesteader

GILES, MARJORIE GORDON-
14976 Fountain House Rd.
Dobbins, CA 95935
Telephone: 916-692-1581
Fax: 919-481-4314
MAILING ADDRESS:
Inkwell
P.O. Box 178
Dobbins, CA 95935
AFFILIATIONS:
NWU, CWC, SWN, PMA,
  COSMEP
PRINCIPAL SUBJECTS:
The Arts
Entertainment
Book Reviews
History
Travel
Journalism
Human Relations
PUBLICATIONS:
Connections Quarterly,
  (Amherst, MA)
Radius, (Mendocino, CA)
YS Regional Arts Newsletter,
  (Marysville, CA)
Appeal Democrat, (Yuba -
  Sutter, CA)
Sacramento Connection, The,
  (Sacramento, CA)
Let's Live Magazine
Christian Science Monitor
The Californians

GILFERT, SHIRLEY
2208 3rd Avenue
Nebraska City, NE 68410

Telephone: 402-873-5629
AFFILIATIONS:
NWG, SCBWI
PRINCIPAL SUBJECTS:
Travel
History
PUBLICATIONS:
Family Motor Coaching
Western RV. News
Ranger Rick

GILINSKY, RHODA M.
188 Wilmot Rd.
New Rochelle, NY 10804
Telephone: 914-235-8144
AFFILIATIONS:
ASJA, EWA
PRINCIPAL SUBJECTS:
Education
Family
Health
Human Interest
Human Relations
Senior Citizens
Social Trends
The Arts
Travel
Women's Interest
Youth
PUBLICATIONS:
New York Times
Working Mother
Publishers Weekly
Reader's Digest

GLASS, JUDITH E.
177 Vineyard Rd.
Huntington, NY 11743
Telephone: 516-669-6263
MAILING ADDRESS:
Glass, Judith
81 Captains Dr.
West Babylon, NY 11704
AFFILIATIONS:
SPJ, NY, FWA
PRINCIPAL SUBJECTS:
Medical
Government
Business & Industry
Architecture
Ecology
Editorial
Education
General Interest
Health
Human Interest
Journalism
Media
Nature
News
Personalities

Women's Interest
PUBLICATIONS:
New York Times
International Medical Tribune
Cardiovascular Reviews and
  Reports
Harper's Bazaar
Journal of Commerce
National Jeweler
Long Islander
Long Island Business News

GLASSER, SELMA
10240 Camarillo St., Ste. 210
Toluca Lake, CA 91602
Telephone: 818-769-4774
AFFILIATIONS:
NCA, NYW, CW
PRINCIPAL SUBJECTS:
The Arts
General Interest
Home & Garden
Humor
Women's Interest
Youth
Education
Advertising
Book Reviews
Entertainment
Family
Health
Hobbies
Human Interest
Human Relations
Marketing
Medical
Movie Reviews
Nature
Psychology
Senior Citizens
PUBLICATIONS:
American Legion
Family Weekly
Good Housekeeping
Playboy
Reader's Digest
Saturday Evening Post
Writer's Digest
L.A. Times
The Writer
Prizewinner
Joan Rivers
San Francisco Examiner
Wall Street Journal
Golden Chances
New York News
Medical World News
N.Y. Times
Jackpotunities
Womens World - 1985
Writer, Inc., The Article, June

1987, Oct 1990
Southern California - Senior
  Life - Monthly Column
Senior Scene Magazine,
  Monthly Column
Of Related Words
Contest Magazine
General Contests
Harpers
In The Company of Poets
  Monthly Column
L.A. Daily News, "The
  Complete Guide to Prize

GLEASNER, DIANA C.
7994 Holly Ct.
Denver, NC 28037
Telephone: 704-483-9301
AFFILIATIONS:
ASJA, SATW, TJG
PRINCIPAL SUBJECTS:
Travel
PUBLICATIONS:
AAA World
Vacations Magazine
Home and Away
Highways
Daily News (N.Y.)
Boston Herald
Bride's Magazine
Globe Pequot Press
San Antonio Express
Coast to Coast
Chicago Sun - Times
Baltimore Sun
Buffalo News
Touring America
T. L. Enterprises
Diversion
Destinations

GLINES, CARROLL V.
7212 Warbler Ln.
Mc Lean, VA 22101
Telephone: 703-356-6648
Fax: 703-356-2418
AFFILIATIONS:
SPJ, ANC, ACW, ANA, AWA
PRINCIPAL SUBJECTS:
Aviation
Business & Industry
Book Reviews
History
Military
PUBLICATIONS:
Professional Pilot
Air Force Magazine
Nations Business
American Legion

Retired Officer
Air Line Pilot
Aviation Heritage Magazine

GLOECKL, ROBYN
2934 Stafford St.
Pittsburgh, PA 15204
Telephone: 412-331-0680
PRINCIPAL SUBJECTS:
Human Interest
PUBLICATIONS:
Pittsburgh Press
Mt. Washington News
Mt. Lebanon News
Pittsburgh Suburban
   Community Newspapers

GOLDFEIN, DONNA
152 28th Avenue
San Francisco, CA 94121
Telephone: 415-752-4445
PRINCIPAL SUBJECTS:
General Interest
Family
Travel

GOLDSTEIN, GREG
124 Regent Drive
Long Beach, NY 11561
Telephone: 516-431-2230
MAILING ADDRESS:
Goldstein, Greg
254 36th St.
Brooklyn, NY 11232
PRINCIPAL SUBJECTS:
Sports
Computer Technology
Entertainment
Business & Industry
Personalities
Human Interest
PUBLICATIONS:
Science Digest
New York Times
Sport
Focus
Baseball Update
Evening Press
Camden Journal

GOLIN, MILTON
3510 Meadow Lane
Glenview, IL 60025
Telephone: 708-446-3100
MAILING ADDRESS:
Milton Golin
Box 36
Glencoe, IL 60022
AFFILIATIONS:
NASW, SJA, SPJ

PRINCIPAL SUBJECTS:
Computer Technology
Electronics
Health
Journalism
Medical
Science
Travel
PUBLICATIONS:
Reader's Digest
Journal of AMA
Catholic Digest
Seventeen
Mademoiselle

GOODHEART, BARBARA
15 Sheffield Ct.
Lincolnshire, IL 60069
Telephone: 708-945-4353
AFFILIATIONS:
ASJA, AMWA, IWOC
PRINCIPAL SUBJECTS:
Medical
Health
General Interest
PUBLICATIONS:
Better Homes & Gardens
Family Weekly
Today's Health
Westways

GOODING, JUDSON
P.O. Box 745, Summer (June -
   October)
Walpole, NH 03608
Telephone: 603-756-4162
MAILING ADDRESS:
Judson Gooding
16, Rue Spontini, Winter
Paris, France, TX 75116
AFFILIATIONS:
ASJA
PRINCIPAL SUBJECTS:
Business & Industry
Architecture
General Interest
Health
Travel
Book Reviews
Editorial
Education
Foreign
Government
History
Journalism
Medical
Social Trends
Urban Affairs
PUBLICATIONS:
Fortune
New York Times Magazine

Reader's Digest
Across the Board
Life
Travel & Leisure
Business And Society
Money
The Atlantic
Constitution
Time Magazine
Omni Magazine
American Health
Forbes
Profiles
Esquire
Archeology

GOODMAN, GERSON W.
259 Bennett Ave.
New York, NY 10040
Telephone: 212-567-4841
PRINCIPAL SUBJECTS:
Business & Industry
PUBLICATIONS:
Brushware

GOODMAN, JACK
6053 S. 23rd E.
Salt Lake Cty, UT 84121
Telephone: 801-277-0193
MAILING ADDRESS:
J. Goodman's City
   View Column
Salt Lake Tribune, 143 S. Main
Salt Lake Cy, UT 84111
PRINCIPAL SUBJECTS:
Book Reviews
Architecture
Travel
The Arts
News
PUBLICATIONS:
New York Times
Newsweek
Salt Lake Tribune (Weekly
   Column - "City View")
United Magazine
Western's World
American Film

GOODRICH, DONNA CLARK
648 S. Pima St.
Mesa, AZ 85210
Telephone: 602-962-6694
PRINCIPAL SUBJECTS:
Religion
Business & Industry
Editorial

PUBLICATIONS:
Arizona Nine to Five
Supervisors Bulletin
Leader
Pathways to God

GOODSELL, JAMES NELSON
330 Dartmouth St., #2 - S
Boston, MA 02116
Telephone: 617-247-4811
AFFILIATIONS:
OPC, CFR, CLAH, SPJ
PRINCIPAL SUBJECTS:
Foreign
Government
History
Aviation
Book Reviews
Editorial
Geography
Journalism
Media
World Affairs
PUBLICATIONS:
Christian Science Monitor, The
New York Herald Tribune
Miami Herald
Baltimore Sun
Chicago Tribune
St. Louis Post - Dispatch
New York Times
Progressive, The
New Republic, The
Nation, The
Hispanic American
   Historical Review
Inter American Review of
   Bibliography
American Historical Review

GOODWIN, DAVE
P.O. Drawer 54-6661
Miami, FL 33154
Telephone: 305-531-0071
Fax: 305-531-5490
AFFILIATIONS:
AAIMCO
PRINCIPAL SUBJECTS:
Business & Industry
Travel
Human Interest
Management
PUBLICATIONS:
Financial Planner
Insurance Journal
Best's Review
Consumers Digest
Boardroom Reports
The Professional Agent
American Agent & Broker
Medical Economics

Miami Herald
Insurance Times
Insurance Advocate
Probe
Insurance Review
Financial Services Times
Life Insurance Sales
Insurance Selling
CPCU Journal
Life Plus Forum

GORDON, BERNARD LUDWIG
Professor, Earth Sciences,
   Northeastern Univ.
Chestnut Hill, MA 02167
Telephone: 617-437-3176
MAILING ADDRESS:
B. L. Gordon
P. O. Box 114
Chestnut Hill, MA 02167
AFFILIATIONS:
AG BB MIRAB EC
PRINCIPAL SUBJECTS:
The Arts
Ecology
General Interest
History
Philosophy
Science
Sports
Youth
Marine
Human Interest
Nature
PUBLICATIONS:
National Fisherman
Aquasphere
Grade Teacher
Sea Frontiers
Field & Stream
Diversion
Natural History
Antiquarian Bookman
Cricket Magazine
The Log of Mystic Seaport
Salt Water Sportsman
Postcard Views

GORDON, SUSAN J.
11 Avondale Rd.
White Plains, NY 10605
Telephone: 914-948-7462
Fax: 914-948-7565
AFFILIATIONS:
ASJA, NWW, AG
PRINCIPAL SUBJECTS:
Family
Youth
Travel
Editorial
Human Relations

Humor
Women's Interest
PUBLICATIONS:
American Baby
Amtrak Express
Expecting
Family Circle
Good Housekeeping
Home
Ladies' Home Journal
McCall's
New York Newsday
New York Times
Reader's Digest
Seventeen
Victoria
Weight Watchers
Woman's Day
Working Mother

GOULD, LARK ELLEN
3551 Pueblo Way
Las Vegas, NV 89109
Telephone: 702-255-4014
AFFILIATIONS:
TRAVEL PRESS
   INTERNATIONAL
PRINCIPAL SUBJECTS:
Government
Travel
Human Interest
Personalities
Ecology
Entertainment
World Affairs
PUBLICATIONS:
Boston Globe, The
Toronto Star, The
Christian Science Monitor, The
Aramco Magazine
Berlitz Travel Guides
International Jewish Monthly
Caribian Travel & Life
Travel Agent Magazine
Denver Post

GRAF, RUDOLF F.
111 Van Etten Blvd.
New Rochelle, NY 10804
Telephone: 914-235-6611
Fax: 914-576-6051
PRINCIPAL SUBJECTS:
Business & Industry
General Interest
Hobbies
Home & Garden
Photography
Science
Computer Technology
Electronics
Video

PUBLICATIONS:
Family Handyman
Mechanix Illustrated
Popular Mechanics
Popular Science
How to Magazine (NRHA)
Times Mirror
Radio Electronics
Reston
Librairie Artheme Fayard,
   France (Paris)
Muszaki Konyvkiado, Hungary
   (Budapest)
Editorial Ramonsopena S.A.,
   Spain (Barcelona)
Editora Tecnoprint LTDA,
   Brazil (Rio de Janeiro)
Editorial Labor S.A., Spain
   (Barcelona)

GRAND, CARMEN T.
3707 S.W. Coronado St.
Portland, OR 97219
Telephone: 503-245-0546
MAILING ADDRESS:
Carmen T. Bernier - Grand
Portland, OR 97219
AFFILIATIONS:
SCBW WW
PRINCIPAL SUBJECTS:
Youth
Foreign
PUBLICATIONS:
Young American
Highlights for Children
The Oregonian

GRANHOLM, JACKSON W.
1516 El Dorado Dr.
Thousand Oaks, CA 91362
Telephone: 805-495-2336
AFFILIATIONS:
AAAS
PRINCIPAL SUBJECTS:
Computer Technology
Electronics
Science
History
Agriculture
Architecture
PUBLICATIONS:
Aeronautical Engineering
   Review
American Nurseryman
Computers & Automation
Design News
Horticulture
National Review
American Mercury
Aviation Age
Datamation

Data Processing
Electronic Equipment
Engineering
Manufacturing Systems
Sacramento Bee
Ventura County Magazine
World War II
Seattle Times
Monterey Life
Also 21 Produced Motion
   Pictures & Videos
Business Digest

GRANT, NANCY S.
3516 West Dogwood Circle
La Grange, KY 40031
Telephone: 502-241-6766
AFFILIATIONS:
ASJA
PRINCIPAL SUBJECTS:
Animals
Agriculture
Nature
Entertainment
Personalities
Youth
PUBLICATIONS:
Farming
Farm and Ranch Living
America Illustrated
Topic
Kentucky Living
Symphony

GRAPES, JOAN A.
1008 W. Mountain Rd.
Cheshire, MA 01225
Telephone: 413-743-2036
AFFILIATIONS:
ASJA
PRINCIPAL SUBJECTS:
Business & Industry
General Interest
PUBLICATIONS:
Bank Teller's Report
Branch Banker's Report
Bank Marketing Report
Berkshire Sampler
Bankers Magazine
Compass
Consumers Digest
Money Maker
Bride's
Easy Living
Dynamic Years
Cosmopolitan
National Enquirer
Tables
Woman's Day
Modern Maturity
Newark Star - Ledger

GRECO, GAIL
5501 Granby Rd.
Rockville, MD 20855
Telephone: 301-990-6760
AFFILIATIONS:
ASJA IACP
PRINCIPAL SUBJECTS:
Home & Garden
Travel
Business & Industry
PUBLICATIONS:
New York Times
Country Living Magazine
USA Today
Bride's Magazine
Corporate Brochures, Videos
Country Home Magazine
Innsider Magazine
AD Week Magazine
Christian Science Monitor
Philadelphia Inquirer
Victoria Accents
Creative Ideas for Living

GREENBERG, JAN
420 Riverside Drive
New York, NY 10025
Telephone: 212-864-3306
Fax: 212-749-7943
AFFILIATIONS:
ATPAM, AJC
PRINCIPAL SUBJECTS:
Advertising
Entertainment
Health
Marketing
Media
Medical
PUBLICATIONS:
Theatre Magazine
Seventeen
Newsday

GREENE, FREDA
6624 Newcastle Ave.
Reseda, CA 91335
Telephone: 818-344-5279
AFFILIATIONS:
ASJA WIM PILA
PRINCIPAL SUBJECTS:
Business & Industry
Foreign
Journalism
Travel
PUBLICATIONS:
Europe, (Magazine of The
  Economic Community)
Los Angeles Times
London Observer
Travel & Leisure
Financial Weekly (UK)

Hong Kong Standard News
Scanorama
Changing Homes - (Regional
  Editor)
Home (Knapp)
International Tax Free
  Trader-UK

GREENGARD, SAMUEL
725 North Kenwood St.
Burbank, CA 91505
Telephone: 818-848-3783
Fax: 818-566-7705
AFFILIATIONS:
ASJA
PRINCIPAL SUBJECTS:
Business & Industry
Computer Technology
General Interest
Geography
Government
Health
Home & Garden
Human Interest
Human Relations
Management
Medical
Men's Interest
Personal Finance
Photography
Psychology
Science
Social Trends
Sports
Urban Affairs
PUBLICATIONS:
Discover
Playboy
Family Circle
Home
Travel & Leisure
American Way
US Air
Los Angeles Times

GREGG, JAMES R.
412 S. Rolling Hills Pl.
Anaheim, CA 92807
Telephone: 714-998-5242
PRINCIPAL SUBJECTS:
Health
Science
Travel
Sports
PUBLICATIONS:
Boating
Field and Stream
Golf Digest
Modern Maturity
Sports Afield
Trailer Life

Travel & Leisure
Westways
Yachting
National Racquet Ball
Orange County Illustrated
American Shot Gunner
L.A. Times - Travel Section
Bike World
Backpacker
Canoeing

GRESHAM, GRITS
942 Williams Ave.
Natchitoches, LA 71457
Telephone: 318-357-8104
Fax: 318-352-4590
AFFILIATIONS:
OWAA, IABW, SA
PRINCIPAL SUBJECTS:
Nature
Travel
Ecology
General Interest
PUBLICATIONS:
Sports Afield
Gentleman's Quarterly
Sports Illustrated
True
Field & Stream
Outdoor Life
Vista
Guns
American Rifleman, The
Gun World
Guns & Ammo
Bassmaster
Southern Outdoors
Western Outdoors
Boating
Outboard
Advertising Age
Camping Journal
Sportsman & His Family
  Outdoors, The
Argosy

GREWELL, BOB
93 E. Columbus St.
Mt Sterling, OH 43143
Telephone: 614-869-2058
AFFILIATIONS:
OWU
PRINCIPAL SUBJECTS:
Photography
PUBLICATIONS:
Petersen's Photographic
Street Rodder
Horse & Horseman
Outdoor Life
Game & Fish
Bow & Arrow

Bow & Hunter
Florida Wild Life
Lake & Travel

GRICE, MARY A.
803 Porter
Wichita, KS 67203
Telephone: 316-942-9641
Fax: 617-332-4760
AFFILIATIONS:
NASW
PRINCIPAL SUBJECTS:
The Arts
Health
Philosophy
Religion
PUBLICATIONS:
Laser Focus World

GRIFFIN, C. W.
4428 E. Shomi St.
Phoenix, AZ 85044
Telephone: 602-496-8124
AFFILIATIONS:
SMW
PRINCIPAL SUBJECTS:
Ecology
Government
Business & Industry
Science
Sports
PUBLICATIONS:
Golf
Harper's, Atlantic Monthly,
  Nation
Saturday Progressive Review
Golf Illustrated

GRIFFIN, KELLY L.
85 Fair Oaks Ct.
Newtown, PA 18940
Telephone: 215-860-1783
PRINCIPAL SUBJECTS:
Human Relations
Health
Women's Interest
Business & Industry
Management

GRIMM, TOM
P.O. Box 1840
Islamorada, FL 33036
Telephone: 305-664-8009
PRINCIPAL SUBJECTS:
General Interest
Photography
Travel
PUBLICATIONS:
Consumer Travel-Worldwide
California Travel

**GROENE, GORDON &
GROENE, JANET**
206 Lake Mamie Rd.
DeLand, FL 32724
Telephone: 904-736-0313
Fax: 904-736-0313
AFFILIATIONS:
ASJA, BWI, SATW, NATJA,
   OWAA
PRINCIPAL SUBJECTS:
Amusements
Automotive
Aviation
Book Reviews
Family
General Interest
Home & Garden
Personal Finance
Photography
Senior Citizens
Sports
Travel
PUBLICATIONS:
Family Motor Coaching
Endless Vacation
Touring America
Anchorage Daily News
Miami Herald
Accent/Travelog
Cruise Travel
Denver Post

GROENE, JANET
206 Lake Mamie Rd.
De Land, FL 32724
Telephone: 904-736-0313
AFFILIATIONS:
ASJA,SATW,BWI,OWAA
PRINCIPAL SUBJECTS:
Travel
Automotive
General Interest
Hobbies
Marine
Aviation
Book Reviews
Family
History
Human Interest
PUBLICATIONS:
Miami Herald
Family Motor Coaching
Boston Herald
Traveland USA
Touring America
Transitions Abroad
Innkeeping World
Worldview Systems
Torrance Daily Breeze
Anchorage Daily News

The Homeowner
Leisure Life
Syndicated Newspaper
   Column, The Southern
   Traveler

GROSS, RONALD
17 Myrtle Dr.
Great Neck, NY 11021
Telephone: 516-487-0235
AFFILIATIONS:
ASJA AG WPI CNP
PRINCIPAL SUBJECTS:
Education
Social Trends
Government
PUBLICATIONS:
Christian Science Monitor
Harper's
The Nation
The New Republic
N.Y. Times Mag., Bk. Review,
   Education Section.
Parents'
Saturday Review
TV Guide
American Education
Social Policy
Change
Commentary
Commonweal
Cultural Affairs

GROSSINGER, TANIA
1 Christopher St., #7E
New York, NY 10014
Telephone: 212-243-5063
AFFILIATIONS:
ASJA
PRINCIPAL SUBJECTS:
General Interest
Travel
Social Trends
PUBLICATIONS:
New York Times Travel Section
Working Woman Magazine
Good Housekeeping
Better Homes and Gardens
Ladies Home Journal
New Choices
Boston Globe
New York Newsday
Newark Star Ledger
Sun Sentinel - Ft. Lauderdale

GROSSMAN, ELLIE
126 W. 73rd St.
New York, NY 10023
AFFILIATIONS:
ASJA

PRINCIPAL SUBJECTS:
Family
General Interest
Health
Human Relations
Personalities
Psychology
Senior Citizens
Women's Interest
PUBLICATIONS:
Ladies' Home Journal
New York Daily News
Weight Watchers Magazine
Cosmopolitan
Newspaper Enterprise
   Association

GUNST, KATHY
126 Old Fields Rd.
South Berwick, ME 03908
Telephone: 207-384-5988
MAILING ADDRESS:
Kathy Gunst
855 Islington St., #224
Portsmouth, NH 03801
PRINCIPAL SUBJECTS:
Travel
Youth
Personalities
PUBLICATIONS:
Food & Wine Magazine
Metropolitan Home Magazine
Film Comment
Diversion Magazine
House Beautiful
New England Monthly
Yankee Magazine
New York Times
Parents
Cook's Magazine, The
Harper's Bazaar
New York Daily News
Bon Appetit Magazine
Maine Times
Parenting Magazine

GYSI, CHUCK
P.O. Box 911
Burlington, IA 52601
Telephone: 319-752-3000
AFFILIATIONS:
RCMA, ARRL, APCO
PRINCIPAL SUBJECTS:
Electronics
Hobbies
General Interest
Automotive
Travel
Computer Technology
PUBLICATIONS:
Popular Communications

RCMA Journal
Grit
Monitor America
Daily Newspapers
Northeast Public Safety and
   Communications
Northeast Scanning News
Trucker's Road Atlas
Bottom Line Personal
Scanner Master
Popular Communications'
   Communications Guide

HAAPOJA, MARGARET A.
347 County Road 70
Bovey, MN 55709
Telephone: 218-247-7830
AFFILIATIONS:
ASJA
PRINCIPAL SUBJECTS:
Book Reviews
Ecology
Education
Family
General Interest
Hobbies
Home & Garden
Human Interest
Nature
Personalities
Senior Citizens
Travel
Women's Interest
PUBLICATIONS:
Modern Maturity
New Choices
Dog World
Common Ground
Organic Gardening
Horticulture
Harrowsmith
Minnesota Calls
Country America
Workbasket
Flower and Garden
The Rotarian
Home & Away
Women's Household
Weekend Gardener
Minnesota Monthly
Minnesota Horticulturist
The Senior Reporter
Countryside

HAAS, ALAN D.
41-33 68th St.
Flushing, NY 11377
Telephone: 718-446-0415
PRINCIPAL SUBJECTS:
Business & Industry
Sports

The Arts
Education
Personalities

HABIBI, MOE
P.O. Box 94147
Oklahoma City, OK 73143
Telephone: 405-478-1142
PRINCIPAL SUBJECTS:
Journalism
PUBLICATIONS:
Absolute
Single Life

HACKETT, BLANCHE
303 Concord St.
Cresskill, NJ 07626
Telephone: 201-569-5886
AFFILIATIONS:
ASJA
PRINCIPAL SUBJECTS:
The Arts
Business & Industry
General Interest
Travel
Women's Interest
History
Home & Garden
Book Reviews
News
Journalism
PUBLICATIONS:
Christian Science Monitor
New York Daily News
N.Y. Times Northeast Outdoors
American Forest
Common Cents
Highlights for Children
Suburbanite, Valley Star,
   Palisades Newspapers
Trailering Guide, Quilt World

HADDOCK, PATRICIA
3193 16th Street
San Francisco, CA 94103
Telephone: 415-863-3917
AFFILIATIONS:
ASJA, AG, SCBW
PRINCIPAL SUBJECTS:
Business & Industry
Management
Marketing
Motivation
PUBLICATIONS:
Woman's Day
Personal Finance
Seventeen
Delta Sky

HAGGITH, DAVID
3100 W. Commodore Wy, 300
Seattle, WA 98199
Telephone: 206-281-7133
AFFILIATIONS:
WIN
PRINCIPAL SUBJECTS:
The Arts
Humor
Religion
Advertising
PUBLICATIONS:
Group Magazine
Baptist Leader, The
Church Teachers
Christian Essence
HIS Magazine
Christian Single
Creation Social Science
Humanities Quarterly
Various Newspapers
Today's Single
Lutheran Layman, The
Rocky Mountain Lutheran
Youth Leader, The
Christian Living
Christian Educators Journal
Bridal Trends

HAIT, PAM
5331 E. MacDonald
Paradise Valley, AZ 85253
Telephone: 602-952-0040
Fax: 602-840-0145
AFFILIATIONS:
ASJA, NATWA
PRINCIPAL SUBJECTS:
Architecture
Ecology
Family
Fashion
Health
Human Interest
Human Relations
Humor
Marketing
Medical
Personalities
The Arts
Travel
Urban Affairs
Women's Interest
PUBLICATIONS:
Omni
Ladies Home Journal
Travel & Leisure
USA Today
Sunset

HALL, JAMES B.
1670 E. 27th Ave.
Eugene, OR 97403
Telephone: 503-342-2975
AFFILIATIONS:
MBNSA
PRINCIPAL SUBJECTS:
General Interest
Education
Travel
PUBLICATIONS:
Atlantic
Esquire
Holiday
Surfer/Monterey Life

HALLADAY, GENEVA
818 N. A Street
Monmouth, IL 61462
Telephone: 309-734-7717
PRINCIPAL SUBJECTS:
Family
Animals
Hobbies
Religion
Family
Women's Interest
PUBLICATIONS:
Highlights For Children
Personal Romances
Farm Wife News

HALPERN, FRANCES
P.O. Box 5657
Montecito, CA 93150
Telephone: 805-969-9827
MAILING ADDRESS:
Frances Halpern Talk Show
   Host
P.O. Box 4458
Santa Barbara, CA 93140
AFFILIATIONS:
ASJA, WNBA, SPJ,
   AG, NA, TSH
PRINCIPAL SUBJECTS:
General Interest
Journalism
Book Reviews
Movie Reviews
Video
PUBLICATIONS:
Seventeen
Westways
Reeves Journal
Plain Truth
The Los Angeles Times
East/West Network
Valley Magazine
Los Angeles Magazine
Palos Verdes

Peninsula News
(Los Angeles) Herald Examiner
The Daily News of Los Angeles

HAMALIAN, LEO
530 E. 90th St.
New York, NY 10128
Telephone: 212-831-6857
PRINCIPAL SUBJECTS:
Amusements
The Arts
Philosophy
Travel
World Affairs
PUBLICATIONS:
The Nation
The New York Times
   Literary Review
Journal of Modern Literature
Journal of Popular Culture
Blackwood's Magazine
Aramco World
American Book Review
Araratan Book Review
Colorado Quarterly
D.C. Gazette
Univ. Of Massachusetts Review
Columbia Magazine
North Dakota Quarterly
The Multicultural Review

HAMILTON, KATIE
P.O. Box 520, 111 West
   Chestnut Street
St Michaels, MD 21663
Telephone: 410-745-5859
Fax: 410-745-6072
AFFILIATIONS:
ASJA, NAREE, NAHWW
PRINCIPAL SUBJECTS:
Home & Garden
PUBLICATIONS:
Washington Post
USA Weekend
Chicago Tribune
Cleveland Plain Dealer
Philadelphia Daily News

HAMILTON, PHD., ELEANOR
P.O. Box 765, 60 E. Robert Dr.
Inverness, CA 94937
Telephone: 415-663-8286
AFFILIATIONS:
ASJA, AMFT
PRINCIPAL SUBJECTS:
Book Reviews
Education
Family
Health
Human Interest
Psychology

Senior Citizens
Social Trends
Women's Interest
Youth
PUBLICATIONS:
Modern Bride
Science
Pt. Reyes Light
Parents

HAMMEL, ERIC
1149 Grand Teton Drive
Pacifica, CA 94044
Telephone: 415-355-6678
Fax: 415-359-3699
AFFILIATIONS:
ASJA
PRINCIPAL SUBJECTS:
Aviation
History
Military
News
PUBLICATIONS:
Leatherneck
World War II
Naval Institute Proceedings
Military History
Marine Corps Gazette

HAMMER, ROGER A.
3900 Glenwood Ave.
Minneapolis, MN 55422
Telephone: 612-374-2120
AFFILIATIONS:
SPJ, SDX, MPC
PRINCIPAL SUBJECTS:
Science
Business & Industry
General Interest
Human Interest
Journalism
News
Sports
Medical
PUBLICATIONS:
The Quill
Daily Newspapers
Business Week
Electronics
ACHR News
UPI/King Features
Appliance
Better Homes & Gardens
The Service Reporter
Aviation Week/Space
   Technology
Hispanic America
American Way

Domestic Engineering/DE
   Journal
Consumer Guide
Read, America! (Quarterly
   Newsletter)

HAMMITT, HARRY
417 Elmwood Ave.
Lynchburg, VA 24503
Telephone: 804-845-5527
Fax: 804-846-6928
AFFILIATIONS:
ASAP
PRINCIPAL SUBJECTS:
Government
PUBLICATIONS:
IRE Journal
Reporters Handbook
SDX FOI Supplement
Quill, The
Government Executive

HANCOCK, M. A.
491 Kimberly Ave., #303
Asheville, NC 28804
Telephone: 704-251-0845
PRINCIPAL SUBJECTS:
Ecology
General Interest
History
Home & Garden
PUBLICATIONS:
Pageant
Reader's Digest
Sports Illustrated
Fate Magazine
Saturday Evening Post
Sports Parade
The American Legion
   Magazine
Progressive Farmer
VFW Magazine
Elk's Magazine

HANLE, ZACK
2 Horatio St.
New York, NY 10014
Telephone: 212-255-8699
AFFILIATIONS:
ASJA, ASME, AG
PRINCIPAL SUBJECTS:
Book Reviews
Health
Travel
PUBLICATIONS:
Bon Appetit

HANSEN, ELIZABETH
2565 Ardath Rd.
La Jolla, CA 92037
Telephone: 619-459-8851

AFFILIATIONS:
ASJA, SATW
PRINCIPAL SUBJECTS:
Journalism
Photography
Travel
Women's Interest
PUBLICATIONS:
Travel & Leisure
Travel Holiday

HARDER, PAUL B.
731 Kala Pt. Dr.
Port Townsend, WA 98368
Telephone: 206-385-4878
AFFILIATIONS:
ASMP, PPA
PRINCIPAL SUBJECTS:
Agriculture
Business & Industry
Management

HARKNESS, CHRIS
706 Beard St., 2
Tallahassee, FL 32303
Telephone: 904-222-0313
PRINCIPAL SUBJECTS:
Marine
Travel
Photography
PUBLICATIONS:
Yacht, The
Sailing Magazine
Small Boat Journal
Sailors' Gazette
Florida Waterways
Bicycling Magazine
Sailor's Guide Publication
Southern Magazine
Boat Journal

HARMAN, HARRY & JEANNE
3105 Country Club Dr.
Valdosta, GA 31602
Telephone: 912-242-3697
AFFILIATIONS:
SATW, ASJA, OPC,
   IFW, TWA, SPJ
PRINCIPAL SUBJECTS:
Travel
Fashion
Sports
Business & Industry
General Interest
PUBLICATIONS:
Toronto Star
Fieldings Guide to the
   Caribbean 1969-1978
Harmans Official Guide to
   Cruise Ships
Atlanta Journal Constitution

Miami Herald
Washington Post
Exxon Travel Guides
Los Angeles Herald Examiner
San Francisco Chronicle
Camden Courier Post
Gannett News Service
Fort Lauderdale News
Hackensack Record
Milwaukee Journal
Boston Herald American
Princeton Features Syndicate
Kansas City Star
Miami News
Going Places
St. Simons/Sea Island Report
Hilton Head Island Report
Virgin Islands Report
   (3 Editions)
Chicago Tribune
Cruise Passenger Network
Caribbean Travel & Life
Midway Magazine
Review Magazine
Prentice Hall Press
Fort Lauderdale News & Sun
   Sentinel
San Diego Tribune

HARMON, MARY
291 Baltic St.
Brooklyn, NY 11201
Telephone: 718-624-5053
AFFILIATIONS:
ASJA
PRINCIPAL SUBJECTS:
Family
Social Trends
PUBLICATIONS:
New York Times
Ladies' Home Journal
Working Mother
McCall's
Mademoiselle

HARRIS, ELEANOR
1456 Altridge Drive
Beverly Hills, CA 90210
Telephone: 213-272-4652
AFFILIATIONS:
SATW
PRINCIPAL SUBJECTS:
Travel
Photography
Senior Citizens
Entertainment
Sports
Women's Interest
General Interest
Architecture
History

The Arts
PUBLICATIONS:
Travel & Leisure
Los Angeles Herald Examiner
  Travel
Los Angeles Times Travel
California Good Life
  Magazine-Dining
Los Angeles Magazine-City
  Guides, Travel
Western's World (inflight)
Chicago Tribune-Travel
Vancouver Sun-Travel
Palm Beach Post-Travel
Daily News-Travel
Newsday-Travel
Westways Magazine-Travel
San Diego Union-Travel
San Francisco Examiner-Travel
Big Valley Magazine City
  Guides, Travel
New West Magazine
New York Post-Travel
Touring & Travel
  (Toronto) Mag.
Connecticut Motorist
  Magazine-Travel
International Travel News
Boston Globe-Travel
Airfair Interline-Travel
Boston Herald American-Travel
Seattle Post Intelligencer-Travel
Tacoma News Tribune-Travel
San Jose Mercury News-Travel
Skylite Magazine - Travel
MD Magazine - Travel
National Motorist Magazine -
  Travel
Globehopper Magazine
  (Toronto) - Travel
Cruise Travel Magazine -
  Travel
Top Priority Magazine - Travel
Calgary Herald - Travel
  (Alberta)
Globe and Mail, The
  (Toronto) - Travel
Senior Life - Travel
San Diego Union
Cruise Travel
International Travel News
Senior Life
Daily News (New York)
Calgary Herald
Tacoma News Tribune
Airfair
American Way
California Senior
  Magazine, The
Trip & Tour
Army/Air Force Times

Senior America News
National Motorist
International Travel News
Globe & Mail, The
Senior American News
Life In The Times
Cruise Travel
Senior Edition
Westways
Trip & Tour
SEI Senior World
Discovery
Globe and Mail, The
Trip & Tour
Silver Kris
City Press
Army Times
Golden Years
Cruise Travel
Senior Life
International Travel News
Jewish Journal, The
Life in The Times
Silver Kris
The Globe and Mail
Trip & Tour
Jewish Journal
Senior Editions
Seniors Cape Cod Forum
Senior Dynamics
Senior Edition USA
Globe and Mail
Senior News Chicago
Mature Times
So. California Senior Life
Silver Kris
National Motorist

HARRIS, JUDITH
31270 Stafford
Beverly Hills, MI 48025
Telephone: 313-646-9444
PRINCIPAL SUBJECTS:
Health
Automotive
Education

HARRIS, PATRICIA
6 Crawford St., #11
Cambridge, MA 02139
Telephone: 617-864-0361
PRINCIPAL SUBJECTS:
The Arts
Travel
PUBLICATIONS:
Boston Globe Magazine
Reader's Digest
Travel Holiday
Fiber Arts
Americas

Los Angeles Times
Yankee
CompuServe

HARSHAM, PHILIP
2057 Kansas Avenue, N.E.
St Petersburg, FL 33703
Telephone: 813-522-1018
AFFILIATIONS:
ASJA
PRINCIPAL SUBJECTS:
Business & Industry
General Interest
Travel
Foreign
PUBLICATIONS:
Medical Economics
Money
Travel & Leisure
Aramco World
N.Y. Times
Life
Datamation
Florida Trend
Louisville Courier Journal

HARTLEY, JEAN AYRES
5020 Winding Way
Sacramento, CA 95841
Telephone: 916-489-0294
Fax: 916-489-0294
AFFILIATIONS:
ASJA, CWC, IPA, IF, TWA
PRINCIPAL SUBJECTS:
Travel
PUBLICATIONS:
Country Accents
Bon Appetit
Country Inns
Discovery
Family Houseboating
Family Weekly
Lady's Circle
Modern Maturity
Off Duty
Acquire
Marathon World
Christian Life
Friends Magazine
NRTA Journal
Friendly Exchange
People On Parade
Glimpses Of Micronesia
Graduate Woman
New Zealand Herald
Chevron USA & Ford Times
Christian Science Monitor
Western Boatman
American West
Military Lifestyle
Travel Holiday

Northern California Home &
  Garden
International Living
International Travel News
New Choices

HARVEY, FRANK
Drakestown Rd., Box 195-F
Hackettstown, NJ 07840
Telephone: 908-852-9113
MAILING ADDRESS:
Frank Harvey
P.O. Box 195 - F
Hackettstown, NJ 07840
AFFILIATIONS:
Author's Guild
PRINCIPAL SUBJECTS:
Aviation
Business & Industry
General Interest
Government
World Affairs
PUBLICATIONS:
Christian Science Monitor
Reader's Digest
Popular Science
Saturday Evening Post

HARVEY, HARRIET
3900 Watson Pl., NW - #B-4H
Washington, DC 20016
Telephone: 202-298-6028
Fax: 202-298-6028

HARWOOD, JAMES
  QUITTNER
2809 Rittenhose St., N.W.
Washington, DC 20015
Telephone: 202-363-5445
MAILING ADDRESS:
7805 Briardale Terrace
Rockville, MD 20855
Telephone: 301-258-2651
PRINCIPAL SUBJECTS:
Automotive
Computer Technology
PUBLICATIONS:
ICIA Market Monitor
NTDRA Dealer News

HASKIN, PHD., JOHN A.
537-B South Garfield
Traverse City, MI 49684
Telephone: 616-946-0299
Fax: 616-941-7030
PRINCIPAL SUBJECTS:
Health
Education
Psychology

HASTINGS, ROBERT A.
198 Pleasant St.
Marblehead, MA 01945
Telephone: 617-631-9700
MAILING ADDRESS:
Robert A. Hastings
P.O. Box 406
Marblehead, MA 01945
PRINCIPAL SUBJECTS:
Travel
Editorial
Business & Industry
Health
Government
Ecology
PUBLICATIONS:
Editor - Publisher, Coast &
    Country
Daily Evening Item, Lynn MA
    (Former Editor)
Area Daily Press

HAUSER, HILLARY
2421 Shelby St.
Summerland, CA 93067
Telephone: 805-969-6699
MAILING ADDRESS:
Hillary Hauser
P.O. Box 988
Summerland, CA 93067
PRINCIPAL SUBJECTS:
Marine
Amusements
Travel
PUBLICATIONS:
National Geographic Magazine
Redbook Magazine
Santa Barbara News - Press
Ocean Science News
Skin Diver Magazine
New Zealand Dive
Christian Science Sentinel
Waterfront
Scuba Times
Esquire
Oceans
PSA Magazine
Westways
Sportscene
Western's World
Submarine (Germany)
First Class
Orange Disc.
Redbook
Carte Blanche
Islands Magazine
Ranger Rick
PSA Magazine

Esquire Magazine
Ocean Realm
Los Angeles Times-Travel
    Section

HAUSMANN, WERNER K.
4332 Post Road
San Diego, CA 92117
Telephone: 619-274-0508
AFFILIATIONS:
NWC, NWC/SCC
PRINCIPAL SUBJECTS:
Journalism

HAY, PHD., VICTORIA
1748 W. Orchid Lane
Phoenix, AZ 85021
Telephone: 602-997-4760
Fax: 602-944-2789
AFFILIATIONS:
ASJA
PRINCIPAL SUBJECTS:
Animals
Book Reviews
Ecology
Editorial
General Interest
History
Journalism
Nature
The Arts
Travel
Women's Interest
PUBLICATIONS:
Petersen's Hunting
Friendly Exchange
LA Daily News
Arizona Highways

HAY, VICTORIA
1748 W. Orchid Lane
Phoenix, AZ 85021
Telephone: 602-997-4760
Fax: 602-944-2789
AFFILIATIONS:
ASJA
PRINCIPAL SUBJECTS:
Book Reviews
Business & Industry
Ecology
General Interest
History
Journalism
Nature
Senior Citizens
PUBLICATIONS:
Arizona Highways
Petersen's Hunting
TWA Ambassador
Friendly Exchange
Sunset

HAZEN, BARBARA SHOOK
108 East 82nd St.
New York, NY 10028
Telephone: 212-288-1253
AFFILIATIONS:
AG, ASJA, SCBW
PRINCIPAL SUBJECTS:
Animals
Ecology
General Interest
Human Relations
Youth
PUBLICATIONS:
Ladies' Home Journal
Holiday
Woman's Day

HEATH, JARRETT A.
P.O. Box 184, Bath Beach
    Station
Brooklyn, NY 11214
Telephone: 718-837-3484
MAILING ADDRESS:
Jarrett A. Heath
P.O. Box 184, Bath Beach Sta.
Brooklyn, NY 11214
AFFILIATIONS:
AG, BWC
PRINCIPAL SUBJECTS:
Medical
Health
Book Reviews
General Interest
Motivation
News
Psychology
Religion
Senior Citizens
PUBLICATIONS:
UCP News
SHR
Christian Single
Rave Reviews
Here's Brooklyn
Brooklyn Graphic
Phoenix
Brooklyn Times
Home Reporter
American Citizen Press
Brooklyn Spectator
Friend to Friend
Handicraft News
Bluebird Robin
Children's World
Century II Magazine (Catholic)

HECHLER, DAVID
P.O. Box 737
Larchmont, NY 10538
Telephone: 914-834-0525
Fax: 914-834-0524

AFFILIATIONS:
ASJA
PRINCIPAL SUBJECTS:
Education
Human Relations
Journalism
News
Psychology
PUBLICATIONS:
The New York Times
Wall Street Journal
Columbia Journalism Review
American Journalism Review
Newsday
Dallas Life Magazine

HECHT, JEFF
525 Auburn St.
Auburndale, MA 02166
Telephone: 617-965-3834
Fax: 617-332-4760
AFFILIATIONS:
NASW, IEEE, AMPS,
    OSA, AGLI
PRINCIPAL SUBJECTS:
Science
Electronics
Nature
PUBLICATIONS:
Omni
New Scientist
Lasers Focus World
Electronics Times
Computers in Physics
Analog Science
    Fiction/Science Fact

HEDDEN, JAY W.
3911 W. 100 Terrace
Shawnee Msn, KS 66207
Telephone: 816-531-5730
AFFILIATIONS:
AEA, NAHWN
PRINCIPAL SUBJECTS:
General Interest
Hobbies
Home & Garden
Business & Industry
PUBLICATIONS:
Workbench
Consumers Digest
Structures Publishing
Creative Homeowners Press

HEILMAN, JOAN RATTNER
812 Stuart Ave.
Mamaroneck, NY 10543
Telephone: 914-698-6429
AFFILIATIONS:
ASJA, AG

PRINCIPAL SUBJECTS:
Health
Medical
Human Relations
Personalities
Travel
Animals
Senior Citizens
PUBLICATIONS:
Parade
Redbook
New Choices
Elks Magazine
Maturity News Service
Travel Smart

HEITZIG, JAMES L.
1585 The Alameda, Ste. 100
San Jose, CA 95126
Telephone: 408-287-9055
Fax: 408-293-7545
AFFILIATIONS:
PPC, PRSA
PRINCIPAL SUBJECTS:
Medical
Science
Business & Industry
PUBLICATIONS:
IBM Corporate Publications
San Jose Mercury News
California Business
UPI Newswire
AP Newswire
Wall Street Journal
Bottom Line Magazine
Life Association News

HELLER, MARION
1301 Washington Street
Hollywood, FL 33019
Telephone: 305-921-7385
PRINCIPAL SUBJECTS:
Travel
Health

HELLMAN, HAL
100 High St.
Leonia, NJ 07605
Telephone: 201-947-5534
AFFILIATIONS:
NASW, ASJA
PRINCIPAL SUBJECTS:
Electronics
General Interest
Medical
Nature
Science
PUBLICATIONS:
Reader's Digest
Omni
Psychology Today

HELM, SYLVIA
285 W. Riverside Dr., #80
New York, NY 10025
Telephone: 212-864-8715
Fax: 212-916-6088
MAILING ADDRESS:
TIAA-CREF
730 Third Ave.
New York, NY 10017
AFFILIATIONS:
ASJA
PRINCIPAL SUBJECTS:
Business & Industry
Women's Interest
Personalities
Computer Technology
Personal Finance
Advertising
Education
Journalism
Medical
News
PUBLICATIONS:
Consumer Reports
Venture Magazine
Woman Magazine
PC Magazine
Village Voice
Sylvia Porters Personal
  Finance Magazine
Newark Star Ledger
Lotus Magazine
ABA Banking Journal
Computers in Banking
Medical Tribune

HELMLINGER, TRUDY
7127 Murdock Way
Carmichael, CA 95608
Telephone: 916-485-4119
AFFILIATIONS:
ASJA
PRINCIPAL SUBJECTS:
Health
Psychology
PUBLICATIONS:
New Woman
Working Woman
Ladies' Home Journal

HEMBREE, DIANA
568 Howard St., 5th Flr.
San Francisco, CA 94105
Telephone: 415-543-1200
Fax: 415-543-8311
AFFILIATIONS:
IRE, NWUMA
PRINCIPAL SUBJECTS:
Women's Interest
Ecology
Foreign

PUBLICATIONS:
Columbia Journalism Review
Ms.
Parenting
Hippocrates
Albuquerque Journal
News America/Times of
  London Syndicate & Pacific
Pacific News Service
Working Mother
Mother Jones
E Magazine
The Progressive

HEMMING, ROY
106 E. 60th St.
New York, NY 10022
Telephone: 212-688-8656
Fax: 212-688-6788
AFFILIATIONS:
OPC, SPJ, AG
PRINCIPAL SUBJECTS:
Entertainment
Travel
Amusements
Book Reviews
Foreign
History
Media
Movie Reviews
The Arts
Travel
Video
PUBLICATIONS:
Video Review Magazine
  (Since 1980)
Stereo Review Magazine
  (Since 1969)
International Herald - Tribune
  (Since 1960s)
N.Y. Times (Since 1960s)
50 Plus Magazine
  (1975 - 1980)
Ovation Magazine (Since 1978)
Scholastic Magazines
  (1954 - 1975)
The Gramophone, 1991
Christian Science Monitor
Entertainment Weekly

HENDERSON, BRUCE B.
P.O. Box 231
Forestville, CA 95436
Telephone: 707-829-0310
Fax: 707-829-2704

HENLEY, ARTHUR
175 Fifth Avenue, #2462
New York, NY 10010
Telephone: 212-263-0136

AFFILIATIONS:
PEN, NASW, ASJA
PRINCIPAL SUBJECTS:
Editorial
Humor
Health
Travel
Human Relations
Medical
Psychology
Senior Citizens
PUBLICATIONS:
Family Health
Ladies' Home Journal
NY Times
Saturday Evening Post
McCall's
Public Affairs Pamphlets
Bride Magazine

HENNESSEE, JUDITH ADLER
3 East 85th St.
New York, NY 10028
Telephone: 212-288-4244
PRINCIPAL SUBJECTS:
Media
Social Trends
PUBLICATIONS:
Manhattan, Inc.
Avenue
Mirabella

HIBBEN, DR. FRANK C.
3005 Campus Blvd., N.E.
Albuquerque, NM 87106
Telephone: 505-255-5119
MAILING ADDRESS:
Dr. Frank C. Hibben
Dept. Of Anthropology, UNM
Albuquerque, NM 87131
AFFILIATIONS:
AAAS, AAA
PRINCIPAL SUBJECTS:
Ecology
General Interest
Science
Sports
History
Human Relations
Nature
Animals
Foreign
PUBLICATIONS:
Field & Stream
Outdoor Life
Reader's Digest
Saturday Evening Post
Scientific American

Sports Afield
American Antiquity
American Archeology
Harper's

HICKS, JUNE L.
14925 Prospect
Dearborn, MI 48126
Telephone: 313-584-0752
PRINCIPAL SUBJECTS:
Home & Garden
Nature
PUBLICATIONS:
The Detroit News
Detroit Monthly
American Horticulturist
Michigan Living

HIGDON, HAL
P.O. Box 1034
Michigan City, IN 46360
Telephone: 219-879-0133
Fax: 219-874-7413
AFFILIATIONS:
ASJA, AG, NASJA
PRINCIPAL SUBJECTS:
Health
General Interest
Sports
The Arts
PUBLICATIONS:
Reader's Digest
Snow Country
Air & Space
Smithsonian
Travel & Leisure
American Health
Runner's World
Boys' Life

HILL, M.T.
1705 Contention Lane
Cottonwood, AZ 86326
Telephone: 602-567-4631
MAILING ADDRESS:
Hill, M.T., Librarian
Beaver Creek School, Box 190
Rimrock, AZ 86335

HILL, NORMAN
210 E. 68th St.
New York, NY 10021
Telephone: 212-734-3799
AFFILIATIONS:
ASJA, AG
PRINCIPAL SUBJECTS:
Business & Industry
Media
The Arts

HINTZ, MARTIN
316 N. Milwaukee St., #502
Milwaukee, WI 53202
Telephone: 414-273-8132
Fax: 414-273-8196
AFFILIATIONS:
SATW, TMTWA, SPJ
PRINCIPAL SUBJECTS:
History
Personalities
Entertainment
Family
Travel
Business & Industry
Amusements
Ecology
Foreign
General Interest
Home & Garden
Geography
Human Interest
Management
News
Religion
Sports
The Arts
World Affairs
PUBLICATIONS:
Chicago Sun Times
Complete Meeting Guide
Milwaukee Journal, Sentinel
Irish American Post
Travel Holiday
Trailer Life
Corporate Report Wisconsin
Wisconsin Trails
Midwest Living
Globe Pequot Press
Travel California
Golf Week
Odyssey

HOCH, DR. DEAN E.
15 Tulane Ave.
Pocatello, ID 83201
Telephone: 208-232-4809
Fax: 208-233-5744
AFFILIATIONS:
ASJA
PRINCIPAL SUBJECTS:
Education
Family
Business & Industry
Humor
Management
Travel
General Interest
PUBLICATIONS:
Readers Digest
Good Housekeeping
Phi Delta Kappa Magazine

Friendly Exchange
Family Handyman
Mother Earth Magazine
Sex Education for Todays
　Teens & Preteens
Boy Raising Secrets Every
　Parent Should Know
Family
Executive Place
Ensign

HOCH, NANCY M.
15 Tulane Ave.
Pocatello, ID 83201
Telephone: 208-232-4809
AFFILIATIONS:
ASJA
PRINCIPAL SUBJECTS:
Business & Industry
Education
Family
General Interest
Humor
Management
Travel
PUBLICATIONS:
Reader's Digest
Good Housekeeping
Phi Delta Kappa Magazine
Friendly Exchange
Family Handyman
Mother Earth Magazine
Sex Education for Today's
　Teens & Pre-Teens

HOCHMAN, GLORIA
44 Trent Road
Wynnewood, PA 19096
Telephone: 215-649-4110
Fax: 215-735-9410
MAILING ADDRESS:
Gloria Hochman
1800 Walnut St., #701
Philadelphia, PA 19102
AFFILIATIONS:
ASJA, SPJ
PRINCIPAL SUBJECTS:
Family
General Interest
Health
Human Relations
Philosophy
Book Reviews
Human Interest
Medical
News
Personalities
Psychology
Social Trends
Women's Interest

PUBLICATIONS:
American Health
Ladies' Home Journal
Reader's Digest
The Philadelphia Inquirer
Toronto Star
San Jose Mercury
TWA Ambassador
Miami Herald
Chicago Tribune

HODGE, ADELE
Box 3960 Merchandise Mart
Chicago, IL 60654
Telephone: 312-332-5483
AFFILIATIONS:
ASMP
PRINCIPAL SUBJECTS:
Business & Industry
Editorial
Entertainment
General Interest
Human Interest
Media
Personalities
The Arts
Video
Women's Interest
PUBLICATIONS:
Redbook
Essence
Chicago Reader
Chicago Sun-Times
Chicago Tribune
Northshore

HOFFMAN, NANCY YANES
16 San Rafael Drive
Rochester, NY 14618
Telephone: 716-385-1515
Fax: 716-385-3858
AFFILIATIONS:
ASJA, NASW, AMWA,
　AASECT, STC, SIECUS
PRINCIPAL SUBJECTS:
Book Reviews
Business & Industry
Editorial
Education
General Interest
Health
Human Interest
Human Relations
Management
Medical
Motivation
Psychology
Science
Senior Citizens
Travel
Women's Interest

PUBLICATIONS:
Southwest Review
Los Angeles Times
Jama
Medical Times
Commonweal
Radiology
Being Well
Gannett Press
California Living

HOLCOMB, GEORGE B.
14220 Chesterfield Dr.
Woodbridge, VA 22191
Telephone: 703-494-5833
MAILING ADDRESS:
OIA/OPA
Rm. 536-A
Washington, DC 20250
PRINCIPAL SUBJECTS:
World Affairs
Agriculture
Foreign
Science
News
Senior Citizens
Health
History
Book Reviews
Education

HOLDER, DENNIS
2821 McKinney, 10
Dallas, TX 75204
Telephone: 214-954-4334
Fax: 214-954-4335
AFFILIATIONS:
PCD
PRINCIPAL SUBJECTS:
Media
Business & Industry
Personalities
Travel
PUBLICATIONS:
Washington Journalism Review
Working Woman
USA Today
Nation's Business
Spirit
Philip Morris Magazine
Texas Business
Texas Monthly
TV Guide
Southpoint

HOLTJE, HERBERT F.
151 Sunset Lane
Tenafly, NJ 07670
Telephone: 201-568-2002
MAILING ADDRESS:
James Peter Associates, Inc.

P.O. Box 772
Tenafly, NJ 07670
AFFILIATIONS:
APA, ASTD
PRINCIPAL SUBJECTS:
Business & Industry

HOLTON, FELICIA
   ANTONELLI
525 Grove St.
Evanston, IL 60201
Telephone: 708-869-7754
AFFILIATIONS:
AG
PRINCIPAL SUBJECTS:
Education
Computer Technology
Science
PUBLICATIONS:
Family Circle
Impact
New York Times Travel
Vista-U.S.A.
University of Chicago
   Magazine

HONE, HARRY
Rte. 658 North
Williamsburg, VA 23128
Telephone: 804-725-2234
MAILING ADDRESS:
Harry Hone
P.O. Box 473
Williamsburg, VA 23187
AFFILIATIONS:
ABWA, NPC
PRINCIPAL SUBJECTS:
Business & Industry
General Interest
Human Relations
Women's Interest
Government
Advertising
Personal Finance
Book Reviews
Editorial
Education
Foreign
Psychology
News
Personalities
Philosophy
Religion
Sales
Senior Citizens
Travel
World Affairs
PUBLICATIONS:
The Hone Report
The Financial Security Digest
Syndicated In Weekly Local

Newspapers (100)
The Money School
Financial Survival In The "80's"
"The Light at The End of The
   Tunnel"
Baja Times (Mexico)
"The Best of The Duck Book"
The Advantage
Money School Monitor, The
Ex Pats International
Sound Money Investor
Delaware Today

HORN, YVONNE MICHIE
134 Country Club Dr.
Santa Rosa, CA 95401
Telephone: 707-525-8302
Fax: 707-545-1338
MAILING ADDRESS:
Yvonne Michie Horn
P.O. Box 7513
Santa Rosa, CA 95407
AFFILIATIONS:
SATW, ASJA, SCPC
PRINCIPAL SUBJECTS:
Travel
PUBLICATIONS:
Islands
Quarterly Review Of Wine
Golf For Women
American Express
   Magazine-Asia

HORNBAKER, ALICE J.
485 McIntosh Dr.
Cincinnati, OH 45252
Telephone: 513-528-6163
AFFILIATIONS:
SPJ, ONWA, OPW
PRINCIPAL SUBJECTS:
Entertainment
Family
General Interest
Humor
Personalities
Women's Interest
Medical
Senior Citizens
Travel
PUBLICATIONS:
Modern Maturity
Writer's Digest
NATR Journal
Cincinnati Sunday Magazine
   Enquirer
Retirement Years
Senior Advocates
Cincinnati Magazine
New York Times
Tristate Sunday Magazine -
   The Cincinnati Enquirer

Byline Across the Nation
People Magazine
IR-TV Guide etc.
Tempo (Feature Section
   Cincinnati Enquirer)
Cincinati Magazine

HORNER, SHIRLEY
1575 Brookside Rd.
Mountainside, NJ 07092
Telephone: 908-232-2804
AFFILIATIONS:
NBCC
PRINCIPAL SUBJECTS:
Book Reviews
General Interest
History
Personalities
Government
PUBLICATIONS:
New York Times,
   New Jersey Weekly
Publishers Weekly

HORNIK-BEER, EDITH LYNN
865 First Ave.
New York, NY 10017
Telephone: 212-421-2391
Fax: 707-829-2704
PRINCIPAL SUBJECTS:
Travel
PUBLICATIONS:
Elle
TWA Ambassador
Newsday
New York Times
Young Miss
New York Style

HORNSTEIN, HAROLD
90 Norton Rd.
Easton, CT 06612
Telephone: 203-268-8128
AFFILIATIONS:
SPJ
PRINCIPAL SUBJECTS:
Health
History
The Arts
Sports
Government
Personalities
Travel
PUBLICATIONS:
Yankee Magazine
New Haven Register
Bridgeport, Conn., Post
New York Times
Westport News

HOROWITZ, SHEL ALAN
P.O. Box 1164
Northampton, MA 01061
Telephone: 413-586-2388
AFFILIATIONS:
NWU, PARW, PWI
PRINCIPAL SUBJECTS:
The Arts
Entertainment
Travel
Computer Technology
Human Interest
Business & Industry
News
Family
Government
General Interest
Advertising
Amusements
Editorial
Journalism
Marketing
Social Trends
PUBLICATIONS:
Business West
Writer, The
Boston Globe
Macworld
Springfield (MA) Union News
Transitions Abroad
Vegetarian Times
Western Massachusetts
 Business & Economic Review
MacGuide
In These Times
Computerland Magazine
Growing Parent
Reach New England
Writer's Digest
Fireside/Simon & Schuster
The Bulletin
Leisure
Beyond Computing
Washington Post

HOTCHKISS, JUDY
951 Edgewood Ave., NE
Atlanta, GA 30307
Telephone: 404-521-9320
AFFILIATIONS:
APC, GWAA
PRINCIPAL SUBJECTS:
Home & Garden
General Interest
PUBLICATIONS:
Atlanta Homes & Lifestyles
Atlanta Journal & Constitution
Atlanta Singles Magazine
Atlanta Magazine

HOUSE, DARLENE
9543 West Outer Dr.
Detroit, MI 48223
Telephone: 313-255-6274
Fax: 313-255-6274
AFFILIATIONS:
WICI
PRINCIPAL SUBJECTS:
Business & Industry
PUBLICATIONS:
Adventure Magazine
Dawn
Ad Crafter

HOUSTON, RUTH
P.O. Box 7129
Elmhurst, NY 11368
Telephone: 718-592-6039
Fax: 718-592-2018
MAILING ADDRESS:
Houston-Burton, Ruth
98-25 H.H. Expy., #10-D
Rego Park, NY 11368
Telephone: 918-271-7840
AFFILIATIONS:
ASJA, FERA, NWU
PRINCIPAL SUBJECTS:
Fashion
Travel
General Interest
Personalities
Social Trends
PUBLICATIONS:
Cosmopolitan
Essence
Natural Science
Enterpreneurial Woman
Black Elegance
Elegant Bride
Brides Today
Class
Ebony Man
Fashion World
Four Seasons Hotel Magazine
Intimate Fashion News
Black Hair & Beauty
Gold Coast Gazette

HOWARD, ELIZABETH M.
43 Old Farm Road
Charlottesvle, VA 22903
Telephone: 804-295-9793
AFFILIATIONS:
ASJA, ITA
PRINCIPAL SUBJECTS:
Advertising
Education
Entertainment
Family
General Interest
Health

Human Interest
Human Relations
Personalities
Psychology
Senior Citizens
Social Trends
The Arts
Women's Interest
Youth
PUBLICATIONS:
The Ladies Home Journal
McCall's
Working Woman
Ms.
USA Today
Good Housekeeping
People
Psychology Today

HOWDEN, D. MURIEL
16 Mira Las Olas
San Clemente, CA 92673
Telephone: 714-498-6026
PRINCIPAL SUBJECTS:
Business & Industry

HOWE, RUSSELL WARREN
P.O. Box 32221
Washington, DC 20007
Telephone: 202-337-1560
Fax: 202-625-1999
MAILING ADDRESS:
Russell Warren Howe
Washington, DC 20007
AFFILIATIONS:
SPJ/SDX WIW
PRINCIPAL SUBJECTS:
Foreign
Government
Aviation
Book Reviews
Editorial
General Interest
Media
Military
World Affairs
PUBLICATIONS:
Foreign Affairs
Harper's
Atlantic, The
Smithsonian, The
Economist, The
Observer Magazine, The
Connoisseur
Travel
Air Force Magazine
Leaders
Penthouse
New Republic, The
Washington Post, The
(Baltimore) Sun

Christian Science Monitor
(London) Sunday Times
(London & Manchester)
 Guardian
Chicago Daily News
Business Tokyo
Northeast International
 Business
New York Times, The
Observer, The
Kyodo News Service
Al-Wasat Magazine

HOWES, CONNIE B.
765 E. Morningside Dr.
Lake Forest, IL 60045
Telephone: 708-234-5548
AFFILIATIONS:
OWAA, NPC
PRINCIPAL SUBJECTS:
Business & Industry
General Interest
Sports
Travel
Women's Interest
PUBLICATIONS:
Better Homes & Gardens
Rand McNally Guides
Field & Stream
Chicago Tribune

HOYT, ERICH
29 Dirleton Ave., No. 11
North Berwick,
 SCOTLAND EH394BE
Telephone: 44-620-3644/
Fax: 4-620-5257
AFFILIATIONS:
ASJA, NASWI,
 TWG, ISWA, OWOC
PRINCIPAL SUBJECTS:
Agriculture
Animals
Book Reviews
Ecology
Foreign
Geography
Marine
Nature
Science
Travel
PUBLICATIONS:
National Geographic
New York Times
International Wildlife
Discover
Reader's Digest
The Guardian (U.K.)
Equinox (Canada)
Cleveland Plain Dealer
Kagaku Asahi (Japan)

HUBBELL, JOHN G.
4004 Queen Ave. S.
Minneapolis, MN 55410
Telephone: 612-927-6146
PRINCIPAL SUBJECTS:
General Interest
Health
Humor
Personalities
Government
Foreign
Medical
PUBLICATIONS:
Reader's Digest
Families
Air Force
Saturday Evening Post
Flying
Catholic Digest

HUFF, DARRELL
P.O. Box AS
Carmel, CA 93921
Telephone: 408-624-8052
PRINCIPAL SUBJECTS:
Computer Technology
General Interest
Health
Hobbies
Home & Garden
Philosophy
Sports
Travel
Architecture
PUBLICATIONS:
Esquire
Harper's
Medical Economics
Popular Mechanics
Popular Science
Reader's Digest
Redbook
Money
Profiles

HUFF, FRANCES N.
Torres & 10th
Carmel, CA 93921
Telephone: 408-624-8052
MAILING ADDRESS:
Frances N. Huff
P.O. Drawer A-S
Carmel, CA 93921
PRINCIPAL SUBJECTS:
Health
Home & Garden
Travel

HUNT, DIANA
8889 Pioneer Trl.
Parker, CO 80134

Telephone: 303-841-8793
AFFILIATIONS:
NASJA
PRINCIPAL SUBJECTS:
Aviation
Sports
Travel
PUBLICATIONS:
Ski Impact
Fodor's Travel Guides
Chronicle Of The Horse
Travel
Yachting
Spur
Viva
Travel Agent
Caminos Del Aire
Denver Post
Travel/Holiday
Rocky Mountain Ski Guide
Commuter Air
Rocky Mountain News
Commuter/Regional
  Airline News
Polo Magazine
Powder

HUNT, JAMES E.
31 Lake Valley Rd.
Morristown, NJ 07960
Telephone: 201-267-5374
AFFILIATIONS:
PRSA, IABC
PRINCIPAL SUBJECTS:
Business & Industry
Health
Education
Computer Technology

HURWOOD, BERNHARDT J.
JCA Literary Agency,
  242 W. 27Th St.
New York, NY 10001
Telephone: 212-807-0888
MAILING ADDRESS:
Bernhardt J. Hurwood
165 West 107th Street/Pnthse
New York, NY 10025
AFFILIATIONS:
AG, ASJA, MWA, WGA
PRINCIPAL SUBJECTS:
Travel
Health
History
Personalities
Medical
Computer Technology
Entertainment
PUBLICATIONS:
New York
Saturday Review

Vogue
U.S. Air
Travelscene
Forum
NY Times
Realities
Harpers Bazaar
Penthouse
Gallery
Scene
Geo.
Travel Weekly
Us
Christian Science Monitor
Genesis
Videogaming & Computer
  Gaming Illustrated
Publishers Weekly
Computer Buyers Guide &
  Handbook
Computer Decisions
Medicine & Computer
MD Magazine
TWA Ambassador
Goodlife
Washington Post
San Jose Mercury News

HYYPIA, ERIK J.
2264-C Spruce St.
Boulder, CO 80302
Telephone: 303-449-5832
Fax: 303-449-8870
PRINCIPAL SUBJECTS:
Travel
Aviation
Computer Technology
Sports
PUBLICATIONS:
Newsday (Travel Section)
Salt Lake Tribune (Travel Sect.)
Pittsburgh Press (Travel Sect.)
Income Opportunities Mag.
Mechanix Illustrated
Science and Mechanics
Home Handyman
  Encyclopedia
Camping Journal
Budget Electronics
Elementary Electronics
Tacoma News
San Jose Mercury News
Ft. Lauderdale Sun Sentinel
India Currents Mag.
Los Angeles Times - Travel
Student Traveler Magazine
Running Times Magazine
Runners World Magazine
British Running Magazine
S. A. Runners
Jogging - Italy Magazine

Wild Sports Magazine
Newsweek
Spiridon (Gdr)
Rocky Mountain News
Denver Post
Westword
Des Moines Register
Boulder Dailey Camera
Student Traveler
Health Treks
Wild Sports Magazine
Las Vegas Review Journal

HYYPIA, JORMA
90 Bowman Dr., N.
Greenwich, CT 06831
AFFILIATIONS:
NAHWW, ACS
PRINCIPAL SUBJECTS:
Amusements
Business & Industry
General Interest
Hobbies
Home & Garden
Science
Sports
Photography
PUBLICATIONS:
Camping Journal
Popular Mechanics
Science & Mechanics
Elementary Electronics
101 Home Plans
Income Opportunities
Today's Homes
Better Building Ideas
Backpacking Journal
HiFi Stereo Buyer's Guide
Budget Electronics
Camping Journal
Radio Electronics
Mechanix Illustrated Home
  Improvements
S&M Complete Handyman

IACONETTI, JOAN
145 Fourth Avenue, #17J
New York, NY 10003
Telephone: 212-254-9311
AFFILIATIONS:
ASJA, ASMP
PRINCIPAL SUBJECTS:
Editorial
Family
Human Relations
Management
Motivation
Travel
Women's Interest
PUBLICATIONS:
Travel & Leisure

New Woman
Ladies Home Journal
Modern Bride
Glamour
Redbook

INGE, ARLINE
1910 Corinth Ave., #1
Los Angeles, CA 90025
Telephone: 310-478-7604
AFFILIATIONS:
SATW, SCRW
PRINCIPAL SUBJECTS:
Amusements
Editorial
Human Interest
Personalities
The Arts
Travel
Women's Interest
PUBLICATIONS:
Bon Appetit
Cuisine
Los Angeles
Westways
Woman's Day
McCalls
Working Mother
Los Angeles Times
Readers' Digest
Modern Maturity

IRA, ALLEN
1636 N. Wells, #2003
Chicago, IL 60614
Telephone: 312-787-6803
AFFILIATIONS:
OWAA
PRINCIPAL SUBJECTS:
The Arts
Business & Industry
Entertainment
General Interest
Health
Personalities
Travel
Youth
Amusements
Book Reviews
Computer Technology
Ecology
Education
Electronics
Family
Fashion
Human Interest
Human Relations
Management
Marketing
Media
Medical

Men's Interest
Motivation
Nature
News
Personal Finance
Physical Fitness
Psychology
Sales
Science
Science
Social Trends
Urban Affairs
PUBLICATIONS:
Ebony
National Enquirer
New York Times (travel)
Plan & Print
Saturday Review
Trailer Life
Writer's Digest
New Times Magazine
American Laundry Digest
Commercial Car Journal
Connecticut Magazine
Dance
Flightline News
New Haven Register
On The Sound
Hospital Progress
Sepia
Merchandising
Chicago Tribune
Gourmet

ISAACS, FLORENCE
175 West 13th St.
New York, NY 10011
Telephone: 212-675-9197
Fax: 212-675-4197
PRINCIPAL SUBJECTS:
Health
Human Relations
Family
Medical
PUBLICATIONS:
Good Housekeeping
Woman's Day
Reader's Digest
New Woman

JACKSON, LESLIE
2801 N. Surrey Dr.
Carrollton, TX 75006
Telephone: 214-416-0308
PRINCIPAL SUBJECTS:
Women's Interest
Family
Business & Industry
Travel
PUBLICATIONS:
Toastmaster, The

Fashion Galleria, The
Dallas Child
Boy's Life Magazine
Dallas Morning News
SR Dallas
Self - Employed America
L. A. Parent
Seattle's Child

JACKSON, WILLIAM S.
115-117 S. Water St.
Hummelstown, PA 17036
Telephone: 717-566-3251
AFFILIATIONS:
SAH, GMW
PRINCIPAL SUBJECTS:
Automotive
Military
PUBLICATIONS:
Motor Trend
Road and Track
Automobile Quarterly
Autocar (English)
Antique Automobile
Autoweek
Classic Car
Bulb Horn

JACOBS, DORRI
784 COLUMBUS AVE., #1 - C
NEW YORK, NY 10025
Telephone: 212-222-4606
AFFILIATIONS:
NWU, EFA, MDF, WASC
PRINCIPAL SUBJECTS:
Management
The Arts
Human Relations
PUBLICATIONS:
Daily News, The
New Woman
Patients Digest
Single Parent, The
Westside Press, The
NYAHP Newsletter, The
Family Circle
Good Looks
Single Times
Cleo
Woman
Sophisticate Beauty Digest
Complete Woman
Our Town
Wisdom's Child/N.Y. Guide
Management Solutions
DVM Newsmagazine
Hong Kong Trainer, The
Modern Veterinary Practice
NYMETRO ASTD Lamplighter
Westsider, The
Training News

President, The
Boardroom Reports
Today's Supervisor
OR Manager
Banking Week
Work Dynamics
Management World
Celibate Woman, The
Management Review
New York Doctor, The
Working Woman
Practical Banker
Journal of Volunteer
  Administration
Leaders Digest
Human Capital

JACOBS, FRANK
4181 Kling St., #63
Burbank, CA 91505
Telephone: 818-845-2929
AFFILIATIONS:
NAHWW, ACS
PRINCIPAL SUBJECTS:
The Arts
Humor
Travel
PUBLICATIONS:
Signature
Mad
Town & Country
Punch
Youths Companion
Playboy

JACOBSON, BEVERLY
12 Thompson Rd.
Shelburne, VT 05482
Telephone: 802-985-9729
AFFILIATIONS:
ASJA, AG, NWU
PRINCIPAL SUBJECTS:
Health
Women's Interest
PUBLICATIONS:
Good Housekeeping
NY Times
Parents
Publishers Weekly
Rotarian
Civil Rights Digest
McCall's
Science Digest
Childworld
New Woman
Savvy
Ladies Home Journal
National Forum
Parade

Seventeen
Medica
Good Food

JACOKES, DIANE
22375 Innsbrook
Northville, MI 48167
Telephone: 313-478-8244
PRINCIPAL SUBJECTS:
Business & Industry
Personalities
Computer Technology
Medical
Science
PUBLICATIONS:
USA Today
Omni
Detroit Monthly
Ford Times
Glass Digest
U.S. Glass
Ann Arbor Scence
Metropolitan Detroit
Detroit News
Flagship Magazine

JAMES JR., JESSE A.
211 Frederick
Bastrop, LA 71220
Telephone: 318-281-1756
PRINCIPAL SUBJECTS:
The Arts
Ecology
Government
Sports
PUBLICATIONS:
American Rifleman
Field and Stream
Southern Living
Sports Afield

JAMES, LAURIE
500 W. 43rd St., #250
New York, NY 11746
Telephone: 516-499-1637
AFFILIATIONS:
DG, PBI
PRINCIPAL SUBJECTS:
History
Education
Women's Interest
PUBLICATIONS:
American Home
Parents'
Camp Fire Girls
Family Circle
Fire Island News

JAMISON, WARREN
40-300 Washington St.,
  Suite J-105
Bermuda Dunes, CA 92201
Telephone: 619-772-2917
Fax: 619-345-8471
AFFILIATIONS:
AG, ASJA
PRINCIPAL SUBJECTS:
Business & Industry
Health
Marketing
Medical
Physical Fitness
Sales
Senior Citizens

JANICKI, EDWARD
37825 Santa Barbara
Mount Clemens, MI 48043
Telephone: 313-463-9756
AFFILIATIONS:
DPC, DAWG, IMP
PRINCIPAL SUBJECTS:
Men's Interest
Business & Industry
Automotive
PUBLICATIONS:
Highway Patrolman Magazine
Automotive News
Better Homes & Gardens
Science & Mechanics

JANIK, CAROLYN
29 Old Coach Road
Basking Ridge, NJ 07920
Telephone: 908-647-4519
Fax: 908-647-7848
PUBLICATIONS:
Home Selling
Woman's Day
House Beautiful
Parade
Redbook
Home Buying
Real Estate Careers

JANSON JR., JOHN J. D.
17831 Whitford Ln.
Huntington Bh, CA 92649
Telephone: 714-840-4743

JENSEN, CHERYL
12700 Lake Ave., #2203
Cleveland, OH 44107
Telephone: 216-226-8990
PRINCIPAL SUBJECTS:
Medical
Senior Citizens
Human Interest

PUBLICATIONS:
Washington Post, The
Ms Magazine
McCall's
Writer's Digest
Better Homes & Gardens

JERISON, IRENE
503 W. Rustic Road
Santa Monica, CA 90402
Telephone: 310-454-9553
Fax: 310-454-3325

JOHNSON, JAN
4897 Abilene St.
Simi, CA 93063
Telephone: 805-522-3221
Fax: 805-522-3221
AFFILIATIONS:
ASJA, NLAPW
PRINCIPAL SUBJECTS:
Education
Family
Health
Human Interest
Human Relations
Humor
Journalism
Philosophy
Psychology
Religion
Social Trends
PUBLICATIONS:
American Baby
Parenting
Los Angeles Times
Changes
Focus on the Family
Christianity Today

JOHNSON, SABEEHA H.
1288 W. Bloomfield
Honeoye Falls, NY 14472
Telephone: 716-624-4169
AFFILIATIONS:
GWAA
PRINCIPAL SUBJECTS:
Nature
Entertainment
General Interest
Health
Home & Garden
Computer Technology
Travel
Women's Interest
Hobbies
Fashion
Personalities
PUBLICATIONS:
Better Homes & Gardens
Consumers Weekly

Australian Women's Weekly
Panorama
Times of India
Real Estate Forum
Wash. Times Magazine
Washingtonian
Country Magazine
Gourmet
Washington Post
Cosmopolitan
Chicago Tribune
Rochester Democrat &
  Chronicle
Upstate Magazine
New York Times
Gannet News Service
Flower & Garden Magazine

JOHNSTON, MELANIE LEE
Johnston Writing & Design
P.O. Box 4674
Scottsdale, AZ 85261
Telephone: 602-451-1087
Fax: 602-661-9574
AFFILIATIONS:
ASJA, AAA
PRINCIPAL SUBJECTS:
Advertising
Book Reviews
Business & Industry
Computer Technology
Electronics
Entertainment
Human Interest
Journalism
Marketing
Media
Personal Finance
Personalities
Senior Citizens
Social Trends
Travel
PUBLICATIONS:
Modern Maturity
Arizona Highways
Chicago Sun-Times
Advertising Age
Successful Meetings
TravelAge

JOLLIFFE, LEE
3700 W. Sugartree Lane
Columbia, MO 65201
Telephone: 314-882-2880
Fax: 314-882-9002
AFFILIATIONS:
ASJA, AEJMC
PRINCIPAL SUBJECTS:
Media
Science
Home & Garden

JOSEPH, JOAN
2155 Ibis Isle #9
Palm Beach, FL 33480
Telephone: 407-588-0075
Fax: 407-588-5082

JOSEPH, LOU
1933 Locust St.
Des Plaines, IL 60018
Telephone: 708-296-5192
Fax: 708-299-7145
AFFILIATIONS:
NASW, AMWA, ISWA, AAAS
PRINCIPAL SUBJECTS:
Health
Science
Medical
PUBLICATIONS:
Better Homes and Gardens
Life & Health
Family Health
Today's Health
Catholic Digest
Prepared Childbirth
Catholic Digest
Consumers Digest
Journal of American Dental
  Association
Amwa Journal

JOURNEY, ALFRED E. 'BUD'
572 Florence Rd.
Libby, MT 59923
Telephone: 406-293-6985
AFFILIATIONS:
ASJA, OWAA, SCRWI, NOWA
PRINCIPAL SUBJECTS:
Family
Men's Interest
Nature
News
Photography
Sports
PUBLICATIONS:
Outdoor Life
Sports Afield
Field & Stream
Canoe
Fodor's Travel/Publicationos
Bugle
Trailer Life

JUDSON, KAREN
60 Lakewood
Fort Dodge, IA 50501
Telephone: 515-573-4708
MAILING ADDRESS:
Judson, Karen
Box 1062
Fort Dodge, IA 50501

PRINCIPAL SUBJECTS:
Health
Hobbies
PUBLICATIONS:
Working Woman
Better Health
In Flight Magazine
Bride

K-TURKEL, JUDI
3006 Gregory St.
Madison, WI 53711
Telephone: 608-231-1003
AFFILIATIONS:
ASJA, AG
PRINCIPAL SUBJECTS:
Computer Technology
Business & Industry
Education
Management
Personal Finance
Science
PUBLICATIONS:
Fortune
Omni
Woman's Day
McCall's
Popular Science
Health

KAHN, ADA PASKIND
2562 Wellington Court
Evanston, IL 60201
AFFILIATIONS:
ASJA, AG, AMWA
PRINCIPAL SUBJECTS:
Book Reviews
Editorial
Family
Health
Human Interest
Human Relations
Humor
Medical
Psychology
Science
Senior Citizens
Social Trends
Women's Interest
PUBLICATIONS:
Psychiatric News
Psychiatric Times
Chicago Medicine

KANIGEL, ROBERT
2643 North Calvert Street
Baltimore, MD 21218
Telephone: 410-467-4163
AFFILIATIONS:
ASJA, NASW, NCIS, SHT

PRINCIPAL SUBJECTS:
Book Reviews
Business & Industry
Education
General Interest
Health
History
Management
Medical
Psychology
Science
Urban Affairs
PUBLICATIONS:
New York Times
Washington Post
Book World
Psychology Today
Los Angeles Times
Health
The Sciences
American Health

KAPLAN, DAVID
568 Howard St., 5th Fl.
San Francisco, CA 94105
Telephone: 415-543-1200
Fax: 415-543-8311
PRINCIPAL SUBJECTS:
World Affairs
PUBLICATIONS:
Technology Review
Village Voice
California
Los Angeles Times
Times Of London
San Francisco Examiner
Hong Kong Standard
Toronto Globe & Mail

KARAS, NICHOLAS
11 Red Oak Rd.
Saint James, NY 11780
Telephone: 516-862-9254
AFFILIATIONS:
IABW, OWAA
PRINCIPAL SUBJECTS:
Family
Men's Interest
Sports
Travel
PUBLICATIONS:
Field and Stream
Outdoor Life
Salt Water Sportsman
Sports Afield
Sports Illustrated
Newsday-Leisure Sports,
  Four/Week
Guide to Saltwater Fishing

KARLIN, ELYSE ZORN
10 Elk Ave.
New Rochelle, NY 10804
Telephone: 914-636-3784
AFFILIATIONS:
ASJA
PRINCIPAL SUBJECTS:
Advertising
Family
PUBLICATIONS:
Bride's
Collector's Clocks and Jewelry
Heritage

KARPEL, CRAIG S.
350 W. 57th St.
New York, NY 10019
Telephone: 000-000-0000
MAILING ADDRESS:
Craig S. Karpel
New York, NY 10019
Telephone: 516-862-9254
AFFILIATIONS:
IABW, OWAA
PRINCIPAL SUBJECTS:
Book Reviews
Travel
Business & Industry
PUBLICATIONS:
Esquire
Harper's
New York Magazine
Playboy
New Republic, The
Village Voice, The
Penthouse

KARTEN, HOWARD A.
40 Woodland Pkwy., Apt. W-5
Randolph, MA 02368
Telephone: 617-986-4869
PRINCIPAL SUBJECTS:
Computer Technology
Business & Industry
PUBLICATIONS:
ABA Banking Journal
PC Magazine Forbes
Computer World

KASS, BENNY L.
1050 17th St., N.W., #100
Washington, DC 20036
Telephone: 202-659-6500
Fax: 202-293-2608
AFFILIATIONS:
NAREE
PRINCIPAL SUBJECTS:
Business & Industry

PUBLICATIONS:
Washington Post -
  Weekly Column
Los Angeles Times

KATZ, RUTH J.
2109 Broadway 10-54
New York, NY 10023
Telephone: 212-870-1471
Fax: 212-799-4040
PRINCIPAL SUBJECTS:
Fashion
Home & Garden
PUBLICATIONS:
New York Magazine
New York Times

KAUFMAN, WALLACE
P.O. Box 1021
Pittsboro, NC 27312
Telephone: 919-542-4072
Fax: 919-540-4072
AFFILIATIONS:
ASJA, AIBS
PRINCIPAL SUBJECTS:
Book Reviews
Business & Industry
Ecology
Editorial
Foreign
Nature
Personal Finance
Science
Travel
PUBLICATIONS:
American Forests
American Health
Audubon
New York Times
National Wildlife
Newsday
Orion
Science Digest
Redbook
Omni
Chicago Tribune

KAVALER, LUCY
103 E. 86 Street
New York, NY 10028
Telephone: 212-427-0948
AFFILIATIONS:
NASW, AMWA, ASJA, NYBPE,
  PEN, AG
PRINCIPAL SUBJECTS:
Ecology
Fashion
General Interest
Health
History
Human Interest

Medical
Nature
Science
Women's Interest
PUBLICATIONS:
Skin Cancer Foundation
  Journal
Female Patient
Primary Cardiology
Hospital Physician
Memories
Self
Cosmopolitan
Smithsonian
Reader's Digest

KAY, JANE HOLTZ
156 Milk Street
Boston, MA 02109
Telephone: 617-426-7261
PRINCIPAL SUBJECTS:
Urban Affairs
Ecology
PUBLICATIONS:
The Nation
New York Times
Boston Globe
Landscape Architecture

KAYE, EVELYN
3031 Fifth St.
Boulder, CO 80304
Telephone: 303-449-8474
AFFILIATIONS:
ASJA, NATJA, CIPA
PRINCIPAL SUBJECTS:
Ecology
Geography
Family
Nature
Travel
Women's Interest
World Affairs
PUBLICATIONS:
Glamour
Parents
Travel & Leisure
Ladies Home Journal
Boston Globe
New York Times
Adventure Travel
McCalls
N.J. Record
Active Times

KEATING, BERN
The Bayou Rd. 141
Greenville, MS 38701
Telephone: 601-334-4088
Fax: 601-334-9607

AFFILIATIONS:
ASJA-AG, TJG
PRINCIPAL SUBJECTS:
History
Travel
World Affairs
Ecology
PUBLICATIONS:
National Geographic
Travel & Leisure
Smithsonian
Town & Country

KEEN, MARJORIE
10 Woods Lane
Parkesburg, PA 19365
Telephone: 215-857-3432
Fax: 215-857-3275
PRINCIPAL SUBJECTS:
Agriculture
Ecology
Travel
PUBLICATIONS:
Mushroom News
Environmental Action
Farm & Ranch Living
Ford New Holland News
Pennsylvania Magazine
The Philadelphia Inquirer
Hoard's Dairyman
Lancaster Farming
Farmshine
Allentown Morning Call
Harrisburg Patriot-News
Lancaster Intelligence Journal
Lancaster New Era
West Chester Daily Local News
Reading Eagle
York Sunday News
Chester County Business &
  Industry
ACC Currents
Public Opinion

KEIL, BILL
6306 S.W. 39th Ave.
Portland, OR 97221
Telephone: 503-244-5289
AFFILIATIONS:
OWAA, NASJA, SAF, NOWA
PRINCIPAL SUBJECTS:
Sports
Nature
Travel
PUBLICATIONS:
Skiing
American Forests
Skiing Trade News
Wood Based Panels
  International
Oregonian, The

Pacific Northwest
Outdoor Life
Sports Afield

KEITH, ALLAN
P.O. Box 882
Mattoon, IL 61938
Telephone: 217-235-0995
PRINCIPAL SUBJECTS:
Government

KELLY, KATE
11 Rockwood Drive
Larchmont, NY 10538
Telephone: 914-834-0602
Fax: 914-833-2368
AFFILIATIONS:
ASJA, AG
PRINCIPAL SUBJECTS:
Advertising
Business & Industry
Education
Family
History
Personal Finance
Women's Interest
PUBLICATIONS:
Sesame St. Parents Guide
Woman's Day
Parents
Redbook
Glamour

KEMPER, SU
25 Rimfire Cir.
Reno, NV 89509
Telephone: 702-746-2121
Fax: 702-746-1850
MAILING ADDRESS:
Su Kemper
P.O. Box 10588
Reno, NV 89510
AFFILIATIONS:
ASMP, AARWBA
PRINCIPAL SUBJECTS:
Automotive
Travel
Editorial
PUBLICATIONS:
Nation's Business
Road & Track Magazine
Autosport (U.K.)
Automobile Magazine
Rombo (Italy)
Off Road Magazine
On Track
Motoring News (U.K.)
Auto Racing USA
VW & Porsche Magazine
Newsweek (Int.)

KEMPTON-SMITH, DEBBI
P.O. Box 1801 FDR Station
New York, NY 10022
Telephone: 212-750-0188
AFFILIATIONS:
MENSA, AFTRA, AG,
 AFA, ASJA
PRINCIPAL SUBJECTS:
Travel
Government
Humor
Psychology
PUBLICATIONS:
Event U.S.A.
The Observer (London)
IBM P.C.
Orbit Video
Good Food
New Yorker
Harper's Bazaar
Taxi
Glamour
Cosmopolitan
New York Magazine
Seventeen

KENEAU, ANDREE DION
17021 E. Jefferson
Detroit, MI 48230
Telephone: 313-882-6762

KIEL, STUART
12 Skylark Lane
Stony Brook, NY 11790
Telephone: 516-751-7080
AFFILIATIONS:
AG
PRINCIPAL SUBJECTS:
Human Interest
Humor
Health
PUBLICATIONS:
The New York Times
Beyond
Ampersand
Newsday
Signet Books
Christian Science Monitor, The
SFWA Bulletin
Authors Guild Bulletin
Art Materials Trade News
Tor Books
Muscle Training Illustrated
Muscular Development
Changes
Bronze Thrills

KIMMERLY, MAUREEN C.
MK Concepts
14529 Saddleback Drive
Carmel, IN 46032

Telephone: 317-580-9628
AFFILIATIONS:
WICI
PRINCIPAL SUBJECTS:
Management
Advertising
History
Family

KING, GAIL
935 Craig Dr.
Henderson, KY 42420
Telephone: 502-826-3209
PUBLICATIONS:
Ohio River
Kentucky History
Quilts
Across The Board
Kentucky Living
The Wall Street Journal
Fabric Art

KINGDOM, GERRY
305 S. William St.
Johnstown, NY 12095
Telephone: 518-762-8653
PRINCIPAL SUBJECTS:
Nature
Sports
Travel
PUBLICATIONS:
Field & Stream, Outdoor Life,
 Travel/Holiday,
Accent
Sports Afield
Saturday Evening Post, The

KITAY, WILLIAM
108 Wilson Pl.
Plainview, NY 11803
Telephone: 516-681-7939
Fax: 516-681-5037
AFFILIATIONS:
AMWA, NASW,
 CBE, ASJA, SPJ
PRINCIPAL SUBJECTS:
Health
Medical
PUBLICATIONS:
Smithsonian
Orthopaedic Review
Orthopaedic Audio-Synopsis
Oncology Guide
Ladies Home Journal
Your Health
Rheumatology Guide
Family Circle

Practical Gastroenterology
American Journal of
 Arthrospopy
Infusion, The Journal of IV
 Therapy

KLAUS, BARBARA
111 Berkshire Rd.
Rockville Ctr, NY 11570
Telephone: 516-678-1363
AFFILIATIONS:
APJ, LIPC, WGA
PRINCIPAL SUBJECTS:
Humor
General Interest
Travel
News
PUBLICATIONS:
New York Times
 (Humor Column)
Newsday
N.Y. Daily News
American Way
Long Island Magazine
Pageant
New York Magazine
Expressions
Chalice
Newsday
 (Humor Column)-Current

KLAVAN, ELLEN
235 Low Rd.
Sharon, CT 06069
Telephone: 203-364-5449
AFFILIATIONS:
ASJA, WIP
PRINCIPAL SUBJECTS:
Family
General Interest
Human Interest
Human Relations
Women's Interest
PUBLICATIONS:
Parents
Working Mother
Woman's Day
Good Housekeeping
American Baby

KLINE, LLOYD W.
P.O. Box 1127
Newark, DE 19715
Telephone: 302-737-3698
AFFILIATIONS:
EPAA
PRINCIPAL SUBJECTS:
Education
Human Interest
Business & Industry
Agriculture

Editorial
Family
General Interest
Health
Human Relations
Journalism
Management
Marketing
Medical
News
Sales
Senior Citizens
PUBLICATIONS:
Delaware Today
PHI Delta Kappan
Home Life
United Church Herald
Today's Catholic Teacher
Media and Methods
Pennsylvania Farmer
Numerous Private Publications
Learning/90
ED Press News
Curriculum Update

KNAPPMAN, ELIZABETH
 FROST
P.O. Box 5
Chester, CT 06412
Telephone: 203-345-Read
Fax: 203-345-3660

KNICELY, FAY
Acworth, NH 03601
Telephone: 603-835-2295
MAILING ADDRESS:
Fay Knicely
P.O. Box 1
Acworth, NH 03601
AFFILIATIONS:
NHADA, CSA
PRINCIPAL SUBJECTS:
General Interest
News
Business & Industry
History
PUBLICATIONS:
N.H. Times
N.H. Business Review
Leisure Weekly
Local Area Newspapers
Vintage Fashion Magazine

KNIGHT, DOUG
P.O. Box 101
North Sutton, NH 03260
Telephone: 603-927-4623
Fax: 603-927-4477
AFFILIATIONS:
ASJA, OWAA, ASC

PRINCIPAL SUBJECTS:
Travel
Ecology
General Interest
Men's Interest
Science
Sports
Nature
Agriculture
Animals
Book Reviews
Business & Industry
Education
Foreign
Health
Hobbies
Home & Garden
Human Interest
Military
Movie Reviews
World Affairs
PUBLICATIONS:
Argosy
Arizona Highways
Field & Stream
Fishing World
Outdoor Life
Popular Mechanics
Popular Science
Saga
Sports Afield
American Hunter
Peterson's Hunting
Sports
Safari
Western Outdoors
True Magazine
Guns Quarterly
Journal of Cybernetics

KNIGHT, MRS. RICHARD
  ALDEN
P.O. Box 207
Montoursville, PA 17754
Telephone: 717-368-8042
Fax: 717-368-8179
AFFILIATIONS:
OWAA
PRINCIPAL SUBJECTS:
Ecology
Men's Interest
Sports

KOCH, JOANNE & LEWIS
343 Dodge
Evanston, IL 60202
Telephone: 708-864-5660
AFFILIATIONS:
ASJA, WP
PRINCIPAL SUBJECTS:
Family

Youth
Human Relations
Human Interest
PUBLICATIONS:
McCalls
Psychology Today
Chicago
Chicago Tribune
Parade
Newsday

KOCIVAR, BEN
330 Greenwich Rd., Rt. 4
Bedford, NY 10506
Telephone: 914-234-3653
AFFILIATIONS:
AIAA, NYAPK,
  NSWA, OMPA, ASJA
PRINCIPAL SUBJECTS:
Aviation
Human Relations
Computer Technology
Automotive
Sports
Travel
PUBLICATIONS:
Family Circle
New York Times
Parade
Popular Science
Yachting
Aeronautics & Astronautics
Flight International
Look
IBM Think
Popular Mechanics
Ford Times
Life
Rudder
Small World
FAA
Cosmopolitan

KOEHLER, MARGARET
  HUDSON
38 River Rd.
East Orleans, MA 02653
Telephone: 508-255-1358
MAILING ADDRESS:
Koehler Associates, Ltd.
P.O. Box 487
East Orleans, MA 02643
AFFILIATIONS:
ASJA, AG, ALA
PRINCIPAL SUBJECTS:
General Interest
History
Travel
PUBLICATIONS:
Bon Appetit
Family Circle

Ford Times
Gourmet
Travel/Holiday
Early American Life
TWA Ambassador
Antiques Journal

KOERNER, THOMAS F.
2357 Tumbletree Way
Reston, VA 22091
Telephone: 703-860-2813
PRINCIPAL SUBJECTS:
Management
Education

KOFRANEK, ANTON M.
Univ. of Calif.,Dept.of
  Environmental Horticulture
Davis, CA 95616
Telephone: 916-752-0130
Fax: 916-752-1819
MAILING ADDRESS:
Anton M. Kofranek
803 Linden Ln.
Davis, CA 95616
AFFILIATIONS:
ASHS, AOS, ISHS
PRINCIPAL SUBJECTS:
Home & Garden
PUBLICATIONS:
Hortscience
Florist's Review
California Agriculture
American Orchid Bulletin
Chronica Horticulture

KOLUS, HOWARD
419 Kent Dr.
Mechanicsburg, PA 17055
Telephone: 717-766-6444
Fax: 717-838-6409
MAILING ADDRESS:
Howard Kolus
P.O. Box 304
Palmyra, PA 17078
PRINCIPAL SUBJECTS:
Journalism
General Interest
PUBLICATIONS:
Aging Magazine
Geisinger Magazine
Lebanon Daily News
Apprise Magazine

KONNER, LINDA
123 Waverly Place, #9E
New York, NY 10011
Telephone: 212-533-5085
AFFILIATIONS:
ASJA

PRINCIPAL SUBJECTS:
Amusements
Entertainment
Health
Human Relations
Humor
Journalism
Motivation
Personalities
Physical Fitness
The Arts
Travel
Video
Women's Interest
PUBLICATIONS:
Redbook
New York Times
TV Guide
Playboy
Woman's Day
New Woman
Travel Holiday
Boston Globe

KOONTZ, KATY
8232 Cambridge Woods Lane
Knoxville, TN 37923
Telephone: 615-693-9845
AFFILIATIONS:
SATW, ASMP, ASJA, TJG
PRINCIPAL SUBJECTS:
Amusements
Ecology
Editorial
Family
Foreign
General Interest
Geography
Health
Home & Garden
Humor
Medical
Nature
Photography
Physical Fitness
Psychology
Travel
Women's Interest
PUBLICATIONS:
New York Times
McCall's
Connoisseur
Outside
Men's Journal
Self
Ski
Snow Country
Special Report
New Woman
Woman's Day

Saturday Evening Post
Travel & Leisure
Garden Design
Shape

KOWAL, JOHN PAUL
125 Bonad Rd.
Brookline, MA 02167
Telephone: 617-325-2640
PRINCIPAL SUBJECTS:
General Interest
Science
Travel
Computer Technology
PUBLICATIONS:
Skin Diver Magazine
Sea Frontiers
Health Magazine
Triton Magazine
The Journal of Popular Culture
Underwater Magazine
Content
The Canadian Journalists
  Magazine
Writer's Digest
Journal of Technical Writing
  and Communications
Photomethods
Photolith
Training Digest
Communications: Journalism
  Education Today
Medical Dimensions
The Compass: A Magazine of
  the Sea
Quill & Scroll
The Rangefinder
Monitor
Technical Photography
Photo Life
Medical Communications
Public Relations Journal
The Boston Globe
Boston Herald
The Union Leader
Better Communication
Lady's Circle
Baby Talk
The Boston Business Journal

KRANISH, ARTHUR
National Press Bldg., Rm. 1079
Washington, DC 20045
Telephone: 202-393-0031
Fax: 202-393-1732
AFFILIATIONS:
AIAA, IEEE, AP
PRINCIPAL SUBJECTS:
Business & Industry
Ecology
General Interest

Government
Science
Travel
Youth
Automotive
Aviation
Book Reviews
Computer Technology
Electronics
Health
Medical
Nature
News
The Arts

KRASNER, MICHAEL F.
295 Turnpike Rd., Apt. 605N.
Westborough, MA 01581
Telephone: 508-366-0254
MAILING ADDRESS:
Michael F. Krasner
P.O. Box 1129
Westborough, MA 01581
AFFILIATIONS:
PCNE
PRINCIPAL SUBJECTS:
News
PUBLICATIONS:
Telegram & Gazette, City Line
  (Worcester, Ma.)

KREDENSER, PETER
2551 Angelo Drive
Los Angeles, CA 90077
Telephone: 310-278-6356
Fax: 310-276-4822
AFFILIATIONS:
ASMP
PRINCIPAL SUBJECTS:
Fashion
Personalities

KREIG, ANDREW, ESQ.
701 Pennsylvania Ave.,
  NW Ph8
Washington, DC 20004
Telephone: 202-638-0070
AFFILIATIONS:
ASJA
PRINCIPAL SUBJECTS:
Book Reviews
Government
Journalism
PUBLICATIONS:
Yankee
Boston Magazine
Boston Globe
Connecticut Magazine
Hartford Courant

KREMEN, BENNETT
151 E. 26th St.
New York, NY 10010
Telephone: 212-689-6671
AFFILIATIONS:
AL, AG
PRINCIPAL SUBJECTS:
The Arts
Business & Industry
General Interest
PUBLICATIONS:
Holiday
The Nation
New York Times
Penthouse
Dissent
Village Voice

KRYMOW, VINCENZINA
6340 Millbank Drive
Centerville, OH 45459
Telephone: 513-434-1518
AFFILIATIONS:
WICI
PRINCIPAL SUBJECTS:
Health
Religion
Senior Citizens
PUBLICATIONS:
NAPMR Quarterly
Catholic Telegraph

KUHN, IRENE CORBALLY
45 Christopher St.
New York, NY 10014
Telephone: 212-242-4541
AFFILIATIONS:
OPC, NYTWAS
PRINCIPAL SUBJECTS:
General Interest
Government
Personalities
Travel
World Affairs
PUBLICATIONS:
Christian Science Monitor
Gourmet
National Review
Reader's Digest
Town and Country
Travel/Holiday Magazine
Emporia (Kansas) Gazette
The Sign
Chicago Tribune
San Francisco Chronicle
Union Leader,
  Manchester, N.H.
Honolulu Star Bulletin
The Citizen
S. F. Examiner
Cosmopolitan

Good Housekeeping
Los Angeles Times
Boston Globe

KUSTANOWITZ, SHULAMIT E.
4 - 27 Karl St.
Fair Lawn, NJ 07410
Telephone: 201-796-8685
AFFILIATIONS:
AOJC
PRINCIPAL SUBJECTS:
Foreign
Human Interest
Travel
Religion
PUBLICATIONS:
The Jerusalem Post
New York Times, The
Record, The
New American, The
Digest (IBM ISG/NAD)
Jewish Standard, The
Travel Weekly
Woman's World Magazine

LACEY, DIANE G.
180-G Overmount Ave.
Little Falls, NJ 07424
Telephone: 201-256-1288
PRINCIPAL SUBJECTS:
Fashion
Health
The Arts
Home & Garden
Business & Industry
PUBLICATIONS:
Home Improvement
Woman's World
Executive Jeweler
Giftware News
Mall Magazines

LADACH, PAULETTE
10278 Vinemont
Dallas, TX 75218
Telephone: 214-321-6427
AFFILIATIONS:
WICI
PRINCIPAL SUBJECTS:
Home & Garden
PUBLICATIONS:
Dallas Morning News

LAGAN, CONSTANCE
  HALLINAN
35 Claremont Ave.
North Babylon, NY 11703
Telephone: 516-661-5181
AFFILIATIONS:
WICI, NLAPW

PRINCIPAL SUBJECTS:
Business & Industry
Management
Women's Interest
Family
Hobbies
Human Interest
PUBLICATIONS:
Entrepreneur
In Business
Home Business News
National Home Business
  Report
Crafts Report, The
Homeworking Mothers
Small Businesswoman's
  Newsletter
Crafts Woman
Professional Quilter, The
See Saw
Creative Person
Library Imagination Paper, The
Long Island Heritage
Long Island Craftsmen's
  Newsletter
Sunstorm
Homemaker, The
Goodfellow Review of Crafts
Quilter's Newsletter Magazine
Cottage - Crafts & Fibers
Workbasket
Quilt
Quilt Almanac (1984) (1985)
Needle & Thread
Country Craftmakers & Hobby
  Magazine
Crafts
Sew News
Cast On
Precious Fibers
Crafts 'N Things
Craft Projects 'N Patterns
Shuttle Spindle & Dyepot
Cross Stitch & Needlepoint
Women's Circle
North Country Craftswoman
Writer's Club Newsletter
Long Island Quilter's Society
  Newsletter
Mother's Money Making
  Manual
Craft & Needlework Age
Parent Connections
Directory of Money Making
  Ideas
Home Business Advisor
Home Sweet Home
Marketing Options Report
  Series for Craftspeople
Teaching for Learning
Self - Employed America

Traditional Quiltworks
Quick & Easy Quilting
Natl Assn of Arts & Crafts
  Magazine
Art & Craft Show Guide
Long Island Parenting News

LAMANGA, JOSEPH
P.O. Box 882
Yonkers, NY 10702
Telephone: 914-963-3260
PRINCIPAL SUBJECTS:
History
Hobbies
Nature

LAMONT, DOUGLAS
2765 N. Kenmore, #1f
Chicago, IL 60614
Telephone: 312-327-8428
AFFILIATIONS:
ASJA
PRINCIPAL SUBJECTS:
Business & Industry
Marketing
Management
World Affairs
PUBLICATIONS:
Harvard Business Review
Fact

LAMPE, DAVID
3508 Great Valley Dr.
Cedar Park, TX 78613
Telephone: 512-258-6875
PRINCIPAL SUBJECTS:
Animals
Architecture
Automotive
Aviation
Business & Industry
Ecology
Family
General Interest
Home & Garden
Human Interest
Medical
Military
Nature
Personalities
Social Trends
The Arts
Travel
PUBLICATIONS:
American Weekly
Argosy
Family Health
Family Weekly
House Beautiful
Medical Opinion
Mother Earth News

National & International Wildlife
Parade
P.M. (Germany)
Popular Science
Reader's Digest
SAGA
Saturday Review
Science Digest
Seventeen
Sports Illustrated
Sunday Telegraph
  Magazine (UK)
Today's Health
Smithsonian
Sci Quest
Sunday Times Colour
  Magazine (UK)
Popular Mechanics
Mosaic (Natl. Science
  Foundation)
Real
Cavalier
Men In Danger
Auto Age
Motor Trend
Ellery Queen Mystery
  Magazine
Diversion
Family Handyman
Mechanix Illustrated
Ultra
The Connoisseur
Manchester Guardian (U.K.)
Holiday
The Reporter
Epicure
Courier (UK)
Homemaker (UK)
Flying
Illustrated (UK)
Lilliput (UK)
The Lion
American Rifleman
Marathon World
Shell News
Motor Trade Executive (UK)
Engineering (UK)
Mayfair (Canada)
Wildlife (UK)
Tidbits (UK)
Weekend (UK)
Reveille (UK)
Reynolds News (UK)
P.M. (Germany)
Discover
BBC Wildlife
The Connoisseur
Discover
Popular Mechanics
Popular Science
The Reporter

Smithsonian
Sunday Times Magazine
  (London)
Telegraph Color Magazine
  (London)
Today's Health

LANDER, KATHLEEN
144 East 36th St., #1-C
New York, NY 10016
Telephone: 212-689-8426
AFFILIATIONS:
WCI
PRINCIPAL SUBJECTS:
Electronics
PUBLICATIONS:
Home Entertainment
The Robb Report
Campus USA
New York Times
Home Video
Country Music
International Herald Tribune
Video World (UK)
Ace International
New Jersey Home & Garden
Newsweek
Good Housekeeping
Newsday
Chicago Tribune
Boston Phoenix
Washington Post
Electronics Retailing
Dealerscope
Consumer Electronics
  Product News
Advertising Age

LANDT, DENNIS
135 E. 39th St.
New York, NY 10016
Telephone: 212-532-8226
AFFILIATIONS:
NAHWW, IMPA
PRINCIPAL SUBJECTS:
Amusements
General Interest
History
Fashion
Travel
Architecture
Personalities
PUBLICATIONS:
Reader's Digest
Sat. Review
Travel Holiday
Realites
Ultra
Town & Country
Harper's Bazaar

Home & Away
Ladies Home Journal
Family Circle

LANDWEHR, SHELDON
345 West 58th St., #412
New York, NY 10019
Telephone: 212-581-0360
Fax: 212-489-1973
AFFILIATIONS:
ASJA, IFWT
PRINCIPAL SUBJECTS:
Travel
PUBLICATIONS:
New York Post
Cue
Penthouse

LANGER, CASSANDRA
32-22 89th St., #605
Flushing, NY 11369
Telephone: 718-476-7834
AFFILIATIONS:
ASJA, NWU, CAA, IAAC
PRINCIPAL SUBJECTS:
Book Reviews
Ecology
Entertainment
Health
Movie Reviews
Nature
The Arts
PUBLICATIONS:
Ms.
American Artist
Womens Art Journal
Woman Artist News
Art Journal

LANGHAM, BARBARA
9501 Capital of Texas Hwy.,
  N., #202
Austin, TX 78759
Telephone: 512-346-2261
Fax: 512-346-4751
AFFILIATIONS:
IABC, PRSA
PRINCIPAL SUBJECTS:
The Arts
Business & Industry
Government
Human Relations
Education
Youth
Health
PUBLICATIONS:
EXXON USA
Tenneco Publications
University of Texas at Austin
  Publications
Texas Child Care Quarterly

Houston Forum Club
Texas Highways
University of Texas System
  Publications
Successful Meetings Magazine
Texas Medicine
Government Technology

LANGWORTH, RICHARD M.
181 Burrage Rd.
Contoocook, NH 03229
Telephone: 603-746-5606
Fax: 603-746-4260
MAILING ADDRESS:
Dragonwyck Publishing, Inc.
P.O. Box 385
Contoocook, NH 03229
AFFILIATIONS:
IABC, PRSA
PRINCIPAL SUBJECTS:
History
Personalities
Automotive
PUBLICATIONS:
American Way
Car Collector
Consumer Guide
National Review
Boy's Life
British Heritage
Manchester Union - Leader

LANKARD, TOM
P.O. Box 162634
Sacramento, CA 95816
Telephone: 916-731-7078
PRINCIPAL SUBJECTS:
Automotive
PUBLICATIONS:
Auto Week Magazine
Automotive News
Auto Magazine

LARBERG, ANN
810 Overhill Rd.
Deland, FL 32720
Telephone: 904-734-1955
PRINCIPAL SUBJECTS:
Travel
History
Education
Science
Youth
Advertising
Book Reviews
Family
General Interest
Health
Medical
News
Photography

Psychology
Religion
Travel
World Affairs
PUBLICATIONS:
Reflections Magazine
Daytona News-Journal
Singles Circle
Christian Single
The Indian Trader
Salesmans Opportunity
Vegetarian Times
Instructor, The
Rangefinder
Technomic Publishers
Southern Baptist Sunday
  School Dept.
Write Way, The
Jobortunity
Mother Earth News
Daytona News Journal
Mother
Earth News
Vegetarian Times
Rangefinder
Instructor
Home Life
Highlights For Children
The Write Way
Media Profiles
Capper's Weekly

LASHUA, MARGERY F.
HCR 32, Box 560
Montpelier, VT 05602
Telephone: 802-223-3929
AFFILIATIONS:
LVW (League Of Vermont
  Writers)
PRINCIPAL SUBJECTS:
History
Social Trends
PUBLICATIONS:
Poems of Great America
  (Vol. II)
Poems of The Great Northeast

LASLEY, PAUL/ELIZABETH
  HARRYMAN
P.O. Box 5256
Beverly Hills, CA 90209
Telephone: 213-935-8101
Fax: 213-935-8101

LASSEN, JEFF
P.O. Box 2545
Carson City, NV 89702
Telephone: 702-883-8936
PRINCIPAL SUBJECTS:
Travel
Hobbies

PUBLICATIONS:
Stamp Collector
The Fun Trader
The Posthorn

LAYNE, MARIE
17 Chambers Crt.
Clifton, NJ 07013
AFFILIATIONS:
AMA, NEA, CMU
PRINCIPAL SUBJECTS:
Family
Health
Philosophy
Religion
Travel
Youth
General Interest
PUBLICATIONS:
Christian Science Monitor
Travel
Home & Health
Listen
Minnesota AAA Motorist
Our Sunday Visitor
Alert
Our Lady of Fatima
North American Voice of
  Fatima
Sunday Digest
My Daily Visitor
Smoke Signals
Parish Family Digest
Upward
Apostolate
Our Family
Marian Helpers Bulletin

LEAS, MARLIN
1951 S. California Ave.
Monrovia, CA 91016
PRINCIPAL SUBJECTS:
Humor

LEAVITT, MARC K.
67 S. Third Ave.
New York, NY 10003
Telephone: 212-721-2140
PUBLICATIONS:
Stars & Stripes
Ashbury Pk. Press, The
News Tribune, The
Associated Press
Pet Dealer Magazine
Ansom

LEBLANC, RENA DICTOR
P.O. Box 68
Woodland Hills, CA 91365
Telephone: 818-887-6053
Fax: 818-884-9795

AFFILIATIONS:
ASJA, PEN, WGAW
PRINCIPAL SUBJECTS:
Animals
Entertainment
Human Interest
Medical
Personalities
Psychology
Science
Senior Citizens
Travel
Women's Interest
PUBLICATIONS:
Reader's Digest
McCall's
Redbook
Ladies Home Journal
Good Housekeeping
New York Times Syndicate
Woman's World
Los Angeles

LEDERER, MURIEL
756 Lincoln Ave.
Winnetka, IL 60093
Telephone: 708-446-5551
Fax: 708-446-5116
AFFILIATIONS:
ASJA
PRINCIPAL SUBJECTS:
Business & Industry
Management
Marketing

LEE, SHIRLEY
22839 Saticoy St.
West Hills, CA 91304
Telephone: 818-992-4137
AFFILIATIONS:
ASJA, HWPC
PRINCIPAL SUBJECTS:
Business & Industry
Ecology
Entertainment
General Interest
Hobbies
Home & Garden
Human Interest
Nature
Personalities
Physical Fitness
The Arts
Travel
Women's Interest
Youth
PUBLICATIONS:
Redbook
Woman's World
Boys' Life
The Christian Science Monitor

Westways
Mature American
Plate World
The Franklin Mint Almanac
Star
Globe
Teen
Vista

LEERBURGER, BENEDICT
338 Heathcote Road
Scarsdale, NY 10583
Telephone: 914-972-2470
Fax: 914-472-4510
AFFILIATIONS:
NASU, ASJA
PRINCIPAL SUBJECTS:
Agriculture
Animals
Automotive
Aviation
Book Reviews
Business & Industry
Computer Technology
Ecology
Education
Education
Foreign
General Interest
Health
Government
Management
Marketing
Medical
Nature
Science
Senior Citizens
Travel
PUBLICATIONS:
Smithsonian
Family Circle
Vis A Vis
Siganture
Encyclopedia Britannica
Popular Science

LEIF, ROBERT
3826 N. Bresee Ave.
Baldwin Park, CA 91706
Telephone: 818-337-4832
AFFILIATIONS:
LAPC
PRINCIPAL SUBJECTS:
General Interest
Video
Men's Interest
Science
Automotive
Aviation
Sports

PUBLICATIONS:
Petersen Publications
Science Digest
Porsche Panorama
Hot Rod
Car Craft
Popular Science

LEMKOWITZ, FLORENCE
7116 First Ave., S.
St Petersburg, FL 33707
Telephone: 813-344-3147
AFFILIATIONS:
National Press Club, SATW
PRINCIPAL SUBJECTS:
General Interest
Humor
Personalities
Travel

LEONARD, GEORGE
P.O. Box 609
Mill Valley, CA 94942
Telephone: 415-383-1480
AFFILIATIONS:
ECE
PRINCIPAL SUBJECTS:
Health
Government
Philosophy
Sports
Ecology
Education
PUBLICATIONS:
Atlantic Monthly
Esquire
Harper's
Readers Digest
Saturday Review
New York
San Francisco Focus
New Age
San Francisco Chronicle
New York Times
Self

LEONARD, JOHN EDWARD
6846 Brian Michael Ct.
Springfield, VA 22153
Telephone: 703-569-8606
AFFILIATIONS:
SPJ, NPPA, IABC, WIW
PRINCIPAL SUBJECTS:
General Interest
Government
Human Interest
Journalism
Urban Affairs

PUBLICATIONS:
Editor & Publisher
Congressional Quarterly
Weekly Report

LESLIE, JACQUES
124 Reed Street
Mill Valley, CA 94941
Telephone: 415-331-2644
Fax: 415-331-1090
PRINCIPAL SUBJECTS:
Computer Technology
Foreign
General Interest
Government
Health
Humor
Journalism
Media
Social Trends
PUBLICATIONS:
The Atlantic
New York Times Magazine
Wired
Los Angeles Times Magazine
Washington Post
Washington Monthly
Reader's Digest
Parenting
Newsweek
Wall Street Journal
Washington Journalism Review

LEVIN, AARON
3000 Chestnut Ave. Suite 102
Baltimore, MD 21211
Telephone: 410-467-8646
AFFILIATIONS:
DCSWA
PRINCIPAL SUBJECTS:
Editorial
Education
Foreign
Health
History
Journalism
Medical
Photography
Science
The Arts
Travel
PUBLICATIONS:
New York Times
Archaeology
Johns Hopkins
Baltimore Sun
Saturday Evening Post

LEVINE, FAYE
20 E. 9th St., #8T
New York, NY 10003

Telephone: 212-473-5392
AFFILIATIONS:
Pen Club
PRINCIPAL SUBJECTS:
Science
Government
Personalities
Religion
The Arts
Women's Interest
Amusements
Book Reviews
Editorial
Education
Entertainment
Foreign
General Interest
History
Human Interest
Humor
Journalism
Medical
News
Social Trends
Urban Affairs
Travel
PUBLICATIONS:
The Atlantic Monthly
Ms.
The New York Times Book
  Review
Newsweek
Penthouse
Rolling Stone
Newsday
New York Post

LEVINSON, ROBIN
282 Greenland Ave.
Trenton, NJ 08638
Telephone: 609-538-0544
AFFILIATIONS:
NASW, SPJ, NFPW
PRINCIPAL SUBJECTS:
Health
Medical
Science
Personalities
Human Interest
PUBLICATIONS:
Times Trenton, The
Odessa American (TX)
Deming Headlight (NM)
New Mexico Business
  Magazine
Albuquerque Tribune (NM)
New York Times Supplements

LEVITSKY, DR. SERGE L.
620 Barrymore Ln.
Mamaroneck, NY 10543

Telephone: 914-698-1247
AFFILIATIONS:
UL, NAE, RSL
PRINCIPAL SUBJECTS:
Business & Industry
Government
History
Personalities
World Affairs
PUBLICATIONS:
Cornell International Law
  Journal
Journal Of Media Law &
  Practice (London)
Americas
Netherlands Review of
  International Law

LEVY, ERIC
1625 Emmons Ave., #6H
Brooklyn, NY 11235
Telephone: 718-646-2344
PRINCIPAL SUBJECTS:
Medical
Health
Human Interest
Business & Industry
News
PUBLICATIONS:
South Queens Forum
Toastmasters Magazine
Modern Floor Coverings
Health & Diet Times
New York Review
Corporate Fitness & Recreation
  Magazine
New York Newsday
Podiatry Management

LEVY, RICHARD C.
P.O. Box 34828
Bethesda, MD 20827
Telephone: 301-469-6481
AFFILIATIONS:
ASJA
PRINCIPAL SUBJECTS:
Amusements
Business & Industry
Electronics
General Interest
Human Interest
Marketing
News
Social Trends
Travel
PUBLICATIONS:
Parade
Philadelphia Inquirer
The Star

Variety
Investor's Digest
Dealerscope

LEW, IRVINA
P.O. Box 5285
Bay Shore, NY 11706
Telephone: 516-666-5705
Fax: 516-666-7489
AFFILIATIONS:
ASJA, NATJA
PRINCIPAL SUBJECTS:
Family
Foreign
Health
Human Interest
Physical Fitness
Senior Citizens
The Arts
Travel
Women's Interest
PUBLICATIONS:
Diversion
Modern Bride
Vis A Vis
Travel Holiday
Ladies Home Journal
New York Times
Newsday
Family Circle

LEWIS, HOWARD R.
132 Hutchin Hill
Bearsville, NY 12409
Telephone: 914-679-2217
MAILING ADDRESS:
Clinical Communications, Inc.
Bearsville, NY 12409
PRINCIPAL SUBJECTS:
Health
Computer Technology
Medical
PUBLICATIONS:
Family Circle
Reader's Digest
Consumer Reports
Good Housekeeping
The People's Medical Manual
Sex And Health
Psychosomatics

LEWIS, JACK
3601 Cambridge St., #163
Las Vegas, NV 89109
Telephone: 702-733-6711
PRINCIPAL SUBJECTS:
Business & Industry
General Interest
History
Hobbies

PUBLICATIONS:
American Mercury
Catholic Digest
Science Digest
Sports Action
Writer's Digest
Police Gazette
Car Life
Management Digest
Motor Life
College & Pro Football
Gambling Times
Chips
Flying
New York Post
Old West
Motor Guide
Commercial Car Journal
Tradition
Motor Thrift
Business Management
Southern Motor Cargo
Grit
Business Review
Today's Secretary
National Parks
May Trends
Collector's World
Toastmaster
Kyle Rote's Sportsform
Modern Woodman
Our Army
Our Navy
Juniors
Boys & Girls
Sir!
Caper
Mr.
Bachelor
Here's How
Adam
Topper
Christian Standard
Listen
Midnight
A.S.T.A. Travel News
Early American Life
Sports Eye
Las Vegas SUN
Gaming International
Environmental Action
Car Collector - Car Craft
Fate

LEWIS, PARNELLS
413 Burke St.
Easton, PA 18042
Telephone: 215-253-6095
AFFILIATIONS:
SPJ

PRINCIPAL SUBJECTS:
News
Sports
Human Interest
PUBLICATIONS:
"On Stream"
United Press
Associated Press
International News.

LICHTENBERG, MARGARET
  KLEE
130 Appleton St., 5d
Boston, MA 02116
Telephone: 617-437-0313
AFFILIATIONS:
WNBA, ASJA
PRINCIPAL SUBJECTS:
Family
Human Relations
Personalities
Women's Interest
Senior Citizens
Medical
PUBLICATIONS:
Mademoiselle
Ms. Magazine
N.Y. Times Book Review
Publishers Weekly
Women Sports
Show
Crawdaddy
The Nation
Working Woman

LIEBERMAN, ROBERT H.
400 Nelson Rd.
Ithaca, NY 14850
Telephone: 607-273-8801
AFFILIATIONS:
AFI, AG
PRINCIPAL SUBJECTS:
Book Reviews
Travel
Government
PUBLICATIONS:
N.Y. Times
Damernas Varld (Sweden)

LILES, BRENDA
P.O. Box 632
Richton, MS 39476
Telephone: 601-788-5794
PRINCIPAL SUBJECTS:
Human Relations

LINDSAY, RAE
364 Mauro Rd.
Englewd Clfs, NJ 07632
Telephone: 201-567-8986

AFFILIATIONS:
APN, NPC, ASJA
PRINCIPAL SUBJECTS:
General Interest
Social Trends
Health
Travel
Youth
Family
Personal Finance
PUBLICATIONS:
Bergen Record
Travel News
Woman's World Magazine

LINSLEY, LESLIE
37-1/2 Union St.
Nantucket, MA 02554
Telephone: 508-228-2855
Fax: 508-325-5836

LIPPERT, JOAN
353 Farragut Ave.
Hastings-On-Hudson,
  NY 10706
Telephone: 914-478-5939
AFFILIATIONS:
ASJA
PRINCIPAL SUBJECTS:
Family
Health
Medical
Physical Fitness
PUBLICATIONS:
Ladies' Home Journal
New Woman
Redbook
Woman's World
Health

LOCKETT-JOHN, SUE
4804 NE 40th
Seattle, WA 98105
Telephone: 206-526-9677
AFFILIATIONS:
WCI
PRINCIPAL SUBJECTS:
Health
Youth
PUBLICATIONS:
Seattle Post Intelli Gencer
Seattle's Child
Christian Parenting Today

LOCKWOOD, GEORGENE
  MULLER
P.O. Box 433, 86 Taunton
  Lake Rd.
Newtown, CT 06470
Telephone: 203-426-8573
Fax: 203-426-4665

AFFILIATIONS:
ASJA, AG, IMPA, IWWG
PRINCIPAL SUBJECTS:
Computer Technology
History
Sports
Women's Interest
PUBLICATIONS:
Quilt Craft
Working Woman
Modern Bride
Country Decorator
Country Victorian Accents
Digital Review
Computer Graphics World

LOEBL, SUZANNE
788 Riverside Dr., Apt. 7E
New York, NY 10032
Telephone: 212-281-4065
AFFILIATIONS:
ASJA, NASW
PRINCIPAL SUBJECTS:
Health
PUBLICATIONS:
The New York Times
Parents
Science Digest
Dial
Rx Being Well

LONDON, BILL
P.O. Box 8152
Moscow, ID 83843
Telephone: 208-882-0127
AFFILIATIONS:
EWA, ASJA, NOWA
PRINCIPAL SUBJECTS:
Travel
Education
Human Interest
The Arts
Business & Industry
Book Reviews
Social Trends
PUBLICATIONS:
Northwest Living
Oh! Idaho
Western Outdoors
Trailerboats
Family Motor Coaching
World & I, The
Americas
Mothering

LOOMIS, JAMIE
1914 Wilson Ln., #203
Mc Lean, VA 22102
Telephone: 703-847-3120
MAILING ADDRESS:
Write Touch, The

P.O. Box 8212
Mc Lean, VA 22106
PRINCIPAL SUBJECTS:
Travel
Journalism
Personalities
Business & Industry
Nature
Medical
PUBLICATIONS:
Restaurants, USA
Fairfax Magazine

LORE, DIANE C.
54 Jerome Ave.
Staten Island, NY 10305
Telephone: 718-981-1234
Fax: 718-981-5679
MAILING ADDRESS:
Staten Island Advance
Staten Island, NY 10305
AFFILIATIONS:
SPJ, NYPC, News Women
  Club of NY
PRINCIPAL SUBJECTS:
Education
Human Interest
News
Government
PUBLICATIONS:
Sunday Advance
Staten Island Advance

LORENZ-FIFE, IRIS
Star Route P.O. Box 172-A
Woodside, CA 94062
Telephone: 415-747-0400
Fax: 415-747-0914
AFFILIATIONS:
ASJA, MCA, IFW, TWA, BWA
PRINCIPAL SUBJECTS:
Book Reviews
Business & Industry
Electronics
Family
Foreign
General Interest
Health
Hobbies
Home & Garden
Human Relations
Humor
Medical
Motivation
Personal Finance
Personalities
Physical Fitness
Psychology
Social Trends
The Arts
Travel

Women's Interest
World Affairs
PUBLICATIONS:
Views News Magazine
Small Business Success
Entrepreneurs
New Business Opportunities
Working Woman
Savvy

LOSCHIAVO, LINDA ANN
24 Fifth Avenue, #611
New York, NY 10011
Telephone: 212-477-0893
Fax: 703-931-8925
AFFILIATIONS:
ASJA, STD
PRINCIPAL SUBJECTS:
Amusements
Book Reviews
Business & Industry
Editorial
Entertainment
Family
Fashion
Foreign
General Interest
Health
Hobbies
Home & Garden
Human Interest
Journalism
Management
Marketing
Medical
Motivation
Movie Reviews
News
Personalities
Physical Fitness
Psychology
Science
Social Trends
Sports
Travel
Women's Interest
PUBLICATIONS:
Cosmopolitan
Better Home & Gardens
Modern Bride
New York News Magazine
New York Post
Seventeen
TWA Ambassador

LYHNE, BOB
247 Fulton St.
Palo Alto, CA 94301
Telephone: 000-000-0000

PRINCIPAL SUBJECTS:
Ecology
Human Interest
Book Reviews

LYNCH, PAT
2 Horatio St., #12N
New York, NY 10014
Telephone: 212-243-6386
PRINCIPAL SUBJECTS:
Journalism
Business & Industry
Travel
PUBLICATIONS:
US News & World Report
  (Former Correspondent)

LYON, DAVID
6 Crawford St., #11
Cambridge, MA 02139
Telephone: 617-864-0361
AFFILIATIONS:
NASW
PRINCIPAL SUBJECTS:
Science
Travel
PUBLICATIONS:
Boston Globe Magazine
Travel - Holiday
Atlantic Monthly
Readers Digest
Americas
Los Angeles Times
Yankee
Financial Times

LYONS, CHRISTINE
515 E 14 St., #9b
New York, NY 10009
Telephone: 212-475-5339
AFFILIATIONS:
ASJA, FPA, EFA
PRINCIPAL SUBJECTS:
Editorial
Family
Foreign
Health
Human Relations
Medical
News
Personalities
Travel
PUBLICATIONS:
Travel Agent Magazine
USA Today
New York Daily News
Bride's
Longevity
Chicago Sun
Boston Herald
Country Living

New York Times
Woman's World
Business Travel News
Incentive Magazine

MACDONALD, SANDY
421 Broadway
Cambridge, MA 02138
Telephone: 617-876-4046
Fax: 617-876-4046
PRINCIPAL SUBJECTS:
Travel
Book Reviews
Video
Family
Amusements
Architecture
Editorial
Education
Entertainment
Home & Garden
Media
The Arts
PUBLICATIONS:
Worth
Family Circle
Parenting
New York Times Book Review
Travel & Leisure
Ski
Family Fun
Child
Country Inns

MACKOWSKI, MAURA J.
7714 Aragorn Court
Hanover, MD 21076
Telephone: 410-519-0018
Fax: 410-519-0017
AFFILIATIONS:
AWA, NAWBO,
  AIAA, SPJ, NSS
PRINCIPAL SUBJECTS:
Science
Computer Technology
Business & Industry
Aviation
PUBLICATIONS:
Final Frontier
AD ASTRA
Illustreret Videnskab (Danish)
St. Louis Post - Dispatch
St. Louis Business Journal
Hispanic Business
CompuServe Magazine
Space Technology
  International (U.K.)
Space Technology Intl (British)
Computer Magazine (Belgian)

MALLETTE, MAL
2419 Silver Fox Ln.
Reston, VA 22091
Telephone: 703-860-2879
AFFILIATIONS:
AC
PRINCIPAL SUBJECTS:
Personalities
Animals
Sports
Travel
Health
Book Reviews
Editorial
Family
General Interest
Journalism
Media
Medical
Physical Fitness
Senior Citizens
Youth
PUBLICATIONS:
Better Homes and Gardens
Christian Science Monitor
Golf Magazine
Sports Illustrated
Time
Saturday Evening Post
Wall Street Journal
Los Angeles Times
St. Louis Post - Dispatch
St. Petersburg Times
Richmond Times - Dispatch
"presstime" Jrnl. of American
  Nwspaper Pub Assn
Handbook for Journalists of
  Central&Eastern Europe

MALOTT, GENE
250 E. Riverview Cir.
Reno, NV 89509
Telephone: 702-786-7419
AFFILIATIONS:
SATW, NFPW
PRINCIPAL SUBJECTS:
Travel
Senior Citizens
Personal Finance
PUBLICATIONS:
Midwest Living
Better Homes & Gardens
Home & Away
Friendly Exchange
Coast to Coast
The Mature Traveler
New York Times Syndicate
US Air Magazine
America West Magazine

MANDELL, PATRICIA
40 Ireland Rd.
Marshfield, MA 02050
Telephone: 617-837-3269
Fax: 617-837-3316
AFFILIATIONS:
ASJA, TJG
PRINCIPAL SUBJECTS:
General Interest
Travel
PUBLICATIONS:
Boston Globe
Denver Post
Washington Post
Baltimore Sun
Miami Herald
Yankee
Family Fun
Yankee Traveler
Americana

MANNERS, DAVID X.
237 East Rocks Rd.
Norwalk, CT 06851
Telephone: 203-846-2079
AFFILIATIONS:
Authors Guild
PRINCIPAL SUBJECTS:
Ecology
Home & Garden
Travel
PUBLICATIONS:
House Beautiful
Popular Science
Reader's Digest

MAPPES, DR. CARL R.
P.O. Box 633
Kimberling Cy, MO 65686
AFFILIATIONS:
ASMP, PPA, IPA
PRINCIPAL SUBJECTS:
General Interest
History
Business & Industry
Humor
Science
Travel
News

MARGOLIS, LYNNE
200 Shadyhill Road
Pittsburgh, PA 15205
Telephone: 412-222-2200
Fax: 412-225-2077
MAILING ADDRESS:
Lynne Margolis
122 S. Main St.
Washington, PA 15301
AFFILIATIONS:
SPJ, SDX

PRINCIPAL SUBJECTS:
The Arts
Entertainment
Human Interest
Journalism
Nature
Advertising
Amusements
Animals
Book Reviews
Ecology
Editorial
Humor
Marketing
Media
Movie Reviews
Personalities
Photography
Social Trends
Travel
Video
Women's Interest
PUBLICATIONS:
The Observer
Centre Daily Times
York Dispatch
York Daily Herald
Pittsburgh Post-Gazette
Pittsburgh News Weekly
Rockflash

MARGOLIUS, ESTHER
74 Davis Rd.
Prt Washingtn, NY 11050
Telephone: 516-944-6277
AFFILIATIONS:
NCL, NCSC
PRINCIPAL SUBJECTS:
Business & Industry
General Interest
Health
Personal Finance

MARKS, EDITH
35 W. 90th St.
New York, NY 10024
Telephone: 212-873-8661
Fax: 202-625-1999
AFFILIATIONS:
SPJWIW
PRINCIPAL SUBJECTS:
Education
General Interest
Health
PUBLICATIONS:
New York Times Travel Section
European Travel & Life

MARKS, JANE
3 Merriam Place
Bronxville, NY 10708

Telephone: 914-961-6061
AFFILIATIONS:
ASJA
PRINCIPAL SUBJECTS:
Family
Youth
Health
PUBLICATIONS:
Parent Magazine

MARKS, JASON
35 W. 90th St.
New York, NY 10024
Telephone: 212-873-9661
MAILING ADDRESS:
Marks, Jason
New York, NY 85100
PRINCIPAL SUBJECTS:
Travel
Women's Interest
PUBLICATIONS:
CEA Forum, The
Literary Review, The
New York Times, The
European Travel & Life

MARQUARDT, DEBORAH
812 Stockley Gardens, #1
Norfolk, VA 23507
Telephone: 804-622-1312
Fax: 804-622-7624
PRINCIPAL SUBJECTS:
Business & Industry
Medical
General Interest
PUBLICATIONS:
Virginia Business Magazine
Radiology Management
Family Circle
The New York Times
The Washington Post

MARSH, SUSAN
199 Ash St., #844
Denver, CO 80220
Telephone: 303-377-5380
MAILING ADDRESS:
Susan Marsh
111 Emerson St.
Denver, CO 80218
AFFILIATIONS:
AVS, AFM
PRINCIPAL SUBJECTS:
The Arts
Ecology
Family
General Interest
Sports
Travel
Senior Citizens

PUBLICATIONS:
Glamour
New York Times
Teaching, K-8
Grit
Denver Post
Grade Teacher
Nordic World
Empire Mag.
Journal of Geography
Music Journals
Trail and Timberline
My Weekly Reader

MARTIN, MILDRED CROWL
850 Webster St., #620
Palo Alto, CA 94301
Telephone: 415-328-8005
AFFILIATIONS:
CWC, NLAP
PRINCIPAL SUBJECTS:
Family
Government
Health
Personalities
Religion
General Interest
Human Relations
PUBLICATIONS:
Bride's Magazine
Family Circle
Parents'
Today's Health

MARTIN, NORMA MILNER
602 Washington St., S. -
Apt. 612
Philadelphia, PA 19106
Telephone: 215-925-4732
PRINCIPAL SUBJECTS:
Photography
Travel
Science
PUBLICATIONS:
Courier Post Cherry Hill,
NJ, The
Allegheny Airwaves
Photographic Society of
America Journal
Pinelands Commission
Newsletter, The
Pinelands Commission Annual
Report

MARZECKI, LONGIN W.
P.O. Box 202
Avenel, NJ 07001
Telephone: 908-634-7021
PRINCIPAL SUBJECTS:
General Interest
Government

History
Travel
Foreign
PUBLICATIONS:
National Fisherman
New York Times
Polish American World
New Brunswick (NJ) Sunday
  Home News
News Tribune, The
Independent - Leader
God's Field

MASARACCHIA, SUSAN
43 Crestview Terr.
Buffalo Grove, IL 60089
Telephone: 708-537-5010
AFFILIATIONS:
PCC, NWC, HCC, NAFE
PRINCIPAL SUBJECTS:
General Interest
Entertainment
Human Relations
Medical
Health
Human Interest
Marketing
Media
Personalities
Photography
Social Trends
Travel
Women's Interest
Youth
PUBLICATIONS:
Suburban Trib.
Chicago's Suburban Today
Daily Herald
Business Today
Calligranews
Sergeants
Contemporary Drama
  Svc./Meriwether Publishing
Progress Notes - Highland
  Park Hospital
Thermometer - Highland Park
  Hospital
Lerner Voice
Allergy Update
Graphic Arts Monthly
Nursing Spectrum (Illinois)
Chicago Tribune
In Business
In Nursing News

MASON, LEE FRANZ
8410 Madeline Dr.
Saint Louis, MO 63114
Telephone: 314-427-6311
AFFILIATIONS:
GWA, WC, NLAP

PRINCIPAL SUBJECTS:
Nature
General Interest
Travel
Photography
PUBLICATIONS:
Christian Science Monitor
St. Louis Post - Dispatch
Kansas City Star, Etc.
Modern Maturity
Catholic Digest
Missouri Life
Flower & Garden
Nature Journal, The
Hearthstone
Safer Motoring
Sunshine
Audubon Bulletins
St. Louis Magazine
Author & Journalist
Harvest Years
Rural Life
Midwest Motorist
Travel Magazine
Missouri Municipal Review
Independent Banker, The
Caribbean Traveler
Bluebird, The
Commerce Magazine
Photographer - Writer, The
Conservationist, The
Workshops
Photography Workshops

MASSEY, R. L.
1302 S. 8th St.
Edinburg, TX 78539
PRINCIPAL SUBJECTS:
Travel
Health
Home & Garden
Hobbies
General Interest
PUBLICATIONS:
Country Victorian
Rock and Gem
Trailer Life
Westways
Lets Live
Oregon Coast

MASSOW, ROSALIND
530 E. 72nd St., Apt. C-21
New York, NY 10021
Telephone: 212-879-4440
AFFILIATIONS:
SATW, NYTW, SD, OPC
PRINCIPAL SUBJECTS:
Travel
Health
General Interest

Women's Interest
Human Interest
Medical
Senior Citizens
PUBLICATIONS:
Modern Bride
N.Y. Times
Parade
New York News Magazine
Star
East/West Publications
Daily News
Medical/Mrs.
Boston Globe
Prov. Journal
Glamor
Toronto Star
Repetitions
Newark Star Ledger
Boston Herald
Travel Agent Magazine

MASTROLIA, LILYAN S.
4706 Cameron Ranch Dr.
Sacramento, CA 95841
Telephone: 916-488-2722
AFFILIATIONS:
NWU, CWC, AMWA, IFW, TWA
PRINCIPAL SUBJECTS:
Computer Technology
Business & Industry
Travel
Health
Amusements
Animals
Book Reviews
Entertainment
Family
General Interest
Hobbies
Human Interest
Human Relations
Humor
Media
Medical
Movie Reviews
Personal Finance
Personalities
Psychology
Science
Senior Citizens
Social Trends
The Arts
Travel
Video
PUBLICATIONS:
California Computer News
Science & Children
The Science Teacher
PC Travel Guide
The Executive

Business Journal
Scaramento To Bee & Union
Crime Monitor

MATHEWS, BEVERLY
2516 Arizona Ave., 4
Santa Monica, CA 90404
Telephone: 310-829-0590
AFFILIATIONS:
IFW&TWA, ASJA, CW
PRINCIPAL SUBJECTS:
Business & Industry
Senior Citizens
Family
Travel
General Interest
Human Interest
Women's Interest
PUBLICATIONS:
New York Newsday
Boston Herald
Boston Globe
LA Times
San Antonio Express-News
Denver Post
Chicago Sun Times
Milwaukee Sentinel
Fresno Bee
Grand Rapids Press
Houston Post
Huntsville Times
Knoxville News-Sentinel
Louisville Courier-Journal
Milwaukee Sentinel
Philadelphia Inquirer
Sacramento Bee
San Francisco Examiner
San Jose Mercury News
St. Paul Pioneer Press
  Dispatch

MATTHEWS, DOWNS
3501 Underwood St.
Houston, TX 77025
Telephone: 713-664-3937
Fax: 713-664-5180
AFFILIATIONS:
ASJA, TJG, IABC, OWAA
PRINCIPAL SUBJECTS:
Animals
Business & Industry
Nature
Science
PUBLICATIONS:
Smithsonian
Popular Photography
Town and Country
Sports Illustrated

Wildlife Conservation
Destination Discovery
Christian Science Monitor
Exxon Lamp

MATURI, RICHARDS J.
1320 Curt Gowdy Drive
Cheyenne, WY 82009
Telephone: 307-638-2254
AFFILIATIONS:
ASJA, AG, WMP, DPC
PRINCIPAL SUBJECTS:
Business & Industry
General Interest
Human Interest
Management
Marketing
Men's Interest
Personal Finance
Fashion
PUBLICATIONS:
Barron's
Your Money
Technical Analysis
New York Times
Kiplinger's Personal
  Finance Mag.
Investigate
Crain's
Akron Beacon
Institutional Investor
Chief Executive
Cleveland Plain Dealer
Cleveland Magazine
Personal Finance
Denver Post
Research
Investor's Business Daily
American History Illustrated
Industry Week
Entrepreneur
Executive Wealth Advisory
American Woman
Area Development
Business Cleveland
Global Finance
Ohio Business
Corporate Cleveland
Executive Living
CSU Magazine
Northern Ohio Live
Medical Tribune
Physician's Financial News
Institutional Research
Independent Business
Your Company
Crain's Cleveland Business
Denver Business Journal

MATUSIK, JO ELLEN
69 Union Ave.
Saratoga Spring, NY 12866
Telephone: 518-583-7425
PRINCIPAL SUBJECTS:
Travel
Personalities
General Interest
History
PUBLICATIONS:
New York Alive
Adirondack Life
Saratoga Style
Local & Regional Newspapers
Vista USA
Old House Journal

MAXWELL, KATIE
4851 Cypress Ave.
Carmichael, CA 95608
Telephone: 916-484-0877
Fax: 916-484-1454
AFFILIATIONS:
CWC, ASJA, NWU, IRE
PRINCIPAL SUBJECTS:
Agriculture
Psychology
Travel
PUBLICATIONS:
Family Motor Coaching
Sacramento Bee
Los Angeles Times
Virtue
Produce News
New York Daily News

MAYER, BARBARA
53 Cross Pond Rd.
Pound Ridge, NY 10576
Telephone: 914-763-5895
AFFILIATIONS:
AG, ASJA
PRINCIPAL SUBJECTS:
Architecture
Family
Home & Garden
Social Trends
The Arts
Women's Interest
PUBLICATIONS:
Elle Decor
Town & Country
Art & Antiques
Better Homes & Gardens

MAYNARD, JOANNA
3428 Hughes Ave.
Girard, OH 44420
Telephone: 216-530-9678
MAILING ADDRESS:
Maynard, JoAnna

3438 Hughes Ave.
Girard, OH 44420
PRINCIPAL SUBJECTS:
Journalism

MAYNARD, MARY
134 Wellesley St.
Weston, MA 02193
Telephone: 617-889-0605
PRINCIPAL SUBJECTS:
Women's Interest
Travel
History
PUBLICATIONS:
Equal Times
Sojourner
New Directions For Women
Ms.
Boston Magazine
Weston Town Crier
Radcliffe Quarterly
Sojourner
New Directions for Women
Downtown Gazette
Middlesex News
Boston Globe, The
Hassle - Free Boston
  (For Women) - Lewis Pub.
Island Hopping in New
  England (Yankee
  Books, Pub.)
Pilgrim Script (Magazine of
  Traveler's Info.)
Open House in New England
  (Yankee Books, Pub.)

MAZIE, DAVID
3308 Glenmoor Drive
Chevy Chase, MD 20815
Telephone: 301-652-6511
Fax: 202-966-8668
AFFILIATIONS:
SPJ, WIW
PRINCIPAL SUBJECTS:
Government
Education
Family
Editorial
Foreign
Human Interest
Senior Citizens
Social Trends
Travel
Urban Affairs
World Affairs
Youth
PUBLICATIONS:
World Bank Reports
Washington Post
Readers Digest

MCCANN, BRIAN & JEAN
Medical News Inc.
2980 Berkshire Rd.
Cleveland, OH 44118
Telephone: 216-932-8027
MAILING ADDRESS:
McCann, Brian & Jean
Medical News Inc.
P.O. Box 8600
Cleveland, OH 44118
Fax: 216-932-8025

MCCARTNEY, LUCINDA L.
P.O. Box 1027
Palmetto, FL 34220
Telephone: 813-746-9071
Fax: 813-749-5141
AFFILIATIONS:
ASJA, NAREE, FOWA, NWC
PRINCIPAL SUBJECTS:
Business & Industry
Ecology
Home & Garden
Management
Marine
Nature
Personal Finance
PUBLICATIONS:
Consumers Digest
Your Money
Sylvia Porter Personal Finance
TWA Ambassador
Family Motor Coaching
Saltwater Sportsman
Southern Rv-Ing

MCCLENDON, SARAH
3133 Connecticut Ave.,
  N.W., #215
Washington, DC 20008
Telephone: 202-483-3791
Fax: 202-483-7918
AFFILIATIONS:
NPC, ANWC, WC, SDC, NFPW
PRINCIPAL SUBJECTS:
Government
Human Interest
Military
Women's Interest
PUBLICATIONS:
Esquire
Penthouse
Pageant
Ladycom
Stars and Stripes
Diplomat
Maturity Outlook

MCCOMB, GORDON
2642 Hope St.
Oceanside, CA 92056

Telephone: 619-941-6632
PRINCIPAL SUBJECTS:
Computer Technology
Video
Media
Photography
PUBLICATIONS:
Popular Science
Omni
Electronics Now
PC Magazine
Family Handyman
Video Magazine
Mac User
MacWorld
Computer Buyer's Guide

MCCORMICK, MICHELE
8273 Plumeria Ave.
Fair Oaks, CA 95628
Telephone: 916-736-6900
MAILING ADDRESS:
Michele McCormick
1529 28th St.
Sacramento, CA 95816
AFFILIATIONS:
ASJA
PRINCIPAL SUBJECTS:
Editorial
General Interest
Health
Humor
Management
Marketing
Military
Senior Citizens
PUBLICATIONS:
Army Times Newspaper
People Magazine
Writer's Digest
International Herald Tribune
Newsweek
Philadelphia Inquirer
Wall Street Journal, The
America West
Navy Times Newspaper
Air Force Times Newspaper

MCDERMOTT, MICHAEL J.
Horsepound Rd.
Carmel, NY 10512
Telephone: 914-225-9426
Fax: 914-225-9472
AFFILIATIONS:
ASJA, MENSA
PRINCIPAL SUBJECTS:
General Interest
Business & Industry
PUBLICATIONS:
Auto Week
Consumer Electronics Daily

Chain Drug Review
Audio Sound &
  Communications
Audio Times
Mass Market Retailers
Crain's New York Business
Video Store Magazine
Sports Illustrated
Popular Mechanics
Continental Profiles
Prodigy

MCDONALD, MAUREEN
820 E. Fifth St.
Royal Oak, MI 48067
Telephone: 313-548-8013
Fax: 313-548-2829
PRINCIPAL SUBJECTS:
Automotive
Business & Industry
PUBLICATIONS:
Automotive News
American Women Motorsports
American Bicyclist
Michigan Living
New York Times
Detroit Free Press
Tampa Bay Magazine
Detroiter

MCDOWELL, LEONARD O.
P.O. Box 593
Florence, AL 35631
Telephone: 205-767-7082
MAILING ADDRESS:
Leonard O. McDowell
Florence, AL 35631
AFFILIATIONS:
SMF
PRINCIPAL SUBJECTS:
Health
Human Relations
Religion
Personalities
PUBLICATIONS:
The Interpreter
Christian Times
Christian Advocate
Pulpit Digest
Today's Youth
Christianity Today
Florence District Connection

MCDOWELL-LYNCH, JUNE
8615 Rockwood Lane, 130
Austin, TX 78757
Telephone: 512-371-9634
PRINCIPAL SUBJECTS:
Foreign
PUBLICATIONS:
Dallas Morning News

MCGRADY JR., PATRICK M.
221 West 82nd St.
New York, NY 10024
Telephone: 212-724-6990
MAILING ADDRESS:
Patrick M. McGrady, Jr.
3111 Paradise Bay Rd.
Port Ludlow, WA 98365
Telephone: 206-437-2291
AFFILIATIONS:
ASJA
PRINCIPAL SUBJECTS:
Health
PUBLICATIONS:
Esquire
Family Circle
Ladies' Home Journal
Reader's Digest
Vogue
Woman's Day

MCKENZIE, J. NORMAN
155 Lansdowne St.
North Quincy, MA 02171
Telephone: 617-328-1635
PRINCIPAL SUBJECTS:
Business & Industry
Government
Sports
Travel
Home & Garden
General Interest
Book Reviews
PUBLICATIONS:
Boating Magazine
Ford Times
Washington Post
Baltimore Sun
Wall Street Journal
Boston Sunday Globe
Boston Herald
Worcester Sun. Telegram
Milwaukee Journal
Cincinnati Enquirer
Motorboat
Newsday
Columbia
Catholic Digest
Elks Magazine
Quihcy Patriot Ledger
Christian Science Monitor
Milwaukee Sentinel
Portland Oregonian
Denver Post
Los Angeles Times
San Francisco Examiner
Dallas Morning News
Delta's Sky
Chicago Sun-Times
The American Way
TV Guide

Grit
Wall Street Journal
Yankee
Buffalo News
Mature Living
Washington (D.C.) Times
Good Old Days
Sports Illustrated
Lutheran Digest
Touring Times
Omaha World-Herald
Philadelphia Inquirer
St. Louis Post-Dispatch
Arizona Republic
Tacoma News-Tribune
Drug Topics
The Army Times
Navy Times
San Jose (CA) Mercury News
Offshore Magazine
San Diego (CA) Union
New Hampshire Profiles
Air Force Times
Providence R.I. Sunday Jrnl.
Christian Single
Detroit Free Press

MCKEON, KEVIN
32 - 15 41st, #E4
Long Is City, NY 11103
Telephone: 718-204-0798
PRINCIPAL SUBJECTS:
General Interest
Social Trends
Government
Business & Industry
PUBLICATIONS:
American Way
Echelon
Delta Sky

MCKEOWN, WM. TAYLOR
2 Park Ave.
New York, NY 10016
Telephone: 212-779-5259
Fax: 212-686-6877
MAILING ADDRESS:
Wm. T. McKeown,
  Cmpt Trvl Inf.
52 Monell Pl.
Beacon, NY 12508
PRINCIPAL SUBJECTS:
Travel
Marine
Nature
PUBLICATIONS:
N.Y. Times
Esquire
Motor Boating & Sailing
Popular Mechanics
NEA

Yachting
Travel/Holiday
Family Handyman
Outdoor Life
Popular Science

MCKINNEY, SALLY BROWN
1014 Lindberg Rd.
West Lafayette, IN 47906
Telephone: 317-497-4456
MAILING ADDRESS:
Syndicated Travel Features
P.O. Box 809
Lafayette, IN 47902
AFFILIATIONS:
SATW
PRINCIPAL SUBJECTS:
Travel
PUBLICATIONS:
Asia Pacific Travel
Pacific Way (New Zealand)
Tours and Resorts
Endless Vacation
New Orleans Times Picayune
Cleveland Plain Dealer
London Free Press (Canada)
The Straits Times (Singapore)
Far East Traveler (Japan)
Women's Out-door Journal
Tai Pan (Hong Kong, Manila)
Purdue Alumnus
Innsider Magazine
Indiana Alumni
LA Times
Boston Globe
S.F. Examiner

MCMAHON, KAREN
1221 Oak Park Blvd.
Cedar Falls, IA 50613
Telephone: 319-277-2255
Fax: 310-277-2255
AFFILIATIONS:
AAE (American Assoc. of
   Agriculture Editors)
PRINCIPAL SUBJECTS:
Agriculture
PUBLICATIONS:
Farm Journal
Hogs Today
Dairy Today

MCMORROW, TOM
245 E. 40th St.
New York, NY 10016
Telephone: 212-490-3642
MAILING ADDRESS:
Tom Mc Morrow
New York, NY 10016

AFFILIATIONS:
The Drama Guild, American
   Theater Critic Asoc.
PRINCIPAL SUBJECTS:
Entertainment
Sports
PUBLICATIONS:
Modern Maturity
TV Guide
New York Sunday News
New York Daily News
New York City Magazine
Smart Living

MCNAIR, MARCIA L.
P.O. Box 1058
Jamaica, NY 11431
Telephone: 718-217-1408
AFFILIATIONS:
SIGMA/DELTA/CHI
PRINCIPAL SUBJECTS:
Human Interest
Education
PUBLICATIONS:
Essence
Ms. Magazine
Black Collegian

MCNEES, PAT
10643 Weymouth St., #204
Bethesda, MD 20814
Telephone: 301-897-8557
Fax: 301-897-8569
AFFILIATIONS:
AG, PEN, ASJA
PRINCIPAL SUBJECTS:
Amusements
Education
Business & Industry
Family
Human Interest
Psychology
Social Trends
Travel
PUBLICATIONS:
Washington Post
New York Magazine
Parents
Savvy

MCPHEE, MARNIE
4203 S.E. Cora St.
Portland, OR 97206
Telephone: 503-775-8951
Fax: 503-235-3549
MAILING ADDRESS:
Marnie McPhee
Portland, OR 97206
AFFILIATIONS:
NWIN

PRINCIPAL SUBJECTS:
Travel
Agriculture
Health
Nature
Marine
Personalities
Ecology
Book Reviews
Women's Interest
Youth
PUBLICATIONS:
Popular Science
Organic Gardening
Country Journal
Oregonian, The
Northwest Magazine
Willamette Week
Weekly, The
Washington Magazine
Oregon Magazine
Willamette Valley Observer
Capital Press
Focus Oregon
National Geographic Traveler
Harrowsmith Country Life
Organic (Sp)
Organic Gardening
New Product News
Prepared Foods
Organic Times
Oregon Coast Magazine
Northwest Travel

MCVAY, ROSANNE
242 E. 15th St.
New York, NY 10003
Telephone: 212-475-6084
AFFILIATIONS:
OPC
PRINCIPAL SUBJECTS:
Senior Citizens
Health
Fashion
Family
PUBLICATIONS:
True Story
Collier's
SEP
Coronet
Medical Economics
Glamour

MEEKER, EUNICE JUCKETT
66 Davids Ln.,P.O. Box 1110
East Hampton, NY 11937
Telephone: 516-324-0645
MAILING ADDRESS:
Timely Travel
P.O. Box 1110
East Hampton, NY 11937

PRINCIPAL SUBJECTS:
Hobbies
Human Relations
History
Travel
Foreign
Family
Fashion
Women's Interest
PUBLICATIONS:
Travel
Los Angeles Times
NY Times
Chattanooga Free Press
Dallas Times Herald
Country
Coast to Coast
Chicago Sun Times
Toronto Star
San Diego Union
American Motorist
Travel Agent Magazine
Country Living
L.A. Times
Cruise Travel
Kaleidoscope TV
Miami Herald
Country Magazine
Maryland Magazine

MENKUS, BELDEN
P.O. Box 129
Hillsboro, TN 37342
Telephone: 615-728-2421
MAILING ADDRESS:
Belden Menkus
Hillsboro, TN 37342
Telephone: 615-728-2853
PRINCIPAL SUBJECTS:
Business & Industry
General Interest
Management
Computer Technology
Religion
PUBLICATIONS:
Journal of Systems
   Management
Banking Journal
Dun's Business Months
Accounting Today
Government Computer News
Inform
Computerworld
Christianity Today

MEOLA, PATRICIA E.
29 Lowell Avenue
Summit, NJ 07901
Telephone: 908-273-4424
Fax: 908-464-0973

AFFILIATIONS:
NJPW, NFPW, NJPC
PRINCIPAL SUBJECTS:
Architecture
Book Reviews
Editorial
Education
Entertainment
Family
General Interest
Government
Hobbies
Home & Garden
Human Interest
Humor
Journalism
Media
Men's Interest
News
Personalities
Travel
Women's Interest
Youth
PUBLICATIONS:
The Star-Ledger
The Independent Press
New York Yankees Magazine
World's Fair Collectors Society
  Magazine
The Herald/Dispatch

MEROWITZ, MORTON J.
71 N. MAPLEMERE RD.
WILLIAMSVILLE, NY 14221
Telephone: 716-631-5684
PRINCIPAL SUBJECTS:
Religion
History
PUBLICATIONS:
Buffalo Jewish Review
Midstream
Religious Education
Journal of the American
  Academy of Religion
Religious Studies Review
Judaism
SEE AD IN SECTION 2

MERWIN, PHILIP DEAN
21 Elm St.
Great Neck, NY 11021
Telephone: 516-487-9209
PRINCIPAL SUBJECTS:
Health, Medical
Personalities
PUBLICATIONS:
The NYU Physician

MESSINEO, JOHN
P.O. Box 1636-A
Ft. Collins, CO 80522

Telephone: 303-482-9349
AFFILIATIONS:
OWAA
PRINCIPAL SUBJECTS:
Agriculture
Animals
Automotive
Book Reviews
Ecology
Nature
Photography
Travel
Youth
PUBLICATIONS:
Canoe
Colorado Outdoors
Rocky Mountain Game & Fish
Farm Pond Harvest
Fur-Fish-Game
Fishing & Hunting News
On The Line
Studio Photography

MESSNER, FRED R.
MESSNER MARKETING
  COMMUNICATIONS
30 RAVINE DR.
WOODCLIFF LAKE, NJ 07675
Telephone: 201-391-5488
Fax: 201-391-0676
AFFILIATIONS:
BPAA, ASCAP
PRINCIPAL SUBJECTS:
Advertising
Marketing
Media
The Arts
PUBLICATIONS:
Advertising Age
Journal of Marketing
Ad Week
Business Marketing

MEYERS, CAROLE
  TERWILLIGER
P.O. Box 6061
Albany, CA 94706
Telephone: 510-527-5849
AFFILIATIONS:
IFWA
PRINCIPAL SUBJECTS:
Family
Travel
PUBLICATIONS:
Oakland Tribune
San Jose Mercury News -
  Columnist
Sacramento Bee
California Living Magazine
San Francisco Magazine

New West Magazine
Oakland Magazine
Parents' Press-Columnist
California Magazine Columnist
Family Circle
Goodlife Magazine-Columnist
San Francisco Focus
  Magazine - Columnist
California Traveler
Family Travel Times
Image Magazine
San Francisco Chronicle
West Magazine
Diablo Magazine
San Francisco Examiner -
  Columnist
SF Magazine
New Choices Magazine
Bay Area Parent
Motorland
Family Fun
Parenting Magazine

MICHAEL, JOYCE EMMETT
440 Lake St.
Crystal Lake, IL 60014
Telephone: 815-477-3661
AFFILIATIONS:
CPC
PRINCIPAL SUBJECTS:
News
Business & Industry
Personalities
News
Science
Entertainment
PUBLICATIONS:
Chicago Tribune
The Reader
Shoot to Miss
Voice of America

MILLER AND MARK ELLIS
  MILLER, JUDITH BRAFFMAN
1149 Partridge Avenue
St. Louis, MO 63130
Telephone: 314-725-1229
AFFILIATIONS:
ASJA, IRE
PRINCIPAL SUBJECTS:
Foreign
General Interest
Government
Health
Human Interest
News
Science
Social Trends
Urban Affairs
Women's Interest
World Affairs

PUBLICATIONS:
America
Chicago Sun-Times
Consumer Reports
Field Newspaper Syndicate
The Humanist
Sepia
King Features Syndicate
Ms.
New York
Oui
St. Louis Post Dispatch
San Jose Mercury News
San Jose Studies
Trial
Woman
Woman's World
USA Today

MILLER, BRUCE
515 Pavonia St.
Sioux City, IA 51101
Telephone: 712-279-5075
Fax: 712-275-5059
AFFILIATIONS:
NPPW
PRINCIPAL SUBJECTS:
Home & Garden
Travel
Business & Industry
Hobbies
Entertainment
Video
The Arts
Fashion
Media
Management
PUBLICATIONS:
Sioux City Journal
Boston Globe

MILLER, CATHERINE
  LANHAM
5140 Gentry Ln.
Carson City, NV 89701
Telephone: 702-883-9618
PRINCIPAL SUBJECTS:
Family
Human Interest
Women's Interest
Youth
Travel
PUBLICATIONS:
Dynamic Maturity
Good Housekeeping
Ladies' Home Journal
McCalls
Harper's Bazaar
House Beautiful
Nevada Appeal,
  (Carson City, Nv)

The Daily Leader,
  (Frederick, Ok)
The Daily News,
  (Greensburg, In)
Photo Marketing Magazine
Bonanza, The, (Incline
  Village, NV)
Carson Chronicle,
  (Carson City, NV)
Prime Times

MILLER, DOROTHY G.
6726 Sulky Ln.
Rockville, MD 20852
Telephone: 301-881-4241
PRINCIPAL SUBJECTS:
Medical
Business & Industry
PUBLICATIONS:
PMA Newsletter
Adolescent Medicine
HLB Newsletter

MILLMAN, SANDY K.
7 Adriance Ave.
Poughkeepsie, NY 12601
Telephone: 212-725-1593
AFFILIATIONS:
GWAA
PRINCIPAL SUBJECTS:
Travel
Sports
Medical
History
Health
Business & Industry
PUBLICATIONS:
N.Y. Post
Newsday
Boston Herald American
Hudson Valley Magazine
Miami Herald
N.Y. Times
Philadelphia Enquirer
Miami News
Denver Post
Hartford Courant
Japan Times
Wall St. Journal
People Magazine
Sporting Goods Business
Diversions
Brooklyn Home Reporter
Kings Courier
Buffalo Courier - Express

MILLNER, CORK
3375 Foothill Road #1011
Carpinteria, CA 93013
Telephone: 805-684-6939

AFFILIATIONS:
ASJA
PRINCIPAL SUBJECTS:
Aviation
Entertainment
Fashion
Personalities
Travel
PUBLICATIONS:
Playboy
Saturday Evening Post
LA Times
Seventeen
Diversion
Delta Sky
Wine World
Wine Country

MILNE, DR. MARGERY
One Garden Lane
Durham, NH 03824
Telephone: 603-868-2794
AFFILIATIONS:
SWG
PRINCIPAL SUBJECTS:
Science
Ecology
Travel
PUBLICATIONS:
Audubon Magazine
National Geographic
New York Times
American Scholar
Arizona Highways
Atlantic Mo.
Christian Science Monitor
Harvard Mag.
Internat'l
Wildlife
London Illustrated News
Sat. Eve. Post
Country Jour.
New Hampshire Profiles
Writer, The
Science
Juveniles
Readers Digest

MILNE, ROBERT SCOTT
Waldorf-Astoria, Suite 1850,
  301 Park Ave.
New York, NY 10022
Telephone: 212-759-6744
Fax: 212-758-9209
AFFILIATIONS:
SATW, TJG, NYTWA, FIJET,
  MA, IFWTWA
PRINCIPAL SUBJECTS:
Book Reviews
Ecology
Foreign

General Interest
Journalism
Marine
Media
The Arts
Travel
PUBLICATIONS:
Travelwriter Marketletter
Atlantic Monthly
Vista USA
Travel Agent
Seventeen
Cruise Travel
Exxon Travel Guide

MINKOW, ROSALIE
69 Essex Court
Prt Washingtn, NY 11050
Telephone: 516-944-8239
MAILING ADDRESS:
R.H. Minkow Associates
AFFILIATIONS:
ASJA, AG
PRINCIPAL SUBJECTS:
Personal Finance
Business & Industry
PUBLICATIONS:
Better Home & Gardens
Working Woman
N.Y. Times

MIRVIS, KENNETH W.
86 Rosedale Road
Watertown, MA 02172
Telephone: 617-924-7122
Fax: 617-923-4195
PRINCIPAL SUBJECTS:
Nature
Education
General Interest
Science
PUBLICATIONS:
Christian Science Monitor
Atlanta Magazine
Old Farmer's Almanac
Boston Globe
Yankee Magazine
Landscape Architecture

MIX, SHELDON A.
18 S. Home Ave.
Park Ridge, IL 60068
Telephone: 708-692-2448
PRINCIPAL SUBJECTS:
Business & Industry
Editorial
Human Interest
History
Sports
Nature
Architecture

Book Reviews
General Interest
Health
History
Hobbies
Management
Travel
PUBLICATIONS:
Baseball Digest
Discover
Chicago Tribune
Christian Science Monitor
American Way (American
  Airlines Magazine)
Milwaukee Journal
Chicago Sun-Times
Wall Street Journal
Toastmaster, The
AB Bookman's Weekly
The Cubs Reader

**MOATES, MARIANNE
  MERRILL**
640 Peckerwood Creek Trail
Sylacauge, AL 35150
Telephone: 205-249-4225
AFFILIATIONS:
ASJA
PRINCIPAL SUBJECTS:
Health
Human Relations
Advertising
Education
Family
Health
Social Trends
Women's Interest
PUBLICATIONS:
Seventeen
Writers Digest
Birmingham News
Mind And Body
Artline

MOFFAT, SHANNON
3484 Cowper Court
Palo Alto, CA 94306
Telephone: 415-494-2810
AFFILIATIONS:
NASW, ASJA, AMWA
PRINCIPAL SUBJECTS:
Health
Science
PUBLICATIONS:
Scientific American Medicine
Hospital Practice
The Stanford Magazine
Modern Medicine

MOLDAFSKY, ANNIE
1787 St. Johns Avenue
Highland Park, IL 60035
Telephone: 708-432-2940
AFFILIATIONS:
ASJA, AG, SPJ
PRINCIPAL SUBJECTS:
Architecture
Family
Foreign
Health
History
Management
Marketing
Men's Interest
Personal Finance
Personalities
Senior Citizens
Social Trends
The Arts
Travel
Women's Interest
Youth
PUBLICATIONS:
Syslvia Porter Personal
  Finance
Consumer's Digest
Family Circle
Working Mother
Success
Chicago Tribune
Milwaukee Journal

MONROE, KEITH
11965 Montana Ave.
Los Angeles, CA 90049
Telephone: 310-826-2685
AFFILIATIONS:
OPC
PRINCIPAL SUBJECTS:
Business & Industry
Entertainment
General Interest
Sports
PUBLICATIONS:
Boys' Life
N.Y. Times
Reader's Digest
Scouting Magazine
Harpers Magazine
New Yorker
The Rotarian Magazine

MONSON, NANCY P.
425 Country Club Lane
Pomona, NY 10970
Telephone: 914-354-2097
Fax: 914-354-8486
AFFILIATIONS:
ASJA

PRINCIPAL SUBJECTS:
Entertainment
Family
General Interest
Health
Hobbies
Human Relations
Medical
Physical Fitness
Psychology
The Arts
Travel
Women's Interest
PUBLICATIONS:
Glamour
Redbook
First for Women
Fitness
New Woman
Health Watch
Beauty

MONTGOMERY, ED
1525 Franklin Dr.
Norman, OK 73072
Telephone: 405-366-4542
AFFILIATIONS:
SPJ
PRINCIPAL SUBJECTS:
Government
Humor
Personalities
Sports
PUBLICATIONS:
Argosy
Field & Stream
Saturday Evening Post

MOON, BEN L.
112 Hamp Chappell Rd.
Carrollton, GA 30117
Telephone: 706-854-8458
PRINCIPAL SUBJECTS:
Business & Industry
Agriculture
Aviation
PUBLICATIONS:
Data Processing (IBM)
Progressive Farmer
Successful Farming
TOM On - Line
Southern Living
Guideposts

MOORE, DIANNE
509 1/2 Lake St.
Cadillac, MI 49601
Telephone: 616-775-9169
MAILING ADDRESS:
Dianne Moore
Cadillac, MI 49601

AFFILIATIONS:
ASJA
PRINCIPAL SUBJECTS:
Family
General Interest
Health
Human Relations
Women's Interest
PUBLICATIONS:
Complete Woman
Women's World
Baby Talk
Business Today
New Choices
Single Parent
Redbook

MORGAN, ARJAY
8815 EDGEWOOD BLVD.
TAMPA, FL 33635
Telephone: 813-885-7760
PRINCIPAL SUBJECTS:
Computer Technology
Marine
Travel
Business & Industry
News
PUBLICATIONS:
Data Bus
American Way
Telephony
Printing Impressions
Tampa Bay Life
Lan Times
Omni; Heavy Truck
Salesman
** (Technology Columnist)**
Food Business
West Coast Woman
Trading Partners
Reuters News Service
Christian Science Monitor

MORGAN, JOHN S.
302 Fox Chapel Rd., #516
Pittsburgh, PA 15238
Telephone: 412-782-4734
MAILING ADDRESS:
John S. Morgan,
  Advcy. Comm.
P.O. Box 11441
Pittsburgh, PA 15238
AFFILIATIONS: PPA
PRINCIPAL SUBJECTS:
Business & Industry
General Interest
Management
PUBLICATIONS:
Litton

MORGAN, MURRAY
4505 S. 376th St., (Trout Lake)
Auburn, WA 98001
Telephone: 206-927-2384
PRINCIPAL SUBJECTS:
Marine
History
PUBLICATIONS:
American Heritage
Esquire
Readers Digest
American West
Harpers
Pacific Northwest Quarterly

MORGAN, NEIL
7930 Prospect Pl.
La Jolla, CA 92037
Telephone: 619-293-1301
Fax: 619-293-2443
MAILING ADDRESS:
San Diego Union-Tribune
P.O. Box 191
San Diego, CA 92112
AFFILIATIONS:
AG, ASMC, SPJ, SATW
PRINCIPAL SUBJECTS:
General Interest
Travel
World Affairs
PUBLICATIONS:
Esquire
Harper's
National Geographic
Reader's Digest
Saturday Review
Travel & Leisure
Copley Newspapers
Westward Tilt

MORLAND, ALVIN
2326 NE 29th St.
Pompano Beach, FL 33064
Telephone: 305-942-7410
Fax: 305-532-5027
AFFILIATIONS:
ASJA, FFWA
PRINCIPAL SUBJECTS:
Travel
History
Military
PUBLICATIONS:
Boston Globe
Houston Post
Miami Herald
New York Newsday
Touring America
Toronto Globe & Mail
Dallas News
Oceans Magazine
American Airlines

Florida Living
Army, Navy, Air Force Times
Stars & Stripes

MORRILL, STEPHEN
2105 Watrous Ave.
Tampa, FL 33606
Telephone: 813-251-8087
Fax: 813-251-8087
AFFILIATIONS:
ASJA
PRINCIPAL SUBJECTS:
Architecture
Ecology
General Interest
History
Home & Garden
Human Interest
Humor
Journalism
Marine
Nature
News
PUBLICATIONS:
New York Times Magazine
Vista
Historic Preservation
Florida Business
Reuters
Business Age
Robb Report
Horizon

MORRIS, GLEN
1306 150th St.
Hammond, IN 46327
Telephone: 219-931-9175
PRINCIPAL SUBJECTS:
Religion
Human Interest
Family
Human Relations
PUBLICATIONS:
Pen Pal Newsletter
Entrepreneur Digest
Mail Order Messenger
Mail Profits Magazine

MORRIS, HAL
6633 Sherbourne Dr.
Los Angeles, CA 90056
Telephone: 213-776-4998
AFFILIATIONS:
ABWA
PRINCIPAL SUBJECTS:
Travel
Business & Industry
General Interest
Personalities
PUBLICATIONS:
The Christian Science Monitor

Business Travel News
USA Today
Independent Banker
Nation's Business
American Way
Family Circle
Destination
TWA Ambassador
Travel & Leisure
Woman's Own

MORRIS, MRS. TERRY
200 Central Park South
New York, NY 10019
Telephone: 212-247-5476
AFFILIATIONS:
ASJA
PRINCIPAL SUBJECTS:
Health
Human Relations
Medical
PUBLICATIONS:
Family Circle
Good Housekeeping
McCall's
Redbook

MOSKIN, J. ROBERT
945 Fifth Ave.
New York, NY 10021
Telephone: 212-288-1166
AFFILIATIONS:
ASJA, OPC, NPC
PRINCIPAL SUBJECTS:
Government
Health
History
Personalities
World Affairs
PUBLICATIONS:
World Press Review
Travel & Leisure
Present Tense
Saturday Review
Look
Reader's Digest
Town & Country

MOSLEY, JEAN BELL
703 E. Rodney Dr.
Cpe Girardeau, MO 63701
Telephone: 314-335-8141
AFFILIATIONS:
GFWC
PRINCIPAL SUBJECTS:
Family
Philosophy
Religion
General Interest
PUBLICATIONS:
Guideposts

Reader's Digest
Southeast Missourian
Tipoff
Daily Word
Southeast Missourian
   Newspaper

MOST, BRUCE W.
2983 S. Willow St.
Denver, CO 80231
Telephone: 303-755-1030
Fax: 303-755-1030
AFFILIATIONS:
ASJA
PRINCIPAL SUBJECTS:
Science
Social Trends
Business & Industry
Personal Finance
PUBLICATIONS:
Parade
Family Weekly
TV Guide
Signature
American Way
Ford Times
Popular Science
Popular Mechanics
Travel & Leisure
Western's World
Modern Maturity
Friends
New York Times, The
Washington Post, The

MOWRY, SERENA BLODGETT
20 Kingswood Dr.
N Stonington, CT 06359
Telephone: 203-535-1940
MAILING ADDRESS:
Serena Blodgett Mowry
N Stonington, CT 06359
PRINCIPAL SUBJECTS:
Government
Education
PUBLICATIONS:
Saturday Evening Post - "Be a
   Sensible Boy"
The Instructor
Croydon Advertiser - "Over the
   Way in the U.S.A."
Croydon
Wall Street Journal, Feb. 1991

MOYLAN, TOM
1715 Elmhurst Dr.
Whitehall, PA 18052
Telephone: 215-799-0839
PRINCIPAL SUBJECTS:
Business & Industry
Science

PUBLICATIONS:
Morning Call, The,
   (Allentown PA)
Emergency Magazine,
   (Carlsbad CA)
Associated Press

MUMMERT, ROGER
7 Evergreen Dr.
Syosset, NY 11791
Telephone: 516-364-8020
Fax: 516-364-8021
PRINCIPAL SUBJECTS:
Travel
Health
Family
Agriculture
Marketing
PUBLICATIONS:
New York Times
New York Magazine
Manhattan, Inc.
Penthouse
Cook's Magazine
Success
Travel & Leisure
Food & Wine
Wine & Food Companion
Sidestreets of The World
Parenting
Omni

MURPHY, RAYMOND J.
184 Sheffield Bldg H
West Palm Bch, FL 33417
Telephone: 407-640-0174
PRINCIPAL SUBJECTS:
Business & Industry
Human Relations
Philosophy
Travel
World Affairs
Education
PUBLICATIONS:
America
Pageant
Parade
Business Education World
Woman's World

MURPHY, WENDY B.
109 Geer Mountain Road
South Kent, CT 06785
Telephone: 203-927-3364
Fax: 203-927-3234
AFFILIATIONS:
ASJA
PRINCIPAL SUBJECTS:
Agriculture
Business & Industry
Health

Home & Garden
Medical
PUBLICATIONS:
Horizon
American Heritage
Cosmopolitan
McCalls
Horticulture
Remedy

NADEL PH.D., LAURIE
1245 East 27 Street
Brooklyn, NY 11210
Telephone: 212-995-9761
Fax: 718-951-0732
AFFILIATIONS:
ASJA
PRINCIPAL SUBJECTS:
Health
Motivation
Physical Fitness
Psychology
Travel
PUBLICATIONS:
Mens Fitness
New Woman
Elle

NADLER, BOB
85 Lake St.
Englewood, NJ 07631
Telephone: 201-568-6250
AFFILIATIONS:
AG, ASJA, NWU
PRINCIPAL SUBJECTS:
Business & Industry
General Interest
Hobbies
Science
Photography
Computer Technology
PUBLICATIONS:
Popular Photography
Photography How-To Guide
American Way
Consumer Guide
Boating
Lakeland Boating
Mechanix Illustrated
N. Y. Times
Popular Mechanics
Playboy
Motorboating & Sailing
Syntax
Info World
Popular Computing
Computor Shopper
Computer Buying World

NANESS, BARBARA
119 Washington Ave.
Staten Island, NY 10314
Telephone: 718-698-6979
AFFILIATIONS:
SPJ
PRINCIPAL SUBJECTS:
Human Interest
Humor
Entertainment
History
PUBLICATIONS:
American Way
Signs of the Times
Staten Island Register
The Stars and Stripes
New York Newsday

NASON, STEPHEN
221 S. Liberty St.
Asheville, NC 28801
Telephone: 704-258-1322
MAILING ADDRESS:
Nason & Associates
P.O. Box 8204
Asheville, NC 28814
PRINCIPAL SUBJECTS:
Business & Industry
Fashion
General Interest
Architecture
Journalism
Management
Media
News
Personal Finance
PUBLICATIONS:
Home Lighting &
  Accessories Mag.
Bedroom Mag.
Nails Mag.
Miniatures Dealer Mag.
Giftware News - Mag.
China, Glass &
  Tableware Mag.
Vows - Magazine
Drapery & Window
  Coverings - Mag.
Farm & Power
  Equipment - Mag.
Party & Paper Retailer - Mag.
Christian Retailing - Mag.
Produce Business - Mag.
WNC Business Journal -
  Newspaper
Souvenir - Mag.
Watch & Clock Review - Mag.
Women's Wear Daily -
  Newspaper
Daily News Record -
  Newspaper

Floor Covering Weekly -
  Newspaper
Gift Reporter - Mag.
Gift & Decorative
  Accessories - Mag.
Fence Industry - Mag.
Swimming Pool Age - Mag.
Convenience
  Store News - Mag.
Convenience Store
  Business - Mag.
Hotel - Motel
  Management - Mag.
Tableware Int'l. - Mag.

NEELY, BONNIE BURGESS
P.O. Box 595, 530 Laurel Lane
Paris, TX 75460
Telephone: 903-785-5171
AFFILIATIONS:
ASJA
PRINCIPAL SUBJECTS:
Amusements
Entertainment
Family
General Interest
Hobbies
Home & Garden
Human Relations
Humor
Nature
Personalities
Physical Fitness
Psychology
Religion
Travel
Video
Women's Interest
Youth

NEELY, WILLIAM
Box 500
Jane Lew, WV 26378
Telephone: 304-884-7500
PRINCIPAL SUBJECTS:
Travel
Men's Interest
Sports
PUBLICATIONS:
Playboy
Sports Illustrated
Motor Trend
Auto Week
Esquire
Car and Driver

NELSON, CHARLES L.
712 South 19th St.
Oxford, MS 38655

NELSON, ED
212 N. Ridgeland Ave.
Oak Park, IL 60302
Telephone: 708-848-1752
MAILING ADDRESS:
Ed
  Nelson/COMMUNICATIONS
Oak Park, IL 60302
AFFILIATIONS:
ASJA
PRINCIPAL SUBJECTS:
Automotive
Government
Editorial
Family
Science
General Interest
Human Relations
News
Youth
Travel
Urban Affairs
Sales
Psychology
Motivation
Military
Marketing
Health
PUBLICATIONS:
Popular Science
Science Digest
esprit
Popular Mechanics
Car And Motor
Computer Help

NELSON, JANET
Finney Farm
Croton-Hdsn, NY 10520
Telephone: 914-271-5453
MAILING ADDRESS:
Janet Nelson
P.O. Box 374
Croton Hdsn, NY 10520
AFFILIATIONS:
ASMP, SATW, GWAA
PRINCIPAL SUBJECTS:
Sports
Health
Photography
Travel
PUBLICATIONS:
The New York Times
Traveler
Skiing
American Health
New York Magazine
Golf Digest
Ski Area Management
Travel & Leisure

NELSON, KAY SHAW
5214 Abingdon Rd.
Bethesda, MD 20816
Telephone: 301-229-7689
AFFILIATIONS:
NPC, ANWC
PRINCIPAL SUBJECTS:
Travel
Women's Interest
PUBLICATIONS:
Family Circle
Gourmet
House and Garden
Washington Post
Americana
Woman's Day
Washington
Country
Cuisine
New York Times
World & I
Washington Post

NEMIRO, BEVERLY
  ANDERSON
23 Polo Club Drive
Denver, CO 80209
Telephone: 303-777-5245
AFFILIATIONS:
ASJA, AG, Denver Women's
  Press Club
PRINCIPAL SUBJECTS:
Human Relations
Travel
Women's Interest
Social Trends
Book Reviews
Personal Finance
Physical Fitness
Senior Citizens
PUBLICATIONS:
Better Homes & Gardens
Sunset
Mature Outlook
Denver Post
Rocky Mtn. News
AAA Rocky Mountain Motorist
Today's Health

NEMIROW-NELSON, JILL
24 Orange Ave.
Clifton, NJ 07013
Telephone: 000-000-0000
PRINCIPAL SUBJECTS:
Health
Youth
Humor
Animals
Fashion
Women's Interest
Media

Physical Fitness
PUBLICATIONS:
Reader's Digest (Canada)
Writer's Digest
Bergen Record
American Health
Bruce Jenner's Better
  Health & Living
TeenAge Magazine
Total Fitness
Fit
Woman's World
Playgirl Magazine
Steppin Out Magazine
Dateline Journal
Nutshell News

NEMSER, CINDY
41 Montgomery Place
Brooklyn, NY 11215
Telephone: 718-857-9456
AFFILIATIONS:
SJA, DD, PEN, ATC
PRINCIPAL SUBJECTS:
Book Reviews
Editorial
Humor
The Arts
Women's Interest
PUBLICATIONS:
Ms.
New York Law Journal
Newsday
Village Voice
Art in America
Arts
The Feminist Art Journal
Artforum

NEUMEYER, KATHLEEN
4936 Carpenter Avenue
Valley Village, CA 91607
Telephone: 818-509-9772
Fax: 818-509-0943
PRINCIPAL SUBJECTS:
Government
Health

NEW, AMY ROFFMANN
1402 West Stottler Ct.
Chandler, AZ 85224
Telephone: 602-786-4302
Fax: 602-786-1776
PRINCIPAL SUBJECTS:
Health
Business & Industry
Computer Technology
PUBLICATIONS:
Better Homes & Gardens
Business Week

Boston Business Journal
Entrepreneur
Ladies Home Journal

NEWCOMB, DUANE G.
18293 Crystal St.
Grass Valley, CA 95945
Telephone: 916-272-8047
AFFILIATIONS:
ASJA, BWA, AG
PRINCIPAL SUBJECTS:
The Arts
Business & Industry
General Interest
Home & Garden
Management
Science
PUBLICATIONS:
Family Circle
Field & Stream
Fishing Tackle Trade News
Parker

NICKLAS, NICK
518 Sheffield Ave.
Aliquippa, PA 15001
Telephone: 412-375-7552
MAILING ADDRESS:
Nick Nicklas
P.O. Box 217
Aliquippa, PA 15001
AFFILIATIONS:
IMPA, AAWBA
PRINCIPAL SUBJECTS:
General Interest
Government
Management
Travel
Automotive
Business & Industry
PUBLICATIONS:
Valley Tribune

NIELSEN, DOLLY
504 Merrick Rd., 1e
Lynbrook, NY 11563
Telephone: 516-593-5584
AFFILIATIONS:
WICI
PRINCIPAL SUBJECTS:
Travel
Home & Garden
PUBLICATIONS:
Travel Weekly
Jax Fax Travel Marketing
Hudson Valley Magazine
Long Island Nightlife
USA Today
Airfair
Signature
Baltimore Sun

N.Y. Daily News
N.Y. Newsday
HFD
New York Times
Caribbean Travel & Life

NORTON, PHILLIP
492 Covey Hill Rd.
Quebec, CN
Telephone: 514-826-4626
MAILING ADDRESS:
Norton, Phillip
P.O. Box 91
Mooers Forks, NY 12959
PRINCIPAL SUBJECTS:
Nature
Travel
Ecology
Sports
PUBLICATIONS:
Rotarian, The
Harrowsmith
Adirondack Life
US
Wilderness Camping
Canadian Geographic
Bicycling!
Cross - Country Skier
Adventure Travel
Time
Philadelphia Inquirer
Travel/Holiday

NOSSAMAN, MICHAEL
7130 Village Dr.
Shawnee Msn, KS 66208
Telephone: 913-432-5856
Fax: 913-432-6399
PRINCIPAL SUBJECTS:
Business & Industry
Government
Urban Affairs
Foreign
Management
Marketing
Military
Sales
PUBLICATIONS:
Tactical Response Magazine
Briefing
Chain Reaction

NOVITZ, CHARLES R.
160 West End Ave.
New York, NY 10023
Telephone: 212-819-1633
Fax: 212-944-8049
MAILING ADDRESS:
36 W. 44th St. #201
NY, NY 10023
Telephone: 212-787-6908

AFFILIATIONS:
SPJ
PRINCIPAL SUBJECTS:
Journalism
Management
Education
Human Interest
News
Business & Industry
Media
Video
Personal Finance
Motivation
PUBLICATIONS:
N.Y. Times
McCall's
Quill
Communicator, The
Family Advocate
Money Call News
Business Journalism Review
The Complete Lawyer

NUWER, HANK
8311 Countryside Lane
Fogelsville, PA 18051
Telephone: 215-285-2996
Fax: 215-285-2413
MAILING ADDRESS:
Hank Nuwer
P.O. Box 776
Fogelsville, PA 18051
AFFILIATIONS:
SPJ
PRINCIPAL SUBJECTS:
Personalities
Youth
Sports
Health
PUBLICATIONS:
Inside Sports
GQ
Saturday Evening Post
Los Angeles Times Syndicate
Success
Outside
Sport
Boston
Country Journal
The Nation
Writers Digest

O'CONNOR, KAREN
5050 La Jolla Bl., #3-B
San Diego, CA 92109
Telephone: 619-483-3184
Fax: 619-483-3184
PRINCIPAL SUBJECTS:
Family
Psychology
Religion

Women's Interest
Youth
PUBLICATIONS:
Reader's Digestt
Young Miss
Seventeen
Christian Herald

O'REILLY, DON
198 Sea Pines Cir.,
   Indigo Lakes
Daytona Beach, FL 32114
Telephone: 904-257-5186
Fax: 904-258-3027
MAILING ADDRESS:
Don O'Reilly
198 Sea Pines Cir.,Indigo Lake
Daytona Beach, FL 32114
AFFILIATIONS:
SPJ, NPC
PRINCIPAL SUBJECTS:
Automotive
Personalities
Sports
History
PUBLICATIONS:
Illustrated Speedway News
Popular Mechanics
Saturday Evening Post
Stock Car Racing Magazine
Daily Newspapers
Racing Pictorial
New York Journal American
Columbus Ohio Dispatch
Flagler Palm Coast
   News-Tribune
National Speed Sport Directory
Auto Racing Guide
Speed Age Magazine
Motor Speed Sports Review
Circle Track
Southern Motor Sports Journal
Motor Trend
Auto Week
Automotive News
Small Cars Magazine
Daytona Beach News-Journal
Indianapolis News
Racing Speedway Style
Racing Super Speedway Style
Inside Auto Racing
Dateline Detroit
Motorcade USA
Washington Post
New London Day

OATIS, JONATHAN W.
135 Pacific Apt. 4
Brooklyn, NY 11201
Telephone: 718-596-4522
MAILING ADDRESS:

Jonathan W. Oatis
Brooklyn, NY 11201
AFFILIATIONS:
SPJ
PRINCIPAL SUBJECTS:
News
General Interest

OCKERSHAUSEN, JANE
101 Washington Ave.,
   Suite 227
Oakmont, PA 15139
Telephone: 412-828-8152
Fax: 412-224-3556
AFFILIATIONS:
SATW, ASJA
PRINCIPAL SUBJECTS:
Travel
PUBLICATIONS:
Pittsburgh Post Gazette
Washington Times
Chicago Tribune
Dallas Times Herald
National Geographic Traveller

OGDEN, SHEPHERD
P.O. Box 76, Barker Road
Londonderry, VT 05148
Telephone: 802-824-5526
Fax: 802-824-3027
AFFILIATIONS:
GWAA, ASJA
PRINCIPAL SUBJECTS:
Agriculture
Book Reviews
Business & Industry
Computer Technology
Ecology
Home & Garden
Management
Marketing
Nature
Photography
Social Trends
Travel
PUBLICATIONS:
Boston Globe
New England Living
Country Living
Country Journal
National Gardening
Organic Gardening
Harrowsmith

OLDS, SALLY WENDKOS
25 N. Washington St.
Prt Washingtn, NY 11050
Telephone: 516-883-7511
AFFILIATIONS:
ASJA, AG

PRINCIPAL SUBJECTS:
Family
Health
Women's Interest
Youth
Human Relationship
Social Trends
Human Interest
PUBLICATIONS:
Woman's Day
Ladies' Home Journal
McCall's
Redbook
New Woman
New York Times

OLECK, HOWARD L.
5940 Pelican Bay Plaza, #301
St Petersburg, FL 33707
Telephone: 813-347-1389
PRINCIPAL SUBJECTS:
General Interest
Government
History
Business & Industry
World Affairs
PUBLICATIONS:
American Bar Assn. Journal
Cleveland Plain Dealer
Pinellas Review

OLLOVE, STEVE
P.O. Box 197
Hamilton, MA 01936
Telephone: 508-468-2632
PRINCIPAL SUBJECTS:
Sports
PUBLICATIONS:
Chicago Sun - Times
New York Post
Detroit News
Pittsburgh Press
Los Angeles Daily News
Daily Racing Form
Atlanta Journal & Constitution
Sports Illustrated for Kids
Sporting News, The
Washington Times

OLNEY, ROSS R.
2335 Sunset Dr.
Ventura, CA 93001
Telephone: 805-643-6741
Fax: 805-643-9247
AFFILIATIONS:
AARWBA
PRINCIPAL SUBJECTS:
Aviation
History
Men's Interest
Personalities

Entertainment
PUBLICATIONS:
Mechanix Illustrated
Discovery
Vista
Workbench
Reader's Digest

OLSEN, J.W.
1130 S. Michigan, Suite 1816
Chicago, IL 60605
Telephone: 312-939-3300
Fax: 312-939-3300
PRINCIPAL SUBJECTS:
Computer Technology
World Affairs

OPPENHEIM M.D., MICHAEL
2366 Veteran Ave.
Los Angeles, CA 90064
Telephone: 310-478-4477
AFFILIATIONS:
ASJA
PRINCIPAL SUBJECTS:
Medical
Health
Science
Book Reviews
PUBLICATIONS:
T.V. Guide
Readers Digest
Cosmopolitan
New York Times
Family Circle
Men's Health
Better Homes & Gardens
Self
McCalls

OPPENHEIMER, ERNEST J.
4/ Central Park South
New York, NY 10019
Telephone: 212-759-8454
AFFILIATIONS:
AG, ASJA
PRINCIPAL SUBJECTS:
Business & Industry
Science
Government
PUBLICATIONS:
Barron's
Pensions & Investments
Wall Street Journal
Petroleum Engineer
  International
New York Times
A Realistic Approach to U.S.
  Engery Independence
Fortune

ORTH, JOAN
401 E. 65th St., Ste. 14J
New York, NY 10021
Telephone: 212-734-9497
MAILING ADDRESS:
Joan Orth, Ste. 14J
401 E. 65th St.
New York, NY 10021
AFFILIATIONS:
NYPC
PRINCIPAL SUBJECTS:
Book Reviews
Travel
Business & Industry
Video

OSTERLING, CHERYL A.
13161 August Dr.
Augusta, MI 49012
Telephone: 616-731-2632

OSTROW, RONALD J.
L.A. Times - 1875 Eye St.,
  N.W.
Washington, DC 20006
Telephone: 202-861-9241
MAILING ADDRESS:
Ronald J. Ostrow
6401 - 81st St.
Cabin John, MD 20818
Telephone: 301-229-0510
PRINCIPAL SUBJECTS:
Government
PUBLICATIONS:
Los Angeles Times
Washington Post News Service
New Republic
Nieman Reports

OWEN, JENNIFER BRYON
380 Wickerberry Lane
Roswell, GA 30075
Telephone: 404-992-8459
Fax: 404-594-0187
AFFILIATIONS:
WICI
PRINCIPAL SUBJECTS:
Business & Industry
Government
Human Relations
Religion
Video
PUBLICATIONS:
Writers Digest
Christian Retailing
Fishing Tackle
Inside Government
Georgia Living

OXFORD, EDWARD
1133 Midland Ave.
Bronxville, NY 10708
Telephone: 914-961-7085
PRINCIPAL SUBJECTS:
History
Travel
PUBLICATIONS:
American History Illustrated
American Legion
Aloha
Irish America

PAAJANEN, ANNETTE LAABS
5916 Walnut Dr.
Minneapolis, MN 55436
Telephone: 612-930-0803
Fax: 612-930-0803
PRINCIPAL SUBJECTS:
Psychology
Education
The Arts
Personal Finance
Photography
Business & Industry

PAANANEN, ELOISE
6348 Cross Woods Drive
Falls Church, VA 22044
Telephone: 703-256-6077
Fax: 619-297-2588
AFFILIATIONS:
ASJA
PRINCIPAL SUBJECTS:
Travel
Military
History
Aviation
PUBLICATIONS:
Washington Post
Marine Corp. Gazette
Times

PALMQUIST, RON
16 Glen Ave.
Portland, ME 04107
Telephone: 207-799-1761
AFFILIATIONS:
SPJ
PRINCIPAL SUBJECTS:
Human Relations
Media
Travel
Journalism
Management
History
PUBLICATIONS:
Maine Sunday Telegram
Pine Tree Flyer (RR Historical
  Scty. of Maine)
Business Digest (Southern

Maine)
Trains Magazine
Rail Classics Magazine
United Press International
  Wire Photo
Model Railroader Magazine
Portland Press Herald

PARADISE, PAUL RICHARD
722 Willow Ave., Apt. 6
Hoboken, NJ 07030
Telephone: 201-656-2042
AFFILIATIONS:
SPJ
PRINCIPAL SUBJECTS:
Animals
Business & Industry
Family
General Interest
Journalism
PUBLICATIONS:
Tropical Fish Hobbyist
  Magazine
Police Product News
Firehouse Magazine
Law & Order Magazine
Parent Guide
P.I. Magazine

PARK, ED
P.O. Box 887
Bend, OR 97709
Telephone: 503-576-2242
AFFILIATIONS:
OWAA, NOWA
PRINCIPAL SUBJECTS:
Book Reviews
Travel
Photography
Animals
Ecology
Journalism
Nature
Senior Citizens
Sports
PUBLICATIONS:
American Hunter
Outdoor Life
Field & Stream
Sports Afield
Western Outdoors
Audubon

PATRICK, MELANIE
  REYNOLDS
1129 Empire Lane
Birmingham, AL 35226
Telephone: 205-823-3435
Fax: 205-823-9406

PAUGH, TOM
250 W. 55th St.
New York, NY 10019
Telephone: 212-649-4000
AFFILIATIONS:
OWAA, ASME
PRINCIPAL SUBJECTS:
Hobbies
Sports
Photography
PUBLICATIONS:
Sports Afield
The Sports Afield Treasury of
    Fly Fishing

PAUST, GIL
142 Douglas Ave.
Yonkers, NY 10703
Telephone: 914-968-1548
PRINCIPAL SUBJECTS:
Animals
General Interest
Hobbies
Marketing
Social Trends
Book Reviews
Nature
Humor
Foreign
Journalism
History
Ecology
PUBLICATIONS:
American Legion
Flying
Field and Stream
Sports Afield
Hunters & Shooters Magazine
Cosmopolitan
Sports Illustrated
Capitalist Reporter
Sportsman
Stag
Adventure Magazine

PAYNE, PEGGY
512 St. Mary's St.
Raleigh, NC 27605
Telephone: 919-833-8021
AFFILIATIONS:
ASJA
PRINCIPAL SUBJECTS:
The Arts
General Interest
Travel
PUBLICATIONS:
McCall's
Travel Holiday
The Washington Post
The Los Angeles Times
Family Circle

Ms.
The New York Times
Travel & Leisure
Cosmopolitan

PEAKE, JACQUELYN
P.O. Box 591, 247 Third St.
Ashland, OR 97520
Telephone: 503-482-6788
AFFILIATIONS:
ASJA
PRINCIPAL SUBJECTS:
General Interest
Travel
PUBLICATIONS:
Travel & Leisure
Travel Holiday
Sunset
Country Journal
Elle Decor
New York Times

PEEPLES, EDWIN A.
Vixen Hill, 1611 Kimberton Rd.
Phoenixville, PA 19460
Telephone: 215-827-7241
AFFILIATIONS:
AG
PRINCIPAL SUBJECTS:
Humor
Ecology
Entertainment
Home & Garden
PUBLICATIONS:
Esquire
Today - Magazine Section
Green Scene
County Lines
Mademoiselle
Elks Magazine, The
Country Journal
Harrowsmith
Town & Country

PEPE, BARBARA
3430 Federal Ave.
Los Angeles, CA 90066
Telephone: 310-391-6683
AFFILIATIONS:
SPJSDC
PRINCIPAL SUBJECTS:
Entertainment
Sports
Travel
The Arts
Women's Interest
PUBLICATIONS:
Us, Playboy, Rolling Stone,
    USA Today
Diversion, American Way

Billboard, Cashbox, Creem
Horizon, Ms., Home Viewer
LA Times, NY Daily News,
    Money

PERLOFF, SUSAN
6389 Overbrook Ave.
Philadelphia, PA 19151
Telephone: 215-879-3101
PRINCIPAL SUBJECTS:
Humor
Medical
Business & Industry
Journalism
PUBLICATIONS:
Philadelphia Inquirer
Washington Post
Ski
San Diego Union
Detroit News
Baltimore Sun
Chicago Tribune
Newsday
Houston Chronicle

PERRY, ERMA
134 Greenwood Ave.
Jenkintown, PA 19046
Telephone: 215-886-9684
Fax: 215-886-9684
MAILING ADDRESS:
(Summer Address)
West Side Road
North Conway, NH 03860
AFFILIATIONS:
SATW, ASJA
PRINCIPAL SUBJECTS:
General Interest
Personalities
Travel
Architecture
Book Reviews
Education
Family
Home & Garden
Nature
The Arts
PUBLICATIONS:
Family Circle
Ford Times
Modern Maturity
Philadelphia Bulletin
New York Times
Grit
Miami Herald
Going Places
Los Angeles Times
San Diego Union
Boston Herald American
Dynamic Years
Success Unlimited

Farm & Ranch Living
Phila Inquirer
Woman's World
Soundings
Hartford Courant
Farm Journal
Flying Colors (Braniff)
Providence Journal
Maine Sunday Telegram
Architectural Digest
Yacht, The
Cruising World
Mid - Atlantic Country
Irish Edition
Fort Myers News Press

PERRY, SUSAN K.
2715 Lakewood Ave.
Los Angeles, CA 90039
Telephone: 213-667-2638
Fax: 213-663-6573
AFFILIATIONS:
ASJA, IWOSC, PEN, NWU
PRINCIPAL SUBJECTS:
Book Reviews
Education
Family
Psychology
Women's Interest
Youth
PUBLICATIONS:
Parenting
Teen
USA Today
LA Times
Family Fun
Valley Magazine
LA Parent
Working World

PETERS, JANE S.
3654 A Flad Ave.
Saint Louis, MO 63110
Telephone: 314-773-3792
AFFILIATIONS:
ASJA
PRINCIPAL SUBJECTS:
Business & Industry
Video
Computer Technology
PUBLICATIONS:
Consumer Digest
Redbook
Buildings
American School & University
St. Louis Magazine
Construction News

PETERSON, FRANKLYNN
3006 Gregory St.
Madison, WI 53711

Telephone: 608-231-1003
AFFILIATIONS:
ASJA, NPC, AG
PRINCIPAL SUBJECTS:
Computer Technology
Business & Industry
Management
PUBLICATIONS:
McCall's
Physician's Management
Popular Science
The Do-It-Yourself Furniture
  Catalog
Popular Mechanics
Omni
Fortune
Parade

PETROWSKI, ELAINE MARTIN
70 Phelps Rd.
Ridgewood, NJ 07450
Telephone: 201-652-4662
Fax: 201-652-3310
MAILING ADDRESS:
Elaine Petrowski
Ridgewood, NJ 07450
Telephone: 201-652-5852
AFFILIATIONS:
ASJA, NAREE
PRINCIPAL SUBJECTS:
Home & Garden
Architecture
Humor
Travel
Women's Interest
PUBLICATIONS:
Good House Keeping
House Beautiful
N.Y. Times
Consumer Digest
Home Mechanix
Decorating/Remodeling
Nj Focus

PFEIFER, LUANNE
1032 Atelier
Sun Valley, ID 83353
Telephone: 310-456-8414
Fax: 310-456-7112
MAILING ADDRESS:
Luanne Pfeifer
3224 Malibu Canyon Rd.
Malibu, CA 90265
AFFILIATIONS:
ASJA, NATJ, NASJA
PRINCIPAL SUBJECTS:
Entertainment
Personalities
Sports
Travel
Physical Fitness

Fashion
Foreign
PUBLICATIONS:
Ski
World Travel
Airline Inflights
L. A. Times Travel Section
California Today Mag
Los Angeles Mag.
California Living Mag.
Westways
Marco Polo Mag. (Hong Kong)
Tournovosti (Moscow, Russia)

PICKENS, THOMAS M.
43 Collins Ct.
Brick, NJ 08724
Telephone: 908-458-0796
MAILING ADDRESS:
Thomas Pickens
P.O. Box 691
Brick, NJ 08723
AFFILIATIONS:
ASJA, SFWA
PRINCIPAL SUBJECTS:
General Interest
Personalities
Sports
Travel
World Affairs
PUBLICATIONS:
American Way
Lively World
Number One
Passages
Creative Lviing
TWA Ambassador
Various

PINES, MAYA
4701 Willard Ave.
Bethesda, MD 20815
Telephone: 301-215-8859
PRINCIPAL SUBJECTS:
Personalities
Science
Education
PUBLICATIONS:
New York Times Magazine
Psychology Today
Science - 85

PINKWAS, STAN
Video Magazine
522 East Fifth Street
New York, NY 10009
Telephone: 212-947-6500
Fax: 212-947-6727
MAILING ADDRESS:
Pinkwas, Stan
Video Magazine

460 W. 34th St.
New York, NY 10001
AFFILIATIONS:
ASJA
PRINCIPAL SUBJECTS:
Computer Technology
Electronics
Entertainment
Media
Video
PUBLICATIONS:
Video Magazine
Metropolis
Village Voice

PITTMAN, RUTH
1422 E. Maple Street
Glendale, CA 91205
Telephone: 818-548-1057
AFFILIATIONS:
ASJA, NWC
PRINCIPAL SUBJECTS:
Business & Industry
Editorial
Family
General Interest
Health
History
Human Interest
Human Relations
Management
Personalities
Women's Interest
PUBLICATIONS:
American Way
Los Angeles
Elks
American Legion
Ford Times
Fedco Reporters
Park Labrea News
Specialty Store Service Bulletin
Cleveland Plain Dealer
Newsday
Catholic Forester

PIZER, VERNON
2206 Newbern Dr.
Valdosta, GA 31602
Telephone: 912-247-0846
AFFILIATIONS:
AG, ASJA, NPC
PRINCIPAL SUBJECTS:
Medical
Travel
Social Trends
Science
Human Interest

PUBLICATIONS:
Esquire
Readers Digest
Washingtonian

PLANT, JANET
821 S. Dwyer Ave., Ste. F
Arlington Hts., IL 60005
Telephone: 708-255-7783
PRINCIPAL SUBJECTS:
Nature
Computer Technology
Health

PLUMEZ, DR. JACQUELINE
  HORNER
90 Beechtree Drive
Larchmont, NY 10538
Telephone: 914-834-1982
AFFILIATIONS:
ASJA
PRINCIPAL SUBJECTS:
Medical
Psychology
Travel
Women's Interest
PUBLICATIONS:
N.Y. Times
Ladies Home Journal
Working Woman
Caribbean Travel & Life
American Baby

PODOLSKY, M. LAWRENCE
400 Davey Glen Rd., #4907
Belmont, CA 94002
Telephone: 415-591-9056
Fax: 415-595-5000
AFFILIATIONS:
ASJA
PRINCIPAL SUBJECTS:
Science
Business & Industry
Travel
Medical
Book Reviews
Family
History
Home & Garden
Nature
Personal Finance
Photography
Social Trends
PUBLICATIONS:
Western Traveler
Journal Am. Med. Assn.
Modern Medicine
Medical Economics
Family Motor Coach Magazine
Cruising World
Independent Living

San Mateo Times
Sports Medicine
Consumers Digest
Consumer Reports
Bay & Delta Yachtsman
Private Practice
Cardiology World
Physicians Travel & Meeting
   Giuide
Publishers Weekly
Contemporary Pediatrics
San Francisco Business Times
Trailer Life Publications
MD Magazine

POGREBIN, LETTY COTTIN
33 W. 67th St.
New York, NY 10023
Telephone: 212-873-1460
Fax: 212-787-5733
PRINCIPAL SUBJECTS:
Social Trends
Women's Interest
Family
News
Religion
PUBLICATIONS:
Ms. Magazine
New York Times
Washington Post
TV Guide
Tikkun
Good Housekeeping
Harpers Bazaar
Bottom Line
N.Y. Times Book Review
N.Y. Times Travel Section
Nation, The
Moment
Newsday
Ladies Home Journal

POGUE, FORREST C.
1600 S. Joyce St.
Arlington, VA 22202
Telephone: 703-521-7890
AFFILIATIONS:
ASJA
PRINCIPAL SUBJECTS:
Government
History
Personalities
PUBLICATIONS:
Army Magazine
World Politics
International Security
American History Illustrated
Look

POLAND, NANCY
7403 Honeywell Lane
Bethesda, MD 20814
Telephone: 202-328-8180
Fax: 202-265-6477
MAILING ADDRESS:
1607 22nd St., N.W.
Washington, DC 20008
Telephone: 301-654-2043
AFFILIATIONS:
ANWC, WICI
PRINCIPAL SUBJECTS:
Book Reviews
Editorial
Foreign
Government
Human Interest
Human Relations
News
Personalities
Social Trends
The Arts
Travel
World Affairs
PUBLICATIONS:
Washington Post
Midwest Quarterly
Harvard Magazine

POLKING, MISS KIRK
529 Constitution Square
Cincinnati, OH 45255
Telephone: 513-528-5262
MAILING ADDRESS:
Miss Kirk Polking
Cincinnati, OH 45255
AFFILIATIONS:
WICI, NFPW, AL
PRINCIPAL SUBJECTS:
Aviation
History
Marine
Science
PUBLICATIONS:
Writer's Magazines
Aviation
Social Science
History
Oceanography
Science

POLVAY, MARINA
9881 E. Bay Harbor Dr., Apt.
   2d Bayharbor
Miami, FL 33154
Telephone: 305-868-9502
MAILING ADDRESS:
Polvay, Marina
12550 Biscayne Blvd., #305
Miami, FL 33181

AFFILIATIONS:
AG
PRINCIPAL SUBJECTS:
General Interest
Travel
Women's Interest
PUBLICATIONS:
Family Circle
Gourmet
New York News
Town & Country
Travel/Holiday
Carte Blanche Magazine
Palm Beach Life
Air Cal Magazine
South Florida Magazine
Cuisine
Bon Appetit
Florida Homes & Gardens
Focus, Millionare Magazine

POMADA, ELIZABETH
1029 Jones St.
San Francisco, CA 94109
Telephone: 415-673-0939
AFFILIATIONS:
ASJA, AG, PEN
PRINCIPAL SUBJECTS:
The Arts
Architecture
Book Reviews
Travel
Home & Garden
PUBLICATIONS:
San Francisco Chronicle
Library Journal
San Francisco Review Of
   Books, McCall's
San Francisco Magazine
Focus Magazine, Library
   Journal

PONZO, MARIE
201 E. 37th St.
New York, NY 10016
Telephone: 212-687-0296
PRINCIPAL SUBJECTS:
The Arts
Travel
PUBLICATIONS:
Opera News
Washington Post
Westways
Wine World
Boston Globe
Aloft
Los Angeles Times
Weight Watchers
Providence Journal

New York City Opera Program
Newsday
Opera Orchestra of New York
   Newsletter

POPHAL, LIN GRENSING-
17889 Stillson Rd.
Chippewa Fls, WI 54729
Telephone: 715-839-1332
AFFILIATIONS:
IABC, UCI
PRINCIPAL SUBJECTS:
Advertising
Business & Industry
Management
Media
PUBLICATIONS:
Small Business Opportunities
Income Opportunities
Manage
I.B.

POSTER, CAROL
English Dept., Tate Hall 107
   Univ. of Missouri
Columbia, MO 65211
Telephone: 314-449-0765
MAILING ADDRESS:
Carol Poster
Tate Hall 107, Univ. of MO
Columbia, MO 65211
Telephone: 801-649-7295
PRINCIPAL SUBJECTS:
Computer Technology
The Arts
Sports
Travel
Ecology
Nature
PUBLICATIONS:
Backpacker
Dance News
Southwest Profiles
Show Business
Women's Sports and Fitness
RV & Camping
PC Resource
Sports Guide, The
Rocky Mountain Sports &
   Fitness
Ski Magazine
Snow Country
Outdoor Woman
Canoe Magazine
Utah Holiday

POWER, CHARLOTTE A.
Rt. 9, Box 38D
Jonesboro, AR 72401
Telephone: 501-935-2087

PRINCIPAL SUBJECTS:
Humor
Medical
Personalities
History
PUBLICATIONS:
Lady's Circle Magazine

PRIBUS, MARILYN
4318 Donnybrook Way
Fair Oaks, CA 95628
Telephone: 916-962-1761

PRYOR, HUBERT
3560 S. Ocean Blvd., 708
Palm Beach, FL 33480
Telephone: 407-585-1328
AFFILIATIONS:
ASME, OPC
PRINCIPAL SUBJECTS:
Senior Citizens
PUBLICATIONS:
Look
Science Digest
Modern Maturity
Science of Mind
Arthritis Today
Palm Beach Post

PUGH JR., JAMES E.
2636 Fairlawn Dr.
Winston Salem, NC 27106
Telephone: 919-768-5208
PRINCIPAL SUBJECTS:
Business & Industry
Science
PUBLICATIONS:
Electronics World
Popular Electronics
Radio Electronics
Science & Mechanics
Popular Mechanics
Field & Stream

PURDY, SUSAN
30 Liberty Avenue
Lindenhurst, NY 11757
Telephone: 516-226-2810
AFFILIATIONS:
ASJA
PRINCIPAL SUBJECTS:
Travel
Women's Interest
Social Trends
PUBLICATIONS:
Womans World
Saturday Evening Post
Good Housekeeping
New York Daily News

Newsweek
Seventeen
Brides
MS

RADCLIFFE, DONALD
1725 W. Thorndale Ave #1 - B
Chicago, IL 60660
Telephone: 312-784-0724
MAILING ADDRESS:
Donald Radcliffe
P.O. Box A-3945
Chicago, IL 60690
AFFILIATIONS:
NASW, AMWA
PRINCIPAL SUBJECTS:
Business & Industry
General Interest
Health
Science
PUBLICATIONS:
Family Health
Incentive Marketing
The Hearing Journal
Medical Observer (Australia)

RAKSTIS, TED J.
7621 Little Paw Paw Lake Rd.
Coloma, MI 49038
Telephone: 616-468-4238
AFFILIATIONS:
ASJA
PRINCIPAL SUBJECTS:
Business & Industry
Management
Social Trends
Marketing
Motivation
Psychology
Sales
Social Trends
PUBLICATIONS:
Teamleader
Reader's Digest
Teamwork
Chicago Tribune Magazine
Chicago Magazine
Elks Magazine
Quality First
Playthings (Chicago Field
  Editor)

RAND, ABBY
11 Riverside Dr.
New York, NY 10023
Telephone: 303-923-3956
AFFILIATIONS:
ASJA, SATW
PRINCIPAL SUBJECTS:
General Interest
Sports

Travel
PUBLICATIONS:
Harper's Bazaar
Ski
Town & Country
Travel & Leisure
Travel Holiday
Glamour
Ultra

RANDOLPH, ELIZABETH
606 Shore Acres Drive
Mamaroneck, NY 10543
Telephone: 914-698-3688
Fax: 914-698-3184
AFFILIATIONS:
ASJA, DWAA, AG
PRINCIPAL SUBJECTS:
Animals
Health
Nature
PUBLICATIONS:
Family Circle
Reader's Digest
Whittle Pamphlets
Rx Being Bell

RANKIN, JEFF
316 Queens Ave., Upper Ste.
00000
Telephone: 519-672-4408
MAILING ADDRESS:
Sirius Productions
P.O. Box 9044, Sub 40
PUBLICATIONS:
Air Forces Mon Thly
Flypast
Le Fana De L'aviation
Flug Revue
Koku - Fan
Scale Models International
Flight International
Finescale Modeler
Air International
London International Air Show
  Programme
Engineering Dimensions
Military Aircraft Serials of North
  America

REARDEN, JIM
413 E. Lee Drive
Homer, AK 99603
Telephone: 907-235-8543
AFFILIATIONS:
ASJA
PRINCIPAL SUBJECTS:
Animals
Aviation
Ecology
Military

Nature
PUBLICATIONS:
National Geographic
Geo
National Wildlife
International Wildlife
Audubon
Outdoor Life
Sports Afield
Field and Stream
Boy's Life
Science Digest
Alaska Magazine
American Legion

REICHEK, MORTON
1 Worchester Drive
Cranbury, NJ 08512
Telephone: 609-395-7039
PRINCIPAL SUBJECTS:
Business & Industry
Foreign
Social Trends
Religion
PUBLICATIONS:
Business Week
Forbes
Newhouse Newspapers
New York Times Magazine
New York Times Book Review
The New Republic
The New Leader
Columbia Journalism Review
Present Tense

REIMER, KATHLEEN
8108 Golden Crest Wy.
Orangevale, CA 95662
Telephone: 916-726-7349
Fax: 916-726-0482
AFFILIATIONS:
ASJA, IFW & TWA
PRINCIPAL SUBJECTS:
Family
General Interest
History
Home & Garden
Nature
Travel
PUBLICATIONS:
New York Times Syndicate
US Air
Toronto Star
Country America
Norwest Park/Travel
Military Lifestyle
Off-Road

REISS, ALVIN H.
408 W. 57th St.
New York, NY 10019

Telephone: 212-245-3850
AFFILIATIONS:
ASJA, AG, MCA
PRINCIPAL SUBJECTS:
The Arts
Business & Industry
Ecology
General Interest
Travel
Amusements
Social Trends
Entertainment
Urban Affairs
Humor
Marketing
PUBLICATIONS:
Esquire
Family Health
American Way
USA Today
Art News
New York Times, Mainliner
Creative Living
Cultural Post
Playbill

REYNOLDS, WILLIAM J.
1000 S. Third Ave.
Sioux Falls, SD 57105
Telephone: 605-334-4391
PRINCIPAL SUBJECTS:
Science
Computer Technology
Personalities
Advertising
PUBLICATIONS:
TWA Ambassador
Travel Leisure
Corporate Report
Friendly Exchange
Link - Up
Western's World
Better Homes & Gardens
Writer's Digest
Alfred Hitchcock's Mystery
 Magazine
Midwest Art
U.S. Art

RICCIUTI, EDWARD R.
177 Roast Meat Hill
Killingworth, CT 06419
Telephone: 203-663-1804
AFFILIATIONS:
OWAA, ASJA
PRINCIPAL SUBJECTS:
Nature
Science
PUBLICATIONS:
Audubon
National Wildlife

International Wildlife
Field & Stream
Outside
Wildlife Conversation

RICHARD, JEROME
1009 W. Blaine
Seattle, WA 98119
Telephone: 206-282-5482
AFFILIATIONS:
ASJA
PRINCIPAL SUBJECTS:
Travel
Ecology
PUBLICATIONS:
Wine Enthusiast
Pacific Discovery
Providence Sunday Journal

RICKEY, GAIL
13114 Holston Hills
Houston, TX 77069
Telephone: 713-440-0353
Fax: 713-440-1902
AFFILIATIONS:
ASJA, NATJA
PRINCIPAL SUBJECTS:
Travel
Business & Industry
PUBLICATIONS:
Sunset
Elegant Bride
Vista USA
Travel Age
Houston Business Journal

RICKS, JACKIE D.
P.O. Box 455
Mineola, TX 75773
Telephone: 903-569-5548
AFFILIATIONS:
SCBWI
PRINCIPAL SUBJECTS:
Religion
Youth
PUBLICATIONS:
The Gifted Child Today
Venture
Focus

RIEGER, TED
P.O. Box 254452
Sacramento, CA 95865
Telephone: 916-362-8280
AFFILIATIONS:
SPJ
PRINCIPAL SUBJECTS:
Ecology
History
Nature
Science

Sports
Travel
PUBLICATIONS:
American Forests
California Explorer
Compass (Continental
 Insurance Magazine)
Home Energy
Indoor Comfort News
Museum Magazine
Sacramento Magazine
Preservation News
Westways
Vineyard & Winery
 Management
Business Journal of
 Sacramento, The
Sierra Heritage

RILLY, CHERYL
20028 Woodmont
Detroit, MI 48225
Telephone: 313-881-4551
MAILING ADDRESS:
Cheryl Rilly
P.O. Box 80816
St Clair Shrs, MI 48080
AFFILIATIONS:
NWC
PRINCIPAL SUBJECTS:
Science
History
Home & Garden
Health
General Interest
Humor
PUBLICATIONS:
Woman's Day
Heritage
Bridal Guide
BusinessWeek Careers
HomeOwners
Casual Living
Airlines
Military Life
Catholic Digest
Silver Circle
Signature
Detroit News

RIVOIRE, JOHN
649 E. 14th St.
New York, NY 10009
Telephone: 212-228-6785
PRINCIPAL SUBJECTS:
Business & Industry
Science
PUBLICATIONS:
Chemical Week

ROBERTS, D.P.M.,
 ELIZABETH H.
210 West 90th Street
New York, NY 10024
Telephone: 212-873-8085
AFFILIATIONS:
MSA, WICI
PRINCIPAL SUBJECTS:
Health
Medical
Physical Fitness
Senior Citizens
PUBLICATIONS:
Consumer Research
Podiatry Management
Nailpro

ROBERTS, JANET M.
16 Stony Brook Ln.
Princeton, NJ 08540
Telephone: 609-921-6114
MAILING ADDRESS:
Janet Roberts
259 W. Johnson St., #45
Philadelphia, PA 19144
Telephone: 215-848-5418
AFFILIATIONS:
MLA, AWP
PRINCIPAL SUBJECTS:
Ecology
The Arts
Travel
Architecture
Book Reviews
Editorial
Family
Hobbies
Home & Garden
Human Interest
Movie Reviews
Nature
Photography
Women's Interest
PUBLICATIONS:
Gifted/Talented Education
Princeton Packet
Wisconsin State Journal
AMA Journal
Manhattan Poetry Review
NJ Autholory
Edith Wharton Journal

ROBINSON, TED
4272 Lakeridge Ct.
Bloomfield, MI 48302
Telephone: 313-855-0452
AFFILIATIONS:
NPC, ASJA, OPC
PRINCIPAL SUBJECTS:
General Interest
Humor

Business & Industry
Sports
PUBLICATIONS:
Hot Rod
Popular Mechanics
Popular Science
Friends

ROCK, MAXINE
370 Valley Green Drive
Atlanta, GA 30342
Telephone: 404-252-9249
Fax: 404-252-9249
AFFILIATIONS:
ASJA, AMWA
PRINCIPAL SUBJECTS:
Health
Medical
Physical Fitness
Senior Citizens
Business & Industry
PUBLICATIONS:
N.Y. Times Magazine
Smithsonian
Woman's Day
McCalls
Inc.
USA Today
Harper's Bazaar
Reader's Digest
Redbook
Acccent

RODDIN, MIKE
5629 Roundtree Dr.
Woodbridge, VA 22193
Telephone: 703-590-5827
MAILING ADDRESS:
Mike Roddin
Woodbridge, VA 22193
AFFILIATIONS:
NWC
PRINCIPAL SUBJECTS:
Medical
Sports
Health
Government
PUBLICATIONS:
Army Times/Navy Times/Air
   Force Times
Army Magazine
Soldier Support Journal
Psych It.
Bozell Midwest
Arnews
Manhattan Mercury
Lakeland Publications
Recruiter Journal

RODNEY, JAMES C.
2571 T.R. 180
Fredericktown, OH 43019
Telephone: 419-768-3492
Fax: 612-421-2000
PRINCIPAL SUBJECTS:
Media
Nature
Science
Human Interest
PUBLICATIONS:
The Atlantic
Country Living
Cinema Quebec
Columbus Dispatch
Guns
Issues & Events
Movie & T.V. Marketing
What's News
Work Life

ROES, NICHOLAS A.
P.O. Box 233
Barryville, NY 12719
Telephone: 914-557-8713
Fax: 914-557-6770
PRINCIPAL SUBJECTS:
Business & Industry
Education
Book Reviews
Health
Health
Home & Garden
Motivation
Youth
Personal Finance
PUBLICATIONS:
Gambling Times
Arizona (AZ Republic
   Sunday Mag)
Business View
Childhood Education
Moneysworth
(Middletown) Times - Herald -
   Record
Suburban News
Central Bergen Reporter
Hackensack News South
River Reporter, The
Manhattan Cooperator
Teacher
Teacher Update
Glamour
TWA Ambassador
Win Magazine

ROESCH, ROBERTA
131 Prospect Ave.
Westwood, NJ 07675
Telephone: 201-664-2635

AFFILIATIONS:
ASJA, AG
PRINCIPAL SUBJECTS:
Family
Health
General Interest
Human Interest
Women's Interest
Psychology
Senior Citizens
PUBLICATIONS:
McCall's
Glamour
Good Housekeeping
New Woman
Reader's Digest
Syndicates
Working Woman
Family Circle
Travel & Leisure
Parents
Us
Consumers Digest

ROESSING, WALTER
1418 Corona Place
Walnut Creek, CA 94596
Telephone: 510-933-6988
Fax: 510-935-4731
AFFILIATIONS:
SATW, ASJA
PRINCIPAL SUBJECTS:
Amusements
Business & Industry
Computer Technology
Family
Foreign
Management
Marine
Men's Interest
Personal Finance
Science
Senior Citizens
Social Trends
Sports
The Arts
Travel
Women's Interest
Youth
PUBLICATIONS:
Parade
Cosmopolitan
Ladies' Home Journal
Copley News Service
Saturday Evening Post
Grit
Boys' Life

ROGAK, LISA
RR2, Box 33B
Enfield, NH 03748

Telephone: 603-632-9275
AFFILIATIONS:
ASJA
PRINCIPAL SUBJECTS:
Travel
Health
Physical Fitness
Women's Interest
History
Animals
Business & Industry
Family
Men's Interest
Home & Garden
PUBLICATIONS:
Readers Digest
New York Magazine
Travel & Leisure
Mademoiselle
Woman's Day
L.A. Times
Boston Globe
N.Y. Daily News

ROGERS, BARBARA
   RADCLIFFE
686 Old Homestead Hwy.
Richmond, NH 03470
Telephone: 603-239-6231
AFFILIATIONS:
ASJA, NATJA, FIJET
PRINCIPAL SUBJECTS:
Book Reviews
Home & Garden
Nature
Travel
PUBLICATIONS:
Yankee
Los Angeles Times
Animal Kingdom
Senior World
London (Ontario) Free Press
Early American Life
Fine Gardening

ROGERS, KRISTA
4712 W 70th Street
Shawnee Mission, KS 66208
Telephone: 913-262-8641
Fax: 913-722-2936
AFFILIATIONS:
WICI
PRINCIPAL SUBJECTS:
Science
Marketing

ROHAN, REBECCA
15001 - 35th Ave. W.,
   Ste. 14 - 104
Lynnwood, WA 98037
Telephone: 206-745-7761

Fax: 206-745-7762
MAILING ADDRESS:
11749 Greenwood Ave. N.
 #310
Seattle, WA 98133
Telephone: 206-365-4354
PRINCIPAL SUBJECTS:
Computer Technology
PUBLICATIONS:
Computer Shopper
Windows Magazine
Compute
Home Office Computing
PC Computing

ROOD, RONALD
R.F.D. 1
Lincoln, VT 05443
Telephone: 802-453-3175
MAILING ADDRESS:
Ronald Rood
R.R. 1 P.O. Box 740
Lincoln, VT 05443
PRINCIPAL SUBJECTS:
History
Youth
Travel
Family
Human Interest
PUBLICATIONS:
Audubon Magazine
National Wildlife
Reader's Digest
Vermont Life
Blair & Ketchum's Country
 Journal
New York Times
Ranger Rick's Nature
 Magazine
Yankee Magazine
Bi - Weekly Commintary on
 Vermont Public Radio

ROSEN, M. DANIEL
20 West 86th St.
New York, NY 10024
Telephone: 212-724-3057
Fax: 212-724-6399
AFFILIATIONS:
ASJA, AG
PRINCIPAL SUBJECTS:
Business & Industry
General Interest
Government
Health
Personalities
World Affairs
Travel
Computer Technology
PUBLICATIONS:
Cosmopolitan

Monsantu Magazine
Family Circle
Financial World
The Nation
New York Times Magazine
Penthouse
Playboy
Beckman Life
TV Guide
Baxter Pace
Exxon Lamp
Discover
Flying
Columbia Journal of World
 Business

ROSENBAUM, HELEN
142 East 33rd St.
New York, NY 10016
Telephone: 212-532-5057
AFFILIATIONS:
ASJA,
PRINCIPAL SUBJECTS:
Entertainment
Fashion
General Interest
Home & Garden
Senior Citizens
Sports
Travel
Women's Interest
Youth
PUBLICATIONS:
The Elks
Modern Maturity
Playbill
New Woman
Bon Appetit
ASTA Travel News

ROSENBERG, SHIRLEY
 SIROTA
116 Fourth St., S.E.
Washington, DC 20003
Telephone: 202-543-1800
AFFILIATIONS:
ASJA, NAGC, WWPR, WNRA,
 Washington Express
PRINCIPAL SUBJECTS:
Health
World Affairs
Journalism
Ecology
Military
PUBLICATIONS:
Parents'
Washington Post
Washington Star
Popular Dynamics Quarterly
Friends
Kiwanis

Companion
Family Weekly
Look

ROSENBLUM, DEBBIE
578-F Water Oak Lane
Agoura Hills, CA 91301
Telephone: 818-879-2113
Fax: 818-597-8428
PRINCIPAL SUBJECTS:
Video
Electronics

ROSENDO, JOSEPH
TRAVELSCOPE
12375 HERBERT ST.
LOS ANGELES, CA 90066
Telephone: 310-397-1787
MAILING ADDRESS:
Rosendo, Joseph (IFTWA)
Travelscope
4230 Del Rey Ave. #203
Marina Del Ray, CA 90292
Fax: 213-245-5438
AFFILIATIONS:
IFTWA
PRINCIPAL SUBJECTS:
Amusements
Book Reviews
Editorial
Entertainment
Foreign
Health
Human Interest
Humor
Men's Interest
The Arts
Travel
PUBLICATIONS:
LA Times
Shape Magazine
Westways Magazine
Washington Post
New York Daily News

ROSENTHAL, ALAN
2470 Bryant Ave.
Evanston, IL 60201
Telephone: 708-328-8023

ROSS, BETTY
5610 Wisconsin Ave. #306
Chevy Chase, MD 20815
Telephone: 301-718-9808
Fax: 301-718-1783
AFFILIATIONS:
ASJA, TJG, SATW
PRINCIPAL SUBJECTS:
The Arts
Travel

Women's Interest
Senior Citizens
PUBLICATIONS:
National Geographic Traveler
Family Circle
Travel Weekly
American Way
US News & World Report
Washington Post
Los Angeles Times
Chicago Tribune
Fodor's Guide To
 Washington, D.C.

ROSS, MARILYN HEIMBERG
209 Church St.
Buena Vista, CO 81211
Telephone: 719-395-2459
MAILING ADDRESS:
Marilyn Heimberg Ross
P.O. Box 1500
Buena Vista, CO 81211
Telephone: 303-395-2227
AFFILIATIONS:
ASJA/AG
PRINCIPAL SUBJECTS:
Human Interest
Business & Industry
General Interest
Journalism
PUBLICATIONS:
Essence
Modern Maturity
Westways
Toastmaster's Magazine
Southwest Airlines Magazine
NRTA Journal
Complete Woman
Executive Female
Publishers Weekly
Signature

ROTHMAN, HOWARD
1280 E. Easter Ave.
Littleton, CO 80122
Telephone: 303-347-0754
Fax: 303-347-1064
AFFILIATIONS:
CAL
PRINCIPAL SUBJECTS:
Business & Industry
Health
Travel
Family
Management
Medical
Physical Fitness
PUBLICATIONS:
Outside Business Magazine
Entrepreneurial Woman
Guest Informant

Kiwanis Magazine
Nation's Business Magazine
Cross Country Skier
Modern Maturity
Shape
Women's Sports & Fitness
Walking
Camping Magazine (UK)
Business and Society Review

ROWLES, GENEVIEVE
1815 South 1100 East
Salt Lake Cty, UT 84105
Telephone: 801-485-8450
Fax: 801-487-5811
AFFILIATIONS:
SATW, ASJA, SPJ
PRINCIPAL SUBJECTS:
Family
History
Photography
Travel

RUBIN, NANCY
8 Avon Rd.
Larchmont, NY 10538
Telephone: 914-834-6841
AFFILIATIONS:
ASJA, AG
PRINCIPAL SUBJECTS:
Book Reviews
Editorial
Education
Family
General Interest
History
Home & Garden
Human Relations
Women's Interest
PUBLICATIONS:
New York Times
Ladies Home Journal
McCalls
Savvy
Travel & Leisure
Parents
Working Mother
L.A. Times
Newsday

RUDOLPH, JOHN K.
126 Old Fields Rd.
South Berwick, ME 03908
Telephone: 617-450-7856
Fax: 617-450-2905
MAILING ADDRESS:
John K. Rudolph
Mail Drop C-20, 1 Norway St.
Boston, MA 02115
PRINCIPAL SUBJECTS:
Business & Industry

Ecology
Travel
Agriculture
Foreign
Government
Journalism
News
Social Trends
Travel
PUBLICATIONS:
New York Times, The
Diversion Magazine
Country Journal
Parenting

RUSSELL, BARBARA
2425 Vail Ave., #A-19
Charlotte, NC 28207
Telephone: 704-375-5548
Fax: 612-929-8580
PRINCIPAL SUBJECTS:
Health
Business & Industry

RUSSELL, FRED
1100 Broad St.
Nashville, TN 37203
Telephone: 615-259-8219
PRINCIPAL SUBJECTS:
Humor
Personalities
Sports
PUBLICATIONS:
Nashville Banner
The Saturday Evening Post
Readers Digest
The Sporting News

SABIN, FRANCENE
103 Connolly Drive
Milltown, NJ 08850
Telephone: 908-821-8633
Fax: 908-297-7977
AFFILIATIONS:
ASJA
PRINCIPAL SUBJECTS:
Animals
Ecology
Education
Family
Health
Human Interest
Human Relations
Medical
Nature
Personalities
Photography
Science
Sports
Travel
Women's Interest

PUBLICATIONS:
Seventeen
Omni
Parade
American Education
Ladies' Home Journal
Family Circle

SAFRAN, CLAIRE
53 Evergreen Ave.
Westport, CT 06880
Telephone: 203-227-6271
AFFILIATIONS:
ASJA, NWU
PRINCIPAL SUBJECTS:
Social Trends
Personalities
Health
PUBLICATIONS:
Readers Digest
Good Housekeeping
Redbook
T.V. Guide
New Choices
McCalls
Ladies Home Journal
Lears

SAKELY, THOMAS
4564 Fifteen Mile
Sterling Hgts., MI 48310
Telephone: 313-979-6794
PRINCIPAL SUBJECTS:
Advertising
Marketing
Business & Industry

SAMBROT, WILLIAM
1839 Oak St.
Napa, CA 94559
Telephone: 212-473-5400
MAILING ADDRESS:
Curtis Brown, LTD.
10 Astor Pl.
New York, NY 10003
PRINCIPAL SUBJECTS:
Aviation
Business & Industry
General Interest
Health
Science
PUBLICATIONS:
Toronto Star Weekly
Argosy
Esquire
Playboy
Reader's Digest
Saturday Evening Post
Seventeen
Talk

SANDEL, SUSAN L.
Y34 Quonnipaug Ln.
Guilford, CT 06437
Telephone: 203-238-8325
MAILING ADDRESS:
Senior News
P.O. Box 853
Rockville, NY 11571
PRINCIPAL SUBJECTS:
Senior Citizens
The Arts
Health
General Interest
PUBLICATIONS:
Senior News, Long Island
Design Magazine
New York Times
D. O. N. Magazine

SAUNDERS, LUCY
2412 E. Stratford Court
Shorewood, WI 53211
Telephone: 414-962-5523
Fax: 414-962-5523
MAILING ADDRESS:
Saunders, Lucy
Shorewood, WI 53211
AFFILIATIONS:
AIWF
PRINCIPAL SUBJECTS:
Business & Industry
PUBLICATIONS:
The Milwaukee Journal
Fancy Food
Restaurants & Institutions
Marketing News
Detroit Free Press
St. Louis Magazine
Chicago Tribune, The
Ford Times Magazine
Showcase Magazine
Gourmet Retailer
Top Shelf Magazine

SAYLOR DOPPENBERG,
  JEAN
1904 Dogwood Dr.
Santa Rosa, CA 95403
Telephone: 707-525-0539
PRINCIPAL SUBJECTS:
Business & Industry
Travel

SCAGNETTI, JACK
5258 Cartwright Ave.
N Hollywood, CA 91601
Telephone: 818-762-3871
MAILING ADDRESS:
Scagnetti, Jack
5330 Lankershim Bl. #210
N. Hollywood, CA 91601

Telephone: 213-762-3871
PRINCIPAL SUBJECTS:
Entertainment
Health
Automotive
Business & Industry
Men's Interest
Sports
PUBLICATIONS:
Mechanix Illustrated
Motor Trend
Popular Science
Golf Tips Magazine
The Peoples Almanac
Sports Parade
Golf Magazine
Golf Digest
Golf Tips
Golf Illustrated

SCHARFENBERGER, JOHN
232 McMakin-McMullen Rd.
Shelbyville, KY 40065
Telephone: 606-257-3740
Fax: 606-257-4017
PRINCIPAL SUBJECTS:
Religion
Business & Industry
PUBLICATIONS:
Crossroads
The Lane Report
Louisville Business First
Modern Maturity

SCHELL, NORMAN B.
63 Birchwood Park Dr.
Jericho, NY 11753
Telephone: 516-935-7504
Fax: 516-935-7504
AFFILIATIONS:
AMWA
PRINCIPAL SUBJECTS:
Health
PUBLICATIONS:
New York State Journal of
    Medicine
Pediatrics
Health Week
Readers Digest

SCHERMERHORN, DERICK D.
322 Spring Hill Rd.
Sharon, NH 03458
Telephone: 603-924-8494
MAILING ADDRESS:
Derick D. Schermerhorn
Sharon, NH 03458
PRINCIPAL SUBJECTS:
Business & Industry
Management
Human Relations

Computer Technology
Ecology
Editorial
History
Health
PUBLICATIONS:
Public Relations Journal
New York State Bar Journal
Printing Paper Quarterly

SCHILLER, ANDREW
1030 N. Kenilworth Ave.
Oak Park, IL 60302
Telephone: 708-383-0993
PRINCIPAL SUBJECTS:
General Interest
Education
PUBLICATIONS:
Harper's
Panorama
American Educator

SCHLEIN, ALAN M.
308 E. Capitol St., #9
Washington, DC 20003
Telephone: 202-544-5893
AFFILIATIONS:
SPJ, IRE, Regional Reporters
    Association
PRINCIPAL SUBJECTS:
Government
Health
PUBLICATIONS:
London Daily Telegraph, V. K.
National Syndicated Column in
    Aging
Money Magazine
People

SCHLICK, JACK
416 Summit Ave.
Burlington, WI 53105
Telephone: 414-763-9475
AFFILIATIONS:
ADS, SDC, NPC
PRINCIPAL SUBJECTS:
Animals
Human Relations
Travel
Automotive
PUBLICATIONS:
Ford Marketing Institute
    Solutions
Sears Apparel Group
    "Momentum"
Pabst Brewing Company
    "Salesmaker"

SCHLOSS, MURIEL
736 Malcolm Ave.
Los Angeles, CA 90024

Telephone: 310-474-1707
AFFILIATIONS:
ASJA, PEN
PRINCIPAL SUBJECTS:
Animals
Family
Human Interest
Human Relations
Science
Travel
General Interest
PUBLICATIONS:
LA Times
Grit
Chicago Sun Times

SCHMITH, CINDY
14903 Sulky Way
Carmel, IN 46032
Telephone: 317-848-2457
PRINCIPAL SUBJECTS:
Family
Religion
PUBLICATIONS:
The Family

SCHNECK, MARCUS H.
4920 Liberty Lane
Allentown, PA 18106
Telephone: 215-481-0160
Fax: 215-481-0160
AFFILIATIONS:
OWAA
PRINCIPAL SUBJECTS:
Animals
Business & Industry
Ecology
Sports
PUBLICATIONS:
Grit
Pennsylvania Magazine
Underwater USA
Pennsylvania Sportsman
Pennsylvania Forests
State College Magazine
Northeast Outdoors
Centre Daily Times
Pennsylvania Game News
Northeast Pennsylvania
    Business Journal
Off Duty
Lutheran, The
Modern Dentalab
Pennsylvania Wildlife &
    Outdoor Digest
Long Island Monthly
Eastern Pennsylvania Business
    Journal

SCHNEIDER-AKER,
    KATHERINE
9212 Cedros Ave.
Van Nuys, CA 91402
Telephone: 818-893-7700
AFFILIATIONS:
IWWG, WWW, TRWS
PRINCIPAL SUBJECTS:
Religion
Women's Interest
PUBLICATIONS:
Womans Newspaper, The
Seek
Daughters of Sarah
L. U. C.
Broomstick
Recovery Now
Daily Meditation

SCHOTT-JONES, ELAINE
140 Caversham Woods
Pittsford, NY 14534
Telephone: 716-383-1797
Fax: 716-383-9062
AFFILIATIONS:
STC, WICI
PRINCIPAL SUBJECTS:
Management
Health
Photography
Computer Technology
Electronics

SCHREIBER, NORMAN
135 Eastern Parkway
Brooklyn, NY 11238
Telephone: 718-636-5992
PRINCIPAL SUBJECTS:
Business & Industry
Entertainment
General Interest
Personalities
Photography
The Arts
Travel
PUBLICATIONS:
Smithsonian
Popular Integrity
Ameican Management Review

SCHULTZ, DODI
152 W. 77th St.
New York, NY 10024
Telephone: 212-362-3153
AFFILIATIONS:
ASJA, AG, NASW, SPJ
PRINCIPAL SUBJECTS:
Health
Medical
Book Reviews

PUBLICATIONS:
Cosmopolitan
Family Circle
Games
Ladies Home Journal
N.Y. Times Magazine
Parade
Parents
Science Digest
Self
Dell Puzzle Magazines
Today's Health
Viva
Woman's World
SciQuest

SCHULTZ, MORTON J.
19 Bedford Rd.
Somerset, NJ 08873
Telephone: 908-247-9187
PRINCIPAL SUBJECTS:
Automotive
Home & Garden
Computer Technology
PUBLICATIONS:
Family Circle
The Family Handyman
Popular Mechanics
The Homeowner
Reader's Digest
Home Mechanix
Popular Science
Motor
Information Week
Consumer Reports
Better Homes & Gardens
Medical Economics
Rudder

SCHWALBERG, CAROL
629 Palisades Ave.
Santa Monica, CA 90402
Telephone: 310-451-0098
AFFILIATIONS:
AG; PEN; NWU
PRINCIPAL SUBJECTS:
General Interest
Humor
Foreign
Travel
Amusements
PUBLICATIONS:
Glamour
Mademoiselle
Playgirl
Working Woman
Los Angeles Times
Various
Redbook

Ladies' Home Journal
Penthouse
Working Woman

SCHWANZ, MICHAEL L.
235 W. 75th St., Apt. 4 - S
New York, NY 10023
Telephone: 212-496-9103
AFFILIATIONS:
SPJ, ASME
PRINCIPAL SUBJECTS:
Sports
Travel
Ecology
Human Interest
Health
PUBLICATIONS:
Sports Afield
Fodor's Travel Guides
United Magazine
Chicago Sun - Times Sunday
  Travel Section
New Jersey Monthly
Self Magazine
Longevity

SCHWARZ, TED
1752 Holyoke 2
Cleveland, OH 44112
Telephone: 216-249-3101
Fax: 216-249-3212
MAILING ADDRESS:
Ted Schwarz
P.O. Box 14609
Cleveland, OH 44144
PRINCIPAL SUBJECTS:
Business & Industry
Medical
Photography
Sports
PUBLICATIONS:
Family Circle
PSA Magazine
Penthouse Forum
Phoenix Magazine
Studio Photography
Reader's Digest
Woman's Day
American Way
Writer's Digest
Physician's Management
Pageant
Black Belt
Stern (Germany)
Rangefinder Magazine, The
Chic
Detroit News
Dental Management
Numismatic News
Coins
Australian Photography

Tucson Magazine
Hustler
Saga
Today's Christian Woman
Seventeen Magazine
Success Magazine
Health Matrix
Cosmopolitan
Woman
Modern Bride

SCOBEY, JOAN
9 Lenox Pl.
Scarsdale, NY 10583
Telephone: 914-723-2747
AFFILIATIONS:
AG, PEN, IWOSC
PRINCIPAL SUBJECTS:
Travel
Human Interest
Humor
Social Trends
PUBLICATIONS:
Family Circle
Ladies Home Journal
McCall's
Reader's Digest
Woman's Day
Travel & Leisure
House & Garden
Food & Wine
Newsday
Christian Science Monitor
Boston Globe
Los Angeles Times
House Beautiful
Bride's

SCOTT, GINI GRAHAM
715 48th Avenue
San Francisco, CA 94121
Telephone: 415-387-1771
Fax: 415-387-1779
AFFILIATIONS:
ASJA; PEN
PRINCIPAL SUBJECTS:
Business & Industry
Education
Entertainment
General Interest
Government
History
Management
Photography
Religion
Social Trends

SEAMAN, BARBARA
110 West End Ave., Apt. 5d
New York, NY 10023
Telephone: 212-580-1838

Fax: 212-580-5083
AFFILIATIONS:
PEN, AG
PRINCIPAL SUBJECTS:
Health
Personalities
Women's Interest
Book Reviews
Family
History
Human Relations
Medical
Social Trends
PUBLICATIONS:
Family Circle
Ms Magazine
Penthouse
Washington Post
Womens Day
Ladies Home Journal
Working Woman
Brides Magazine
Omni Magazine
Good Housekeeping
Social Policy
Playgirl
New York Magazine
Village Voice
New York Times
Cosmopolitan
Newsday

SEAMANS, ANDY
1921 Westmoreland St.
Mc Lean, VA 22101
Telephone: 703-356-4826
Fax: 703-356-4826
MAILING ADDRESS:
"The Answer Man"
Mc Lean, VA 22101
AFFILIATIONS:
SPJ
PRINCIPAL SUBJECTS:
History
Geography
Family
General Interest
Government
Animals
Entertainment
Education
Religion
Sales
Travel
The Arts
PUBLICATIONS:
Detroit News
Manchester (NH) Union Leader
Indianapolis News
(Waterbury, Conn.) Republican
  & American

Orange County (Calif.) Register
San Diego Union
Arizona Republic
Washington Times

SECUNDA, VICTORIA
4 Hardscrabble Circle
Armonk, NY 10504
Telephone: 914-273-5694
Fax: 914-273-1760
AFFILIATIONS:
AG, ASJA
PRINCIPAL SUBJECTS:
Family
Human Relations
Media
Psychology
Women's Interest
PUBLICATIONS:
Woman's Day
New Woman
Harper's Bazaar
TV Guide
Glamour
Redbook
Cosmopolitan

SEIDEN, OTHNIEL J.
3654 S. Oneida Way
Denver, CO 80237
Telephone: 303-758-5405
Fax: 303-758-4124
PRINCIPAL SUBJECTS:
Medical
Advertising
History
Video
Foreign
Health

SEITEL, FRASER PAUL
12 King Pl.
Closter, NJ 07624
Telephone: 212-552-4503
Fax: 201-784-1446
MAILING ADDRESS:
Emerald Ptnrs.
177 Main St., Ste. 215
Fort Lee, NJ 07024
Telephone: 201-784-8880
PRINCIPAL SUBJECTS:
Sports
Business & Industry
Travel
General Interest
Humor
Management
Marketing
PUBLICATIONS:
US Banker
New York Times

SERVINO, CAROL
1080 Valley St.
Astoria, OR 97103
Telephone: 503-325-2863
AFFILIATIONS:
NFPW, OPW
PRINCIPAL SUBJECTS:
Family
Youth
Health
Personalities
PUBLICATIONS:
Oregonian
Peninsula Magazine,
   (Sequim, Wa.)
Daily World, The,
   (Aberdeen, Wa.)
Herald Journal, The,
   (Logan, Utah)
Press and Sunday Press, The,
   (Atlantic City, N.J.)
Northwest Magazine,
   (Portland, Oregon)
Sentinal, The, Portland,
   Oregon

SHAKESPEARE, MARGARET
304 W. 89th St.
New York, NY 10024
Telephone: 212-799-5877
Fax: 313-884-5326
AFFILIATIONS:
ASJA
PRINCIPAL SUBJECTS:
Travel
The Arts
Personalities
Health
PUBLICATIONS:
New York Times
New York Woman
Gourmet
American Way
Working Woman

SHAPIRO, CECILE
RFD 77
Cavendish, VT 05142
Telephone: 802-226-7677
Fax: 802-226-7677
AFFILIATIONS:
AG, ASJA, GWAA
PRINCIPAL SUBJECTS:
The Arts
Home & Garden
Book Reviews
PUBLICATIONS:
House & Garden
Americana
Artnews

Cleveland Plain Dealer
Publishers Weekly
New York Times

SHAPIRO, PATRICIA
   GOTTLIEB
121 Coulter Ave.
Ardmore, PA 19003
Telephone: 215-649-3924
AFFILIATIONS:
ASJA
PRINCIPAL SUBJECTS:
Family
Health
Human Interest
Management
Medical
Psychology
Women's Interest
PUBLICATIONS:
New Woman
Philadelphia
Philadelphia Inquirer
Applause
Baltimore Sun
Chicago Sun Times

SHAW, EVA
1758 Yourell Ave.
Carlsbad, CA 92008
Telephone: 619-729-1326
Fax: 619-434-5630
AFFILIATIONS:
ASJA
PRINCIPAL SUBJECTS:
Animals
Health
Hobbies
Human Interest
Humor
Personalities
Physical Fitness
Senior Citizens
Women's Interest
PUBLICATIONS:
LA Times
Weight Watchers
Jewish Journal
Shape
Business Today
San Diego Union
Let's Live
Sunset

SHEFFE, EDWARD D.
247 E. 28th St.
New York, NY 10016
Telephone: 212-685-4191
Fax: 212-689-9091
MAILING ADDRESS:
Edward D. Sheffe

AFFILIATIONS:
ASJA, SDX/SPJ
PRINCIPAL SUBJECTS:
Business & Industry
Travel
Editorial
Computer Technology
PUBLICATIONS:
Esquire
Philadelphia Magazine
Backpacker
Nashville Tennessean
Appalachian Journal (AMC)
Outside
Madison Avenue
Chicago Tribune
Adventure Travel

SHEIN, ARN
6816 R. Hyde Park Dr.
San Diego, CA 92119
PRINCIPAL SUBJECTS:
Motivation
Sports
Personalities
PUBLICATIONS:
Beckett Publication
Catholic Digest
El Centinella
Evangel
Finance
Guideposts
Homelife
Legacies
Liguorian
Los Angeles Times
Modern Maturity
Modern Woodmen
Quiet Hour
Reader's Digest
San Diego Union Tribune
Signs of the Times
Venture
Winning
The Writer

SHELDON, GEORGE
P.O. Box 158
Mount Joy, PA 17552
Telephone: 717-653-9614
Fax: 717-653-8348
AFFILIATIONS:
ASJA
PRINCIPAL SUBJECTS:
Business & Industry
Computer Technology
General Interest
Hobbies
Journalism
Marketing
Personalities

Photography
The Arts
Travel
PUBLICATIONS:
PC World
PAQ
PA Game News

SHEMANSKI, FRANCES
2211 Lodovick Avenue
Bronx, NY 10469
Telephone: 718-798-7408
AFFILIATIONS:
SATW, WYTWA, NEWSPAPER
  WOMEN CLUB OF NY
PRINCIPAL SUBJECTS:
Entertainment
The Arts
Travel
PUBLICATIONS:
Newark Star Ledger
Dallas Morning News
Boston Globe
Chicago Tribune
Philadelphia Inquirer
Washington Post
Adventure Road

SHEPARD, SUSAN J.
68 Jack's Bridge Rd.
Woodbury, CT 06798
Telephone: 203-263-2168
MAILING ADDRESS:
Susan J. Shepard
P.O. Box 259
Woodbury, CT 06798
PRINCIPAL SUBJECTS:
Government
Agriculture
PUBLICATIONS:
Litchfield County Times, The
AI Expert
Computer Language
Language Technology
PC Tech Journal
New Age Journal
Citrus Grower

SHERMAN, SIGNE L.
648 Halo Dr. Angel Is.
Troy, MT 59935
Telephone: 406-295-5139
Fax: 406-295-5303
MAILING ADDRESS:
Signe L. Sherman
648 Halo Dr. Angel Island
Troy, MT 59935
PRINCIPAL SUBJECTS:
Business & Industry
Science
Photography

PUBLICATIONS:
Barron's Weekly
The Chemist; The New Fibers
The Journal of Nutrition
The Journal of
  Pharmacology and
Experimental Therapeutics
Chemical Products and
  Chemical News, (London)

SHERWOOD, HUGH C.
109 N. Broadway #L6
White Plains, NY 10603
Telephone: 914-949-6876
AFFILIATIONS:
ASJA
PRINCIPAL SUBJECTS:
Business & Industry
Personal Finance
Management
PUBLICATIONS:
Harper's Bazaar
Nation's Business
Town & Country
Industry Week
AMA News
Physician's Management
Dental Management
Euromoney

SHEVIS, JIM
2587 Viking Dr.
Herndon, VA 22071
Telephone: 202-619-4415
AFFILIATIONS:
SPJ, SEJ
PRINCIPAL SUBJECTS:
News
Human Interest
PUBLICATIONS:
Christian Science Monitor
World Affairs
Virginia Cardinal
Washington Post
Fairfax Journal
Abroad
Herndon Observer

SHIMBERG, ELAINE FANTLE
100 S. Ashley Dr., Ste. 820
Tampa, FL 33602
Telephone: 813-221-9673
Fax: 813-223-2615
MAILING ADDRESS:
Elaine Fantle Shimberg
Tampa, FL 33602
Telephone: 813-258-1161
AFFILIATIONS:
ASJA, AMWA, NASW
PRINCIPAL SUBJECTS:
Family

General Interest
Health
Medical
Women's Interest
Youth
PUBLICATIONS:
Essence
Glamour
Lady's Circle
Seventeen
Highlights For Children
Writer's Digest
Milwaukee Journal
Tampa Tribune
St. Petersburg Times

SHIPLER, GUY
Capitol Press Room,
  Capitol Bldg.
Carson City, NV 89710
Telephone: 702-882-3535
MAILING ADDRESS:
Guy Shipler
P.O. Box 642
Carson City, NV 89702
Telephone: 702-882-7666
PRINCIPAL SUBJECTS:
General Interest
Government
PUBLICATIONS:
Sports Illustrated
Time
People
Nevada Magazine
McGraw-Hill Magazines
Sacramento Bee
Gaining Business Magazine
Las Vegas Business Press
Henderson Home News

SHUBIN, SEYMOUR
122 Harrogate Rd.
Wynnewood, PA 19096
Telephone: 215-649-4325
MAILING ADDRESS:
Shubin, Seymour
Wynnewood, PA 19096
AFFILIATIONS:
ASJA, AG
PRINCIPAL SUBJECTS:
General Interest
Health
Humor
Personalities
PUBLICATIONS:
Argosy
Family Circle
Reader's Digest
Redbook

Saga
Emergency Medicine
Saturday Evening Post

SIEGEL, DOROTHY
4-11 Kenneth Ave.
Fair Lawn, NJ 07410
Telephone: 201-791-6275
AFFILIATIONS:
ASJA, SCBW
PRINCIPAL SUBJECTS:
General Interest
Health
Home & Garden
Personalities
Travel
Education
Family
Medical
Women's Interests
Youth
Journalism
PUBLICATIONS:
Family Circle
Good Housekeeping
McCall's
Parents'
Reader's Digest
Redbook
American Education
Money
Travel
Vista/USA
Weight Watchers
Woman's Day
Ladies Home Journal
NJ Monthly

SIEGEL, MARY ELLEN
75-68 195th Street
Fresh Meadows, NY 11366
Telephone: 718-465-1908
Fax: 412-224-3556
AFFILIATIONS:
ASJA, NASW
PRINCIPAL SUBJECTS:
Health
Family
Human Relations
Senior Citizens
Physical Fitness

SIEGEL, PAULA M.
235 W. 102 St. #5l
New York, NY 10025
Telephone: 212-662-2429
Fax: 212-222-8143
AFFILIATIONS:
ASJA
PRINCIPAL SUBJECTS:
Family

Health
Human Relations
Medical
Physical Fitness
Psychology
Women's Interest
PUBLICATIONS:
Redbook
Working Mother
Self
Glamour
Parenting
Bazaar
Mademoiselle
Beauty

SILBAR, HOWARD J.
3260 Bradford NE
Grand Rapids, MI 49546
Telephone: 616-949-0557
AFFILIATIONS:
AFA
PRINCIPAL SUBJECTS:
Business & Industry
Family
General Interest
History
Travel
PUBLICATIONS:
AAA Motorist
Grand Rapids Magazine
Grand Rapids Press
Chicago Daily News
Woodworking Furniture Digest
Ann Arbor Daily News

SILBERMAN, ARLENE
535 E. 86th St., Apt. 2a
New York, NY 10028
Telephone: 212-744-9644
AFFILIATIONS:
ASJA
PRINCIPAL SUBJECTS:
Education
Youth
Family
General Interest
Human Relations
PUBLICATIONS:
Good Housekeeping
Ladies' Home Journal
McCall's
Pageant
Reader's Digest
Redbook
Woman's Day

SILBEY, PAULA J.
41 Mt. Airy Rd.
Saugerties, NY 12477
Telephone: 914-246-7820

Fax: 914-246-4007
AFFILIATIONS:
ASJA, EFA
PRINCIPAL SUBJECTS:
Advertising
Amusements
Business & Industry
Entertainment
Family
Fashion
Foreign
General Interest
Health
Human Interest
Journalism
Marketing
News
Personalities
Sales
Senior Citizens
The Arts
Travel
Women's Interest
PUBLICATIONS:
Newsweek
House Beautiful
Woman's Day
Weight Watchers
Connoisseur
Instrumentalist
Stagebill
Musical America

SILVA, KATE
P.O. Box 1667
Dayton, NV 89403
Telephone: 702-246-0278
PRINCIPAL SUBJECTS:
Travel
Advertising

SINBERG, STAN
39 Roque Morals Ct.
Mill Valley, CA 94941
Telephone: 510-382-7311
Fax: 415-883-5458
MAILING ADDRESS:
Sinberg, Stan
150 Alameda Del Plado
Novato, CA 94949
PRINCIPAL SUBJECTS:
Computer Technology
Humor

SISCO, PAUL C.
1705 DeSales St., N.W.
Washington, DC 20036
Telephone: 202-887-7889
Fax: 202-887-7891
MAILING ADDRESS:
Sisco, Paul C.

Washington, DC 20036
AFFILIATIONS:
SPJ, RNDA, NATAS
PRINCIPAL SUBJECTS:
Foreign
General Interest
News

SKLAR, DUSTY
1043 Wilson Ave.
Teaneck, NJ 07666
Telephone: 201-836-7182
AFFILIATIONS:
ASJA, IWWG
PRINCIPAL SUBJECTS:
General Interest
Health
Humor
Personalities
Philosophy
The Arts
Family
Book Reviews
Youth
PUBLICATIONS:
Cosmopolitan
Family Weekly
Modern Maturity
The Nation
Self
N.Y. Sunday News Magazine
Virginia Quarterly Review
Playgirl
NY Sunday Times

SKLAREWITZ, NORMAN
321 S. San Vicente Blvd.,
  Rm. 504
Los Angeles, CA 90048
Telephone: 310-275-2630
MAILING ADDRESS:
Sklarewitz Norman
P.O. Box 5385
Beverly Hills, CA 90209
AFFILIATIONS:
ASJA, SATW
PRINCIPAL SUBJECTS:
Business & Industry
Travel
Aviation
PUBLICATIONS:
Frequent Flyer
Business Travel News
International Business
Los Angeles Daily News
Jet Cargo News
CFO Magazine
Silver Kris
Far East Traveler
Aircraft Maintenance
  International

Travel Agent Magazine
Communication World
Beverly Hills Life
Boy's Life
Photo District News
Amusement Business
Public Relations Journal
Westways
Far East Traveller
Relax Magazine

SLATE, LIBBY
6316 W. 6th St.
Los Angeles, CA 90048
Telephone: 213-939-5807
AFFILIATIONS:
SPJ, IWSC
PRINCIPAL SUBJECTS:
Amusements
Entertainment
Personalities
Sports
Women's Interest
The Arts
Human Interest
PUBLICATIONS:
Los Angeles Times
US
Emmy
Performing Arts
American Premiere
Skating
Canadian Skater
McGill's Survey of Cinema/&
  Cinema Annuals
Young Miss
Hollywood Reporter
Essence
Skating

SLATTERY, WILLIAM J.
P.O. Box 239
Jamestown, RI 02835
Telephone: 401-423-2674
AFFILIATIONS:
Authors Guild
PRINCIPAL SUBJECTS:
Amusements
Business & Industry
General Interest
Humor
PUBLICATIONS:
Argosy
Cosmopolitan
Esquire
Genesis
New York Times
Penthouse
Signature
True
TV Guide

Writer's Digest
Playboy Press
Rudder
Audience
NY Daily News Sunday
  Magazine
Providence Journal Sunday
  Magazine
Providence Journal Book
  Review
Boston Magazine
Good Food
Cruising World

SLEAR, TOM
328 Beach Dr.
Annapolis, MD 21403
Telephone: 410-268-4773
Fax: 410-263-1462
AFFILIATIONS:
ASJA
PRINCIPAL SUBJECTS:
Sports
Physical Fitness
Personal Finance
Business & Industry
Military
PUBLICATIONS:
Ms.
Boys' Life
Baltimore Sun
Hartford Courent, The
Times Journal

SLOME, JESSE R.
32504 Carrie Pl.
Thousand Oaks, CA 91361
Telephone: 818-592-3777
PRINCIPAL SUBJECTS:
Business & Industry
Personal Finance
Travel
Hobbies
PUBLICATIONS:
Business Age
New York Times
Associated Press/U.P.I.
Copley News Service
Money

SMALL, SYLVIA ADAMSON
3142 Ashbury Ln.
Rex, GA 30273
Telephone: 404-968-0923
PRINCIPAL SUBJECTS:
Human Relations
News
Personalities
Entertainment
Photography
Home & Garden

PUBLICATIONS:
Southern Homes Magazine
Association Executive, The
Metro South Magazine
Georgia Journal
Photo District News

SMITH, BEVERLY BUSH
24302 Ontario Lane
Lake Forest, CA 92630
Telephone: 714-458-8981
AFFILIATIONS:
Intl.Food,Wine,Travel Writers,
  So.Ca.Rest.Writers
PRINCIPAL SUBJECTS:
Health
Management
Human Interest
Travel
Religion
PUBLICATIONS:
Los Angeles Times
The Lookout

SMITH, CARIN A., DVM
19691 Highway 209
Leavenworth, WA 98826
Telephone: 509-763-2052
Fax: 509-763-2112
AFFILIATIONS:
AVMA, ASJA, Pac NWW
PRINCIPAL SUBJECTS:
Animals
Business & Industry
Medical
Science
Women's Interest
PUBLICATIONS:
Journal of the Am. Vet. Med.
  Assoc.
Horse Illustrated
Veterinary Economics
Cat Lover's
Assoc. for Women
  Veterinarian's Bulletin
Pure-bred Dogs-AKC Gazette

SMITH, LEE A.
1210 Oak St., #2
Kenova, WV 25530
Telephone: 304-453-6217
MAILING ADDRESS:
Lee A. Smith
1210 Oak St., 2
Kenova, WV 25530
PRINCIPAL SUBJECTS:
Personalities
Fashion
The Arts
PUBLICATIONS:
Hearthstone Magazine

US News & World Report
Huntington Quarterly
Libido (Literary Journal)

SMITH, LIZ
160 E. 38th St., Ste. 26A
New York, NY 10016
Telephone: 212-490-3153
PRINCIPAL SUBJECTS:
Amusements
Entertainment
General Interest
Philosophy
PUBLICATIONS:
Cosmopolitan
Ladies' Home Journal
Vogue
New York Newsday
McCalls
Redbook
H. Bazaar
N. Y. Times
Esquire
New York Magazine
Sports Illustrated
Parade

SMITH, RICHARD AUSTIN
Cove Nook Farm, Brook St.
Groton, CT 06340
Telephone: 203-536-8182
MAILING ADDRESS:
Richard Austin Smith
P.O. Box 9191, NOANK Station
Groton, CT 06340
AFFILIATIONS:
AL, NPC
PRINCIPAL SUBJECTS:
Aviation
Business & Industry
Government
Personalities
PUBLICATIONS:
Fortune
Reader's Digest
Sports Illustrated
Time
Life
Finance (French)

SMITH, RUTH BAYARD
99 Glenwood Avenue
Leonia, NJ 07605
Telephone: 201-944-4969
AFFILIATIONS:
ASJA
PRINCIPAL SUBJECTS:
Book Reviews
Education
General Interest
Health

History
Human Interest
Human Relations
Journalism
Media
Social Trends
Women's Interest
PUBLICATIONS:
Boston Globe
New York Times
Folio
New Jersey Monthly

SOHN, DAVID A.
1909 Lincoln St., No. A-1
Evanston, IL 60201
Telephone: 708-491-1929
Fax: 708-491-1929
PRINCIPAL SUBJECTS:
Amusements
The Arts
General Interest
Philosophy
Education
Media
PUBLICATIONS:
Film News
Media & Methods
Take One Magazine
Change Magazine
Literary Cavalcade
English Journal
Language Arts
Chicago Tribune

SOLOMON, GOODY L.
1712 Taylor St., N.W.
Washington, DC 20011
Telephone: 202-723-2477
Fax: 202-882-9335
MAILING ADDRESS:
Washington, DC 20011
AFFILIATIONS:
SPJ
PRINCIPAL SUBJECTS:
Health
Human Interest
Agriculture
Family
Ecology
Nature
The Arts
Video
Women's Interest
PUBLICATIONS:
Journal Newpapers, The
Milwaukee Journal
Philadelphia Inquirer
Boston Globe
Press Telegram/Long Beach
Gannett News Service

Changing Times
Working Woman
Washington Woman
Readers Digest
Newsletter, The Food & Drug
  Letter
AAA Potomac
Consumer Reports

SOMAN, SHIRLEY CAMPER
40 West 77th St. - 15B
New York, NY 10024
Telephone: 212-787-8722
Fax: 212-787-8781
AFFILIATIONS:
ASJA, NASW, ACSW, AG
PRINCIPAL SUBJECTS:
Book Reviews
Education
Family
General Interest
Government
Health
History
Human Interest
Human Relations
Medical
Personalities
Psychology
Science
Senior Citizens
Social Trends
The Arts
Travel
Urban Affairs
Women's Interest
World Affairs
Youth
PUBLICATIONS:
Springfield (MA) Union-News
Good Housekeeping
Home Office Computing
Longevity

SOSIN, MARK
681 S.W. 15th St.
Boca Raton, FL 33486
Telephone: 407-368-5556
Fax: 407-391-3004
AFFILIATIONS:
ASJA, OWAA, SEOPA
PRINCIPAL SUBJECTS:
Hobbies
Sports
Travel
Ecology
PUBLICATIONS:
Boys' Life
Field & Stream
Fishing World
Outdoor Life

Popular Mechanics
Saltwater Sportsman
Sports Afield
Boating
Fly Fisherman
Yachting
Reader's Digest

SOTER, TOM
1264 Amsterdam Avenue, #3B
New York, NY 10027
Telephone: 212-316-4916
Fax: 212-316-4916
AFFILIATIONS:
ASJA, NWU
PRINCIPAL SUBJECTS:
Book Reviews
Entertainment
General Interest
Health
Human Interest
Media
Movie Reviews
News
The Arts
Video
PUBLICATIONS:
Americana
Backstage
Chelsea-Clinton News
The Dial
Diversion
East Side Express
Entertainment Weekly
Firehouse
Fuji Magazine
INTV Journal
Joe Franklin's Nostalgia
LA Times Syndicate
Management Review
Men's Fitness
Men's Guide to Fashion
Men's Health
Millimeter
Movieline
New York Newsday
New York Observer
New York Times Syndicate
San Francisco Chronicle
Southwest Airlines Spirit
Starlog
Television Engineering
Urban Backpacker
Video Magazine
Video Times
World Screen News

SPANO SR., JOHN J.
10700 Pine Haven Terr.
Rockville, MD 20852
Telephone: 301-231-4804

AFFILIATIONS:
NPC
PRINCIPAL SUBJECTS:
General Interest
Government
Business & Industry
Science
PUBLICATIONS:
Chemical Week
Wall Street Journal
Democrat
Editor & Publisher Magazine
Business Week
Chemical Marketing Reporter

SPANO, SUSAN
23 Barrow St., Apt. 2B
New York, NY 10014
Telephone: 212-242-7961
Fax: 212-242-7961
AFFILIATIONS:
EFA
PRINCIPAL SUBJECTS:
Editorial
The Arts
Travel
Women's Interest
PUBLICATIONS:
New York Times Book Review
Newsday
The Bloomsbury Review
New York Times Travel
  Section, The
Woman's Day
Fodor's Travel Guides
British Heritage
New Woman

SPATTER, SAM
45 Wyoming St.
Pittsburgh, PA 15211
Telephone: 412-481-1892
PRINCIPAL SUBJECTS:
Home & Garden
PUBLICATIONS:
Pittsburgh Post-Gazette
National Real Estate Investor
Christian Science Monitor (No
  Longer Stringer)
Scripps - Howard News
  Service
New York Times

SPIOTTA-DIMARE, LOREN
341 West End Rd.
South Orange, NJ 07079
Telephone: 201-761-0397
AFFILIATIONS:
DWA, NJPW
PRINCIPAL SUBJECTS:
Animals

PUBLICATIONS:
Better Homes & Gardens
American Health
New Choices
Ladies Home Journal
Animals

SPRING, BOB & NORMA
18961 Marine View Cir., S.W.
Seattle, WA 98166
Telephone: 206-242-1249
AFFILIATIONS:
SATW
PRINCIPAL SUBJECTS:
Travel
PUBLICATIONS:
Ford Times
Vista
Fodor's Travel Guides
Discovery Magazine
Chicago Tribune
Seattle Times Roto
Los Angeles Times
San Francisco Examiner
Eastern Airlines Review
The Seattle Post Intelligencer
Houston Chronicle
Dallas Morning News
San Jose Mercury News
Independent Press Telegram
Sacramento Bee
Sacramento Union
Mexico City News
Michigan Living (AAA)
Home & Away (AAA)
Travel/Holiday
Cruise Travel
Senior World Publications
San Diego Union & Trib.
St. Petersburg Independent
Tampa Tribune
New York News Magazine
Senior Life Magazine
Arizona Republic
Palm Beach Post
Boston Globe
News/Sun Sentinal
Exxon Travel Guide
Houston Post
San Antonio Express News
Salt Lake Tribune
Toronto Star
Contra Cost Times
L.A. Daily Breeze
Tacoma News Tribune
Oregonian
Childrens Press

SPRINGER, P. GREGORY
206 Wood
Urbana, IL 61801

Telephone: 217-344-8479
AFFILIATIONS:
ATCA
PRINCIPAL SUBJECTS:
Entertainment
The Arts
Human Relations
Advertising
Book Reviews
Editorial
Men's Interest
Movie Reviews
PUBLICATIONS:
American Film
Quill, The
Writer's Digest
Variety
Advocate
Info World
Nation's Business
New York Times

ST. JOHN, TERRY
1533 Vermont
Houston, TX 77006
Telephone: 713-524-3712
Fax: 713-524-9637
AFFILIATIONS:
PRSA, WICI
PRINCIPAL SUBJECTS:
Sports
Business & Industry

STACK, ROBERT
425 Madison Ave.
New York, NY 10017
Telephone: 212-750-3434
Fax: 212-750-3435
PRINCIPAL SUBJECTS:
Entertainment
Sports
Personalities
Business & Industry

STAR, JACK
18 Wilson Ct.
Park Forest, IL 60466
Telephone: 708-748-6992
PRINCIPAL SUBJECTS:
General Interest
Geography
Health
Media
Personal Finance
Travel
Architecture
Aviation
Book Reviews
Computer Technology
PUBLICATIONS:
North Shore Magazine

Reader's Digest
Chicago Tribune Travel
   Section
Chicago Tribune Magazine
Chicago Magazine
New York News Magazine
Lufthansa Magazine
Chicago Tribune Travel
   Section
Ford Times

STAUB, MOLLY AROST
4740 S. Ocean Blvd.,
   Suite 1001
Boca Raton, FL 33487
Telephone: 407-392-5222
Fax: 407-367-1261
AFFILIATIONS:
ASJA
PRINCIPAL SUBJECTS:
Ecology
Personalities
Travel
PUBLICATIONS:
The Miami Herald
McCalls
Bridal Guide
Travel & Leisure

STEIN, HERBERT G.
WQED 4802 Fifth Ave.
Pittsburgh, PA 15213
Telephone: 412-622-1300
AFFILIATIONS:
SPJ
PRINCIPAL SUBJECTS:
Human Relations
Journalism
PUBLICATIONS:
Pittsburgh Magazine
Pittsburgh Post - Gazette

STEIN, M. L.
369 Seville Way
Long Beach, CA 90814
Telephone: 310-597-1159
Fax: 310-597-1776
AFFILIATIONS:
ASJA, SPJ
PRINCIPAL SUBJECTS:
Business & Industry
General Interest
Travel
Media
PUBLICATIONS:
Better Homes & Gardens
Nation
New York Times
Saturday Review
Travel
L. A. Times

Chicago Tribune
Editor & Publisher
Clipper
Boston Globe
Toronto Globe & Mail
Houston Post
San Diego Union
Newsday
Ozark
Columbia Journalism Review
Raleigh News & Observer
St. Petersburg Times
Columbia Journalism Review
The Quill
La Opinion

STEINBERG, JANET
900 Adams Crossing #9200
Cincinnati, OH 45202
Telephone: 513-241-1093
AFFILIATIONS:
SATW, MTWA, IFW&TWA,
   SPJ, ASJA
PRINCIPAL SUBJECTS:
Fashion
Personalities
Travel
Women's Interest
PUBLICATIONS:
Consumers Digest
Travel & Leisure
Cincinnati Enquirer
Columbus Dispatch
LA Times
Boston Globe
Silver Circle
Michigan Living

STEINER, SHARI
20 Prescott Ct.
San Francisco, CA 94133
Telephone: 415-398-8093
Fax: 415-986-4429
AFFILIATIONS:
ASJA, PEN
PRINCIPAL SUBJECTS:
Travel
Women's Interest
Business & Industry
Computer Technology
Personal Finance
Photography
PUBLICATIONS:
Family Weekly
Glamour Magazine
Playgirl Magazine
Carte Blanche Magazine
Ladies Home Journal
Readers Digest
Cosmopolitan
Saturday Review Of Literature

Publisher's Weekly
Travel International
Commercial Real Estate
   Newsletter (Editor)

STEPHEN, RAE
5 Riverside Drive, #7F
New York, NY 10023
Telephone: 212-769-2362
PRINCIPAL SUBJECTS:
Health
Religion
Travel
PUBLICATIONS:
Elle
Modern Maturity
Mademoiselle
Playboy
Spy
Cosmopolitan
Travel & Leisure

STEWART-LALE, CISSY
3900 White Settlement Road,
   #101
Fort Worth, TX 76107
Telephone: 817-624-2588
AFFILIATIONS:
WICI
PRINCIPAL SUBJECTS:
History
Human Relations
PUBLICATIONS:
Aura Magazine

STICH, SALLY
3227 S. Niagara
Denver, CO 80224
Telephone: 303-757-3765
Fax: 303-757-3765
AFFILIATIONS:
ASJA
PRINCIPAL SUBJECTS:
Entertainment
Family
General Interest
Home & Garden
Human Interest
Humor
Psychology
PUBLICATIONS:
Redbook
Ladies Home Journal
Modern Maturity
Parents
Denver Post
Washington Post

STICKLER, JOHN C.
8300 N. McCarty Rd.
Tucson, AZ 85704

Telephone: 602-797-3131
Fax: 602-797-3131
AFFILIATIONS:
ASJA, SATW
PRINCIPAL SUBJECTS:
Business & Industry
Architecture
Travel
Advertising
Book Reviews
Marketing
Business & Industry
Social Trends
Management
PUBLICATIONS:
Advertising Age
New York Times
Editor & Publisher
Media
Journal of Applied
  Management
Pacific Travel News
Business Week
The Asia Magazine
The Asia Mail
Travel/Holiday
AdVentures
American Credit Union News
Southwest Profile
Tucson Lifestyle
Tennis USA
Tennis Week
City Magazine (Tucson)
International Advertiser
Capitol Times (Arizona)

STITT, ABBY
9229 - 132 Village Glen Dr.
San Diego, CA 92123
Telephone: 619-571-5335
AFFILIATIONS:
AMWA
PRINCIPAL SUBJECTS:
Women's Interest
General Interest
Health
Science
Youth
Social Trends
PUBLICATIONS:
Emergency Medicine
Self
Mothers Manual
Harper's Bazaar
Playgirl
Journal Of Sex Education &
  Therapy

STOCKER, JOSEPH
1609 W. Keim Dr.
Phoenix, AZ 85015

Telephone: 602-249-1101
AFFILIATIONS:
ASJA APHA SSSS
PRINCIPAL SUBJECTS:
Animals
Government
History
Philosophy
Travel
PUBLICATIONS:
Boys' Life
Elks Magazine
The Nation
Creative Living
American Education
Reader's Digest
Redbook
Parade
Family Circle
American Legion Magazine
Arizona Highways

STODDARD, BROOKE C.
1206 Prince St.
Alexandria, VA 22314
Telephone: 703-548-7891
Fax: 703-548-7891
AFFILIATIONS:
ASJA
PRINCIPAL SUBJECTS:
Business & Industry
Computer Technology
Personal Finance
PUBLICATIONS:
Washington Post
Baltimore Sun
Historic Preservation
Mid-Atlantic Country
Chicago Sun-Times
National Geographic World

STREHLOW, LORETTA
N76 W7292 Linden St.
Cedarburg, WI 53012
Telephone: 414-375-0194
AFFILIATIONS:
WFOP, CWW
PRINCIPAL SUBJECTS:
The Arts
Entertainment
Travel
General Interest

STRESHINSKY, SHIRLEY G.
50 Kenyon Ave.
Kensington, CA 94708
Telephone: 510-526-1976
Fax: 510-527-7740
MAILING ADDRESS:
Shirley Streshinsky
Box 674

Berkeley, CA 94701
AFFILIATIONS:
AG
PRINCIPAL SUBJECTS:
General Interest
Travel
PUBLICATIONS:
Glamour
Ladies Home Journal
McCall's
Conde Nast Traveler
Audubon
Reader's Digest
Redbook
Woman's Day
Travel & Leisure
Silver Kris (Singapore Airlines)
San Francisco Examiner
San Francisco Chronicle

STRICKLER, CAROLYN J.
960 San Pasqual St.
Pasadena, CA 91106
Telephone: 818-584-6885
AFFILIATIONS:
PEN
PRINCIPAL SUBJECTS:
History
Travel
PUBLICATIONS:
Westways
Mankind Magazine
Ford's Travel Guides
Los Angeles Times
Chevron USA

STRUGATCH, WARREN
57 Forest Ave.
Valley Stream, NY
Telephone: 516-872-3657
AFFILIATIONS:
SPJ, NWU SABEW, NYBPE
PRINCIPAL SUBJECTS:
Business & Industry
Travel
The Arts
Government
PUBLICATIONS:
American Banker
New York Times
Newsday

STUART, ANNE ELIZABETH
10 Azel Road
Braintree, MA 02184
Telephone: 617-849-0647
AFFILIATIONS:
NWU
PRINCIPAL SUBJECTS:
Health
Medical

Media
The Arts
Human Interest
PUBLICATIONS:
Boston Magazine
Prelude Magazine
Newsday
MacMillan Health Care
  Information Publications
Conquering Endometriosis
Patriot Ledger, The,
  (Quincy, MA)
Knickerbocker News, The,
  (Albany NY)
Star - Gazette, The,
  (Elmira NY)
Minneapolis Tribune, The
Woman's Day
Herald & News - Tribune,
  (Duluth, MN)
State Journal, The,
  (Lansing MI)
Seventeen
Boston Woman

STUART, KIEL
12 Skylark Lane
Stony Brook, NY 11790
AFFILIATIONS:
AG, SFWA, WA
PRINCIPAL SUBJECTS:
Humor
Physical Fitness
PUBLICATIONS:
New York Times
Newsday
Christian Science Monitor
Commodore Computers
Beyond
Ampersand
NRB
Keystrokes

SULLIVAN, GEORGE
330 East 33rd. St.
New York, NY 10016
Telephone: 212-689-9745
Fax: 212-683-8064
AFFILIATIONS:
ASJA, PEN, AG
PRINCIPAL SUBJECTS:
Sports
Military
History
Hobbies

SWANN, CHRISTOPHER
1641 Hillcrest Rd.
Santa Barbara, CA 93103
Telephone: 805-965-3122

PRINCIPAL SUBJECTS:
Marine
Science
Computer Technology
PUBLICATIONS:
Popular Science
PSA
Exxon - USA
America Illustrated
Time/Life Books
Skin Diver

SZUPROWICZ, BOHDAN O.
8200 Kennedy Blvd., E.
North Bergen, NJ 07047
Telephone: 201-868-0881
AFFILIATIONS:
AG, ASJA
PRINCIPAL SUBJECTS:
Aviation
Business & Industry
Computer Technology
Education
Foreign
Media
PUBLICATIONS:
Barron's Weekly
Military Review
Datamation
National Investments &
   Finance (India)
Usine Nouvelle (France)
New Scientist (UK)
Mini-Micro Systems
Computerworld
Air Transport World
China Business Review
Christian Science Monitor
Newsday
Denver Post
Financial Post(Canada)
The Bulletin (Australia)
Canadian Business
Dun's Review
Investment Dealers Digest
High Technology
Fact, The Money Management
   Magazine
Finance Week (South Africa)
Bull & Bear
California Business
Systems International (UK)
Les Affairs (Canada)
Zerouno (Italy)
OI Informatique (France)
Oficinas (Spain)
Asia Computer Week
   (Singapore)
Canadian Datasystems
Journal of Expert Systems
MIS Week

PC Woche (Germany)
Angewandte Informatik
   (Germany)
Australian Computerworld
Wall Street Micro Investor
Supergrowth Technology USA
Management Technology
Dataweek (South Africa)
Business & Technology
   Consultant
Automatica e Instrumentation
   (Spain)
Kapital (Norway)

TAJER, JOSIE
18535 Queensbury Drive
Livonia, MI 48152
Telephone: 313-464-3449
PRINCIPAL SUBJECTS:
Humor
Animals
Sports
Personal Finance
PUBLICATIONS:
Detroit Free Press
Woman's World
Toledo Blade
Detroit Magazine
Mature Living
Lollipops Magazine
Polish American News
Great Lakes Boating
Lakeland Boating

TAMIS, VALERIE B.
P.O. Box 3202
Fort Lee, NJ 07024
Telephone: 201-947-1331
AFFILIATIONS:
ASJA
PRINCIPAL SUBJECTS:
General Interest
Human Interest
Travel
Women's Interest
PUBLICATIONS:
Bride's
Endless Vacation
USAir
NJ Monthly
Buffalo News
Winston-Salem Journal
Anchorage Daily News
Modern Bride

TANNE, JANICE HOPKINS
251 Central Parkk West
New York, NY 10024
Telephone: 212-799-1622
Fax: 212-877-3298

AFFILIATIONS:
AAAAS, AMWA, ASJA, AG
PRINCIPAL SUBJECTS:
Health
Medical
Men's Interest
Physical Fitness
Psychology
Science
Urban Affairs
Women's Interest
PUBLICATIONS:
New York
British Medical Journal
American Health
Associated Press Newsfeatures
Family Circle
Mademoiselle
Mirabella
New York Times
Reader's Digest
Redbook
Self
Vogue
Woman's Day

TANNER, OGDEN
51 Lambert Rdd.
New Canaan, CT 06840
Telephone: 203-966-4384
Fax: 203-966-4384
PRINCIPAL SUBJECTS:
Ecology
Nature
Home & Garden
Urban Affairs

TAUB, HARALD J.
22960 Calabash St.
Woodland Hls, CA 91364
Telephone: 818-225-8528
PRINCIPAL SUBJECTS:
Health

TAYLOR, GARY
7245 Hillcroft, No. 45
Houston, TX 77081
Telephone: 713-981-4971
Fax: 713-771-0752
AFFILIATIONS:
ASJA
PRINCIPAL SUBJECTS:
Business & Industry
General Interest
Government
Medical
Sports
Personal Finance

PUBLICATIONS:
National Law Journal
Money
USA Today
N.Y. Times

TAYLOR, THEODORE
1856 Catalina St.
Laguna Beach, CA 92651
Telephone: 714-494-6294
AFFILIATIONS:
WG, AMPAS
PRINCIPAL SUBJECTS:
Government
Sports
Youth
PUBLICATIONS:
Argosy
Ladies Home Journal
McCall's
Redbook
New York Times Magazine

TEEVAN, CATHERINE J.
184 Garden St.
Roslyn Hts, NY 11577
Telephone: 516-621-5232
MAILING ADDRESS:
Catherine J. Teevan
11577
PRINCIPAL SUBJECTS:
Home & Garden
PUBLICATIONS:
Housewares Merchandising
Prof'l Furniture Merchant
Apparel Industry Magazine
Inside Furniture (Fairchild,
   defunct)
American Building Supplies
   (Gralla, Charleson;
defunct)
HBA Perspectives
Health Care Systems (Gralla)
New York Times, The (Long
   Island Section)
Suburbia Today (Gannett)

TEGELER, DOROTHY
P.O. Box 51234
Phoenix, AZ 85076
Telephone: 602-759-7872
PRINCIPAL SUBJECTS:
Book Reviews
Medical
Family
Health
Education
Psychology
General Interest
Travel

PUBLICATIONS:
Golf Digest
Advertising Age
Kiwanis
USA Today
Medical World News
Northeast

TEMKO, FLORENCE
5050 La Jolla Blvd., P - C
San Diego, CA 92109
Telephone: 619-483-5122
AFFILIATIONS:
AG, ASJA
PRINCIPAL SUBJECTS:
The Arts
Hobbies
Education
Journalism
PUBLICATIONS:
Boston Globe
Lakeville Journal
Berkshire Eagle
Crafts Magazine
New York Sunday Times
Creative Crafts
Camp Director's Guide
Ebony Jr.
Faces (Magazine)
Yarn Market News
World & I, The (Magazine)
SKY (Magazine)

TERRES, JOHN K.
1118 Sourwood Drive
Chapel Hill, NC 27514
Telephone: 919-942-9906
MAILING ADDRESS:
Dr. John K. Terres
118 Sourwood Drive
Chapel Hill, NC 27514
PRINCIPAL SUBJECTS:
Animals
Ecology
General Interest
Nature
PUBLICATIONS:
Audubon Magazine
New York Times
Sports Illus.
Bird Watcher's Digest
Birder's World
National Wildlife
USAIR Magazine
Living Bird, The
Linnaean Soc News Letter
Woman's Day

TESSINA, PHD., TINA B.
P.O. Box 4884,
1055 Junipero Ave.
Long Beach, CA 90804
Telephone: 310-438-8077
AFFILIATIONS:
ASJA, AAMFT
PRINCIPAL SUBJECTS:
Family
Human Relations
Psychology
Senior Citizens
Women's Interest
PUBLICATIONS:
New Woman
Odyssey
In Context
The Therapist
New Age Journal

THOMPSON, JACQUELINE
100 Bay St. Landing, Suite 7F
Staten Island, NY 10301
Telephone: 718-273-3229
AFFILIATIONS:
ASJA
PRINCIPAL SUBJECTS:
Business & Industry
Fashion
General Interest
Personal Finance
Physical Fitness
PUBLICATIONS:
New York Magazine
Forbes
Working Woman
Fortune
Bride's

THOMSON, PEGGY
23 Grafton St.
Chevy Chase, MD 20815
Telephone: 301-656-3630
PRINCIPAL SUBJECTS:
History
Personalities
Animals
Nature
The Arts
PUBLICATIONS:
Smithsonian
American Education
The Living Wilderness
Washington Post

TONNESSEN, DIANA
2390 NW 18 Place
Gainesville, FL 32605
Telephone: 904-375-7164
AFFILIATIONS:
ASJA, NASW, AMWA

PRINCIPAL SUBJECTS:
Health
Medical
Physical Fitness
Women's Interest
PUBLICATIONS:
Health
Glamour
Self
McCalls
American Baby

TOWLE, LISA H.
110 Dutchess Dr.
Cary, NC 27513
Telephone: 919-481-3943
Fax: 919-481-4314
AFFILIATIONS:
SPJ
PRINCIPAL SUBJECTS:
Education
Religion
General Interest
Business & Industry
Health
PUBLICATIONS:
Time Magazine
Life
New York Times, The
Boston Phoenix, The
Parents Magazine
Parenting Magazine
American Retailer Magazine
Good Housekeeping Magazine
North Carolina Magazine
Triangle Corp. Report

TRASOBARES, CAESAR M.
556 E. 12th St.
Hialeah, FL 33010
Telephone: 305-888-6622
AFFILIATIONS:
ASJA
PRINCIPAL SUBJECTS:
The Arts
Business & Industry
PUBLICATIONS:
Art International

TRILLING, DIANA
35 Claremont Ave.
New York, NY 10027
Telephone: 212-662-5469
PRINCIPAL SUBJECTS:
The Arts
Government
Philosophy
Social Trends
PUBLICATIONS:
New York Times

American Scholar
Redbook
Partisan Review
Vanity Fair

TROMBETTI, STEVEN E.
P.O. Box 1436 Fdr. Sta.
New York, NY 10150
Telephone: 212-832-9065
Fax: 212-832-9065
AFFILIATIONS:
SATW
PRINCIPAL SUBJECTS:
Travel
Home & Garden
Amusements
Entertainment
Men's Interest
PUBLICATIONS:
Advertising Age
Midtown Magazine
Woman Traveler, The
Lodging Magazine
SATW Travel Writer
New York Daily News

TRUBO, RICHARD
3612 Hamilton St.
Irvine, CA 92714
Telephone: 714-786-3248
AFFILIATIONS:
ASMP
PRINCIPAL SUBJECTS:
Health
Science
PUBLICATIONS:
Parade
TV Guide
Los Angeles Times
Chicago Tribune
Woman's Day
Good Housekeeping
Glamour
American Health
Mademoiselle
Family Circle
Self
Cosmopolitan
Medical World News

TRUSSO, JOSEPH
65 Witch Tree Rd.
Woodstock, NY 12498
Telephone: 914-679-7421
PRINCIPAL SUBJECTS:
Ecology
Government
Computer Technology
Education
PUBLICATIONS:
Smithsonian

Newsday
Marine Aquarist
The Guardian (London)
Phototherapy Quarterly
L. A. Times
Washington Post

TUPPER, MARGO
2024 Franklin Ave.
Mc Lean, VA 22101
Telephone: 703-534-6330
AFFILIATIONS:
NPC
PRINCIPAL SUBJECTS:
Human Interest
Family
Business & Industry
Home & Garden
Human Relations
General Interest
Senior Citizens
Travel
PUBLICATIONS:
Good Housekeeping
Parade
Redbook
Washington Post
Washington Star

TURECAMO, DORRINE
6400 Barrie Road, #1107
Edina, MN 55435
Telephone: 612-929-7692
Fax: 612-929-8580
AFFILIATIONS:
ASJA
PRINCIPAL SUBJECTS:
Book Reviews
Business & Industry
Education
Family
Health
Humor
Management
Religion
Social Trends
The Arts
Youth
PUBLICATIONS:
Family Circle
Savvy
Self
Working Woman
Ladies Home Journal
Los Angeles Examiner

TUTHILL JR., OLIVER W.
3022 NE 140th St. #401
Seattle, WA 98125
Telephone: 206-364-9202

AFFILIATIONS:
ASJA
PRINCIPAL SUBJECTS:
Editorial
Entertainment
Government
Human Interest
Human Relations
Journalism
Marketing
Movie Reviews
News
Philosophy
Photography
Psychology
Sales
Sports
World Affairs
PUBLICATIONS:
Marketing
Gallery
Pentax Life
Inside Sports
Baseball Digest
The Ring
Boxing Beat
Sporting

UCHITELLE, ROBERT
655 Irving Park Rd.
Chicago, IL 60613
Telephone: 312-472-7071
Fax: 312-472-7071
PRINCIPAL SUBJECTS:
Senior Citizens
PUBLICATIONS:
Engineer & Mining Journal
Demolition Age

ULRICH, ELISE VONS
330 East 49th Street
New York, NY 10017
Telephone: 212-752-1965
AFFILIATIONS:
ASJA
PRINCIPAL SUBJECTS:
Fashion
Health
Men's Interest
Physical Fitness
Travel
Women's Interest
PUBLICATIONS:
Health, Beauty and Travel
Business Week
Health
McCalls
Men's Fitness
Nature & Health
Sunday Women Plus
USA Today

URROWS, HENRY AND
   ELIZABETH
720 Broadway
Longboat Key, FL 34228
Telephone: 813-383-9319
Fax: 813-383-3694
AFFILIATIONS:
PEN, ASJA, NASW
PRINCIPAL SUBJECTS:
Book Reviews
Business & Industry
Computer Technology
Education
Electronics
Foreign
Government
Health
Media
Medical
Personalities
Science
Senior Citizens
Social Trends
The Arts
Travel
Urban Affairs
World Affairs
PUBLICATIONS:
Harvard
MIT Technology Review
Manufacturing Systems
CD-Rom World
Computers in Libraries
Document Management
Document Image Automation
Foundation News
Chem Matters
MD Magazine
College Board Review
InfoWorld
Computer World
InfoSystems
International Management
PC Week
Popular Computing
Creative Computing
AB Bookman's Weekly
Think
Educational and Industrial
   Television
American Bankerb

VALENTI, DAN
P.O. Box 1845
Pittsfield, MA 01202
Telephone: 413-448-6342
Fax: 413-447-9520
PRINCIPAL SUBJECTS:
Religion
Travel
Entertainment

Sports
Media
Education
Book Reviews
PUBLICATIONS:
Boston Globe
Mart Magazine
S.F. Chronicle

VAN COLLIE, SHIMON-CRAIG
1400 Hearst Ave.
Berkeley, CA 94702
Telephone: 510-843-7213
Fax: 510-843-4253
AFFILIATIONS:
ASJA
PRINCIPAL SUBJECTS:
Computer Technology
Sports
Medical
Entertainment
Editorial

VAN DILLEN, LAILEE
410 Severn Lane
Burlingame, CA 94010
Telephone: 415-347-6015
AFFILIATIONS:
ASJA
PRINCIPAL SUBJECTS:
Book Reviews
Education
Media
Personalities
PUBLICATIONS:
Tennis
The Californians

VANDERTUIN, VICTORIA E.
62091 Valley View Cir.
Joshua Tree, CA 92252
Telephone: 619-366-2833
AFFILIATIONS:
NAPRA
PRINCIPAL SUBJECTS:
Religion
PUBLICATIONS:
Cosmic Star
New Age World News
Polaris Digest

VIORST, MILTON
3432 Ashley Terrace, N.W.
Washington, DC 20008
Telephone: 202-966-8676
Fax: 202-966-5328
AFFILIATIONS:
SPJ, PEN
PRINCIPAL SUBJECTS:
World Affairs
Government

Book Reviews
Editorial
Foreign
History
News
PUBLICATIONS:
New Yorker
Washington Post
N.Y. Times

VOLLMAR, ALICE M.
5115 Dupont Ave., S.
Minneapolis, MN 55419
Telephone: 612-825-3187
AFFILIATIONS:
NWC
PRINCIPAL SUBJECTS:
Travel
Photography
Family
General Interest
PUBLICATIONS:
Travel & Leisure
Travel - Holiday
Midwest Living
Home & Away
Trailer Life
Ladies' Home Journal
Endless Vacation
Twins Magazine

VOTANO, PAUL A.
163 Pennsylvania Ave.
Tuckahoe, NY 10707
Telephone: 914-793-4896
Fax: 914-337-3752
PRINCIPAL SUBJECTS:
Entertainment
General Interest
Personalities
Sports

WAGNER, BILL
17 6th St., SE
Watertown, SD 57201
Telephone: 605-886-6132
PRINCIPAL SUBJECTS:
Agriculture
Business & Industry
PUBLICATIONS:
America
Our Sunday Visitor
Incentive Marketing
Counselor, The
Foremens' Letter
Innkeeping World
Nursing Homes
Construction Foreman
Utility Foreman

RE
S.D. Union Farmer
NFO Reporter

WALKER, DR. MORTON
Freelance Communications
484 High Ridge Road
Stamford, CT 06905
Telephone: 203-322-1551
Fax: 203-322-4656
AFFILIATIONS:
ASJA, NWU
PRINCIPAL SUBJECTS:
Book Reviews
Ecology
Health
Marine
Medical
Nature
Physical Fitness
Psychology
Senior Citizens
Travel

WALKER, GLADYS H.
618a Erie Ln.
Stratford, CT 06497
Telephone: 203-378-9653
AFFILIATIONS:
ASJA, WICI
PRINCIPAL SUBJECTS:
Health
Human Interest
Women's Interest
Business & Industry
Family
Medical
Social Trends
PUBLICATIONS:
New York Times
Interior Design
Los Angeles Times
Architectural Record
American Baby

WALTER, CLAIRE
630 Spruce St.
Boulder, CO 80302
Telephone: 303-442-7709
Fax: 303-440-5660
AFFILIATIONS:
ASTW, ASJA
PRINCIPAL SUBJECTS:
Business & Industry
Personalities
Sports
Travel
Aviation
PUBLICATIONS:
Military Lifestyle
Skiing

Travel & Leisure
Skiing Trade News
Ski Area Management
Wilderness Trails
Wine Country International
Denver Post
Business Travel News

WALTER, EUGENE
161 Grand Blvd.
Mobile, AL 36607
Telephone: 205-479-9828
AFFILIATIONS:
Pres Wil.Ins./Bd of Food Art
   Mag/Ed Brd of Par Rev
PRINCIPAL SUBJECTS:
Amusements
The Arts
Home & Garden
Personalities
Travel
Journalism
PUBLICATIONS:
Azalea City News

WALTERS GROUP
315 W. 70th St., Ste. 6C
New York, NY 10023
Telephone: 212-580-8833
MAILING ADDRESS:
J. Walters, Walters Grp, Inc.
315 W. 70 St., Ste. 6c
New York, NY 10023
Telephone: 212-580-8850
PRINCIPAL SUBJECTS:
Human Relations
General Interest
Journalism
Medical
Health
PUBLICATIONS:
Cosmopolitan
National Enquirer
Forum Magazine
National Star
Medical Tribune
Vogue
Medical World News
Details
Penthouse
Playboy
Longevity

WALTON, CHELLE KOSTER
936 Main St.
Sanibel, FL 33957
Telephone: 813-472-4893
MAILING ADDRESS:
Chelle Koster Walton
P.O. Box 242
Sanibel, FL 33957

AFFILIATIONS:
SATW, ASJA
PRINCIPAL SUBJECTS:
Travel
Nature
History
The Arts
PUBLICATIONS:
Islands
Miami Herald
Los Angeles Herald - Examiner
Ft. Lauderdale News
Detroit News
Caribbean Travel & Life
Guest Informant

WANG, JULIE C.
373 Park Avenue South
New York, NY 10016
Telephone: 212-685-1900
Fax: 212-685-2714

WARREN, CAMERON A.
25 Rimfire Cir.
Reno, NV 89509
Telephone: 702-746-2121
Fax: 702-746-1850
MAILING ADDRESS:
Cam Warren Assoc.
P. O. Box 10588
Reno, NV 89510
AFFILIATIONS:
ASMP
PRINCIPAL SUBJECTS:
General Interest
Business & Industry
Sports
PUBLICATIONS:
Road & Track
PV4 Magazine
Off-Road Magazine
Sports Car
Auto Week
Automobile Year
On Track
Newsweek (Int. Ed.)

WARREN, DAVID
7317 Chesterfield Rd.
Crystal Lake, IL 60012
Telephone: 815-459-6255
MAILING ADDRESS:
David Warren
400 E. Randolph Rm. #3306
Chicago, IL 60601
PRINCIPAL SUBJECTS:
Business & Industry
Family
Home & Garden
Management
History

PUBLICATIONS:
Family Circle
Home Mechanix
The Office
Popular Mechanics
Popular Science
Woman's Day
Workbench
Newspapers
Family Handyman
Electrical World
Personal Publishing

WATLINGTON, JERILYNN
Ridge Rd., P.O. Box 35
Monmouth Jct, NJ 08852
Telephone: 908-329-6241
MAILING ADDRESS:
Jerilynn Watlington
Ridge Rd, P.O. Box 35
Monmouth Jct., NJ 08852
PRINCIPAL SUBJECTS:
Health
Family
Journalism
Physical Fitness
Psychology
Social Trends
The Arts
PUBLICATIONS:
Bestways
Total Fitness
Collegiate Career Woman
Gifted Children Newsletter
Parenting
Wedding Photography
  International
Writer, The
Entrepreneur
WDS (Writers Digest School)
  Forum
Bridal Guide
Bridal Fair
Better Health & Living
Teleflora's Flowers
Woman's World
GM's In Motion
Byline
Writer's Inspirational Markets
  News
TeenAge

WATSON, DELMAR
6762 Hawthorn Ave.
Los Angeles, CA 90028
Telephone: 213-466-3377
Fax: 213-466-3378
AFFILIATIONS:
MPC
PRINCIPAL SUBJECTS:
General Interest

Photography
Aviation
Personalities
Sports
Entertainment

WEHRWEIN, AUSTIN C.
2309 Carter Ave.
Saint Paul, MN 55108
Telephone: 612-645-9894
AFFILIATIONS:
AL, OPC, ASJA
PRINCIPAL SUBJECTS:
Government
Education
PUBLICATIONS:
Washington Post
Minneapolis Star
National Law Journal
London Economist
Chronicle of Higher Education
Education Week
Boston Globe

WEINSTEIN, GRACE W.
8 BRAYTON ST.
ENGLEWOOD, NJ 07631
Telephone: 201-568-4295
Fax: 201-894-1890
AFFILIATIONS:
ASJA
PRINCIPAL SUBJECTS:
Business & Industry
Human Relations
Personal Finance
Senior Citizens
PUBLICATIONS:
Good Housekeeping
Working Mother
Kiplinger's Personal Finance
Money
Woman's Day
Newark Star-Ledger
New York Daily News

WEISBERG, JACOB
16126 Lomacitas Lane
Whittier, CA 90603
Telephone: 714-589-1723
MAILING ADDRESS:
Jacob Weisberg
31861 Via Pavo Real
San Juan Capo, CA 92679
PRINCIPAL SUBJECTS:
Business & Industry
Health
Management
Human Relations

PUBLICATIONS:
Marketing Times
Arthritis News Today
Housekeeping Almanac

WEISS, FRED E.
One Edgewater Plaza, Ste. 216
Staten Island, NY 10305
Telephone: 718-981-9000
PRINCIPAL SUBJECTS:
Business & Industry
Ecology
PUBLICATIONS:
Land Development/Raw Land
  to Profit

WELCH, RANDY
1325 E. 10th Avenue, #9
Denver, CO 80218
Telephone: 303-831-8532
AFFILIATIONS:
ASJA
PRINCIPAL SUBJECTS:
Advertising
Business & Industry
General Interest
Government
Human Interest
Journalism
Management
News
Religion
Travel
PUBLICATIONS:
Sports Illustrated
Travel & Leisure
Working Woman
Savvy
Business Week
US News & World Report
New Choices

WESLEY, MARX
3 Butler
Irvine, CA 92715
Telephone: 714-786-9377
AFFILIATIONS:
WEA, APA
PRINCIPAL SUBJECTS:
Ecology
Nature
Sports
Government
General Interest
PUBLICATIONS:
Reader's Digest
Oceans
Smithsonian
Audubon

California Journal
Coast and Ocean
EPA Journal

WESSEL, MORRIS A.
61 Elmwood Rd.
New Haven, CT 06515
Telephone: 203-387-4604
AFFILIATIONS:
ASJA
PRINCIPAL SUBJECTS:
General Interest
Health
Youth
Medical
PUBLICATIONS:
Family Health
Parents
Working Mother
Ladies Home Journal
New York Times - (Conn.
  Section)

WESTEN, ROBIN
3 Shadow Lawn
Brattleboro, VT 05301
Telephone: 802-257-1426
AFFILIATIONS:
ASJA, WG
PRINCIPAL SUBJECTS:
Family
General Interest
Human Relations
Psychology
Women's Interest
PUBLICATIONS:
New Woman
Cosmopolitan
Glamour
Savvy
Us
American Baby
Brides
First

WESTGATE, ROBERT D.
1425 17th St., N.W., 401
Washington, DC 20036
Telephone: 202-332-9088
PRINCIPAL SUBJECTS:
Senior Citizens
Business & Industry
Family
Government
Travel
World Affairs
Health
PUBLICATIONS:
Washington Post
Popular Science
Single Parent

Horizons
Topic
America Illustrated
Changing Times
Mature Outlook
Ocean Science News
Nation's Health, The

WESTHEIMER, MARY
5831 N. 46th Pl.
Phoenix, AZ 85018
Telephone: 602-952-9434
Fax: 602-952-8314
AFFILIATIONS:
AAA
PRINCIPAL SUBJECTS:
Business & Industry
Health
Advertising
Humor
General Interest
Marketing
The Arts
Social Trends
Travel
Women's Interest
PUBLICATIONS:
Columbia Journalism Review
USA Today
Amer. West Airlines Magazine -
   Contributing Editor
Good News America
Phoenix Business Journal
Phoenix Magazine

WESTON, CAROL
545 West End Ave. 11E
New York, NY 10024
Telephone: 212-724-1311
AFFILIATIONS:
ASJA
PRINCIPAL SUBJECTS:
Book Reviews
Family
Youth
PUBLICATIONS:
LHJ
Seventeen
YM
McCalls
Redbook
New York Times

WHALEY, PEGGY
Whaley & Associates
414 Southland Drive
Dalton, GA 30720
Telephone: 706-278-8577
Fax: 706-278-8577
MAILING ADDRESS:
Whaley, Peggy

Whaley & Associates
P.O. Box 205
Dalton, GA 30722
AFFILIATIONS:
NYBPE
PRINCIPAL SUBJECTS:
Home & Garden
Business & Industry
PUBLICATIONS:
ATI Magazine
Carpet & Rug Industry
Southeast Floor Covering
Dalton Carpet Journal
Daily Citizen
Modern Floor Covering

WHALIN, W. TERRY
8637 Dornel Rd.
Eden Prairie, MN 55344
Telephone: 612-828-9618
Fax: 612-944-8353
MAILING ADDRESS:
W. Terry Whalin, Editorial
Eden Prairie, MN 55344
AFFILIATIONS:
SPJ, SCBW
PRINCIPAL SUBJECTS:
Family
Hobbies
Human Interest
Personalities
Religion
Book Reviews
Computer Technology
Journalism
PUBLICATIONS:
Today's Christian Woman
Bookstore Journal
Focus on the Family's
   Clubhouse
Teens Today
Christian Parenting Today
The Christian Communicator
Christian Single
Christian Reader, The
Marriage Partnership
Charisma

WHITE, BARBARA
Rossway Rd.
Plsnt Vlly, NY 12569
Telephone: 914-635-2361
MAILING ADDRESS:
Barbara White
P.O. Box 237A
Plsnt Vlly, NY 12569
PRINCIPAL SUBJECTS:
General Interest
Hobbies

PUBLICATIONS:
Antiques and the Arts Weekly
Valley Bulletin

WHITFORD, JAMES
5 Sunrise Terr.
Staten Island, NY 10304
Telephone: 718-981-3052
PRINCIPAL SUBJECTS:
Business & Industry
Health
Video
Personal Finance
Management

WHITLEY, SHARON
5666 Meredith Avenue
San Diego, CA 92120
Telephone: 619-583-7346
Fax: 619-583-7346
AFFILIATIONS:
ASJA, NLAPW, SDPC
PRINCIPAL SUBJECTS:
Editorial
Education
Family
General Interest
Health
History
Hobbies
Home & Garden
Human Interest
Humor
Journalism
Medical
Personal Finance
Personalities
Photography
Psychology
Religion
Senior Citizens
Social Trends
Travel
Women's Interest
PUBLICATIONS:
Reader's Digest
Writer's Digest
New Woman
American Woman
Woman's Own
New Body
Catholic Digest
Los Angeles Times Magazine

WHITNALL, JACK
8 N. 26th Ave.
Yakima, WA 98902
Telephone: 509-452-1426
Fax: 509-453-7072
MAILING ADDRESS:
Photo-Grammetrics

Yakima, WA 98902
AFFILIATIONS:
ASP
PRINCIPAL SUBJECTS:
Photography
Media
Science
PUBLICATIONS:
Mechanix Illustrated
The Insurance Adjuster
Western Conservation
Forest Industries
Life
Time
Fortune
Photomethods
Claims
Functional Photography

WILCOX, CHARLOTTE
10485 Sunrise Road
Harris, MN 55032
Telephone: 612-674-4819
Fax: 612-674-4819
MAILING ADDRESS:
Charlotte Wilcox
PRINCIPAL SUBJECTS:
Religion
Agriculture
Nature
News
Youth

WILKES, RALPH S.
48 W. Lake Rd.
Branchport, NY 14418
Telephone: 315-595-6676
AFFILIATIONS:
NAHWW
PRINCIPAL SUBJECTS:
Home & Garden
PUBLICATIONS:
Home Mechanix
Popular Mechanics
Popular Science
Handyman
Workbench
Homeowner
American Woodworker

WILKINSON, PAMELA L.
148 Hillside Drive
Georgetown, KY 40324
Telephone: 502-868-9990
MAILING ADDRESS:
Georgetown News
218 E. Main
Georgetown, KY 40324
AFFILIATIONS:
SPJ

PRINCIPAL SUBJECTS:
History
Animals
General Interest
Human Interest
Travel
Entertainment
PUBLICATIONS:
Kentucky Images Magazine
West Virginia Hillbilly
Chief Justice, Vol. 46, The
Parthenon, The
Georgetown News

WILLIAMS, RUSSELL J.
102 Winthrop Ave.
Albany, NY 12203
Telephone: 518-489-4578
MAILING ADDRESS:
Russ Williams
Albany, NY 12203
PRINCIPAL SUBJECTS:
The Arts
Education
Travel
Government
Nature
PUBLICATIONS:
Library Journal
College Review Service
Whitehall Times
University Review
914 Entertainment Guide
Colorado North Review
New Mexico Philatelist
Blueline
Whitehall Independent
Bullet, The
North Country
Gates to the City
Albany Times Union: Sunday
   Perspective
Glens Falls Post - Star
Northern Tier Sportman
Adirondack Echoes

WILLISTEIN, PAUL
101 N. 6th St.
Allentown, PA 18101
Telephone: 215-820-6562
AFFILIATIONS:
SDC, ASSFE
PRINCIPAL SUBJECTS:
Entertainment
The Arts
PUBLICATIONS:
Morning Call
Los Angeles Times Wire
   Service
Performance Magazine
Charlotte Observer

San Francisco Chronicle
New Brunswick Home News
Winnepeg, Canada Daily
Times - Mirror News Service
Akron Beacon Journal
New York Daily News
Philadelphia Daily News
Associated Press
New York Times News Service
Miami Herald
Hartford Courant

WILSON, KATHY
P.O. Box 134
Joice, IA 50446
PRINCIPAL SUBJECTS:
Youth

WILSON, ROBERT L.
One Juniata St.
Lewistown, PA 17044
Telephone: 717-242-1493
PRINCIPAL SUBJECTS:
Editorial
General Interest

WINTER, RUTH
44 Holly Dr.
Short Hills, NJ 07078
Telephone: 201-376-8385
Fax: 201-376-0199
AFFILIATIONS:
ASJA, AMWD, NASW, NFPW
PRINCIPAL SUBJECTS:
Health
Science
Human Interest
Women's Interest
PUBLICATIONS:
Family Circle
Good Housekeeping
American Health
Reader's Digest
Omni
Woman's Day
Success
Working Woman
Good Housekeeping
Omni
Us
Parade
Harpers Bazaar

WISE, CHRISTY
2404 20th St NW
Washington, DC 20009
Telephone: 202-667-7069
AFFILIATIONS:
NPC, WIW, NAREE
PRINCIPAL SUBJECTS:
World Affairs

Travel
Business & Industry
PUBLICATIONS:
Wall Street Journal, The
San Francisco Examiner
Oakland Tribune
Crain's New York Business
Corporate Travel
Mid - Atlantic Country
New York Times

WOLF, MARVIN J.
13237 Warren Ave.
Los Angeles, CA 90066
Telephone: 310-391-1105
Fax: 310-391-1105

WOLFE, DARRELL K.
710 E. Lakeshore Dr.
Ocoee, FL 34761
Telephone: 407-877-2258
PRINCIPAL SUBJECTS:
General Interest
Health
Religion
Computer Technology
Editorial
History

WOLKOMIR, RICHARD AND
   JOYCE ROGERS
   WOLKOMIR
Calais Stage
Montpelier, VT 05602
Telephone: 802-223-6762
AFFILIATIONS:
ASJA, NWU
PRINCIPAL SUBJECTS:
Animals
Ecology
Education
General Interest
Health
Human Interest
Humor
Medical
Psychology
Science
Social Trends
Travel
PUBLICATIONS:
Smithsonian
Reader's Digest
National Wildlife
Playboy
McCall's
National Geographic
Woman's Day
Omni

WOLLMAN, JANE
1933 18th St.
Santa Monica, CA 90404
Telephone: 310-392-5057
MAILING ADDRESS:
Jane Wollman
Santa Monica, CA 90404
AFFILIATIONS:
SPJ
PRINCIPAL SUBJECTS:
Entertainment
Health
Science
PUBLICATIONS:
New York Times, The
Esquire
USA Today
New York Daily News, The
Newsday
TV Guide
Washington Post, The
Orange County Register
L.A. Executive
Emmy Magazine

WOLLMAN, PHYLLIS
401 E. 74th St.
New York, NY 10021
Telephone: 212-744-5443
AFFILIATIONS:
NASW
PRINCIPAL SUBJECTS:
Health
Science
PUBLICATIONS:
Science Digest
Associated Press
Newspaper Enterprise Assoc.
Medical Dimensions
Medical Tribune
Emergency Medicine
AMA News
OMNI
Popular Computing
Sciquest
Popular Mechanics
American Health
New York Times
Economist, The
Technology Review

WOMACK, ROCKY
Rt. 1 Box 159
Victoria, VA 23974
Telephone: 804-696-2270
PRINCIPAL SUBJECTS:
Agriculture
Business & Industry
General Interest
Health
Editorial

Education
PUBLICATIONS:
Flue - Cured Tobacco
   Farmer, The
Peanut Farmer, The
Radford News Journal, The
Intercom
Mountainside
Progressive Farmer
Rodeo News
Cooperative Farmer
Carolina Cooperator
The Daily Times News
Thalhimers Today
Danville Register, The

WOOD, SHARON M.
3953 S.E. Grant Street
Portland, OR 97214
Telephone: 503-238-9842
AFFILIATIONS:
ASJA, NWI, OWC
PRINCIPAL SUBJECTS:
Architecture
Education
General Interest
History
Journalism
Science
PUBLICATIONS:
Oceans
Oregon Business
National Fisherman
Horizon Inflight
The Oregonian
Marine Digest

WOODARD, BERT
2540 Chesterfield Ave.
Charlotte, NC 28205
Telephone: 704-332-9060
AFFILIATIONS:
SPJ
PRINCIPAL SUBJECTS:
Human Interest
Amusements
Editorial
Journalism
News
Personalities
PUBLICATIONS:
Golfweek
Sports Page, The
ACC Baseball Tournament
   Program
Wake Forest Football Game
   Programs
Wake Forest Media Guide

Deacons, The
Drag Racing Today
Wake Forest Basketball Game
   Program

WOODRUM, LINDA
4212 Firebrick Lane
Dallas, TX 75287
Telephone: 214-248-4580
MAILING ADDRESS:
Linda Foley Woodrum, Inc.
PUBLICATIONS:
Better Homes & Gardens
The Dallas Morning News

WOODSON, R. DODGE
RR 2 Box 3154
Bowdoinham, ME 04008
Telephone: 207-666-8235
AFFILIATIONS:
AG, ASJA, ASTD
PRINCIPAL SUBJECTS:
Business & Industry
General Interest
Hobbies
Home & Garden
Management
Marketing
Personal Finance
Photography
PUBLICATIONS:
Outdoor Life
Financial Freedom
Fur-Fish-Game
Northeast Outdoors
Journal of Light Construction
Trailway News
Eastern BowHunter

WOOG, DAN
301 Post Rd., E.
Westport, CT 06880
Telephone: 203-227-1755
Fax: 203-226-6087
AFFILIATIONS:
NLGJA
PRINCIPAL SUBJECTS:
General Interest
Business & Industry
Sports
Education
Family
Human Relations
Social Trends
Travel
Youth
PUBLICATIONS:
American Way
Soccer America

USA Today
New York Times
Sports Illustrated

WORKMAN, BARBARA L.
28121 37th Ave, S.
Auburn, WA 98001
Telephone: 206-244-1562
PRINCIPAL SUBJECTS:
Human Interest
Business & Industry
Women's Interest
PUBLICATIONS:
Northwest Passage
Seattle Post Intelligence
   Newspaper
Seattle Times Newspaper
Science of Mind Magazine
Writer's Digest

WORTH, HELEN
1701 Owensville Rd.
Charlottesvle, VA 22901
Telephone: 804-296-4380
MAILING ADDRESS:
Helen Worth
Charlottesvle, VA 22901
AFFILIATIONS:
AL, ASJA
PRINCIPAL SUBJECTS:
Entertainment
PUBLICATIONS:
Harper's Bazaar
Talk Magazine
Liquor Store Magazine
New York Magazine
Modern Bride
Town & Village Newspaper
Manhattan Park West
   Newspaper
Games Magazine
Charlottesville Albermarle
   Almanac
C - Ville Review
Parent's Magazine
Washington Post
INA Syndicate
The Wine Enthusiast
Household Management
   Magazine Group
House Beautiful
Life in The Times
Wine Times
Wine West
Charlottesville Albemarle
   Observer
Brides Today

WRIGHT JR., ED
22770 S. Tamiami Trail, #237,
   Estero Wood Village
Estero, FL 33928
Telephone: 813-495-9469
MAILING ADDRESS:
Ed Wright, Jr.
22770 S. Tamiami Trail, #237
Estero, FL 33928
AFFILIATIONS:
SCN
PRINCIPAL SUBJECTS:
Business & Industry
Personalities
Government
General Interest
PUBLICATIONS:
Christian Science Monitor
Southern Magazine
Forest Hills Journal,
   (Cincinnati, Ohio)
Community Journal,
   (Cincinnati, Ohio)
Courier - Tribune,
   (Asheboro, N.C.)
Bladen Journal,
   (Elizabethtown, N.C.)
Cheraw Chronicle
Charlotte Observer
Wilmington Star - News
Southern Lumberman
Souvenir
Produce News
Food People
Pizza & Pasta

WRIGHT, SYLVIA HOEHNS
9363 Hoehns Rd.
Glen Allen, VA 23060
Telephone: 804-672-6007
AFFILIATIONS:
NPW
PRINCIPAL SUBJECTS:
Business & Industry
Management
Motivation
PUBLICATIONS:
Journal of System
   Management
Data Management
Your Computer Career
Office, The
Better Business Bureau
   Newsletter

WUCHERER, RUTH
3370A S. 12th St.
Milwaukee, WI 53215
Telephone: 414-483-6689
MAILING ADDRESS:
Ruth Wucherer

Milwaukee, WI 53215
AFFILIATIONS:
IWWG
PRINCIPAL SUBJECTS:
Business & Industry
General Interest
Travel
Women's Interest
Book Reviews
Advertising
Animals
Movie Reviews
Editorial
History
Senior Citizens
The Arts
PUBLICATIONS:
Accent
Milwaukee Journal
Mature America
The Lutheron
Good Reading Magazine

WULFF, JOAN SALVATO
Beaverkill Rd., HCR 1 Box 141
Lew Beach, NY 12758
Telephone: 914-439-3798
Fax: 914-439-3083
MAILING ADDRESS:
Joan S. Wulff
Beaverkill Rd., HCR 1 Bx 141
Lew Beach, NY 12758
AFFILIATIONS:
OWAA
PRINCIPAL SUBJECTS:
Sports
Hobbies
PUBLICATIONS:
Outdoor Life, Field & Stream
Sports Afield
Fly Rod and Reel
Fly Fisherman

YAGER, JAN
P.O. Box 8038,
Ridgeway Station
Stanford, CT 06905
Telephone: 203-329-8738
MAILING ADDRESS:
Jan Yager (aka J.L. Barkas)
P.O. Box 8038, Ridgeway Stn.
Stamford, CT 06905
AFFILIATIONS:
ASJA, CPC
PRINCIPAL SUBJECTS:
Business & Industry
Social Trends
Human Relations
Travel
PUBLICATIONS:
Family Circle

Family Health
Family Weekly
Glamour
Harper's Magazine
McCall's
The New York Times
Opera News
Redbook
The New Leader
Newsday
Modern Bride
Los Angeles Times
Seventeen
Chicago Tribune
New York Daily News
Independent News Alliance
 (INA)
New Woman
Parade

YARBROUGH, CAROLYN J.
29351 Summerset Dr.
Sun City, CA 92586
Telephone: 909-672-2492
AFFILIATIONS:
SATW
PRINCIPAL SUBJECTS:
Travel
Photography
PUBLICATIONS:
Far East Traveler Magazine
Houston Post Travel Section &
 Traveler Magazine
San Diego Union
San Diego Tribune
Fishing World
Pacific Travel News
TravelAge East
TravelAge Mid - America
TravelAge Southeast
TravelAge West
Travel - Holiday
Writer's West
Boston Globe
Buffalo News
Chicago Tribune
Copley Press
Dallas Morning News
Denver Post
Detroit News
Los Angeles Times
Miami Herald
Portland Oregonian
San Antonio Express - News
San Francisco Examiner
Western Outdoors
OAG Sales Guide on San
 Diego
Pacific Travel News Sales
 Guide on Fiji
Oakland Tribune (Travel

Section)
Toronto Star
Orlando Sentinel
Baltimore Sun
Worcester Telegram
Tours & Resorts Magazine
Cruise Travel Magazine
OAG Sales Guide on Southern
 California
Arizona Daily Star
Columbian, The
 (Vancouver WA)
Vancouver Sun (Canada)
Alameda Newspaper Group
Ft. Myers News - Press
Gainesville Sun
London (Canada) Free Press
Los Angeles Herald - Examiner
Knoxville News - Sentinel
New Orleans Picayune
Toronto Globe - Mail
Good Reading Magazine
San Diego Magazine
Riverside Press - Enterprise
TravelAge Sales Guide on Baja
 California
Aurora Beacon - News
London Canada Free Press
Springfield MA Sunday
 Republican
Baja Times
Monterey Herald
Mesa Tribune
Grand Rapids Press

YARMON, MORTON
35 Sutton Place
New York, NY 10022
Telephone: 212-755-3487
Fax: 212-755-3488
AFFILIATIONS:
ASJA
PRINCIPAL SUBJECTS:
Business & Industry
General Interest
Advertising
Book Reviews
Computer Technology
Ecology
Family
Health
Human Relations
Media
Personal Finance
Social Trends
The Arts
PUBLICATIONS:
Better Homes And Gardens
Good Housekeeping
Parade

Redbook
50-plus
Palm Beach Life Magazine

YOUNG, DONALD
166 E. 61st St., #3 - C
New York, NY 10021
Telephone: 212-593-0010
AFFILIATIONS:
ASPP
PRINCIPAL SUBJECTS:
History
Government
World Affairs
Nature
Ecology
Travel
PUBLICATIONS:
American Roulette
Adventure In Politics
The Great American Desert
Saturday Review
World Almanac
Backpacking Journal
Adventure Travel
MD

YOUNG, WARREN R.
39 N. Greenwich Rd.
Armonk, NY 10504
Telephone: 914-273-8456
AFFILIATIONS:
AGAL
PRINCIPAL SUBJECTS:
Aviation
General Interest
Health
Human Interest
PUBLICATIONS:
New York Times (special
 features)
Reader's Digest
Smithsonian
Life
McCalls

YUDKIN, MARCIA
P.O. Box 1310
Boston, MA 02117
Telephone: 617-266-1613
MAILING ADDRESS:
Marcia Yudkin
Boston, MA 02117
AFFILIATIONS:
AG
PRINCIPAL SUBJECTS:
Women's Interest
Motivation
Psychology
Social Trends

PUBLICATIONS:
Ms.
Psychology Today
New York Times Magazine
New Age Journal
US Air Magazine
TWA Ambassador
Cosmopolitan

ZATZ, ARLINE
77 Woodside Avenue
Metuchen, NJ 08840
Telephone: 908-494-9258
Fax: 908-494-9258
AFFILIATIONS:
OWAA, ASJA, NJPW, NFPW
PRINCIPAL SUBJECTS:
Amusements
Animals
Book Reviews
Education
Family
General Interest
Health
Home & Garden
Human Interest
Medical
Nature
Personalities
Photography
Physical Fitness
Senior Citizens
Sports
Travel
PUBLICATIONS:
New York Times
Philadelphia Inquirer
New York Daily News
New York Post
Asbury Park Press
Trailer Life

ZEILLER, WARREN
5016 S.W. 72nd Ave.
Miami, FL 33155
Telephone: 305-661-9446
AFFILIATIONS:
AAZPA
PRINCIPAL SUBJECTS:
Animals
PUBLICATIONS:
Natural History

ZIMMERMAN, DAVID R.
121 E. 26th St.
New York, NY 10010
Telephone: 212-545-0088
AFFILIATIONS:
ASJA, NASW, PEN
PRINCIPAL SUBJECTS:
Ecology

Health
Medical
Science
Media
PUBLICATIONS:
Audubon, Etc.
Ladies Home Journal
NY Times Magazine
Smithsonian
Woman's Day
American Health
Glamour
Mosaic
Science 83
Good Housekeeping
Family Circle
PROBE

ZOBEL, LOUISE PURWIN
23350 Sereno Ct., Villa 30
Cupertino, CA 95014
Telephone: 510-691-0300
Fax: 415-691-0700
MAILING ADDRESS:
Louise Purwin Zobel
Cupertino, CA 95014
Telephone: 415-691-0300
AFFILIATIONS:
ASJA
PRINCIPAL SUBJECTS:
Family
General Interest
Travel
Home & Garden
Human Relations
PUBLICATIONS:
American Home
Better Homes and Gardens
Brides Magazine
Christian Science Monitor
House Beautiful
Medical Economics
Modern Maturity
Parents
San Francisco Magazine
Weight Watcher's Magazine
Westways
Writers Digest
Going Places
Off Duty
Aramco World
The Writer
Travel Age West
Accent
Los Angeles Times (travel
   section)
Realities
Mankind
Sacramento Weekender
San Jose Mercury News
   (Travel Section)

Relax
New England Review
California Today
Long Island's Newsday
Home and Highway
Kansas City Star (Travel
   Section)
Trip and Tour
Overseas Life
Northwest Today
Seattle Time Magazine
World Voyager
Denver Post Magazine
Palo Alto Times
Oxnard Press-Courier
Peninsula Living
Progress
The Woman
Independent Woman
Forward
Christian Home
Together
The Educational Forum
Friends
Peninsula Midweek
Presbyterian Life
Home Life
Young Miss
Mother's Manual
Lady's Circle
Forbes
Woman's Day
United Press
Mature Years
San Francisco Examiner
   (Travel Section)
Van Nuys Daily News (Travel
   Section)
Asbury Park Press (Travel
   Section)
Long Island Newsday (Travel
   Section)
Traveling Times
Southbay Accent
Toronto Sun (Travel Section)
Peninsula Times Tribune
   (Travel Section)
Palo Alto Weekly
ASU Travel Guide
California Traveler
Tacoma News Tribune (Travel
   Section)
Providence Journal (Travel
   Section)
Woodall's Retirement Directory
San Diego Union (Travel
   Section)
Oakland Tribune (Travel
   Section)
Peninsula Magazine
Edmonton, Alberta, Journal

(Travel Section)
Anchorage Daily News (Travel
   Section)
Waterbury, CT., Sunday
   Republican (Travel Section)
Stanford Magazine
Appelton Post Crescent (Travel
   Section)
Stockton Record (Travel
   Section)
San Antonio Express News
   (Travel Section)

ZOLLMAN, JOSEPH
25 E. Penn St.
Long Beach, NY 11561
Telephone: 516-431-6697
AFFILIATIONS:
IPPC
PRINCIPAL SUBJECTS:
Hobbies
PUBLICATIONS:
Canadian Stamp News
Stamps Magazine
Stamp Collector
Linn's Stamp News
Mekeels Stamp News
South Shore Record
   (Hewlett, N.Y.)
Huntsville Times -
   (Huntsville, Alabama)

ZURCHER, MARVIN
412 Wabash St.
Berne, IN 46711
Telephone: 219-589-3555
AFFILIATIONS:
HW
PRINCIPAL SUBJECTS:
Photography
Nature
News
Women's Interest
Men's Interest
Hobbies
General Interest
Book Reviews
Animals
Sports
PUBLICATIONS:
Zurchers National Bowhunting
   Magazine
Archer World Magazine
Michigans Archer Magazine
Shooting Industry Magazine
Mich. Bow Hunter
Western Bowhunter Magazine
Great Lakes Bowhunter
Indy Sports Magazine

Regional News Papers
International Bowhunting
Northwoods Call Magazine

ZWEIG, PHILLIP L.
330 E. 38th St., #16Q
New York, NY 10016
Telephone: 212-490-0811
MAILING ADDRESS:
Phillip L. Zweig
New York, NY 10016
PRINCIPAL SUBJECTS:
Business & Industry
General Interest
Sports
Personal Finance
PUBLICATIONS:
American Banker
NY Times
Wall Street Journal
Financial World
Corporate Finance Magazine
Institutional Investor
Avenue
Journal of Commerce
Yachting Magazine
Newsday

ZWICKER, DENISE ALLEN
2712 Carolina Way
Houston, TX 77005
Telephone: 713-665-8512
Fax: 713-665-1280
AFFILIATIONS:
WICI
PRINCIPAL SUBJECTS:
Business & Industry
Medical
General Interest
Advertising

Section 4
INDEX OF FREELANCE PHOTOGRAPHERS BY SUBJECT

ADVERTISING

ABRAHAM, JOE
ABRAMSON, DEAN
ACKROYD, HUGH S.
ACOSTA, JOSE'
ADAMS, EDDIE
ADAMS, JANET L.
ADAMS, JANET L.
AIOSA, VINCENT
ALDRICH, JAY
ALKALAY, MORRIS
ALLAN PRICE
ALLEN, ED
ALLEN, J. J.
ALLEN, TIM
ALTMAN, DAVID M.
AMBORN, JOHN E.
ANDERSON, RICHARD
APTON, BILL
ARDEN, MICHAEL
ARPADI, ALLEN G.
ART OF FINE PHOTOGRAPHY
ASCHERMAN, JR., HERBERT
ASHE, BILL
AUEL, ADAM
AUSTIN, MILES
AVERY, RON
BADGER, BOBBY
BAER, GORDON
BAER, RHODA
BAILEY, ROBERT
BAKER, BOBBE CLINTON
BAKER, JULIE
BAKKE, ERIC
BAPTIE, FRANK
BARAG, MARC
BARBAGALLO, ANTONINO
BARBALACE PHOTOGRAPHY
BARDIN, KEITH
BARLEY, BILL
BARNES, MICHELLE A.
BARON, JAMES J.
BARRETT, CHARLES
BARRON, DAVID
 M./OXYGEN GROUP
BARROS, ROBERT
 PHOTOGRAPHY INC.
BARTRUFF, DAVE
BAXLEY, KIRK
BAYER, DANIEL

BAYLES, DAL
BECHTOLD, CHARLES
BECK, PETER
 PHOTOGRAPHY
BEDNARSKI, PAUL S.
BEKKER, PHILIP
BELLENIS, JOHN
BENKERT, CHRISTINE
BENYAS, BOB
BERGERON, JOSEPH
BERMAN, MICHAEL
BERNSTEIN, ALAN
BEVILACQUA, JOE
BIEGUN, RICHARD
BISCHOFF, KARL
BISHOP, G. ROBERT
BISHOP, RANDA
BITTERS, DAVID
BLAKESBERG, JAY
BLOCH, STEVEN
BLOCK, RAY
BOBBE, LELAND
BOGACZ, MARK F.
BOWDEN, BOB
BRANDON, RANDY
BRAUN, BOB
BROMLEY, DONALD
BROOKS, CHARLES W.
BROWN, JIM
BUCK, BRUCE
BURLINGAME, JACK
BURNS, STEVE
BURY, SUSAN
BUSCH, SCHERLEY
BUSH, CHAN
BUSHUE, KATHY
BUTLER, TIM
BUTTON DOWN
 PRODUCTIONS LTD.
BUZBY, SHERRIE
CALDWELL, JIM
CAMPBELL, THOMAS S.
CAMPBELL, TOM
CARR, KATHLEEN THORMOD
CARRIKER, RONALD
 PHOTOGRAPHY
CARROLL, TOM
CARRUZZA
CASTANEDA, LUIS
CERNY, PAUL
CHAMPAGNE, BARRY

CHARETTE, MARK
CHARLES, CINDY
CHESLER, KEN
CHEW, JOHN T.
CHIKA
CHINITZ, ADAM
CHURCH, DENNIS
CLARK, H. DEAN
CLARK, JUNEBUG
CLARKSON, FRANK
CLARKSON, RICHARD C.
CLARKSON, ROBERT NOEL
CLEFF, BERNIE
CLEMENTS, STEPHEN P.
CLYMER, JONATHAN
COHEN, ANDY
COHEN, DAN
COLEMAN, GENE
COLMAN III, BEN
COMET, RENEE
CONRAD, CHRISTOPHER
COOKE, JERRY
COOKE, JOHN DR.
COONRAD, JORDAN
COOPER, TOM
CORY, JEFF
COSTE, KURT
COX, DENNIS
CRANE, ARNOLD
CRAWFORD, PAT
CROFOOT, RON
CROKE, THOMAS J.
CROSBY, A. DAVID
CURTIS, JOHN
CURTIS, STEVEN
DAKAN, LEW
DANIELS, JOSEPHUS
DARNELL, MITCHELL
DARRYL, JACOBSON
DAVIDSON, CAMERON
DAVIS, DEE
DE CASSERES, JOSEPH
DECRUYENAERE, HOWARD
DEGABRIELE PHOTOGRAPHY
DEGGINGER, PHIL
DEITS, KATIE
DELLA GROTTA, VIVIENNE
DEMPSAY, SAY
DENUTO, ELLEN
DEUTSCH, JACK
DEVAULT, JIM

DIAZ, ARMANDO
DIETZ, CRAIG
DIMARCO, JR., SAL
DORSEY, RON
 PHOTOGRAPHY
DOUGLAS, KEITH
DOWNIE, DANA
DRAKE, JEANNE
DRESSLER, BRIAN
DRISCOLL, W. M.
DUFRESNE, WALTER
DUHON, MIKE
DUNMIRE, LARRY
DUNOFF, RICH
DYER, ED
EASTERLY, LIBBY
EBERT, BOB
EDELMAN, HARRY
EDSON, STEVEN
ELAKMAN, MARC
ELBINGER, DOUGLAS
ELDER, THOM
ELLMAN, ELAINE
ELLZEY, BILL
EMMERICH, DON
ENGELMANN, SUZANNE J.
ESCOSA, JOHN
ESTY, ANDREA
EYLE, NICOLAS EDWARD
FABRICIUS, DAGMAR
FAIRCLOTH, JANE G.
FARR, JULIE
FARRELL, BILL
FEILING, DAVID A.
FIELDS, BRUCE
FINLEY, DOUG
FIREBAUGH, STEVE
FISHER PHOTOGRAPHY
FLEMING, LARRY
FLETCHER, T. MIKE
FLOTTE, LUCIEN
FORBERT, DAVID J.
FORDEN, J. PATRICK
FOSTER, KEVIN
FOURRE, LIZA
FRANCIA, ANTHONY L.
FRANZEN, DAVID
FRENCH, PETER
FRICK, KEN
FRIESE, RICK
FRISCH, STEPHEN

FRITZ, BRUCE
FRITZ, GERARD
FRITZ, TOM
FRY III, GEORGE B.
FUKUHARA, RICHARD
  YUTAKA
FUSCO, PAUL
GAGE, HAL
GALLIAN, DIRK
GAMAGE, DOUGLAS C.
GARIK, ALICE
GARLAND, MICHAEL E.
GAROFALO, JOHN
  CLEVELAND
GEER, GARRY
GEFTER, JUDITH
GENTILE, SR., ARTHUR
GERCZYNSKI, TOM
GIAMMATTEO, JOHN
GLASS, BRUCE
GLASSMAN, KEITH
GNASS, JEFF
GOLDBLATT, STEVEN
GOODHEIM, JANIS
GOODMAN, LISA J.
GORDON, FRANK
GORE, ARNOLD
GORIN, BART
GORNICK JR., ALAN
GOTFRYD, BERNARD
GOTTLIEB, STEVEN
GRAHAM, A. MICHAEL
GRAHAM, STEPHEN
GRANNIS, BOB
GREEN-ARMYTAGE,
  STEPHEN
GREENBERG, CHIP
GREENBLATT, WILLIAM D.
GRIGG, ROGER
GRIMES, BILLY
GUBIN, MARK
GURAVICH, DAN
HACKNEY, KERRY
HALL, DON
HALPERN, DAVID
HALSTEAD, DIRCK
HAMILTON, CHRIS
HAND, RAY PHOTOGRAPHY
HANDLEY, ROBERT E.
HARLAN, BRUCE
HARMON, TIM
HARP, DAVID
HARRINGTON, JOHN
HARRINGTON, TY
HARRIS, CHRISTOPHER R.
HARTMANN, W. GEOFFREY
HEBBERD, LINDSAY
HEDRICH-BLESSING
HENRY, GEORGE T.
HEWETT, RICHARD R.
HEWITT, SCOTT

HILL, DAN SCOTT
HILL, JACKSON
HIRSCH, KAREN I.
HITT, WESLEY
HOEBERMAN, MATHEW &
  KRISTIN
HOFFMAN, ROB
HOLLENBECK, CLIFF/KEVIN
  MORRIS
HOLLYMAN, TOM
HOLTEL, JOHN P.
HOLZ, WILLIAM
HOSS, RONALD P.
HOUSER, DAVE G.
HOUSER, ROBERT
HOWARD, CARL
HUBBELL, WILLIAM
HUCKABY, JERRY
HUGHES, JOHN
HUMPHRIES, JR., H.
  GORDON
HUNTER, FIL
HUNTZINGER, ROBERT
IRVIN, MARCUS
JACKSON, DON
JACOBSON, RANDALL C.
JALBERT, PAUL
JERNIGAN, JOHN E.
JOHNSON & JOHNSON
  STUDIO
JOHNSON, FOREST
JOHNSON, J. SAM
JOHNSTON, GREG
JONES, LOU
JORDAN, JOE F.
JOUBERT PHOTOGRAPHY,
  LARRY
KAMP, ERIC
KANOWSKY, KEN
KAPLAN, B. PETER
KARALES, JAMES
KASPER, KEN
KASTEN, JERRY
KATZMAN, MARK
KAUFMAN, ELLIOTT
KEENAN, JOHN C.
KELLEY, TOM
KENNEDY, M. LEWIS
KENTON, BASIA
KHORNAK, LUCILLE
KIDD, CHUCK
KIEFFER, JOHN
KILBORN, BILL
KINCAID, CLARK L.
KINETIC CORPORATION (G.
  RAYMOND SCHUHMANN)
KING, KATHLEEN
KING, TOM
KIRKENDALL/SPRING
  PHOTOGRAPHERS
KOLLODGE, KENNETH

KONIG, THIA
KONRATH, G. FRANK
KOROPP, ROBERT
KRASKA, MARK
KRATT, K.C.
KRAVITZ, TOM
KRUBNER, RALPH
KUHLMAN, CHRIS
LABUA, FRANK
LE GRAND, PETER
LEDUC, LYLE
LEE, LARRY
LEE, ROBERT II
  PHOTOGRAPHY
LEIBER, N. GREGORY
LENTZ & ASSOCIATES
LESTER, PETER
LEVITON, DREW B.
LEVITON, JOYCE B.
LEVY, BURT
LEVY, PATRICIA BARRY
LEVY, RON
LEWIS, G. BRAD
LEY, RUSSELL
LIEBERMAN, ARCHIE
LILLIBRIDGE, DAVID C.
LINCK, TONY
LINDQUIST, NILS
LISSY, DAVID
LITSEY, LLOYD
LOHBECK, STEPHEN
LOMEO, ANGELO & SONJA
  BULLATY
LONGWOOD, MARC D.
LONNINGE, LARS
LORD, JIM
LORENZ, ROBERT
LOTT, HAL
LOYST, KEN
LUCE, DON
LUKOWICZ, JEROME
MACKENZIE, MAXWELL
MAGIC LANTERN STUDIOS
MAHONEY, BOB
MAKRIS, DAVID
MALLINSON, PETER A.
MARES-MANTON,
  ALEXANDER
MARGERIN, BILL
MARKATOS, JERRY
MAROON, FRED J.
MARX, RICHARD
MASON, STEPHEN
MASSIE, KIM
MASSON, LISA
MAY, CLYDE
MCBRIDE, TOM
MCCLAIN, RICK
  PHOTOGRAPHY
MCCLUSKEY, D. THOMAS
MCCRIRICK, FLIP

MCCUTCHEON, JR., SHAW
MCGEE, E. ALAN
MCGEE, TONY
MCGLYNN, DAVID
MCGUIRE, JOSEPH W.
MCKAY, DOUG
MCKEE, MICHAEL
MCNEILL, BRIAN
MCVICKER, SAM
MEANS, LISA
MENDELSOHN, DAVID
MENDLOWITZ, BENJAMIN
METRISIN, JIM
MICHELSON, ERIC
MIGLAVS, MR. JANIS
MIHALEVICH, MICHAEL
MIHOVIL, ROBERT JOHN
MILLER PHOTOGRAPHY, INC.
MILLER, DAVID P.
MILLER, MELABEE M.
MILLER, ROGER
  PHOTO, LTD.
MILMOE, JAMES O.
MILNE, ROBERT
MISHLER, CLARK JAMES
MODRICKER, DARREN
MOONEY, CHRIS
MOONEY, KEVIN O.
MOORE, MICHAEL
MOORE, RIC
MORELAND, MIKE
MORGENSTEIN, RICHARD
MORRIS, JEFF
MORRIS, PAUL
MOSS, GARY
MOSS, HOWARD
MOULIN, THOMAS
MULLEN, EDWARD F.
NANCE, ANCIL
NANO, ED
NELSON, BRUCE G.
NERONI, ROBERT
NESTE, ANTHONY
NETZER, DON
NEWMAN, ARNOLD
NEY, NANCY
NIKAS, GREG
NORTON, MICHAEL
NORTON, PEARL
O'BYRNE, WILLIAM M.
OBREMSKI, GEORGE
OMER, DAVID
ORANS, MURIEL
ORDERS, KAREN
ORRICO, CHARLES J.
OTSUKI, TOSHI
OWEN, SIGRID
PAIGE, PETER
PALMIERI, JORGE
PANAYIOTOU, PETER
PARAS, MICHAEL

PAZOVSKI, KAZIK
PEARSE, DON
PETERSON JR., CHESTER
PETERSON, JR., CHESTER
PETERSON, LEE
PHAM, DIEM K.
PHILIBA, ALLAN
PHILLIPS, JAMES
PHOTO RESOURCE HAWAII
PHOTO, COMM
PHOTOGRAPHIC DESIGNS
PHOTOGRAPHIC IMPACT
PHOTOGRAPHY UNLIMITED
PHOTOSMITH
PLATTETER, GEORGE
PLUMMER, DOUG
POHLMAN STUDIOS
POLSKY, JOEL
POLUMBAUM, TED
PORTNOY, LEWIS
POST, GEORGE
POWELL, TODD B.
PRESTON, LOUISA
PRICE, CLAYTON J.
PRICE, GREG
PUTNAM, DON
QUARTUCCIO, DOM
QUICKSILVER
  PHOTOGRAPHY
RAFKIND, ANDREW J.
REED, GEOFF
REID, SEAN
REMINGTON, GEORGE
RENNIE, BRIAN H.
RENO, KENT
REVETTE, DAVID
RICARDEL, VINCENT J.
RICH, BERNI
RICH, BERNI
RICHARDSON, DAVID C.
RIECKS, DAVID
RILEY, GEORGE
RILEY, JON
ROBINSON, BILL
ROBINSON, MIKE
ROGERS, CHUCK
ROLO PHOTOGRAPHY
ROSENBLUM, BERNARD
ROSSI, DAVID A.
ROWIN, STANLEY
RUHE, GEORGE-EDWARD
RUSSELL, MARC
RYCUS, JEFFREY A.
SACHA, BOB
SALVO, CHRIS
SANDBANK, HENRY
SANFORD, ERIC M.
SARCONE, JOE
SATTERWHITE, AL
SAVILLE, LYNN
SAYLOR, TED

SCHAMP, J. BROUGH
SCHANUEL, ANTHONY
SCHIERSTEDT, NEIL
SCHIFF, NANCY RICA
SCHLANGER, IRV
SCHLUETER, MICHAEL K.
SCHMIDT, DIANE JOY
SCHNEIDER, JOHN
SCHWELIK, FRANK
SCOCOZZA, VICTOR
SCORY, RAYMOND G.
SEEGER, STEPHEN E.
SEITZ, SEPP
SEYMOUR, RONALD
SHAKOOR, RA
SHANEFF, CARL
SHERMAN, BOB
SHIELDS-MARLEY
  PHOTOGRAPHY
SHIER, DEANN
SHRIKHANDE, DEVENDRA
SHROUT, BILL & KATHRYN E.
SHULTZ, LAURA
SHULTZ, LAURA MAXWELL
SIBLEY, SCOTT
SICKLES PHOTO-REPORTING
  SERVICE
SIEGEL, R. MYLES
  PHOTOGRAPHY
SILLA, JON
SIMS, MARK
SINKLER, PAUL
SIRLIN, TED
SISSON, BOB
SLATER, EDWARD
SMELTZER, ROBERT
SMELTZER, ROBERT
SMITH, DAVID L.
SNYDER, LEE F.
SOCHUREK, HOWARD J.
SOLOMON, RON
SOMOZA, GERARDO
SPEARS, PHILLIP
SPEYER, LARS
STALVIG, MURLYN A.
STAWNIAK, JIM
STEELE, MAX
STEELE, W. RICHARD
STEIN-MASON STUDIO
STEWARDSON, JOE
STEWART, ED
STOCK PHOTOS HAWAII
STONE, TONY IMAGES
STORMZAND, JOHN
STOVER, DAVID
STRASSER, JOEL
STRATFORD, JIM
STREANO, VINCENT C.
STREET, PARK
STRESHINSKY, TED
STROMBERG, BRUCE

SUMMER PRODUCTIONS
SUMNER
  PHOTOGRAPHY INC.
SVEHLA, JAMES C.
SWARTZ, FRED
SWETNAM, JIM
SWOGER, ARTHUR
TADDER, MORTON
TATEM, MIKE
TAXEL, BARNEY
TAYLOR, RANDY G.
TENIN, BARRY
TESADA, DAVID X.
THATCHER, CHARLES R.
THILL, NANCY
THOMPSON, MICHAEL S.
TOLBERT, BRIAN R.
TORREZ, BOB
TOTO , JOE
TRENKA, BUD
TROXELL, W. H.
TRUSLOW, B.
TUCKER, MORT
ULMER, DAVID
UPITIS, ALVIS
URBINA, WALT
VAN DE VEN, MARY
VANCE, JIM
VANDER SCHUIT
  STUDIO INC.
VANMARTER, ROBERT
WACHTER, JERRY
WADDELL, ROBERT M.
WADE, ROGER
WAGGONER, MIKE
WAGNER, ANDREW A.
WAKEFIELD'S OF KANSAS
  CITY, INC.
WAPINSKI, DAVID
WARD, JERRY
WARTELL, BOB
WASHNIK, ANDY
WATERSUN, DAVID
WEAVER, MARTHA
WECKLER, CHAD
WEIDLEIN, PETER
WELSH, STEVE
WESTHEIMER, BILL
WHELESS, ROB
WHITAKER, GREG
WHITENTON, CARY
WIEN JEFFREY
WILLIAMS, HAL
WILLIAMS, JAY S.
WILLIAMS, RON STUDIO
WILLITS, PAT L.
WINTER, NITA
WIRONEN
WISSER, BILL
WOLF, JACK
WOLFE, DAN

WOOD, ANTHONY B.
WOOD, TED
WOOLFE, RAYMOND G.
WRISLEY, BARD
WRISTEN, DONALD F.
WYMAN, JAKE
YARBROUGH, CARL
YAWORSKI, DON
YONKER, THOMAS
  PHOTOGRAPHY
ZAHNER, DAVID
ZAKE, BRUCE

AGRICULTURE

ALBINO, JOSEPH X.
ALLEN, JOHN O.
ARRUZA, TONY
BALLIS, GEORGE
BARBALACE PHOTOGRAPHY
BARON, JAMES J.
BEATTY, DAVID E.
BECK, PETER
  PHOTOGRAPHY
BENNETT, ROBERT J.
BERG, MARGARET C.
BISHOP, G. ROBERT
BOWEN, JOHN
COLEMAN, GENE
COLMAN III, BEN
CORY, JEFF
COX, DENNIS
CURTIS, STEVEN
DECRUYENAERE, HOWARD
DEGGINGER, DR. E. R.
DEGGINGER, PHIL
DODGE, LARRY
DOWNIE, DANA
ELK III, JOHN
ELLZEY, BILL
ENGELMANN, SUZANNE J.
ENGH, ROHN
FAIRCLOTH, JANE G.
FARR, JULIE
FINLEY, DOUG
FIREBAUGH, STEVE
FLEMING, LARRY
FORDEN, J. PATRICK
FRISCH, STEPHEN
FRITZ, BRUCE
GARIK, ALICE
GIBSON, MARK & AUDREY
GOODMAN, LISA J.
GORDON, FRANK
GRAHAM, A. MICHAEL
GREEN-ARMYTAGE,
  STEPHEN
GUBIN, MARK
GURAVICH, DAN
HANDS, BRUCE
HARDEN, CLIFF

HARDER, PAUL B.
HARMON, TIM
HARP, DAVID
HARTMANN, W. GEOFFREY
HOLT, SAXON
JOHNSON, EVERETT C.
KASHI, ED
KASPER, KEN
KIDD, CHUCK
KIEFFER, JOHN
KNIGHT, DOUG
KONRATH, G. FRANK
KUPER, HOLLY
LEVY, PATRICIA BARRY
LIEBERMAN, ARCHIE
MARVY, JIM
MAY, RONALD W.
MCKAY, DOUG
MCMULLIN, FOREST
MENZEL, PETER
MESSINEO, JOHN
MIHALEVICH, MICHAEL
MIHOVIL, ROBERT JOHN
MILLER PHOTOGRAPHY, INC.
MILLER, JOE
MOON, BEN L.
MOORE, DAN
MUSCHENETZ, ROLAND &
  KAREN
MYERS, FRED
O'BYRNE, WILLIAM M.
ODYSSEY PRODUCTIONS
ORANS, MURIEL
PAZOVSKI, KAZIK
PETERSON JR., CHESTER
PETERSON, JR., CHESTER
PHANEUF, ART
PHELAN, JOHN
PHOTO RESOURCE HAWAII
PLACE, CHARLES
POERTNER, KENNETH C.
PORTNOY, LEWIS
PRATT, DIANE
PRESTON, LOUISA
RAFKIND, ANDREW J.
RIECKS, DAVID
RYCUS, JEFFREY A.
SCHLUETER, MICHAEL K.
SCHMID, BERT
SEEGER, STEPHEN E.
SHRIKHANDE, DEVENDRA
SICKLES PHOTO-REPORTING
  SERVICE
SIEGEL, R. MYLES
  PHOTOGRAPHY
STARR, ASHBY
  PHOTOGRAPHER
STEWARDSON, JOE
STOCK PHOTOS HAWAII
STONE, TONY IMAGES
STORMZAND, JOHN

TESADA, DAVID X.
THOMPSON, MICHAEL S.
TINKER, LESTER
TREYBIG, CYNTHIA
ULMER, DAVID
UPITIS, ALVIS
WAPINSKI, DAVID
WATERSUN, DAVID
WEAKS, BILL S.
WHITAKER, GREG
WHITENTON, CARY
WHITMIRE, KENNETH L.
WILSON, DOUG M.
WITHEY, GARY S.
WOOLFE, RAYMOND G.
YAMASHITA, MICHAEL S.

AMUSEMENTS

ALEKANDROWICZ, FRANK
ALLEN, MARIETTE PATHY
BLINKOFF, RICHARD
BOLSTER, MARK
CARLEBACH, MICHAEL L.
CASSILL, KAY
CASTANEDA, LUIS
COOKE, JERRY
COX, DENNIS
CROMER, PEGGO
DE ZANGER, ARIE
DOFF, A. F.
EBERT, BOB
FANSLER, EARL
FINLEY, DOUG
FLOTTE, LUCIEN
GAMMA LIAISON INC.
GEFTER, JUDITH
GESCHEIDT, ALFRED
GORDON, FRANK
HARMON, TIM
HEBBERD, LINDSAY
HENRY, GEORGE T.
JAMES, GRANT R.
KIDD, CHUCK
KLASS, RUBIN & ERIKA
  PHOTOGRAPHY
NADLER, BOB
ORANS, MURIEL
PHOTOGRAPHY UNLIMITED
PORTNOY, LEWIS
REED, GEOFF
RICCA, ANTONIO D.
SANDBANK, HENRY
SEEGER, STEPHEN E.
SETON, CHARLES
SIEGEL, R. MYLES
  PHOTOGRAPHY
SPEYER, LARS
STOCK PHOTOS HAWAII
STORMZAND, JOHN
TURNER, PETE

WAPINSKI, DAVID
WHITMIRE, KENNETH L.
WIEN JEFFREY
WOODALLEN
  PHOTOGRAPHERS
YARBROUGH, BOB

ANIMALS

ADAMS, JANET L.
ALKALAY, MORRIS
BARNES, MICHELLE A.
BARON, JAMES J.
BARRON, DAVID M./OXYGEN
  GROUP
BEVAN, PAT
BISHOP, G. ROBERT
BITTERS, DAVID
BROWN, JAMES
BROWN-ROSNER, SHEREE
BRUNDEGE, BARBARA A.
BULL, DAVID
BURGESS, MICHELE A.
BUSH, DARRYL W.
BUSHUE, KATHY
CASTANEDA, LUIS
CHANDOHA, WALTER
CHIN, RUTH
CLARK, H. DEAN
CLEMENTS, STEPHEN P.
COHEN, ANDY
COOKE, JERRY
COOKE, JOHN DR.
DEGABRIELE PHOTOGRAPHY
DEGGINGER, PHIL
DEMPSAY, SAY
DOMINIS, JOHN
DOUGLASS, DARREN
DRAKE, JEANNE
FACTOR, BEVERLY
FLOTTE, LUCIEN
FULTON, CONRAD JAMES
GARRISON, RON
GEER, GARRY
GIANNINI, GEMMA
GNASS, JEFF
GOVE, GEOFFREY
GRAHAM, A. MICHAEL
GREEN-ARMYTAGE,
  STEPHEN
GRIMM, MICHELE
GUBIN, MARK
HARDEN, CLIFF
HARMON, TIM
HARP, DAVID
HIGHTON, SCOTT
HIRSCH, KAREN I.
JACKSON, DON
JERNIGAN, JOHN E.
JOHNSTON, GREG
KAEHLER, WOLFGANG

KANOWSKY, KEN
KAPLAN, B. PETER
KASPER, KEN
KEATING, FRANKE
KLASS, RUBIN & ERIKA
  PHOTOGRAPHY
KOLLODGE, KENNETH
LATHROPE, WILMA
LEE, ROBERT II
  PHOTOGRAPHY
LEVY, RON
LOYST, KEN
MCBRIDE, TOM
MCCARTNEY, SUSAN
MENZEL, PETER
MESSINEO, JOHN
MONTGOMERY PICTURES
MYERS, TOM
O'TOOLE, TOM AND JOANNE
OLIVE, JIM
ORANS, MURIEL
PEARCE, ADDEE
PETERSON, LEE
PHOTO RESOURCE HAWAII
POST, JOHN
PRESTON, LOUISA
REED, GEOFF
RIECKS, DAVID
ROBERTS, JANET M.
RYCUS, JEFFREY A.
SAVILLE, LYNN
SISSON, BOB
SMITH, BRADLEY
STAMATES, JIM
STEINGROVE, JACK
STONE, TONY IMAGES
STORMZAND, JOHN
TARR, CHARLES J.
TOTO , JOE
TREYBIG, CYNTHIA
WAGNER, ANDREW A.
WALKER, HARRY M.
WAPINSKI, DAVID
WILLIS, CLIFF
WOOLFE, RAYMOND G.
WU, NORBERT
YARBROUGH, BOB
YOUNG, DONALD
ZILLIOUX, JOHN

ARCHITECTURE

ABRABEN, E. 'MANNY'
ABRAHAM, JOE
ACKROYD, HUGH S.
ADAMS, JANET L.
ADAMS, STEVEN
ALEKANDROWICZ, FRANK
ARDEN, MICHAEL
ARNDT, DIANE
AUPIED, STEVEN

BABBITT, SHARON
BAER, GORDON
BAER, MORLEY
BAILEY, ROBERT
BARAG, MARC
BARBALACE PHOTOGRAPHY
BARDIN, KEITH
BARLEY, BILL
BARON, JAMES J.
BARRETT, CHARLES
BARTH, HARRY
BARTRUFF, DAVE
BASCOM, WILLIAM A.
BAXLEY, KIRK
BAYER, DANIEL
BECHTOLD, CHARLES
BEDNARSKI, PAUL S.
BEKKER, PHILIP
BELLENIS, JOHN
BERNSTEIN, MARION
BERRY & HOMER
  PHOTOGRAPHICS
BISCHOFF, KARL
BOHON, ED
BRADY ARCHITECTURAL
  PHOTOGRAPHY
BRANDON, RANDY
BRAUN, BOB
BRINK, STEVEN
BRIZZI, ANDREA
BROWNE, TURNER
BURLINGAME, JACK
BUSCH, SCHERLEY
CABANBAN, ORLANDO R.
CAPOTOSTO, JOHN J.
CARLEBACH, MICHAEL L.
CARROLL, HANSON
CARRUTHERS, ROBERT J.
CASTANEDA, LUIS
CAVANAUGH, JAMES
CERNY, PAUL
CHARLES, FREDERICK
CHESLER, DONNA & KEN
CHESLER, KEN
CHEW, JOHN T.
CLARKSON, FRANK
CLEFF, BERNIE
COHEN, ANDY
COLEMAN, PH.D., REV.
  CHERYL L.
COLLINS, SHELDAN
COLTON, ROBERT
CONNER, GARY
CORY, JEFF
COSTE, KURT
COX, DENNIS
CRAWFORD, PAT
CROKE, THOMAS J.
CROMER, PEGGO
CROSBY, A. DAVID
CURTIS, STEVEN

D'ADDIO, JAMES
DAVIDSON, DARWIN K.
DE CASSERES, JOSEPH
DECRUYENAERE, HOWARD
DEGGINGER, PHIL
DEITS, KATIE
DEMPSAY, SAY
DIETZ, CRAIG
DOLIN, IRVING
DOMINIS, JOHN
DORSEY, RON
  PHOTOGRAPHY
DOUGLAS, KEITH
DOWNIE, DANA
DRESSLER, BRIAN
DUFRESNE, WALTER
DYER, ED
EBERT, BOB
EDELMAN, HARRY
ELAKMAN, MARC
ELBINGER, DOUGLAS
ELK III, JOHN
ELLZEY, BILL
EMMERICH, DON
FANSLER, EARL
FARR, JULIE
FARRELL, BILL
FEILING, DAVID A.
FIREBAUGH, STEVE
FISHER PHOTOGRAPHY
FLOTTE, LUCIEN
FORBERT, DAVID J.
FORDEN, J. PATRICK
FORMISANO-MAYERI, YONI
FOWLEY, DOUGLAS
FRANCIA, ANTHONY L.
FRANZEN, DAVID
FREEMAN, TINA
FRENCH, PETER
FRIESE, RICK
FRISCH, STEPHEN
FRITZ, TOM
GARIK, ALICE
GARLAND, MICHAEL E.
GARRETT, KENNETH
GEFTER, JUDITH
GEIGER, K. WILLIAM
GELLER, ALAN
GENTILE, SR., ARTHUR
GERCZYNSKI, TOM
GIAMMATTEO, JOHN
GIBSON, MARK & AUDREY
GLASS, BRUCE
GOHLICH, ED
GOLDBERG, JEFF
GOODHEIM, JANIS
GOODMAN, LISA J.
GORDON, FRANK
GOTTLIEB, STEVEN
GRAHAM, A. MICHAEL
GRAHAM, STEPHEN

GREEN-ARMYTAGE,
  STEPHEN
GREENBERG, STANLEY
GRUBB, ROBERT B.
GUBIN, MARK
HALL, DON
HALL, JOHN M.
HALSEY, TERRY
HAMPSON PHOTOGRAPHY
HANDLEY, ROBERT E.
HARDEN, CLIFF
HARKEY, JOHN J.
HARLAN, BRUCE
HARMON PHOTOGRAPHERS
HARMON, TIM
HARTMANN, W. GEOFFREY
HEBBERD, LINDSAY
HEDRICH-BLESSING
HELSPER, MANFRED
HENTE, JERRY L.
HEWITT, SCOTT
HILL, JACKSON
HILLYER, JONATHON
HIRSCH, KAREN I.
HOFFMAN, ROB
HOUSER, DAVE G.
HUBBELL, WILLIAM
HUMPHRIES, JR., H.
  GORDON
JAMES, GRANT R.
JERNIGAN, JOHN E.
JONES, LOU
KANOWSKY, KEN
KAPLAN, HOWARD N.
KAUFMAN, ELLIOTT
KENNEDY, M. LEWIS
KENTON, BASIA
KHANLIAN, RICHARD
KIDD, CHUCK
KINCAID, CLARK L.
KINETIC CORPORATION (G.
  RAYMOND SCHUHMANN)
KOENIG, GEA
KOLLODGE, KENNETH
KOROPP, ROBERT
KOTECKI, STAN
KRASKA, MARK
KRUBNER, RALPH
KUHLMAN, CHRIS
LANGENBACH, RANDOLPH
LEVIN, AARON
LEVY, BURT
LEWELLYN, JON
LEY, RUSSELL
LINCK, TONY
LITSEY, LLOYD
LOTT, HAL
MACKENZIE, MAXWELL
MAGIC LANTERN STUDIOS
MAGID, JEROME
MARKATOS, JERRY

MARVY, JIM
MASSON, LISA
MAY, CLYDE
MCCLAIN, RICK
  PHOTOGRAPHY
MCCUTCHEON, JR., SHAW
MCGEE, E. ALAN
MCGEE, TONY
MCGLYNN, DAVID
MCGUIRE, JOSEPH W.
MCKAY, DOUG
MCKEE, MICHAEL
MCLEMORE, BILL
MCNEELY, BURTON
MCNEILL, BRIAN
METRISIN, JIM
MIGLAVS, MR. JANIS
MIHALEVICH, MICHAEL
MIHOVIL, ROBERT JOHN
MILLER, MELABEE M.
MOORE, MICHAEL
MORELAND, MIKE
MUNCH, ERIC
MURPHY, MICHAEL
NERONI, ROBERT
NIEMAN, WILLIAM
NORTON, MICHAEL
ODYSSEY PRODUCTIONS
OLIVE, JIM
ORANS, MURIEL
PAIGE, PETER
PAZOVSKI, KAZIK
PEARCE, ADDEE
PEARSE, DON
PEARSON, CHARLES R.
PERRON, ROBERT
PETERSEN, JON B.
PETERSON, LEE
PHILIBA, ALLAN
PHILLIPS, ROBIN H.
PHOTOSMITH
PISANO, ROBERT
PLATTETER, GEORGE
PORTNOY, LEWIS
POSEY, MIKE
POST, GEORGE
POST, JOHN
POWELL, TODD B.
PROUD, B.
QUARTUCCIO, DOM
QUICKSILVER
  PHOTOGRAPHY
RAFKIND, ANDREW J.
RANDLETT, MARY
REED, GEOFF
REMINGTON, GEORGE
REVETTE, DAVID
RICARDEL, VINCENT J.
RICH, BERNI
RIECKS, DAVID
RILEY, JON

RIZZO, RION
ROBERTS, JANET M.
ROBINSON, BILL
ROLLAND, GUY A.
ROLO PHOTOGRAPHY
ROSENBLUM, BERNARD
RUSSELL, GAIL
RUSSELL, MARC
RYBISKI JR., A. J.
RYCUS, JEFFREY A.
SALMOIRAGHI, FRANCO
SANFORD, ERIC M.
SARCONE, JOE
SARNACKI, MICHAEL
SAYLOR, TED
SCHAMP, J. BROUGH
SCHATZ, BOB
SCHMID, BERT
SCHNEIDER, JOHN
SCORY, RAYMOND G.
SEEGER, STEPHEN E.
SETON, CHARLES
SHIER, DEANN
SHRIKHANDE, DEVENDRA
SIBLEY, SCOTT
SIMS, MARK
SMALLING, WALTER
SMITH, D. LYNN
SMITH, ROBIN B.
SOLOMON, RON
SOMOZA, GERARDO
SPEARS, PHILLIP
SPILLERS, MICHAEL
STARR, ASHBY
  PHOTOGRAPHER
STAWNIAK, JIM
STEELE, MAX
STEIN-MASON STUDIO
STEWART, ED
STIERER, DENNIS
STONE, TONY IMAGES
STRASSER, JOEL
STREET, PARK
STROUSS, SARAH
SUMNER
  PHOTOGRAPHY INC.
SVEHLA, JAMES C.
SWANSON, BOB
SWETNAM, JIM
TADDER, MORTON
TARLETON, GARY
TAXEL, BARNEY
TESADA, DAVID X.
THIGPEN, ALEXANDER G.
THILL, NANCY
TOLBERT, BRIAN R.
TRENKA, BUD
TREYBIG, CYNTHIA
TUCKER, HOWARD
TUCKER, MORT
UPITIS, ALVIS

VANDER SCHUIT
  STUDIO INC.
WADDELL, ROBERT M.
WADE, HARRY
WADE, ROGER
WAGNER, ANDREW A.
WALKER, JESSIE
WALLEN, JONATHAN
WAPINSKI, DAVID
WARD, JERRY
WARTELL, BOB
WATERSUN, DAVID
WEIDLEIN, PETER
WELSH, STEVE
WHELESS, ROB
WHITE, GEORGE
WHITENTON, CARY
WILLIAMS, JAY S.
WILLIG, WILLIAM J.
WILSON, BURTON
WILSON, JAMES F.
WIRONEN
WOLLIN, WILLIAM
WOOD, RICHARD
WOODALLEN
  PHOTOGRAPHERS
WOOLFE, RAYMOND G.
WRISTEN, DONALD F.
WYNER, ISAIAH
YARBROUGH, BOB
YAWORSKI, DON

AUTOMOTIVE

ABRAMSON, DEAN
ASHE, BILL
ASQUINI, JAY
AVERY, RON
BEDNARSKI, PAUL S.
BUTTON DOWN
  PRODUCTIONS LTD.
COHEN, ANDY
COX, DENNIS
CRAWFORD, PAT
DAVIS, HOWARD
DECRUYENAERE, HOWARD
DIMARCO, JR., SAL
DOLIN, IRVING
ELBINGER, DOUGLAS
ELDER, JIM
ESTY, ANDREA
FELT, JIM
FINLEY, DOUG
GENTILE, SR., ARTHUR
GROENE, GORDON
HALL, DON
HARMON, TIM
HEWITT, SCOTT
HUNTZINGER, ROBERT
KAPLAN, B. PETER
KINETIC CORPORATION (G.

RAYMOND SCHUHMANN)
KLASS, RUBIN & ERIKA
  PHOTOGRAPHY
KRASKA, MARK
LUCE, DON
MARVY, JIM
MCCRIRICK, FLIP
MESSINEO, JOHN
MILLER PHOTOGRAPHY, INC.
NORTON, MICHAEL
ORRICO, CHARLES J.
POST, JOHN
RENNIE, BRIAN H.
SCHATZ, BOB
SCHIERSTEDT, NEIL
SCHLANGER, IRV
SHRIKHANDE, DEVENDRA
SIEGEL, R. MYLES
  PHOTOGRAPHY
STONE, TONY IMAGES
STORMZAND, JOHN
TENIN, BARRY
TORREZ, BOB
UPITIS, ALVIS
WADDELL, ROBERT M.
WAGNER, ANDREW A.
WAPINSKI, DAVID
WARREN, CAM
WEDLAKE, JIM
WILLIAMS, HAL
WOOLFE, RAYMOND G.
WRISTEN, DONALD F.

AVIATION

ACKROYD, HUGH S.
AVERETT, GERALD L.
BAILEY, ROBERT
BARON, JAMES J.
BAXLEY, KIRK
BAYER, DANIEL
BEATTY, DAVID E.
BENNETT, ROBERT J.
BOLESTA, ALAN
BRANDON, RANDY
BURROUGHS, ROBERT
BURY, SUSAN
BUSHUE, KATHY
CAMPBELL, TOM
CAVANAUGH, JAMES
CHESLER, DONNA & KEN
COLTON, ROBERT
CONNER, GARY
COONRAD, JORDAN
CORY, JEFF
DAKAN, LEW
DAVIDSON, CAMERON
DAVIS, DAVE
DEGABRIELE PHOTOGRAPHY
DELANO, JON
DOWNIE, DANA

ESTY, ANDREA
FANSLER, EARL
FARRELL, BILL
FELT, JIM
FINLEY, DOUG
FIREBAUGH, STEVE
GAMMA LIAISON INC.
GANDY, SKIP
GEIGER, WILLIAM K.
GENTILE, SR., ARTHUR
GERCZYNSKI, TOM
GOLD, GARY
GOLD, SAMMY
GOOD, JAY
GRAHAM, STEPHEN
GROENE, GORDON
HALL, DON
HAMPSON PHOTOGRAPHY
HARMON, TIM
HEDRICH-BLESSING
HIGHTON, SCOTT
HITT, WESLEY
HUCKABY, JERRY
JACOBY, RAY
JOHNSON, DONALD
JORDAN, JOE F.
KAPLAN, B. PETER
KILBORN, BILL
KLASS, RUBIN & ERIKA
  PHOTOGRAPHY
LINCK, TONY
LOYST, KEN
MAHIEU, TED
MASTROIANNI, ROGER
MATHIESON, GREG E.
MAY, RONALD W.
MCGRAIL, JOHN
MENZEL, PETER
MIHALEVICH, MICHAEL
MILLMAN, LESTER J.
MOON, BEN L.
MOORE, DAN
MOORE, MICHAEL
MUNSON, RUSSELL
PETERSON JR., CHESTER
PETERSON, JR., CHESTER
PHILLIPS, ROBIN H.
PORTNOY, LEWIS
PRITCHETT, LAUREN
  LAVONNE
QUARTUCCIO, DOM
REID, SEAN
RENNIE, BRIAN H.
RYCHETNIK, JOSEPH S.
RYCUS, JEFFREY A.
SATTERWHITE, AL
SAYLOR, TED
SCHAMP, J. BROUGH
SCHANUEL, ANTHONY
SEEGER, STEPHEN E.
SHANEFF, CARL

SHIELDS-MARLEY
  PHOTOGRAPHY
SHIER, DEANN
SOCHUREK, HOWARD J.
STALVIG, MURLYN A.
STEELE, GEOFF
STONE, TONY IMAGES
STOTT, BARRY
SUGAR, JAMES A.
SUMMER PRODUCTIONS
SWARTZ, FRED
TARCHALA, JOHN
THIGPEN, ALEXANDER G.
TRENKA, BUD
TUCKER, HOWARD
TUCKER, MORT
VAN DE VEN, MARY
WADDELL, ROBERT M.
WAGNER, ANDREW A.
WAPINSKI, DAVID
WEAKS, BILL S.
WHITE, GEORGE
WHITMIRE, KENNETH L.
WOODALLEN
  PHOTOGRAPHERS
YAMASHITA, MICHAEL S.

BOOK REVIEWS

ASCHERMAN, JR., HERBERT
HARMON, TIM
JACOBS, JR., LOU
KEMPER, BART
KIDD, CHUCK
LEVY, PATRICIA BARRY
LOYST, KEN
MESSINEO, JOHN
PECHTER, ALESE
PECHTER, MORTON H.
PETERSON, JR., CHESTER
PRESTON, LOUISA
PUTNAM, SARAH
ROLO PHOTOGRAPHY
RYCHETNIK, JOSEPH S.
SCHMIDT, DIANE JOY
SIBLEY, SCOTT
STORMZAND, JOHN
VAN RIPER, FRANK A.
WOOLFE, RAYMOND G.

BUSINESS & INDUSTRY

ABRAHAM, JOE
ADAMS, STEVEN
ALBINO, JOSEPH X.
ALEKANDROWICZ, FRANK
ALLEN, TIM
AMBORN, JOHN E.
AMER, TOMMY
APTON, BILL
ARNDT, DIANE

ARRUZA, TONY
ASQUINI, JAY
AUEL, ADAM
AVERETT, GERALD L.
AVERY, RON
BAER, RHODA
BAGG, ALAN
BAKER, JULIE
BAKKE, ERIC
BARBAGALLO, ANTONINO
BARNELL, JOE
BARNES, BILLY
BARON, JAMES J.
BARRON, DAVID M./OXYGEN
  GROUP
BARROS, ROBERT
  PHOTOGRAPHY INC.
BARTRUFF, DAVE
BAYER, DANIEL
BAYLES, DAL
BAYLES, DAL
BECK, PETER
  PHOTOGRAPHY
BEDNARSKI, PAUL S.
BEGLEITER, STEVEN H.
BENKERT, CHRISTINE
BENYAS, BOB
BERG, MARGARET C.
BITTERS, DAVID
BLACK, BILLY
BLAKESBERG, JAY
BOGACZ, MARK F.
BOHON, ED
BOLSTER, MARK
BRANDON, RANDY
BRAUN, BOB
BRIGNOLO, JOSEPH B.
BRINK, STEVEN
BROMLEY, DONALD
BURNS, STEVE
BUSH, DARRYL W.
BUTLER, TIM
CALDWELL, JIM
CAMPBELL, THOMAS S.
CAMPBELL, TOM
CARRIKER, RONALD
  PHOTOGRAPHY
CAVANAUGH, JAMES
CENDROWSKI, DWIGHT
CERNY, PAUL
CHAMPAGNE, BARRY
CHARLES, CINDY
CHARLES, FREDERICK
CHIN, RUTH
CLARK, H. DEAN
CLYMER, JONATHAN
COLLINS, ARLENE
COLMAN III, BEN
COLTON, ROBERT
COONRAD, JORDAN
CORY, JEFF

COSTE, KURT
COX, DENNIS
CURTIS, STEVEN
DANTZIC, JERRY
DECRUYENAERE, HOWARD
DEGABRIELE PHOTOGRAPHY
DEGGINGER, DR. E. R.
DEGGINGER, PHIL
DEVAULT, JIM
DIETZ, CRAIG
DIMARCO, JR., SAL
DORSEY, RON
  PHOTOGRAPHY
DOWNIE, DANA
DRESSLER, BRIAN
DREYER, PETER
DUNMIRE, LARRY
DUNOFF, RICH
DYER, ED
EDELMAN, HARRY
ELBINGER, DOUGLAS
ENGLISH, MELISSA HAYES
FARKAS, ALAN
FARR, JULIE
FARRELL, BILL
FEILING, DAVID A.
FELT, JIM
FINLEY, DOUG
FIREBAUGH, STEVE
FISHER PHOTOGRAPHY
FORDEN, J. PATRICK
FOSTER, KEVIN
FOWLEY, DOUGLAS
FRANZEN, DAVID
FREEMAN, DAVIS
FREEMAN, ROLAND
FRITZ, BRUCE
FRITZ, GERARD
FULTON, CONRAD JAMES
FUSCO, PAUL
GAMMA LIAISON INC.
GANDY, SKIP
GARIK, ALICE
GAROFALO, JOHN
  CLEVELAND
GARRETT, KENNETH
GEER, GARRY
GEFTER, JUDITH
GIAMMATTEO, JOHN
GIBSON, MARK & AUDREY
GIPE, JON
GLASS, BRUCE
GLASSMAN, KEITH
GOLD, GARY
GOLDBLATT, STEVEN
GOOD, JAY
GOODMAN, LISA J.
GORRILL, ROBERT B.
GOVE, GEOFFREY
GRAHAM, STEPHEN
GREEN-ARMYTAGE,

STEPHEN
GREENBERG, CHIP
GREENBLATT, WILLIAM D.
GREHAN, FARRELL
GRIGG, ROGER
GUBIN, MARK
HALPERN, DAVID
HAND, RAY PHOTOGRAPHY
HANSEN, BARBARA
HARDEN, CLIFF
HARKEY, JOHN J.
HARMON, TIM
HARRIS, CHRISTOPHER R.
HENRY, GEORGE T.
HERBST, JOHN
HIGHSMITH, CAROL
HIGHTON, SCOTT
HILL, JACKSON
HIRNELSEN, RICHARD
HIRSCH, KAREN I.
HODGE, ADELE
HOFFMAN, ROB
HOLLENBECK, CLIFF/KEVIN
  MORRIS
HOLT, WALTER
HOOS, GERALD WILLIAM
HOSS, RONALD P.
HOUSER, ROBERT
HOWARD, CARL
HUCKABY, JERRY
HUGHES, JOHN
IRVIN, MARCUS
ISAACS, LEE
ISAACS, ROBERT A.
IWASAKI, RICH
JOHNSON, DONALD
JONES, BRENT
JORDAN, G. STEVE
KAMP, ERIC
KAPLAN, B. PETER
KASHI, ED
KASPER, KEN
KEENAN, JOHN C.
KELLY, TONY
KEMPER, BART
KENNEDY, M. LEWIS
KHANLIAN, RICHARD
KILBORN, BILL
KINCAID, CLARK L.
KIRKENDALL/SPRING
  PHOTOGRAPHERS
KONRATH, G. FRANK
KOTECKI, STAN
KRATT, K.C.
KUHLMAN, CHRIS
KUPER, HOLLY
LABUA, FRANK
LAVINE, ARTHUR
LEE, LARRY
LEE, ROBERT II
  PHOTOGRAPHY

LEIPZIG, ARTHUR
LEVIN, AARON
LEVY, BURT
LEVY, PATRICIA BARRY
LEWELLYN, JON
LEWIS, VICKIE
LEY, RUSSELL
LIEBERMAN, ARCHIE
LINCK, TONY
LISSY, DAVID
LONGWOOD, MARC D.
LORENZ, ROBERT
MAHI, MIEKO SUE
MAHIEU, TED
MAHONEY, BOB
MANHEIM, MICHAEL PHILIP
MAPPES, CARL R.
MARES-MANTON,
  ALEXANDER
MASTROIANNI, ROGER
MATT, PHIL
MATTHEWS, CYNTHIA
MAXWELL, CHIP
MAY, RONALD W.
MAYLEN III, DAVID
MCALLISTER, BRUCE
MCCOY, DAN J.
MCGEE, TONY
MCGRAIL, JOHN
MCKAY, DOUG
MCKEE, MICHAEL
MCMULLIN, FOREST
MCNEILL, BRIAN
MCVICKER, SAM
MENDELSOHN, DAVID
MENZEL, PETER
MIGLAVS, MR. JANIS
MIHALEVICH, MICHAEL
MIHOVIL, ROBERT JOHN
MILLER PHOTOGRAPHY, INC.
MILLMAN, LESTER J.
MISHLER, CLARK JAMES
MOBERLEY, CONNIE
MOON, BEN L.
MOORE, MICHAEL
MOORE, RIC
MORELAND, MIKE
MORGENSTEIN, RICHARD
MORRIS, PAUL
MORROW, CHRISTOPHER W.
MOSS, GARY
MURPHY, MICHAEL
MYERS, FRED
NEUFELD, WILLIAM
NIKAS, GREG
NORTON, MICHAEL
O'BYRNE, WILLIAM M.
OLIVE, JIM
ORANS, MURIEL
ORRICO, CHARLES J.
PAGANELLI, MANUELLO

PALMIERI, JORGE
PARAS, MICHAEL
PATTERSON, MARION
PAWLICK, JOHN
PETERSON, JR., CHESTER
PHELAN, JOHN
PHILLIPS, JAMES
PHOTOGRAPHIC DESIGNS
PLACE, CHARLES
PLATTETER, GEORGE
PLUMMER, DOUG
POGGENPOHL, ERIC
POLSKY, JOEL
POLUMBAUM, TED
PORTNOY, LEWIS
PRESTON, L. STEVE
PRICE, GREG
PROUD, B.
PSZENICA, JUDITH
PUTNAM, DON
PUTNAM, SARAH
QUICKSILVER
  PHOTOGRAPHY
RAFKIND, ANDREW J.
RAICHE, BOB
REDIC, BILL
REED, GEOFF
REID, SEAN
REISS, RAY
REVETTE, DAVID
RICH, BERNI
RIECKS, DAVID
RILEY, JON
ROBINSON, MIKE
ROGERS, CHUCK
ROGOWSKI, TIM
ROSSI, DAVID A.
ROWAN, N. R.
ROWIN, STANLEY
RUNION, BRITT
RUSSELL, MARC
RYBISKI JR., A. J.
RYCUS, JEFFREY A.
SALVO, CHRIS
SAYLOR, TED
SCHANUEL, ANTHONY
SCHATZ, BOB
SCHLEICHER, BILL
SCHLUETER, MICHAEL K.
SCHMIDT, DIANE JOY
SCHWARZ, IRA J.
SCHWARZ, MICHAEL A.
SCHWELIK, FRANK
SCIOLETTI, JODY
SCORY, RAYMOND G.
SEEGER, STEPHEN E.
SEYMOUR, RONALD
SHANEFF, CARL
SHIELDS-MARLEY
  PHOTOGRAPHY
SHRIKHANDE, DEVENDRA

SHULTZ, LAURA
SIBLEY, SCOTT
SIEGEL, R. MYLES
  PHOTOGRAPHY
SMITH, BRIAN
SNOW, ANDY
SORCE, WAYNE
SPEARS, PHILLIP
STARR, ASHBY
  PHOTOGRAPHER
STEINER, CLYDE
STEWARDSON, JOE
STIERER, DENNIS
STOCK PHOTOS HAWAII
STONE, TONY IMAGES
STORMZAND, JOHN
STOVER, DAVID
STRATFORD, JIM
STRESHINSKY, TED
STROMBERG, BRUCE
SWANSON, BOB
SWARTZ, FRED
TARCHALA, JOHN
TARLETON, GARY
TATEM, MIKE
TAXEL, BARNEY
TAYLOR, RANDY G.
TESADA, DAVID X.
THOMAS, CLARK
TOLBERT, BRIAN R.
TRENKA, BUD
TRUSLOW, B.
TUCKER, HOWARD
TUCKER, MORT
URSILLO, CATHERINE
VANDER SCHUIT
  STUDIO INC.
WADDELL, ROBERT M.
WAGGONER, MIKE
WAGNER, ANDREW A.
WALKER, HARRY M.
WALLEN, JONATHAN
WAPINSKI, DAVID
WATERSUN, DAVID
WECKLER, CHAD
WEINTRAUB, DAVID
WELSH, STEVE
WERNER, PERRY
WESTHEIMER, BILL
WHEELER, NIK
WHITE, GEORGE
WHITMAN, ALAN
WHITMORE, KEN
WILLIS, CLIFF
WILLITS, PAT L.
WILSON, DOUG M.
WISSER, BILL
WOLF, JACK
WOLMAN, BARON
WOOD, ANTHONY B.
WOOD, RICHARD

WRISLEY, BARD
WRISTEN, DONALD F.
WYMAN, JAKE
YONKER, THOMAS
  PHOTOGRAPHY
YOUNG-WOLFF, DAVID
ZAVODNY, STEVEN
ZILLIOUX, JOHN

COMPUTER TECHNOLOGY

AIOSA, VINCENT
ARPADI, ALLEN G.
AVERY, RON
BAER, RHODA
BARON, JAMES J.
BARROS, ROBERT
  PHOTOGRAPHY INC.
BERG, MARGARET C.
BLOCH, STEVEN
BOGACZ, MARK F.
BOLSTER, MARK
BURROUGHS, ROBERT
CAMPBELL, TOM
CARROLL, TOM
CHAMPAGNE, BARRY
CHARLES, CINDY
COGSWELL, JENNIFER D.
COLMAN III, BEN
COSTE, KURT
COX, DENNIS
CRAWFORD, PAT
DARNELL, MITCHELL
EMMERICH, DON
FINLEY, DOUG
FIREBAUGH, STEVE
FOSTER, KEVIN
FOSTER, LEE
FRITZ, BRUCE
FRITZ, GERARD
GAGE, HAL
GEFTER, JUDITH
GIBSON, MARK & AUDREY
GOODMAN, LISA J.
GOVE, GEOFFREY
GREENBERG, CHIP
GROTTA, SALLY WEINER
HARMON, TIM
HARTMANN, W. GEOFFREY
HILL, JACKSON
HUNTER, FIL
IRVIN, MARCUS
JACOBSON, RANDALL C.
JALBERT, PAUL
JOUBERT PHOTOGRAPHY,
  LARRY
KEMPER, BART
KENNEDY, M. LEWIS
KONRATH, G. FRANK
KOWAL, JOHN PAUL
LEVIN, AARON

LEY, RUSSELL
LONGWOOD, MARC D.
LORENZ, ROBERT
MAKRIS, DAVID
MAY, RONALD W.
MCCOY, DAN J.
MCGLYNN, DAVID
MCGRAIL, JOHN
MCKAY, DOUG
MCNEILL, BRIAN
MENZEL, PETER
MEYERS, EDWARD
MIGLAVS, MR. JANIS
MIHALEVICH, MICHAEL
MILLER PHOTOGRAPHY, INC.
MISHLER, CLARK JAMES
MOLENHOUSE, CRAIG
MOON, BEN L.
MOONEY, CHRIS
MORRIS, JEFF
NADLER, BOB
NELSON, ROBIN
OMER, DAVID
PETERSON JR., CHESTER
PETERSON, JR., CHESTER
PICKERELL, JAMES H.
POST, GEORGE
PRICE, CLAYTON J.
QUICKSILVER
  PHOTOGRAPHY
REDIC, BILL
RIECKS, DAVID
RILEY, JON
ROGERS, CHUCK
ROLO PHOTOGRAPHY
ROSSI, DAVID A.
ROWIN, STANLEY
RYCUS, JEFFREY A.
SCHLANGER, IRV
SCHMIDT, DIANE JOY
SCHWARZ, IRA J.
SEITZ, SEPP
SHOLIK, STAN
SIBLEY, SCOTT
SLATER, EDWARD
STEINER, CLYDE
STEWARDSON, JOE
STONE, TONY IMAGES
SUGAR, JAMES A.
TAXEL, BARNEY
TESADA, DAVID X.
THILL, NANCY
THILL, NANCY
UNIPHOTO PICTURE
  AGENCY
URBINA, WALT
VANDER SCHUIT
  STUDIO INC.
VENDITTI, JAMES VINCENT
WAPINSKI, DAVID
WELSH, STEVE

WILLIS, CLIFF
WRISTEN, DONALD F.

ECOLOGY

ACOSTA, JOSE'
ALBINO, JOSEPH X.
ALDRICH, JAY
ALEKANDROWICZ, FRANK
ANDERSON, GORDON
AUEL, ADAM
BAKER, BOBBE CLINTON
BAKER, JOHN
BARON, JAMES J.
BARR, IAN
BERNSTEIN, MARION
BITTERS, DAVID
BRANDON, RANDY
BRAUN, ERNEST
BULL, DAVID
BURNS, STEVE
BUSHUE, KATHY
CARDACINO, MICHAEL
COLMAN III, BEN
COOKE, JOHN DR.
COOPER, TOM
CORY, JEFF
COX, DENNIS
DAVIDSON, CAMERON
DAVIS, DAVE
DECRUYENAERE, HOWARD
DEGABRIELE PHOTOGRAPHY
DEMPSAY, SAY
DEVORE III, NICHOLAS
DODGE, LARRY
DOUGLASS, DARREN
DOWNIE, DANA
DRAKE, JEANNE
ELK III, JOHN
FARR, JULIE
FARRELL, BILL
FINLEY, DOUG
FLOTTE, LUCIEN
FORBERT, DAVID J.
FOXX, JEFFREY JAY
FRENCH, PETER
GARIK, ALICE
GIBSON, MARK & AUDREY
GNASS, JEFF
GOLD, GARY
GOODMAN, LISA J.
GOVE, GEOFFREY
GREEN-ARMYTAGE,
  STEPHEN
GRESHAM, GRITS
GROTTA, SALLY WEINER
HALPERN, DAVID
HARP, DAVID
HERRON, MATT
HIGHTON, SCOTT
HOFFMAN, ROB

HOUSER, DAVE G.
JACKSON, DON
JOHNSON, TREVE
KANOWSKY, KEN
KAPLAN, B. PETER
KASPER, KEN
KIDD, CHUCK
KIRCHHEIMER, GABE
KLASS, RUBIN & ERIKA
  PHOTOGRAPHY
KONRATH, G. FRANK
KUHLMAN, CHRIS
LEE, CAROL
LEVY, RON
LEWIS, G. BRAD
LONGWOOD, MARC D.
MCCARTNEY, SUSAN
MCMULLIN, FOREST
MCNEILL, BRIAN
MESSINEO, JOHN
MOONEY, CHRIS
MYERS, TOM
NORTON, PHILLIP
ODYSSEY PRODUCTIONS
ORANS, MURIEL
PECHTER, ALESE
PECHTER, MORTON H.
PERRON, ROBERT
PETERSON, LEE
PHOTO RESOURCE HAWAII
PLUMMER, DOUG
PRATT, VERNA E.
PRESTON, LOUISA
PRIER, ALLEN
PRITCHETT, LAUREN
  LAVONNE
QUARTUCCIO, DOM
REID, SEAN
RIECKS, DAVID
RIEGER, TED
ROBERTS, JANET M.
ROLLAND, GUY A.
ROLO PHOTOGRAPHY
RYAN, DAVID
RYCUS, JEFFREY A.
SALMOIRAGHI, FRANCO
SANGER, DAVID
SCHEIDEGGER, FRANCIS
SCHEIDEGGER, FRANCIS
SCHERMEISTER, PHIL
SCHLUETER, MICHAEL K.
SCHMID, BERT
SCHMIDT, DIANE JOY
SIBLEY, SCOTT
SISSON, BOB
SPIEGEL, TED
STAMATES, JIM
STEINGROVE, JACK
STEWARDSON, JOE
STIERER, DENNIS
STOCK PHOTOS HAWAII

STONE, TONY IMAGES
STORMZAND, JOHN
STRATFORD, DENIS
TAXEL, BARNEY
TENIN, BARRY
TORREZ, BOB
TREYBIG, CYNTHIA
UNIPHOTO PICTURE
  AGENCY
VAUGHN, GREG
WADDELL, ROBERT M.
WAGNER, ANDREW A.
WAPINSKI, DAVID
WATERSUN, DAVID
WITHEY, GARY S.
WOOD, RICHARD
WU, NORBERT

EDITORIAL

ABRAMSON, DEAN
ACOSTA, JOSE'
ADAMS, EDDIE
ADELMAN, BOB
ALDRICH, JAY
ALEKANDROWICZ, FRANK
ALLEN, J. J.
ALLEN, MARIETTE PATHY
ALPER, BARBARA
AMER, TOMMY
ANCONA, GEORGE
ANDERSON, RICHARD
ARNDT, DIANE
ARRUZA, TONY
ART OF FINE PHOTOGRAPHY
ASHE, BILL
BAER, GORDON
BAER, RHODA
BAGG, ALAN
BAKER, BOBBE CLINTON
BAKER, JULIE
BAKKE, ERIC
BARAG, MARC
BARBAGALLO, ANTONINO
BARBALACE PHOTOGRAPHY
BARCELLONA, MARIANNE
BARNELL, JOE
BARNES, MICHELLE A.
BARON, JAMES J.
BARRETT, CHARLES
BARRINGTON, CAROL
BAUMEL, KEN
BAYER, DANIEL
BAYLES, DAL
BECHTOLD, CHARLES
BECK, PETER
  PHOTOGRAPHY
BENKERT, CHRISTINE
BENNETT, ROBERT J.
BERNSTEIN, MARION
BEVAN, PAT

BISHOP, RANDA
BITTERS, DAVID
BLAKESBERG, JAY
BLOCH, STEVEN
BLOCK, RAY
BOBBE, LELAND
BOGACZ, MARK F.
BOHON, ED
BOLSTER, MARK
BORDNICK, BARBARA
BRANDON, RANDY
BRAUN, BOB
BROMLEY, DONALD
BROOKS, CHARLES W.
BROWN, JAMES
BROWN-ROSNER, SHEREE
BRUNDEGE, BARBARA A.
BUCK, BRUCE
BUDROW, NANCY
BULL, DAVID
BURGESS, MICHELE A.
BURNS, STEVE
BUSCH, SCHERLEY
BUSH, DARRYL W.
BUSHUE, KATHY
BUZBY, SHERRIE
CALDWELL, JIM
CAMPBELL, J. KENT
CAPOTOSTO, JOHN J.
CARR, KATHLEEN THORMOD
CASTANEDA, LUIS
CENDROWSKI, DWIGHT
CERNY, PAUL
CHANDOHA, WALTER
CHAPUT, SIMON
CHARLES, CINDY
CHIKA
CLARKSON, FRANK
CLARKSON, ROBERT NOEL
CLEFF, BERNIE
COGSWELL, JENNIFER D.
COHEN, ANDY
COHEN, DAN
COLEMAN, GENE
COLLINS, ARLENE
COLMAN III, BEN
COMET, RENEE
CONNER, GARY
CONRAD, CHRISTOPHER
COOPER, ED
COOPER, TOM
CORSALE, LORRAINE
CORY, JEFF
COX, DENNIS
CRAWFORD, PAT
CROKE, THOMAS J.
CROSBY, A. DAVID
CURTIS, STEVEN
D'ADDIO, JAMES
DARRYL, JACOBSON
DAUMAN, HENRI

DAVIDSON, CAMERON
DAVIS, DAVE
DE CASSERES, JOSEPH
DE ZANGER, ARIE
DECRUYENAERE, HOWARD
DEGGINGER, PHIL
DELANO, JON
DEMPSAY, SAY
DEUTSCH, JACK
DIAZ, ARMANDO
DIBARTOLOMEO, GAREN
DIMARCO, JR., SAL
DOWNEY, CHARLES
DOWNIE, DANA
DRESSLER, BRIAN
DREYER, PETER
DUFRESNE, WALTER
DUNOFF, RICH
DYER, ED
ELAKMAN, MARC
ELK III, JOHN
ELLMAN, ELAINE
ELLZEY, BILL
EMMERICH, DON
ENGELMANN, SUZANNE J.
ESCOSA, JOHN
ESTY, ANDREA
FABRICIUS, DAGMAR
FARRELL, BILL
FINLEY, DOUG
FIREBAUGH, STEVE
FISHER PHOTOGRAPHY
FISHER, RAY
FLEMING, LARRY
FLETCHER, T. MIKE
FLORET, EVELYN
FLOTTE, LUCIEN
FORDEN, J. PATRICK
FORMISANO-MAYERI, YONI
FOSTER, LEE
FOURRE, LIZA
FOXX, JEFFREY JAY
FRANZEN, DAVID
FREEMAN, ROLAND
FREEMAN, TINA
FRENCH, PETER
FRICK, KEN
FRIEDMAN, RICK
FRIESE, RICK
FRISCH, STEPHEN
FRITZ, BRUCE
FUKUHARA, RICHARD
  YUTAKA
FULTON, CONRAD JAMES
FUSCO, PAUL
FUSS, EDUARDO
GAMMA LIAISON INC.
GARIK, ALICE
GARLAND, MICHAEL E.
GAROFALO, JOHN
  CLEVELAND

GARRETT, KENNETH
GEER, GARRY
GEFTER, JUDITH
GEIGER, K. WILLIAM
GEIGER, WILLIAM K.
GENTILE, SR., ARTHUR
GETLEN, DAVID
GIBSON, MARK & AUDREY
GLASSMAN, KEITH
GNASS, JEFF
GOLDBLATT, STEVEN
GOOD, JAY
GOODHEIM, JANIS
GOODMAN, LISA J.
GRAHAM, A. MICHAEL
GRAHAM, STEPHEN
GREEN-ARMYTAGE,
  STEPHEN
GREEN-ARMYTAGE,
  STEPHEN
GRIMES, BILLY
GUBIN, MARK
GWINN, BETH
HALL, JOHN M.
HALSEY, TERRY
HALSTEAD, DIRCK
HAND, RAY PHOTOGRAPHY
HANDS, BRUCE
HARBRON, PATRICK
HARLAN, BRUCE
HARMON, TIM
HARP, DAVID
HARRINGTON, JOHN
HARRINGTON, TY
HARRIS, CHRISTOPHER R.
HARTMANN, W. GEOFFREY
HAWK, DARYL
HAWTHORNE, ANN
HEBBERD, LINDSAY
HEDRICH-BLESSING
HELLER, MICHAEL
HEWITT, SCOTT
HIGHTON, SCOTT
HILL, JACKSON
HIRSCH, KAREN I.
HITT, WESLEY
HOEBERMAN, MATHEW &
  KRISTIN
HOFFMAN, ROB
HOLBROOKE, ANDREW
HOLLAND, JAMES R.
HOLLENBECK, CLIFF/KEVIN
  MORRIS
HOLLYMAN, TOM
HOLTEL, JOHN P.
HOOS, GERALD WILLIAM
HORSTED, PAUL
HOUSER, DAVE G.
HOUSER, ROBERT
HOWARD, CARL
HUMPHRIES, JR., H.

GORDON
HUNTER, FIL
ISAACS, ROBERT A.
IWASAKI, RICH
JACOBS, JR., LOU
JAMES, GRANT R.
JEFFERSON, LOUISE E.
JOHNSON, DONALD
JOHNSON, EVERETT C.
JOHNSON, FOREST
JOHNSON, J. SAM
JOHNSON, TREVE
JOHNSTON, GREG
JONES, BRENT
JOUBERT PHOTOGRAPHY,
  LARRY
KAEHLER, WOLFGANG
KALE, WALTER
KALUZNY, ZIGY
KAPLAN, B. PETER
KATZMAN, MARK
KAYE, ROD
KEHRWALD, RICHARD
KEMPER, BART
KEMPER, SUSAN M.
KENNEDY, M. LEWIS
KENTON, BASIA
KERMANI, SHAHN
KHORNAK, LUCILLE
KIDD, CHUCK
KING, KATHLEEN
KIRCHHEIMER, GABE
KLASS, RUBIN & ERIKA
  PHOTOGRAPHY
KOENIG, GEA
KOLLODGE, KENNETH
KONRATH, G. FRANK
KOONTZ, KATY
KOROPP, ROBERT
KRAVITZ, TOM
KRUEGER, BOB
KUPER, HOLLY
LABUA, FRANK
LAMONT, DANIEL E., JR.
LAVINE, ARTHUR
LE GRAND, PETER
LEDUC, LYLE
LEE, CAROL
LEE, LARRY
LEE, ROBERT II
  PHOTOGRAPHY
LEIBER, N. GREGORY
LEVIN, AARON
LEVITON, DREW B.
LEVITON, JOYCE B.
LEVY, PATRICIA BARRY
LEVY, RON
LEWIS, G. BRAD
LEWIS, VICKIE
LEY, RUSSELL
LIEBERMAN, ARCHIE

LINCK, TONY
LISSY, DAVID
LITSEY, LLOYD
LONGWOOD, MARC D.
LORD, JIM
LORENZ, ROBERT
LOTT, HAL
LOYST, KEN
LUKOWICZ, JEROME
MACKENZIE, MAXWELL
MACWEENEY, ALEN
MAGID, JEROME
MAHI, MIEKO SUE
MAHONEY, BOB
MANONI, EILEEN
MARES-MANTON,
   ALEXANDER
MARGERIN, BILL
MARKATOS, JERRY
MAROON, FRED J.
MASSIE, KIM
MASSON, LISA
MASTROIANNI, ROGER
MATT, PHIL
MATTHEWS, CYNTHIA
MCCARTHY, MARGARET
MCCUTCHEON, JR., SHAW
MCDARRAH, FRED W.
MCGINTY, KATHIE
MCGLYNN, DAVID
MCGRATH, NORMAN
MCKAY, DOUG
MCMULLIN, FOREST
MCNEILL, BRIAN
MEANS, LISA
MELTZER, LEE
MENNENGA, JERRY
MERIDETH, PAUL L.
MICHELSON, ERIC
MIGLAVS, MR. JANIS
MIHALEVICH, MICHAEL
MIHOVIL, ROBERT JOHN
MILLER PHOTOGRAPHY, INC.
MILLER, JOE
MILLER, MELABEE M.
MILLER, ROGER
   PHOTO, LTD.
MILLMAN, LESTER J.
MISHLER, CLARK JAMES
MITCHELL, JACK
MODRICKER, DARREN
MOONEY, KEVIN O.
MORGENSTEIN, RICHARD
MORRIS, PAUL
MORROW, CHRISTOPHER W.
MOSER, DAVID W.
MOSS, GARY
MOSS, HOWARD
MUSCHENETZ, ROLAND &
   KAREN
NANCE, ANCIL

NANO, ED
NELSON, ROBIN
NETZER, DON
NEWMAN, ARNOLD
NORTON, MICHAEL
OBREMSKI, GEORGE
ORANS, MURIEL
ORDERS, KAREN
ORRICO, CHARLES J.
OTSUKI, TOSHI
OUZER, LOUIS
PAGANELLI, MANUELLO
PALMIERI, JORGE
PARAS, MICHAEL
PAWLICK, JOHN
PAYNE, SHELBY
PECHTER, ALESE
PECHTER, MORTON H.
PERESS, GILLES
PEREZ, MARTY
PETT, LAURENCE J.
PHAM, DIEM K.
PHANEUF, ART
PHOTO RESOURCE HAWAII
PHOTOGRAPHIC IMPACT
PHOTOSMITH
PITOU, CINDY
PLATTETER, GEORGE
PLUMMER, DOUG
POGGENPOHL, ERIC
POLUMBAUM, TED
POOR, SUZANNE
PORTNOY, LEWIS
POST, JOHN
POWELL, TODD B.
POWER, CHARLOTTE A.
PRESTON, LOUISA
PRICE, GREG
PRINCE, NORMAN
PROUD, B.
PSZENICA, JUDITH
PUTNAM, SARAH
QUARTUCCIO, DOM
RAFKIND, ANDREW J.
RANTZMAN, KAREN
   STAFFORD
REED, GEOFF
REILLY, JOHN
RENO, KENT
RICARDEL, VINCENT J.
RICHARDSON, DAVID C.
RIECKS, DAVID
RILEY, GEORGE
ROBINSON, BILL
ROBINSON, MIKE
ROLO PHOTOGRAPHY
ROMANO, PATRICK J.
ROSSI, DAVID A.
ROWAN, N. R.
ROWIN, STANLEY
RUBIN, JANICE

RUHE, GEORGE-EDWARD
RYAN, DAVID
RYCHETNIK, JOSEPH S.
RYCUS, JEFFREY A.
SACHA, BOB
SALMOIRAGHI, FRANCO
SALVO, CHRIS
SANDBANK, HENRY
SAVILLE, LYNN
SCHAMP, J. BROUGH
SCHIERSTEDT, NEIL
SCHIFF, NANCY RICA
SCHLUETER, MICHAEL K.
SCHMID, BERT
SCHMIDT, DIANE JOY
SCHWARZ, IRA J.
SCHWARZ, MICHAEL A.
SCHWELIK, FRANK
SCIOLETTI, JODY
SEITZ, ART
SELIGMAN, PAUL
SETON, CHARLES
SEYMOUR, RONALD
SHANEFF, CARL
SHERMAN, BOB
SHERMAN, RON
SHIELDS-MARLEY
   PHOTOGRAPHY
SHIER, DEANN
SHRIKHANDE, DEVENDRA
SHROUT, BILL & KATHRYN E.
SHULTZ, LAURA
SHULTZ, LAURA MAXWELL
SIBLEY, SCOTT
SIMS, MARK
SISSON, BOB
SMELTZER, ROBERT
SMITH, BRIAN
SMITH, ROBIN B.
SMITH, ROGER B.
SNOW, ANDY
SNYDER, LEE F.
SOMOZA, GERARDO
STAMATES, JIM
STARR, ASHBY
   PHOTOGRAPHER
STAWNIAK, JIM
STEELE, MAX
STEINER, LISL
STEWARDSON, JOE
STIERER, DENNIS
STOCK PHOTOS HAWAII
STONE, ERIKA
STONE, TONY IMAGES
STORMZAND, JOHN
STOVER, DAVID
STRATFORD, JIM
STREET, PARK
STRESHINSKY, TED
STROMBERG, BRUCE
SVEHLA, JAMES C.

SWARTZ, FRED
SWOGER, ARTHUR
TADDER, MORTON
TAGGART, MARK J.
TANNENBAUM, ALLAN
TARLETON, GARY
TARR, CHARLES J.
TAXEL, BARNEY
TAYLOR, RANDY G.
TENIN, BARRY
TESADA, DAVID X.
THATCHER, CHARLES R.
THOMAS, CLARK
THOMPSON, MICHAEL S.
TORREZ, BOB
TOTO , JOE
TRENKA, BUD
ULMER, DAVID
UPITIS, ALVIS
VARTOOGIAN, JACK
VAUGHN, GREG
WADDELL, ROBERT M.
WADE, ROGER
WAGNER, ANDREW A.
WALKER, HARRY M.
WALKER, JESSIE
WALLEN, JONATHAN
WAPINSKI, DAVID
WARD, JERRY
WATERSUN, DAVID
WELLS, DAVID H.
WERNER, PERRY
WESTHEIMER, BILL
WHEELER, NIK
WHITE, GEORGE
WHITMAN, ALAN
WHITMIRE, KENNETH L.
WHITMORE, KEN
WILLIAMS III, ZANE
WILLIAMS, HAL
WILLIS, CLIFF
WINTER, NITA
WOLF, JACK
WOLFE, DAN
WOOD, TED
WRISLEY, BARD
WRISTEN, DONALD F.
WYMAN, IRA
WYNER, ISAIAH
WYROSTOK, CHUCK
YAMASHITA, MICHAEL S.
YARBROUGH, CARL
YONKER, THOMAS
   PHOTOGRAPHY
ZAKE, BRUCE
ZAVODNY, STEVEN

EDUCATION

ABRAMSON, DEAN
ADAMS, JANET L.

ALBINO, JOSEPH X.
ALDRICH, JAY
ANCONA, GEORGE
ANDERSON, RICHARD
ARPADI, ALLEN G.
ART OF FINE PHOTOGRAPHY
AVERY, RON
BARNES, BILLY
BARNES, MICHELLE A.
BARON, JAMES J.
BARROS, ROBERT
  PHOTOGRAPHY INC.
BAYLES, DAL
BEKKER, PHILIP
BERG, MARGARET C.
BERNSTEIN, MARION
BEVAN, PAT
BLOCK, RAY
BROWN-ROSNER, SHEREE
BUTLER, TIM
CENDROWSKI, DWIGHT
CHARLES, CINDY
COHEN, STUART
COLMAN III, BEN
CORY, JEFF
COX, DENNIS
CROMER, PEGGO
DELLA GROTTA, VIVIENNE
DEMPSAY, SAY
DIMARCO, JR., SAL
ELBINGER, DOUGLAS
ENGELMANN, SUZANNE J.
ENGH, ROHN
FAIRCLOTH, JANE G.
FARR, JULIE
FISHER PHOTOGRAPHY
FITZHUGH, SUSIE
FLOTTE, LUCIEN
FORBERT, DAVID J.
FREEMAN, JOHN
FRISCH, STEPHEN
GIBSON, MARK & AUDREY
GNASS, JEFF
GRAHAM, A. MICHAEL
GRIMES, BILLY
HARMON, TIM
HARTMANN, ERICH
HEBBERD, LINDSAY
HERRON, MATT
HILL, JACKSON
HIRSCH, KAREN I.
HOLT, WALTER
HOUSER, ROBERT
ISAACS, ROBERT A.
JOHNSON, TREVE
KAPLAN, B. PETER
KASPER, KEN
KIDD, CHUCK
KONRATH, G. FRANK
LEVIN, AARON
LEVY, PATRICIA BARRY

LORENZ, ROBERT
MASSON, LISA
MCALLISTER, BRUCE
MCBRIDE, TOM
MCCUTCHEON, STEVE
MIGLAVS, MR. JANIS
MIHALEVICH, MICHAEL
MUSCHENETZ, ROLAND &
  KAREN
ODYSSEY PRODUCTIONS
ORANS, MURIEL
PHOTO RESOURCE HAWAII
PHOTOGRAPHIC DESIGNS
PHOTOSMITH
PRICE, GREG
PRINCE, NORMAN
RAFKIND, ANDREW J.
RANTZMAN, KAREN
  STAFFORD
RIECKS, DAVID
ROLO PHOTOGRAPHY
RUST, GREGORY E.
RYCUS, JEFFREY A.
SCHMIDT, DIANE JOY
SEEGER, STEPHEN E.
SELIGMAN, PAUL
SIBLEY, SCOTT
SISSON, BOB
SITEMAN, FRANK
SPEARS, PHILLIP
STARR, ASHBY
  PHOTOGRAPHER
STEWARDSON, JOE
STONE, ERIKA
STONE, TONY IMAGES
STORMZAND, JOHN
STREET, PARK
STROMBERG, BRUCE
SUDOW, ELLYN
TAXEL, BARNEY
TRENKA, BUD
WAPINSKI, DAVID
WARD, JERRY
WHITE-FALCON, REGINA E.
WHITMAN, ALAN
WINTER, NITA
WOOD, ANTHONY B.
WOOD, RICHARD

ELECTRONICS

BAYER, DANIEL
CARROLL, TOM
COOKE, JOHN DR.
COX, DENNIS
DIMARCO, JR., SAL
DOUGLAS, KEITH
ELAKMAN, MARC
ELBINGER, DOUGLAS
EMMERICH, DON
FINLEY, DOUG

FLOTTE, LUCIEN
FOSTER, KEVIN
FRITZ, GERARD
FRY III, GEORGE B.
GOODMAN, LISA J.
HARMON, TIM
HUNTER, FIL
KONRATH, G. FRANK
MAY, RONALD W.
MCNEILL, BRIAN
MIHALEVICH, MICHAEL
MILLER PHOTOGRAPHY, INC.
MORRIS, JEFF
NELSON, ROBIN
PICKERELL, JAMES H.
PRICE, CLAYTON J.
QUARTUCCIO, DOM
ROLO PHOTOGRAPHY
ROSSI, DAVID A.
ROWIN, STANLEY
SCHLANGER, IRV
SCHMIDT, DIANE JOY
SCHNEIDER, JOHN
SEEGER, STEPHEN E.
SHOLIK, STAN
SLATER, EDWARD
STONE, TONY IMAGES
TAXEL, BARNEY
TAYLOR, RANDY G.
UNIPHOTO PICTURE
  AGENCY
VENDITTI, JAMES VINCENT
WAPINSKI, DAVID

ENTERTAINMENT

AARON, RICHARD E.
ADAMS, EDDIE
ART OF FINE PHOTOGRAPHY
BAYER, DANIEL
BILKER, HARVEY L.
BLAKESBERG, JAY
BLOCK, RAY
BROMLEY, DONALD
BROWN-ROSNER, SHEREE
BUTTON DOWN
  PRODUCTIONS LTD.
CAMPBELL, TOM
CARTER, WILLIAM
CHARLES, FREDERICK
CHIKA
CLARKSON, ROBERT NOEL
COHEN, ANDY
CORY, JEFF
COX, DENNIS
DAUMAN, HENRI
DELANO, JON
DRESSLER, BRIAN
ELLMAN, ELAINE
ENGELMANN, SUZANNE J.
FISHER, RAY

FLOTTE, LUCIEN
FRENCH, PETER
FRIEDMAN, IRV
FULTON, CONRAD JAMES
GAMMA LIAISON INC.
GARLAND, MICHAEL E.
GOOD, JAY
GORDON, FRANK
GROSS, ALEX LLOYD
HALSTEAD, DIRCK
HARBRON, PATRICK
HARMON, TIM
HARRINGTON, JOHN
HIRSCH, KAREN I.
HODGE, ADELE
HOLZ, WILLIAM
HUCKABY, JERRY
JEFFRY, MISS ALIX
KAYE, ROD
KEMPER, BART
KIDD, CHUCK
KNIGHT, DOUG
KONRATH, G. FRANK
LEIALOHA, MARK
LESTER, PETER
MASTROIANNI, ROGER
MATHIESON, GREG E.
MCGLYNN, DAVID
MIHALEVICH, MICHAEL
MILLER PHOTOGRAPHY, INC.
MITCHELL, JACK
MODRICKER, DARREN
MORRIS, JEFF
MOSS, HOWARD
PECHTER, ALESE
PECHTER, MORTON H.
PEREZ, MARTY
PETT, LAURENCE J.
PHOTOGRAPHY UNLIMITED
POLSKY, JOEL
PRICE, GREG
QUARTUCCIO, DOM
QUICKSILVER
  PHOTOGRAPHY
REED, GEOFF
REMINGTON, GEORGE
RIECKS, DAVID
ROBERTS, EBET
ROSENBLUM, BERNARD
ROSSI, DAVID A.
RYCUS, JEFFREY A.
SCHMIDT, DIANE JOY
SEEGER, STEPHEN E.
SELIGMAN, PAUL
SHAKOOR, RA
SIBLEY, SCOTT
SMETZER, DONALD
SOMOZA, GERARDO
STAWNIAK, JIM
STOCK PHOTOS HAWAII
STORMZAND, JOHN

STREET, PARK
SUDOW, ELLYN
TAYLOR, RANDY G.
TENIN, BARRY
UNIPHOTO PICTURE
  AGENCY
VARTOOGIAN, JACK
WACHTER, JERRY
WADDELL, ROBERT M.
WAGNER, ANDREW A.
WAPINSKI, DAVID
WARD, JERRY
WEIL, KAREN
WHITAKER, GREG
WHITMAN, ALAN
WHITMORE, KEN
WILLIAMS, HAL
WILLITS, PAT L.
WILSON, BURTON
WOLMAN, BARON
YARBROUGH, BOB
ZAHNER, DAVID

FAMILY

ADAMS, JANET L.
ALKALAY, MORRIS
ALLEN, MARIETTE PATHY
ALPER, BARBARA
ANCONA, GEORGE
ART OF FINE PHOTOGRAPHY
ASCHERMAN, JR., HERBERT
BAER, GORDON
BAKER, BOBBE CLINTON
BARAG, MARC
BARON, JAMES J.
BECK, PETER
  PHOTOGRAPHY
BEVAN, PAT
BLINKOFF, RICHARD
BOLSTER, MARK
BRADY ARCHITECTURAL
  PHOTOGRAPHY
BROWN-ROSNER, SHEREE
BURY, SUSAN
CHURCH, DENNIS
COOPER, TOM
COOPER, TOM
COX, DENNIS
DECRUYENAERE, HOWARD
DEITS, KATIE
DELLA GROTTA, VIVIENNE
DIETZ, CRAIG
DOWNIE, DANA
EMMERICH, DON
ENGH, ROHN
EPSTEIN, LARRY
FAIRCLOTH, JANE G.
FORMISANO-MAYERI, YONI
FOSTER, KEVIN
FOURRE, LIZA

GAROFALO, JOHN
  CLEVELAND
GEFTER, JUDITH
GERCZYNSKI, TOM
GOODMAN, LISA J.
GREEN-ARMYTAGE,
  STEPHEN
HARMON, TIM
HARRINGTON, TY
HARTMANN, ERICH
HICKS, JAMES
HIRSCH, KAREN I.
HUCKABY, JERRY
HUMPHRIES, JR., H.
  GORDON
JOUBERT PHOTOGRAPHY,
  LARRY
KAPLAN, B. PETER
KASHI, ED
KASPER, KEN
KHORNAK, LUCILLE
KIDD, CHUCK
KING, KATHLEEN
KONRATH, G. FRANK
KUPER, HOLLY
LATHROPE, WILMA
LEE, ROBERT II
  PHOTOGRAPHY
LESTER, PETER
LEVY, PATRICIA BARRY
LEVY, RON
LISSY, DAVID
MIGLAVS, MR. JANIS
MILJAKOVICH, HELEN
MILLER, JOE
MISHLER, CLARK JAMES
MOSS, GARY
MULLEN, EDWARD F.
NELSON, ROBIN
PALMIERI, JORGE
PHANEUF, ART
PHOTO RESOURCE HAWAII
PITOU, CINDY
POOR, SUZANNE
PUTNAM, SARAH
RANTZMAN, KAREN
  STAFFORD
REED, GEOFF
RIECKS, DAVID
ROBINSON, MIKE
ROSSI, DAVID A.
RYCUS, JEFFREY A.
SAVILLE, LYNN
SCHLUETER, MICHAEL K.
SCHMIDT, DIANE JOY
SEEGER, STEPHEN E.
SETON, CHARLES
SIBLEY, SCOTT
SMETZER, DONALD
SMITH, ROBIN B.
SORRELL, RONDA

SPEARS, PHILLIP
STOCK PHOTOS HAWAII
STONE, ERIKA
STONE, TONY IMAGES
STORMZAND, JOHN
STREET, PARK
SUDOW, ELLYN
THOMPSON, MICHAEL S.
TOTO , JOE
URBINA, WALT
WAKEFIELD'S OF KANSAS
  CITY, INC.
WAPINSKI, DAVID
WATERSUN, DAVID
WESTERGAARD, FRED
WHITE, GEORGE
WILLIAMS, HAL
WINTER, NITA
WOLVOVITZ, ETHEL
WOOD, ANTHONY B.
WOOLFE, RAYMOND G.

FASHION

ACOSTA, JOSE'
ADAMS, EDDIE
ALDRICH, JAY
ALLEN, TIM
ANDERSON, RICHARD
ARDEN, MICHAEL
ASCHERMAN, JR., HERBERT
BADGER, BOBBY
BANKHEAD, GARY
BARBAGALLO, ANTONINO
BEDNARSKI, PAUL S.
BENKERT, CHRISTINE
BERNSTEIN, ALAN
BITTERS, DAVID
BLINKOFF, RICHARD
BLINKOFF, RICHARD
BLOCK, RAY
BOLSTER, MARK
BORDNICK, BARBARA
BUCK, BRUCE
BUSCH, SCHERLEY
BUTTON DOWN
  PRODUCTIONS LTD.
CAMPBELL, TOM
CARRIKER, RONALD
  PHOTOGRAPHY
CHINITZ, ADAM
COHEN, ANDY
CORY, JEFF
COSTE, KURT
CROMER, PEGGO
CROSBY, A. DAVID
DEL AMO, TOMAS
DENUTO, ELLEN
DEREX, DAVID
DEUTSCH, JACK
DEVORE III, NICHOLAS

DOUGLAS, KEITH
DRISCOLL, W. M.
DUBLER, DOUGLAS W.
DYER, ED
ELAKMAN, MARC
ELBINGER, DOUGLAS
ELDER, JIM
ELLMAN, ELAINE
EMMERICH, DON
FANSLER, EARL
FARRELL, BILL
FEILING, DAVID A.
FLORET, EVELYN
FLOTTE, LUCIEN
FOURRE, LIZA
GARIK, ALICE
GORRILL, ROBERT B.
GUBIN, MARK
HANDLEY, ROBERT E.
HILL, JACKSON
HUCKABY, JERRY
HUGHES, JOHN
HUGLIN, GREG
HUMPHRIES, JR., H.
  GORDON
HUNTZINGER, ROBERT
JACOBSON, RANDALL C.
KENNEDY, M. LEWIS
KENTON, BASIA
KHORNAK, LUCILLE
KING, KATHLEEN
KONRATH, G. FRANK
KOTECKI, STAN
KRATT, K.C.
LABUA, FRANK
LE GRAND, PETER
LORD, JIM
MACWEENEY, ALEN
MAROON, FRED J.
MASON, STEPHEN
MATHIESON, GREG E.
MCGLYNN, DAVID
MCGUIRE, JOSEPH W.
METRISIN, JIM
MILLER PHOTOGRAPHY, INC.
MILNE, ROBERT
MODRICKER, DARREN
MOORE, MICHAEL
NERONI, ROBERT
NESTE, ANTHONY
NEY, NANCY
NICCOLINI, DIANORA
OTSUKI, TOSHI
PALMIERI, JORGE
PRICE, GREG
QUICKSILVER
  PHOTOGRAPHY
REMINGTON, GEORGE
RENNIE, BRIAN H.
REVETTE, DAVID
ROBERTS, JANET M.

ROBINSON, BILL
ROBINSON, MIKE
ROSSI, DAVID A.
ROWIN, STANLEY
RYCUS, JEFFREY A.
SAVILLE, LYNN
SCHLANGER, IRV
SCHNEIDER, JOHN
SCHRAMM, FRANK
SCHWARZ, TED
SHAKOOR, RA
SIMS, MARK
SMITH, ALLEN
SNYDER, LEE F.
SOMOZA, GERARDO
STEELE, MAX
STEELE, W. RICHARD
STIERER, DENNIS
STORMZAND, JOHN
STOTT, BARRY
SUMNER
  PHOTOGRAPHY INC.
TAGGART, MARK J.
TATE, TED
TATEM, MIKE
TORREZ, BOB
TURNER, PETE
VANCE, DAVID
VANCE, JIM
VANDER SCHUIT
  STUDIO INC.
VEGTER, BRIAN S.
WADDELL, ROBERT M.
WADE, HARRY
WAPINSKI, DAVID
WATERSUN, DAVID
WECKLER, CHAD
WEIL, KAREN
WHIPPLE III, GEORGE C.
WHITENTON, CARY
WILLIAMS, RON STUDIO
WISSER, BILL
WOOLFE, RAYMOND G.
WORD, TROY
WRISTEN, DONALD F.
ZAHNER, DAVID

FOOD/DIET

ALLEN, TIM
ASHE, BILL
AUPIED, STEVEN
BABBITT, SHARON
BAKER, JULIE
BEKKER, PHILIP
BENKERT, CHRISTINE
BERGERON, JOSEPH
BISHOP, G. ROBERT
BOGACZ, MARK F.
BORDEN, LESLYE MICHLIN
BROWN, JAMES

BROWNE, TURNER
BRUNDEGE, BARBARA A.
BUTTON DOWN
  PRODUCTIONS LTD.
CHANDOHA, WALTER
CHARLES, FREDERICK
COLEMAN, GENE
COMET, RENEE
CONRAD, CHRISTOPHER
CRAWFORD, PAT
DAVIS, HOWARD
DEITS, KATIE
DOMINIS, JOHN
FICALORA, TONI
FIELDS, BRUCE
FIELDS, BRUCE
FINLEY, DOUG
FORDEN, J. PATRICK
FRANZEN, DAVID
GLASSMAN, KEITH
GRAHAM, A. MICHAEL
GREGG, BARRY
HARMON, TIM
HOOS, GERALD WILLIAM
HUBBELL, WILLIAM
HUNTER, FIL
JERNIGAN, JOHN E.
KASPER, KEN
KELLEY, TOM
KIRCHHEIMER, GABE
KOROPP, ROBERT
KRATT, K.C.
LOTT, HAL
MAGID, JEROME
MARGERIN, BILL
MARVY, JIM
MARVY, JIM
MASSON, LISA
MAY, CLYDE
METRISIN, JIM
MILLER PHOTOGRAPHY, INC.
MOORE, RIC
NANO, ED
NERONI, ROBERT
OBREMSKI, GEORGE
OMER, DAVID
ORANS, MURIEL
OSWALD, JAN
PEARSON, CHARLES R.
PETERSON, LEE
POLSKY, JOEL
PROUD, B.
RAFKIND, ANDREW J.
RENNIE, BRIAN H.
RILEY, JON
ROBERTS, JANET M.
RUSSELL, MARC
RYCHETNIK, JOSEPH S.
SANDBANK, HENRY
SCHATZ, BOB
SCHLANGER, IRV

SCOCOZZA, VICTOR
SCOCOZZA, VICTOR
SHIELDS-MARLEY
  PHOTOGRAPHY
SHOLIK, STAN
STEELE, MAX
STONE, TONY IMAGES
TARCHALA, JOHN
TOLBERT, BRIAN R.
VANCE, JIM
VANDER SCHUIT
  STUDIO INC.
WAPINSKI, DAVID
WATERSUN, DAVID
WHITENTON, CARY
WOLFE, DAN

FOREIGN

ABRAMSON, DEAN
ALEKANDROWICZ, FRANK
ART OF FINE PHOTOGRAPHY
ASCHERMAN, JR., HERBERT
BADER, KATE
BAKER, BOBBE CLINTON
BARCELLONA, MARIANNE
BARNELL, JOE
BARON, JAMES J.
BISHOP, RANDA
BOLESTA, ALAN
CARRUTHERS, ROBERT J.
CASTANEDA, LUIS
CHIKA
CHIN, RUTH
CORY, JEFF
COX, DENNIS
CRANE, ARNOLD
DEGGINGER, PHIL
DELANO, JON
DEMPSAY, SAY
DIMARCO, JR., SAL
DOWNIE, DANA
ELK III, JOHN
EMMERICH, DON
ENGELMANN, SUZANNE J.
FACTOR, BEVERLY
FIREBAUGH, STEVE
FLOTTE, LUCIEN
FOURRE, LIZA
FRENCH, PETER
GAMMA LIAISON INC.
GEIGER, K. WILLIAM
GIAMMATTEO, JOHN
GOODE, PAUL B.
GOODMAN, LISA J.
GOVE, GEOFFREY
GRAHAM, STEPHEN
GRIFFIN, ARTHUR L.
GRIMM, MICHELE
GUBIN, MARK
HARMON, TIM

HARRINGTON III, BLAINE
HARRINGTON, TY
HARTMANN, W. GEOFFREY
HAWK, DARYL
HAWTHORNE, ANN
HEBBERD, LINDSAY
HILL, JACKSON
HIRSCH, KAREN I.
HOLBROOKE, ANDREW
HOUSER, DAVE G.
IWASAKI, RICH
JEFFERSON, LOUISE E.
KANOWSKY, KEN
KAPLAN, B. PETER
KASHI, ED
KIRKENDALL/SPRING
  PHOTOGRAPHERS
KOONTZ, KATY
KRUBNER, RALPH
LEE, LARRY
LEE, ROBERT II
  PHOTOGRAPHY
LEVY, RON
LEWIS, G. BRAD
LOYST, KEN
LUKOWICZ, JEROME
MAHONEY, BOB
MARES-MANTON,
  ALEXANDER
MATHIESON, GREG E.
MCCARTNEY, SUSAN
MCCUTCHEON, JR., SHAW
MCGLYNN, DAVID
MENDLOWITZ, BENJAMIN
MIGLAVS, MR. JANIS
MUSCHENETZ, ROLAND &
  KAREN
NERONI, ROBERT
O'BYRNE, WILLIAM M.
ODYSSEY PRODUCTIONS
ORANS, MURIEL
PARSONS, KIMBERLY
PAWLICK, JOHN
PEARCE, ADDEE
PERESS, GILLES
PETT, LAURENCE J.
PHANEUF, ART
PHILIBA, ALLAN
PHOTO RESOURCE HAWAII
PLUMMER, DOUG
POERTNER, KENNETH C.
POLUMBAUM, TED
POST, JOHN
POWELL, TODD B.
PROUD, B.
QUARTUCCIO, DOM
RANTZMAN, KAREN
  STAFFORD
RIECKS, DAVID
ROBERTS, JANET M.
RUDOLPH, NANCY

SALMOIRAGHI, FRANCO
SANFORD, ERIC M.
SANGER, DAVID
SCHAMP, J. BROUGH
SCHMID, BERT
SCHMIDT, DIANE JOY
SIBLEY, SCOTT
SILBERT, LAYLE
SISSON, BOB
SMETZER, DONALD
STEELE, MAX
STEINGROVE, JACK
STOCK PHOTOS HAWAII
STONE, TONY IMAGES
STORMZAND, JOHN
STREET, PARK
SUMMER PRODUCTIONS
TARR, CHARLES J.
TAYLOR, RANDY G.
THOMPSON, MICHAEL S.
WAPINSKI, DAVID
WHITAKER, GREG
WHITE-FALCON, REGINA E.
WOOD, RICHARD
WRISLEY, BARD
WRISTEN, DONALD F.
YAMASHITA, MICHAEL S.
YONKER, THOMAS
  PHOTOGRAPHY

GENERAL INTEREST

ABRAMSON, DEAN
ADELMAN, BOB
AIOSA, VINCENT
ALBINO, JOSEPH X.
ALLAN PRICE
ALLEN, ED
ALLEN, J. J.
ALPER, BARBARA
AMBORN, JOHN E.
ANCONA, GEORGE
ATKESON, RAY
AVERETT, GERALD L.
BAER, GORDON
BAILEY, ROBERT
BAKER, JULIE
BARAG, MARC
BARCELLONA, MARIANNE
BARDIN, KEITH
BARLEY, BILL
BARON, JAMES J.
BARRINGTON, CAROL
BAXLEY, KIRK
BAYER, DANIEL
BEATTY, DAVID E.
BENNETT, ROBERT J.
BENTON, VIRGINIA M.
BERG, MARGARET C.
BERNSTEIN, MARION
BIGGS, KEN

BLAKESBERG, JAY
BONNEY, LORRAINE G.
BRADY ARCHITECTURAL
  PHOTOGRAPHY
BRAUN, ERNEST
BROOKS, CHARLES W.
BROWN, JIM
CAPOTOSTO, JOHN J.
CARLEBACH, MICHAEL L.
CARROLL, TOM
CASSILL, KAY
CASTANEDA, LUIS
CENDROWSKI, DWIGHT
CHIKA
CIRONE, BETTINA
CLARK, JUNEBUG
COHEN, ANDY
COLMAN III, BEN
CONDIT, DONALD G.
CONLEY, CHARLES R.
CORY, JEFF
COX, DENNIS
CRANE, ARNOLD
CROMER, PEGGO
CURLER, BERNICE
DAKAN, LEW
DARRYL, JACOBSON
DAVIS, DAVE
DE CASSERES, JOSEPH
DEGABRIELE PHOTOGRAPHY
DEGGINGER, DR. E. R.
DEITS, KATIE
DELANO, JON
DEMPSAY, SAY
DIAZ, ARMANDO
DIMARCO, JR., SAL
DODGE, LARRY
DOFF, A. F.
DORSEY, RON
  PHOTOGRAPHY
DOWNEY, CHARLES
DOWNIE, DANA
ELBINGER, DOUGLAS
ELDER, JIM
ELK III, JOHN
ELLZEY, BILL
ESCOSA, JOHN
FAIRCLOTH, JANE G.
FANSLER, EARL
FEILING, DAVID A.
FICALORA, TONI
FIELDS, BRUCE
FISHER PHOTOGRAPHY
FISHER, RAY
FLEMING, LARRY
FLETCHER, T. MIKE
FLOTTE, LUCIEN
FORBERT, DAVID J.
FORDEN, J. PATRICK
FRANZEN, DAVID
FREEMAN, JOHN

FRENCH, PETER
FRICK, KEN
FRIEDMAN, IRV
FRIESE, RICK
FRY III, GEORGE B.
FUKUHARA, RICHARD
  YUTAKA
FUSS, EDUARDO
GAMMA LIAISON INC.
GARLAND, MICHAEL E.
GEFTER, JUDITH
GEIGER, K. WILLIAM
GESCHEIDT, ALFRED
GETLEN, DAVID
GIBSON, MARK & AUDREY
GOLD, SAMMY
GOOD, JAY
GOODMAN, LISA J.
GORDON, FRANK
GORE, ARNOLD
GORNICK JR., ALAN
GORRILL, ROBERT B.
GOTFRYD, BERNARD
GRANNIS, BOB
GREEN-ARMYTAGE,
  STEPHEN
GREHAN, FARRELL
GRIMES, BILLY
GROENE, GORDON
GROSS, ALEX LLOYD
GROTTA, SALLY WEINER
GRUBB, ROBERT B.
GUBIN, MARK
GURAVICH, DAN
HALPERN, DAVID
HAMPSON PHOTOGRAPHY
HANDLEY, ROBERT E.
HANDS, BRUCE
HARDER, PAUL B.
HARMON PHOTOGRAPHERS
HARMON, TIM
HARRINGTON, JOHN
HARRINGTON, TY
HAWK, DARYL
HELLER, MICHAEL
HENRY, LOWELL
HEWITT, SCOTT
HIGHT, GEORGE C.
HIRSCH, KAREN I.
HOEBERMAN, MATHEW &
  KRISTIN
HOLLAND, JAMES R.
HORSTED, PAUL
HUCKABY, JERRY
HURST, NORMAN
ISAACS, ROBERT A.
JACOBY, RAY
JAMES, GRANT R.
JERNIGAN, JOHN E.
JOHNSON, EVERETT C.
JOHNSON, TREVE

JORDAN, JOE F.
JOUBERT PHOTOGRAPHY,
  LARRY
KALE, WALTER
KAPLAN, AL
KASPER, KEN
KEENAN, JOHN C.
KEMPER, BART
KIDD, CHUCK
KILBORN, BILL
KIRCHHEIMER, GABE
KIRKENDALL/SPRING
  PHOTOGRAPHERS
KLASS, RUBIN & ERIKA
  PHOTOGRAPHY
KOROPP, ROBERT
KOTECKI, STAN
KOWAL, JOHN PAUL
KRUEGER, BOB
LANE, WALTER B.
LANGE, ED
LEE, ROBERT II
  PHOTOGRAPHY
LENTZ & ASSOCIATES
LESTER, PETER
LEVITON, DREW B.
LEVITON, JOYCE B.
LEVY, PATRICIA BARRY
LEVY, RON
LEWELLYN, JON
LIEBERMAN, ARCHIE
LOCKWOOD, LEE
LOMEO, ANGELO & SONJA
  BULLATY
LOYST, KEN
MALLINSON, PETER A.
MANHEIM, MICHAEL PHILIP
MAPPES, CARL R.
MARCUS, HELEN
MARIEN, ROBERT
MAROON, FRED J.
MARSCHALL, FREDERIC
MASSIE, KIM
MATT, PHIL
MCCUTCHEON, JR., SHAW
MCCUTCHEON, STEVE
MCGUIRE, JOSEPH W.
MCKAY, DOUG
MCLEMORE, BILL
MENDLOWITZ, BENJAMIN
MICHELSON, ERIC
MIGLAVS, MR. JANIS
MIHALEVICH, MICHAEL
MILJAKOVICH, HELEN
MILLER, DAVID P.
MOBERLEY, CONNIE
MORROW, CHRISTOPHER W.
MOSS, HOWARD
MULLEN, EDWARD F.
MYERS, FRED
MYERS, TOM

NADLER, BOB
NORTON, PEARL
O'BYRNE, WILLIAM M.
ORRICO, CHARLES J.
PANTAGES, TOM
PAWLICK, JOHN
PAYNE, SHELBY
PEARCE, ADDEE
PECHTER, ALESE
PECHTER, MORTON H.
PETERSEN, JON B.
PETERSON, JR., CHESTER
PETERSON, LEE
PETT, LAURENCE J.
PHANEUF, ART
PHILLIPS, ROBIN H.
PHOTO RESOURCE HAWAII
PHOTO, COMM
PHOTOGRAPHY UNLIMITED
PLATTETER, GEORGE
POERTNER, KENNETH C.
POOR, SUZANNE
POST, JOHN
PRATT, VERNA E.
PRICE, GREG
PRINCE, NORMAN
PSZENICA, JUDITH
RANDLETT, MARY
RANTZMAN, KAREN
 STAFFORD
REPP, DAVE
RIECKS, DAVID
RIVELLI, WILLIAM
ROGERS, CHUCK
ROLO PHOTOGRAPHY
ROSSI, DAVID A.
ROTHSCHILD, NORMAN
RYBISKI JR., A. J.
RYCUS, JEFFREY A.
SANFORD, ERIC M.
SAVILLE, LYNN
SAXE, ARNOLD J.
SAYLOR, TED
SCHEIDEGGER, FRANCIS
SCHLEICHER, BILL
SCHMID, BERT
SCHMIDT, DIANE JOY
SCHWARTZ, GEORGE J.
SCIOLETTI, JODY
SCOCOZZA, VICTOR
SELIGMAN, PAUL
SEYMOUR, RONALD
SHELTON, SYBIL
SHERMAN, RON
SHRIKHANDE, DEVENDRA
SIBLEY, SCOTT
SICKLES PHOTO-REPORTING
 SERVICE
SIEVERS, ALVIN M.
SMITH, D. LYNN
STECKER, ELINOR H.

STEIN-MASON STUDIO
STEINER, LISL
STOCK PHOTOS HAWAII
STORMZAND, JOHN
STOVER, DAVID
STRASSER, JOEL
STRATFORD, JIM
STREET, PARK
STROUSS, SARAH
SWETNAM, JIM
TADDER, MORTON
TARCHALA, JOHN
TARR, CHARLES J.
TAYLOR, RANDY G.
TOLBERT, BRIAN R.
TROXELL, W. H.
VENDITTI, JAMES VINCENT
WAGNER, ANDREW A.
WAPINSKI, DAVID
WARD, JERRY
WEAKS, BILL S.
WHITE, GEORGE
WINTER, NITA
WOLFE, DAN
WOOD, ANTHONY B.
WOODALLEN
 PHOTOGRAPHERS
WRISTEN, DONALD F.
WYMAN, IRA

GEOGRAPHY

ACOSTA, JOSE'
ALEKANDROWICZ, FRANK
ALLEN, JOHN O.
ATKESON, RAY
BADER, KATE
BAER, GORDON
BARON, JAMES J.
BERNSTEIN, MARION
BRANDON, RANDY
BROOKS, RICHARD
 WEYMOUTH
CARROLL, TOM
CARTER, WILLIAM
CASTANEDA, LUIS
COHEN, STUART
COONRAD, JORDAN
COOPER, ED
CORY, JEFF
COX, DENNIS
CURLER, BERNICE
CURTIS, STEVEN
DE ZANGER, ARIE
DEGGINGER, DR. E. R.
DEMPSAY, SAY
DEVORE III, NICHOLAS
DOWNIE, DANA
ELK III, JOHN
ELLZEY, BILL
ENGELMANN, SUZANNE J.

FIREBAUGH, STEVE
FOXX, JEFFREY JAY
FRENCH, PETER
GARLAND, MICHAEL E.
GIBSON, MARK & AUDREY
GNASS, JEFF
GORDON, FRANK
GORNICK JR., ALAN
GORRILL, ROBERT B.
GOVE, GEOFFREY
GREEN-ARMYTAGE,
 STEPHEN
HARDEN, CLIFF
HARMON, TIM
HARP, DAVID
HARRINGTON, TY
HAWKINS, WALT
HESS, HARRY
HIGHT, GEORGE C.
HIRSCH, KAREN I.
HISER, DAVID
HOLLENBECK, CLIFF/KEVIN
 MORRIS
HOUSER, DAVE G.
JOHNSON, NEIL
JOHNSON, TREVE
KAEHLER, WOLFGANG
KANOWSKY, KEN
KEHRWALD, RICHARD
KIRKENDALL/SPRING
 PHOTOGRAPHERS
KRUBNER, RALPH
LEE, LARRY
LEE, ROBERT II
 PHOTOGRAPHY
LEVY, RON
LEWIS, G. BRAD
MATHIESON, GREG E.
MCBRIDE, TOM
MCCUTCHEON, STEVE
MILNE, ROBERT
MONTGOMERY PICTURES
NORTON, PHILLIP
ODYSSEY PRODUCTIONS
ORANS, MURIEL
PANTAGES, TOM
PATTERSON, MARION
PETERSON, LEE
QUARTUCCIO, DOM
RANDLETT, MARY
REID, SEAN
ROLLAND, GUY A.
ROLO PHOTOGRAPHY
RYAN, DAVID
RYCHETNIK, JOSEPH S.
RYCUS, JEFFREY A.
SCHMID, BERT
SCHMIDT, DIANE JOY
SEEGER, STEPHEN E.
SIBLEY, SCOTT
SLAUGHTER, PAUL

SMETZER, DONALD
SPIEGEL, TED
SPRING, BOB & IRA
STAMATES, JIM
STEINGROVE, JACK
STONE, TONY IMAGES
STORMZAND, JOHN
STRATFORD, DENIS
STREET, PARK
TROXELL, W. H.
VAUGHN, GREG
WAPINSKI, DAVID
WHEELER, NIK
WITHEY, GARY S.
YAMASHITA, MICHAEL S.

GOVERNMENT

BERNSTEIN, MARION
BROWN-ROSNER, SHEREE
BUDROW, NANCY
CARROLL, TOM
CHARETTE, MARK
CLARKSON, ROBERT NOEL
CORY, JEFF
COX, DENNIS
CURTIS, STEVEN
DIMARCO, JR., SAL
FICALORA, TONI
FLETCHER, T. MIKE
FRIEDMAN, RICK
GAMMA LIAISON INC.
GOTTLIEB, STEVEN
GRAHAM, STEPHEN
HARMON, TIM
HARRINGTON, JOHN
HARRINGTON, TY
HENRY, LOWELL
HIRSCH, KAREN I.
JORDAN, JOE F.
KAPLAN, AL
KEITH, ALLAN
KIDD, CHUCK
KRAFFT, LOUISE
LOCKWOOD, LEE
MAASS, ROBERT
MAROON, FRED J.
MATHIESON, GREG E.
MCCUTCHEON, STEVE
MILJAKOVICH, HELEN
MILLER, DAVID P.
PANTAGES, TOM
RIECKS, DAVID
ROBERTS, JANET M.
ROLO PHOTOGRAPHY
ROSENBLUM, BERNARD
RYCUS, JEFFREY A.
SCHEIDEGGER, FRANCIS
SCHMIDT, DIANE JOY
SCHWARZ, IRA J.
SIRLIN, TED

SMITH, D. LYNN
STEELE, GEOFF
STORMZAND, JOHN
UNIPHOTO PICTURE
  AGENCY
WAPINSKI, DAVID

HEALTH

ADAMS, JANET L.
ANDERSON, RICHARD
BAER, GORDON
BAER, RHODA
BAKER, JULIE
BARDIN, KEITH
BARNES, BILLY
BARON, JAMES J.
BERLAND, THEODORE
BERNSTEIN, MARION
BOGACZ, MARK F.
BUSCH, SCHERLEY
BUTTON DOWN
  PRODUCTIONS LTD.
CLARKSON, FRANK
COHEN, ANDY
COLEMAN, GENE
COLEMAN, PH.D., REV.
  CHERYL L.
CORY, JEFF
COSTE, KURT
COX, DENNIS
CRANE, ARNOLD
CURTIS, STEVEN
DEITS, KATIE
DOWNIE, DANA
DRESSLER, BRIAN
ENGELMANN, SUZANNE J.
FARRELL, BILL
FITZHUGH, SUSIE
FOSTER, KEVIN
FOURRE, LIZA
FREEMAN, DAVIS
FRITZ, GERARD
GOOD, JAY
GORDON, FRANK
GOVE, GEOFFREY
HALL, DON
HARMON, TIM
HARTMANN, ERICH
HERRON, MATT
HILL, JACKSON
HIRNELSEN, RICHARD
JONES, BRENT
JONES, LOU
KASHI, ED
KASPER, KEN
KAYE, ROD
KIDD, CHUCK
KIRCHHEIMER, GABE
KONRATH, G. FRANK
KOTECKI, STAN

KUHLMAN, CHRIS
LESTER, PETER
LISSY, DAVID
LUKOWICZ, JEROME
MCKAY, DOUG
MENZEL, PETER
MILLER, DAVID P.
MOSS, GARY
NELSON, JANET
NELSON, ROBIN
OLIVE, JIM
ORRICO, CHARLES J.
PALMIERI, JORGE
PETERSON, JR., CHESTER
PLUMMER, DOUG
POLSKY, JOEL
PREUSS, KAREN
PRICE, CLAYTON J.
PROUD, B.
PUTNAM, SARAH
RAFKIND, ANDREW J.
RANTZMAN, KAREN
  STAFFORD
REMINGTON, GEORGE
RIECKS, DAVID
ROBINSON, MIKE
ROLO PHOTOGRAPHY
RYCUS, JEFFREY A.
SAVILLE, LYNN
SCHIFF, NANCY RICA
SCHLEICHER, BILL
SCHMID, BERT
SCHMIDT, DIANE JOY
SEEGER, STEPHEN E.
SEYMOUR, RONALD
SIBLEY, SCOTT
STIERER, DENNIS
STOCK PHOTOS HAWAII
STONE, TONY IMAGES
STORMZAND, JOHN
STREET, PARK
STROMBERG, BRUCE
TAXEL, BARNEY
TENIN, BARRY
UNIPHOTO PICTURE
  AGENCY
UPITIS, ALVIS
URBINA, WALT
WAPINSKI, DAVID
WATERSUN, DAVID
WHITAKER, GREG
WHITE, GEORGE
WINTER, NITA
WISSER, BILL
WOOD, ANTHONY B.
WU, NORBERT

HISTORY

ALEKANDROWICZ, FRANK
BARBALACE PHOTOGRAPHY

BONNEY, LORRAINE G.
BUDROW, NANCY
CHARLES, FREDERICK
COGSWELL, JENNIFER D.
COX, DENNIS
DIMARCO, JR., SAL
DOUGLASS, DARREN
EBERT, BOB
ELK III, JOHN
ENGELMANN, SUZANNE J.
FORBERT, DAVID J.
GEIGER, K. WILLIAM
GEIGER, WILLIAM K.
GNASS, JEFF
GOLDBERG, JEFF
GORDON, FRANK
GOVE, GEOFFREY
GREENFIELD, LAUREN
GUBIN, MARK
HARP, DAVID
HARRINGTON, TY
HEBBERD, LINDSAY
HERRON, MATT
JOHNSON, NEIL
KLASS, RUBIN & ERIKA
  PHOTOGRAPHY
LAMAGNA, JOSEPH
LANGENBACH, RANDOLPH
LEVIN, AARON
MASSON, LISA
MATHIESON, GREG E.
MUNCH, ERIC
ODYSSEY PRODUCTIONS
PLACE, CHARLES
POLK, MILBRY
REID, SEAN
RICH, BERNI
ROBERTS, JANET M.
ROME, STUART
RYCHETNIK, JOSEPH S.
SALMOIRAGHI, FRANCO
SELIGMAN, PAUL
SHRIKHANDE, DEVENDRA
SIBLEY, SCOTT
SPIEGEL, TED
STORMZAND, JOHN
UNIPHOTO PICTURE
  AGENCY
WAGNER, ANDREW A.
WALLEN, JONATHAN
WAPINSKI, DAVID
YAMASHITA, MICHAEL S.
YARBROUGH, BOB

HOBBIES

ACOSTA, JOSE'
BARNELL, JOE
BAYER, DANIEL
BOLSTER, MARK
COX, DENNIS

DANTZIC, JERRY
DAVIS, DAVE
DOUGLASS, DARREN
DOWNIE, DANA
GEFTER, JUDITH
GRESHAM, GRITS
HAWKINS, WALT
HENRY, GEORGE T.
HIRSCH, KAREN I.
HOEBERMAN, MATHEW &
  KRISTIN
KAPLAN, B. PETER
KEMPER, BART
KIDD, CHUCK
KIRKENDALL/SPRING
  PHOTOGRAPHERS
LAMAGNA, JOSEPH
LEVY, RON
LORENZ, ROBERT
LOYST, KEN
PORTNOY, LEWIS
RIECKS, DAVID
SCHEIDEGGER, FRANCIS
SCHMIDT, DIANE JOY
SLATER, EDWARD
STOCK PHOTOS HAWAII
STONE, TONY IMAGES
STORMZAND, JOHN
STRATFORD, DENIS
WAGNER, ANDREW A.
WAPINSKI, DAVID

HOME & GARDEN

BAKER, BOBBE CLINTON
BAKER, JULIE
BARNES, BILLY
BELLENIS, JOHN
BENKERT, CHRISTINE
BISCHOFF, KARL
BISHOP, RANDA
BITTERS, DAVID
BRAUN, BOB
BROWNE, TURNER
CHANDOHA, WALTER
CHESLER, DONNA & KEN
CONRAD, CHRISTOPHER
COOPER, TOM
COSTE, KURT
COX, DENNIS
DECRUYENAERE, HOWARD
DEGGINGER, PHIL
DIETZ, CRAIG
DOWNIE, DANA
DRESSLER, BRIAN
DUFRESNE, WALTER
DUHON, MIKE
ENGELMANN, SUZANNE J.
FARR, JULIE
FORBERT, DAVID J.
FREEMAN, TINA

GARIK, ALICE
GARLAND, MICHAEL E.
GIANNINI, GEMMA
GIBSON, MARK & AUDREY
GOHLICH, ED
GOODMAN, LISA J.
GRAHAM, A. MICHAEL
GREENBERG, STANLEY
GROENE, GORDON
HALL, JOHN M.
HAMPSON PHOTOGRAPHY
HARP, DAVID
HEDRICH-BLESSING
HOLT, SAXON
JERNIGAN, JOHN E.
KAPLAN, B. PETER
KASPER, KEN
KENNEDY, M. LEWIS
KENTON, BASIA
KLASS, RUBIN & ERIKA
   PHOTOGRAPHY
KRUBNER, RALPH
KUHLMAN, CHRIS
LEE, ROBERT II
   PHOTOGRAPHY
LEVY, BURT
LEWIS, G. BRAD
LOTT, HAL
MACKENZIE, MAXWELL
MASSON, LISA
MCCARTNEY, SUSAN
MCGEE, TONY
MIGLAVS, MR. JANIS
MILLER PHOTOGRAPHY, INC.
MILLER, MELABEE M.
MORELAND, MIKE
MOSS, GARY
OBREMSKI, GEORGE
ORANS, MURIEL
ORDERS, KAREN
PAZOVSKI, KAZIK
PEARCE, ADDEE
PERRON, ROBERT
PRATT, DIANE
PRATT, VERNA E.
PRESTON, LOUISA
PROUD, B.
RANDLETT, MARY
RANTZMAN, KAREN
   STAFFORD
RIECKS, DAVID
ROBERTS, JANET M.
RUSSELL, MARC
RYCUS, JEFFREY A.
SALMOIRAGHI, FRANCO
SCHAMP, J. BROUGH
SCHLUETER, MICHAEL K.
SCHMIDT, DIANE JOY
SCHNEIDER, JOHN
SEEGER, STEPHEN E.
SHIELDS-MARLEY

PHOTOGRAPHY
SHRIKHANDE, DEVENDRA
SIBLEY, SCOTT
SISSON, BOB
STEELE, GEOFF
STEWARDSON, JOE
STONE, TONY IMAGES
STORMZAND, JOHN
STROUSS, SARAH
SWANSON, BOB
TAYLOR, CURTICE
THOMPSON, MICHAEL S.
TRENKA, BUD
VANDER SCHUIT
   STUDIO INC.
WADDELL, ROBERT M.
WAGNER, ANDREW A.
WALKER, JESSIE
WAPINSKI, DAVID
WATERSUN, DAVID
WESTERGAARD, FRED
WHITAKER, GREG
WIRONEN
WOLLIN, WILLIAM
WRISTEN, DONALD F.
YARBROUGH, BOB

HUMAN INTEREST

ABRAMSON, DEAN
ACKROYD, HUGH S.
ALDRICH, JAY
ALEKANDROWICZ, FRANK
ALLEN, ED
ALLEN, J. J.
ALLEN, MARIETTE PATHY
ALPER, BARBARA
AMER, TOMMY
ARDEN, MICHAEL
ASCHERMAN, JR., HERBERT
AUSTIN, MILES
BAER, GORDON
BAGG, ALAN
BALLIS, GEORGE
BARCELLONA, MARIANNE
BARDIN, KEITH
BARNES, BILLY
BARNES, MICHELLE A.
BARRETT, CHARLES
BAUMAN, MARGARET
BAYLES, DAL
BENNETT, ROBERT J.
BENYAS, BOB
BERNSTEIN, MARION
BEVAN, PAT
BILKER, HARVEY L.
BLIZZARD, WILLIAM C.
BRADY ARCHITECTURAL
   PHOTOGRAPHY
BRANDON, RANDY
BRAUN, ERNEST

BRESCOLL, JAMES
BROWN-ROSNER, SHEREE
BRUNDEGE, BARBARA A.
BUDROW, NANCY
BURGESS, MICHELE A.
BUTTON DOWN
   PRODUCTIONS LTD.
CARDACINO, MICHAEL
CASSILL, KAY
CASTANEDA, LUIS
CHESTER, MARK S.
CHIKA
CHIN, RUTH
CIRONE, BETTINA
CLEFF, BERNIE
COHEN, ANDY
COLBROTH, RON
COLMAN III, BEN
COLTON, ROBERT
CONLEY, CHARLES R.
CORSALE, LORRAINE
COX, DENNIS
CROKE, THOMAS J.
CURTIS, STEVEN
DAVIS, DAVE
DAVIS, DEE
DEGABRIELE PHOTOGRAPHY
DEMPSAY, SAY
DEVAULT, JIM
DIAZ, ARMANDO
DIMARCO, JR., SAL
DODGE, LARRY
DOFF, A. F.
DOWNIE, DANA
DUMBAR, ARNOLD
DUNOFF, RICH
EBERT, BOB
ELLMAN, ELAINE
ELLMAN, FAYE
ENGH, ROHN
ENGLISH, MELISSA HAYES
FABRICIUS, DAGMAR
FANSLER, EARL
FEILING, DAVID A.
FLEMING, LARRY
FOSTER, KEVIN
FRENCH, PETER
FRICK, KEN
FRIEDMAN, IRV
FULTON, CONRAD JAMES
FUSCO, PAUL
GAMAGE, DOUGLAS C.
GAMMA LIAISON INC.
GEFTER, JUDITH
GEIGER, K. WILLIAM
GIBSON, MARK & AUDREY
GIPE, JON
GOODMAN, LISA J.
GOOLSBY, JOHN
GOTTLIEB, STEVEN
GREHAN, FARRELL

HANDS, BRUCE
HARLAN, BRUCE
HARMON, TIM
HARRINGTON, TY
HAWK, DARYL
HAWKINS, WALT
HEBBERD, LINDSAY
HELLER, MICHAEL
HENRY, GEORGE T.
HILL, JACKSON
HIRSCH, KAREN I.
HOLLAND, JAMES R.
HOLT, WALTER
HORSTED, PAUL
HOUSER, ROBERT
HUCKABY, JERRY
JACKSON, DON
JALBERT, PAUL
JOHNSON, EVERETT C.
JOHNSON, NEIL
JOUBERT PHOTOGRAPHY,
   LARRY
KAHANA, YORAM
KALE, WALTER
KEENAN, JOHN C.
KEMPER, BART
KERMANI, SHAHN
KIDD, CHUCK
KLASS, RUBIN & ERIKA
   PHOTOGRAPHY
KNIGHT, DOUG
KONIG, THIA
KONRATH, G. FRANK
KOTECKI, STAN
KRAMER, DANIEL
KRUEGER, BOB
LEE, ROBERT II
   PHOTOGRAPHY
LEIPZIG, ARTHUR
LEVY, PATRICIA BARRY
LEVY, RON
LEWELLYN, JON
LOMEO, ANGELO & SONJA
   BULLATY
LOYST, KEN
MAASS, ROBERT
MAHI, MIEKO SUE
MANONI, EILEEN
MARX, RICHARD
MAYLEN III, DAVID
MCCLELLAND, KIRK
MCCUTCHEON, STEVE
MCKAY, DOUG
MCKEE, MICHAEL
MCNEELY, BURTON
MCVICKER, SAM
MEYERS, EDWARD
MILJAKOVICH, HELEN
MILLER PHOTOGRAPHY, INC.
MILLER, DAVID P.
MISHLER, CLARK JAMES

MONTGOMERY PICTURES
MOORE, BARBARA
MOORE, MICHAEL
MORGENSTEIN, RICHARD
MOSS, GARY
MOSS, HOWARD
MULLEN, EDWARD F.
NORTON, MICHAEL
PAYNE, SHELBY
PEARCE, ADDEE
PETERSON, LEE
PETT, LAURENCE J.
PHANEUF, ART
PHOTOSMITH
PICKERELL, JAMES H.
PITOU, CINDY
POERTNER, KENNETH C.
POST, JOHN
PREUSS, KAREN
PRINCE, NORMAN
PSZENICA, JUDITH
RANTZMAN, KAREN
  STAFFORD
REDIC, BILL
REID, SEAN
REMINGTON, GEORGE
RICH, BERNI
RIECKS, DAVID
ROBERTS, JANET M.
ROBINSON, MIKE
ROGERS, DAVID
ROGOWSKI, TIM
ROLO PHOTOGRAPHY
ROSSI, DAVID A.
RUDOLPH, NANCY
RUST, GREGORY E.
RYCUS, JEFFREY A.
SALMOIRAGHI, FRANCO
SARCONE, JOE
SARNACKI, MICHAEL
SATTERWHITE, AL
SAVILLE, LYNN
SCHANUEL, ANTHONY
SCHEIDEGGER, FRANCIS
SCHLEICHER, BILL
SCHMIDT, DIANE JOY
SCHWARTZ, JERI
SCHWARZ, IRA J.
SCIOLETTI, JODY
SELIGMAN, PAUL
SEYMOUR, RONALD
SHIELDS-MARLEY
  PHOTOGRAPHY
SHULTZ, LAURA MAXWELL
SIBLEY, SCOTT
SIRLIN, TED
SMELTZER, ROBERT
SMITH, ROBIN B.
SOMOZA, GERARDO
SPEYER, LARS
STALVIG, MURLYN A.

STEELE, W. RICHARD
STIERER, DENNIS
STONE, TONY IMAGES
STORMZAND, JOHN
STOVER, DAVID
STREET, PARK
SWARTZ, FRED
SWETNAM, JIM
TAGGART, MARK J.
TAYLOR, RANDY G.
TORREZ, BOB
VARNEY, FRANK
WADDELL, ROBERT M.
WAGNER, ANDREW A.
WALKER, HARRY M.
WAPINSKI, DAVID
WATERSUN, DAVID
WELLS, DAVID H.
WHITAKER, GREG
WHITE, GEORGE
WILLIS, CLIFF
WINTER, NITA
WOLLIN, WILLIAM
WOLMAN, BARON
WOLVOVITZ, ETHEL
WRISTEN, DONALD F.
YARBROUGH, BOB
YONKER, THOMAS
  PHOTOGRAPHY

HUMAN RELATIONS

ALLEN, MARIETTE PATHY
ART OF FINE PHOTOGRAPHY
BAER, GORDON
BARAG, MARC
BARCELLONA, MARIANNE
BARON, JAMES J.
BERNSTEIN, MARION
BOBBE, LELAND
BOGACZ, MARK F.
BRADY ARCHITECTURAL
  PHOTOGRAPHY
BROWN-ROSNER, SHEREE
BUTLER, TIM
CASTANEDA, LUIS
COHEN, ANDY
COLMAN III, BEN
CORSALE, LORRAINE
COX, DENNIS
CURTIS, STEVEN
ELLMAN, ELAINE
FARR, JULIE
FOSTER, KEVIN
FRENCH, PETER
FRICK, KEN
FULTON, CONRAD JAMES
GAMMA LIAISON INC.
GEFTER, JUDITH
GOODMAN, LISA J.
HARMON, TIM

HARRINGTON, TY
HARTMANN, ERICH
HARTMANN, W. GEOFFREY
HIRSCH, KAREN I.
HOEBERMAN, MATHEW &
  KRISTIN
HOUSER, ROBERT
JOHNSON, TREVE
JONES, VALERIA
JOUBERT PHOTOGRAPHY,
  LARRY
KIDD, CHUCK
KONRATH, G. FRANK
LESTER, PETER
LEVY, PATRICIA BARRY
MCCLUSKEY, D. THOMAS
MIGLAVS, MR. JANIS
MOSS, GARY
MYERS, TOM
NORTON, MICHAEL
PETT, LAURENCE J.
PHANEUF, ART
PHOTO RESOURCE HAWAII
PHOTO, COMM
PUTNAM, SARAH
RANTZMAN, KAREN
  STAFFORD
REED, GEOFF
RENO, KENT
ROBERTS, JANET M.
ROBINSON, MIKE
ROLO PHOTOGRAPHY
ROSSI, DAVID A.
ROWAN, N. R.
ROWIN, STANLEY
RYCUS, JEFFREY A.
SAVILLE, LYNN
SCHMIDT, DIANE JOY
SCHWELIK, FRANK
SCIOLETTI, JODY
SEEGER, STEPHEN E.
SEYMOUR, RONALD
SHULTZ, LAURA MAXWELL
SIBLEY, SCOTT
STONE, TONY IMAGES
STORMZAND, JOHN
STOVER, DAVID
STREET, PARK
SUMMER PRODUCTIONS
TAXEL, BARNEY
TORREZ, BOB
VANCE, JIM
WAPINSKI, DAVID
WATERSUN, DAVID
WELLS, DAVID H.
WHITAKER, GREG
WHITE, GEORGE
WILLIS, CLIFF
WOLLIN, WILLIAM
WOOD, ANTHONY B.
WRISTEN, DONALD F.

YONKER, THOMAS
  PHOTOGRAPHY

HUMOR

ASCHERMAN, JR., HERBERT
BEVAN, PAT
BLOCH, STEVEN
BRANDON, RANDY
COHEN, ANDY
DONDERO, DON
FINLEY, DOUG
FLOTTE, LUCIEN
FRICK, KEN
HARBRON, PATRICK
HARMON, TIM
ISAACS, ROBERT A.
JOHNSON & JOHNSON
  STUDIO
KONRATH, G. FRANK
LEVY, RON
MANHEIM, MICHAEL PHILIP
MEYERS, EDWARD
MOORE, MICHAEL
PETERSON, LEE
POERTNER, KENNETH C.
POWER, CHARLOTTE A.
REED, GEOFF
REID, SEAN
RENO, KENT
RIECKS, DAVID
RYCHETNIK, JOSEPH S.
SAVILLE, LYNN
STOCK PHOTOS HAWAII
STONE, TONY IMAGES
STORMZAND, JOHN
TOTO , JOE
WAPINSKI, DAVID
WILLIAMS, HAL
WRISTEN, DONALD F.

JOURNALISM

ACOSTA, JOSE'
ADELMAN, BOB
ALDRICH, JAY
ALEKANDROWICZ, FRANK
ALLEN, J. J.
ALLEN, MARIETTE PATHY
ALPER, BARBARA
ANDERSON, RICHARD
ART OF FINE PHOTOGRAPHY
AVERETT, GERALD L.
BAER, GORDON
BAGG, ALAN
BAKER, BOBBE CLINTON
BAKKE, ERIC
BARBAGALLO, ANTONINO
BARCELLONA, MARIANNE
BARLEY, BILL
BARNELL, JOE

BARTRUFF, DAVE
BASCOM, WILLIAM A.
BAUMAN, MARGARET
BAYER, DANIEL
BERRY & HOMER
  PHOTOGRAPHICS
BEVAN, PAT
BOWDEN, BOB
BRANDON, RANDY
BRESCOLL, JAMES
BROOKS, CHARLES W.
BROWN, JIM
BROWNE, TURNER
BRUNDEGE, BARBARA A.
BUSH, DARRYL W.
BUZBY, SHERRIE
CARROLL, TOM
CENDROWSKI, DWIGHT
CHAMBERLAIN JR.,
  ROBERT M.
CHARLES, CINDY
CHIKA
CHURCH, DENNIS
COHEN, ANDY
COONRAD, JORDAN
CORSALE, LORRAINE
COX, DENNIS
CRAMER, BILL
CRANDALL, ALISSA
CROKE, THOMAS J.
CURTIS, STEVEN
DEGABRIELE PHOTOGRAPHY
DELANO, JON
DIMARCO, JR., SAL
DOBRZYCKI, MARY
DOFF, A. F.
DOMINIS, JOHN
DONDERO, DON
DUNMIRE, LARRY
ELDER, THOM
ELLMAN, ELAINE
ELLMAN, FAYE
EMMERICH, DON
ENGELMANN, SUZANNE J.
FISHER PHOTOGRAPHY
FLEMING, LARRY
FLORET, EVELYN
FORDEN, J. PATRICK
FREEMAN, JOHN
FRENCH, PETER
FRICK, KEN
FRIEDMAN, IRV
FRITZ, BRUCE
GAMAGE, DOUGLAS C.
GAMMA LIAISON INC.
GANDY, SKIP
GAROFALO, JOHN
  CLEVELAND
GEFTER, JUDITH
GEIGER, K. WILLIAM
GIPE, JON

GLEASNER, BILL
GOLD, SAMMY
GOOD, JAY
GOTFRYD, BERNARD
GREENBLATT, WILLIAM D.
GREWELL, BOB
GROSS, ALEX LLOYD
GUBIN, MARK
HALL, DON
HALSTEAD, DIRCK
HANSEN, BARBARA
HARMON PHOTOGRAPHERS
HARMON, TIM
HARRINGTON, JOHN
HARRINGTON, TY
HARTMANN, W. GEOFFREY
HELLER, MICHAEL
HESS, HARRY
HEWETT, RICHARD R.
HIGHTON, SCOTT
HILL, JACKSON
HIRSCH, KAREN I.
HISER, DAVID
HITT, WESLEY
HOLLYMAN, TOM
HOUSER, ROBERT
HUCKABY, JERRY
KALUZNY, ZIGY
KAPLAN, AL
KAPLAN, B. PETER
KATZ, MARTY
KEATING, FRANKE
KEENAN, JOHN C.
KELLY, TONY
KEMPER, BART
KERMANI, SHAHN
KIDD, CHUCK
KIRCHHEIMER, GABE
KONRATH, G. FRANK
LAMONT, DANIEL E., JR.
LANE, WALTER B.
LANGE, ED
LEE, CAROL
LEE, ROBERT II
  PHOTOGRAPHY
LEVIN, AARON
LEVY, RON
LEWIS, G. BRAD
LEWIS, VICKIE
LIFTIN, JOAN
LILLIBRIDGE, DAVID C.
LOCKWOOD, LEE
LOYST, KEN
MACWEENEY, ALEN
MAHI, MIEKO SUE
MAHONEY, BOB
MARCUS, HELEN
MAROON, FRED J.
MATHIESON, GREG E.
MATT, PHIL
MCALLISTER, BRUCE

MCCLUSKEY, D. THOMAS
MCCUTCHEON, JR., SHAW
MCGLYNN, DAVID
MCKAY, DOUG
MCMULLIN, FOREST
MENDLOWITZ, BENJAMIN
MENNENGA, JERRY
MENZEL, PETER
MERIDETH, PAUL L.
MICHELSON, ERIC
MIGLAVS, MR. JANIS
MIHOVIL, ROBERT JOHN
MILLER PHOTOGRAPHY, INC.
MOONEY, CHRIS
MOORE, MICHAEL
MORGENSTEIN, RICHARD
MORROW, CHRISTOPHER W.
MOSER, DAVID W.
MOSS, GARY
NELSON, ROBIN
NORTON, PEARL
OPPERSDORFF, MATHIAS
PAYNE, SHELBY
PECHTER, ALESE
PECHTER, MORTON H.
PERESS, GILLES
PEREZ, MARTY
PETERSON, JR., CHESTER
PETT, LAURENCE J.
PHILLIPS, ROBIN H.
PHOTOGRAPHY UNLIMITED
PHOTOSMITH
PITOU, CINDY
POLK, MILBRY
POOR, SUZANNE
PRESTON, JIM
PSZENICA, JUDITH
REED, GEOFF
REESE, KAY
RICH, BERNI
RICHARDSON, DAVID C.
RIECKS, DAVID
ROLO PHOTOGRAPHY
ROWIN, STANLEY
RUBINGER, DAVID D.
RUHE, GEORGE-EDWARD
RUST, GREGORY E.
RYCUS, JEFFREY A.
SACHA, BOB
SCHIERSTEDT, NEIL
SCHLEICHER, BILL
SCHMID, BERT
SCHMIDT, DIANE JOY
SCHWARZ, IRA J.
SCIOLETTI, JODY
SELIGMAN, PAUL
SETON, CHARLES
SHERMAN, BOB
SHERMAN, RON
SHIELDS-MARLEY
  PHOTOGRAPHY

SHRIKHANDE, DEVENDRA
SHULTZ, LAURA MAXWELL
SIBLEY, SCOTT
SICKLES PHOTO-REPORTING
  SERVICE
SIRLIN, TED
SISSON, BOB
SLATER, EDWARD
SOCHUREK, HOWARD J.
SOMOZA, GERARDO
SORCE, WAYNE
STEELE, MAX
STEINER, LISL
STEWARDSON, JOE
STORMZAND, JOHN
STRATFORD, JIM
STREANO, VINCENT C.
SVEHLA, JAMES C.
SWANSON, DICK
TANNENBAUM, ALLAN
TATEM, MIKE
TAXEL, BARNEY
TAYLOR, RANDY G.
TENIN, BARRY
TESADA, DAVID X.
TORREZ, BOB
TOUCHTON, KEN
TRENKA, BUD
UPITIS, ALVIS
URSILLO, CATHERINE
VAN RIPER, FRANK A.
WACHTER, JERRY
WADDELL, ROBERT M.
WAGNER, ANDREW A.
WAPINSKI, DAVID
WEINTRAUB, DAVID
WELLS, DAVID H.
WERNER, PERRY
WHEELER, NIK
WHITMIRE, KENNETH L.
WILLIS, CLIFF
WILLITS, PAT L.
WINTER, NITA
WOOD, RICHARD
WOOLFE, RAYMOND G.
WYMAN, IRA
YAMASHITA, MICHAEL S.
YONKER, THOMAS
  PHOTOGRAPHY

LOUISIANA LIFE

BROWNE, TURNER

MANAGEMENT

ASCHERMAN, JR., HERBERT
BOLSTER, MARK
BUDROW, NANCY
CARROLL, TOM
COX, DENNIS

DEGABRIELE PHOTOGRAPHY
DIMARCO, JR., SAL
DOWNIE, DANA
DRESSLER, BRIAN
FISHER, RAY
FLEMING, LARRY
GOLDBLATT, STEVEN
GOODMAN, LISA J.
HARMON, TIM
HARRINGTON, TY
KIDD, CHUCK
KONRATH, G. FRANK
LEVY, PATRICIA BARRY
LONGWOOD, MARC D.
MCKAY, DOUG
MIGLAVS, MR. JANIS
ROLO PHOTOGRAPHY
ROWIN, STANLEY
RYCUS, JEFFREY A.
SCHMIDT, DIANE JOY
SHRIKHANDE, DEVENDRA
SIBLEY, SCOTT
STARR, ASHBY
  PHOTOGRAPHER
STONE, TONY IMAGES
STORMZAND, JOHN
WAPINSKI, DAVID

MARINE

ABRAMSON, DEAN
ACKROYD, HUGH S.
ALKALAY, MORRIS
ANDERSON, JOHN D.
BAILEY, ROBERT
BAYER, DANIEL
BERMAN, MICHAEL
BITTERS, DAVID
BLACK, BILLY
BRANDON, RANDY
BROWN, JIM
BULL, DAVID
BUSHUE, KATHY
CARR, KATHLEEN THORMOD
CARROLL, HANSON
CHESLER, DONNA & KEN
CHESLER, KEN
CHINITZ, ADAM
CORY, JEFF
CROKE, THOMAS J.
DEGABRIELE PHOTOGRAPHY
DEGGINGER, PHIL
DEMPSAY, SAY
DOUGLASS, DARREN
ELDER, JIM
EMMERICH, DON
ESTY, ANDREA
FACTOR, BEVERLY
FINLEY, DOUG
FLOTTE, LUCIEN
FRENCH, PETER

FRIESE, RICK
FRISCH, STEPHEN
GANDY, SKIP
GORDON, FRANK
GORNICK JR., ALAN
GRAHAM, A. MICHAEL
GUBIN, MARK
HALL, DON
HAMPSON PHOTOGRAPHY
HANDS, BRUCE
HARDEN, CLIFF
HARKNESS, CHRIS
HARMON, TIM
HARP, DAVID
HARRINGTON, TY
HIGHTON, SCOTT
HIRSCH, KAREN I.
HOFFMAN, ROB
JOHNSON, FOREST
JOHNSTON, GREG
KAPLAN, HOWARD N.
KASPER, KEN
KING, TOM
KLASS, RUBIN & ERIKA
  PHOTOGRAPHY
KUHLMAN, CHRIS
LEVY, RON
LOHBECK, STEPHEN
LOYST, KEN
MCCUTCHEON, JR., SHAW
MCGRAIL, JOHN
MCNEELY, BURTON
MENDLOWITZ, BENJAMIN
MIHALEVICH, MICHAEL
MILLER PHOTOGRAPHY, INC.
MOORE, MICHAEL
MOSS, HOWARD
MUSCHENETZ, ROLAND &
  KAREN
O'BYRNE, WILLIAM M.
ODYSSEY PRODUCTIONS
PECHTER, ALESE
PECHTER, MORTON H.
PETERSON, LEE
PHOTO RESOURCE HAWAII
POGGENPOHL, ERIC
PRESTON, LOUISA
RANDLETT, MARY
REED, GEOFF
REID, SEAN
REILLY, JOHN
ROMANO, PATRICK J.
ROTMAN, JEFFREY
SCHLEICHER, BILL
SCHLUETER, MICHAEL K.
SHIER, DEANN
SIBLEY, SCOTT
SISSON, BOB
STEINGROVE, JACK
STONE, TONY IMAGES
SUMNER PHOTOGRAPHY

INC.
TANNENBAUM, ALLAN
TENIN, BARRY
THIGPEN, ALEXANDER G.
TORREZ, BOB
VAN DE VEN, MARY
WADDELL, ROBERT M.
WAGNER, ANDREW A.
WAPINSKI, DAVID
WATERSUN, DAVID
WEYDIG, KATHY
WHITE, GEORGE
WHITE-FALCON, REGINA E.
WHITMIRE, KENNETH L.
WOOLFE, RAYMOND G.
WU, NORBERT
YARBROUGH, BOB

MARKETING

ASCHERMAN, JR., HERBERT
ASQUINI, JAY
BAKKE, ERIC
BARBAGALLO, ANTONINO
BARON, JAMES J.
BEVAN, PAT
BISCHOFF, KARL
BOGACZ, MARK F.
BUDROW, NANCY
BUTTON DOWN
  PRODUCTIONS LTD.
CARROLL, TOM
CHAMPAGNE, BARRY
COHEN, DAN
COLMAN III, BEN
CONRAD, CHRISTOPHER
COX, DENNIS
DEGABRIELE PHOTOGRAPHY
DIETZ, CRAIG
DOWNIE, DANA
EASTERLY, LIBBY
EMMERICH, DON
FINLEY, DOUG
FRENCH, PETER
GAMMA LIAISON INC.
GEER, GARRY
GETLEN, DAVID
GNASS, JEFF
GOODMAN, LISA J.
HALL, DON
HARMON, TIM
HARRINGTON, JOHN
HARRINGTON, TY
HARTMANN, W. GEOFFREY
HIGHTON, SCOTT
HILL, JACKSON
HIRSCH, KAREN I.
HITT, WESLEY
HOLLENBECK, CLIFF/KEVIN
  MORRIS
JOUBERT PHOTOGRAPHY,

LARRY
KAUFMAN, ELLIOTT
KONRATH, G. FRANK
KOTECKI, STAN
KRATT, K.C.
KUHLMAN, CHRIS
LEVY, BURT
LONGWOOD, MARC D.
LOTT, HAL
MATHIESON, GREG E.
MCKAY, DOUG
MIGLAVS, MR. JANIS
MIHALEVICH, MICHAEL
MILLER PHOTOGRAPHY, INC.
MILLER, MELABEE M.
MORGENSTEIN, RICHARD
MORRIS, JEFF
MOSS, HOWARD
NORTON, MICHAEL
ORANS, MURIEL
PHOTOGRAPHIC DESIGNS
PITOU, CINDY
POLSKY, JOEL
QUARTUCCIO, DOM
QUICKSILVER
  PHOTOGRAPHY
RAFKIND, ANDREW J.
RILEY, JON
ROBINSON, MIKE
ROLO PHOTOGRAPHY
ROSSI, DAVID A.
RYCUS, JEFFREY A.
SAVILLE, LYNN
SCHLANGER, IRV
SCHMIDT, DIANE JOY
SCHWELIK, FRANK
SHIELDS-MARLEY
  PHOTOGRAPHY
SHRIKHANDE, DEVENDRA
SLATER, EDWARD
SPEARS, PHILLIP
STEWARDSON, JOE
STOCK PHOTOS HAWAII
STONE, TONY IMAGES
STREET, PARK
SVEHLA, JAMES C.
TAXEL, BARNEY
TESADA, DAVID X.
THILL, NANCY
WAGNER, ANDREW A.
WAKEFIELD'S OF KANSAS
  CITY, INC.
WAPINSKI, DAVID
WARD, JERRY
WHITE, GEORGE
WOOD, ANTHONY B.
YONKER, THOMAS
  PHOTOGRAPHY

MEDIA

BROWN-ROSNER, SHEREE
BUSCH, SCHERLEY
BUTLER, TIM
CHIKA
COHEN, DAN
COLMAN III, BEN
COX, DENNIS
DEGABRIELE PHOTOGRAPHY
DEMPSAY, SAY
DENUTO, ELLEN
DIMARCO, JR., SAL
EASTERLY, LIBBY
FINLEY, DOUG
FISHER PHOTOGRAPHY
FLOTTE, LUCIEN
FRENCH, PETER
FRITZ, BRUCE
GEFTER, JUDITH
GOODMAN, LISA J.
GOOLSBY, JOHN
GOVE, GEOFFREY
GUBIN, MARK
HARMON, TIM
HARRINGTON, JOHN
HARTMANN, W. GEOFFREY
HAWK, DARYL
HELLER, MICHAEL
HIGHTON, SCOTT
KAYE, ROD
KERMANI, SHAHN
KIDD, CHUCK
KONRATH, G. FRANK
LOYST, KEN
MATHIESON, GREG E.
MAYERS, MARK M./AT
  AGENZIA
MCBRIDE, TOM
MCBRIDE, TOM
MIHOVIL, ROBERT JOHN
MILLER PHOTOGRAPHY, INC.
MILLER, ROGER
  PHOTO, LTD.
MOSS, HOWARD
NELSON, ROBIN
NICCOLINI, DIANORA
NORTON, MICHAEL
OMER, DAVID
ORANS, MURIEL
POLSKY, JOEL
PORTNOY, LEWIS
QUARTUCCIO, DOM
REID, SEAN
RIECKS, DAVID
ROLO PHOTOGRAPHY
ROSENBLUM, BERNARD
ROSSI, DAVID A.
RYCUS, JEFFREY A.
SARNACKI, MICHAEL
SCHIERSTEDT, NEIL

SCHWARZ, IRA J.
SELIGMAN, PAUL
SHIELDS-MARLEY
  PHOTOGRAPHY
SHRIKHANDE, DEVENDRA
STEWARDSON, JOE
STORMZAND, JOHN
SVEHLA, JAMES C.
TRENKA, BUD
UNIPHOTO PICTURE
  AGENCY
WAGNER, ANDREW A.
WAPINSKI, DAVID
WARD, JERRY
WATERSUN, DAVID
WEIL, KAREN
WHITE-FALCON, REGINA E.
YONKER, THOMAS
  PHOTOGRAPHY

MEDICAL

ACKROYD, HUGH S.
ANDERSON, RICHARD
ART OF FINE PHOTOGRAPHY
BAER, GORDON
BAKER, JULIE
BARBALACE PHOTOGRAPHY
BARON, JAMES J.
BARROS, ROBERT
  PHOTOGRAPHY INC.
BAYLES, DAL
BERNSTEIN, MARION
BILKER, HARVEY L.
BLOCK, RAY
CARRIKER, RONALD
  PHOTOGRAPHY
CENDROWSKI, DWIGHT
CLARKSON, FRANK
CLYMER, JONATHAN
COHEN, DAN
COLMAN III, BEN
CORSALE, LORRAINE
CORY, JEFF
COSTE, KURT
COX, DENNIS
CRANE, ARNOLD
CROSBY, A. DAVID
CURTIS, STEVEN
DEGABRIELE PHOTOGRAPHY
DEITS, KATIE
DIMARCO, JR., SAL
DOUGLASS, DARREN
DOWNEY, CHARLES
DOWNIE, DANA
DUNOFF, RICH
EISMAN, JAMIE
ENGELMANN, SUZANNE J.
FINLEY, DOUG
FOSTER, KEVIN
FOURRE, LIZA

FOWLEY, DOUGLAS
FREEMAN, DAVIS
FRISCH, STEPHEN
FRITZ, BRUCE
GEFTER, JUDITH
GEIGER, K. WILLIAM
GOODMAN, LISA J.
GOVE, GEOFFREY
HALL, DON
HILL, JACKSON
HUMPHRIES, JR., H.
  GORDON
KAPLAN, B. PETER
KASPER, KEN
KENNEDY, M. LEWIS
KIDD, CHUCK
KNIGHT, DOUG
KONRATH, G. FRANK
KOTECKI, STAN
KUHLMAN, CHRIS
LONGWOOD, MARC D.
MATT, PHIL
MCCOY, DAN J.
MCNEILL, BRIAN
MIHALEVICH, MICHAEL
MIHOVIL, ROBERT JOHN
MILLER PHOTOGRAPHY, INC.
MITCHELL, BENN
MOORE, RIC
MORELAND, MIKE
MORGENSTEIN, RICHARD
MURPHY, MICHAEL
NELSON, BRAD
NELSON, ROBIN
NERONI, ROBERT
NICCOLINI, DIANORA
OBREMSKI, GEORGE
ORRICO, CHARLES J.
PETERSON, LEE
PLUMMER, DOUG
PORTNOY, LEWIS
POWER, CHARLOTTE A.
PRESTON, LOUISA
PRICE, CLAYTON J.
PROUD, B.
RAFKIND, ANDREW J.
RANTZMAN, KAREN
  STAFFORD
REED, GEOFF
REMINGTON, GEORGE
REVETTE, DAVID
RILEY, JON
ROSSI, DAVID A.
RYCUS, JEFFREY A.
SCHIFF, NANCY RICA
SCHMIDT, DIANE JOY
SEEGER, STEPHEN E.
SEITZ, SEPP
SEYMOUR, RONALD
SHOLIK, STAN
STEWARDSON, JOE

STONE, TONY IMAGES
TAXEL, BARNEY
TESADA, DAVID X.
TRENKA, BUD
UNIPHOTO PICTURE
  AGENCY
UPITIS, ALVIS
WAPINSKI, DAVID
WEYDIG, KATHY
WHITAKER, GREG
WHITE, GEORGE
WOOD, ANTHONY B.
WOOD, RICHARD

MEN'S INTEREST

ACOSTA, JOSE'
ARDEN, MICHAEL
BARBAGALLO, ANTONINO
BARDIN, KEITH
BUTTON DOWN
  PRODUCTIONS LTD.
CAMPBELL, TOM
CARROLL, TOM
CORY, JEFF
COX, DENNIS
DRESSLER, BRIAN
FINLEY, DOUG
GAMMA LIAISON INC.
GARLAND, MICHAEL E.
HIRSCH, KAREN I.
KASPER, KEN
KIDD, CHUCK
KONRATH, G. FRANK
MOSS, GARY
NORTON, MICHAEL
PRICE, GREG
QUICKSILVER
  PHOTOGRAPHY
REID, SEAN
REMINGTON, GEORGE
RYCUS, JEFFREY A.
SHRIKHANDE, DEVENDRA
SIBLEY, SCOTT
SILLA, JON
STEWARDSON, JOE
STONE, TONY IMAGES
STORMZAND, JOHN
TARR, CHARLES J.
TORREZ, BOB
TRENKA, BUD
WAGNER, ANDREW A.
WAPINSKI, DAVID
WHITAKER, GREG
WHITE, GEORGE

MILITARY

ALBINO, JOSEPH X.
BAYER, DANIEL
COONRAD, JORDAN

COOPER, TOM
CORY, JEFF
DAVIDSON, CAMERON
FLOTTE, LUCIEN
GAMMA LIAISON INC.
HARRINGTON, JOHN
HARRINGTON, TY
KAPLAN, B. PETER
KEMPER, BART
KLASS, RUBIN & ERIKA
  PHOTOGRAPHY
MAHONEY, BOB
MATHIESON, GREG E.
MOORE, MICHAEL
PHOTO RESOURCE HAWAII
PRITCHETT, LAUREN
  LAVONNE
RYCHETNIK, JOSEPH S.
SHIELDS-MARLEY
  PHOTOGRAPHY
STEWARDSON, JOE
STORMZAND, JOHN
SUMMER PRODUCTIONS
TAGGART, MARK J.
WAPINSKI, DAVID

MOTIVATION

BROWN-ROSNER, SHEREE
BRUNDEGE, BARBARA A.
CARROLL, TOM
COGSWELL, JENNIFER D.
KIDD, CHUCK
MCKAY, DOUG
PORTNOY, LEWIS
STOCK PHOTOS HAWAII
STONE, TONY IMAGES
STORMZAND, JOHN
WAPINSKI, DAVID

MOVIE REVIEWS

BARROS, ROBERT
  PHOTOGRAPHY INC.
GAMMA LIAISON INC.
KEMPER, BART
TAYLOR, RANDY G.
WADDELL, ROBERT M.

NATURE

ACOSTA, JOSE'
ALBINO, JOSEPH X.
ALEKANDROWICZ, FRANK
ALLEN, JOHN O.
ANDERSON, GORDON
ASHWOOD, PHILIP
ATKESON, RAY
AUEL, ADAM
BADER, KATE
BAER, MORLEY

BAKER, BOBBE CLINTON
BAKER, JOHN
BALLIS, GEORGE
BARNES, MICHELLE A.
BARTRUFF, DAVE
BAYER, DANIEL
BERNSTEIN, MARION
BEVAN, PAT
BITTERS, DAVID
BLIZZARD, WILLIAM C.
BOBBE, LELAND
BONNEY, LORRAINE G.
BOWDEN, BOB
BOWEN, JOHN
BOWEN, JOHN
BRANDON, RANDY
BROOKS, CHARLES W.
BROOKS, RICHARD
  WEYMOUTH
BRUNDEGE, BARBARA A.
BUDROW, NANCY
BULL, DAVID
BURGESS, MICHELE A.
BURROUGHS, ROBERT
BUSH, DARRYL W.
BUSHUE, KATHY
BUTLER, TIM
CARR, KATHLEEN THORMOD
CARROLL, HANSON
CARROLL, TOM
CARTER, BILL
CARTER, WILLIAM
CASTANEDA, LUIS
CHANDOHA, WALTER
CHARETTE, MARK
CHIN, RUTH
CLEMENTS, STEPHEN P.
COHEN, ANDY
COLEMAN, GENE
COLMAN III, BEN
COOKE, JERRY
COOKE, JOHN DR.
COONRAD, JORDAN
COOPER, ED
CORY, JEFF
CRANDALL, ALISSA
DALY, MICHAEL KEVIN
DAVIS, DAVE
DECRUYENAERE, HOWARD
DEGABRIELE PHOTOGRAPHY
DEGGINGER, DR. E. R.
DEMPSAY, SAY
DEVORE III, NICHOLAS
DODGE, LARRY
DOLIN, IRVING
DOMINIS, JOHN
DORSEY, RON
  PHOTOGRAPHY
DOWNIE, DANA
DRAKE, JEANNE
DUHL, DAVID

DUMBAR, ARNOLD
EBERT, BOB
EISBERG, JON
ELK III, JOHN
ELLMAN, ELAINE
ELLZEY, BILL
EMMERICH, DON
ENGELMANN, SUZANNE J.
FACTOR, BEVERLY
FAIRCLOTH, JANE G.
FARR, JULIE
FARRELL, BILL
FIELDS, BRUCE
FINLEY, DOUG
FIREBAUGH, STEVE
FORBERT, DAVID J.
FOSTER, LEE
FOSTER, NICHOLAS
FRENCH, PETER
FRICK, KEN
FRITZ, BRUCE
FUSS, EDUARDO
GANDY, SKIP
GARIK, ALICE
GARLAND, MICHAEL E.
GARRISON, RON
GEFTER, JUDITH
GETLEN, DAVID
GIBSON, MARK & AUDREY
GNASS, JEFF
GOVE, GEOFFREY
GRAHAM, A. MICHAEL
GREHAN, FARRELL
GRESHAM, GRITS
GRIMES, BILLY
GRIMM, MICHELE
GUBIN, MARK
GURAVICH, DAN
HALPERN, DAVID
HANDS, BRUCE
HARMON, TIM
HARP, DAVID
HARRINGTON, TY
HARRIS, CHRISTOPHER R.
HAWK, DARYL
HAWKINS, WALT
HAWTHORNE, ANN
HIGHT, GEORGE C.
HIGHTON, SCOTT
HIRSCH, KAREN I.
HISER, DAVID
HOFFMAN, ROB
HORSTED, PAUL
HUBBELL, WILLIAM
JACKSON, DON
JACOBS, JR., LOU
JEFFERSON, LOUISE E.
JOHNSON, EVERETT C.
JOHNSON, J. SAM
JOHNSON, TREVE
JOHNSTON, GREG

JOUBERT PHOTOGRAPHY,
  LARRY
KAEHLER, WOLFGANG
KANOWSKY, KEN
KAPLAN, B. PETER
KASPER, KEN
KASTEN, JERRY
KEHRWALD, RICHARD
KHANLIAN, RICHARD
KIDD, CHUCK
KIEFFER, JOHN
KIRCHHEIMER, GABE
KIRKENDALL/SPRING
  PHOTOGRAPHERS
KLAGES, WALTER W.
KLASS, RUBIN & ERIKA
  PHOTOGRAPHY
KNIGHT, DOUG
KOENIG, GEA
KOLLODGE, KENNETH
KOROPP, ROBERT
KUHLMAN, CHRIS
LABUA, FRANK
LAMAGNA, JOSEPH
LATHROPE, WILMA
LEDUC, LYLE
LEE, CAROL
LEE, ROBERT II
  PHOTOGRAPHY
LEIBER, N. GREGORY
LEVY, BURT
LEVY, RON
LEWIS, G. BRAD
LOMEO, ANGELO & SONJA
  BULLATY
LONGWOOD, MARC D.
LOTT, HAL
MACKENZIE, MAXWELL
MARIEN, ROBERT
MCBRIDE, TOM
MCCARTNEY, SUSAN
MCCOY, DAN J.
MCCRIRICK, FLIP
MCCUTCHEON, STEVE
MCGLYNN, DAVID
MCGRAIL, JOHN
MESSINEO, JOHN
MIGLAVS, MR. JANIS
MIHALEVICH, MICHAEL
MILLER PHOTOGRAPHY, INC.
MILLER, DAVID P.
MILLER, JOE
MILLER, ROGER
  PHOTO, LTD.
MILMOE, JAMES O.
MISHLER, CLARK JAMES
MONTGOMERY PICTURES
MOORE, MICHAEL
MUENCH, DAVID
MULLEN, EDWARD F.
MUSCHENETZ, ROLAND &

KAREN
MYERS, TOM
NELSON, BRAD
NIEMAN, WILLIAM
OBREMSKI, GEORGE
ODYSSEY PRODUCTIONS
OLIVE, JIM
ORDERS, KAREN
PARSONS, KIMBERLY
PATTERSON, MARION
PAWLICK, JOHN
PEARCE, ADDEE
PECHTER, ALESE
PECHTER, MORTON H.
PETERSON, LEE
PHILIBA, ALLAN
PHOTO RESOURCE HAWAII
PLUMMER, DOUG
POERTNER, KENNETH C.
POLK, MILBRY
PRATT, VERNA E.
PRESTON, LOUISA
PRIER, ALLEN
PRINCE, NORMAN
QUARTUCCIO, DOM
RAFKIND, ANDREW J.
RANDLETT, MARY
RANTZMAN, KAREN
 STAFFORD
REED, GEOFF
REID, SEAN
RICCA, ANTONIO D.
RIEGER, TED
ROBERTS, JANET M.
ROGOWSKI, TIM
ROLLAND, GUY A.
ROSSI, DAVID A.
ROTHSCHILD, NORMAN
RUSSELL, MARC
RYCUS, JEFFREY A.
RYDEN, MIKE & SARA
SABELLA, JILL
SANFORD, ERIC M.
SANGER, DAVID
SCHANUEL, ANTHONY
SCHERMEISTER, PHIL
SCHMID, BERT
SCHMIDT, DIANE JOY
SCHWARTZ, GEORGE J.
SELIGMAN, PAUL
SEYMOUR, RONALD
SHANEFF, CARL
SHIELDS-MARLEY
 PHOTOGRAPHY
SINKLER, PAUL
SISSON, BOB
SLATER, EDWARD
SLAUGHTER, PAUL
SMITH, BRADLEY
SNOW, ANDY
SNYDER, LEE F.

SOMOZA, GERARDO
SORRELL, RONDA
SPRING, BOB & IRA
STAMATES, JIM
STEELE, W. RICHARD
STEINGROVE, JACK
STOCK PHOTOS HAWAII
STONE, TONY IMAGES
STORMZAND, JOHN
STRASSER, JOEL
SWANSON, BOB
SWANSON, DICK
TAXEL, BARNEY
TESADA, DAVID X.
THOMPSON, MICHAEL S.
TINKER, LESTER
TORREZ, BOB
TREYBIG, CYNTHIA
ULMER, DAVID
VAN DE VEN, MARY
VANMARTER, ROBERT
VAUGHN, GREG
VOLPE, ANTHONY
WADE, ROGER
WAGNER, ANDREW A.
WALKER, HARRY M.
WALLEN, JONATHAN
WAPINSKI, DAVID
WATERSUN, DAVID
WEINTRAUB, DAVID
WHELESS, ROB
WHITAKER, GREG
WHITE, GEORGE
WHITENTON, CARY
WHITMIRE, KENNETH L.
WILLIAMS III, ZANE
WILLIAMS III, ZANE
WITHEY, GARY S.
WOLLIN, WILLIAM
WOOD, RICHARD
WOOD, TED
WRISTEN, DONALD F.
YARBROUGH, BOB
YOUNG, DONALD
ZAVODNY, STEVEN
ZILLIOUX, JOHN

NATURE PHOTOGRAPHY

DIETRICH, DICK

NEWS

ALDRICH, JAY
BAER, GORDON
BASCOM, WILLIAM A.
BAUMAN, MARGARET
BAYER, DANIEL
BAYLES, DAL
BEATTY, DAVID E.
BENNETT, ROBERT J.

BEVAN, PAT
BILKER, HARVEY L.
BITTERS, DAVID
BLOCH, STEVEN
BROWN-ROSNER, SHEREE
BUSH, DARRYL W.
BUTLER, TIM
BUZBY, SHERRIE
CAMPBELL, THOMAS S.
CHIKA
CHIN, RUTH
CLARKSON, RICHARD C.
COHEN, ANDY
CONLEY, CHARLES R.
CORSALE, LORRAINE
CORY, JEFF
COX, DENNIS
CRAMER, BILL
CROKE, THOMAS J.
DELANO, JON
DEWALD, DAVID
DIMARCO, JR., SAL
DOUGLASS, DARREN
DOWNIE, DANA
DUMOFF, ALAN M., PH.D.
EDELMAN, HARRY
ELDER, THOM
ELLMAN, ELAINE
ENGELMANN, SUZANNE J.
FINNIGAN, VINCE
FLEMING, LARRY
FORDEN, J. PATRICK
FRIEDMAN, RICK
GAMMA LIAISON INC.
GEFTER, JUDITH
GROSS, ALEX LLOYD
GUBIN, MARK
HARMON, TIM
HARRINGTON, TY
HELLER, MICHAEL
HOLBROOKE, ANDREW
JONES, VALERIA
KAPLAN, B. PETER
KEENAN, JOHN C.
KEMPER, BART
KENNERLY, DAVID HUME
KIDD, CHUCK
KIRCHHEIMER, GABE
KONRATH, G. FRANK
KUPER, HOLLY
LEIBER, N. GREGORY
LEVY, PATRICIA BARRY
LEWIS, G. BRAD
LIEBERMAN, KEN
MAGID, JEROME
MANONI, EILEEN
MASTROIANNI, ROGER
MATHIESON, GREG E.
MATT, PHIL
MCKAY, DOUG
MENNENGA, JERRY

MIHOVIL, ROBERT JOHN
MILLER PHOTOGRAPHY, INC.
MILLMAN, LESTER J.
MOSS, GARY
MYERS, TOM
NELSON, ROBIN
ORDERS, KAREN
PERESS, GILLES
PEREZ, MARTY
PETT, LAURENCE J.
PHOTO, COMM
PITOU, CINDY
POOR, SUZANNE
PSZENICA, JUDITH
REID, SEAN
REILLY, JOHN
REPP, DAVE
RICH, BERNI
ROLO PHOTOGRAPHY
RUHE, GEORGE-EDWARD
RYCUS, JEFFREY A.
SARCONE, JOE
SAXE, ARNOLD J.
SCHIERSTEDT, NEIL
SCHMIDT, DIANE JOY
SCIOLETTI, JODY
SELIGMAN, PAUL
SHERMAN, BOB
SHIELDS-MARLEY
 PHOTOGRAPHY
SIBLEY, SCOTT
SOMOZA, GERARDO
STAWNIAK, JIM
STEELE, W. RICHARD
STEWARDSON, JOE
STORMZAND, JOHN
STRATFORD, JIM
SVEHLA, JAMES C.
TANNENBAUM, ALLAN
TAYLOR, RANDY G.
TORREZ, BOB
TROXELL, W. H.
UNIPHOTO PICTURE
 AGENCY
WAPINSKI, DAVID
WARD, JERRY
WERNER, PERRY
WRISTEN, DONALD F.
YONKER, THOMAS
 PHOTOGRAPHY

PERSONAL FINANCE

BUTTON DOWN
 PRODUCTIONS LTD.
CARROLL, TOM
COX, DENNIS
FINLEY, DOUG
KASPER, KEN
KONRATH, G. FRANK
LEVY, PATRICIA BARRY

MCKAY, DOUG
PETERSON JR., CHESTER
ROLO PHOTOGRAPHY
SIBLEY, SCOTT
WAPINSKI, DAVID

PERSONALITIES

ADAMS, STEVEN
ADELMAN, BOB
ALEKANDROWICZ, FRANK
ALPER, BARBARA
ART OF FINE PHOTOGRAPHY
ASCHERMAN, JR., HERBERT
BADGER, BOBBY
BAER, GORDON
BAER, RHODA
BANKHEAD, GARY
BARCELLONA, MARIANNE
BARNES, BILLY
BARNES, BILLY
BARRETT, CHARLES
BECK, PETER
  PHOTOGRAPHY
BEVAN, PAT
BISHOP, G. ROBERT
BITTERS, DAVID
BLACK, BILLY
BLOCK, RAY
BORDNICK, BARBARA
BROWN-ROSNER, SHEREE
BUSCH, SCHERLEY
BUSH, DARRYL W.
BUTLER, TIM
BUTTON DOWN
  PRODUCTIONS LTD.
CAMPBELL, TOM
CARR, KATHLEEN THORMOD
CARROLL, TOM
CHURCH, DENNIS
CIRONE, BETTINA
CLARK, H. DEAN
COX, DENNIS
CURTIS, STEVEN
DAUMAN, HENRI
DEGABRIELE PHOTOGRAPHY
DEMPSAY, SAY
DEREX, DAVID
DEVAULT, JIM
DEVORE III, NICHOLAS
DIETZ, CRAIG
DOWNIE, DANA
DRESSLER, BRIAN
ELLMAN, ELAINE
ENGELMANN, SUZANNE J.
FISHER PHOTOGRAPHY
FORDEN, J. PATRICK
FORMISANO-MAYERI, YONI
FREEMAN, DAVIS
FRY III, GEORGE B.
FULTON, CONRAD JAMES

GAMMA LIAISON INC.
GEFTER, JUDITH
GEIGER, K. WILLIAM
GOTFRYD, BERNARD
GOTTLIEB, STEVEN
GREEN-ARMYTAGE,
  STEPHEN
GREGG, BARRY
GROSS, ALEX LLOYD
GUBIN, MARK
GWINN, BETH
HALL, DON
HALSTEAD, DIRCK
HANSEN, BARBARA
HARMON, TIM
HARRINGTON, JOHN
HARRINGTON, TY
HARTMANN, W. GEOFFREY
HAWK, DARYL
HEWITT, SCOTT
HIRSCH, KAREN I.
HODGE, ADELE
HOLLYMAN, TOM
HUCKABY, JERRY
HUMPHRIES, JR., H.
  GORDON
HUNTRESS, DIANE
JONES, VALERIA
KAHANA, YORAM
KAPLAN, B. PETER
KASHI, ED
KHORNAK, LUCILLE
KIDD, CHUCK
KING, KATHLEEN
KONRATH, G. FRANK
KRATT, K.C.
LEVY, PATRICIA BARRY
LOYST, KEN
LUKOWICZ, JEROME
MACWEENEY, ALEN
MAHONEY, BOB
MANHEIM, MICHAEL PHILIP
MASTROIANNI, ROGER
MATHIESON, GREG E.
MATT, PHIL
MCKAY, DOUG
MELTZER, LEE
MISHLER, CLARK JAMES
MODRICKER, DARREN
MOORE, MICHAEL
MORGENSTEIN, RICHARD
MOSER, DAVID W.
MOSS, GARY
NEWMAN, ARNOLD
NEY, NANCY
OBREMSKI, GEORGE
ORDERS, KAREN
OUZER, LOUIS
PAGANELLI, MANUELLO
PAYNE, SHELBY
PECHTER, ALESE

PECHTER, MORTON H.
PERESS, GILLES
PETT, LAURENCE J.
PHANEUF, ART
PITOU, CINDY
PRICE, GREG
PSZENICA, JUDITH
PUTNAM, DON
QUICKSILVER
  PHOTOGRAPHY
RANDLETT, MARY
REED, GEOFF
RIECKS, DAVID
ROBERTS, JANET M.
SACHA, BOB
SARNACKI, MICHAEL
SCHERMEISTER, PHIL
SCHIFF, NANCY RICA
SCHLANGER, IRV
SCHMIDT, DIANE JOY
SCIOLETTI, JODY
SEITZ, ART
SHAKOOR, RA
SHRIKHANDE, DEVENDRA
SIBLEY, SCOTT
SILBERT, LAYLE
SILLA, JON
SIMS, MARK
SMITH, BRADLEY
STEELE, GEOFF
STORMZAND, JOHN
STREET, PARK
SUDOW, ELLYN
SUMMER PRODUCTIONS
SUMNER
  PHOTOGRAPHY INC.
TAXEL, BARNEY
TAYLOR, RANDY G.
TENIN, BARRY
TRENKA, BUD
TRUSLOW, B.
UNIPHOTO PICTURE
  AGENCY
VANCE, DAVID
VANDER SCHUIT
  STUDIO INC.
WAGNER, ANDREW A.
WAKEFIELD'S OF KANSAS
  CITY, INC.
WAPINSKI, DAVID
WATERSUN, DAVID
WESTERGAARD, FRED
WHIPPLE III, GEORGE C.
WHITE-FALCON, REGINA E.
WRISTEN, DONALD F.

PHILOSOPHY

ASCHERMAN, JR., HERBERT
CURTIS, STEVEN
HARMON, TIM

SINKLER, PAUL
STORMZAND, JOHN
WAPINSKI, DAVID
WRISLEY, BARD

PHOTOGRAPHY

ABRABEN, E. 'MANNY'
ACOSTA, JOSE'
ADAMS, JANET L.
ALDRICH, JAY
ALLISON, GLEN
ALTMAN, DAVID M.
AMBORN, JOHN E.
ANDERSON, JOHN D.
ARPADI, ALLEN G.
ASCHERMAN, JR., HERBERT
ASHWOOD, PHILIP
AUEL, ADAM
AUPIED, STEVEN
BADER, KATE
BADGER, BOBBY
BAER, GORDON
BAKER, BOBBE CLINTON
BARAG, MARC
BARBAGALLO, ANTONINO
BARR, IAN
BARTH, HARRY
BASCOM, WILLIAM A.
BAYER, DANIEL
BAYLES, DAL
BEGLEITER, STEVEN H.
BEKKER, PHILIP
BELLENIS, JOHN
BELLIS, PHIL
BENTON, VIRGINIA M.
BENYAS, BOB
BERG, MARGARET C.
BERRY & HOMER
  PHOTOGRAPHICS
BILKER, HARVEY L.
BIRDWHISTELL, REIS
BISHOP, G. ROBERT
BLOCK, RAY
BOBBE, LELAND
BOGACZ, MARK F.
BOLSTER, MARK
BORDNICK, BARBARA
BOYER, DALE
BRADY ARCHITECTURAL
  PHOTOGRAPHY
BRAUN, BOB
BROWN, CONNIE
BROWN, JIM
BROWN-ROSNER, SHEREE
BROWNE, TURNER
BRUNDEGE, BARBARA A.
BUDROW, NANCY
BURGESS, MICHELE A.
BURNS, STEVE
BURY, SUSAN

BUSH, CHAN
BUSHUE, KATHY
BUTTON DOWN
  PRODUCTIONS LTD.
CAMPBELL, TOM
CARROLL, TOM
CARRUZZA
CARTER, BILL
CARTER, WILLIAM
CASTANEDA, LUIS
CAVANAUGH, JAMES
CENDROWSKI, DWIGHT
CHAMPAGNE, BARRY
CHANDOHA, WALTER
CHAPUT, SIMON
CHARLES, CINDY
CHESLER, KEN
CHEW, JOHN T.
CHIKA
CHINITZ, ADAM
CHURCH, DENNIS
CLARK, H. DEAN
COGSWELL, JENNIFER D.
COHEN, STUART
COLEMAN, GENE
COOKE, JOHN DR.
COOPER, ED
COX, DENNIS
CRANDALL, ALISSA
CRANE, ARNOLD
CRAWFORD, PAT
CROFOOT, RON
CURTIS, JOHN
CURTIS, STEVEN
DAKAN, LEW
DANTZIC, JERRY
DAVIS, HOWARD
DE ZANGER, ARIE
DEGABRIELE PHOTOGRAPHY
DEL AMO, TOMAS
DELANO, JON
DENUTO, ELLEN
DEVAULT, JIM
DIBARTOLOMEO, GAREN
DIMARCO, JR., SAL
DOBRZYCKI, MARY
DORF, MYROM JAY
DOUGLASS, DARREN
DOWNIE, DANA
DRESSLER, BRIAN
DRISCOLL, W. M.
DUNMIRE, LARRY
EDSON, STEVEN
ELBINGER, DOUGLAS
ELLZEY, BILL
EMMERICH, DON
ENGELMANN, SUZANNE J.
FACTOR, BEVERLY
FARKAS, ALAN
FEILING, DAVID A.
FISHER PHOTOGRAPHY

FISHER, RAY
FLEMING, LARRY
FLORET, EVELYN
FLOTTE, LUCIEN
FORBERT, DAVID J.
FORDEN, J. PATRICK
FOSTER, KEVIN
FOSTER, LEE
FOXX, JEFFREY JAY
FREEMAN, DAVIS
FREEMAN, JOHN
FREEMAN, ROLAND
FREEMAN, TINA
FRENCH, PETER
FRIEDMAN, RICK
FRITZ, BRIAN
FRITZ, TOM
FRY III, GEORGE B.
GAMMA LIAISON INC.
GARLAND, MICHAEL E.
GEER, GARRY
GEFTER, JUDITH
GEIGER, K. WILLIAM
GENTILE, SR., ARTHUR
GERCZYNSKI, TOM
GIAMMATTEO, JOHN
GIBSON, MARK & AUDREY
GLASSMAN, KEITH
GLEASNER, BILL
GOLD, GARY
GOLDBERG, JEFF
GOLDBLATT, STEVEN
GOOD, JAY
GOODMAN, LISA J.
GORE, ARNOLD
GORRILL, ROBERT B.
GOVE, GEOFFREY
GREWELL, BOB
GRIMES, BILLY
GRIMM, MICHELE
GROTTA, SALLY WEINER
GUBIN, MARK
GWINN, BETH
HAILEY, JASON
HALL, DON
HALL, JOHN M.
HAMILTON, CHRIS
HAMILTON, JOHN R.
HAMILTON, JOHN R.
HARKNESS, CHRIS
HARMON PHOTOGRAPHERS
HARMON, TIM
HARP, DAVID
HARRINGTON, TY
HARRIS, CHRISTOPHER R.
HATHON, ELIZABETH
HAWK, DARYL
HAWKINS, WALT
HEDSPETH, JERRY
HENTE, JERRY L.
HESS, HARRY

HICKS, JAMES
HICKS, NORM
HILL, JACKSON
HIRSCH, KAREN I.
HITT, WESLEY
HOOS, GERALD WILLIAM
HOUSER, DAVE G.
HUBBELL, WILLIAM
HUNTER, FIL
HUNTZINGER, ROBERT
IRVIN, MARCUS
JACKSON, DON
JACOBS, JR., LOU
JACOBY, RAY
JEFFRY, MISS ALIX
JOHNSON, TREVE
JONES, BRENT
JONES, DAWSON L.
JONES, SPENCER
KAMP, ERIC
KAPLAN, B. PETER
KATZMAN, MARK
KAYE, ROD
KERMANI, SHAHN
KETCHUM, LARRY
KHORNAK, LUCILLE
KIDD, CHUCK
KIEFFER, JOHN
KINETIC CORPORATION (G.
  RAYMOND SCHUHMANN)
KING, KATHLEEN
KIRKENDALL/SPRING
  PHOTOGRAPHERS
KLASS, RUBIN & ERIKA
  PHOTOGRAPHY
KONRATH, G. FRANK
KOROPP, ROBERT
KRAMER, DANIEL
KRUBNER, RALPH
KUHLMAN, CHRIS
KUPER, HOLLY
LABUA, FRANK
LAMAGNA, JOSEPH
LAVINE, ARTHUR
LEE, LARRY
LEE, ROBERT II
  PHOTOGRAPHY
LEVITON, DREW B.
LEVITON, JOYCE B.
LEWIS, G. BRAD
LEY, RUSSELL
LIGHTFOOT III, ROBERT M.
LOCKWOOD, LEE
LORD, JIM
LOUIS SR., THOMAS
LOUIS, THOMAS SR.
LOYST, KEN
MACWEENEY, ALEN
MAGID, JEROME
MAHI, MIEKO SUE
MANONI, EILEEN

MARCUS, HELEN
MARES-MANTON,
  ALEXANDER
MARKATOS, JERRY
MARSCHALL, FREDERIC
MARVY, JIM
MARX, RICHARD
MASON, STEPHEN
MASSON, LISA
MAXWELL, CHIP
MAY, RONALD W.
MAYLEN III, DAVID
MCALLISTER, BRUCE
MCBRIDE, TOM
MCCARTHY, MARGARET
MCCARTNEY, SUSAN
MCCLAIN, RICK
  PHOTOGRAPHY
MCCLUSKEY, D. THOMAS
MCCUTCHEON, JR., SHAW
MCGEE, E. ALAN
MCGLYNN, DAVID
MCKAY, DOUG
MCKNIGHT, DARLENE
MCMULLIN, FOREST
MCNAMARA, DAVE
MCNEELY, BURTON
MEANS, LISA
MELTZER, LEE
MENDELSOHN, DAVID
MERIDETH, PAUL L.
MESSINEO, JOHN
MICHELSON, ERIC
MIGLAVS, MR. JANIS
MIHALEVICH, MICHAEL
MIHOVIL, ROBERT JOHN
MILJAKOVICH, HELEN
MILLER PHOTOGRAPHY, INC.
MILLER, ROGER
  PHOTO, LTD.
MOLENHOUSE, CRAIG
MOONEY, CHRIS
MOONEY, KEVIN O.
MOORE, BARBARA
MOORE, MICHAEL
MOORE, RIC
MORGAN, BRUCE
MORGENSTEIN, RICHARD
MORRIS, JEFF
MORRIS, PAUL
MOSS, GARY
MUMMA, KEITH
NADLER, BOB
NELSON, BRAD
NELSON, BRUCE G.
NELSON, JANET
NELSON, ROBIN
NETZER, DON
NEUBAUER, JOHN
NEUFELD, WILLIAM
NICCOLINI, DIANORA

O'BYRNE, WILLIAM M.
OBREMSKI, GEORGE
ODYSSEY PRODUCTIONS
ORANS, MURIEL
ORDERS, KAREN
ORRICO, CHARLES J.
PANAYIOTOU, PETER
PARAS, MICHAEL
PAZOVSKI, KAZIK
PEARCE, ADDEE
PEARSE, DON
PEREZ, MARTY
PETERSON, JR., CHESTER
PETERSON, LEE
PETT, LAURENCE J.
PHAM, DIEM K.
PHILLIPS, JAMES
PHOTO, COMM
PHOTOGRAPHIC DESIGNS
PLUMMER, DOUG
POHLMAN STUDIOS
POLK, MILBRY
PORTNOY, LEWIS
PORTOGALLO, JOSEPH A.
POST, GEORGE
PRATT, DIANE
PRATT, VERNA E.
PRESTON, JIM
PRESTON, LOUISA
PRICE, GREG
PROBST, KEN
PROUD, B.
Q, PATRICIA & MIKE
QUARTUCCIO, DOM
QUICKSILVER
  PHOTOGRAPHY
RAFKIND, ANDREW J.
RAICHE, BOB
RANTZMAN, KAREN
  STAFFORD
REESE, KAY
REID, SEAN
REILLY, JOHN
REMINGTON, GEORGE
RICHARDSON, DAVID C.
RIECKS, DAVID
RILEY, JON
ROBERTS, JANET M.
ROBINSON, MIKE
ROGERS, CHUCK
ROLLAND, GUY A.
ROME, STUART
ROSSI, DAVID A.
ROTMAN, JEFFREY
ROWAN, N. R.
ROWIN, STANLEY
RUHE, GEORGE-EDWARD
RYCHETNIK, JOSEPH S.
RYCUS, JEFFREY A.
RYDEN, MIKE & SARA
SABELLA, JILL

SALMOIRAGHI, FRANCO
SANGER, DAVID
SARCONE, JOE
SARNACKI, MICHAEL
SAVILLE, LYNN
SCHLANGER, IRV
SCHMID, BERT
SCHMIDT, DIANE JOY
SCHWARZ, IRA J.
SCIOLETTI, JODY
SEEGER, STEPHEN E.
SELIGMAN, PAUL
SEYMOUR, RONALD
SHERMAN, RON
SHIELDS-MARLEY
  PHOTOGRAPHY
SHRIKHANDE, DEVENDRA
SHROUT, BILL & KATHRYN E.
SIBLEY, SCOTT
SISSON, BOB
SLATER, EDWARD
SMALLING, WALTER
SMITH, DAVID L.
SMITH, ROGER B.
SOMOZA, GERARDO
STACY H. GEIKEN
  PHOTOGRAPHY
STAWNIAK, JIM
STECKER, ELINOR H.
STEINER, LISL
STOCK PHOTOS HAWAII
STORMZAND, JOHN
STOTT, BARRY
STOVER, DAVID
STRASSER, JOEL
STREANO, VINCENT C.
STREET, PARK
STRESHINSKY, TED
STROUSS, SARAH
SUDOW, ELLYN
SUGAR, JAMES A.
SUMMER PRODUCTIONS
SVEHLA, JAMES C.
SWANSON, BOB
TARCHALA, JOHN
TARR, CHARLES J.
TATEM, MIKE
TAXEL, BARNEY
TAYLOR, RANDY G.
TEGARDEN, SHANE
  PHOTOGRAPHY
TENIN, BARRY
TESADA, DAVID X.
TOLBERT, BRIAN R.
TORREZ, BOB
TRENKA, BUD
TRUSLOW, B.
URBINA, WALT
VAN RIPER, FRANK A.
VANDER SCHUIT
  STUDIO INC.

VANMARTER, ROBERT
VAUGHN, GREG
VOLPE, ANTHONY
WADDELL, ROBERT M.
WADE, HARRY
WADE, ROGER
WAGNER, ANDREW A.
WAKEFIELD'S OF KANSAS
  CITY, INC.
WALTER, BILL
WAPINSKI, DAVID
WARD, JERRY
WARTELL, BOB
WASHNIK, ANDY
WEAKS, BILL S.
WEAVER, MARTHA
WECKLER, CHAD
WEDLAKE, JIM
WELLS, DAVID H.
WELSH, STEVE
WHELESS, ROB
WHITAKER, GREG
WHITE, GEORGE
WHITMAN, ALAN
WIEN, STEVEN
WILLIS, CLIFF
WILLITS, PAT L.
WITHEY, GARY S.
WOLLIN, WILLIAM
WOOLFE, RAYMOND G.
WORD, TROY
WRIGHT, TIMOTHY
WRISTEN, DONALD F.
YAMASHITA, MICHAEL S.
ZINTECK, DONALD S.

PHYSICAL FITNESS

ACOSTA, JOSE'
ARDEN, MICHAEL
BARBAGALLO, ANTONINO
BARDIN, KEITH
BARON, JAMES J.
BARROS, ROBERT
  PHOTOGRAPHY INC.
BEGLEITER, STEVEN H.
BOLSTER, MARK
BUTTON DOWN
  PRODUCTIONS LTD.
COLMAN III, BEN
CORY, JEFF
COX, DENNIS
DALY, MICHAEL KEVIN
DAVIS, DAVE
DEGABRIELE PHOTOGRAPHY
DOUGLASS, DARREN
ENGELMANN, SUZANNE J.
FIREBAUGH, STEVE
FRENCH, PETER
FRITZ, GERARD
GETLEN, DAVID

GIBSON, MARK & AUDREY
GOODE, PAUL B.
GORDON, FRANK
GREEN-ARMYTAGE,
  STEPHEN
HARRINGTON, TY
HIRSCH, KAREN I.
KAPLAN, B. PETER
KAYE, ROD
KIDD, CHUCK
KONRATH, G. FRANK
LEVY, BURT
LISSY, DAVID
MCKAY, DOUG
MOORE, MICHAEL
NELSON, JANET
NORTON, MICHAEL
PETERSON JR., CHESTER
PETERSON, JR., CHESTER
POOR, SUZANNE
PORTNOY, LEWIS
POWELL, TODD B.
QUICKSILVER
  PHOTOGRAPHY
ROLO PHOTOGRAPHY
RYCUS, JEFFREY A.
SCHLANGER, IRV
SCHMID, BERT
SCHMIDT, DIANE JOY
SHRIKHANDE, DEVENDRA
STOCK PHOTOS HAWAII
STONE, TONY IMAGES
STORMZAND, JOHN
TARR, CHARLES J.
URBINA, WALT
VANDER SCHUIT
  STUDIO INC.
WAGNER, ANDREW A.
WAPINSKI, DAVID
WATERSUN, DAVID

PSYCHOLOGY

ALLEN, MARIETTE PATHY
ANDERSON, RICHARD
BAER, GORDON
CARROLL, TOM
COX, DENNIS
GOVE, GEOFFREY
HARMON, TIM
PALMIERI, JORGE
SAVILLE, LYNN
SCHMIDT, DIANE JOY
STONE, TONY IMAGES
STORMZAND, JOHN
TAXEL, BARNEY
WAPINSKI, DAVID
WHITE-FALCON, REGINA E.
WINTER, NITA
WRISTEN, DONALD F.

RELIGION

ALBINO, JOSEPH X.
ALEKANDROWICZ, FRANK
ANDERSON, RICHARD
BARTRUFF, DAVE
BITTERS, DAVID
CARROLL, TOM
COLEMAN, PH.D., REV.
  CHERYL L.
CORY, JEFF
COX, DENNIS
DECRUYENAERE, HOWARD
DOWNIE, DANA
ELK III, JOHN
FRENCH, PETER
GOOLSBY, JOHN
HARMON, TIM
HARTMANN, ERICH
KIRCHHEIMER, GABE
MILLER, JOE
RIECKS, DAVID
SCHMID, BERT
SCHMIDT, DIANE JOY
STEELE, MAX
STORMZAND, JOHN
TAXEL, BARNEY
WAPINSKI, DAVID
WHITE, GEORGE
WHITMAN, ALAN
WRISTEN, DONALD F.

SALES

CARROLL, TOM
COX, DENNIS
DEMPSAY, SAY
HUCKABY, JERRY
KIDD, CHUCK
KOTECKI, STAN
MASSON, LISA
MILLER PHOTOGRAPHY, INC.
MOORE, RIC
PHOTOGRAPHIC DESIGNS
PORTNOY, LEWIS
SCHMIDT, DIANE JOY
SCHWELIK, FRANK
STONE, TONY IMAGES
STORMZAND, JOHN
TAXEL, BARNEY
TESADA, DAVID X.
WAPINSKI, DAVID

SCIENCE

ALBINO, JOSEPH X.
BARON, JAMES J.
BAYER, DANIEL
BOGACZ, MARK F.
BOWDEN, BOB
BOWEN, JOHN

CARRUTHERS, ROBERT J.
CHINITZ, ADAM
COOKE, JOHN DR.
COX, DENNIS
CURTIS, STEVEN
DEGABRIELE PHOTOGRAPHY
DEGGINGER, DR. E. R.
DIMARCO, JR., SAL
DUMOFF, ALAN M., PH.D.
EISMAN, JAMIE
FINLEY, DOUG
FIREBAUGH, STEVE
FRIEDMAN, RICK
FRISCH, STEPHEN
FRITZ, BRUCE
FRITZ, GERARD
GAMMA LIAISON INC.
GARLAND, MICHAEL E.
GURAVICH, DAN
HARMON, TIM
JOHNSON, TREVE
JONES, LOU
KAPLAN, B. PETER
KASHI, ED
KASPER, KEN
KASTEN, JERRY
KEMPER, BART
KIDD, CHUCK
KONRATH, G. FRANK
KOWAL, JOHN PAUL
LEVIN, AARON
LONGWOOD, MARC D.
LORENZ, ROBERT
MAPPES, CARL R.
MARIEN, ROBERT
MATT, PHIL
MAY, RONALD W.
MCCOY, DAN J.
MENZEL, PETER
NADLER, BOB
NELSON, BRAD
ODYSSEY PRODUCTIONS
ORANS, MURIEL
PANTAGES, TOM
PRICE, CLAYTON J.
RIECKS, DAVID
RIEGER, TED
ROSENBLUM, BERNARD
ROWIN, STANLEY
SACHA, BOB
SCHMIDT, DIANE JOY
SEEGER, STEPHEN E.
SEITZ, SEPP
SISSON, BOB
SOCHUREK, HOWARD J.
STREET, PARK
VAUGHN, GREG
WAGNER, ANDREW A.
WAPINSKI, DAVID
WOOD, ANTHONY B.

SENIOR CITIZENS

ADAMS, JANET L.
ANDERSON, RICHARD
BAKER, JULIE
BARBAGALLO, ANTONINO
BARDIN, KEITH
BARON, JAMES J.
BARROS, ROBERT
  PHOTOGRAPHY INC.
BERNSTEIN, MARION
BILKER, HARVEY L.
BROWN-ROSNER, SHEREE
CAMPBELL, TOM
CARROLL, TOM
COHEN, ANDY
COLEMAN, PH.D., REV.
  CHERYL L.
COX, DENNIS
DEGABRIELE PHOTOGRAPHY
DOWNIE, DANA
ENGELMANN, SUZANNE J.
FISHER PHOTOGRAPHY
FORBERT, DAVID J.
GEFTER, JUDITH
GERCZYNSKI, TOM
GORDON, FRANK
GRAHAM, A. MICHAEL
HALL, DON
HARMON, TIM
HARRINGTON, TY
HARTMANN, ERICH
HIRSCH, KAREN I.
HUMPHRIES, JR., H.
  GORDON
JERNIGAN, JOHN E.
JOHNSON, EVERETT C.
KAPLAN, B. PETER
KASPER, KEN
LEE, ROBERT II
  PHOTOGRAPHY
LEVY, PATRICIA BARRY
LISSY, DAVID
MIGLAVS, MR. JANIS
MIHALEVICH, MICHAEL
NELSON, ROBIN
NORTON, MICHAEL
PETT, LAURENCE J.
PHANEUF, ART
QUICKSILVER
  PHOTOGRAPHY
REED, GEOFF
ROLO PHOTOGRAPHY
RYCHETNIK, JOSEPH S.
SCHIFF, NANCY RICA
SCHLUETER, MICHAEL K.
SCHMIDT, DIANE JOY
SEEGER, STEPHEN E.
SELIGMAN, PAUL
STEELE, MAX
STONE, ERIKA

STONE, TONY IMAGES
STORMZAND, JOHN
STREET, PARK
TAXEL, BARNEY
UNIPHOTO PICTURE
  AGENCY
WAPINSKI, DAVID
WATERSUN, DAVID
WESTERGAARD, FRED
WINTER, NITA
WOOD, ANTHONY B.

SOCIAL TRENDS

ADAMS, EDDIE
ALLEN, MARIETTE PATHY
BAER, GORDON
BARDIN, KEITH
BARON, JAMES J.
BLAKESBERG, JAY
BLANKENBURG, BEN
BOLSTER, MARK
BROWNE, TURNER
BUTTON DOWN
  PRODUCTIONS LTD.
CARROLL, TOM
COGSWELL, JENNIFER D.
COX, DENNIS
DALY, MICHAEL KEVIN
DEGABRIELE PHOTOGRAPHY
DIMARCO, JR., SAL
DOWNIE, DANA
DRESSLER, BRIAN
DUNOFF, RICH
FOXX, JEFFREY JAY
GIBSON, MARK & AUDREY
GOODMAN, LISA J.
HARMON, TIM
HARRINGTON, TY
HATHON, ELIZABETH
HOUSER, ROBERT
KERMANI, SHAHN
KIRCHHEIMER, GABE
LEVY, PATRICIA BARRY
MORGENSTEIN, RICHARD
MURPHY, MICHAEL
NELSON, ROBIN
PALMIERI, JORGE
PSZENICA, JUDITH
RANTZMAN, KAREN
  STAFFORD
ROLO PHOTOGRAPHY
SCHATZ, BOB
SCHERMEISTER, PHIL
SCHMIDT, DIANE JOY
SELIGMAN, PAUL
SIBLEY, SCOTT
SOMOZA, GERARDO
STONE, TONY IMAGES
STORMZAND, JOHN
STREET, PARK

TOLBERT, BRIAN R.
UNIPHOTO PICTURE
  AGENCY
WAGNER, ANDREW A.
WAPINSKI, DAVID
WHIPPLE III, GEORGE C.
WINTER, NITA
YAMASHITA, MICHAEL S.
YONKER, THOMAS
  PHOTOGRAPHY

SPORTS

ABRAMSON, DEAN
ACOSTA, JOSE'
ALKALAY, MORRIS
ALLAN PRICE
ALLEN, J. J.
ARRUZA, TONY
BAKKE, ERIC
BARBAGALLO, ANTONINO
BARON, JAMES J.
BAUMEL, KEN
BAYER, DANIEL
BAYLES, DAL
BEVAN, PAT
BLACK, BILLY
BLANKENBURG, BEN
BLIZZARD, WILLIAM C.
BOGACZ, MARK F.
BONNEY, LORRAINE G.
BROWN, JIM
BROWN-ROSNER, SHEREE
BUDROW, NANCY
BURROUGHS, ROBERT
BUSH, DARRYL W.
BUTTON DOWN
  PRODUCTIONS LTD.
BUZBY, SHERRIE
CARROLL, HANSON
CASTANEDA, LUIS
CHAMBERLAIN JR.,
  ROBERT M.
CHIKA
CLARKSON, RICHARD C.
CLEMENTS, STEPHEN P.
COLMAN III, BEN
COLTON, ROBERT
COOKE, JERRY
COONRAD, JORDAN
COOPER, TOM
CORY, JEFF
CROKE, THOMAS J.
DALY, MICHAEL KEVIN
DANDO, MARK
DAVIS, DAVE
DAVIS, DEE
DE ZANGER, ARIE
DEGABRIELE PHOTOGRAPHY
DEWALD, DAVID
DIMARCO, JR., SAL

DOWNEY, CHARLES
DUNMIRE, LARRY
EDSON, STEVEN
EISBERG, JON
ELDER, JIM
EMMERICH, DON
ENGELMANN, SUZANNE J.
ESTY, ANDREA
FAIRCLOTH, JANE G.
FARKAS, ALAN
FLEMING, LARRY
FLOTTE, LUCIEN
FORSTER, DANIEL
FRENCH, PETER
GALLIAN, DIRK
GAMAGE, DOUGLAS C.
GARIK, ALICE
GETLEN, DAVID
GIANNINI, GEMMA
GIBSON, MARK & AUDREY
GOLD, GARY
GORDON, FRANK
GOVE, GEOFFREY
GREEN-ARMYTAGE,
  STEPHEN
GRESHAM, GRITS
GROENE, GORDON
GROSS, ALEX LLOYD
HAMILTON, CHRIS
HARKNESS, CHRIS
HARMON, TIM
HARRISON, HOWARD
HIRSCH, KAREN I.
HITT, WESLEY
HUGLIN, GREG
HUNTRESS, DIANE
JOHNSON, DONALD
JOHNSON, J. SAM
JOHNSON, NEIL
KAPLAN, AL
KAPLAN, B. PETER
KAYE, ROD
KEMPER, SUSAN M.
KING, TOM
KNIGHT, DOUG
KRAFFT, LOUISE
KRUEGER, BOB
LEVY, BURT
LIEBERMAN, KEN
LISSY, DAVID
LOUIS SR., THOMAS
LOYST, KEN
MANONI, EILEEN
MATTHEWS, CYNTHIA
MAYERS, MARK M./AT
  AGENZIA
MCCLAIN, RICK
  PHOTOGRAPHY
MCCLUSKEY, D. THOMAS
MCCRIRICK, FLIP
MCKAY, DOUG

MCNEELY, BURTON
METRISIN, JIM
MIHALEVICH, MICHAEL
MOLENHOUSE, CRAIG
MOONEY, CHRIS
NADLER, BOB
NELSON, JANET
NESTE, ANTHONY
NORTON, PHILLIP
OMER, DAVID
PAWLICK, JOHN
PECHTER, ALESE
PECHTER, MORTON H.
PETERSON JR., CHESTER
PETERSON, LEE
PHANEUF, ART
PHOTO RESOURCE HAWAII
PHOTO, COMM
PHOTOGRAPHY UNLIMITED
PORTNOY, LEWIS
POST, JOHN
POWELL, TODD B.
PRESTON, LOUISA
PRITCHETT, LAUREN
  LAVONNE
QUICKSILVER
  PHOTOGRAPHY
RAFKIND, ANDREW J.
REDIC, BILL
REED, GEOFF
REILLY, JOHN
REMINGTON, GEORGE
RIEGER, TED
RUST, GREGORY E.
RYCUS, JEFFREY A.
SALLAZ, WILLIAM R.
SARNACKI, MICHAEL
SATTERWHITE, AL
SCHIERSTEDT, NEIL
SCHMIDT, DIANE JOY
SCHWARTZ, GEORGE J.
SCIOLETTI, JODY
SEITZ, ART
SEITZ, ART
SELIGMAN, PAUL
SHERMAN, BOB
SHERMAN, RON
SHIER, DEANN
SHRIKHANDE, DEVENDRA
SLATER, EDWARD
SMITH, ROBIN B.
SOLOMON, CHUCK
SOMOZA, GERARDO
STEWARDSON, JOE
STOCK PHOTOS HAWAII
STONE, TONY IMAGES
STORMZAND, JOHN
STOTT, BARRY
STRATFORD, JIM
STREANO, VINCENT C.
SUDOW, ELLYN

SVEHLA, JAMES C.
SWARTZ, FRED
TADDER, MORTON
TENIN, BARRY
TORREZ, BOB
TRENKA, BUD
TREYBIG, CYNTHIA
VAUGHN, GREG
VEGTER, BRIAN S.
VENDITTI, JAMES VINCENT
WACHTER, JERRY
WADDELL, ROBERT M.
WAGGONER, MIKE
WAGNER, ANDREW A.
WAPINSKI, DAVID
WARD, JERRY
WARTELL, BOB
WATERSUN, DAVID
WESTERGAARD, FRED
WHITAKER, GREG
WILLIAMS, HAL
WILLIS, CLIFF
WOLMAN, BARON
WOOD, TED
WOOLFE, RAYMOND G.
WRISTEN, DONALD F.
YARBROUGH, CARL
ZAKE, BRUCE

THE ARTS

ADELMAN, BOB
ALLEN, MARIETTE PATHY
ARNDT, DIANE
ART OF FINE PHOTOGRAPHY
ASCHERMAN, JR., HERBERT
BAER, GORDON
BAGG, ALAN
BAKER, BOBBE CLINTON
BALLIS, GEORGE
BARBAGALLO, ANTONINO
BARCELLONA, MARIANNE
BARDIN, KEITH
BARRETT, CHARLES
BARTRUFF, DAVE
BECHTOLD, CHARLES
BEKKER, PHILIP
BENKERT, CHRISTINE
BENYAS, BOB
BERK, OTTO
BERNSTEIN, MARION
BLAKESBERG, JAY
BORNEFELD, WILLIAM
BRAUN, BOB
BUTTON DOWN
  PRODUCTIONS LTD.
CAHEN, ROBERT
CALDWELL, JIM
CAMPBELL, TOM
CARR, KATHLEEN THORMOD
CARTER, WILLIAM

CASSILL, KAY
CASTANEDA, LUIS
CHARLES, FREDERICK
CHESLER, DONNA & KEN
CIRONE, BETTINA
CLARKSON, RICHARD C.
CLEFF, BERNIE
COGSWELL, JENNIFER D.
COLLINS, SHELDAN
COLMAN III, BEN
COX, DENNIS
CRANE, ARNOLD
CROMER, PEGGO
CURTIS, STEVEN
DANIELS, JOSEPHUS
DANTZIC, JERRY
DAUMAN, HENRI
DAVIS, DEE
DE CASSERES, JOSEPH
DEGABRIELE PHOTOGRAPHY
DELANO, JON
DEMPSAY, SAY
DENUTO, ELLEN
DEVORE III, NICHOLAS
DIETZ, CRAIG
DOLIN, IRVING
DOWNIE, DANA
DRESSLER, BRIAN
EDSON, STEVEN
ELBINGER, DOUGLAS
FINLEY, DOUG
FISHER PHOTOGRAPHY
FISHER, RAY
FORBERT, DAVID J.
FORDEN, J. PATRICK
FOSTER, NICHOLAS
FREEMAN, TINA
FRENCH, PETER
FRIEDMAN, IRV
FULTON, CONRAD JAMES
GAGE, HAL
GAMMA LIAISON INC.
GARIK, ALICE
GARLAND, MICHAEL E.
GEFTER, JUDITH
GOLDBERG, JEFF
GOODE, PAUL B.
GOODMAN, LISA J.
GOTFRYD, BERNARD
GOVE, GEOFFREY
HAILEY, JASON
HALL, DON
HALL, JOHN M.
HAMILTON, CHRIS
HAMILTON, JOHN R.
HAMPSON PHOTOGRAPHY
HARBRON, PATRICK
HARMON, TIM
HARTMANN, ERICH
HENRY, GEORGE T.
HEWITT, SCOTT

HIRSCH, KAREN I.
HOLLYMAN, TOM
HOUSER, ROBERT
HURST, NORMAN
JEFFRY, MISS ALIX
JELEN, TOM
JOHNSON, NEIL
JONES, LOU
KAPLAN, B. PETER
KEMPER, BART
KHANLIAN, RICHARD
KHORNAK, LUCILLE
KIDD, CHUCK
KOLLODGE, KENNETH
KONIG, THIA
KONRATH, G. FRANK
KOROPP, ROBERT
LANE, WALTER B.
LEE, ROBERT II
 PHOTOGRAPHY
LENTZ & ASSOCIATES
LEVIN, AARON
LEVY, PATRICIA BARRY
LEWIS, G. BRAD
MACWEENEY, ALEN
MAHI, MIEKO SUE
MARCUS, HELEN
MARKATOS, JERRY
MASSON, LISA
MASTROIANNI, ROGER
MATT, PHIL
MAY, RONALD W.
MAYLEN III, DAVID
MCCARTHY, MARGARET
MCGRAIL, JOHN
MCKAY, DOUG
MCKEE, MICHAEL
MCKNIGHT, DARLENE
MCLEMORE, BILL
MIGLAVS, MR. JANIS
MIHOVIL, ROBERT JOHN
MILLER PHOTOGRAPHY, INC.
MILMOE, JAMES O.
MITCHELL, JACK
MOORE, MICHAEL
MOORE, RIC
MORGENSTEIN, RICHARD
MORRIS, JEFF
MUNCH, ERIC
NICCOLINI, DIANORA
ORDERS, KAREN
OSWALD, JAN
OUZER, LOUIS
PALMIERI, JORGE
PEARCE, ADDEE
POST, GEORGE
POST, JOHN
PRICE, CLAYTON J.
PRINCE, NORMAN
PSZENICA, JUDITH
PUTNAM, SARAH

RANDLETT, MARY
RANTZMAN, KAREN
 STAFFORD
REED, GEOFF
RIECKS, DAVID
ROBERTS, EBET
ROBERTS, JANET M.
ROBINSON, MIKE
ROME, STUART
ROSENBLUM, BERNARD
ROSSI, DAVID A.
ROTHSCHILD, NORMAN
RUHE, GEORGE-EDWARD
RUSSELL, MARC
RYCUS, JEFFREY A.
SACHA, BOB
SALMOIRAGHI, FRANCO
SANDBANK, HENRY
SARCONE, JOE
SCHMIDT, DIANE JOY
SCHRAMM, FRANK
SEEGER, STEPHEN E.
SELIGMAN, PAUL
SHIELDS-MARLEY
 PHOTOGRAPHY
SHRIKHANDE, DEVENDRA
SIBLEY, SCOTT
SMITH, ALLEN
SMITH, BRADLEY
SOMOZA, GERARDO
SPEYER, LARS
SPIEGEL, TED
STARR, ASHBY
 PHOTOGRAPHER
STECKER, ELINOR H.
STIERER, DENNIS
STONE, TONY IMAGES
STORMZAND, JOHN
STRASSER, JOEL
STREET, PARK
SUDOW, ELLYN
SVEHLA, JAMES C.
TAXEL, BARNEY
THILL, NANCY
TURNER, PETE
VAN RIPER, FRANK A.
VARTOOGIAN, JACK
VENDITTI, JAMES VINCENT
WADDELL, ROBERT M.
WADE, HARRY
WAGNER, ANDREW A.
WAPINSKI, DAVID
WATERSUN, DAVID
WHITAKER, GREG
WHITE-FALCON, REGINA E.
WILLIAMS III, ZANE
WOOLFE, RAYMOND G.
YAMASHITA, MICHAEL S.

TRAVEL

ABRAMSON, DEAN
ACOSTA, JOSE'
ALBINO, JOSEPH X.
ALEKANDROWICZ, FRANK
ALKALAY, MORRIS
ALLISON, GLEN
ALPER, BARBARA
ANCONA, GEORGE
ARNDT, DIANE
ARNDT, DIANE
ARRUZA, TONY
ASCHERMAN, JR., HERBERT
ASHWOOD, PHILIP
AUBRY, DANIEL
BADER, KATE
BAKER, BOBBE CLINTON
BAKKE, ERIC
BARBALACE PHOTOGRAPHY
BARCELLONA, MARIANNE
BARDIN, KEITH
BARNELL, JOE
BARNES, BILLY
BARON, JAMES J.
BARRINGTON, CAROL
BARRON, DAVID M./OXYGEN
 GROUP
BARTRUFF, DAVE
BAYER, DANIEL
BEDNARSKI, PAUL S.
BELLENIS, JOHN
BENNETT, ROBERT J.
BENTON, VIRGINIA M.
BERG, MARGARET C.
BERLAND, THEODORE
BERMAN, MICHAEL
BERNSTEIN, MARION
BEVAN, PAT
BISCHOFF, KARL
BISHOP, RANDA
BLACK, BILLY
BLANKENBURG, BEN
BLINKOFF, RICHARD
BLOCH, STEVEN
BOHON, ED
BOLESTA, ALAN
BOLSTER, MARK
BOWEN, JOHN
BOYER, DALE
BRANDON, RANDY
BRAUN, BOB
BRIZZI, ANDREA
BROOKS, CHARLES W.
BROWN, JIM
BRUNDEGE, BARBARA A.
BURGESS, MICHELE A.
BUSCH, SCHERLEY
BUTTON DOWN
 PRODUCTIONS LTD.
CAHEN, ROBERT

CALDWELL, JIM
CAMPBELL, J. KENT
CAMPBELL, TOM
CARDACINO, MICHAEL
CARR, KATHLEEN THORMOD
CARROLL, TOM
CARTER, BILL
CARTER, WILLIAM
CASSILL, KAY
CASTANEDA, LUIS
CHAMPAGNE, BARRY
CHESTER, MARK S.
CHIN, RUTH
CIRONE, BETTINA
COGSWELL, JENNIFER D.
COHEN, DAN
COHEN, STUART
COLBROTH, RON
COLLINS, ARLENE
COLMAN III, BEN
CONNER, GARY
COOKE, JERRY
COOKE, JOHN DR.
COOPER, ED
CORY, JEFF
COX, DENNIS
CRANDALL, ALISSA
CRANE, ARNOLD
CROMER, PEGGO
CURLER, BERNICE
CURTIS, STEVEN
D'ADDIO, JAMES
DAKAN, LEW
DANIELS, JOSEPHUS
DANTZIC, JERRY
DARRYL, JACOBSON
DAVIS, DAVE
DE CASSERES, JOSEPH
DECRUYENAERE, HOWARD
DEGABRIELE PHOTOGRAPHY
DEGGINGER, DR. E. R.
DELANO, JON
DELLA GROTTA, VIVIENNE
DEMPSAY, SAY
DEVORE III, NICHOLAS
DIAZ, ARMANDO
DIMARCO, JR., SAL
DODGE, LARRY
DOLIN, IRVING
DORSEY, RON
  PHOTOGRAPHY
DOUGLASS, DARREN
DOWNIE, DANA
DRESSLER, BRIAN
EDELMAN, HARRY
EDSON, STEVEN
EISBERG, JON
ELBINGER, DOUGLAS
ELDER, JIM
ELK III, JOHN
ELLMAN, FAYE

ELLZEY, BILL
EMMERICH, DON
ENGELMANN, SUZANNE J.
EPSTEIN, LARRY
ESTY, ANDREA
FEILING, DAVID A.
FINLEY, DOUG
FIREBAUGH, STEVE
FISHER PHOTOGRAPHY
FISHER, RAY
FLEMING, LARRY
FLOTTE, LUCIEN
FORBERT, DAVID J.
FORDEN, J. PATRICK
FORSTER, DANIEL
FOSTER, LEE
FOSTER, NICHOLAS
FOURRE, LIZA
FOXX, JEFFREY JAY
FRANZEN, DAVID
FRENCH, PETER
FRIEDMAN, RICK
FRIEDMAN, RONALD A.
FRIESE, RICK
GAGE, HAL
GAMAGE, DOUGLAS C.
GARLAND, MICHAEL E.
GEFTER, JUDITH
GEIGER, K. WILLIAM
GEIGER, WILLIAM K.
GELLER, ALAN
GERCZYNSKI, TOM
GETLEN, DAVID
GIBSON, MARK & AUDREY
GLEASNER, BILL
GNASS, JEFF
GOOD, JAY
GOODMAN, LISA J.
GORDON, FRANK
GORNICK JR., ALAN
GOTTLIEB, STEVEN
GOVE, GEOFFREY
GRAHAM, A. MICHAEL
GRAHAM, STEPHEN
GREEN-ARMYTAGE,
  STEPHEN
GREENFIELD, LAUREN
GREHAN, FARRELL
GRESHAM, GRITS
GRIFFIN, ARTHUR L.
GRIMM, MICHELE
GROENE, GORDON
GROTTA, SALLY WEINER
GUBIN, MARK
GURAVICH, DAN
HALL, DON
HALPERN, DAVID
HAMILTON, CHRIS
HANDS, BRUCE
HANSEN, BARBARA
HARKNESS, CHRIS

HARMON, TIM
HARP, DAVID
HARRINGTON, JOHN
HARRINGTON, TY
HARTMANN, W. GEOFFREY
HAWK, DARYL
HAWTHORNE, ANN
HEBBERD, LINDSAY
HESS, HARRY
HIGHT, GEORGE C.
HIGHTON, SCOTT
HILL, JACKSON
HIRSCH, KAREN I.
HITT, WESLEY
HOEBERMAN, MATHEW &
  KRISTIN
HOLBROOKE, ANDREW
HOLLAND, JAMES R.
HOLLENBECK, CLIFF/KEVIN
  MORRIS
HOLLYMAN, TOM
HORSTED, PAUL
HOSS, RONALD P.
HOUSER, DAVE G.
HOUSER, ROBERT
HUNTRESS, DIANE
JACKSON, DON
JACOBS, JR., LOU
JOHNSON, EVERETT C.
JOHNSTON, GREG
JONES, LOU
KAEHLER, WOLFGANG
KAHANA, YORAM
KALUZNY, ZIGY
KAMP, ERIC
KANOWSKY, KEN
KAPLAN, B. PETER
KASPER, KEN
KASTEN, JERRY
KEATING, FRANKE
KEMPER, BART
KEMPER, SUSAN M.
KENTON, BASIA
KERR, GEORGE
KIDD, CHUCK
KIEFFER, JOHN
KIRCHHEIMER, GABE
KIRKENDALL/SPRING
  PHOTOGRAPHERS
KLAGES, WALTER W.
KLASS, RUBIN & ERIKA
  PHOTOGRAPHY
KNIGHT, DOUG
KOENIG, GEA
KONIG, THIA
KONRATH, G. FRANK
KOONTZ, KATY
KOWAL, JOHN PAUL
KRUBNER, RALPH
LABUA, FRANK
LEDUC, LYLE

LEE, CAROL
LEE, LARRY
LEE, ROBERT II
  PHOTOGRAPHY
LEIBER, N. GREGORY
LEVIN, AARON
LEVY, PATRICIA BARRY
LEVY, RON
LEWIS, G. BRAD
LOHBECK, STEPHEN
LOMEO, ANGELO & SONJA
  BULLATY
LONGWOOD, MARC D.
LOTT, HAL
LOYST, KEN
MACKENZIE, MAXWELL
MACWEENEY, ALEN
MAHIEU, TED
MANHEIM, MICHAEL PHILIP
MAPPES, CARL R.
MARCUS, HELEN
MARES-MANTON,
  ALEXANDER
MAROON, FRED J.
MARVY, JIM
MASSIE, KIM
MASSON, LISA
MCALLISTER, BRUCE
MCCARTHY, MARGARET
MCCARTNEY, SUSAN
MCCOY, DAN J.
MCCUTCHEON, JR., SHAW
MCKAY, DOUG
MCNEELY, BURTON
MENDLOWITZ, BENJAMIN
MENZEL, PETER
MERIDETH, PAUL L.
MESSINEO, JOHN
MEYERS, EDWARD
MIGLAVS, MR. JANIS
MIHALEVICH, MICHAEL
MILLER, ROGER PHOTO,
  LTD.
MISHLER, CLARK JAMES
MITCHELL, BENN
MOBERLEY, CONNIE
MOONEY, KEVIN O.
MOORE, MICHAEL
MOSS, GARY
MOSS, HOWARD
MULLEN, EDWARD F.
MUSCHENETZ, ROLAND &
  KAREN
MYERS, TOM
NELSON, JANET
NELSON, ROBIN
NERONI, ROBERT
NIKAS, GREG
NORTON, PHILLIP
O'TOOLE, TOM AND JOANNE
OBREMSKI, GEORGE

ODYSSEY PRODUCTIONS
OPPERSDORFF, MATHIAS
ORANS, MURIEL
PALMIERI, JORGE
PANAYIOTOU, PETER
PARSONS, KIMBERLY
PATTERSON, MARION
PAWLICK, JOHN
PAYNE, SHELBY
PEARCE, ADDEE
PECHTER, ALESE
PECHTER, MORTON H.
PETERSON, JR., CHESTER
PETT, LAURENCE J.
PHAM, DIEM K.
PHANEUF, ART
PHILIBA, ALLAN
PHOTO RESOURCE HAWAII
PICKERELL, JAMES H.
PLACE, CHARLES
PLATTETER, GEORGE
PLUMMER, DOUG
POOR, SUZANNE
PORTNOY, LEWIS
POST, JOHN
POWELL, TODD B.
PRATT, DIANE
PRESTON, LOUISA
PREUSS, KAREN
PRICE, GREG
PRINCE, NORMAN
PROUD, B.
QUARTUCCIO, DOM
RANTZMAN, KAREN
  STAFFORD
REED, GEOFF
REID, SEAN
RENNIE, BRIAN H.
RIECKS, DAVID
RIEGER, TED
ROBERTS, JANET M.
ROBINSON, BILL
ROGERS, CHUCK
ROGERS, DAVID
ROLLAND, GUY A.
ROLO PHOTOGRAPHY
ROTHSCHILD, NORMAN
ROWAN, N. R.
ROWIN, STANLEY
RUDOLPH, NANCY
RUHE, GEORGE-EDWARD
RUNION, BRITT
RUSS, WILLIAM
RYAN, DAVID
RYCUS, JEFFREY A.
SACHA, BOB
SALMOIRAGHI, FRANCO
SANFORD, ERIC M.
SANFORD, RON
SANGER, DAVID
SATTERWHITE, AL

SCHAMP, J. BROUGH
SCHANUEL, ANTHONY
SCHATZ, BOB
SCHERMEISTER, PHIL
SCHLUETER, MICHAEL K.
SCHMID, BERT
SCHMIDT, DIANE JOY
SCHWARTZ, GEORGE J.
SEITZ, ART
SELIGMAN, PAUL
SETON, CHARLES
SHANEFF, CARL
SHERMAN, BOB
SHRIKHANDE, DEVENDRA
SIBLEY, SCOTT
SILBERT, LAYLE
SIMS, MARK
SLAUGHTER, PAUL
SMITH, BRIAN
SMITH, ROBIN B.
SOCHUREK, HOWARD J.
SOLOMON, RON
STAWNIAK, JIM
STEELE, GEOFF
STEELE, MAX
STEELE, W. RICHARD
STEINER, CLYDE
STEINGROVE, JACK
STEWARDSON, JOE
STIERER, DENNIS
STOCK PHOTOS HAWAII
STONE, TONY IMAGES
STORMZAND, JOHN
STOTT, BARRY
STOVER, DAVID
STREANO, VINCENT C.
STREET, PARK
STRESHINSKY, TED
STROMBERG, BRUCE
SUMNER
  PHOTOGRAPHY INC.
SWARTZ, FRED
TANNENBAUM, ALLAN
TARR, CHARLES J.
TAXEL, BARNEY
TAYLOR, CURTICE
TAYLOR, RANDY G.
TENIN, BARRY
TESADA, DAVID X.
THILL, NANCY
THOMPSON, MICHAEL S.
TORREZ, BOB
TRENKA, BUD
TREYBIG, CYNTHIA
TROXELL, W. H.
TURNER, PETE
ULMER, DAVID
UPITIS, ALVIS
URBINA, WALT
URSILLO, CATHERINE
VANDER SCHUIT STUDIO

INC.
VARTOOGIAN, JACK
VAUGHN, GREG
WACHTER, JERRY
WADDELL, ROBERT M.
WAGGONER, MIKE
WAGNER, ANDREW A.
WALKER, HARRY M.
WALLEN, JONATHAN
WAPINSKI, DAVID
WARREN, CAM
WATERSUN, DAVID
WEDLAKE, JIM
WEINTRAUB, DAVID
WERNER, PERRY
WEYDIG, KATHY
WHEELER, NIK
WHITAKER, GREG
WHITE, GEORGE
WHITE-FALCON, REGINA E.
WHITENTON, CARY
WHITMAN, ALAN
WHITMIRE, KENNETH L.
WILLIAMS III, ZANE
WILLIAMS, HAL
WILSON, DOUG M.
WINIKER, BARRY M.
WOLLIN, WILLIAM
WOLMAN, BARON
WOOD, TED
WOOLFE, RAYMOND G.
WRISTEN, DONALD F.
YAMASHITA, MICHAEL S.
YARBROUGH, BOB
YARBROUGH, CARL
YONKER, THOMAS
  PHOTOGRAPHY
YOUNG, DONALD

URBAN AFFAIRS

COLBROTH, RON
COLMAN III, BEN
CORY, JEFF
COX, DENNIS
CURTIS, STEVEN
DEMPSAY, SAY
DOWNIE, DANA
ELBINGER, DOUGLAS
FINNIGAN, VINCE
FORDEN, J. PATRICK
GIBSON, MARK & AUDREY
GRAHAM, A. MICHAEL
HARMON, TIM
HARRINGTON, TY
JEFFERSON, LOUISE E.
KENNEDY, M. LEWIS
KIRCHHEIMER, GABE
KONRATH, G. FRANK
KRUBNER, RALPH
LEVIN, AARON

MCCUTCHEON, STEVE
MCKAY, DOUG
MILLER PHOTOGRAPHY, INC.
MOSS, GARY
NELSON, ROBIN
PETT, LAURENCE J.
ROLLAND, GUY A.
ROLO PHOTOGRAPHY
RUHE, GEORGE-EDWARD
SCHMIDT, DIANE JOY
SCHWARZ, TED
SELIGMAN, PAUL
SIBLEY, SCOTT
STARR, ASHBY
  PHOTOGRAPHER
STEELE, MAX
STORMZAND, JOHN
TAXEL, BARNEY
TRENKA, BUD
WAPINSKI, DAVID
WINTER, NITA

VIDEO

BEATTY, DAVID E.
BROWN-ROSNER, SHEREE
CHEW, JOHN T.
COGSWELL, JENNIFER D.
COSTE, KURT
DEMPSAY, SAY
FINNIGAN, VINCE
FOXX, JEFFREY JAY
FREEMAN, ROLAND
GOVE, GEOFFREY
GRAHAM, STEPHEN
HARMON, TIM
HIGHTON, SCOTT
HILL, DAN SCOTT
HOWARD, CARL
KASTEN, JERRY
MARX, RICHARD
MAYERS, MARK M./AT
  AGENZIA
MCCOY, DAN J.
MOORE, MICHAEL
MOSS, HOWARD
MOULIN, THOMAS
PETERSON, LEE
QUARTUCCIO, DOM
RAFKIND, ANDREW J.
REMINGTON, GEORGE
SELIGMAN, PAUL
SETON, CHARLES
STECKER, ELINOR H.
SUMMER PRODUCTIONS
THATCHER, CHARLES R.
VEGTER, BRIAN S.
WADDELL, ROBERT M.
WAPINSKI, DAVID

WOMEN'S INTEREST

ADAMS, JANET L.
ADAMS, STEVEN
ARNDT, DIANE
BAER, GORDON
BARBAGALLO, ANTONINO
BARDIN, KEITH
BEVAN, PAT
BITTERS, DAVID
BRUNDEGE, BARBARA A.
CARROLL, TOM
COGSWELL, JENNIFER D.
COLEMAN, PH.D., REV.
  CHERYL L.
DEMPSAY, SAY
DOWNIE, DANA
ENGELMANN, SUZANNE J.
FANSLER, EARL
FINLEY, DOUG
FISHER PHOTOGRAPHY
FLOTTE, LUCIEN
GAMMA LIAISON INC.
GARIK, ALICE
GEFTER, JUDITH
GIBSON, MARK & AUDREY
GOODE, PAUL B.
HALL, DON
HERRON, MATT
HIRSCH, KAREN I.
KAPLAN, B. PETER
KASPER, KEN
KERMANI, SHAHN
KONRATH, G. FRANK
KUPER, HOLLY
LABUA, FRANK
LEVY, PATRICIA BARRY
LEWIS, VICKIE
MAHI, MIEKO SUE
MARIEN, ROBERT
MILLER, DAVID P.
MOSS, GARY
NELSON, ROBIN
NEY, NANCY
NORTON, MICHAEL
PHOTO RESOURCE HAWAII
POOR, SUZANNE
PRESTON, LOUISA
PUTNAM, SARAH
QUICKSILVER
  PHOTOGRAPHY
REMINGTON, GEORGE
ROBERTS, JANET M.
RYCUS, JEFFREY A.
SAVILLE, LYNN
SCHMIDT, DIANE JOY
SHIELDS-MARLEY
  PHOTOGRAPHY
SORRELL, RONDA
STONE, TONY IMAGES
SUDOW, ELLYN

SUMMER PRODUCTIONS
TAXEL, BARNEY
THILL, NANCY
TORREZ, BOB
WAPINSKI, DAVID
WHITAKER, GREG
WHITE, GEORGE
WHITE-FALCON, REGINA E.
WRISTEN, DONALD F.

WORLD AFFAIRS

BAER, GORDON
CARROLL, TOM
CORY, JEFF
DEMPSAY, SAY
ELBINGER, DOUGLAS
ENGELMANN, SUZANNE J.
GAMMA LIAISON INC.
HARMON, TIM
HARRINGTON, JOHN
HOLBROOKE, ANDREW
KASHI, ED
KERMANI, SHAHN
KONRATH, G. FRANK
LEDUC, LYLE
LEY, RUSSELL
MARES-MANTON,
  ALEXANDER
MATHIESON, GREG E.
MATT, PHIL
ORRICO, CHARLES J.
PERESS, GILLES
PETT, LAURENCE J.
RANTZMAN, KAREN
  STAFFORD
RIECKS, DAVID
ROBERTS, JANET M.
ROLO PHOTOGRAPHY
RUHE, GEORGE-EDWARD
SARNACKI, MICHAEL
SCHMIDT, DIANE JOY
STORMZAND, JOHN
TAXEL, BARNEY
TAYLOR, RANDY G.
WAGNER, ANDREW A.
WAPINSKI, DAVID
WHITAKER, GREG

YOUTH

ANCONA, GEORGE
BAER, GORDON
BARON, JAMES J.
BAYER, DANIEL
BENNETT, ROBERT J.
BITTERS, DAVID
BUTTON DOWN
  PRODUCTIONS LTD.
CHINITZ, ADAM
COLEMAN, PH.D., REV.

CHERYL L.
COX, DENNIS
DE ZANGER, ARIE
DEMPSAY, SAY
DOWNIE, DANA
FAIRCLOTH, JANE G.
FARR, JULIE
FITZHUGH, SUSIE
FORMISANO-MAYERI, YONI
FRENCH, PETER
GOVE, GEOFFREY
GRAHAM, A. MICHAEL
GREENFIELD, LAUREN
HARTMANN, W. GEOFFREY
HUMPHRIES, JR., H.
  GORDON
KAPLAN, B. PETER
KIDD, CHUCK
KIRCHHEIMER, GABE
KLEMM, STEPHEN
KONRATH, G. FRANK
LATHROPE, WILMA
MANONI, EILEEN
MESSINEO, JOHN
MIGLAVS, MR. JANIS
MOORE, BARBARA
NORTON, MICHAEL
PECHTER, ALESE
PECHTER, MORTON H.
PHANEUF, ART
PREUSS, KAREN
RAFKIND, ANDREW J.
RANTZMAN, KAREN
  STAFFORD
REED, GEOFF
REMINGTON, GEORGE
RIECKS, DAVID
ROBERTS, JANET M.
ROLO PHOTOGRAPHY
ROSSI, DAVID A.
RYCUS, JEFFREY A.
SAVILLE, LYNN
SCHLUETER, MICHAEL K.
SCHMIDT, DIANE JOY
SHELTON, SYBIL
SIBLEY, SCOTT
STEELE, GEOFF
STEELE, MAX
STEINER, LISL
STOCK PHOTOS HAWAII
STONE, ERIKA
STONE, TONY IMAGES
STORMZAND, JOHN
STREANO, VINCENT C.
STREET, PARK
SUDOW, ELLYN
TAXEL, BARNEY
TORREZ, BOB
TOTO , JOE
WAGNER, ANDREW A.
WAPINSKI, DAVID

WATERSUN, DAVID
WHITAKER, GREG
WHITE, GEORGE
WINTER, NITA

Professional Services

PHOTOGRAPHERS

Section 6
FREELANCE PHOTOGRAPHERS

AARON, RICHARD E.
P.O. Box 97
Santa Monica, CA 90406
Telephone: 310-395-5064
Fax: 310-395-3855
AFFILIATIONS:
ASMP
PRINCIPAL SUBJECTS:
Entertainment
PUBLICATIONS:
New York Times
Time
Playboy
People
Newsweek
US
Rolling Stone
Spin

ABRABEN, E. 'MANNY'
6463 LaCosta Drive (405)
Boca Raton, FL 33433
Telephone: 407-750-7570
MAILING ADDRESS:
ARCHITECTURAL
  PHOTOGRAPHY
Boca Raton, FL 33433
AFFILIATIONS:
AIA, RIBA, PPA
PRINCIPAL SUBJECTS:
Architecture
Photography

ABRAHAM, JOE
5859 W. 34th St.
Houston, TX 77092
Telephone: 713-688-9000
Fax: 718-688-8010
AFFILIATIONS:
ASMP
PRINCIPAL SUBJECTS:
Business & Industry
Advertising
Architecture
PUBLICATIONS:
Town & Country
Computer Graphics World
Houston Chronicle
Houston Post

ABRAMSON, DEAN
P.O. Box 610, 37 Main St.
Raymond, ME 04071
Telephone: 207-655-7386
AFFILIATIONS:
ASMP
PRINCIPAL SUBJECTS:
Advertising
Automotive
Editorial
Education
Foreign
General Interest
Human Interest
Marine
Sports
Travel
PUBLICATIONS:
Time
US News & World Report
Forbes
Nat'l. GEO Traveler
Enterpreneur
Yankee
Newsweek
Travel & Leisure

ACKROYD, HUGH S.
3840 NW Yeon Ave.
Portland, OR 97210
Telephone: 503-227-5694
Fax: 503-227-1740
MAILING ADDRESS:
P.O. Box 10101
Portland, OR 97210
Telephone: 503-222-1858
AFFILIATIONS:
ASMP, PPI, CPO
PRINCIPAL SUBJECTS:
Advertising
Aviation
Human Interest
Architecture
Marine
Medical
PUBLICATIONS:
Business Week
Fortune
National Geographic
Life
Medical World

Nat. Enquirer
Star Weekly
MacLean's Canada & Toronto
  Saturday Night
US News and World Report

ACOSTA, JOSE'
11548 Corliss Ave., North
Seattle, WA 98133
Telephone: 206-367-7861
Fax: 206-367-7861
AFFILIATIONS:
ASMP
PRINCIPAL SUBJECTS:
Advertising
Ecology
Editorial
Fashion
Geography
Hobbies
Journalism
Men's Interest
Nature
Photography
Physical Fitness
Sports
Travel
PUBLICATIONS:
Horizon Air Mag.
Rock & Ice
Diversions
Bazaar
Butterick Patterns
Phillip Morris
Sports Physician
Maupintour Brouture

ADAMS, EDDIE
2059 Huntington Ave., #1407
Alexandria, VA 22303
Telephone: 703-960-5810
Fax: 703-960-9618
PRINCIPAL SUBJECTS:
Advertising
Editorial
Entertainment
Fashion
Social Trends

ADAMS, JANET L.
Adams Studio, The
215 King Ave.
Columbus, OH 43201
Telephone: 614-297-7575
Fax: 614-297-7594
AFFILIATIONS:
ASMP
PRINCIPAL SUBJECTS:
Advertising
Advertising
Animals
Architecture
Education
Family
Health
Photography
Senior Citizens
Women's Interest
PUBLICATIONS:
Cosmopolitan
Living Single
Columbus Monthly

ADAMS, STEVEN
5813 St. Johns Ave.
Minneapolis, MN 55424
Telephone: 612-922-5267
MAILING ADDRESS:
ADAMS PHOTOGRAPHY
Edina, MN 55424
AFFILIATIONS:
PP of A; MPPA
PRINCIPAL SUBJECTS:
Personalities
Business & Industry
Women's Interest
Architecture
PUBLICATIONS:
Ad Week

ADELMAN, BOB
151 W. 28th St.
New York, NY 10001
Telephone: 212-736-0537
AFFILIATIONS:
ASMP
PRINCIPAL SUBJECTS:
Editorial
General Interest
Journalism

Personalities
The Arts
PUBLICATIONS:
Newsweek
Life
Time
The London Times Magazine
Stern
The New York Times Magazine

AIOSA, VINCENT
5 West 31st
New York, NY 10001
Telephone: 212-563-1859
AFFILIATIONS:
ASMP, PPI
PRINCIPAL SUBJECTS:
General Interest
Advertising
Computer Technology
PUBLICATIONS:
New York Times
Playboy
Nat. Lampoon
TV Guide
Life

ALBINO, JOSEPH X.
221 Hillbrook Rd.
Syracuse, NY 13219
Telephone: 315-487-5710
MAILING ADDRESS:
JOSEPH X. ALBINO
P.O. Box 21
Camillus, NY 13031
PRINCIPAL SUBJECTS:
Travel
Agriculture
Nature
Education
Business & Industry
Ecology
General Interest
Military
Religion
Science

ALDRICH, JAY
P.O. Box 1807
Minden, NV 89423
Telephone: 702-782-4383
AFFILIATIONS:
ASMP
PRINCIPAL SUBJECTS:
Advertising
Ecology
Editorial
Education
Fashion
Human Interest
Journalism

News
Photography
PUBLICATIONS:
Time
New York Times
Quick (Germany)
San Francisco Chronicle
Nevada Magazine
Motorland
Adventure West
Westways

ALEKANDROWICZ, FRANK
343 Canterbury Road
Bay Village, OH 44140
Telephone: 216-871-5081
AFFILIATIONS:
ASMP, PJ, NPPA
PRINCIPAL SUBJECTS:
Amusements
Architecture
Business & Industry
Ecology
Editorial
Foreign
Geography
History
Human Interest
Journalism
Nature
Personalities
Religion
Travel
PUBLICATIONS:
Nation's Business
Business Week
Fortune
Esquire
Newsweek
Time
Life
Popular Mechanics
Akron Beacon-Journal
Erie Times-News
Elyria Chronicle/Telegram

ALKALAY, MORRIS
18645 Collins St., #21
Tarzana, CA 91356
Telephone: 818-774-0653
AFFILIATIONS:
ASMP
PRINCIPAL SUBJECTS:
Advertising
Animals
Family
Marine
Sports
Travel

ALLAN PRICE
110 Greene St.
New York, NY 10012
Telephone: 212-925-2722
MAILING ADDRESS:
ALLEN PRICE
  PHOTOGRAPHY
110 Green St.
New York, NY 10012
PRINCIPAL SUBJECTS:
Advertising
Sports
General Interest
PUBLICATIONS:
Time Mag.
People
New York Times
New York Post
Daily News, The
TV Guide
Associated Press
UPI
ET Tonight
Amsterdamn News
AD Week
Broadcasting

ALLEN, ED
3231 Industrial Rd.
Las Vegas, NV 89109
Telephone: 702-732-2211
MAILING ADDRESS:
SO. NEV. NEWS
  BUREAU, INC.
P. O. Box 14847
Las Vegas, NV 89114
Telephone: 702-735-2222
AFFILIATIONS:
PPA
PRINCIPAL SUBJECTS:
Advertising
General Interest
Human Interest
PUBLICATIONS:
Time
Fortune

ALLEN, J. J.
630 S. Central Ave.
Hapeville, GA 30354
Telephone: 404-767-7011
MAILING ADDRESS:
FLAIR PHOTOGRAPHIC
P.O. Box 82134
Hapeville, GA 30354
AFFILIATIONS:
PPA
PRINCIPAL SUBJECTS:
Advertising
Editorial
General Interest

Human Interest
Journalism
Sports
PUBLICATIONS:
Range Finder, The,
  Photography & Writing

ALLEN, JOHN O.
1341 Northwestern Ave.
W Lafayette, IN 47906
Telephone: 317-463-9614
AFFILIATIONS:
PPA
PRINCIPAL SUBJECTS:
Agriculture
Geography
Nature

ALLEN, MARIETTE PATHY
100 Riverside Dr., #15AB
New York, NY 10024
Telephone: 212-496-0655
AFFILIATIONS:
ASMP, PWP
PRINCIPAL SUBJECTS:
Amusements
Editorial
Family
Human Interest
Human Relations
Journalism
Psychology
Social Trends
The Arts
PUBLICATIONS:
American Photography
Stern
New York Woman
Philadelphia Magazine
Soho News
Village Voice
Dance Magazine
Penthouse Forum

ALLEN, TIM
1118 Jenks Ave.
Panama City, FL 32401
Telephone: 904-763-5795
Fax: 904-785-3508
AFFILIATIONS:
ASMP
PRINCIPAL SUBJECTS:
Fashion
Food/Diet
Advertising
Business & Industry

ALLISON, GLEN
P.O. Box 641485
Los Angeles, CA 90064
Telephone: 310-842-4962

AFFILIATIONS:
ASMP
PRINCIPAL SUBJECTS:
Photography
Travel
PUBLICATIONS:
Travel/Holiday
Sunset
Westways
Los Angeles Times
New York Times
House & Garden
Architectural Digest
House Beautiful

ALPER, BARBARA
202 W. 96th St., #2E
New York, NY 10025
Telephone: 212-316-6518
Fax: 212-316-1259
AFFILIATIONS:
ASMP
PRINCIPAL SUBJECTS:
Editorial
Family
General Interest
Human Interest
Journalism
Personalities
Travel
PUBLICATIONS:
Los Angeles Times
American Lawyer
L'Express
Creative Camera

ALTMAN, DAVID M.
4159-A Botanical
St. Louis, MO 63110
Telephone: 314-664-5483
AFFILIATIONS:
ASMP
PRINCIPAL SUBJECTS:
Advertising
Photography
PUBLICATIONS:
St. Louis Post-Dispatch

AMBORN, JOHN E.
263 Tomahawk Trail, S.E.
Cedar Rapids, IA 52403
Telephone: 319-366-4121
PRINCIPAL SUBJECTS:
Advertising
General Interest
Business & Industry
Photography
PUBLICATIONS:
Business & Industry Magazines
  & Publications
Time

AMDAL, PHILIP
618 W. McGraw St.
Seattle, WA 98119
Telephone: 206-281-0054
Fax: 206-286-1025
AFFILIATIONS:
ASMP
PUBLICATIONS:
Computer Technology
Medical
Science
Sports

AMER, TOMMY
1858 Westerly Terrace
Los Angeles, CA 90026
Telephone: 213-664-7624
AFFILIATIONS:
ASMP
PRINCIPAL SUBJECTS:
Editorial
Human Interest
Business & Industry

ANCONA, GEORGE
Route 10 Box 94g
Santa Fe, NM 87501
Telephone: 505-471-8755
PRINCIPAL SUBJECTS:
Family
Editorial
Education
General Interest
Travel
Youth
PUBLICATIONS:
New York Magazine

ANDERSON, GORDON
264 Brookridge
Palmer Lake, CO 80133
Telephone: 719-481-3737
MAILING ADDRESS:
P.O. Box 918
Palmer Lake, CO 80133
PRINCIPAL SUBJECTS:
Nature
Ecology
PUBLICATIONS:
Sierra
National Geographic Traveler
Wild America
Wilderness
Outside
Backpacker

ANDERSON, JOHN D.
6460 Byrnes Rd.
Vacaville, CA 95687
Telephone: 707-448-4926
Fax: 505-471-8755

AFFILIATIONS:
ASMP
PRINCIPAL SUBJECTS:
Photography
Marine

ANDERSON, RICHARD
6637 Winnebago
St. Louis, MO 63109
Telephone: 314-823-0160
PRINCIPAL SUBJECTS:
Advertising
Editorial
Education
Fashion
Health
Journalism
Medical
Psychology
Religion
Senior Citizens

APTON, BILL
577 Howard St.
San Francisco, CA 94105
Telephone: 415-861-1840
AFFILIATIONS:
ASMP
PRINCIPAL SUBJECTS:
Advertising
Business & Industry
PUBLICATIONS:
Business Week
Fortune
Town & Country
San Francisco Magazine
Better Homes & Gardens
PC World

ARDEN, MICHAEL
14568 Greenleaf St.
Sherman Oaks, CA 91403
Telephone: 310-274-2064
Fax: 310-274-2064
AFFILIATIONS:
ASMP, PPA
PRINCIPAL SUBJECTS:
Advertising
Architecture
Fashion
Human Interest
Men's Interest
Physical Fitness
PUBLICATIONS:
Interior Design
Designers West
Global Architecture
Architectural Record
Los Angeles Magazine
California Muscle

ARNDT, DIANE
400 Central Park West
New York, NY 10025
Telephone: 212-866-1902
AFFILIATIONS:
ASMP, ASPP, PWP
PRINCIPAL SUBJECTS:
Editorial
Architecture
Business & Industry
The Arts
Travel
Travel
Women's Interest
PUBLICATIONS:
M-H World
Fortune
Architectural Record
Business Week
Manhattan Spirit

ARPADI, ALLEN G.
5846 Waterman Blvd.
St. Louis, MO 63112
Telephone: 314-863-6643
Fax: 314-863-6643
AFFILIATIONS:
ASMP, SPE
PRINCIPAL SUBJECTS:
Advertising
Computer Technology
Education
Photography
PUBLICATIONS:
New York Magazine

ARRUZA, TONY
25D Edmor Rd.
West Palm Bch, FL 33405
Telephone: 407-832-5978
Fax: 407-832-1503
MAILING ADDRESS:
P.O. Box 6155
West Palm Beach, FL 33405
AFFILIATIONS:
ASMP
PRINCIPAL SUBJECTS:
Agriculture
Travel
Sports
Editorial
Business & Industry
PUBLICATIONS:
Financial World
Travel Holiday
Islands
Power & Motor Yacht
GEO
Readers Digest
Los Angeles Times
Popular Photography

ART OF FINE
  PHOTOGRAPHY
Art of Fine Photography
P.O. Box 2028
Newport Beach, CA 92660
Telephone: 714-548-1815
Fax: 714-645-5537
MAILING ADDRESS:
Art of Fine Photography
340 Cherry Tree Ln.
Newport Beach, CA 92660
AFFILIATIONS:
ASMP, PPA, PPC, PPOC
PRINCIPAL SUBJECTS:
Advertising
Editorial
Education
Entertainment
Family
Foreign
Human Relations
Journalism
Medical
Personalities
The Arts

ASCHERMAN, JR.,
  HERBERT
1846 Coventry Village
Cleveland Heights, OH 44118
Telephone: 216-321-0055
Fax: 216-321-4372
AFFILIATIONS:
ASMP, PPA
PRINCIPAL SUBJECTS:
Advertising
Book Reviews
Family
Fashion
Foreign
Human Interest
Humor
Management
Marketing
Personalities
Philosophy
Photography
The Arts
Travel
PUBLICATIONS:
Petersons Photographic
Ohio Magazine
Cleveland Magazine
Northern Ohio Live
Town & Country

ASHE, BILL
534 West 35th St.
New York, NY 10001
Telephone: 212-695-6473

AFFILIATIONS:
ASMP, IMPA
PRINCIPAL SUBJECTS:
Advertising
Automotive
Editorial
Food/Diet
PUBLICATIONS:
Audio Magazine
New York Times Magazine
Time
Newsweek
Popular Mechanics
Stereo Review
Car Stereo Review
Esquire
American Banker

ASHWOOD, PHILIP
7421 Sanford Road
Calcium, NY 13616
Telephone: 315-788-9363
AFFILIATIONS:
ASMP, APPA
PRINCIPAL SUBJECTS:
Nature
Photography
Travel

ASQUINI, JAY
29628 Munger
Livonia, MI 48154
Telephone: 313-421-0980
Fax: 313-421-6825
AFFILIATIONS:
ASMP
PRINCIPAL SUBJECTS:
Automotive
Business & Industry
Marketing
PUBLICATIONS:
Automotive Industries
Time

ATKESON, RAY
3215 N.W. Yeon
Portland, OR 97210
Telephone: 503-226-0762
Fax: 503-295-1868
MAILING ADDRESS:
RAY ATKESON
P.O. Box 10306
Portland, OR 97210
PRINCIPAL SUBJECTS:
General Interest
Geography
Nature
PUBLICATIONS:
Natural History Mag.
National Geographic

AUBRY, DANIEL
365 First Avenue
New York, NY 10010
Telephone: 212-598-4191
AFFILIATIONS:
ASMP
PRINCIPAL SUBJECTS:
Travel

AUEL, ADAM
3985 Bradwater St.
Fairfax, VA 22031
Telephone: 703-323-4799
Fax: 703-560-7238
MAILING ADDRESS:
ADAM AUEL PHOTOGRAPHY
Fairfax, VA 22031
AFFILIATIONS:
ASMP
PRINCIPAL SUBJECTS:
Photography
Advertising
Business & Industry
Ecology
Nature
PUBLICATIONS:
Washington Post
Annual Reports

AUPIED, STEVEN
2000 Clearview Pkwy., 100
Metairie, LA 70001
Telephone: 504-455-2176
MAILING ADDRESS:
OPA PRODUCTIONS
200 Clearview Pkwy., 100
Metaire, LA 70001
AFFILIATIONS:
PPA, PPLA
PRINCIPAL SUBJECTS:
Architecture
Photography
Food/Diet
PUBLICATIONS:
Louisianna Life Magazine
Love & Marriage
Wedding Guide

AUSTIN, MILES
402 West Broad St.
Westfield, NJ 07090
Telephone: 908-232-1155
Fax: 908-232-5444
MAILING ADDRESS:
AUSTIN PHOTOGRAPHY
Westfield, NJ 07090
AFFILIATIONS:
ASMP;PPOFA;CPP
PRINCIPAL SUBJECTS:
Advertising
Human Interest

PUBLICATIONS:
Professional Photography
Star Ledger
Range Finder

AVERETT, GERALD L.
4132 Ridgerest Dr.
Springfield, MO 65807
Telephone: 417-883-0619
AFFILIATIONS:
PPA
PRINCIPAL SUBJECTS:
General Interest
Business & Industry
Journalism
Aviation

AVERY, RON
11821 Mississippi Ave.
Los Angeles, CA 90025
Telephone: 310-477-1632
MAILING ADDRESS:
AVERY STUDIO
Los Angeles, CA 90025
PRINCIPAL SUBJECTS:
Advertising
Education
Automotive
Business & Industry
Computer Technology
PUBLICATIONS:
T.V. Guide
Life
Time

BABBITT, SHARON
3219 Milan
Houston, TX 77006
Telephone: 713-523-8757
PRINCIPAL SUBJECTS:
Food/Diet
Architecture

BADER, KATE
RD 1, Box 110D
East Nassau, NY 12062
Telephone: 718-786-1440
AFFILIATIONS:
ASMP, PWP, ASPP
PRINCIPAL SUBJECTS:
Foreign
Geography
Nature
Photography
Travel
PUBLICATIONS:
GEO
National Geographic World
Time

The New York Times
Fotopro
'10,000 Eyes': ASMP's
   Celebration Of The 150th Ann

BADGER, BOBBY
1355 Chemical St.
Dallas, TX 75207
Telephone: 214-634-0222
Fax: 214-634-1115
AFFILIATIONS:
ASMP
PRINCIPAL SUBJECTS:
Fashion
Personalities
Photography
Advertising
PUBLICATIONS:
American Way
"D" Magazine
Select Magazine

BAER, GORDON
18 E. Fourth St.
Cincinnati, OH 45202
Telephone: 513-381-4466
Fax: 513-621-4556
AFFILIATIONS:
ASMP, NPPA
PRINCIPAL SUBJECTS:
Advertising
Architecture
Editorial
Family
General Interest
Geography
Health
Human Interest
Human Relations
Journalism
Medical
News
Personalities
Photography
Psychology
Social Trends
The Arts
Women's Interest
World Affairs
Youth
PUBLICATIONS:
Time
Fortune
Forbes
National Geographic World
   Magazine
Child Magazine
Parent
Parade

BAER, MORLEY
8205 Carmel Valley Rd.
Carmel, CA 93923
Telephone: 408-624-3530
MAILING ADDRESS:
MORLEY BAER
P.O. Box 222537
Carmel, CA 93922
AFFILIATIONS:
ASMP, FOP
PRINCIPAL SUBJECTS:
Nature
Architecture
PUBLICATIONS:
Architectural Record
House & Garden
House Beautiful
Progressive Architecture

BAER, RHODA
3006 Military Rd., NW
Washington, DC 20015
Telephone: 202-364-8480
Fax: 202-362-7318
AFFILIATIONS:
ASMP
PRINCIPAL SUBJECTS:
Business & Industry
Advertising
Computer Technology
Editorial
Health
Personalities
PUBLICATIONS:
Fortune
Inc.
Smithsonian
Working Woman

BAGG, ALAN
3230 Lathrop Ave.
Racine, WI 53405
Telephone: 414-554-1938
AFFILIATIONS:
PPA, OWAA
PRINCIPAL SUBJECTS:
The Arts
Editorial
Business & Industry
Journalism
Human Interest

BAILEY, ROBERT
10500 Northwest Frwy., #200
Houston, TX 77092
Telephone: 713-956-1235
Fax: 713-956-8269
MAILING ADDRESS:
HARPER LEIPER
   STUDIOS INC.
Telephone: 713-890-2277

AFFILIATIONS:
PPA, TPP
PRINCIPAL SUBJECTS:
Advertising
Aviation
General Interest
Architecture
Marine
PUBLICATIONS:
Time
Architectural Forum
The Professional Photographer
Pittsburgh Plate
   Glass Magazine
Black's Guide
Houston Post
Houston Business Journal
Houston Magazine

BAKER, BOBBE CLINTON
1119 Ashburn Ave., E.
College Station, TX 77840
Telephone: 409-696-7185
AFFILIATIONS:
ASMP, MPCA
PRINCIPAL SUBJECTS:
Advertising
Ecology
Editorial
Family
Foreign
Home & Garden
Journalism
Nature
Photography
The Arts
Travel
PUBLICATIONS:
Newsweek
Progressive Farmer
Texas Monthly
Farm Journal

BAKER, JOHN
6511 N.W. Valley View Rd.
Kansas City, MO 64152
Telephone: 913-492-0792
AFFILIATIONS:
ASMP
PRINCIPAL SUBJECTS:
Nature
Ecology
PUBLICATIONS:
Photo Marketing
   Magazine, Oct. 1992
Various Trane Publications

BAKER, JULIE
Baker, Julie Photography
P.O. Box 4581
San Diego, CA 92164

Telephone: 619-233-5233
AFFILIATIONS:
ASMP
PRINCIPAL SUBJECTS:
Advertising
Business & Industry
Editorial
Food/Diet
General Interest
Health
Home & Garden
Medical
Senior Citizens
PUBLICATIONS:
San Diego Union-Tribune
Senior World
Supermarket News
Price Club Journal

BAKKE, ERIC
23575 Currant Drive
Golden, CO 80401
Telephone: 303-526-9495
PRINCIPAL SUBJECTS:
Business & Industry
Sports
Journalism
Travel
Advertising
Marketing
Editorial

BALLIS, GEORGE
35751 Oak Spring Dr.
Tollhouse, CA 93667
Telephone: 209-855-3710
PRINCIPAL SUBJECTS:
Agriculture
Human Interest
Nature
The Arts
PUBLICATIONS:
Vogue
Life
Sunset

BANKHEAD, GARY
1245 W. 18th, Studio C
Houston, TX 77008
Telephone: 713-861-4030
Fax: 713-868-7409
AFFILIATIONS:
ASMP
PRINCIPAL SUBJECTS:
Fashion
Personalities

BAPTIE, FRANK
1426 9th Street, North
St Petersburg, FL 33704
Telephone: 813-823-7319

Fax: 813-821-6106
AFFILIATIONS:
ASMP
PRINCIPAL SUBJECTS:
Advertising

BARAG, MARC
3401 W. Penn St.
Philadelphia, PA 19129
Telephone: 215-848-6391
AFFILIATIONS:
ASMP, PP of A
PRINCIPAL SUBJECTS:
Advertising
Architecture
Editorial
Family
General Interest
Human Relations
Photography

BARBAGALLO, ANTONINO
Barbagallo, Antonino
  Photography
250 N. Goodman St.
Rochester, NY 14607
Telephone: 716-271-4656
Fax: 716-271-8299
AFFILIATIONS:
ASMP
PRINCIPAL SUBJECTS:
Advertising
Business & Industry
Editorial
Fashion
Journalism
Marketing
Men's Interest
Photography
Physical Fitness
Senior Citizens
Sports
The Arts
Women's Interest

BARBALACE PHOTOGRAPHY
Barbalace Photography
1420 S. Lincoln St.
Aberdeen, SD 57401
Telephone: 605-229-4570
AFFILIATIONS:
ASMP, MPCA
PRINCIPAL SUBJECTS:
Advertising
Agriculture
Architecture
Editorial
History
Medical
Travel

BARCELLONA, MARIANNE
175 5th Ave., #2422
New York, NY 10010
Telephone: 212-463-9717
AFFILIATIONS:
ASMP, NPPA
PRINCIPAL SUBJECTS:
Editorial
Foreign
General Interest
Human Interest
Human Relations
Journalism
Personalities
The Arts
Travel
PUBLICATIONS:
People
Fortune
New York Times
Entertainment Weekly
Time
Sports Illustrated For Kids
Forbes
Life

BARDIN, KEITH
Bardin, Keith Studio
1027 Dragon St.
Dallas, TX 75207
Telephone: 214-744-2222
Fax: 214-748-1463
AFFILIATIONS:
ASMP
PRINCIPAL SUBJECTS:
Advertising
Architecture
General Interest
Health
Human Interest
Men's Interest
Physical Fitness
Senior Citizens
Social Trends
The Arts
Travel
Women's Interest
PUBLICATIONS:
Fortune
Texas Monthly
Woman's Day

BARLEY, BILL
71 Crystal Springs Dr.
Lexington, SC 29073
Telephone: 803-755-1554
Fax: 803-755-3711
MAILING ADDRESS:
P.O. Box 280005
Columbia, SC 29228

AFFILIATIONS:
ASMP
PRINCIPAL SUBJECTS:
Advertising
General Interest
Journalism
Architecture
PUBLICATIONS:
N.Y. Times
USA Magazines
Corporate & Trade Publications
American Showcase
Black Enterprise
Car Audio Magazine
Time

BARNELL, JOE
556 Silk Oak Drive
Venice, FL 34293
Telephone: 813-493-2723
AFFILIATIONS:
ASMP, PACA
PRINCIPAL SUBJECTS:
Business & Industry
Editorial
Foreign
Hobbies
Journalism
Travel
PUBLICATIONS:
Reader's Digest
Newsweek

BARNES, BILLY
313 Severin St.
Chapel Hill, NC 27516
Telephone: 919-942-6350
Fax: 919-942-6350
AFFILIATIONS:
ASMP
PRINCIPAL SUBJECTS:
Business & Industry
Personalities
Travel
Education
Personalities
Human Interest
Health
Home & Garden
PUBLICATIONS:
Business Week
Time
Fortune
Compuserve
Woman's Day
New York Times
U.S. News & World Report
Working Woman

BARNES, MICHELLE A.
P.O. Box 771613
Eagle River, AK 99577
Telephone: 907-688-4178
AFFILIATIONS:
ASMP/ALASKA
  WOMENS PRESS
PRINCIPAL SUBJECTS:
Education
Human Interest
Nature
Advertising
Animals
Editorial
PUBLICATIONS:
National Geographic
Outside Magazine
American Lawyer
National Wildlife Federation
  Magazine

BARON, JAMES J.
Baron Photography
  And Image Finders
812 Huron, Suite 314
Cleveland, OH 44115
Telephone: 216-781-7729
Fax: 216-781-7729
AFFILIATIONS:
ASMP, PPA
PRINCIPAL SUBJECTS:
Advertising
Agriculture
Animals
Architecture
Aviation
Business & Industry
Computer Technology
Ecology
Editorial
Education
Family
Foreign
General Interest
Geography
Health
Human Relations
Marketing
Medical
Physical Fitness
Science
Senior Citizens
Social Trends
Sports
Travel
Youth
PUBLICATIONS:
The Cleveland Plain Dealer
Ohio Magazine

Cleveland Magazine
Corporate Cleveland Magazine
Home & Away Magazine

BARR, IAN
2640 SW 19th St.
Ft Lauderdale, FL 33312
Telephone: 305-563-3290
Fax: 305-563-7341
PRINCIPAL SUBJECTS:
Ecology
Photography

BARRETT, CHARLES
Barrett, Charles Photography
1800 15th St., #204
Denver, CO 80202
Telephone: 303-595-4850
Fax: 303-534-1608
PRINCIPAL SUBJECTS:
Advertising
Architecture
Editorial
Human Interest
Personalities
The Arts
PUBLICATIONS:
Denver Post
Colorado Creative
Spectrum Magazine
The Prospector
Advertising & Marketing
   Review (Denver)
Good News

BARRINGTON, CAROL
5323 Lookout Mountain Dr.
Houston, TX 77069
Telephone: 713-444-6598
AFFILIATIONS:
ASMP, SATW, SPJ, ASJA
PRINCIPAL SUBJECTS:
Editorial
General Interest
Travel
PUBLICATIONS:
Texas Highways
Houston Chronicle
Chicago Tribune
Sunset
Dallas Morning News

BARRON, DAVID M./OXYGEN
   GROUP
247 Dutton Rd.
Sudbury, MA 01776
Telephone: 508-443-7423
Fax: 508-443-7461
AFFILIATIONS:
ASMP

PRINCIPAL SUBJECTS:
Advertising
Animals
Business & Industry
Travel
PUBLICATIONS:
Geographic Travel
Discover
Science Magazine
Earthwatch
Harvard Magazine
Delta Sky
NE Journal Of Medicine/The
   World & I

BARROS, ROBERT
   PHOTOGRAPHY INC.
Barros, Robert
   Photography Inc.
E. 1813 Sprague Avenue
Spokane, WA 99202
Telephone: 509-535-6455
Fax: 509-535-2829
AFFILIATIONS:
ASMP
PRINCIPAL SUBJECTS:
Advertising
Business & Industry
Computer Technology
Education
Medical
Movie Reviews
Physical Fitness
Senior Citizens
PUBLICATIONS:
ASMP-Silver Book
American Showcase
Parents Magazine
Northwest Graphic Arts And
   Photography Index

BARTH, HARRY
3700 S. Crysler
Independence, MO 64055
Telephone: 816-252-9429
AFFILIATIONS:
PPA, PPM, GKC
PRINCIPAL SUBJECTS:
Architecture
Photography
PUBLICATIONS:
PPA Magazine
Flower & Garden Magazine
Missouri Life Magazine

BARTRUFF, DAVE
524 San Anselmo Ave.
San Anselmo, CA 94960
Telephone: 415-457-1482
Fax: 415-457-0399
MAILING ADDRESS:

DAVE BARTRUFF/
   ARTISTRY INTL.
San Anselmo, CA 94960
AFFILIATIONS:
ASMP, SATW
PRINCIPAL SUBJECTS:
Advertising
Religion
Journalism
Travel
Architecture
Business & Industry
Nature
The Arts
PUBLICATIONS:
Travel and Leisure
The Lutheran Magazine
New York Times
World & I
Bon Appetit
Motorland
Endless Vacations
Better Homes & Gardens
Adventure Road
Hemispheres

BASCOM, WILLIAM A.
35 Magnolia Dr.
St. Louis, MO 63124
Telephone: 314-997-2533
AFFILIATIONS:
ASMP
PRINCIPAL SUBJECTS:
Architecture
Journalism
News
Photography
PUBLICATIONS:
Christian Science Monitor
St. Louis Post Dispatch

BAUMAN, MARGARET
8100 Lamplighter Circle
Anchorage, AK 99502
Telephone: 907-349-7917
Fax: 907-248-7454
MAILING ADDRESS:
Alaska Journal Of Commerce
3710 Woodland Dr., Suite 2100
Anchorage, AK 99517
AFFILIATIONS:
ASMP, APC
PRINCIPAL SUBJECTS:
Human Interest
Journalism
News

BAUMEL, KEN
RR1, Box 306
Milford, PA 18337
Telephone: 717-686-2900

AFFILIATIONS:
ASMP
PRINCIPAL SUBJECTS:
Editorial
Sports
PUBLICATIONS:
The Village Voice
Natural Health
Ladies Home Journal
Signature
Art & Antique
Middleton Record
News Eagle

BAXLEY, KIRK
1552 Walton Way
Augusta, GA 30904
Telephone: 706-724-7759
Fax: 706-724-7749
MAILING ADDRESS:
FITZ - SYMMS
   PHOTOGRAPHY
Augusta, GA 30904
Telephone: 706-722-2944
AFFILIATIONS:
ASMP, NPPA, PAI
PRINCIPAL SUBJECTS:
Architecture
Aviation
General Interest
Advertising

BAYER, DANIEL
5325 Cochran St., #207
Simi Valley, CA 93063
Telephone: 805-581-9436
AFFILIATIONS:
ASMP
PRINCIPAL SUBJECTS:
Advertising
Architecture
Aviation
Business & Industry
Editorial
Electronics
Entertainment
General Interest
Hobbies
Journalism
Marine
Military
Nature
News
Photography
Science
Sports
Travel
Youth
PUBLICATIONS:
Ad Week
Disney News Reel

US Naval Institute
'Proceedings'
Aviation Week
Petersons Pro Sports

BAYLES, DAL
4431 N. 64th St.
Milwaukee, WI 53218
Telephone: 414-464-8917
PRINCIPAL SUBJECTS:
Education
Business & Industry
Photography
Advertising
Editorial
News
Human Interest
Business & Industry
Sports
Medical
PUBLICATIONS:
Nation's Business Magazine
Business Week Magazine
Inc. Magazine
Black Enterprise Magazine
USA Today
US News & World Report
  Magazine
Newsweek Magazine
USA Weekend Magazine
Woman's World Magazine
Time Magazine
New York Times

BEATTY, DAVID E.
1287 Wabash Ave.
Springfield, IL 62704
Telephone: 217-787-4747
Fax: 217-787-4865
AFFILIATIONS:
ITVA
PRINCIPAL SUBJECTS:
Aviation
General Interest
News
Agriculture
Video

BECHTOLD, CHARLES
65 Avenel Street
Avenel, NJ 07001
Telephone: 908-750-3619
AFFILIATIONS:
ASMP
PRINCIPAL SUBJECTS:
Advertising
Architecture
Editorial
The Arts
PUBLICATIONS:
The Clarion

BECK, PETER
  PHOTOGRAPHY
Beck, Peter Photography
906 W. Minnehaha Pkwy.
Minneapolis, MN 55419
Telephone: 612-882-6115
Fax: 612-882-7117
AFFILIATIONS:
ASMP
PRINCIPAL SUBJECTS:
Advertising
Agriculture
Business & Industry
Editorial
Family
Personalities
PUBLICATIONS:
Time
Business Week
Forbes
Ladies Home Journal
Working Mother
Money
Financial World
Scholastic

BEDNARSKI, PAUL S.
1500 Woodbridge, Suite 201
Detroit, MI 48207
Telephone: 313-259-6565
Fax: 313-259-6566
MAILING ADDRESS:
PAUL S. BEDNARSKI
  PHOTOGRAPHICS
AFFILIATIONS:
ASMP
PRINCIPAL SUBJECTS:
Advertising
Architecture
Automotive
Business & Industry
Fashion
Travel
PUBLICATIONS:
Detroit Monthly
House & Garden
New Changes
Time
Woman's Day

BEGLEITER, STEVEN H.
303 Park Ave. S., #512
New York, NY 10010
Telephone: 212-475-7498
PRINCIPAL SUBJECTS:
Business & Industry
Physical Fitness
Photography

BEKKER, PHILIP
Art Institute of Atlanta
5070 Trimble Rd.
Atlanta, GA 30342
Telephone: 404-847-9777
Fax: 404-847-9777
AFFILIATIONS:
ASMP
PRINCIPAL SUBJECTS:
Advertising
Architecture
Education
Food/Diet
Photography
The Arts
PUBLICATIONS:
Graphis Photo
Graphis Poster
The Workbook
American Showcase
Erotic Art by Living Artists
Colorfoto (Germany)
Atlanta Homes & Lifestyles

BELLENIS, JOHN
2 Northedge Road
Hamilton, MA 01982
Telephone: 508-468-5045
Fax: 508-468-5055
AFFILIATIONS:
ASMP
PRINCIPAL SUBJECTS:
Advertising
Architecture
Home & Garden
Photography
Travel
PUBLICATIONS:
Departures Magazine
British 'Tailor'
'City & Country Homes'
  Magazine

BELLIS, PHIL
1032 Maine
Quincy, IL 62301
Telephone: 217-222-2405
MAILING ADDRESS:
MAXWELL & BELLIS
  PHOTOGRAPHERS &
  FRAMERS
Quincy, IL 62301
AFFILIATIONS:
P.P. of Amer.
PRINCIPAL SUBJECTS:
Photography
PUBLICATIONS:
Time
Overdrive Magazine
Sports Illustrated

BENKERT, CHRISTINE
27 N. 4th St., Suite 50
Minneapolis, MN 55401
Telephone: 612-340-9503
Fax: 612-344-1988
AFFILIATIONS:
ASMP
PRINCIPAL SUBJECTS:
Advertising
Business & Industry
Editorial
Fashion
Food/Diet
Home & Garden
The Arts
PUBLICATIONS:
Elle
Self
Better Home & Gardens
Ms.
Low Review
Hearth & Home
American Crafts

BENNETT, ROBERT J.
310 Edgewood St.
Bridgeville, DE 19933
Telephone: 302-337-3347
Fax: 302-337-3444
MAILING ADDRESS:
CUSTOM CRAFT STUDIOS
Bridgeville, DE 19933
AFFILIATIONS:
ASMP, NPPA, PPA
PRINCIPAL SUBJECTS:
Aviation
News
Human Interest
Youth
Agriculture
Travel
General Interest
Editorial
PUBLICATIONS:
National Geography World
National Gardening
Sun - Globe, Etc.
Readers Digest
Ladies Home Journal
Country Living
Progressive Farmer

BENTON, VIRGINIA M.
113 Covington Ave.
Opp, AL 36467
Telephone: 205-493-3218
MAILING ADDRESS:
VIRGINIA BENTON
P.O. Box 31
Opp, AL 36467
Telephone: 205-493-3184

AFFILIATIONS:
PPA, PPMA, OPP
PRINCIPAL SUBJECTS:
General Interest
Travel
Photography
PUBLICATIONS:
Water Well Press
Opp News
Andalusia Star News
Montgomery Advertiser
Dothan Eagle
Textile Publications
Alumni News University
  Of Montevallo

BENYAS, BOB
5597 Apple Ridge Trail
West Bloomfield, MI 48322
Telephone: 313-626-6014
Fax: 313-548-4492
AFFILIATIONS:
PP of A, NPPA
PRINCIPAL SUBJECTS:
Photography
Advertising
Business & Industry
Human Interest
The Arts
PUBLICATIONS:
Time
Life
U.S. News & World Report

BERG, MARGARET C.
1753 Charleston Lane
Encinitas, CA 92024
Telephone: 619-753-0787
AFFILIATIONS:
NPPA, ASPP, NWC
PRINCIPAL SUBJECTS:
Business & Industry
Agriculture
General Interest
Education
Travel
Computer Technology
Photography
PUBLICATIONS:
Silver Burdett
American Demographics
Modern Business Reports
Marketing Letter
Computers in Health Care

BERGERON, JOSEPH
516 Natchez St.
New Orleans, LA 70130
Telephone: 504-522-7503
AFFILIATIONS:
PP of A, ASP, ASMP

PRINCIPAL SUBJECTS:
Advertising
Food/Diet
PUBLICATIONS:
Sports Illustrated
Bride
Better Homes And Gardens
N. Y. Times
Southern Living
News Day

BERK, OTTO
303 Park Ave., So.
New York, NY 10010
Telephone: 212-677-8075
PRINCIPAL SUBJECTS:
The Arts

BERLAND, THEODORE
P.O. Box 597602
Chicago, IL 60659
Telephone: 312-274-2792
AFFILIATIONS:
AMWA, SDX, NASW
PRINCIPAL SUBJECTS:
Health
Travel
PUBLICATIONS:
Time
B H & G
Parade
Reader's Digest
American Health
Consumer's Digest

BERMAN, MICHAEL
P.O. Box 75,
  49 S. Cedar Brook Rd.
Cedar Brook, NJ 08018
Telephone: 609-561-4188
AFFILIATIONS:
ASMP
PRINCIPAL SUBJECTS:
Advertising
Marine
Travel
PUBLICATIONS:
Power & Motor Yacht
Small Boat Journal
Cruising World
Sailing World
Professional Boat Builder
Sailing
Chesapeake Bay Magazine
Caribbean Travel & Life

BERNSTEIN, ALAN
6766 NW 43 Pl.
Coral Springs, FL 33067
Telephone: 305-753-1071

AFFILIATIONS:
ASMP
PRINCIPAL SUBJECTS:
Advertising
Fashion
PUBLICATIONS:
New York Times
GQ
Glamour
Mademoiselle

BERNSTEIN, MARION
110 W. 96th St., #7D
New York, NY 10025
Telephone: 212-663-6674
PRINCIPAL SUBJECTS:
Architecture
Ecology
Editorial
Education
General Interest
Geography
Government
Health
Human Interest
Human Relations
Medical
Nature
Senior Citizens
The Arts
Travel
PUBLICATIONS:
Village Voice
Environs
Garbage
Livable City
Metropolis
New York Times
New York Daily News

BERRY & HOMER
  PHOTOGRAPHICS
2035 Richmond St.
Philadelphia, PA 19125
Telephone: 215-423-6363
AFFILIATIONS:
APA, ASP, PPA
PRINCIPAL SUBJECTS:
Architecture
Photography
Journalism
PUBLICATIONS:
Several Local & National
  Publications

BEVAN, PAT
2100 S. Quebec St.
Arlington, VA 22204
Telephone: 703-553-8990
AFFILIATIONS:
ASMP

PRINCIPAL SUBJECTS:
Animals
Editorial
Education
Family
Human Interest
Humor
Journalism
Marketing
Nature
News
Personalities
Sports
Travel
Women's Interest
PUBLICATIONS:
The Beacon
The Diamondback
Columbia Magazine
AFSCME In Action
AFSCME International
  Magazine

BEVILACQUA, JOE
202 E. 42nd St.
New York, NY 10017
Telephone: 212-490-0355
Fax: 212-490-9082
AFFILIATIONS:
ASMP, APA
PRINCIPAL SUBJECTS:
Advertising

BIEGUN, RICHARD
56 Cherry Ave.
West Sayville, NY 11796
Telephone: 516-567-2645
Fax: 516-244-7175
PRINCIPAL SUBJECTS:
Advertising

BIGGS, KEN
1147 N. Hudson Ave.
Los Angeles, CA 90038
Telephone: 310-462-7739
AFFILIATIONS:
ASMP
PRINCIPAL SUBJECTS:
General Interest
PUBLICATIONS:
Pop Photography
Modern Photography
Kodak Publications

BILKER, HARVEY L.
4 Sylvan Blvd.
Howell, NJ 07731
Telephone: 908-364-0394
AFFILIATIONS:
SFWA

PRINCIPAL SUBJECTS:
Entertainment
Human Interest
Medical
News
Photography
Senior Citizens
PUBLICATIONS:
New York Times
Time, Inc.
Emergency Magazine
Petersen's Photographic
 Magazine
Asbury Park Press
 (New Jersey)
Tri - Town News
Star - Ledger (New Jersey)

BIRDWHISTELL, REIS
771 Monroe Dr.
Atlanta, GA 30308
Telephone: 404-872-0690
Fax: 404-873-2104
PRINCIPAL SUBJECTS:
Photography

BISCHOFF, KARL
1201 1st Ave. S.
Seattle, WA 98134
Telephone: 206-587-4007
Fax: 206-233-0558
AFFILIATIONS:
ASMP, AIGA, SME, SDA
PRINCIPAL SUBJECTS:
Advertising
Architecture
Home & Garden
Marketing
Travel
PUBLICATIONS:
Architectural Digest
Architecture Record
Interiors
Travel & Leisure

BISHOP, G. ROBERT
5622 Delmar, #103 W.
St. Louis, MO 63112
Telephone: 314-367-8787
Fax: 314-367-4262
AFFILIATIONS:
ASMP
PRINCIPAL SUBJECTS:
Advertising
Agriculture
Animals
Food/Diet
Personalities
Photography
PUBLICATIONS:
Time

Newsweek
Sports Illustrated
Money
Forbes
Fortune
Family Circle
Business Week

BISHOP, RANDA
59 W. 12th St.
New York, NY 10011
Telephone: 212-206-1122
AFFILIATIONS:
ASMP
PRINCIPAL SUBJECTS:
Home & Garden
Advertising
Editorial
Foreign
Travel
PUBLICATIONS:
National Geographic Society
Travel & Leisure
L.A. Times
GEO
Relax
Caribbeen Travel & Life

BITTERS, DAVID
Bitters, David Studio
P.O. Box 322, 178
 St. George St.
Duxbury, MA 02331
Telephone: 617-934-2838
Fax: 617-934-9176
AFFILIATIONS:
ASMP, ASPP
PRINCIPAL SUBJECTS:
Advertising
Animals
Business & Industry
Ecology
Editorial
Fashion
Home & Garden
Marine
Nature
News
Personalities
Religion
Women's Interest
Youth
PUBLICATIONS:
Ocean Spray
Fleet Bank
Focus on the Family
Yankee Magazine
Country
Woman's World
Ropes & Gray

BLACK, BILLY
160 Sakonnet Point Road
Little Compton, RI 02837
Telephone: 401-635-2891
Fax: 401-635-2891
AFFILIATIONS:
ASMP, ASAP
PRINCIPAL SUBJECTS:
Business & Industry
Marine
Personalities
Sports
Travel
PUBLICATIONS:
Sports Illustrated
People
Sail
Sailing World
Yachting
Sailing
Cruising World
Showboats International

BLAKESBERG, JAY
P.O. Box 460054
San Francisco, CA 94146
Telephone: 415-550-1035
Fax: 415-648-5994
PRINCIPAL SUBJECTS:
Advertising
Business & Industry
Editorial
Entertainment
General Interest
The Arts
Social Trends

BLANKENBURG, BEN
P.O. Box X
Dillon, CO 80435
Telephone: 303-468-1235
Fax: 303-468-8545
AFFILIATIONS:
ASMP, NASS
PRINCIPAL SUBJECTS:
Sports
Social Trends
Travel

BLINKOFF, RICHARD
147 W. 15th St.
New York, NY 10011
Telephone: 212-620-7883
AFFILIATIONS:
PPA, CLC
PRINCIPAL SUBJECTS:
Family
Fashion
Amusements
Travel
Fashion

PUBLICATIONS:
Family Circle
Ladies Home Journal
Cosmopolitan
Woman's Day
American Baby Magazine
Seventeen Magazine

BLIZZARD, WILLIAM C.
11 Riverside Glen
Winfield, WV 25213
Telephone: 304-755-0094
MAILING ADDRESS:
WILLIAM C. BLIZZARD
Box 11, Riverside Mbl. Hm. Ct.
Winfield, WV 25213
AFFILIATIONS:
ASMP/NWU
PRINCIPAL SUBJECTS:
Human Interest
Nature
Sports
PUBLICATIONS:
Inside Sports
Cosmopolitan
Reader's Digest
American Youth
Dynamic Years
U.S. News And World Report
Smithsonian (Photos)
The Nation
High Fidelity/Musical America
Collectibles Illustrated
Friends Magazine (Chevrolet)
Harvest (Campbell's Soup)
Reader's Digest Books
 (Photos)
NRTA Journal
Popular Mechanics
Off Hours (Medical -
 Recreation)
Woman's World
 (Assignment Photos)

BLOCH, STEVEN
431 N.W. Flanders
Portland, OR 97209
Telephone: 503-224-8018
AFFILIATIONS:
ASMP
PRINCIPAL SUBJECTS:
Advertising
Computer Technology
Editorial
Humor
News
Travel
PUBLICATIONS:
Money Magazine
Fairchild Publications

Lears
Business Week
Mac World

BLOCK, RAY
231 W. 29th St., #601
New York, NY 10001
Telephone: 212-967-9470
AFFILIATIONS:
ASMP
PRINCIPAL SUBJECTS:
Advertising
Editorial
Education
Entertainment
Fashion
Medical
Personalities
Photography
PUBLICATIONS:
People
Down Beat
Village Voice
New York Daily News
Cortlandt Forum
National Examiner
Manhattan Arts

BOBBE, LELAND
51 W. 28th St.
New York, NY 10001
Telephone: 212-685-5238
Fax: 212-685-1033
AFFILIATIONS:
ASMP
PRINCIPAL SUBJECTS:
Advertising
Editorial
Human Relations
Nature
Photography

BOGACZ, MARK F.
11 Pondview Place
Tyngsborough, MA 01879
Telephone: 508-649-3886
Fax: 508-649-6621
AFFILIATIONS:
ASMP
PRINCIPAL SUBJECTS:
Advertising
Business & Industry
Computer Technology
Editorial
Food/Diet
Health
Human Relations
Marketing
Photography
Science
Sports

PUBLICATIONS:
Time
Boston Globe
Concord Monitor
Progressive Grocer
Top Shelf
Supermarket Business
Business New Hampshire

BOHON, ED
43-23 Colden St., 27n
Flushing, NY 11355
Telephone: 718-359-2450
AFFILIATIONS:
ASMP
PRINCIPAL SUBJECTS:
Architecture
Editorial
Travel
Business & Industry
PUBLICATIONS:
Guideposts
Travel & Leisure
Popular Photography
National Geographic
Nikon World
Flying
TWA Ambassador

BOLESTA, ALAN
11 Riverside Dr., 13-SE
New York, NY 10023
Telephone: 212-873-1932
AFFILIATIONS:
ASMP
PRINCIPAL SUBJECTS:
Aviation
Travel
Foreign
PUBLICATIONS:
Town & Country
Travel & Leisure
Diversions
Caribbean Travel & Life

BOLSTER, MARK
2200 California Ave.
Pittsburgh, PA 15212
Telephone: 412-231-3757
Fax: 412-231-0930
AFFILIATIONS:
ASMP
PRINCIPAL SUBJECTS:
Amusements
Business & Industry
Computer Technology
Editorial
Family
Fashion
Hobbies
Management

Photography
Physical Fitness
Social Trends
Travel
PUBLICATIONS:
Business Week
Forbes
Inc.
D & B Reports
Geography
Information Week
Mid Atlantic Country

BONNEY, LORRAINE G.
P.O. Box 129
Kelly, WY 83011
Telephone: 307-733-6392
MAILING ADDRESS:
BONNEY, LORRIANE G.
Kelly, WY 83011
AFFILIATIONS:
ASJA, OWAA
PRINCIPAL SUBJECTS:
General Interest
Sports
Nature
History
PUBLICATIONS:
Teton Magazine
Alaska Magazine
McMurdo Antartic Sun - Times
American Geographic
  Publishing
Appalachia
American Alpine Club
  Newsletter
Wyoming Backroads

BORDEN, LESLYE MICHLIN
6056 Corbin Ave.
Tarzana, CA 91356
Telephone: 818-342-2811
Fax: 818-343-9548
AFFILIATIONS:
ASMP, AIWF
PRINCIPAL SUBJECTS:
Food/Diet
PUBLICATIONS:
LA Times
Long Beach Press
San Francisco Chronicle
Chicago Tribune
Ft. Lauderdale Sun
Baltimore Sun
Family Circle
Cooking Light

BORDNICK, BARBARA
39 E. 19th St.
New York, NY 10003
Telephone: 212-533-1180

AFFILIATIONS:
ASMP, APA
PRINCIPAL SUBJECTS:
Fashion
Editorial
Personalities
Photography
PUBLICATIONS:
Geo
American Health
Life
Horizon
Newsweek
McCalls
Ladies
Home Journal
Redbook
Seventeen
Vogue
Avenue (Holland)
American Photographer
German Photography
Zoom
Lear's

BORNEFELD, WILLIAM
586 Hollywood Place
Saint Louis, MO 63119
Telephone: 314-962-5596
PRINCIPAL SUBJECTS:
The Arts

BOWDEN, BOB
P.O. Box 328
Nassau, DE 19969
Telephone: 302-645-4370
Fax: 305-583-2529
AFFILIATIONS:
PP of A
PRINCIPAL SUBJECTS:
Journalism
Nature
Science
Advertising
PUBLICATIONS:
Professional Photographers of
  America

BOWEN, JOHN
176 Halai Street
Hilo, HI 96720
Telephone: 808-935-2885
Fax: 808-935-7033
MAILING ADDRESS:
P.O. Box 1115
Hilo, HI 96721
AFFILIATIONS:
ASMP
PRINCIPAL SUBJECTS:
Nature
Agriculture

Nature
Science
Travel
PUBLICATIONS:
N.Y. Times
People Magazine
Woman's World

BOYER, DALE
P.O. Box 391535
Mountain View, CA 94039
Telephone: 415-964-3771
PRINCIPAL SUBJECTS:
Photography
Travel

BRADY ARCHITECTURAL
  PHOTOGRAPHY
Brady Architectural
  Photography
3939 Turnagain Blvd. E.
Anchorage, AK 99517
Telephone: 907-248-7500
Fax: 907-243-1684
AFFILIATIONS:
ASMP
PRINCIPAL SUBJECTS:
Architecture
Family
General Interest
Human Interest
Human Relations
Photography
PUBLICATIONS:
Alaska Gas & Oil Magazine
Architectural Digest
Sweets Catalogue
Alaska Business Monthly
Architectural Records

BRANDON, RANDY
700 W. 58th Aveneue, Suite D
Anchorage, AK 99518
Telephone: 907-783-2773
Fax: 907-783-2773
MAILING ADDRESS:
RANDY BRANDON
P.O. Box 1010
Girdwood, AK 99587
AFFILIATIONS:
ASMP
PRINCIPAL SUBJECTS:
Advertising
Architecture
Aviation
Business & Industry
Ecology
Editorial
Geography
Human Interest
Humor

Journalism
Marine
Nature
Travel
PUBLICATIONS:
Discover
Vogue
Sports Illustrated
Newsweek
National Geographic
National Wildlife
Playboy
Reader's Digest
Time
Vista
Esquire
Anchorage Daily News
Discover
Vogue
Sports Illustrated
Newsweek
National Geographic
National Wildlife
Playboy
Reader's Digest
Time
Vista
Esquire
Anchorage Daily News

BRAUN, BOB
3536 Edgewater Dr., #1
Orlando, FL 32804
Telephone: 407-425-7921
Fax: 407-841-4534
MAILING ADDRESS:
BOB BROWN
P.O. Box 547755
Orlando, FL 32854
AFFILIATIONS:
ASMP
PRINCIPAL SUBJECTS:
Editorial
Architecture
Business & Industry
Photography
Advertising
Home & Garden
Travel
The Arts
PUBLICATIONS:
Architectural Digest
Architectural Record
Antiques Magazine
Florida Designers Quarterly
MD Magazine
Professional Remodeling
Perfect Home
Better Homes & Gardens
Form & Function
Professional Builder

"Orlando" Magazine
Florida Builder
Metro Magazine

BRAUN, ERNEST
P.O. Box 627
San Anselmo, CA 94979
Telephone: 510-454-2791
AFFILIATIONS:
ASMP
PRINCIPAL SUBJECTS:
General Interest
Human Interest
Ecology
PUBLICATIONS:
Life
Audobon
Outdoor Photography
Fortune

BRESCOLL, JAMES
1315 West Roosevelt Road
Wheaton, IL 60187
Telephone: 708-665-1115
PRINCIPAL SUBJECTS:
Human Interest
Journalism

BRIGNOLO, JOSEPH B.
11 Oak Gate Drive
Hendersonvlle, NC 28739
Telephone: 704-696-3374
Fax: 704-696-3376
PRINCIPAL SUBJECTS:
Business & Industry
PUBLICATIONS:
American Photographer

BRINK, STEVEN
509 Devon Pl.
West Islip, NY 11795
Telephone: 516-661-5535
PRINCIPAL SUBJECTS:
Architecture
Business & Industry
PUBLICATIONS:
Babylon Beacon
Graphic
South Hampton Living
Suffolk Living

BRIZZI, ANDREA
405 W. 23rd St., #9B
New York, NY 10011
Telephone: 212-627-2341
AFFILIATIONS:
ASMP
PRINCIPAL SUBJECTS:
Architecture
Travel

PUBLICATIONS:
Interiors
Meeting News
Newsweek
Audio Video Interiors
Travel & Leisure

BROMLEY, DONALD
4455 N. Ashland
Chicago, IL 60640
Telephone: 312-334-3340
Fax: 312-334-5703
AFFILIATIONS:
ASMP
PRINCIPAL SUBJECTS:
Business & Industry
Editorial
Advertising
Entertainment
PUBLICATIONS:
Register Representative
Chicago Reader
Chicago Magazine
Family Business

BROOKS, CHARLES W.
800 Luttrell St.
Knoxville, TN 37917
Telephone: 615-525-4501
Fax: 615-546-1341
AFFILIATIONS:
ASMP
PRINCIPAL SUBJECTS:
Advertising
Editorial
General Interest
Journalism
Nature
Travel
PUBLICATIONS:
Time
Fortune
Parade
U.S. News & World Report
Sports Illustrated
Business Week
Prevention
Newsweek

BROOKS, RICHARD
  WEYMOUTH
2995 Woodside Rd., Ste. 400
Woodside, CA 94062
Telephone: 415-855-7100
PRINCIPAL SUBJECTS:
Geography
Nature
PUBLICATIONS:
Time/Life

BROWN, CONNIE
17 Ridgemont
Adrian, MI 49221
Telephone: 517-423-4129
AFFILIATIONS:
PPA, PPM, MTPPA
PRINCIPAL SUBJECTS:
Photography
PUBLICATIONS:
Range Finder
PPA Magazine

BROWN, JAMES
1349 E. McMillan St.
Cincinnati, OH 45206
Telephone: 513-221-1144
Fax: 569-860-8608
MAILING ADDRESS:
JAMES F. BROWN
  PHOTOGRAPHY
Cincinnati, OH 45206
Telephone: 513-321-0232
AFFILIATIONS:
ASMP
PRINCIPAL SUBJECTS:
Editorial
Animals
Food/Diet

BROWN, JIM
7964 S.E. Double Tree Dr.
Hobe Sound, FL 33455
Telephone: 407-283-2469
AFFILIATIONS:
ASMP
PRINCIPAL SUBJECTS:
Advertising
General Interest
Journalism
Marine
Photography
Sports
Travel
PUBLICATIONS:
Sail
Cruising World
Nautical Quarterly
National Geographic World
Time

BROWN-ROSNER, SHEREE
603 Joy Blvd.
Baldwin, NY 11510
Telephone: 516-868-6920
Fax: 516-485-0420
MAILING ADDRESS:
SHEREE BROWN-ROSNER
200 North Franklin St.
Hempstead, NY 11550
AFFILIATIONS:
ASMP, PPA

PRINCIPAL SUBJECTS:
Animals
Editorial
Education
Entertainment
Family
Government
Human Interest
Human Relations
Media
Motivation
News
Personalities
Photography
Senior Citizens
Sports
Video
PUBLICATIONS:
Newsday
Victorian Homes Magazine
Post Parade Magazine
Self Magazine
Photo District News
Art & Antiques Magazine
ASMP-LI Newsletter
Newsday
Victorian Homes Magazine
Post Parade Magazine
Self Magazine
Photo District News
Art & Antiques Magazine
ASMP-LI Newsletter

BROWNE, TURNER
137 30th Ave.
Seattle, WA 98122
Telephone: 206-322-0837
AFFILIATIONS:
ASMP
PRINCIPAL SUBJECTS:
Home & Garden
Architecture
Journalism
Food/Diet
Photography
Social Trends
Louisiana Life
PUBLICATIONS:
Designer's West
Country Inns
Creative Ideas
People
Natural History
Smithsonian
Southern Hearts

BRUNDEGE, BARBARA A.
P.O. Box 24571
San Jose, CA 95154
Telephone: 408-265-4627

AFFILIATIONS:
ASMP, OWAA
PRINCIPAL SUBJECTS:
Animals
Editorial
Food/Diet
Human Interest
Journalism
Motivation
Nature
Photography
Travel
Women's Interest
PUBLICATIONS:
National Geographic World
Smithsonian
Equinex
Outdoor Photographer
The Atlantic
Walking
Audubon
Sierra Club Books & More

BRYANT, D. DONNE
4036 Irvine St.
Baton Rouge, LA 70808
Telephone: 504-387-1620
Fax: 504-383-2951
MAILING ADDRESS:
DOUGLAS DONNE BRYANT
P.O. Box 80155
Baton Rouge, LA 70898
AFFILIATIONS:
ASPP
PUBLICATIONS:
OAS Americas Magazine
America Magazine
Bride's Magazine
Caribbean Travel
Endless Vacation
Southern Travel
World and I Magazine
Diversion
Discovery
Amoco Traveler
Viajando
Newsweek
New York Times

BUCK, BRUCE
39 W. 14th St.
New York, NY 10011
Telephone: 212-645-1022
AFFILIATIONS:
ASMP, APNY
PRINCIPAL SUBJECTS:
Advertising
Editorial
Fashion
PUBLICATIONS:
Cosmopolitan Magazine

Glamour
Simplicity Pattern Co.
New Body Magazine
American Woman

BUDROW, NANCY
600 S.W. 10th Ave., #424
Portland, OR 97205
Telephone: 503-225-0292
Fax: 503-227-7224
AFFILIATIONS:
ASMP, OPW, NASJA, NWWI
PRINCIPAL SUBJECTS:
Editorial
Government
History
Human Interest
Management
Marketing
Nature
Photography
Sports
PUBLICATIONS:
Las Vegas Magazine
Christian Science Monitor
Nordic West
The Oregonian
NW Magazine
Balloon Life
The Racer West
Ski Oregon

BULL, DAVID
6513 Carmen St.
Metairie, LA 70003
Telephone: 504-887-9633
Fax: 504-736-0464
AFFILIATIONS:
ASMP, AAUS
PRINCIPAL SUBJECTS:
Animals
Ecology
Editorial
Marine
Nature
PUBLICATIONS:
Parade
World & I
Texas Parks & Wildlife
Environment Magazine
Underwater USA
Health Magazine
Enterpreneur

BURGESS, MICHELE A.
20741 Catamaran Ln.
Huntington Beac, CA 92646
Telephone: 714-536-6104
Fax: 714-536-6578
AFFILIATIONS:
SATW

PRINCIPAL SUBJECTS:
Travel
Animals
Editorial
Photography
Human Interest
Nature
PUBLICATIONS:
Travel & Leisure
Travel Holiday
Westways
Inflight Magazines (American,
    Delta, Alaska)
MotorHome
Trailer Life
Cruise Travel
Vogue
Tours & Resorts
Vista/USA
MD
Glamour
Essence
Far East Traveler
Nissan Discovery
Northwest Magazine
Off Duty
Bridal Guide
Houston Chronicle
Los Angeles Herald - Examiner
Portland Oregonian
Relax

BURLINGAME, JACK
One Crandall St.
Binghamton, NY 13905
Telephone: 607-722-4487
AFFILIATIONS:
PPA
PRINCIPAL SUBJECTS:
Advertising
Architecture

BURNS, STEVE
P.O. Box 175
Westwood, NJ 07675
Telephone: 201-358-1890
AFFILIATIONS:
ASMP
PRINCIPAL SUBJECTS:
Photography
Business & Industry
Advertising
Editorial
Ecology
PUBLICATIONS:
Inc. Magazine
Ford Dealer World
NCR Alpha
Corporate Showcase 8,9,10

BURROUGHS, ROBERT
6713 Bardonia Street
San Diego, CA 92119
Telephone: 619-469-6922
Fax: 619-469-6922
AFFILIATIONS:
ASMP, NPPA
PRINCIPAL SUBJECTS:
Aviation
Sports
Nature
Computer Technology
PUBLICATIONS:
N.Y. Times
Business Week
Forbes
Newsweek
Time

BURY, SUSAN
8 Linda Lane
Bethel, CT 06801
Telephone: 203-743-5761
PRINCIPAL SUBJECTS:
Advertising
Aviation
Family
Photography
PUBLICATIONS:
Business Digest

BUSCH, SCHERLEY
Busch, Scherley Photography
4186 Pamona Ave.
Miami, FL 33133
Telephone: 305-661-6605
Fax: 305-443-5124
AFFILIATIONS:
ASMP
PRINCIPAL SUBJECTS:
Advertising
Architecture
Editorial
Fashion
Health
Media
Personalities
Travel
PUBLICATIONS:
A.P.
Miami Herald
New Miami Magazine
South Florida Magazine

BUSH, CHAN
P.O. Box 819
Montrose, CA 91021
Telephone: 818-957-6558
MAILING ADDRESS:
CHAN BUSH PHOTOGRAPHY
Montrose, CA 91021

PRINCIPAL SUBJECTS:
Photography
Advertising
PUBLICATIONS:
Life
Random House
Golf Digest
Geo Magazine
Ford Times
L.A. Times
Datsun Discovery
Automobile
Golf Illustrated
Business Week
Car & Driver
Popular Science
Family Circle

BUSH, DARRYL W.
2568 24th Ave.
San Francisco, CA 94116
Telephone: 415-664-5247
PRINCIPAL SUBJECTS:
Editorial
News
Business & Industry
Personalities
Sports
Nature
Animals
Journalism
PUBLICATIONS:
Marine World Africa USA
San Francisco
    Chronicle/Examiner
Los Angeles Times
Shaklee Alive

BUSHUE, KATHY
Bushue, Kathy Photography
P.O. Box 190851
Anchorage, AK 99519
Telephone: 907-272-7887
Fax: 907-277-5902
AFFILIATIONS:
ASMP, APW
PRINCIPAL SUBJECTS:
Advertising
Aviation
Ecology
Editorial
Marine
Nature
Photography
Animals
PUBLICATIONS:
Newsweek
Audubon
National Wildlife
Natural History
Life Magazine

Field & Stream
Time
National Geographic World

BUTLER, TIM
8509 Summerfield Ln.
Huntersville, NE 28078
Telephone: 704-948-0641
AFFILIATIONS:
PP of A, ITVA
PRINCIPAL SUBJECTS:
Advertising
Business & Industry
Education
Human Relations
Media
Nature
News
Personalities

BUTTON DOWN
    PRODUCTIONS LTD.
Button Down Productions Ltd.
925 W. Cullom
Chicago, IL 60613
Telephone: 312-525-6661
Fax: 708-437-6402
AFFILIATIONS:
ASMP
PRINCIPAL SUBJECTS:
Advertising
Automotive
Entertainment
Fashion
Food/Diet
Health
Human Interest
Marketing
Men's Interest
Personal Finance
Personalities
Photography
Physical Fitness
Social Trends
Sports
The Arts
Travel
Youth
PUBLICATIONS:
Chicago Magazine
Business Week
Chicago Tribune Magazine

BUZBY, SHERRIE
1891 Vineway Dr., Unit 32
Canton, MI 48188
Telephone: 313-397-2440
AFFILIATIONS:
NPPA, MPPA, WICI
PRINCIPAL SUBJECTS:
Journalism

Sports
Editorial
Advertising
News
PUBLICATIONS:
Phoenix Magazine
Sunset Magazine
Ann Arbor News
Philadelphia Daily News
Observer & Eccentric
  Newspapers

CABANBAN, ORLANDO R.
531 S. Plymouth Ct.
Chicago, IL 60605
Telephone: 312-922-1836
AFFILIATIONS:
ASMP
PRINCIPAL SUBJECTS:
Architecture
PUBLICATIONS:
Progressive Architecture
Architectural Record
Interiors Magazine

CAHEN, ROBERT
2725 Ralston Avenue
Burlingame, CA 94010
Telephone: 415-342-6333
Fax: 415-342-6334
PRINCIPAL SUBJECTS:
The Arts
Travel

CALDWELL, JIM
101 W. Drew Ave.
Houston, TX 77006
Telephone: 713-527-9121
Fax: 713-527-9121
MAILING ADDRESS:
CALDWELL PHOTOGRAPHY
Houston, TX 77006
AFFILIATIONS:
ASMP
PRINCIPAL SUBJECTS:
Business & Industry
Advertising
Editorial
The Arts
Travel

CAMPBELL, J. KENT
86 University Ave.
Rochester, NY 14610
Telephone: 716-482-0550
Fax: 716-482-5648
AFFILIATIONS:
PPA, PPSNY,GRPP
PRINCIPAL SUBJECTS:
Editorial
Travel

PUBLICATIONS:
Transeat
Business Week
Red Book

CAMPBELL, THOMAS S.
772 San Antonio Dr.
Atlanta, GA 30306
Telephone: 404-885-3316
Fax: 404-885-3900
AFFILIATIONS:
PPFA
PRINCIPAL SUBJECTS:
Business & Industry
Advertising
News

CAMPBELL, TOM
2018 Meadow Valley Terrace
Los Angeles, CA 90039
Telephone: 213-661-9288
Fax: 213-661-0079
AFFILIATIONS:
ASMP, PPA, APA
PRINCIPAL SUBJECTS:
Advertising
Aviation
Business & Industry
Computer Technology
Entertainment
Fashion
Men's Interest
Personalities
Photography
Senior Citizens
The Arts
Travel
PUBLICATIONS:
Travel & Leisure
Time
National Geographic
Fleguert Flyer
Professional Photographer
Studio Photographs
US Air Magazine
Hosseblad Magazine

CAPOTOSTO, JOHN J.
P.O. Box 445
East Northport, NY 11731
Telephone: 516-462-6228
Fax: 516-462-5793
AFFILIATIONS:
GRPP,PPSNY,PPA
PRINCIPAL SUBJECTS:
Architecture
Editorial
General Interest
PUBLICATIONS:
Woodworker

CARDACINO, MICHAEL
20 Ridge Rd.
Douglaston, NY 11363
Telephone: 718-224-0426
Fax: 718-631-0308
PRINCIPAL SUBJECTS:
Ecology
Human Interest
Travel

CARLEBACH, MICHAEL L.
3634 Bayview Road
Miami, FL 33133
Telephone: 305-446-4075
AFFILIATIONS:
ASMP, PPA
PRINCIPAL SUBJECTS:
Architecture
General Interest
Amusements
PUBLICATIONS:
Time
Newsweek
Fortune
Business Week

CARR, KATHLEEN THORMOD
2126 Green Hill Rd.
Sebastopol, CA 95473
Telephone: 707-829-5649
Fax: 707-829-5649
AFFILIATIONS:
ASMP
PRINCIPAL SUBJECTS:
Advertising
Editorial
Marine
Nature
Personalities
The Arts
Travel
PUBLICATIONS:
Prevention Magazine
Utne Reader
Outdoor Photographer
U.S. News & World Report
New Age Journal
Psychology Today
Esquire
San Francisco Magazine

CARRIKER, RONALD
  PHOTOGRAPHY
Carriker, Ronald Photography
P.O. Box 24187
Winston-Salem, NC 27114
Telephone: 919-765-3852
Fax: 919-765-3960
AFFILIATIONS:
ASMP

PRINCIPAL SUBJECTS:
Advertising
Business & Industry
Fashion
Medical
PUBLICATIONS:
Medical Economics

CARROLL, HANSON
New Boston Rd.
Norwich, VT 05055
Telephone: 802-649-1094
AFFILIATIONS:
ASMP
PRINCIPAL SUBJECTS:
Architecture
Marine
Nature
Sports
PUBLICATIONS:
Better Homes & Gardens
Field & Stream
Smithsonian
O T Life
Farm Journal
Sports Illustrated

CARROLL, TOM
Carroll, Tom Photography, Inc.
26712 Calle Los Alamos
Capistrano Beach, CA 92624
Telephone: 714-493-2665
Fax: 714-493-0758
AFFILIATIONS:
ASMP, ADS
PRINCIPAL SUBJECTS:
Advertising
Computer Technology
Electronics
General Interest
Geography
Government
Journalism
Management
Marketing
Men's Interest
Motivation
Nature
Personal Finance
Personalities
Photography
Psychology
Religion
Sales
Senior Citizens
Social Trends
Travel
Women's Interest
World Affairs

CARRUTHERS, ROBERT J.
60 Phyllis Dr.
Patchogue, NY 11772
Telephone: 516-289-2485
Fax: 516-289-0322
AFFILIATIONS:
ASMP, PPA
PRINCIPAL SUBJECTS:
Architecture
Science
Foreign

CARRUZZA
162 N. State St.
Chicago, IL 60601
Telephone: 312-782-2462
Fax: 312-782-4090
MAILING ADDRESS:
MARSHALL
   PHOTOGRAPHER, INC.
Chicago, IL 60601
Telephone: 312-725-3926
PRINCIPAL SUBJECTS:
Advertising
Photography

CARTER, BILL
39 E. 12th St.
New York, NY 10003
Telephone: 212-505-6088
AFFILIATIONS:
ASMP
PRINCIPAL SUBJECTS:
Nature
Travel
Photography
PUBLICATIONS:
Popular Photography
Modern Photography
Life

CARTER, WILLIAM
809 San Antonio Rd.
Palo Alto, CA 94303
Telephone: 415-858-2040
AFFILIATIONS:
ASMP, IB
PRINCIPAL SUBJECTS:
Geography
Nature
Travel
Photography
The Arts
Entertainment
PUBLICATIONS:
Life
New York Times
Time
Sunset
Los Angeles Times

CASSILL, KAY
22 Boylston Ave.
Providence, RI 02906
Telephone: 401-751-4949
AFFILIATIONS:
ASJA, AG, AWP
PRINCIPAL SUBJECTS:
The Arts
General Interest
Human Interest
Amusements
Travel
PUBLICATIONS:
Cosmopolitan
Ladies Home Journal
People Magazine
McCalls
Viva
Marathon World
Discovery
Yankee
American Artist
Smithsonian
Saturday Review
Better Homes And Gardens

CASTANEDA, LUIS
14778 SW 81 St.
Miami, FL 33193
Telephone: 305-387-1267
Fax: 305-387-1267
AFFILIATIONS:
ASMP
PRINCIPAL SUBJECTS:
Advertising
Amusements
Animals
Architecture
Editorial
Foreign
General Interest
Geography
Human Interest
Human Relations
Nature
Photography
Sports
The Arts
Travel
PUBLICATIONS:
Dance Magazine
Photo District News
Color Foto (Germany)
Geomundo (Latin
   America-USA-Mexico)
Gente/Viajes (Spain)

CAVANAUGH, JAMES
32 Calvin Ct., South
Tonawanda, NY 14150
Telephone: 716-838-8018

Fax: 716-838-8022
AFFILIATIONS:
ASMP
PRINCIPAL SUBJECTS:
Architecture
Aviation
Business & Industry
Photography
PUBLICATIONS:
Business Week
Reader's Digest
Rangefinder

CENDROWSKI, DWIGHT
2870 Easy St.
Ann Arbor, MI 48104
Telephone: 313-971-3107
Fax: 313-971-9232
AFFILIATIONS:
ASMP
PRINCIPAL SUBJECTS:
Business & Industry
Editorial
Education
General Interest
Journalism
Medical
Photography
PUBLICATIONS:
Crain's Detroit Business
Corporate Detroit
Chrysler Times
Mothering Magazine

CERNY, PAUL
5200 Wood Street
Zephyrhills, FL 33541
Telephone: 800-788-5134
Fax: 813-782-4386
MAILING ADDRESS:
5200 Wood St.
Zephyr Hills, FL 33541
Telephone: 813-782-4386
AFFILIATIONS:
ASMP, PPA
PRINCIPAL SUBJECTS:
Business & Industry
Advertising
Architecture
Editorial
PUBLICATIONS:
Shell Oil Co. Annual Report
Water Well Journal
Newsweek
Time
Business Week
Travel & Leisure
U.S. Journal/Medical
   Economic Magazine

CHAMBERLAIN JR.,
   ROBERT M.
420 W. Francis St.
Aspen, CO 81611
Telephone: 303-925-7509
AFFILIATIONS:
ASMP
PRINCIPAL SUBJECTS:
Journalism
Sports
PUBLICATIONS:
Ski
Skier's Gazette
Mountain Gazette
Aspen Illustrated News
Aspen Times
Western Skier
Skier's Digest
Sunset
Pacific Sun
Majority Of One
Powder
Journey West
Aspen Magazine
Women's Wear Daily
Rogue
Telluride Times
City Sports Monthly
Cruising World
Skiing

CHAMPAGNE, BARRY
Champagne, Barry
   Photography, Inc.
18119 Lake Bend Dr.
Houston, TX 77084
Telephone: 713-463-4264
Fax: 713-463-4264
AFFILIATIONS:
ASMP
PRINCIPAL SUBJECTS:
Advertising
Business & Industry
Computer Technology
Marketing
Photography
Travel
PUBLICATIONS:
Texas Sourcebook

CHANDOHA, WALTER
50 Spring Hill Rd.
Annandale, NJ 08801
Telephone: 908-782-3666
AFFILIATIONS:
ASMP, GWAA
PRINCIPAL SUBJECTS:
Animals
Nature
Home & Garden
Editorial

Food/Diet
Photography
PUBLICATIONS:
National Geographic
Family Circle
Woman's Day
Ladies Home Journal
McCall's
House Beautiful
Forbes
N.Y. Times
Parade
Country Journal
Horticulture
House & Garden
Peterson's Photographic
Money
Organic Gardening
Womans World
Architectural Digest
Good Housekeeping
Flower & Garden
Home Mechanix
World & I
Westin

CHAPUT, SIMON
25 Mercer St.
New York, NY 10013
Telephone: 212-334-1848
Fax: 212-274-1620
MAILING ADDRESS:
CHOPUT, SIMON
P.O. Box 2029, Canal St. Sta.
New York, NY 10013
AFFILIATIONS:
F.P.A., ASMP
PRINCIPAL SUBJECTS:
Editorial
Photography
PUBLICATIONS:
Smithsonian Air & Space
New Age Journal
New York Times
T.V. Guide
Le Figaro (France)
Front Cover (G.B.)

CHARETTE, MARK
1701 N. Potomac St.
Arlington, VA 22205
Telephone: 703-532-3495
PRINCIPAL SUBJECTS:
Government
Nature
Advertising

CHARLES, CINDY
Charles, Cindy Photographer
1129 Folsom Street
San Francisco, CA 94103

AFFILIATIONS:
ASMP
PRINCIPAL SUBJECTS:
Advertising
Business & Industry
Computer Technology
Editorial
Education
Journalism
Photography
PUBLICATIONS:
Time
Forbes
International Business
Computer World

CHARLES, FREDERICK
254 Park Avenue, South, 7f
New York, NY 10010
Telephone: 212-505-0686
PRINCIPAL SUBJECTS:
Architecture
Entertainment
Food/Diet
Business & Industry
History
The Arts
PUBLICATIONS:
Newsweek
Fortune
Time
Businessweek
New York Magazine

CHESLER, DONNA & KEN
6941 NW 12th St.
Plantation, FL 33313
Telephone: 305-581-6489
Fax: 305-581-3678
AFFILIATIONS:
PPA, PAPI
PRINCIPAL SUBJECTS:
Home & Garden
Architecture
Aviation
The Arts
Marine
PUBLICATIONS:
Power & Motor Yacht
View on Design
Florida Builders
Show Boats International

CHESLER, KEN
6941 NE 12th St.
Plantation, FL 33313
Telephone: 305-581-6489
Fax: 305-581-3678
AFFILIATIONS:
PP of A

PRINCIPAL SUBJECTS:
Architecture
Photography
Marine
Advertising
PUBLICATIONS:
Showboats International
Yachts Premiere
Power & Motor Yachts
Florida Design
Audio-Video Interiors
Palm Beach Life

CHESTER, MARK S.
P.O. Box 640501
San Francisco, CA 94164
Telephone: 415-922-7512
AFFILIATIONS:
ASMP, SPE
PRINCIPAL SUBJECTS:
Travel
Human Interest
PUBLICATIONS:
"The Photographer As Travel
   Writer"
Exhibition Catalogs

CHEW, JOHN T.
P.O. Box 382
Wayne, PA 19087
Telephone: 215-688-9431
AFFILIATIONS:
ASMP
PRINCIPAL SUBJECTS:
Advertising
Architecture
Photography
Video
PUBLICATIONS:
Sotheby's Preview

CHIKA
Chika
P.O. Box 930
Beverly Hills, CA 90213
Telephone: 310-276-8884
Fax: 310-276-8884
AFFILIATIONS:
ASMP, FPC
PRINCIPAL SUBJECTS:
Advertising
Editorial
Entertainment
Foreign
General Interest
Human Interest
Journalism
Media
News
Photography
Sports

PUBLICATIONS:
New York Daily News
Nikkan Sports Paper (Japan)
L'Equipe
Sports Illustrated (Japan)
World Boxing (Japan)

CHIN, RUTH
1007 N. Tillotson Ave.
Muncie, IN 47304
Telephone: 317-284-4582
Fax: 317-284-4582
MAILING ADDRESS:
RUTH CHIN
1007 N. Tillotson
Muncie, IN 47304
AFFILIATIONS:
ASMP,NFPW,MTWA
PRINCIPAL SUBJECTS:
Animals
Human Interest
Nature
News
Travel
Foreign
Business & Industry
PUBLICATIONS:
Travel/Holiday
Reader's Digest Books
Ceramics Monthly
Trailer Life Publications
Retirement Living
Muncie Star Weekly Column
United Press International
Meridian Publications
Webb Co. Publications
Ford Times
News & Views
Online Today
Indiana Horizons
Farm Futures

CHINITZ, ADAM
43 W. 24th St., #3B
New York, NY 10010
Telephone: 212-727-7506
Fax: 212-243-7878
AFFILIATIONS:
ASMP
PRINCIPAL SUBJECTS:
Advertising
Fashion
Marine
Photography
Science
Youth
PUBLICATIONS:
Interview
Harper's Bazzar
New York Magazine
Wall Street Journal

W Magazine
Art News
Art & Antique
Daily News Sunday Magazine

CHURCH, DENNIS
301 S. Bedford St., #6
Madison, WI 53703
Telephone: 608-255-2726
Fax: 608-255-2482
AFFILIATIONS:
ASMP
PRINCIPAL SUBJECTS:
Advertising
Family
Journalism
Personalities
Photography
PUBLICATIONS:
Better Homes & Gardens
American Lawyer
Managers Magazine
Milwaukee Journal
American Druggist
Chicago Tribune

CHWATSKY, ANN
111 Fourth Ave., 7c
New York, NY 10003
Telephone: 212-673-5689
Fax: 516-678-5080
AFFILIATIONS:
ASMP, PP of A, PWP
PUBLICATIONS:
Architectural Digest
Glamour
Machete
Metropolitan Home
Newsday
New York Times
Time

CIRONE, BETTINA
260 W. 52nd St.
New York, NY 10019
Telephone: 212-262-3062
AFFILIATIONS:
PPA
PRINCIPAL SUBJECTS:
Personalities
The Arts
Travel
General Interest
Human Interest
PUBLICATIONS:
People
US
Daily News
N. Y. Times
N. Y. Post
Ladies Home Journal

Cosmopolitan
Vogue
Playboy
Bunte (Germany)
Travel/Holiday
Travel Agent
Gente
Revista
Sunday (London)
Epoca
Oggi (Italy)
Blick (Switzerland)
American Photographer
Scope (South Africa)
Hola (Spain)
Vanidades (South America)
Geo Mundo
Photo District News
American Photographer
Quick (Germany)
Globe
Annabella
Gioia
Panorama
Bolero
Eva Express
ID Press
Norsk Ukeblad
Saxon & Linds
Allers
Husmodern
Min Varld
Garbo
Doce
Hitkrant
Grazia
Novella 2000
Heiwa Shuppan
USA Today
Hello! (London)

CLARK, H. DEAN
5315 FM 1960 W.
Houston, TX 77069
Telephone: 713-537-6262
AFFILIATIONS:
ASMP
PRINCIPAL SUBJECTS:
Advertising
Animals
Business & Industry
Personalities
Photography
PUBLICATIONS:
Oil & Gas Journal
Houston Chronicle
Houston Post

CLARK, JUNEBUG
36264 Freedom Rd.
Farmington, MI 48335

Telephone: 313-478-3666
AFFILIATIONS:
ASMP
PRINCIPAL SUBJECTS:
Advertising
General Interest
PUBLICATIONS:
Time
Life
People
Newsweek
National Geographic

CLARKSON, FRANK
855 Islington Street, #111
Portsmouth, NH 03801
Telephone: 603-427-0006
Fax: 603-427-0273
MAILING ADDRESS:
FRANK CLARKSON
P.O. Box 148
Portsmouth, NH 03802-0148
AFFILIATIONS:
ASMP
PRINCIPAL SUBJECTS:
Advertising
Architecture
Editorial
Health
Medical
PUBLICATIONS:
Inc.
Yankee
Harrowsmith Country Life
Down East
New England Business
Historic Preservation
Inc.
Yankee
Harrowsmith Country Life
Down East
New England Business
Historic Preservation

CLARKSON, RICHARD C.
3200 Cherry Creek South
  Drive, The Citadel, #650
Denver, CO 80209
Telephone: 303-744-2538
Fax: 303-744-2556
AFFILIATIONS:
ASMP, NPPA
PRINCIPAL SUBJECTS:
News
Sports
The Arts
Advertising
PUBLICATIONS:
Sports Illustrated
Time
Life

Runner's World
The Runner
Playboy
Money
Fortune
National Geographic
Stern
New York Times Magazine

CLARKSON, ROBERT NOEL
401 North Hoback Street
Helena, MT 59601
Telephone: 406-442-2046
Fax: 406-442-2046
AFFILIATIONS:
ASMP
PRINCIPAL SUBJECTS:
Entertainment
Government
Editorial
Advertising
PUBLICATIONS:
Parade
ABA Journal

CLEFF, BERNIE
715 Pine St.
Philadelphia, PA 19106
Telephone: 215-922-4246
AFFILIATIONS:
ASMP
PRINCIPAL SUBJECTS:
Advertising
Editorial
Human Interest
The Arts
Architecture
PUBLICATIONS:
Fortune
Smithsonian
National Sculpture Review
Business Week
Forbes
Venture
Farm Journal
The Cape May Handbook
Changing Times
Medical Economics

CLEMENTS, STEPHEN P.
725 N. 77th
Seattle, WA 98103
Telephone: 206-784-1154
Fax: 206-782-4460
AFFILIATIONS:
ASMP, NOWA
PRINCIPAL SUBJECTS:
Advertising
Animals
Nature
Sports

PUBLICATIONS:
Backpacker
Outside

CLYMER, JONATHAN
180-F Central Avenue
Englewood, NJ 07631
Telephone: 201-568-1760
AFFILIATIONS:
ASMP
PRINCIPAL SUBJECTS:
Advertising
Business & Industry
Medical

COGSWELL, JENNIFER D.
Stockslides
6 Overlook Rd.
Waltham, MA 02154
Telephone: 617-891-5849
Fax: 617-891-9696
AFFILIATIONS:
ISMP, NEPA, ITVA, WIF&V
PRINCIPAL SUBJECTS:
Computer Technology
Editorial
History
Motivation
Photography
Social Trends
The Arts
Travel
Video
Women's Interest
PUBLICATIONS:
Changing Times Magazine
Ogden Leisure Times

COHEN, ANDY
4611 S. Univeristy Dr., #251
Davie, FL 33328
Telephone: 305-967-6742
Fax: 305-967-6743
AFFILIATIONS:
ASMP
PRINCIPAL SUBJECTS:
Advertising
Animals
Architecture
Automotive
Editorial
Entertainment
Fashion
General Interest
Health
Human Interest
Human Relations
Humor
Journalism
Nature
News

Senior Citizens
PUBLICATIONS:
Birdtalk
Wildlife Conservation
Das Tier (Germany)
American Cagebird

COHEN, DAN
1003 Justin Ln., #2093
Austin, TX 78757
Telephone: 512-458-1659
AFFILIATIONS:
ASMP
PRINCIPAL SUBJECTS:
Advertising
Editorial
Marketing
Media
Medical
Travel

COHEN, STUART
P.O. Box 2007
Salem, MA 01970
Telephone: 617-631-7150
AFFILIATIONS:
ASMP, ASPP
PRINCIPAL SUBJECTS:
Education
Geography
Photography
Travel
PUBLICATIONS:
Fortune
Ski
Endless Vacation
Boston Magazine
Trade Publications
Educational Materials

COLBERT, JUDY
12411 Sexton Lane
Bowie, MD 20715
Telephone: 301-262-0177
PUBLICATIONS:
Washington Post
Prince George's Magazine
Recreation Register
Bowie News
Evening Capital
Bowie Blade
Women In Advertising And
  Marketing
Business of Travel
Health - Handicap
American Way
Boston Globe
AAA World
San Diego Union
Oakland Tribune
St. Petersburg Times

Baltimore Sun
Newsday
Providence Journal
Charlotte Observer
San Antonio Express - News
Review
Washington Post
Prince George's Magazine
Women in Advertising &
  Marketing
Akron Beacon Journal
Corridor
Vocational Biographies
WDS Forum
Pool & Spa News
Travel Woman

COLBROTH, RON
8610 Battailles Court
Annandale, VA 22003
Telephone: 703-978-5879
Fax: 703-978-1319
AFFILIATIONS:
ASMP, NPPA
PRINCIPAL SUBJECTS:
Travel
Urban Affairs
Human Interest
PUBLICATIONS:
National Geographic Treweller
Washington Post
U.S. News & World Report
Sky
Esquire (Japan)
Alona
Wing Span (Japan)

COLEMAN, GENE
250 W. 27th St.
New York, NY 10001
Telephone: 212-691-4752
Fax: 212-633-6537
AFFILIATIONS:
ASMP
PRINCIPAL SUBJECTS:
Advertising
Agriculture
Editorial
Food/Diet
Health
Nature
Photography
PUBLICATIONS:
Gentlemen's Quarterly
Cigar Aficionado
Longevity
Rolling Stone
Stereo Review
Sound & Image
Living Well
Food Arts

COLEMAN, PH.D.,
  REV. CHERYL L.
2261 Market St., Ste. 238
San Francisco, CA 94114
Telephone: 415-863-1527
Fax: 415-552-6615
AFFILIATIONS:
ASMP
PRINCIPAL SUBJECTS:
Architecture
Health
Religion
Senior Citizens
Women's Interest
Youth
PUBLICATIONS:
U.L.C. News

COLLINS, ARLENE
64 N. Moore St., 3e
New York, NY 10013
Telephone: 212-431-9117
Fax: 212-226-8466
AFFILIATIONS:
ASMP
PRINCIPAL SUBJECTS:
Editorial
Business & Industry
Travel
PUBLICATIONS:
New York Times
American Lawyer
NCR
World Press Review

COLLINS, SHELDAN
26 Clifton Terrace
Weehawken, NJ 07087
Telephone: 201-867-6297
Fax: 201-867-6047
PRINCIPAL SUBJECTS:
The Arts
Architecture

COLMAN III, BEN
1660 Broadway
Ann Arbor, MI 48105
Telephone: 313-741-8037
AFFILIATIONS:
ASMP
PRINCIPAL SUBJECTS:
Advertising
Agriculture
Business & Industry
Computer Technology
Ecology
Editorial
Education
General Interest
Human Interest
Human Relations

Marketing
Media
Medical
Nature
Physical Fitness
Sports
The Arts
Travel
Urban Affairs
PUBLICATIONS:
Parade
Paddler

COLTON, ROBERT
1700 York Ave.
New York, NY 10128
Telephone: 212-831-3953
AFFILIATIONS:
ASMP
PRINCIPAL SUBJECTS:
Human Interest
Sports
Architecture
Aviation
Business & Industry
PUBLICATIONS:
Penthouse

COMET, RENEE
Comet, Renee Photography
410 8th Street, N.W., #302
Washington, DC 20004
Telephone: 202-347-3408
Fax: 202-393-0080
AFFILIATIONS:
ASMP
PRINCIPAL SUBJECTS:
Advertising
Editorial
Food/Diet
PUBLICATIONS:
Washington Post Magazine
Washingtonian
Islands Magazine
Maryland Magazine
Esquire Magazine
GQ Magazine
Eating Well Magazine

CONDIT, DONALD G.
1632 S.E. 10th
Portland, OR 97214
Telephone: 503-232-7723
Fax: 503-231-9816
AFFILIATIONS:
PPA,CPO,PAF,PMA
PRINCIPAL SUBJECTS:
General Interest
PUBLICATIONS:
Glamour
Seventeen

Sunset
True
Ski
Vogue
Architectural Digest

CONLEY, CHARLES R.
Tempe, AZ 85281
Telephone: 602-966-1882
MAILING ADDRESS:
P.O. Box 3116
Tempe, AZ 85280
AFFILIATIONS:
PPA,CPO,PAF,PMA
PRINCIPAL SUBJECTS:
General Interest
Human Interest
News
PUBLICATIONS:
Sports Illustrated
Playboy
Mechanic Illustrated

CONNER, GARY
1331 Amherst Ave., 14
Los Angeles, CA 90025
Telephone: 310-447-1602
PRINCIPAL SUBJECTS:
Editorial
Aviation
Architecture
Travel
PUBLICATIONS:
AIA Journal
Daily Variety
Palm Springs Magazine
Phi Delta Kappa Journal
Puerto Rico Magazine
Architectural Record

CONRAD, CHRISTOPHER
333 2nd Ave. West
Seattle, WA 98119
Telephone: 206-284-5663
Fax: 206-281-9156
AFFILIATIONS:
ASMP
PRINCIPAL SUBJECTS:
Advertising
Editorial
Food/Diet
Home & Garden
Marketing
PUBLICATIONS:
Wall Street Journal
T.V. Guide
Restaurant Business
New York Times
House & Garden

COOKE, JERRY
175 Further Lane
East Hampton, NY 11937
Telephone: 516-324-3375
MAILING ADDRESS:
JERRY COOKE INC.
P.O. Box 770
East Hampton, NY 11937
PRINCIPAL SUBJECTS:
Animals
Amusements
Sports
Travel
Advertising
Nature

COOKE, JOHN DR.
P.O. Box 171
Dutch Flat, CA 95714
Telephone: 916-389-2167
AFFILIATIONS:
ASMP
PRINCIPAL SUBJECTS:
Advertising
Animals
Ecology
Electronics
Nature
Photography
Science
Travel
PUBLICATIONS:
National Geographic
Natural History
Omni
Science
Ranger Rider
International Wildlife

COONRAD, JORDAN
P.O. Box 2878
Alameda, CA 94501
Telephone: 510-769-9766
AFFILIATIONS:
ASMP; PPA
PRINCIPAL SUBJECTS:
Advertising
Aviation
Business & Industry
Geography
Journalism
Military
Nature
Sports
PUBLICATIONS:
Air & Space
Flying
Golf
National Geogrpahic

Oceans
Omni
U.S. New & World Report

COOPER, ED
P.O. Box G
El Verano, CA 95433
Telephone: 707-996-1934
AFFILIATIONS:
ASMP
PRINCIPAL SUBJECTS:
Editorial
Geography
Nature
Photography
Travel
PUBLICATIONS:
National Geographic
Audubon
Outside
Sunset
Modern Maturity

COOPER, TOM
7795 Fairview, 2
Boise, ID 83704
Telephone: 208-323-0022
Fax: 208-377-1117
PRINCIPAL SUBJECTS:
Advertising
Ecology
Editorial
Family
Family
Home & Garden
Military
Sports
PUBLICATIONS:
Texas Monthly
Idaho Statesman

CORSALE, LORRAINE
1 Montgomery Place
Brooklyn, NY 11215
Telephone: 718-789-7088
PRINCIPAL SUBJECTS:
Editorial
Human Interest
Human Relations
Journalism
Medical
News
PUBLICATIONS:
Smithsonian Magazine
Town & Country
New York Times Magazine

CORY, JEFF
Impact Image
352 SW 15 Rd., Nr1
Miami, FL 33129

Telephone: 305-285-0261
Fax: 305-285-0261
AFFILIATIONS:
ASMP
PRINCIPAL SUBJECTS:
Advertising
Agriculture
Architecture
Aviation
Business & Industry
Ecology
Editorial
Education
Entertainment
Fashion
Foreign
General Interest
Geography
Government
Health
Marine
Medical
Men's Interest
Military
Nature
News
Physical Fitness
Religion
Sports
Travel
Urban Affairs
World Affairs

COSTE, KURT
929 Julia Street
New Orleans, LA 70113
Telephone: 504-523-6060
Fax: 504-525-2993
AFFILIATIONS:
ASMP
PRINCIPAL SUBJECTS:
Advertising
Architecture
Business & Industry
Computer Technology
Fashion
Health
Home & Garden
Medical
Video
PUBLICATIONS:
Better Homes
Where Magazines
10,000 Eyes
Passion
Times Picayune

COX, DENNIS
22111 Cleveland, #211
Dearborn, MI 48124
Telephone: 313-561-1842

Fax: 313-561-1842
AFFILIATIONS:
ASMP, ASPP
PRINCIPAL SUBJECTS:
Advertising
Agriculture
Amusements
Architecture
Automotive
Business & Industry
Computer Technology
Ecology
Editorial
Education
Electronics
Entertainment
Family
Foreign
General Interest
Geography
Government
Health
History
Hobbies
Home & Garden
Human Interest
Human Relations
Journalism
Management
Marketing
Media
Medical
Men's Interest
News
Personal Finance
Personalities
Photography
Physical Fitness
Psychology
Religion
Sales
Science
Senior Citizens
Social Trends
The Arts
Travel
Urban Affairs
Youth
PUBLICATIONS:
Forbes
Business Week
Newsweek
Midwest Living
Smithsonian
Historic Preservation
Money
Time

CRAMER, BILL
301 N. 3rd St.
Philadelphia, PA 19106

Telephone: 215-922-4155
PRINCIPAL SUBJECTS:
Journalism
News

CRANDALL, ALISSA
6200 Bubbling Brook
Anchorage, AK 99516
Telephone: 907-346-1001
Fax: 907-346-1001
AFFILIATIONS:
APW, ASMP
PRINCIPAL SUBJECTS:
Journalism
Nature
Photography
Travel
PUBLICATIONS:
Alaska Magazine
Outdoor Photographer
   Magazine
BBC Wildlife Magazine
Outside Magazine
Smithsonian Magazine
Equinox Magazine

CRANE, ARNOLD
680 N. Lakeshore Drive, #1202
Chicago, IL 60611
Telephone: 312-337-5544
Fax: 312-337-5747
AFFILIATIONS:
ASMP, NPPA
PRINCIPAL SUBJECTS:
Advertising
Foreign
General Interest
Health
Medical
Photography
The Arts
Travel
PUBLICATIONS:
Life
Look
Chicago Magazine
Chicago Sun Times
Chicago Tribune

CRAWFORD, PAT
918 Lady St.
Columbia, SC 29201
Telephone: 803-799-0894
Fax: 803-779-3394
MAILING ADDRESS:
PAT CRAWFORD
P.O. Box 2322
Columbia, SC 29201
AFFILIATIONS:
ASMP, CCAS

PRINCIPAL SUBJECTS:
Advertising
Architecture
Automotive
Computer Technology
Editorial
Food/Diet
Photography
PUBLICATIONS:
People
T.V. Guide
Law Practice Mgt.
SC Lawyer
People
T.V. Guide
Law Practice Mgt.
SC Lawyer

CROFOOT, RON
6140 Wayzata Blvd.
Minneapolis, MN 55416
Telephone: 612-546-0643
Fax: 612-546-1862
AFFILIATIONS:
ASMP
PRINCIPAL SUBJECTS:
Advertising
Photography
PUBLICATIONS:
Archive
Communication Arts

CROKE, THOMAS J.
95 Davenport Street
Taunton, MA 02780
Telephone: 508-822-3808
Fax: 508-822-8202
MAILING ADDRESS:
THOMAS J. CROKE
P.O. Box 786
Taunton, MA 02780
AFFILIATIONS:
ASMP
PRINCIPAL SUBJECTS:
Advertising
Architecture
Editorial
Human Interest
Journalism
Marine
News
Sports

CROMER, PEGGO
1206 Andora Ave.
Coral Gables, FL 33146
Telephone: 305-667-3722
MAILING ADDRESS:
PEGGO CROMER
Coral Gables, FL 33146

AFFILIATIONS:
PPA, ASMP
PRINCIPAL SUBJECTS:
The Arts
Education
Fashion
General Interest
Amusements
Travel
Architecture
PUBLICATIONS:
Good Houskeeping
Designers Quarterly
Children of the World
Amerika
World and I, The
Vanidades
Dance Magazine
Horizon
Womens World
Frontline Graphics
Progressive Grocers Magazine

CROSBY, A. DAVID
P.O. Box 25878
Greenville, SC 29616
Telephone: 803-232-4403
Fax: 803-232-0773
AFFILIATIONS:
ASMP
PRINCIPAL SUBJECTS:
Advertising
Architecture
Editorial
Fashion
Medical

CURLER, BERNICE
8156 Waikiki Dr.
Fair Oaks, CA 95628
Telephone: 916-967-7114
AFFILIATIONS:
ASJA, CWC, SHS
PRINCIPAL SUBJECTS:
General Interest
Geography
Travel
PUBLICATIONS:
House Beautiful
Writer's Digest
Lady's Circle
McCalls
Modern Maturity
Progressive Woman
Small World
American Girl
Young Miss
Canadian Home
Mature Years
Christian Science Monitor
Success Unlimited

The Lamp
Grit
Sacramento Union Weekender
California Today
National Enquirer
National Star
Lifestyle
Popular Craft
Sacramento Magazine
United Church Herald
Points
Dairy Scope
Nebraska Electric Farmer
Progressive Grocer
The Merchandiser
Modern Romances
Plaza Digest Corp.
Ace
Parent's Magazine
Enterprises
Ideal
Dauntless
West Ways

CURTIS, JOHN
27 Drydock Ave.
Boston, MA 02210
Telephone: 617-261-7675
Fax: 617-261-7676
AFFILIATIONS:
ASMP
PRINCIPAL SUBJECTS:
Photography
Advertising
PUBLICATIONS:
Time
Vogue
Newsweek
Boston Globe
N.Y. Times

CURTIS, STEVEN
341 N. 14th St.
Kansas City, KS 66102
Telephone: 913-321-4222
Fax: 913-321-9014
AFFILIATIONS:
ASMP, SCP
PRINCIPAL SUBJECTS:
Advertising
Agriculture
Architecture
Business & Industry
Editorial
Geography
Government
Health
Human Interest
Human Relations
Journalism
Medical

Personalities
Philosophy
Photography
Science
The Arts
Travel
Urban Affairs
PUBLICATIONS:
Ingram's
American Banker
The Family Therapy Networker
Stages
Fidelity Focus
Borderline
Assemblage/K.C.
   Art Institute Mag.

D'ADDIO, JAMES
12 E. 22nd Street
New York, NY 10010
Telephone: 212-533-0668
Fax: 212-533-0813
AFFILIATIONS:
ASMP
PRINCIPAL SUBJECTS:
Travel
Editorial
Architecture
PUBLICATIONS:
House Beautiful
Interior Design
New York Times Magazine
Progressive Architecture

DAKAN, LEW
900 Scott Ave., LPR
Estes Park, CO 80517
Telephone: 303-586-5638
MAILING ADDRESS:
Estes Park, CO 80517
AFFILIATIONS:
PPOFA
PRINCIPAL SUBJECTS:
Aviation
General Interest
Advertising
Photography
Travel
PUBLICATIONS:
Housing-Greeley
   Tribune-Aerials
Guns-Estes Park
   Trail-Gazette-Scenics
Better Homes & Gardens
Westways
Home & Away
Travel - Holiday
Southern Living
Texas Monthly
Sunset
Holiday Inns

DALY, MICHAEL KEVIN
P.O. Box 3675
Eugene, OR 97403
Telephone: 503-342-8337
AFFILIATIONS:
ASMP
PRINCIPAL SUBJECTS:
Sports
Physical Fitness
Social Trends
Nature
PUBLICATIONS:
Esquire
Sports Illustrated
Outside Mag.
American Health
Time
Islands
Cosmopolitan
Parade

DANDO, MARK
8613 East Delaware Ave.
Richland, MI 49083
Telephone: 616-629-4004
PRINCIPAL SUBJECTS:
Sports
PUBLICATIONS:
Jet Skier Magazine
Splash

DANIELS, JOSEPHUS
Su Vecino Ct., Dolores & 6th
Carmel, CA 93921
Telephone: 408-625-3316
MAILING ADDRESS:
JOSEPHUS DANIELS
P.O. Box 7418
Carmel, CA 93921
AFFILIATIONS:
ASMP
PRINCIPAL SUBJECTS:
Advertising
The Arts
Travel
PUBLICATIONS:
Horizons Magazine
Life Magazine
Time/Life Annual Report
New York Times
Orientations (Hong Kong)
American Medical Assoc.
   Journal

DANTZIC, JERRY
910 President St.
Brooklyn, NY 11215
Telephone: 718-789-7478
AFFILIATIONS:
ASMP

PRINCIPAL SUBJECTS:
Photography
Business & Industry
Hobbies
The Arts
Travel
PUBLICATIONS:
New York Times
Readers Digest
Life
Amphoto Miranda Manual
Holiday
Look
Life
T.V. Guide

DARNELL, MITCHELL
Darnell, Mitchell Photography
1925 Forbes Ave.
Pittsburgh, PA 15219
Telephone: 412-765-3634
AFFILIATIONS:
ASMP
PRINCIPAL SUBJECTS:
Advertising
Computer Technology
PUBLICATIONS:
Seventeen
New York Times Magazine
Pittsburgh Magazine
Mademoiselle

DARRYL, JACOBSON
11 W. 19th St., 6th Fl.
New York, NY 10011
Telephone: 212-633-0300
MAILING ADDRESS:
SUPERSTOCK INC.
New York, NY
Telephone: 908-354-5436
AFFILIATIONS:
ASPP
PRINCIPAL SUBJECTS:
Advertising
Editorial
General Interest
Travel
PUBLICATIONS:
Time
Newsweek
Vogue
Readers Digest

DAUMAN, HENRI
4 East 88th St.
New York, NY 10128
Telephone: 212-860-3804
Fax: 212-860-3805
AFFILIATIONS:
ASMP

PRINCIPAL SUBJECTS:
Editorial
Entertainment
Personalities
The Arts
PUBLICATIONS:
Life
NY Times
Arts & Leisure
Town & Country

DAVIDSON, CAMERON
863 North Abingdon Street
Arlington, VA 22203
Telephone: 703-812-0571
Fax: 703-812-0563
AFFILIATIONS:
ASMP
PRINCIPAL SUBJECTS:
Advertising
Aviation
Ecology
Editorial
Military
PUBLICATIONS:
National Geographic
Smithsonian
American Way
Military Lifestyle
U.S. News & World Report
Audubon

DAVIDSON, DARWIN K.
R.R. 1 Box 549
Deer Isle, ME 04627
Telephone: 800-247-6667
Fax: 207-348-7768
MAILING ADDRESS:
DARWIN K. DAVIDSON
RR 1 Box 549
Deer Isle, ME 04627
Telephone: 207-348-2234
AFFILIATIONS:
ASMP
PRINCIPAL SUBJECTS:
Architecture
PUBLICATIONS:
House Beautiful
Woman's Day
Interior Design
Interiors
Designer's Kitchens & Baths
Southern Accents
Colonial Homes
House Beautiful Special
　Publications
Home
Colonial Homes
Archtectural Lighting

DAVIS, DAVE
5715 N. 13th St.
Phoenix, AZ 85014
Telephone: 602-266-9851
AFFILIATIONS:
ASMP
PRINCIPAL SUBJECTS:
Aviation
Editorial
General Interest
Human Interest
Travel
Nature
Ecology
Sports
Physical Fitness
Hobbies
PUBLICATIONS:
Family Circle
Cosmopolitain
N.Y. Magazine
Fortune
Barron

DAVIS, DEE
641 Fogg St., #206
Nashville, TN 37203
Telephone: 615-259-1575
MAILING ADDRESS:
234 Summit Ridge Drive
Nashville, TN 37215
Telephone: 615-297-1579
AFFILIATIONS:
ASMP
PRINCIPAL SUBJECTS:
The Arts
Human Interest
Advertising
Sports
PUBLICATIONS:
Nashville Business & Life
　Styles Magazine
Music Row Magazine
Country America Magazine
The Tennessean

DAVIS, HOWARD
19 East 21st Street
Baltimore, MD 21218
Telephone: 410-625-3838
Fax: 410-625-3839
AFFILIATIONS:
ASMP
PRINCIPAL SUBJECTS:
Photography
Automotive
Food/Diet
PUBLICATIONS:
Philadelphia Inquirer

Washington Post
Medical Economics
National Observer

DE CASSERES, JOSEPH
418 Calhoun St., N.W.
Atlanta, GA 30318
Telephone: 404-872-4480
AFFILIATIONS:
ASMP, SPE
PRINCIPAL SUBJECTS:
Advertising
Architecture
The Arts
Editorial
General Interest
Travel
PUBLICATIONS:
New York Times
Atlanta Journal - Constitution
Atlanta Magazine
Vogue
Harpers Bazaar
Notre Dame
　Magazine/Newsletter
Emory University Literary
　Magazine
Atlanta Symphony
　programs & PR
Dance Magazine
Atlanta Ballet Programs & PR
Southern Ballet
　Programs & PR
Georgia Tech Architecture
　bulletins/journals
Elle - Italian

DE ZANGER, ARIE
P.O. Box 41
Sugar Loaf, NY 10981
Telephone: 914-469-4498
Fax: 914-469-4729
PRINCIPAL SUBJECTS:
Editorial
Photography
Geography
Amusements
Sports
Youth
PUBLICATIONS:
Women's Day
Bon Appetit Magazine
American Heritage
Americana Magazine
Redbook
Esquire

DECRUYENAERE,
　HOWARD
2417 N. Park Blvd.
Santa Ana, CA 92706

Telephone: 714-997-4446
AFFILIATIONS:
ASMP
PRINCIPAL SUBJECTS:
Advertising
Agriculture
Architecture
Automotive
Business & Industry
Ecology
Editorial
Family
Home & Garden
Nature
Religion
Travel

DEGABRIELE
  PHOTOGRAPHY
DeGabriele Photography
900 1st Ave. S., #305
Seattle, WA 98134
Telephone: 206-624-9928
Fax: 206-624-8048
AFFILIATIONS:
ASMP
PRINCIPAL SUBJECTS:
Advertising
Animals
Aviation
Business & Industry
Ecology
General Interest
Human Interest
Journalism
Management
Marine
Marketing
Media
Medical
Nature
Personalities
Photography
Physical Fitness
Science
Senior Citizens
Social Trends
Sports
The Arts
Travel
PUBLICATIONS:
ASMP Silver Book #7
CA Annual

DEGGINGER, DR. E. R.
40 Laura Ln.
Morristown, NJ 07960
Telephone: 201-267-4165
MAILING ADDRESS:
COLOR - PIC, INC.
Morristown, NJ 07960

AFFILIATIONS:
ASMP, PSA
PRINCIPAL SUBJECTS:
General Interest
Geography
Business & Industry
Nature
Travel
Agriculture
Science
PUBLICATIONS:
Audubon
Natl. Geographic
National/Intl. Wildlife

DEGGINGER, PHIL
189 Johnson Rd.
Morris Plains, NJ 07950
Telephone: 201-455-1733
Fax: 916-984-0660
AFFILIATIONS:
ASMP
PRINCIPAL SUBJECTS:
Advertising
Agriculture
Animals
Architecture
Business & Industry
Editorial
Foreign
Home & Garden
Marine

DEITS, KATIE
2001 Bomar Drive, Suite 4
North Palm Beach, FL 33408
Telephone: 407-775-3399
Fax: 407-622-2727
AFFILIATIONS:
ASMP, PPA, FPP,
  PPGPB, PAPI
PRINCIPAL SUBJECTS:
Advertising
Architecture
Family
Food/Diet
General Interest
Health
Medical
PUBLICATIONS:
Woman's World
Palm Beach Post (Florida)
People
Popular Photography
Elegance

DEL AMO, TOMAS
2525 Arapahoe, Suite E4-320
Boulder, CO 80302
Telephone: 303-444-5137

AFFILIATIONS:
ASMP, PPB
PRINCIPAL SUBJECTS:
Fashion
Photography
PUBLICATIONS:
Modern Bride
Eating Right & Living Well
Woman's World

DELANO, JON
227 Chris Columbus Dr.,
  #235-B
Jersey City, NJ 07302
Telephone: 201-309-2110
AFFILIATIONS:
ASMP, NPPA, PPA
PRINCIPAL SUBJECTS:
Aviation
Editorial
Entertainment
Foreign
General Interest
Journalism
News
Photography
The Arts
Travel
PUBLICATIONS:
People
New York Times
New York Magazine
Life
New York Post
Daily News
Leatherneck
Architectual Digest

DELLA GROTTA,
  VIVIENNE
700 Concha Loma Dr.
Carpinteria, CA 93013
Telephone: 805-684-1339
MAILING ADDRESS:
VIVIENNE DELLA GROTTA
P.O. Box 927
Carpinteria, CA 93014
AFFILIATIONS:
ASMP
PRINCIPAL SUBJECTS:
Advertising
Family
Travel
Education
PUBLICATIONS:
World Of Children (UNICEF)
Deutsche Bundpost, Hamburg
Parents Magazine
Weekly Reader
  (Xerox Ed. Pub.)
National Enquirer

PTA Today
Young Children
Good Housekeeping
Christian Science Monitor

DEMPSAY, SAY
1384 Shoreline Drive
Santa Barbara, CA 93109
PRINCIPAL SUBJECTS:
Advertising
Animals
Architecture
Ecology
Editorial
Education
Foreign
General Interest
Geography
Human Interest
Marine
Media
Nature
Personalities
Sales
The Arts
Travel
Urban Affairs
Video
Women's Interest
World Affairs
Youth

DENUTO, ELLEN
24 Mill Street, #203
Paterson, NJ 07501
Telephone: 201-881-0614
AFFILIATIONS:
ASMP
PRINCIPAL SUBJECTS:
Advertising
Fashion
Media
Photography
The Arts
PUBLICATIONS:
The New York Times
The Star Ledger
Foto Magazine
The Minolta Mirror
Shuesha Publications

DEREX, DAVID
210 Route 4 East
Paramus, NJ 07652
Telephone: 201-909-0600
Fax: 201-909-0005
AFFILIATIONS:
ASMP
PRINCIPAL SUBJECTS:
Fashion
Personalities

PUBLICATIONS:
Vogue
Soap Opera Digest
Cosmopolitan

DEUTSCH, JACK
48 W. 21, 12th Fl.
New York, NY 10010
Telephone: 212-633-1424
AFFILIATIONS:
ASMP
PRINCIPAL SUBJECTS:
Advertising
Editorial
Fashion
PUBLICATIONS:
Vogue Knitting
Bridal Guide
European Travel & Life
Interview
Paper

DEVAULT, JIM
2400 Sunset Place
Nashville, TN 37212
Telephone: 615-269-4538
Fax: 615-269-0202
AFFILIATIONS:
ASMP
PRINCIPAL SUBJECTS:
Personalities
Advertising
Business & Industry
Human Interest
Photography
PUBLICATIONS:
Ad Week
Financial World
Forbes
Fortune

DEVORE III, NICHOLAS
1280 Ute Ave.
Aspen, CO 81611
Telephone: 303-925-2317
Fax: 303-925-2420
MAILING ADDRESS:
DEVORE III NICHOLAS
P.O. Box 0-3
Aspen, CO 81612
AFFILIATIONS:
ASMP, NPPA
PRINCIPAL SUBJECTS:
The Arts
Fashion
Travel
Nature
Geography
Personalities
Ecology

PUBLICATIONS:
National Geographic Magazine
Natural History Magazine
GEO
Outside
Fortune
New York Times
Travel & Leisure
Food & Wine
Atlantic
Chicago Tribune
Stern
Conde Nast Traveler
Islands
Bunte
Aspen Magazine
Darkroom Photography
World & I
Life Magazine

DEWALD, DAVID
211 S. Beverly
Casper, WY 82609
Telephone: 307-234-5941
AFFILIATIONS:
NPPA, PP of A
PRINCIPAL SUBJECTS:
News
Sports
PUBLICATIONS:
U.S. News & World Report
Old West Trail Guide
NRTA Journal

DIAZ, ARMANDO
19 S. Park
San Francisco, CA 94107
Telephone: 415-495-3552
AFFILIATIONS:
ASMP, APA
PRINCIPAL SUBJECTS:
Advertising
Editorial
General Interest
Human Interest
Travel

DIBARTOLOMEO, GAREN
3801 Hanlin Way
Weirton, WV 26062
Telephone: 304-748-0877
Fax: 304-748-3766
AFFILIATIONS:
ASMP, AIGA
PRINCIPAL SUBJECTS:
Editorial
Photography
PUBLICATIONS:
Arizona Highways

Entrepreneur Magazine
Cortlandt Forum
First Magazine

DIETRICH, DICK
702 W. Solano Dr.
Phoenix, AZ 85013
Telephone: 602-246-8079
Fax: 602-246-2557
MAILING ADDRESS:
DIETRICH STOCK
  PHOTO INC.
PRINCIPAL SUBJECTS:
Nature Photography

DIETZ, CRAIG
510 1/2 Gravier
New Orleans, LA 70130
Telephone: 504-523-3630
AFFILIATIONS:
ASMP
PRINCIPAL SUBJECTS:
Advertising
Architecture
Business & Industry
Family
Home & Garden
Marketing
Personalities
The Arts
PUBLICATIONS:
Time
Newsweek
New York Newsday
London Sunday Times

DIMARCO, JR., SAL
P.O. Box 502
Drexel Hill, PA 19026
Telephone: 215-789-3239
Fax: 215-853-3007
AFFILIATIONS:
ASMP, WHNPA, SPJ, NPPA
PRINCIPAL SUBJECTS:
Advertising
Automotive
Business & Industry
Editorial
Education
Electronics
Foreign
General Interest
Government
History
Human Interest
Journalism
Management
Media
Medical
News
Photography

Science
Social Trends
Sports
Travel
PUBLICATIONS:
Time
The New York Times
Industry Week
Fortune
Forbes
Business Week
Readers Digest
Life
Nation's Business

DOBRZYCKI, MARY
Imagery Source, Inc.
4648 N. Sayre Ave.
Harwood Heights, IL 60656
Telephone: 312-775-8814
AFFILIATIONS:
NPPA, ASMP
PRINCIPAL SUBJECTS:
Journalism
Photography
PUBLICATIONS:
Vanity Fair
Time
Ebony
New York Times
Chicago Sun-Times
Chicago Tribune
San Francisco Examiner
Denver Post

DODGE, LARRY
1919 Hwy 271
Helmville, MT 59843
Telephone: 406-793-5682
MAILING ADDRESS:
BIG SKY MAGIC
P.O. Box 60
Helmville, MT 59843
PRINCIPAL SUBJECTS:
Travel
General Interest
Human Interest
Agriculture
Ecology
Nature
PUBLICATIONS:
Montana Magazine
U.S. News & World Report
Nomos Magazine
Reason Magazine
Wall Street Journal
Libertarian Party News
Readers Digest
Trout Magazine

DOFF, A. F.
35 Constellation Rd.
Levittown, NY 11756
Telephone: 516-731-5230
PRINCIPAL SUBJECTS:
General Interest
Human Interest
Amusements
Journalism

DOLIN, IRVING
124 Ludlow St.
New York, NY 10002
Telephone: 212-473-4006
AFFILIATIONS:
IMPA
PRINCIPAL SUBJECTS:
Architecture
Nature
Travel
The Arts
Automotive
PUBLICATIONS:
Time
Harper's Bazaar
Fortune
N.Y. Times Magazine
Esquire
Sport
Popular Photography
Modern Photography
Road & Track
Car & Driver
Scholastic
True
Holiday
Life
Popular Mechanics
Stereo Review
Automobile

DOMINIS, JOHN
252 W. 102nd St.
New York, NY 10025
Telephone: 212-222-9890
AFFILIATIONS:
ASMP
PRINCIPAL SUBJECTS:
Animals
Architecture
Food/Diet
Journalism
Nature
PUBLICATIONS:
Life
Traveler
National Geographic
Time
People
Fortune
Architectural Digest

Working Woman
Smithsonian
Connoiseur
House Beautiful

DONDERO, DON
2755 Pioneer Dr.
Reno, NV 89509
Telephone: 702-825-7348
MAILING ADDRESS:
D. DONDERO
Box 52
Reno, NV 89510
AFFILIATIONS:
ASMP, NPPA
PRINCIPAL SUBJECTS:
Humor
Journalism
PUBLICATIONS:
Fortune
National Enquirer
Time
Life
SI
New York Times
L.A. Times
AP & UPI
People
Der Spiegel

DORF, MYROM JAY
205 W. 19th St.
New York, NY 10011
Telephone: 212-255-2020
Fax: 212-255-2020
AFFILIATIONS:
APA, ASMP
PRINCIPAL SUBJECTS:
Photography

DORNHEIM, BETTY
15 Hamilton Ave.
Bronxville, NY 10708
Telephone: 914-337-0396

DORSEY, RON
  PHOTOGRAPHY
Dorsey, Ron Photography
2715 Stacy Ln.
Austin, TX 78704
Telephone: 512-441-8445
AFFILIATIONS:
ASMP
PRINCIPAL SUBJECTS:
Advertising
Architecture
Business & Industry
General Interest
Nature
Travel

PUBLICATIONS:
House Beautiful
Architectural Digest
Play Boy
Country Living
Woman's World
Parade

DOUGLAS, KEITH
Douglas, Keith Photo
405 NE 8th St.
Ft. Lavo, FL 33304
Telephone: 305-763-5883
Fax: 305-763-5085
AFFILIATIONS:
ASMP
PRINCIPAL SUBJECTS:
Advertising
Architecture
Electronics
Fashion
PUBLICATIONS:
ASMP Silver Books
Showcase (America)
  13,14,15,16

DOUGLASS, DARREN
1227 Bonnie Brae
Pomona, CA 91767
Telephone: 909-625-2598
AFFILIATIONS:
ASMP, OWA
PRINCIPAL SUBJECTS:
Animals
Ecology
History
Hobbies
Marine
Medical
News
Photography
Physical Fitness
Travel
PUBLICATIONS:
Skin Diver
Pacific Diver
Westways
Underwater USA
Vista USA
Ocean Realm
Rodale's Scuba Diving
Outdoors Unlimited

DOWNEY, CHARLES
Telephone: 909-866-6566
MAILING ADDRESS:
CHARLES DOWNEY
P.O. Box 406
Fawnskin, CA 92333
AFFILIATIONS:
ASJA

PRINCIPAL SUBJECTS:
Editorial
General Interest
Medical
Sports
PUBLICATIONS:
Better Homes & Gardens
Black Enterprise
Cavalier
Playboy
Kiwanis
Mechanix Illustrated
Modern Maturity
Money Magazine
National Enquirer
Woman's World
Mc Call's
Science '82
Inflight Magazines
Overseas Magazines in
  Australia & Germany
American Way
American Legion
Diversion
Readers Digest
Los Angeles Times
Washington Post
Monitor Radio
Boys' Life
Men's Fitness
Woman's Day

DOWNIE, DANA
P.O. Box 19313
Oakland, CA 94619
Telephone: 510-261-1660
Fax: 510-261-1661
AFFILIATIONS:
ASMP, SMPS
PRINCIPAL SUBJECTS:
Advertising
Agriculture
Architecture
Aviation
Business & Industry
Ecology
Editorial
Family
Foreign
General Interest
Geography
Health
Hobbies
Home & Garden
Human Interest
Management
Marketing
Medical
Nature
News
Personalities

Photography
Religion
Senior Citizens
Social Trends
The Arts
Travel
Urban Affairs
Women's Interest
Youth
PUBLICATIONS:
Time
Newsweek
National New York Times
Forbes
Des Moines Iowa Register

DRAKE, JEANNE
Wildlife & Sporting
  Photography
8032 Hackberry Drive
Las Vegas, NV 89123
Telephone: 702-361-0060
Fax: 702-896-7402
AFFILIATIONS:
ASMP, OWAA
PRINCIPAL SUBJECTS:
Advertising
Animals
Ecology
Nature
PUBLICATIONS:
Natioanl Geographic World
Wildlife Conservation
Petersens Hunting
Outdoor Life
Hunting Horizons
Terre Sauvage
Das Dier

DRESSLER, BRIAN
111 Northway Road, Suite A
Columbia, SC 29201
Telephone: 803-254-7171
Fax: 803-254-7707
AFFILIATIONS:
ASMP
PRINCIPAL SUBJECTS:
Advertising
Architecture
Business & Industry
Editorial
Entertainment
Health
Home & Garden
Management
Men's Interest
Personalities
Photography
Social Trends
The Arts
Travel

PUBLICATIONS:
Time
Newsweek
Fortune
Forbes
Focus On Family
Focus On Health
Architectural Record

DREYER, PETER
916 Pleasant St., 11
Norwood, MA 02062
Telephone: 617-762-8550
Fax: 617-326-0712
AFFILIATIONS:
ASMP
PRINCIPAL SUBJECTS:
Editorial
Business & Industry

DRISCOLL, W. M.
P.O. Box 8195
Dallas, TX 75205
Telephone: 214-363-8429
AFFILIATIONS:
ASMP, PPA
PRINCIPAL SUBJECTS:
Advertising
Fashion
Photography
PUBLICATIONS:
Swimwear Illustrated
Swimsuit International
Dallas Observer
Plain Talk

DUBLER, DOUGLAS W.
162 E. 92nd St.
New York, NY 10128
Telephone: 212-410-6300
Fax: 212-996-8901
AFFILIATIONS:
ASMP
PRINCIPAL SUBJECTS:
Fashion
PUBLICATIONS:
Vogue
Cosmopolitan
Playboy
Time
TV Guide
Harpers Bazaar
Glamour
Self
Madamoiselle
Vogue (Italian)
LEI
Cosmopolitan (British)
Amica
Redbook

DUFRESNE, WALTER
31 Montgomery Place
Brooklyn, NY 11215
Telephone: 718-622-1901
Fax: 718-622-1901
AFFILIATIONS:
ASMP, SPE
PRINCIPAL SUBJECTS:
Architecture
Home & Garden
Editorial
Advertising

DUHL, DAVID
817 Kent Road
Nashville, TN 37214
Telephone: 615-885-0822
AFFILIATIONS:
ASMP
PRINCIPAL SUBJECTS:
Nature
PUBLICATIONS:
Outside
National Geographic World

DUHON, MIKE
807 Rochow
Houston, TX 77019
Telephone: 713-529-4333
Fax: 713-529-6868
AFFILIATIONS:
ASMP
PRINCIPAL SUBJECTS:
Advertising
Home & Garden

DUMBAR, ARNOLD
713 S. Fin
Yuma, CO 80759
Telephone: 303-848-2326
Fax: 303-848-2326
AFFILIATIONS:
PPA, DDC, ASMP
PRINCIPAL SUBJECTS:
Human Interest
Nature
PUBLICATIONS:
Farm & Ranch Living
Vista
Midwest Motorist
Runners World

DUMOFF, ALAN M., PH.D.
P.O. Box 147
Hammonton, NJ 08037
Telephone: 800-533-4348
Fax: 800-327-3006
AFFILIATIONS:
NPPA, ASMP, EPIC, SIFPD,
  IAAI, N.J.-IAAI, IFDA

PRINCIPAL SUBJECTS:
News
Science
PUBLICATIONS:
Photo Journal
Law & Enforcement
IAAI-Journ.

DUNMIRE, LARRY
509 - B 35th St.
Newport Beach, CA 92663
Telephone: 714-673-4058
Fax: 714-673-1471
MAILING ADDRESS:
LARRY DUNMIRE
P.O. Box 338
Balboa Island, CA 92662
Telephone: 808-737-8488
AFFILIATIONS:
PCA
PRINCIPAL SUBJECTS:
Advertising
Journalism
Sports
Photography
Business & Industry
PUBLICATIONS:
Motor Boating & Sailing
Boating-Western's
  World-Lakeland Boating
Sea Magazine
Pacific Skipper-Carte Blanche,
  Holiday
Saltwater Sportsman-The
  Executive, Aircal Mag.
Pan Am Clipper
Mainliner Mag.-Pentax
  Life Mag.
New Worlds Magazine
Motor Boat
Yachting
Sail
Outside Magazine
Boote (Germany)
Segling (Sweden)
US Air, Triathlon Magazine
Windsong Magazine
Waterfront
Aloha
Palm Springs Life
Discover Hawaii
Women's Sports
Power & Motor Yacht

DUNOFF, RICH
1313 Delmont Ave.
Havertown, PA 19083
Telephone: 215-642-6137
AFFILIATIONS:
ASMP

PRINCIPAL SUBJECTS:
Advertising
Human Interest
Business & Industry
Social Trends
Medical
Editorial
PUBLICATIONS:
Fortune
Ladies Home Journal
Good Housekeeping
Architectural Digest
Applause
PA. Gazette

DYER, ED
414 Brandy Lane
Mechanicsburg, PA 17055
Telephone: 717-737-6618
AFFILIATIONS:
ASMP, PPA
PRINCIPAL SUBJECTS:
Architecture
Business & Industry
Advertising
Editorial
Fashion

EASTERLY, LIBBY
6320 N. MacArthur Blvd.,
  #2078
Irving, TX 75036
Telephone: 214-444-8896
AFFILIATIONS:
ASMP, DMA
PRINCIPAL SUBJECTS:
Advertising
Marketing
Media
PUBLICATIONS:
American Heart Assoc.
News Magazine

EBERT, BOB
P.O. Box 2881
Honolulu, HI 96802
Telephone: 808-531-1560
MAILING ADDRESS:
PACIFIC PRODUCTIONS
Honolulu, HI 96802
Telephone: 808-737-8488
AFFILIATIONS:
PCA
PRINCIPAL SUBJECTS:
Architecture
Human Interest
Amusements
Nature
Advertising
History

PUBLICATIONS:
National Geographic
Life
Fortune

EDELMAN, HARRY
2790 McCully Rd.
Allison Park, PA 15101
Telephone: 412-486-8822
Fax: 412-486-8755
AFFILIATIONS:
ASMP
PRINCIPAL SUBJECTS:
Travel
News
Advertising
Architecture
Business & Industry
PUBLICATIONS:
USA Today
Inc. (Magazine)
P.C. Week
Venture
U.S. News & World Report
Time
PC Week
MAC Week
Town & Country

EDSON, STEVEN
25 Otis Street
Watertown, MA 02172
Telephone: 617-924-2212
AFFILIATIONS:
ASMP
PRINCIPAL SUBJECTS:
Advertising
Photography
Sports
The Arts
Travel
PUBLICATIONS:
LA Times
Ray Guns
Sun Expert
Details
Interview
Spin
Better Homes & Garden
New York Times

EISBERG, JON
741 Drum Point Road
Brick, NJ 08723
Telephone: 908-477-9682
Fax: 518-434-6185
PRINCIPAL SUBJECTS:
Travel
Sports
Nature

EISMAN, JAMIE
1833 Old Gulph Rd.
Villanova, PA 19085
Telephone: 215-527-0114
Fax: 215-527-7689
AFFILIATIONS:
ASMP
PRINCIPAL SUBJECTS:
Medical
Science

ELAKMAN, MARC
1456 N.E. 29th Street
Pompano Beach, FL 33064
Telephone: 305-979-6969
MAILING ADDRESS:
MARC ELAKMAN
P.O. Box 5156
Lighthouse Point, FL 33074
AFFILIATIONS:
ASMP
PRINCIPAL SUBJECTS:
Advertising
Architecture
Editorial
Electronics
Fashion

ELBINGER, DOUGLAS
Elbinger Studios, Inc.
220 Albert St.
East Lansing, MI 48823
Telephone: 517-332-3026
Fax: 517-332-3027
AFFILIATIONS:
ASMP, PPA
PRINCIPAL SUBJECTS:
Advertising
Architecture
Automotive
Business & Industry
Education
Electronics
Fashion
General Interest
Photography
The Arts
Travel
Urban Affairs
World Affairs
PUBLICATIONS:
Time
Newsweek
Sports Illustrated
Popular Photography
Washington Post
New York Times
Detroit Free Press

ELDER, JIM
P.O. Box 1600
Jackson, WY 83001
Telephone: 307-733-3555
Fax: 307-733-7890
AFFILIATIONS:
ASMP,OWAA,IMAGE
PRINCIPAL SUBJECTS:
Fashion
General Interest
Marine
Sports
Travel
Automotive
PUBLICATIONS:
NY Times Travel
Chevy Outdoors
Pho Pro
Pan-AM Clipper
Better Homes & Gardens
Signature
Road and Track
Motorhome
Trailer Life
Ski Doo Snowmobiles
Time
AAA World
In-Fisherman
Newsweek
Sports Illustrated
Holiday

ELDER, THOM
140 N. La Brea Ave.
Los Angeles, CA 90036
Telephone: 213-931-7707
AFFILIATIONS:
ASMP
PRINCIPAL SUBJECTS:
News
Advertising
Journalism
PUBLICATIONS:
USA Today
People
AP

ELK III, JOHN
3163 Wisconsin St.
Oakland, CA 94602
Telephone: 510-531-7469
Fax: 510-531-7469
AFFILIATIONS:
ASMP, ASPP
PRINCIPAL SUBJECTS:
Agriculture
Architecture
Ecology
Editorial
Foreign
General Interest

Geography
History
Nature
Religion
Travel
PUBLICATIONS:
Nature Conservancy
Sierra
National Geographic World
Motorland
Home and Away
Oklahoma Today
Outdoor Photographer
Travel And Leisure

ELLMAN, ELAINE
60 Gramercy Park
New York, NY 10010
Telephone: 212-674-8850
AFFILIATIONS:
ASMP, APA, SPJ
PRINCIPAL SUBJECTS:
Advertising
Editorial
Entertainment
Fashion
Human Interest
Human Relations
Journalism
Nature
News
Personalities
PUBLICATIONS:
Vogue
Glamour
The Village Voice
Lear's
The New York Times Magazine
Entertainment Weekly
Vibe

ELLMAN, FAYE
270 W. 25 St.
New York, NY 10001
Telephone: 212-243-3759
Fax: 212-741-3985
AFFILIATIONS:
NPPA, ASMP
PRINCIPAL SUBJECTS:
Journalism
Travel
Human Interest

ELLZEY, BILL
P.O. Box 1171
Telluride, CO 81435
Telephone: 303-728-4584
Fax: 303-626-5049
AFFILIATIONS:
ASMP, PPA

PRINCIPAL SUBJECTS:
Advertising
Agriculture
Architecture
Editorial
General Interest
Geography
Nature
Photography
Travel
PUBLICATIONS:
USA Today
Diversion
New York Times
Endless Vacations
Travel Holiday
Detroit Free Press
Snow Country
Texas Monthly

EMMERICH, DON
11940 W. 22nd Place
Lakewood, CO 80215
Telephone: 303-757-5299
Fax: 303-237-0348
MAILING ADDRESS:
DON EMMERICH
7200 E. Hampden, #102
Denver, CO 80224
AFFILIATIONS:
PPA, ASMP
PRINCIPAL SUBJECTS:
Advertising
Architecture
Computer Technology
Editorial
Electronics
Family
Fashion
Foreign
Journalism
Marine
Marketing
Nature
Photography
Sports
Travel
PUBLICATIONS:
Brides Magazine
Sports Illustrated
Professional Photography
Time/Life
Rangefinder
Lens
Studio Photography
Brides Magazine
Sports Illustrated
Professional Photography
Time/Life

Rangefinder
Lens
Studio Photography

ENGELMANN, SUZANNE J.
1609 Lance Rd.
Jupiter, FL 33469
Telephone: 407-747-7676
AFFILIATIONS:
ASMP
PRINCIPAL SUBJECTS:
Advertising
Agriculture
Editorial
Education
Entertainment
Foreign
Geography
Health
History
Home & Garden
Journalism
Medical
Nature
News
Personalities
Photography
Physical Fitness
Senior Citizens
Sports
Travel
Women's Interest
World Affairs
PUBLICATIONS:
New York Times
Travel & Leisure

ENGH, ROHN
Pine Lake Farm
Osceola, WI 54020
Telephone: 715-248-3800
Fax: 715-248-7394
MAILING ADDRESS:
EGNH ROHN
Osceola, WI 54020
AFFILIATIONS:
SATW,ASPP,NPP
PRINCIPAL SUBJECTS:
Agriculture
Family
Education
Human Interest
PUBLICATIONS:
Redbook
Parents
People

ENGLISH, MELISSA HAYES
1195 Woods Circle, N.E.
Atlanta, GA 30324
Telephone: 404-261-7650

Fax: 404-261-7650
AFFILIATIONS:
ASMP
PRINCIPAL SUBJECTS:
Business & Industry
Human Interest
PUBLICATIONS:
Fortune Magazine
Atlanta Magazine
Tables Magazine

EPSTEIN, LARRY
5155 Earle St.
Fremont, CA 94536
Telephone: 510-797-0696
PRINCIPAL SUBJECTS:
Family
Travel
PUBLICATIONS:
Tri-City Tidings

ESCOSA, JOHN
1133 Rivermet
Fort Wayne, IN 46805
Telephone: 219-422-8625
PRINCIPAL SUBJECTS:
Advertising
Editorial
General Interest
PUBLICATIONS:
Inc. Magazine
Indiana Business
Farm & Ranch Living

ESTY, ANDREA
26861 Trabuco Rd, #E-234
Mission Viego, CA 92691
Telephone: 714-757-9848
AFFILIATIONS:
ASMP
PRINCIPAL SUBJECTS:
Advertising
Automotive
Aviation
Editorial
Marine
Sports
Travel
PUBLICATIONS:
Motor Trend
Outdoors
Racer
Sports Illustrated
Newsweek
People
National Geographic Traveler

EYLE, NICOLAS EDWARD
205 Onondaga Ave.
Syracuse, NY 13207
Telephone: 315-422-6231

AFFILIATIONS:
ASMP
PRINCIPAL SUBJECTS:
Advertising
PUBLICATIONS:
Governing
EPRI
Forbes
You Magazine

FABRICIUS, DAGMAR
1150 Fifth Ave.
New York, NY 10128
Telephone: 212-860-0880
Fax: 212-860-0880
AFFILIATIONS:
ASMP, APA
PRINCIPAL SUBJECTS:
Editorial
Advertising
Human Interest
PUBLICATIONS:
Time
Newsweek
International Press

FACTOR, BEVERLY
Factor, Beverly Photography
P.O. Box 4136
Laguna Beach, CA 92652
Telephone: 714-499-5710
Fax: 714-499-0581
AFFILIATIONS:
ASMP
PRINCIPAL SUBJECTS:
Animals
Foreign
Marine
Nature
Photography

FAIRCLOTH, JANE G.
1008 East Blvd.
Charlotte, NC 28203
Telephone: 704-333-5330
Fax: 704-332-3431
AFFILIATIONS:
ASMP, ASPP
PRINCIPAL SUBJECTS:
Advertising
Agriculture
Education
Family
General Interest
Nature
Sports
Youth
PUBLICATIONS:
Duke Power Annual Report
BB & T Annual Report

FANSLER, EARL
414 Baxter Ave., Ste. 100
Louisville, KY 40204
Telephone: 502-587-6443
Fax: 502-587-9157
MAILING ADDRESS:
EARL FANSLER
　PHOTOGRAPHERS, INC.
414 Baxter Ave., #100
Louisville, KY 40204
AFFILIATIONS:
PPA
PRINCIPAL SUBJECTS:
Architecture
Aviation
General Interest
Human Interest
Amusements
Fashion
Women's Interest
PUBLICATIONS:
Wall Street Journal
Life
Time

FARKAS, ALAN
114 St. Paul Street
Rochester, NY 14604
Telephone: 716-232-1124
Fax: 716-954-7164
AFFILIATIONS:
ASMP
PRINCIPAL SUBJECTS:
Business & Industry
Photography
Sports
PUBLICATIONS:
Forbes
Success

FARR, JULIE
135 W. Market St.
Scranton, PA 18508
Telephone: 717-961-8523
Fax: 717-341-0615
AFFILIATIONS:
ASMP, PPA
PRINCIPAL SUBJECTS:
Advertising
Agriculture
Architecture
Business & Industry
Ecology
Education
Home & Garden
Human Relations
Nature
Youth

PUBLICATIONS:
Impressions
NEPA Business Journal
Hospital News

FARRELL, BILL
2450 Central Ave. G
Boulder, CO 80301
Telephone: 303-442-3917
Fax: 303-442-3937
MAILING ADDRESS:
THE PHOTO WORKS INC.
2450 Central Ave. G.
Boulder, CO 80301
AFFILIATIONS:
ASMP, PPA, PPBC
PRINCIPAL SUBJECTS:
Advertising
Architecture
Aviation
Business & Industry
Ecology
Editorial
Fashion
Health
Nature
PUBLICATIONS:
C.I.O. Magazine
Electronic Design News
Fortune Magazine
Telephony
Life Magazine
Time

FEILING, DAVID A.
7804 Ravenswood Lane
Manlius, NY 13104
Telephone: 315-682-7937
AFFILIATIONS:
ASMP
PRINCIPAL SUBJECTS:
Advertising
Architecture
Business & Industry
Fashion
General Interest
Human Interest
Photography
Travel

FELT, JIM
1316 S.E. 12th Ave.
Portland, OR 97214
Telephone: 503-238-1748
Fax: 503-236-6014
MAILING ADDRESS:
JIM FELT
P.O. Box 5063
Portland, OR 97208

PRINCIPAL SUBJECTS:
Business & Industry
Automotive
Aviation

FICALORA, TONI
11 Janet Terrace
Irvington, NY 10533
Telephone: 914-591-7344
Fax: 914-591-8055
AFFILIATIONS:
PPA,BPA,ASMP,DGA
PRINCIPAL SUBJECTS:
Food/Diet
General Interest
Government

FIELDS, BRUCE
71 Greene St.
New York, NY 10012
Telephone: 212-431-8852
Fax: 212-941-9352
AFFILIATIONS:
ASMP, APA
PRINCIPAL SUBJECTS:
General Interest
Nature
Food/Diet
Advertising
Food/Diet
PUBLICATIONS:
Vogue
Harpers Bazaar
Town & Country
Architectural Digest
Gentlemen's Quarterly
L' Officiel
New Yorker
New York Magazine
New York Times
Art Direction
Parents
McCall's
Members
Mirabella
Psychology Today

FINLEY, DOUG
355 Rt. 46
Mine Hill, NJ 07801
Telephone: 201-584-2553
AFFILIATIONS:
ASMP
PRINCIPAL SUBJECTS:
Advertising
Agriculture
Amusements
Automotive
Aviation
Business & Industry
Computer Technology

Ecology
Editorial
Electronics
Food/Diet
Humor
Marine
Marketing
Media
Medical
Men's Interest
Nature
Personal Finance
Science
The Arts
Travel
Women's Interest
PUBLICATIONS:
Time Magazine
Teen Magazine
Numerous Annual Reports
N.J. Source
Chocolatier Magazine

FINNIGAN, VINCE
806 Maryland Ave., N.E.
Washington, DC 20002
Telephone: 202-544-2945
AFFILIATIONS:
PPA,WHNPA,NPPA
PRINCIPAL SUBJECTS:
News
Urban Affairs
Video
PUBLICATIONS:
Forbes
Business Week
News Week
U.S. Banker

FIREBAUGH, STEVE
6750 55th Ave. S.
Seattle, WA 98118
Telephone: 206-721-5151
AFFILIATIONS:
ASMP
PRINCIPAL SUBJECTS:
Advertising
Agriculture
Architecture
Aviation
Business & Industry
Computer Technology
Editorial
Foreign
Geography
Nature
Physical Fitness
Science
Travel
PUBLICATIONS:
Fortune

Gourmet
Business Week
Texaco Today
Boeing Annual Report
Audobon
Communication Arts
Science

FISHER PHOTOGRAPHY
Fisher Photography
2234 Cathedral Avenue N.W.
Washington, DC 20008
Telephone: 202-232-3781
AFFILIATIONS:
ASMP, ASPP
PRINCIPAL SUBJECTS:
Advertising
Architecture
Business & Industry
Editorial
Education
General Interest
Journalism
Media
Personalities
Photography
Senior Citizens
The Arts
Travel
Women's Interest
PUBLICATIONS:
Parade
Car & Driver
The Washington Post
Smithsonian
Electronic Business
Engineering News Record
Wonderful West Virginia

FISHER, RAY
10700 S.W. 72nd Court
Miami, FL 33156
Telephone: 305-665-7659
AFFILIATIONS:
NPPA,ASMP, PAI
PRINCIPAL SUBJECTS:
Editorial
General Interest
Management
Photography
The Arts
Travel
Entertainment
PUBLICATIONS:
Time
Forbes
Playboy
Life
N.Y. Times
Reader's Digest

FITZHUGH, SUSIE
3406 Chestnut Avenue
Baltimore, MD 21211
Telephone: 410-243-6112
Fax: 410-243-0205
AFFILIATIONS:
ASMP
PRINCIPAL SUBJECTS:
Youth
Education
Health
PUBLICATIONS:
Life
Audubon
Washington Post Magazine

FLEMING, LARRY
P.O. Box 3823
Wichita, KS 67201
Telephone: 316-267-0780
AFFILIATIONS:
ASMP
PRINCIPAL SUBJECTS:
Advertising
Agriculture
Editorial
General Interest
Human Interest
Journalism
Management
News
Photography
Sports
Travel
PUBLICATIONS:
Forbes
Fortune
Business Week
Midwest Living
Time
Success
Farm Journal

FLETCHER, T. MIKE
7467 Kingsbury Blvd.
Saint Louis, MO 63130
Telephone: 314-721-2279
AFFILIATIONS:
NPPA
PRINCIPAL SUBJECTS:
Advertising
Editorial
General Interest
Government
PUBLICATIONS:
Time Magazine
People
Fortune
Business Week
Forbes

FLORET, EVELYN
3 E. 80th St.
New York, NY 10021
Telephone: 212-472-3179
AFFILIATIONS:
ASMP
PRINCIPAL SUBJECTS:
Editorial
Fashion
Journalism
Photography
PUBLICATIONS:
People
Time
Avenue
Sports Illustrated

FLOTTE, LUCIEN
5 West 31st St., 8th Fl.
New York, NY 10001
Telephone: 212-564-9670
AFFILIATIONS:
ASMP
PRINCIPAL SUBJECTS:
Advertising
Amusements
Animals
Architecture
Ecology
Editorial
Education
Electronics
Entertainment
Fashion
Foreign
General Interest
Humor
Marine
Media
Military
Photography
Sports
Travel
Women's Interest
PUBLICATIONS:
Elle
Home Magazine
Pop Photo
Stereo Review
Car & Driver
Guitar Magazine
Sony Magazine
Musician Magazine

FORBERT, DAVID J.
6 Whitewood Rd.
White Plains, NY 10603
Telephone: 914-592-9451
Fax: 914-592-9451
AFFILIATIONS:
ASMP, ASPP, PAI

PRINCIPAL SUBJECTS:
Advertising
General Interest
Travel
The Arts
Photography
Architecture
Ecology
Education
History
Home & Garden
Nature
Senior Citizens
PUBLICATIONS:
Readers Digest
National Geographic Mag.
American Express
Newsweek

FORDEN, J. PATRICK
P.O. Box 77334
San Francisco, CA 94107
Telephone: 415-441-1250
Fax: 415-441-1197
AFFILIATIONS:
ASMP
PRINCIPAL SUBJECTS:
Advertising
Agriculture
Architecture
Business & Industry
Editorial
Food/Diet
General Interest
Journalism
News
Personalities
Photography
The Arts
Travel
Urban Affairs
PUBLICATIONS:
Newsweek
Time
US News & World Report
Paris Match (France)
Le Point (France)
Epoca (Italy)
Elle (France)

FORMISANO-MAYERI, YONI
84 Southwood Drive
Orinda, CA 94563
Telephone: 510-254-2000
Fax: 510-254-5029
AFFILIATIONS:
ASMP, APA
PRINCIPAL SUBJECTS:
Architecture
Editorial
Family

Personalities
Youth
PUBLICATIONS:
Rolling Stone
Architectural Record Review
Northern California
Home & Garden
Diablo
Sunset

FORSTER, DANIEL
124 Green End Ave.
Middletown, RI 02840
Telephone: 401-847-4866
Fax: 401-846-5574
AFFILIATIONS:
ASMP
PRINCIPAL SUBJECTS:
Sports
Travel
PUBLICATIONS:
Time
Sports Illustated
Life
Outside

FOSTER, KEVIN
P.O. Box 68520,
  8081 Zionsville Rd.
Indianapolis, IN 46268
Telephone: 800-428-4220
Fax: 317-872-2635
AFFILIATIONS:
ASMP
PRINCIPAL SUBJECTS:
Advertising
Business & Industry
Computer Technology
Electronics
Family
Health
Human Interest
Human Relations
Medical
Photography
PUBLICATIONS:
USA Today
Time

FOSTER, LEE
P.O. Box 5715
Berkeley, CA 94705
Telephone: 510-549-2202
AFFILIATIONS:
ASMP, SATW
PRINCIPAL SUBJECTS:
Computer Technology
Editorial
Nature
Photography
Travel

PUBLICATIONS:
Travel & Leisure
New York Times
Canadian
San Jose Mercury
Farm Family America

FOSTER, NICHOLAS
143 Claremolnt Rd.
Bernardsville, NJ 07924
Telephone: 908-766-7526
AFFILIATIONS:
ASMP
PRINCIPAL SUBJECTS:
Nature
Travel
The Arts
PUBLICATIONS:
Life
Popular Photography

FOSTER, RANDY
809 Main St.
Creighton, NE 68729
Telephone: 402-358-3293
MAILING ADDRESS:
RANDY FOSTER
Box 7
Creighton, NE 68729
Telephone: 402-358-5396
AFFILIATIONS:
PPN, PPA
PUBLICATIONS:
Farm Journal

FOURRE, LIZA
840 Ford Centre, 420 N. 5th St.
Minneapolis, MN 55401
Telephone: 612-338-1790
Fax: 612-338-7395
AFFILIATIONS:
ASMP, MCIPA
PRINCIPAL SUBJECTS:
Advertising
Editorial
Family
Fashion
Foreign
Health
Medical
Travel
PUBLICATIONS:
Minnesota Monthly
On Location
Caugill News
Pulse Magazine
The Power of Dress

FOWLEY, DOUGLAS
103 N. Hite Ave.
Louisville, KY 40206

Telephone: 502-897-7222
Fax: 502-897-7636
AFFILIATIONS:
ASMP
PRINCIPAL SUBJECTS:
Medical
Business & Industry
Architecture

FOXX, JEFFREY JAY
307 Park Place
Brooklyn, NY 11238
Telephone: 718-783-2043
Fax: 718-622-0065
AFFILIATIONS:
ASMP
PRINCIPAL SUBJECTS:
Ecology
Editorial
Geography
Photography
Social Trends
Travel
Video
PUBLICATIONS:
Living Maya
Turquoise Trail:
  Jewelry & Culture

FRANCIA, ANTHONY L.
3747 S. Kenilworth
Berwyn, IL 60402
Telephone: 708-788-8669
PRINCIPAL SUBJECTS:
Architecture
Advertising

FRANZEN, DAVID
15 Hekili St., #100
Kailua, HI 96734
Telephone: 808-261-9998
Fax: 808-262-4456
AFFILIATIONS:
ASMP
PRINCIPAL SUBJECTS:
Advertising
Architecture
Business & Industry
Editorial
Food/Diet
General Interest
Travel
PUBLICATIONS:
Town & Country
Forbes
Sunset
Designers West
Architectural Record
Interiors
Aloha

FREEMAN, DAVIS
365 Wheeler St.
Seattle, WA 98109
Telephone: 206-284-1767
AFFILIATIONS:
ASMP
PRINCIPAL SUBJECTS:
Business & Industry
Health
Medical
Personalities
Photography
PUBLICATIONS:
New York Times
Newsweek
Fame
US News & World Report

FREEMAN, JOHN
TX Christian Univ.,
  P.O. Box 30793
Fort Worth, TX 76129
Telephone: 817-921-7630
Fax: 817-921-7333
MAILING ADDRESS:
P.O. Box 30793
Fort Worth, TX 76129
AFFILIATIONS:
ITVA, SMPTE,BEA
PRINCIPAL SUBJECTS:
Education
General Interest
Photography
Journalism
PUBLICATIONS:
Journal of Film & Video

FREEMAN, ROLAND
117 Ingraham Street, NW
Washington, DC 20011
Telephone: 202-882-7764
Fax: 202-829-6814
PRINCIPAL SUBJECTS:
Photography
Editorial
Business & Industry
Video

FREEMAN, TINA
1040 Magazine St.
New Orleans, LA 70130
Telephone: 504-523-3000
Fax: 504-581-4397
AFFILIATIONS:
ASMP
PRINCIPAL SUBJECTS:
Architecture
Editorial
Home & Garden
Photography
The Arts

PUBLICATIONS:
New York Tinmes Magazine
Home & Garden
Art & Antiques
Southern Accents
Architectural Digest
The Connoisseur
Country Life
Elle Decoration
Elle Decor
Forbes

FRENCH, PETER
P.O. Box 100
Kamuela, HI 96743
Telephone: 808-884-5588
Fax: 808-885-5655
AFFILIATIONS:
ASMP
PRINCIPAL SUBJECTS:
Advertising
Architecture
Ecology
Editorial
Entertainment
Foreign
General Interest
Geography
Human Interest
Human Relations
Journalism
Marine
Marketing
Media
Nature
Photography
Physical Fitness
Religion
Sports
The Arts
Travel
Youth
PUBLICATIONS:
Travel/Leisure
Geo.
Islands
Travel/Holiday
Adventure/West
Nat. Geographic
Tennis
Bicycling

FRICK, KEN
66 Northmoor Pl.
Columbus, OH 43214
Telephone: 614-263-9955
AFFILIATIONS:
ASMP
PRINCIPAL SUBJECTS:
Advertising
Editorial

General Interest
Human Interest
Human Relations
Humor
Journalism
Nature

FRIEDMAN, IRV
1326 S.E. Vestridge Lane
Port St. Lucie, FL 34952
Telephone: 407-335-9388
AFFILIATIONS:
ASMP, SPE, FPPI
PRINCIPAL SUBJECTS:
Entertainment
General Interest
Human Interest
Journalism
The Arts
PUBLICATIONS:
Miami Herald
Port St. Lucie News
Focus Magazine
Treasure Coast
  Pictorial
Fort Pierce
  Tribune
Palm Beach Post
Around Towne

FRIEDMAN, RICK
133 BEACONSFIELD RD.,
  STE. 11
BROOKLINE, MA 02146
Telephone: 617-734-8125
Fax: 617-734-4557
AFFILIATIONS:
ASMP, NPPA
PRINCIPAL SUBJECTS:
Editorial
Government
News
Photography
Science
Travel
PUBLICATIONS:
Time
Newsweek
US News &
  World Report
Discover
New York Times
Business Week
Travel & Leisure
Science
Time
Newsweek

FRIEDMAN, RONALD A.
6400 Falkirk Rd.
Baltimore, MD 21239
Telephone: 410-377-7484
PRINCIPAL SUBJECTS:
Travel

FRIES, JANET
4439 Ellicott St., N.W.
Washington, DC 20016
Telephone: 202-362-4443
AFFILIATIONS:
ASMP
PUBLICATIONS:
Washingtonian Magazine
Washington Post
New York Times
American Lawyer Magazine
Corporate Finance Magazine

FRIESE, RICK
P.O. Box 31658
Palm Beach Gardens,
  FL 33420
Telephone: 407-627-8989
Fax: 407-624-3961
AFFILIATIONS:
ASMP
PRINCIPAL SUBJECTS:
Advertising
Architecture
Editorial
General Interest
Marine
Travel
PUBLICATIONS:
Architectural Digest
The Robb Report
Yachting
Sail
Cruising World
Boat International
Canadian Yachting

FRISCH, STEPHEN
480 Gate 5 Rd., Studio 258
Sausalito, CA 94965
Telephone: 415-332-4545
AFFILIATIONS:
ASMP, ASPP
PRINCIPAL SUBJECTS:
Advertising
Agriculture
Architecture
Editorial
Education
Marine
Medical
Science
PUBLICATIONS:
National Geographic

Time
Life
Fortune

FRITZ, BRIAN
1246 Daryl Ln.
Northbrook, IL 60062
Telephone: 708-272-9459
PRINCIPAL SUBJECTS:
Photography

FRITZ, BRUCE
10 Quinn Circle
Madison, WI 53713
Telephone: 608-222-5299
Fax: 608-222-5230
AFFILIATIONS:
ASMP, NPPA
PRINCIPAL SUBJECTS:
Advertising
Agriculture
Business & Industry
Computer Technology
Editorial
Journalism
Media
Medical
Nature
Science
PUBLICATIONS:
National Geographic
Time
Newsweek
US
New York Times
Stern
Barrons
USA Today

FRITZ, GERARD
1306 Matthews Plantation Dr.
Matthews, NC 28105
Telephone: 704-841-8181
Fax: 704-841-8181
AFFILIATIONS:
ASMP, PPA
PRINCIPAL SUBJECTS:
Advertising
Business & Industry
Computer Technology
Electronics
Health
Physical Fitness
Science
PUBLICATIONS:
Business North Carolina
US News & World Report
The Charlotte Observer
Charlotte Magazine

FRITZ, TOM
2930 W. Clybourn
Milwaukee, WI 53208
Telephone: 414-344-8300
Fax: 414-344-6155
AFFILIATIONS:
ASMP
PRINCIPAL SUBJECTS:
Advertising
Architecture
Photography
PUBLICATIONS:
American Showcase

FRY III, GEORGE B.
10 Maple Ave.
Atherton, CA 94027
Telephone: 415-323-7663
Fax: 415-323-9835
MAILING ADDRESS:
GEORGE B. FRY III
P.O. Box 2465
Menlo Park, CA 94026
AFFILIATIONS:
ASMP, PAPA
PRINCIPAL SUBJECTS:
Advertising
Electronics
General Interest
Personalities
Photography
PUBLICATIONS:
SI For Kids
SI For Kids

FUKUHARA, RICHARD
  YUTAKA
1032 - 2 W. Taft Ave.
Orange, CA 92665
Telephone: 714-998-8790
Fax: 718-998-0545
AFFILIATIONS:
ASMP, APA
PRINCIPAL SUBJECTS:
Advertising
Editorial
General Interest
PUBLICATIONS:
Westways Magazine
Home Magazine
L.A. Times
Occidental Annual Report
Popular Photography
Modern Maturity
IEEE Magazine

FULTON, CONRAD JAMES
5916 Vesper Ave.
Van Nuys, CA 91411
Telephone: 818-989-2072

AFFILIATIONS:
ASMP, EPIC
PRINCIPAL SUBJECTS:
Editorial
Human Relations
Business & Industry
Animals
Human Interest
Personalities
Entertainment
The Arts
PUBLICATIONS:
Calif. Builder & Engineer Mag.
Tatteler Mag.
Review Mag.
Dodge News
Valley Times Newspaper
Town & Country
The U.S.A. Magazine In Russia
Ultra Magazine
Archituctural Digest
USIA Information Service
Louvre Museum Catalog
Los Angeles Times
Herald Examiner
Beverly Hills Citizen News
Valley Times
Daily News
B H People
Santa Monica Outlook
Society West
Dodge News
Town & Country
Palm Beach Life
Holiday
Architectural Digest
Tattler
Rogers & Cowan
Capitol Records
KFAC Radio
President Nixon
President Ford
Premier of Japan
John Wayne
Agnes Moorhead
George Harrison
Mayor Bradley
Bob Hope
Helen Hayes
Donald O'Connor
Gene Kelly
Gov. Reagan
Gov. Brown

FUSCO, PAUL
72 Spring St.
New York, NY 10012
Telephone: 212-966-9200
MAILING ADDRESS:
PAUL FUSCO/MAGNUM
  PHOTOS

P.O. Box 1427
Mill Valley, CA 94942
AFFILIATIONS:
ASMP
PRINCIPAL SUBJECTS:
Advertising
Editorial
Business & Industry
Human Interest
PUBLICATIONS:
Life
N.Y.T. Magazine
AM. Health
Hippocrates
Time
Newsweek
Esquire
Money
People

FUSS, EDUARDO
P.O. Box 8400
Santa Fe, NM 87504
Telephone: 505-988-9172
AFFILIATIONS:
ASMP
PRINCIPAL SUBJECTS:
Editorial
General Interest
Nature
PUBLICATIONS:
Smithsonian Magazine
Audubon
Modern Maturity
Arizona Highways
Reader's Digest
New York Times
Bunte Illustrierte
Airone

GAGE, HAL
2008 E. Northern Lights
Anchorage, AK 99508
Telephone: 907-272-4356
AFFILIATIONS:
ASMP, MPCA
PRINCIPAL SUBJECTS:
Advertising
Computer Technology
The Arts
Travel
PUBLICATIONS:
Alaska Magazine
Alaska Quarterly Review
Wall Street Review

GALLIAN, DIRK
P.O. Box 541
Lotus, CA 95651
Telephone: 800-562-3342
Fax: 713-868-2414

PRINCIPAL SUBJECTS:
Sports
Advertising

GAMAGE, DOUGLAS C.
26 Glen St.
Riverside, RI 02915
Telephone: 401-433-4475
AFFILIATIONS:
ASMP, MP
PRINCIPAL SUBJECTS:
Advertising
Human Interest
Journalism
Sports
Travel
PUBLICATIONS:
E. Providence Post
Life Magazine
Yankee Magazine
Time Magazine
New England Business
 Magazine

GAMMA LIAISON INC.
11 E. 26th St.
New York, NY 10010
Telephone: 212-447-2500
Fax: 212-447-2534
PRINCIPAL SUBJECTS:
Amusements
Aviation
Business & Industry
Editorial
Entertainment
Foreign
General Interest
Government
Human Interest
Human Relations
Journalism
Marketing
Men's Interest
Military
Movie Reviews
News
Personalities
Photography
Science
The Arts
Women's Interest
World Affairs

GANDY, SKIP
302 E. Davis Blvd.
Tampa, FL 33606
Telephone: 813-253-0340
Fax: 813-251-0731
AFFILIATIONS:
ASMP

PRINCIPAL SUBJECTS:
Marine
Business & Industry
Nature
Journalism
Aviation
PUBLICATIONS:
Popular Mechanics
Fordtimes
Boating
Financial Planning

GARIK, ALICE
P.O. Box 147
East Arlington, VT 05252
Telephone: 802-375-1079
AFFILIATIONS:
AP/NY
PRINCIPAL SUBJECTS:
Advertising
Agriculture
Architecture
Business & Industry
Ecology
Editorial
Fashion
Home & Garden
Nature
Sports
The Arts
Women's Interest
PUBLICATIONS:
World Magazine
Ms

GARLAND, MICHAEL E.
26 Avenue 28
Venice, CA 90291
Telephone: 310-827-0670
AFFILIATIONS:
ASMP
PRINCIPAL SUBJECTS:
Advertising
Architecture
Editorial
Entertainment
General Interest
Geography
Home & Garden
Men's Interest
Nature
Photography
Science
The Arts
Travel
PUBLICATIONS:
Time
Newsweek
Esquire
Premiere
U.S.

Home
Money
L.A. Style

GAROFALO, JOHN
 CLEVELAND
10743 Lake Forest Drive
Manassas, VA 22111
Telephone: 703-368-3861
Fax: 703-361-9232
AFFILIATIONS:
ASMP, NPPA
PRINCIPAL SUBJECTS:
Family
Journalism
Editorial
Business & Industry
Advertising
PUBLICATIONS:
Detroit Free Press
Washington Post
Washington Times
Newsday

GARRETT, KENNETH
P.O. Box 208
Broad Run, VA 22014
Telephone: 703-347-5848
Fax: 703-347-2601
PRINCIPAL SUBJECTS:
Editorial
Business & Industry
Architecture

GARRISON, RON
Zoo Drive, Balboa Park
San Diego, CA 92112
Telephone: 619-231-1515
Fax: 619-231-1725
MAILING ADDRESS:
PHOTO LAB,
 SAN DIEGO ZOO
P.O. Box 551
San Diego, CA 92112
AFFILIATIONS:
ASMP
PRINCIPAL SUBJECTS:
Animals
Nature
PUBLICATIONS:
Earthwatch Magazine
BBC Wildlife Magazine
National Geographic Books
Weekly Reader Magazine
Discover Magazine
World Book
Disney Publications
National Enquirer
Das Tier Magazine (German)

GEER, GARRY
183 Saint Paul St., #404
Rochester, NY 14604
Telephone: 716-232-2393
Fax: :716-262-996
AFFILIATIONS:
ASMP/WNY
PRINCIPAL SUBJECTS:
Advertising
Animals
Business & Industry
Editorial
Marketing
Photography

GEFTER, JUDITH
1725 Clemson Road
Jacksonville, FL 32217
Telephone: 904-733-5498
AFFILIATIONS:
ASMP
PRINCIPAL SUBJECTS:
Advertising
Amusements
Architecture
Business & Industry
Computer Technology
Editorial
Family
General Interest
Hobbies
Human Interest
Human Relations
Journalism
Media
Medical
Nature
News
Personalities
Photography
Senior Citizens
The Arts
Travel
Women's Interest
PUBLICATIONS:
Life
Time
Newsweek
Fortune
Forbes
Cosmopolitan
Money
Sports Illustrated

GEIGER, K. WILLIAM
4944 Quebec St., N.W.
Washington, DC 20016
Telephone: 202-244-7245
AFFILIATIONS:
ASMP

PRINCIPAL SUBJECTS:
Architecture
Editorial
Foreign
General Interest
History
Human Interest
Journalism
Medical
Personalities
Photography
Travel
PUBLICATIONS:
National Geographic
Smithsonian
Country Journal
Mid-Atlantic Country
Outside
Historic Preservation
National Parks
C-Span Quarterly

GEIGER, WILLIAM K.
4944 Quebec St., N.W.
Washington, DC 20016
Telephone: 202-244-7245
MAILING ADDRESS:
GEIGER PHOTOGRAPHY
Washington, DC 20016
PRINCIPAL SUBJECTS:
Aviation
Editorial
History
Travel
PUBLICATIONS:
Travel & Leisure
Outside
Denver Post
National Geographic
Washington Post
Historical Preservation

GELLER, ALAN
1360 Lombard
San Francisco, CA 94109
Telephone: 415-775-2497
AFFILIATIONS:
ASMP
PRINCIPAL SUBJECTS:
Architecture
Travel
PUBLICATIONS:
Sunset Magazine
San Francisco Chronicle
Builder Magazine

GENTILE, SR., ARTHUR
P.O. Box 32188
Charlotte, NC 28232
Telephone: 704-358-5856
Fax: 704-358-5865

AFFILIATIONS:
ASMP
PRINCIPAL SUBJECTS:
Photography
Aviation
Architecture
Advertising
Automotive
Editorial
PUBLICATIONS:
Time
Newsweek
People
Southern Accents
The Charlotte Observer
Parade
Readers Digest

GERCZYNSKI, TOM
2211 N. 7th Ave.
Phoenix, AZ 85007
Telephone: 602-252-9229
Fax: 602-271-9355
AFFILIATIONS:
ASMP
PRINCIPAL SUBJECTS:
Advertising
Architecture
Aviation
Family
Photography
Senior Citizens
Travel
PUBLICATIONS:
Elle
Dance
Popular Mechanics
Better Homes & Gardens
New Choices
Arizona Highways

GESCHEIDT, ALFRED
175 Lexington Ave.
New York, NY 10016
Telephone: 212-889-4023
AFFILIATIONS:
ASMP,JEC, ASL
PRINCIPAL SUBJECTS:
General Interest
Amusements
PUBLICATIONS:
Woman's Day
Esquire
Time Magazine
Psychlogy Today
New York Magazine
Parade
Psychology Today
Madison Ave.
New York Times, The

GETLEN, DAVID
60 Gramercy Park
New York, NY 10010
Telephone: 212-475-6940
Fax: 212-475-6940
AFFILIATIONS:
ASMP
PRINCIPAL SUBJECTS:
Editorial
General Interest
Marketing
Nature
Physical Fitness
Sports
Travel
PUBLICATIONS:
Runners World
World Tennis
Stern
Running Times
New York Running News
Ultra Sport
Vogue

GIAMMATTEO, JOHN
343 Jackson Hill RD.
Middlefield, CT 06455
Telephone: 203-349-3743
Fax: 203-349-8110
AFFILIATIONS:
ASMP
PRINCIPAL SUBJECTS:
Advertising
Architecture
Business & Industry
Foreign
Photography

GIANNINI, GEMMA
117 Monument Avenue
Barrington, IL 60010
Telephone: 708-381-1840
AFFILIATIONS:
ASMP, ASPP
PRINCIPAL SUBJECTS:
Animals
Sports
Home & Garden
PUBLICATIONS:
Horses Illustrated
Equus
Hunter & Sporthorse
The Sentinel

GIBSON, MARK & AUDREY
GIBSON COLOR
  PHOTOGRAPHY
112 N. WASHINGTON DR.
MT. SHASTA, CA 96067
Telephone: 916-926-5966
Fax: 916-926-5968

AFFILIATIONS:
ASMP
PRINCIPAL SUBJECTS:
Agriculture
Architecture
Business & Industry
Computer Technology
Ecology
Editorial
Education
General Interest
Geography
Home & Garden
Human Interest
Nature
Photography
Physical Fitness
Social Trends
Sports
Travel
Urban Affairs
Women's Interest
PUBLICATIONS:
National Geographic Traveler
Travel & Leisure
Delta Sky
Chevron USA Odyssey
AAA Travel Publications

GIBSON, RALPH
630 Central Ave.
New Providence, NJ 07974
PRINCIPAL SUBJECTS:
Editorial

GIPE, JON
6747 N. 10th St.
Phoenix, AZ 85014
Telephone: 602-230-8266
Fax: 602-230-1570
PRINCIPAL SUBJECTS:
Journalism
Human Interest
Business & Industry

GLASS, BRUCE
6200 Gulfton, #1003
Houston, TX 77081
Telephone: 713-772-4150
AFFILIATIONS:
ASMP
PRINCIPAL SUBJECTS:
Advertising
Architecture
Business & Industry

GLASSMAN, KEITH
365 1st Ave.
New York, NY 10010
Telephone: 212-353-1214
Fax: 212-353-1675

AFFILIATIONS:
ASMP
PRINCIPAL SUBJECTS:
Advertising
Business & Industry
Editorial
Food/Diet
Photography

GLEASNER, BILL
7994 Holly Ct.
Denver, NC 28037
Telephone: 704-483-9301
AFFILIATIONS:
ASMP, SATW, TJG
PRINCIPAL SUBJECTS:
Journalism
Photography
Travel
PUBLICATIONS:
National Geographic Traveler
American Way
New York Times
San Antonio Express News
Toronto Star
Touring America

GNASS, JEFF
P.O. Box 3400
Sisters, OR 97759
Telephone: 503-389-4301
Fax: 503-389-4602
AFFILIATIONS:
ASMP, ASPP
PRINCIPAL SUBJECTS:
Advertising
Animals
Ecology
Editorial
Education
Geography
History
Marketing
Nature
Travel
PUBLICATIONS:
Alaska Airlines
Disneyland Creative Services
Eastman Kodak
GEO
Holland America
IBM
Nike
Revlon

GOGNO, ANITA
1345 Timber Lane
Hatfield, PA 19440
Telephone: 215-855-3863
Fax: 303-442-3937

GOHLICH, ED
102 Tunapuna Lane
Coronado, CA 92118
Telephone: 619-423-4237
Fax: 619-423-0493
AFFILIATIONS:
ASMP
PRINCIPAL SUBJECTS:
Architecture
Home & Garden
PUBLICATIONS:
Architectural Record
Better Homes & Gardens
Designers West
Kitchen & Bath Ideas
Bedroom & Bath Ideas

GOLD, GARY
454 North Pearl Street
Albany, NY 12204
Telephone: 518-434-4887
Fax: 518-434-6185
AFFILIATIONS:
ASMP, PPA, ARPA
PRINCIPAL SUBJECTS:
Business & Industry
Aviation
Ecology
Photography
Sports

GOLD, SAMMY
4238 S. Alameda St.
Crp Christi, TX 78412
Telephone: 512-992-7400
AFFILIATIONS:
PPA, ASP, TPPA
PRINCIPAL SUBJECTS:
Aviation
General Interest
Journalism
PUBLICATIONS:
Wendy's Magazine,
   August 1987
USA Today

GOLDBERG, JEFF
201 East 12th St. #404
New York, NY 10003
Telephone: 212-505-1285
AFFILIATIONS:
ASMP, AL
PRINCIPAL SUBJECTS:
Architecture
History
Photography
The Arts
PUBLICATIONS:
Newsweek
Time
Interiors

Architecture
Architectural Record
Interior Design

GOLDBLATT, STEVEN
32 S. Strawberry St.
Philadelphia, PA 19106
Telephone: 215-925-3825
Fax: 215-925-1925
AFFILIATIONS:
ASMP, PPA
PRINCIPAL SUBJECTS:
Business & Industry
Editorial
Management
Photography
Advertising
PUBLICATIONS:
Newsweek
N. Y. Times
National Geographic
Business Week
Philadelphia Magazine
Nation's Business Magazine

GOOD, JAY
20901 NE 26 Ave.
N. Miami Beach, FL 33180
Telephone: 305-935-4884
Fax: 305-935-9225
AFFILIATIONS:
ASMP
PRINCIPAL SUBJECTS:
Aviation
Business & Industry
Editorial
Entertainment
General Interest
Health
Journalism
Photography
Travel
PUBLICATIONS:
The Village Voice
New York Magazine
South Florida Magazine
Newsweek
Texas Monthly Magazine
Life Magazine
Good Housekeeping
Harpers' Bazaar

GOODE, PAUL B.
165 W. 83rd St., Apt. 41
New York, NY 10024
Telephone: 212-874-0713
PRINCIPAL SUBJECTS:
Foreign
The Arts
Women's Interest
Physical Fitness

GOODHEIM, JANIS
P.O. Box 3616
Boise, ID 83703
Telephone: 208-336-9518
AFFILIATIONS:
ASMP
PRINCIPAL SUBJECTS:
Editorial
Architecture
Advertising
PUBLICATIONS:
Signs

GOODMAN, LISA J.
7 Garrett Rd.
Wilmington, DE 19809
Telephone: 302-792-2141
Fax: 302-792-2140
AFFILIATIONS:
ASMP
PRINCIPAL SUBJECTS:
Advertising
Agriculture
Architecture
Business & Industry
Computer Technology
Ecology
Editorial
Electronics
Family
Foreign
General Interest
Home & Garden
Human Interest
Human Relations
Management
Marketing
Media
Medical
Photography
Social Trends
The Arts
Travel

GOOLSBY, JOHN
P.O. Box 146
Mira Loma, CA 91752
Telephone: 909-685-5530
AFFILIATIONS:
PPA, WPI
PRINCIPAL SUBJECTS:
Media
Religion
Human Interest
PUBLICATIONS:
Coverage of PPA Conventions
   1990, 1991, 1992
The Rangefinder

GORDON, FRANK
5977 Laurel St.
New Orleans, LA 70115
Telephone: 504-899-9793
Fax: 504-899-6240
AFFILIATIONS:
ASMP, GNOCC
PRINCIPAL SUBJECTS:
Advertising
Agriculture
Amusements
Architecture
Entertainment
General Interest
Geography
Health
History
Marine
Physical Fitness
Senior Citizens
Sports
Travel
PUBLICATIONS:
Yachting
Sailing
Sail
National Geographic
Black's List
Louisiana Life
New Orleans Magazine
Travel

GORE, ARNOLD
316 N. Milwaukee St.
Milwaukee, WI 53202
Telephone: 414-271-7646
MAILING ADDRESS:
ARNOLD GORE, INC.
Milwaukee, WI 53202
Telephone: 414-964-8891
PRINCIPAL SUBJECTS:
Advertising
Photography
General Interest
PUBLICATIONS:
Time
Fortune
Business Week

GORIN, BART
126 11th Ave.
New York, NY 10011
Telephone: 212-727-7344
AFFILIATIONS:
ASMP
PRINCIPAL SUBJECTS:
Advertising

GORNICK JR., ALAN
4200 Camino Real
Los Angeles, CA 90065

Telephone: 213-223-8914
Fax: 213-221-9935
AFFILIATIONS:
ASMP, IATSE 659
PRINCIPAL SUBJECTS:
General Interest
Geography
Marine
Travel
Advertising
PUBLICATIONS:
Photographic
Skin Diver
Let's Live
Sea Frontiers
Sea Secrets
American Rifleman
American Marksman
Gun Week
Precision Shooting
International Photographer
Model Airplane News

GORRILL, ROBERT B.
70 Gladstone St.
Squantum, MA 02171
Telephone: 617-328-4012
Fax: 617-328-4012
MAILING ADDRESS:
R. B. GORRILL/BOB BARRY
   STUDIO
P. O. Box 206
North Quincy, MA 02171
AFFILIATIONS:
ASMP
PRINCIPAL SUBJECTS:
Photography
General Interest
Geography
Fashion
Business & Industry
PUBLICATIONS:
Boston Sunday Globe
Boston Herald Magazine
Dynamic Years
The Patriot Ledger
The Quincy Sun
Modern Maturity

GOTFRYD, BERNARD
46 Wendover Rd.
Flushing, NY 11375
Telephone: 718-261-8039
AFFILIATIONS:
ASMP
PRINCIPAL SUBJECTS:
General Interest
Advertising
Journalism
Personalities
The Arts

PUBLICATIONS:
Newsweek
Latin American & USIA Publ.
Schweitzer Illustrierte
Stern
Bunte
Epoca
Der Spiegel
Editora Abril
N.Y. Mag
Forbes
Insight
Focus
McCalls - Vanity Fair
Applause
Special Report
New York Times
Life Magazine
Burda
Vanity Fair
WJR
World Press
Changing Times
Weltwoche Magazine
English Forward-Weekly
   Tabloid
Literay Cavalcade
Jewish Monthly
Congress Monthly
Lifestyles
Dan's Paper
Parade Mag.
People
Scholastic
Essence

GOTTLIEB, STEVEN
3601 East-West Hwy.
Chevy Chase, MD 20815
Telephone: 301-951-9648
Fax: 301-951-9649
AFFILIATIONS:
ASMP
PRINCIPAL SUBJECTS:
Advertising
Architecture
Government
Human Interest
Personalities
Travel

GOVE, GEOFFREY
117 Waverly Pl., S.E.
New York, NY 10011
Telephone: 212-260-6051
AFFILIATIONS:
ASMP, ASPP, SPE
PRINCIPAL SUBJECTS:
Animals
Business & Industry
Computer Technology

Ecology
Foreign
Geography
Health
History
Media
Medical
Nature
Photography
Psychology
Sports
The Arts
Travel
Video
Youth
PUBLICATIONS:
Psychology Today
Sports Illustrated

GRAHAM, A. MICHAEL
771 N.W. 122 St.
N. Miami, FL 33168
Telephone: 305-681-7601
Fax: 305-687-8438
PRINCIPAL SUBJECTS:
Advertising
Agriculture
Animals
Architecture
Editorial
Education
Food/Diet
Home & Garden
Marine
Nature
Senior Citizens
Travel
Urban Affairs
Youth
PUBLICATIONS:
Bird Talk
Seafood Leader
Miami Times

GRAHAM, STEPHEN
1120 W. Stadium Blvd., #2
Ann Arbor, MI 48103
Telephone: 313-761-6888
Fax: 313-761-1416
PRINCIPAL SUBJECTS:
Advertising
Architecture
Aviation
Business & Industry
Editorial
Foreign
Government
Travel
Video
PUBLICATIONS:
Corporate Detroit

Fortune
New Choices
Building Ideas
Eye Weekly-Toronto
Internal Medicine News
Victorian Homes

GRANNIS, BOB
4044R Hillsboro Rd.
Nashville, TN 37215
Telephone: 615-383-3432
MAILING ADDRESS:
GRANNIS PHOTOGRAPHY
Nashville, TN 37215
Telephone: 615-646-3656
AFFILIATIONS:
TPPA, PPA, SEP
PRINCIPAL SUBJECTS:
Advertising
General Interest

GREEN-ARMYTAGE,
  STEPHEN
171 West 57th St., 7a
New York, NY 10019
Telephone: 212-247-6314
PRINCIPAL SUBJECTS:
Advertising
Personalities
Business & Industry
Sports
Family
Agriculture
Animals
Architecture
Ecology
Editorial
Editorial
General Interest
Geography
Travel
Physical Fitness
PUBLICATIONS:
Sports Illustrated
Good Housekeeping
Fortune
Smithsonian

GREENBERG, CHIP
Greenberg, Chip Studios Inc.
325 High St.
Metuchen, NJ 08840
Telephone: 908-548-5612
AFFILIATIONS:
ASMP
PRINCIPAL SUBJECTS:
Advertising
Business & Industry
Computer Technology

GREENBERG, STANLEY
136 Dean St.
Brooklyn, NY 11217
Telephone: 718-522-0056
PRINCIPAL SUBJECTS:
Architecture
Home & Garden

GREENBLATT, WILLIAM D.
20 Nantucket Ln.
Saint Louis, MO 63132
Telephone: 314-554-1000
Fax: 314-289-1977
MAILING ADDRESS:
WILLIAM GREENBLATT
  PHOTOGRAPHY
St. Louis, MO 63132
AFFILIATIONS:
NPPA/IRE/ASMP/SPJ
PRINCIPAL SUBJECTS:
Journalism
Business & Industry
Advertising

GREENFIELD, LAUREN
15 - 24th Ave.
Venice, CA 90291
Telephone: 310-821-5924
AFFILIATIONS:
ASMP, NPPA
PRINCIPAL SUBJECTS:
Travel
History
Youth
PUBLICATIONS:
Newsweek
Life
Time
National Geographic
L.A. Times Magazine

GREGG, BARRY
84 University, Suite 210
Seattle, WA 98101
Telephone: 206-285-8695
Fax: 206-622-8089
MAILING ADDRESS:
GREGG BARRY STUDIO
AFFILIATIONS:
ASMP
PRINCIPAL SUBJECTS:
Food/Diet
Personalities
PUBLICATIONS:
American Showcase

GREHAN, FARRELL
5 E. 22nd St. (22L)
New York, NY 10010
Telephone: 212-677-3999

AFFILIATIONS:
ASMP
PRINCIPAL SUBJECTS:
General Interest
Human Interest
Business & Industry
Nature
Travel
PUBLICATIONS:
Travel & Leisure
World & I, The
Sabbna Revue
Holland Herald

GRESHAM, GRITS
942 Williams Ave.
Natchitoches, LA 71457
Telephone: 318-357-8104
Fax: 318-352-4590
AFFILIATIONS:
OWAA
PRINCIPAL SUBJECTS:
Ecology
Travel
Hobbies
Nature
Sports
PUBLICATIONS:
Sports Afield
Gentleman's Quarterly
Sports Illustrated
Field & Stream
Outdoor Life

GREWELL, BOB
93 E. Columbus St.
Mt Sterling, OH 43143
Telephone: 614-869-2058
PRINCIPAL SUBJECTS:
Photography
Journalism
PUBLICATIONS:
Modern Photography
Darkroom Techniques
Petersen's Photographic
Darkroom Photography
Popular Mechanics
Field & Stream
Outdoor Life
Petersen's Hunting
Harris Outdoor Publications
Bow & Arrow
Bow Hunter
Archery World
Deer & Deer Hunting
Gun World
Gun's Magazine
Fins & Feathers
North American Hunter
Midwest Outdoors
Ohio Fisherman

Texas Fisherman
Outdoor Journal
Horse & Horseman
Game & Fish Publications
Ontario Out of Doors

GRIFFIN, ARTHUR L.
22 Euclid Ave.
Winchester, MA 01890
Telephone: 617-729-2690
AFFILIATIONS:
ASMP, NPP
PRINCIPAL SUBJECTS:
Foreign
Travel

GRIGG, ROGER
P.O. Box 52851
Atlanta, GA 30355
Telephone: 404-876-4748
AFFILIATIONS:
ASMP, IABC
PRINCIPAL SUBJECTS:
Business & Industry
Advertising
PUBLICATIONS:
Time
Los Angeles Times

GRIMES, BILLY
P.O. Box 5125 WSB
Gainesville, GA 30504
Telephone: 404-899-9975
AFFILIATIONS:
ASMP, NPPA
PRINCIPAL SUBJECTS:
Advertising
Editorial
Education
General Interest
Photography
Nature
PUBLICATIONS:
Fortune
Time
Business Week
Forbes
T.V. Guide
Discover
Newsweek
Parade
US News & World Report

GRIMM, MICHELE
P.O. Box 1840
Islamorada, FL 33036
Telephone: 305-664-8009
Fax: 305-664-5509
AFFILIATIONS:
SATW

PRINCIPAL SUBJECTS:
Photography
Travel
Animals
Foreign
Nature
PUBLICATIONS:
Orange Coast Magazine
Travel Editor,
    Orange Coast Magazine
Away for the Weekend
    Southern California

GROENE, GORDON
206 Lake Mamie Rd.
De Land, FL 32724
Telephone: 904-736-0313
AFFILIATIONS:
ASJA, BWI
PRINCIPAL SUBJECTS:
Aviation
General Interest
Travel
Sports
Automotive
Home & Garden
PUBLICATIONS:
Traveland U.S.A.
Touring America
The Southern Traveler
Family Motor Coaching
Miami Herald
Photography

GROSS, ALEX LLOYD
2500 Knights Rd., #20-01
Bensalem, PA 19020
Telephone: 215-639-8306
Fax: 215-881-8397
AFFILIATIONS:
NPPA
PRINCIPAL SUBJECTS:
Entertainment
General Interest
Journalism
News
Personalities
Sports
PUBLICATIONS:
Philadelphia Inquirer
Philadelphia Daily News
New York Times
Buck County Courier Times
Camden County Courier Post
Sterlings Magazines

GROTTA, SALLY WEINER
609 East Philadelphia Ave.
Boyertown, PA 19512
Telephone: 215-367-9496
Fax: 215-367-7130

AFFILIATIONS:
ASMP, TSM
PRINCIPAL SUBJECTS:
Computer Technology
Ecology
General Interest
Photography
Travel
PUBLICATIONS:
Time
Islands
The Robb Report
Popular Science
Computer Shopper
Photo Pro
Home Office Computing

GRUBB, ROBERT B.
6744 Lawnton Ave.
Philadelphia, PA 19126
Telephone: 215-548-0869
Fax: 215-548-7069
MAILING ADDRESS:
BOB GRUBB & SON
    PHOTOGRAPHY INC.
Philadelphia, PA 19126
Telephone: 215-548-1592
AFFILIATIONS:
PPA, SCPP
PRINCIPAL SUBJECTS:
Architecture
General Interest

GUBIN, MARK
2893 S. Delaware
Milwaukee, WI 53207
Telephone: 414-482-0640
Fax: 414-481-9320
AFFILIATIONS:
ASMP
PRINCIPAL SUBJECTS:
Advertising
Agriculture
Animals
Architecture
Business & Industry
Editorial
Fashion
Foreign
General Interest
History
Journalism
Marine
Media
Nature
News
Personalities
Photography
Travel
PUBLICATIONS:
Time

US News
Forbes
People
Stern
Family Circle
Architectural Digest
Newsweek

GURAVICH, DAN
407 Rebecca Drive
Greenville, MS 38701
Telephone: 601-335-2444
Fax: 601-332-9528
MAILING ADDRESS:
DAN GURAVICH
P.O. Box 891
Greenville, MS 38702
AFFILIATIONS:
SATW, TSG, ASMP
PRINCIPAL SUBJECTS:
Advertising
General Interest
Nature
Science
Travel
Agriculture
PUBLICATIONS:
Life
Outdoor Photography
Time
Audubon
Smithsonian
Natural History
Wild Life
Sports Afield
Sports Illustrated
Natural History
Canadian Geography
Popular Photography
Creative Living
Philip Morris Magazine

GWINN, BETH
2610 Oakland Ave.
Nashville, TN 37212
Telephone: 615-385-0917
Fax: 615-297-5754
MAILING ADDRESS:
BETH GWINN
P.O. Box 22817
Nashville, TN 37202
AFFILIATIONS:
ASMP
PRINCIPAL SUBJECTS:
Editorial
Personalities
Photography
PUBLICATIONS:
U.S. Magazine
Time Magazine
Locus

People
Guitar Player
U.S. Magazine
Time Magazine
Locus
People
Guitar Player

HACKNEY, KERRY
8609 N.W. 66th St.
Miami, FL 33166
Telephone: 305-592-3664
AFFILIATIONS:
ASMP
PRINCIPAL SUBJECTS:
Advertising

HADJOLIAN, SERGE
30 Central Park, S., Ste. 8B
New York, NY 10019
Telephone: 212-371-9696
Fax: 212-755-0199
AFFILIATIONS:
ASMP, ISP, ASPP
PUBLICATIONS:
Human Behavior
Journal Of Personality
    Assessment

HAILEY, JASON
4121 Redwood Ave., #101
Los Angeles, CA 90066
Telephone: 310-301-9592
Fax: 310-301-9592
AFFILIATIONS:
PP OF A, ASP
PRINCIPAL SUBJECTS:
Photography
The Arts
PUBLICATIONS:
Trade & Consumer Mag.
Art Publications
Designer's West
Graphis
Camercraftsmen of
    America - Book

HALL, DON
2922 Hyde Park Street
Sarasota, FL 34239
Telephone: 813-365-6161
Fax: 813-365-6161
AFFILIATIONS:
ASMP
PRINCIPAL SUBJECTS:
Advertising
Architecture
Automotive
Aviation
Health
Journalism

Marine
Marketing
Medical
Personalities
Photography
Senior Citizens
The Arts
Travel
Women's Interest
PUBLICATIONS:
Life
Time
Newsweek
People
Working Woman
Savvy
50 + Magazine
Builder Magazine

HALL, JOHN M.
500 West 58, #3F
New York, NY 10019
Telephone: 212-757-0369
Fax: 212-956-1462
PRINCIPAL SUBJECTS:
Architecture
Editorial
Home & Garden
Photography
The Arts
PUBLICATIONS:
Home & Garden
Elle Decor
House Beautiful
New York Time Magazine
Colonial Homes
World of Interiors
Vogue Decoration
Architectural Record

HALPERN, DAVID
7420 East 70th Street
Tulsa, OK 74133
Telephone: 918-252-4973
Fax: 918-252-5710
AFFILIATIONS:
ASMP
PRINCIPAL SUBJECTS:
Advertising
Business & Industry
Ecology
General Interest
Nature
Travel

HALSEY, TERRY
6210 A Royalton
Houston, TX 77081
Telephone: 713-661-0976
Fax: 713-661-0976

AFFILIATIONS:
PPA
PRINCIPAL SUBJECTS:
Architecture
Editorial

HALSTEAD, DIRCK
3332 'P' St. N.W.
Washington, DC 20036
Telephone: 202-338-2028
MAILING ADDRESS:
Time Magazine
1050 Connecticut Ave. N.W.
Washington, DC 20036
PRINCIPAL SUBJECTS:
Advertising
Editorial
Entertainment
Journalism
Personalities
PUBLICATIONS:
Time
Life
Time
Life

HAMILTON, CHRIS
485 Little Road
Marietta, GA 30067
Telephone: 404-971-2024
Fax: 404-971-5837
MAILING ADDRESS:
CHRIS HAMILTON
6595-G Roswell Rd., #675
Atlanta, GA 30328
AFFILIATIONS:
ASMP
PRINCIPAL SUBJECTS:
Advertising
Photography
Sports
The Arts
Travel
PUBLICATIONS:
Sports Illustrated
Kid Sport Magazine
Interior Design Magazine
Sports Illustrated
Kid Sport Magazine
Interior Design Magazine

HAMILTON, JOHN R.
1455 W. 172nd St.
Gardena, CA 90247
Telephone: 213-321-9992
Fax: 310-523-3306
AFFILIATIONS:
ASMP
PRINCIPAL SUBJECTS:
Photography
The Arts

Photography
PUBLICATIONS:
Time, Life
TV GUIDE
US
Sports Illustrated

HAMMID, TINO
6305 Yucca St., Suite 500
Los Angeles, CA 90028
Telephone: 213-461-8017
Fax: 213-461-6588
PUBLICATIONS:
Modern Jeweler
Audubon

HAMPSON PHOTOGRAPHY
1201 Gilbert
Shreveport, LA 71101
Telephone: 318-222-4572
MAILING ADDRESS:
HAMPSON, FRANK
00000
AFFILIATIONS:
A.S.M.P. #659,PP of
   A,SWPA,PP of L
PRINCIPAL SUBJECTS:
Architecture
Aviation
General Interest
Home & Garden
Marine
The Arts
PUBLICATIONS:
Wall Street Journal

HAND, RAY PHOTOGRAPHY
Hand, Ray Photography
10921 Shady Trail, #100
Dallas, TX 75220
Telephone: 214-351-2488
Fax: 214-351-2499
AFFILIATIONS:
ASMP
PRINCIPAL SUBJECTS:
Advertising
Business & Industry
Editorial
PUBLICATIONS:
Travel & Leisure
Tennis Magazine
D Magazine

HANDLEY, ROBERT E.
1920 E. Croxton Ave.
Bloomington, IL 61701
Telephone: 309-828-4661
Fax: 309-662-1920
AFFILIATIONS:
PPA,ASP, ASMP

PRINCIPAL SUBJECTS:
Advertising
Architecture
Fashion
General Interest
PUBLICATIONS:
Sylvia Porters Financial
   Magazine
Medical Economics
Penthouse
PC World

HANDS, BRUCE
211 Elk Range Way
Darby, MT 59829
Telephone: 406-821-4550
Fax: 406-821-4550
AFFILIATIONS:
ASMP
PRINCIPAL SUBJECTS:
Agriculture
Editorial
General Interest
Human Interest
Marine
Nature
Travel
PUBLICATIONS:
Forbes
Lears
Modern Maturity
Countryside
Historic Perservation
Alaska
Pacific Northwest
Sunset

HANSEN, BARBARA
48 Monroe Ave., #2
Larchmont, NY 10538
Telephone: 212-822-1676
AFFILIATIONS:
ASMP
PRINCIPAL SUBJECTS:
Personalities
Business & Industry
Travel
Journalism
PUBLICATIONS:
Los Angeles Times
Miami Herald
New York Times
Time
USA Today
Washington Post

HARBRON, PATRICK
666 Greenwich St., #746
New York, NY 10014
Telephone: 212-967-2111

AFFILIATIONS:
ASMP, IATSE
PRINCIPAL SUBJECTS:
Editorial
Entertainment
Humor
The Arts
PUBLICATIONS:
Esquire
Entertainment Weekly
Time
Los Angeles Time Magazine
Worth
Rolling Stone
Musician
Buzz

HARDEN, CLIFF
1769 Cheshire Bridge Rd., N.E.
Atlanta, GA 30324
Telephone: 404-872-1769
AFFILIATIONS:
PPA
PRINCIPAL SUBJECTS:
Agriculture
Animals
Architecture
Geography
Business & Industry
Marine

HARDER, PAUL B.
731 Kala Pt. Dr.
Port Townsend, WA 98368
Telephone: 206-385-4878
Fax: 206-385-4874
AFFILIATIONS:
PPA, SEPPA
PRINCIPAL SUBJECTS:
Agriculture
General Interest

HARKEY, JOHN J.
90 Larch St.
Providence, RI 02906
Telephone: 401-272-5703
PRINCIPAL SUBJECTS:
Architecture
Business & Industry

HARKNESS, CHRIS
706 Beard St., 2
Tallahassee, FL 32303
Telephone: 904-222-0313
MAILING ADDRESS:
CHRIS HARKNESS
706 Benad St., 2
Tallahassee, FL 32303
PRINCIPAL SUBJECTS:
Marine
Sports

Travel
Photography
PUBLICATIONS:
Sailing Magazine
Bicycling Magazine
Small Boat Journal
Sailors' Gazette
Florida Waterways
Sailor's Guide Publication
Yacht, The
Southern Magazine
Boat Journal

HARLAN, BRUCE
52922 Camellia Dr.
South Bend, IN 46637
Telephone: 219-631-7350
Fax: 219-273-6992
MAILING ADDRESS:
BRUCE HARLON
  PHOTOGRAPHY
South Bend, IN 46637
Telephone: 219-272-2904
AFFILIATIONS:
ASMP, PPA, NPPA
PRINCIPAL SUBJECTS:
Advertising
Architecture
Editorial
Human Interest
PUBLICATIONS:
Forbes
Time
Newsweek
Fortune
Victorian Accents

HARMON PHOTOGRAPHERS
14330 S. Tamiami Trail
Fort Myers, FL 33912
Telephone: 813-482-6728
Fax: 813-482-6722
MAILING ADDRESS:
JUDY HARMON & KAREN
  HARMON
AFFILIATIONS:
PPA, PMA
PRINCIPAL SUBJECTS:
Architecture
General Interest
Journalism
Photography

HARMON, TIM
380 S.E. Spokane St., #200
Portland, OR 97202
Telephone: 503-236-3213
Fax: 503-233-2529
MAILING ADDRESS:
TIM HARMON
P.O. Box 82454

Portland, OR 97202
AFFILIATIONS:
ASMP
PRINCIPAL SUBJECTS:
Advertising
Agriculture
Amusements
Animals
Architecture
Automotive
Aviation
Book Reviews
Business & Industry
Computer Technology
Editorial
Education
Electronics
Entertainment
Family
Food/Diet
Foreign
General Interest
Geography
Government
Health
Human Interest
Human Relations
Humor
Journalism
Management
Marine
Marketing
Media
Nature
News
Personalities
Philosophy
Photography
Psychology
Religion
Science
Senior Citizens
Social Trends
Sports
The Arts
Travel
Urban Affairs
Video
World Affairs
PUBLICATIONS:
Newsweek
Time/Life
Bunte
Der Speigel
Harvard Business Review
Newsweek
Time/Life
Bunte
Der Speigel
Harvard Business Review

HARP, DAVID
6027 Pinehurst Rd.
Baltimore, MD 21212
Telephone: 410-433-9242
Fax: 410-435-2042
AFFILIATIONS:
ASMP
PRINCIPAL SUBJECTS:
Advertising
Agriculture
Animals
Ecology
Editorial
Geography
History
Home & Garden
Marine
Nature
Photography
Travel
PUBLICATIONS:
National Geographic Islands
Sierra Magazine
Mid Atlantic
Sea Frontiers
Washingtonian

HARRINGTON III, BLAINE
2 Virginia Avenue
Danbury, CT 06810
Telephone: 203-798-2866
PRINCIPAL SUBJECTS:
Foreign

HARRINGTON, JOHN
700 Fourth St., N.E.
Washington, DC 20002
Telephone: 800-544-4577
Fax: 202-544-4578
AFFILIATIONS:
ASMP, MPCA, NPPA, PPA,
  ASPP, WHNPA
PRINCIPAL SUBJECTS:
Advertising
Editorial
Entertainment
General Interest
Government
Journalism
Marketing
Media
Military
Personalities
Travel
World Affairs
PUBLICATIONS:
U.S. News & World Report
Newsweek
Stern
Der Speigel
People

U.S. Magazine
Who Magazine
Elle
Vogue
Seventeen

HARRINGTON, TY
29 Merwin Ln.
Wilton, CT 06897
Telephone: 203-438-2340
Fax: 203-438-2340
AFFILIATIONS:
ASMP, NPC
PRINCIPAL SUBJECTS:
Advertising
Editorial
Family
Foreign
General Interest
Geography
Government
History
Human Interest
Human Relations
Journalism
Management
Marine
Marketing
Military
Nature
News
Personalities
Photography
Physical Fitness
Senior Citizens
Social Trends
Travel
Urban Affairs
PUBLICATIONS:
Smithsonian
National Geographic
Wall Street Journal
Discovery
Yankee
New York Times

HARRIS, CHRISTOPHER R.
P.O. Box 193
Lascassas, TN 37085
Telephone: 615-890-0985
Fax: 615-898-5682
MAILING ADDRESS:
CHRISTOPHER R. HARRIS
RA-TV/Photo Box 58 MTSU
Murfreesboro, TN 37132
AFFILIATIONS:
NPPA, AEJMC
PRINCIPAL SUBJECTS:
Editorial
Business & Industry
Photography

Nature
Advertising
PUBLICATIONS:
Time
Newsweek
N.Y.Times
Esquire
Life
Fortune
People

HARRISON, HOWARD
150 W. 22nd St.
New York, NY 10011
Telephone: 212-989-9233
Fax: 212-463-9118
PRINCIPAL SUBJECTS:
Sports

HARTMANN, ERICH
117 W. 78th St.
New York, NY 10024
Telephone: 212-724-5381
Fax: 212-595-3047
AFFILIATIONS:
ASMP
PRINCIPAL SUBJECTS:
Education
Family
Health
Human Relations
Religion
Senior Citizens
The Arts
PUBLICATIONS:
Fortune
Newsweek
Time
Business Week
New York Times Magazine

HARTMANN, W. GEOFFREY
2622 Grist Mill Rd.
Little Rock, AR 72207
Telephone: 501-228-9290
AFFILIATIONS:
ASMP
PRINCIPAL SUBJECTS:
Advertising
Agriculture
Architecture
Computer Technology
Editorial
Foreign
Human Relations
Journalism
Marketing
Media
Personalities
Travel
Youth

PUBLICATIONS:
Newsweek
Time
Business Week

HATHON, ELIZABETH
8 Greene St.
New York, NY 10013
Telephone: 212-219-0685
Fax: 212-219-0289
AFFILIATIONS:
ASMP, APA
PRINCIPAL SUBJECTS:
Photography
Social Trends

HAWK, DARYL
8 Bossy Ln.
Wilton, CT 06897
Telephone: 203-834-9595
AFFILIATIONS:
ASMP, MPPI
PRINCIPAL SUBJECTS:
Editorial
Foreign
General Interest
Human Interest
Media
Nature
Personalities
Photography
Travel
PUBLICATIONS:
Peterson Photographics
Popular Photography
Progressive Architecture

HAWKINS, WALT
P.O. Box 828
Temple, TX 76503
Telephone: 817-778-3232
Fax: 817-778-3535
AFFILIATIONS:
SWPA, PPA, TPPA
PRINCIPAL SUBJECTS:
Geography
Hobbies
Human Interest
Nature
Photography

HAWTHORNE, ANN
649 C. Street S.E., #402
Washington, DC 20003
Telephone: 202-543-1636
AFFILIATIONS:
ASMP
PRINCIPAL SUBJECTS:
Editorial
Foreign
Nature

Travel
PUBLICATIONS:
Air & Space
Destination Discovery
Harpers
Time
Newsweek
National Geographic
Appalachia

HEBBERD, LINDSAY
306 Steeplechase Drive
Irving, TX 75062
Telephone: 214-717-5151
Fax: 214-717-0955
AFFILIATIONS:
ASMP
PRINCIPAL SUBJECTS:
Advertising
Amusements
Architecture
Editorial
Education
Foreign
History
Human Interest
Travel
PUBLICATIONS:
Communication Arts
Life
Travel & Leisure
GEO Magazine
Innerasia

HEDRICH-BLESSING
11 W. Illinois
Chicago, IL 60610
Telephone: 312-321-1151
Fax: 312-321-1165
MAILING ADDRESS:
MICHAEL O.
HOULAHON/HEDRICH
BLESSING
Chicago, IL 60610
AFFILIATIONS:
SMPS, AIA
PRINCIPAL SUBJECTS:
Advertising
Architecture
Aviation
Editorial
Home & Garden
PUBLICATIONS:
Interior Design
Interiors
Architecture
Progressive Architecture
Architectural Record
Corporate Design & Realty
Inland Architect
Metropolitan Home

Better Homes & Gardens
Connoissuer
Most Shelter Magazines
Chicago
U.S.A. Today
Professional Builder
Chicago Tribune

HEDSPETH, JERRY
Rt. 2 Box 168
Conway, NC 27820
Telephone: 919-585-0394
AFFILIATIONS:
PPA, PPNC
PRINCIPAL SUBJECTS:
Photography

HELLER, MICHAEL
Heller Photography
62 Acca bonac St.
East Hampton, NY 11937
Telephone: 516-324-2061
AFFILIATIONS:
ASMP, IFPA, FPA
PRINCIPAL SUBJECTS:
Editorial
General Interest
Human Interest
Journalism
Media
News
PUBLICATIONS:
Penthouse Magazine
Firehouse Magazine
Modern Times Magazine
Long Island Newsday
New York Times
Fire Times
Music Connection

HELSPER, MANFRED
1220 E. Campbell Ave.
Gilbert, AZ 85234
Telephone: 602-926-3467
Fax: 602-926-4235
AFFILIATIONS:
PPA, APPA, PPPA
PRINCIPAL SUBJECTS:
Architecture

HENRY, GEORGE T.
2325 Grande Ave., S.E.
Cedar Rapids, IA 52403
Telephone: 319-363-5389
Fax: 319-362-8391
AFFILIATIONS:
PP of A
PRINCIPAL SUBJECTS:
Advertising
Hobbies
Human Interest

Amusements
Business & Industry
The Arts

HENRY, LOWELL
403 W. Maple St.
Maquoketa, IA 52060
Telephone: 319-652-3226
Fax: 319-362-8391
AFFILIATIONS:
PP of A
PRINCIPAL SUBJECTS:
General Interest
Government

HENTE, JERRY L.
3902 Glen Oaks Manor Dr.
Sarasota, FL 34232
Telephone: 813-366-5258
AFFILIATIONS:
PPA, SP
PRINCIPAL SUBJECTS:
Photography
Architecture
PUBLICATIONS:
The Professional Photographer
Range Finder

HERBST, JOHN
1115 W. 4th Street
Little Rock, AR 72201
Telephone: 501-374-1746
MAILING ADDRESS:
BEN RED STUDIO, INC.
Little Rock, AR 72201
PRINCIPAL SUBJECTS:
Business & Industry

HERON, MICHAL
28 West 71st Street
New York, NY 10023
Telephone: 212-787-1272
Fax: 212-721-0844
AFFILIATIONS:
ASMP, APA, ASPP
PUBLICATIONS:
US Family Life

HERRON, MATT
P.O. Box 1860
Sausalito, CA 94966
Telephone: 510-479-6994
Fax: 415-479-6995
PRINCIPAL SUBJECTS:
Education
Ecology
Women's Interest
History
Health

HESS, HARRY
H.C. 4 Box 106x56
New Braunfels, TX 78133
Telephone: 512-964-3771
AFFILIATIONS:
PPA, RPE
PRINCIPAL SUBJECTS:
Geography
Travel
Journalism
Photography
PUBLICATIONS:
Oil & Gas Journal
Drilling
Petroleum Engineer
Ocean Industry
Offshore
Texas Contractor
Engineering News/Record

HEWETT, RICHARD R.
5725 Buena Vista Terr.
Los Angeles, CA 90042
Telephone: 213-254-4577
AFFILIATIONS:
ASMP
PRINCIPAL SUBJECTS:
Advertising
Journalism

HEWITT, SCOTT
2011 N. Franklin St.
Wilmington, DE 19802
Telephone: 302-426-0182
AFFILIATIONS:
ASMP
PRINCIPAL SUBJECTS:
Architecture
Automotive
Editorial
Advertising
General Interest
Personalities
The Arts
PUBLICATIONS:
Delaware Today
Road Racer Illustrated

HICKS, JAMES
1558-121 Rossville Ave.
Frankfort, IN 46041
Telephone: 317-654-5948
MAILING ADDRESS:
J & C PHOTOGRAPHY
Frankfort, IN 46041
AFFILIATIONS:
P.P. of A.
PRINCIPAL SUBJECTS:
Family
Photography

HICKS, NORM
1871 Milden Rd.
Columbus, OH 43221
Telephone: 614-442-5650
Fax: 614-442-8012
PRINCIPAL SUBJECTS:
Photography

HIGHSMITH, CAROL
3299 K St., NW #404
Washington, DC 20007
Telephone: 202-347-0910
PRINCIPAL SUBJECTS:
Business & Industry

HIGHT, GEORGE C.
434 Live Oak Lp., N.E.
Albuquerque, NM 87122
Telephone: 505-294-2578
AFFILIATIONS:
ASMP
PRINCIPAL SUBJECTS:
Geography
Nature
Travel
General Interest
PUBLICATIONS:
Arizona Hiways
"America Illustrations"
Nathan Ferdinand
    Publications-(France)
New Mexico Magazine
Numerous Western Indian &
    Southwest Publications
Philips CD-1

HIGHTON, SCOTT
996 McCue Ave.
San Carlos, CA 94070
Telephone: 415-592-5277
Fax: 415-592-5277
AFFILIATIONS:
ASMP, NPPA, ASPP
PRINCIPAL SUBJECTS:
Animals
Aviation
Business & Industry
Ecology
Editorial
Journalism
Marine
Marketing
Media
Nature
Travel
Video
PUBLICATIONS:
Stern
GEO
AOPA Pilot

Millimeter
Panorama
Smithsonian (Air & Space)

HILL, DAN SCOTT
5235-H Fox Hunt Dr.
Greensboro, NC 27407
Telephone: 919-855-6651
AFFILIATIONS:
ASMP
PRINCIPAL SUBJECTS:
Advertising
Video
PUBLICATIONS:
House & Garden
House Beautiful

HILL, JACKSON
Southern Lights
  Photography, Inc.
901 Carondelet St.
New Orleans, LA 70130
Telephone: 504-524-0200
AFFILIATIONS:
ASMP, NPPA
PRINCIPAL SUBJECTS:
Advertising
Architecture
Business & Industry
Computer Technology
Editorial
Education
Fashion
Foreign
Health
Human Interest
Journalism
Marketing
Medical
Photography
Travel
PUBLICATIONS:
Forbes
Fortune
Time
Business Week
Money Magazine
American Way Magazine
Entrepreneur
Reader's Digest

HILLYER, JONATHON
2604 Parkside Dr.
Atlanta, GA 30305
Telephone: 404-841-6679
Fax: 404-841-9088
MAILING ADDRESS:
JONATHON HILLYER
Atlanta, GA 30305
AFFILIATIONS:
ASMP

PRINCIPAL SUBJECTS:
Architecture
PUBLICATIONS:
Architecture
Architectural Record
Progressive Architecture
Southern Accents

HIRNELSEN, RICHARD
306 S. Washington, Suite 218
Royal Oak, MI 48067
Telephone: 313-399-2410
Fax: 313-399-2214
AFFILIATIONS:
ASMP
PRINCIPAL SUBJECTS:
Health
Business & Industry
PUBLICATIONS:
Newsweek
Time

HIRSCH, KAREN I.
4170 N. Marine Dr., #6G
Chicago, IL 60613
Telephone: 312-440-5011
Fax: 312-751-3502
AFFILIATIONS:
ASMP
PRINCIPAL SUBJECTS:
Advertising
Animals
Architecture
Business & Industry
Editorial
Education
Entertainment
Family
Foreign
General Interest
Geography
Government
Hobbies
Human Interest
Human Relations
Journalism
Marine
Marketing
Men's Interest
Nature
Personalities
Photography
Physical Fitness
Senior Citizens
Sports
The Arts
Travel
Women's Interest
PUBLICATIONS:
Chicago Tribune
Chicago Sun Times

Chicago Magazine
Where Magazine
Sail Magazine
Advertising Age
Travel Holiday
Inland Architecture

HISER, DAVID
319F AABC
Aspen, CO 81611
Telephone: 303-925-2179
Fax: 303-925-2420
MAILING ADDRESS:
DAVID HISER
Aspen, CO 81611
AFFILIATIONS:
ASMP
PRINCIPAL SUBJECTS:
Journalism
Geography
Nature
PUBLICATIONS:
National Geographic
Outside
Time
Geo
Forbes

HITT, WESLEY
600 Boyle Building
Little Rock, AR 72201
Telephone: 501-375-5091
Fax: 501-376-2584
AFFILIATIONS:
ASMP
PRINCIPAL SUBJECTS:
Advertising
Aviation
Editorial
Journalism
Marketing
Photography
Sports
Travel
PUBLICATIONS:
Newsweek
Time
Nation's Business

HODGE, ADELE
P.O. Box 3960,
  Merchandise Mart
Chicago, IL 60611
Telephone: 312-828-0611
AFFILIATIONS:
ASMP
PRINCIPAL SUBJECTS:
Entertainment
Business & Industry
Personalities

PUBLICATIONS:
Merchandise Mart
Redbook
Essence

HOEBERMAN, MATHEW &
  KRISTIN
Hoebermann Studio, Inc.,
  49 W. 44th St.
New York, NY 10036
Telephone: 212-840-2678
Fax: 212-840-2678
AFFILIATIONS:
ASMP, PPA
PRINCIPAL SUBJECTS:
Advertising
Editorial
General Interest
Hobbies
Travel
Human Relations
PUBLICATIONS:
Harris Publications
New York "Times"
Newsweek (Covers)

HOFFMAN, ROB
Phoenix Group Inc.
105 Space Park Dr.
Nashville, TN 37211
Telephone: 615-834-0534
Fax: 615-646-1540
AFFILIATIONS:
ASMP
PRINCIPAL SUBJECTS:
Advertising
Architecture
Business & Industry
Ecology
Editorial
Marine
Nature
PUBLICATIONS:
Time
US News & World Reviews
Design West
A.I.A. Journal
Sweets
Architectural Record

HOLBROOKE, ANDREW
50 W. 29th St.
New York, NY 10001
Telephone: 212-889-5995
Fax: 212-889-3438
AFFILIATIONS:
ASMP
PRINCIPAL SUBJECTS:
Editorial
Foreign
News

Travel
World Affairs
PUBLICATIONS:
Life
Time
Newsweek
The New York Times
U.S. News & World Report
Smithsonian
GEO
Travel & Leisure
Philadelphia Inquirer Magazine
Boston Globe Magazine
Fortune
Forbes
Natural History Magazine
American Photography

HOLLAND, JAMES R.
5 Brimmer St.
Boston, MA 02108
Telephone: 617-720-0324
Fax: 617-720-0324
AFFILIATIONS:
PP Of A,ASMP
PRINCIPAL SUBJECTS:
Editorial
General Interest
Human Interest
Travel
PUBLICATIONS:
National Geographic
U. S. News & World Report
Paris Match
Stern
N. Y. Times Magazine
Time Magazine
The Amazon
Mr. Pops
Tanglewood

HOLLENBECK, CLIFF/KEVIN
  MORRIS
2223 Second Ave.
Seattle, WA 98121
Telephone: 206-682-6300
Fax: 206-441-0743
MAILING ADDRESS:
HOLLENBECK/MORRIS
P.O. Box 4247, Pioneer Sq.
Seattle, WA 98104
AFFILIATIONS:
ASMP,SATW,PPA
PRINCIPAL SUBJECTS:
Advertising
Editorial
Travel
Business & Industry
Geography
Marketing

PUBLICATIONS:
National Geographic Books
Sunset
Time-Life
Newspapers
Advertising Agencies
Airlines
Resorts

HOLLYMAN, TOM
300 E. 40th St.
New York, NY 10016
Telephone: 212-867-2383
AFFILIATIONS:
ASMP
PRINCIPAL SUBJECTS:
Advertising
Editorial
Journalism
Personalities
The Arts
Travel
PUBLICATIONS:
Town & Country
Travel Holiday
Travel & Leisure

HOLT, SAXON
601 22nd St.
San Francisco, CA 94107
Telephone: 415-695-7788
MAILING ADDRESS:
HOLT, SAXON W.
2745 Elmwood Ave.
Berkeley, CA 94705
Telephone: 510-843-7788
PRINCIPAL SUBJECTS:
Home & Garden
Agriculture

HOLT, WALTER
P.O. Box 936
Media, PA 19063
Telephone: 215-565-1977
AFFILIATIONS:
ASMP,SACA
PRINCIPAL SUBJECTS:
Education
Business & Industry
Human Interest
PUBLICATIONS:
Medical World News
Womens World
Time

HOLTEL, JOHN P.
339 Congress Park Dr.
Dayton, OH 45459
Telephone: 513-436-3686
Fax: 513-436-9551

AFFILIATIONS:
ASMP
PRINCIPAL SUBJECTS:
Advertising
Editorial
PUBLICATIONS:
Parade Magazine
Newsweek

HOLZ, WILLIAM
7630 W. Norton Ave.
Los Angeles, CA 90046
Telephone: 213-656-4061
AFFILIATIONS:
ASMP
PRINCIPAL SUBJECTS:
Entertainment
Advertising

HOOS, GERALD WILLIAM
1035 Wesley Ave.
Evanston, IL 60202
Telephone: 708-475-6400
Fax: 708-475-6418
AFFILIATIONS:
MIPA, NIR/SAAC
PRINCIPAL SUBJECTS:
Photography
Food/Diet
Business & Industry
Editorial
PUBLICATIONS:
Life
World Book
Plate World
Good Housekeeping
Better Homes & Gardens
The Norshore Magazine
Chicago Magazine
Range Finder
Popular Photog.
Modern Photog.
Packaging Digest
Industrial Photography
Review, The
Time
Playboy
Mustang Monthly
Tracks
Saturday Evening Post
Ebony
Archetural Digest
Concrete Trader, The
E.R.N.
U.S. News
PEI Journal
Fancy Foods
Darkroom Techniques
Chromatography Illustrated
Photomethods
Professional Photographer

Kodak Studio Light
Analytical Standards
Brunswick Technetics
PCI Journal
New York Construction News
Old Car Weekly
Hemings Motor News
Ford Buyer's Guide
Mustang Illustrated
The Automotive Humorist

HORSTED, PAUL
31702 Peavine St.
Dowagiac, MI 49047
Telephone: 616-782-7478
AFFILIATIONS:
ASMP, OWAA
PRINCIPAL SUBJECTS:
Editorial
General Interest
Human Interest
Nature
Travel
PUBLICATIONS:
Life
USA Today
Travel Holiday
Business Week

HOSS, RONALD P.
303 Union Station,
  P.O. Box 5935
Vancouver, WA 98660
Telephone: 503-228-3016
PRINCIPAL SUBJECTS:
Travel
Business & Industry
Advertising
PUBLICATIONS:
Travel Age West
Advertising Age
Portland Daily Journal of
  Commerce
Vancouver, Wa., Columbian

HOUSER, DAVE G.
P.O. Box 1371, #510
Ruidoso, NM 88345
Telephone: 505-354-2500
Fax: 505-354-2525
AFFILIATIONS:
SATW, ASMP
PRINCIPAL SUBJECTS:
Advertising
Architecture
Ecology
Editorial
Foreign
Geography
Photography
Travel

PUBLICATIONS:
Chevron USA/Odyssey
Cruises & Tours
Delta Sky
Diversion
Endless Vacations
Islands
New York
Travel/Holiday

HOUSER, ROBERT
P.O. Box 299
Litchfield, CT 06759
Telephone: 203-567-4241
Fax: 203-567-3789
AFFILIATIONS:
ASMP
PRINCIPAL SUBJECTS:
Advertising
Business & Industry
Editorial
Education
Human Interest
Human Relations
Journalism
Social Trends
The Arts
Travel

HOWARD, CARL
27 Huckleberry Ln.
Ballston Lake, NY 12019
Telephone: 518-877-7615
MAILING ADDRESS:
CARL HOWARD
Ballston Lake, NY 12019
AFFILIATIONS:
ASMP
PRINCIPAL SUBJECTS:
Editorial
Advertising
Business & Industry
Video
PUBLICATIONS:
Time Life
Popular Science
N. Y. Times
Art Forum
America Illustrated
Datamation
USIA "America"
Parenting
Black & Decker

HUBBELL, WILLIAM
R.R. 1, Box 2375
Litchfield, ME 04350
Telephone: 207-582-3000
AFFILIATIONS:
ASMP, MPPA

PRINCIPAL SUBJECTS:
Advertising
Architecture
Food/Diet
Nature
Photography
PUBLICATIONS:
Life
National Geographic
Connecticut Magazine

HUCKABY, JERRY
10 Hill St.
Morristown, NJ 07960
Telephone: 201-984-1046
AFFILIATIONS:
ASMP, PPA
PRINCIPAL SUBJECTS:
Advertising
Aviation
Business & Industry
Entertainment
Family
Fashion
General Interest
Human Interest
Journalism
Personalities
Sales
PUBLICATIONS:
New York TimesAtlanta Journal

HUGHES, JOHN
2616 Columbine Dr.
Durango, CO 81301
Telephone: 303-259-0862
Fax: 303-259-2690
MAILING ADDRESS:
JOHN HUGHES,
   PHOTOGRAPHER
Box 1470
Durango, CO 81302
PRINCIPAL SUBJECTS:
Advertising
Fashion
Business & Industry
PUBLICATIONS:
National Inquirer
Gas Magazine
Houston Magazine

HUGLIN, GREG
1427 Greenworth Place
Santa Barbara, CA 93108
Telephone: 805-969-0990
Fax: 805-969-0990
AFFILIATIONS:
ASMP
PRINCIPAL SUBJECTS:
Sports
Fashion

PUBLICATIONS:
Outside
Women's Sports & Fitness
Men's Health
Runners World
Cosmopolitan
Windsurfing
Bazaar
Allure

HUMPHRIES, JR.,
   H. GORDON
The Gallery Studios
1579 Broad River Rd.
Columbia, SC 29210
Telephone: 803-772-3535
Fax: 803-731-4600
AFFILIATIONS:
PPA, ASMP
PRINCIPAL SUBJECTS:
Advertising
Architecture
Editorial
Family
Fashion
Medical
Personalities
Senior Citizens
Youth
PUBLICATIONS:
Southern Exposure
Southern Accents
National Historic Perservation
   Trust.

HUNTER, FIL
2402 Mt. Vernon Ave.
Alexandria, VA 22301
Telephone: 703-836-2910
Fax: 703-836-3012
AFFILIATIONS:
ASMP, VPPA
PRINCIPAL SUBJECTS:
Advertising
Computer Technology
Editorial
Electronics
Food/Diet
Photography
PUBLICATIONS:
Time-Life Books
Nation's Business
U.S. News
Electrical Contractor
Life
Symphony Magazine

HUNTRESS, DIANE
3337 W. 23rd Ave.
Denver, CO 80211
Telephone: 303-480-0219

Fax: 303-480-0218
PRINCIPAL SUBJECTS:
Personalities
Travel
Sports
PUBLICATIONS:
Family Circle
Time
Successful Meetings
American Photographer
Ski Magazine
Denver Post

HUNTZINGER, ROBERT
1524 Old Bethlehem Rd.
Pleasant Valley, PA 18951
Telephone: 215-346-8000
Fax: 215-346-6765
AFFILIATIONS:
ASMP
PRINCIPAL SUBJECTS:
Advertising
Automotive
Fashion
Photography
PUBLICATIONS:
Sports Ilustrated
Woman's Day

HURST, NORMAN
53 Mount Auburn St.
Cambridge, MA 02138
Telephone: 617-491-6888
Fax: 617-661-0439
PRINCIPAL SUBJECTS:
The Arts
General Interest
PUBLICATIONS:
Harvard Magazine
Parade
Boston Globe

IRVIN, MARCUS
4210 Hawthorne Ave.
Dallas, TX 75219
Telephone: 214-249-2891
Fax: 214-948-8465
PRINCIPAL SUBJECTS:
Business & Industry
Advertising
Photography
Computer Technology

ISAACS, LEE
629 22nd Ave., South
Birmingham, AL 35205
Telephone: 205-324-7334
AFFILIATIONS:
ASMP, PAPA
PRINCIPAL SUBJECTS:
Business & Industry

ISAACS, ROBERT A.
1646 Mary Ave.
Sunnyvale, CA 94087
Telephone: 408-245-1690
MAILING ADDRESS:
ROBERT A. ISAACS
Sunnyvale, CA 94087
AFFILIATIONS:
ASMP, PAPA
PRINCIPAL SUBJECTS:
Editorial
Business & Industry
General Interest
Education
Humor
PUBLICATIONS:
Time
Life
Business Week
Fortune
Inc.
Electronic Business
Personal Computing
IEEE Spectrum

IWASAKI, RICH
431 NW Flanders
Portland, OR 97209
Telephone: 503-242-1380
Fax: 503-223-8685
PRINCIPAL SUBJECTS:
Business & Industry
Editorial
Foreign
PUBLICATIONS:
Fortune
Forbes
Business Week
Newsweek

JACKSON, DON
240 Vila Rd.
Forestville, CA 95436
Telephone: 707-887-1332
Fax: 707-887-9811
AFFILIATIONS:
ASMP
PRINCIPAL SUBJECTS:
Advertising
Animals
Ecology
Human Interest
Nature
Photography
Travel
PUBLICATIONS:
Santa Rosa Press Democrat
California Scenio
Sierra Club Publication

Audubon Publication
Mono Lake Community
    Publication
San Francisco Chronicle

JACOBS, JR., LOU
296 Avenida Andorra
Cathedral City, CA 92234
Telephone: 619-324-5505
AFFILIATIONS:
ASMP
PRINCIPAL SUBJECTS:
Book Reviews
Editorial
Nature
Photography
Travel
PUBLICATIONS:
Chevron Magazine
Ford Times
Rangefinder
Audobon
Petersens Photographic
Friends

JACOBSON, RANDALL C.
7911 Halsey
Lenexar, KS 66215
Telephone: 913-492-5902
AFFILIATIONS:
ASMP
PRINCIPAL SUBJECTS:
Advertising
Computer Technology
Fashion
PUBLICATIONS:
Women's Wear Daily
Kansas City Star
'PRE' Magazine
Time
Wall Street Journal
PC World
Popular Science

JACOBY, RAY
908 Oakdale Dr.
Oklahoma City, OK 73127
Telephone: 405-787-2022
PRINCIPAL SUBJECTS:
Aviation
General Interest
Photography

JALBERT, PAUL
6 Wisina Court
Medford, NJ 08055
Telephone: 609-654-8877
Fax: 609-654-1431
AFFILIATIONS:
PPA-DVGPA

PRINCIPAL SUBJECTS:
Human Interest
Computer Technology
Advertising

JAMES, GRANT R.
116 Walt Whitman Blvd.
Cherry Hill, NJ 08003
Telephone: 609-795-0322
AFFILIATIONS:
PPA
PRINCIPAL SUBJECTS:
Architecture
Editorial
General Interest
Amusements

JEFFERSON, LOUISE E.
West St.
Litchfield, CT 06759
Telephone: 203-567-3356
MAILING ADDRESS:
LOUISE E. JEFFERSON
West St., P.O. Box 464
Litchfield, CT 06759
AFFILIATIONS:
PPA, CPDV
PRINCIPAL SUBJECTS:
Editorial
Foreign
Nature
Urban Affairs
PUBLICATIONS:
Greenwich Review
Sat. Review Of Literature
Viewfinders (Photography) -
    Dodd - Mead

JEFFRY, MISS ALIX
P.O. Box 13594
Albuquerque, NM 87192
Telephone: 505-294-5916
PRINCIPAL SUBJECTS:
Entertainment
Photography
The Arts
PUBLICATIONS:
New York Times
Chicago Tribune
Newsweek
Time
Opera News
American Theatre

JELEN, TOM
P.O. Box 115
Arlington Hts, IL 60006
Telephone: 708-612-0994
Fax: 713-460-9553
PRINCIPAL SUBJECTS:
The Arts

JERNIGAN, JOHN E.
1820 E. Silver Spgs. Blvd.
Ocala, FL 32670
Telephone: 904-732-7927
Fax: 904-732-5040
MAILING ADDRESS:
JOHN E. JERNIGAN
Ocala, FL 32670
Telephone: 904-732-5040
AFFILIATIONS:
FPPA, SEPA, PPA
PRINCIPAL SUBJECTS:
Advertising
Animals
Architecture
General Interest
Food/Diet
Home & Garden
Senior Citizens
PUBLICATIONS:
Central Florida Magazine
Blood Horse, The
Thoroughbred Record
Bon Appetit
Florida Trend

JOHNSON & JOHNSON
    STUDIO
Johnson & Johnson Studio
4205 Waterscape Dr.
Palmer Harbor, FL 34685
Telephone: 800-331-0332
AFFILIATIONS:
ASMP
PRINCIPAL SUBJECTS:
Advertising
Humor
PUBLICATIONS:
Workbook 93
Single Image

JOHNSON, DONALD
562 Cumberland Ave.
Portland, ME 04101
Telephone: 207-774-8850
AFFILIATIONS:
PPA, NPPA, CIPNE
PRINCIPAL SUBJECTS:
Aviation
Business & Industry
Editorial
Sports

JOHNSON, EVERETT C.
12150 Cathedral Drive
Lake Ridge, VA 22192
Telephone: 703-494-8483
AFFILIATIONS:
ASMP
PRINCIPAL SUBJECTS:
Agriculture

Editorial
General Interest
Human Interest
Nature
Senior Citizens
Travel
PUBLICATIONS:
Fodor's Travel Guides
Mid Atlantic Country Magazine
Woman's World Magazine
Journal Of Housing
EPA Journal
Journal-Painters
  & Allied Trades
Fairfax-Magazine Of Va.
The Researcher's Guide To
  Am. Geneology (Cover)
Potomac Electric Power
  Company Annual Report

JOHNSON, FOREST
7200 SW 129th St.
Miami, FL 33156
Telephone: 305-251-1300
Fax: 305-251-5511
AFFILIATIONS:
ASMP, APA
PRINCIPAL SUBJECTS:
Advertising
Editorial
Marine
PUBLICATIONS:
Boating
Motor Boating & Sailing
Robb Report
Car & Driver
Power & Motoryacht
Yachting
Showboats International
Salt Water Sportsman

JOHNSON, J. SAM
P.O. Box 2008
Palm Beach, FL 33480
Telephone: 407-582-4576
AFFILIATIONS:
ASMP, PPA, SPPA
PRINCIPAL SUBJECTS:
Advertising
Editorial
Nature
Sports
PUBLICATIONS:
American Bell
Palm Beach Life
Medical Economics
Time

JOHNSON, NEIL
124 E. Prosepect
Shreveport, LA 71104

Telephone: 318-221-2299
AFFILIATIONS:
ASMP
PRINCIPAL SUBJECTS:
Sports
History
The Arts
Geography
Human Interest

JOHNSON, TREVE
509 Carmel Ave.
Albany, CA 94706
Telephone: 510-527-6766
AFFILIATIONS:
ASMP, IAPP
PRINCIPAL SUBJECTS:
Ecology
Editorial
Education
General Interest
Geography
Human Relations
Nature
Photography
Science

JOHNSTON, GREG
12914 S.W. 132nd Ct.
Miami, FL 33186
Telephone: 305-233-9353
Fax: 305-233-9604
AFFILIATIONS:
ASMP
PRINCIPAL SUBJECTS:
Advertising
Animals
Editorial
Marine
Nature
Travel
PUBLICATIONS:
Skin Diver
Travel Holiday
Sport Diver
Endless Vacation
Rodale's Publications
Caribbean Sports & Travel
In-Flight Magazines
Travel of Leisure

JONES, BRENT
9121 South Merrill Avenue
Chicago, IL 60617
Telephone: 312-933-1174
Fax: 312-221-6255
MAILING ADDRESS:
9121 S. Merritt Ave.
Chicago, IL 61617
AFFILIATIONS:
ASPP

PRINCIPAL SUBJECTS:
Business & Industry
Health
Editorial
Photography
PUBLICATIONS:
Time Newsweek (April 11,
  1983 Cover), USA Today,
US News & World Report,
  Ebony, Black Enterprise,
Chicago Magazine, Chicago
  Sun-Times, Tribune
(Chgo.) Magazine &
  Newspaper
Guideposts
Parade

JONES, DAWSON L.
23 N. Walnut St.
Dayton, OH 45449
Telephone: 513-859-7799
MAILING ADDRESS:
DAWSON JONES, INC.
P.O. Box 520
Mt. Orab, OH 45154
AFFILIATIONS:
ASMP
PRINCIPAL SUBJECTS:
Photography
PUBLICATIONS:
Inc Magazine
Information Age
Venture Magazine
Success Magazine
Entrepreneur Magazine

JONES, LOU
22 Randolph St.
Boston, MA 02118
Telephone: 617-426-6335
Fax: 617-695-9022
MAILING ADDRESS:
LOU JONES
Boston, MA 02118
AFFILIATIONS:
APA, ASMP, ASPP
PRINCIPAL SUBJECTS:
Travel
Advertising
Architecture
Health
The Arts
Science
PUBLICATIONS:
US News
Financial World
Business Week
Fortune
Time
National Geographic
Esquire, Inc.

JONES, SPENCER
23 Leonard Street, Studio 5
New York, NY 10013
Telephone: 212-941-8165
Fax: 212-941-1699
AFFILIATIONS:
ASMP-APA
PRINCIPAL SUBJECTS:
Photography

JONES, VALERIA
116 M.L.K. Blvd.
Atlantic City, NJ 08401
Telephone: 609-348-8656
AFFILIATIONS:
ASMP
PRINCIPAL SUBJECTS:
Human Relations
News
Personalities

JORDAN, G. STEVE
116 West 72nd St., 15a
New York, NY 10023
Telephone: 212-724-7309
Fax: 216-391-3922
AFFILIATIONS:
ASMP, ASPP
PRINCIPAL SUBJECTS:
Business & Industry

JORDAN, JOE F.
1621 E. North St.
Greenville, SC 29607
Telephone: 803-235-6243
MAILING ADDRESS:
JOE F JORDAN
  PHTGRPHR, INC.
P.O. Box 756
Greenville, SC 29602
Telephone: 803-232-8371
AFFILIATIONS:
PPA, COC, SCPPA
PRINCIPAL SUBJECTS:
Advertising
Aviation
General Interest
Government
PUBLICATIONS:
Textile World
America's Textile Reporter
Time Magazine
Greenville Magazine
Sports Style Magazine

JOUBERT PHOTOGRAPHY,
  LARRY
Joubert Photography, Larry
728 Auburn Street, #G-4
Whitman, MA 02382
Telephone: 617-447-1178

AFFILIATIONS:
ASMP
PRINCIPAL SUBJECTS:
Advertising
Computer Technology
Editorial
Family
General Interest
Human Interest
Human Relations
Marketing
Nature
PUBLICATIONS:
Boston Magazine
Computer Buying World
  Magazine
Digital Review Magazine
American Lawyer Magazine

KAEHLER, WOLFGANG
13641 NE 42nd St.
Bellevue, WA 98005
Telephone: 206-881-6581
AFFILIATIONS:
ASMP, NPPA
PRINCIPAL SUBJECTS:
Animals
Editorial
Geography
Nature
Travel
PUBLICATIONS:
GEO
Time-Live
Audubon
Natural History
Intern. Wildlife
National Geographic

KAHANA, YORAM
1441 N. Mc Cadden Pl.
Los Angeles, CA 90028
Telephone: 213-469-2020
Fax: 213-469-0880
MAILING ADDRESS:
KAHAPTA, YORAM
P.O. Box 93368
Los Angeles, CA 90093
AFFILIATIONS:
ASMP,SATW/ASPP/TJG
PRINCIPAL SUBJECTS:
Personalities
Human Interest
Travel

KALE, WALTER
1916 B. Wilmette Ave.
Wilmette, IL 60091
Telephone: 708-256-2034
MAILING ADDRESS:
CHICAGO TRIBUNE

435 N. Michigan Ave.
Chicago, IL 60611
Telephone: 312-256-2034
AFFILIATIONS:
CPPA
PRINCIPAL SUBJECTS:
Editorial
General Interest
Human Interest
PUBLICATIONS:
Time
Newsweek
Chicago Tribune

KALUZNY, ZIGY
4700 Strass Dr.
Austin, TX 78731
Telephone: 512-452-4463
Fax: 512-452-9560
AFFILIATIONS:
ASMP
PRINCIPAL SUBJECTS:
Editorial
Travel
Journalism
PUBLICATIONS:
Forbes
People
Time
Life
Newsweek
Business Week
GEO
American Way
Travel & Leisure
Stern
Der Spiegel
Interior
NY Times

KAMP, ERIC
43 Clinton Street
Sea Cliff, NY 11579
Telephone: 516-676-1071
Fax: 516-676-1071
AFFILIATIONS:
ASMD
PRINCIPAL SUBJECTS:
Advertising
Business & Industry
Travel
Photography

KANOWSKY, KEN
P.O. Box 133,
  119 Mt. Adams Hwy.
Glenwood, WA 98619
Telephone: 800-952-8110
Fax: 509-364-3689
AFFILIATIONS:
ASMP

PRINCIPAL SUBJECTS:
Advertising
Animals
Architecture
Ecology
Foreign
Geography
Nature
Travel
PUBLICATIONS:
Outdoor Photographer
Sea Frontiers
Motor Home Marketing
Diamond/Cosa Science
  Journal
American Survival
Guide/Facets
Nature Photographer

KAPLAN, AL
P.O. Box 611373
Miami, FL 33261
Telephone: 305-891-7595
AFFILIATIONS:
ASMP
PRINCIPAL SUBJECTS:
General Interest
Journalism
Sports
Government
PUBLICATIONS:
U. S. News & World Report
Chic
New Shelter
Miami Magazine

KAPLAN, B. PETER
7 East 20th St., Ste. 4R
New York, NY 10003
Telephone: 212-995-5000
Fax: 212-995-5698
AFFILIATIONS:
ASMP, NBM
PRINCIPAL SUBJECTS:
Advertising
Animals
Automotive
Aviation
Business & Industry
Ecology
Editorial
Education
Family
Foreign
Hobbies
Home & Garden
Journalism
Medical
Military
Nature
News

Personalities
Photography
Physical Fitness
Science
Senior Citizens
Sports
The Arts
Travel
Women's Interest
Youth
PUBLICATIONS:
Time
Life
Newsweek
Geo
Smithsonian
Audubon

KAPLAN, HOWARD N.
610 Green Bay Rd.
Highland Park, IL 60035
Telephone: 708-433-6666
Fax: 708-433-5154
AFFILIATIONS:
ASMP
PRINCIPAL SUBJECTS:
Architecture
Marine
PUBLICATIONS:
Time
Newsweek
Architectural Digest
Architectural Record
Progressive Architecture
Chicago Magazine
Casa Vogue

KARALES, JAMES
217 Cleveland Dr.
Croton-Hdsn, NY 10520
Telephone: 212-799-2483
PRINCIPAL SUBJECTS:
Advertising
PUBLICATIONS:
Look
Life

KASHI, ED
824 Florida Street
San Francisco, CA 94110
Telephone: 415-641-4636
Fax: 415-641-5381
AFFILIATIONS:
ASMP
PRINCIPAL SUBJECTS:
Agriculture
Business & Industry
Family
Foreign
Health
Personalities

Science
World Affairs
PUBLICATIONS:
National Geographic
Time
Newsweek
Fortune
Discover
Business Week
Forbes
N.Y Times Magazine

KASPER, KEN
1232 Cobbs St.
Drexel Hill, PA 19026
Telephone: 215-789-7033
Fax: 215-446-0108
AFFILIATIONS:
ASMP, PPA
PRINCIPAL SUBJECTS:
Advertising
Agriculture
Animals
Business & Industry
Ecology
Education
Family
Food/Diet
General Interest
Health
Home & Garden
Marine
Medical
Men's Interest
Nature
Personal Finance
Science
Senior Citizens
Travel
Women's Interest

KASTEN, JERRY
1120 Metro Crest, Suite 200A
Carrollton, TX 75006
Telephone: 214-416-4133
AFFILIATIONS:
ASMP
PRINCIPAL SUBJECTS:
Advertising
Nature
Travel
Video
Science
PUBLICATIONS:
Dallas Morning News
Dallas Times Herald
Texas Game & Fish Magazine
Plano Star Courier
Richardson Daily News
U.S. Army I & E

KATZ, MARTY
Box 141
Brooklandvl, MD 21022
Telephone: 410-484-3500
MAILING ADDRESS:
MARTY KATZ
Brooklandville, MD 21022
AFFILIATIONS:
ASMP, NPPA
PRINCIPAL SUBJECTS:
Journalism
PUBLICATIONS:
Life Magazine
Time Magazine
Newsweek Magazine
N. Y. Times
Business Week
Annual Reports
Foreign Magazines
Fortune Magazine
Barron's

KATZMAN, MARK
710 North Tucker, Suite 512
Saint Louis, MO 63101
Telephone: 314-241-3811
AFFILIATIONS:
ASMP
PRINCIPAL SUBJECTS:
Editorial
Photography
Advertising
PUBLICATIONS:
Time
Newsweek
Forbes
Fortune
Business Week
Rolling Stone
Inc.
Money

KAUFMAN, ELLIOTT
255 W. 90th St., Apt. 5C
New York, NY 10024
Telephone: 212-496-0860
Fax: 212-496-9104
AFFILIATIONS:
ASMP, APA/NY, AIA
PRINCIPAL SUBJECTS:
Advertising
Architecture
Marketing
PUBLICATIONS:
Architecture
Progressice Architecture
Interior Design
Interiors
HG-House Beautiful
Wind (Japan)

KAYE, ROD
680 Medlock Rd.
Decatur, GA 30033
Telephone: 404-320-6798
AFFILIATIONS:
ASMP, ASMP
PRINCIPAL SUBJECTS:
Editorial
Entertainment
Health
Media
Photography
Physical Fitness
Sports
PUBLICATIONS:
American Photo
Outdoor Photographer
Fitness Swimwear
Atlanta Magazine
Atlantic Sport & Fitness

KEATING, FRANKE
141 Bayou Rd.
Greenville, MS 38701
Telephone: 601-334-4088
AFFILIATIONS:
SATW, ASMP,TJG
PRINCIPAL SUBJECTS:
Journalism
Travel
Animals
PUBLICATIONS:
National Geographic Society
Travel & Leisure
Town & Country
Ford Times

KEEGAN, MARCIA
823 Don Diego
Santa Fe, NM 87501
Telephone: 505-989-9590
Fax: 404-872-6773
AFFILIATIONS:
ASMP, PPA
PUBLICATIONS:
Foreign
Travel
Human Interest

KEENAN, JOHN C.
2849 Glenmore Ave.
Pittsburgh, PA 15216
Telephone: 412-341-4079
AFFILIATIONS:
PPA
PRINCIPAL SUBJECTS:
Advertising
General Interest
Human Interest
Business & Industry
Journalism

News
PUBLICATIONS:
Pittsburgh Press
Pittsburgh Post Gazette
N. Y. Times
Pittsburgh Catholic
Pittsburgher Magazine

KEHRWALD, RICHARD
32 S. Main St.
Sheridan, WY 82801
Telephone: 307-674-4679
AFFILIATIONS:
NPPA NPAGP PPA
PRINCIPAL SUBJECTS:
Geography
Nature
Editorial
PUBLICATIONS:
Time
Newsweek
Business Week
Fortune
N. Y. Times

KEITH, ALLAN
P.O. Box 882
Mattoon, IL 61938
Telephone: 217-235-0995
PRINCIPAL SUBJECTS:
Government

KELLEY, TOM
2472 Eastman Ave.,
  Studios 35 and 36
Ventura, CA 93003
Telephone: 805-658-9908
Fax: 805-658-8355
AFFILIATIONS:
ASMP, APA
PRINCIPAL SUBJECTS:
Advertising
Food/Diet
PUBLICATIONS:
TV Guide
Playboy
L. A. Times
Sunset
Life
Bon Appetite
New Yorker

KELLY, TONY
1311 Main
Evanston, IL 60202
Telephone: 708-864-0488
AFFILIATIONS:
ASMP, SPJ, SND
PRINCIPAL SUBJECTS:
Business & Industry
Journalism

PUBLICATIONS:
Time
Life
Fortune
Paris Match

KEMPER, BART
3000 JULY ST., #101
BATON ROUGE, LA 70808
Telephone: 504-387-6488
Fax: 504-387-4162
AFFILIATIONS:
NPPA, SPJ, ASMP
PRINCIPAL SUBJECTS:
Book Reviews
Business &
  Industry
Computer
  Technology
Editorial
Entertainment
General Interest
Hobbies
Human Interest
Journalism
Military
Movie Reviews
News
Science
The Arts
Travel
PUBLICATIONS:
Writer's Digest
Salute Magazine
Baton Rouge
  Advocate
Baton Rouge
  State-Times
2AM Magazine
Quantum
Associated Press
SEE AD IN SECTION 5

KEMPER, SUSAN M.
25 Rimfire Circle
Reno, NV 89509
Telephone: 702-746-2121
Fax: 702-746-1850
MAILING ADDRESS:
P.O. Box 10588
Reno, NV 89510
AFFILIATIONS:
ASMP
PRINCIPAL SUBJECTS:
Sports
Travel
Editorial
PUBLICATIONS:
Newsweek

Off Road
On Track
ABA Journal

KENNEDY, M. LEWIS
Kennedy Photo Graphics
2700 Seventh Ave., South
Birmingham, AL 35233
Telephone: 205-252-2700
Fax: 205-252-2701
AFFILIATIONS:
ASMP, SMPS, PRCA
PRINCIPAL SUBJECTS:
Advertising
Architecture
Business & Industry
Computer Technology
Editorial
Fashion
Home & Garden
Medical
Urban Affairs
PUBLICATIONS:
Architecture
Business Alabama
Black Enterprise
Progressive Architecture
Photo District News
Birmingham

KENNERLY, DAVID HUME
4006 Dixie Canyon Ave.
Van Nuys, CA 91423
Telephone: 818-906-8700
Fax: 818-960-3000
MAILING ADDRESS:
TANNER & MAINSTREAM
1086 Wilshire Blvd., 10th Fl.
Los Angeles, CA 90024
AFFILIATIONS:
ASMP, WHNP
PRINCIPAL SUBJECTS:
News
PUBLICATIONS:
Life
Time
People
Fortune
U.S. News & World Report

KENTON, BASIA
1341 Ocean Ave., Suite 355
Santa Monica, CA 90401
Telephone: 310-395-2443
Fax: 415-388-3345
AFFILIATIONS:
ASMP
PRINCIPAL SUBJECTS:
Editorial
Architecture
Advertising

Travel
Home & Garden
Fashion
PUBLICATIONS:
LA Style
LA Times Magazine
Aspen Magazine
Self
Connoisseur

KERMANI, SHAHN
109 Minna St., #210
San Francisco, CA 94105
Telephone: 415-567-6073
AFFILIATIONS:
ASMP, NPPA
PRINCIPAL SUBJECTS:
Editorial
Human Interest
Journalism
Media
Photography
Social Trends
Women's Interest
World Affairs
PUBLICATIONS:
Life Magazine
Time
Newsweek
People
Paris Match
Le Figaro

KERR, GEORGE
401 W. 2nd St.
Reno, NV 89503
Telephone: 702-786-4999
MAILING ADDRESS:
GEORGE KERR,
  DBA GROUP III
620 Richards Way
Sparks, NV 89431
Telephone: 702-358-6757
PRINCIPAL SUBJECTS:
Travel

KETCHUM, LARRY
530 Pylon Dr.
Raliegh, NC 27606
Telephone: 919-856-1860
Fax: 919-856-0672
AFFILIATIONS:
ASMP
PRINCIPAL SUBJECTS:
Photography
PUBLICATIONS:
D & B Reports

KHANLIAN, RICHARD
Rt. 7, Box 129aa
Santa Fe, NM 87505

Telephone: 505-984-1420
AFFILIATIONS:
ASMP
PRINCIPAL SUBJECTS:
Architecture
Business & Industry
Nature
The Arts
PUBLICATIONS:
N.Y. Times
N.M. Magazine
Albuquerque
  Journal
Albuquerque
  Tribune
New Mexico
  Architecture

KHORNAK, LUCILLE
425 East 58th St.
New York, NY 10022
Telephone: 212-593-0933
AFFILIATIONS:
ASMP
PRINCIPAL SUBJECTS:
Advertising
Editorial
Family
Fashion
Personalities
Photography
The Arts
PUBLICATIONS:
Vogue
New York Times
Omni
Time

KIDD, CHUCK
HC62, Box 39
Gilbertville, MA 01031
Telephone: 413-477-8529
Fax: 413-477-6691
AFFILIATIONS:
ASMP
PRINCIPAL SUBJECTS:
Advertising
Agriculture
Amusements
Architecture
Book Reviews
Ecology
Editorial
Education
Entertainment
Family
General Interest
Government
Health
Hobbies
Human Interest

Human Relations
Journalism
Management
Media
Medical
Men's Interest
Motivation
Nature
News
Personalities
Photography
Physical Fitness
Sales
Science
The Arts
Travel
Youth
PUBLICATIONS:
Country Living
Country Journal
Yankee Magazine
Old House Magazine
Peterson's Photographic

KIEFFER, JOHN
4548 Beachcomber Court
Boulder, CO 80301
Telephone: 303-530-3357
Fax: 303-530-0274
AFFILIATIONS:
ASMP
PRINCIPAL SUBJECTS:
Advertising
Agriculture
Nature
Photography
Travel
PUBLICATIONS:
New York Times
Summit Magazine
Photo District News
The Conservationist

KILBORN, BILL
109 E. New Haven
Melbourne, FL 32901
Telephone: 407-727-8290
AFFILIATIONS:
PPA
PRINCIPAL SUBJECTS:
Advertising
General Interest
Business & Industry
Aviation
PUBLICATIONS:
The Professional Photgrapher
Rangefinder, The
Soaring Magazine
British Soaring Journal

KINCAID, CLARK L.
1015 Washington Ave., #201
St. Louis, MO 63101
Telephone: 314-231-5215
Fax: 314-231-4124
AFFILIATIONS:
ASMP
PRINCIPAL SUBJECTS:
Advertising
Architecture
Business & Industry
PUBLICATIONS:
Palete 93
St. Louis Magazine

KINETIC CORPORATION (G.
    RAYMOND SCHUHMANN)
Distillery Commons 240
Louisville, KY 40206
Telephone: 502-583-1679
Fax: 502-583-1104
AFFILIATIONS:
ONPA,PPA,NPPA
PRINCIPAL SUBJECTS:
Advertising
Architecture
Automotive
Photography
PUBLICATIONS:
Better Homes & Gardens
House & Home
Working Woman
Good Housekeeping
Kodak International
Gourmet
Glamour

KING, KATHLEEN
King, Kathleen
    Photography, Inc.
1916 Pike Place, #527
Seattle, WA 98101
Telephone: 206-443-2800
AFFILIATIONS:
ASMP
PRINCIPAL SUBJECTS:
Advertising
Editorial
Family
Fashion
Personalities
Photography
PUBLICATIONS:
Vogue
Mademoiselle
Glamour
Forbes
Washington CEO
The Weekly
Fortune, Inc.
Interview

Golf
Greater Seattle
View

KING, TOM
7401 Chancery Lane
Orlando, FL 32809
Telephone: 407-856-0618
Fax: 407-876-0210
AFFILIATIONS:
ASMP
PRINCIPAL SUBJECTS:
Advertising
Marine
Sports
PUBLICATIONS:
Sports Illustrated
National Geographic World
American Photographer
Popular Photography
Boating
Water Ski

KIRCHHEIMER, GABE
720 Fort Washington Ave.
New York, NY 10040
Telephone: 212-927-6324
AFFILIATIONS:
ASMP
PRINCIPAL SUBJECTS:
Ecology
Editorial
Food/Diet
General Interest
Health
Journalism
Nature
News
Religion
Social Trends
Travel
Urban Affairs
Youth
PUBLICATIONS:
Time
Daily News
Adweek
High Times

KIRKENDALL/SPRING
    PHOTOGRAPHERS
Kirkendall/Spring
    Photographers
18819 Olympic View Dr.
Edmonds, WA 98020
Telephone: 206-776-4685
Fax: 206-776-4685
AFFILIATIONS:
ASMP
PRINCIPAL SUBJECTS:
Advertising

Business & Industry
Foreign
General Interest
Geography
Hobbies
Nature
Photography
Travel
PUBLICATIONS:
Childrens Press
Backpacker
Outside
Word Book

KLAGES, WALTER W.
703 E. Main St.
Enterprise, OR 97828
Telephone: 503-426-3239
MAILING ADDRESS:
WALTER W. KLAGES,
    PP/MSTR PHTG
P.O. Box 208
Enterprise, OR 97828
AFFILIATIONS:
PPA,PP/ORE, ASP
PRINCIPAL SUBJECTS:
Nature
Travel
PUBLICATIONS:
PP Of Amer Mag-Infocus-Ore
    Farm-Range Finder
Oregon Bar Assoc. Mag.
Farm & Ranch Living
Pilot Magazine
Art West Magazine
Farm Journal 88

KLASS, RUBIN & ERIKA
    PHOTOGRAPHY
Klass, Rubin & Erika
    Photography
5200 N. Federal Hwy., #2
Fort Lauderdale, FL 33308
Telephone: 305-565-1612
Fax: 305-565-1612
AFFILIATIONS:
ASMP, ASPP
PRINCIPAL SUBJECTS:
Amusements
Animals
Automotive
Aviation
Ecology
Editorial
General Interest
History
Home & Garden
Human Interest
Marine
Military

Nature
Photography
Travel

KLEMM, STEPHEN
2380 W. 5th St.
Lincoln, IL 62656
Telephone: 217-735-5332
PRINCIPAL SUBJECTS:
Youth
PUBLICATIONS:
Commercial News Letters &
 Brochures

KNIGHT, DOUG
123 Huminy Pot Rd.
North Sutton, NH 03260
Telephone: 603-427-4477
MAILING ADDRESS:
DOUG KNIGHT
Box 101
North Sutton, NH 03260
Telephone: 603-927-4477
AFFILIATIONS:
OWAA,ASC,ASJA
PRINCIPAL SUBJECTS:
Travel
Entertainment
Human Interest
Nature
Medical
Sports
Agriculture
PUBLICATIONS:
Popular Science
True
Outdoor Life
Argosy
Popular Mechanics
Field & Stream
American Sportsman
Safari
Sport
Sports Afield
American Hunter
American Rifleman
Hunting
Arizona Highways
Outdoor Sports Life

KOENIG, GEA
463 West St. D-948
New York, NY 10014
Telephone: 212-243-3248
AFFILIATIONS:
ASMP, SATW,NYTW
PRINCIPAL SUBJECTS:
Travel
Nature
Architecture
Editorial

PUBLICATIONS:
Relax
Travel & Leisure
Travel Holiday
Providence Journal
Boston Herald
Newark Star Ledger
New York Post

KOLLODGE, KENNETH
Alaska Chromes, Inc.
433 Fairbanks St.
Fairbanks, AK 99709
Telephone: 907-479-4106
Fax: 907-479-9597
AFFILIATIONS:
ASMP, ASPP
PRINCIPAL SUBJECTS:
Advertising
Animals
Architecture
Editorial
Nature
The Arts
PUBLICATIONS:
Sierra Club
Natural History
Alaska Magazine

KONIG, THIA
2347 Roanoke Dr.
Boise, ID 83712
Telephone: 208-345-0134
AFFILIATIONS:
ASMP
PRINCIPAL SUBJECTS:
The Arts
Travel
Human Interest
Advertising
PUBLICATIONS:
American Photo
Outside
Photo District News
Polaroid Guide

KONRATH, G. FRANK
7518 West Madison Street
Forest Park, IL 60130
Telephone: 708-366-1770
Fax: 708-366-1771
AFFILIATIONS:
ASMP
PRINCIPAL SUBJECTS:
Advertising
Agriculture
Business & Industry
Computer Technology
Ecology
Editorial
Education

Electronics
Entertainment
Family
Fashion
Health
Human Interest
Human Relations
Humor
Journalism
Management
Marketing
Media
Medical
Men's Interest
News
Personal Finance
Personalities
Photography
Physical Fitness
Science
The Arts
Travel
Urban Affairs
Women's Interest
World Affairs
Youth
PUBLICATIONS:
Chicago Parent Magazine
Wednesday Journal
Billboard Magazine
Chicago Tribune
Moody Magazine
Screen Magazine
Vegetarian Times
Industrial Photography
 Magazine

KOONTZ, KATY
8232 Cambridge Woods Ln.
Knoxville, TN 37923
Telephone: 615-693-9845
AFFILIATIONS:
ASMP, SATW
PRINCIPAL SUBJECTS:
Editorial
Foreign
Travel
PUBLICATIONS:
Delta Sky
McCall's
Shape
Travel Life
Westways
Garden Design
Abbey Press
Physicians Lifestyle Magazine

KOROPP, ROBERT
24326 Winder Pl.
Golden, CO 80403
Telephone: 303-642-7800

Fax: 303-642-0154
AFFILIATIONS:
ASMP, CPAC
PRINCIPAL SUBJECTS:
Advertising
Architecture
Editorial
Food/Diet
General Interest
Nature
Photography
The Arts
PUBLICATIONS:
Life Magazine
Time Magazine
Petersen's Photograpic
International Photography
The Professional Photographer
Bluegrass
Colorado Homes & Lifestyles
New Hampshire Profiles

KOTECKI, STAN
278 Appletree Ct.
Buffalo Grove, IL 60089
Telephone: 708-541-8011
Fax: 708-541-8011
AFFILIATIONS:
ASMP
PRINCIPAL SUBJECTS:
Architecture
Business & Industry
Fashion
General Interest
Health
Human Interest
Marketing
Medical
Sales
PUBLICATIONS:
Guideposts
Hasselblad Forum

KOWAL, JOHN PAUL
125 Bonad Rd.
Brookline, MA 02167
Telephone: 617-325-2640
AFFILIATIONS:
OWAA, ASC, ASJ
PRINCIPAL SUBJECTS:
General Interest
Science
Travel
Computer Technology
PUBLICATIONS:
The Boston Globe
The Boston Herald
The Boston Business Journal
The Union Leader
Better Communication
Public Relations Quarterly

Journal Of Technical Writing
  And Communication
Writer's Digest
Photomethods
IEEE Transactions On
  Professional Communication
Ladies' Circle
The Press
WDS Forum
Diver Magazine (Canada &
  England)
New Haven INFO Magazine

KRAFFT, LOUISE
3215 Valley Drive
Alexandria, VA 22302
Telephone: 703-998-8648
PRINCIPAL SUBJECTS:
Sports
Government

KRAMER, DANIEL
110 W. 86th St.
New York, NY 10024
Telephone: 212-873-7777
AFFILIATIONS:
ASMP, DGA
PRINCIPAL SUBJECTS:
Photography
Human Interest
PUBLICATIONS:
Business Week
Fortune Magazine
New York Magazine
People Magazine
Life Magazine
Connoisseur Magazine
America Illustrated
American Heritage
Food & Wine Magazine
Horizon Magazine
Reader's Digest
Signature Magazine
Time Magazine
Time Life Books
T.V. Guide
Paris Match
Stern
Manchete
Newsweek
Art in America
Rolling Stone
Forbes Magazine
Money Magazine
Entertainment Weekly

KRASKA, MARK
Kraska, Mark Photography
2899 E. Big Beaver, #291
Troy, MI 48083
Telephone: 313-545-2722

AFFILIATIONS:
ASMP, USGTA/ACD
PRINCIPAL SUBJECTS:
Advertising
Architecture
Automotive
PUBLICATIONS:
Newsweek
Time
Sports Illustrated
Golf Digest
Friends
Architecture
Detroit News

KRATT, K.C.
64 Amherst St.
Buffalo, NY 14207
Telephone: 716-876-8275
Fax: 716-874-3074
AFFILIATIONS:
ASMP, AAF
PRINCIPAL SUBJECTS:
Advertising
Business & Industry
Fashion
Food/Diet
Marketing
Personalities
PUBLICATIONS:
Elle Decor
Metropolitan Home
Metropolis

KRAVITZ, TOM
3447 Motor Ave., Ste. C
Los Angeles, CA 90034
Telephone: 310-838-1531
Fax: 310-838-1436
MAILING ADDRESS:
TOM KRAVITZ
P.O Box 1307
Culver City, CA 90232
PRINCIPAL SUBJECTS:
Editorial
Advertising
PUBLICATIONS:
People
Time
US News & World Report

KRUBNER, RALPH
4 Juniper Court
Jackson, NJ 08527
Telephone: 908-364-3640
AFFILIATIONS:
ASMP-NJ, ASPP
PRINCIPAL SUBJECTS:
Advertising
Architecture
Foreign

Geography
Home & Garden
Photography
Travel
Urban Affairs
PUBLICATIONS:
Womens World Magazine
AAA Maps & Guidebooks
Insight (Cover)
TV Guide
NJ Monthly (Adv.)
Destinations

KRUEGER, BOB
P.O. Box 1841
Aspen, CO 81612
Telephone: 303-923-3078
AFFILIATIONS:
NPPA,ASMP
PRINCIPAL SUBJECTS:
Editorial
General Interest
Human Interest
Sports
PUBLICATIONS:
Audubon
Aspen Mag.
Boys Life
Business Week
Country Journal
Country Roads
Country Music
Denver Post
Guitar Player
L.A. Times
Newsweek
N.Y. Times
Outside
Pacific Press Serv.
Parade
Popular Photography
Rolling Stone
Skiing
Travel & Leisure
Us
Womens World
Ballet West

KUHLMAN, CHRIS
Kuhlman, Chris Photography
12403-B Scarsdale
Houston, TX 77089
Telephone: 713-484-8600
Fax: 713-481-6782
MAILING ADDRESS:
Chris Kuhlman Photography
1002 Todville
Seabrook, TX 77586
AFFILIATIONS:
ASMP

PRINCIPAL SUBJECTS:
Advertising
Architecture
Business & Industry
Ecology
Health
Home & Garden
Marine
Marketing
Medical
Nature
Photography

KUPER, HOLLY
5522 Anita Street
Dallas, TX 75206
Telephone: 214-827-4494
AFFILIATIONS:
ASMP, NPPA
PRINCIPAL SUBJECTS:
Agriculture
Business & Industry
Editorial
Family
News
Photography
Women's Interest
PUBLICATIONS:
Business Week
Forbes
Fortune
Farm Journal Publications
USA Today
Nations Business

LABUA, FRANK
377 Hil-Ray Ave.
Wyckoff, NJ 07481
Telephone: 201-783-6318
AFFILIATIONS:
ASMP
PRINCIPAL SUBJECTS:
Advertising
Business & Industry
Editorial
Fashion
Nature
Photography
Travel
Women's Interest
PUBLICATIONS:
Travel/Holiday
Travel & Leisure
Popular Photography
Vogue
Details
Woman's World

LAMAGNA, JOSEPH
P.O. Box 882
Yonkers, NY 10702

Telephone: 914-963-3260
MAILING ADDRESS:
JOSEPH LAMAGNA
Yonkers, NY 10702
PRINCIPAL SUBJECTS:
Nature
Hobbies
History
Photography
PUBLICATIONS:
NY State Outdoor Recreation
  Guide
Southern NY Sportsman
Entertainer
Mountain Eagle, The
Mirror - Recorder
Bob Zwirz's Fishing/Boating
  Guide
Yonkers Home News & Times

LAMONT, DANIEL E., JR.
Lamont, Dan Photography
P.O. Box 9323
Seattle, WA 93109-9323
Telephone: 206-285-9049
AFFILIATIONS:
ASMP
PRINCIPAL SUBJECTS:
Editorial
Journalism
PUBLICATIONS:
Smithsonian
Audubon
New York Times Sunday
  Magazine
Life
Time
Newsweek
Derspiegl
US News & World Report

LANE, WALTER B.
34 York St.
Gettysburg, PA 17325
Telephone: 717-334-5513
AFFILIATIONS:
ASMP USSW NPPA
PRINCIPAL SUBJECTS:
General Interest
Journalism
The Arts
PUBLICATIONS:
Life
Time

LANGE, ED
700 Robinson Rd.
Topanga, CA 90290
Telephone: 310-455-1000
Fax: 310-455-2007

AFFILIATIONS:
PPA,ASMP, LA PR
PRINCIPAL SUBJECTS:
General Interest
Journalism
PUBLICATIONS:
Life
Vogue
L. A. Times
Time Mag.
Life Mag.
Elysium Journal of the Senses
  (Jots)
Nudism Today
Life Styles
Nudist Idea, The
"Jots" (Journal of the Senses)
N & N Magazine

LANGENBACH, RANDOLPH
6446 Harwood Ave.
Oakland, CA 94618
Telephone: 510-428-2252
Fax: 510-428-0810
AFFILIATIONS:
ASMP
PRINCIPAL SUBJECTS:
Architecture
History
PUBLICATIONS:
Life
Time
American Heritage
Architecture
Progressive Architecture

LATHROPE, WILMA
1590 Garden Ave.
Holly Hill, FL 32117
Telephone: 904-672-2130
Fax: 904-673-1281
AFFILIATIONS:
ASMP, FPP
PRINCIPAL SUBJECTS:
Animals
Family
Nature
Youth
PUBLICATIONS:
Daytona Beach News Journal

LAVINE, ARTHUR
17614 Marymount Place
San Diego, CA 92128
Telephone: 619-674-5718
MAILING ADDRESS:
ARTHUR LAVINE
San Diego, CA 92128
AFFILIATIONS:
ASMP,PAI

PRINCIPAL SUBJECTS:
Business & Industry
Editorial
Photography
PUBLICATIONS:
Business Week
Forbes
Time
Fortune
New York Times Magazine
Chase Manhattan Annual
  Reports
Newsweek
Life
Look
Esquire
Glamour
Redbook
ABA Banking Journal

LE GRAND, PETER
1620 West Lunt Ave.
Chicago, IL 60626
Telephone: 312-274-9523
Fax: 312-274-9517
AFFILIATIONS:
ASMP
PRINCIPAL SUBJECTS:
Advertising
Editorial
Fashion
PUBLICATIONS:
Fortune
Boat & Motor Dealer
Chicago Magazine
Crain's Chicago Business

LEDUC, LYLE
320 East 42nd St.
New York, NY 10017
Telephone: 212-697-9216
Fax: 212-727-8130
AFFILIATIONS:
ASMP
PRINCIPAL SUBJECTS:
Advertising
Editorial
Nature
Travel
World Affairs
PUBLICATIONS:
John Deere: 'The Furrow'
Emphasis Magazine
National Geographic
Travel-Holiday

LEE, CAROL
P.O. Box 4087
Christiansted, ST.CROIX 00822
Telephone: 809-773-5412
Fax: 809-773-5412

AFFILIATIONS:
ASMP, CTO
PRINCIPAL SUBJECTS:
Ecology
Editorial
Journalism
Nature
Travel
PUBLICATIONS:
Travel & Leisure
Audubon
Caribbean Travel & Life
Natural History
New York Times
Caribbean Travel News
Caribbean World
Miami Herald

LEE, LARRY
P.O. Box 4688
North Hollywood, CA 91607
Telephone: 805-259-1226
Fax: 805-259-1226
AFFILIATIONS:
ASMP
PRINCIPAL SUBJECTS:
Advertising
Business & Industry
Editorial
Foreign
Geography
Photography
Travel

LEE, ROBERT II
  PHOTOGRAPHY
Lee, Robert II Photography
1512 Northlin Dr.
St. Louis, MO 63122
Telephone: 314-965-5832
Fax: 314-821-5632
AFFILIATIONS:
ASMP
PRINCIPAL SUBJECTS:
Advertising
Animals
Business & Industry
Editorial
Family
Foreign
General Interest
Geography
Home & Garden
Human Interest
Journalism
Nature
Photography
Senior Citizens
The Arts
Travel

PUBLICATIONS:
Britannica
New York Times
Womans World Magazine
Guest Informant

LEIALOHA, MARK
1045 17th St.
San Francisco, CA 94107
Telephone: 415-864-5520
Fax: 415-431-5647
AFFILIATIONS:
ASMP
PRINCIPAL SUBJECTS:
Entertainment
PUBLICATIONS:
Guitar Player
New York Times
Newsweek
Propaganda
Rolling Stone
Spin
Time
Vox
VOX (England)
Ill Venerdi (Italy)
RIP (Spain)
Music Connection

LEIBER, N. GREGORY
Photoquest)P.O. Box 1688
Jacksonville,
Or, 97530 503-770-80
AFFILIATIONS:
ASMP, NPPA
PRINCIPAL SUBJECTS:
Advertising
Editorial
Nature
News
Travel
PUBLICATIONS:
The Oregonian
NEA Today
Northwest Magazine

LEIPZIG, ARTHUR
378 Glen Ave.
Sea Cliff, NY 11579
Telephone: 516-676-6016
Fax: 516-671-4385
PRINCIPAL SUBJECTS:
Human Interest
Business & Industry

LENTZ & ASSOCIATES
1000-104 Brighthurst Dr.
Raleigh, NC 27605
Telephone: 919-828-6761
MAILING ADDRESS:
LENTZ & ASSOCIATES, INC.

P. O. Box 6181
Raleigh, NC 27628
Telephone: 919-828-2233
AFFILIATIONS:
ITVA
PRINCIPAL SUBJECTS:
Advertising
General Interest
The Arts

LESTER, PETER
1401 Surrey Lane
Wynnewood, PA 19096
Telephone: 215-649-6038
AFFILIATIONS:
ASMP
PRINCIPAL SUBJECTS:
Advertising
Entertainment
Family
General Interest
Health
Human Relations
PUBLICATIONS:
Philadelphia Magazine
Philadelphia Inquirer

LEVIN, AARON
3000 Chestnut Ave., #102
Baltimore, MD 21211
Telephone: 410-467-8646
AFFILIATIONS:
ASMP
PRINCIPAL SUBJECTS:
Architecture
Business & Industry
Computer Technology
Editorial
Education
History
Journalism
Science
The Arts
Travel
Urban Affairs
PUBLICATIONS:
New York Times
Baltimore Sun
Saturday Evening Post
Archeology
Hopkins Magazine

LEVITON, DREW B.
1271 Roxboro Dr., N.E.
Atlanta, GA 30324
Telephone: 404-237-7766
AFFILIATIONS:
ASMP, BDP
PRINCIPAL SUBJECTS:
Advertising
Editorial

General Interest
Photography
PUBLICATIONS:
Business Week
Forbes
Fortune
Time
People
Life
Newsweek

LEVITON, JOYCE B.
1271 Roxboro Dr., N.E.
Atlanta, GA 30324
Telephone: 404-237-7766
Fax: 404-237-8882
AFFILIATIONS:
IAWWW, NWC
PRINCIPAL SUBJECTS:
Advertising
Editorial
General Interest
Photography
PUBLICATIONS:
Business Week
Fortune
Time
People
Life

LEVY, BURT
1101 Stinson Boulevard
Minneapolis, MN 55413
Telephone: 612-331-4014
Fax: 612-331-3421
AFFILIATIONS:
ASMP, MCIPA
PRINCIPAL SUBJECTS:
Advertising
Architecture
Business & Industry
Home & Garden
Marketing
Nature
Physical Fitness
Sports
PUBLICATIONS:
AIA Journal
Metropolitan Home
Minneapolis Star & Tribune
Voyager Press
Studio Photography Magazine

LEVY, PATRICIA BARRY
3389 W. 29th Ave.
Denver, CO 80211
Telephone: 303-458-6692
Fax: 303-458-5363
AFFILIATIONS:
ASMP

PRINCIPAL SUBJECTS:
Advertising
Agriculture
Book Reviews
Business & Industry
Editorial
Education
Family
General Interest
Human Interest
Human Relations
Management
News
Personal Finance
Personalities
Senior Citizens
Social Trends
The Arts
Travel
Women's Interest
PUBLICATIONS:
Newsweek
Business Week
Forbes
Computer World
Inc.
U.S. News & World Report
Working Woman

LEVY, RON
P.O. Box 3416
Soldotna, AK 99669
Telephone: 907-262-7899
MAILING ADDRESS:
RON LEVY
Kendanemken Rd.
Soldotna, AK 99669
AFFILIATIONS:
ASMP, PPA
PRINCIPAL SUBJECTS:
Advertising
Animals
Ecology
Editorial
Family
Foreign
General Interest
Geography
Hobbies
Human Interest
Humor
Journalism
Marine
Nature
Travel
PUBLICATIONS:
Fame
Time
Northern Telecom
People
Alaska

Fame
Time
Northern Telecom
People
Alaska

LEWELLYN, JON
10702 S. Western Ave.
Chicago, IL 60643
Telephone: 312-239-2239
AFFILIATIONS:
PPA
PRINCIPAL SUBJECTS:
Architecture
General Interest
Human Interest
Business & Industry

LEWIS, G. BRAD
RR2, Box 4774
Pahoa, HI 96778
Telephone: 808-965-7584
AFFILIATIONS:
ASMP
PRINCIPAL SUBJECTS:
Advertising
Ecology
Editorial
Foreign
Geography
Home & Garden
Journalism
Nature
News
Photography
The Arts
Travel
PUBLICATIONS:
Time
Life
Newsweek
Omni
Stern
Sierra
Forbes
Outside

LEWIS, VICKIE
1435 Corcoran St., NW, #6
Washington, DC 20009
Telephone: 202-328-9099
AFFILIATIONS:
ASMP,WHNPA
PRINCIPAL SUBJECTS:
Business & Industry
Journalism
Women's Interest
Editorial
PUBLICATIONS:
People
Stern

N.Y. Times
Time-Life Books
National Geographic World

LEY, RUSSELL
Russell Studios
103 Ardale St.
Boston, MA 02131
Telephone: 617-325-2500
AFFILIATIONS:
ASMP
PRINCIPAL SUBJECTS:
Advertising
Architecture
Business & Industry
Computer Technology
Editorial
Photography
World Affairs

LIEBERMAN, ARCHIE
P.O. Box 61
Scales Mound, IL 61075
Telephone: 815-845-2443
AFFILIATIONS:
CPC, SPJ
PRINCIPAL SUBJECTS:
Advertising
Agriculture
Editorial
General Interest
Business & Industry
PUBLICATIONS:
North Shore Magazine
Chicago Magazine
Look
Life
Time

LIEBERMAN, KEN
118 West 22nd St.
New York, NY 10011
Telephone: 212-633-0500
Fax: 212-675-8269
AFFILIATIONS:
ASMP,PAI,NYPPA
PRINCIPAL SUBJECTS:
Sports
News
PUBLICATIONS:
Art In America

LIFTIN, JOAN
One Fifth Avenue #16G
New York, NY 10003
Telephone: 212-475-1489
PRINCIPAL SUBJECTS:
Journalism

LIGHTFOOT III, ROBERT M.
311 Good Ave.
Des Plaines, IL 60016
Telephone: 708-297-5447
Fax: 708-297-5448
PRINCIPAL SUBJECTS:
Photography
PUBLICATIONS:
Time
Tribune
The N.Y. Times
Fortune
Newsweek
Stern
Ovation
Popular Photography

LILLIBRIDGE, DAVID C.
Rte. 4, P.O. Box 1172
Burlington, CT 06013
Telephone: 203-673-9786
AFFILIATIONS:
ASMP
PRINCIPAL SUBJECTS:
Advertising
Journalism
PUBLICATIONS:
American Machinist
Modern Machine Shop
Spectra
N.C. Shopowner
Security Mag.

LINCK, TONY
2100 Linwood Ave., Ste. 19Y
Fort Lee, NJ 07024
Telephone: 201-944-5454
MAILING ADDRESS:
LINCK TONY
2100 Linwood Ave., Ste. 19 - Y
Fort Lee, NJ 07024
AFFILIATIONS:
ASMP,AWA,OPC
PRINCIPAL SUBJECTS:
Aviation
Editorial
Advertising
Business & Industry
Architecture
PUBLICATIONS:
Time
Life
American Heritage
Aviation International News

LINDQUIST, NILS
264 Fenway Road
Columbus, OH 43214
Telephone: 614-888-4788
Fax: 614-888-3959

AFFILIATIONS:
ASMP, AWA, OPC
PRINCIPAL SUBJECTS:
Advertising
PUBLICATIONS:
National Geographic
National Safety News

LISSY, DAVID
14472 Applewood Ridge Rd.
Golden, CO 80401
Telephone: 303-277-0232
Fax: 303-277-1508
AFFILIATIONS:
ASMP
PRINCIPAL SUBJECTS:
Advertising
Business & Industry
Editorial
Family
Health
Physical Fitness
Senior Citizens
Sports
PUBLICATIONS:
Sports Illustrated
Newsweek
Time
Nation's Business
Ski
Sport
Outside

LITSEY, LLOYD
Photolitsey
2201 W. Markham
Little Rock, AR 72205
Telephone: 501-375-9534
Fax: 501-375-6329
AFFILIATIONS:
ASMP
PRINCIPAL SUBJECTS:
Advertising
Architecture
Editorial
PUBLICATIONS:
Arkansas Times
Vogue
Giftware News
Playboy
Builder
Arkansas Business
Forbes

LOCKWOOD, LEE
27 Howland Rd.
West Newton, MA 02165
Telephone: 617-965-6343
AFFILIATIONS:
AG, NWU

PRINCIPAL SUBJECTS:
General Interest
Government
Journalism
Photography
PUBLICATIONS:
Life
Look
Nat'l Geographic
Fortune
Time
Newsweek
N.Y. Review of Books
Horticulture
Smithsonian
New York Times Magazine
Nation, The
London Times, The
Paris Match

LOHBECK, STEPHEN
6 Harvest Wind Ct.
Saint Louis, MO 63128
Telephone: 314-845-9511
Fax: 314-894-8595
AFFILIATIONS:
ASMP, MPCA
PRINCIPAL SUBJECTS:
Advertising
Marine
Travel

LOMEO, ANGELO & SONJA
  BULLATY
336 Central Park W.
New York, NY 10025
Telephone: 212-663-2122
AFFILIATIONS:
ASMP, PAI, PWP
PRINCIPAL SUBJECTS:
General Interest
Human Interest
Nature
Travel
Advertising
PUBLICATIONS:
Outdoor Photographer
Life
Country Journal
Travel & Leisure
Popular Photography
Modern Photography
Zoom

LONGWOOD, MARC D.
Longwood, Marc Photography
11553 Soda Springs Way
Sacramento, CA 95670
Telephone: 916-635-0652
AFFILIATIONS:
ASMP

PRINCIPAL SUBJECTS:
Advertising
Business & Industry
Computer Technology
Ecology
Editorial
Management
Marketing
Medical
Nature
Science
Travel
PUBLICATIONS:
Business Week
PC World
LA Times

LONNINGE, LARS
Lonninge Studio Inc., Lars
121 West 19 Street
New York, NY 10011
Telephone: 212-627-0100
Fax: 212-633-8144
AFFILIATIONS:
APA, ASMP
PRINCIPAL SUBJECTS:
Advertising

LORD, JIM
P.O. Box 879
Fair Lawn, NJ 07410
Telephone: 201-796-5282
Fax: 201-794-0971
AFFILIATIONS:
ASMP
PRINCIPAL SUBJECTS:
Advertising
Editorial
Fashion
Photography
PUBLICATIONS:
Newsweek
New York Times
Philadelphia Inquirer
Nikon Photo International

LORENZ, ROBERT
80 Fourth Ave., #302
New York, NY 10003
Telephone: 212-505-8483
Fax: 212-995-8090
AFFILIATIONS:
APNY, ASMP, ASPP
PRINCIPAL SUBJECTS:
Advertising
Business & Industry
Computer Technology
Editorial
Education
Hobbies
Science

PUBLICATIONS:
Scholastic: Choires
Matu Power
Science World
Scholastic News
Digital Review
Stereo Review

LOTT, HAL
5320 Gulfton #8
Houston, TX 77081
Telephone: 713-661-2595
Fax: 713-661-2597
AFFILIATIONS:
ASMP, ASID
PRINCIPAL SUBJECTS:
Advertising
Architecture
Editorial
Food/Diet
Home & Garden
Marketing
Nature
Travel
PUBLICATIONS:
Southern Accents
Creative Ideas
Southern Living
Country Homes
Kitchen & Bath
Houston Met

LOUIS SR., THOMAS
487 Caulfield Ave.
Woodbury, NJ 08096
Telephone: 609-845-6837
AFFILIATIONS:
PP OF A
PRINCIPAL SUBJECTS:
Photography
Sports
PUBLICATIONS:
Gloucester County Times
Courier Post, Gannett Division
Suburban Press

LOUIS, THOMAS SR.
487 Caulfield Ave.
Woodbury, NJ 08096
Telephone: 609-845-6837
AFFILIATIONS:
PPA
PRINCIPAL SUBJECTS:
Photography

LOYST, KEN
P.O. Box 83727
San Diego, CA 92138
Telephone: 619-697-0703
Fax: 619-697-0123

AFFILIATIONS:
ASMP, NAUI
PRINCIPAL SUBJECTS:
Advertising
Animals
Aviation
Book Reviews
Editorial
Foreign
General Interest
Hobbies
Human Interest
Journalism
Marine
Media
Personalities
Photography
Sports
Travel
PUBLICATIONS:
Discover Diving Magazine
Sources Magazine
Dive Retailer
Scuba Trade
SRA Journal

LUCE, DON
1547 St. Clair Ave.
Cleveland, OH 44114
Telephone: 216-781-1547
Fax: 216-781-8462
AFFILIATIONS:
ASMP, AIGA
PRINCIPAL SUBJECTS:
Advertising
Automotive
PUBLICATIONS:
Stereo Review
Photo Pro
Car & Driver
Automotive News
Sylvia Porters Personal
  Finance

LUKOWICZ, JEROME
122 Arch Street
Philadelphia, PA 19106
Telephone: 215-922-7122
AFFILIATIONS:
ASMP
PRINCIPAL SUBJECTS:
Advertising
Editorial
Health
Personalities
Foreign
PUBLICATIONS:
Annual Reports
Corporate Magazines &
  Newsletters

MAASS, ROBERT
166 E. 7 Street
New York, NY 10009
Telephone: 212-473-5612
PRINCIPAL SUBJECTS:
Human Interest
Government

MACKENZIE, MAXWELL
Architectural Photographer
2641 Garfield St. NW
Washington, DC 20008
Telephone: 202-232-6684
AFFILIATIONS:
ASMP
PRINCIPAL SUBJECTS:
Advertising
Architecture
Editorial
Home & Garden
Nature
Travel
PUBLICATIONS:
Architecture
Architectural Record
Better Homes & Garden
Business Interiors
Historic Preservation
Home
Interior Design
Interiors
Landscape Architecture
Professional Office Design
Progressive Architecture
Restaurant Business
Travel & Leisure

MACWEENEY, ALEN
171 1st Ave.
New York, NY 10003
Telephone: 212-473-2500
Fax: 212-473-2250
AFFILIATIONS:
ASMP, APA
PRINCIPAL SUBJECTS:
Editorial
Fashion
Journalism
Personalities
Photography
The Arts
Travel
PUBLICATIONS:
Life
Esquire
The New York Times
GQ Travel & Leisure

MADERE, JOHN
187 Boston Post Rd., Box 340
Old Lyme, CT 06371

Telephone: 203-434-3338
Fax: 203-434-5824
MAILING ADDRESS:
15 Swanswood Lane
Old Lyme, CT 06371
PUBLICATIONS:
Business & Industry

MAGIC LANTERN STUDIOS
Magic Lantern Studios
7440 Sepulveda Blvd., #303
Van Nuys, CA 91405
Telephone: 818-786-1756
Fax: 818-993-0373
AFFILIATIONS:
ASMP
PRINCIPAL SUBJECTS:
Advertising
Architecture
PUBLICATIONS:
Playboy
Architectural Digest
Gentlemen's Companion
Gentleman's Quarterly
Designer's West

MAGID, JEROME
13358 Victoria
Royal Oak, MI 48070
Telephone: 313-545-5212
AFFILIATIONS:
ASMP
PRINCIPAL SUBJECTS:
Architecture
Editorial
Food/Diet
News
Photography
PUBLICATIONS:
Time
Newsweek
Business Week
Ward's Auto World

MAGRO, BENJAMIN
2 Mechanic Street
Camden, ME 04843
Telephone: 207-236-4774
AFFILIATIONS:
ASMP, NEPA
PUBLICATIONS:
Boston Globe
N.Y. Times
Country Homes
Christian Science Monitor
Good Housekeeping
Antipies Magazine
Yankee Magazine

MAHI, MIEKO SUE
5857 Inwood Dr., #17
Houston, TX 77057
Telephone: 713-296-2987
Fax: 713-871-0728
AFFILIATIONS:
ASMP, ITVA
PRINCIPAL SUBJECTS:
Business & Industry
Editorial
Human Interest
Journalism
Photography
The Arts
Women's Interest
PUBLICATIONS:
Oil & Gas Journal
Offshore Oil Management
Petroleum Engineering
  International
Gulf Coast Oil World
Oil & Gas Investor

MAHIEU, TED
P.O. Box 245
Pebble Beach, CA 93953
Telephone: 408-626-6903
Fax: 408-625-1828
AFFILIATIONS:
ASMP
PRINCIPAL SUBJECTS:
Aviation
Business & Industry
Travel

MAHONEY, BOB
347 Cameco Circle
Liverpool, NY 13090
Telephone: 315-652-7870
AFFILIATIONS:
ASMP, NPPA
PRINCIPAL SUBJECTS:
Advertising
Business & Industry
Editorial
Foreign
Journalism
Military
Personalities
PUBLICATIONS:
Time
Newsweek
Forbes
Business Week
USA Today
New York Times

MAKRIS, DAVID
6 Scott Court
Poughkeepsie, NY 12601
Telephone: 914-462-4502

AFFILIATIONS:
ASMP, APA, APNY
PRINCIPAL SUBJECTS:
Computer Technology
Advertising
PUBLICATIONS:
Manufacturers Mart
New York Outdoors
Hudson Valley Magazine
Photo District News

MALLINSON, PETER A.
28 N. Colony St.
Wallingford, CT 06492
Telephone: 203-265-0244
PRINCIPAL SUBJECTS:
Advertising
General Interest

MANHEIM, MICHAEL PHILIP
P.O. Box 35
Marblehead, MA 01945
Telephone: 617-631-3560
Fax: 617-631-2888
MAILING ADDRESS:
MANAHEIM, MICHAEL
Marblehead, MA 01945
AFFILIATIONS:
ASMP, ASPP, SATW
PRINCIPAL SUBJECTS:
Humor
Travel
General Interest
Personalities
Business & Industry

MANONI, EILEEN
8-B Risk Ave.
Summit, NJ 07901
Telephone: 908-522-0078
AFFILIATIONS:
NFPW, NJPA
PRINCIPAL SUBJECTS:
Editorial
Human Interest
News
Photography
Sports
Youth
PUBLICATIONS:
Forbes Newspapers, Inc.
North Jersey Newspapers, Inc.
Venture Inward Magazine

MAPPES, CARL R.
P.O. Box 633
Kimberling Cy, MO 65686
Telephone: 417-739-5384
MAILING ADDRESS:
Kimberling Cy, MO 65686
Telephone: 414-739-5384

AFFILIATIONS:
ASMP,PPA,RPS
PRINCIPAL SUBJECTS:
General Interest
Business & Industry
Science
Travel
PUBLICATIONS:
International Who's Who of
 Intellectuals

MARCUS, HELEN
120 E. 75th St.
New York, NY 10021
Telephone: 212-879-6903
Fax: 212-517-2159
MAILING ADDRESS:
MARCUS GROUP, INC., THE
New York, NY 10021
AFFILIATIONS:
ASMP,ASPP,PWP,
 APA ALGA, OPC
PRINCIPAL SUBJECTS:
The Arts
Photography
General Interest
Journalism
Travel
PUBLICATIONS:
Publishers Weekly
Gourmet
Time
N. Y. Times
Food & Wine
Guidepost
Fortune
Diversion
Town & Country
Vanity Fair

MARES-MANTON,
 ALEXANDER
3233 N.E. 92nd St.
Seattle, WA 98115
Telephone: 206-522-4089
Fax: 206-522-4173
AFFILIATIONS:
ASMP
PRINCIPAL SUBJECTS:
Advertising
Business & Industry
Editorial
Foreign
Photography
Travel
World Affairs
PUBLICATIONS:
Business Week
Forbes
Fortune
Money

MARGERIN, BILL
41 W. 25th Street, 8th Flr.
New York, NY 10010
Telephone: 212-645-1532
AFFILIATIONS:
ASMP
PRINCIPAL SUBJECTS:
Advertising
Editorial
Food/Diet
PUBLICATIONS:
Modern Bride

MARIEN, ROBERT
3101 Riverside Dr.
Burbank, CA 91505
Telephone: 818-842-3777
Fax: 818-566-7380
MAILING ADDRESS:
ROBERT MARIEN,
 RO MA STOCK
10153 1/2 Riverside Dr., 564
N Hollywood, CA 91602
Telephone: 818-566-8528
AFFILIATIONS:
PACA, ASMP
PRINCIPAL SUBJECTS:
Nature
Science
General Interest
Women's Interest
PUBLICATIONS:
Tourism Compani of Puerto
 Rico Magazine
"Que Pasa" Magazine in
 Puerto Rico
Locations Magazine, Ad
 Campaign for Puerto Rico
Woman's World
Foto Kem Industries,
 Corporate Brochure

MARKATOS, JERRY
Rt. 2, Box 419
Pittsboro, NC 27312
Telephone: 919-542-2139
AFFILIATIONS:
ASMP
PRINCIPAL SUBJECTS:
Advertising
Architecture
Editorial
The Arts
Photography
PUBLICATIONS:
Fine Home Building
GTE Together Magazine
AIA Magazine

01 Informatique (France)
Family Health International
 Annual Reports
Country Journal Magazine

MAROON, FRED J.
2725 P St. NW
Washington, DC 20007
Telephone: 202-337-0337
Fax: 202-337-8672
AFFILIATIONS:
ASMP, ASPP, PWP
PRINCIPAL SUBJECTS:
Advertising
Editorial
Fashion
General Interest
Government
Journalism
Travel
PUBLICATIONS:
Travel And Leisure
Town And Country
Newsweek
Time
Life
E. F. Hutton Corporate
 Annual Report

MARSCHALL, FREDERIC
331 Crescent Ave.
Buffalo, NY 14214
Telephone: 716-835-5839
AFFILIATIONS:
PPA, PPSNY, PA
PRINCIPAL SUBJECTS:
General Interest
Photography
PUBLICATIONS:
The Professional Photographer
PPSNY Journal
Studio Photography
University Review
Lens Magazine (1987)

MARVY, JIM
41 12TH Ave., N.
Hopkins, MN 55343
Telephone: 612-935-0307
Fax: 612-933-2061
AFFILIATIONS:
ASMP, PPA, apa
PRINCIPAL SUBJECTS:
Photography
Food/Diet
Architecture
Agriculture
Food/Diet
Travel
Automotive

MARX, RICHARD
130 W. 25th St.
New York, NY 10001
Telephone: 212-929-8880
Fax: 212-727-2856
MAILING ADDRESS:
RICHARD MARX STUDIO
New York, NY 10001
AFFILIATIONS:
ASMP
PRINCIPAL SUBJECTS:
Human Interest
Video
Photography
Advertising
PUBLICATIONS:
New York Times
Woman's Wear Daily
Bath Products
New York Magazine

MASON, STEPHEN
P.O. Box 3284
Ketchum, ID 83340
Telephone: 208-788-2543
Fax: 208-788-2543
AFFILIATIONS:
ASMP
PRINCIPAL SUBJECTS:
Fashion
Photography
Advertising
PUBLICATIONS:
Vogue
GQ
Shape
Self
Field & Stream
Outdoor Life

MASSIE, KIM
452 Whitfield Rd.
Accord, NY 12404
Telephone: 914-687-7744
AFFILIATIONS:
ASMP
PRINCIPAL SUBJECTS:
Advertising
Editorial
General Interest
Travel
PUBLICATIONS:
Time
Newsweek
Sports Illustrated
New York Times
Look Magazine

MASSON, LISA
3122 S. Abingdon St.
Arlington, VA 22206

Telephone: 703-379-1401
Fax: 703-379-1403
AFFILIATIONS:
ASMP, IFDA
PRINCIPAL SUBJECTS:
Advertising
Architecture
Editorial
Education
Food/Diet
History
Home & Garden
Photography
Sales
The Arts
Travel
PUBLICATIONS:
Southern Accents Magazine
Woman's Day
Annapoltian Magazine
Home
American History Illustrated
Kiplingers
Washington Post Home
  Section
U.S. News & World Report

MASTROIANNI, ROGER
4614 Prospect Ave.
Cleveland, OH 44103
Telephone: 216-391-3917
Fax: 216-391-3922
AFFILIATIONS:
ASMP;BLACK STAR
PRINCIPAL SUBJECTS:
Aviation
Business & Industry
Editorial
Entertainment
News
The Arts
Personalities
PUBLICATIONS:
Business Week
Forbes
Fortune
Time
N.Y. Times
U.S.A. Today
New York Magazine

MATHIESON, GREG E.
6601 Ashmore Lane
Contreville, VA 22020
Telephone: 703-968-0030
Fax: 703-968-0040
AFFILIATIONS:
WHNPA, NPPA,
  USMCCA, ASMP
PRINCIPAL SUBJECTS:
Aviation

Entertainment
Fashion
Foreign
Geography
Government
History
Journalism
Marketing
Media
Military
News
Personalities
World Affairs
PUBLICATIONS:
· Life
Time
Newsweek
US News & World Report
Forbes
Fortune
Paris Match
USA Today

MATT, PHIL
P.O. Box 10406
Rochester, NY 14610
Telephone: 716-461-5977
AFFILIATIONS:
ASMP
PRINCIPAL SUBJECTS:
Business & Industry
Editorial
General Interest
Journalism
Medical
News
Personalities
Science
The Arts
World Affairs
PUBLICATIONS:
Time Magazine
The New York Times
Newsweek
Fortune
Barron's
Business Week
USA Today
US News & World Report

MATTHEWS, CYNTHIA
200 E. 78th St.
New York, NY 10021
Telephone: 212-288-7349
Fax: 212-879-0508
AFFILIATIONS:
ASMP
PRINCIPAL SUBJECTS:
Editorial
Business & Industry
Sports

PUBLICATIONS:
Town & Country
Time
Newsweek
Forbes
Sports Illustrated
New York Magazine

MAXWELL, CHIP
P.O. Box 151844
Tampa, FL 33684
Telephone: 813-875-1752
AFFILIATIONS:
ASMP
PRINCIPAL SUBJECTS:
Photography
Business & Industry

MAY, CLYDE
1037 Monroe Dr., N.E.
Atlanta, GA 30306
Telephone: 404-873-4329
AFFILIATIONS:
ASMP, APA
PRINCIPAL SUBJECTS:
Advertising
Architecture
Food/Diet

MAY, RONALD W.
P.O. Box 8359
Ft. Wayne, IN 46898
Telephone: 219-483-7872
Fax: 219-483-7872
AFFILIATIONS:
ASMP
PRINCIPAL SUBJECTS:
Agriculture
Aviation
Business & Industry
Computer Technology
Electronics
Photography
Science
The Arts

MAYERS, MARK M./AT
  AGENZIA
P.O. Box 144342
Coral Springs, FL 33114
Telephone: 305-663-9296
Fax: 305-663-9260
MAILING ADDRESS:
MARK M. MAYERS/AT
  AGENZIA
4901 S.W. 74th Court
Miami, FL 33155
AFFILIATIONS:
ASMP
PRINCIPAL SUBJECTS:
Media

Sports
Video
PUBLICATIONS:
Matchball
Tennis Oggi
Fitness
Vista Magazine
Matchball
Tennis Oggi
Fitness
Vista Magazine

MAYLEN III, DAVID
14231 W. 11 Mile Rd.
Oak Park, MI 48237
Telephone: 313-542-3287
Fax: 313-542-3287
AFFILIATIONS:
PP of A, MMNPA
PRINCIPAL SUBJECTS:
Business & Industry
Photography
The Arts
Human Interest
PUBLICATIONS:
Omni Magazine
Popular Photography
Art Glass Magazine
Detroit Free Press
The Uptown Review
The Pinconning Journal

MCALLISTER, BRUCE
P.O. Box 109
Boulder, CO 80306
Telephone: 303-444-9484
Fax: 303-444-5052
AFFILIATIONS:
ASMP
PRINCIPAL SUBJECTS:
Business & Industry
Education
Photography
Journalism
Travel
PUBLICATIONS:
London Daily Mail
Denver Post
Air & Space/Smithsonian
New York Times
Shell News
Successful Farming

MCBRIDE, TOM
2051 Colorado Gulch
Helena, MT 59601
Telephone: 406-443-5286
AFFILIATIONS:
MPPA, PPA
PRINCIPAL SUBJECTS:
Advertising

Animals
Photography
Media
Geography
Education
Nature
Media
PUBLICATIONS:
Quest
Out Side
East West Journal
The Range Finder
The Montana Magazine
Changing Times & (The
   Kiplinger Magazine)
Montana Out Doors
The New Age Journal
Readers' Digest
Kodak Studio Light
Tri Quarterly

MCCARTHY, MARGARET
247 West 30 St., 9 Fl.
New York, NY 10001
Telephone: 212-239-3221
Fax: 212-239-3221
AFFILIATIONS:
ASMP
PRINCIPAL SUBJECTS:
Photography
The Arts
Editorial
Travel
PUBLICATIONS:
N.Y. Times Travel Sec.
Westchester/Gannet
   Newspapers

MCCARTNEY, SUSAN
Rm. 1608, 902 Broadway
New York, NY 10010
Telephone: 212-533-0660
MAILING ADDRESS:
Photo Researchers Inc.
60 East 56th Street
New York City, NY 10021
AFFILIATIONS:
ASMP
PRINCIPAL SUBJECTS:
Animals
Ecology
Foreign
Home & Garden
Nature
Photography
Travel
PUBLICATIONS:
Life
National Geographic Traveler
Travel & Leisure
Travel/Holiday

Geo
Popular Photography
Womans Day
New York Times
Life
National Geographic Traveler
Travel & Leisure
Travel/Holiday
Geo
Popular Photography
Womans Day
New York Times

MCCLAIN, RICK
   PHOTOGRAPHY
McClain, Rick Photography
2212 So. West Temple, #6
Salt Lake City, UT 84115
Telephone: 800-728-9656
Fax: 801-487-2112
AFFILIATIONS:
ASMP
PRINCIPAL SUBJECTS:
Advertising
Architecture
Photography
Sports
PUBLICATIONS:
Vista USA
Arizona Highways
Fountain Magazine
Better Nutrition
The World & I
M.D. Magazine

MCCLELLAND, KIRK
1652 El Dorado Ave.
San Jose, CA 95126
Telephone: 408-241-6927
AFFILIATIONS:
ASMP, MPCA
PRINCIPAL SUBJECTS:
Human Interest

MCCLUSKEY, D. THOMAS
2343 Illinois Rd.
Northbrook, IL 60062
Telephone: 708-272-5632
AFFILIATIONS:
IABC, ASMP
PRINCIPAL SUBJECTS:
Advertising
Human Relations
Journalism
Photography
Sports

MCCOY, DAN J.
1079 Main St.
Housatonic, MA 01236
Telephone: 413-274-6211

Fax: 413-274-6689
MAILING ADDRESS:
RAINBOW
P.O. Box 573
Housatonic, MA 01236
AFFILIATIONS:
ASMP, PACA
PRINCIPAL SUBJECTS:
Science
Nature
Medical
Computer Technology
Travel
Business & Industry
Video
PUBLICATIONS:
Geo (French & German)
Omni
Longevity
Discover
Smithsonian
Time
Newsweek
Paris-Match
Newton (Japanese)
Manchete (Brazil)
Panorama (Holland)
Stern (Germany)
Science et Vie (France)
New York Times Magazine
National Geographic - Book
   Division
World & I
Epoca (Italy)
U.S. News & World Report

MCCRIRICK, FLIP
1265 Lupine Way
Golden, CO 80401
Telephone: 303-526-1890
AFFILIATIONS:
ASMP
PRINCIPAL SUBJECTS:
Advertising
Automotive
Nature
Sports
PUBLICATIONS:
Skiing
Ski Tech
Ski Racing
Road & Track
Car & Driver
Automobile
Off Road
Motor Trend

MCCUTCHEON,
   JR., SHAW
2100 N.W. 30th Rd.
Boca Raton, FL 33431

Telephone: 407-998-9736
Fax: 407-998-9737
AFFILIATIONS:
ASMP
PRINCIPAL SUBJECTS:
Advertising
Architecture
Editorial
Foreign
General Interest
Journalism
Marine
Photography
Travel
PUBLICATIONS:
Travel/Holiday
Conde Nast Traveller
Yankee
People
Boating
Motor Boating & Sailing
Islands
Yachting

MCCUTCHEON, STEVE
3363 Lakeside Dr.
Anchorage, AK 99515
Telephone: 907-344-1370
Fax: 907-344-5343
MAILING ADDRESS:
ALASKA PICTORIAL SERVICE
P.O. Box 190144
Anchorage, AK 99519
AFFILIATIONS:
ASMP, ACC, ASPP
PRINCIPAL SUBJECTS:
Education
General Interest
Government
Human Interest
Nature
Geography
Urban Affairs
PUBLICATIONS:
National Geographic
Coal Age
Flying Mag
AOPA Pilot
Alaska Magazine
Alaska Journal
Alaska Geographic
New York Times
Chicago Tribune
Los Angeles Times
Audubon Mag
Ranger Rick
Anchorage Times
Fairbanks News Miner
Ketchikan News
Atlante-Italy
Tier Freund-Germany

Das Tier-Germany
Alaska Construction
  & Oil Report
Forbes Magazine
Musical World
I B M Corp Magazine
National Wildlife Magazine
Newsweek
U S News & World Report
Pipeline & Gas Journal
Watersports Magazine
Pacific Fisherman
American Bar Journal
Allyn & Bacon Text Books
Wm. C. Brown
  Publishers Texts
Denoyer Gepart Texts
D C Heath
Readers Digest Magazine
Time Life
German Geo Magazine
National Academy Sciences
Alaska Miner Journal
British Science & Technology

MCDARRAH, FRED W.
36 Cooper Sq.
New York, NY 10003
Telephone: 212-475-3333
Fax: 212-254-5547
MAILING ADDRESS:
VILLAGE VOICE NEWSPAPER
36 Cooper Square
New York, NY 10003
AFFILIATIONS:
ASMP, ACC, ASPP
PRINCIPAL SUBJECTS:
Editorial

MCGEE, E. ALAN
1816 Briarwood Ind. Ct.
Atlanta, GA 30329
Telephone: 404-633-1286
Fax: 404-633-1572
AFFILIATIONS:
ASMP, APPA
PRINCIPAL SUBJECTS:
Architecture
Advertising
Photography
PUBLICATIONS:
Architectural Record
Interior Design
Interiors
Better Homes & Gardens
Brides
Home
Bldg. Design & Construction
Popular Science
Woman's Day
McCall's

Metropolitan Home
Progressive Architecture
Builder
Engineering Specifier
Architecture
Atlanta Magazine

MCGEE, TONY
212 Norton Road
Mount Holly, NC 28120
Telephone: 704-827-0050
MAILING ADDRESS:
TONY MCGEE
  PHOTOGRAPHY
AFFILIATIONS:
PPNC, PPA, WPI
PRINCIPAL SUBJECTS:
Architecture
Business & Industry
Advertising
Home & Garden
PUBLICATIONS:
Carolina Bride

MCGINTY, KATHIE
199 Bleecker St.
New York, NY 10012
Telephone: 212-924-4277
Fax: 212-675-1163
AFFILIATIONS:
ASMP, AAP
PRINCIPAL SUBJECTS:
Editorial
PUBLICATIONS:
American Photographer
Child Magazine
Fitness Magazine

MCGLYNN, DAVID
80 Fourth Ave., #7
New York, NY 10003
Telephone: 212-982-8181
PRINCIPAL SUBJECTS:
Advertising
Architecture
Computer Technology
Editorial
Entertainment
Fashion
Foreign
Journalism
Nature
Photography
PUBLICATIONS:
Life
New York
New York Times
Entertainment Weekly
TV Guide
Met. Home
Travel & Leisure

Traveler
Glamour
Interview

MCGRAIL, JOHN
Ste. C-2, 1200
  New Rodgers Rd. #840
Bristol, PA 19007
Telephone: 215-781-3990
Fax: 215-781-3904
AFFILIATIONS:
ASMP, IAPP
PRINCIPAL SUBJECTS:
Computer Technology
Nature
The Arts
Aviation
Business & Industry
Marine
PUBLICATIONS:
Business Week
Financial World
Fortune
Life
Money
Newsweek
People
Scientific American
Smithsonian
Time
U.S. News & World Report
Aviation Week & Space
  Technology

MCGRATH, NORMAN
164 W. 79th St.
New York, NY 10024
Telephone: 212-799-6422
Fax: 212-799-1285
AFFILIATIONS:
APA, ASMP
PRINCIPAL SUBJECTS:
Editorial
PUBLICATIONS:
Architectural Digest
N.Y. Times
Life Magazine
Architectural Record

MCGUIRE, JOSEPH W.
3148 N. Pennsylvania St.
Indianapolis, IN 46205
Telephone: 317-923-1122
Fax: 317-923-7634
AFFILIATIONS:
ASMP, PPA
PRINCIPAL SUBJECTS:
Advertising
Architecture
Fashion
General Interest

PUBLICATIONS:
SI
USNWR
Saturday Evening Post
Arc. Forum
Eng. News Record
USA Today
Sat. Eve. Post

MCKAY, DOUG
516 S. Hanley
St. Louis, MO 63105
Telephone: 314-863-7167
Fax: 314-727-8305
AFFILIATIONS:
ASMP
PRINCIPAL SUBJECTS:
Advertising
Agriculture
Architecture
Business & Industry
Computer Technology
Editorial
General Interest
Health
Human Interest
Journalism
Management
Marketing
Motivation
News
Personal Finance
Personalities
Photography
Physical Fitness
Sports
The Arts
Travel
Urban Affairs
PUBLICATIONS:
Senior Golf Magazine
Nothern Telecom Connections
Black Enterprise
Food Management
Wall Street Journal
Chemical Monthly

MCKEE, MICHAEL
117 S.W. Sixth Street (Studio)
Topeka, KS 66603
Telephone: 913-235-3260
AFFILIATIONS:
AAF, ASMP
PRINCIPAL SUBJECTS:
Business & Industry
Advertising
Architecture
The Arts
Human Interest
PUBLICATIONS:
Network Magazine

National Law Journal
Covlandt Forum
Santa Fe Railway News
Woman Wear Daily
Kansas Bankers Magazine

MCKNIGHT, DARLENE
113 Marion Ave.
Punta Gorda, FL 33950
Telephone: 813-639-6115
MAILING ADDRESS:
DARLENE TOTAL PHOTO
  ART PROD.
113 W. Marion Ave.
Punta Gorda, FL 33950
AFFILIATIONS:
PP of FI
PRINCIPAL SUBJECTS:
Photography
The Arts
PUBLICATIONS:
Tempo Magazine

MCLEMORE, BILL
7040 E. Main St.
Scottsdale, AZ 85251
Telephone: 602-945-3937
Fax: 602-941-3804
AFFILIATIONS:
PPA, ASMP
PRINCIPAL SUBJECTS:
Architecture
General Interest
The Arts
PUBLICATIONS:
American Indian Arts Mag.
Uniques
Art In America
Phx. Home & Garden
Scottsdale Quarterly
AZ Trends
Cubs Vine Line

MCMULLIN, FOREST
183 Saint Paul St.
Rochester, NY 14604
Telephone: 716-262-3944
Fax: 716-232-8839
AFFILIATIONS:
ASMP
PRINCIPAL SUBJECTS:
Agriculture
Business & Industry
Editorial
Ecology
Journalism
Photography
PUBLICATIONS:
Time
Forbes
Audubon

Scientific American
USA Today
Ladies Home Journal

MCNAMARA, DAVE
2317 Orbit
Corpus Christi, TX 78409
Telephone: 512-241-4029
PRINCIPAL SUBJECTS:
Photography
PUBLICATIONS:
Range Finder
Professional Photographers

MCNEELY, BURTON
P.O. Box 338
Land O Lakes, FL 34639
Telephone: 813-996-3025
AFFILIATIONS:
ASMP
PRINCIPAL SUBJECTS:
Architecture
Human Interest
Marine
Sports
Travel
Photography
PUBLICATIONS:
Life
Time
Saturday Evening Post
National Geographic
Sport Diver
Motorboat
True
Argosy
Sports Illustrated

MCNEILL, BRIAN
McNeill, Brian Photography
1511 Cowpath Road
Hatfield, PA 19440
Telephone: 215-368-3326
Fax: 215-368-6807
AFFILIATIONS:
ASMP
PRINCIPAL SUBJECTS:
Advertising
Architecture
Business & Industry
Computer Technology
Ecology
Editorial
Electronics
Medical

MCVICKER, SAM
P.O. Box 880
Dunedin, FL 34697
Telephone: 813-734-9660

PRINCIPAL SUBJECTS:
Advertising
Business & Industry
Human Interest

MEANS, LISA
5915 Anita
Dallas, TX 75206
Telephone: 214-826-4979
Fax: 214-826-4045
AFFILIATIONS:
ASMP
PRINCIPAL SUBJECTS:
Advertising
Editorial
Photography

MELTZER, LEE
1 Barstow Rd., #P-20
Great Neck, NY 11021
Telephone: 516-487-5002
Fax: 516-487-5002
AFFILIATIONS:
ASMP
PRINCIPAL SUBJECTS:
Editorial
Personalities
Photography
PUBLICATIONS:
Industry Week
Building Design & Construction
Gift & Stationery Business
Measurements & Control
  Magazine

MENDELSOHN, DAVID
15 Tall Pines Rd.
Durham, NH 03824
Telephone: 603-659-2530
AFFILIATIONS:
ASMP
PRINCIPAL SUBJECTS:
Business & Industry
Advertising
Photography
PUBLICATIONS:
Fortune Magazine
Forbes
Time
Life
Nations Business

MENDLOWITZ, BENJAMIN
Rt. 175, P.O. Box 14
Brooklin, ME 04616
Telephone: 207-359-2131
AFFILIATIONS:
ASMP
PRINCIPAL SUBJECTS:
Advertising
Foreign

General Interest
Journalism
Marine
Travel
PUBLICATIONS:
Nautical Quarterly
Sail
Yachting
Connoisseur
New York Times Magazine
Wooden Boat
Atlantic Monthly

MENNENGA, JERRY
23142 Leonora Dr.
Woodland Hls, CA 91367
Telephone: 805-897-7871
PRINCIPAL SUBJECTS:
Editorial
News
Journalism
PUBLICATIONS:
Los Angeles Times
Newsweek
Time

MENZEL, PETER
199 Kreuzer Lane
Napa, CA 94559
Telephone: 707-255-3528
Fax: 707-255-4720
AFFILIATIONS:
ASMP, NPPA
PRINCIPAL SUBJECTS:
Agriculture
Animals
Aviation
Business & Industry
Computer Technology
Health
Journalism
Science
Travel
PUBLICATIONS:
National Geographic
Life
Time
Business Week
Omni
U.S. News & World Report
Discover

MERIDETH, PAUL L.
1506 W. Augusta Blvd.
Chicago, IL 60622
Telephone: 312-772-7333
Fax: 312-772-7333
AFFILIATIONS:
ASMP
PRINCIPAL SUBJECTS:
Editorial

Journalism
Photography
Travel
PUBLICATIONS:
Life Mag.
New York Times
Forbes
Fortune
U.S. News

MESSINEO, JOHN
P.O. Box 1636-A
Ft. Collins, CO 80522
Telephone: 303-482-9349
AFFILIATIONS:
OWAA
PRINCIPAL SUBJECTS:
Agriculture
Animals
Automotive
Book Reviews
Ecology
Nature
Photography
Travel
Youth
PUBLICATIONS:
Newsweek
Business Week
Successful Farming
Canoe
Colorado Outdoors
Rocky Mountain Game & Fish
Farm Pond Harvest
Feed Management
On The Line
Technical Photography

METRISIN, JIM
16102 Huntmers Ave.
Cleveland, OH 44110
Telephone: 216-621-6366
MAILING ADDRESS:
Zena Photography
633 Huron Rd.
Cleveland, OH 44115
AFFILIATIONS:
ASMP
PRINCIPAL SUBJECTS:
Advertising
Architecture
Fashion
Food/Diet
Sports
PUBLICATIONS:
Northern Ohio Live
Corporate Cleveland
Restaurant Hospitality
The Cleveland Edition
Northern Ohio Live

Corporate Cleveland
Restaurant Hospitality
The Cleveland Edition

MEYERS, EDWARD
61-68 77 St., Middle Village
New York City, NY 11379
Telephone: 718-426-6221
Fax: 718-426-1481
PRINCIPAL SUBJECTS:
Travel
Human Interest
Computer Technology
Humor

MICHELSON, ERIC
Michelson, Eric Studio, Inc.
7 Birchwood Dr.
Huntington Station,
  NY 11746-3901
Telephone: 516-271-3361
Fax: 516-271-3361
AFFILIATIONS:
ASMP, NPPA
PRINCIPAL SUBJECTS:
Advertising
Editorial
General Interest
Journalism
Photography
PUBLICATIONS:
L. I. Newsday
New York Times

MIGLAVS, MR. JANIS
525 First St., #104
Lake George, OR 97034
Telephone: 503-635-5616
AFFILIATIONS:
ASMP
PRINCIPAL SUBJECTS:
Advertising
Architecture
Business & Industry
Computer Technology
Editorial
Education
Family
Foreign
General Interest
Home & Garden
Human Relations
Journalism
Management
Marketing
Nature
Photography
Senior Citizens
The Arts
Travel
Youth

PUBLICATIONS:
National Geographic
National Wildlife
Harrowsmith
Modern Maturity
Travel/Holiday
National Geographic Traveler

MIHALEVICH, MICHAEL
Mihalevich Photography
4482 S.W. Bowsprit Drive
Lee's Summit, MO 64082
Telephone: 816-537-7770
Fax: 816-537-7770
AFFILIATIONS:
ASMP
PRINCIPAL SUBJECTS:
Advertising
Agriculture
Architecture
Aviation
Business & Industry
Computer Technology
Editorial
Education
Electronics
Entertainment
General Interest
Marine
Marketing
Medical
Nature
Photography
Senior Citizens
Sports
Travel

MIHOVIL, ROBERT JOHN
Mihovil Photography
2402 Church St.
Galveston, TX 77550
Telephone: 409-763-3951
Fax: 409-763-6244
AFFILIATIONS:
ASMP, NPPA
PRINCIPAL SUBJECTS:
Advertising
Agriculture
Architecture
Business & Industry
Editorial
Journalism
Media
Medical
News
Photography
The Arts
PUBLICATIONS:
People
Newsweek
National Geographic

USA Today
New York Times
Boston Globe
D-Magazine
Houston Metropolitan
  Magazine
The Houston Chronicle
Houston Post

MILJAKOVICH, HELEN
114 7TH Ave., (3C)
New York, NY 10011
Telephone: 212-242-0646
AFFILIATIONS:
PPA, ASMP, PWP
PRINCIPAL SUBJECTS:
Family
General Interest
Government
Human Interest
Photography
PUBLICATIONS:
Time
Coronet
Pageant
Cosmopolitan
Hollywood Reporter
McCalls
Glamor
Infinity
West
Popular Photography
Opera News
Dance Magazine
Modern Photography
The New York Times
The L. A. Times
Downtown

MILLER
  PHOTOGRAPHY, INC.
Miller Photography, Inc.
212 N. Main
Tulsa, OK 74103
Telephone: 918-587-2505
Fax: 918-587-2505
AFFILIATIONS:
ASMP
PRINCIPAL SUBJECTS:
Advertising
Agriculture
Automotive
Business & Industry
Computer Technology
Editorial
Electronics
Entertainment
Fashion
Food/Diet
Home & Garden
Human Interest

Journalism
Marine
Marketing
Media
Medical
Nature
News
Photography
Sales
The Arts
Urban Affairs
PUBLICATIONS:
Wall Street Journal
Newsweek
U.S. News & World Report

MILLER, DAVID P.
One Penrita Rd.
Lockport, NY 14094
Telephone: 716-433-5842
MAILING ADDRESS:
DAVID P. MILLER
Lockport, NY 14094
AFFILIATIONS:
PP OF A,PPSNY
PRINCIPAL SUBJECTS:
Advertising
General Interest
Government
Human Interest
Nature
Women's Interest
Health
PUBLICATIONS:
Mechanics Illustrated

MILLER, JOE
Miller, Joe Photography
508 1st St. S.
Buffalo, MN 55313
Telephone: 612-682-6704
AFFILIATIONS:
ASMP, WPI
PRINCIPAL SUBJECTS:
Agriculture
Editorial
Family
Nature
Religion
PUBLICATIONS:
Let's Live
Road Rider
Decision
Central Minnesota Catholic

MILLER, MELABEE M.
29 Beechwood Place
Hillside, NJ 07205
Telephone: 908-527-9121
AFFILIATIONS:
ASMP, ASID

PRINCIPAL SUBJECTS:
Advertising
Architecture
Editorial
Home & Garden
Marketing
PUBLICATIONS:
New Jersey Monthly
The Star-Ledger
Woman's Day
Interiors
Interior Design
House Beautiful
Kitchen & Bath Business

MILLER, ROGER
   PHOTO, LTD.
Miller, Roger Photo, Ltd.
1411 Hollins Street,
   Union Square
Baltimore, MD 21223
Telephone: 410-566-1222
Fax: 410-233-1241
AFFILIATIONS:
ASMP, FII
PRINCIPAL SUBJECTS:
Advertising
Editorial
Media
Nature
Photography
Travel

MILLMAN, LESTER J.
Affil, Photographic Services
P.O. Box 61H
Scarsdale, NY 10583
Telephone: 914-946-2097
AFFILIATIONS:
ASMP
PRINCIPAL SUBJECTS:
Aviation
Business & Industry
Editorial
News
PUBLICATIONS:
Time
Newsweek
New York Times
Bunte Illustrated
Stern
St. Louis Post Dispatch
People

MILMOE, JAMES O.
14900 Cactus Circle
Golden, CO 80401
Telephone: 303-279-4364
AFFILIATIONS:
ASMP

PRINCIPAL SUBJECTS:
Advertising
Nature
The Arts
PUBLICATIONS:
Fortune
New York Times
Womans Day
Art In America
Domus

MILNE, ROBERT
400 East Pine, 215
Seattle, WA 98122
Telephone: 206-329-3757
AFFILIATIONS:
ASMP
PRINCIPAL SUBJECTS:
Geography
Fashion
Advertising

MISHLER, CLARK JAMES
1238 G St.
Anchorage, AK 99501
Telephone: 907-279-8847
Fax: 907-258-0579
AFFILIATIONS:
ASMP
PRINCIPAL SUBJECTS:
Advertising
Business & Industry
Computer Technology
Editorial
Family
Human Interest
Nature
Personalities
Travel
PUBLICATIONS:
National Geographic Magazine
U.S. News & World Report
CA Magazine
GEO
Newsweek
Alaska Magazine

MITCHELL, BENN
75 Bank Street
New York, NY 10014
Telephone: 212-255-8686
PRINCIPAL SUBJECTS:
Travel
Medical

MITCHELL, JACK
356 E. 74th St.
New York, NY 10021
Telephone: 212-737-8940
AFFILIATIONS:
ASMP

PRINCIPAL SUBJECTS:
Editorial
Entertainment
The Arts
PUBLICATIONS:
New York Times
Rolling Stone
Newsweek
Time
Entertainment Weekly
Harper's Bazaar
Vanity Fair
Dance Magazine

MOBERLEY, CONNIE
215 Asbury St.
Houston, TX 77007
Telephone: 713-864-4111
AFFILIATIONS:
ASMP
PRINCIPAL SUBJECTS:
General Interest
Business & Industry
Travel

MODRICKER, DARREN
50 Lexington Ave., #159
New York, NY 10010
Telephone: 212-978-8877
AFFILIATIONS:
ASMP
PRINCIPAL SUBJECTS:
Advertising
Editorial
Entertainment
Fashion
Personalities
PUBLICATIONS:
EMI Records
Met-Life

MOLENHOUSE, CRAIG
P.O. Box 7678
Van Nuys, CA 91409
Telephone: 818-901-9306
Fax: 818-901-0433
AFFILIATIONS:
ASMP
PRINCIPAL SUBJECTS:
Sports
Computer Technology
Photography
PUBLICATIONS:
Sports Illustrated
LA Dodgers Inc.
USA Today
Fortune
Business Week
Money
Financial World
News Media Showcase

MONTGOMERY
  PICTURES
P.O. Box 722
Las Vegas, NM 87701
Telephone: 505-425-3146
MAILING ADDRESS:
MRS. C. M.
  MONTGOMERY, OWNER
Las Vegas, NM 87701
AFFILIATIONS:
NWC, PPA
PRINCIPAL SUBJECTS:
Animals
Geography
Human Interest
Nature
PUBLICATIONS:
New Mexico Magazine
Decision Magazine
Ideals
Arizona Highways
Sunset Magazine
Denver Post
New Mexico Journal of
  Archaelogy

MOON, BEN L.
112 Hamp Chappell Rd.
Carrollton, GA 30117
Telephone: 706-854-8458
PRINCIPAL SUBJECTS:
Business & Industry
Computer Technology
Agriculture
Aviation
PUBLICATIONS:
Progressive Farmer
Successful Farming
Tom On - Line
Southern Living
Guideposts

MOONEY, CHRIS
1838 E. 6th Street
Tucson, AZ 85719
Telephone: 602-624-1121
Fax: 602-791-2003
AFFILIATIONS:
ASMP, NPPA
PRINCIPAL SUBJECTS:
Advertising
Computer Technology
Ecology
Journalism
Photography
Sports
PUBLICATIONS:
Bicycling
Sports Illustrated
McCalls
American Lawyer

Penthouse
USA Today
Popular Science
People

MOONEY, KEVIN O.
511 North Noble St.
Chicago, IL 60622
Telephone: 312-738-1816
Fax: 312-738-1596
AFFILIATIONS:
ASMP
PRINCIPAL SUBJECTS:
Advertising
Editorial
Photography
Travel
PUBLICATIONS:
Worth
Forbes
Fortune
Chicago Magazine
Parenting
Life
National Geographic
Runner's World

MOORE, BARBARA
1671 Parkcrest Cir., #301
Reston, VA 22090
Telephone: 703-471-4175
MAILING ADDRESS:
REFLEXIONS PHOTOGRAPHY
P.O. Box 960
Herndon, VA 22070
PRINCIPAL SUBJECTS:
Youth
Human Interest
Photography
PUBLICATIONS:
Reston Connection
Reston Times
Reston Directory
Washington Post
Center Stage

MOORE, DAN
1029 N. Wichita, #9
Wichita, KS 67203
Telephone: 316-264-4168
Fax: 316-264-7506
AFFILIATIONS:
ASMP
PRINCIPAL SUBJECTS:
Agriculture
Aviation
PUBLICATIONS:
Flying Magazine
Flight International
Pro Pilot

Restaurant Business
The Wichitan Magazine
KS Magazine

MOORE, MICHAEL
P.O. Box 183
Ballentine, SC 29002
Telephone: 803-732-6377
AFFILIATIONS:
ASMP
PRINCIPAL SUBJECTS:
Advertising
Architecture
Aviation
Business & Industry
Fashion
Human Interest
Humor
Journalism
Marine
Military
Nature
Personalities
Photography
Physical Fitness
The Arts
Travel
Video

MOORE, RIC
Moore, Ric Photographs
323 De La Mare Ave.
Fairhope, AL 36532
Telephone: 205-990-8622
Fax: 205-990-8019
AFFILIATIONS:
ASMP
PRINCIPAL SUBJECTS:
Advertising
Business & Industry
Food/Diet
Medical
Photography
Sales
The Arts

MORATH, INGE
72 Spring St.,
  c/o Magnum Photos
New York, NY 10012
Telephone: 212-966-9200
Fax: 212-941-9325
PUBLICATIONS:
Atlantic Monthly
Life
Newsweek
Du Magazine
Paris Match
Geo. Vogue
New York Times Magazine
New York Magazine

People Magazine
Sunday Observer
London Sunday Times
Traveller, The
Aperture
Art In America
Marie Claire
Camera Austria
Ogonek Moscow
Aperture
Sunday Observer
Newmag
El Europeo

MORELAND, MIKE
160 Roswell Farms Ln.
Roswell, GA 30075
Telephone: 404-993-6059
Fax: 404-642-7446
AFFILIATIONS:
ASMP, PPA, GPPA
PRINCIPAL SUBJECTS:
Advertising
Architecture
Business & Industry
Home & Garden
Medical
PUBLICATIONS:
Better Homes & Gardens
Country Home
Victorian Magazine
Home Magazine
Woman's World
Redbook
Country Accents
Builder Magazine

MORGAN, BRUCE
315 W. Sunrise Hwy.
Freeport, NY 11520
Telephone: 516-546-2034
Fax: 516-546-2054
AFFILIATIONS:
ASMP, PPA
PRINCIPAL SUBJECTS:
Photography
PUBLICATIONS:
New York Times & Magazine
Liparent
Daily News & Post
Sport Magazine

MORGAN, RICKEY L.
2145 W. Wilshire, 3
Phoenix, AZ 85009
Telephone: 602-254-0882

MORGENSTEIN, RICHARD
826 Moultrie St.
San Francisco, CA 94110
Telephone: 415-648-3408

AFFILIATIONS:
ASMP
PRINCIPAL SUBJECTS:
Advertising
Business & Industry
Editorial
Human Interest
Journalism
Marketing
Medical
Personalities
Photography
Social Trends
The Arts
PUBLICATIONS:
Business Week
Forbes
L. A. Times
Time-Life Books
Wine & Spirits
Inc. Magazine
Medical Economics
Global Finance

MORRIS, JEFF
Morris Graphics
2813 White Oak Drive
Nashville, TN 37215
Telephone: 615-269-5473
AFFILIATIONS:
ASMP
PRINCIPAL SUBJECTS:
Advertising
Computer Technology
Electronics
Entertainment
Marketing
Photography
The Arts
PUBLICATIONS:
Tennesee CPA

MORRIS, PAUL
770 N.E. 75th St.
Miami, FL 33138
Telephone: 305-757-6700
Fax: 305-758-8150
PRINCIPAL SUBJECTS:
Business & Industry
Editorial
Advertising
Photography
PUBLICATIONS:
AR 92;94, 15 & 13
American Showcase

MORROW,
  CHRISTOPHER W.
2A Ike Noble Dr.
Canton, NY 13617
Telephone: 315-386-1202

MAILING ADDRESS:
CHRISTOPHER MORROW
P.O. Box 309
Canton, NY 13617
AFFILIATIONS:
ASMP, ASPP
PRINCIPAL SUBJECTS:
Editorial
General Interest
Journalism
Business & Industry
PUBLICATIONS:
U.S. News & World Report
Smithsonian Magazine
Family Circle
CIO Magazine
Boston Business Magazine
Inc. Magazine
Modern Maturity
Mac Week

MOSER, DAVID W.
109 Brookmead Rd.
Wayne, PA 19087
Telephone: 215-222-6660
AFFILIATIONS:
ASMP
PRINCIPAL SUBJECTS:
Editorial
Journalism
Personalities
PUBLICATIONS:
Parade
Photographer's Forum
Business Week

MOSS, GARY
4 E. Holly St., #207
Pasadena, CA 91103
Telephone: 213-255-2404
Fax: 213-255-2457
AFFILIATIONS:
APA, ASMP
PRINCIPAL SUBJECTS:
Advertising
Business & Industry
Editorial
Family
Health
Home & Garden
Human Interest
Human Relations
Journalism
Men's Interest
News
Personalities
Photography
Travel
Urban Affairs
Women's Interest

PUBLICATIONS:
New York Times Magazine
LA Times Magazine
Newsweek
TV Guide
Time
Inc. Magazine
Mens Health
Success

MOSS, HOWARD
P.O. Box 1394
Miami, FL 33138
Telephone: 305-751-MOSS
Fax: 305-759-0024
AFFILIATIONS:
ASMP, PPA
PRINCIPAL SUBJECTS:
Advertising
Editorial
Entertainment
General Interest
Human Interest
Marine
Marketing
Media
Travel
Video
PUBLICATIONS:
Newsweek
Travel & Leisure
Miami Mag.
Ebony
Scuba Sports
Earthtreks

MOULIN, THOMAS
526 Second St.
San Francisco, CA 94107
Telephone: 415-541-9452
Fax: 415-541-9451
AFFILIATIONS:
PPA, WPI
PRINCIPAL SUBJECTS:
Advertising
Video
PUBLICATIONS:
DuPont Magazine
Pacific Tel Mag

MUENCH, DAVID
P.O. Box 30500
Santa Barbara, CA 93130
Telephone: 805-967-4488
Fax: 805-967-4268
AFFILIATIONS:
ASMP
PRINCIPAL SUBJECTS:
Nature
PUBLICATIONS:
Life

National Geographic
Audubon
Natural History
National Parks Of America
Ancient America

MULLEN, EDWARD F.
810 Ponce de Leon Blvd.
Clearwater, FL 34616
Telephone: 813-585-1763
AFFILIATIONS:
ASMP, BPI
PRINCIPAL SUBJECTS:
Advertising
Family
General Interest
Human Interest
Nature
Travel
PUBLICATIONS:
Orlando Magazine
Homes International

MUMMA, KEITH
7000 Portage Road,
  Unit 9817-189-1
Kalamazoo, MI 49001
Telephone: 616-329-3742
Fax: 616-323-5180
AFFILIATIONS:
ASMP
PRINCIPAL SUBJECTS:
Photography
PUBLICATIONS:
Newsweek
Chemical Week
Business Week
Upjohn
International Child Care
Kalamazoo Gazette
Womans Day
Nikon

MUNCH, ERIC
4254 Tenth St.
Calumet, MI 49913
Telephone: 906-337-5084
AFFILIATIONS:
PP of A, MPPA
PRINCIPAL SUBJECTS:
Architecture
History
The Arts
PUBLICATIONS:
American Heritage

MUNSON, RUSSELL
458 Broadway, 5th Floor
New York, NY 10013
Telephone: 212-226-8875
Fax: 212-941-6061

AFFILIATIONS:
ASMP
PRINCIPAL SUBJECTS:
Aviation
PUBLICATIONS:
Flying
Time
Fortune
Money
Popular Mechanics

MURPHY, MICHAEL
3200 S. Westshore Blvd.
Tampa, FL 33629
Telephone: 813-831-1210
Fax: 813-837-5686
AFFILIATIONS:
ASMP
PRINCIPAL SUBJECTS:
Business & Industry
Architecture
Medical
Social Trends
PUBLICATIONS:
Newsweek

MUSCHENETZ, ROLAND &
  KAREN
1156 9th St.
Los Osos, CA 93402
Telephone: 805-528-1434
Fax: 805-528-5531
AFFILIATIONS:
ASMP, ASPP
PRINCIPAL SUBJECTS:
Agriculture
Editorial
Education
Foreign
Marine
Nature
Travel
PUBLICATIONS:
Audubon
Smithsonian
Sunset
Guide Post
Elle
Quick
Gong
Country Journal

MYERS, FRED
114 Regent Lane
Florence, AL 35630
Telephone: 205-766-4802
AFFILIATIONS:
ASMP

PRINCIPAL SUBJECTS:
Agriculture
General Interest
Business & Industry

MYERS, TOM
1737 Markham Way
Sacramento, CA 95818
Telephone: 916-443-8886
Fax: 916-443-0465
AFFILIATIONS:
ASMP, NPPA, CAPA
PRINCIPAL SUBJECTS:
Animals
General Interest
Human Relations
Nature
News
Travel
Ecology
PUBLICATIONS:
National Geographic
National Wildlife

NADLER, BOB
85 Lake St.
Englewood, NJ 07631
Telephone: 201-568-6250
AFFILIATIONS:
ASJA, AG
PRINCIPAL SUBJECTS:
General Interest
Amusements
Photography
Computer Technology
Science
Sports
PUBLICATIONS:
American Way
Boating
Playboy
Consumer Guide
Mechanix Illustrated
Modern Photography
New York Times
Motor Boating & Sailing
Petersen's Photographic
Popular Photography
Popular Mechanics
Commodore Microcomputers
InfoWorld
Popular Computing
Syntax
Computer Shopper
Computer Buying World
"Personal Computing"
PC Sources
Window Sources
Info World Direct

NANCE, ANCIL
Nance, Ancil Photographs
600 SW Tenth 530 The Galleria
Portland, OR 97205
Telephone: 503-223-9534
Fax: 503-241-9520
AFFILIATIONS:
ASMP
PRINCIPAL SUBJECTS:
Advertising
Editorial
PUBLICATIONS:
Runners World
Sports Illustrated
Sunset

NANO, ED
3413 Rocky River Dr.
Cleveland, OH 44111
Telephone: 216-941-3373
AFFILIATIONS:
ASMP
PRINCIPAL SUBJECTS:
Advertising
Editorial
Food/Diet
PUBLICATIONS:
Fortune
Business Week
Forbes
Time
Life
Parade

NELSON, BRAD
2195 E. 3970 South
Salt Lake City, UT 84124
Telephone: 801-277-8110
Fax: 801-585-3300
AFFILIATIONS:
ASMP, BPA
PRINCIPAL SUBJECTS:
Medical
Nature
Photography
Science
PUBLICATIONS:
Newsweek
Life
Time
Discover

NELSON, BRUCE G.
8931 Ridgeland Dr.
Miami, FL 33157
Telephone: 305-233-1491
Fax: 305-256-2677
AFFILIATIONS:
ASMP
PRINCIPAL SUBJECTS:
Advertising

Photography
PUBLICATIONS:
Modern Bride
The Miami Herald

NELSON, JANET
Finney Farm
Croton-Hdsn, NY 10520
Telephone: 914-271-5453
MAILING ADDRESS:
JANET NELSON
P.O. Box 374
Croton Hdsn, NY 10520
AFFILIATIONS:
ASMP,SATW,NEOWA,GWAA
PRINCIPAL SUBJECTS:
Sports
Travel
Photography
Health
Physical Fitness
PUBLICATIONS:
The New York Times
Conde Nast Traveler
American Health
New York Magazine
Ski Area Management
Travel & Leisure

NELSON, ROBIN
2512 Summerchase Drive
Woodstock, GA 30188
Telephone: 404-871-4431
AFFILIATIONS:
ASMP
PRINCIPAL SUBJECTS:
Computer Technology
Editorial
Electronics
Family
Health
Journalism
Media
Medical
News
Photography
Senior Citizens
Social Trends
Travel
Urban Affairs
Women's Interest
PUBLICATIONS:
Newsweek
Time
Forbes
Fortune
Business Week
Barrons
Womans World
Glamour

NERONI, ROBERT
120 N. 3rd St.
Philadelphia, PA 19106
Telephone: 215-923-8829
Fax: 215-923-6894
AFFILIATIONS:
ASMP
PRINCIPAL SUBJECTS:
Advertising
Architecture
Fashion
Food/Diet
Foreign
Medical
Travel
PUBLICATIONS:
Woman's Day
Town & Country
Architectural Digest
Philadelphia Magazine

NESTE, ANTHONY
P.O. Box 602
Deer Park, NY 11729
Telephone: 516-667-3453
Fax: 516-254-2263
AFFILIATIONS:
ASMP, NYPPA
PRINCIPAL SUBJECTS:
Sports
Advertising
Fashion
PUBLICATIONS:
Sports Illustrated
N.Y. Times
Home Box Office
Entertainment Weekly
New York Magazine

NETZER, DON
Don Netzer Adv. & Corp.
  Photography
2510 Southwell, #107
Dallas, TX 75229
Telephone: 214-247-4115
Fax: 214-247-4115
AFFILIATIONS:
ASMP, IABC
PRINCIPAL SUBJECTS:
Advertising
Editorial
Photography

NEUBAUER, JOHN
1525 S. Arlington Ridge Rd.
Arlington, VA 22202
Telephone: 703-920-8895
Fax: 703-521-9304
AFFILIATIONS:
PPA

PRINCIPAL SUBJECTS:
Photography
PUBLICATIONS:
Time
Newsweek
U. S. News & World Report
Money
Der Speigel
Bunte
Smithsonian
Stern
Changing Times
People
Friends Magazine
American Way
House & Gardens
Family Weekly
Parade
Horticulture
Garden Design
Odyssey

NEUFELD, WILLIAM
265 Grove St.
Teaneck, NJ 07666
Telephone: 201-836-6006
PRINCIPAL SUBJECTS:
Photography
Business & Industry

NEUMANN, WILLIAM
96 Carmita Ave.
Rutherford, NJ 07070
Telephone: 212-691-7405
Fax: 212-691-7889
PUBLICATIONS:
New York Times Jazz Artists
Inc. Entrepreneur of The Year

NEWMAN, ARNOLD
39 W. 67th St., Studio 102
New York, NY 10023
Telephone: 212-877-4510
Fax: 212-799-0358
AFFILIATIONS:
ASMP
PRINCIPAL SUBJECTS:
Advertising
Personalities
Editorial
PUBLICATIONS:
Look
Holiday
Travel & Leisure
Town & Country
Vanity Fair
Newsweek
Time
Esquire
Fortune

Life
Time
Harpers Bazaar

NEY, NANCY
108 E. 16th St.
New York, NY 10003
Telephone: 212-260-4300
Fax: 212-260-0403
AFFILIATIONS:
ASMP
PRINCIPAL SUBJECTS:
Advertising
Fashion
Personalities
Women's Interest
PUBLICATIONS:
New York Times Magazine
Vogue
Gourmet
Glamour
Mademoisselle
Cosmopolitan
Victoria

NICCOLINI, DIANORA
356 E. 78th St.
New York, NY 10021
Telephone: 212-288-1698
MAILING ADDRESS:
DIANORA NICCOLINI
New York, NY 10021
AFFILIATIONS:
ASMP, AIVF, BPA
PRINCIPAL SUBJECTS:
Medical
Photography
Media
The Arts
Fashion
PUBLICATIONS:
New York Times
Village Voice
Popular Photograghy
Functional Photography
N. Y. Photo District News
PWP Times
Backstage
Show Business

NIEMAN, WILLIAM
411 4th Street, S.
Wisc Rapids, WI 54494
Telephone: 715-424-1870
AFFILIATIONS:
PPA, WPPA
PRINCIPAL SUBJECTS:
Architecture
Nature
PUBLICATIONS:
Wisconsin Builders Architect

Inova
Peterson Photography
Popular Photography
Photo Methods

NIKAS, GREG
Drawer 690
Ipswich, MA 01938
Telephone: 508-356-0018
PRINCIPAL SUBJECTS:
Business & Industry
Advertising
Travel

NORTON, MICHAEL
3106 N. 16th St.
Phoenix, AZ 85016
Telephone: 602-274-8834
Fax: 602-274-8828
AFFILIATIONS:
ASMP, PSCA
PRINCIPAL SUBJECTS:
Advertising
Architecture
Automotive
Business & Industry
Editorial
Human Interest
Human Relations
Marketing
Media
Men's Interest
Physical Fitness
Senior Citizens
Women's Interest
Youth
PUBLICATIONS:
PC Week
Guitar Player Magazine
Forbes
Parade
Computerworld
UPS Corporate Magazine
Frito-Lay Corporate Magazine
IBM Corporate Magazine
AT & T Corporate Magazine

NORTON, PEARL
875 Cowan Rd.
Burlingame, CA 94010
Telephone: 415-697-0766
MAILING ADDRESS:
P.O. Box 545
Burlingame, CA 94011
AFFILIATIONS:
PPA, PMA
PRINCIPAL SUBJECTS:
Advertising
General Interest
Journalism

PUBLICATIONS:
Telephony
DuPont News

NORTON, PHILLIP
P.O. Box 91
Mooers Forks, NY 12959
Telephone: 514-826-4626
PRINCIPAL SUBJECTS:
Geography
Ecology
Sports
Travel
PUBLICATIONS:
Rotarian, The
Harrowsmith
New Farm, The
Associated Press
Pennsylvania Naturalist, The
Adirondack Life
Christian Herald

O'BYRNE, WILLIAM M.
P.O. Box 517
Boothbay Harbor, ME 04538
Telephone: 207-633-5623
AFFILIATIONS:
ASMP
PRINCIPAL SUBJECTS:
Advertising
Agriculture
Business & Industry
Foreign
General Interest
Marine
Photography
PUBLICATIONS:
Caterpillar World
Energy

O'TOOLE, TOM AND JOANNE
Travel
  Journalists/Photographers
4603 Wood St.
Willoughby, OH 44094
Telephone: 216-942-2455
AFFILIATIONS:
SATW, TJG, MTWA, NPC
PRINCIPAL SUBJECTS:
Animals
Travel

OBREMSKI, GEORGE
Obremski Studio
1200 Broadway
New York, NY 10001
Telephone: 212-684-2933
PRINCIPAL SUBJECTS:
Advertising
Editorial
Food/Diet

Home & Garden
Medical
Nature
Personalities
Photography
Travel
PUBLICATIONS:
Travel & Leisure
Natural History
Architectural Digest
Travel Holiday
Food & wine

ODYSSEY PRODUCTIONS
Odyssey Productions
2633 N. Greenview
Chicago, IL 60614
Telephone: 312-883-1965
Fax: 312-883-0929
AFFILIATIONS:
ASMP, ASPP
PRINCIPAL SUBJECTS:
Agriculture
Architecture
Ecology
Education
Foreign
Geography
History
Marine
Nature
Photography
Science
Travel
PUBLICATIONS:
Los Angeles Times Magazine
GEO (France)
Kids Discover Magazine
National Geographic
Travel Holiday
Hemispheres

OLIVE, JIM
3115 D'Amico
Houston, TX 77019
Telephone: 713-526-7599
Fax: 713-520-1700
MAILING ADDRESS:
3115 D' Amico
Houston, TX 77019
AFFILIATIONS:
ASMP
PRINCIPAL SUBJECTS:
Animals
Architecture
Business & Industry
Health
Nature
PUBLICATIONS:
Time
Life

GEO (Germany)
Businessweek
Stern
Field & Stream
Nation's Business

OMER, DAVID
Box 4849
Austin, TX 78765
Telephone: 512-479-0643
MAILING ADDRESS:
DAVID OMER
306 W. 16th St.
Austin, TX 78701
AFFILIATIONS:
ASMP
PRINCIPAL SUBJECTS:
Advertising
Computer Technology
Food/Diet
Media
Sports
PUBLICATIONS:
Texas Monthly
Sports Illustrated
In-Line
Texas Monthly
Sports Illustrated
In-Line

OPPERSDORFF, MATHIAS
P.O. Box 590
Wakefield, RI 02880
Telephone: 401-783-5389
PRINCIPAL SUBJECTS:
Travel
Journalism

ORANS, MURIEL
Horticultural Photography
1810 Circle Pl. N.W.
Corvalis, OR 97330
Telephone: 503-758-1216
Fax: 503-758-1216
AFFILIATIONS:
ASMP, GW
PRINCIPAL SUBJECTS:
Advertising
Agriculture
Amusements
Animals
Architecture
Business & Industry
Ecology
Editorial
Education
Food/Diet
Foreign
Geography
Home & Garden
Marketing

Media
Photography
Science
Travel
PUBLICATIONS:
National Arbor Day Journal
Home Base
Better Homes & Gardens

ORDERS, KAREN
501 N. 36th St., #151
Seattle, WA 98103
Telephone: 206-776-2720
AFFILIATIONS:
ASMP
PRINCIPAL SUBJECTS:
Advertising
Editorial
Home & Garden
Nature
News
Personalities
Photography
The Arts
PUBLICATIONS:
Seattle Times
Columns Magazine
University Week
U. of W. Pres. Report
Wa. State Bar News
PC Magazine
B.A. Publications

ORRICO, CHARLES J.
72 Barry Lane
Syosset, NY 11791
Telephone: 516-364-9826
Fax: 516-364-9826
AFFILIATIONS:
ASMP
PRINCIPAL SUBJECTS:
Advertising
Automotive
Business & Industry
Editorial
General Interest
Health
Medical
Photography
World Affairs
PUBLICATIONS:
Parents Magazine
Signature Magazine
Long Island Magazine
Newsday
Fitness Magazine

OSBURN, KEN
6330 Middle Lake Rd.
Clarkston, MI 48346
Telephone: 313-620-0757

Fax: 516-676-1071
PUBLICATIONS:
Editorial
Business & Industry
Advertising

OSWALD, JAN
921 Santa Fe Drive
Denver, CO 80204
Telephone: 303-893-8038
AFFILIATIONS:
ASMP
PRINCIPAL SUBJECTS:
The Arts
Food/Diet

OTSUKI, TOSHI
334 East 22nd Street
New York, NY 10010
Telephone: 212-533-3960
Fax: 212-529-0533
AFFILIATIONS:
ASMP
PRINCIPAL SUBJECTS:
Editorial
Fashion
Advertising
PUBLICATIONS:
Hearst Magazines

OUZER, LOUIS
111 East Ave., Suite 102
Rochester, NY 14604
Telephone: 716-454-7582
AFFILIATIONS:
ASMP, NYPPA
PRINCIPAL SUBJECTS:
The Arts
Editorial
Personalities

OWEN, SIGRID
221 E. 31 St.
New York, NY 10016
Telephone: 212-686-5190
Fax: 212-686-5186
PRINCIPAL SUBJECTS:
Advertising

PAGANELLI, MANUELLO
6003 Curtier Dr.
Alexandria, VA 22310
Telephone: 703-719-9567
Fax: 703-719-9567
PRINCIPAL SUBJECTS:
Editorial
Personalities
Business & Industry
PUBLICATIONS:
Forbes
Business Week

Modern Maturity
Me World
Parade
Entertainment Weekly

PAIGE, PETER
269 Parkside Rd.
Harrington Park, NJ 07640
Telephone: 201-767-3150
Fax: 201-767-9263
AFFILIATIONS:
ASMP
PRINCIPAL SUBJECTS:
Advertising
Architecture
PUBLICATIONS:
Interior Design
Architectural Digest
Metropolitan Home
Interiors Magazine
Architectural Record
Progressive Architecture
Architecture
Hospitality Design

PALMIERI, JORGE
Photography/Studio 21
516 1/2 8th St. SE
Washington, DC 20003
Telephone: 202-543-3326
AFFILIATIONS:
ASMP, WCP
PRINCIPAL SUBJECTS:
Advertising
Business & Industry
Editorial
Family
Fashion
Health
Psychology
Social Trends
The Arts
Travel
PUBLICATIONS:
Life Magazine
French Vogue
One Magazine
Broadcasting Magazine

PANAYIOTOU, PETER
4025 Harvard Terrace
Skokie, IL 60076
Telephone: 708-677-1733
Fax: 708-677-1733
AFFILIATIONS:
ASMP
PRINCIPAL SUBJECTS:
Advertising
Photography
Travel

PANTAGES, TOM
34 Centre St.
Concord, NH 03301
Telephone: 603-224-1489
Fax: 603-226-1831
AFFILIATIONS:
ASPP, NEOWA
PRINCIPAL SUBJECTS:
Science
Government
Geography
General Interest
PUBLICATIONS:
Scientific American
Harvard Magazine

PARAS, MICHAEL
668 Ave. of The Americas
New York, NY 10010
Telephone: 212-243-8546
Fax: 212-243-8547
PRINCIPAL SUBJECTS:
Advertising
Editorial
Photography
Business & Industry

PARSONS, KIMBERLY
435 Brannan Street, Suite 203
San Francisco, CA 94107
Telephone: 415-543-8983
Fax: 415-543-2199
AFFILIATIONS:
ASMP
PRINCIPAL SUBJECTS:
Foreign
Travel
Nature

PATTERSON, MARION
P.O. Box 842
Menlo Park, CA 94026
Telephone: 415-854-3678
MAILING ADDRESS:
MARION PATTERSON
Menlo Park, CA 94026
Telephone: 213-652-3099
AFFILIATIONS:
ASMP, SPE
PRINCIPAL SUBJECTS:
Geography
Nature
Travel
Business & Industry

PAWLICK, JOHN
7 Henshaw Terr.
W. Roxbury, MA 02132
Telephone: 617-327-0117
AFFILIATIONS:
ASMP, NPPA

PRINCIPAL SUBJECTS:
Business & Industry
Editorial
Foreign
General Interest
Nature
Sports
Travel
PUBLICATIONS:
NY Times
Boston Globe
Boston Herald
National Law Journal
MacLeans
Natural History

PAYNE, SHELBY
640 Wrightwood, #315
Chicago, IL 60614
Telephone: 312-929-5448
PRINCIPAL SUBJECTS:
General Interest
Human Interest
Editorial
Journalism
Travel
Personalities
PUBLICATIONS:
Pulitzer Newspapers

PAZOVSKI, KAZIK
1310 Pendleton St., 713
   Pendleton Arts Center
Cincinnati, OH 45210
Telephone: 513-281-0030
AFFILIATIONS:
ASMP, SPE
PRINCIPAL SUBJECTS:
Advertising
Agriculture
Architecture
Home & Garden
Photography
PUBLICATIONS:
Sat. Eve. Post
Farm Quarterly
Farm Journal
Successful Farming
McCalls
Mechanix Illustrustator
Medical Economies
N.Y. Times

PEARCE, ADDEE
10501 WILSHIRE BLVD.
   #1006
LOS ANGELES, CA
   90024-6307
Telephone: 310-474-1314
AFFILIATIONS:
ASMP

PRINCIPAL SUBJECTS:
Animals
Architecture
Foreign
General Interest
Home & Garden
Human Interest
Nature
Photography
The Arts
Travel
PUBLICATIONS:
Activewear Magazine
ASMP Magazine
(Southern Ca)

PEARSE, DON
223 Parham Road
Springfield, PA 19064
Telephone: 215-328-3179
Fax: 215-543-7764
AFFILIATIONS:
ASMP, MLA
PRINCIPAL SUBJECTS:
Advertising
Architecture
Photography
PUBLICATIONS:
Architectural Digest
Hospitality
Home Magazine
Philadelphia Magazine
Delaware Today
Delaware Valley

PEARSON, CHARLES R.
1542 Deception Rd.
Anacortes, WA 98221
Telephone: 206-293-8361
Fax: 206-293-0627
AFFILIATIONS:
ASMP
PRINCIPAL SUBJECTS:
Architecture
Food/Diet
PUBLICATIONS:
Architectural Digest
Interiors
Better Homes & Gardens
Business Week
Family Circle
Fortune
Good Housekeeping
Ladies Home Journal
McCalls
Parents
Time
Woman's Day
Elle

PECHTER, ALESE
P.O. Box 670
Delray Beach, FL 33447
Telephone: 407-272-3252
Fax: 407-272-3266
AFFILIATIONS:
ASMP, NPPA
PRINCIPAL SUBJECTS:
Book Reviews
Ecology
Editorial
Entertainment
General Interest
Journalism
Marine
Nature
Personalities
Sports
Travel
Youth
PUBLICATIONS:
Forbes
New York Times
Conde Nast Traveler
Disney Adventures
Sports Illustrated For Kids
Tennis
National Geographic World
Underwater USA
Skin Diver

PECHTER, MORTON H.
P.O. Box 670
Delray Beach, FL 33447
Telephone: 407-272-3252
Fax: 407-272-3266
AFFILIATIONS:
ASMP, NPPA
PRINCIPAL SUBJECTS:
Book Reviews
Ecology
Editorial
Entertainment
General Interest
Journalism
Marine
Nature
Personalities
Sports
Travel
Youth
PUBLICATIONS:
Forbes
New York Times
Cande Nast Traveler
National Geographic World
Disney Adventures
Sports Illustrated For Kids
Tennis
Underwater USA
Skin Diver

PERESS, GILLES
Magnum Photos
72 Spring St.
New York, NY 10012
Telephone: 212-966-9200
AFFILIATIONS:
ASMP
PRINCIPAL SUBJECTS:
Editorial
Foreign
Journalism
News
Personalities
World Affairs
PUBLICATIONS:
New York Times
The Independent
Tempo
London Sunday Times
American Photo
Stern

PEREZ, MARTY
9940 S. Oakley
Chicago, IL 60643
Telephone: 312-779-5440
AFFILIATIONS:
ASMP
PRINCIPAL SUBJECTS:
Editorial
Entertainment
Journalism
News
Photography
PUBLICATIONS:
New City
Chicago Reader
The Rocket
Spin
The Bob
Puncture
Tower Pulse
Reflex

PERRON, ROBERT
119 Chestnut St.
Branford, CT 06405
Telephone: 203-481-2004
MAILING ADDRESS:
Box 309
Branford, CT 06405
Telephone: 203-481-5041
AFFILIATIONS:
ASMP, ASPP
PRINCIPAL SUBJECTS:
Architecture
Home & Garden
Ecology
PUBLICATIONS:
House Beautiful
Progressive Architecture

Architectural Record
Garden Design
Nature Conservancy Mag.
Remodeling
The New York Times
Builder
Audubon Magazine
Home Mechanix
Family Circle
Oceans
Sierra Club Bulletin
Connecticut Magazine
Woman's Day

PETERSEN, JON B.
628 E. 3rd
Tulsa, OK 74120
Telephone: 918-585-2509
Fax: 913-227-3880
AFFILIATIONS:
PPA
PRINCIPAL SUBJECTS:
Architecture
General Interest
PUBLICATIONS:
Prophotos I
Saturday Review
Progressive Architecture
Architecture Magazine
P.P. of A. Magazine

PETERSON JR., CHESTER
P.O. Box 71
Lindsborg, KS 67456
Telephone: 913-227-3880
AFFILIATIONS:
ASMP,AAEA,NATL.
  WRITERS CLUB
PRINCIPAL SUBJECTS:
Advertising
Agriculture
Aviation
Sports
Computer Technology
Personal Finance
Physical Fitness
PUBLICATIONS:
Flight Training Magazine
AOPA Pilot
Magazine Design & Production
Photo District News
Solutions
Farm Journal
Air Progress

PETERSON, JR., CHESTER
P.O. Box 71
Lindsborg, KS 67456
Telephone: 913-227-3880
Fax: 913-227-3880

AFFILIATIONS:
AAEA, ASMP
PRINCIPAL SUBJECTS:
Agriculture
Aviation
Computer Technology
Business & Industry
Advertising
Health
Book Reviews
General Interest
Journalism
Travel
Physical Fitness
Photography
PUBLICATIONS:
Successful Farming
Farm Journal
Private Pilot
Air Progress

PETERSON, LEE
Peterson, Lee Studio B/MCD
11717 Sorrento Valley Rd.
San Diego, CA 92121
Telephone: 619-455-0873
AFFILIATIONS:
ASMP, SDUPS
PRINCIPAL SUBJECTS:
Advertising
Animals
Architecture
Ecology
Food/Diet
General Interest
Geography
Human Interest
Humor
Marine
Medical
Nature
Photography
Sports
Video
PUBLICATIONS:
Communication Arts
Skin Diver
Discover Diving
Insurance Journal
American Photography
Travel & Leisure
S.D. Union-Trib.
Scripps Medical Journal

PETT, LAURENCE J.
5907 Cahill Ave.
Tarzana, CA 91356
Telephone: 818-344-9453
Fax: 818-344-9453
AFFILIATIONS:
ASMP

PRINCIPAL SUBJECTS:
Editorial
Entertainment
Foreign
General Interest
Human Interest
Human Relations
Journalism
News
Personalities
Photography
Senior Citizens
Travel
Urban Affairs
World Affairs
PUBLICATIONS:
Los Angeles Times
Herald-Examiner
New York Times
Kansas City Star
New York Post
Newsweek

PHAM, DIEM K.
18630 Bushard St.
Fountain Valley, CA 92708
Telephone: 714-963-7023
AFFILIATIONS:
APA, ASMP, WAGGGS
PRINCIPAL SUBJECTS:
Advertising
Editorial
Photography
Travel

PHANEUF, ART
HCR 75, Box 168
Plainfield, NH 03781
Telephone: 603-675-9268
Fax: 603-675-9268
AFFILIATIONS:
ASMP
PRINCIPAL SUBJECTS:
Agriculture
Editorial
Family
Foreign
General Interest
Human Interest
Human Relations
Personalities
Senior Citizens
Sports
Travel
Youth
PUBLICATIONS:
Network World
Science Digest
Rotorways

Scholastic
Vermont Life
Restaurant Business

PHELAN, JOHN
4387 Laclede
Saint Louis, MO 63108
Telephone: 314-534-7777
Fax: 314-534-7777
AFFILIATIONS:
ASMP
PRINCIPAL SUBJECTS:
Business & Industry
Agriculture

PHILIBA, ALLAN
3501 Cherryhill Drive
Orlando, FL 32822
Telephone: 407-381-5000
Fax: 407-381-3818
AFFILIATIONS:
ASMP, ASSPP
PRINCIPAL SUBJECTS:
Advertising
Travel
Architecture
Foreign
Nature
PUBLICATIONS:
AAA Today
Travel & Leisure
Caribbean Travel & Life
Modern Maturity
Town & Country
New York Times Sunday
   Travel Section

PHILLIPS, JAMES
Northern Exposure
   Photography
11406 Cedar Ln.
Beltsville, MD 20705
Telephone: 301-595-0349
Fax: 301-595-3391
AFFILIATIONS:
ASMP
PRINCIPAL SUBJECTS:
Advertising
Business & Industry
Photography

PHILLIPS, ROBIN H.
1505 S. Florida Ave.
Lakeland, FL 33803
Telephone: 813-683-8853
AFFILIATIONS:
PPA, FPP, MFPP
PRINCIPAL SUBJECTS:
Architecture
Aviation
General Interest

Journalism
PUBLICATIONS:
Official Photographer
   (Miss USA 1984 - 85)
Official Photographer
   (Miss Teen USA 1983)

PHOTO RESOURCE HAWAII
Photo Resource Hawaii
1146 Fort St., #207
Honolulu, HI 96813
Telephone: 808-599-7773
Fax: 808-599-7754
AFFILIATIONS:
ASMP
PRINCIPAL SUBJECTS:
Advertising
Agriculture
Animals
Ecology
Editorial
Education
Family
Foreign
General Interest
Human Relations
Marine
Military
Nature
Sports
Travel
Women's Interest
PUBLICATIONS:
National Geographic Traveler
Better Homes & Gardens
Life
Travel & Leisure
Sunset
Honolulu Magazine
Sierra
The World & I

PHOTO, COMM
3142 Ashbury Lane
Atlanta, GA 30273
Telephone: 404-261-6894
PRINCIPAL SUBJECTS:
Photography
Human Relations
Advertising
News
Sports
General Interest
PUBLICATIONS:
Georgia Journal Magazine
Associated Press
United Press Inter.
Local Papers
Association Executive, The

Metro South Magazine
Atlanta Journal & Constitution
Runner Magazine

PHOTOGRAPHIC DESIGNS
Photographic Designs
70 Strawberry Hill Ave., F3A
Stanford, CT 06902
Telephone: 203-348-7997
Fax: 203-977-8312
AFFILIATIONS:
EWN, ASMP, WICI
PRINCIPAL SUBJECTS:
Advertising
Business & Industry
Education
Marketing
Photography
Sales
PUBLICATIONS:
Business Week
House & Garden

PHOTOGRAPHIC IMPACT
Photographic Impact
126 11th Ave.
New York, NY 10011
Telephone: 212-206-7962
AFFILIATIONS:
APANY, ASMPNY
PRINCIPAL SUBJECTS:
Advertising
Editorial

PHOTOGRAPHY UNLIMITED
3662 S. Westshore Blvd.
Tampa, FL 33629
Telephone: 813-839-7710
MAILING ADDRESS:
PHOTOGRAPHY, UNLIMITED
Tampa, FL 33629
AFFILIATIONS:
PPA, BPA, ASMP
PRINCIPAL SUBJECTS:
Advertising
General Interest
Amusements
Journalism
Sports
Entertainment
PUBLICATIONS:
Newsweek
U. S. News & World Report
Tampa Times
Tampa Tribune
Morrison Manor
Florida Trend
Tampa Magazine
Time Magazine

PHOTOSMITH
Photosmith
39 E. Court
Cincinnati, OH 45202
Telephone: 513-651-3105
AFFILIATIONS:
ASMP
PRINCIPAL SUBJECTS:
Advertising
Architecture
Editorial
Education
Human Interest
Journalism
PUBLICATIONS:
Forbes
Ohio Magazine
Cincinnati Magazine
Childrens Hospital Annual
  Report
US Shoe Annual Report
Sister of Charity Health Care
  Annual Report

PICKERELL, JAMES H.
110 Frederick Ave., E - Bay
Rockville, MD 20850
Telephone: 301-251-0720
Fax: 301-309-0941
AFFILIATIONS:
PPA/FPA/SSPA
PRINCIPAL SUBJECTS:
Electronics
Human Interest
Computer Technology
Travel
PUBLICATIONS:
Newsweek
Life
Time
National Geographic
Saturday Evening Post
Fortune
Business Week
Forbes
U.S. News & World Report
Ebony
McCalls
True
Cosmopolitan
Esquire
Argosy
Parade
Family Weekly
New York Times Magazine
Aviation Week
Popular Mechanics
Paris Match
Der Stern (Germany)
Daily Telegraph Magazine
  (London)

Quick (Germany)
Sir + Er (Switzerland)
Expresso (Italy)
Medical World News
Farm Journal
CBS News
ABC News

PISANO, ROBERT
7527 15th Ave., N.E.
Seattle, WA 98115
Telephone: 206-525-3500
Fax: 206-525-2234
AFFILIATIONS:
ASMP
PRINCIPAL SUBJECTS:
Architecture
PUBLICATIONS:
Architectural Digest
Architectural Record
Designers West
Custom Home

PITOU, CINDY
4007 Thacher Rd.
Ojai, CA 93023
Telephone: 805-646-6263
AFFILIATIONS:
ASMP
PRINCIPAL SUBJECTS:
Editorial
Family
Human Interest
Journalism
Marketing
News
Personalities
PUBLICATIONS:
People
New York Times
Savvy
Discover
Country America
Health

PLACE, CHARLES
2940 Lomita Rd.
Santa Barbara, CA 93105
Telephone: 805-682-6089
AFFILIATIONS:
ASMP
PRINCIPAL SUBJECTS:
Business & Industry
Travel
History
Agriculture
PUBLICATIONS:
Time
Travel & Leisure

National Geographic
Smithsonian
Sail

PLATTETER, GEORGE
33 Branchbrook Dr.
Henrietta, NY 14467
Telephone: 716-334-1533
AFFILIATIONS:
ASMP
PRINCIPAL SUBJECTS:
Advertising
Architecture
Editorial
General Interest
Travel
Business & Industry
PUBLICATIONS:
Forbes
Fortune
Business Week

PLUMMER, DOUG
501 N. 36th St., #409
Seattle, WA 98103
Telephone: 206-789-8174
Fax: 206-782-7190
AFFILIATIONS:
ASMP, ASPP
PRINCIPAL SUBJECTS:
Advertising
Business & Industry
Ecology
Editorial
Foreign
Health
Medical
Nature
Photography
Travel
PUBLICATIONS:
American Lawyer
Outside
Time
US News & World Report
Audubon
Sierra
Elle
Harper's Bazaar

POERTNER, KENNETH C.
613 Hillview Dr.
Boise, ID 83712
Telephone: 208-336-0499
AFFILIATIONS:
ASMP
PRINCIPAL SUBJECTS:
General Interest
Agriculture
Human Interest
Foreign

Humor
Nature
PUBLICATIONS:
Farm & Ranch Living
Tops News

POGGENPOHL, ERIC
340 South Pleasant St.
Amherst, MA 01002
Telephone: 413-256-0948
Fax: 413-549-6401
AFFILIATIONS:
ASMP
PRINCIPAL SUBJECTS:
Business & Industry
Editorial
Marine
PUBLICATIONS:
Forbes
Motorboating & Sailing
American Lawyer
Washington Post
Nations Business

POHLMAN STUDIOS
535 N. 27th St.
Milwaukee, WI 53208
Telephone: 414-342-6363
MAILING ADDRESS:
P.O. Box 08296
Milwaukee, WI 53208
PRINCIPAL SUBJECTS:
Advertising
Photography
PUBLICATIONS:
Oster
Harley Davidson
Regalware
Sunbeam
Shopko

POKEMPNER, MARC
1453 W. Addison St.
Chicago, IL 06613
Telephone: 312-525-4567
AFFILIATIONS:
ASMP, ILPPN
PUBLICATIONS:
New York Times Magazine
Newsweek
Time
People
Money
Fortune
Forbes
Business Week
Rolling Stone
Downbeat
Chicago Magazine
Chicago Reader
Village Voice

Stern
Manchete
Paris Match

POLK, MILBRY
P.O. Box 716
Palisades, NY 10964
Telephone: 914-365-0297
PRINCIPAL SUBJECTS:
Photography
Nature
History
Journalism
PUBLICATIONS:
Fortune
Mademoiselle
Quest

POLSKY, JOEL
Polsky, Joel Photography
1426 N.E. 151st St., #104
Seattle, WA 98155
Telephone: 206-365-4866
AFFILIATIONS:
ASMP, AAF
PRINCIPAL SUBJECTS:
Advertising
Business & Industry
Entertainment
Food/Diet
Health
Marketing
Media

POLUMBAUM, TED
326 Harvard St.
Cambridge, MA 02139
Telephone: 617-491-4947
Fax: 617-491-4948
AFFILIATIONS:
ASMP
PRINCIPAL SUBJECTS:
Editorial
Business & Industry
Advertising
Foreign

POOR, SUZANNE
280 Bloomfield Avenue
Verona, NJ 07044
Telephone: 201-857-5161
Fax: 201-857-5282
AFFILIATIONS:
ASMP
PRINCIPAL SUBJECTS:
Editorial
Family
General Interest
Journalism
News
Physical Fitness

Travel
Women's Interest
PUBLICATIONS:
New York Times
NJ Monthly
Ad Talk
Exposure
Newark Star Ledger
Montclair (NJ) Times

PORTNOY, LEWIS
#5 Carole Lane
St. Louis, MO 63131
Telephone: 314-567-5700
Fax: 314-567-5704
AFFILIATIONS:
ASMP
PRINCIPAL SUBJECTS:
Advertising
Agriculture
Amusements
Architecture
Aviation
Business & Industry
Editorial
Hobbies
Media
Medical
Motivation
Photography
Physical Fitness
Sales
Sports
Travel
PUBLICATIONS:
Time
Life
Sports Illustrated
Business Week
Heartland
St. Louis Post Dispatch

PORTOGALLO, JOSEPH A.
34 E. 30th St.
New York, NY 10016
Telephone: 212-725-8910
Fax: 212-725-5642
AFFILIATIONS:
ASMP
PRINCIPAL SUBJECTS:
Photography
PUBLICATIONS:
N. Y. Times Magazine
Car & Driver
Diabetes Forecast

POSEY, MIKE
3524 Canal St.
New Orleans, LA 70119
Telephone: 504-488-8000

AFFILIATIONS:
ASMP, PPA
PRINCIPAL SUBJECTS:
Architecture

POST, GEORGE
5835 Bouquet Ave.
Richmond, CA 94805
Telephone: 510-237-0197
Fax: 510-236-0519
AFFILIATIONS:
ASMP, MAPP
PRINCIPAL SUBJECTS:
Advertising
Architecture
Computer Technology
Photography
The Arts
PUBLICATIONS:
Popular Photography
Camera & Darkroom
American Craft
Northern California Homes &
   Gardens
Image (San Francisco
   Examiner)
Niche
Sky & Telescope

POST, JOHN
P.O. Box 211
Hermosa Beach, CA 90254
Telephone: 310-376-4448
AFFILIATIONS:
ASMP
PRINCIPAL SUBJECTS:
Animals
Architecture
Automotive
Editorial
Foreign
General Interest
Human Interest
Sports
The Arts
Travel
PUBLICATIONS:
City Sports
Splash
Runners World
10,000 Eyes

POWELL, TODD B.
P.O. Box 2279
Breckenridge, CO 80424
Telephone: 303-453-0469
Fax: 303-453-0469
AFFILIATIONS:
ASMP, NASJA
PRINCIPAL SUBJECTS:
Advertising

Architecture
Editorial
Foreign
Physical Fitness
Sports
Travel
PUBLICATIONS:
Ski
Skiing
National Geographic Traveler

POWER, CHARLOTTE A.
Rt. 9, P.O. 38D
Jonesboro, AR 72401
Telephone: 501-935-2087
PRINCIPAL SUBJECTS:
Medical
Editorial
Humor
PUBLICATIONS:
Lady's Circle Magazine

PRATT, DIANE
Rd. 1 Box 220
Blairstown, NJ 07825
Telephone: 908-459-5815
Fax: 908-459-5815
AFFILIATIONS:
ASMP
PRINCIPAL SUBJECTS:
Agriculture
Home & Garden
Photography
Travel
PUBLICATIONS:
Morris County Magazine
Warren County Companion
  Magazine

PRATT, VERNA E.
7446 E. 20th Ave.
Anchorage, AK 99504
Telephone: 907-333-8212
Fax: 907-333-4989
MAILING ADDRESS:
VERNA E. PRATT
P.O. Box 210087
Anchorage, AK 99521
AFFILIATIONS:
ASMP
PRINCIPAL SUBJECTS:
Ecology
General Interest
Home & Garden
Nature
Photography
PUBLICATIONS:
Alaska Outdoors
Times
Alaska Outdoors
Times

PRESTON, JIM
4747 Southwest Freeway
Houston, TX 77027
Telephone: 713-840-5883
Fax: 713-840-6722
MAILING ADDRESS:
J. PRESTON, POST, THE
P.O. Box 4747
Houston, TX 77210
AFFILIATIONS:
ASMP
PRINCIPAL SUBJECTS:
Journalism
Photography
PUBLICATIONS:
Houston Post, The
Worcester Telegram & Gazette

PRESTON, L. STEVE
610 Stealey Ave.
Clarksburg, WV 26301
Telephone: 304-622-5671
AFFILIATIONS:
PPA, WVPP, UPPA
PRINCIPAL SUBJECTS:
Business & Industry

PRESTON, LOUISA
220 Redwood Hwy. #159
Mill Valley, CA 94941
Telephone: 415-381-2716
AFFILIATIONS:
ASMP
PRINCIPAL SUBJECTS:
Advertising
Agriculture
Animals
Book Reviews
Ecology
Editorial
Home & Garden
Marine
Medical
Nature
Photography
Sports
Travel
Women's Interest
PUBLICATIONS:
GEO Magazine
'10,000 Eyes' Photo Book
New York Times
Underwater USA
Oceansports Magazine
Independent Journal
Defenders of Wildlife

PREUSS, KAREN
369 11th Ave.
San Francisco, CA 94118
Telephone: 415-752-7545

AFFILIATIONS:
ASMP
PRINCIPAL SUBJECTS:
Health
Travel
Human Interest
Youth
PUBLICATIONS:
Motorland
San Francisco Examiner
Compass Reading
Relax
Chronicle of Higher Education

PRICE, CLAYTON J.
205 West 19th St.
New York, NY 10011
Telephone: 212-929-7721
AFFILIATIONS:
ASMP
PRINCIPAL SUBJECTS:
Advertising
Computer Technology
Electronics
Health
Medical
Science
The Arts
PUBLICATIONS:
Parade
Life
National Geographic
U.S. News & World Rept.

PRICE, GREG
14 Cayuga Rd.
Cranford, NJ 07016
Telephone: 908-245-1711
MAILING ADDRESS:
GREG PRICE
P.O. Box 665
Cranford, NJ 07016
AFFILIATIONS:
ASMP, APNJ
PRINCIPAL SUBJECTS:
Advertising
Business & Industry
Editorial
Education
Entertainment
Fashion
General Interest
Men's Interest
Personalities
Photography
Travel
PUBLICATIONS:
World Guide to Nude Beaches
  & Recreation
Nude And Natural
The Event

The Cranford Chronicle
Videography
Price Club Journal
World Guide to Nude Beaches
  & Recreation
Nude And Natural
The Event
The Cranford Chronicle
Videography
Price Club Journal

PRIER, ALLEN
P.O. Box 90537
Anchorage, AK 99509
Telephone: 907-349-2767
AFFILIATIONS:
ASMP, IAPP
PRINCIPAL SUBJECTS:
Nature
Ecology
PUBLICATIONS:
Newsweek
Outside
Modern Maturity
Sunset

PRINCE, NORMAN
3245 25th St.
San Francisco, CA 94110
Telephone: 415-821-6595
AFFILIATIONS:
ASPP, ASMP
PRINCIPAL SUBJECTS:
The Arts
Editorial
General Interest
Human Interest
Nature
Travel
Education
PUBLICATIONS:
Sunset Magazine
Chevron USA Odyssey
  Magazine
Geo Magazine
Mexicana Airlines
Harry Abrams
National Geographic World
  Books
Travel/Holiday

PRITCHETT, LAUREN
  LAVONNE
2201 Mohala Way
Honolulu, HI 96822
Telephone: 808-941-8265
MAILING ADDRESS:
P.O. Box 61668
Honolulu, HI 96822
PRINCIPAL SUBJECTS:
Aviation

Military
Sports
Ecology
PUBLICATIONS:
Surfing Magazine
Volleyball Magazine
Surfer Magazine
Flipper Magazine (Japan)
National Geographic World

PROBST, KEN
842 Folsom St. 375
San Francisco, CA 94107
Telephone: 415-821-6212
PRINCIPAL SUBJECTS:
Photography
PUBLICATIONS:
Vanity Fair
Allure
New York Magazine
Buzz
Redbook
Family Circle

PROUD, B.
900 W. 21st St.
Wilmington, DE 19802
Telephone: 302-429-9345
AFFILIATIONS:
ASMP
PRINCIPAL SUBJECTS:
Architecture
Business & Industry
Editorial
Food/Diet
Foreign
Health
Home & Garden
Medical
Photography
Travel
PUBLICATIONS:
House Beautiful
Mid-Atlantic Country
New Choices
Reader's Digest
Entrepreneur
Delaware Today
Washingtonian

PSZENICA, JUDITH
2 Scribner Ave.
Norwalk, CT 06854
Telephone: 203-866-2929
AFFILIATIONS:
ASMP, NPPA
PRINCIPAL SUBJECTS:
Business & Industry
Editorial
General Interest
Human Interest

Journalism
News
Personalities
Social Trends
The Arts
PUBLICATIONS:
New York Times
Entrepeneur Magazine
Business Week
Forbes
Financial World
Scholastic

PUTNAM, DON
P.O. Box 120623
Nashville, TN 37212
Telephone: 800-458-6706
Fax: 800-438-6706
MAILING ADDRESS:
P.O. Box 836
Athens, AL 35611
AFFILIATIONS:
ASMP, ISES
PRINCIPAL SUBJECTS:
Business & Industry
Advertising
Personalities
PUBLICATIONS:
Elle
Rolling Stone
People
Country Music
Billboard
London Sunday Times

PUTNAM, SARAH
8 Newell St.
Cambridge, MA 02140
Telephone: 617-547-3758
Fax: 617-547-3758
AFFILIATIONS:
ASMP, ASPP
PRINCIPAL SUBJECTS:
Book Reviews
Business & Industry
Editorial
Family
Health
Human Relations
The Arts
Women's Interest
PUBLICATIONS:
Time
Business Week
Fortune
N.Y. Times
U.S. News & World Report
Parenting

Q, PATRICIA & MIKE
1972 Lincoln Hwy.
Edison, NJ 08817
Telephone: 908-287-1234
AFFILIATIONS:
PPA
PRINCIPAL SUBJECTS:
Photography
PUBLICATIONS:
"The Manual of Slide
 Duplicating"-Amphoto
"Professional Portraiture"
 Amphoto
Prof. Photographer
 Magazine-Byes.
Amphoto Publishers:"Manual
 Of Slide Duplicating"
"Professional Portrait
 Photography"
Photo Methods

QUARTUCCIO, DOM
410 W. 24th St., #9M
New York, NY 10011
Telephone: 212-727-7329
Fax: 212-691-4265
AFFILIATIONS:
ASMP
PRINCIPAL SUBJECTS:
Advertising
Architecture
Aviation
Ecology
Editorial
Electronics
Entertainment
Foreign
Geography
Marketing
Media
Nature
Photography
Travel
Video

QUICKSILVER
 PHOTOGRAPHY
Quicksilver Photography
66 W. Whittier St.
Columbus, OH 43206
Telephone: 614-443-6530
Fax: 614-443-0599
PRINCIPAL SUBJECTS:
Advertising
Architecture
Business & Industry
Computer Technology
Entertainment
Fashion
Marketing
Men's Interest

Personalities
Photography
Physical Fitness
Senior Citizens
Sports
Women's Interest

RAFKIND, ANDREW J.
ANDREW RAFKIND
 PHOTOGRAPHY
1702 FAIRVIEW AVE.
BOISE, ID 83702
Telephone: 208-344-9918
Fax: 208-343-3837
AFFILIATIONS:
ASMP
PRINCIPAL SUBJECTS:
Advertising
Agriculture
Architecture
Business & Industry
Editorial
Education
Food/Diet
Health
Marketing
Medical
Nature
Photography
Sports
Video
Youth
PUBLICATIONS:
Time
Newsweek
Travel & Leisure
Forbes
Inc.
Parade
Weekly Reader
NEA Today
Time
Newsweek
Travel & Leisure
Forbes
Inc.
Parade
Weekly Reader
NEA Today

RAICHE, BOB
305 Stark Ln.
Manchester, NH 03102
Telephone: 603-623-7912
Fax: 603-626-1088
AFFILIATIONS:
PPA, NHPPA, PPA & E
PRINCIPAL SUBJECTS:
Business & Industry
Photography

PUBLICATIONS:
Production News
The Professional
  Photographer Mag.
The Union Leader
New Hampshire Sunday News
N H Business Review

RANDLETT, MARY
P.O. Box 10536
Bainbridge Is, WA 98110
Telephone: 206-842-3935
AFFILIATIONS:
ASMP
PRINCIPAL SUBJECTS:
Architecture
General Interest
Geography
Nature
Home & Garden
Marine
Personalities
The Arts
PUBLICATIONS:
Far Field, The
Writing's & Reflections
Architectual Record Book of
  Vacation House's
Beautiful Northwest
Contemporary American Poetry
My Life & Times
House Next Door
Mountain In The Clouds
Spires of Form
New as a Wave
Northwest Traditions
Arts of Asia
Sunset Magazine
Architectual Record
Progressive Architecture
Art in America
Art News Space
  Design - Japan
Exxon USA
Seattle Times Pictorial
Puget Soundings
Sporting Classics
Good Housekeeping
Playboy
Time
New York Times
London Observer
Christian Science Monitor

RANKIN, JEFF
316 Queens Ave.,
  Upper Ste. 00000
Telephone: 519-672-4408
Fax: 215-857-3275
MAILING ADDRESS:
SIRIUS PRODUCTIONS

P.O. Box 9044, Sub 40
00000
Telephone: 215-857-3432
PUBLICATIONS:
Air Forces Monthly
Flypast
Le Fana De L'aviation
Flug Revue
Koku - Fan
Scale Models International
Flight International
Finescale Modeler
Air International
London International Air Show
  Programme
Engineering Dimensions
Military Aircraft Serials of North
  America

RANTZMAN, KAREN
  STAFFORD
130 Media Avenue
Half Moon Bay, CA 94109
Telephone: 415-726-3998
AFFILIATIONS:
ASMP, MA
PRINCIPAL SUBJECTS:
Editorial
Education
Family
Foreign
General Interest
Health
Home & Garden
Human Interest
Human Relations
Medical
Nature
Photography
Social Trends
The Arts
Travel
World Affairs
Youth
PUBLICATIONS:
San Francisco Examiner
  (Image Magazine)
California Farmer
Sunset Travel Guide
  (Hawaii & SE Asia)
Mac Week
USA Today
Architectural Record

REDIC, BILL
841 Thirteenth St.
Oakmont, PA 15139
Telephone: 412-826-1818
Fax: 412-826-1818
AFFILIATIONS:
ASMP

PRINCIPAL SUBJECTS:
Business & Industry
Computer Technology
Human Interest
Sports

REED, GEOFF
29 Prospect St.
Keyport, NJ 07735
Telephone: 908-888-7758
Fax: 908-264-4590
AFFILIATIONS:
ASMP, NPPA
PRINCIPAL SUBJECTS:
Advertising
Amusements
Animals
Architecture
Business & Industry
Editorial
Entertainment
Family
Human Relations
Humor
Journalism
Marine
Medical
Nature
Personalities
Senior Citizens
Sports
The Arts
Travel
Youth
PUBLICATIONS:
U.N. Chronicle
The Wine Spectator
The New Jersey Star Ledger
The Daily Record
Southwest Art
San Diego Magazine
The L.A. Times

REESE, KAY
225 Central Park West
New York, NY 10024
Telephone: 212-799-1133
MAILING ADDRESS:
KAY REESE &
  ASSOCIATES, INC.
New York, NY 10024
AFFILIATIONS:
ASMP
PRINCIPAL SUBJECTS:
Journalism
Photography
PUBLICATIONS:
ASMP Magazine Newsletter
Photo Magazine

REID, SEAN
200 W. 34th Avenue, #431
Anchorage, AK 99503
Telephone: 907-338-4250
AFFILIATIONS:
PRSA, ASMP
PRINCIPAL SUBJECTS:
Advertising
Aviation
Business & Industry
Ecology
Geography
History
Human Interest
Humor
Marine
Media
Men's Interest
Nature
News
Photography
Travel
PUBLICATIONS:
Alaska Magazine
Alaska Business Monthly
Alaska Geographic

REILLY, JOHN
Creative Camera Inc.
7151 Warner Ave., Ste. #432
Huntington Beach, CA 92647
Telephone: 714-377-0369
AFFILIATIONS:
ASMP, NPI, PPOC, APA, PIC
PRINCIPAL SUBJECTS:
Editorial
Marine
News
Photography
Sports

REISS, RAY
2144 N. Leavitt
Chicago, IL 60647
Telephone: 312-384-3245
Fax: 312-384-3252
AFFILIATIONS:
ASMP
PRINCIPAL SUBJECTS:
Business & Industry

REMINGTON, GEORGE
1455 West 29th Street
Cleveland, OH 44113
Telephone: 216-241-1440
Fax: 216-241-1424
AFFILIATIONS:
CPD
PRINCIPAL SUBJECTS:
Advertising
Architecture

Entertainment
Fashion
Health
Human Interest
Medical
Men's Interest
Photography
Sports
Video
Women's Interest
Youth
PUBLICATIONS:
Cleveland Plain Dealer

RENNIE, BRIAN H.
1442 N. Hundley St.
Anaheim, CA 92806
Telephone: 714-630-7965
Fax: 714-666-2586
AFFILIATIONS:
PPA
PRINCIPAL SUBJECTS:
Aviation
Food/Diet
Travel
Advertising
Fashion
Automotive
PUBLICATIONS:
Outside Mag.
Climbing Mag.
New Homes Mag.
Orange Coast Magazine
Register Newspaper
Climbing Mag.

RENO, KENT
125 Calumet Ave.
San Anselmo, CA 94960
Telephone: 415-453-4599
AFFILIATIONS:
ASMP, MAPP
PRINCIPAL SUBJECTS:
Advertising
Editorial
Human Relations
Humor

REPP, DAVE
510 S. Mitchell
Bloomington, IN 47401
Telephone: 812-332-6235
AFFILIATIONS:
NPPA
PRINCIPAL SUBJECTS:
General Interest
News
PUBLICATIONS:
Time
Audubon
Newsweek

Quest
USA Today
Sweet's Catalog

REVETTE, DAVID
111 Sunset Ave.
Syracuse, NY 13208
Telephone: 315-422-1558
Fax: 315-422-1555
AFFILIATIONS:
ASMP, MPCA
PRINCIPAL SUBJECTS:
Advertising
Architecture
Business & Industry
Fashion
Medical
PUBLICATIONS:
New Choices
American Showcase 13, 14, 15

RICARDEL, VINCENT J.
310 E. Capitol St., NE, SE
Washington, DC 20003
Telephone: 202-547-2527
Fax: 202-546-1231
PRINCIPAL SUBJECTS:
Editorial
Advertising
Architecture

RICCA, ANTONIO D.
P.O. Box 903
Escondido, CA 92033
Telephone: 619-745-1139
AFFILIATIONS:
NPPA, PPA
PRINCIPAL SUBJECTS:
Amusements
Nature
PUBLICATIONS:
Cover Girls Models
Glamorous Models
Lapidary Journal
The Professional Photographer
Amateur Screen &
    Photography

RICH, BERNI
1595 E. 22nd St.
Cleveland, OH 44114
Telephone: 216-621-7566
AFFILIATIONS:
PPA, GCGA
PRINCIPAL SUBJECTS:
Advertising
Architecture
Human Interest
Journalism
News
History

Advertising
Business & Industry
PUBLICATIONS:
IBM In-House Magazines
Time
U.S. News & World Report
Copper Topics
Appliance Manufacturer
LTV Steel "Reporter"

RICHARDSON, DAVID C.
528 Ave. F, #A
Redondo Beach, CA 90277
Telephone: 310-543-1215
Fax: 310-543-1215
AFFILIATIONS:
ASMP
PRINCIPAL SUBJECTS:
Advertising
Editorial
Journalism
Photography
PUBLICATIONS:
Sail Magazine
LA Times
Golf Digest
Daily Breeze

RIECKS, DAVID
1270 Lafayette Circle
Urbana, IL 61801
Telephone: 217-333-9435
Fax: 217-244-7503
AFFILIATIONS:
ASMP, SPE
PRINCIPAL SUBJECTS:
Advertising
Agriculture
Animals
Architecture
Business & Industry
Computer Technology
Ecology
Editorial
Education
Entertainment
Family
Foreign
General Interest
Government
Health
Hobbies
Home & Garden
Human Interest
Humor
Journalism
Media
Personalities
Photography
Religion
Science

The Arts
Travel
World Affairs
Youth
PUBLICATIONS:
Omni
Farm Journal
Farm Futures
Progressive Farmer
Illinois Quarterly
Illinois Research
Chicago Tribune

RIEGER, TED
P.O. Box 254452
Sacramento, CA 95865
Telephone: 916-362-8280
AFFILIATIONS:
SPJ
PRINCIPAL SUBJECTS:
Ecology
Nature
Science
Sports
Travel
PUBLICATIONS:
Compass (Continental
    Insurance Magazine)
Indoor Comfort News
Sacramento Magazine
Sacramento Union, The
Preservation News
Westways
Vineyard & Winery
    Management
Sierra Heritage

RILEY, GEORGE
415 Sisquisic Trail
Yarmouth, ME 04096
Telephone: 207-846-5787
Fax: 207-846-5787
MAILING ADDRESS:
P.O. Box 1025
Yarmouth, ME 04096
Telephone: 207-846-6262
AFFILIATIONS:
ASMP
PRINCIPAL SUBJECTS:
Advertising
Editorial
PUBLICATIONS:
PC Week
Money
Boston
Travel & Leisure
Country Journal
Boston Globe
Nikon

RILEY, JON
Riley & Riley Photography
1078 Tunnel Rd.
Asheville, NC 28805
Telephone: 704-299-9018
Fax: 704-299-4431
AFFILIATIONS:
ASMP
PRINCIPAL SUBJECTS:
Advertising
Architecture
Business & Industry
Computer Technology
Food/Diet
Marketing
Medical
Photography
PUBLICATIONS:
Time
Forbes
Americana
House & Garden
Popular Photography
Country Home
Business Week

RIVELLI, WILLIAM
303 Park Ave S.
New York, NY 10010
Telephone: 212-254-0990
Fax: 212-254-0922
AFFILIATIONS:
PPA, GCGA, ASMP, AIGA
PRINCIPAL SUBJECTS:
General Interest

RIZZO, RION
Creative Sources Photography
6095 Lake Forrest Dr., #100
Atlanta, GA 30328
Telephone: 404-843-2141
Fax: 404-250-1807
AFFILIATIONS:
ASMP
PRINCIPAL SUBJECTS:
Architecture
PUBLICATIONS:
Interior Designs
Interiors
Progressive Architecture
Architecture
Architectural Record
Contract Magazine
Building Design & Construction
Professional Builder &
  Remodeler

ROBBINS, ROB
322 Chimney Rock, 209
Tyler, TX 75703
Telephone: 903-561-4709

PUBLICATIONS:
Advertising
Sports
News
General Interest

ROBERTS, EBET
245 West 107th Street, 10c
New York, NY 10025
Telephone: 212-316-3696
PRINCIPAL SUBJECTS:
The Arts
Entertainment
PUBLICATIONS:
N.Y. Times
Rolling Stone
Newsweek
Time
People
Playboy
Village Voice
USA Today

ROBERTS, JANET M.
259 W. Johnson St. Apt. 4S
Philadelphia, PA 19144
Telephone: 215-848-5418
PRINCIPAL SUBJECTS:
Animals
Architecture
Ecology
Fashion
Food/Diet
Foreign
Government
History
Home & Garden
Human Interest
Human Relations
Nature
Personalities
Photography
The Arts
Travel
Women's Interest
World Affairs
Youth
PUBLICATIONS:
The Princeton Packet
  (Princeton, NJ)

ROBINSON, BILL
Robinson, Bill Photography
4654 Newport St.
San Diego, CA 92107
Telephone: 619-224-9426
Fax: 619-224-9426
MAILING ADDRESS:
Robinson, Bill Photography
P.O. Box 6624
San Diego, CA 92166

AFFILIATIONS:
ASMP
PRINCIPAL SUBJECTS:
Advertising
Architecture
Editorial
Fashion
Travel
PUBLICATIONS:
Progressive Architecture
Sunset
Designers West
Architecture
The Designer
Baja Explorer
San Diego Magazine
Home Magazine
Progressive Architecture
Sunset
Designers West
Architecture
The Designer
Baja Explorer
San Diego Magazine
Home Magazine

ROBINSON, MIKE
2413 Sarah Street
Pittsburgh, PA 15203
Telephone: 412-431-4102
Fax: 412-381-5332
AFFILIATIONS:
ASMP
PRINCIPAL SUBJECTS:
Advertising
Business & Industry
Editorial
Family
Fashion
Health
Human Interest
Human Relations
Marketing
Photography
The Arts
PUBLICATIONS:
Time
Pittsburgh Magazine

ROGERS, CHUCK
2708 Janellen Drive
Atlanta, GA 30345
Telephone: 404-633-0105
Fax: 404-633-7138
AFFILIATIONS:
ASMP
PRINCIPAL SUBJECTS:
Advertising
Business & Industry
Computer Technology
General Interest

Photography
Travel
PUBLICATIONS:
Life
Fortune
Women's Wear Daily
Forbes
Aviation Week
Paris Match

ROGERS, DAVID
P.O. Box 121557
Nashville, TN 37212
Telephone: 615-262-1658
AFFILIATIONS:
ASMP-NPPA
PRINCIPAL SUBJECTS:
Human Interest
Travel

ROGOWSKI, TIM
214 E. 8th Street
Cincinnati, OH 45202
Telephone: 513-621-3826
Fax: 513-621-3833
AFFILIATIONS:
ASMP
PRINCIPAL SUBJECTS:
Business & Industry
Human Interest
Nature

ROLLAND, GUY A.
P.O. Box 34172
Phoenix, AR 85067
Telephone: 602-997-9771
AFFILIATIONS:
ASMP, PPA
PRINCIPAL SUBJECTS:
Architecture
Ecology
Geography
Nature
Photography
Travel
Urban Affairs
PUBLICATIONS:
Travel Holiday
America West
Phoenix Business Journal

ROLO PHOTOGRAPHY
Rolo Photography
214 W. 17th St.
New York, NY 10011
Telephone: 22-691-8355/
Fax: 2-691-8356
AFFILIATIONS:
ASMP, APA
PRINCIPAL SUBJECTS:
Advertising

Architecture
Book Reviews
Computer Technology
Ecology
Editorial
Education
Electronics
General Interest
Geography
Government
Health
Human Interest
Human Relations
Journalism
Management
Marketing
Media
News
Personal Finance
Physical Fitness
Senior Citizens
Social Trends
Travel
Urban Affairs
World Affairs
Youth
PUBLICATIONS:
Fortune
Parents
City Sports
Travel & Leisure
Vanity Fair
Newsday
Mix Magazine
M Magazine

ROMANO, PATRICK J.
12362 Hyannis Ct.
Saint Louis, MO 63146
Telephone: 314-434-0978
AFFILIATIONS:
GWAA
PRINCIPAL SUBJECTS:
Marine
Editorial
PUBLICATIONS:
Bell Telephone-Southwestern
Family Circle-Supermarkets

ROME, STUART
Drexel Univ., Dept. of Interiors
  & Graphic Studies
Philadelphia, PA 19104
Telephone: 215-895-2385
MAILING ADDRESS:
STUART ROME
253 N. 3rd Street
Philadelphia, PA 19106
AFFILIATIONS:
ASMP, SPE

PRINCIPAL SUBJECTS:
History
Photography
The Arts
PUBLICATIONS:
Apeture Magazine
Newsweek
Time
Apeture Magazine
Newsweek
Time

ROSENBLUM, BERNARD
Rosenblum Gallery, The, 224
  W. Overland
El Paso, TX 79901
Telephone: 915-532-4455
Fax: 915-532-4455
AFFILIATIONS:
PPA, RPS, EPIC
PRINCIPAL SUBJECTS:
Advertising
Government
Science
Architecture
Entertainment
Media
The Arts
PUBLICATIONS:
Time
Forbes
Sunset
Northwest Inflight Mag.
Print Mag.
El Paso Magazine
Houston Post, Houston Texas
Texas Monthly

ROSSI, DAVID A.
Photo Associates
121 Central Avenue
Westfield, NJ 07050
Telephone: 908-232-8300
Fax: 908-232-8301
PRINCIPAL SUBJECTS:
Advertising
Business & Industry
Computer Technology
Editorial
Electronics
Entertainment
Family
Fashion
General Interest
Human Interest
Human Relations
Marketing
Media
Medical
Nature

Photography
The Arts
Youth

ROTHSCHILD, NORMAN
4 PARK AVE., #17G
NEW YORK, NY 10016
Telephone: 212-684-0432
AFFILIATIONS:
ASMP
PRINCIPAL SUBJECTS:
The Arts
General Interest
Nature
Travel
PUBLICATIONS:
Popular Photography
Stern (Germany)
New York
Leica Fotografie
  (Germany)
Foto Magazine
  (Germany)
Foto Popular (Germany)
Fotoheft
U.S. Camera
Colorfoto (Germany)
Shutterbug

ROTMAN, JEFFREY
14 Cottage Ave.
Somerville, MA 02144
Telephone: 617-666-0874
MAILING ADDRESS:
LANE, MARIA
Somerville, MA 02144
PRINCIPAL SUBJECTS:
Marine
Photography
PUBLICATIONS:
Telegraph (England)
Smithsonian
GEO (France & Germany)
Paris Match (France)
International Wildlife
Weiner (Germany)

ROWAN, N. R.
106 E. 6th St.
Clifton, NJ 07011
Telephone: 201-340-2284
PRINCIPAL SUBJECTS:
Photography
Editorial
Travel
Business & Industry
Human Relations
PUBLICATIONS:
New York Times
New York Daily News

National Gerographic
USA Today
Newsweek
Discover

ROWIN, STANLEY
791 Tremont St. #W515
Boston, MA 02118
Telephone: 617-437-0641
Fax: 617-437-0641
AFFILIATIONS:
ASMP
PRINCIPAL SUBJECTS:
Advertising
Business & Industry
Computer Technology
Editorial
Electronics
Fashion
Human Relations
Journalism
Management
Photography
Science
Travel
PUBLICATIONS:
Glamour
Scientific American
Entrepreneur
New York Times
Governing
Washington Post
Information Week

RUBIN, JANICE
705 E. 16th Street
Houston, TX 77008
Telephone: 713-868-6060
PRINCIPAL SUBJECTS:
Editorial
PUBLICATIONS:
Newsweek
Town & Country
Forbes
Smithsonian

RUBINGER, DAVID D.
16 Bustenai St.
Jerusalem, ISRAEL 93229
Telephone: 972-2-632074
Fax: 972-2-669-55
MAILING ADDRESS:
Time Jerusalem Pkt
1271 Ave. of the Americas
New York, NY 10020
AFFILIATIONS:
ASMP, FPAI
PRINCIPAL SUBJECTS:
Journalism
PUBLICATIONS:
Time

Life
People
Time
Life
People

RUDOLPH, NANCY
35 West 11th St.
New York, NY 10011
Telephone: 212-989-0392
AFFILIATIONS:
ASMP
PRINCIPAL SUBJECTS:
Travel
Foreign
Human Interest
PUBLICATIONS:
N.Y. Times Magazine
Cosmopolitan
Harpers
Food & Wine
Synergy

RUHE, GEORGE-EDWARD
85 Buckingham Street
Hartford, CT 06106
Telephone: 212-330-7653
Fax: 203-247-1690
AFFILIATIONS:
ASMP, APA
PRINCIPAL SUBJECTS:
Advertising
Editorial
Journalism
News
Photography
The Arts
Travel
Urban Affairs
World Affairs
PUBLICATIONS:
Hartford Courant
Pacific Northwest Magazine
Seattle Times

RUNION, BRITT
7409 Chancery Ln.
Orlando, FL 32809
Telephone: 407-857-0491
Fax: 407-857-0492
AFFILIATIONS:
ASMP, PPA
PRINCIPAL SUBJECTS:
Business & Industry
Travel
PUBLICATIONS:
Money Magazine
Fortune
Inc.

RUSS, WILLIAM
818 E. Forost Hills
Durham, NC 27707
Telephone: 919-733-7242
Fax: 919-733-8582
MAILING ADDRESS:
WILLIAM RUSS
430 N. Salisbury St.
Raleigh, NC 27611
AFFILIATIONS:
ASMP
PRINCIPAL SUBJECTS:
Travel
PUBLICATIONS:
Atlanta Const.
New York Times
Southern Living
Forbes
Golden Years
Destinations
Atlanta Const.
New York Times
Southern Living
Forbes
Golden Years
Destinations

RUSSELL, GAIL
P.O. Box 241
Taos, NM 87571
Telephone: 505-776-8474
Fax: 505-758-7244
MAILING ADDRESS:
GAIL RUSSELL
Taos, NM 87571
AFFILIATIONS:
PPA, TAA
PRINCIPAL SUBJECTS:
Architecture
PUBLICATIONS:
Saturday Review
U.S. Camera Annual
New York Times
New Age
Southwest Art
New Mexico Magazine
Rio Grande Magazine
East West Journal
Crosswinds
Guest Life
Unique Homes
Continental Airlines Magazine
Boston Globe

RUSSELL, MARC
Russell, Marc Studio Inc.
36 East 12th Street
New York, NY 10003
Telephone: 212-505-7916
AFFILIATIONS:
ASMP

PRINCIPAL SUBJECTS:
Advertising
Architecture
Business & Industry
Food/Diet
Home & Garden
Nature
The Arts
PUBLICATIONS:
Photo Dist. News
Metropolis
NT Times
Select

RUST, GREGORY E.
Xavier University,
   3800 Victory Pkwy.
Cincinnati, OH 45207
Telephone: 513-745-3433
AFFILIATIONS:
ASMP, UPAA
PRINCIPAL SUBJECTS:
Education
Human Interest
Journalism
Sports

RYAN, DAVID
463 8th Ave., #4
San Francisco, CA 94118
Telephone: 415-752-8277
MAILING ADDRESS:
UNIPHOTO PICTURE
   AGENCY
463 8th Ave, #4
San Francisco, CA 94118
PRINCIPAL SUBJECTS:
Geography
Travel
Ecology
Editorial
PUBLICATIONS:
Time
U.S. News
S.F. Examiner & Chronicle
Islands
Natural History
Newsweek
GEO
N.Y. Times
Travel/Holiday
L.A. Times
Wash. Post
Nation's Business
Vogue

RYBISKI JR., A. J.
425 10th St.
Lake Charles, LA 70601
Telephone: 318-433-5498

AFFILIATIONS:
SPA
PRINCIPAL SUBJECTS:
Architecture
General Interest
Business & Industry

RYCHETNIK, JOSEPH S.
P.O. Box 5030
Palm Springs, CA 92263
Telephone: 619-322-7252
AFFILIATIONS:
ASMP
PRINCIPAL SUBJECTS:
Aviation
Book Reviews
Editorial
Food/Diet
Geography
History
Humor
Military
Photography
Senior Citizens
PUBLICATIONS:
Time
Sports Illustrated
Outdoor Life
Guns
Rifle
The American Rifleman
Gun Digest
Naval Institute Proceedings
Military History
Aviation
Flying
Leatherneck
Alta Vista
Alaska
Ford Times
RV Times
American Blade
Explorers Journal

RYCUS, JEFFREY A.
Rycus Associates Photography
274 Marconi Blvd., Ste. 330
Columbus, OH 43215
Telephone: 614-461-6633
Fax: 614-461-8391
AFFILIATIONS:
ASMP
PRINCIPAL SUBJECTS:
Advertising
Agriculture
Animals
Architecture
Aviation
Business & Industry
Computer Technology
Ecology

Editorial
Education
Entertainment
Family
Fashion
General Interest
Geography
Government
Health
Home & Garden
Human Interest
Human Relations
Journalism
Management
Marketing
Media
Medical
Men's Interest
Nature
News
Photography
Physical Fitness
Sports
The Arts
Travel
Women's Interest
Youth
PUBLICATIONS:
Changing Times
New York Magazine
Fortune
GEO
Time-Life
Better Homes & Gardens
People
Working Woman

RYDEN, MIKE & SARA
1205 Birch St.
Montrose, CO 81401
Telephone: 303-249-2703
AFFILIATIONS:
ASMP
PRINCIPAL SUBJECTS:
Nature
Photography

SABELLA, JILL
2607 9th Ave., W.
Seattle, WA 98119
Telephone: 206-285-4794
Fax: 206-284-8161
AFFILIATIONS:
ASMP
PRINCIPAL SUBJECTS:
Photography
Nature
PUBLICATIONS:
Daydreams
Nature American

SACHA, BOB
12 West 96th St.
New York City, NY 10025
Telephone: 212-749-4128
AFFILIATIONS:
ASMP, NPPA
PRINCIPAL SUBJECTS:
Advertising
Editorial
Journalism
Personalities
Science
The Arts
Travel
PUBLICATIONS:
Life
Audubon
National Geographic
Fortune
Money

SALLAZ, WILLIAM R.
P.O. Box 280947,
   9031 W. Arizona Dr.
Lakewood, CO 80228
Telephone: 303-763-8822
Fax: 303-763-8822
AFFILIATIONS:
ASMP, NPPA
PRINCIPAL SUBJECTS:
Sports
PUBLICATIONS:
Sports Illustrated
Outside
Newsweek
Powder Magazine
The Sporting News

SALMOIRAGHI, FRANCO
P.O. Box 61708 -
   Manoa Station
Honolulu, HI 96839
Telephone: 808-955-3581
AFFILIATIONS:
ASMP
PRINCIPAL SUBJECTS:
Architecture
Ecology
Editorial
Foreign
History
Home & Garden
Human Interest
Photography
The Arts
Travel
PUBLICATIONS:
Islands
East West
Gulliver (Japan)
Pacifica (Continental Airlines)

Elle
L.A. Style
Honolulu

SALVO, CHRIS
5447 Kingfisher
Houston, TX 77096
Telephone: 713-721-5000
PRINCIPAL SUBJECTS:
Business & Industry
Advertising
Editorial

SANDBANK, HENRY
140 Old Saw Mill River Rd.
Hawthorne, NY 10532
Telephone: 914-747-2510
Fax: 914-747-4034
MAILING ADDRESS:
HENRY SANDBANK
Hawthorne, NY 10532
AFFILIATIONS:
PPLA
PRINCIPAL SUBJECTS:
Advertising
Editorial
Food/Diet
Amusements
The Arts
PUBLICATIONS:
Commercial

SANFORD, ERIC M.
110 Shaw St.
Manchester, NH 03104
Telephone: 603-624-0122
AFFILIATIONS:
ASMP, NPPA, CIPNE, PPYA
PRINCIPAL SUBJECTS:
Advertising
General Interest
Nature
Foreign
Architecture
Travel
PUBLICATIONS:
Time
Xerox Publications
Newsweek
Modern Maturity
World Book
Yankee
Unique Homes Magazine
Reader's Digest Books
Rand McNally

SANFORD, RON
599 Oregon St.
Gridley, CA 95948
Telephone: 916-846-4687
Fax: 916-846-4687

MAILING ADDRESS:
RON SANFORD
P.O. Box 248
Gridley, CA 95948
AFFILIATIONS:
ASMP
PRINCIPAL SUBJECTS:
Travel
PUBLICATIONS:
Life
Time
Newsweek
National Geographic

SANGER, DAVID
920 Evelyn Ave.
Albany, CA 94706
Telephone: 510-526-0800
Fax: 510-526-0800
AFFILIATIONS:
ASMP, BATW
PRINCIPAL SUBJECTS:
Ecology
Foreign
Nature
Photography
Travel
PUBLICATIONS:
Sierra
Rock & Ice
Regional Parks
Diablo Watch
Mt. Diablo News

SARCONE, JOE
1515 College St.
Columbus, MS 39701
Telephone: 601-328-7384
MAILING ADDRESS:
JOE SARCONE
P.O. Box 1
Columbus, MS 39703
PRINCIPAL SUBJECTS:
Advertising
Architecture
Human Interest
News
The Arts
Photography
PUBLICATIONS:
Colonial Homes
Mississippi Magazine
Today in Mississippi

SARNACKI, MICHAEL
802 W. 4th
Royal Oak, MI 48067
Telephone: 313-541-2210
Fax: 313-548-1149
AFFILIATIONS:
ASMP

PRINCIPAL SUBJECTS:
Architecture
Human Interest
Media
Personalities
Photography
Sports
World Affairs

SATTERWHITE, AL
P.O. Box 398
Concord, VA 24538
Telephone: 804-332-1818
PRINCIPAL SUBJECTS:
Aviation
Sports
Human Interest
Travel
Advertising
PUBLICATIONS:
Sports Illustrated
Car & Driver
Life
Time
Travel & Leisure

SAVILLE, LYNN
440 Riverside Drive, #45
New York, NY 10027
Telephone: 212-932-1854
AFFILIATIONS:
ASMP
PRINCIPAL SUBJECTS:
Advertising
Animals
Editorial
Family
Fashion
General Interest
Health
Human Interest
Human Relations
Humor
Marketing
Photography
Psychology
Women's Interest
Youth
PUBLICATIONS:
Time
Newsweek
Panorama (Italy)
Studio (France)
Newsday
Expecting Magazine
Daily News
Barron's

SAXE, ARNOLD J.
436 Arlington Rd.
Cedarhurst, NY 11516

Telephone: 516-374-4406
MAILING ADDRESS:
A. J. SAXE
P.O. Box 341
Cedarhurst, NY 11516
AFFILIATIONS:
NPPA
PRINCIPAL SUBJECTS:
General Interest
News
PUBLICATIONS:
Associated Press
New York Post
Brooklyn Heights Press
Brooklyn Daily Bulletin
American Cowboy
Lacrosse
Campus Life
ASCE News
New Horizons
New York Times
New York News
United Press
Newsday
Journal of the National
  Medical Assoc.
American Teacher
Present Tense
Insight Magazine

SAYLOR, TED
2312 Farwell Dr.
Tampa, FL 33603
Telephone: 813-879-5636
AFFILIATIONS:
PPA
PRINCIPAL SUBJECTS:
Advertising
Architecture
Aviation
General Interest
Business & Industry
PUBLICATIONS:
TV Guide
Life
Time
Builder
Sailing

SCHAMP, J. BROUGH
3616 Ednor Rd.
Baltimore, MD 21218
Telephone: 410-235-0840
AFFILIATIONS:
ASMP
PRINCIPAL SUBJECTS:
Advertising
Architecture
Aviation
Editorial
Foreign

Home & Garden
Travel
PUBLICATIONS:
Architecture
Sun Magazine
Mid-Atlantic Country
Style Magazine
Baltimore Magazine

SCHANUEL, ANTHONY
10901 Oasis Dr.
Saint Louis, MO 63123
Telephone: 314-849-3495
Fax: 314-849-3495
PRINCIPAL SUBJECTS:
Human Interest
Aviation
Advertising
Business & Industry
Travel
Nature
PUBLICATIONS:
Forbes
Field & Stream
Graphic Arts Monthly

SCHATZ, BOB
112 Second Avenue, North
Nashville, TN 37201
Telephone: 615-254-7197
Fax: 615-254-7198
AFFILIATIONS:
ASMP
PRINCIPAL SUBJECTS:
Business & Industry
Architecture
Automotive
Food/Diet
Travel
Social Trends
PUBLICATIONS:
Financial World
Success
Spur
Equus
Travel/Holiday
New York Times Travel Section
Outdoor Illustrated
Town & Country
Business Week

SCHEIDEGGER, FRANCIS
207A N. Kirkwood Rd.
Saint Louis, MO 63122
Telephone: 314-965-2410
AFFILIATIONS:
PPA, SLDA, KCC
PRINCIPAL SUBJECTS:
General Interest
Human Interest
Ecology

Hobbies
Ecology
Government
PUBLICATIONS:
St. Louis Post-Dispatch
St. Louis Globe-Democrat
Construction News Review
Kirkwood-Webster Times
St. Louis County Journals

SCHERMEISTER, PHIL
233 Winding Way
San Francisco, CA 94112
Telephone: 415-587-4706
AFFILIATIONS:
ASMP
PRINCIPAL SUBJECTS:
Ecology
Nature
Personalities
Social Trends
Travel
PUBLICATIONS:
National Geographic
Life
Time

SCHIERSTEDT, NEIL
6933 West 29th Place
Berwyn, IL 60402
Telephone: 708-788-1567
AFFILIATIONS:
ASMP, AIGA
PRINCIPAL SUBJECTS:
Advertising
Automotive
Editorial
Journalism
Media
News
Sports

SCHIFF, NANCY RICA
24 West 30th Street
New York, NY 10001
Telephone: 212-679-9444
AFFILIATIONS:
ASMP
PRINCIPAL SUBJECTS:
Advertising
Editorial
Health
Medical
Personalities
Senior Citizens
PUBLICATIONS:
Newsweek
Business Week
Forbes
Working Mother

Working Women
New York Times Magazine
People

SCHLANGER, IRV
946 Cherokee Rd.
Huntingdon Valley, PA 19006
Telephone: 215-663-0663
AFFILIATIONS:
ASMP, PPA
PRINCIPAL SUBJECTS:
Advertising
Automotive
Computer Technology
Electronics
Fashion
Food/Diet
Marketing
Personalities
Photography
Physical Fitness

SCHLEICHER, BILL
125 Barclay St., Rm. 730
New York, NY 10007
Telephone: 212-815-1529
Fax: 212-815-7535
AFFILIATIONS:
PPA, ILCA
PRINCIPAL SUBJECTS:
General Interest
Human Interest
Journalism
Marine
Business & Industry
Health
PUBLICATIONS:
New York Magazine
New York News (Sunday &
  Daily)

SCHLUETER, MICHAEL K.
4038 Southbridge
St. Peters, MO 63376
Telephone: 314-926-8181
Fax: 314-928-8196
AFFILIATIONS:
ASMP, PPA
PRINCIPAL SUBJECTS:
Advertising
Agriculture
Business & Industry
Ecology
Editorial
Family
Home & Garden
Marine
Senior Citizens
Travel

Youth
PUBLICATIONS:
St. Louis Home & Garden
  Magazine

SCHMID, BERT
P.O. Box 336
Scarsdale, NY 10583
Telephone: 914-723-8033
Fax: 914-723-8033
AFFILIATIONS:
ASMP, MPCA
PRINCIPAL SUBJECTS:
Agriculture
Architecture
Ecology
Editorial
Foreign
General Interest
Geography
Health
Journalism
Nature
Photography
Physical Fitness
Religion
Travel
PUBLICATIONS:
New York Times
Geo Magazine
Travel Holiday Magazine
Westchester Magazine
Animal Lovers, Seafood Leaver
Woman's World

SCHMIDT, DIANE JOY
4601 E. Skyline Dr., #909
Tucson, AZ 85718
Telephone: 602-299-4329
AFFILIATIONS:
ASMP
PRINCIPAL SUBJECTS:
Advertising
Book Reviews
Business & Industry
Computer Technology
Ecology
Editorial
Education
Electronics
Entertainment
Family
Foreign
General Interest
Geography
Government
Health
Hobbies
Home & Garden
Human Interest
Human Relations

Journalism
Management
Marketing
Medical
Nature
News
Personalities
Photography
Physical Fitness
Psychology
Religion
Sales
Science
Senior Citizens
Social Trends
Sports
The Arts
Travel
Urban Affairs
Women's Interest
World Affairs
Youth
PUBLICATIONS:
Forbes
Time
Chicago Tribune
Travel & Leisure
Town & Country
Parade End
Chicago Magazine

SCHNEIDER, JOHN
5102 Autumncrest Dr.
Greensboro, NC 27407
Telephone: 919-855-0261
Fax: 919-855-0261
AFFILIATIONS:
ASMP
PRINCIPAL SUBJECTS:
Advertising
Architecture
Electronics
Fashion
Home & Garden
PUBLICATIONS:
Architectural Digest
House & Garden
Southern Living

SCHRAMM, FRANK
59 Bank Street
New York, NY 10014
Telephone: 212-807-1390
Fax: 212-807-1111
AFFILIATIONS:
ASMP
PRINCIPAL SUBJECTS:
Fashion
The Arts
PUBLICATIONS:
Vogue

L.A. Style
Harper's Bazaar
Interview
New York Times
Le Monde
Liberation (Paris)

SCHWARTZ, GEORGE J.
P.O. Box 413
Bend, OR 97709
Telephone: 503-389-4062
PRINCIPAL SUBJECTS:
General Interest
Nature
Sports
Travel
PUBLICATIONS:
Greeting cards

SCHWARTZ, JERI
N114 W16776 Crown Dr.
Germantown, WI 53022
Telephone: 414-255-5536
AFFILIATIONS:
WRWA, PW
PRINCIPAL SUBJECTS:
Human Interest
PUBLICATIONS:
Milwaukee Journal
Milwaukee Sentinel
N. Y. Daily News
The Instructor
Wisconsin Week-End
Christian Science Monitor
WI Sports Parade (On Staff)
German Town News

SCHWARZ, IRA J.
5525 Devon Rd.
Bethesda, MD 20814
Telephone: 301-986-1681
Fax: 301-718-3635
AFFILIATIONS:
ASMP, WHNPA, NPC
PRINCIPAL SUBJECTS:
Business & Industry
Computer Technology
Editorial
Government
Human Interest
Journalism
Media
Photography
PUBLICATIONS:
Newsweek
US News & World Report
Reuters News Picture Service
The Associated Press
The New York Times
The Boston Globe
Newsday

SCHWARZ, MICHAEL A.
422 Sterling Street
Atlanta, GA 30307
Telephone: 404-584-8141
Fax: 404-521-9489
AFFILIATIONS:
ASMP, NPPA
PRINCIPAL SUBJECTS:
Editorial
Business & Industry
PUBLICATIONS:
Fortune
Forbes
Times
U.S. News & World Report
USA Today

SCHWARZ, TED
1752 Holyoke 2
Cleveland, OH 44112
Telephone: 216-249-3101
MAILING ADDRESS:
TED SCHWARZ
P.O. Box 14609
Cleveland, OH 44114
PRINCIPAL SUBJECTS:
Urban Affairs
Fashion
PUBLICATIONS:
Stern (Germany)
Amphoto
Studio Photography
Tucson Magazine
Black Belt
Success Magazine
Family Circle
Rangefinder Magazine, The
Physician's Management
Today's Christian Woman
Focal Pross

SCHWELIK, FRANK
1311 Mian Avenue
Cleveland, OH 44113
Telephone: 216-579-1211
Fax: 216-579-0697
AFFILIATIONS:
ASMP
PRINCIPAL SUBJECTS:
Advertising
Business & Industry
Editorial
Human Relations
Marketing
Sales
PUBLICATIONS:
Medical Market News
Supermarket News

SCIOLETTI, JODY
61 Lee Street
Marblehead, MA 01945
Telephone: 617-639-1664
MAILING ADDRESS:
JODY SCIOLETTI
P.O. Box 534
Swampscott, MA 01907
AFFILIATIONS:
ASMP, NPPA, BPPA
PRINCIPAL SUBJECTS:
Business & Industry
Editorial
General Interest
Human Interest
Human Relations
Journalism
News
Personalities
Photography
Sports
PUBLICATIONS:
Boston Globe
Boston Herald
People Magazine
Boston Globe
Boston Herald
People Magazine

SCOCOZZA, VICTOR
42 West 24th Street
New York, NY 10010
Telephone: 212-627-2177
Fax: 212-633-0380
AFFILIATIONS:
ASMP
PRINCIPAL SUBJECTS:
Food/Diet
General Interest
Advertising
Food/Diet
PUBLICATIONS:
Seventeen
Bon Appetit
Womens Day
Good House Keeping
McCalls
Country Living
Redbook

SCORY, RAYMOND G.
236 Elmwood Circle
Cheshire, CT 06410
Telephone: 203-272-2336
MAILING ADDRESS:
INDUSTRIAL PHOTO
 SERVICE, INC.
P.O. Box 361
Cheshire, CT 06410
AFFILIATIONS:
PPA, CPPA, PPANE

PRINCIPAL SUBJECTS:
Advertising
Business & Industry
Architecture
PUBLICATIONS:
Iron Age
Connecticut Industry
Metal Working
The Professional Photography
Industrial Photography
The Blue Book Electrical
Professional Photography
Industrial Photography Annual
Quality
The Professional Photographer

SEEGER, STEPHEN E.
Seeger, Stephen Photography
2931 Irving Blvd., #101
Dallas, TX 75247
Telephone: 214-634-1309
Fax: 214-631-2216
AFFILIATIONS:
ASMP, DSVC
PRINCIPAL SUBJECTS:
Advertising
Agriculture
Amusements
Architecture
Aviation
Business & Industry
Education
Electronics
Entertainment
Family
Geography
Health
Home & Garden
Human Relations
Medical
Photography
Science
Senior Citizens
The Arts
PUBLICATIONS:
USAA Magazine & Newsletter
Chemical Week
Studio Photographer
D Magazine
Texas Monthly
Architectural Digest
Home & Garden

SEITZ, ART
1905 N. Atlantic Blvd., Tower
 House - E
Ft Lauderdale, FL 33305
Telephone: 305-563-0060
AFFILIATIONS:
ASMP, USTWA, NPPA

PRINCIPAL SUBJECTS:
Sports
Travel
Editorial
Personalities
Sports
PUBLICATIONS:
Time
Town And Country
Sports Illustrated
Tennis
Seventeen
Paris Match
Playboy
Tennis
Golf Digest
People
Stern
Paris Match
Red Book
Travel & Leisure
N.Y. Times Magazine
USA Today

SEITZ, SEPP
117 E. 24th Street, #9A
New York, NY 10010
Telephone: 212-505-9917
AFFILIATIONS:
ASMP
PRINCIPAL SUBJECTS:
Advertising
Computer Technology
Medical
Science
PUBLICATIONS:
Time
Fortune
Stern
New York Times Magazine

SELIGMAN, PAUL
163 W. 17th St.
New York, NY 10011
Telephone: 212-242-5688
AFFILIATIONS:
ASMP
PRINCIPAL SUBJECTS:
Editorial
Education
Entertainment
General Interest
History
Human Interest
Journalism
Media
Nature
News
Photography
Senior Citizens
Social Trends

Sports
The Arts
Travel
Urban Affairs
Video
PUBLICATIONS:
Time
Newsweek
Life
The New York Times
People
Smithsonian
Audubon
Opera News

SELKIRK, NEIL
515 West 19 St.
New York, NY 10011
Telephone: 212-243-6778

SETON, CHARLES
257 Mamaroneck Ave.
Mamaroneck, NY 10543
Telephone: 914-381-2530
AFFILIATIONS:
ASMP, PAI
PRINCIPAL SUBJECTS:
Amusements
Architecture
Editorial
Family
Journalism
Travel
Video
PUBLICATIONS:
Popular Photography
Travel & Leisure
Geography
Gourmet

SEYMOUR, RONALD
1625 N. Milwaukee Ave.
Chicago, IL 60647
Telephone: 312-235-0161
Fax: 312-235-9649
AFFILIATIONS:
ASMP
PRINCIPAL SUBJECTS:
Advertising
Business & Industry
Editorial
General Interest
Health
Human Interest
Human Relations
Medical
Nature
Photography

SHAKOOR, RA
Shakoor Studio
13243 G Fiji Way
Marina Del Rey, CA 90292
Telephone: 310-827-2555
Fax: 310-827-5606
AFFILIATIONS:
ASMP
PRINCIPAL SUBJECTS:
Advertising
Entertainment
Fashion
Personalities
PUBLICATIONS:
Harper's Bazaar
Vogue
GQ & L'Espresso (Italian)
Interview
Metro
Essence
Ebony
Up Scale

SHANEFF, CARL
1200 College Walk, Rm. 105
Honolulu, HI 96817
Telephone: 808-533-3010
Fax: 808-545-2374
AFFILIATIONS:
ASMP
PRINCIPAL SUBJECTS:
Nature
Aviation
Advertising
Business & Industry
Editorial
Travel
PUBLICATIONS:
Architectural Digest
Hawaii Business Magazine
Business Week
Travel & Leisure

SHELTON, SYBIL
416 Valleyview Rd.
Englewood, NJ 07631
Telephone: 201-568-8684
AFFILIATIONS:
ASMP, ASPP
PRINCIPAL SUBJECTS:
General Interest
Youth
PUBLICATIONS:
N. Y. Times
Newsweek
U. S. News & World Report
MD Magazine
Woman's World

SHERMAN, BOB
1166 N.E. 182nd St.
Miami, FL 33162
Telephone: 305-944-2111
AFFILIATIONS:
ASMP, NPAA
PRINCIPAL SUBJECTS:
Advertising
Editorial
Journalism
News
Sports
Travel
PUBLICATIONS:
Life
Time
People
USA Today
Paris Match
Newsweek
Bunte
NY Times

SHERMAN, RON
P.O. Box 28656
Atlanta, GA 30358
Telephone: 404-993-7197
Fax: 404-993-6106
AFFILIATIONS:
ASMP, NPPA
PRINCIPAL SUBJECTS:
Editorial
General Interest
Journalism
Sports
Photography
PUBLICATIONS:
Life
Time
Newsweek
Businessweek
New York Times Magazine
Venture
Inside Sports
Sports Illustrated
Forbes

SHIELDS-MARLEY
  PHOTOGRAPHY
Shields-Marley Photography
117 South Victory
Little Rock, AR 72201
Telephone: 501-372-6148
Fax: 501-371-9517
PRINCIPAL SUBJECTS:
Advertising
Aviation
Business & Industry
Editorial
Food/Diet
Home & Garden

Human Interest
Journalism
Marketing
Media
Military
Nature
News
Photography
The Arts
Women's Interest
PUBLICATIONS:
Architectural Record
Architectural/Design
  Collaborators
Southern Living
Arkansas Times
Arkansas Homes
Kitchen & Bath Concepts
The American Architectural
  Photographer

SHIER, DEANN
2904 Pacific Hwy.
San Diego, CA 92101
Telephone: 619-291-2123
Fax: 619-291-2143
AFFILIATIONS:
ASMP, SDCC
PRINCIPAL SUBJECTS:
Advertising
Architecture
Aviation
Editorial
Marine
Sports
PUBLICATIONS:
Yachting
U.S. News
Forbes
San Diego Magazine
Motorboat & Sailing
Wings West

SHOLIK, STAN
1946 E. Blair Ave.
Santa Ana, CA 92705
Telephone: 714-250-9275
Fax: 714-756-2623
AFFILIATIONS:
ASMP
PRINCIPAL SUBJECTS:
Medical
Computer Technology
Electronics
Food/Diet
PUBLICATIONS:
Professional Photographer,
  The Aug '84

Studio Photography,
January, 1987
Forbes, June, 1987
View Camera July/August 92

SHRIKHANDE, DEVENDRA
1814 1/2 18th St.
Cody, WY 82414
Telephone: 307-527-6868
AFFILIATIONS:
ASMP
PRINCIPAL SUBJECTS:
Advertising
Agriculture
Architecture
Automotive
Business & Industry
Editorial
General Interest
History
Home & Garden
Journalism
Management
Marketing
Media
Men's Interest
Personalities
Photography
Physical Fitness
Sports
The Arts
Travel
PUBLICATIONS:
Esquire
Inc.
Gourmet
Field & Stream
Sports Afield

SHROUT, BILL & KATHRYN E.
Isle Aux Oies River, 11434
Murray Rd.
Theodore, AL 36582
Telephone: 205-973-1379
AFFILIATIONS:
ASMP
PRINCIPAL SUBJECTS:
Advertising
Editorial
Photography
PUBLICATIONS:
National Geographic
Southern Living
Business Week
Saturday Evening Post
Time, Inc.

SHULTZ, LAURA
201 Wyandotte, 207
Kansas City, MO 64105
Telephone: 816-474-7929

PRINCIPAL SUBJECTS:
Editorial
Advertising
Business & Industry

SHULTZ, LAURA MAXWELL
201 Wyandotte
Kansas City, MO 64105
Telephone: 816-474-7929
AFFILIATIONS:
ASMP
PRINCIPAL SUBJECTS:
Advertising
Editorial
Human Interest
Human Relations
Journalism
PUBLICATIONS:
Time
U.S. News
Mac Week
USA Today

SIBLEY, SCOTT
Photo International
817 Folsom St.
San Francisco, CA 94107
Telephone: 415-978-5485
Fax: 415-978-5453
AFFILIATIONS:
ASMP, PMA
PRINCIPAL SUBJECTS:
Advertising
Architecture
Book Reviews
Business & Industry
Computer Technology
Ecology
Editorial
Education
Entertainment
Family
Foreign
General Interest
Geography
Health
History
Home & Garden
Human Interest
Human Relations
Journalism
Management
Marine
Men's Interest
News
Personal Finance
Personalities
Photography
Social Trends
The Arts
Travel

Urban Affairs
Youth
PUBLICATIONS:
New York Times
Le Figaro
Town & Country
Sailing
National Geographic World
Modern Bride
Florist
SN

SICKLES PHOTO-REPORTING
SERVICE
11 Park Rd., Box 98
Maplewood, NJ 07040
Telephone: 201-763-6355
Fax: 201-763-4473
MAILING ADDRESS:
SICKLES PHOTO -
REPORTING SVC.
P.O. Box 98
Maplewood, NJ 07040
Telephone: 201-763-3543
AFFILIATIONS:
IABC
PRINCIPAL SUBJECTS:
Agriculture
General Interest
Journalism
Advertising
PUBLICATIONS:
Annual Reports
Company Publications
Brochures-Direct Mail,Ads

SIEGEL, DICK
13700 Valley View Rd., 156
Eden Prairie, MN 55344
Fax: 612-934-8771
MAILING ADDRESS:
R. MYLES SIEGEL
PHOTOGRAPHY

SIEGEL, R. MYLES
PHOTOGRAPHY
Siegel, R. Myles Photography
13700 Valley View Rd., #156
Eden Prairie, MN 55344
Telephone: 612-934-4120
Fax: 612-934-8771
AFFILIATIONS:
ASMP
PRINCIPAL SUBJECTS:
Advertising
Agriculture
Amusements
Automotive
Business & Industry

SIEVERS, ALVIN M.
1055 Raisher Dr.
Saint Louis, MO 63130
Telephone: 314-725-3449
MAILING ADDRESS:
SIEVERS PHOTOGRAPHERS
Saint Louis, MO 63130
AFFILIATIONS:
PPA, MPA, SLPA
PRINCIPAL SUBJECTS:
General Interest

SILBERT, LAYLE
505 LaGuardia Pl., 16c
New York, NY 10012
Telephone: 212-677-0947
AFFILIATIONS:
ASMP
PRINCIPAL SUBJECTS:
Personalities
Foreign
Travel
PUBLICATIONS:
Time
People
N.Y. Times

SILLA, JON
400 South Graham Street
Charlotte, NC 28202
Telephone: 704-377-8694
Fax: 704-377-8695
AFFILIATIONS:
ASMP
PRINCIPAL SUBJECTS:
Advertising
Men's Interest
Personalities
PUBLICATIONS:
Trade Magazine

SIMS, MARK
Sims, Mark Photographics, Inc.
1631 15th St., 5th Fl.
Denver, CO 80202
Telephone: 303-573-6713
MAILING ADDRESS:
MARK SIMS
Mark Sims Photographics, Inc.
P.O. Box 480543
Denver, CO 80248
AFFILIATIONS:
ASMP, DAF
PRINCIPAL SUBJECTS:
Advertising
Architecture
Editorial
Fashion
Personalities
Travel

PUBLICATIONS:
Rocky Mountain News
Colorado Homes & Lifestyles
Rocky Mountain News
Colorado Homes & Lifestyles

SINKLER, PAUL
420 N. 5th St., #516
Minneapolis, MN 55401
Telephone: 612-343-0325
Fax: 612-343-0908
AFFILIATIONS:
ASMP
PRINCIPAL SUBJECTS:
Advertising
Nature
Philosophy
PUBLICATIONS:
Star Tribune

SIRLIN, TED
2020 I Street
Sacramento, CA 95814
Telephone: 916-444-8464
Fax: 916-442-8131
AFFILIATIONS:
PPA
PRINCIPAL SUBJECTS:
Advertising
Government
Human Interest
Journalism
PUBLICATIONS:
Easy Living
Studio Light (Kodak
    Publication)
The Rangefinder
The Professional Photographer
Camera Craftsman of America

SISSON, BOB
P.O. Box 1649
Englewood, FL 34295
Telephone: 813-475-0757
AFFILIATIONS:
WHMP, BPA, SPSE
PRINCIPAL SUBJECTS:
Advertising
Animals
Ecology
Editorial
Education
Foreign
Home & Garden
Journalism
Marine
Nature
Photography
Science

SITEMAN, FRANK
136 Pond St.
Winchester, MA 01890
Telephone: 617-729-3742
PRINCIPAL SUBJECTS:
Education

SLATER, EDWARD
3601 W. Commercial Blvd.,
    #33
Ft. Lauderdale, FL 33309
Telephone: 305-486-7117
Fax: 305-486-7118
AFFILIATIONS:
ASMP, PACA, ASPP
PRINCIPAL SUBJECTS:
Advertising
Computer Technology
Electronics
Hobbies
Journalism
Marketing
Nature
Photography
Sports
PUBLICATIONS:
National Geographic
Newsweek
Time
National Wildlife
Florida Trends

SLAUGHTER, PAUL
1300 Calle Giraso
Santa Fe, NM 87501
Telephone: 505-988-3179
Fax: 505-986-8008
AFFILIATIONS:
ASMP
PRINCIPAL SUBJECTS:
Travel
Geography
Nature
PUBLICATIONS:
Time
National Geographic Books
Travel & Leisure
Islands
Popular Photography
Los Angeles Time
Image Magazine
    (S.F. Examiner)

SMALLING, WALTER
1541 Eighth Street, N.W.
Washington, DC 20001
Telephone: 202-234-2438
Fax: 202-667-4894
PRINCIPAL SUBJECTS:
Architecture
Photography

SMELTZER, ROBERT
207-A Chick Hampton Bldg., 1
    Chick Springs Dr.
Greenville, SC 29609
Telephone: 803-235-2186
AFFILIATIONS:
ASMP
PRINCIPAL SUBJECTS:
Advertising
Editorial
Human Interest
Advertising
PUBLICATIONS:
Trade Publications
Business Week
Daily News Record
American Lawyer
Textile World
Textile Industries
Medical Economics
ACTWU
Quick Frozen Foods
Time-Life
Readers Digest

SMETZER, DONALD
2534 N. Burling St.
Chicago, IL 60614
Telephone: 312-327-1716
AFFILIATIONS:
ASMP, ASPP
PRINCIPAL SUBJECTS:
Family
Foreign
Geography
Entertainment
PUBLICATIONS:
Life
Stern
Bunte
Time
Newsweek
People

SMITH, ALLEN
622 N 16th St.
Grnd Junction, CO 81501
Telephone: 303-245-2019
AFFILIATIONS:
ASMP
PRINCIPAL SUBJECTS:
Fashion
The Arts

SMITH, BRADLEY
5858 Desert View Dr.
La Jolla, CA 92037
Telephone: 619-454-4321
AFFILIATIONS:
ASMP, ASPP

PRINCIPAL SUBJECTS:
Animals
The Arts
Nature
Personalities
PUBLICATIONS:
Smithsonian Magazine
San Diego Magazine
Playboy Magazine
Natural History Magazine
Life Magazine

SMITH, BRIAN
7 Glenley Terrace
Boston, MA 02135
Telephone: 617-926-8311
Fax: 617-926-1714
AFFILIATIONS:
ASMP
PRINCIPAL SUBJECTS:
Editorial
Business & Industry
Travel
PUBLICATIONS:
Business Week
Forbes
Fortune
Money

SMITH, D. LYNN
2900 Photo Ave.
Fort Worth, TX 76107
Telephone: 817-732-4444
MAILING ADDRESS:
GORDON SMITH/
    M. PHOTO. CR. CPP
Fort Worth, TX 76107
Telephone: 817-292-4444
AFFILIATIONS:
TPSN, PPA, SWPPA
PRINCIPAL SUBJECTS:
General Interest
Government
Architecture
PUBLICATIONS:
U.S. News (Ads)
PP of A. Magazine (Article on
    Photography)
Popular Mechanics (Article on
    Photography)

SMITH, DAVID L.
Smith, David L. Photography
420 Gold Way
Pittsburgh, PA 15213
Telephone: 412-687-7500
Fax: 412-621-9030
AFFILIATIONS:
ASMP
PRINCIPAL SUBJECTS:
Advertising

Photography
PUBLICATIONS:
Winged Head
Executive Report
Black Box Catalog
Plastics Engineering
Laser World
Pittsburgh Magazine
Cosmopolitan
Gift Reporter

SMITH, ROBIN B.
P.O. Box 4244
Aspen, CO 81612
Telephone: 303-923-6810
AFFILIATIONS:
ASMP
PRINCIPAL SUBJECTS:
Architecture
Editorial
Family
Human Interest
Sports
Travel
PUBLICATIONS:
Ski
Travel & Leisure
Delta Digest
Coastal Journal
Christian Science Monitor

SMITH, ROGER B.
267 Oxford St., #605
Rochester, NY 14607
Telephone: 716-442-4388
AFFILIATIONS:
ASMP, PHOTONET
PRINCIPAL SUBJECTS:
Editorial
Photography
PUBLICATIONS:
New York Times
Time
Rolling Stone
U.S. Air Magazine

SNOW, ANDY
322 S. Paterson Blvd.
Dayton, OH 45402
Telephone: 513-461-2930
PRINCIPAL SUBJECTS:
Business & Industry
Editorial
Nature
PUBLICATIONS:
Business Week
Forbes
Fortune
Newsweek
PC World
Time

SNYDER, LEE F.
4150 Studio D, 112th Ter. N.
Clearwater, FL 34622
Telephone: 800-741-3686
Fax: 813-572-6394
AFFILIATIONS:
ASMP
PRINCIPAL SUBJECTS:
Advertising
Editorial
Fashion
Nature
PUBLICATIONS:
St. Petersburg Times
LA Times
Birder's World
Newsweek
New York Times Syndicate
Birding Magazine
Continental News/Features
Wildbird Magazine
US Air Magazine
Delta Sky Magazine
Private Clubs Magazine

SOCHUREK, HOWARD J.
Howard Sochurek, Inc.
Delray Bch, FL 33483
Telephone: 407-243-3691
MAILING ADDRESS:
HOWARD SOCHUREK, INC.
25 Seabreeze Ave.
Delray Beach, FL 33483
AFFILIATIONS:
ASMP
PRINCIPAL SUBJECTS:
Advertising
Aviation
Journalism
Science
Travel
PUBLICATIONS:
Time
Life
Fortune
Nat. Geographic
Smithsonian
Technology
Discover
Newsweek, US News & World
   Report

SOLOMON, CHUCK
67 Hudson Street, Suite 3d
New York, NY 10013
Telephone: 212-349-0608
AFFILIATIONS:
ASMP
PRINCIPAL SUBJECTS:
Sports

PUBLICATIONS:
NY Times
Sports Illustrated
Time

SOLOMON, RON
149 West Montgomery Street
Baltimore, MD 21230
Telephone: 410-539-0403
Fax: 410-539-4343
AFFILIATIONS:
ASMP
PRINCIPAL SUBJECTS:
Advertising
Architecture
Travel
PUBLICATIONS:
Interior Design
Contract, Travel
Design West
Interiors
Southern Accents
Architecture

SOMOZA, GERARDO
247 W. 30th St., 6th Fl.
New York, NY 10001
Telephone: 212-868-0612
Fax: 212-868-2818
AFFILIATIONS:
OP-NY & LA
PRINCIPAL SUBJECTS:
Advertising
Architecture
Editorial
Entertainment
Fashion
Human Interest
Journalism
Nature
News
Photography
Social Trends
Sports
The Arts
PUBLICATIONS:
German Elle
Forbes
Time & Time Int.
People
Photo (American)
Allure
Moda (Italy)
Bunte (Germany)

SORCE, WAYNE
20 Henry St./5G
Brooklyn, NY 11201
Telephone: 718-237-0497
PRINCIPAL SUBJECTS:
Journalism

Business & Industry
PUBLICATIONS:
Life Magazine
Time Magazine
Fortune Magazine
Modern Photography
Bunta
Money Magazine
Discover Magazine
Smithsonian Magazine
Actual Magazine
Nations Business
Newton
Stern
Europea
Readers Digest
Paris Match
Playboy
Manchette
Review Magazine

SORRELL, RONDA
215 N. Arendell Ave.
Zebulon, NC 27597
Telephone: 919-269-0888
Fax: 919-269-4536
AFFILIATIONS:
PMP
PRINCIPAL SUBJECTS:
Family
Women's Interest
Nature

SPEARS, PHILLIP
Creative Sources Photography
6095 Lake Forrest Drive, #100
Atlanta, GA 30328
Telephone: 404-843-2141
Fax: 404-250-1807
AFFILIATIONS:
ASMP
PRINCIPAL SUBJECTS:
Advertising
Architecture
Business & Industry
Education
Family
Marketing
PUBLICATIONS:
Atlanta Magazine
Business Atlanta
Jacksonville Today
Historic Preservation
Diversion
Southern Homes

SPEYER, LARS
698 Kendall Ave.
Palo Alto, CA 94306
Telephone: 415-493-2869

AFFILIATIONS:
ASMP
PRINCIPAL SUBJECTS:
Advertising
The Arts
Human Interest
Amusements

SPIEGEL, TED
9 Laurie Lane
South Salem, NY 10590
Telephone: 914-763-3668
AFFILIATIONS:
ASMP, NPPA
PRINCIPAL SUBJECTS:
Ecology
Geography
History
The Arts
PUBLICATIONS:
National Geographic Magazine
U.S. Congress/Office Of
  Technology Assesment
Time-Life Publications
Signature Magazine
Rockefeller Foundation
  Publications

SPILLERS, MICHAEL
421 E. 69th Terrace
Kansas City, MO 64131
Telephone: 816-444-0882
PRINCIPAL SUBJECTS:
Architecture

SPRING, BOB & IRA
18819 Olympic View Dr.
Edmonds, WA 98020
Telephone: 206-776-4685
Fax: 206-776-4685
AFFILIATIONS:
ASPP
PRINCIPAL SUBJECTS:
Geography
Nature
PUBLICATIONS:
Reader's Digest

STACY H. GEIKEN
  PHOTOGRAPHY
Stacy H. Geiken Photography
431 Monterey Ave., #2
Los Gatos, CA 95030
Telephone: 408-395-7786
Fax: 408-395-3316
AFFILIATIONS:
ASMP, IABC
PRINCIPAL SUBJECTS:
Photography
PUBLICATIONS:
Forbes

Runner's World
California
Open Systems Today
Running Times
Measure Magazine
Stanford Magazine

STALVIG, MURLYN A.
1998 Princeton Ave.
St. Paul, MN 55105
Telephone: 612-699-4433
PRINCIPAL SUBJECTS:
Advertising
Aviation
Human Interest

STAMATES, JIM
Low Impact Wildlife
  Photography
P.O. Box 11211,
  2790 Blitzen Rd.
South Lake Taho, CA 96155
Telephone: 916-577-4101
Fax: 916-577-5204
AFFILIATIONS:
ASMP
PRINCIPAL SUBJECTS:
Animals
Ecology
Editorial
Geography
Nature
PUBLICATIONS:
Sierra Heritage
Falcon Press
International Paper

STARR, ASHBY
  PHOTOGRAPHER
4416 MAYCREST AVE.
LOS ANGELES, CA 90032
Telephone: 213-223-7247
AFFILIATIONS:
ASMP
PRINCIPAL SUBJECTS:
Agriculture
Architecture
Business & Industry
Editorial
Education
Management
The Arts
Urban Affairs
SEE AD IN SECTION 5

STAWNIAK, JIM
On Sight Photography
314 N. Highland Ave.
Atlanta, GA 30307
Telephone: 404-659-5457
Fax: 404-659-5457

AFFILIATIONS:
ASMP, APG
PRINCIPAL SUBJECTS:
Advertising
Architecture
Editorial
Entertainment
News
Photography
Travel
PUBLICATIONS:
Vanity Fair
Georgia Trend
Forbes
Glamour
Gourmet Retailer
Business Atlanta
Health
Heartland USA

STECKER, ELINOR H.
1633 Broadway
New York, NY 10019
Telephone: 212-767-6368
Fax: 212-767-5629
MAILING ADDRESS:
POPULAR PHOTOGRAPHY
New York, NY 10019
Telephone: 914-948-8099
PRINCIPAL SUBJECTS:
General Interest
The Arts
Video
Photography
PUBLICATIONS:
The New York Times
Filmmakers Newsletter
Time
Popular Photography
US Air Magazine
Lens

STEELE, GEOFF
6053 25th Rd., N.
Arlington, VA 22207
Telephone: 703-533-1450
MAILING ADDRESS:
STEEL, GEOFF
3205 N. Columbus St.
Arlington, VA 22207
PRINCIPAL SUBJECTS:
Aviation
Youth
Home & Garden
Personalities
Travel
Government
PUBLICATIONS:
General Motors World
Washington Post

Soaring Magazine
Associated Press Photo Wire
United Press Photowire
Weekly Reader

STEELE, MAX
770 Walnut, Unit C
Boulder, CO 80302
Telephone: 303-443-2357
AFFILIATIONS:
ASMP, AIA, AIGA, SEGD
PRINCIPAL SUBJECTS:
Advertising
Architecture
Editorial
Fashion
Food/Diet
Foreign
Journalism
Religion
Senior Citizens
Travel
Urban Affairs
Youth
PUBLICATIONS:
AIA Calender

STEELE, W. RICHARD
822 Lowell Ave.
Toms River, NJ 08753
Telephone: 908-341-0411
AFFILIATIONS:
NPPA, NPPNJ
PRINCIPAL SUBJECTS:
Advertising
Human Interest
Nature
News
Fashion
Travel
PUBLICATIONS:
Time
Life

STEIN-MASON STUDIO
348 Newbury St.
Boston, MA 02115
Telephone: 617-536-8227
AFFILIATIONS:
MA, MTC, CPA
PRINCIPAL SUBJECTS:
Advertising
Architecture
General Interest
PUBLICATIONS:
Annual Reports-Analog
  Devices-C.River Breeding Lab
Sports Illustrated
Time

Business Week
People Magazine
Fortune

STEINER, CLYDE
20 Prescott Ct.
San Francisco, CA 94133
Telephone: 415-398-8093
Fax: 415-986-4429
AFFILIATIONS:
MA, MTC, CPPA
PRINCIPAL SUBJECTS:
Computer Technology
Business & Industry
Travel
PUBLICATIONS:
San Jose Mercury
Compass
Copley News Service
Computer Press Association
Semaphore - (Editor)
Publishers Weekly

STEINER, LISL
'El Repecho' Trinity Pass
Pound Ridge, NY 10576
Telephone: 914-764-5538
Fax: 914-764-5959
AFFILIATIONS:
ASMP
PRINCIPAL SUBJECTS:
Editorial
General Interest
Journalism
Photography
Youth
PUBLICATIONS:
Time
Life
Newsweek
O'Cruzeiro (Latin America)

STEINGROVE, JACK
146 N. Sunrise Dr.
Tavernier, FL 33070
Telephone: 305-852-6004
Fax: 206-285-5037
MAILING ADDRESS:
Zegrahm Expeditions
1414 Dexter Ave. N.
Seattle, WA 98109
AFFILIATIONS:
ASMP, MPCA
PRINCIPAL SUBJECTS:
Animals
Ecology
Foreign
Geography
Marine
Nature
Travel

PUBLICATIONS:
GEO
Oceans
Calypso Log
National Geography
GEO
Oceans
Calypso Log
National Geography

STEWARDSON, JOE
903 Glen Arden Way NE
Atlanta, GA 30306
Telephone: 404-875-4239
AFFILIATIONS:
ASMP
PRINCIPAL SUBJECTS:
Advertising
Agriculture
Business & Industry
Computer Technology
Ecology
Editorial
Education
Home & Garden
Journalism
Marketing
Media
Medical
Men's Interest
Military
News
Sports
Travel
PUBLICATIONS:
USA Today
Nations Business
U.S. News & World Report

STEWART, ED
5950 Westward
Houston, TX 77081
Telephone: 713-988-0775
AFFILIATIONS:
PP Of A, HAC
PRINCIPAL SUBJECTS:
Architecture
Advertising

STIERER, DENNIS
145 Chestnut St.
Lockport, NY 14094
Telephone: 716-439-8444
Fax: 716-439-8444
AFFILIATIONS:
NPPA
PRINCIPAL SUBJECTS:
Business & Industry
Architecture
Ecology
Editorial

Fashion
Health
Human Interest
The Arts
Travel
PUBLICATIONS:
R.N. Magazine
Boston Globe Magazine
National Geographic - World
Caribbean Travel
Insight

STOCK PHOTOS HAWAII
Stock Photos Hawaii
1128 Nuuanu Avenue,
 Suite 250
Honolulu, HI 96817
Telephone: 808-538-1389
Fax: 808-537-9111
AFFILIATIONS:
ASMP
PRINCIPAL SUBJECTS:
Advertising
Agriculture
Amusements
Business & Industry
Ecology
Editorial
Entertainment
Family
Foreign
General Interest
Health
Hobbies
Humor
Marketing
Motivation
Nature
Photography
Physical Fitness
Sports
Travel
Youth
PUBLICATIONS:
Travel & Leisure
National Geographic
Sunset
Hemispheres
Wall St. Journal
Conde Nast's Traveller
Brides & Modern Bride
Travel/Holiday

STONE, ERIKA
327 E. 82nd St.
New York, NY 10028
Telephone: 212-737-6435
Fax: 212-737-6814
AFFILIATIONS:
ASMP, ASPP, PWP

PRINCIPAL SUBJECTS:
Editorial
Education
Family
Senior Citizens
Youth

STONE, TONY IMAGES
Stone, Tony Images
6100 Wilshire Blvd., #1250
Los Angeles, CA 90048
Telephone: 213-938-1700
Fax: 213-938-0731
AFFILIATIONS:
PACA, ASPP, ASMP
PRINCIPAL SUBJECTS:
Advertising
Agriculture
Animals
Architecture
Automotive
Aviation
Business & Industry
Computer Technology
Ecology
Editorial
Education
Electronics
Family
Food/Diet
Foreign
Geography
Health
Hobbies
Home & Garden
Human Interest
Human Relations
Humor
Management
Marine
Marketing
Medical
Men's Interest
Motivation
Nature
Physical Fitness
Psychology
Sales
Senior Citizens
Social Trends
Sports
The Arts
Travel
Women's Interest
Youth
PUBLICATIONS:
Communication Arts
Art Direction
Archive
Photo District News
Confetti

Applied Arts
Folio
Print

STORMZAND, JOHN
3097 Lincolnview
Auburn Hills, MI 48326
Telephone: 810-299-4739
AFFILIATIONS:
ASMP
PRINCIPAL SUBJECTS:
Advertising
Agriculture
Amusements
Animals
Automotive
Book Reviews
Business & Industry
Ecology
Editorial
Education
Entertainment
Family
Fashion
Foreign
General Interest
Geography
Government
Health
History
Hobbies
Home & Garden
Human Interest
Human Relations
Humor
Journalism
Management
Media
Men's Interest
Military
Motivation
Nature
News
Personalities
Philosophy
Photography
Physical Fitness
Psychology
Religion
Sales
Senior Citizens
Social Trends
Sports
The Arts
Travel
Urban Affairs
World Affairs
Youth
PUBLICATIONS:
Time Magazine
New York Times

Los Angeles Times
Detroit News
USA Today
Boston Globe
World & I
US News & World Report
People Magazine

STOTT, BARRY
2427 Chamonix Ln.
Vail, CO 81657
Telephone: 303-476-5774
AFFILIATIONS:
ASMP, PPA
PRINCIPAL SUBJECTS:
Aviation
Fashion
Travel
Photography
Sports
PUBLICATIONS:
N.Y. Times
Time
Newsweek
Sports Illustrated
Travel & Leisure
Signature
Fortune
Money
Mainliner
Denver Post
Business & Commercial
   Aviation
Aviation Convention News
Aviation Consumer
Aviation Safety
Air Progress

STOVER, DAVID
Stover, David Photography
15 East Main St., 2nd Floor
Richmond, VA 23219
Telephone: 804-782-0988
AFFILIATIONS:
ASMP
PRINCIPAL SUBJECTS:
Advertising
Business & Industry
Editorial
General Interest
Human Interest
Human Relations
Photography
Travel
PUBLICATIONS:
Field & Stream
Fortune
Richmond Surroundings
Parade Magazine

STRASSER, JOEL
519 W. 22nd St.
Sioux Falls, SD 57105
Telephone: 605-332-7651
MAILING ADDRESS:
STEVE PAREZO
Sioux Falls, SD 57105
AFFILIATIONS:
ASMP, PP of A,
PRINCIPAL SUBJECTS:
Advertising
Architecture
The Arts
General Interest
Nature
Photography
PUBLICATIONS:
Architectural Record
Progressive Architecture
Farm & Ranch Living
Farm Journal
Applied Photography
Studio Light
Range Finder
US News
Reader Digest

STRATFORD, DENIS
24 Raspberry Cir.
Durango, CO 81301
Telephone: 303-385-7465
PRINCIPAL SUBJECTS:
Hobbies
Geography
Ecology

STRATFORD, JIM
1218 Cleburne St.
Greensboro, NC 27408
Telephone: 919-274-0909
Fax: 919-279-8371
AFFILIATIONS:
ASMP
PRINCIPAL SUBJECTS:
Advertising
Business & Industry
Editorial
General Interest
Journalism
News
Sports
PUBLICATIONS:
Time
Newsweek
US News & World Report
Fortune
Parents
Family Circle
Business Week
Dupont World

STREANO, VINCENT C.
1549 Deception Rd.
Anacortes, WA 98221
Telephone: 206-293-4525
Fax: 206-293-2411
MAILING ADDRESS:
VINCE STREANO
P.O. Box 488
Anacortes, WA 98221
AFFILIATIONS:
APA, ASMP
PRINCIPAL SUBJECTS:
Advertising
Youth
Travel
Journalism
Sports
Photography
PUBLICATIONS:
Smithsonian Magazine
Sports Illustrated
National Geographic
People Magazine
Forbes Magazine
Time Magazine
Fortune

STREET, PARK
3200 Bonnie Rd.
Austin, TX 78703
Telephone: 512-477-3572
Fax: 512-477-3572
AFFILIATIONS:
ASMP
PRINCIPAL SUBJECTS:
Advertising
Architecture
Editorial
Education
Entertainment
Family
Foreign
General Interest
Geography
Health
Human Interest
Human Relations
Marketing
Personalities
Photography
Science
Senior Citizens
Social Trends
The Arts
Travel
Youth
PUBLICATIONS:
Communication Arts
Guitar Player

Downbeat
Musician
Guitar World

STRESHINSKY, TED
50 Kenyon Avenue
Kensington, CA 94708
Telephone: 510-526-0921
Fax: 510-527-7740
MAILING ADDRESS:
TED STRESHINSKY
P. O. Box 674
Berkeley, CA 94701
Telephone: 510-526-1976
AFFILIATIONS:
ASMP, APA, ASPP
PRINCIPAL SUBJECTS:
Advertising
Editorial
Business & Industry
Travel
Photography
PUBLICATIONS:
Fortune
Money
Business Week
People
Time
Esquire
Smithsonian
Life
Der Spiegel
Stern
London Observer
Sports Illustrated
GEO
Travel and Leisure
Conde Nast Traveller

STROMBERG, BRUCE
P.O. Box 2052
Philadelphia, PA 19103
Telephone: 215-545-0842
AFFILIATIONS:
ASMP
PRINCIPAL SUBJECTS:
Advertising
Business & Industry
Editorial
Education
Health
Travel
PUBLICATIONS:
N.Y. Times
Time
Life
Business Week
Penthouse
Philadelphia

STROUSS, SARAH
Strouss, Sarah Photography
524 Warner Road
Hubbard, OH 44425
Telephone: 216-568-0203
Fax: 216-568-0205
AFFILIATIONS:
ASMP
PRINCIPAL SUBJECTS:
Architecture
General Interest
Home & Garden
Photography
PUBLICATIONS:
Progressive Grocer
Ohio Magazine
Building Designer Construction
Restaurant News
Archtypes
USA Today

SUDOW, ELLYN
1091 Old Cedar Rd.
McLean, VA 22102
Telephone: 703-827-0007
AFFILIATIONS:
ASMP, ASPP
PRINCIPAL SUBJECTS:
Education
Entertainment
Family
Personalities
Photography
Sports
The Arts
Women's Interest
Youth
PUBLICATIONS:
Kennedy Center News
Washington Life
Providence Journal
Potomac School Bulletin

SUGAR, JAMES A.
45 Midway Avenue
Mill Valley, CA 94941
Telephone: 415-388-3344
Fax: 415-388-3345
AFFILIATIONS:
ASMP, WHNPA
PRINCIPAL SUBJECTS:
Computer Technology
Photography
Aviation
PUBLICATIONS:
National Geographic
Smithsonian Air & Space
Flying
Newsweek

Time
Sports Illustrated
National Geographic Traveller
  & World Magazine

SUMMER PRODUCTIONS
Summer Productions
P.O. Box 124
Livermore, CA 94550
Telephone: 510-933-8268
Fax: 510-933-8268
AFFILIATIONS:
ASMP
PRINCIPAL SUBJECTS:
Advertising
Aviation
Foreign
Human Relations
Military
Personalities
Video
Women's Interest
Photography
PUBLICATIONS:
Womans World
High Society
World & I

SUMNER
  PHOTOGRAPHY INC.
Sumner Photography Inc.
7765 S.W. 144th St.
Miami, FL 33158
Telephone: 305-256-8654
Fax: 305-256-1504
AFFILIATIONS:
ASMP
PRINCIPAL SUBJECTS:
Advertising
Architecture
Fashion
Marine
Personalities
Travel
PUBLICATIONS:
Travel & Leisure
Playboy
Time
House & Garden
Life
Yachting
Showboats

SVEHLA, JAMES C.
900 Jackson
Naperville, IL 60566
Telephone: 708-953-9358
AFFILIATIONS:
NPPA, IPPA
PRINCIPAL SUBJECTS:
Advertising

Architecture
Editorial
Journalism
Marketing
Media
News
Photography
Sports
The Arts
PUBLICATIONS:
Chicago Tribune

SWANSON, BOB
Swanson Images
259 Clara St.
San Francisco, CA 94107
Telephone: 415-495-6507
Fax: 415-495-6531
AFFILIATIONS:
ASMP, APA
PRINCIPAL SUBJECTS:
Architecture
Business & Industry
Home & Garden
Nature
Photography
PUBLICATIONS:
Architectural Record
Interiors
Better Homes & Gardens
Northern California Home &
  Garden
Phoenix Home & Garden
Southwest Passages West

SWANSON, DICK
6122 Wiscasset Rd.
Bethesda, MD 20816
Telephone: 202-965-1185
Fax: 301-229-7033
AFFILIATIONS:
ASMP,WHNPA
PRINCIPAL SUBJECTS:
Journalism
Nature
PUBLICATIONS:
Annual Reports
National Geographic
Washington Post

SWARTZ, FRED
135 S. La Brea
Los Angeles, CA 90036
Telephone: 213-939-2789
AFFILIATIONS:
ASMP
PRINCIPAL SUBJECTS:
Advertising
Editorial
Human Interest
Sports

Travel
Aviation
Business & Industry
PUBLICATIONS:
Time
Fortune
Business Week
Sports Illustrated
Dun's Business Monthly
IBM Outlook
Woman's World

SWETNAM, JIM
108 W. 19th St.
Kansas City, MO 64108
Telephone: 816-421-6484
AFFILIATIONS:
PPA
PRINCIPAL SUBJECTS:
Advertising
Architecture
General Interest
Human Interest

SWOGER, ARTHUR
61 Savoy St.
Providence, RI 02906
Telephone: 401-331-0440
AFFILIATIONS:
ASMP, ASPP
PRINCIPAL SUBJECTS:
Editorial
Advertising
PUBLICATIONS:
New York Times Magazine
Natural History

TADDER, MORTON
1010 Morton St.
Baltimore, MD 21201
Telephone: 410-837-7427
Fax: 410-837-1414
AFFILIATIONS:
PP of A, ASMP, SG
PRINCIPAL SUBJECTS:
Advertising
Architecture
Editorial
General Interest
Sports

TAGGART, MARK J.
P.O. Box 1061
Bethany Beach, DE 19930
Telephone: 302-530-3860
AFFILIATIONS:
ASMP
PRINCIPAL SUBJECTS:
Fashion

Editorial
Human Interest
Military

TANNENBAUM, ALLAN
182 Duane St.
New York, NY 10013
Telephone: 212-431-9797
Fax: 212-431-9796
MAILING ADDRESS:
322 8th Ave.
New York, NY 10001
AFFILIATIONS:
ASMP
PRINCIPAL SUBJECTS:
Journalism
News
Editorial
Travel
Marine
PUBLICATIONS:
Time
Newsweek
Life
Stern
U.S. News
Vanity Fair
New York Magazine

TANNER, PETER
3862 West 33 Ave.
Telephone: 604-667-1602
PUBLICATIONS:
Sports
Family

TARCHALA, JOHN
4549 Dickman Rd.
Battle Creek, MI 49015
Telephone: 616-968-0044
Fax: 616-968-8899
AFFILIATIONS:
NAVA, PPM
PRINCIPAL SUBJECTS:
Aviation
Food/Diet
General Interest
Business & Industry
Photography
PUBLICATIONS:
1001 Home Ideas Magazine
  Cover
Better Homes & Garden
Black Family
Elias Menus
Archway Nat'l Trade Ads
Annual Reports

General Foods
Kelloggs Boxes
MI Dept. of
  Commerce/Communications
  Group

TARLETON, GARY
P.O. Box 183
Corvallis, OR 97339
Telephone: 503-752-3759
Fax: 617-547-3758
AFFILIATIONS:
ASMP, AIA
PRINCIPAL SUBJECTS:
Editorial
Architecture
Business & Industry
PUBLICATIONS:
Architecture Record
Fine Homebuilding
Newsweek
Builder

TARR, CHARLES J.
418 B Street, Fourth Floor
Santa Rosa, CA 95401
Telephone: 707-546-5858
AFFILIATIONS:
ASMP
PRINCIPAL SUBJECTS:
Animals
Editorial
Foreign
General Interest
Men's Interest
Photography
Physical Fitness
Travel

TATE, TED
23945 Mercantile Rd.
Cleveland, OH 44122
Telephone: 216-360-8283
MAILING ADDRESS:
TATE PHOTOGRAPHY
  STUDIOS
Cleveland, OH 44122
AFFILIATIONS:
CGA,CCB,BBB,PP of A,ASMP
PRINCIPAL SUBJECTS:
Fashion

TATEM, MIKE
6256 S. Albion Way
Littleton, CO 80121
Telephone: 303-770-6080
MAILING ADDRESS:
MIKE TATEM,
  PHOTOGRAPHIC
Littleton, CO 80121

AFFILIATIONS:
PPA, ASMP
PRINCIPAL SUBJECTS:
Advertising
Fashion
Business & Industry
Journalism
Photography
PUBLICATIONS:
TV
Holiday
Living
The Bride
Vogue
Flash Photography
House Beautiful
Architectural Forum
U. S. Camera
Modern Photography
Radio & T.V. Mirror
Harper's Bazaar
Magnavox
Motorola
American Photographer
Photo Tech Topics
Photo/Techniques

TAXEL, BARNEY
4614 Prospect Ave.
Cleveland, OH 44103
Telephone: 216-431-2400
Fax: 216-431-6922
AFFILIATIONS:
ASMP
PRINCIPAL SUBJECTS:
Advertising
Architecture
Business & Industry
Computer Technology
Ecology
Editorial
Education
Electronics
Health
Human Relations
Journalism
Marketing
Medical
Nature
Personalities
Photography
Psychology
Religion
Sales
Senior Citizens
The Arts
Travel
Urban Affairs
Women's Interest
World Affairs
Youth

PUBLICATIONS:
The New York Times
The New York Times Magazine
Natural Health
Independent Business
Governing
The Wall Street Journal
Millimeter
Avenues
The Plain Dealer Magazine

TAYLOR, CURTICE
29 E. 22 Social Trends.
New York, NY 10010
Telephone: 212-473-6886
Fax: 212-477-1190
AFFILIATIONS:
ASMP
PRINCIPAL SUBJECTS:
Home & Garden
Travel
PUBLICATIONS:
House Beautiful
Elle Decor
Vogue
Decorating & Remodeling
Interior Design
House & Garden

TAYLOR, RANDY G.
International News Service
555 N.E. 34th St., #1502
Miami, FL 33137
Telephone: 305-573-5200
AFFILIATIONS:
ASMP
PRINCIPAL SUBJECTS:
Advertising
Business & Industry
Editorial
Electronics
Entertainment
Foreign
General Interest
Human Interest
Journalism
Movie Reviews
News
Personalities
Photography
Travel
World Affairs
PUBLICATIONS:
Time
Newsweek
People
Us
Life
Traveler

Forbes
Business Week
National Geographic

TEGARDEN, SHANE
  PHOTOGRAPHY
Tegarden, Shane Photography
310 OE St.
Kihei, HI 96753
Telephone: 808-874-0100
Fax: 808-874-8722
AFFILIATIONS:
ASMP, PPA
PRINCIPAL SUBJECTS:
Photography

TENIN, BARRY
111 Hills Point Rd.
Westport, CT 06880
Telephone: 203-226-9396
MAILING ADDRESS:
P.O. Box 2660
Westport, CT 06880
AFFILIATIONS:
ASMP
PRINCIPAL SUBJECTS:
Advertising
Editorial
Automotive
Photography
Sports
Ecology
Entertainment
Health
Journalism
Marine
Personalities
Travel
PUBLICATIONS:
Time
Sports Illustrated
People
National Geographic
Business Week
Car & Driver
Fortune
Yachting

TESADA, DAVID X.
12036 W. Brandt Pl.
Littleton, CO 80127
Telephone: 303-979-0171
Fax: 303-979-0171
AFFILIATIONS:
ASMP
PRINCIPAL SUBJECTS:
Advertising
Agriculture
Architecture
Business & Industry
Computer Technology

Editorial
Journalism
Marketing
Medical
Nature
Photography
Sales
Travel
PUBLICATIONS:
Corporate Showcase
Modern Maturity
Info World
Prevention
Time

THATCHER, CHARLES R.
7007 Pasadena Ave.
Dallas, TX 75214
Telephone: 214-634-9444
Fax: 214-634-9495
AFFILIATIONS:
ASMP
PRINCIPAL SUBJECTS:
Advertising
Editorial
Video
PUBLICATIONS:
Fortune
Forbes
Business Week
Premier
New York Times
Inc.
London Observer
Der Spiegel

THIGPEN, ALEXANDER G.
2105 Vivian Dr.
Mobile, AL 36693
Telephone: 205-666-2851
Fax: 205-666-2852
MAILING ADDRESS:
THIGPEN PHOTOGRAPHY
P.O. Box 9242
Mobile, AL 36691
AFFILIATIONS:
ASMP, IMPA
PRINCIPAL SUBJECTS:
Architecture
Aviation
Marine
PUBLICATIONS:
Architectural Record
Colliers
Sports Afield
Natl. Geo.
Time
Newsweek Magazine (1992)
Sports Illustrated

THILL, NANCY
780 South Federal Street
Chicago, IL 60605
Telephone: 312-939-7770
AFFILIATIONS:
ASMP, APAC
PRINCIPAL SUBJECTS:
Advertising
Architecture
Computer Technology
Marketing
The Arts
Travel
Women's Interest
Computer Technology
PUBLICATIONS:
Newsweek
National Equirer
American Health
National Geographic

THOMAS, CLARK
235 Lauderdale Rd.
Nashville, TN 37205
Telephone: 615-269-7700
AFFILIATIONS:
ASMP
PRINCIPAL SUBJECTS:
Editorial
Business & Industry
PUBLICATIONS:
People Magazine
Country Music Magazine
CBS Records Album Covers
Journal of Country Music
U.S. News & World Report
American Airlines Magazine
Venture
Parents Magazine

THOMPSON, MICHAEL S.
1980 Monroe St.
Eugene, OR 97405
Telephone: 503-485-0805
AFFILIATIONS:
ASMP
PRINCIPAL SUBJECTS:
Advertising
Agriculture
Editorial
Family
Foreign
Home & Garden
Nature
Travel
PUBLICATIONS:
Sunset Magazine
Horticulture Magazine
Life Magazine
Agricultural Research

Organic Gardening
American Horticulturist
Better Homes & Gardens

TINKER, LESTER
426 County Road 223
Durango, CO 81301
Telephone: 303-247-2132
MAILING ADDRESS:
LESTER TINKER
AFFILIATIONS:
API
PRINCIPAL SUBJECTS:
Agriculture
Nature
PUBLICATIONS:
Pentecostal Evangol
Directions Magazine
Frontier Times
Old West
Hartford Agent
Arizona Highways
Grit
Ideals
Country
Farm & Ranch Living
War Cry

TOLBERT, BRIAN R.
911 State St.
Lancaster, PA 17603
Telephone: 717-393-0918
Fax: 717-393-1560
MAILING ADDRESS:
BRT PHOTO
  ILLUSTRATIONS, INC.
Lancaster, PA 17603
Telephone: 717-569-7733
AFFILIATIONS:
PPA, ASMP, LCC
PRINCIPAL SUBJECTS:
Advertising
Architecture
General Interest
Business & Industry
Photography
Food/Diet
Social Trends
PUBLICATIONS:
Food Management
Time
Newsweek
New Yorker
Readers Digest
Wall St. Journal
American Home
Sunday N.Y. Times
House & Garden
Forbes
Early American Life
Computer - Decision Magazine

Sylvia Porter's Money
  Magazine
Architectural Digest
Organic Gardening
Popular Science

TORREZ, BOB
1329 Voltaire Dr.
Riverside, CA 92506
Telephone: 909-280-8455
Fax: 909-780-4757
AFFILIATIONS:
ASMP, NPPA, PPA
PRINCIPAL SUBJECTS:
Advertising
Automotive
Ecology
Editorial
Fashion
Human Interest
Human Relations
Journalism
Marine
Men's Interest
Nature
News
Photography
Sports
Travel
Women's Interest
Youth
PUBLICATIONS:
Sport
Sports Ilustrated
Surfer
Time
Runners World
Orange Coast
Petersons Pro-Football-Pro
  Basketball

TOTO , JOE
Joe Toto Inc.
17 East 64th Street, 3rd Flr.
New York, NY 10021
Telephone: 212-628-4824
Fax: 212-628-5562
PRINCIPAL SUBJECTS:
Advertising
Animals
Editorial
Family
Humor
Youth

TOUCHTON, KEN
1100 NE 28th Terrace
Pompano Beach, FL 33062
Telephone: 305-785-0104
AFFILIATIONS:
ASMP

PRINCIPAL SUBJECTS:
Journalism
PUBLICATIONS:
Street Gangs of America
Religion in America
America's Cup 92

TRENKA, BUD
Trenka, Bud Photographics
960 Hope Street, #1-E
Stamford, CT 06907
Telephone: 203-323-7506
AFFILIATIONS:
ASMP, SCC
PRINCIPAL SUBJECTS:
Advertising
Architecture
Aviation
Business & Industry
Editorial
Education
Home & Garden
Journalism
Media
Medical
Men's Interest
Personalities
Photography
Sports
Travel
Urban Affairs
PUBLICATIONS:
Corporate Finance
Unique Homes
Stamford Advocate
Wilton Journal
Junior League Magazine

TREYBIG, CYNTHIA
3737 Hughes Drive
Kingsport, TN 37660
Telephone: 615-349-4218
AFFILIATIONS:
ASMP
PRINCIPAL SUBJECTS:
Nature
Animals
Ecology
Architecture
Agriculture
Travel
Sports
PUBLICATIONS:
El Cameo Leader News
Kingsport Time News
Running Journal

TROXELL, W. H.
Box 610
Flagstaff, AZ 86002
Telephone: 602-526-3806

AFFILIATIONS:
ASMP
PRINCIPAL SUBJECTS:
General Interest
News
Travel
Advertising
Geography
PUBLICATIONS:
Sunset
Sea & Pacific
Trade Journals
Ariz. Hiways

TRUSLOW, B.
855 Islington St.
Portsmouth, NH 03801
Telephone: 603-436-4600
Fax: 603-430-9102
AFFILIATIONS:
ASMP
PRINCIPAL SUBJECTS:
Business & Industry
Advertising
Photography
Personalities
PUBLICATIONS:
New England Monthly
New England Living

TUCKER, HOWARD
1616 St. Clair
Cleveland, OH 44114
Telephone: 216-696-4616
Fax: 216-696-4620
PRINCIPAL SUBJECTS:
Architecture
Aviation
Business & Industry

TUCKER, MORT
1616 St. Clair Ave.
Cleveland, OH 44114
Telephone: 216-696-4616
PRINCIPAL SUBJECTS:
Architecture
Advertising
Aviation
Business & Industry

TURNER, PETE
P.O. Box 203
Wainslott, NY 11975
Telephone: 516-537-2434
AFFILIATIONS:
ASMP
PRINCIPAL SUBJECTS:
The Arts
Fashion
Amusements
Travel

PUBLICATIONS:
Foto (Stockholm)
Foto (Germany)
Photo (Italy)
Photo (Paris)
Photo World (USA)
Modern Photography Annual
   (USA)
Time Life Photography (USA)
Communication Arts (USA)
Photo World (Penthouse)
   (USA)
Zoom (France)
Photographie (Germany)
Mainliner Magazine (USA)
Photographer's Forum (USA)
Foto Magazine (Germany)
Il Fotografo (Italy)
Omni (USA)
Studio Photography (USA)
Today's Photographer (USA)
American Photographer (USA)
Camera Magazine
   (Great Britain)
Nikon World Annual (Japan)

ULMER, DAVID
669 Castle Cliff Rd.
Ballwin, MO 63021
Telephone: 314-394-1686
AFFILIATIONS:
ASMP
PRINCIPAL SUBJECTS:
Advertising
Agriculture
Editorial
Nature
Travel
PUBLICATIONS:
European Travel & Life
Audubon
Natural History
St. Louis Commerce
Sierra
Canoe

UNIPHOTO PICTURE
   AGENCY
3307 M St. N.W.
Washington, DC 20007
Telephone: 800-345-0546
Fax: 202-338-5578
MAILING ADDRESS:
UNIPHOTO, INC.
3205 Grace St., NW
Washington, DC 20007
AFFILIATIONS:
NPPA
PRINCIPAL SUBJECTS:
Computer Technology
Ecology

Electronics
Entertainment
Government
Health
History
Media
Senior Citizens
Medical
News
Personalities
Social Trends
PUBLICATIONS:
Nations Business
U. S. News World Report
U. S. Air/Amtrak Travel
   Brochures
USA Today
Business Week
(On) Cable Magazine
Modern Maturity
Washington Trade Association
   Publications
Science '85

UPITIS, ALVIS
620 Morgan Ave. S.
Minneapolis, MN 55405
Telephone: 612-374-9375
AFFILIATIONS:
ASMP
PRINCIPAL SUBJECTS:
Advertising
Agriculture
Architecture
Automotive
Editorial
Health
Journalism
Medical
Travel

URBINA, WALT
1113 E. Carson St.
Pittsburgh, PA 15203
Telephone: 412-481-9650
AFFILIATIONS:
ASMP
PRINCIPAL SUBJECTS:
Advertising
Computer Technology
Family
Health
Photography
Physical Fitness
Travel
PUBLICATIONS:
Time
Vanity Fair
PGH Magazine

URSILLO, CATHERINE
1040 Park Ave.
New York, NY 10028
Telephone: 212-722-9297
Fax: 212-860-7527
PRINCIPAL SUBJECTS:
Travel
Journalism
Business & Industry
PUBLICATIONS:
Diversions
N.Y. Times; Travel & Leisure
N.Y. Times Magazine

VAN DE VEN, MARY
949 Prospect St.
Honolulu, HI 96822
Telephone: 808-536-7731
Fax: 808-545-2031
AFFILIATIONS:
ASMP
PRINCIPAL SUBJECTS:
Advertising
Marine
Aviation
Nature
PUBLICATIONS:
Hawaii Magazine
Smithsonian Air & Space
N.Y. Times
Range Finder Magazine

VAN RIPER, FRANK A.
Goodman/Van Riper
   Photography
3502 Quesada St. Newsweek
Washington, DC 20015
Telephone: 202-362-8103
Fax: 202-362-1898
AFFILIATIONS:
ADM, SNF, ASMP
PRINCIPAL SUBJECTS:
Book Reviews
Journalism
Photography
The Arts
PUBLICATIONS:
New York Daily News
Rolling Stone
New Republic
Nieman Reports
Saturday Evening Post
Washington Post

VANCE, DAVID
150 Nw 164 St.
Miami, FL 33169
Telephone: 305-354-2083
Fax: 305-354-2085
AFFILIATIONS:
ASMP, APA

PRINCIPAL SUBJECTS:
Fashion
Personalities
PUBLICATIONS:
Workbook
Single Image

VANCE, JIM
3321 Lake Trail
Metairie, LA 70003
Telephone: 504-888-9132
AFFILIATIONS:
ASMP, PPLA
PRINCIPAL SUBJECTS:
Advertising
Fashion
Food/Diet
Human Relations
PUBLICATIONS:
Times Picayune
Chef's Magazine

VANDER SCHUIT
   STUDIO INC.
Vander Schuit Studio Inc.
751 Turquoise St.
San Diego, CA 92104
Telephone: 619-539-7337
Fax: 619-539-2081
AFFILIATIONS:
ASMP, APA
PRINCIPAL SUBJECTS:
Advertising
Architecture
Business & Industry
Computer Technology
Fashion
Food/Diet
Home & Garden
Personalities
Photography
Physical Fitness
Travel
PUBLICATIONS:
Better Homes & Gardens
Metropolitan Home
Country Home
House & Garden
Home Magazine
San Diego Magazine

VANMARTER, ROBERT
1209 Alstott Drive South
Howell, MI 48843
Telephone: 517-546-1923
AFFILIATIONS:
ASMP
PRINCIPAL SUBJECTS:
Photography
Nature
Advertising

VARNEY, FRANK
612 Washington St.
Denver, CO 80203
Telephone: 303-830-0644
PRINCIPAL SUBJECTS:
Human Interest
PUBLICATIONS:
Glamour
Ladies Home Journal

VARTOOGIAN, JACK
262 W. 107th St., #6-A
New York, NY 10025
Telephone: 212-663-1341
Fax: 212-865-4229
AFFILIATIONS:
ASMP
PRINCIPAL SUBJECTS:
Editorial
Entertainment
The Arts
Travel
PUBLICATIONS:
New York Times
Time
Newsweek
People
Entertainment Weekly
New York Magazine
Dance
Rolling Stone

VAUGHN, GREG
2960 Alder St.
Eugene, OR 97405
Telephone: 503-485-8597
Fax: 503-343-2681
AFFILIATIONS:
ASMP
PRINCIPAL SUBJECTS:
Ecology
Editorial
Geography
Nature
Photography
Science
Sports
Travel
PUBLICATIONS:
National Geographic
Travel & Leisure
Sierra
Natural History
National Wildlife
Ranger Rick
Islands
U.S. News & World Report

VEGTER, BRIAN S.
1431 Gilbert Ave.
Downers Grove, IL 60515-4514

Telephone: 708-852-2267
AFFILIATIONS:
ASMP
PRINCIPAL SUBJECTS:
Fashion
Sports
Video
PUBLICATIONS:
The Loupe
Contact Sheet

VENDITTI, JAMES VINCENT
950 Broadway
Bedford, OH 44146
Telephone: 216-232-7575
MAILING ADDRESS:
JAMES V. VENDITTI
Cleveland, OH 44146
Telephone: 216-232-1044
AFFILIATIONS:
PPA, PPO, EPIC, RI
PRINCIPAL SUBJECTS:
General Interest
Computer Technology
Electronics
Sports
The Arts
PUBLICATIONS:
The Professional Photographer
Cleveland Press
Cleveland Plain Dealer
Bedford Times Register
The Rotarian Magazine
   (International)
The Purchasing Magazine
Studio Light
Range Finder

VOLPE, ANTHONY
Route 9w, P.O. Box 598
Marlboro, NY 12542
Telephone: 914-236-4034
AFFILIATIONS:
PPA,WPI,HVPPSNY
PRINCIPAL SUBJECTS:
Nature
Photography

WACHTER, JERRY
1410 Bare Hills Ave.
Baltimore, MD 21209
Telephone: 410-466-3866
AFFILIATIONS:
ASMP
PRINCIPAL SUBJECTS:
Advertising
Journalism
Sports
Travel
Entertainment

PUBLICATIONS:
Sports Illustrated
Sport
Business Week
Modern Maturity
Medical Economics

WADDELL, ROBERT M.
4150 St. Clair Ave.
Studio City, CA 91604
Telephone: 818-980-0383
Fax: 818-980-0383
AFFILIATIONS:
ASMP, APA
PRINCIPAL SUBJECTS:
Advertising
Architecture
Automotive
Aviation
Business & Industry
Ecology
Editorial
Entertainment
Fashion
Home & Garden
Human Interest
Journalism
Marine
Movie Reviews
Photography
Sports
The Arts
Travel
Video
PUBLICATIONS:
L.A. Times Magazine
Stern
Home
Der Spiegal
Vogue

WADE, HARRY
4216 Webster St.
Oakland, CA 94609
Telephone: 510-652-1595
AFFILIATIONS:
ASMP
PRINCIPAL SUBJECTS:
Architecture
The Arts
Photography
Fashion
PUBLICATIONS:
Life

WADE, ROGER
P.O. Box 1130
Condon, MT 59826
Telephone: 406-754-2793
Fax: 406-754-2793

AFFILIATIONS:
ASMP
PRINCIPAL SUBJECTS:
Advertising
Architecture
Editorial
Nature
Photography
PUBLICATIONS:
Log Home Living
Log Home Guide
Whitefish Magazine
Timber Frame Annual
Glacier Country Travel Guide

WAGGONER, MIKE
Photography
118 Omao St.
Kailua, HI 96734
Telephone: 808-263-3646
Fax: 808-263-3646
MAILING ADDRESS:
Mike Waggoner Photography
P.O. Box 849
Kailua, HI 96734
PRINCIPAL SUBJECTS:
Advertising
Business & Industry
Sports
Travel
PUBLICATIONS:
Surfer Magazine
Aloha Magazine
Action Sports Retailer
Surfer Magazine
Aloha Magazine
Action Sports Retailer

WAGNER, ANDREW A.
Wagner, Andrew A.
   Photography
P.O. Box 176
Sewickley, PA 15143
Telephone: 412-741-1118
Fax: 412-741-8815
AFFILIATIONS:
ASMP, GPCVB
PRINCIPAL SUBJECTS:
Advertising
Animals
Architecture
Automotive
Aviation
Business & Industry
Ecology
Editorial
Entertainment
General Interest
History
Hobbies
Home & Garden

Human Interest
Journalism
Marine
Marketing
Media
Men's Interest
Nature
Personalities
Photography
Physical Fitness
Science
Social Trends
Sports
The Arts
Travel
World Affairs
Youth
PUBLICATIONS:
Profiles
Sky
New York Times
Pittsburgh Magazine

WAKEFIELD'S OF KANSAS
 CITY, INC.
Wakefield's of Kansas City, Inc.
804 West 63rd Street
Kansas City, MO 64113
Telephone: 816-523-5995
AFFILIATIONS:
ASMP
PRINCIPAL SUBJECTS:
Advertising
Family
Marketing
Personalities
Photography
PUBLICATIONS:
Computer Age
People
Midwest Motorist
Saturday Evening Post

WALKER, HARRY M.
6828 Cape Lisburne
Anchorage, AK 99504
Telephone: 907-338-7288
Fax: 907-338-7288
AFFILIATIONS:
ASMP
PRINCIPAL SUBJECTS:
Animals
Business & Industry
Editorial
Human Interest
Nature
Travel
PUBLICATIONS:
Discover
Alaska
Alaska Geographic

Pacific Northwest
Minerals Today
Americana
Guidepost
Backpacker

WALKER, JESSIE
241 Fairview Road
Glencoe, IL 60022
Telephone: 708-835-0522
AFFILIATIONS:
ASMP, WICI
PRINCIPAL SUBJECTS:
Architecture
Editorial
Home & Garden
PUBLICATIONS:
Country Living
Good Housekeeping
House Beautiful
Decorating/Remodeling
Home
Better Homes & Garden
Country Living Gardner
BH & G Kitchen & Bath Ideas

WALLEN, JONATHAN
41 Lewis Parkway
Yonkers, NY 10705
Telephone: 914-476-8674
Fax: 914-476-8677
AFFILIATIONS:
ASMP
PRINCIPAL SUBJECTS:
Travel
Nature
Editorial
Architecture
Business & Industry
History
PUBLICATIONS:
Colonial Homes
National Geographic Traveller
Woman's Day
Antiques

WALTER, BILL
104 S. Francisca
Redondo Beach, CA 90277
Telephone: 310-542-8850
AFFILIATIONS:
PPA, CPP
PRINCIPAL SUBJECTS:
Photography
PUBLICATIONS:
American Survival Guide
Shooting Sportsman
South Bay Magazine

WAPINSKI, DAVID
476 E. South Temple, #139
Salt Lake City, UT 84111
Telephone: 801-355-3932
Fax: 801-355-3932
AFFILIATIONS:
ASMP
PRINCIPAL SUBJECTS:
Advertising
Agriculture
Amusements
Animals
Architecture
Automotive
Aviation
Business & Industry
Computer Technology
Ecology
Editorial
Education
Electronics
Entertainment
Family
Fashion
Food/Diet
Foreign
General Interest
Geography
Government
Health
History
Hobbies
Home & Garden
Human Interest
Human Relations
Humor
Journalism
Management
Marine
Marketing
Media
Medical
Men's Interest
Military
Motivation
Nature
News
Personal Finance
Personalities
Philosophy
Photography
Physical Fitness
Psychology
Religion
Sales
Science
Senior Citizens
Social Trends
Sports
The Arts
Travel

Urban Affairs
Video
Women's Interest
World Affairs
Youth

WARD, JERRY
1537 S. Carrollton Ave.
New Orleans, LA 70118
Telephone: 504-861-1112
Fax: 504-865-5621
AFFILIATIONS:
ASMP, CASE
PRINCIPAL SUBJECTS:
Advertising
Architecture
Editorial
Education
Entertainment
General Interest
Marketing
Media
News
Photography
Sports
PUBLICATIONS:
Sports Illustrated
The Sporting News
The Washington Post
Chicago Tribune

WARREN, CAM
P.O. Box 10588
Reno, NV 89510
Telephone: 702-746-2121
Fax: 702-746-1850
AFFILIATIONS:
ASMP, MPG
PRINCIPAL SUBJECTS:
Automotive
Travel
PUBLICATIONS:
Newsweek International
Road & Track
Car & Driver
Automobile Year

WARTELL, BOB
20 Frasco Rd.
Santa Fe, NM 87505
Telephone: 505-986-1543
Fax: 505-988-3609
AFFILIATIONS:
PPA, ASMD
PRINCIPAL SUBJECTS:
Photography
Architecture
Sports
Advertising

WASHNIK, ANDY
Washnik, Andy Studio
145 Woodland Ave.
Westwood, NJ 07675
Telephone: 201-664-0441
Fax: 201-664-6464
AFFILIATIONS:
ASMP, APA
PRINCIPAL SUBJECTS:
Advertising
Photography
PUBLICATIONS:
American Showcase

WATERSUN, DAVID
Watersun Photography
1295 South Kihei Road, #2002
Kihei Maui, HI 96753
Telephone: 808-879-3318
Fax: 808-879-3318
AFFILIATIONS:
ASMP, PPA
PRINCIPAL SUBJECTS:
Advertising
Agriculture
Architecture
Business & Industry
Ecology
Editorial
Family
Fashion
Food/Diet
Health
Home & Garden
Human Interest
Human Relations
Marine
Media
Nature
Personalities
Physical Fitness
Senior Citizens
Sports
The Arts
Travel
Youth

WEAKS, BILL S.
502 S. Broadway
Plainview, TX 79072
Telephone: 806-296-0828
AFFILIATIONS:
PP of A, ASP
PRINCIPAL SUBJECTS:
Agriculture
Aviation
General Interest
Photography
PUBLICATIONS:
Progressive Farmer
Farmer Stockman

WEAVER, MARTHA
319 Ash
Lockhart, TX 78644
Telephone: 512-398-7571
AFFILIATIONS:
PPA
PRINCIPAL SUBJECTS:
Advertising
Photography

WECKLER, CHAD
210 East 63 Street 10
New York, NY 10021
Telephone: 212-355-1135
PRINCIPAL SUBJECTS:
Fashion
Business & Industry
Photography
Advertising
PUBLICATIONS:
Interview
Woman's Day
Fortune
Business Week
American Vogue

WEDLAKE, JIM
750 Jossman Rd.
Ortonville, MI 48462
Telephone: 313-627-2711
AFFILIATIONS:
ASMP
PRINCIPAL SUBJECTS:
Automotive
Photography
Travel
PUBLICATIONS:
U.S. News & World Report
Business Week
Time
Action Track

WEIDLEIN, PETER
19 Vanderbilt Road
W Hartford, CT 06119
Telephone: 203-231-9009
Fax: 203-231-9128
PRINCIPAL SUBJECTS:
Architecture
Advertising
PUBLICATIONS:
Business Week
Photo Design
Single Image Vol. 1-9
Workbook
NY Gold, Vol. 1+2

WEIL, KAREN
41 Octavia, #10
San Francisco, CA 94102
Telephone: 415-564-4933

PRINCIPAL SUBJECTS:
Entertainment
Fashion
Media
PUBLICATIONS:
American Music Press
Fad Magazine
Sin Magazine
Independent Biker
Bam Magazine

WEINTRAUB, DAVID
1728 Union St., Suite 105
San Francisco, CA 94123
Telephone: 415-931-7776
Fax: 415-931-7776
AFFILIATIONS:
ASMP
PRINCIPAL SUBJECTS:
Business & Industry
Journalism
Nature
Travel
PUBLICATIONS:
Audubon
Smithsonian
Entrepreneur
ABA Journal
Associated Press
New York Times
Sierra
Newsweek

WELLS, DAVID H.
23 Kuhn Road
Layton, NJ 07851
Telephone: 201-948-0609
Fax: 201-948-0609
AFFILIATIONS:
ASMP, NPPA
PRINCIPAL SUBJECTS:
Editorial
Human Interest
Human Relations
Journalism
Photography
PUBLICATIONS:
New York Times
Philadelphia Inquirer
L.A. Times
National Geographic
U.S.A. Today
Time Magazine
Life Magazine
Newsweek

WELSH, STEVE
1191 Grove St.
Boise, ID 83702
Telephone: 208-336-5541
Fax: 208-336-5579

AFFILIATIONS:
ASMP
PRINCIPAL SUBJECTS:
Advertising
Architecture
Business & Industry
Computer Technology
Photography
PUBLICATIONS:
Entrepeneur
Business Week
Lady's Home Journal
Reader's Digest
Texaco Magazine
Boise Cascade A.R.
Chevroy Magazine

WERNER, PERRY
259 Continental Avenue
River Edge, NJ 07661
Telephone: 201-967-7306
PRINCIPAL SUBJECTS:
Journalism
News
Travel
Business & Industry
Editorial
PUBLICATIONS:
N.Y. Times
Forbes
Financial World
Business Week
American Lawyer

WESTERGAARD, FRED
FM 9 (South) Box 148
Waskom, TX 75692
Telephone: 903-687-2630
AFFILIATIONS:
ASMP
PRINCIPAL SUBJECTS:
Family
Home & Garden
Personalities
Senior Citizens
Sports
PUBLICATIONS:
Reader's Digest
Horse & Rider
Horseman
Shreveport Magazine
Natural Food & Farming
Organic Gardening
Shreveport Journal

WESTHEIMER, BILL
167 Spring St., 3w
New York, NY 10012
Telephone: 212-431-6360
Fax: 212-431-5496

PRINCIPAL SUBJECTS:
Business & Industry
Editorial
Advertising

WEYDIG, KATHY
Weydig, Kathy Photography
P.O. Box 3058
Fairfield, CT 06430
Telephone: 203-333-3483
Fax: 203-926-8974
AFFILIATIONS:
ASMP
PRINCIPAL SUBJECTS:
Medical
Marine
Travel

WHEELER, NIK
7444 Woodrow Wilson Drive
Los Angeles, CA 90046
Telephone: 310-850-0234
Fax: 213-850-5721
AFFILIATIONS:
ASMP, SATW
PRINCIPAL SUBJECTS:
Editorial
Geography
Journalism
Travel
Business & Industry
PUBLICATIONS:
National Geographic
Geo
Life
Time
Newsweek
Stern
Bunte
Paris Match
People
Intl. Wildlife
Travel & Leisure
Signature
Travel/Holiday
Island
Gourmet

WHELESS, ROB
3039 Amwiler Rd., #114
Atlanta, GA 30360
Telephone: 404-729-1066
Fax: 404-729-1163
AFFILIATIONS:
ASMP
PRINCIPAL SUBJECTS:
Advertising
Architecture
Nature
Photography

PUBLICATIONS:
Wall St. Journal
Newsweek
Architectural Digest
Byte
Professional Builder
Security Magazine
Menus Today
Intech

WHIPPLE III, GEORGE C.
5 Tudor City Place, Studio 325
New York, NY 10017
Telephone: 212-219-0202
Fax: 212-949-6263
AFFILIATIONS:
ASMP
PRINCIPAL SUBJECTS:
Fashion
Social Trends
Personalities
PUBLICATIONS:
The New York Times Magazine
Playboy
Harpers Bazaar

WHITAKER, GREG
Whitaker, Greg Photography
P.O. Box 1693
Nashville, IN 47448
Telephone: 812-988-8808
Fax: 812-988-8808
AFFILIATIONS:
ASMP
PRINCIPAL SUBJECTS:
Advertising
Agriculture
Entertainment
Foreign
Health
Home & Garden
Human Interest
Human Relations
Medical
Men's Interest
Nature
Photography
Sports
The Arts
Travel
Women's Interest
World Affairs
Youth
PUBLICATIONS:
Inc. Magazine
Musician Magazine
Black Enterprise Magazine
IB Magazine

WHITE, GEORGE
Location Photography
2125 N.E. 81st Street
Seattle, WA 98115
Telephone: 206-525-1862
Fax: 206-525-1862
AFFILIATIONS:
ASMP
PRINCIPAL SUBJECTS:
Architecture
Aviation
Business & Industry
Editorial
Family
General Interest
Health
Human Interest
Human Relations
Marine
Marketing
Medical
Men's Interest
Nature
Photography
Religion
Travel
Women's Interest
Youth
PUBLICATIONS:
Forbes Magazine
Glamour Magazine
Parent Magazine
Special Report Magazine
Construction Data Magazine
Pacific N.W. Magazine
Chevion USA Odyssey
   Magazine

WHITE-FALCON, REGINA E.
Winter Gardens,
   P.O. Box 545932
Surfside, FL 33154
Telephone: 305-865-1982
AFFILIATIONS:
ASMP
PRINCIPAL SUBJECTS:
Education
Foreign
Marine
Media
Personalities
Psychology
The Arts
Travel
Women's Interest

WHITENTON, CARY
9918 McCullough Aveneue
San Antonio, TX 78216
Telephone: 210-341-9404

AFFILIATIONS:
ASMP
PRINCIPAL SUBJECTS:
Advertising
Agriculture
Architecture
Fashion
Food/Diet
Nature
Travel
PUBLICATIONS:
Business Week
Texas Monthly
Time
Newsweek

WHITMAN, ALAN
P.O. Box 6466
Mobile, AL 36660
Telephone: 205-460-0400
Fax: 205-344-8586
AFFILIATIONS:
ASMP
PRINCIPAL SUBJECTS:
Editorial
Photography
Travel
Education
Religion
Entertainment
Business & Industry

WHITMIRE, KENNETH L.
8 N. 8th Ave.
Yakima, WA 98902
Telephone: 509-248-6700
Fax: 509-575-3080
AFFILIATIONS:
PPA, PPW
PRINCIPAL SUBJECTS:
Agriculture
Editorial
Amusements
Journalism
Nature
Marine
Travel
Aviation
PUBLICATIONS:
Nat. Geographic
Washington Post
Sports Illustrated
The Good Fruitgrower

WHITMORE, KEN
P.O. Box 49373,
   1038 N. Kenter
Los Angeles, CA 90049
Telephone: 310-472-4337
MAILING ADDRESS:
P.O. Box 49373

Los Angeles, CA 90049
AFFILIATIONS:
ASMP
PRINCIPAL SUBJECTS:
Business & Industry
Entertainment
Editorial
PUBLICATIONS:
Dole Food Company Annual
  Report
T.V. Guide
Time
Readers Digest
Entertainment Weekly
Fortune
Family Circle

WIEN JEFFREY
29 W. 38th St.
New York, NY 10018
Telephone: 212-354-8024
Fax: 212-354-8025
PRINCIPAL SUBJECTS:
Advertising
Amusements

WIEN, STEVEN
2739 West 79 Street, #16
Miami, FL 33016
Telephone: 305-828-7400
Fax: 305-828-6419
AFFILIATIONS:
ASMP
PRINCIPAL SUBJECTS:
Photography
PUBLICATIONS:
Jewelers Showcase
Harpers Bazaar
Duty-Free
Vogue
Bloomingdales Catalogue

WILLIAMS III, ZANE
101 S. Franklin St.
Madison, WI 53703
Telephone: 608-256-5776
AFFILIATIONS:
ASMP
PRINCIPAL SUBJECTS:
Editorial
Travel
Nature
The Arts
Nature
PUBLICATIONS:
Travel & Leisure
Americana
People
Wisconsin Trails
Winsconsin

WILLIAMS, HAL
P.O. Box 10436
Aspen, CO 81612
Telephone: 303-963-3912
Fax: 305-925-8949
AFFILIATIONS:
ASMP
PRINCIPAL SUBJECTS:
Advertising
Automotive
Editorial
Entertainment
Family
Humor
Sports
Travel
PUBLICATIONS:
Snow Country
Travel & Leisure
Air Destinations
Bicycling

WILLIAMS, JAY S.
Box 694
Kimberton, PA 19442
Telephone: 215-983-3025
Fax: 215-983-3026
MAILING ADDRESS:
JAY S. WILLIAMS
Kimberton, PA 19442
AFFILIATIONS:
ASMP, PP of A
PRINCIPAL SUBJECTS:
Advertising
Architecture
PUBLICATIONS:
Trade Publications
Corporate Publications

WILLIAMS, RON STUDIO
Williams, Ron Studio
105-A Space Park Dr.
Nashville, TN 37211
Telephone: 615-331-2500
PRINCIPAL SUBJECTS:
Advertising
Fashion

WILLIG, WILLIAM J.
1511 Glenwood Ave.
Fort Wayne, IN 46805
Telephone: 219-483-0188
PRINCIPAL SUBJECTS:
Architecture

WILLIS, CLIFF
9740 Mueck Terr.
St. Louis, MO 63119
Telephone: 314-968-2068
AFFILIATIONS:
ASMP

PRINCIPAL SUBJECTS:
Animals
Business & Industry
Computer Technology
Editorial
Human Interest
Human Relations
Journalism
Photography
Sports
PUBLICATIONS:
Compuserve
Outside
L.A. Times

WILLITS, PAT L.
10889 Wilshire Blvd., #1229
Los Angeles, CA 90024
Telephone: 310-443-6585
AFFILIATIONS:
ASMP
PRINCIPAL SUBJECTS:
Advertising
Business & Industry
Entertainment
Journalism
Photography
PUBLICATIONS:
Occidental Petroleum Annual
  Reports
The News Circle Magazine

WILSON, BURTON
703 W. 32nd Street
Austin, TX 78705
Telephone: 512-453-8341
AFFILIATIONS:
ASMP
PRINCIPAL SUBJECTS:
Entertainment
Architecture

WILSON, DOUG M.
10133 N.E. 113th Pl.
Kirkland, WA 98033
Telephone: 206-822-8604
Fax: 206-823-4907
AFFILIATIONS:
ASMP
PRINCIPAL SUBJECTS:
Travel
Business & Industry
Agriculture

WILSON, JAMES F.
P.O. Box 50142
Dallas, TX 75250
Telephone: 214-823-6542
AFFILIATIONS:
ASMP

PRINCIPAL SUBJECTS:
Architecture
PUBLICATIONS:
Interior Design
Architecture
Progressive Architecture
Elle Decor

WINIKER, BARRY M.
173 W. 78th St.
New York, NY 10024
Telephone: 212-580-0841
AFFILIATIONS:
SATW
PRINCIPAL SUBJECTS:
Travel
PUBLICATIONS:
Los Angeles Times
New York Times
Chicago Tribune
Washington Post
Newsday
San Francisco Examiner And
  Chronicle

WINTER, NITA
Winter, Nita Photography
9 Ridge Way
Corte Madera, CA 94925-1337
Telephone: 415-927-4300
Fax: 415-927-3800
AFFILIATIONS:
ASMP, NPPA, ASPP
PRINCIPAL SUBJECTS:
Advertising
Editorial
Education
Family
General Interest
Health
Human Interest
Journalism
Psychology
Senior Citizens
Social Trends
Urban Affairs
Youth
PUBLICATIONS:
Parenting
Sesame Street Magazine
Creative Classroom
Parent's Digest
Ladies Home Journal
Sierra Magazine
Geriatric Consulting
San Francisco Chronicle
San Francisco Examiner
Family Circle Magazine

WIRONEN
180 Linus Allain Ave.
Gardner, MA 01440
Telephone: 508-632-1714
Fax: 508-630-3174
MAILING ADDRESS:
WIRONEN, INC.
Gardner, MA 01440
AFFILIATIONS:
PMA
PRINCIPAL SUBJECTS:
Advertising
Architecture
Home & Garden
PUBLICATIONS:
House Beautiful
Furniture World
Boston Globe
Country Woman
Yankee
Furniture Today
New Yorker

WISSER, BILL
1525 Euclid Ave., #19
Miami Beach, FL 33139
Telephone: 305-672-2448
Fax: 305-672-2448
AFFILIATIONS:
ASMP
PRINCIPAL SUBJECTS:
Advertising
Fashion
Business & Industry
Health
PUBLICATIONS:
People
Family Circle
Women's World
Time
Newsweek
Bell Atlantic Brochures

WITHEY, GARY S.
938-C 5th Ave. West
West Fargo, ND 58078
Telephone: 701-282-0466
AFFILIATIONS:
ASMP
PRINCIPAL SUBJECTS:
Agriculture
Ecology
Geography
Nature
Photography
PUBLICATIONS:
Audubon
U.S. News & World Report
Landscape Architecture
GEO

Reader's Digest
Smithsonian Guide to Hist.
  America
Children's Television Workshop

WOLF, JACK
1546 Powers Run Rd.
Pittsburgh, PA 15238
Telephone: 412-963-7915
PRINCIPAL SUBJECTS:
Advertising
Business & Industry
Editorial

WOLFE, DAN
39 E. Walnut St.
Pasadena, CA 91103
Telephone: 818-584-4000
AFFILIATIONS:
PMA
PRINCIPAL SUBJECTS:
Advertising
Editorial
Food/Diet
General Interest
PUBLICATIONS:
Bon Appetit Magazine
Better Homes & Gardens
Redbook Magazine
Time Magazine
Playboy Magazine
Newsweek Magazine

WOLLIN, WILLIAM
P.O. Box 510011
Melbourne Beach, FL 32951
Telephone: 407-727-8483
Fax: 407-727-8433
AFFILIATIONS:
PPA,SEOPA,OWCA,WOLA,AGL
OW
PRINCIPAL SUBJECTS:
Architecture
Travel
Nature
Home & Garden
Human Interest
Human Relations
Photography
PUBLICATIONS:
Time
Life
Field & Stream
Outdoor Life
Sports Afield
Arch. Record
Arch. Forum
House & Home
Holiday
Saturday Evening Post

WOLMAN, BARON
735 Shiloh Canyon
Santa Rosa, CA 95403
Telephone: 707-545-1221
Fax: 707-545-0909
MAILING ADDRESS:
BARON WOLMAN PHOTO
P.O. Box 6699
Santa Rosa, CA 95406
AFFILIATIONS:
ASMP
PRINCIPAL SUBJECTS:
Business & Industry
Travel
Human Interest
Sports
Entertainment
PUBLICATIONS:
Money
Fortune
Vogue
Playboy
Time
Smithsonian
Newsweek
Rolling Stone
Conde' Nast Traveler
Life
Smithsonian Air & Space
Travel & Leisure

WOLVOVITZ, ETHEL
305 Ocean Pkwy.
Brooklyn, NY 11218
Telephone: 718-851-3162
AFFILIATIONS:
ASMP
PRINCIPAL SUBJECTS:
Human Interest
Family
PUBLICATIONS:
Lears
American Health
Special Report
Coraiere Della Sera (Italy)

WOOD, ANTHONY B.
Wood, Anthony B.
  Photography
213 Fairview Terrace
Belmont Hills, PA 19004
Telephone: 215-667-8779
AFFILIATIONS:
ASMP
PRINCIPAL SUBJECTS:
Advertising
Business & Industry
Education
Family
General Interest
Health

Human Relations
Marketing
Medical
Science
Senior Citizens
PUBLICATIONS:
Photo Review
10,000 Eyes

WOOD, RICHARD
169 O'Brien Hwy.
Cambridge, MA 02141
Telephone: 617-661-6856
Fax: 617-738-1575
AFFILIATIONS:
ASMP
PRINCIPAL SUBJECTS:
Architecture
Business & Industry
Ecology
Education
Foreign
Journalism
Medical
Nature
PUBLICATIONS:
Time
Omni
Fortune
Manchete
Newsweek
Cosmopolitan
Technology Illustrated
Business Week
High Technology
Harvard Alumni
Forbes
Discover
Electronic Business
Personal Computing
Horticulture
Electronics Purchasing
Working Woman
Digital Review
US

WOOD, TED
P.O. Box 2908,
  86 E. Hansen Ave.
Jackson, WY 83001
Telephone: 307-733-7916
Fax: 307-733-7916
AFFILIATIONS:
ASMP
PRINCIPAL SUBJECTS:
Advertising
Editorial
Nature
Sports
Travel

PUBLICATIONS:
Newsweek
Vanity Fair
Time
Outside
Smithsonian
Sports Illustrated
National Wildlife

WOODALLEN
  PHOTOGRAPHERS
3505 Louisiana St.
Houston, TX 77002
Telephone: 713-526-1747
Fax: 713-526-1750
AFFILIATIONS:
ASMP, PPA
PRINCIPAL SUBJECTS:
Architecture
Aviation
General Interest
Amusements
PUBLICATIONS:
Houston Monthly
Houston City
Oil & Gas Journal

WOOLFE, RAYMOND G.
Hawk's Nest Farm,
  Rte. 1 Box 1020
Troy, VA 22974
Telephone: 804-295-0606
Fax: 804-979-4681
MAILING ADDRESS:
R. WOOLFE/CONCEPTS
  PUBL/PHOTOS
P.O. Box 5561
Charlottesvle, VA 22905
AFFILIATIONS:
ASMP, NG PEI
PRINCIPAL SUBJECTS:
Advertising
Fashion
Sports
Travel
Agriculture
Animals
Architecture
Automotive
Book Reviews
Marine
Journalism
Family
Photography
The Arts
PUBLICATIONS:
Equus
Blood-Horse
Thoroughbred Record
Spur
Pacemaker (U.K.)

Daily Racing Form
Travel & Leisure
Practical Horseman
Town & Country
Commonwealth Magazine (Va.)
Southern Living
The Chronicle Of The Horse
Sports Illustrated
Military History
Field & Stream
Time
DuPont (Co.) Magazine
Sporting Clays Magazine
New Dominion (Va.) Magazine
POLO Magazine
METRO - TURF (A Daily
  Racing Form Publication)
Boating Magazine

WORD, TROY
78 Fifth Ave.
New York, NY 10011
Telephone: 212-366-5442
Fax: 212-366-5645
AFFILIATIONS:
ASMP
PRINCIPAL SUBJECTS:
Fashion
Photography
PUBLICATIONS:
Glamour
Mademoiselle
Mirabella
British Elle
Italian Elle
Spanish Vogue
American Photo
Details

WRIGHT, TIMOTHY
P.O. Box 8296
Richmond, VA 23226
Telephone: 804-272-1439
Fax: 804-330-7390
AFFILIATIONS:
ASMP
PRINCIPAL SUBJECTS:
Photography
PUBLICATIONS:
New York Times
Business Week
Associated Press
Wildlife Conservation Magazine
National Wildlife Magazine
Washington Post
Time

WRISLEY, BARD
P.O. Box 1021
Dahlonega, GA 30533
Telephone: 404-525-2928

Fax: 404-864-6622
AFFILIATIONS:
ASMP
PRINCIPAL SUBJECTS:
Advertising
Business & Industry
Editorial
Foreign
Philosophy
PUBLICATIONS:
Business Week
Forbes
Newsweek
Home Mechanics
Southern Accents
Georgia Trend
Business Atlanta
Atlanta Magazine

WRISTEN, DONALD F.
2025 Levee St.
Dallas, TX 75207
Telephone: 214-748-5317
AFFILIATIONS:
ASMP
PRINCIPAL SUBJECTS:
Advertising
Architecture
Automotive
Business & Industry
Computer Technology
Editorial
Fashion
Foreign
General Interest
Home & Garden
Human Interest
Human Relations
Humor
Nature
News
Personalities
Photography
Psychology
Religion
Sports
Travel
Women's Interest
PUBLICATIONS:
Architectural Digest
Veranda
Entrepreneur
Texas Highways
Photo District News
D Magazine
Dallas Morning News
Texas Society CPA

WU, NORBERT
165 Ivy Drive
Orinda, CA 94563

Telephone: 510-376-8418
Fax: 510-376-8864
AFFILIATIONS:
ASMP, ASPP
PRINCIPAL SUBJECTS:
Marine
Ecology
Animals
Health
PUBLICATIONS:
National Geographic
Audubon
Harper's
International Wildlife
Natural History
New York Times Magazine
Omni
Outside
Smithsonian

WYMAN, IRA
14 Crane Ave.
Peabody, MA 01960
Telephone: 508-535-2880
AFFILIATIONS:
ASMP, NPPA, BPPA
PRINCIPAL SUBJECTS:
Editorial
General Interest
Journalism
PUBLICATIONS:
Newsweek
Time
N.Y. Times
Business Week
Us Magazine
People
Discover
Money Magazine
Fortune Magazine

WYMAN, JAKE
P.O. Box M85
Hoboken, NJ 07030
Telephone: 201-420-8462
AFFILIATIONS:
ASMP, NPPA
PRINCIPAL SUBJECTS:
Advertising
Business & Industry
PUBLICATIONS:
Fortune
Business Week
Travel & Leisure
GQ
Rolling Stone
New England Monthly

WYNER, ISAIAH
70 Greene Street- #4
New York, NY 10012

Telephone: 212-226-4845
PRINCIPAL SUBJECTS:
Editorial
Architecture

WYROSTOK, CHUCK
Clay Route, Box 89-C
Spencer, WV 25276
Telephone: 304-927-2978
Fax: 304-927-3650
PRINCIPAL SUBJECTS:
Editorial
PUBLICATIONS:
Newsday
New York Daily News
Appalachia Magazine
Unity Magazine
Goldenseal-West Virginia State
    Magazine

YAMASHITA, MICHAEL S.
25 Roxiticus Road
Mendham, NJ 07945
Telephone: 201-543-4473
Fax: 201-543-4469
AFFILIATIONS:
ASMP, NPPA
PRINCIPAL SUBJECTS:
Agriculture
Aviation
Editorial
Foreign
Geography
History
Journalism
Photography
Social Trends
The Arts
Travel
PUBLICATIONS:
National Geographic
GEO
National Geographic Traveler
Travel & Leisure

YARBROUGH, BOB
29351 Summerset Dr.
Sun City, CA 92586
Telephone: 909-672-2492
MAILING ADDRESS:
BOB B. YARBROUGH
    PHOTOGRAPHERS
89351 Summerset Dr.
Sun City, CA 92586
PRINCIPAL SUBJECTS:
Travel
Nature
History
Animals
Entertainment
Marine

Amusements
Human Interest
Home & Garden
Architecture
PUBLICATIONS:
Tours & Resorts Magazine
Cruise Travel Magazine
San Diego Convention &
    Visitors Bureau
TravelAge Publications Sales
    Guides
Good Reading
American Heritage
Far East Traveler Magazine
Caribbean Travel & Life
Airfair Magazine
Leisure World
Miscellaneous Promotional
    Brochures
Interval's Traveler Magazine
San Diego Magazine
Tour & Travel News
Baja Times
Ogilvy & Mather - Promotional
    Brochure
Sheraton Corp. - Promotional
    Brochure
The Pointe Resorts -
    Promotional Brochure
Business Tokyo
Coastal Advertising
Purple Pansy - Framed Photos
White Sheet
Adventure Road
Monterey Herald
Holidays With Style
Italtours
Taste of the Town
Docufile
Insights

YARBROUGH, CARL
811 Mapleton Ave.
Boulder, CO 80304
Telephone: 303-444-1500
Fax: 303-444-6279
AFFILIATIONS:
ASMP
PRINCIPAL SUBJECTS:
Advertising
Editorial
Sports
Travel
PUBLICATIONS:
Sports Illustrated
Womens Sports & Fitness
American Photo
Outdoor & Travel Photography
Ski
Bicycling Guide

YAWORSKI, DON
600 White Oak Lane
Kansas City, MO 64116
Telephone: 816-454-4011
Fax: 816-454-4011
AFFILIATIONS:
ASMP, PPA
PRINCIPAL SUBJECTS:
Advertising
Architecture
PUBLICATIONS:
Successful Farming
Industrial Photography
Time

YONKER, THOMAS
    PHOTOGRAPHY
Yonker, Thomas Photography
P.O. Box 2001
Grand Rapids, MI 49501
Telephone: 616-897-5493
Fax: 616-459-4299
AFFILIATIONS:
ASMP
PRINCIPAL SUBJECTS:
Advertising
Business & Industry
Editorial
Foreign
Human Interest
Human Relations
Journalism
Marketing
Media
News
Social Trends
Travel
PUBLICATIONS:
Dow Jones
Avon
Upjohn
Michcon
Contact

YOUNG, DONALD
166 E. 61st St., Apt. 3 - C
New York, NY 10021
Telephone: 212-593-0010
MAILING ADDRESS:
DONALD YOUNG
New York, NY 10021
AFFILIATIONS:
ASPP
PRINCIPAL SUBJECTS:
Nature
Animals
Travel
PUBLICATIONS:
Reader's Digest Books
Popular Photography
The Great American Desert

Backpacking Journal
Adventure Travel
MD
American Southwest, The
Journeys in Science
Amtrak Express
National Parks
E: The Environmental
    Magazine
Sierra Annual Report

YOUNG-WOLFF, DAVID
2621 28th St., 3
Santa Monica, CA 90405
Telephone: 310-452-1054
PRINCIPAL SUBJECTS:
Business & Industry

ZAHNER, DAVID
145 West 78th
New York City, NY 10024
Telephone: 212-362-9829
AFFILIATIONS:
ASMP
PRINCIPAL SUBJECTS:
Advertising
Entertainment
Fashion
PUBLICATIONS:
Vogue
'W'
Interview
Town & Country

ZAKE, BRUCE
633 Huron Rd.
Cleveland, OH 44115
Telephone: 216-694-3686
AFFILIATIONS:
ASMP
PRINCIPAL SUBJECTS:
Editorial
Advertising
Sports
PUBLICATIONS:
Fortune
Time
Newsweek

ZAVODNY, STEVEN
2456 S. Clayton
Denver, CO 80210
Telephone: 303-756-1344
AFFILIATIONS:
ASMP
PRINCIPAL SUBJECTS:
Business & Industry
Editorial
Nature
PUBLICATIONS:
Denver Business Journal

Colorado Business Magazine
Westwood
Rocky Mountain News

ZILLIOUX, JOHN
9127 Southwest 96 Avenue
Miami, FL 33176
Telephone: 305-270-1270
AFFILIATIONS:
ASMP
PRINCIPAL SUBJECTS:
Nature
Animals
Business & Industry

ZINTECK, DONALD S.
1045 Elmwood Avenue
Buffalo, NY 14222
Telephone: 716-885-7112
Fax: 716-885-7113
AFFILIATIONS:
ASMP
PRINCIPAL SUBJECTS:
Photography

Section 7
INDEX OF PROFESSIONAL SPEAKERS BY SUBJECT

ADVERTISING

AMBROSIUS, RICHARD, CEO
BEALS, GARY
BERMAN, HELEN
BILKER, HARVEY L.
BRUN, DONALD J.
BYERS, MARY
CARSON, TERRENCE J.
DALY, JOHN J.
DEAN, HARVEY D.
DOORNICK, ROBERT
DORSEY, CALVIN
FARRELL, ROBERT E.
FINGEROTE, PAUL S.
FINK, MARTHA
FLETCHER, JERRY L.
FLICKINGER, BONNIE G.
GALLAGHER, BILL
 'GUERRILLA', PH.D.
GIOIA, JOYCE L.
GOOZE, MITCHELL
GORBY, JOHN C.
HALTER, 'DIAMOND' JIM
HAMEROFF, EUGENE J.
HASKELL, JOHN S.
HELITZER, MELVIN
KAINE, JACK W.
KENNEDY, DAN S.
KNOLL, HERBERT E. JR.
KOJM, KURT BARNABY
KRAMER, ROBERT G.
LERMAN, KENNETH B.
MATTIMORE, BRYAN W.
MCNAIR, J. FRANK
MILLER, ANNE
MILLER, MADELYN
MYERS, GERRY
PALMQUIST, RICHARD
PETERSEN, KRISTELLE
PISCOPO, MARIA
REYNOLDS, PATRICK
ROOS, JAMES P.
ROSS, MARILYN
ROSS, TOM
ROUSH, SHERYL L.
SABAH, JOE
SABAH, JUDY
SEDACCA, ROSALIND
SELWYN, PADI
SHERMAN, RALPH

SUMMEY, MIKE
SWANSON, DAVID
TEPPER, BRUCE
UKER, DON
WALTERS, DOTTIE
WEST, KEN
WHALIN, GEORGE
WHITE, BARTON C.
WILLIAMS, JOHN R., LCDR
WILSON, JUSTIN
YAMBERT, CONSTANCE
 DEAN
YOUNG, WOODY

AGRICULTURE

ATKINS, CHANDLER PH.D.
BIRK, RON
BLAKELY, DON & MIKE
COATES, MARTY
CUROE, JOHN
CUTLER, MARY LOUISE
 (DTM)
DEL CASTILLO, JANET
EMMERICH, ROXANNE
EVANS, ROBERT MAYER
HARRISON, GENE
JOHNSON, HUB, PH.D.
KAINE, JACK W.
LAMB, WILLIAM CARROLL
LEICHTY, MARLENE A.
MAAS, GARY
MCKAIN, SCOTT
METZGER, RICK L.
MINNICK, DALEH
O'CONNOR, JERRY
REEDER, RANDALL, C.
REESE, MONTE
ROTRAMEL, RICK
SCHREINER, CAROL D.
SMITH, ROY L.
TROUT, SHIRLEY

AMUSEMENTS

ADAMS, KENNETH R.
BURNS, PAT
DOORNICK, ROBERT
GRANGER, SUSAN
MAAS, GARY
O'CONNOR, JERRY

RICHARDS, RAMONA

ANIMALS

ANFINSON, STACIE A.
BENNIE, MARK
DEL CASTILLO, JANET
DILLON, ILENE L.
FLICKINGER, BONNIE G.
LEGATT, HADASSA PH.D.
MORSCHER, BETSY, PH.D.
RICHARDS, RAMONA
SOARES, DR. CECLIA J.

ARCHITECTURE

ALFORD, RON
DVORAK, ROBERT REGIS
FLICKINGER, BONNIE G.
KNACKSTEDT, MARY V.
LISK, THOM
OXLEY, ROBERT R.
PETERSEN, KRISTELLE
PISCOPO, MARIA
ROBERTS, JANET M.
SCHOEMAN, MARILYN

AUTOMOTIVE

BILLINGS-HARRIS, LENDRA
CHARBONNEAU, JOS. J.
DECKER, DON B.
HOLCOMB, JANE, PH.D.
KAINE, JACK W.
LEONE, RAY
LOSYK, BOB
LOUDEN, STEPHEN H.
MARTH, ROALD D.
MCKINLEY, MICHAEL P.
 (CPAE)
MYERS, GERRY
ROACH-KILCUP, DONNA L.
SHAPIRO, DON
SHELTON, LEE
THOMAS, ELAINE J.
WALLACE, KEN
WILSON, JERRY R.

AVIATION

ASHLEY, JAMES
BLAKELY, DON & MIKE
CUMMINGS, BETH A.
GUTRIDGE, DON FOSTER
HARRAL, CHAS
HOOD, RALPH
JENSEN, JAY R.
KAINE, JACK W.
LAND, PETER A.
MAAS, GARY
POYNTER, DAN
PUTNAM, HOWARD D.
ROSSITER, SHERRY KNIGHT
SIRESS, JIM
SUCKOW, BOB
WILLIAMS, JIM, CAPT.
WILLIAMS, JOHN R., LCDR

BUSINESS & INDUSTRY

ABBOTT, DR. LINDA M.C.
ABELSON, HAL
ABRAMS-MINTZER, BARBARA
ALBERT, WILLIAM C.
ALCORN, PAT
ALESANDRINI, KATHRYN,
 PH.D.
ALLEN, ELIZABETH 'BETSY'
ASHLEY, JAMES
ASIJA, S. PAL
ATKINS, CHANDLER PH.D.
BAILEY, ROBERT L.
BAKER, LARRY D., DR.
BAKER, LEN
BALL, JIM
BARNHILL, ROBERT E. III
BASSETT, LAWRENCE
 (LARRY) C. (CMC)
BEAUBIEN, ELAINE
 ESTERVIG
BENNIE, MARK
BERG, DR. DEANNA
BERNS, FRED
BETHEL, SHEILA MURRAY
BIECH, ELAINE
BLACK, JERRY
BLAKELY, DON & MIKE
BOCK, WALLY
BOLTON, DENNY

BOOHER, DIANNA
BORDEAUX, DARLENE B.
BOWMAN, FOREST
BOWMAN, ROBIN
BOYCE, BETTY L.
  ENTERPRISES
BOYLE, VIRGINIA, PHD.
BROWN, KATHY &
  ASSOCIATES
BROWN, MARLENE B., M.S.
BUDD, NANCY
BURG, BOB
BURGE, JOAN M.
BURRUS, DANIEL
CALHOON, JOE
CARLINO, ANDY
CAROLAN, SHIRLEY M.
CARSON, GAYLE, DR.
CARTER, ARNOLD 'NICK'
CASE, BOB
CHINN, C. EARL
CHRISTOPHER, SYLVIA
COLOMBO, GEORGE W.
CONDON, GWEN
CONLON, PETER J., JR.
CONNOR, TIM
CONSTANT, RUTH L.
CORCORAN, DENISE M
CORNWELL, ART
CRAWFORD, SALLY L.
CROWSON, GATHA ROMINE
CRUMPTON, DEBRA J.
DACEY, JUDITH E., CPA
DAVIDSON, JEFF
  (MBA) (CMC)
DAVIS, RONALD L.
DAWSON, ROGER
  PRODUCTIONS, INC.
DEAL, LUISA
DELVES, JOHN A.
DEROSE, ROLAND
DOMITRECZ, STEVE
DONADIO, PATRICK J.
DORSEY, IVORY
DUNN, MARIANNE
DUPONT, M. KAY
DVORAK, ROBERT REGIS
DWYER, DAWN
EAGLE, MARK
EINSTEIN ALIVE
EMMERICH, ROXANNE
ENEN, JACK
EVANS, ROBERT MAYER
FIELDER GROUP, THE
FIORE, JAMES
FISHER, DONNA
FLETCHER, TANA
FOUNTAIN, ELEANOR A.
FRANK, MIKE, (CPAE)
FRIED, N. ELIZABETH, PH.D
FRIEDMAN, SIDNEY A.

FRIPP, PATRICIA
FRITZ, DR. BOB
GABRIELSEN, RON (CCM)
GAGE, RANDY
GALLAGHER, BILL
  'GUERRILLA', PH.D.
GALLAGHER, CATHY L.
GARRETT, A. MILTON
GEBHARDT, MARK D.
GEE, BOBBIE
GERAGHTY, BARBARA
GERMANN, DOUGLAS D.
GILLESPIE, JEFFREY A.
GIOIA, JOYCE L.
GITTERMAN, HEIDI
GOLBERT, GLORIA
GORDEN, DAVE
GREENE-DAVIDSON, SUSAN
GREIF, ED
GRIESSMAN, GENE, PH.D.
GROSS, T. SCOTT
GUTRIDGE, DON FOSTER
HALVERSON, DEAN
HARRIS, MELVA J.
HATHAWAY, PATTI
HAWKINS, KATHLEEN
HAWLEY, CASEY FITTS
HELVEY, EDWARD P., JR.
HEMPHILL, BARBARA
HENNING, MIKE
HERBSTER, DOUGLAS DR.
HERMAN, ROGER E., (CMC)
HILL, JOANNE K.
HIXON, GEORGE G.
HODGES, WILLIAM N.
HOLCOMB, JANE, PH.D.
HOOSER, PHILLIP VAN
HORVATH, DENNIS D.
HORVATH, TERRI
HUMPHRIES, ANN
  CHADWELL
HUNT, D. TRINIDAD
HUNTER, WILLIAM L.
HUTTER, V. ROSAN
INGRAM, ROBERT
ISLER, MARK
ISRAELOV, RHODA
JABLONSKI, JOSEPH R.
JENSEN, JAY R.
JOHNSON, HUB, PH.D.
JONES, DEWITT
JUTKINS, RAY W.
KAHN, SANFORD
KAINE, JACK W.
KAPLAN, STEVE
KAYE, STEVE
KEELER, JOHN A.
KENNEDY, DAN S.
KLEIN, RUTH L.
KLINKENBERG, HILDA
KOJM, KURT BARNABY

KOLTIN, ALLAN DAVID, CPA
KRATOWICZ, M. J.
KUTSKO, JIM
LAFRENIERE, DONNA
LAJOYCE CHATWELL
  LAWTON
LAND, PETER A.
LARSEN, LARRY L.
LATTA, MARIE B. M.ED.
LAUGHLIN, LEWIS E.
LAWSON, KAREN
LEACH, LYNNE C.
LEAPTROTT, NAN S.
LEFKOWITZ, HAL
LEONE, RAY
LERMAN, KENNETH B.
LETOURNEAU, TOM
LINKLETTER, ART
LISK, THOM
LITTLE, ERLENE
LLOYD, JOAN
LONG, BRIAN G.
LOSSY, RELLA
LOSYK, BOB
LOVELESS, KATHY
LOWE, PETER
LUBOTSKY, TERRY
LYTLE, TOBI L.
MANNING, MARILYN, PH.D.
MARINO, MIKE JR. 'IN
  PERSON'
MARKEL, GERALDINE PH.D.
MARTH, ROALD D.
MATTIMORE, BRYAN W.
MAYNARD, MICHAEL
MCARDLE, KEVIN J.
MCARTHUR, GILBERT B.
MCCOY, DORIS L., PH.D.
MCCUISTION, DENNIS
MCDONALD, THOMAS, PH.D.
MCKAIN, SCOTT
MCKINLEY, MICHAEL P.
  (CPAE)
MCLAUGHLIN, KENNETH
MCNAIR, J. FRANK
MEISENHEIMER, JIM
MERCHANT, RONALD
MILLER, ANNE
  PROMOTIONS, INC.
MILLER, VALERIE J. S.
MINER-WARGO, NANETTE
MINNINGER, JOAN
MONTEFUSCO, JR.,
  MICHAEL T.
MOORE, JAMES F.
MOORE, LAURIE
MORAN, KEVIN M.
MORGAN, REBECCA
MORRISEY, GEORGE L.
MORRISON, ANN M.
MORRISON, JAMES N.

MORROW, PEGGY &
  ASSOCIATES
MORTELL, ART
MOSER, MILTON J.
MYERS, JANET L.
NABERS, MARY SCOTT
NELSON, SANDRA
NORTON, GEORGE M.
OLSON, HARRY A.
OSMAN, WALI M. PH.D.
OUTLAW, KEMILEE K.
OXLEY, ROBERT R.
PALMEN, RALPH H.
PATTERSON, BILL
PATTISON, POLLY
PENNINGTON, RANDY G.
PETERSEN, GLORIA
PETERSEN, KRISTELLE
PETERSON, THERESA L.
PHILLIPS, RICK
PINKSTAFF, MARLENE
  ARTHUR
PINSKEY, RALEIGH
POLLAR, ODETTE
POSTEN, ROBERT
PRIGAL, KENNETH B.K.
PUTNAM, HOWARD D.
PUTZIER, JOHN
RAEL, RON, CPA
RANDOLPH, ROBERT M.
RASBAND, JUDITH
RAST, EDWARD
REAVES, CHUCK
RECKNER, JERALD
  (JERRY) H.
REED, DAVE
REED, DEBRA J.
REID, T.J.
REZEK, GEOFFREY R.
  (CFPIM) (CPM)
RHODE, JIM
RICHARDSON, DAVID W.
RICHARDSON, DR. ARTHUR
RIDGWAY, JO
RIGSBEE, ED
RINKE, WOLF J., PH.D.
RITSCHER, JIM
ROBINSON, EMMET
ROHLANDER, DAVID
ROSE, ALBERT L.
ROSENBAUM, JERRY, CLU
ROSENBERG, DEANNE
ROSENBERG, RICHARD
ROSS, KENNETH
ROSS, MARILYN
ROSS, TOM
RUDNICKI, BARBARA A.
RUSSELL, RAY L., DR.
RYAN, LYNN
SALINGER, TONY
SASSI, PAULA A.

SAUBY, RON
SCANNELL, EDWARD E.
SCHEESSELE, WILLIAM
SCHENK, GEORGE
SCHMIDT, JOY A.
SCHOEMAN, MARILYN
SCHWARTZ, FRANCIE
SCHWARZ, BARB
SCOTT, BLACKIE
SCOTT, GINI
  GRAHAM, PH.D., J.D.
SEARCY, RHODA M.
SEDACCA, ROSALIND
SELAME, ELINOR
SELWYN, PADI
SEVERIN, THOMAS J.
SHAPIRO, BARRY M.
SHAPIRO, DON
SHEA, CHARLENE
SHELTON, LEE
SHIELDS, LINDA
SHUH, AL & ASSOCIATES
SIEGFRIED, CHARLOTTE
SILVER, SUSAN
SIMS, D. PHILLIP
SMITH, WALTER D.
SNYDER, MARILYN
SORENTINO, PHIL
SPENGLER, CHRISTINE J.
  (CPS/CAM)
SPRINKLE, G. K.
STARK, PETER BARRON
STARKEY, JUDITH A.
STATON, BILL
STAUB, JAMES R.
STEIL, LYMAN K. (MANNY),
  DR. (CPAE)
STEIN, CAROLYN
STEIN, SANDY
STEPHANI, SUSAN
STRIKE, LOUIS N.
SWANSON, DAVID
TAHIR, ELIZABETH
TAYLOR, BRUCE J.
TAYLOR, PAULA R., M.A.
TEPPER, BRUCE
THOMAS, ELAINE J.
THOMPSON, BILLIE
TINGLEY, JUDITH C.
TOOPER, VIRGINIA, ED.D.
TRUAX, PAMELA
TURLA, PETER
TURNER, ROSLYN A.
TUROCK, ART
TURPIN, BEN
TWEED, STEPHEN C.
UHLER, JAY, C.P.C
UHLER, MATTHEW
VASQUEZ, SABINE GROSS
VOTH, ERIC R.
WALLACE, KEN

WALTERS, DOTTIE
WATSON, JEAN
WAYMON, LYNNE
WEISEL, JACQUES
WEISS, ALAN PH.D.
WELLNITZ, CRAIG
WELLS, D. BRENT J.D.
WESNER, ERIC C.
WEST, KEN
WHITE, SOMERS
WIGGLE, PHILIP LAWRENCE
WIKLUND, PATRICIA PH.D.
WILCOX, CHUCK
WILDE, LARRY
WILLIAMS, MIKKI
WILSON, KAREN
WILSON, LARRY
WILSON, STEVE
WOLF, JOHN M. 'JACK' PH.D.
WOOD, BETTY
WOODCOCK, DAVID
WYSS, O'NEILL
YOHO, DAVID
YOUNG, DOUG
YOUNG, WOODY
ZICK, BERNARD HALE
ZINGER, JIM
ZYETZ, ALICE

COMMUNICATIONS

ALESSANDRA, DR. TONY
BALL, PATRICIA
BARON, JUDY KAPLAN
BEAUBIEN, ELAINE
  ESTERVIG
BETHEL, BILL
BLOCH, ANN
BRODY, MARJORIE
BROOKS, EVE
BROWN, TRACY
BRUNER, HELEN L.C.S.W.
BURNELL, IVAN G.
CAMPER, NATALIE K., PH.D.
CARMODY, KATHY
COFFEE, GERALD
DRAKE, CAROL
DUPONT, M. KAY
FIELDER GROUP, THE
FISHER, DONNA
GAULKE, SUE MACK
GEDALIAH, ROBERT
GRANGER, SUSAN
GRANT, CAROL
HABER, DR. MEL
HARLAN, RAY
HAWKINS, KATHLEEN
HELSTEIN, IVY
HILLMAN, RALPH E.
HODGES, WILLIAM N.
JABLONSKI, JOSEPH R.

JACOBS, ANITA I.
JOHNSON, BILL L.
KAY, ANDREA
KELLER, KAY D.
KING, CHRIS
LAMON, DANA
LEACH, LYNNE C.
LEWISON-SINGER, RITA
LOSSY, RELLA
LOWELL TRAINING &
  CONSULTING
MCKENZIE, SAMUEL
MERRITT, CONNIE
METCALF, ED, DR.
MILIOS, RITA
MINER, DAVID LEE
MOWBRAY, CATHERINE
MULLER, DAVE
PATTERSON, BILL
PETERSON, THERESA L.
QUINN, BEVERLY CARLSON
RIDGWAY, JO
RIFENBARY, JAY C.
ROACH, MARY BETH
SABAH, JUDY
SABINE, ELIZABETH
SCOTT, SUSAN
SHULTS, JOHN A.
SJODIN, TERRI
SMITH, CARL T.
STERN, DEBRA
TABERS, JOE
TURLEY, JOYCE
VARGA, MARI PAT
VAUGHAN, SUZANNE
WADE, BOB ED.D.
WALLACE, JOANNE
WILKINS, WALLACE PH.D.
WILSON, KAREN

**COMPUTER
TECHNOLOGY**

ALESANDRINI,
  KATHRYN, PH.D.
ALLEN, GORDIE
ANFINSON, STACIE A.
ASIJA, S. PAL
BARBER, JIM
BLACKMAN, JEFF, J.D.
BOYCE, BETTY L.
  ENTERPRISES
BROWN, MARLENE B., M.S.
BURRUS, DANIEL
COLOMBO, GEORGE W.
DOMITRECZ, STEVE
EAGLE, MARK
EVANS, ROBERT MAYER
FRITZ, DR. BOB
GILLESPIE, JEFFREY A.
GIOIA, JOYCE L.

GOOZE, MITCHELL
HORVATH, DENNIS D.
JJ LAUDERBAUGH
KARTEN, NAOMI
KOLTIN, ALLAN DAVID, CPA
KRATOWICZ, M. J.
MARTH, ROALD D.
MATTIMORE, BRYAN W.
MAYNARD, MICHAEL
MCMAHON, MICHAEL
METCALF, ED, DR.
MONK, ART
MORTELL, ART
PATTISON, POLLY
PEPPER, MICHAEL J.
POSTEN, ROBERT
RADTKE, RICHARD L.
RADTKE, RICHARD, L.
SANDROS, DON
SILVER, SUSAN
SNYDER, MARILYN
SPENGLER, CHRISTINE J.
  (CPS/CAM)
TAILLON, YAHZDI

ECOLOGY

ANFINSON, STACIE A.
CUMMINGS, DR. RITA J.
DEE, EMILY
JABLONSKI, JOSEPH R.
KOJM, KURT BARNABY
LENZ, BOB
LONGFELLOW, LAYNE A.,
  PH.D.
MCCOY, DORIS L., PH.D.
O'CONNOR, JERRY
RADTKE, RICHARD L.
RADTKE, RICHARD, L.
RICHARDS, RAMONA
ROBERTS, JANET M.
SIMONS, EDWARD A.
VARMA, VISH
WILLIAMS, JOHN R., LCDR

EDUCATION

ABBOTT, DR. LINDA M.C.
ACERS, PATSY
ALESANDRINI, KATHRYN,
  PH.D.
ALFORD, RON
ANFINSON, STACIE A.
ARLEQUE, LILLIAN, ED.D.
ASHLEY, JAMES
ATKINS, CHANDLER PH.D.
AUSTIN, EMORY
BELGUM, MERRILYN
BENNETT, LOIS E.,
  M.ED.,M.A.
BENNIE, MARK

BERG, DR. DEANNA
BIRK, RON
BISHOP, VENNA
BISSELL, BEN
BLAKELY, DON & MIKE
BLOCH, ANN
BOOHER, DIANNA
BOWMAN, FOREST
BOYCE, BETTY L.
  ENTERPRISES
BOYLE, VIRGINIA, PHD.
BRACKETT, SHIRLEY
BROWN, KATHY &
  ASSOCIATES
BROWN, LINDEE S.
BROWN, MARLENE B., M.S.
BROWN, RICHARD R.
BRUN, DONALD J.
BURRUS, DANIEL
BUTLER, JENNIFER
CABRERA, JIMMY
CANFIELD, JACK
CARMODY, KATHY
CAROLAN, SHIRLEY M.
CARTER, ARNOLD 'NICK'
CHESTER, ERIC
COEY, NANCY
CORTIS, BRUNO, MD
COUCH, DR. BOB E., PH.D.
CROWSON, GATHA ROMINE
CUMMINGS, DR. RITA J.
DEAL, LUISA
DEE, EMILY
DEMKO, DAVID J.
DEPOYSTER, BOBBY
  R., ED.D
DEROSE, ROLAND
DOCKERY, WALLENE T.
DOORNICK, ROBERT
DUBIN, BURT
DVORAK, ROBERT REGIS
DWYER, DAWN
DYGERT, CHARLES B., PH.D
ECK, ARLENE
EINSTEIN ALIVE
ELIAS, JEFF
EMMERICH, ROXANNE
FIELDER GROUP, THE
FLICKINGER, E. G.
FOTIADES, VALLA D.
FOUNTAIN, ELEANOR A.
FRAGER, STANLEY R. PHD
FRESHOUR, FRANK W.
GABRIELSEN, RON (CCM)
GALLAGHER, CATHY L.
GLICK, BARBARA
GOETZMAN,
  RICHARD K., PH.D.
GOLBERT, GLORIA
GOOD, PERRY
GORDEN, DAVE

GORDON, CONNI
GREEN, LILA
GREENE, IDA
GRIESSMAN, GENE, PH.D.
HADAWAY, GEORGE W.
HARLAN, RAY
HARPER, JEANNE M.
HATHAWAY, PATTI
HATTON, J. DUEY
HAVEY, CAROL V.
HAWKINS, KATHLEEN
HELSTEIN, IVY
HELVEY, EDWARD P., JR.
HENLEY-SMITH, LINDA
HERBSTER, DOUGLAS DR.
HERMAN, JEFF
HEROLD, MORT
HOLCOMB, JANE, PH.D.
HOOPER, DR. DON W.
HUGHES, LADDIE W.
HUNDERTMARK, JERI
HUNT, D. TRINIDAD
HURLEY, CARL E., ED.D.
  (CPAE)
HUTTER, V. ROSAN
ISLER, MARK
JACOBS, ANITA I.
JONES, MARILYN K., DDS
KARPOVICH, MICHAEL S.
KEELAN, JIM
KICK, FRAN
KIENE, ANDREA L.
KLEIN, RUTH L.
KOTZ, STEVE
KRATOWICZ, M. J.
KURZWEG, MARY KAY
LADDIE, W. HUGHES
LAIPPLY, BOB
LEA, DIXIE PH.D.
LEBEAU, CALENE
LEGATT, HADASSA PH.D.
LEMKE, RAYMOND
LENZ, BOB
LEONE, RAY
LEWISON-SINGER, RITA
LINKLETTER, ART
LINQUIST, LUANN
LITTLE, ERLENE
LITTLEFIELD, HENRY M.
LLOYD, JOAN
LOCKRIDGE, ALICE
LOVELESS, KATHY
LUBOTSKY, TERRY
LUCHT, CHARLES
LUETHY, DR. GERRY
LYTLE, TOBI L.
MAINELLA, MARK T.
MANNING, MARILYN, PH.D.
MARKEL, GERALDINE PH.D.
MATTIMORE, BRYAN W.
MCCARTY, DR. HANOCH

MCCORMICK, MS. PATRICIA
MCCOY, DORIS L., PH.D.
MCILVAIN, TED L.
MCLAUGHLIN, KENNETH
MCNAIR, J. FRANK
MCNEIL, MICHAEL R. (BCSW)
MERCHANT, RONALD
METZGER, RICK L.
MEYERS, PAMELA, PH.D.
MILIOS, RITA
MILLER, ANNE
  PROMOTIONS, INC.
MILLER, JOHNNY
MORAN, KEVIN M.
MORRISON, ANN M.
MORSCHER, BETSY, PH.D.
MORTELL, ART
MYERS, JEFFRY W.
NIELSEN, RICK J.
O'CONNOR, JERRY
OUTLAW, KEMILEE K.
PATTERSON, BILL
PELLEY, JIM
PESUT, TIM S.
PETERSON, THERESA L.
POLK, JANE M.
RADDE, PAUL O.
RADTKE, RICHARD L.
RADTKE, RICHARD, L.
RAST, EDWARD
REEDER, RANDALL, C.
RENSTROM, GREGORY
REUM, EARL, DR.
RICHARDS, RAMONA
RICHARDSON, DR. ARTHUR
RISBERG, GREG
ROBERTS, JANET M.
ROBERTS, KATHI
RUSSELL, RAY L., DR.
SASSI, PAULA A.
SCANLON, DERALEE R.D.
SCANNELL, EDWARD E.
SCHOEMAN, MARILYN
SCHREINER, CAROL D.
SCHWAB, PATT, DR.
SEARCY, RHODA M.
SHAPIRO, DON
SHELTON, LEE
SHUH, AL & ASSOCIATES
SIMMS, STEVE
SIMON, BARBARA J.
SIMS, D. PHILLIP
SMITH, CARL T.
SMITH, DIANE ELLINGSON
SNYDER, MARILYN
SOMMER, BOBBE, PH.D.
SPENGLER, CHRISTINE J.
  (CPS/CAM)
STAUB, JAMES R.
STEIL, LYMAN K. (MANNY),
  DR. (CPAE)

STEIN, SANDY
STENNES, BARBARA
STEVENS, SUZANNE H.
STEWART, LAURIE A.
SUTTON, JAMES D., DR.
SUTTON, SUZY
SWANSON, DAVID
SWARTZ, JOHN C.
TANSEY, DR. DAVE
TEPPER, BRUCE
THOMAS, ELAINE J.
THOMPSON, BILLIE
TOOPER, VIRGINIA, ED.D.
TROUT, SHIRLEY
TRUAX, PAMELA
TURLEY, JOYCE
VAUGHAN, SUZANNE
WAGNER, JOHN P.
WALLACE, KEN
WANGBERG, 'DR. LOU'
WARNER, CAROLYN
WEISEL, JACQUES
WEISS, BONNIE
WELLNITZ, CRAIG
WEST, KEN
WIKLUND, PATRICIA PH.D.
WILCOX, CHUCK
WILLIAMSON, JOHN S.
WILSON, LARRY
WOLF, JOHN M. 'JACK' PH.D.
WOODS, RHONDA B.
WYSS, O'NEILL
YOUNG, BILL
ZIMMERMAN, TOM
ZINGER, JIM
ZYETZ, ALICE

ELECTRONICS

GOOZE, MITCHELL
KEELER, JOHN A.
MAYNARD, MICHAEL
WILSON, STEVE

ENTERTAINMENT

ABAGNALE, FRANK W.
ACERS, PATSY
ADAMS, KENNETH R.
ANDERSON, DALE L.
ANFINSON, STACIE A.
BELGUM, MERRILYN
BENNETT, LOIS E.,
  M.ED.,M.A.
BERGER, RUTH
BILKER, HARVEY L.
BLAKELY, DON & MIKE
BOYLE, VIRGINIA, PHD.
BROWN, KATHY &
  ASSOCIATES
BROWN, LINDEE S.

BURNS, KAREN
CARSON, TERRENCE J.
CARTER, ARNOLD 'NICK'
COLLINS, PEGGY
CUROE, JOHN
DE GRAVELLES, ROU
DEAN, BONNIE 'THE MOTION
  COACH'
DEROSE, ROLAND
DOORNICK, ROBERT
DVORAK, ROBERT REGIS
EAGLES, GIL
EASON, W.H.
FIELDER GROUP, THE
FISHER, MARY
FLICKINGER, E. G.
FRIPP, PATRICIA
GARBISCH, WALTER E.
GLICKSTEIN, LEE
GORDON, CONNI
GRANGER, SUSAN
GUTRIDGE, DON FOSTER
HANSON, JERRY
HELITZER, MELVIN
HENLEY-SMITH, LINDA
HENRY, ROBERT H.
HEROLD, MORT
HICKMAN, ANDY L.
HOOD, RALPH
HURLEY, CARL
  E., ED.D. (CPAE)
HYKEN, SHEP A.
HYKEN, SHEP A.
IRVIN, DALE
JAMES, MERLIN R.
JOLLEY, WILLIE 'THE
  INSPIRTAINER'
KARSCHNER, GRAY DON
KILPATRICK, KURT
LAMB, WILLIAM CARROLL
LEE, CLIFFORD M., DR.
LEGATT, HADASSA PH.D.
LEICHTY, MARLENE A.
LINKLETTER, ART
MARINO, MIKE JR. 'IN
  PERSON'
MCKAIN, SCOTT
MENTA, SISTER
  ANGELICA M.
MILLER, ANNE
  PROMOTIONS, INC.
MORTELL, ART
NIELSEN, RICK J.
NIKAM, S. G. 'NIK', MD
  (FACC) (FACP)
O'CONNOR, JERRY
OECHSLI, MATTHEW J.
OSTARO, DHRUV
OUTLAW, KEMILEE K.
PARINELLO, AL
PINSKEY, RALEIGH

POTUCK, MARK W.
RAETHER, EDIE
RICHARDS, RAMONA
ROSS, BOB
SASSI, PAULA A.
SCOTT, BLACKIE
SHELTON, LEE
SHERMAN, RALPH
SHUH, AL & ASSOCIATES
SKOGLUND, ROBERT
SMITH, ROY L.
STACY, GAYLON
THOMAS, DIAN
TOOPER, VIRGINIA, ED.D.
TYRA, STEVE
VELLIOTES, GEORGE
WADE, ALLAN L.
WARD, AUDREY PEELE
WEISS, BONNIE
WELLNITZ, CRAIG
WENOS, GAIL (CPAE)
WHITE, STAN
WILLIAMS, MIKKI
WILSON, JUSTIN
ZIMMERMAN, TOM
ZINGER, JIM

FAMILY

ABAGNALE, FRANK W.
ACERS, PATSY
ALCORN, PAT
ANFINSON, STACIE A.
ARLEQUE, LILLIAN, ED.D.
BAKER, HELEN JOYCE
BALL, DR. ROBERT R.
BASSETT, LAWRENCE
  (LARRY) C. (CMC)
BELGUM, MERRILYN
BENDER, BEV
BENNETT, LOIS E.,
  M.ED.,M.A.
BENNIE, MARK
BISHOP, VENNA
BISSELL, BEN
BLAKELY, DON & MIKE
BORDEAUX, DARLENE B.
BOYD, LORRIE DR.
BRACKETT, SHIRLEY
BRANDAU, KARLA
BRODER, MICHAEL S. PHD
BROWN, KATHY &
  ASSOCIATES
BRUNER, HELEN L.C.S.W.
BUDD, NANCY
BURNELL, IVAN G.
CAMPBELL, SANDRA JONES
CARMODY, KATHY
CARSON, RICHARD D.
CARTER, ARNOLD 'NICK'
COPELAND, GARY R.

COUCH, DR. BOB E., PH.D.
CREEL, JOANNE P.
CROWSON, GATHA ROMINE
CUNNINGHAM, DOYLE
CUROE, JOHN
DEAN, BONNIE 'THE MOTION
  COACH'
DEE, EMILY
DEMKO, DAVID J.
DENNY, JEAN
DEROSE, ROLAND
DILLON, ILENE L.
DRAKE, CAROL
DWYER, DAWN
EGGLESTON, JULIA
EMMETT, RITA
FARRELL, ROBERT E.
FISHER, MARY
FISHER, SANDRA L.
FLICKINGER, E. G.
FORZANO, RICK E.
FRAZEE, LINDA
FRESHOUR, FRANK W.
GLICK, BARBARA
GOLBERT, GLORIA
GOLLIVER, JOY J.
GORDEN, DAVE
GREEN, LILA
HARDY, MARC
HARPER, JEANNE M.
HATHAWAY, PATTI
HAVEY, CAROL V.
HEADLEY, WILLIAM
HELSTEIN, IVY
HENNING, MIKE
HERRON, SANDRA
  WHITACRE
HIGGS, LIZ CURTIS
HILL, JOANNE K.
HUNDERTMARK, JERI
JACKSON, LUAN
JAMES, DIANA L.
JASIM, JANIE
JENSEN, JAY R.
JOHNSON, JENYCE
KARPOVICH, MICHAEL S.
KELLER, KAY D.
KINNARD, MELLY
KURZWEG, MARY KAY
LAIPPLY, BOB
LAIPPLY, SANDY
LEA, DIXIE PH.D.
LEE, CLIFFORD M., DR.
LEICHTY, MARLENE A.
LENZ, BOB
LEWIS-WILLIAMS, MYRA
LINKLETTER, ART
LINQUIST, LUANN
LITTAUER, FLORENCE
LITTAUER, MARITA
LLOYD, HERB J.

LOVERDE, MARY
LUETHY, DR. GERRY
MASUMOTO, PAT
MAYNE, MAVIS
MCCLARY, CLEBE
MCCOY, DORIS L., PH.D.
MCILVAIN, TED L.
MCNEIL, MICHAEL R. (BCSW)
MEEKS, DAVID &
  ASSOCIATES
MERCHANT, RONALD
MILLER, REV. MARILYN K.
MINNINGER, JOAN
MORRISON, JAMES N.
NELSON, SANDRA
NICHOLSON, SHERYL
O'CONNOR, CAROL
O'HARA, CAROL
OUTLAW, KEMILEE K.
PAGE, SUSAN
PENNER, SHEBA
PETTY, DR. CHARLES V.
RADTKE, RICHARD, L.
RAETHER, EDIE
RASBAND, JUDITH
RHOADES, ROGER A.
RICHARDS, RAMONA
ROBERTS, JANET M.
ROLFE, RANDY
SCANLON, DERALEE R.D.
SCHWARTZ, ELAINE
SCOTT, BLACKIE
SCOTT, SUSAN
SEARCY, RHODA M.
SMITH, HAROLD IVAN
SMITH, J. THOMAS
SOARES, DR. CECLIA J.
SOMMER, BOBBE, PH.D.
SPENCER, DUFFY, PH.D.
STEIL, LYMAN K. (MANNY),
  DR. (CPAE)
STEVENS, SUZANNE H.
STEWART, LAURIE A.
SUCKOW, BOB
SUMMER, SHIRLEY
SUTTON, JAMES D., DR.
SWARTZ, JOHN C.
THOMAS, DIAN
THOMPSON, BILLIE
TROUT, SHIRLEY
UHLER, JAY, C.P.C
UHLER, MATTHEW
VAUGHAN, SUZANNE
VERRI, ROSEMARY
WALKER, ANNE
WALLACE, KEN
WAREHAM, GWENDOLYN
WEISBERG, JACOB
WENOS, GAIL (CPAE)
WHARTON, MARCIA M.
WIKLUND, PATRICIA PH.D.

WILHELM, DOROTHY
WOOD, BETTY
ZIMMERMAN, DR. ALAN R.
ZIMMERMAN, TOM

FASHION

BOILEAU & ASSOCIATES
BROWN, KATHY ASSOC
BUTLER, JENNIFER
CHEN, NANCY
DWYER, DAWN
FLICKINGER, BONNIE G.
FOTIADES, VALLA D.
HARDY, BETTY
HUNTTING, SHERRY E.
KAHN, RITA
KING, CHRIS
LITTAUER, MARITA
MEYERS, PAMELA, PH.D.
MORROW, PEGGY &
  ASSOCIATES
PETERSEN, GLORIA
POOSER, DORIS
RASBAND, JUDITH
REID, T.J.
RICHARDS, RAMONA
SCANLON, DERALEE R.D.
SEGEL, RICK
TARTARELLA, KATHY
TYRA, STEVE
WALLACE, JOANNE
WILLIAMS, JOHN R., LCDR

FOOD/DIET

ARTERBURN, STEPHEN
BEAUBIEN, ELAINE
  ESTERVIG
BRECHT, ANN M.
CALMES, MARYLEE
CRACKOWER, SYDNEY, M.D.
CSOLKOVITS, ERNEST A.
CUMMING, CANDY
CUMMINGS, DR. RITA J.
DEAL, SHELDON C.
EPSTEIN-SHEPHERD,
  DR. BEE
FRAZEE, LINDA
GILLARD, JUDY
GRANT, CAROL
GROPPEL, JACK L. PH.D.
JENSEN, JAY R.
JEPPESEN, LYNDA
  FRANCE MBA
JOHNSON, DR. JOYCE
JONES, MARILYN K., DDS
KVITKA, ELAINE
LEA, DIXIE PH.D.
LITTAUER, MARITA
LOCKRIDGE, ALICE

MALAINY, DON
MEYERS, PAMELA, PH.D.
MILLER, ANNE
  PROMOTIONS, INC.
MILLER, MADELYN
MORRIS, WILLIAM C.
MURRAY, JOAN
NEWSOME, PAULA R.
NIENSTEDT, JOHN F.
PICKERING, WAYNE
PODANY, SUE
PROUT, LINDA L., M.S.
PYFER, HOWARD R. M.D.
REYNOLDS, PATRICK
ROLFE, RANDY
RYBACK, DAVID, DR.
SANFORD, JAMES VIKING
SCANLON, DERALEE R.D.
SEARCY, RHODA M.
THOMAS, DIAN
TYRA, STEVE
TYRIAN, CHARLIE
WAREHAM, GWENDOLYN
WILSON, JUSTIN
ZINGER, JIM

GEOGRAPHY

FOSTER, LARRY J.
WARNER, CAROLYN

GOVERNMENT

BENNIE, MARK
BLACKWELL, JOEL
BROWN, MARLENE B., M.S.
CHILDRESS, GENE W.
DALY, JOHN J.
DEROSE, ROLAND
DUNN, MARIANNE
FLICKINGER, E. G.
GABRIELSEN, RON (CCM)
HARRAL, CHAS
HERBSTER, DOUGLAS DR.
HERMAN, ROGER E., (CMC)
HOLCOMB, JANE, PH.D.
HUGHES, LADDIE W.
ISLER, MARK
JABLONSKI, JOSEPH R.
KOJM, KURT BARNABY
LADDIE, W. HUGHES
LAND, PETER A.
LITTAUER, FLORENCE
LITTLEFIELD, HENRY M.
LOVELESS, KATHY
MANNING, MARILYN, PH.D.
MORRISON, ANN M.
NABERS, MARY SCOTT
NIENSTEDT, JOHN F.
OUTLAW, KEMILEE K.
PETERSON, THERESA L.

SIMONS, EDWARD A.
SPRINKLE, G. K.
SUMMEY, MIKE
SWARTZ, JOHN C.
THOMAS, JEFFERY M.
VELLIOTES, GEORGE
WANGBERG, 'DR. LOU'
WEST, KEN
WIENER, VALERIE
WIKLUND, PATRICIA PH.D.

HEALTH

ALFORD, RON
ANDERSON, DALE L.
ARTERBURN, STEPHEN
BAKER, HELEN JOYCE
BARRETT, DIANNE
  E. R.N., M.A.
BASSETT, LAWRENCE
  (LARRY) C. (CMC)
BELGUM, MERRILYN
BERGER, RUTH
BILKER, HARVEY L.
BOYD, LORRIE DR.
BRAHAM, BARBARA J.
BRANDAU, KARLA
BRAVERMAN, TERRY
BRECHT, ANN M.
BRILES, DR. JUDITH
BROWN, KATHY &
  ASSOCIATES
BUDD, NANCY
BUTTS, JIMMIE K.
CALMES, MARYLEE
CAMPBELL, SANDRA JONES
CARMODY, KATHY
CARR, SHARON
CARSON, RICHARD D.
CASE, BOB
CORTIS, BRUNO, MD
CRACKOWER, SYDNEY, M.D.
CUMMING, CANDY
CUMMINGS, DR. RITA J.
CUNNINGHAM, DOYLE
CUROE, JOHN
CUTLER, MARY LOUISE
  (DTM)
DEAL, SHELDON C.
DEE, EMILY
DEROSE, ROLAND
DILLON, ILENE L.
DRAKE, DEBBIE
DRENCH, MEREDITH E. PHD
DVORAK, ROBERT REGIS
DWYER, DAWN
EMMETT, RITA
EPSTEIN-SHEPHERD,
  DR. BEE
FIELDER GROUP, THE
FISHER, MARY

FISHER, SANDRA L.
FLICKINGER, E. G.
FOREMAN, ED
FOSTER, WILLIAM E.
FRAGER, STANLEY R. PHD
FRAZEE, LINDA
FRINGS,
  CHRISTOPHER S., PH.D.
GARGANTA, KATHLEEN T.
GESELL, IZZY
GILLARD, JUDY
GLICK, BARBARA
GLICKSTEIN, LEE
GOLBERT, GLORIA
GOLDMAN, CONNIE
GOLDTRAP, GEORGE
GRANT, CAROL
GREEN, LILA
GROPPEL, JACK L. PH.D.
HAGESETH, CHRISTIAN III
HALPERN, STEVEN
HALVERSON, DEAN
HARMON, SHIRLEY
HARPER, JEANNE M.
HARRAL, CHAS
HENLEY-SMITH, LINDA
HICKMAN, ANDY L.
HIGGS, LIZ CURTIS
HUGHES, LADDIE W.
INGRAM, ROBERT
INTERNATIONAL INSTITUTE
  OF REFLEXOLOGY
JACKSON, LUAN
JENSEN, JAY R.
JEPPESEN, LYNDA
  FRANCE MBA
JOHNSON, DR. JOYCE
JONES, MARILYN K., DDS
KLEIN, ALLEN
KLEINE-KRACHT, ANN E.
KVITKA, ELAINE
LADDIE, W. HUGHES
LAFRENIERE, DONNA
LAND, PETER A.
LATTA, MARIE B. M.ED.
LEBEAU, CALENE
LEICHTY, MARLENE A.
LEVIN, ROGER P.
LINQUIST, LUANN
LITTLE, ERLENE
LLOYD, HERB J.
LOCKRIDGE, ALICE
LONGFELLOW,
  LAYNE A., PH.D.
MACALUSO, SISTER MARY
  CHRISTELLE, RSM, PH.D
MALAINY, DON
MANNING, MARILYN, PH.D.
MCCOY, DORIS L., PH.D.
MCGHEE, PAUL E., PH.D.
MEYER, BILL

MEYERS, PAMELA, PH.D.
MILIOS, RITA
MILLER, ANNE
  PROMOTIONS, INC.
MILLER, REV. MARILYN K.
MORAN, KEVIN M.
MOREL, LIN M.
MORRIS, WILLIAM C.
MORSCHER, BETSY, PH.D.
MYERS, JEFFRY W.
NELSON, DAVID N., P.T.
NEWMAN, RICHARD D.
NEWSOME, PAULA R.
NIKAM, S. G. 'NIK', MD
  (FACC) (FACP)
NORTON, KEN
OBERG, BILL
OLDAK, EMILY
OLESEN, ERIK L.
OUTLAW, KEMILEE K.
PARKER, LARRY R.
PATTON, RICHARD M.
PETSCHULAT, DR. NEUB
PICKERING, WAYNE
PILGRIM, M. SUSAN
PLUMMER, RICHARD E., DR.
PODANY, SUE
POLK, JANE M.
POTUCK, MARK W.
PROUT, LINDA L., M.S.
PYFER, HOWARD R. M.D.
RADDE, PAUL O.
RAETHER, EDIE
RAFINSKI, MARCIA
REYNOLDS, PATRICK
RHOADES, ROGER A.
RHODE, JIM
RICHARDS, RAMONA
RISBERG, GREG
RITCHIE, JAN
ROACH-KILCUP, DONNA L.
ROBERTS, RONALD H. PH.D.
ROLFE, RANDY
ROSS, JO-ANN
RYBACK, DAVID, DR.
SABINE, ELIZABETH
SANDFORD, VIRGINIA A.
SASSI, PAULA A.
SCANLON, DERALEE R.D.
SCHLAMOWITZ, KEVAN, DR.
SCHREINER, CAROL D.
SCHUSTER, DIANE L.
SEARCY, RHODA M.
SIMON, BARBARA J.
SLADE, TOM
SMITH, DIANE ELLINGSON
SMITH, RICHARD Q.
SOARES, DR. CECLIA J.
SOMMER, BOBBE, PH.D.
SPENCER, DUFFY, PH.D.
STEWART, ROD

STILLWAGON, GLENN, DR.
SUCKOW, BOB
SUTTON, JAMES D., DR.
TAYLOR, MEREDITH
TEPLITZ, JERRY V., DR.
TICE, PATRICIA K.
TREJO, WILLIE
TYRIAN, CHARLIE
UDELL, BARBARA A.
ULLMAN, DANA M.P.H.
USELDINGER, RONALD E.
VAUGHAN, SUZANNE
VELLIOTES, GEORGE
WAREHAM, GWENDOLYN
WARZECHA, MARY M.
WATSON, DONNA S.
WATSON, DR. DONNA S.
WERNER, STAN 'THE HAND'
WILKINS, WALLACE PH.D.
WILLIAMS, MIKKI
WILSON, STEVE
WINSLOW, EDWINA
WOLINSKI, KIM
YAMAMOTO, GARY K.
YOUNG, GARY A.
ZARE, NANCY C., DR.
ZIMMERMAN, TOM
ZINGER, JIM

HISTORY

ADAMS, KENNETH R.
ARCHBALD, RALPH (CPAE)
BOWMAN, FOREST
DENNY, JEAN
FLICKINGER, BONNIE G.
GRIESSMAN, GENE, PH.D.
KARSCHNER, GRAY DON
LAUFER, JOSEPH M.
LITTLEFIELD, HENRY M.
SLOTKIN, FRAN S.
SMITH, ROY L.
SPENGLER, CHRISTINE J.
  (CPS/CAM)
SWARTZ, JOHN C.

HOBBIES

CLIFFE, ROGER W.
DEROSE, ROLAND
GORDON, CONNI
LAIPPLY, SANDY
LEICHTY, MARLENE A.
MILLER, MADELYN
REUM, EARL, DR.
THOMAS, DIAN

HOME & GARDEN

BARRETT, DIANNE
  E. R.N., M.A.
BOYD, LORRIE DR.
DILLON, ILENE L.
ELIAS, JEFF
FLICKINGER, BONNIE G.
HOXWORTH, STEVE
KNACKSTEDT, MARY V.
LEICHTY, MARLENE A.
LITTAUER, MARITA
MONJI, MICHAEL A.
O'HARA, CAROL
OXLEY, ROBERT R.
ROBERTS, JANET M.

HUMAN RELATIONS

ABBOTT, DR. LINDA M.C.
ABELSON, HAL
ACERS, PATSY
ACKERMANN, LINDA HOLT
ALBERT, WILLIAM C.
ALESSANDRA, DR. TONY
ALEXANDER, BOB
ALLEN, ELIZABETH 'BETSY'
ANDERSON, KARE
ARCHBALD, RALPH (CPAE)
ARTERBURN, STEPHEN
ASHLEY, JAMES
ATKINS, CHANDLER PH.D.
AUSTIN, EMORY
BAKER, LARRY D., DR.
BAKER, LEN
BALL, DR. ROBERT R.
BALL, PATRICIA
BALZER, ALVIN L.
BARNHILL, ROBERT E. III
BARRON, LAURA
BARROWS, SYDNEY BIDDLE
BASSETT, LAWRENCE
  (LARRY) C. (CMC)
BATES, LARRY
BEARDEN, JIM
BEATTY, MAURA CLELAND
BEAUBIEN, ELAINE
  ESTERVIG
BENNIE, MARK
BERG, DR. DEANNA
BERGER, FRANCINE
BERGER, RUTH
BIECH, ELAINE
BIGGS, DICK
BISHOP, VENNA
BISSELL, BEN
BLAKELY, DON & MIKE
BOLING, DUTCH
BOOHER, DIANNA
BOWMAN, FOREST
BOWMAN, ROBIN

BRACKETT, SHIRLEY
BRILES, DR. JUDITH
BRITTON, TOM
BRODY, MARJORIE
BROWN, KATHY &
  ASSOCIATES
BROWN, MARLENE B., M.S.
BROWN, TRACY
BROWNELL, EILEEN O.
BRUNER, HELEN L.C.S.W.
BUCARO, FRANK C.
BUDD, NANCY
BURG, BOB
BURGE, JOAN M.
BURROUGHS, HENRIETTA J.
BUTLER, JENNIFER
CAMPBELL, SANDRA JONES
CAMPER, NATALIE K., PH.D.
CANFIELD, JACK
CARLE, GILDA PHD
CARMODY, KATHY
CARSON, GAYLE, DR.
CARSON, RICHARD D.
CARTER, ARNOLD 'NICK'
CARUSO, JOSEPH A.
CASE, BOB
CHILDRESS, GENE W.
CHRISTOPHER, SYLVIA
COFFEE, GERALD
CONLEY, JEFF
CONNOR, TIM
CORNYN-SELBY, ALYCE
CORTIS, BRUNO, MD
COUCH, DR. BOB E., PH.D.
CRACKOWER, SYDNEY, M.D.
CRAWFORD, SALLY L.
CREEL, JOANNE P.
CROWSON, GATHA ROMINE
CSOLKOVITS, ERNEST A.
DAVIS, RONALD L.
DAWSON, ROGER
  PRODUCTIONS, INC.
DEAL, LUISA
DEAN, BONNIE 'THE MOTION
  COACH'
DEL CASTILLO, JANET
DEROSE, ROLAND
DILLON, ILENE L.
DIRESTA, DIANE
DOHERTY, BILL
DONADIO, PATRICK J.
DORSEY, IVORY
DRAKE, CAROL
DRENCH, MEREDITH E. PHD
DUNN, GLORIA
DUNN, MARIANNE
DUPONT, M. KAY
DWYER, DAWN
ELVES, CONRAD
EMMERICH, ROXANNE

EPSTEIN-SHEPHERD, DR. BEE
EVERDING, MARIA
FIELDER GROUP, THE
FIORE, NEIL A., PH.D.
FISHER, MARY
FLICKINGER, E. G.
FOREMAN, ED
FOSTER, WILLIAM E.
FOTIADES, VALLA D.
FOUNTAIN, ELEANOR A.
FOX, JOAN G.
FRAGER, STANLEY R. PHD
FRANKLIN, CARLEEN
FRESHOUR, FRANK W.
FRIED, N. ELIZABETH, PH.D
FRIPP, PATRICIA
FYOCK, CATHERINE D.
GABRIELSEN, RON (CCM)
GALLAGHER, CATHY L.
GARGANTA, KATHLEEN T.
GARLAND, BARRY
GERAGHTY, BARBARA
GESELL, IZZY
GIOIA, JOYCE L.
GLICK, BARBARA
GOLBERT, GLORIA
GOLLIVER, JOY J.
GORDEN, DAVE
GORDON, CONNI
GRANGER, SUSAN
GRANT, CAROL
GRANT, LYNELLA F.
GREENE, IDA
GREENE-DAVIDSON, SUSAN
GREGG, ROBERT E.
GRIESSMAN, GENE, PH.D.
GRIFFIN, TOM
GROSS, T. SCOTT
GUTRIDGE, DON FOSTER
HARDY, MARC
HARMON, SHIRLEY
HARPER, JEANNE M.
HARRIS, MELVA J.
HATHAWAY, PATTI
HAVEY, CAROL V.
HAWKINS, KATHLEEN
HELITZER, MELVIN
HELSTEIN, IVY
HENLEY-SMITH, LINDA
HERMAN, ROGER E., (CMC)
HERRON, SANDRA WHITACRE
HIGHTSHOE, NANCY
HILL, JOANNE K.
HODGES, WILLIAM N.
HOOSER, PHILLIP VAN
HORKEY, DONNA L.
HOWLEY, C. JOE
HULL, MIRIAM B.

HUMPHRIES, ANN CHADWELL
HUNDERTMARK, JERI
HUNT, D. TRINIDAD
HURLEY, CARL E., ED.D. (CPAE)
INGRAM, ROBERT
ISLER, MARK
JACK, BARBARA M.
JACKSON, LUAN
JACOBS, ELLEN
JAMES, DIANA L.
JAMES, LARRY
JAMES, MERLIN R.
JASIM, JANIE
JENSEN, JAY R.
JEPPESEN, LYNDA FRANCE MBA
JJ LAUDERBAUGH
JOHNSON, HUB, PH.D.
JOHNSON, JENYCE
JOHNSON, KAY B.
KAPLAN, STEVE
KARR, RONALD E.
KARTEN, NAOMI
KEELAN, JIM
KELLER, KAY D.
KENNEDY, DAN S.
KERLEY, WILLIAM C.
KING, CHRIS
KING, HARLEY
KINNARD, MELLY
KLEIN, RUTH L.
KLINKENBERG, HILDA
KOJM, KURT BARNABY
KOPP, KRISTIN
KRATOWICZ, M. J.
KURZWEG, MARY KAY
LAND, PETER A.
LAWSON, KAREN
LEAPTROTT, NAN S.
LEBEAU, CALENE
LEE, CLIFFORD M., DR.
LEICHTY, MARLENE A.
LEMKE, RAYMOND
LENZ, BOB
LEONE, RAY
LETOURNEAU, TOM
LEWIS-WILLIAMS, MYRA
LINQUIST, LUANN
LIPNACK, MARTIN I.
LITTAUER, FLORENCE
LITTLE, ERLENE
LLOYD, HERB J.
LLOYD, JOAN
LONG, BRIAN G.
LOSSY, RELLA
LOVERDE, MARY
LUBOTSKY, TERRY
LUETHY, DR. GERRY
LYFORD, LOIS

LYTLE, TOBI L.
MAAS, GARY
MACALUSO, SISTER MARY CHRISTELLE, RSM, PH.D
MAILE, LISA
MALLERY, SUZY
MANNERING, DENNIS E.
MANNERING, WENDY K.
MANNING, MARILYN, PH.D.
MARINO, MIKE JR. 'IN PERSON'
MASUMOTO, PAT
MATSCHEK, CHERYL A.
MAYNE, MAVIS
MCCOY, DORIS L., PH.D.
MCILVAIN, TED L.
MCKAIN, SCOTT
MCKINLEY, MICHAEL P. (CPAE)
MCNAIR, J. FRANK
MCNEIL, MICHAEL R. (BCSW)
MEEKS, DAVID & ASSOCIATES
MENTA, SISTER ANGELICA M.
MERCER, MICHAEL W., PH.D.
MERRITT, CONNIE
MICHAEL, ANGIE
MILLER, ANNE PROMOTIONS, INC.
MILLER, ANNE PROMOTIONS, INC.
MILLER, JOHNNY
MINER, DAVID LEE
MINER-WARGO, NANETTE
MINNINGER, JOAN
MOHNEY, DR. NELL W.
MORAN, KEVIN M.
MORRISON, ANN M.
MORRISON, JAMES N.
MORROW, PEGGY & ASSOCIATES
MORTELL, ART
MOWBRAY, CATHERINE
MULVANEY, MAUREEN
MUNGAVAN, THOMAS E.
NATIONAL TRAUMA SERVICES
NELSON, SANDRA
NELSON, WILLIE
NICHOLSON, SHERYL
NIELSEN, RICK J.
NIENSTEDT, JOHN F.
NORTON, KEN
O'CONNOR, CAROL
OAKLEY, ED
OLSON, HARRY A.
OUTLAW, KEMILEE K.
OXLEY, ROBERT R.
PAGANO, BARBARA L.
PAGE, SUSAN

PALMEN, RALPH H.
PATTERSON, BILL
PAULSON, TERRY L., PH.D. (CPAE)
PEARL, LYNN
PENNER, SHEBA
PERSONS, HAROLD D. 'HAL'
PETERSEN, GLORIA
PETERSEN, KRISTELLE
PHILLIPS, RICK
PINKSTAFF, MARLENE ARTHUR
PLUMMER, RICHARD E., DR.
PODANY, SUE
POLK, JANE M.
POLLAR, ODETTE
PRIESKORN, JOHN PH.D.
PRIGAL, KENNETH B.K.
PUTZIER, JOHN
RADDE, PAUL O.
RAETHER, EDIE
RAFINSKI, MARCIA
RANDOLPH, ROBERT M.
RASBAND, JUDITH
RAST, EDWARD
RECKNER, JERALD (JERRY) H.
REYNOLDS, ROSE CELLINO
RHOADES, ROGER A.
RHODES, ROY, ED.D.
RICHARDS, RAMONA
RICHARDSON, DAVID W.
RICHARDSON, DR. ARTHUR
RIGSBEE, ED
RINKE, WOLF J., PH.D.
RISBERG, GREG
RISSER, RITA
RITCHIE, JAN
RITSCHER, JIM
ROBERT, CAVETT
ROBERTS, KATHI
ROBERTS, RONALD H. PH.D.
ROGERS, LOUISA
ROLFE, RANDY
ROSENBAUM, JERRY, CLU
ROSENBERG, DEANNE
ROSSITER, SHERRY KNIGHT
ROUSH, SHERYL L.
RUDNICKI, BARBARA A.
RUSSELL, RAY L., DR.
RYAN, LYNN
RYBACK, DAVID, DR.
SANFORD, JAMES VIKING
SASSI, PAULA A.
SCANNELL, EDWARD E.
SCHACK, POLLY
SCHLAMOWITZ, KEVAN, DR.
SCHREINER, CAROL D.
SCHWARTZ, ELAINE
SCHWARTZ, FRANCIE
SCOBEY, SALLY

SCOTT, GINI
  GRAHAM, PH.D., J.D.
SCOTT, SUSAN
SEARCY, RHODA M.
SEDACCA, ROSALIND
SHAPIRO, BARRY M.
SHEA, CHARLENE
SHELTON, LEE
SHELTON, SANDRA A.
SIBERT, DENNIS G.
SIEGFRIED, CHARLOTTE
SILVER, IDORA
SIMON, BARBARA J.
SIMS, D. PHILLIP
SIRESS, JIM
SLADE, TOM
SLOTKIN, FRAN S.
SMITH, HAROLD IVAN
SMITH, J. THOMAS
SNYDER, MARILYN
SOARES, DR. CECLIA J.
SOMMER, BOBBE, PH.D.
SPENCER, DUFFY, PH.D.
SPENGLER, CHRISTINE J.
  (CPS/CAM)
STALEY, MICHAEL F.
STARKEY, JUDITH A.
STARR, ROBERT BRUCE
STEIL, LYMAN K. (MANNY),
  DR. (CPAE)
STEIN, CAROLYN
STEIN, SANDY
STEPHANI, SUSAN
STERN, DEBRA
STEWART, LAURIE A.
STOLTZFUS, D. LEE, PH.D.
SUCKOW, BOB
SUMMER, SHIRLEY
SUTTON, SUZY
SWANSON, DAVID
SWINDELL, GENE
TABERS, JOE
TAHIR, ELIZABETH
TAILLON, YAHZDI
TAYLOR, MEREDITH
TEPLITZ, JERRY V., DR.
THOMAS, ELAINE J.
TICE, PATRICIA K.
TINGLEY, JUDITH C.
TOOPER, VIRGINIA, ED.D.
TOWNSEND, BRIAN
TSCHOHL, JOHN
TURNER, ROSLYN A.
TYRIAN, CHARLIE
UDELL, BARBARA A.
UHLAR, BOB & CARLA
  GOLDEN
VARGA, MARI PAT
VASSALLO, WANDA
VAUGHAN, SUZANNE
VINING, EARLENE

WADE, BOB ED.D.
WALKER, ANNE
WALLACE, KEN
WALTHER, GEORGE R.
  (CPAE)
WARD, AUDREY PEELE
WARREN, JOHN
WARZECHA, MARY M.
WATSON, JEAN
WAYMON, LYNNE
WEISEL, JACQUES
WEISS, ALAN PH.D.
WELLS, D. BRENT J.D.
WELLS, THELMA &
  ASSOCIATES
WHARTON, MARCIA M.
WHITE, SOMERS
WIKLUND, PATRICIA PH.D.
WILCOX, CHUCK
WILKINS, WALLACE PH.D.
WILKINSON, BRUCE S.
WILLIAMS, MIKKI
WILLIAMSON, JOHN S.
WILSON, CAROL ANN
WILSON, JUSTIN
WILSON, STEVE
WOLINSKI, KIM
WOODRUFF, DAVIS M.
YAMAMOTO, GARY K.
YAMBERT, CONSTANCE
  DEAN
YOUNG, DOUG
ZEZZA, MYRNA
ZIMMERMAN, DR. ALAN R.
ZIMMERMAN, TOM
ZINGER, JIM
ZYETZ, ALICE

HUMOR

ABELSON, HAL
ACERS, PATSY
ANDERSON, DALE L.
ANFINSON, STACIE A.
ARCHBALD, RALPH (CPAE)
ARNETTE, NICK
ARTERBURN, STEPHEN
ASIJA, S. PAL
ATKINSON, WILLIAM C.
AUSTIN, EMORY
BAKER, LEN
BARBER, JIM
BASSETT, LAWRENCE
  (LARRY) C. (CMC)
BELGUM, MERRILYN
BENDER, BEV
BERG, DR. DEANNA
BERGER, RUTH
BIRK, RON
BISSELL, BEN
BLAKELY, DON & MIKE

BLOCH, ANN
BLOCH, ROBERT H.
BOLING, DUTCH
BOURQUE, RONALD J.
BOWMAN, FOREST
BOWMAN, ROBIN
BOYD, LORRIE DR.
BRANDON, STEVE
BRAVERMAN, TERRY
BROWN, KATHY &
  ASSOCIATES
BROWN, MARLENE B., M.S.
BROWN, RICHARD R.
BURNS, KAREN
BURTON, BEN
BUTTS, JIMMIE K.
BUXMAN, KARYN
CAMPBELL, SANDRA JONES
CARMODY, KATHY
CARTER, ARNOLD 'NICK'
CHESTER, ERIC
COATES, MARTY
COLLINS, PEGGY
CONDON, GWEN
CORNYN-SELBY, ALYCE
COUCH, DR. BOB E., PH.D.
COX, DANNY, CPAE
CRAWFORD, MADISON
CRIST, LYLE
CROWSON, GATHA ROMINE
CUMMING, CANDY
CUMMINGS, BETH A.
CUNNINGHAM, DOYLE
CUROE, JOHN
DAVIS, DARRYL
DEAN, HARVEY D.
DELVES, JOHN A.
DENTINGER, RON
DEPOYSTER, BOBBY R.,
  ED.D
DERRICK, FLETCHER C. JR.
DOORNICK, ROBERT
EAGLE, MARK
EASON, W.H.
FARRELL, ROBERT E.
FIELDER GROUP, THE
FISHER, MARY
FLECK, JAMES R.
FLICKINGER, E. G.
FORZANO, RICK E.
GANNETT, MARYE D.
GERAGHTY, BARBARA
GESELL, IZZY
GLICKSTEIN, LEE
GLINER, ART
GOLDTRAP, GEORGE
GORDEN, DAVE
GORDON, CONNI
GREEN, LILA
GREENE, TAG
HAGESETH, CHRISTIAN III

HARBIN, CHARLES
HARDY, MARC
HARRAL, CHAS
HATTON, J. DUEY
HAVEY, CAROL V.
HEADLEY, WILLIAM
HELITZER, MELVIN
HENLEY-SMITH, LINDA
HENRY, ROBERT H.
HERSEY, ROSS V.
HICKMAN, ANDY L.
HIGGS, LIZ CURTIS
HOLDER, VERN
HOPE, LUCILLE
HOXWORTH, STEVE
HURLEY, CARL E., ED.D.
  (CPAE)
HYKEN, SHEP A.
IRVIN, DALE
JANSEN, ROBERT H.
JASIM, JANIE
JOHNSON, HUB, PH.D.
KAHN, RITA
KARPOVICH, MICHAEL S.
KAYE, STEVE
KEELAN, JIM
KELLEY, JIM
KENNEDY, DAN S.
KERLEY, WILLIAM C.
KILPATRICK, KURT
KINDE, JOHN E.
KLEIN, ALLEN
KLEINE-KRACHT, ANN E.
KLOCK, JOSEPH P.
LAMB, WILLIAM CARROLL
LARSON, JOE
LASKIN, JACK
LEE, CLIFFORD M., DR.
LEICHTY, MARLENE A.
LENZ, BOB
LINKLETTER, ART
LISK, THOM
LITTAUER, FLORENCE
LLOYD, HERB J.
LOVELESS, KATHY
MACALUSO, SISTER MARY
  CHRISTELLE, RSM, PH.D
MARINO, MIKE JR. 'IN
  PERSON'
MASQUELIER, ROGER
MASUMOTO, PAT
MATTIMORE, BRYAN W.
MCARTHUR, GILBERT B.
MCCOY, DORIS L., PH.D.
MCGHEE, PAUL E., PH.D.
MCKINLEY,
  MICHAEL P. (CPAE)
MEADES, KEN
MENTA, SISTER
  ANGELICA M.

MILLER, ANNE
  PROMOTIONS, INC.
MILLER, JOHNNY
MILLER, MADELYN
MILNER, ANITA CHEEK
MINER, DAVID LEE
MINNICK, DALEH
MOODY, ROY E.
MORAN, KEVIN M.
MORTELL, ART
MURDOCK, KEN
NIELSEN, RICK J.
NIKAM, S. G. 'NIK', MD
  (FACC) (FACP)
NUNES, MARIANNA
O'CONNOR, JERRY
OLDAK, EMILY
OSTARO, DHRUV
OUTLAW, KEMILEE K.
PARINELLO, AL
PARKER, DON
PAULSON, TERRY
  L., PH.D. (CPAE)
PETERSEN, KRISTELLE
PETITJEAN, DAVE
PETTY, DR. CHARLES V.
PHILPOT, JOHN
PICKERING, DAVE
PICKERING, WAYNE
POTUCK, MARK W.
PULLIAM, LINDA
RADKE, DALE L.
RAETHER, EDIE
REESE, MONTE
REYNOLDS, ROSE CELLINO
RHODES, ROY, ED.D.
RICHARDS, RAMONA
ROACH, MARY BETH
ROBERT, CAVETT
ROBERT, LEE E.
ROBERTS, KATHI
ROBISON, AUBRY, JR.
ROSE, ALBERT L.
ROSS, BOB
ROSS, KENNETH
ROTRAMEL, RICK
SAUBY, RON
SCHACK, POLLY
SCHERER, GEORGE
SCHIAVO, 'FANTASTIC FRED'
SCHREINER, CAROL D.
SCHWAB, PATT, DR.
SCOTT, BLACKIE
SCOTT, SUSAN
SEGEL, RICK
SHELTON, LEE
SHERMAN, RALPH
SHUH, AL & ASSOCIATES
SIMMS, STEVE
SKOGLUND, ROBERT
SLADE, TOM

SMITH, ROY L.
SORENTINO, PHIL
STACY, GAYLON
STARR, ROBERT BRUCE
STAUB, JAMES R.
STAUTER, ROGER
STEWART, ROD
SUTTON, SUZY
TAYLOR, MEREDITH
THOMAS, CLIFF, R.PH.
TISDALE, J. WAYNE
TOMCZAK, LARRY-MR.
  VERSATILITY
TOOPER, VIRGINIA, ED.D.
TOWNSEND, BRIAN
TREJO, WILLIE
TROUT, SHIRLEY
TYRA, STEVE
TYRIAN, CHARLIE
UDELL, BARBARA A.
VASSALLO, WANDA
VAUGHAN, SUZANNE
VELLIOTES, GEORGE
VERRI, ROSEMARY
WAGNER, JOHN P.
WALKER, ANNE
WARD, AUDREY PEELE
WATSON, JEAN
WEISS, BONNIE
WELLNITZ, CRAIG
WENOS, GAIL (CPAE)
WHITE, STAN
WILDE, LARRY
WILHELM, DOROTHY
WILKHOLM, MARIOU S.
WILKINSON, BRUCE S.
WILLIAMS, MIKKI
WILSON, JUSTIN
WILSON, STEVE
WOLINSKI, KIM
WOOD, BETTY
WOOLF, REESA, PH.D.
YAMBERT, CONSTANCE
  DEAN
ZIMMERMAN, TOM
ZINGER, JIM
ZUMM, TOM

JOURNALISM

ANDERSON, KARE
BILKER, HARVEY L.
BLACKWELL, JOEL
BURGETT, GORDON
EVANS, ROBERT MAYER
GIOIA, JOYCE L.
HAMPTON, LOU
HARBIN, CHARLES
HELITZER, MELVIN
HERMAN, JEFF
JANSEN, ROBERT H.

KILPATRICK, KURT
KING, CHRIS
LEAPTROTT, NAN S.
MATTIMORE, BRYAN W.
MCCOY, DORIS L., PH.D.
MILLER, MADELYN
O'HARA, CAROL
PATTERSON, BILL
ROSS, MARILYN
ROSS, TOM
ROUSH, SHERYL L.
SCOBEY, SALLY
THOMAS, ELAINE J.
WEISS, ALAN PH.D.
WIENER, VALERIE

MANAGEMENT

ABBOTT, DR. LINDA M.C.
ABELSON, HAL
ABRAMS-MINTZER, BARBARA
ACKERMANN, LINDA HOLT
ALBERT, WILLIAM C.
ALCORN, PAT
ALESANDRINI, KATHRYN,
  PH.D.
ALEXANDER, BOB
ALFORD, RON
ANDERSON, KARE
ANDERSON, LESTER W.
ARCEMENT, BILLY
ARNOLD, BILL
ARNSTEIN, SAM
ASHLEY, JAMES
ATKINS, CHANDLER PH.D.
AUN, MICHAEL A.
AUSTIN, EMORY
BAILEY, ROBERT L.
BAKER, LARRY D., DR.
BAKER, LEN
BALZER, ALVIN L.
BARNHILL, ROBERT E. III
BASSETT, LAWRENCE
  (LARRY) C. (CMC)
BATES, LARRY
BEARDEN, JIM
BEAUBIEN, ELAINE
  ESTERVIG
BENNIE, MARK
BERG, DR. DEANNA
BERGER, FRANCINE
BETHEL, SHEILA MURRAY
BIECH, ELAINE
BILLINGS-HARRIS, LENDRA
BISSELL, BEN
BLACK, JERRY
BLAKELY, DON & MIKE
BLOHOWIAK, DON
BOCK, WALLY
BOLTON, DENNY
BORDEAUX, DARLENE B.

BOURQUE, RONALD J.
BOWMAN, FOREST
BOWMAN, ROBIN
BOYD, LORRIE DR.
BRANDAU, KARLA
BRITTON, TOM
BROWN, KATHY &
  ASSOCIATES
BROWN, MARLENE B., M.S.
BROWN, TRACY
BRUN, DONALD J.
BUCARO, FRANK C.
BURNELL, IVAN G.
BURRUS, DANIEL
BUSSEY, TROY D.
CALHOON, JOE
CAMPER, NATALIE K., PH.D.
CARLINO, ANDY
CARR, SHARON
CARSON, GAYLE, DR.
CARTER, ARNOLD 'NICK'
CARTER, CHERIE-SCOTT
CARTER, STEVEN L.
CARUSO, JOSEPH A.
CASE, BOB
CHARBONNEAU, JOS. J.
CHILDRESS, GENE W.
CHITWOOD, ROY E.
CHRISTOPHER, SYLVIA
COATES, MARTY
COLE, P. CHRISTIAN
COLOMBO, GEORGE W.
CONLEY, JEFF
CONLON, PETER J., JR.
CONNOR, TIM
COOK, ETHEL M.
COPELAND, GARY R.
CORNWELL, ART
CORNYN-SELBY, ALYCE
COTTLE, DAVID W.
COX, DANNY, CPAE
CRAWFORD, MADISON
CRAWFORD, SALLY L.
CROWSON, GATHA ROMINE
CRUMPTON, DEBRA J.
CSOLKOVITS, ERNEST A.
CUSTER, CHUCK
DAFFRON, RAY
DALY, JOHN J.
DAVEY, JUDY
DAVIES, KENT R.
DAVIS, KEVIN F.
DAVIS, RONALD L.
DAWSON, ROGER
  PRODUCTIONS, INC.
DEAL, LUISA
DEAN, HARVEY D.
DECKER, DON B.
DEROSE, ROLAND
DIDONATO, RALPH
DOHERTY, BILL
DONADIO, PATRICK J.

DORSEY, IVORY
DOUGLASS, DR. MERRILL
DUBIN, BURT
DUNN, GLORIA
DUNN, MARIANNE
DYGERT, CHARLES B., PH.D
EAGLES, GIL
ECK, ARLENE
EINSTEIN ALIVE
EMMERICH, ROXANNE
EPSTEIN-SHEPHERD,
　DR. BEE
EVANS, ROBERT MAYER
FARRELL, ROBERT E.
FIELDER GROUP, THE
FILIPPO, LOU 'COACH'
FINK, MARTHA
FIORE, JAMES
FIORE, NEIL A., PH.D.
FLATT, VERNE
FLECK, JAMES R.
FLETCHER, JERRY L.
FOUNTAIN, ELEANOR A.
FRANK, MIKE, (CPAE)
FRAZEE, LINDA
FRESHOUR, FRANK W.
FRIEDMAN, SIDNEY A.
FRINGS, CHRISTOPHER
　S., PH.D.
FRIPP, PATRICIA
FRITZ, DR. BOB
FYOCK, CATHERINE D.
GABRIELSEN, RON (CCM)
GALLAGHER, BILL
　'GUERRILLA', PH.D.
GANNETT, MARYE D.
GARLAND, BARRY
GARRETT, A. MILTON
GERAGHTY, BARBARA
GILLARD, JUDY
GILLESPIE, JEFFREY A.
GITTERMAN, HEIDI
GOLBERT, GLORIA
GOOD, PERRY
GORBY, JOHN C.
GORDEN, DAVE
GREENE, TAG
GREENE-DAVIDSON, SUSAN
GREGG, ROBERT E.
GREIF, ED
GRIFFIN, TOM
GUTRIDGE, DON FOSTER
HADAWAY, GEORGE W.
HADDEN, RICHARD
HALTER, 'DIAMOND' JIM
HAMPTON, LOU
HARDY, MARC
HARLAN, RAY
HARRIS, MELVA J.
HARRISON, GENE
HATHAWAY, PATTI

HEDRICK, LUCY H.
HEMPHILL, BARBARA
HENNIG, JAMES F., PH.D
HENNING, MIKE
HERBSTER, DOUGLAS DR.
HERMAN, ROGER E. CMC
HERMAN, ROGER E., (CMC)
HEROLD, MORT
HIGHTOWER, KATHIE J.
HIGHTSHOE, NANCY
HILL, JOANNE K.
HIXON, GEORGE G.
HODGES, WILLIAM N.
HOLCOMB, JANE, PH.D.
HOLTON, CHER
HOOPER, DR. DON W.
HOOSER, PHILLIP VAN
HORKEY, DONNA L.
HOWLEY, C. JOE
HUFFMAN, CARL E., JR.
HULL, MIRIAM B.
HUMPHRIES, ANN
　CHADWELL
HUNT, D. TRINIDAD
HUNTER, WILLIAM L.
HUTSON, DON
INGRAM, ROBERT
JABLONSKI, JOSEPH R.
JACOBS, ANITA I.
JAMES, MERLIN R.
JEFFRIES, ELIZABETH
JENSEN, JAY R.
JEPPESEN, LYNDA
　FRANCE MBA
JJ LAUDERBAUGH
JOHNSON, BILL L.
JOHNSON, CAROL
JOHNSON, HUB, PH.D.
JOHNSON, JENYCE
JOHNSON, KAY B.
KABACHNICK, TERRI
KAPLAN, STEVE
KARR, RONALD E.
KARTEN, NAOMI
KAYE, STEVE
KEELAN, JIM
KEELER, JOHN A.
KELLEY, JIM
KERLEY, WILLIAM C.
KHERA, SHIV
KIENE, ANDREA L.
KINNARD, MELLY
KLEIN, RUTH L.
KLINKENBERG, HILDA
KLOCK, JOSEPH P.
KNACKSTEDT, MARY V.
KNOX, DAVID S.
KOJM, KURT BARNABY
KOLTIN, ALLAN DAVID, CPA
KOPP, KRISTIN
KOTZ, STEVE

KRAMER, ROBERT G.
KRATOWICZ, M. J.
KUTSKO, JIM
LABRANCHE, GARY A. (CAE)
LAND, PETER A.
LARSEN, LARRY L.
LATTA, MARIE B. M.ED.
LAWSON, KAREN
LEACH, LYNNE C.
LEBEAU, CALENE
LEE, BILL
LEEDS, DOROTHY
LEFKOWITZ, HAL
LEMKE, RAYMOND
LEONE, RAY
LERMAN, KENNETH B.
LETOURNEAU, TOM
LEVIN, ROGER P.
LEVOY, ROBERT P.
LISK, THOM
LITTAUER, MARITA
LLOYD, HERB J.
LLOYD, JOAN
LOFY, CARL
LONG, BRIAN G.
LONGFELLOW,
　LAYNE A., PH.D.
LONTOS, PAM
LOSYK, BOB
LOUDEN, STEPHEN H.
LOVELESS, KATHY
LYTLE, TOBI L.
MALLERY, SUZY
MARKEL, GERALDINE PH.D.
MARTH, ROALD D.
MASUMOTO, PAT
MATSCHEK, CHERYL A.
MATTIMORE, BRYAN W.
MAYNARD, MICHAEL
MCARDLE, KEVIN J.
MCARTHUR, GILBERT B.
MCCLAIN, BRENDA H.
MCCOY, DORIS L., PH.D.
MCDONALD, THOMAS, PH.D.
MCILVAIN, TED L.
MCKAIN, SCOTT
MCKINLEY, MICHAEL
　P. (CPAE)
MCNAIR, J. FRANK
MERCER, MICHAEL W., PH.D.
MERRITT, CONNIE
METCALF, ED, DR.
MEYER, BILL
MICALE, FRANCES A.
MILLER, ANNE
　PROMOTIONS, INC.
MILLER, JOHNNY
MILLER, REV. MARILYN K.
MILLER, VALERIE J. S.
MILTEER, LEE
MITCHELL, HERBERT E.

MONK, ART
MONTEFUSCO, JR.,
　MICHAEL T.
MOODY, ROY E.
MOORE, JAMES F.
MOORE, LAURIE
MORAN, KEVIN M.
MOREL, LIN M.
MORGAN, DONALD R.
MORGAN, REBECCA
MORRISEY, GEORGE L.
MORRISON, ANN M.
MORRISON, JAMES N.
MORROW, PEGGY &
　ASSOCIATES
MORTELL, ART
MOSER, MILTON J.
MUNGAVAN, THOMAS E.
MURRAY, MARCELLA
MYERS, JANET L.
NABERS, MARY SCOTT
NASH, LINDA J.
NELSON, SANDRA
NICHOLSON, SHERYL
NORTON, GEORGE M.
OAKLEY, ED
OECHSLI, MATTHEW J.
OLESEN, ERIK L.
OLSON, HARRY A.
OSMAN, WALI M. PH.D.
OUTLAW, KEMILEE K.
OUTLAW, WAYNE
OXLEY, ROBERT R.
PALMEN, RALPH H.
PALMQUIST, RICHARD
PANHORST, DON, DR.
PARISSE, ALAN J.
PARKER, CHARLES E.
PATTERSON, BILL
PAULSON, TERRY L., PH.D.
　(CPAE)
PAYNE, THOMAS E.
PEARL, LYNN
PENNINGTON, RANDY G.
PETERSEN, GLORIA
PETERSON, THERESA L.
PHILLIPS, RICK
PICKERING, DAVE
PINKSTAFF, MARLENE
　ARTHUR
POLLAR, ODETTE
PRIGAL, KENNETH B.K.
PUTNAM, HOWARD D.
PUTZIER, JOHN
RADDE, PAUL O.
RAEL, RON, CPA
RAETHER, EDIE
RALSTON, JOHN
RANDOLPH, ROBERT M.
RASBAND, JUDITH
RAST, EDWARD

REAVES, CHUCK
RECKNER, JERALD
  (JERRY) H.
REED, DAVE
REED, DEBRA J.
REUM, EARL, DR.
REYNOLDS, ROSE CELLINO
REZEK, GEOFFREY R.
  (CFPIM) (CPM)
RHODE, JIM
RHODES, ROY, ED.D.
RICH, SUSAN A.
RICHARDSON, DAVID W.
RIFENBARY, JAY C.
RIGSBEE, ED
RINKE, WOLF J., PH.D.
RITCHIE, JAN
RITSCHER, JIM
ROBERTS, JERRY W.
ROBERTS, KATHI
ROGERS, LOUISA
ROHLANDER, DAVID
ROOS, JAMES P.
ROSE, ALBERT L.
ROSENBAUM, JERRY, CLU
ROSENBERG, DEANNE
ROSENBERG, RICHARD
ROSS, BOB
ROSSITER, SHERRY KNIGHT
ROTRAMEL, RICK
ROUSOPOULOS, DENO
RUDNICKI, BARBARA A.
RUSSELL, RAY L., DR.
RYAN, LYNN
SALINGER, TONY
SANBORN, MARK H.
SANDLIN, RUSSELL
SASSI, PAULA A.
SAUER, JOHN R.
SCANNELL, EDWARD E.
SCHACK, POLLY
SCHENK, GEORGE
SCHMIDT, JOY A.
SCHWAB, PATT, DR.
SCHWARTZ, FRANCIE
SCHWARZ, BARB
SCOTT, GINI GRAHAM,
  PH.D., J.D.
SEARCY, RHODA M.
SHAPIRO, DON
SHARP, SALLY O.
SHEA, CHARLENE
SHELTON, LEE
SHELTON, SANDRA A.
SHUH, AL & ASSOCIATES
SIBERT, DENNIS G.
SIEGFRIED, CHARLOTTE
SILVER, SUSAN
SIMON, BARBARA J.
SIMS, D. PHILLIP
SIRESS, JIM

SMITH, WALTER D.
SOARES, DR. CECLIA J.
SORENTINO, PHIL
SPENCER, DUFFY, PH.D.
SPENGLER, CHRISTINE J.
  (CPS/CAM)
STARK, PETER BARRON
STARKEY, JUDITH A.
STAUB, JAMES R.
STEIL, LYMAN K. (MANNY),
  DR. (CPAE)
STEIN, CAROLYN
STEIN, SANDY
STENNES, BARBARA
STERN, DEBRA
STEWART, MIKE
STOLTZFUS, D. LEE, PH.D.
STONE, D. CONWAY
STRIKE, LOUIS N.
SUCKOW, BOB
SUMMER, SHIRLEY
SWINDELL, GENE
TABERS, JOE
TAHIR, ELIZABETH
TANSEY, DR. DAVE
TAYLOR, PAULA R., M.A.
TEPLITZ, JERRY V., DR.
TEPPER, BRUCE
THOMAS, ELAINE J.
TREJO, WILLIE
TURLA, PETER
TURNER, ROSLYN A.
TUROCK, ART
TWEED, STEPHEN C.
TYRIAN, CHARLIE
TYTER, RICHARD
UDELL, BARBARA A.
UHLER, JAY, C.P.C
URBASHICH, HERM
VAN DYKE, FLAVIL Q.
VARMA, VISH
VASQUEZ, SABINE GROSS
VETTER PRODUCTIVITY
VOTH, ERIC R.
WADE, BOB ED.D.
WAGNER, JOHN P.
WALKER, ANNE
WALL, KEVIN DONALD
WALLACE, KEN
WALSH, PATRICIA ANN, ED.D.
WANGBERG, 'DR. LOU'
WARNER, CAROLYN
WATSON, DONNA S.
WATSON, DR. DONNA S.
WATSON, JEAN
WAYMON, LYNNE
WEISBERG, JACOB
WEISEL, JACQUES
WEISS, ALAN PH.D.
WENOS, GAIL (CPAE)
WESNER, ERIC C.

WETMORE, DONALD E.
WEXLER, PHILLIP S.
WEYLMAN, C. RICHARD
WHALIN, GEORGE
WHITE, SOMERS
WHITT, JIM
WIGGLE, PHILIP LAWRENCE
WIKLUND, PATRICIA PH.D.
WILDFOGEL, JEFFREY PH.D.
WILKINSON, BRUCE S.
WILLIAMS, JIM, CAPT.
WILLIAMS, JOHN R., LCDR
WILLIAMS, MIKKI
WILSON, KAREN
WILSON, LARRY
WILSON, STEVE
WOLD, BARBARA
WOLF, JOHN M. 'JACK' PH.D.
WOODRUFF, DAVIS M.
YAMAMOTO, GARY K.
YAMBERT, CONSTANCE
  DEAN
YELLEN, PAMELA G.
YOHO, DAVID
YOUNG, DOUG
YOUNG, WOODY
ZARE, NANCY C., DR.
ZICK, BERNARD HALE
ZIMMERMAN, DR. ALAN R.
ZIMMERMAN, TOM
ZINGER, JIM
ZYETZ, ALICE

MARKETING

ACKERMANN, LINDA HOLT
ALCORN, PAT
ALFORD, RON
AMBROSIUS, RICHARD, CEO
ANDERSON, KARE
ANDERSON, LESTER W.
ARTERBURN, STEPHEN
ATKINS, CHANDLER PH.D.
BALZER, ALVIN L.
BARNHILL, ROBERT E. III
BARRERA, RICK
BARROWS, SYDNEY BIDDLE
BEALS, GARY
BEAUBIEN, ELAINE
  ESTERVIG
BERNS, FRED
BESDANSKY, BRENDA
BETHEL, BILL
BIECH, ELAINE
BILLUE, STAN
BLACK, JERRY
BLACKMAN, JEFF, J.D.
BLACKWELL, JOEL
BLOCH, ROBERT H.
BOILEAU & ASSOCIATES
BOLTON, DENNY

BORDEAUX, DARLENE B.
BOYAN, LEE
BRITTON, TOM
BRUN, DONALD J.
BUDD, NANCY
BURGETT, GORDON
BUSSEY, TROY D.
BYERS, MARY
CARTER, ARNOLD 'NICK'
CARUSO, JOSEPH A.
CHITWOOD, ROY E.
COATES, MARTY
CORCORAN, DENISE M
CORNWELL, ART
COTTLE, DAVID W.
CROWSON, GATHA ROMINE
CUSTER, CHUCK
DACEY, JUDITH E., CPA
DAFFRON, RAY
DAVIDSON,
  JEFF (MBA) (CMC)
DAVIS, RONALD L.
DEAN, BONNIE 'THE MOTION
  COACH'
DEMKO, DAVID J.
DONALDSON, KEITH
DOORNICK, ROBERT
ELIAS, JEFF
EMMERICH, ROXANNE
ENEN, JACK
EVANS, ROBERT MAYER
FARRELL, ROBERT E.
FIELDER GROUP, THE
FINGEROTE, PAUL S.
FINK, MARTHA
FISHER, DONNA
FLETCHER, JERRY L.
FORZANO, RICK E.
FRANK, MIKE, (CPAE)
FRESHOUR, FRANK W.
FRIEDMAN, SIDNEY A.
FRIPP, PATRICIA
GABRIELSEN, RON (CCM)
GAGE, RANDY
GALLAGHER, BILL
  'GUERRILLA', PH.D.
GARFINKEL, DAVID
GERAGHTY, BARBARA
GIOIA, JOYCE L.
GITTERMAN, HEIDI
GOOZE, MITCHELL
GORDEN, DAVE
GRANGER, SUSAN
HALTER, 'DIAMOND' JIM
HALVERSON, DEAN
HAMEROFF, EUGENE J.
HASKELL, JOHN S.
HAWLEY, CASEY FITTS
HELVEY, EDWARD P., JR.
HENNIG, JAMES F., PH.D
HERBSTER, DOUGLAS DR.

HEROLD, MORT
HIGHTOWER, KATHIE J.
HILL, JOANNE K.
HIXON, GEORGE G.
HODGES, WILLIAM N.
HUMPHRIES, ANN
  CHADWELL
HYDEN, HOWARD E.
HYKEN, SHEP A.
JABLONSKI, JOSEPH R.
JAMES, MERLIN R.
JEPPESEN, LYNDA
  FRANCE MBA
JOHNSON, BILL L.
JUTKINS, RAY W.
KAHN, RITA
KAINE, JACK W.
KARR, RONALD E.
KEELER, JOHN A.
KENNEDY, DAN S.
KERLEY, WILLIAM C.
KILPATRICK, KURT
KING, HARLEY
KINNARD, MELLY
KLEIN, RUTH L.
KLOCK, JOSEPH P.
KNACKSTEDT, MARY V.
KNOLL, HERBERT E. JR.
KOJM, KURT BARNABY
KOLTIN, ALLAN DAVID, CPA
KRAMER, ROBERT G.
KRATOWICZ, M. J.
LARSEN, LARRY L.
LEEDS, DOROTHY
LEFKOWITZ, HAL
LEICHTY, MARLENE A.
LERMAN, KENNETH B.
LETOURNEAU, TOM
LEVIN, ROGER P.
LEVOY, ROBERT P.
LEWISON-SINGER, RITA
LILLY, SAM, PH.D.
LISK, THOM
LONG, BRIAN G.
LOUDEN, STEPHEN H.
LOVELESS, KATHY
LOWE, PETER
MAILE, LISA
MALLERY, SUZY
MARINO, MIKE JR. 'IN
  PERSON'
MARTH, ROALD D.
MASQUELIER, ROGER
MASUMOTO, PAT
MATSCHEK, CHERYL A.
MATTIMORE, BRYAN W.
MAYNARD, MICHAEL
MCCLAIN, BRENDA H.
MCDONALD, THOMAS, PH.D.
MCKAIN, SCOTT
MCNAIR, J. FRANK

MEYER, BILL
MICHAEL, ANGIE
MILLER, ANNE
  PROMOTIONS, INC.
MILLER, MADELYN
MILLER, VALERIE J. S.
MITCHELL, HERBERT E.
MONK, ART
MOORE, LAURIE
MORTELL, ART
MYERS, GERRY
MYERS, JANET L.
NASH, LINDA J.
OECHSLI, MATTHEW J.
OSMAN, WALI M. PH.D.
OUTLAW, WAYNE
OXLEY, ROBERT R.
PALMQUIST, RICHARD
PALUMBO, JOHN A.
PATTISON, POLLY
PEARL, LYNN
PESUT, TIM S.
PETERSEN, KRISTELLE
PETERSON, CAROL C.
PILLOW, JOHN G. (MHS)
PINSKEY, RALEIGH
POOSER, DORIS
POSTEN, ROBERT
PRICE, BETTE
PRICE, DON L.
PRIGAL, KENNETH B.K.
PUTNAM, HOWARD D.
REAVES, CHUCK
RECKNER, JERALD
  (JERRY) H.
REED, DAVE
REZEK, GEOFFREY R.
  (CFPIM) (CPM)
RHODE, JIM
RICHARDSON, DAVID W.
RICHARDSON, DR. ARTHUR
RIGSBEE, ED
ROBERT, CAVETT
ROOS, JAMES P.
ROSENBERG, RICHARD
ROSS, MARILYN
ROSS, TIMOTHY G.
ROSS, TOM
RYAN, LYNN
SABAH, JOE
SABAH, JUDY
SANDLIN, RUSSELL
SASSI, PAULA A.
SCANNELL, EDWARD E.
SCHENK, GEORGE
SCOTT, GINI GRAHAM, PH.D.,
  J.D.
SEARCY, RHODA M.
SEDACCA, ROSALIND
SEGEL, RICK
SELAME, ELINOR

SELWYN, PADI
SHANNON, SHARON L.
SHAPIRO, DON
SHELTON, LEE
SLUTSKY, JEFF
STEIL, LYMAN K. (MANNY),
  DR. (CPAE)
STEWART, DAVID
STRIKE, LOUIS N.
SULLIVAN, TERRY
SUMMEY, MIKE
SWANSON, DAVID
TAHIR, ELIZABETH
TARTARELLA, KATHY
TEPPER, BRUCE
THOMAS, ELAINE J.
TISDALE, J. WAYNE
TRUAX, PAMELA
TSCHOHL, JOHN
TURPIN, BEN
TWEED, STEPHEN C.
VAN DYKE, FLAVIL Q.
VARMA, VISH
WALTERS, DOTTIE
WANGBERG, 'DR. LOU'
WARZECHA, MARY M.
WEISBERG, JACOB
WEISS, ALAN PH.D.
WEISS, BONNIE
WESNER, ERIC C.
WEXLER, PHILLIP S.
WEYLMAN, C. RICHARD
WHALIN, GEORGE
WHITE, BARTON C.
WHITE, SOMERS
WIENER, VALERIE
WILLIAMS, JOHN R., LCDR
WILLIAMS, MIKKI
WILSON, JERRY R.
WOLD, BARBARA
WOODCOCK, DAVID
WOODS, RHONDA B.
YAMBERT, CONSTANCE
  DEAN
YELLEN, PAMELA G.
YOHO, DAVID
YOUNG, DOUG
YOUNG, WOODY
ZAKIAN, ALICE L.
ZICK, BERNARD HALE
ZINGER, JIM

MEDIA

ALESANDRINI,
  KATHRYN, PH.D.
AMBROSIUS, RICHARD, CEO
ANDERSON, KARE
BEALS, GARY
BERNS, FRED
BILKER, HARVEY L.

BLACKWELL, JOEL
BRODER, MICHAEL S. PHD
BRUN, DONALD J.
BURGETT, GORDON
BURROUGHS, HENRIETTA J.
BYERS, MARY
CUTLER, MARY
  LOUISE (DTM)
DONADIO, PATRICK J.
DORSEY, CALVIN
FINGEROTE, PAUL S.
FLETCHER, JERRY L.
FLETCHER, TANA
FRIED, N. ELIZABETH, PH.D
GERAGHTY, BARBARA
GORBY, JOHN C.
GORDON, CONNI
GRANGER, SUSAN
HAMPTON, LOU
HELVEY, EDWARD P., JR.
KAINE, JACK W.
KENNEDY, DAN S.
KILPATRICK, KURT
KOJM, KURT BARNABY
MALLERY, SUZY
MCCOY, DORIS L., PH.D.
MCCUISTION, DENNIS
MCGHEE MEDIA
  ASSOCIATES
MILLER, MADELYN
MORRISON, JAMES N.
MORSCHER, BETSY, PH.D.
NUELL, JOY
PALMQUIST, RICHARD
PARINELLO, AL
PATTERSON, BILL
PETERSEN, KRISTELLE
PHILPOT, JOHN
PINSKEY, RALEIGH
RICHARDS, RAMONA
ROSS, TIMOTHY G.
SCANLON, DERALEE R.D.
SCOBEY, SALLY
SHERMAN, RALPH
SIMENTON, PHILIP R.
STEIN, CAROLYN
THOMAS, DIAN
WEISS, BONNIE
WIENER, VALERIE
WILKINSON, BRUCE S.
WILSON, KAREN
YAMBERT, CONSTANCE
  DEAN
ZINGER, JIM

MEDICAL

ABRAMS-MINTZER, BARBARA
ANDERSON, DALE L.
BILKER, HARVEY L.
BLAKELY, DON & MIKE

BROWN, KATHY &
    ASSOCIATES
BUXMAN, KARYN
CRACKOWER, SYDNEY, M.D.
CROWSON, GATHA ROMINE
CUMMINGS, DR. RITA J.
DERRICK, FLETCHER C. JR.
DRENCH, MEREDITH E. PHD
FIELDER GROUP, THE
GARGANTA, KATHLEEN T.
GORDEN, DAVE
GREEN, LILA
HUTTER, V. ROSAN
JEPPESEN, LYNDA
    FRANCE MBA
JOHNSON, KAY B.
JONES, MARILYN K., DDS
LINQUIST, LUANN
LOVERDE, MARY
MATSCHEK, CHERYL A.
MAYNE, MAVIS
MERRITT, CONNIE
NELSON, DAVID N., P.T.
NEWSOME, PAULA R.
NICHOLSON, SHERYL
OBERG, BILL
OUTLAW, KEMILEE K.
PELLEY, JIM
PYFER, HOWARD R. M.D.
REYNOLDS, PATRICK
ROBERTS, KATHI
ROBERTS, RONALD H. PH.D.
SCANLON, DERALEE R.D.
SEARCY, RHODA M.
SHELTON, LEE
SILVER, IDORA
SLADE, TOM
SMITH, DIANE ELLINGSON
STALEY, MICHAEL F.
SUTTON, JAMES D., DR.
TROUT, SHIRLEY
ULLMAN, DANA M.P.H.
VELLIOTES, GEORGE
WARD, AUDREY PEELE
WAREHAM, GWENDOLYN
WERNER, STAN 'THE HAND'
WILSON, STEVE

MILITARY

CHINN, C. EARL
DEROSE, ROLAND
GABRIELSEN, RON (CCM)
HARDY, MARC
HARRAL, CHAS
JABLONSKI, JOSEPH R.
JAMES, MERLIN R.
JENSEN, JAY R.
LITTLEFIELD, HENRY M.
NIENSTEDT, JOHN F.
RIFENBARY, JAY C.

ROSE, ALBERT L.
SCOTT, CHARLES W.
    (CHUCK), COL.
SUCKOW, BOB
TYRIAN, CHARLIE

MOTIVATION

ABAGNALE, FRANK W.
ABELSON, HAL
ABRAMS-MINTZER, BARBARA
ACKERMANN, LINDA HOLT
ALEXANDER, BOB
ALLEN, ELIZABETH 'BETSY'
ANDERSON, DALE L.
ANDERSON, KARE
ANDERSON, LESTER W.
ARCEMENT, BILLY
ARLEQUE, LILLIAN, ED.D.
ARTERBURN, STEPHEN
ASHLEY, JAMES
ATKINS, CHANDLER PH.D.
ATKINSON, WILLIAM C.
AUN, MICHAEL A.
AUSTIN, EMORY
BAKER, LARRY D., DR.
BAKER, LEN
BALL, DR. ROBERT R.
BALL, JIM
BARBER, JIM
BARKER, JOCK
BARNHILL, ROBERT E. III
BARON, JUDY KAPLAN
BARRERA, RICK
BASSETT, LAWRENCE
    (LARRY) C. (CMC)
BATES, LARRY
BEARDEN, JIM
BEATTY, MAURA CLELAND
BEAUBIEN, ELAINE
    ESTERVIG
BELGUM, MERRILYN
BENDER, BEV
BENNETT, LOIS E.,
    M.ED.,M.A.
BENNIE, MARK
BERG, DR. DEANNA
BERGER, FRANCINE
BERGER, RUTH
BERNS, FRED
BETHEL, SHEILA MURRAY
BIECH, ELAINE
BILLUE, STAN
BIRK, RON
BISHOP, VENNA
BISSELL, BEN
BLACK, JERRY
BLACKMAN, JEFF, J.D.
BLAKELY, DON & MIKE
BLOCH, ANN
BOLING, DUTCH

BOLTON, DENNY
BOOHER, DIANNA
BORDEAUX, DARLENE B.
BOURQUE, RONALD J.
BOWMAN, FOREST
BOWMAN, ROBIN
BOYAN, LEE
BOYD, LORRIE DR.
BOYLE, VIRGINIA, PHD.
BRAHAM, BARBARA J.
BRANDAU, KARLA
BRAVERMAN, TERRY
BRILES, DR. JUDITH
BRITTON, TOM
BRODER, MICHAEL S. PHD
BRODY, MARJORIE
BROOKS, EVE
BROWN, KATHY &
    ASSOCIATES
BROWN, LINDEE S.
BROWN, MARLENE B., M.S.
BROWN, RICHARD R.
BROWN, TRACY
BROWNELL, EILEEN O.
BRUN, DONALD J.
BRUNER, HELEN L.C.S.W.
BUCARO, FRANK C.
BUDD, NANCY
BURGE, JOAN M.
BURNELL, IVAN G.
BURNS, PAT
BURZYNSKI, LINDA L.
BUSSEY, TROY D.
BUTLER, JENNIFER
BUXMAN, KARYN
CABRERA, JIMMY
CALHOON, JOE
CALMES, MARYLEE
CAMPBELL, SANDRA JONES
CANFIELD, JACK
CARLE, GILDA PHD
CARLINO, ANDY
CARMODY, KATHY
CAROLAN, SHIRLEY M.
CARR, SHARON
CARTER, ARNOLD 'NICK'
CARTER, SHERIE-SCOTT
CARUSO, JOSEPH A.
CASE, BOB
CHARBONNEAU, JOS. J.
CHESTER, ERIC
CHILDRESS, GENE W.
CHINN, C. EARL
CHITWOOD, ROY E.
CHRISTOPHER, SYLVIA
COATES, MARTY
COEY, NANCY
COFFEE, GERALD
CONLEY, JEFF
CONNOR, TIM
CONSTANT, RUTH L.
COOK, ETHEL M.

COPELAND, GARY R.
CORCORAN, DENISE M
CORNWELL, ART
COTTLE, DEBRA
COUCH, DR. BOB E., PH.D.
COX, DANNY, CPAE
CRACKOWER, SYDNEY, M.D.
CRAWFORD, MADISON
CRAWFORD, SALLY L.
CREEL, JOANNE P.
CRIST, LYLE
CROWSON, GATHA ROMINE
CRUMPTON, DEBRA J.
CSOLKOVITS, ERNEST A.
CUMMINGS, BETH A.
CUNNINGHAM, DOYLE
D'ANDREA, JOSEPH J.
DAFFRON, RAY
DAVEY, JUDY
DAVIES, KENT R.
DAVIS, DARRYL
DAVIS, RONALD L.
DAWSON, ROGER
    PRODUCTIONS, INC.
DEAL, LUISA
DEAN, BONNIE 'THE MOTION
    COACH'
DEAN, HARVEY D.
DECARLO, LINDA
DECKER, DON B.
DEE, EMILY
DEL CASTILLO, JANET
DELVES, JOHN A.
DEMKO, DAVID J.
DEPOYSTER,
    BOBBY R., ED.D
DEROSE, ROLAND
DOCKERY, WALLENE T.
DOHERTY, BILL
DONADIO, PATRICK J.
DONALDSON, KEITH
DORSEY, IVORY
DRAKE, CAROL
DUNN, GLORIA
DVORAK, ROBERT REGIS
DWYER, DAWN
DYGERT, CHARLES B., PH.D
EAGLES, GIL
ECK, ARLENE
EGGLESTON, JULIA
EINSTEIN ALIVE
EMMETT, RITA
FARRELL, ROBERT E.
FETTIG, ART
FIELDER GROUP, THE
FIORE, JAMES
FIORE, NEIL A., PH.D.
FISHER, DONNA
FISHER, MARY
FISHER, SANDRA L.
FLICKINGER, E. G.

FOREMAN, ED
FORZANO, RICK E.
FOTIADES, VALLA D.
FOUNTAIN, ELEANOR A.
FOX, JOAN G.
FRAGER, STANLEY R. PHD
FRANK, MIKE, (CPAE)
FRANKLIN, CARLEEN
FRAZEE, LINDA
FRESHOUR, FRANK W.
FRIEDMAN, SIDNEY A.
FRINGS,
   CHRISTOPHER S., PH.D.
FRIPP, PATRICIA
FRYAR, HAL
FUTCH, KEN
GABRIELSEN, RON (CCM)
GALLAGHER, BILL
   'GUERRILLA', PH.D.
GALLAGHER, CATHY L.
GANNETT, MARYE D.
GARGANTA, KATHLEEN T.
GARLAND, BARRY
GEDAN, IRA
GEE, BOBBIE
GERAGHTY, BARBARA
GERMANN, DOUGLAS D.
GESELL, IZZY
GILBERT, ROB, PH.D
GILLARD, JUDY
GIOIA, JOYCE L.
GITTERMAN, HEIDI
GLICK, BARBARA
GOETZMAN,
   RICHARD K., PH.D.
GOLBERT, GLORIA
GOLDMAN, CONNIE
GOLLIVER, JOY J.
GOOD, PERRY
GOOZE, MITCHELL
GORDEN, DAVE
GORDON, CONNI
GRANGER, SUSAN
GRANGER, VIRGINIA M.
GRANT, CAROL
GREEN, LILA
GREENE, IDA
GREENE, TAG
GREENE-DAVIDSON, SUSAN
GREIF, ED
GRIESSMAN, GENE, PH.D.
GRIFFIN, TOM
GROPPEL, JACK L. PH.D.
GUTRIDGE, DON FOSTER
HADAWAY, GEORGE W.
HAIGH, LESLEE
HALTER, 'DIAMOND' JIM
HANSEN, MARK VICTOR
HARDY, BETTY
HARDY, MARC
HARMON, SHIRLEY

HARPER, JEANNE M.
HARRAL, CHAS
HARRIS, MELVA J.
HARRISON, GENE
HATHAWAY, PATTI
HATTON, J. DUEY
HAVEY, CAROL V.
HAYASHI, MIKE
HEADLEY, WILLIAM
HENLEY-SMITH, LINDA
HENNIG, JAMES F., PH.D
HENRY, ROBERT H.
HEROLD, MORT
HERRON, SANDRA
   WHITACRE
HERSEY, ROSS V.
HERSEY, WILLIAM
HIGGS, LIZ CURTIS
HILL, JOANNE K.
H!XON, GEORGE G.
HODGES, WILLIAM N.
HOLDER, VERN
HOLTON, CHER
HOOD, RALPH
HOOPER, DR. DON W.
HOOSER, PHILLIP VAN
HORVATH, TERRI
HOWLEY, C. JOE
HOXWORTH, STEVE
HUBER, MARCY
HUFFMAN, CARL E., JR.
HULL, MIRIAM B.
HUMPHRIES, ANN
   CHADWELL
HUNDERTMARK, JERI
HUNT, D. TRINIDAD
HUNTER, C. ROY
HURLEY, CARL E.,
   ED.D. (CPAE)
HUTSON, DON
HYKEN, SHEP A.
INGRAM, ROBERT
JACK, BARBARA M.
JACOBS, ANITA I.
JAMES, DIANA L.
JAMES, LARRY
JAMES, MERLIN R.
JASIM, JANIE
JENSEN, JAY R.
JEPPESEN, LYNDA
   FRANCE MBA
JJ LAUDERBAUGH
JOHNSON, BILL L.
JOHNSON, HUB, PH.D.
JOLLEY, WILLIE 'THE
   INSPIRTAINER'
JOY, PAM
KAHN, RITA
KAINE, JACK W.
KARPOVICH, MICHAEL S.
KARR, RONALD E.

KARSCHNER, GRAY DON
KAYE, STEVE
KEEFFE, CAROL
KEELER, JOHN A.
KELLER, KAY D.
KELLEY, JIM
KENNEDY, DAN S.
KERLEY, WILLIAM C.
KHERA, SHIV
KICK, FRAN
KIENE, ANDREA L.
KILPATRICK, KURT
KING, CHRIS
KING, HARLEY
KINNARD, MELLY
KLEIN, RUTH L.
KLOCK, JOSEPH P.
KNACKSTEDT, MARY V.
KNOX, DAVID S.
KOJM, KURT BARNABY
KOLTIN, ALLAN DAVID, CPA
KOPP, KRISTIN
KOTZ, STEVE
KRATOWICZ, M. J.
KURZWEG, MARY KAY
KUTSKO, JIM
LABRANCHE, GARY A. (CAE)
LAFRENIERE, DONNA
LAIPPLY, BOB
LAIPPLY, SANDY
LAMB, WILLIAM CARROLL
LAMON, DANA
LAND, PETER A.
LARSEN, LARRY L.
LARSON, JOE
LATTA, MARIE B. M.ED.
LEACH, LYNNE C.
LEBEAU, CALENE
LEE, CLIFFORD M., DR.
LEEDS, DOROTHY
LEGATT, HADASSA PH.D.
LEICHTY, MARLENE A.
LEMKE, RAYMOND
LENZ, BOB
LEONE, RAY
LERMAN, KENNETH B.
LETOURNEAU, TOM
LEVIN, ROGER P.
LEWIS-WILLIAMS, MYRA
LILLY, SAM, PH.D.
LINKLETTER, ART
LISK, THOM
LITTAUER, MARITA
LITTLE, ERLENE
LITTLEFIELD, HENRY M.
LLOYD, HERB J.
LLOYD, JOAN
LONGFELLOW,
   LAYNE A., PH.D.
LONTOS, PAM
LOSYK, BOB

LOVELESS, KATHY
LOVERDE, MARY
LOWE, PETER
LOWELL TRAINING &
   CONSULTING
LUCHT, CHARLES
LYFORD, LOIS
LYTLE, TOBI L.
MAAS, GARY
MACALUSO, SISTER MARY
   CHRISTELLE, RSM, PH.D
MAILE, LISA
MAINELLA, MARK T.
MALAINY, DON
MANNERING, DENNIS E.
MANNING, MARILYN, PH.D.
MARINO, MIKE JR. 'IN
   PERSON'
MARTH, ROALD D.
MASQUELIER, ROGER
MASUMOTO, PAT
MATSCHEK, CHERYL A.
MAYFIELD, TERRY L.
MAYNARD, MICHAEL
MCARTHUR, GILBERT B.
MCCARTY, DR. HANOCH
MCCLARY, CLEBE
MCCORMICK, MS. PATRICIA
MCCOY, DORIS L., PH.D.
MCDONALD, THOMAS, PH.D.
MCILVAIN, TED L.
MCKAIN, SCOTT
MCKENZIE, SAMUEL
MCKINLEY, MICHAEL
   P. (CPAE)
MCKINNEY, ANNE M., J.D.
MCNAIR, J. FRANK
MEADES, KEN
MEEKS, DAVID &
   ASSOCIATES
MEISENHEIMER, JIM
MENTA, SISTER
   ANGELICA M.
MERCER, MICHAEL W., PH.D.
MERCHANT, RONALD
MERRITT, CONNIE
METCALF, ED, DR.
METZGER, RICK L.
MEYER, BILL
MICALE, FRANCES A.
MILLER, ANNE
   PROMOTIONS, INC.
MILLER, JOHNNY
MILLER, MADELYN
MILLER, REV. MARILYN K.
MILLER, VALERIE J. S.
MILTEER, LEE
MINER, DAVID LEE
MINNICK, DALEH
MITCHELL, W.
MOHNEY, DR. NELL W.

MOODY, ROY E.	PRICE, BETTE	SANDLIN, RUSSELL	STEVENS, SUZANNE H.
MOORE, JAMES F.	PRICE, DON L.	SANFILIPPO, BARBARA	STEWART, DAVID
MORAN, KEVIN M.	PRIESKORN, JOHN PH.D.	SANFORD, JAMES VIKING	STEWART, LAURIE A.
MOREL, LIN M.	PRIGAL, KENNETH B.K.	SASSI, PAULA A.	STEWART, ROD
MOREO, JUDI	PROUT, LINDA L., M.S.	SAUBY, RON	STOLTZFUS, D. LEE, PH.D.
MORGAN, DONALD R.	PUTZIER, JOHN	SAUER, JOHN R.	STONE, D. CONWAY
MORRIS, WILLIAM C.	RADDE, PAUL O.	SCANNELL, EDWARD E.	SUCKOW, BOB
MORRISON, ANN M.	RADTKE, RICHARD L.	SCHENK, GEORGE	SUKENICK, RON D.
MORTELL, ART	RAEL, RON, CPA	SCHIAVO, 'FANTASTIC FRED'	SULLIVAN, TERRY
MULVANEY, MAUREEN	RAETHER, EDIE	SCHLAMOWITZ, KEVAN, DR.	SUMMER, SHIRLEY
MUNGAVAN, THOMAS E.	RAFINSKI, MARCIA	SCHMIDT, JOY A.	SUTTON, SUZY
MURDOCK, KEN	RANDOLPH, ROBERT M.	SCHOEMAN, MARILYN	SWANSON, DAVID
MURRAY, MARCELLA	RASBAND, JUDITH	SCHREINER, CAROL D.	SWINDELL, GENE
MYERS, JANET L.	RAST, EDWARD	SCHULTZ, KAREN ROSE	TANSEY, DR. DAVE
MYERS, JEFFRY W.	REAGAN, MICHAEL R.	SCHUSTER, DIANE L.	TAYLOR, MEREDITH
MYRICK, SUE	(CPC/CPS)	SCHWARTZ, ARNOLD L.	TAYLOR, PAULA R., M.A.
NABERS, MARY SCOTT	REAVES, CHUCK	SCHWARTZ, FRANCIE	TEPLITZ, JERRY V., DR.
NASH, LINDA J.	RECKNER, JERALD	SCOBEY, SALLY	TEPPER, BRUCE
NELSON, SANDRA	(JERRY) H.	SCOTT, CHARLES W.	TERRY, ELLEN
NELSON, WILLIE	REED, DEBRA J.	(CHUCK), COL.	THOMAS, CLIFF, R.PH.
NEWMAN, RICHARD D.	REESE, MONTE	SCOTT, SUSAN	TISDALE, J. WAYNE
NEWSOME, PAULA R.	RENSTROM, GREGORY	SEARCY, RHODA M.	TOMCZAK, LARRY-MR.
NICHOLSON, SHERYL	REUM, EARL, DR.	SHARP, SALLY O.	VERSATILITY
NIELSEN, RICK J.	REYNOLDS, PATRICK	SHEA, CHARLENE	TREJO, WILLIE
NIENSTEDT, JOHN F.	RHOADES, ROGER A.	SHELTON, LEE	TROUT; SHIRLEY
NORTON, KEN	RHODES, ROY, ED.D.	SHELTON, SANDRA A.	TURNER, ROSLYN A.
NUNES, MARIANNA	RICH, SUSAN A.	SHUH, AL & ASSOCIATES	TUROCK, ART
O'CONNOR, CAROL	RICHARDS, RAMONA	SHULTS, JOHN A.	TURPIN, BEN
O'DOOLEY, PATRICK	RICHARDSON, DAVID W.	SIBERT, DENNIS G.	TYRIAN, CHARLIE
OAKLEY, ED	RICHARDSON, TIM	SILVER, IDORA	TYTER, RICHARD
OBERG, BILL	RIFENBARY, JAY C.	SIMMS, STEVE	UDELL, BARBARA A.
OLDAK, EMILY	RINKE, WOLF J., PH.D.	SIMON, BARBARA J.	UHLAR, BOB & CARLA
OLSON, HARRY A.	RISBERG, GREG	SIMS, D. PHILLIP	GOLDEN
OSMAN, WALI M. PH.D.	RITCHIE, JAN	SIRESS, JIM	UHLER, JAY, C.P.C
OSTARO, DHRUV	RITSCHER, JIM	SKOGLUND, ROBERT	UHLER, MATTHEW
OUTLAW, KEMILEE K.	ROACH, MARY BETH	SLADE, TOM	UKER, DON
OXLEY, ROBERT R.	ROBERT, CAVETT	SLOTKIN, FRAN S.	USELDINGER, RONALD E.
PAGANO, BARBARA L.	ROBERT, LEE E.	SMART, DOUG	VAN DYKE, FLAVIL Q.
PAGE, SUSAN	ROBERTS, KATHI	SMITH, CARL T.	VARGA, MARI PAT
PALMQUIST, RICHARD	ROBISON, AUBRY, JR.	SMITH, DIANE ELLINGSON	VASQUEZ, SABINE GROSS
PARINELLO, AL	ROGERS, LOUISA	SMITH, HAROLD IVAN	VAUGHAN, SUZANNE
PARISSE, ALAN J.	ROHLANDER, DAVID	SMITH, J. THOMAS	VINING, EARLENE
PARKER, LARRY R.	ROLFE, RANDY	SMITH, RICHARD Q.	WADE, ALLAN L.
PAULSON, TERRY	ROSE, ALBERT L.	SMITH, ROY L.	WADE, BOB ED.D.
L., PH.D. (CPAE)	ROSENBAUM, JERRY, CLU	SMITH, WALTER D.	WALKER, ANNE
PAYNE, JUDY	ROSENBERG, DEANNE	SNYDER, MARILYN	WALLACE, JOANNE
PAYNE, THOMAS E.	ROSENBERG, RICHARD	SOMMER, BOBBE, PH.D.	WALLACE, KEN
PEARL, LYNN	ROSS, KENNETH	SORENTINO, PHIL	WALSH, PATRICIA ANN, ED.D.
PENNER, SHEBA	ROSSITER, SHERRY KNIGHT	SPENCER, DUFFY, PH.D.	WALTERS, DOTTIE
PEPPER, MICHAEL J.	ROTRAMEL, RICK	SPENGLER, CHRISTINE J.	WALTHER, GEORGE
PETERSEN, GLORIA	ROUSH, SHERYL L.	(CPS/CAM)	R. (CPAE)
PETERSEN, KRISTELLE	ROUSOPOULOS, DENO	STACY, GAYLON	WANGBERG, 'DR. LOU'
PETERSEN, RUTH KAY	RUDNICKI, BARBARA A.	STALEY, MICHAEL F.	WARD, AUDREY PEELE
PETSCHULAT, DR. NEUB	RUSSELL, RAY L., DR.	STARR, ROBERT BRUCE	WAREHAM, GWENDOLYN
PICKERING, DAVE	RYAN, LYNN	STAUB, JAMES R.	WARREN, JOHN
PILGRIM, M. SUSAN	SABAH, JUDY	STAUTER, ROGER	WARZECHA, MARY M.
PILLOW, JOHN G. (MHS)	SABINE, ELIZABETH	STEIN, CAROLYN	WATSON, DONNA S.
PLUMMER, RICHARD E., DR.	SADOVSKY, ANNE	STEIN, SANDY	WATSON, DR. DONNA S.
PODANY, SUE	SALINGER, TONY	STENNES, BARBARA	WATSON, JEAN
POLK, JANE M.	SANBORN, MARK H.	STEPHANI, SUSAN	WEISEL, JACQUES
POTUCK, MARK W.	SANDFORD, VIRGINIA A.	STERN, DEBRA	WEISS, ALAN PH.D.

WELLS, THELMA &
  ASSOCIATES
WENOS, GAIL (CPAE)
WERNER, STAN 'THE HAND'
WEYLMAN, C. RICHARD
WHARTON, MARCIA M.
WHITE, SOMERS
WHITE, STAN
WHITT, JIM
WIKLUND, PATRICIA PH.D.
WILCOX, CHUCK
WILDE, LARRY
WILDFOGEL, JEFFREY PH.D.
WILHELM, DOROTHY
WILKHOLM, MARIOU S.
WILKINS, WALLACE PH.D.
WILKINSON, BRUCE S.
WILLIAMS, JIM, CAPT.
WILLIAMS, MIKKI
WILSON, JERRY R.
WILSON, JUSTIN
WILSON, LARRY
WOLD, BARBARA
WOLINSKI, KIM
WOOD, BETTY
WOODCOCK, DAVID
WOOLF, REESA, PH.D.
WYSS, O'NEILL
YAMAMOTO, GARY K.
YAMBERT, CONSTANCE
  DEAN
YOHO, DAVID
YOUNG, DOUG
YOUNG, WOODY
ZAKIAN, ALICE L.
ZEZZA, MYRNA
ZICK, BERNARD HALE
ZIMMERMAN, DR. ALAN R.
ZIMMERMAN, TOM
ZINGER, JIM
ZUMM, TOM

NATURE

BOYD, LORRIE DR.
CUMMINGS, DR. RITA J.
DEAL, SHELDON C.
DEE, EMILY
DILLON, ILENE L.
MCCOY, DORIS L., PH.D.
RADTKE, RICHARD L.
ROBERTS, JANET M.
SCANLON, DERALEE R.D.
SUMMER, SHIRLEY
VARMA, VISH

PERSONAL FINANCE

ACERS, PATSY
ALFORD, RON
ARTERBURN, STEPHEN

BARNHILL, ROBERT E. III
BRILES, DR. JUDITH
BURGETT, GORDON
CARSON, TERRENCE J.
CONLON, PETER J., JR.
DACEY, JUDITH E., CPA
DAVIDSON, JEFF
  (MBA) (CMC)
DAVIS, DARRYL
ELIAS, JEFF
FIORE, JAMES
FLICKINGER, BONNIE G.
FOSTER, LARRY J.
FRIEDMAN, SIDNEY A.
GARTON-GOOD, JULIE
GREENWOOD, RON
HAVEY, CAROL V.
HERBSTER, DOUGLAS DR.
HESSE, DOUGLAS G.
HOXWORTH, STEVE
ISRAELOV, RHODA
JENSEN, JAY R.
KATELHON, GERALD P.
KEEFFE, CAROL
KERLEY, WILLIAM C.
KERSTETTER, KERRY M.
KOPP, KRISTIN
LEVY, JEFFREY G.
LOWE, PETER
MCARTHUR, GILBERT B.
MCKINNEY, ANNE M., J.D.
MCMAHON, MICHAEL
MILLER, ANNE
  PROMOTIONS, INC.
MILLER, REV. MARILYN K.
MONJI, MICHAEL A.
PALUMBO, JOHN A.
PAPE, GLENN
PESUT, TIM S.
RAEL, RON, CPA
RIDGWAY, JO
ROBERTS, BRUCE A.
ROHLANDER, DAVID
SAUBY, RON
STATON, BILL
SUMMER, SHIRLEY
TOMCZAK, LARRY-MR.
  VERSATILITY
WHITE, SOMERS
WILLEY, ALLAN D.
WILLIAMS, JIM, CAPT.
WILSON, CAROL ANN
WORDHOUSE, PHYLLIS J.
WYSS, O'NEILL
ZICK, BERNARD HALE

PHILOSOPHY

ANFINSON, STACIE A.
ARTERBURN, STEPHEN
BENNIE, MARK

BISHOP, VENNA
BLAKELY, DON & MIKE
BROWN, LINDEE S.
BRUN, DONALD J.
BUCARO, FRANK C.
CARTER, ARNOLD 'NICK'
CSOLKOVITS, ERNEST A.
DEAL, SHELDON C.
DILLON, ILENE L.
FLICKINGER, E. G.
GOLDMAN, CONNIE
GRANT, LYNELLA F.
GUTRIDGE, DON FOSTER
HERBSTER, DOUGLAS DR.
ISLER, MARK
JOHNSON, HUB, PH.D.
JUTKINS, RAY W.
KERLEY, WILLIAM C.
KOJM, KURT BARNABY
KOPP, KRISTIN
LENZ, BOB
LOVERDE, MARY
LYTLE, TOBI L.
MCKAIN, SCOTT
MILIOS, RITA
MORTELL, ART
MYERS, JEFFRY W.
OUTLAW, KEMILEE K.
RICHARDS, RAMONA
SIMON, BARBARA J.
STARR, ROBERT BRUCE
SUMMER, SHIRLEY
TURPIN, BEN
TYRIAN, CHARLIE
UHLAR, BOB & CARLA
  GOLDEN
WALLACE, KEN
WERNER, STAN 'THE HAND'
WEST, KEN
YOUNG, DOUG
ZEZZA, MYRNA
ZIMMERMAN, DR. ALAN R.

PHOTOGRAPHY

BILKER, HARVEY L.
HORVATH, DENNIS D.
HORVATH, TERRI
JONES, DEWITT
PISCOPO, MARIA
RICHARDS, RAMONA
ROBERTS, JANET M.
ROSENBERG, RICHARD
TROUT, SHIRLEY
WILLIAMS, JOHN R., LCDR

PHYSICAL FITNESS

BORCHELT, FREDERICK E.
CARTER, ARNOLD 'NICK'
CASE, BOB

CUMMING, CANDY
CUMMINGS, DR. RITA J.
DEAL, SHELDON C.
DEAN, BONNIE 'THE MOTION
  COACH'
DEROSE, ROLAND
DONALDSON, KEITH
DVORAK, ROBERT REGIS
FISHER, SANDRA L.
GRANT, CAROL
GROPPEL, JACK L. PH.D.
HAYES, STEPHEN K.
INTERNATIONAL INSTITUTE
  OF REFLEXOLOGY
JEPPESEN, LYNDA
  FRANCE MBA
JOHNSON, DR. JOYCE
KVITKA, ELAINE
LINKLETTER, ART
LOCKRIDGE, ALICE
MILLER, ANNE
  PROMOTIONS, INC.
MILLER, MADELYN
MORRIS, WILLIAM C.
MORSCHER, BETSY, PH.D.
MYERS, JEFFRY W.
PODANY, SUE
PYFER, HOWARD R. M.D.
REYNOLDS, PATRICK
ROACH-KILCUP, DONNA L.
RYBACK, DAVID, DR.
SCANLON, DERALEE R.D.
SEARCY, RHODA M.
STRIKE, LOUIS N.
SUCKOW, BOB
TEPLITZ, JERRY V., DR.
TYRIAN, CHARLIE
USELDINGER, RONALD E.
WILLIAMS, MIKKI
YOUNG, GARY A.

PSYCHOLOGY

ABBOTT, DR. LINDA M.C.
ALESANDRINI, KATHRYN,
  PH.D.
ANDERSON, DALE L.
ANDERSON, KARE
ARTERBURN, STEPHEN
ATKINS, CHANDLER PH.D.
BALL, DR. ROBERT R.
BARRETT, DIANNE
  E. R.N., M.A.
BENNETT, LOIS E.,
  M.ED.,M.A.
BENNIE, MARK
BERG, DR. DEANNA
BERGER, RUTH
BISHOP, VENNA
BISSELL, BEN
BLAKELY, DON & MIKE

BOYD, LORRIE DR.
BRODER, MICHAEL S. PHD
BROWNELL, EILEEN O.
BRUNER, HELEN L.C.S.W.
BUTLER, JENNIFER
CALMES, MARYLEE
CAMPBELL, SANDRA JONES
CANFIELD, JACK
CARLE, GILDA PHD
CARMODY, KATHY
CARSON, RICHARD D.
CARTER, ARNOLD 'NICK'
CHRISTOPHER, SYLVIA
COPELAND, GARY R.
CORNYN-SELBY, ALYCE
CREEL, JOANNE P.
CROWSON, GATHA ROMINE
CSOLKOVITS, ERNEST A.
DAVIS, DARRYL
DECKER, DON B.
DILLON, ILENE L.
DOORNICK, ROBERT
DRENCH, MEREDITH E. PHD
DWYER, DAWN
FIELDER GROUP, THE
FIORE, NEIL A., PH.D.
FLICKINGER, BONNIE G.
FOUNTAIN, ELEANOR A.
FRAGER, STANLEY R. PHD
FRAZEE, LINDA
FRESHOUR, FRANK W.
GALLAGHER, BILL
  'GUERRILLA', PH.D.
GARBISCH, WALTER E.
GESELL, IZZY
GILBERT, ROB, PH.D
GIOIA, JOYCE L.
GLICK, BARBARA
GOLDMAN, CONNIE
GOOD, PERRY
GRANGER, SUSAN
GRANGER, VIRGINIA M.
GREEN, LILA
GREENE, IDA
GRIESSMAN, GENE, PH.D.
GUTRIDGE, DON FOSTER
HAGESETH, CHRISTIAN III
HARPER, JEANNE M.
HARRAL, CHAS
HATHAWAY, PATTI
HAVEY, CAROL V.
HAYES, STEPHEN K.
HELSTEIN, IVY
HERBSTER, DOUGLAS DR.
HERRON, SANDRA
  WHITACRE
HODGES, WILLIAM N.
JAMES, DIANA L.
KARPOVICH, MICHAEL S.
KARTEN, NAOMI
KERLEY, WILLIAM C.

KICK, FRAN
KLEIN, RUTH L.
KLOCK, JOSEPH P.
KNACKSTEDT, MARY V.
KOPP, KRISTIN
LEE, BILL
LEICHTY, MARLENE A.
LEMKE, RAYMOND
LENZ, BOB
LINQUIST, LUANN
LISK, THOM
LITTAUER, FLORENCE
LITTAUER, MARITA
LOWE, PETER
LUETHY, DR. GERRY
LYTLE, TOBI L.
MANNING, MARILYN, PH.D.
MARKEL, GERALDINE PH.D.
MATSCHEK, CHERYL A.
MATTIMORE, BRYAN W.
MCCARTY, DR. HANOCH
MCCOY, DORIS L., PH.D.
MCDONALD, THOMAS, PH.D.
MCGHEE, PAUL E., PH.D.
MCNAIR, J. FRANK
MCNEIL, MICHAEL R. (BCSW)
MENTA, SISTER
  ANGELICA M.
MERCER, MICHAEL W., PH.D.
MILIOS, RITA
MILLER, ANNE
  PROMOTIONS, INC.
MINNINGER, JOAN
MORRISON, ANN M.
NATIONAL TRAUMA
  SERVICES
NELSON, WILLIE
O'CONNOR, CAROL
OBERG, BILL
OLESEN, ERIK L.
OLSON, HARRY A.
OUTLAW, KEMILEE K.
PAGE, SUSAN
PARKER, CHARLES E.
PESUT, TIM S.
PILGRIM, M. SUSAN
POLK, JANE M.
PUTZIER, JOHN
RADDE, PAUL O.
RAETHER, EDIE
RAFINSKI, MARCIA
RASBAND, JUDITH
RENSTROM, GREGORY
RHOADES, ROGER A.
RHODES, ROY, ED.D.
RICHARDS, RAMONA
RITCHIE, JAN
ROBERTS, JERRY W.
ROBERTS, KATHI
ROBERTS, RONALD H. PH.D.
ROSENBAUM, JERRY, CLU

ROSENBERG, DEANNE
ROSSITER, SHERRY KNIGHT
RYBACK, DAVID, DR.
SANFORD, JAMES VIKING
SASSI, PAULA A.
SCHLAMOWITZ, KEVAN, DR.
SCHWARTZ, ELAINE
SCOTT, GINI
  GRAHAM, PH.D., J.D.
SCOTT, SUSAN
SEARCY, RHODA M.
SHANNON, SHARON L.
SIMON, BARBARA J.
SIMS, D. PHILLIP
SMITH, J. THOMAS
SOARES, DR. CECILIA J.
SOMMER, BOBBE, PH.D.
STEIL, LYMAN K. (MANNY),
  DR. (CPAE)
STERN, DEBRA
STOLTZFUS, D. LEE, PH.D.
STONE, D. CONWAY
SUMMER, SHIRLEY
SUTTON, JAMES D., DR.
SWANSON, DAVID
THOMPSON, BILLIE
TINGLEY, JUDITH C.
TYRIAN, CHARLIE
UHLER, JAY, C.P.C
VAUGHAN, SUZANNE
WAGNER, JOHN P.
WALL, KEVIN DONALD
WAREHAM, GWENDOLYN
WEISS, ALAN PH.D.
WEISS, BONNIE
WERNER, STAN 'THE HAND'
WHARTON, MARCIA M.
WIKLUND, PATRICIA PH.D.
WILDFOGEL, JEFFREY PH.D.
WILKHOLM, MARIOU S.
WILKINS, WALLACE PH.D.
WILSON, STEVE
WOLF, JOHN M. 'JACK' PH.D.
WOLINSKI, KIM
ZIMMERMAN, DR. ALAN R.
ZIMMERMAN, TOM
ZINGER, JIM

RELIGION

ANDERSON, DALE L.
BAKER, HELEN JOYCE
BALL, DR. ROBERT R.
BARNHILL, ROBERT E. III
BENNETT, LOIS E.,
  M.ED.,M.A.
BIRK, RON
BISHOP, VENNA
BORCHELT, FREDERICK E.
BROWN, KATHY &
  ASSOCIATES

BROWN, LINDEE S.
CARTER, ARNOLD 'NICK'
CROWSON, GATHA ROMINE
DEROSE, ROLAND
DILLON, ILENE L.
DWYER, DAWN
FARRELL, ROBERT E.
FLICKINGER, BONNIE G.
GIOIA, JOYCE L.
HARPER, JEANNE M.
HAYES, STEPHEN K.
HEADLEY, WILLIAM
HERRON, SANDRA
  WHITACRE
JACKSON, LUAN
JACOBS, ANITA I.
JAMES, DIANA L.
JENSEN, JAY R.
KERLEY, WILLIAM C.
KOJM, KURT BARNABY
LAUFER, JOSEPH M.
LEE, CLIFFORD M., DR.
LENZ, BOB
LISK, THOM
LITTAUER, FLORENCE
LITTAUER, MARITA
LITTLEFIELD, HENRY M.
LLOYD, HERB J.
LOWE, PETER
MAYNE, MAVIS
MCCLARY, CLEBE
MCNAIR, J. FRANK
MENTA, SISTER
  ANGELICA M.
MILLER, REV. MARILYN K.
MOHNEY, DR. NELL W.
NIELSEN, RICK J.
OBERG, BILL
OLSON, HARRY A.
OUTLAW, KEMILEE K.
RADKE, DALE L.
RHOADES, ROGER A.
ROBERTS, JANET M.
RUSSELL, RAY L., DR.
SAUBY, RON
SCHULTZ, KAREN ROSE
SLADE, TOM
SMITH, HAROLD IVAN
STONE, D. CONWAY
SUCKOW, BOB
SUTTON, JAMES D., DR.
TAILLON, YAHZDI
TREJO, WILLIE
TROUT, SHIRLEY
UHLAR, BOB & CARLA
  GOLDEN
VASSALLO, WANDA
WALL, KEVIN DONALD
WALLACE, JOANNE
WEISS, ALAN PH.D.
WENOS, GAIL (CPAE)

WILSON, JERRY R.
YOUNG, WOODY

SALES

ALESSANDRA, DR. TONY
ALEXANDER, BOB
ALLEN, ELIZABETH 'BETSY'
ALLEN, GORDIE
ANDERSON, LESTER W.
ARNSTEIN, SAM
AUN, MICHAEL A.
BACHRACH, WILLIAM
BAKER, LEN
BALZER, ALVIN L.
BARKER, JOCK
BARNHILL, ROBERT E. III
BARRERA, RICK
BARRON, LAURA
BASSETT, LAWRENCE
  (LARRY) C. (CMC)
BEARDEN, JIM
BENDER, BEV
BENNIE, MARK
BERG, DR. DEANNA
BERGER, FRANCINE
BERGER, RUTH
BERMAN, HELEN
BESDANSKY, BRENDA
BETHEL, BILL
BETHEL, SHEILA MURRAY
BILLINGS-HARRIS, LENDRA
BILLUE, STAN
BISHOP, VENNA
BLACKMAN, JEFF, J.D.
BLAKELY, DON & MIKE
BLOCH, ROBERT H.
BOILEAU & ASSOCIATES
BOLTON, DENNY
BOYAN, LEE
BRITTON, TOM
BROOKS, EVE
BRUN, DONALD J.
BUDD, NANCY
BURG, BOB
BURNS, PAT
BURRUS, DANIEL
BURZYNSKI, LINDA L.
BUSSEY, TROY D.
BUTLER, JENNIFER
CABRERA, JIMMY
CALHOON, JOE
CANFIELD, JACK
CARLINO, ANDY
CARR, SHARON
CARSON, GAYLE, DR.
CARTER, ARNOLD 'NICK'
CARUSO, JOSEPH A.
CHARBONNEAU, JOS. J.
CHITWOOD, ROY E.
COATES, MARTY

COLOMBO, GEORGE W.
CONDON, GWEN
CONNOR, TIM
COTTLE, DEBRA
COUCH, DR. BOB E., PH.D.
CRAWFORD, SALLY L.
CROWSON, GATHA ROMINE
CSOLKOVITS, ERNEST A.
D'ANDREA, JOSEPH J.
DAFFRON, RAY
DAVEY, JUDY
DAVIDSON,
  JEFF (MBA) (CMC)
DAVIS, DARRYL
DAVIS, KEVIN F.
DAVIS, RONALD L.
DAWSON, ROGER
  PRODUCTIONS, INC.
DEAN, BONNIE 'THE MOTION
  COACH'
DEAN, HARVEY D.
DECKER, DON B.
DEROSE, ROLAND
DIDONATO, RALPH
DOHERTY, BILL
DONADIO, PATRICK J.
DONALDSON, KEITH
DOORNICK, ROBERT
DORSEY, CALVIN
DORSEY, IVORY
DUBIN, BURT
DVORAK, ROBERT REGIS
ECK, ARLENE
EGGLESTON, JULIA
EINSTEIN ALIVE
ELVES, CONRAD
EMMERICH, ROXANNE
FILIPPO, LOU 'COACH'
FINK, MARTHA
FLETCHER, JERRY L.
FORZANO, RICK E.
FOUNTAIN, ELEANOR A.
FOX, JOAN G.
FRACASSI, LINDA F.
FRANK, MIKE, (CPAE)
FRESHOUR, FRANK W.
GABRIELSEN, RON (CCM)
GALLAGHER, BILL
  'GUERRILLA', PH.D.
GALLAGHER, CATHY L.
GARFINKEL, DAVID
GEDALIAH, ROBERT
GEDAN, IRA
GEE, BOBBIE
GERAGHTY, BARBARA
GILLESPIE, JEFFREY A.
GIOIA, JOYCE L.
GITTERMAN, HEIDI
GOLBERT, GLORIA
GOOZE, MITCHELL
GREENE, TAG

GREIF, ED
GUTIERREZ, JUAN F.
GUTRIDGE, DON FOSTER
HALTER, 'DIAMOND' JIM
HALVERSON, DEAN
HANSEN, MARK VICTOR
HANSON, JERRY
HARBIN, CHARLES
HASKELL, JOHN S.
HAWLEY, CASEY FITTS
HELVEY, EDWARD P., JR.
HENNIG, JAMES F., PH.D
HERBSTER, DOUGLAS DR.
HEROLD, MORT
HIGHTSHOE, NANCY
HIXON, GEORGE G.
HODGES, WILLIAM N.
HOLDER, VERN
HORVATH, DENNIS D.
HOWLEY, C. JOE
HOXWORTH, STEVE
HULL, MIRIAM B.
HUMPHRIES, ANN
  CHADWELL
HUNTER, C. ROY
HUNTER, WILLIAM L.
HUTSON, DON
HYKEN, SHEP A.
HYKEN, SHEP A.
JACK, BARBARA M.
JACOBS, ELLEN
JAMES, MERLIN R.
JANSEN, ROBERT H.
JASIM, JANIE
JEPPESEN, LYNDA
  FRANCE MBA
JOHNSON, BILL L.
JOHNSON, CAROL
JOY, PAM
JUTKINS, RAY W.
KABACHNICK, TERRI
KAHN, RITA
KARR, RONALD E.
KENNEDY, DAN S.
KHERA, SHIV
KILPATRICK, KURT
KING, CHRIS
KING, HARLEY
KLEIN, RUTH L.
KLOCK, JOSEPH P.
KNOLL, HERBERT E. JR.
KNOX, DAVID S.
KOJM, KURT BARNABY
KOLTIN, ALLAN DAVID, CPA
KOTZ, STEVE
KRAMER, ROBERT G.
KUTSKO, JIM
LAIPPLY, SANDY
LARSEN, LARRY L.
LEACH, LYNNE C.
LEE, BILL

LEEDS, DOROTHY
LEFKOWITZ, HAL
LEICHTY, MARLENE A.
LEMKE, RAYMOND
LEONE, RAY
LERMAN, KENNETH B.
LETOURNEAU, TOM
LEVIN, ROGER P.
LINKLETTER, ART
LISK, THOM
LLOYD, HERB J.
LONTOS, PAM
LOSSY, RELLA
LOWE, PETER
LOWELL TRAINING &
  CONSULTING
LYTLE, TOBI L.
MAAS, GARY
MANNERING, DENNIS E.
MARINO, MIKE JR. 'IN
  PERSON'
MARTH, ROALD D.
MASUMOTO, PAT
MATSCHEK, CHERYL A.
MATTIMORE, BRYAN W.
MAYFIELD, TERRY L.
MAYNARD, MICHAEL
MCARDLE, KEVIN J.
MCDONALD, THOMAS, PH.D.
MCNAIR, J. FRANK
MEADES, KEN
MEISENHEIMER, JIM
MERCER, MICHAEL W., PH.D.
MEYER, BILL
MICALE, FRANCES A.
MILLER, ANNE
MILLER, ANNE
  PROMOTIONS, INC.
MILLER, JOHNNY
MILLER, MADELYN
MILTEER, LEE
MINNICK, DALEH
MITCHELL, HERBERT E.
MONK, ART
MOORE, LAURIE
MOREO, JUDI
MORGAN, REBECCA
MORTELL, ART
MURDOCK, KEN
MYERS, JANET L.
NASH, LINDA J.
NEWMAN, RICHARD D.
NICHOLSON, SHERYL
NIENSTEDT, JOHN F.
NUNES, MARIANNA
OECHSLI, MATTHEW J.
OUTLAW, KEMILEE K.
OUTLAW, WAYNE
OXLEY, ROBERT R.
PALMQUIST, RICHARD
PALUMBO, JOHN A.

PARISSE, ALAN J.
PARKER, CHARLES E.
PAYNE, THOMAS E.
PEARL, LYNN
PEOPLES, DAVID
PETERSEN, KRISTELLE
PETERSEN, RUTH KAY
PHILLIPS, RICK
PILLOW, JOHN G. (MHS)
POOSER, DORIS
POPYK, BOB
PRICE, DON L.
PUTNAM, HOWARD D.
RAETHER, EDIE
RAST, EDWARD
REAGAN, MICHAEL R.
  (CPC/CPS)
REAVES, CHUCK
RECKNER, JERALD
  (JERRY) H.
REED, DAVE
RENSTROM, GREGORY
RHODES, ROY, ED.D.
RICHARDSON, DAVID W.
RIFENBARY, JAY C.
RIGSBEE, ED
ROACH, MARY BETH
ROBERT, CAVETT
ROBERT, LEE E.
ROBERTS, KATHI
ROBINSON, EMMET
ROHLANDER, DAVID
ROOS, JAMES P.
RYAN, LYNN
SABAH, JOE
SADOVSKY, ANNE
SANDLIN, RUSSELL
SANDROS, DON
SANFILIPPO, BARBARA
SANFORD, JAMES VIKING
SCHEESSELE, WILLIAM
SCHENK, GEORGE
SCHWARTZ, ARNOLD L.
SCHWARTZ, FRANCIE
SCHWARZ, BARB
SCOTT, GINI
  GRAHAM, PH.D., J.D.
SEARCY, RHODA M.
SHANNON, SHARON L.
SHAPIRO, DON
SHARP, SALLY O.
SHELTON, LEE
SHERMAN, RALPH
SHUH, AL & ASSOCIATES
SIMMS, STEVE
SJODIN, TERRI
SLADE, TOM
SMART, DOUG
SMITH, CARL T.
SMITH, MARK S. A., CPC
SMITH, RICHARD Q.

SOBCZAK, ART J.
STAUTER, ROGER
STEIL, LYMAN K.
  (MANNY), DR. (CPAE)
STEIN, CAROLYN
STENNES, BARBARA
STEPHANI, SUSAN
STEWART, DAVID
STEWART, MIKE
STOLTZFUS, D. LEE, PH.D.
STONE, D. CONWAY
STRIKE, LOUIS N.
SUKENICK, RON D.
SULLIVAN, TERRY
SUMMEY, MIKE
SWANSON, DAVID
SWINDELL, GENE
TARASAVAGE, EDWARD B.
  (CHA) (CFBE)
TEPLITZ, JERRY V., DR.
TEPPER, BRUCE
TERRY, ELLEN
THOMAS, ELAINE J.
THOMAS, JEFFERY M.
TOMCZAK, LARRY-MR.
  VERSATILITY
TRUAX, WILLIAM J.
TUROCK, ART
TURPIN, BEN
TYRIAN, CHARLIE
UDELL, BARBARA A.
VERRI, ROSEMARY
WALLACE, KEN
WALTERS, DOTTIE
WALTHER,
  GEORGE R. (CPAE)
WANGBERG, 'DR. LOU'
WAYMON, LYNNE
WEISEL, JACQUES
WEISS, ALAN PH.D.
WESNER, ERIC C.
WEXLER, PHILLIP S.
WEYLMAN, C. RICHARD
WHALIN, GEORGE
WHITE, BARTON C.
WHITE, SOMERS
WIGGLE, PHILIP LAWRENCE
WILCOX, CHUCK
WILDFOGEL, JEFFREY PH.D.
WILKINS, WALLACE PH.D.
WILLIAMS, JOHN R., LCDR
WILLIAMS, MIKKI
WILLIAMSON, JOHN S.
WILSON, JERRY R.
WILSON, KAREN
WILSON, LARRY
WOLD, BARBARA
WOLF, JOHN M. 'JACK' PH.D.
WOODS, RHONDA B.
YAMBERT, CONSTANCE
  DEAN

YOHO, DAVID
YOUNG, DOUG
YOUNG, WOODY
ZAKIAN, ALICE L.
ZELL, LEONARD
  PROFESSIONAL SALES
  TRAINING
ZIMMERMAN, DR. ALAN R.
ZINGER, JIM
ZUMM, TOM

SCIENCE

JONES, MARILYN K., DDS
MURRAY, JOAN
O'CONNOR, JERRY
PATTON, RICHARD M.
RADTKE, RICHARD L.
RADTKE, RICHARD, L.
UNDERWOOD, RICHARD W.
VARMA, VISH

SENIOR CITIZENS

ACERS, PATSY
AMBROSIUS, RICHARD, CEO
BASSETT, LAWRENCE
  (LARRY) C. (CMC)
BELGUM, MERRILYN
BETHEL, BILL
BISHOP, VENNA
BROWN, KATHY &
  ASSOCIATES
BRUNER, HELEN L.C.S.W.
BUDD, NANCY
CHINN, C. EARL
CONLON, PETER J., JR.
CUROE, JOHN
DEE, EMILY
DEMKO, DAVID J.
DILLON, ILENE L.
FIELDER GROUP, THE
FIORE, JAMES
FYOCK, CATHERINE D.
GANNETT, MARYE D.
GESELL, IZZY
GOLDMAN, CONNIE
GRANGER, VIRGINIA M.
GREEN, LILA
GREENWOOD, RON
HAYASHI, MIKE
HEADLEY, WILLIAM
HERBSTER, DOUGLAS DR.
HEROLD, MORT
HILL, JOANNE K.
JAMES, DIANA L.
JANSEN, ROBERT H.
KING, HARLEY
LAFRENIERE, DONNA
LEBEAU, CALENE
LEICHTY, MARLENE A.

LEMKE, RAYMOND
LINKLETTER, ART
LINQUIST, LUANN
LUBOTSKY, TERRY
LUETHY, DR. GERRY
LYFORD, LOIS
MCCRASY, C. WILEY
MCKINNEY, ANNE M., J.D.
MOHNEY, DR. NELL W.
NOLAN, THOMAS L. JR.
O'CONNOR, CAROL
O'HARA, CAROL
OUTLAW, KEMILEE K.
PETSCHULAT, DR. NEUB
RASBAND, JUDITH
RISCH, THEODORE 'TED'
ROSS, MARILYN
ROSS, TOM
RUSSELL, RAY L., DR.
RYAN, LYNN
SANDFORD, VIRGINIA A.
SCANLON, DERALEE R.D.
SMITH, HAROLD IVAN
STEIN, SANDY
SUCKOW, BOB
THOMAS, ELAINE J.
TURPIN, BEN
WATSON, JEAN
WEISBERG, JACOB
WEISS, BONNIE
WOOD, BETTY

SOCIAL TRENDS

BASSETT, LAWRENCE
  (LARRY) C. (CMC)
BLACKMAN, JEFF, J.D.
BOCK, WALLY
CREEL, JOANNE P.
CROWSON, GATHA ROMINE
DAVIDSON,
  JEFF (MBA) (CMC)
DEE, EMILY
DEMKO, DAVID J.
DOORNICK, ROBERT
EVANS, ROBERT MAYER
EVERDING, MARIA
GERAGHTY, BARBARA
GIOIA, JOYCE L.
GOLLIVER, JOY J.
GRANT, LYNELLA F.
GRIESSMAN, GENE, PH.D.
HAVEY, CAROL V.
HERMAN, ROGER E. CMC
HERMAN, ROGER E., (CMC)
HUGHES, LADDIE W.
HUMPHRIES, ANN
  CHADWELL
INGRAM, ROBERT
KING, CHRIS
LADDIE, W. HUGHES

LENZ, BOB
LERMAN, KENNETH B.
LOVELESS, KATHY
LYTLE, TOBI L.
MALLERY, SUZY
MCCOY, DORIS L., PH.D.
MOREL, LIN M.
MORRISON, ANN M.
MORTELL, ART
NABERS, MARY SCOTT
OUTLAW, KEMILEE K.
PAULSON, TERRY
  L., PH.D. (CPAE)
PETERSEN, KRISTELLE
POOSER, DORIS
PULLIAM, LINDA
PUTZIER, JOHN
RAETHER, EDIE
RAST, EDWARD
REYNOLDS, PATRICK
ROSS, MARILYN
SCHWARTZ, ELAINE
SCOTT, GINI
  GRAHAM, PH.D., J.D.
SIMON, BARBARA J.
SLOTKIN, FRAN S.
SMITH, HAROLD IVAN
SPENCER, DUFFY, PH.D.
STARR, ROBERT BRUCE
TARTARELLA, KATHY
ULLMAN, DANA M.P.H.
VELLIOTES, GEORGE
WIKLUND, PATRICIA PH.D.
WILSON, BOB
WOOLF, REESA, PH.D.
YAMAMOTO, GARY K.
YOUNG, BILL
ZIMMERMAN, TOM

TRAVEL

ABAGNALE, FRANK W.
ACKERMANN, LINDA HOLT
BAKER, LEN
BLAKELY, DON & MIKE
BURGETT, GORDON
COLLINS, PEGGY
DILLON, ILENE L.
FINK, MARTHA
FIORE, JAMES
FLICKINGER, BONNIE G.
FOSTER, WILLIAM E.
JUTKINS, RAY W.
KAHN, RITA
LAUFER, JOSEPH M.
LINKLETTER, ART
MCCOY, DORIS L., PH.D.
MILLER, MADELYN
MOWBRAY, CATHERINE
NORTON, GEORGE M.
O'HARA, CAROL

PALUMBO, JOHN A.
PUTNAM, HOWARD D.
RADTKE, RICHARD L.
RADTKE, RICHARD, L.
RASBAND, JUDITH
ROBERTS, JANET M.
ROSS, MARILYN
ROSS, TOM
SAUBY, RON
WHITE, SOMERS
WILLIAMS, JIM, CAPT.
WILLIAMS, JOHN R., LCDR

VIDEO

BESDANSKY, BRENDA
CARSON, TERRENCE J.
GERAGHTY, BARBARA
GORDON, CONNI
HELVEY, EDWARD P., JR.
MCCOY, DORIS L., PH.D.
SCOBEY, SALLY

WORLD AFFAIRS

ASHLEY, JAMES
BENNIE, MARK
EAGLE, MARK
ENEN, JACK
EVANS, ROBERT MAYER
FLICKINGER, BONNIE G.
HARDY, MARC
HUGHES, LADDIE W.
HUMPHRIES, ANN
  CHADWELL
ISLER, MARK
LADDIE, W. HUGHES
LEAPTROTT, NAN S.
MERCHANT, RONALD
NABERS, MARY SCOTT
OSMAN, WALI M. PH.D.
OUTLAW, KEMILEE K.
ROBERTS, JANET M.
SCOTT, CHARLES W.
  (CHUCK), COL.
STARKEY, JUDITH A.
TRUAX, PAMELA
WEST, KEN
WHITE, SOMERS
WOODCOCK, DAVID

YOUTH

AUSTIN, EMORY
BASSETT, LAWRENCE
  (LARRY) C. (CMC)
BENNIE, MARK
BORCHELT, FREDERICK E.
BROWN, KATHY &
  ASSOCIATES
CARSON, RICHARD D.

CHESTER, ERIC
CREEL, JOANNE P.
CROWSON, GATHA ROMINE
CUNNINGHAM, DOYLE
DAVEY, JUDY
DEAN, BONNIE 'THE MOTION
  COACH'
DEPOYSTER,
  BOBBY R., ED.D
DILLON, ILENE L.
DWYER, DAWN
FIELDER GROUP, THE
FLICKINGER, BONNIE G.
FLICKINGER, E. G.
GERAGHTY, BARBARA
GOOD, PERRY
GUTRIDGE, DON FOSTER
HALTER, 'DIAMOND' JIM
HARPER, JEANNE M.
HATTON, J. DUEY
JACOBS, ANITA I.
JOHNSON, JENYCE
KARPOVICH, MICHAEL S.
KICK, FRAN
LAIPPLY, BOB
LAIPPLY, SANDY
LENZ, BOB
LINKLETTER, ART
LLOYD, HERB J.
LUETHY, DR. GERRY
MAINELLA, MARK T.
MARINO, MIKE JR. 'IN
  PERSON'
MCILVAIN, TED L.
MCNAIR, J. FRANK
MILIOS, RITA
MILLER, ANNE
  PROMOTIONS, INC.
MILLER, REV. MARILYN K.
MORRIS, WILLIAM C.
NEWMAN, RICHARD D.
NIELSEN, RICK J.
OLDAK, EMILY
OUTLAW, KEMILEE K.
PAULSON, TERRY
  L., PH.D. (CPAE)
REYNOLDS, PATRICK
RICHARDS, RAMONA
ROBERTS, KATHI
RUSSELL, RAY L., DR.
SMITH, DIANE ELLINGSON
SOARES, DR. CECLIA J.
STARR, ROBERT BRUCE
STEVENS, SUZANNE H.
STEWART, LAURIE A.
SUTTON, JAMES D., DR.
TANSEY, DR. DAVE
TREJO, WILLIE
TROUT, SHIRLEY
TYTER, RICHARD
UHLER, MATTHEW

VAUGHAN, SUZANNE
VELLIOTES, GEORGE
WARD, AUDREY PEELE
ZIMMERMAN, TOM

Professional Services

PROFESSIONAL
SPEAKERS

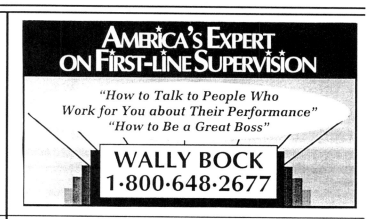

John S. Haskell

Professional Marketing

Consultant & Speaker

1700 Mandeville Canyon Road

Los Angeles, California 90049

310·476·3355   FAX: 310·471·7721

MEMBER OF THE NATIONAL SPEAKERS ASSOCIATION

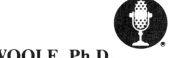

AICI Association of Image Consultants International

NANCY CHEN, AICI
VP-MARKETING '92-'93
Optimal Image
5 Hill & Tree Court
Melville, NY 11747
(516) 692-4116

KENNETH W. ROSS
President

ORGANIZATIONAL SOLUTIONS, INC.

723 Carlene Drive
Bridgewater, NJ 08807

(908) 218-3713

The EnterTrainer

REESA WOOLF, Ph.D.
ENTERTAINING BUSINESS SPEAKER

- Memorable Content -
  Upbeat Delivery
- Stress Reduction Using Humor
- Morale Building and
  Motivational Topics

(410) 358-7100
(800) 76Woolf
FX # (410) 358-0340
3711 Seven Mile Lane
Baltimore, MD 21208

CRAIG CONROY
Professional Speaker

(412) 443-6876

2925 E. Bardonner Road
Gibsonia, PA 15044

Etiquette International

Hilka Klinkenberg
President

254 East 68th Street
Suite 18A
New York, NY 10021
(212) 628-7209
Fax: (212) 628-7290

MEMBER

NATIONAL
SPEAKERS
ASSOCIATION

DON SANDROS & Associates
Sales Automation Consulting

Don Sandros

4950 FM 1960 W - Suite C-324
Houston, Texas 77069

(713) 580-2672
Fax: (713) 580-7978

*"Anything
you can do
You can do
better."*

DeAnne Rosenberg, Inc.
28 Fifer Lane, Lexington, MA 02173
TEL: (617) 862-6117
FAX: (617) 863-8613

 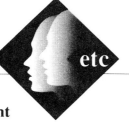
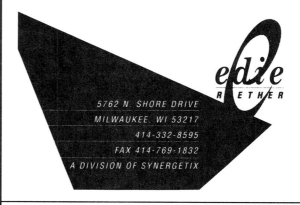

Ethel M. Cook
Principal

*Office Management
Consulting and Training*

(617) 275-2326
Fax: (617) 275-7136

4 Hilda Road
Bedford, MA 01730

U-R "SOMEBODY" SEMINARS, INC.
9130 N. Joyce Ave.
P.O. Box 24028
Milwaukee, WI 53223
(414) 354-0552

"SOMEBODY" SEMINARS, INC.

Committed To Personal And Professional "SOMEBODY-NESS"
JACQUELYN NELSON - VP

KATHLEEN TORPEY GARGANTA
R.D.H., M.D.P.H.

29 HOLLY LANE ■ *SOMERSET, MA 02726*
(508) 672-2010   **(800) 359-3920**

LIZ TAHIR & ASSOCIATES

ELIZABETH TAHIR
PRESIDENT

CONSULTANTS IN NATIONAL & INTERNATIONAL
MARKETING & RETAIL MANAGEMENT
SUITE 2500 · 201 ST. CHARLES AVE. NEW ORLEANS, LA. 70170
(504) 569-1670   FAX (504) 524-7979

LaJoyce Chatwell Lawton
President

P.O. Box 21401
Oklahoma City OK 73156 USA
Telephone/FAX 405/755-0012

International Business Protocol Consultants

Bette Price

Marketing, Communications & Leadership

14821 Le Grande Dr. ▼ Dallas, Texas 75244 ▼ 214-404-0787
▼ FAX 214-991-0368

**SPEAKERS &
SEMINAR
RESOURCES**

Dennis E. Horvath

9220 North College Ave.
Indianapolis, IN 46240
(317) 844-6869

Rose Cellino Reynolds

(918) 459-0440

8086 South Yale • Suite 145
Tulsa, Oklahoma 74136-9060

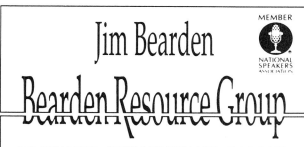

THE PERFORMANCE EDGE

Linda L. Prout, MS

304 Joyce Way
Mill Valley
CA 94941
415/381-6333

Patricia Remele
President

8426 Sparger Street
McLean, Virginia 22102
703-893-3777

Madelyn Miller
Speaker & Marketing Consultant

Madelyn Miller, Inc.
Notables And Quotables
P.O. Box 743242
Dallas, Texas 75243
214-341-0033

PROFESSIONAL SPEAKER

804·460·1818
FAX: 804·460·3675

Lee Milteer

P.O. Box 5653
Virginia Beach, VA
23455

The Raleigh Group, Ltd.
and
Zen of Hype Seminars

1223 Wilshire Blvd., #502

Santa Monica, CA 90403

Voice 310 998.0055
Fax   310 998.0034

MEMBER

NATIONAL SPEAKERS ASSOCIATION

Heart Of The Business Seminars, Inc.

Dr. Keith A. Robinson
President

1200 Binz, Suite 1360
Houston, Texas 77004-6927

Phone (713) 528-5000
Fax (713) 529-1112

Section 9
PROFESSIONAL SPEAKERS

ABAGNALE,
FRANK W. CSP
P.O. Box 701290
Tulsa, OK 74136
Telephone: 800-237-7443
Fax: 918-492-4110
ASSOCIATION
 MEMBERSHIP:
Natl. Speakers Assn.
Platform Speakers
PRINCIPAL TOPICS:
Entertainment
Family
Motivation
Travel
TYPICAL AUDIENCE:
Corporate
Association

ABBOTT, DR. LINDA M.C.
1455 W. Menlo
Fresno, CA 93711
Telephone: 209-439-4588
Fax: 209-449-0612
ASSOCIATION
 MEMBERSHIP:
Natl. Speakers Assn.
PRINCIPAL TOPICS:
Business & Industry
Education
Human Relations
Management
Psychology
TYPICAL AUDIENCE:
Corporate
Association
Institutional

ABELSON, HAL
13180 Cleveland Ave., #234
N. Ft. Myers, FL 33903
Telephone: 813-995-2400
Fax: 813-997-0456
PRINCIPAL TOPICS:
Business & Industry
Human Relations
Humor
Management
Motivation
TYPICAL AUDIENCE:
Association

ABRAMS-MINTZER,
BARBARA
4019A OTONO Drive
Santa Barbara, Ca 93110
Telephone: 805-964-7546
REPRESENTED BY:
Keynote Speakers Bureau
ASSOCIATION
 MEMBERSHIP:
Natl. Speakers Assn.
PRINCIPAL TOPICS:
Business & Industry
Management
Medical
Motivation
TYPICAL AUDIENCE:
Corporate
Association

ACERS, PATSY
Bag-Lady Financial Seminars
1413 E. Sims
Edmond, OK 73013
Telephone: 405-348-8058
Fax: 405-348-3811
MAILING ADDRESS:
Bag-Lady Financial Seminars
P.O. Box 20213
Edmond, OK 73083
ASSOCIATION
 MEMBERSHIP:
Natl. Speakers Assn.
Oklahoma Speakers
PRINCIPAL TOPICS:
Education
Entertainment
Family
Human Relations
Humor
Personal Finance
Senior Citizens
TYPICAL AUDIENCE:
Corporate
Association
Fraternal

ACKERMANN, LINDA
HOLT
521 Highland Avenue
Manhattan Beach, CA 90266
Telephone: 310-376-6549

Fax: 310-376-6549
ASSOCIATION
 MEMBERSHIP:
Natl. Speaker
PRINCIPAL TOPICS:
Human Relations
Management
Marketing
Motivation
Travel
TYPICAL AUDIENCE:
Corporate
Association

ACOSTA, JOSE'
P.O. Box 1234, 11548 Corlis
 Ave, North
Seatle, WA 98133
Telephone: 206-367-7861
Fax: 206-367-7861

ADAMS, KENNETH R.
Adams, Ken
5370 Point View Way
Sparks, NV 89431
Telephone: 702-331-6201
ASSOCIATION
 MEMBERSHIP:
Natl. Speakers Assn.
PRINCIPAL TOPICS:
Amusements
Entertainment
History
TYPICAL AUDIENCE:
Corporate
Fraternal

AGRICULTURAL SPEAKERS
NETWORK
Agricultural Speakers Network
4040 Vincennes Circle, #500
Indianapolis, IN 46268
Telephone: 800-222-1556
Fax: 317-875-0507

ALBERT, WILLIAM C.
2232 S. Don Carlos St.
Mesa, AZ 85202
Telephone: 602-897-6119

ASSOCIATION
 MEMBERSHIP:
Natl. Speakers Assn.
American Society For Training
 & Development
PRINCIPAL TOPICS:
Business & Industry
Human Relations
Management
TYPICAL AUDIENCE:
Corporate
Government

ALCORN, PAT
7957 Olentangy River Rd.
Worthington, OH 43235
Telephone: 614-436-2815
Fax: 614-436-2080
ASSOCIATION
 MEMBERSHIP:
Natl. Speakers Assn.
PRINCIPAL TOPICS:
Business & Industry
Family
Management
Marketing
TYPICAL AUDIENCE:
Association

ALESANDRINI, KATHRYN,
PH.D.
P.O. Box 2805, 23715 W.
 Malibu Rd. Ste. 284
Malibu, CA 90265
Telephone: 310-457-3111
Fax: 310-457-8175
REPRESENTED BY:
Santa Barbara Speakers
The Speaker & Celebrity
 Agency
ASSOCIATION
 MEMBERSHIP:
Natl. Speakers Assn.
PRINCIPAL TOPICS:
Business & Industry
Computer Technology
Education
Management
Media
Psychology

TYPICAL AUDIENCE:
Corporate
Association

ALESSANDRA, DR.
  TONY   CSP
P.O. Box 2767
La Jolla, Ca 92038
Telephone: 800-222-4383
Fax: 619-459-0435
ASSOCIATION
  MEMBERSHIP:
Natl. Speakers Assn.
PRINCIPAL TOPICS:
Human Relations
Sales
Communications
TYPICAL AUDIENCE:
Corporate
Association

ALEXANDER, BOB
1341 Dockside Pl.
Sarasota, FL 34242
Telephone: 813-349-0087
ASSOCIATION
  MEMBERSHIP:
Natl. Speakers Assn.
Toastmasters
ASLA
PRINCIPAL TOPICS:
Human Relations
Management
Motivation
Sales
TYPICAL AUDIENCE:
Corporate
General Public

ALFORD, RON
Disaster Masters Inc.
146-23 61 Rd.
New York, NY 11367-1203
Telephone: 718-939-5800
Fax: 718-939-1398
ASSOCIATION
  MEMBERSHIP:
Natl. Speakers Assn.
PRINCIPAL TOPICS:
Architecture
Education
Health
Management
Marketing
Personal Finance
TYPICAL AUDIENCE:
Corporate
General Public

ALLEN, ELIZABETH
  'BETSY'
725 Piikoi St., #704
Honolulu, HI 96814
Telephone: 808-521-3123
Fax: 808-545-5200
ASSOCIATION
  MEMBERSHIP:
Natl. Speakers Assn.
ASTD
PRINCIPAL TOPICS:
Business & Industry
Human Relations
Motivation
Sales
TYPICAL AUDIENCE:
Corporate
Association

ALLEN, GORDIE
P.O. Box 400
Killarney, FL 34740-0400
Telephone: 800-548-4571
ASSOCIATION
  MEMBERSHIP:
Natl. Speakers Assn.
Toastmasters
PRINCIPAL TOPICS:
Computer Technology
Sales
TYPICAL AUDIENCE:
Corporate
Association

AMBROSIUS, RICHARD,
  CEO
Phoenix Systems Inc.
525 West 22nd Street
Sioux Falls, SD 57105
Telephone: 800-657-4388
Fax: 605-339-0408
ASSOCIATION
  MEMBERSHIP:
American Marketing
PRINCIPAL TOPICS:
Advertising
Marketing
Media
Senior Citizens
TYPICAL AUDIENCE:
Corporate
Association

ANDERSON, DALE L.
2982 W. Owasso Blvd.
Roseville, MN 55113
Telephone: 612-484-5162
Fax: 612-486-8860
ASSOCIATION
  MEMBERSHIP:
Natl. Speakers Assn.

PRINCIPAL TOPICS:
Entertainment
Health
Humor
Medical
Motivation
Psychology
Religion
TYPICAL AUDIENCE:
Corporate
Association
Health-Care

ANDERSON, KARE
Anderson
  Negotiations/Comms
321 Karen Way
Tiburon, CA 94920-2046
Telephone: 415-389-9746
ASSOCIATION
  MEMBERSHIP:
Natl. Speakers Assn.
Toastmasters
PRINCIPAL TOPICS:
Human Relations
Journalism
Management
Marketing
Media
Motivation
Psychology
TYPICAL AUDIENCE:
Corporate
Association

ANDERSON, LESTER W.
5155 Cralyn Ct.
Duluth, GA 30136
Telephone: 404-729-9969
ASSOCIATION
  MEMBERSHIP:
Natl. Speakers
Platform Speakers
PRINCIPAL TOPICS:
Management
Marketing
Motivation
Sales
TYPICAL AUDIENCE:
Corporate
Association

ANFINSON, STACIE A.
8423 Calle Buena Vista
Scottsdale, AZ 85255
Telephone: 602-585-4891
MAILING ADDRESS:
Arizona State University
Tempe, AZ 85287

ASSOCIATION
  MEMBERSHIP:
Natl. Speakers Assn.
PRINCIPAL TOPICS:
Animals
Computer Technology
Ecology
Education
Entertainment
Family
Humor
Philosophy
TYPICAL AUDIENCE:
Fraternal

ARCEMENT, BILLY
108 S. Magnolia Dr.
Donaldsonville, La 70346
Telephone: 504-473-4346
Fax: 504-473-0555
ASSOCIATION
  MEMBERSHIP:
Natl. Speakers Assn.
PRINCIPAL TOPICS:
Management
Motivation
TYPICAL AUDIENCE:
Corporate
Association
Institutional

ARCHBALD, RALPH
  (CPAE)   CSP
P.O. Box 40178
Phildelphia, PA 19106
Telephone: 215-238-0871
Fax: 215-238-9102
ASSOCIATION
  MEMBERSHIP:
Natl. Speakers Assn.
PRINCIPAL TOPICS:
History
Human Relations
Humor
TYPICAL AUDIENCE:
Corporate
Association
General

ARLEQUE, LILLIAN, ED.D.
48 Pleasant St.
Andover, MA 01810
Telephone: 508-683-7381
ASSOCIATION
  MEMBERSHIP:
Natl. Speakers Assn.
PRINCIPAL TOPICS:
Education
Family

Motivation
TYPICAL AUDIENCE:
Association

ARNETTE, NICK
P.O. Box 361180
Los Angeles, CA 90036-9580
Telephone: 800-456-1950
REPRESENTED BY:
Exposures To
   Excellence
Five Star Speakers Bureau
ASSOCIATION
   MEMBERSHIP:
Natl. Speakers Assn.
PRINCIPAL TOPICS:
Humor
TYPICAL AUDIENCE:
Association

ARNOLD, BILL   CSP
2330 Perkins Rd.
Arlington, TX 76016
Telephone: 817-457-6559
Fax: 817-457-2619
ASSOCIATION
   MEMBERSHIP:
Natl. Speakers Assn.
PRINCIPAL TOPICS:
Management
TYPICAL AUDIENCE:
Corporate

ARNSTEIN, SAM
1415 Western Ave., #600
Seattle, WA 98101
Telephone: 800-367-5537
Fax: 206-622-4371
ASSOCIATION
   MEMBERSHIP:
Natl. Speakers Assn.
PRINCIPAL TOPICS:
Management
Sales
TYPICAL AUDIENCE:
Corporate
Association

ARTERBURN, STEPHEN
570 Glennetre, #107
Laguna Beach, CA 92651
Telephone: 714-494-8383
Fax: 714-494-1272
ASSOCIATION
   MEMBERSHIP:
Natl. Speakers Assn.
PRINCIPAL TOPICS:
Food/Diet
Health
Human Relations
Humor

Marketing
Motivation
Personal Finance
Philosophy
Psychology
TYPICAL AUDIENCE:
Corporate

ASHLEY, JAMES
1035 Spanish River Road,
   #116
Boca Raton, FL 33432
Telephone: 407-367-7258
ASSOCIATION
   MEMBERSHIP:
Natl. Speakers Assn.
PRINCIPAL TOPICS:
Aviation
Business & Industry
Education
Human Relations
Management
Motivation
World Affairs
TYPICAL AUDIENCE:
Corporate

ASIJA, S. PAL
7 Woonsocket Ave.
Shelton, CT 06484
Telephone: 203-924-9538
Fax: 203-924-9956
ASSOCIATION
   MEMBERSHIP:
Natl. Speakers Assn.
Platform Speakers
Toastmasters
PRINCIPAL TOPICS:
Business & Industry
Computer Technology
Humor
TYPICAL AUDIENCE:
Corporate
Individuals

ATKINS, CHANDLER PH.D.
1108 Antigua Rd.
Lake George, NY 12845
Telephone: 518-668-2153
Fax: 518-745-1433
ASSOCIATION
   MEMBERSHIP:
Natl. Speakers Assn.
APS
SIOP
PRINCIPAL TOPICS:
Agriculture
Business & Industry
Education
Human Relations
Management

Marketing
Motivation
Psychology
TYPICAL AUDIENCE:
Corporate

ATKINSON, WILLIAM C.
1026 Monroe Dr., N.E.
Atlanta, GA 30306
Telephone: 800-869-3926
Fax: 800-869-8880
REPRESENTED BY:
Happy Talk
ASSOCIATION
   MEMBERSHIP:
Natl. Speakers Assn.
PRINCIPAL TOPICS:
Humor
Motivation
TYPICAL AUDIENCE:
Corporate
Association

AUN, MICHAEL A.
2901 E. Irco Bronson Memorial
   Hwy., #D
Kissimmee, FL 34744
Telephone: 407-870-0030
Fax: 407-870-2088
ASSOCIATION
   MEMBERSHIP:
Natl. Speakers Assn.
Toastmasters
PRINCIPAL TOPICS:
Management
Motivation
Sales
TYPICAL AUDIENCE:
Corporate
Association
Fraternal
Institutional

AUSTIN, EMORY
Austin, Emory & Company
5509 Mallard Dr.
Charlotte, NC 28227
Telephone: 704-567-8000
Fax: 704-537-6016
REPRESENTED BY:
National Speakers Bureau
National Speakers Forum
ASSOCIATION
   MEMBERSHIP:
Natl. Speakers Assn.
Carolinas Speakers
PRINCIPAL TOPICS:
Education
Human Relations
Humor
Management

Motivation
Youth
TYPICAL AUDIENCE:
Corporate
Association

BACHRACH, WILLIAM
Bachrach & Associates
7777 Fay Ave., Ste. K
La Jolla, CA 92037
Telephone: 619-558-3200
Fax: 619-277-9654
REPRESENTED BY:
A.M. Enterprises
Financial Services Speakers
   Network
ASSOCIATION
   MEMBERSHIP:
Natl. Speakers Assn.
PRINCIPAL TOPICS:
Sales
TYPICAL AUDIENCE:
Corporate
Association

BAILEY, ROBERT L.
6445 Meadowbrook Circle
Worthington, OH 43085
Telephone: 614-885-9378
ASSOCIATION
   MEMBERSHIP:
Natl. Speakers Assn.
PRINCIPAL TOPICS:
Business & Industry
Management
TYPICAL AUDIENCE:
Corporate
Association

BAKER, HELEN JOYCE
1434 Janice St.
Spring Valley, Ca 91977
Telephone: 619-466-8436
ASSOCIATION
   MEMBERSHIP:
Natl. Speakers Assn.
PRINCIPAL TOPICS:
Family
Health
Religion
TYPICAL AUDIENCE:
General

BAKER, LARRY D., DR.
The Time Management
   Center Inc.
P.O. Box 6398
Chesterfield, MO 63006-6398
Telephone: 314-230-0900
Fax: 314-230-0576

ASSOCIATION
  MEMBERSHIP:
Natl. Speakers Assn.
PRINCIPAL TOPICS:
Business & Industry
Human Relations
Management
Motivation
TYPICAL AUDIENCE:
Corporate

BAKER, LEN
3003 N. Central, Ste. 2208
Phoenix, AZ 85012
Telephone: 602-279-6010
Fax: 602-279-0110
REPRESENTED BY:
Exposures To Excellence
Agricultural Speakers Network
ASSOCIATION
  MEMBERSHIP:
Natl. Speakers Assn.
Toastmasters
PRINCIPAL TOPICS:
Business & Industry
Human Relations
Humor
Management
Motivation
Sales
Travel
TYPICAL AUDIENCE:
Corporate
Association

BALL, DR. ROBERT R.
1127 Commons Dr.
Sacramento, CA 95825
Telephone: 916-922-3255
ASSOCIATION
  MEMBERSHIP:
Natl. Speakers Assn.
PRINCIPAL TOPICS:
Family
Human Relations
Motivation
Psychology
Religion
TYPICAL AUDIENCE:
Corporate
Association

BALL, JIM
1889 Preston White Dr., #115
Reston, Va 22091
Telephone: 703-620-1900
Fax: 703-620-1103
ASSOCIATION
  MEMBERSHIP:
Natl. Speakers Assn.

PRINCIPAL TOPICS:
Business & Industry
Motivation
TYPICAL AUDIENCE:
Corporate

BALL, PATRICIA   CSP
Corporate Communications
9875 Northbridge Rd.
St. Louis, MO 63124
Telephone: 314-966-5452
Fax: 314-966-6511
REPRESENTED BY:
Jordan International
  Enterprises
5 Star Speakers Bureau
ASSOCIATION
  MEMBERSHIP:
Natl. Speakers Assn.
PRINCIPAL TOPICS:
Human Relations
Communications
TYPICAL AUDIENCE:
Corporate
Association

BALZER, ALVIN L.
P.O. Box 722285
Houston, Tx 77272
Telephone: 713-261-7747
Fax: 713-499-4610
ASSOCIATION
  MEMBERSHIP:
Natl. Speakers Assn.
PRINCIPAL TOPICS:
Human Relations
Management
Marketing
Sales
TYPICAL AUDIENCE:
Corporate
Association

BARBER, JIM
1101 N.W. 78 Ave.
Plantation, FL 33322
Telephone: 305-476-9252
Fax: 305-424-0309
ASSOCIATION
  MEMBERSHIP:
Natl. Speakers Assn.
Toastmasters
PRINCIPAL TOPICS:
Computer Technology
Humor
Motivation
TYPICAL AUDIENCE:
Corporate
Association

BARKER, JOCK
Real Estate By Barker Ent.
P.O. Box 2003
Dillon, CO 80435
Telephone: 303-468-8400
Fax: 303-468-6039
ASSOCIATION
  MEMBERSHIP:
Natl. Speakers Assn.
PRINCIPAL TOPICS:
Motivation
Sales
TYPICAL AUDIENCE:
Corporate
Association

BARNHILL, ROBERT E. III
P.O. Box 2583
Lubbock, TX 79408
Telephone: 806-794-1282
Fax: 806-794-1283
MAILING ADDRESS:
4413 82nd Street
Lubbock, TX 79408
ASSOCIATION
  MEMBERSHIP:
Natl. Speakers Assn.
Toastmasters
PRINCIPAL TOPICS:
Business & Industry
Human Relations
Management
Marketing
Motivation
Personal Finance
Religion
Sales
TYPICAL AUDIENCE:
Association

BARON, JUDY KAPLAN
6046 Cornerstone Ct. W., #208
San Diego, CA 92121
Telephone: 619-558-7400
REPRESENTED BY:
Speak, Inc.
ASSOCIATION
  MEMBERSHIP:
Natl. Speakers Assn.
Amer. Society for Training &
  Dev.
PRINCIPAL TOPICS:
Motivation
Communications
TYPICAL AUDIENCE:
Corporate
Association

BARONE, ROZANNE
2907 Quail Valley East
Missouri City, TX 77489

Telephone: 713-267-3921
MAILING ADDRESS:
P.O. Box 570384
Missouri City, TX 77489

BARRERA, RICK   CSP
P.O. Box 8164
La Jolla, CA 92038
Telephone: 619-456-4050
Fax: 619-456-4059
PRINCIPAL TOPICS:
Marketing
Motivation
Sales
TYPICAL AUDIENCE:
Corporate
Association

BARRETT, DIANNE
  E. R.N., M.A.
735 Sunnyhill Dr.
Los Angeles, CA 90065
Telephone: 213-223-6578
Fax: 805-925-5625
ASSOCIATION
  MEMBERSHIP:
Natl. Speakers Assn.
PRINCIPAL TOPICS:
Health
Home & Garden
Psychology
TYPICAL AUDIENCE:
Association
Fraternal

BARRON, LAURA
8316 Hunter Hill Dr.
Knoxville, TN 37923
Telephone: 615-690-4187
ASSOCIATION
  MEMBERSHIP:
Natl. Speakers Assn.
Speakers USA
American Society of Training &
  Development
PRINCIPAL TOPICS:
Human Relations
Sales
TYPICAL AUDIENCE:
Corporate
Association

BARROWS, SYDNEY
  BIDDLE
210 W. 70th St., #209
New York, NY 10023
Telephone: 212-496-2936
ASSOCIATION
  MEMBERSHIP:
Natl. Speakers Assn.

PRINCIPAL TOPICS:
Human Relations
Marketing
TYPICAL AUDIENCE:
Corporate
Association
Women's Groups

BASSETT, LAWRENCE
  (LARRY) C. (CMC)
1 Ilana Ln.
Thornwood, NY 10594
Telephone: 914-769-3721
Fax: 914-747-4037
ASSOCIATION
  MEMBERSHIP:
Natl. Speakers Assn.
Inst. of Mgmt. Conslts.
Amer. Arbitration Assoc.
American Society of Training &
  Development
PRINCIPAL TOPICS:
Business & Industry
Family
Health
Human Relations
Humor
Management
Motivation
Sales
Senior Citizens
Social Trends
Youth
TYPICAL AUDIENCE:
Corporate
Association
Fraternal

BATES, LARRY
8049 Dunfield Ave.
Los Angeles, Ca (Zip)
Telephone: 310-670-3762
ASSOCIATION
  MEMBERSHIP:
Natl. Speakers Assn.
Toastmasters
PRINCIPAL TOPICS:
Human Relations
Management
Motivation
TYPICAL AUDIENCE:
Corporate
Association
Fraternal

BEALS, GARY
8546 Chevy Chase Dr.
La Mesa, CA 91941
Telephone: 619-463-5050
Fax: 619-463-5097

ASSOCIATION
  MEMBERSHIP:
Natl. Speakers Assn.
PRINCIPAL TOPICS:
Advertising
Marketing
Media
TYPICAL AUDIENCE:
Corporate
Association

BEARDEN, JIM
P.O. BOX 161902
AUSTIN, TX 78716
Telephone: 512-263-2582
Fax: 512-263-5336
ASSOCIATION
  MEMBERSHIP:
Natl. Speakers Assn.
PRINCIPAL TOPICS:
Human Relations
Management
Motivation
Sales
TYPICAL AUDIENCE:
Corporate
Association
SEE AD IN SECTION 8

BEATTY, MAURA
  CLELAND
8760-A Research Blvd., #387
Austin, Tx 78758
Telephone: 512-794-0622
Fax: 512-794-0677
REPRESENTED BY:
Kitty McVay Talent Agency
  (Austin, Tx)
ASSOCIATION
  MEMBERSHIP:
Natl. Speakers Assn.
Natl. Assn. Of Alcohol & Drug
  Abuse Counselors
Meeting Planners Intl.
PRINCIPAL TOPICS:
Human Relations
Motivation
TYPICAL AUDIENCE:
Corporate
Association
Institutional

BEAUBIEN, ELAINE
  ESTERVIG
6520 York Heights
Waterloo, WI 53594
Telephone: 414-478-2811
ASSOCIATION
  MEMBERSHIP:
Natl. Speakers Assn.

PRINCIPAL TOPICS:
Business & Industry
Food/Diet
Human Relations
Management
Marketing
Motivation
Communications
TYPICAL AUDIENCE:
Corporate
Association

BELGUM, MERRILYN
191 Hartman Circle
Fridley, MI 55432
Telephone: 612-257-1191
ASSOCIATION
  MEMBERSHIP:
Natl. Speakers Assn.
PRINCIPAL TOPICS:
Education
Entertainment
Family
Health
Humor
Motivation
Senior Citizens
TYPICAL AUDIENCE:
Corporate
Association
Fraternal

BENDER, BEV
P.O. Box 347335
San Francisco, Ca 94134
Telephone: 415-239-2708
ASSOCIATION
  MEMBERSHIP:
Natl. Speakers Assn.
Toastmasters
PRINCIPAL TOPICS:
Family
Humor
Motivation
Sales
TYPICAL AUDIENCE:
Association

BENNETT, LOIS E.,
  M.ED.,M.A.
4443 N. Highway 67, Suite B
Florissant, MO 63034
Telephone: 314-355-7774
ASSOCIATION
  MEMBERSHIP:
Natl. Speakers
NAPSS
PRINCIPAL TOPICS:
Education
Entertainment
Family

Motivation
Psychology
Religion
TYPICAL AUDIENCE:
Association
Fraternal
Institutional

BENNIE, MARK
5055 Jeffreys, #A-209
Las Vegas, NV 89119
Telephone: 702-798-7005
Fax: 702-736-6881
REPRESENTED BY:
5 Star Speakers
Trainees & Consultants
ASSOCIATION
  MEMBERSHIP:
Natl. Speakers Assn.
PRINCIPAL TOPICS:
Animals
Business & Industry
Education
Government
Human Relations
Management
Motivation
Philosophy
Psychology
Sales
World Affairs
Youth
Family
TYPICAL AUDIENCE:
Corporate
Association

BERG, DR. DEANNA
1202 Calibre Creek Pkwy.
Roswell, GA 30076
Telephone: 404-552-2569
Fax: 404-998-6646
REPRESENTED BY:
The Learning Circle
Jordan International
Odenwald Connection
ASSOCIATION
  MEMBERSHIP:
Natl. Speakers Assn.
PRINCIPAL TOPICS:
Business & Industry
Education
Human Relations
Humor
Management
Motivation
Psychology
Sales
TYPICAL AUDIENCE:
Corporate
Association

BERGER, FRANCINE CSP
Speechworks, Inc.
20 Hawkins Rd.
Stony Brook, NY 11790-1811
Telephone: 516-751-8549
Fax: 516-751-8689
ASSOCIATION
  MEMBERSHIP:
Natl. Speakers Assn.
PRINCIPAL TOPICS:
Human Relations
Management
Motivation
Sales
TYPICAL AUDIENCE:
Corporate

BERGER, RUTH
2530 Crawford Ave., #104
Evanston, IL 60201
Telephone: 708-676-4900
Fax: 708-676-4900
REPRESENTED BY:
Contemporary Forum
ASSOCIATION
  MEMBERSHIP:
Natl. Speakers Assn.
Toastmasters
PRINCIPAL TOPICS:
Entertainment
Health
Human Relations
Humor
Motivation
Psychology
Sales
TYPICAL AUDIENCE:
Corporate
Association
Fraternal

BERMAN, HELEN
Berman, Helen & Assoc.
12021 Wilshire Blvd., #177
Los Angeles, CA 90025
Telephone: 310-820-7312
Fax: 310-312-9757
ASSOCIATION
  MEMBERSHIP:
Natl. Speakers Assn.
PRINCIPAL TOPICS:
Advertising
Sales
TYPICAL AUDIENCE:
Corporate
Association

BERNS, FRED
Power Promotion
148 G St. S.W.
Washington, DC 20024

Telephone: 202-484-1840
Fax: 202-484-1846
ASSOCIATION
  MEMBERSHIP:
Natl. Speakers Assn.
PRINCIPAL TOPICS:
Business & Industry
Marketing
Media
Motivation
TYPICAL AUDIENCE:
Corporate
Association
Fraternal

BESDANSKY, BRENDA
Speakers World
1537 Franklin St.
San Francisco, CA 94109
Telephone: 415-474-1610
REPRESENTED BY:
Speakers World
ASSOCIATION
  MEMBERSHIP:
Natl. Speakers Assn.
IGAB
PRINCIPAL TOPICS:
Marketing
Sales
Video
TYPICAL AUDIENCE:
Association

BETHEL, BILL
1376 Vancouver Ave.
Burlingame, CA 94010
Telephone: 800-548-8001
Fax: 415-2365
REPRESENTED BY:
National Speakers Bureau
Keynote Speakers
Speakers Guide
ASSOCIATION
  MEMBERSHIP:
Natl. Speakers Assn.
National Writers Club
California Writers Club
PRINCIPAL TOPICS:
Marketing
Sales
Senior Citizens
Communications
TYPICAL AUDIENCE:
Corporate
Association

BETHEL, SHEILA MURRAY
1376 Vancouver Avenue
Burlingame, CA 94010
Telephone: 800-548-8001
Fax: 415-344-2365

REPRESENTED BY:
Natl. Speakers Bureau, Inc.
Speakers Guild, Inc.
The Speakers Bureau, Inc.
Speakers Plus, Inc.
Speakers Worldwide, Inc.
California Speakers Bureau
Keynote Speakers, Inc.
Natl. Speakers Forum, Inc.
Jordan Enterprises/SLSS Inc.
Southwest Speakers Bureau
  Inc.
Superior Speakers Bureau, Inc.
Corporate Training Assurance
Educators Network Inc.
Cassidy & Fishman Inc.
Eagles Talent Associates Inc.
Motivational Speakers &
  Entertainment
Lordly & Dame Inc.
Keppler Associates, Inc.
Sandra Ford Agency
Leader Enterprises, Inc.
Prefered Speakers Inc.
Alexander Agency
CC& L Speakers Group
Jack Morton Productions, Inc.
Hudson Agency Inc.
Speakers Bureau Unlimited
Creative Meetings, Inc.
Speak Inc.
Carlson Companies
Uniglobe Main Events
Trans Global Institute
Resource Group Of America
Koegel Group Impact
  Speakers
Tarkenton Speaker Bureau
International Speakers Bureau
Cappa & Graham
High Point Marketing
ASSOCIATION
  MEMBERSHIP:
Natl. Speakers Assn.
PRINCIPAL TOPICS:
Business & Industry
Management
Motivation
Sales
TYPICAL AUDIENCE:
Corporate
Association

BIECH, ELAINE
EBB Associates
816 Cass St., P.O. Box 657
Portage, WI 53901
Telephone: 608-742-5005
Fax: 608-742-8657
REPRESENTED BY:
Speakers Mart, (Madison, Wi)

The Oldenwald Connection,
  (Dallas, Tx)
ASSOCIATION
  MEMBERSHIP:
Natl. Speakers Assn.
PRINCIPAL TOPICS:
Business & Industry
Human Relations
Management
Marketing
Motivation
TYPICAL AUDIENCE:
Corporate

BIGGS, DICK
420 Market Place, #108
Roswell, GA 30075
Telephone: 404-998-5452
Fax: 404-998-5513
ASSOCIATION
  MEMBERSHIP:
Natl. Speakers Assn.
PRINCIPAL TOPICS:
Human Relations
TYPICAL AUDIENCE:
Corporate
Association
General Public

BILKER, HARVEY L.
4 Sylvan Blvd.
Howell, NJ 07731
Telephone: 908-364-0394
PRINCIPAL TOPICS:
Advertising
Entertainment
Health
Journalism
Media
Medical
Photography
TYPICAL AUDIENCE:
Corporate
Association
Fraternal
Educational

BILLINGS-HARRIS,
  LENDRA
2411 W. Mission Dr., #822
Chandler, AZ 85224
Telephone: 602-963-4540
Fax: 602-963-4540
MAILING ADDRESS:
P.O. Box 1002
Tempe, AZ 85280
REPRESENTED BY:
Gold
Walters International

ASSOCIATION
  MEMBERSHIP:
Natl. Speakers Assn.
ASTD
PRINCIPAL TOPICS:
Automotive
Management
Sales
TYPICAL AUDIENCE:
Corporate

BILLUE, STAN　　　　　　CSP
228 Park Avenue North, Suite J
Winter Park, FL 32789
Telephone: 407-668-4058
ASSOCIATION
  MEMBERSHIP:
Natl. Speakers Assn.
PRINCIPAL TOPICS:
Marketing
Motivation
Sales
TYPICAL AUDIENCE:
Corporate
Association

BIRK, RON
101 W. Mimosa
San Marcos, TX 78666
Telephone: 512-396-0767
REPRESENTED BY:
5-Star
Circa, Texas
ASSOCIATION
  MEMBERSHIP:
Natl. Speakers Assn.
PRINCIPAL TOPICS:
Agriculture
Education
Humor
Motivation
Religion
TYPICAL AUDIENCE:
Association
Fraternal

BISHOP, VENNA
Angelic Possibilities
P.O. Box 700662
San Jose, CA 95170
Telephone: 800-995-8099
Fax: 408-725-8099
ASSOCIATION
  MEMBERSHIP:
Natl. Speakers Assn.
PRINCIPAL TOPICS:
Education
Family
Human Relations
Motivation
Philosophy

Psychology
Religion
Sales
Senior Citizens
TYPICAL AUDIENCE:
Association
Religious

BISSELL, BEN
8618 Old Carriage Ct.
Knoxville, TN 37923
Telephone: 804-272-2979
ASSOCIATION
  MEMBERSHIP:
Natl. Speakers Assn.
PRINCIPAL TOPICS:
Education
Family
Human Relations
Humor
Management
Motivation
Psychology
TYPICAL AUDIENCE:
Corporate

BLACK, JERRY
2306 Brookway Dr.
Geneva, IL 60134
Telephone: 708-232-4228
ASSOCIATION
  MEMBERSHIP:
Natl. Speakers Assn.
PRINCIPAL TOPICS:
Business &
  Industry
Management
Marketing
Motivation
TYPICAL AUDIENCE:
Corporate
Association

BLACKMAN,
  JEFF, J.D.　　　　　　CSP
2130 Warwick Lane
Glenview, IL 60025
Telephone: 708-998-0688
Fax: 708-998-0675
ASSOCIATION
  MEMBERSHIP:
Natl. Speakers Assn.
PRINCIPAL TOPICS:
Computer Technology
Marketing
Motivation
Sales
Social Trends
TYPICAL AUDIENCE:
Corporate
Association

BLACKWELL, JOEL
20462 Chartwell Center
Davidson, NC 28036
Telephone: 704-892-9798
MAILING ADDRESS:
P.O. Box 2008
Cornelius, NC 28031
ASSOCIATION
  MEMBERSHIP:
Natl. Speakers Assn.
PRINCIPAL TOPICS:
Government
Journalism
Marketing
Media
TYPICAL AUDIENCE:
Association

BLAKELY, DON & MIKE
Swing Riders, The
3404 Fairway Drive
Wharton, TX 77488
Telephone: 409-532-4502
Fax: 409-532-4223
ASSOCIATION
  MEMBERSHIP:
Natl. Speakers Assn.
PRINCIPAL TOPICS:
Agriculture
Aviation
Business & Industry
Education
Entertainment
Family
Human Relations
Humor
Management
Medical
Motivation
Philosophy
Psychology
Sales
Travel
TYPICAL AUDIENCE:
Corporate
Association

BLOCH, ANN
WRITING WORKOUT
27 BIRCHWOOD LN.
LENOX, MA 01240
Telephone: 413-637-0958
Fax: 413-637-4757
ASSOCIATION
  MEMBERSHIP:
Natl. Speakers Assn.
Toastmasters
PRINCIPAL TOPICS:
Education
Humor
Motivation

Communications
TYPICAL AUDIENCE:
Corporate
Association

BLOCH, ROBERT H.
CAVALIER ENTERPRISES
27 BIRCHWOOD LANE
Lenox, MA 01240
Telephone: 413-637-0958
MAILING ADDRESS:
Cavalier Enterprises
P.O. Box 267
Lenoxdale, MA 01242
Fax: 413-637-4757
ASSOCIATION
  MEMBERSHIP:
Natl. Speakers Assn.
Platform Speakers
PRINCIPAL TOPICS:
Humor
Marketing
Sales
TYPICAL AUDIENCE:
Corporate

BLOHOWIAK, DON
P.O. Box 791
Princeton Junction, NJ 08550
Telephone: 609-799-4477
Fax: 609-799-4477
REPRESENTED BY:
JR Assoc. (Princeton NJ)
ASSOCIATION
  MEMBERSHIP:
Natl. Speakers Assn.
PRINCIPAL TOPICS:
Management
TYPICAL AUDIENCE:
Corporate
Association

BOCK, WALLY
1441 FRANKLIN ST.
OAKLAND, CA 94612
Telephone: 510-835-8566
Fax: 510-835-8531
ASSOCIATION
  MEMBERSHIP:
Natl. Speakers Assn.
PRINCIPAL TOPICS:
Business & Industry
Management
Social Trends
TYPICAL AUDIENCE:
Corporate
Association
SEE AD IN SECTION 8

BOILEAU & ASSOCIATES
Boileau & Associates
P.O. Box 502
Cardiff by the Sea, CA 92007
Telephone: 619-753-5870
Fax: 619-753-5871
ASSOCIATION
 MEMBERSHIP:
Natl. Speakers Assn.
Toastmasters
PRINCIPAL TOPICS:
Fashion
Marketing
Sales
TYPICAL AUDIENCE:
Corporate
Association

BOLING, DUTCH
2730 Devine St.
Columbia, SC 29205
Telephone: 803-799-0328
Fax: 803-799-2305
PRINCIPAL TOPICS:
Human Relations
Humor
Motivation
TYPICAL AUDIENCE:
Corporate
Association

BOLTON, DENNY
Jungle Rules Seminars
101 Twin Oaks Trail
Dripping Springs, TX 78620
Telephone: 800-256-8268
Fax: 512-858-1620
ASSOCIATION
 MEMBERSHIP:
Natl. Speakers Assn.
PRINCIPAL TOPICS:
Business & Industry
Management
Marketing
Motivation
Sales
TYPICAL AUDIENCE:
Corporate
Association
General Public

BOOHER, DIANNA   CSP
804 Overlake
Euless, TX 76039
Telephone: 817-545-4534
Fax: 817-545-5522
MAILING ADDRESS:
1010 W. Euless Blvd., #150
Euless, TX 76040

REPRESENTED BY:
Washington Speakers
 Bureau
Five Star Speakers
Trainers & Consult.
ASSOCIATION
 MEMBERSHIP:
Natl. Speakers Assn.
PRINCIPAL TOPICS:
Business & Industry
Education
Human Relations
Motivation
TYPICAL AUDIENCE:
Corporate
Association

BORCHELT,
 FREDERICK E.
30 Maplewood Rd.
Worcester, MA 01602
Telephone: 508-757-7656
ASSOCIATION
 MEMBERSHIP:
Natl. Speakers Assn.
Toastmasters
PRINCIPAL TOPICS:
Physical Fitness
Religion
Youth
TYPICAL AUDIENCE:
Fraternal
Institutional

BORDEAUX, DARLENE B.
2201 Gates Ave., #4
Redondo Beach, CA 90278
Telephone: 310-370-4328
Fax: 310-542-2044
MAILING ADDRESS:
P.O. Box 2674
Rancho Palos Verdes, CA
 90274
REPRESENTED BY:
The Management Institute
ASSOCIATION
 MEMBERSHIP:
American Society of Training &
 Development
PRINCIPAL TOPICS:
Business & Industry
Family
Management
Marketing
Motivation
TYPICAL AUDIENCE:
Corporate
Association

BOURQUE, RONALD J.
19 Cole Rd.
Salem, NH 03079
Telephone: 603-898-1871
Fax: 603-894-6539
ASSOCIATION
 MEMBERSHIP:
Natl. Speakers Assn.
PRINCIPAL TOPICS:
Humor
Management
Motivation
TYPICAL AUDIENCE:
Corporate

BOWMAN, FOREST
1266 Crestwood Drive
Morgantown, WV 26505
Telephone: 304-599-7004
MAILING ADDRESS:
West Virginia Univ. College Of
 Law, P.O. Box 6130
Morgantown, WV 26506
ASSOCIATION
 MEMBERSHIP:
Natl. Speakers Assn.
PRINCIPAL TOPICS:
Business & Industry
Education
History
Human Relations
Humor
Management
Motivation
TYPICAL AUDIENCE:
Association

BOWMAN, ROBIN
1100 N.W. Loop 410, #219
San Antonio, Tx 78213
Telephone: 210-349-4767
Fax: 210-349-5426
ASSOCIATION
 MEMBERSHIP:
Natl. Speakers Assn.
PRINCIPAL TOPICS:
Business & Industry
Human Relations
Humor
Management
Motivation
TYPICAL AUDIENCE:
Corporate

BOYAN, LEE
1010 South Ocean Blvd.,
 #1507
Pompano Beach, FL 33062
Telephone: 305-785-3017
Fax: 305-785-0507

ASSOCIATION
 MEMBERSHIP:
Natl. Speakers Assn.
PRINCIPAL TOPICS:
Marketing
Motivation
Sales
TYPICAL AUDIENCE:
Corporate

BOYCE, BETTY L.
 ENTERPRISES
Boyce, Betty L. Enterprises
360 Sharry Lane
Santa Maria, Ca 93455
Telephone: 805-937-4353
Fax: 805-934-1765
ASSOCIATION
 MEMBERSHIP:
Natl. Speakers Assn.
Toastmasters
Authors Guild
PRINCIPAL TOPICS:
Business & Industry
Computer Technology
Education
TYPICAL AUDIENCE:
Association
Institutions

BOYD, LORRIE DR.
12555 Euclid St., #25
Garden Grove, CA 92640
Telephone: 714-636-5457
ASSOCIATION
 MEMBERSHIP:
Natl. Speakers Assn.
PRINCIPAL TOPICS:
Family
Health
Home & Garden
Humor
Management
Motivation
Nature
Psychology
TYPICAL AUDIENCE:
Corporate

BOYLE, VIRGINIA, PHD.
532 W. LADONNA DR.
TEMPE, AZ 85283
Telephone: 602-838-3770
Fax: 602-496-9200
ASSOCIATION
 MEMBERSHIP:
Natl. Speakers Assn.
PRINCIPAL TOPICS:
Business & Industry
Education
Entertainment

Motivation
TYPICAL AUDIENCE:
Corporate
Association
Fraternal
General Public

BRACKETT, SHIRLEY
Relationships
5831 Williamson
Dearborn, Mi 48126
Telephone: 313-581-8209
ASSOCIATION
  MEMBERSHIP:
Natl. Speakers Assn.
PRINCIPAL TOPICS:
Education
Family
Human Relations
TYPICAL AUDIENCE:
Association

BRAHAM, BARBARA J.
1143 Neil Ave.
Columbus, OH 43201
Telephone: 614-291-0155
Fax: 614-299-3434
REPRESENTED BY:
Speakers Unlimited
ASSOCIATION
  MEMBERSHIP:
Natl. Speakers Assn.
PRINCIPAL TOPICS:
Health
Motivation
TYPICAL AUDIENCE:
Corporate
Association

BRANDAU, KARLA
Life Power Dynamics
4985 Chartley Cir.
Lilburn, GA 30247
Telephone: 404-923-0883
Fax: 404-921-1446
MAILING ADDRESS:
Life Power Dynamics
P.O. Box 450802
Atlanta, GA 30345
REPRESENTED BY:
Speaker Connect USA
ASSOCIATION
  MEMBERSHIP:
Natl. Speakers Assn.
ASTD
NAFE
PRINCIPAL TOPICS:
Family
Health
Management

Motivation
TYPICAL AUDIENCE:
Corporate
Association

BRANDON, STEVE
5722 Hickory Plaza, Bldg. A2
Nashville, TN 37211
Telephone: 615-333-3492
Fax: 615-333-3495
REPRESENTED BY:
Creative Directions (Nashville)
ASSOCIATION
  MEMBERSHIP:
Natl. Speakers Assn.
PRINCIPAL TOPICS:
Humor
TYPICAL AUDIENCE:
Corporate

BRAVERMAN, TERRY
3595 Grand View Blvd.
Los Angeles, CA 90066
Telephone: 310-397-6543
Fax: 310-397-6543
REPRESENTED BY:
Debra Lilly
Andrea Temel
JNJ
Goldstar
Standing Ovation
ASSOCIATION
  MEMBERSHIP:
Natl. Speakers Assn.
American Society of Training &
  Development
PRINCIPAL TOPICS:
Health
Humor
Motivation
TYPICAL AUDIENCE:
Corporate

BRECHT, ANN M.
4307 Cheyenne Dr.
Laramie, WY 82070
Telephone: 307-742-4641
ASSOCIATION
  MEMBERSHIP:
Natl. Speakers Assn.
Toastmasters
PRINCIPAL TOPICS:
Food/Diet
Health
TYPICAL AUDIENCE:
Corporate
Association

BRILES, DR. JUDITH
P.O. Box 22021
Denver, CO 80222

Telephone: 303-745-4590
Fax: 303-745-4595
REPRESENTED BY:
Kepplers
Wash Speakers Bureau
Lynn Campbell Agency
ASSOCIATION
  MEMBERSHIP:
Natl. Speakers Assn.
PRINCIPAL TOPICS:
Health
Human Relations
Motivation
Personal Finance
TYPICAL AUDIENCE:
Corporate
Association
Institutional

BRITTON, TOM
18350 Arbor Terrace
Spring, TX 77388
Telephone: 713-443-6660
Fax: 713-868-6711
MAILING ADDRESS:
P.O. Box 671232
Houston, TX 77267
REPRESENTED BY:
Speaker Source International
American Speakers
  International
ASSOCIATION
  MEMBERSHIP:
Natl. Speakers Assn.
PRINCIPAL TOPICS:
Human Relations
Management
Marketing
Motivation
Sales
TYPICAL AUDIENCE:
Corporate
Association

BRODER,
  MICHAEL S. PHD
255 S. 17th St., 29th Fl.
Phildelphia, PA 19103
Telephone: 215-545-7000
Fax: 215-545-7011
REPRESENTED BY:
Nightingale Conant
ASSOCIATION
  MEMBERSHIP:
Natl. Speakers Assn.
Toastmasters
PRINCIPAL TOPICS:
Family
Media
Motivation
Psychology

TYPICAL AUDIENCE:
Corporate
Association

BRODY, MARJORIE
Brody Communications
1200 Melrose Ave.
Melrose Park, PA 19126
Telephone: 215-635-4420
Fax: 215-635-3511
ASSOCIATION
  MEMBERSHIP:
Natl. Speakers Assn.
Toastmasters
ASTD
PRINCIPAL TOPICS:
Human Relations
Motivation
Communications
TYPICAL AUDIENCE:
Corporate
Association
Fraternal

BROOKS, EVE
Brooks, E.R. Associates
P.O. Box 2802
Farmington Hills, Mi 48333
Telephone: 313-835-4575
ASSOCIATION
  MEMBERSHIP:
Natl. Speakers Assn.
Professional Speakers Assn. Of
  Mich.
PRINCIPAL TOPICS:
Motivation
Sales
Communications
TYPICAL AUDIENCE:
Corporate
Association

BROWN, KATHY &
  ASSOCIATES
Brown, Kathy & Associates
9108 Trotters Lane
Woodbury, Mi 55125
Telephone: 612-730-1109
Fax: 612-730-1108
REPRESENTED BY:
Key Seminars
Speakers Plus
The Speakers Bureau
National Speakers Bureau, Inc.
ASSOCIATION
  MEMBERSHIP:
Natl. Speakers Assn.
NAFE (Natl. Assoc. of Female
  Exec.)
PRINCIPAL TOPICS:
Business & Industry

Education
Entertainment
Family
Fashion
Health
Human Relations
Humor
Management
Medical
Motivation
Religion
Senior Citizens
Youth
TYPICAL AUDIENCE:
Association

BROWN, LINDEE S.
P.O. Box 88
Montebello, Ca 90640
Telephone: 213-723-1341
Fax: 213-728-9684
ASSOCIATION
  MEMBERSHIP:
Natl. Speakers Assn.
Toastmasters
PRINCIPAL TOPICS:
Education
Entertainment
Motivation
Philosophy
Religion
TYPICAL AUDIENCE:
Association
Fraternal

BROWN,
  MARLENE B., M.S.
Marmel Consulting Firm
P.O. Box 83, 53 White St.,
  Ste. 305
Clark Mills, NY 13321-0083
Telephone: 315-853-5092
Fax: 315-853-4636
ASSOCIATION
  MEMBERSHIP:
Natl. Speakers Assn.
ASTD
PRINCIPAL TOPICS:
Business & Industry
Computer Technology
Education
Government
Human Relations
Humor
Management
Motivation
TYPICAL AUDIENCE:
Corporate
Association

BROWN, RICHARD R.
Rt. 1, Box 256
Evergreen, Al 36401
Telephone: 205-564-2881
ASSOCIATION
  MEMBERSHIP:
Natl. Speakers Assn.
Alabama Speakers
PRINCIPAL TOPICS:
Education
Humor
Motivation
TYPICAL AUDIENCE:
Corporate
Association
Fraternal

BROWN, TRACY
Person To Person Consulting
P.O. Box 150761
Arlington, Tx 76015
Telephone: 817-467-5753
Fax: 817-467-4509
ASSOCIATION
  MEMBERSHIP:
Natl. Speakers Assn.
PRINCIPAL TOPICS:
Human Relations
Management
Motivation
Communications
TYPICAL AUDIENCE:
Corporate
Association

BROWNELL, EILEEN O.
9540 Westbourne Ct., #A
Cypress, CA 90630
Telephone: 714-821-1460
REPRESENTED BY:
Promark
ASSOCIATION
  MEMBERSHIP:
Natl. Speakers Assn.
California Park & Recreation
  Society
PRINCIPAL TOPICS:
Human Relations
Motivation
Psychology
TYPICAL AUDIENCE:
Corporate
Association
Government

BRUN, DONALD J.   CSP
219 Broadway, #449
Laguna Beach, CA 92651
Telephone: 714-494-4960

ASSOCIATION
  MEMBERSHIP:
Natl. Speakers Assn.
PRINCIPAL TOPICS:
Advertising
Education
Management
Marketing
Media
Motivation
Philosophy
Sales
TYPICAL AUDIENCE:
Corporate
Association

BRUNER, HELEN L.C.S.W.
910 Colusa Ave., #5
Berkeley, CA 94707
Telephone: 510-527-0951
ASSOCIATION
  MEMBERSHIP:
Natl. Speakers Assn.
PRINCIPAL TOPICS:
Family
Human Relations
Motivation
Psychology
Senior Citizens
Communications
TYPICAL AUDIENCE:
Association

BUCARO, FRANK C.
722 Canyon Ln.
Elgin, IL 60123
Telephone: 708-697-1587
Fax: 708-697-1505
ASSOCIATION
  MEMBERSHIP:
Natl. Speakers Assn.
PRINCIPAL TOPICS:
Human Relations
Management
Motivation
Philosophy
TYPICAL AUDIENCE:
Corporate
Association

BUDD, NANCY
Budd, Nancy &
  Associates
7508 N. 20th Street
Phoenix, AZ 85020
Telephone: 602-997-2480
Fax: 602-861-1741
ASSOCIATION
  MEMBERSHIP:
Natl. Speakers Assn.
Toastmasters

PRINCIPAL TOPICS:
Business & Industry
Family
Health
Human Relations
Marketing
Motivation
Sales
Senior Citizens
TYPICAL AUDIENCE:
Corporate

BURG, BOB
Burg Communications Inc.
P.O. Box 7002
Jupiter, FL 33468-7002
Telephone: 800-726-3667
Fax: 407-575-2304
ASSOCIATION
  MEMBERSHIP:
Natl. Speakers Assn.
PRINCIPAL TOPICS:
Business & Industry
Human Relations
Sales
TYPICAL AUDIENCE:
Corporate
Association

BURGE, JOAN M.
Office Dymanics
P.O. Box 1039, 3980
  Breckinridge Dr.
Okemos, Mi 48864
Telephone: 517-342-6467
ASSOCIATION
  MEMBERSHIP:
Natl. Speakers Assn.
American Society Of Training &
  Development
PRINCIPAL TOPICS:
Business & Industry
Human Relations
Motivation
TYPICAL AUDIENCE:
Corporate
Association

BURGETT, GORDON
3863 Cherry Hill Rd.
Santa Maria, CA 93455
Telephone: 805-937-8711
Fax: 805-937-3035
MAILING ADDRESS:
P.O. Box 6405
Santa Maria, CA 93456
ASSOCIATION
  MEMBERSHIP:
Natl. Speakers Assn.
PRINCIPAL TOPICS:
Journalism

Marketing
Media
Personal Finance
Travel
TYPICAL AUDIENCE:
Association
Institutional

BURNELL, IVAN G.
Main Street, Box 277
Center Ossipee, NH 03814
Telephone: 603-539-4795
Fax: 603-539-5417
ASSOCIATION
  MEMBERSHIP:
Natl. Speakers Assn.
PRINCIPAL TOPICS:
Communications
Family
Management
Motivation
TYPICAL AUDIENCE:
Corporate
Association
Fraternal
General Public

BURNS, KAREN
P.O. Box 21418
Reno, NV 89515
Telephone: 702-849-2299
Fax: 702-849-2191
ASSOCIATION
  MEMBERSHIP:
Natl. Speakers Assn.
PRINCIPAL TOPICS:
Entertainment
Humor
TYPICAL AUDIENCE:
Corporate

BURNS, PAT
3857 Birch Street, #414
Newport Beach, Ca 92660
Telephone: 714-557-3030
Fax: 714-557-3030
ASSOCIATION
  MEMBERSHIP:
Natl. Speakers Assn.
PRINCIPAL TOPICS:
Amusements
Motivation
Sales
TYPICAL AUDIENCE:
Corporate
Association

BURROUGHS,
  HENRIETTA J.
Personalized Broadcasting
  Service
2680 Bayshore Parkway, #200
Mountain View, CA 94043
Telephone: 415-965-3982
ASSOCIATION
  MEMBERSHIP:
Natl. Speakers Assn.
PRINCIPAL TOPICS:
Human Relations
Media
TYPICAL AUDIENCE:
Corporate
Association

BURRUS, DANIEL　　　　CSP
P.O. Box 26413
Milwaukee, WI 53005
Telephone: 414-774-7790
Fax: 414-774-8330
REPRESENTED BY:
Washington Speakers Bureau
National Speakers Bureau
ASSOCIATION
  MEMBERSHIP:
Natl. Speakers Assn.
PRINCIPAL TOPICS:
Business & Industry
Computer Technology
Education
Management
Sales
TYPICAL AUDIENCE:
Corporate
Association

BURTON, BEN　　　　　CSP
#10 Queens Row
Hot Springs, AR 71901
Telephone: 501-623-6496
Fax: 501-623-0216
ASSOCIATION
  MEMBERSHIP:
Natl. Speakers Assn.
PRINCIPAL TOPICS:
Humor
TYPICAL AUDIENCE:
Corporate
Association

BURZYNSKI, LINDA L.
7140 Poole Jones Rd.
Frederick, MD 21702
Telephone: 301-695-4632
ASSOCIATION
  MEMBERSHIP:
Natl. Speakers Assn.
PRINCIPAL TOPICS:
Motivation

Sales
TYPICAL AUDIENCE:
Corporate

BUSSEY, TROY D.　　　　CSP
7020 125th Ave. S.E.
Renton, WA 98056
Telephone: 206-226-4158
ASSOCIATION
  MEMBERSHIP:
Natl. Speakers Assn.
PRINCIPAL TOPICS:
Management
Marketing
Motivation
Sales
TYPICAL AUDIENCE:
Corporate
Association
State & Federal Agencies

BUTLER, JENNIFER
511 S. Arden
Los Angeles, Ca 90020
Telephone: 213-931-2626
ASSOCIATION
  MEMBERSHIP:
Natl. Speakers Assn.
PRINCIPAL TOPICS:
Education
Fashion
Human Relations
Motivation
Psychology
Sales
TYPICAL AUDIENCE:
Corporate

BUTTS, JIMMIE K.
6801 Phillips Ct.
Raleigh, NC 27607
Telephone: 919-851-1929
ASSOCIATION
  MEMBERSHIP:
Natl. Speakers Assn.
PRINCIPAL TOPICS:
Health
Humor
TYPICAL AUDIENCE:
Corporate
Association

BUXMAN, KARYN
Rt. 3, Box 180 AA
Hannibal, Mo 63401
Telephone: 314-221-2670
REPRESENTED BY:
Journal Of Nursing Jocularity
American Association Of
  Therapeutic Humor

ASSOCIATION
  MEMBERSHIP:
Natl. Speakers Assn.
PRINCIPAL TOPICS:
Humor
Medical
Motivation
TYPICAL AUDIENCE:
Corporate
Association

BYERS, MARY
92 Cottonwood
Chatham, Il 62629
Telephone: 217-483-5856
Fax: 217-483-5856
REPRESENTED BY:
Capital City Speakers Bureau
ASSOCIATION
  MEMBERSHIP:
Natl. Speakers Assn.
PRINCIPAL TOPICS:
Advertising
Marketing
Media
TYPICAL AUDIENCE:
Association

CABRERA, JIMMY　　　CSP
1827 Roanwood Dr.
Houston, TX 77090
Telephone: 713-537-0032
Fax: 713-537-9242
ASSOCIATION
  MEMBERSHIP:
Natl. Speakers Assn.
PRINCIPAL TOPICS:
Education
Motivation
Sales
TYPICAL AUDIENCE:
Corporate
Association

CALHOON, JOE　　　　CSP
Box 15065
Lenexa, KS 66285
Telephone: 913-888-7488
Fax: 913-888-9283
ASSOCIATION
  MEMBERSHIP:
Natl. Speakers Assn.
PRINCIPAL TOPICS:
Business & Industry
Management
Motivation
Sales
TYPICAL AUDIENCE:
Corporate
Association

CALMES, MARYLEE
13812 N.E. 40th St.
Bellevue, Wa 98005
Telephone: 206-869-5271
ASSOCIATION
  MEMBERSHIP:
Natl. Speakers Assn.
PRINCIPAL TOPICS:
Food/Diet
Health
Motivation
Psychology
TYPICAL AUDIENCE:
Association

CAMPBELL, SANDRA
  JONES
P.O. Box 5323
Indian Rocks Beach, Fl 34635
Telephone: 813-593-1616
ASSOCIATION
  MEMBERSHIP:
Natl. Speakers Assn.
PRINCIPAL TOPICS:
Family
Health
Human Relations
Humor
Motivation
Psychology
TYPICAL AUDIENCE:
Corporate
Association
Fraternal

CAMPER, NATALIE
  K., PH.D.
1117 Baylston Street
Chestnut Hill, Ma 02167
Telephone: 617-232-2260
Fax: 617-232-0047
PRINCIPAL TOPICS:
Human Relations
Management
Communications
TYPICAL AUDIENCE:
Corporate
Association
Fraternal

CANFIELD, JACK   CSP
6035 Bristol Pkwy.
Culver City, CA 90230
Telephone: 310-337-9222
Fax: 310-337-7465
REPRESENTED BY:
Walters Bureau
Jostens
ASSOCIATION
  MEMBERSHIP:
Natl. Speakers Assn.
PRINCIPAL TOPICS:
Education
Human Relations
Motivation

Psychology
Sales
TYPICAL AUDIENCE:
Corporate
Association

CARLE, GILDA PHD
Interchange Communications
  Training Inc.
117 De Haven Dr.
Yonkers, NY 10703
Telephone: 914-378-1233
ASSOCIATION
  MEMBERSHIP:
Natl. Speakers Assn.
PRINCIPAL TOPICS:
Human Relations
Motivation
Psychology
TYPICAL AUDIENCE:
Corporate
Association
Fraternal

CARLINO, ANDY
9230 Cypress Hollow Dr.
Palm Beach Gardens, FL
  33418
Telephone: 407-626-0676
Fax: 407-676-8333
ASSOCIATION
  MEMBERSHIP:
Natl. Speakers Assn.
PRINCIPAL TOPICS:
Business & Industry
Management
Motivation
Sales
TYPICAL AUDIENCE:
Corporate

CARMODY, KATHY
LIGHT ATTITUDES
7609 HIGHLANDER DR.
ANCHORAGE, AK 99518
Telephone: 907-344-8579
Fax: 907-344-8579
ASSOCIATION
  MEMBERSHIP:
Natl. Speakers Assn.
American Seminar Leaders
PRINCIPAL TOPICS:
Education
Family
Health
Human Relations
Humor
Motivation
Psychology
Communications
TYPICAL AUDIENCE:
Association
SEE AD IN SECTION 8

CAROLAN, SHIRLEY M.
The Word Master
3203 Jose Court
Hayward, CA 94542
Telephone: 510-733-5124
Fax: 510-886-3416
ASSOCIATION
  MEMBERSHIP:
Natl. Speakers Assn.
Toastmasters
PRINCIPAL TOPICS:
Business & Industry
Education
Motivation
TYPICAL AUDIENCE:
Corporate
Association
Fraternal
Institutional

CARR, SHARON
2800 Prescott Dr.
Carrollton, TX 75006
Telephone: 214-416-1677
Fax: 214-416-1414
ASSOCIATION
  MEMBERSHIP:
Natl. Speakers Assn.
North Texas Speakers
PRINCIPAL TOPICS:
Health
Management
Motivation
Sales
TYPICAL AUDIENCE:
Association

CARSON,
  GAYLE, DR.   CSP
2957 Flamingo Dr.
Miami Beach, FL 33140
Telephone: 305-534-8846
Fax: 305-534-8846
ASSOCIATION
  MEMBERSHIP:
Natl. Speakers Assn.
PRINCIPAL TOPICS:
Business & Industry
Human Relations
Management
Sales
TYPICAL AUDIENCE:
Corporate
Association

CARSON, RICHARD D.
7424 Greenville Ave., #113
Dallas, Tx 75231
Telephone: 214-363-0788
ASSOCIATION
  MEMBERSHIP:
Natl. Speakers Assn.
PRINCIPAL TOPICS:
Family
Health

Human Relations
Psychology
Youth
TYPICAL AUDIENCE:
Association

CARSON, TERRENCE J.
201 Village Commons
Sewickley, PA 15143
Telephone: 412-741-8588
Fax: 412-741-0833
PRINCIPAL TOPICS:
Advertising
Entertainment
Personal Finance
Video
TYPICAL AUDIENCE:
Corporate

CARTER, ARNOLD
  'NICK'   CSP
Nightingale-Conant Corp.
1315 Glenwood Ave.
Deerfiled, IL 60015
Telephone: 800-572-2770
Fax: 708-647-7145
MAILING ADDRESS:
Nightingale-Conant Corp.
7300 N. Lehigh Ave.
Niles, IL 60714
REPRESENTED BY:
Nightingale-Conant Speakers &
  Trainers Bureau
ASSOCIATION
  MEMBERSHIP:
Natl. Speakers Assn.
Toastmasters
Professional Speakers of
  Illinois

PRINCIPAL TOPICS:
Business & Industry
Education
Entertainment
Family
Human Relations
Humor
Management
Marketing
Motivation
Philosophy
Physical Fitness
Psychology
Religion
Sales
TYPICAL AUDIENCE:
Corporate
Association
Fraternal
Institutional

CARTER CHERIE-SCOTT CSP
145 CANON DRIVE
P.O. BOX 30052
SANTA BARBARA, CA 93105

Telephone: 805-563-0789
Fax: 805-563-1028
REPRESENTED BY:
Walters S.B. Speakers
Bureau
ASSOCIATION
 MEMBERSHIP:
Natl. Speakers Assn.
PRINCIPAL TOPICS:
Management
Motivation
TYPICAL AUDIENCE:
Corporate
Association

CARTER, STEVEN L.
65 Woodwind Dr.
Spartanburg, SC 29302
Telephone: 803-573-5234
Fax: 803-573-6085
ASSOCIATION
 MEMBERSHIP:
Natl. Speakers Assn.
PRINCIPAL TOPICS:
Management
TYPICAL AUDIENCE:
Corporate

CARUSO, JOSEPH A.
3171 Palmetto Ct.
Trenton, MI 48183
Telephone: 313-692-0544
Fax: 313-671-7625
ASSOCIATION
 MEMBERSHIP:
Natl. Speakers Assn.
PRINCIPAL TOPICS:
Human Relations
Management
Marketing
Motivation
Sales
TYPICAL AUDIENCE:
Corporate
Association

CASE, BOB
2913 Madison Rd.
Cincinnati, OH 45209
Telephone: 513-631-4438
ASSOCIATION
 MEMBERSHIP:
Natl. Speakers Assn.
Toastmasters
Speakers USA
PRINCIPAL TOPICS:
Business & Industry
Health
Human Relations
Management
Motivation
Physical Fitness
TYPICAL AUDIENCE:
Corporate
Association

CHARBONNEAU, JOS. J.
400 Ginger Court
Southlake, Tx 76092
Telephone: 817-329-2128
Fax: 817-421-0713
REPRESENTED BY:
Winner's Circle
Exposures To Excellence
Linkie Seltzer
ASSOCIATION
 MEMBERSHIP:
Natl. Speakers Assn.
PRINCIPAL TOPICS:
Automotive
Management
Motivation
Sales
TYPICAL AUDIENCE:
Corporate
Association

CHEN NANCY
S. HILL & TREE CT.
MELVILLE, NY 11747
Telephone: 516-696-4116
ASSOCIATION
 MEMBERSHIP:
ASTD
Natl. Speakers Assn.
PRINCIPAL TOPICS:
Fashion
TYPICAL AUDIENCE:
Corporate
Association
Fraternal
SEE AD IN SECTION 8

CHESTER, ERIC
7250 W. 8th Pl.
Lakewood, CO 80215
Telephone: 303-239-9999
Fax: 303-239-9901
ASSOCIATION
 MEMBERSHIP:
Natl. Speakers Assn.
PRINCIPAL TOPICS:
Education
Humor
Motivation
Youth
TYPICAL AUDIENCE:
Association
Institutional

CHILDRESS, GENE W.
99 Wildwood
Versailles, Ky 40383
Telephone: 606-873-7744
ASSOCIATION
 MEMBERSHIP:
Natl. Speakers Assn.
American Society Training &
 Development
PRINCIPAL TOPICS:
Government

Human Relations
Management
Motivation
TYPICAL AUDIENCE:
Corporate
Association
Fraternal
Institutional

CHINN, C. EARL
13745 Rostrata Rd.
Poway, Ca 92064
Telephone: 619-487-6198
Fax: 619-487-4695
ASSOCIATION
 MEMBERSHIP:
Natl. Speakers Assn.
Toastmasters
ASTD
PRINCIPAL TOPICS:
Business & Industry
Military
Motivation
Senior Citizens
TYPICAL AUDIENCE:
Corporate
Association
Fraternal
Institutions

CHITWOOD, ROY E.   CSP
1960 E. Grand Ave.
El Segundo, CA 90245
Telephone: 800-488-4629
Fax: 310-640-2269
ASSOCIATION
 MEMBERSHIP:
Natl. Speakers Assn.
PRINCIPAL TOPICS:
Management
Marketing
Motivation
Sales
TYPICAL AUDIENCE:
Corporate
Association
Fraternal

CHRISTOPHER, SYLVIA
7400 Boneta Rd.
Wadsworth, OH 44281
Telephone: 216-334-4389
ASSOCIATION
 MEMBERSHIP:
Natl. Speakers Assn.
International Speakers Network
PRINCIPAL TOPICS:
Business & Industry
Human Relations
Management
Motivation
Psychology
TYPICAL AUDIENCE:
Corporate
Association

CLIFFE, ROGER W.
511 S. 2nd St.
Dekalb, IL 60115
Telephone: 815-756-6649
Fax: 815-756-1575
MAILING ADDRESS:
P.O. Box 116
Dekalb, IL 60115
ASSOCIATION
 MEMBERSHIP:
Natl. Speakers Assn.
American Society For Training
 & Development
PRINCIPAL TOPICS:
Hobbies
TYPICAL AUDIENCE:
Association

COATES, MARTY
2325 Darden Dr.
Florence, SC 29501
Telephone: 803-679-9755
Fax: 803-678-9826
REPRESENTED BY:
Agriculatural Speakers Network
Exposures to Excellence
B & R Management
Speakers & More
ASSOCIATION
 MEMBERSHIP:
Natl. Speakers Assn.
PRINCIPAL TOPICS:
Agriculture
Humor
Management
Marketing
Motivation
Sales
TYPICAL AUDIENCE:
Corporate
Association

COEY, NANCY
4705 Twinwood Ct.
Raleigh, NC 27613
Telephone: 919-848-9743
REPRESENTED BY:
Jostens, McKinney & Assoc.
ASSOCIATION
 MEMBERSHIP:
Natl. Speakers Assn.
PRINCIPAL TOPICS:
Education
Motivation
TYPICAL AUDIENCE:
Association
Institutional

COFFEE, GERALD   CSP
98-1247 Kaawumanu St., #306
Aiea, HI 96701
Telephone: 808-488-1776
Fax: 808-488-0901

ASSOCIATION
  MEMBERSHIP:
Natl. Speakers Assn.
PRINCIPAL TOPICS:
Communications
Human Relations
Motivation
TYPICAL AUDIENCE:
Corporate
Association
Fraternal
Educational
Religious

COLE, P. CHRISTIAN
2 Smith Farm Road
Stratham, NH 03885
Telephone: 603-772-3454
Fax: 603-772-7376
PRINCIPAL TOPICS:
Management
TYPICAL AUDIENCE:
Corporate
Association

COLLINS, PEGGY
3404 Willowood
Bartlesville, OK 74006
Telephone: 918-333-8395
MAILING ADDRESS:
P.O. Box 2202
Bartlesville, OK 74005
ASSOCIATION
  MEMBERSHIP:
Natl. Speakers Assn.
International Training In
  Communication
PRINCIPAL TOPICS:
Entertainment
Humor
Travel
TYPICAL AUDIENCE:
Association

COLOMBO, GEORGE W.
40 Back River Rd.
Merrimack, NH 03054
Telephone: 603-429-2306
Fax: 603-429-2306
ASSOCIATION
  MEMBERSHIP:
Natl. Speakers Assn.
PRINCIPAL TOPICS:
Business & Industry
Computer Technology
Management
Sales
TYPICAL AUDIENCE:
Corporate

CONDON, GWEN
1093 AIA, #210
St. Augustine Beach, Fl 32084
Telephone: 904-471-4141
Fax: 904-471-4201
ASSOCIATION
  MEMBERSHIP:
Natl. Speakers Assn.
North Florida Professional
  Speakers Assn.
PRINCIPAL TOPICS:
Business & Industry
Humor
Sales
TYPICAL AUDIENCE:
Corporate
Association

CONLEY, JEFF
The Zig Zigler Corporation
3330 Earhart
Carrollton, TX 75006
Telephone: 800-527-0306
Fax: 214-991-1853
REPRESENTED BY:
The Zig Ziglar Corporation's
  Speaker Bureau
PRINCIPAL TOPICS:
Human Relations
Management
Motivation
TYPICAL AUDIENCE:
Corporate

CONLON, PETER J., JR.
3330 MATLOCK RD.,
  STE. 210
ARLINGTON, TX 76015
Telephone: 817-465-3565
ASSOCIATION
  MEMBERSHIP:
Natl. Speakers Assn.
PRINCIPAL TOPICS:
Business & Industry
Management
Personal Finance
Senior Citizens
TYPICAL AUDIENCE:
Corporate
Association

CONNOR, TIM   CSP
433 W. Briar Pl., #2C
Chicago, IL 60657
Telephone: 312-296-2277
Fax: 312-296-2772
REPRESENTED BY:
Nash Speakers
Caf Speakers
Preferred Speak

Speak Inc.
ASSOCIATION
  MEMBERSHIP:
Natl. Speakers Assn.
PRINCIPAL TOPICS:
Business & Industry
Human Relations
Management
Motivation
Sales
TYPICAL AUDIENCE:
Corporate
Association

CONSTANT, RUTH L.
108 Spokane
Victoria, TX 77904
Telephone: 512-578-0762
MAILING ADDRESS:
1501 Mockingbird, #404
Victoria, TX 77904
ASSOCIATION
  MEMBERSHIP:
Natl. Speakers Assn.
PRINCIPAL TOPICS:
Business & Industry
Motivation
TYPICAL AUDIENCE:
Corporate
Association
Fraternal

COOK, ETHEL M.
4 HILDA ROAD
BEDFORD, MA 01730
Telephone: 617-275-2326
Fax: 617-275-7136
ASSOCIATION
  MEMBERSHIP:
Natl. Speakers Assn.
PRINCIPAL TOPICS:
Management
Motivation
TYPICAL AUDIENCE:
Corporate
Association
SEE AD IN SECTION 8

COPELAND, GARY R.
9963 E. Mexico Avenue
Denver, CO 80231
Telephone: 303-368-4099
Fax: 303-368-8089
ASSOCIATION
  MEMBERSHIP:
Natl. Speakers Assn.
PRINCIPAL TOPICS:
Family
Management
Motivation
Psychology

TYPICAL AUDIENCE:
Corporate
Association
Religious

CORCORAN, DENISE M
1110 Polynesia Dr., #116
Foster City, CA 94404
Telephone: 415-341-1477
ASSOCIATION
  MEMBERSHIP:
Natl. Speakers
Toastmasters
PRINCIPAL TOPICS:
Business & Industry
Marketing
Motivation
TYPICAL AUDIENCE:
Association

CORNWELL, ART
The Boardroom
19 Country Club Beach
Rockford, IL 61103
Telephone: 815-962-7100
MAILING ADDRESS:
The Boardroom
202 W. State St., Ste. 918
Rockford, IL 61101
ASSOCIATION
  MEMBERSHIP:
Natl. Speakers Assn.
PRINCIPAL TOPICS:
Business & Industry
Management
Marketing
Motivation
TYPICAL AUDIENCE:
Corporate
Association
Fraternal

CORNYN-SELBY, ALYCE
1928 S.E. Ladd Ave.
Portland, OR 97214
Telephone: 503-232-0433
ASSOCIATION
  MEMBERSHIP:
Natl. Speakers Assn.
Oregon Speakers
PRINCIPAL TOPICS:
Human Relations
Humor
Management
Psychology
TYPICAL AUDIENCE:
Corporate
Association

CORTIS, BRUNO, MD
7605 1/2 W. North Ave.
River Forest, IL 60305
Telephone: 708-366-0117
Fax: 708-366-0710
ASSOCIATION
  MEMBERSHIP:
Natl. Speakers Assn.
PRINCIPAL TOPICS:
Education
Health
Human Relations
TYPICAL AUDIENCE:
Corporate
Association

COTTLE, DAVID W.
13899 Biscayne Blvd., #141
Miami, FL 33181
Telephone: 305-940-5400
Fax: 305-947-9305
ASSOCIATION
  MEMBERSHIP:
Natl. Speakers Assn.
PRINCIPAL TOPICS:
Management
Marketing
TYPICAL AUDIENCE:
Association

COTTLE, DEBRA
1169 S. Plymouth Ct., #120
Chicago, Il 60605
Telephone: 312-922-8016
ASSOCIATION
  MEMBERSHIP:
Natl. Speakers Assn.
PRINCIPAL TOPICS:
Motivation
Sales
TYPICAL AUDIENCE:
Association

COUCH, DR.
  BOB E., PH.D.
130 Donella
San Antonio, TX 78232
Telephone: 210-494-1769
Fax: 210-545-1704
MAILING ADDRESS:
COUCH, DR. BOB E. PHD
P.O. Box 160055
San Antonio, TX 78280
ASSOCIATION
  MEMBERSHIP:
Natl. Speakers Assn.
Toastmasters
PRINCIPAL TOPICS:
Education
Family
Human Relations

Humor
Motivation
Sales
TYPICAL AUDIENCE:
Corporate
Association

COX, DANNY, CPAE
17381 BONNER DR.,
  STE. 101
TUSTIN, CA 92680
Telephone: 714-838-3030
REPRESENTED BY:
Washington Speakers
  Bureau
National Speakers Bureau
ASSOCIATION
  MEMBERSHIP:
Natl. Speakers Assn.
Speakers Roundtable
PRINCIPAL TOPICS:
Humor
Management
Motivation
TYPICAL AUDIENCE:
Corporate
Association

CRACKOWER, SYDNEY, M.D.
701 ROBLEY DR., STE. 100
LAFAYETTE, LA 70503
Telephone: 318-893-7921
MAILING ADDRESS:
203 S. Jefferson St.
Abbeville, LA 70510
Fax: 318-893-1190
ASSOCIATION
  MEMBERSHIP:
Natl. Speakers Assn.
PRINCIPAL TOPICS:
Food/Diet
Health
Human Relations
Medical
Motivation
TYPICAL AUDIENCE:
Corporate
Association

CRAWFORD, MADISON
3422 Oakwood Dr.
Bettendorf, IA 52722
Telephone: 319-359-5525
REPRESENTED BY:
North American Speakers
  Bureau
ASSOCIATION
  MEMBERSHIP:
Natl. Speakers

American Society of Quality
  Control
PRINCIPAL TOPICS:
Humor
Management
Motivation
TYPICAL AUDIENCE:
Corporate
Association

CRAWFORD, SALLY L.
Crawford & Associates Inc.
6250 River Rd., Ste. 12-150
Rosemont, IL 60018
Telephone: 708-698-6670
Fax: 708-698-6992
PRINCIPAL TOPICS:
Business & Industry
Human Relations
Management
Motivation
Sales
TYPICAL AUDIENCE:
Corporate
Association

CREEL, JOANNE P.
23 Nottingham Drive
Yarmouthport, Ma 02675
Telephone: 508-362-5136
Fax: 508-430-0820
ASSOCIATION
  MEMBERSHIP:
Natl. Speakers Assn.
Toastmasters
PRINCIPAL TOPICS:
Family
Human Relations
Motivation
Psychology
Social Trends
Youth
TYPICAL AUDIENCE:
Association
Fraternal

CRIST, LYLE   CSP
2550 Belleflower
Alliance, OH 44601
Telephone: 216-821-0241
REPRESENTED BY:
Speakers Unlimited
ASSOCIATION
  MEMBERSHIP:
Natl. Speakers Assn.
PRINCIPAL TOPICS:
Humor
Motivation
TYPICAL AUDIENCE:
Corporate
Association

CROWSON, GATHA
  ROMINE
Crowson Productions Inc.
Rte. 12, Box 58, 12430
  Lakeview Dr.
Athens, AL 35611
Telephone: 205-729-6476
Fax: 205-772-8888
ASSOCIATION
  MEMBERSHIP:
Natl. Speakers Assn.
PRINCIPAL TOPICS:
Business & Industry
Education
Family
Human Relations
Humor
Management
Marketing
Medical
Motivation
Psychology
Religion
Sales
Social Trends
Youth
TYPICAL AUDIENCE:
Corporate
Association
Fraternal
Civic
Religious

CRUMPTON, DEBRA J.
1501 El Camino Ave., #209
Sacramento, Ca 95815
Telephone: 916-649-6872
Fax: 916-649-0439
ASSOCIATION
  MEMBERSHIP:
Natl. Speakers Assn.
PRINCIPAL TOPICS:
Business & Industry
Management
Motivation
TYPICAL AUDIENCE:
Corporate
Association

CSOLKOVITS, ERNEST A.
16910 West 10 Mile Road
Southfield, MI 48075
Telephone: 313-559-1224
Fax: 313-559-4850
MAILING ADDRESS:
D.E.L.T.A. Motiveaction
  Institute
Southfield, MI 48075
ASSOCIATION
  MEMBERSHIP:
Natl. Speakers Assn.

PRINCIPAL TOPICS:
Food/Diet
Human Relations
Management
Motivation
Philosophy
Psychology
Sales
TYPICAL AUDIENCE:
Corporate
Association
Fraternal

CUMMING, CANDY
3089 C Clairemont Dr., #325
San Diego, CA 92117
Telephone: 619-292-1296
REPRESENTED BY:
The Podium
Speak Inc.
ASSOCIATION
  MEMBERSHIP:
Natl. Speakers Assn.
PRINCIPAL TOPICS:
Food/Diet
Health
Humor
Physical Fitness
TYPICAL AUDIENCE:
Corporate
Association
Spouse Programs

CUMMINGS, BETH A.
307 4th St. S.W.
Great Falls, MT 59404
Telephone: 406-761-7708
MAILING ADDRESS:
Cummings, Beth, A. Propeller
P.O. Box 328
Great Falls, MT 59403
ASSOCIATION
  MEMBERSHIP:
Natl. Speakers Assn.
PRINCIPAL TOPICS:
Aviation
Humor
Motivation
TYPICAL AUDIENCE:
Corporate
Association

CUMMINGS, DR. RITA J.
7200 E. Hampden, #101
Denver, CO 80224
Telephone: 303-756-2737
ASSOCIATION
  MEMBERSHIP:
Natl. Speakers Assn.
PRINCIPAL TOPICS:
Ecology

Education
Food/Diet
Health
Medical
Nature
Physical Fitness
TYPICAL AUDIENCE:
Association
Fraternal

CUNNINGHAM, DOYLE
12410 Brookgreen Dr.
Louisville, Ky 40243
Telephone: 502-245-1930
ASSOCIATION
  MEMBERSHIP:
Natl. Speakers Assn.
Toastmasters
Kentucky Speakers
PRINCIPAL TOPICS:
Family
Health
Humor
Motivation
Youth
TYPICAL AUDIENCE:
Association

CUROE, JOHN
P.O. Box 1212
Dubuque, IA 52004
Telephone: 319-582-8763
ASSOCIATION
  MEMBERSHIP:
Natl. Speakers Assn.
Toastmasters
PRINCIPAL TOPICS:
Agriculture
Entertainment
Family
Health
Humor
Senior Citizens
TYPICAL AUDIENCE:
Association

CUSTER, CHUCK
12620 S.E. 26th Place
Bellevue, WA 98005
Telephone: 206-641-0644
Fax: 206-562-6673
ASSOCIATION
  MEMBERSHIP:
Natl. Speakers Assn.
PRINCIPAL TOPICS:
Management
Marketing
TYPICAL AUDIENCE:
Corporate
Association

CUTLER, MARY LOUISE
  (DTM)
965 Grace St.
Northville, MI 48167
Telephone: 313-349-8855
REPRESENTED BY:
Schoolcraft Community
  College, (Livonia, Mi)
ASSOCIATION
  MEMBERSHIP:
Natl. Speakers Assn.
Toastmasters
Professional Speakers Assoc.
  of Michigan
PRINCIPAL TOPICS:
Agriculture
Health
Media
TYPICAL AUDIENCE:
Association

D'ANDREA, JOSEPH J.
28 Arbor Lane
Dix Hills, NY 11746
Telephone: 516-421-3220
Fax: 516-427-7800
MAILING ADDRESS:
P.O. Box 1408
Melville, NY 11747
ASSOCIATION
  MEMBERSHIP:
Natl. Speakers Assn.
Toastmasters
LI Speakers
LI Progressive Speakers
PRINCIPAL TOPICS:
Motivation
Sales
TYPICAL AUDIENCE:
Corporate
Association
Fraternal

DACEY, JUDITH E., CPA
11018-112 Old St.
  Augustine Rd.
Jacksonville, FL 32257
Telephone: 904-260-0483
Fax: 904-260-0348
ASSOCIATION
  MEMBERSHIP:
Natl. Speakers Assn.
PRINCIPAL TOPICS:
Business & Industry
Marketing
Personal Finance
TYPICAL AUDIENCE:
Association

DAFFRON, RAY
3188 Dolly Ridge Dr.
Birmingham, AL 35243
Telephone: 205-960-2228
Fax: 205-870-3502
MAILING ADDRESS:
P.O. Box 43092
Birmingham, AL 35243
ASSOCIATION
  MEMBERSHIP:
Natl. Speakers Assn.
PRINCIPAL TOPICS:
Management
Marketing
Motivation
Sales
TYPICAL AUDIENCE:
Corporate
Association

DALY, JOHN J.
Daly Associates, Inc.
5616 Grove St., #101
Chevy Chase, MD 20815
Telephone: 301-656-2510
Fax: 301-656-8069
REPRESENTED BY:
French & Assoc.
Five Star
Capital
Dupree Jordan Etc.
ASSOCIATION
  MEMBERSHIP:
Natl. Speakers Assn.
PRINCIPAL TOPICS:
Advertising
Government
Management
TYPICAL AUDIENCE:
Corporate
Association

DAVEY, JUDY
P.O. Box 868
Cary, NC 27512
Telephone: 919-481-0087
Fax: 919-469-2812
ASSOCIATION
  MEMBERSHIP:
Natl. Speakers Assn.
PRINCIPAL TOPICS:
Management
Motivation
Sales
Youth
TYPICAL AUDIENCE:
Corporate
Association

DAVIDSON, JEFF (MBA)
  (CMC)
2417 Honeysuckle Rd.
Chapel Hill, NC 27514
Telephone: 919-932-1996
Fax: 919-932-9982
REPRESENTED BY:
Washington Speakers Forum
PRINCIPAL TOPICS:
Business & Industry
Marketing
Personal Finance
Sales
Social Trends
TYPICAL AUDIENCE:
Association
General Public
Corporate

DAVIES, KENT R.
P.O. Box 975
Anacortes, WA 98221
Telephone: 206-293-0235
Fax: 206-299-9236
PRINCIPAL TOPICS:
Management
Motivation
TYPICAL AUDIENCE:
Association

DAVIS, DARRYL
16 Hewlett Point Ave.
East Rockaway, NY 11518
Telephone: 800-395-3905
Fax: 516-599-4344
ASSOCIATION
  MEMBERSHIP:
Natl. Speakers Assn.
PRINCIPAL TOPICS:
Humor
Motivation
Personal Finance
Psychology
Sales
TYPICAL AUDIENCE:
Corporate
Association

DAVIS, KEVIN F.
696 San Ramon Valley Blvd.,
  #340
Danville, CA 94526
Telephone: 510-831-0922
REPRESENTED BY:
Blanchard Training &
  Development
ASSOCIATION
  MEMBERSHIP:
Natl. Speakers Assn.
PRINCIPAL TOPICS:
Management

Sales
TYPICAL AUDIENCE:
Corporate

DAVIS, RONALD L.   CSP
1865 Miner St.
Des Plaines, IA 60016
Telephone: 708-298-7300
Fax: 708-803-4523
ASSOCIATION
  MEMBERSHIP:
Natl. Speakers Assn.
Platform Speakers

PRINCIPAL TOPICS:
Business & Industry
Human Relations
Management
Marketing
Motivation
Sales
TYPICAL AUDIENCE:
Corporate
Association

DAWSON, ROGER
  PRODUCTIONS, INC.   CSP
Dawson, Roger Productions,
  Inc.
1661 Hanover Drive, #215
City Of Industry, CA 91748
Telephone: 800-932-9766
Fax: 818-854-3591
REPRESENTED BY:
Washington Speakers Bureau
Nightingdale Conant
ASSOCIATION
  MEMBERSHIP:
Natl. Speakers Assn.
Toastmasters
PRINCIPAL TOPICS:
Business & Industry
Human Relations
Management
Motivation
Sales
TYPICAL AUDIENCE:
Corporate
Association

DE GRAVELLES, ROU
225 Carnation Ave.
Corona De Mar, CA 92625
Telephone: 714-675-7196
ASSOCIATION
  MEMBERSHIP:
Natl. Speakers Assn.
Toastmasters
American Society for Training
  & Development
American Society of Trial

Consultants
PRINCIPAL TOPICS:
Entertainment
TYPICAL AUDIENCE:
Corporate

DEAL, LUISA
P.O. Box 207
La Jolla, CA 92038
Telephone: 619-454-1781
Fax: 619-454-2587
REPRESENTED BY:
Speak, Inc.
ASSOCIATION
  MEMBERSHIP:
Natl. Speakers Assn.
PRINCIPAL TOPICS:
Business & Industry
Education
Human Relations
Management
Motivation
TYPICAL AUDIENCE:
Corporate
Association
Fraternal

DEAL, SHELDON C.
1001 N. Swan
Tucson, AZ 85711
Telephone: 602-323-7133
Fax: 602-323-8252
ASSOCIATION
  MEMBERSHIP:
Natl. Speakers Assn.
PRINCIPAL TOPICS:
Food/Diet
Health
Nature
Philosophy
Physical Fitness
TYPICAL AUDIENCE:
Association

DEAN, BONNIE 'THE
  MOTION COACH'
Starlite & Associates
11823 Purslane Cir.
Fountain Valley, CA 92708
Telephone: 714-531-7035
Fax: 714-531-1903
ASSOCIATION
  MEMBERSHIP:
Natl. Speakers Assn.
PRINCIPAL TOPICS:
Entertainment
Family
Human Relations
Marketing
Motivation
Physical Fitness

Sales
Youth
TYPICAL AUDIENCE:
Corporate
Association
General Public

DEAN, HARVEY D.
3037 S. Shirk Rd.
Visalia, Ca 93277
Telephone: 209-651-2820
Fax: 209-651-1429
REPRESENTED BY:
Five Star (Kansas City, Ks)
ASSOCIATION
  MEMBERSHIP:
Natl. Speakers Assn.
PRINCIPAL TOPICS:
Advertising
Humor
Management
Motivation
Sales
TYPICAL AUDIENCE:
Corporate
Association

DECAMP, DONALD D.
183 Middle St.
Portland, ME 04112
Telephone: 207-773-6387

DECARLO, JOE
3520 Cadillac, #B
Costa Mesa, Ca 92626
Telephone: 714-751-2787
Fax: 714-751-0126

DECARLO, LINDA
319 East 24 St., Apt. #20E
New York, NY 10010
Telephone: 212-679-0562
PRINCIPAL TOPICS:
Motivation
TYPICAL AUDIENCE:
Corporate
Association
General Public

DECKER, DON B.
1018 Maxwell Ave.
Evansville, IN 47711
Telephone: 812-423-2336
ASSOCIATION
  MEMBERSHIP:
Natl. Speakers Assn.
Toastmasters
PRINCIPAL TOPICS:
Automotive
Management
Motivation

Psychology
Sales
TYPICAL AUDIENCE:
Corporate

DEE, EMILY
2822 Jackson St.
Sioux City, IA 51104
Telephone: 712-258-8343
ASSOCIATION
   MEMBERSHIP:
Natl. Speakers Assn.
PRINCIPAL TOPICS:
Ecology
Education
Family
Health
Motivation
Nature
Senior Citizens
Social Trends
TYPICAL AUDIENCE:
Corporate
Association
General

DEL CASTILLO, JANET
3708 Crystal Bch. Rd.
Winter Haven, FL 33880
Telephone: 813-299-8448
Fax: 813-293-2749
ASSOCIATION
   MEMBERSHIP:
Natl. Speakers Assn.
PRINCIPAL TOPICS:
Agriculture
Animals
Human Relations
Motivation
TYPICAL AUDIENCE:
General

DELVES, JOHN A.
4860 Moon Road
Powder Springs, GA 30073
Telephone: 404-439-7561
Fax: 404-439-7862
ASSOCIATION
   MEMBERSHIP:
Natl. Speakers Assn.
PRINCIPAL TOPICS:
Business & Industry
Humor
Motivation
TYPICAL AUDIENCE:
General

DEMKO, DAVID J.
21946 Pine Trace
Boca Raton, FL 33428
Telephone: 305-237-4159

ASSOCIATION
   MEMBERSHIP:
Platform Speakers
Master Teacher:Trainer of
   Trainers Project
PRINCIPAL TOPICS:
Education
Family
Marketing
Motivation
Senior Citizens
Social Trends
TYPICAL AUDIENCE:
Corporate
Association

DENNY, JEAN
P.O. Box 104583
Jefferson City, MO 65110
Telephone: 314-893-3336
Fax: 314-635-1216
ASSOCIATION
   MEMBERSHIP:
Natl. Speakers Assn.
Toastmasters
PRINCIPAL TOPICS:
Family
History
TYPICAL AUDIENCE:
Corporate
Association
Fraternal

DENTINGER, RON
P.O. Box 151
Dodgeville, WI 53533
Telephone: 608-935-2417
ASSOCIATION
   MEMBERSHIP:
Natl. Speakers Assn.
PRINCIPAL TOPICS:
Humor
TYPICAL AUDIENCE:
Corporate
Association
Fraternal
General Public

**DEPOYSTER, BOBBY R.,
   ED.D**
P.O. Box 524
Richton, MS 39476
Telephone: 601-788-6581
Fax: 601-788-9391
REPRESENTED BY:
Ben Franklin
ASSOCIATION
   MEMBERSHIP:
Natl. Speakers Assn.
Platform Speakers

PRINCIPAL TOPICS:
Education
Humor
Motivation
Youth
TYPICAL AUDIENCE:
Association
Education Groups

DEROSE, ROLAND
1521 Tejana Mesa Pl., N.E.
Albuquerque, NM 87112
Telephone: 505-298-9150
Fax: 505-846-2371
ASSOCIATION
   MEMBERSHIP:
Natl. Speakers Assn.
Platform Speakers
Toastmasters
PRINCIPAL TOPICS:
Business & Industry
Education
Entertainment
Family
Government
Health
Hobbies
Human Relations
Management
Military
Motivation
Physical Fitness
Religion
Sales
TYPICAL AUDIENCE:
Corporate
Association
Fraternal

**DERRICK,
   FLETCHER C. JR.**
216 Calhoun St.
Charleston, SC 29401
Telephone: 803-577-7374
Fax: 803-722-4370
PRINCIPAL TOPICS:
Humor
Medical
TYPICAL AUDIENCE:
Corporate
Association

DIDONATO, RALPH
33521 Avenida Calita
San Juan Capistrano, CA
   92675
Telephone: 714-661-8482
Fax: 714-365-5690
ASSOCIATION
   MEMBERSHIP:
Natl. Speakers Assn.

ASTD
PRINCIPAL TOPICS:
Management
Sales
TYPICAL AUDIENCE:
Corporate
Association

DILLON, ILENE L.
115A Redwood Road
Fairfax, Ca 94930
Telephone: 415-454-5363
Fax: 415-454-5363
ASSOCIATION
   MEMBERSHIP:
Natl. Speakers Assn.
PRINCIPAL TOPICS:
Animals
Family
Health
Home & Garden
Human Relations
Nature
Philosophy
Psychology
Religion
Senior Citizens
Travel
Youth
TYPICAL AUDIENCE:
Association
Fraternal
General Public

DIRESTA, DIANE
DiResta Communications
885 Third Ave., Ste. 2900
New York, NY 10022
Telephone: 212-230-3296
Fax: 718-447-7720
REPRESENTED BY:
The Motivators
ASSOCIATION
   MEMBERSHIP:
Natl. Speakers Assn.
Platform Speakers
PRINCIPAL TOPICS:
Human Relations
TYPICAL AUDIENCE:
Corporate
Association

DOCKERY, WALLENE T.
8125 Meadow Glen Dr.
Germantown, TN 38138
Telephone: 901-755-7297
Fax: 901-753-2192
ASSOCIATION
   MEMBERSHIP:
Natl. Speakers Assn.
Tenn. Organization of

Professional Speakers
PRINCIPAL TOPICS:
Education
Motivation
TYPICAL AUDIENCE:
Corporate
Association

DOHERTY, BILL
11586 U.S. Highway One, #79
North Palm Beach, Fl 33408
Telephone: 407-627-5081
REPRESENTED BY:
Five Star
PRINCIPAL TOPICS:
Human Relations
Management
Motivation
Sales
TYPICAL AUDIENCE:
Corporate

DOMITRECZ, STEVE
The Computer Training Ctr.,
   #100, 1550 Valley Ctr.
Bethlehem, PA 18017
Telephone: 215-974-8522
Fax: 215-974-8167
ASSOCIATION
   MEMBERSHIP:
Natl. Speakers Assn.
PRINCIPAL TOPICS:
Business & Industry
Computer Technology
TYPICAL AUDIENCE:
Corporate
Association

DONADIO, PATRICK J.
7851 Gordon Circle
Columbus, OH 43235
Telephone: 614-761-7614
ASSOCIATION
   MEMBERSHIP:
Natl. Speakers
Toastmasters
Ohio Speakers Forum
PRINCIPAL TOPICS:
Business & Industry
Human Relations
Management
Media
Motivation
Sales
TYPICAL AUDIENCE:
Corporate
Association
Institutional

DONALDSON, KEITH
2540 Severn Ave.
Metairie, LA 70002
Telephone: 504-832-1747
ASSOCIATION
   MEMBERSHIP:
Natl. Speakers Assn.
PRINCIPAL TOPICS:
Marketing
Motivation
Physical Fitness
Sales
TYPICAL AUDIENCE:
Association

DOORNICK, ROBERT
611 Broadway, #422
New York, NY 10012
Telephone: 212-982-8001
Fax: 212-982-8000
MAILING ADDRESS:
International Robotics, Inc.
611 Broadway
New York, NY 10012
ASSOCIATION
   MEMBERSHIP:
Natl. Speakers Assn.
PRINCIPAL TOPICS:
Advertising
Amusements
Education
Entertainment
Humor
Marketing
Psychology
Sales
Social Trends
TYPICAL AUDIENCE:
Corporate
Association

DORSEY, CALVIN
2049 Vista Drive
Lewisville, TX 75067
Telephone: 214-316-0288
Fax: 214-315-3845
ASSOCIATION
   MEMBERSHIP:
Natl. Speakers Assn.
PRINCIPAL TOPICS:
Advertising
Media
Sales
TYPICAL AUDIENCE:
Corporate

DORSEY, IVORY
1401 Peachtree St., N.E.
Atlanta, GA 30309
Telephone: 404-881-6777
Fax: 404-881-6967

ASSOCIATION
   MEMBERSHIP:
Natl. Speakers Assn.
PRINCIPAL TOPICS:
Business & Industry
Human Relations
Management
Motivation
Sales
TYPICAL AUDIENCE:
Corporate
Association
General

DOUGLASS, DR. MERRILL
1401 Johnson Ferry Rd., #328
Marietta, Ga 30062
Telephone: 404-973-3977
ASSOCIATION
   MEMBERSHIP:
Natl. Speakers Assn.
PRINCIPAL TOPICS:
Management
TYPICAL AUDIENCE:
Corporate

DRAKE, CAROL
Communication Dynamics
1753 E. Shaleh Meadows Rd.,
   #75
Salt Lake City, UT 84117
Telephone: 811-278-1580
Fax: 811-277-9838
ASSOCIATION
   MEMBERSHIP:
Natl. Speakers Assn.
Platform Speakers
Trainer
PRINCIPAL TOPICS:
Family
Human Relations
Motivation
Communications
TYPICAL AUDIENCE:
Corporate
Association

DRAKE, DEBBIE
P.O. Box 370124
Denver, CO 80237
Telephone: 619-429-8707
ASSOCIATION
   MEMBERSHIP:
Natl. Speakers Assn.
Toastmasters
PRINCIPAL TOPICS:
Health
TYPICAL AUDIENCE:
Corporate
Association

DRENCH,
   MEREDITH E. PHD
56 Hickory Dir.
East Greenwich, RI 02818
Telephone: 401-885-5656
Fax: 401-885-5656
ASSOCIATION
   MEMBERSHIP:
Natl. Speakers Assn.
PRINCIPAL TOPICS:
Health
Human Relations
Medical
Psychology
TYPICAL AUDIENCE:
Corporate
Association
Fraternal
Academic

DUBIN, BURT
Box 6543
Kingman, AZ 86402
Telephone: 602-753-7546
Fax: 602-753-7554
ASSOCIATION
   MEMBERSHIP:
Natl. Speakers Assn.
PRINCIPAL TOPICS:
Education
Management
Sales
TYPICAL AUDIENCE:
Association

DUNN, GLORIA
Esteem Dynamics Unlimited
1991 Magellan Drive
Oakland, Ca 94611
Telephone: 510-339-6877
Fax: 510-339-2643
ASSOCIATION
   MEMBERSHIP:
Natl. Speakers Assn.
PRINCIPAL TOPICS:
Human Relations
Management
Motivation
TYPICAL AUDIENCE:
Corporate
Association

DUNN, MARIANNE
2767 Beechmont Drive
Dallas, Tx 75228
Telephone: 214-321-7537
Fax: 214-320-0468
ASSOCIATION
   MEMBERSHIP:
Natl. Speakers Assn.

PRINCIPAL TOPICS:
Business & Industry
Government
Human Relations
Management
TYPICAL AUDIENCE:
Corporate
Association

DUPONT, M. KAY   CSP
The Communication
  Connection
2137 Mt. Vernon Road
Atlanta, GA 30338
Telephone: 404-395-7483
ASSOCIATION
  MEMBERSHIP:
Natl. Speakers Assn.
Toastmasters
PRINCIPAL TOPICS:
Business & Industry
Communications
Human Relations
TYPICAL AUDIENCE:
Corporate
Association

DVORAK, ROBERT REGIS
624 Ruisseau Francais Ave.
Half Moon Bay, CA 94019
Telephone: 415-726-1906
Fax: 415-726-1906
PRINCIPAL TOPICS:
Architecture
Business & Industry
Education
Entertainment
Health
Motivation
Physical Fitness
Sales
TYPICAL AUDIENCE:
Corporate

DWYER, DAWN
Dynamic Seminars
P.O. Box 1565
Lomita, CA 90717
Telephone: 310-787-9660
ASSOCIATION
  MEMBERSHIP:
Natl. Speakers Assn.
PRINCIPAL TOPICS:
Business & Industry
Education
Family
Fashion
Health
Human Relations
Motivation
Psychology

Religion
Youth
TYPICAL AUDIENCE:
Corporate
General Public

DYGERT, CHARLES B.,
  PH.D   CSP
P.O. Box 28124
Columbus, OH 43288
Telephone: 614-870-0024
Fax: 614-870-3136
ASSOCIATION
  MEMBERSHIP:
Natl. Speakers Assn.
PRINCIPAL TOPICS:
Education
Management
Motivation
TYPICAL AUDIENCE:
Corporate
Association
Fraternal
Education

EAGLE, MARK
32 West 40th St.
New York, NY 10018
Telephone: 212-764-2810
Fax: 212-764-2811
MAILING ADDRESS:
Beta Service Bureau
9 East 38th St.
New York, NY 10016
ASSOCIATION
  MEMBERSHIP:
Natl. Speakers Assn.
PRINCIPAL TOPICS:
Business & Industry
Computer Technology
Humor
World Affairs
TYPICAL AUDIENCE:
Corporate
Association

EAGLES, GIL   CSP
P.O. Box 859
Short Hills, NJ 07078
Telephone: 201-376-3737
Fax: 201-376-3660
ASSOCIATION
  MEMBERSHIP:
Natl. Speakers Assn.

PRINCIPAL TOPICS:
Entertainment
Management
Motivation

TYPICAL AUDIENCE:
Corporate
Association

EASON, W.H.
P.O. Box 50
Basalt, CO 81621
Telephone: 303-927-3197
Fax: 303-927-3749
ASSOCIATION
  MEMBERSHIP:
Natl. Speakers Assn.
PRINCIPAL TOPICS:
Entertainment
Humor
TYPICAL AUDIENCE:
Corporate
Association
Fraternal

ECK, ARLENE
1205 Murmac Lane
Westerville, OH 43081
Telephone: 614-895-7727
REPRESENTED BY:
Speakers Unlimited
ASSOCIATION
  MEMBERSHIP:
Natl. Speakers Assn.
PRINCIPAL TOPICS:
Education
Management
Motivation
Sales
TYPICAL AUDIENCE:
Corporate
Association

EGGLESTON, JULIA
1235 S. Gilbert, #3
Mesa, Az 85204
Telephone: 602-981-3878
Fax: 602-892-3482
ASSOCIATION
  MEMBERSHIP:
Natl. Speakers Assn.
PRINCIPAL TOPICS:
Family
Motivation
Sales
TYPICAL AUDIENCE:
Corporate
Association

EINSTEIN ALIVE
Einstein Alive
10565 Caminito Banyon
San Diego, CA 92131
Telephone: 800-748-6967
Fax: 800-621-9050

ASSOCIATION
  MEMBERSHIP:
Natl. Speakers Assn.
Meeting Planners International
American Society of Training &
  Development
Natl. Science Teachers
Natl. Association For Gifted
  Children
PRINCIPAL TOPICS:
Business & Industry
Education
Management
Motivation
Sales
TYPICAL AUDIENCE:
Corporate
Association

ELIAS, JEFF
1000 E. Campbell Rd., #110
Richardson, TX 75081
Telephone: 214-699-8383
Fax: 214-699-8387
ASSOCIATION
  MEMBERSHIP:
Natl. Speakers Assn.
PRINCIPAL TOPICS:
Education
Home & Garden
Marketing
Personal Finance
TYPICAL AUDIENCE:
Association
Fraternal

ELVES, CONRAD
1750 112th N.E., #D155
Bellevue, WA 98004
Telephone: 206-453-8069
Fax: 206-454-6786
PRINCIPAL TOPICS:
Human Relations
Sales
TYPICAL AUDIENCE:
Corporate

EMMERICH, ROXANNE
210 McClellan St., #201
Wausau, WI 54401
Telephone: 715-842-4779
Fax: 715-845-3298
MAILING ADDRESS:
P.O. Box 2003
Wausau, WI 54402
REPRESENTED BY:
Prefer Direct Contact
ASSOCIATION
  MEMBERSHIP:
Natl. Speakers Assn.
WI Professional Speakers

Association
PRINCIPAL TOPICS:
Agriculture
Business & Industry
Education
Human Relations
Management
Marketing
Sales
TYPICAL AUDIENCE:
Corporate
Association

EMMETT, RITA
3125 Sarah St.
Franklin Park, Il 60131
Telephone: 708-671-4890
Fax: 708-451-1652
ASSOCIATION
  MEMBERSHIP:
Natl. Speakers Assn.
Platform Speakers
Toastmasters
Professional Speakers Of
  Illinois
PRINCIPAL TOPICS:
Family
Health
Motivation
TYPICAL AUDIENCE:
Corporate
Association
Schools

ENEN, JACK
5137 Meadow Crest Drive
Dallas, TX 75229
Telephone: 214-361-8782
Fax: 214-361-9192
ASSOCIATION
  MEMBERSHIP:
Natl. Speakers Assn.
PRINCIPAL TOPICS:
Business & Industry
Marketing
World Affairs
TYPICAL AUDIENCE:
Corporate
Association

EPSTEIN-SHEPHERD, DR.
  BEE
8600 Carmel Valley Road
Carmel, CA 93923
Telephone: 408-624-3188
Fax: 408-625-0611
MAILING ADDRESS:
P.O. Box 221383
Carmel, CA 93923

ASSOCIATION
  MEMBERSHIP:
Natl. Speakers Assn.
PRINCIPAL TOPICS:
Food/Diet
Health
Human Relations
Management
TYPICAL AUDIENCE:
Corporate
Association
General Public

EVANS, ROBERT
  MAYER   CSP
120 W. Wieuca Rd., N.W.
Atlanta, GA 30327
Telephone: 404-255-3254
Fax: 404-252-2639
REPRESENTED BY:
Eleven
ASSOCIATION
  MEMBERSHIP:
Natl. Speakers Assn.
PRINCIPAL TOPICS:
Agriculture
Business & Industry
Computer Technology
Journalism
Management
Marketing
Social Trends
World Affairs
TYPICAL AUDIENCE:
Corporate
Association

EVERDING, MARIA
12973 Fiddle Creek Lane
St. Louis, MI 63131
Telephone: 314-965-1261
Fax: 314-965-1261
ASSOCIATION
  MEMBERSHIP:
Natl. Speakers Assn.
PRINCIPAL TOPICS:
Human Relations
Social Trends
TYPICAL AUDIENCE:
Corporate
Association

EX, CAREN (LCSW)
4711 Golf Rd., #806
Skokie, IL 60076
Telephone: 708-677-4664

FARRELL, ROBERT E.
4120 N.E. Beaumont St.
Portland, OR 97212
Telephone: 503-684-2803

Fax: 503-620-6149
MAILING ADDRESS:
12725 S.W. 66th
Portland, OR 97223
ASSOCIATION
  MEMBERSHIP:
Natl. Speakers Assn.
PRINCIPAL TOPICS:
Advertising
Family
Humor
Management
Marketing
Motivation
Religion
TYPICAL AUDIENCE:
Corporate
Association

FETTIG, ART
36 Fairview Ave.
Battle Creek, MI 49017
Telephone: 800-441-7676
Fax: 616-965-4522
ASSOCIATION
  MEMBERSHIP:
Natl. Speakers Assn.
PRINCIPAL TOPICS:
Motivation
TYPICAL AUDIENCE:
Corporate
Association

**FIELDER GROUP, THE
RT. 2, BOX 372
GILBERTSVILLE, KY 42044
Telephone: 502-362-7129
Fax: 502-362-7130
ASSOCIATION
  MEMBERSHIP:
Natl. Speakers Assn.
Tenn. Speakers
PRINCIPAL TOPICS:
Business & Industry
Education
Entertainment
Health
Human Relations
Humor
Management
Marketing
Medical
Motivation
Psychology
Senior Citizens
Youth
Communications
TYPICAL AUDIENCE:
Corporate**

Association
Fraternal
SEE AD IN SECTION 8

FILIPPO, LOU 'COACH'
P.O. Box 7622
Louisville, KY 40257
Telephone: 502-339-8691
Fax: 502-327-8886
ASSOCIATION
  MEMBERSHIP:
Natl. Speakers Assn.
KY Speakers
PRINCIPAL TOPICS:
Management
Sales
TYPICAL AUDIENCE:
Corporate
Association

FINGEROTE, PAUL S.
482 Alvalado St.
Monterey, Ca 93940
Telephone: 408-649-4499
Fax: 408-649-1104
ASSOCIATION
  MEMBERSHIP:
Natl. Speakers Assn.
American Association Of
  Advertising Agencies
PRINCIPAL TOPICS:
Advertising
Marketing
Media
TYPICAL AUDIENCE:
Corporate
Association
Fraternal

FINK, MARTHA
109 Lake Merced Hill
San Francisco, CA 94132
Telephone: 415-333-4540
Fax: 415-333-4541
MAILING ADDRESS:
P.O. Box 3514
Daly City, CA 94015
ASSOCIATION
  MEMBERSHIP:
Natl. Speakers Assn.
Platform Speakers
Toastmasters
PRINCIPAL TOPICS:
Advertising
Management
Marketing
Sales
Travel
TYPICAL AUDIENCE:
Association

FIORE, JAMES
Fiore, James Ph.D. &
  Associates
265 Thompson Mill Road
Newtown, PA 18940
Telephone: 215-598-3481
Fax: 215-598-0907
REPRESENTED BY:
National American Sales And
  Seminar
ASSOCIATION
  MEMBERSHIP:
Natl. Speakers Assn.
Platform Speakers
PRINCIPAL TOPICS:
Business & Industry
Management
Motivation
Personal Finance
Senior Citizens
Travel
TYPICAL AUDIENCE:
Corporate

FIORE, NEIL A., PH.D.
908 Tulare Ave.
Berkeley, Ca 94707
Telephone: 510-525-2673
ASSOCIATION
  MEMBERSHIP:
Natl. Speakers Assn.
PRINCIPAL TOPICS:
Human Relations
Management
Motivation
Psychology
TYPICAL AUDIENCE:
Corporate
Association
Institutional

FISHER, DONNA
3000 WESLAYAN STE. 105
HOUSTON, TX 77027
Telephone: 713-589-1989
Fax: 713-622-0102
ASSOCIATION
  MEMBERSHIP:
Natl. Speakers Assn.
PRINCIPAL TOPICS:
Business & Industry
Marketing
Motivation
Communications
TYPICAL AUDIENCE:
Corporate
Association
SEE AD IN SECTION 8

FISHER, MARY
Five Star Speakers, Trainers,
  Consultants
8685 W. 96th Street
Overland Park, KS 66212
Telephone: 913-648-6480
Fax: 913-648-6484
REPRESENTED BY:
Fiver Star Speakers, Trainers &
  Consultants
ASSOCIATION
  MEMBERSHIP:
Natl. Speakers Assn.
ASTD
PRINCIPAL TOPICS:
Entertainment
Family
Health
Human Relations
Humor
Motivation
TYPICAL AUDIENCE:
Corporate
Association

FISHER, SANDRA L.
535 East 86th St.
New York, NY 10028
Telephone: 212-744-5900
Fax: 212-879-0032
REPRESENTED BY:
JR Associates
Capitol Speakers
ASSOCIATION
  MEMBERSHIP:
Natl. Speakers Assn.
PRINCIPAL TOPICS:
Family
Health
Physical Fitness
Motivation
TYPICAL AUDIENCE:
Corporate
Association

FLATT, VERNE
11107 Wurzbach Rd., #103
San Antonio, TX 78230
Telephone: 210-691-2264
Fax: 210-691-0011
ASSOCIATION
  MEMBERSHIP:
Natl. Speakers Assn.
PRINCIPAL TOPICS:
Management
TYPICAL AUDIENCE:
Corporate

FLECK, JAMES R.
415 Blue River Court, #1
Columbia City, In 46725

Telephone: 219-248-8278
Fax: 219-244-3083
ASSOCIATION
  MEMBERSHIP:
Natl. Speakers Assn.
Natl. Speakers (Indiana
  Chapter)
PRINCIPAL TOPICS:
Humor
Management
TYPICAL AUDIENCE:
General

FLETCHER, JERRY L.
Z-Axis Marketing, Inc.
17387 SW Canyon Dr.
Lake Oswego, OR 97034
Telephone: 503-636-4113
REPRESENTED BY:
Portland Speakers Bureau
ASSOCIATION
  MEMBERSHIP:
Natl. Speakers Assn.
Oregon Speakers/The Center
  For Business
  Communications
PRINCIPAL TOPICS:
Advertising
Management
Marketing
Media
Sales
TYPICAL AUDIENCE:
Corporate
Association

FLETCHER, TANA
P.O. Box 12
Brookeville, MD 20833
Telephone: 301-774-8566
Fax: 301-774-8566
ASSOCIATION
  MEMBERSHIP:
American Business Women's
PRINCIPAL TOPICS:
Business & Industry
Media
TYPICAL AUDIENCE:
Corporate
Association

FLICKINGER, BONNIE G.
Rainbow Lectures
31 Nottingham Terrace
Buffalo, NY 14216
Telephone: 716-875-8335
REPRESENTED BY:
Program Associates
ASSOCIATION
  MEMBERSHIP:
Natl. Speakers

Platform Speakers
Washington Independent
  Writers
National League of American
  Pen Women
PRINCIPAL TOPICS:
Advertising
Animals
Architecture
Fashion
History
Home & Garden
Personal Finance
Psychology
Religion
Travel
World Affairs
Youth
TYPICAL AUDIENCE:
Fraternal

FLICKINGER, E. G.
P.O. Box 15488
North Hollywood, CA 91615
Telephone: 818-764-4493
ASSOCIATION
  MEMBERSHIP:
Natl. Speakers Assn.
Toastmasters
PRINCIPAL TOPICS:
Education
Entertainment
Family
Government
Health
Human Relations
Humor
Motivation
Philosophy
Youth
TYPICAL AUDIENCE:
Corporate
Fraternal

FORBES, EVE-LYN
3622 Nassau Drive
Augusta, GA 30909
Telephone: 706-738-6141
Fax: 667-0074

FOREMAN, ED
14135 Midway Rd., #250,
  L.B.#7
Dallas, TX 75244
Telephone: 214-458-8855
Fax: 214-458-7503
REPRESENTED BY:
Natl. Speakers Bureau
French & Associates
Success Speakers Service
JR Associates

ASSOCIATION
  MEMBERSHIP:
Natl. Speakers Assn.
PRINCIPAL TOPICS:
Health
Human Relations
Motivation
TYPICAL AUDIENCE:
Corporate
Association

FORZANO, RICK E.
3216 Interlaken Rd.
Orchard Lake, MI 48323
Telephone: 313-682-7981
Fax: 313-682-7984
ASSOCIATION
  MEMBERSHIP:
Natl. Speakers Assn.
PRINCIPAL TOPICS:
Family
Humor
Marketing
Motivation
Sales
TYPICAL AUDIENCE:
Corporate
Association

FOSTER, LARRY J.
5527 Harbor Town
Dallas, TX 75287
Telephone: 214-661-0101
Fax: 214-661-5500
ASSOCIATION
  MEMBERSHIP:
Natl. Speakers Assn.
PRINCIPAL TOPICS:
Geography
Personal Finance
TYPICAL AUDIENCE:
Corporate
Association

FOSTER, WILLIAM E.
1424 Judson Ave.
Evanston, IL 60201
Telephone: 708-491-8880
Fax: 708-491-4659
MAILING ADDRESS:
Athletic Director, Northwestern
  University
1501 Central St.
Evanston, IL 60208
ASSOCIATION
  MEMBERSHIP:
Natl. Speakers Assn.
PRINCIPAL TOPICS:
Health
Human Relations

Travel
TYPICAL AUDIENCE:
Corporate

FOTIADES, VALLA D.
P.O. Box 812 - West Side
  Station
Worcester, MA 01602
Telephone: 508-799-9860
REPRESENTED BY:
Bogart Communications
ASSOCIATION
  MEMBERSHIP:
Natl. Speakers Assn.
Toastmasters
PRINCIPAL TOPICS:
Education
Fashion
Human Relations
Motivation
TYPICAL AUDIENCE:
Association
Fraternal

FOUNTAIN, ELEANOR A.
Fountain Associates
1919 Lebanon Drive
Atlanta, Ga 30324
Telephone: 404-876-4072
ASSOCIATION
  MEMBERSHIP:
Natl. Speakers Assn.
PRINCIPAL TOPICS:
Business & Industry
Education
Human Relations
Management
Motivation
Psychology
Sales
TYPICAL AUDIENCE:
Corporate
Association
Fraternal
Institutional
Educational

FOX, JOAN G.
P.O. Box 42754
Cincinnati, Oh 45242
Telephone: 513-793-9582
ASSOCIATION
  MEMBERSHIP:
Natl. Speakers Assn.
PRINCIPAL TOPICS:
Human Relations
Motivation
Sales

FRACASSI, LINDA F.
P.O. Box 572
Englishtown, NJ 07726
Telephone: 908-577-1118
ASSOCIATION
  MEMBERSHIP:
Natl. Speakers Assn.
PRINCIPAL TOPICS:
Sales
TYPICAL AUDIENCE:
Corporate

FRAGER, STANLEY R.
  PHD
3906 Dupont Sq., S.
Louisville, KY 40207
Telephone: 502-893-6654
Fax: 502-895-0000
ASSOCIATION
  MEMBERSHIP:
Natl. Speakers Assn.
PRINCIPAL TOPICS:
Education
Health
Human Relations
Motivation
Psychology
TYPICAL AUDIENCE:
Corporate
Association

FRANK,
  MIKE, (CPAE)   CSP
P.O. Box 27225
Columbus, OH 43227
Telephone: 614-864-3703
Fax: 614-864-3876
ASSOCIATION
  MEMBERSHIP:
Natl. Speakers Assn.
PRINCIPAL TOPICS:
Business & Industry
Management
Marketing
Motivation
Sales
TYPICAL AUDIENCE:
Corporate
Association

FRANKLIN, CARLEEN
Excelerators, The
1631 S.E. 24th Blvd.
Okeechobee, FL 34974
Telephone: 813-467-5350
Fax: 407-770-1857
ASSOCIATION
  MEMBERSHIP:
Natl. Speakers Assn.
Women In Communication
NAFE

Florida Speakers
PRINCIPAL TOPICS:
Human Relations
Motivation
TYPICAL AUDIENCE:
Association

FRAZEE, LINDA
Positive Imagery
11410 Elmshorn Way
Laurel, Md 20708
Telephone: 301-317-0060
Fax: 301-317-9795
ASSOCIATION
  MEMBERSHIP:
Natl. Speakers Assn.
PRINCIPAL TOPICS:
Family
Food/Diet
Health
Management
Motivation
Psychology
TYPICAL AUDIENCE:
Corporate
Association
Fraternal

FRESHOUR, FRANK W.
804 Sandringham Ln.
Lutz, FL 33549
Telephone: 813-949-8814
REPRESENTED BY:
Speakers Connection
ASSOCIATION
  MEMBERSHIP:
Speakers USA
American Society of Training &
  Development
International Listening
PRINCIPAL TOPICS:
Education
Family
Human Relations
Management
Marketing
Motivation
Psychology
Sales
TYPICAL AUDIENCE:
Corporate
Association

FRIED, N. ELIZABETH,
  PH.D
5590 Dumfries Ct. W.
Dublin, OH 43017
Telephone: 614-766-9800
ASSOCIATION
  MEMBERSHIP:
Natl. Speakers Assn.

Society of Human Relations
  Management
PRINCIPAL TOPICS:
Business & Industry
Human Relations
Media
TYPICAL AUDIENCE:
Corporate
Association

FRIEDMAN, SIDNEY A.
200 S. Broad St.
Philadelphia, PA 19102
Telephone: 215-875-8700
Fax: 215-875-0068
ASSOCIATION
  MEMBERSHIP:
Natl. Speakers Assn.
Platform Speakers
Toastmasters
PRINCIPAL TOPICS:
Business & Industry
Management
Marketing
Motivation
Personal Finance
TYPICAL AUDIENCE:
Corporate
Association

FRINGS, CHRISTOPHER S.,
  PH.D.
633 Winwood Drive
Birmingham, Al 35226
Telephone: 205-823-5044
Fax: 205-823-2339
ASSOCIATION
  MEMBERSHIP:
Natl. Speakers Assn.
PRINCIPAL TOPICS:
Health
Management
Motivation
TYPICAL AUDIENCE:
Corporate
Association

FRIPP, PATRICIA   CSP
527 Hugo Street
San Francisco, CA 94122
Telephone: 415-753-6556
Fax: 415-753-0914
REPRESENTED BY:
National Speakers Bureau
Speakers Unlimited
ASSOCIATION
  MEMBERSHIP:
Natl. Speakers Assn.
PRINCIPAL TOPICS:
Business & Industry
Entertainment

Human Relations
Management
Marketing
Motivation
TYPICAL AUDIENCE:
Corporate
Association
Spouse Programs

FRITZ, DR. BOB
7724 Gueniveire Way
Citrus Heights, CA 95610
Telephone: 916-965-7910
Fax: 916-965-7910
REPRESENTED BY:
Management Institute
ASSOCIATION
  MEMBERSHIP:
Natl. Speakers Assn.
PRINCIPAL TOPICS:
Business & Industry
Computer Technology
Management
TYPICAL AUDIENCE:
Corporate

FRYAR, HAL
7810 Sunset Lane
Indianapolis, In 46260
Telephone: 317-255-4282
ASSOCIATION
  MEMBERSHIP:
Natl. Speakers Assn.
PRINCIPAL TOPICS:
Motivation
TYPICAL AUDIENCE:
Association
Fraternal

FUTCH, KEN   CSP
2684 Coldwater Canyon Dr.
Tucker, Ga 30084
Telephone: 404-939-6200
ASSOCIATION
  MEMBERSHIP:
Natl. Speakers Assn.
PRINCIPAL TOPICS:
Motivation
TYPICAL AUDIENCE:
Corporate
Association

FYOCK, CATHERINE D.
3501 Locust St.
Prospect, KY 40059
Telephone: 502-228-3869
Fax: 502-228-8533
MAILING ADDRESS:
P.O. Box 905
Prospect, KY 40059

ASSOCIATION
  MEMBERSHIP:
Natl. Speakers Assn.
PRINCIPAL TOPICS:
Human Relations
Management
Senior Citizens
TYPICAL AUDIENCE:
Corporate
Association
Institutional

GABRIELSEN, RON (CCM)
The Experience Connection
3725 Ventura Cir., #204
Brookfield, WI 53045
Telephone: 414-781-4832
REPRESENTED BY:
Associated Speakers
Options Unlimited
An Open Mind
ASSOCIATION
  MEMBERSHIP:
Natl. Speakers Assn.
PRINCIPAL TOPICS:
Business & Industry
Education
Government
Human Relations
Management
Marketing
Military
Motivation
Sales
TYPICAL AUDIENCE:
Corporate
Association

GAGE, RANDY
7501 East Treasure Dr., Lobby
No. Bay Village, FL 33141
Telephone: 305-864-6658
Fax: 305-864-1398
ASSOCIATION
  MEMBERSHIP:
Natl. Speakers Assn.
PRINCIPAL TOPICS:
Business & Industry
Marketing
TYPICAL AUDIENCE:
Corporate

GALLAGHER, BILL
  'GUERRILLA', PH.D.   CSP
741 N. Circle
Diamond Springs, CA 95619
Telephone: 800-800-8086
Fax: 916-622-6075
ASSOCIATION
  MEMBERSHIP:
Natl. Speakers Assn.

PRINCIPAL TOPICS:
Advertising
Business & Industry
Management
Marketing
Motivation
Psychology
Sales
TYPICAL AUDIENCE:
Corporate
Association

GALLAGHER, CATHY L.
Gallagher & Associates
P.O. Box 23256
Milwaukee, WI 53223
Telephone: 414-354-5496
Fax: 414-355-2436
ASSOCIATION
  MEMBERSHIP:
Natl. Speakers Assn.
PRINCIPAL TOPICS:
Business & Industry
Human Relations
Motivation
Sales
Education
TYPICAL AUDIENCE:
Corporate
Personal

GANNETT, MARYE D.
6800 Baltimore Ave.
University Park, MD 20782
Telephone: 301-864-7262
ASSOCIATION
  MEMBERSHIP:
Natl. Speakers Assn.
Toastmasters
PRINCIPAL TOPICS:
Humor
Management
Motivation
Senior Citizens
TYPICAL AUDIENCE:
Fraternal
Business

GARBISCH, WALTER E.
6715 W. English Meadows
Greenfield, WI 53220
Telephone: 414-282-5667
MAILING ADDRESS:
P.O. Box 28837
Milwaukee, WI 53228
REPRESENTED BY:
Associated Speakers Inc.
ASSOCIATION
  MEMBERSHIP:
Natl. Speakers Assn.

PRINCIPAL TOPICS:
Entertainment
Psychology
TYPICAL AUDIENCE:
Corporate
Association
Fraternal
Conventions & After-Dinner
　Programs

GARDNER, DEBBIE
7 Survive Institute, 7265
　Kenwood Rd.
Cincinnati, Oh 45236
Telephone: 513-791-7453

GARFINKEL, DAVID
2075 21st Ave.
San Francisco, CA 94116
Telephone: 415-564-4475
Fax: 415-564-4599
ASSOCIATION
　MEMBERSHIP:
Natl. Speakers Assn.
PRINCIPAL TOPICS:
Marketing
Sales
TYPICAL AUDIENCE:
Corporate
Association
Small Business

GARGANTA, KATHLEEN T.
MANAGEMENT & TRAINING
**　ENTERPRISES**
29 HOLLY LANE
SOMERSET, MA 02726
Telephone: 508-672-2010
Fax: 800-359-3920
ASSOCIATION
**　MEMBERSHIP:**
Natl. Speakers Assn.
PRINCIPAL TOPICS:
Health
Human Relations
Medical
Motivation
TYPICAL AUDIENCE:
Association
SEE AD IN SECTION 8

GARLAND, BARRY
14101-149th Pl., S.E.
Renton, WA 98059
Telephone: 206-622-1231
ASSOCIATION
　MEMBERSHIP:
Natl. Speakers Assn.
PRINCIPAL TOPICS:
Human Relations
Management

Motivation
TYPICAL AUDIENCE:
Corporate
Government

GARRETT, A. MILTON
9117 Atkinson N.E.
Albuquerque, NM 87112
Telephone: 505-275-3772
Fax: 505-294-8999
ASSOCIATION
　MEMBERSHIP:
Natl. Speakers Assn.
PRINCIPAL TOPICS:
Business & Industry
Management
TYPICAL AUDIENCE:
Corporate
Association

GARTON-GOOD, JULIE
934 Palermo Ave.
Miami, Fl 33134
Telephone: 305-443-1524
Fax: 305-443-5243
ASSOCIATION
　MEMBERSHIP:
Natl. Speakers Assn.
NAREE
PRINCIPAL TOPICS:
Personal Finance
TYPICAL AUDIENCE:
Association

GAULKE, SUE MACK
4261 Chamberlin Drive
Hood River, Or 97031
Telephone: 503-354-2902
ASSOCIATION
　MEMBERSHIP:
Natl. Speakers Assn.
American Society Training &
　Development
PRINCIPAL TOPICS:
Communications
TYPICAL AUDIENCE:
Corporate

GEBHARDT, MARK D.
Career Masters
P.O. Box 951475
Lake Mary, FL 32795
Telephone: 407-862-9299
Fax: 407-788-3837
ASSOCIATION
　MEMBERSHIP:
Natl. Speakers Assn.
PRINCIPAL TOPICS:
Business & Industry
TYPICAL AUDIENCE:
General

GEDALIAH, ROBERT
Gedaliah Communications
200 West 90th Street
New York, NY 10024
Telephone: 212-580-7406
Fax: 212-580-0957
ASSOCIATION
　MEMBERSHIP:
Natl. Speakers Assn.
PRINCIPAL TOPICS:
Communications
Sales
TYPICAL AUDIENCE:
Corporate
Association

GEDAN, IRA
Gedan, Ira Associates
P.O. Box 8588
Coral Springs, FL 33075
Telephone: 305-345-5811
ASSOCIATION
　MEMBERSHIP:
Natl. Speakers Assn.
PRINCIPAL TOPICS:
Motivation
Sales
TYPICAL AUDIENCE:
Corporate

GEE, BOBBIE　　　　CSP
1540 So. Coast Hwy., #206
Laguna Beach, CA 92651
Telephone: 800-462-4386
Fax: 714-497-9155
REPRESENTED BY:
Bernstein & Associates
ASSOCIATION
　MEMBERSHIP:
Natl. Speakers Assn.
PRINCIPAL TOPICS:
Business & Industry
Motivation
Sales
TYPICAL AUDIENCE:
Corporate
Association

GERAGHTY, BARBARA
Idea Quest
14252 Culver Dr. A633
Irvine, CA 92714
Telephone: 714-552-0401
REPRESENTED BY:
Convention Connection
Gail Stewart Enterprises
ASSOCIATION
　MEMBERSHIP:
Natl. Speakers Assn.
PRINCIPAL TOPICS:
Business & Industry

Human Relations
Humor
Management
Marketing
Media
Motivation
Sales
Social Trends
Video
Youth
TYPICAL AUDIENCE:
Corporate
Association

GERMANN, DOUGLAS D.
Acquisition Resources, Inc.
415 Lincoln Way West
Mishawaka, IN 46544
Telephone: 219-262-0600
PRINCIPAL TOPICS:
Business & Industry
Motivation
TYPICAL AUDIENCE:
Corporate

GESELL, IZZY
P.O. Box 962
Northampton, MA 01061
Telephone: 413-586-2634
Fax: 413-586-2634
ASSOCIATION
　MEMBERSHIP:
Natl. Speakers Assn.
PRINCIPAL TOPICS:
Health
Human Relations
Humor
Motivation
Psychology
Senior Citizens
TYPICAL AUDIENCE:
Association

GILBERT, ROB, PH.D
The Center For Sports Success
91 Belleville Avenue, #7
Bloomfield, NJ 07003
Telephone: 201-743-4428
Fax: 201-680-4323
REPRESENTED BY:
The Speakers Bureau
ASSOCIATION
　MEMBERSHIP:
Natl. Speakers Assn.
PRINCIPAL TOPICS:
Motivation
Psychology
TYPICAL AUDIENCE:
Corporate
Association

GILLARD, JUDY
696 N. Hermosa Dr.
Palm Springs, CA 92262
Telephone: 619-320-5983
Fax: 619-325-1625
REPRESENTED BY:
Speakers Bureau Unlimited
ASSOCIATION
  MEMBERSHIP:
Natl. Speakers Assn.
PRINCIPAL TOPICS:
Food/Diet
Health
Management
Motivation
TYPICAL AUDIENCE:
Corporate
Association

GILLESPIE, JEFFREY A.
1455 S. Reynolds, Ste. 262
Toledo, OH 43615
Telephone: 419-389-8262
ASSOCIATION
  MEMBERSHIP:
Natl. Speakers Assn.
PRINCIPAL TOPICS:
Business & Industry
Computer Technology
Management
Sales
TYPICAL AUDIENCE:
Corporate

GIOIA, JOYCE L.
43 Gladstone Rd.
New Rochelle, NY 10804
Telephone: 914-636-6964
Fax: 914-235-0598
ASSOCIATION
  MEMBERSHIP:
Natl. Speakers Assn.
PRINCIPAL TOPICS:
Advertising
Business & Industry
Computer Technology
Human Relations
Journalism
Marketing
Motivation
Psychology
Religion
Sales
Social Trends
TYPICAL AUDIENCE:
Corporate
Association

GITTERMAN, HEIDI
P.O. Box 497
Tiburon, CA 94920

Telephone: 415-435-2260
Fax: 415-435-6499
ASSOCIATION
  MEMBERSHIP:
Natl. Speakers Assn.
PRINCIPAL TOPICS:
Business & Industry
Management
Marketing
Motivation
Sales
TYPICAL AUDIENCE:
Corporate
Association

GLICK, BARBARA
144 Wellington Road
Northbrook, IL 60062
Telephone: 312-498-9979
Fax: 708-559-1234
ASSOCIATION
  MEMBERSHIP:
Natl. Speakers Assn.
Professional Speakers of
  Illinois
American Society of Training &
  Development
PRINCIPAL TOPICS:
Education
Family
Health
Human Relations
Motivation
Psychology
TYPICAL AUDIENCE:
Corporate
Association

GLICKSTEIN, LEE
2078 21st Ave.
San Francisco, CA 94116
Telephone: 415-731-6640
ASSOCIATION
  MEMBERSHIP:
Natl. Speakers Assn.
PRINCIPAL TOPICS:
Entertainment
Health
Humor
TYPICAL AUDIENCE:
Association

GLINER, ART
8902 Maine Avenue
Silver Spring, Md 20910
Telephone: 301-588-3561
ASSOCIATION
  MEMBERSHIP:
Natl. Speakers Assn.
Toastmasters

PRINCIPAL TOPICS:
Humor
TYPICAL AUDIENCE:
Corporate
Association

GODEK, GREGORY J.P.
402 Front St.
Wymouth, MA 02188
Telephone: 617-340-1300
Fax: 617-340-1301

GOETZMAN, RICHARD K.,
  PH.D.
2028 17th Ave., N.W.
Rochester, Mn 55901
Telephone: 507-282-0941
ASSOCIATION
  MEMBERSHIP:
Natl. Speakers Assn.
Minnesota Speakers
PRINCIPAL TOPICS:
Education
Motivation
TYPICAL AUDIENCE:
Corporate
Association
Educational

GOLBERT, GLORIA
255 Union Blvd., Ste. 120
Lakewood, CO 80228
Telephone: 303-988-4970
Fax: 303-320-7534
REPRESENTED BY:
Zoe Resources
ASSOCIATION
  MEMBERSHIP:
Natl. Speakers Assn.
PRINCIPAL TOPICS:
Business & Industry
Education
Family
Health
Human Relations
Management
Motivation
Sales
TYPICAL AUDIENCE:
Associations
Health Care Professionals

GOLDMAN, CONNIE
Connie Goldman Productions
926 Second St., #201
Santa Monica, CA 90403
Telephone: 310-393-6801
Fax: 310-393-1051
ASSOCIATION
  MEMBERSHIP:
Natl. Speakers Assn.

PRINCIPAL TOPICS:
Health
Motivation
Philosophy
Psychology
Senior Citizens
TYPICAL AUDIENCE:
Fraternal
Seniors

GOLDTRAP, GEORGE
1003 Heritage Village
Madison, TN 37115
Telephone: 800-594-7554
Fax: 615-865-2041
REPRESENTED BY:
Happy Talk
Speaker Connect USA
ASSOCIATION
  MEMBERSHIP:
Natl. Speakers Assn.
Inti Group of Agents &
  Bureaus
PRINCIPAL TOPICS:
Health
Humor
TYPICAL AUDIENCE:
Corporate
Association

GOLLIVER, JOY J.
Ignite the Community Spirit
500 W. Roy W
Seattle, WA 98119
Telephone: 206-283-4385
ASSOCIATION
  MEMBERSHIP:
Natl. Speakers Assn.
PRINCIPAL TOPICS:
Family
Human Relations
Motivation
Social Trends
TYPICAL AUDIENCE:
Corporate
Association

GOOD, PERRY
Perry Good Group, The
203 W. Weaver St.
Carrboro, NC 27510
Telephone: 919-942-8491
Fax: 919-942-3760
MAILING ADDRESS:
Perry Good Group, The
P.O. Box 3021
Chapel Hill, NC 27515
ASSOCIATION
  MEMBERSHIP:
Natl. Speakers Assn.

PRINCIPAL TOPICS:
Education
Management
Motivation
Psychology
Youth
TYPICAL AUDIENCE:
Corporate
Association
Institutional

GOOZE, MITCHELL
2700 Augustine Dr., #242
Santa Clara, Ca 95054
Telephone: 800-947-0140
Fax: 408-727-3949
ASSOCIATION
  MEMBERSHIP:
Natl. Speakers Assn.
PRINCIPAL TOPICS:
Advertising
Computer Technology
Electronics
Marketing
Motivation
Sales
TYPICAL AUDIENCE:
Corporate
Association

GORBY, JOHN C.   CSP
Britt, Douglas Co.
1503 Shoreline Dr.
St. Charles, IL 60174
Telephone: 708-377-0018
Fax: 708-377-0199
ASSOCIATION
  MEMBERSHIP:
Natl. Speakers Assn.
PRINCIPAL TOPICS:
Advertising
Management
Media
TYPICAL AUDIENCE:
Corporate
Association

GORDEN, DAVE   CSP
P.O. BOX 150
PIGEON FORGE, TN 37868
Telephone: 615-428-3131
Fax: 615-429-3369
ASSOCIATION
  MEMBERSHIP:
Natl. Speakers Assn.
PRINCIPAL TOPICS:
Business & Industry
Education
Family
Human Relations
Humor

Management
Marketing
Medical
Motivation
TYPICAL AUDIENCE:
Corporate
Association

GORDON, CONNI   CSP
Gordon Creative Research
  Center
427-22 St.
Miami Beach, FL 33139
Telephone: 305-532-1001
Fax: 305-532-5811
REPRESENTED BY:
Wedgewood Productions
ASSOCIATION
  MEMBERSHIP:
Natl. Speakers Assn.
PRINCIPAL TOPICS:
Education
Entertainment
Hobbies
Human Relations
Humor
Media
Motivation
Video
TYPICAL AUDIENCE:
Corporate
Association

GRAHAM, GORDON
1741 N. Ivar, #213
Los Angeles, CA 90028
Telephone: 213-466-7787

GRANGER, SUSAN
CRN International & American
  Movie Classics
124 Cross Highway
Westport, CT 06880
Telephone: 203-227-0080
Fax: 203-227-0603
REPRESENTED BY:
Potomac Speakers Bureau
Cassidy & Fishman
American Program Bureau
Florida Speakers Bureau
Washington Speakers Bureau
ASSOCIATION
  MEMBERSHIP:
Natl. Speakers Assn.
America Theatre Critics
Drama Desk
Outer Critics Circle
Ct. Critics Circle
PRINCIPAL TOPICS:
Amusements

Entertainment
Human Relations
Marketing
Media
Motivation
Psychology
Communications
TYPICAL AUDIENCE:
Corporate
Association

GRANGER, VIRGINIA M.
924 E. Westchester Dr.
Tempe, AZ 85283
Telephone: 602-897-1302
ASSOCIATION
  MEMBERSHIP:
Natl. Speakers Assn.
Toastmasters
PRINCIPAL TOPICS:
Motivation
Psychology
Senior Citizens
TYPICAL AUDIENCE:
Seniors

GRANT, CAROL
1103 JOHNSON AVE.
SAN LUIS OBISPO, CA 93401
Telephone: 805-546-8278
Fax: 805-541-2853
ASSOCIATION
  MEMBERSHIP:
Natl. Speakers Assn.
PRINCIPAL TOPICS:
Food/Diet
Health
Human Relations
Motivation
Physical Fitness
Communications
TYPICAL AUDIENCE:
Corporate
SEE AD IN SECTION 8

GRANT, LYNELLA F.
10245 Evia Linda #222
Scottsdale, AZ 85258
Telephone: 602-451-0790
Fax: 602-451-0794
ASSOCIATION
  MEMBERSHIP:
Natl. Speakers Assn.
Toastmasters
PRINCIPAL TOPICS:
Human Relations
Philosophy
Social Trends
TYPICAL AUDIENCE:
Corporate

GREEN, LILA
2125 Nature Cove
Ann Arbor, MI 48104
Telephone: 313-677-1517
Fax: 313-677-1517
REPRESENTED BY:
American Program Bureau
Michigan Speakers Bureau
ASSOCIATION
  MEMBERSHIP:
Natl. Speakers Assn.
Platform Speakers
PRINCIPAL TOPICS:
Education
Family
Health
Humor
Medical
Motivation
Psychology
Senior Citizens
TYPICAL AUDIENCE:
Association

GREENE, IDA
People Skills International
2910 Baily Ave.
San Diego, CA 92105
Telephone: 619-262-9951
Fax: 619-262-0505
REPRESENTED BY:
Podium
ASSOCIATION
  MEMBERSHIP:
Natl. Speakers Assn.
Platform Speakers
PRINCIPAL TOPICS:
Education
Human Relations
Motivation
Psychology
TYPICAL AUDIENCE:
Association
Fraternal

GREENE, TAG
P.O. Box 5006
Bellevue, WA 98009
Telephone: 206-643-4444
Fax: 206-957-1758
ASSOCIATION
  MEMBERSHIP:
Natl. Speakers
Platform Speakers
Toastmasters
PRINCIPAL TOPICS:
Humor
Management
Motivation
Sales

GREENE-DAVIDSON,
  SUSAN
Greene-Davidson
12520 A1 Westheimer, Ste. 112
Houston, TX 77077
Telephone: 713-558-1053
Fax: 713-558-1044
ASSOCIATION
  MEMBERSHIP:
Natl. Speakers Assn.
PRINCIPAL TOPICS:
Business & Industry
Human Relations
Management
Motivation
TYPICAL AUDIENCE:
Corporate
Association

GREENWOOD, RON
Greenwood & Greenwood
100 Spear St., #930
San Francisco, CA 94105
Telephone: 415-957-9980
Fax: 415-882-9604
ASSOCIATION
  MEMBERSHIP:
Natl. Speakers Assn.
PRINCIPAL TOPICS:
Personal Finance
Senior Citizens
TYPICAL AUDIENCE:
Corporate
Association

GREGG, ROBERT E.
315 Wisconsin Ave.
Madison, WI 53703
Telephone: 608-256-1020
Fax: 608-255-9389
ASSOCIATION
  MEMBERSHIP:
Natl. Speakers Assn.
PRINCIPAL TOPICS:
Human Relations
Management
TYPICAL AUDIENCE:
Corporate
Association
Institutional

GREIF, ED
Greif, Ed & Company Inc.
P.O. Box 40247
Overland Park, KS 66204
Telephone: 913-236-6083
Fax: 913-236-6701
ASSOCIATION
  MEMBERSHIP:
Natl. Speakers]
Institute Of Management

Consultants
PRINCIPAL TOPICS:
Business & Industry
Management
Motivation
Sales
TYPICAL AUDIENCE:
Corporate
Association

GRIESSMAN, GENE, PH.D.
505-1421 Peachtree St., N.E.
Atlanta, Ga 30309
Telephone: 404-872-3054
Fax: 404-872-4243
REPRESENTED BY:
Atlanta Speakers
Speaker Connect
ASSOCIATION
  MEMBERSHIP:
Natl. Speakers Assn.
PRINCIPAL TOPICS:
Business & Industry
Education
History
Human Relations
Motivation
Psychology
Social Trends
TYPICAL AUDIENCE:
Corporate
Association
Educational

GRIFFIN, TOM
1526 Marblehead Dr.
Lewisville, TX 75067
Telephone: 214-221-7036
MAILING ADDRESS:
Texas Instruments
2501 S. hwy. 121
Lewisville, TX 75067
ASSOCIATION
  MEMBERSHIP:
Natl. Speakers Assn.
North Texas Speakers
PRINCIPAL TOPICS:
Human Relations
Management
Motivation
TYPICAL AUDIENCE:
Association
Fraternal

GROPPEL, JACK L. PH.D.
5700 Saddlebrook Way
Wesley Chapel, FL 33543
Telephone: 813-973-8022
Fax: 813-973-8019

ASSOCIATION
  MEMBERSHIP:
Natl. Speakers Assn.
PRINCIPAL TOPICS:
Food/Diet
Health
Motivation
Physical Fitness
TYPICAL AUDIENCE:
Corporate
Association
Sport

GROSS, T. SCOTT
HCR 1, Box 561
Center Point, TX 78010
Telephone: 210-634-2122
REPRESENTED BY:
Master Media
ASSOCIATION
  MEMBERSHIP:
Natl. Speakers Assn.
PRINCIPAL TOPICS:
Business & Industry
Human Relations
TYPICAL AUDIENCE:
Corporate

GUTIERREZ,
  JUAN F.   CSP
Kaset International
8875 Hiden River Parkway
Tampa, FL 33637
Telephone: 813-977-8875
Fax: 813-971-3511
ASSOCIATION
  MEMBERSHIP:
Natl. Speakers Assn.
PRINCIPAL TOPICS:
Sales
TYPICAL AUDIENCE:
Corporate
Association

GUTRIDGE, DON FOSTER
P.O. Box 42223
Santa Barbara, CA 93140
Telephone: 805-984-4519
ASSOCIATION
  MEMBERSHIP:
Natl. Speakers Assn.
PRINCIPAL TOPICS:
Aviation
Business & Industry
Entertainment
Human Relations
Management
Motivation
Philosophy
Psychology
Sales

Youth
TYPICAL AUDIENCE:
Corporate
Association

HABER, DR. MEL
254-39 Bates Road
Little Neck, NY 11363
Telephone: 718-279-3143
ASSOCIATION
  MEMBERSHIP:
Natl. Speakers Assn.
PRINCIPAL TOPICS:
Communications
TYPICAL AUDIENCE:
Corporate
Association

HADAWAY, GEORGE W.
9726 Farralone Ave., #G
Chatsworth, CA 91311
Telephone: 818-882-4137
Fax: 818-727-1617
ASSOCIATION
  MEMBERSHIP:
Natl. Speakers Assn.
PRINCIPAL TOPICS:
Education
Management
Motivation
TYPICAL AUDIENCE:
Corporate

HADDEN, RICHARD
4741 Atlantic Blvd., #C
Jacksonville, FL 32207
Telephone: 904-396-9796
Fax: 904-396-9798
ASSOCIATION
  MEMBERSHIP:
Natl. Speakers Assn.
American Society of Training &
  Development
PRINCIPAL TOPICS:
Management
TYPICAL AUDIENCE:
Corporate
Association

HAGESETH, CHRISTIAN III
1113 Stoney Hill Dr.
Ft. Collins, CO 80525
Telephone: 303-221-2209
PRINCIPAL TOPICS:
Health
Humor
Psychology
TYPICAL AUDIENCE:
Corporate
Association

HAIGH, LESLEE
824 S.E. 209
Gresham, OR 97030
Telephone: 503-666-2202
REPRESENTED BY:
Read Speakers Bureau
ASSOCIATION
 MEMBERSHIP:
Natl. Speakers Assn.
Toastmasters
PRINCIPAL TOPICS:
Motivation
TYPICAL AUDIENCE:
Women's Groups

HALPERN, STEVEN
524 San Anselmo Ave., #700
San Anselmo, Ca 94960
Telephone: 415-485-5321
Fax: 415-485-1312
ASSOCIATION
 MEMBERSHIP:
Natl. Speakers Assn.
PRINCIPAL TOPICS:
Health
TYPICAL AUDIENCE:
Association
General

HALTER, 'DIAMOND' JIM
J.J.O. Inc.
P.O. Box 2902
Valdosta, GA 31604
Telephone: 912-241-8286
MAILING ADDRESS:
J.J.O. Inc.
1199 St. Augustine Rd.
Valdosta, GA 31601
ASSOCIATION
 MEMBERSHIP:
Natl. Speakers Assn.
Platform Speakers
Rotary International
PRINCIPAL TOPICS:
Advertising
Management
Marketing
Motivation
Sales
Youth
TYPICAL AUDIENCE:
Corporate
Schools
Civic

HALVERSON, DEAN
3315 Fairway Dr.
Cato, WI 54206
Telephone: 414-683-5940
Fax: 414-683-5950
MAILING ADDRESS:

Leede Research Group, The
1332 S. 26th St.
Wauitowoc, WI 54220
ASSOCIATION
 MEMBERSHIP:
Natl. Speakers Assn.
PRINCIPAL TOPICS:
Business & Industry
Health
Marketing
Sales
TYPICAL AUDIENCE:
Corporate
Association

HAMEROFF, EUGENE J.
P.O. Box 411
Jupiter, FL 33468
Telephone: 407-747-2264
Fax: 407-575-0866
MAILING ADDRESS:
212 US One, #25
Tequesca, FL 33469
ASSOCIATION
 MEMBERSHIP:
Natl. Speakers Assn.
PRINCIPAL TOPICS:
Advertising
Marketing
TYPICAL AUDIENCE:
Corporate
Association

HAMPTON, LOU
4200 Wisconsin Ave., N.W.,
 #106
Washington, DC 20016
Telephone: 202-686-2020
Fax: 202-363-4941
REPRESENTED BY:
Management Institute
Int'l. Speaker Network
ASSOCIATION
 MEMBERSHIP:
Natl. Speakers Assn.
PRINCIPAL TOPICS:
Journalism
Management
Media
TYPICAL AUDIENCE:
Corporate
Association

HANSEN, MARK
 VICTOR   CSP
P.O. Box 7665
Newport Beach, CA 92658
Telephone: 714-759-9304
Fax: 714-722-6912

ASSOCIATION
 MEMBERSHIP:
Natl. Speakers Assn.
PRINCIPAL TOPICS:
Motivation
Sales
TYPICAL AUDIENCE:
Association

HANSON, JERRY   CSP
208 No. 29th St., #214
Billings, MT 59101
Telephone: 406-245-0404
Fax: 406-245-3897
ASSOCIATION
 MEMBERSHIP:
Natl. Speakers Assn.
PRINCIPAL TOPICS:
Entertainment
Sales
TYPICAL AUDIENCE:
Corporate
Association

HARBIN, CHARLES
27 Linda Lane
Kissimmee, FL 34744
Telephone: 800-594-3741
Fax: 407-846-8972
MAILING ADDRESS:
P.O. Box 29
Kissimmee, FL 34742
ASSOCIATION
 MEMBERSHIP:
Natl. Speakers Assn.
Suncoast Speakers
PRINCIPAL TOPICS:
Humor
Journalism
Sales
TYPICAL AUDIENCE:
Corporate
Association
Fraternal

HARDY, BETTY
3717 Piping Rock Lane
Houston, TX 77027-4031
Telephone: 713-622-3368
ASSOCIATION
 MEMBERSHIP:
Natl. Speakers Assn.
PRINCIPAL TOPICS:
Fashion
Motivation
TYPICAL AUDIENCE:
Corporate
Association
Fraternal

HARDY, MARC
58485 Hilly Lane
Elkhart, IN 46517
Telephone: 219-295-7600
Fax: 219-534-4937
ASSOCIATION
 MEMBERSHIP:
Natl. Speakers
Toastmasters
PRINCIPAL TOPICS:
Family
Human Relations
Humor
Management
Military
Motivation
World Affairs
TYPICAL AUDIENCE:
Association
Fraternal

HARLAN, RAY
17544 E. WESLEY PL.
AURORA, CO 80013-4174
Telephone: 303-671-5833
Fax: 303-368-9095
REPRESENTED BY:
Speakers Unlimited
Prism
Educators Network
ASSOCIATION
 MEMBERSHIP:
Natl. Speakers Assn.
National Writers Club
PRINCIPAL TOPICS:
Education
Management
Communications
TYPICAL AUDIENCE:
Corporate
Governmental
SEE AD IN SECTION 8

HARMON, SHIRLEY
89 Lombardy Lane
Orinda, CA 94563
Telephone: 510-253-0465
Fax: 510-253-0563
ASSOCIATION
 MEMBERSHIP:
Natl. Speakers Assn.
Platform Speakers
PRINCIPAL TOPICS:
Health
Human Relations
Motivation
TYPICAL AUDIENCE:
Corporate
Association

HARPER, JEANNE M.
1113 Elizabeth Ave.,
  P.O. Box 735
Marinette, WI 54143
Telephone: 715-735-9549
Fax: 715-735-0324
REPRESENTED BY:
Ann Miller Promotions
Associated Speakers
The Speakers Mart
PRINCIPAL TOPICS:
Education
Family
Health
Human Relations
Motivation
Psychology
Religion
Youth
TYPICAL AUDIENCE:
Corporate
Institutional
Association

HARRAL, CHAS
1146 N. Kirchoff Drive
Mesa, Az 85203
Telephone: 602-969-8504
Fax: 602-834-4354
REPRESENTED BY:
America's Top Performers
ASSOCIATION
  MEMBERSHIP:
Natl. Speakers Assn.
PRINCIPAL TOPICS:
Aviation
Government
Health
Humor
Military
Motivation
Psychology
TYPICAL AUDIENCE:
Corporate
Association
Fraternal

HARRIS, MELVA J.
Harris Development
  Consultants
834 Jamestown Rd.
East Windsor, NJ 08520
Telephone: 609-448-3424
ASSOCIATION
  MEMBERSHIP:
Natl. Speakers Assn.
PRINCIPAL TOPICS:
Business & Industry
Human Relations
Management
Motivation

TYPICAL AUDIENCE:
Corporate
Association

HARRISON, GENE
Quest Management
  Consultants
1472 Farrand Rd.
Fallbrook, Ca 92028
Telephone: 619-723-2706
Fax: 619-728-1982
REPRESENTED BY:
Agricultural Speakers Network
Walter's Intl. Speakers Bureau
ASSOCIATION
  MEMBERSHIP:
Natl. Speakers Assn.
AMA Presidents
PRINCIPAL TOPICS:
Agriculture
Management
Motivation
TYPICAL AUDIENCE:
Corporate
Association

HASKELL, JOHN S.
1700 MANDEVILLE
  CANYON RD.
LOS ANGELES, CA 90049
Telephone: 310-476-3355
Fax: 310-471-7721
REPRESENTED BY:
Kinsbury Enterprises
ASSOCIATION
  MEMBERSHIP:
Natl. Speakers Assn.
PRINCIPAL TOPICS:
Advertising
Marketing
Sales
TYPICAL AUDIENCE:
Association
SEE AD IN SECTION 8

HATHAWAY, PATTI
Hathaway Group, The
1016 Woodglen Road
Westerville, OH 43081
Telephone: 614-523-3633
REPRESENTED BY:
Speakers Unlimited
Action Entertainmen
ASSOCIATION
  MEMBERSHIP:
Natl. Speakers Assn.
PRINCIPAL TOPICS:
Business & Industry
Education
Family
Human Relations

Management
Motivation
Psychology
TYPICAL AUDIENCE:
Corporate
Association

HATTON, J. DUEY
908 East Lee
Sherwood, Ak 72116
Telephone: 501-835-1749
REPRESENTED BY:
Access Speakers Bureau, Inc.
International Speakers
  Network, Inc.
ASSOCIATION
  MEMBERSHIP:
Natl. Speakers Assn.
Toastmasters
PRINCIPAL TOPICS:
Education
Humor
Motivation
Youth
TYPICAL AUDIENCE:
Corporate
Association
Fraternal
Educational

HAVEY, CAROL V.
122 South Ashland Ave.
La Grange, IL 60525
Telephone: 708-482-3669
ASSOCIATION
  MEMBERSHIP:
Natl. Speakers Assn.
PRINCIPAL TOPICS:
Education
Family
Human Relations
Humor
Motivation
Personal Finance
Psychology
Social Trends
TYPICAL AUDIENCE:
Women

HAWKINS, KATHLEEN
National Mangmt. Institute
3209 Lakewood Lane
Flower Mound, Tx 75028
Telephone: 817-491-9681
Fax: 817-491-9681
PRINCIPAL TOPICS:
Business & Industry
Education
Human Relations
Communications

TYPICAL AUDIENCE:
Corporate
Association

HAWLEY, CASEY FITTS
690 Hardage Farm Drive
Marietta, GA 30064
Telephone: 404-419-7260
Fax: 404-419-7261
ASSOCIATION
  MEMBERSHIP:
Natl. Speakers Assn.
PRINCIPAL TOPICS:
Business & Industry
Marketing
Sales
TYPICAL AUDIENCE:
Corporate
Association

HAYASHI, MIKE
501 W. Encanto Blvd.
Phoenix, Az 85003
Telephone: 602-252-6808
REPRESENTED BY:
Florida Speakers Bureau
ASSOCIATION
  MEMBERSHIP:
Natl. Speakers Assn.
ASTD
PRINCIPAL TOPICS:
Motivation
Senior Citizens
TYPICAL AUDIENCE:
Corporate
Association

HAYES, STEPHEN K.
Nine Gates Institute
P.O. Box 160
Germantown, OH 45327
Telephone: 513-855-2293
ASSOCIATION
  MEMBERSHIP:
Natl. Speakers Assn.
PRINCIPAL TOPICS:
Physical Fitness
Psychology
Religion
TYPICAL AUDIENCE:
Association

HEADLEY, WILLIAM
P.O. Box 298
Worthington, OH 43085
Telephone: 614-888-3550
ASSOCIATION
  MEMBERSHIP:
International Platform Speakers
Ohio Speakers Forum

PRINCIPAL TOPICS:
Family
Humor
Motivation
Religion
Senior Citizens
TYPICAL AUDIENCE:
Corporate
Association
Fraternal
Academic
Religious

HEDRICK, LUCY H.
29 Sound Beach Ave.
Old Greenwich, CT 06870
Telephone: 203-637-1051
ASSOCIATION
 MEMBERSHIP:
Natl. Speakers Assn.
PRINCIPAL TOPICS:
Management
TYPICAL AUDIENCE:
Corporate
Association
Fraternal

HELITZER, MELVIN
Scripps School of Journalism
Ohio University
Athens, OH 45701
Telephone: 614-593-2607
Fax: 614-593-2592
REPRESENTED BY:
Mike Frank
Speakers Unlimited
ASSOCIATION
 MEMBERSHIP:
Natl. Speakers Assn.
PRINCIPAL TOPICS:
Advertising
Entertainment
Human Relations
Humor
Journalism
TYPICAL AUDIENCE:
Corporate
Association
Institutional

HELSTEIN, IVY
27 Georgian Lane
Great Neck, NY 11024
Telephone: 516-487-4456
ASSOCIATION
 MEMBERSHIP:
Natl. Speakers Assn.
PRINCIPAL TOPICS:
Education
Family
Human Relations

Psychology
Communications
TYPICAL AUDIENCE:
General Public

HELVEY, EDWARD P., JR.
461 Layside Dr., #100
Winchester, Va 22602
Telephone: 703-877-2717
Fax: 703-877-1572
ASSOCIATION
 MEMBERSHIP:
Natl. Speakers Assn.
PRINCIPAL TOPICS:
Business & Industry
Education
Marketing
Media
Sales
Video
TYPICAL AUDIENCE:
Corporate
Association

HEMPHILL, BARBARA
Hemphill & Associates Inc.
1464 Garner Station Blvd.
 #330
Raleigh, NC 27603-3634
Telephone: 919-834-8510
Fax: 919-834-8710
ASSOCIATION
 MEMBERSHIP:
Natl. Speakers Assn.
PRINCIPAL TOPICS:
Business & Industry
Management
TYPICAL AUDIENCE:
Corporate

HENLEY-SMITH, LINDA
1806 W. Lawrence Lane
Phoenix, Az 85021
Telephone: 800-325-2844
ASSOCIATION
 MEMBERSHIP:
Natl. Speakers Assn.
PRINCIPAL TOPICS:
Education
Entertainment
Health
Human Relations
Humor
Motivation
TYPICAL AUDIENCE:
Corporate
Association
Institutional

HENNIG, JAMES F.,
 PH.D CSP
Henning, J.F. Associates
1044 Ernst Dr.
Green Bay, WI 54304
Telephone: 414-499-5550
Fax: 414-499-1729
ASSOCIATION
 MEMBERSHIP:
Natl. Speakers Assn.
PRINCIPAL TOPICS:
Management
Marketing
Motivation
Sales
TYPICAL AUDIENCE:
Corporate
Association

HENNING, MIKE CSP
Henning Family Business
 Center
1006 N. Pembroke Court
Effingham, IL 62401
Telephone: 217-342-3728
ASSOCIATION
 MEMBERSHIP:
Natl. Speakers Assn.
Toastmasters
PRINCIPAL TOPICS:
Business & Industry
Family
Management
TYPICAL AUDIENCE:
Corporate
Association

HENRY, ROBERT H. CSP
331 Graystone Lane
Auburn, AL 36830
Telephone: 205-821-2415
MAILING ADDRESS:
P.O. Box 3055
Auburn, AL 36831
REPRESENTED BY:
Speakers
 Unlimited
DuPree Jordans
Esther Eaples
ASSOCIATION
 MEMBERSHIP:
Natl. Speakers Assn.
PRINCIPAL TOPICS:
Entertainment
Humor
Motivation
TYPICAL AUDIENCE:
Corporate
Association

HERBSTER, DOUGLAS
 DR.
3565 Airport Rd.
Belgrade, MT 59714
ASSOCIATION
 MEMBERSHIP:
Natl. Speakers Assn.
PRINCIPAL TOPICS:
Business & Industry
Education
Government
Management
Marketing
Personal Finance
Philosophy
Psychology
Sales
Senior Citizens
TYPICAL AUDIENCE:
Corporate
Association
Public Schools

HERMAN, JEFF
500 Greenwich St.
New York, NY 10013
Telephone: 212-941-0540
Fax: 212-941-0614
ASSOCIATION
 MEMBERSHIP:
Natl. Speakers Assn.
PRINCIPAL TOPICS:
Education
Journalism
TYPICAL AUDIENCE:
Association

**HERMAN, ROGER
 E. CMC CSP
19 NORTH MAIN ST.
RITTMAN, OH 44270
Telephone: 216-927-3566
Fax: 216-925-4356
REPRESENTED BY:
Several
ASSOCIATION
 MEMBERSHIP:
Natl. Speakers Assn.
PRINCIPAL TOPICS:
Management
Social Trends
TYPICAL AUDIENCE:
Corporate
Association
Government
SEE AD IN SECTION 8**

HEROLD, MORT
18658 Golfview Dr.
Hazel Crest, IL 60429
Telephone: 708-798-3730

ASSOCIATION
  MEMBERSHIP:
Natl. Speakers Assn.
PRINCIPAL TOPICS:
Education
Entertainment
Management
Marketing
Motivation
Sales
Senior Citizens
TYPICAL AUDIENCE:
Corporate
Association

HERRON, SANDRA
  WHITACRE
12651 Tunstall St.
Garden Grove, CA 92645
Telephone: 714-971-4222
ASSOCIATION
  MEMBERSHIP:
Natl. Speakers
Toastmasters
PRINCIPAL TOPICS:
Family
Human Relations
Motivation
Psychology
Religion
TYPICAL AUDIENCE:
Association
Fraternal

HERSEY, ROSS V.   CSP
P.O. Box 126
Waynesboro, VA 22980
Telephone: 703-942-9424
Fax: 703-943-8247
ASSOCIATION
  MEMBERSHIP:
Natl. Speakers Assn.
PRINCIPAL TOPICS:
Humor
Motivation
TYPICAL AUDIENCE:
Corporate
Association

HERSEY, WILLIAM
Memory Lane
Norton, MA 02766
Telephone: 508-285-3041
Fax: 508-339-3482
ASSOCIATION
  MEMBERSHIP:
Natl. Speakers Assn.
PRINCIPAL TOPICS:
Motivation
TYPICAL AUDIENCE:
Corporate

HESSE, DOUGLAS G.
1025 Old Roswell Rd., #104
Roswell, Ga 30076
Telephone: 404-992-4444
Fax: 404-587-2531
ASSOCIATION
  MEMBERSHIP:
Natl. Speakers Assn.
PRINCIPAL TOPICS:
Personal Finance
TYPICAL AUDIENCE:
Corporate

HICKMAN, ANDY L.
P.O. Box 181569
Dallas, TX 75218
Telephone: 214-328-5277
Fax: 214-852-6717
REPRESENTED BY:
Exposures To Excellence
ASSOCIATION
  MEMBERSHIP:
Natl. Speakers Assn.
PRINCIPAL TOPICS:
Entertainment
Health
Humor
TYPICAL AUDIENCE:
Corporate
Association

HIGGS, LIZ CURTIS   CSP
P.O. Box 43577
Louisville, KY 40253
Telephone: 502-254-5454
Fax: 502-254-5455
ASSOCIATION
  MEMBERSHIP:
Natl. Speakers Assn.
PRINCIPAL TOPICS:
Family
Health
Humor
Motivation
TYPICAL AUDIENCE:
Corporate
Association

HIGHTOWER, KATHIE J.
38415 Reed Rd.
Nehalem, OR 97131
Telephone: 503-368-7036
ASSOCIATION
  MEMBERSHIP:
Natl. Speakers Assn.
Toastmasters
PRINCIPAL TOPICS:
· Management
Marketing
TYPICAL AUDIENCE:
Corporate

Association
Military
Government

HIGHTSHOE, NANCY
P.O. Box 11846
St. Louis, MO 63105
Telephone: 314-862-7808
Fax: 314-862-0904
ASSOCIATION
  MEMBERSHIP:
Natl. Speakers Assn.
PRINCIPAL TOPICS:
Human Relations
Management
Sales
TYPICAL AUDIENCE:
Corporate
Association
Institutional

HILL, JOANNE K.
Horizons Unlimited
59999 Myrtle Rd.
South Bend, IN 46614
Telephone: 219-289-3526
ASSOCIATION
  MEMBERSHIP:
Natl. Speakers Assn.
Toastmasters
Natl. Assoc. for Self-Employed
PRINCIPAL TOPICS:
Business & Industry
Family
Human Relations
Management
Marketing
Motivation
Senior Citizens
TYPICAL AUDIENCE:
Association
Religious

HILLMAN, RALPH E.
MTSU, Box 373
Murfreesboro, Tn 37132
Telephone: 615-898-2271
Fax: 615-898-5826
REPRESENTED BY:
Happy Talk
ASSOCIATION
  MEMBERSHIP:
Natl. Speakers Assn.
PRINCIPAL TOPICS:
Communications
TYPICAL AUDIENCE:
Association

HILTON, HERMINE
Kessler Management
10747 Wilshire Blvd., #807
Los Angeles, CA 90024
Telephone: 310-824-3333
Fax: 310-470-2111
REPRESENTED BY:
World Class Speakers Bureau
TYPICAL AUDIENCE:
Corporate
Association

HIXON, GEORGE G.
12611 Pawnee Lane
Shawnee Mission, KS 66209
Telephone: 913-491-9897
ASSOCIATION
  MEMBERSHIP:
Natl. Speakers Assn.
PRINCIPAL TOPICS:
Business & Industry
Management
Marketing
Motivation
Sales
TYPICAL AUDIENCE:
Corporate
Association

HODGES, WILLIAM N.
P.O. Box 22
Fairborn, OH 45324
Telephone: 513-878-9701
Fax: 513-878-4718
ASSOCIATION
  MEMBERSHIP:
Natl. Speakers
Toastmasters
Professional Speaker Guild
PRINCIPAL TOPICS:
Business & Industry
Human Relations
Management
Marketing
Motivation
Psychology
Sales
Communications
TYPICAL AUDIENCE:
Corporate
Association
Institutional

HOFSTETTER, CATHI S.
2427 E. Bethel Dr.
Anaheim, CA 92806
Telephone: 714-772-8311
Fax: 714-772-1197

HOLCOMB, JANE, PH.D.
7805 W. 80th Street
Playa del Rey, Ca 90293
Telephone: 310-821-7624
ASSOCIATION
 MEMBERSHIP:
Natl. Speakers Assn.
ASTD
PRINCIPAL TOPICS:
Automotive
Business & Industry
Education
Government
Management
TYPICAL AUDIENCE:
Corporate
Association

HOLDER, VERN
Holder & Associates
2005 Running Branch Rd.
Edmond, Ok 73013
Telephone: 405-341-4355
ASSOCIATION
 MEMBERSHIP:
Natl. Speakers Assn.
Oklahoma Speakers
PRINCIPAL TOPICS:
Humor
Motivation
Sales
TYPICAL AUDIENCE:
Corporate
Association

HOLTON, CHER   CSP
Holton Consulting Group, Inc.,
 The
4704 Little Falls Dr., #300
Raleigh, NC 27609
Telephone: 919-783-7088
ASSOCIATION
 MEMBERSHIP:
Natl. Speakers Assn.
American Society of Training &
 Development
PRINCIPAL TOPICS:
Management
Motivation
TYPICAL AUDIENCE:
Corporate

HOOD, RALPH   CSP
P.O. Box 4817
Huntsville, AL 35815
Telephone: 205-881-2907
Fax: 205-882-1361
ASSOCIATION
 MEMBERSHIP:
Natl. Speakers Assn.

PRINCIPAL TOPICS:
Aviation
Entertainment
Motivation
TYPICAL AUDIENCE:
Association

HOOPER, DR. DON W.
323 Ballantine
Houston, Tx 77015
Telephone: 713-455-7235
Fax: 713-676-2022
ASSOCIATION
 MEMBERSHIP:
Natl. Speakers Assn.
PRINCIPAL TOPICS:
Education
Management
Motivation
TYPICAL AUDIENCE:
Corporate

HOOSER, PHILLIP
 VAN   CSP
P.O. Box 5094
Ocala, FL 34478
Telephone: 904-368-7609
Fax: 904-368-7786
ASSOCIATION
 MEMBERSHIP:
Natl. Speakers Assn.
PRINCIPAL TOPICS:
Business & Industry
Human Relations
Management
Motivation
TYPICAL AUDIENCE:
Corporate
Association

HOPE, LUCILLE
P.O. Box 24404
Ft. Lauderdale, FL 33307
Telephone: 305-563-1338
Fax: 305-564-3034
ASSOCIATION
 MEMBERSHIP:
Natl. Speakers Assn.
Toastmasters
PRINCIPAL TOPICS:
Humor
TYPICAL AUDIENCE:
Corporate
Association

HOPKINS, TOM   CSP
7531 E. 2nd St.
Scottsdale, AZ 85251
Telephone: 800-528-0446
Fax: 602-949-0786

MAILING ADDRESS:
P.O. Box 1969
Scottsdale, AZ 85252

HORKEY, DONNA L.
5950 W. Oakland Pk. Blvd.,
 #310
Ft. Lauderdale, FL 33313
Telephone: 305-485-0390
Fax: 305-485-0327
ASSOCIATION
 MEMBERSHIP:
Natl. Speakers Assn.
Society For Human Resource
 Management
PRINCIPAL TOPICS:
Human Relations
Management
TYPICAL AUDIENCE:
Corporate

HORVATH, DENNIS D.
9220 NORTH COLLEGE AVE.
INDIANAPOLIS, IN 46240
Telephone: 317-844-6869
Fax: 317-844-0669
REPRESENTED BY:
Speakers & Seminar
 Resources
ASSOCIATION
 MEMBERSHIP:
Natl. Speakers Assn.
Toastmasters
PRINCIPAL TOPICS:
Business & Industry
Computer Technology
Photography
Sales
TYPICAL AUDIENCE:
Corporate
Association
SEE AD IN SECTION 8

HORVATH, TERRI
9220 N. College Ave.
Indianapolis, IN 46240
Telephone: 317-844-6869
Fax: 317-844-0669
REPRESENTED BY:
Speakers & Seminar
 Resources
ASSOCIATION
 MEMBERSHIP:
Platform Speakers
Toastmasters
PRINCIPAL TOPICS:
Business & Industry
Motivation
Photography
TYPICAL AUDIENCE:
Association

HOWLEY, C. JOE
461 Meridian
Crystal Lake, IL 60014
Telephone: 815-459-5164
Fax: 815-459-5169
MAILING ADDRESS:
555 Oakwood Ave.
Lake Zurich, IL 60047
ASSOCIATION
 MEMBERSHIP:
Natl. Speakers Assn.
Prof. Speakers of Illinois
PRINCIPAL TOPICS:
Human Relations
Management
Motivation
Sales
TYPICAL AUDIENCE:
Corporate

HOXWORTH, STEVE
15 Spinning Wheel, #400
Hinsdale, IL 60521
Telephone: 708-325-0717
Fax: 708-325-0728
ASSOCIATION
 MEMBERSHIP:
Natl. Speakers
Toastmasters
PRINCIPAL TOPICS:
Home & Garden
Humor
Motivation
Personal Finance
Sales
TYPICAL AUDIENCE:
Association
Fraternal

HUBER, MARCY
Center For Language Training
24310 Moulton Pkwy. C-1,
 #260
Laguna Hills, CA 92653-3306
Telephone: 714-770-4466
ASSOCIATION
 MEMBERSHIP:
Natl. Speakers Assn.
PRINCIPAL TOPICS:
Motivation
TYPICAL AUDIENCE:
Corporate
Senior Citizens

HUFFMAN, CARL E., JR.
213 Wilcox Dr.
Bartlett, IL 60103
Telephone: 708-483-8997
Fax: 708-483-8931
MAILING ADDRESS:
HUFFMAN, CARL E.

P.O. Box 8357
Bartlett, IL 60103
REPRESENTED BY:
Associated Speakers Bureau
  (Wisconsin)
ASSOCIATION
  MEMBERSHIP:
Natl. Speakers Assn.
Toastmasters
PRINCIPAL TOPICS:
Management
Motivation
TYPICAL AUDIENCE:
Corporate
Association

HUGHES, LADDIE W.
1690 Edgewood Dr.
Palo Alto, Ca 94303
Telephone: 415-323-9916
ASSOCIATION
  MEMBERSHIP:
Natl. Speakers Assn.
Intl. Platform
PRINCIPAL TOPICS:
Education
Government
Health
Social Trends
World Affairs
TYPICAL AUDIENCE:
Association
Fraternal

HULL, MIRIAM B.
225 S. Swoope Ave., #210
Maitland, Fl 32751
Telephone: 407-628-0669
Fax: 407-539-2133
ASSOCIATION
  MEMBERSHIP:
Natl. Speakers Assn.
PRINCIPAL TOPICS:
Human Relations
Management
Motivation
Sales
TYPICAL AUDIENCE:
Corporate
Association

HUMPHRIES, ANN
  CHADWELL
629 S. Brick Rd.
Columbia, SC 29223
Telephone: 803-736-1934
Fax: 803-736-6073
MAILING ADDRESS:
P.O. Box 69530
Columbia, SC 69530

ASSOCIATION
  MEMBERSHIP:
Natl. Speakers Assn.
PRINCIPAL TOPICS:
Business & Industry
Human Relations
Management
Marketing
Motivation
Sales
Social Trends
World Affairs
TYPICAL AUDIENCE:
Corporate
Association

HUNDERTMARK, JERI
360 Keller Hill Rd.
Mooresville, IN 46158
Telephone: 317-831-2192
ASSOCIATION
  MEMBERSHIP:
Natl. Speakers Assn.
Indiana Chapter-NSA
PRINCIPAL TOPICS:
Education
Family
Human Relations
Motivation
TYPICAL AUDIENCE:
Corporate
Association
Parents

HUNT, D. TRINIDAD
47-430 Hui Nene St.
Kaneohe, HI 96744
Telephone: 808-239-4431
Fax: 808-239-2482
ASSOCIATION
  MEMBERSHIP:
Natl. Speakers Assn.
Hawaii Speakers
PRINCIPAL TOPICS:
Business & Industry
Education
Human Relations
Management
Motivation
TYPICAL AUDIENCE:
Corporate

HUNTER, C. ROY
30640 Pacific Hwy. S., #E
Federal Way, WA 98003
Telephone: 206-946-3218
MAILING ADDRESS:
Alliance Hypnotherpy Inc.
Federal Way, WA 98003
REPRESENTED BY:
Benson Corporate Seminars

ASSOCIATION
  MEMBERSHIP:
Natl. Speakers Assn.
PRINCIPAL TOPICS:
Motivation
Sales
TYPICAL AUDIENCE:
Corporate
Association

HUNTER, WILLIAM L.
Pavilions at Greentree
  Suite 408
Marlton, NJ 08053
Telephone: 609-596-9545
Fax: 609-428-5236
ASSOCIATION
  MEMBERSHIP:
Natl. Speakers Assn.
PRINCIPAL TOPICS:
Business & Industry
Management
Sales
TYPICAL AUDIENCE:
Corporate
Association

HUNTTING, SHERRY E.
3913 Toronto Road
Cameron Park, CA 95682
Telephone: 716-677-1282
ASSOCIATION
  MEMBERSHIP:
Natl. Speakers Assn.
PRINCIPAL TOPICS:
Fashion
TYPICAL AUDIENCE:
Association
Government
Small Business

HURLEY, CARL E., ED.D.
  (CPAE)   CSP
McKinney Associates, Inc.
1380 Fontaine
Lexington, KY 40502
Telephone: 502-583-8222
MAILING ADDRESS:
HURLEY, CARL E., ED.D.,
  CPAE
McKinney Associates, Inc.
P.O. Box 5162
Louisville, KY 40255-0162
REPRESENTED BY:
McKinney
  Associates
ASSOCIATION
  MEMBERSHIP:
Natl. Speakers Assn.
PRINCIPAL TOPICS:
Education

Entertainment
Human Relations
Humor
Motivation
TYPICAL AUDIENCE:
General
Corporate
Association

HUTSON, DON   CSP
871 Ridgeway Loop, #102
Memphis, TN 38120
Telephone: 800-647-9166
Fax: 901-767-5959
ASSOCIATION
  MEMBERSHIP:
Natl. Speakers Assn.
PRINCIPAL TOPICS:
Management
Motivation
Sales
TYPICAL AUDIENCE:
Corporate
Association

HUTTER, V. ROSAN
Horizons Unlimited
5008 Butternut Rd.
Durham, NC 27707
Telephone: 919-489-0123
ASSOCIATION
  MEMBERSHIP:
Natl. Speakers Assn.
American Society of Training &
  Development
PRINCIPAL TOPICS:
Business & Industry
Education
Medical
TYPICAL AUDIENCE:
Association
Institutional

HYDEN, HOWARD E.
7415 Hyde Park Dr.
Minneapolis, MN 55439
Telephone: 612-942-0980
Fax: 612-943-1398
ASSOCIATION
  MEMBERSHIP:
Natl. Speakers
Platform Speakers
PRINCIPAL TOPICS:
Marketing
TYPICAL AUDIENCE:
Corporate
Association

**HYKEN, SHEP A.
(SHEPARD
  PRESENTATIONS)**

897 FEE FEE RD.
ST. LOUIS, MO 63043
Telephone: 314-576-6600
Fax: 314-576-2807
ASSOCIATION
  MEMBERSHIP:
Natl. Speakers Assn.
PRINCIPAL TOPICS:
Entertainment
Humor
Motivation
Sales
TYPICAL AUDIENCE:
Corporate
Association
SEE AD IN SECTION 8

INGRAM, ROBERT
935 Poplar Ave.
Sunnyvale, CA 94086
Telephone: 408-773-1744
Fax: 415-852-2907
ASSOCIATION
  MEMBERSHIP:
Natl. Speakers Assn.
American Society of Training &
  Development
PRINCIPAL TOPICS:
Business & Industry
Health
Human Relations
Management
Motivation
Social Trends
TYPICAL AUDIENCE:
Corporate
Association

INTERNATIONAL INSTITUTE
  OF REFLEXOLOGY
International Institute of
  Reflexology
5650 1st Ave., N.
St. Petersburg, FL 33710
Telephone: 813-343-4811
Fax: 813-381-2807
PRINCIPAL TOPICS:
Health
Physical Fitness
TYPICAL AUDIENCE:
Association

IRVIN, DALE   CSP
5712 Dunham Rd.
Downers Grove, IL 60516
Telephone: 708-852-7695
Fax: 708-852-9889
MAILING ADDRESS:
P.O. Box 9061
Downers Grove, IL 60515

REPRESENTED BY:
Natl. Speakers Forum
Capitol Speakers Bureau
The Speaker Network
Jorden International
Speaker Connect
Speakers Unlimited
Agricultural Speakers Network
Associated Speakers
The Speakers Bureau
Preferred Speakers
National Speakers Bureau
Speakers International
Chicago Speakers Bureau
Five Star Speakers Bureau
North American Speakers
  Bureau
Access Speakers
  Bureau
Speakers Source
Standing Ovations
Speak Inc.
Great Speakers!
ASSOCIATION
  MEMBERSHIP:
Natl. Speakers Assn.
PRINCIPAL TOPICS:
Entertainment
Humor
TYPICAL AUDIENCE:
Corporate
Association

ISLER, MARK
8019 Haskell Ave.
Van Nuys, CA 91406
Telephone: 818-994-1088
ASSOCIATION
  MEMBERSHIP:
Natl. Speakers Assn.
PRINCIPAL TOPICS:
Business & Industry
Education
Government
Human Relations
Philosophy
World Affairs
TYPICAL AUDIENCE:
Fraternal

ISRAELOV, RHODA
201 N. Illinois, #400
Indianapolis, IN 46204
Telephone: 317-237-3055
Fax: 317-237-3111
ASSOCIATION
  MEMBERSHIP:
Natl. Speakers Assn.
Toastmasters
PRINCIPAL TOPICS:
Business & Industry

Personal Finance
TYPICAL AUDIENCE:
Corporate
Association
General Public

JABLONSKI, JOSEPH R.
2004 WHITE CLOUD, N.E.
ALBUQUERQUE, NM 87112
Telephone: 505-299-3983
Fax: 505-299-5788
MAILING ADDRESS:
P.O. Box 13591
Albuquerque, NM 87192
ASSOCIATION
  MEMBERSHIP:
Natl. Speakers Assn.
PRINCIPAL TOPICS:
Business & Industry
Ecology
Government
Management
Marketing
Military
Communications
TYPICAL AUDIENCE:
Corporate
Association

JACK, BARBARA M.
6415 S. 'M' Street
Tacoma, WA 98408
Telephone: 206-473-3727
ASSOCIATION
  MEMBERSHIP:
Natl. Speakers Assn.
PRINCIPAL TOPICS:
Human Relations
Motivation
Sales
TYPICAL AUDIENCE:
Corporate
Association
Education

JACKSON, LUAN
1256 Briar Hill Dr.
Lapeer, MI 48446
Telephone: 313-664-4641
MAILING ADDRESS:
456 S. Main St.
Lapeer, MI 48446
ASSOCIATION
  MEMBERSHIP:
Natl. Speakers Assn.
PRINCIPAL TOPICS:
Family
Health
Human Relations
Religion

TYPICAL AUDIENCE:
Fraternal
Religious

JACOBS, ANITA I.
Natl. Center for Effective
  Speaking
1504 Jefferson Street
Teaneck, NJ 07666
Telephone: 201-801-0630
Fax: 201-801-0241
REPRESENTED BY:
Jordan International
Management Institute
National Practice Institute
United Jewish Appeal
ASSOCIATION
  MEMBERSHIP:
Natl. Speakers
Platform Speakers
PRINCIPAL TOPICS:
Education
Management
Motivation
Religion
Youth
Communications
TYPICAL AUDIENCE:
Corporate
Association

JACOBS, ELLEN
11333 N. 92nd St., #2097
Scottsdale, AZ 85260
Telephone: 602-860-4925
PRINCIPAL TOPICS:
Human Relations
Sales
TYPICAL AUDIENCE:
Corporate

JAMES, DIANA L.
86-P Calle Aragon
Laguna Hills, CA 92653
Telephone: 714-770-8266
Fax: 714-770-1864
MAILING ADDRESS:
23010 Lake Forest Dr., #302
Laguna Hills, CA 92653
REPRESENTED BY:
Class Speakers
Dottie Walters
ASSOCIATION
  MEMBERSHIP:
Natl. Speakers Assn.
Toastmasters
PRINCIPAL TOPICS:
Family
Human Relations
Motivation
Psychology

Religion
Senior Citizens
TYPICAL AUDIENCE:
Association

JAMES, LARRY
Career Assurance Network
8086 South Yale, #300
Tulsa, OK 74136
Telephone: 918-744-9223
Fax: 918-747-3185
ASSOCIATION
  MEMBERSHIP:
Natl. Speakers Assn.
PRINCIPAL TOPICS:
Human Relations
Motivation
TYPICAL AUDIENCE:
Corporate
Association

JAMES, MERLIN R.
MiRe Co. Productions
3984 Blenheim Street
Ft. Myers, Fl 33919
Telephone: 813-433-2769
Fax: 813-482-1828
ASSOCIATION
  MEMBERSHIP:
Natl. Speakers Assn.
Platform Speakers
PRINCIPAL TOPICS:
Entertainment
Human Relations
Management
Marketing
Military
Motivation
Sales
TYPICAL AUDIENCE:
Corporate
Association

JANSEN, ROBERT H.
7332 W. State St., #3
Wauwatosa, WI 53213
Telephone: 414-258-5720
Fax: 414-258-5721
ASSOCIATION
  MEMBERSHIP:
Natl. Speakers Assn.
PRINCIPAL TOPICS:
Humor
Journalism
Sales
Senior Citizens
TYPICAL AUDIENCE:
General Audiences

JASIM, JANIE   CSP
1743 Green Crest Dr.
Victoria, MN 55386
Telephone: 612-443-3086
Fax: 612-443-3081
REPRESENTED BY:
Speakers Bureau
ASSOCIATION
  MEMBERSHIP:
Natl. Speakers Assn.
PRINCIPAL TOPICS:
Family
Human Relations
Humor
Motivation
Sales
TYPICAL AUDIENCE:
Corporate
Association
General Public

JEFFRIES,
  ELIZABETH   CSP
P.O. Box 24495
Louisville, KY 40224
Telephone: 502-339-1600
Fax: 502-339-1232
ASSOCIATION
  MEMBERSHIP:
Natl. Speakers Assn.
PRINCIPAL TOPICS:
Management
TYPICAL AUDIENCE:
Association

JENSEN, JAY R.
3869 Cherry Hill Rd.
Santa Maria, CA 93455
Telephone: 805-937-0869
ASSOCIATION
  MEMBERSHIP:
Natl. Speakers Assn.
PRINCIPAL TOPICS:
Aviation
Business & Industry
Family
Food/Diet
Health
Human Relations
Management
Military
Motivation
Personal Finance
Religion
TYPICAL AUDIENCE:
Corporate
Association
Fraternal

JEPPESEN, LYNDA FRANCE
  MBA
Keyes
234 E. 3900 S., #1
Salt Lake City, UT 84107
Telephone: 801-261-1777
Fax: 801-261-3153
ASSOCIATION
  MEMBERSHIP:
Natl. Speakers Assn.
Toastmasters
PRINCIPAL TOPICS:
Food/Diet
Health
Human Relations
Management
Marketing
Medical
Motivation
Physical Fitness
Sales
TYPICAL AUDIENCE:
Corporate

JJ LAUDERBAUGH
JJ Lauderbaugh
189 Altura Vista Dr.
Los Gatos, CA 95030
Telephone: 408-866-7673
ASSOCIATION
  MEMBERSHIP:
Natl. Speakers Assn.
PRINCIPAL TOPICS:
Computer Technology
Human Relations
Management
Motivation
TYPICAL AUDIENCE:
Corporate
Association

JOHNSON, BILL L.   CSP
7502 N. 10th St.
Phoenix, AZ 85020
Telephone: 602-943-1624
REPRESENTED BY:
Corporate
Association
PRINCIPAL TOPICS:
Management
Marketing
Motivation
Sales
Communications

JOHNSON, CAROL
Recruiting Network, The
1375 E. Schaumburg Rd.,
  #240
Schaumburg, IL 60194
Telephone: 708-529-8487

Fax: 708-529-9926
ASSOCIATION
  MEMBERSHIP:
Natl. Speakers Assn.
PRINCIPAL TOPICS:
Management
Sales
TYPICAL AUDIENCE:
Association

JOHNSON, DR. JOYCE
Johnson, Joyce Nutrition
1800 W. Katella, #102
Orange, CA 92667
Telephone: 714-532-1111
ASSOCIATION
  MEMBERSHIP:
Natl. Speakers Assn.
PRINCIPAL TOPICS:
Food/Diet
Health
Physical Fitness
TYPICAL AUDIENCE:
Corporate
Association

JOHNSON, HUB, PH.D.
RR. 1, Box 194A
Flora, In 46929
Telephone: 219-967-4454
Fax: 219-722-8601
REPRESENTED BY:
Speakers & Seminar
  Resources
ASSOCIATION
  MEMBERSHIP:
Natl. Speakers Assn.
PRINCIPAL TOPICS:
Agriculture
Business & Industry
Human Relations
Humor
Management
Motivation
Philosophy
TYPICAL AUDIENCE:
Corporate
Association
Fraternal

JOHNSON, JENYCE
1108 Woodsmans Ct., #2
Chesapeake, Va 23320
Telephone: 804-436-2534
Fax: 804-436-2534
ASSOCIATION
  MEMBERSHIP:
Natl. Speakers Assn.
ASTD
NSPI

PRINCIPAL TOPICS:
Family
Human Relations
Management
Youth
TYPICAL AUDIENCE:
General

JOHNSON, KAY B.
245-B North Hawthorne Road
Winston-Salem, NC 27104
Telephone: 919-725-9465
Fax: 919-723-8374
ASSOCIATION
  MEMBERSHIP:
Natl. Speakers Assn.
PRINCIPAL TOPICS:
Human Relations
Management
Medical
TYPICAL AUDIENCE:
Corporate
Association

JOLLEY, WILLIE 'THE
  INSPIRTAINER'
P.O. Box 55459,
  5711 13th St. N.W.
Washington, DC 20040
Telephone: 202-723-8863
Fax: 202-722-1180
ASSOCIATION
  MEMBERSHIP:
Natl. Speakers Assn.
PRINCIPAL TOPICS:
Entertainment
Motivation
TYPICAL AUDIENCE:
Corporate
Association
Scholls/Colleges

JONES, DEWITT
Box 698
Redwood Valley, CA 95470
Telephone: 707-463-1081
Fax: 707-463-1088
REPRESENTED BY:
Great Speakers
ASSOCIATION
  MEMBERSHIP:
Natl. Speakers Assn.
PRINCIPAL TOPICS:
Business & Industry
Photography
TYPICAL AUDIENCE:
Corporate
Association

JONES, MARILYN K., DDS
2077 S. Gessner, Ste. 129
Houston, TX 77063-1127
Telephone: 713-977-1010
ASSOCIATION
  MEMBERSHIP:
Natl. Speakers Assn.
Toastmasters
PRINCIPAL TOPICS:
Education
Food/Diet
Health
Medical
Science
TYPICAL AUDIENCE:
Corporate
Association

JOY, PAM
440 York Dr.
Benicia, CA 94510
Telephone: 707-745-1411
Fax: 707-745-1411
ASSOCIATION
  MEMBERSHIP:
Natl. Speakers Assn.
PRINCIPAL TOPICS:
Motivation
Sales
TYPICAL AUDIENCE:
Corporate

JUTKINS, RAY W.
Rockingham Rance
Roll, AZ 85347
Telephone: 602-785-9400
Fax: 602-785-9356
REPRESENTED BY:
California Speakers Bureau
ASSOCIATION
  MEMBERSHIP:
Natl. Speakers
Direct Mktg.
Business/Professional
  Advertising
PRINCIPAL TOPICS:
Business & Industry
Marketing
Philosophy
Sales
Travel
TYPICAL AUDIENCE:
Corporate
Association

KABACHNICK, TERRI
160 West St.
Cromwell, Ct 06416
Telephone: 203-635-6543
Fax: 203-635-0477

REPRESENTED BY:
Keynote Speakers
National Speakers Forum
ASSOCIATION
  MEMBERSHIP:
Natl. Speakers Assn.
PRINCIPAL TOPICS:
Management
Sales
TYPICAL AUDIENCE:
Corporate
Association

KAFOURY, JEANNINE
P.O. Box 22803
Milwaukie, OR 97269-2803
Telephone: 503-659-0482
Fax: 503-233-4045

KAHN, RITA
P.O. Box 420024
San Diego, CA 92142
Telephone: 619-278-8145
ASSOCIATION
  MEMBERSHIP:
Natl. Speakers Assn.
Toastmasters
PRINCIPAL TOPICS:
Fashion
Humor
Marketing
Motivation
Sales
Travel
TYPICAL AUDIENCE:
Association
Fraternal
Women's Groups

KAHN, SANFORD
3041 E. 3rd St., #2
Long Beach, CA 90814
Telephone: 310-434-4695
ASSOCIATION
  MEMBERSHIP:
Natl. Speakers Assn.
PRINCIPAL TOPICS:
Business & Industry
TYPICAL AUDIENCE:
Association

KAINE, JACK W.
911 Main St., 1100 Commerce
  Tower
Kansas City, MO 64105
Telephone: 816-471-0404
Fax: 816-471-5277
ASSOCIATION
  MEMBERSHIP:
Natl. Speakers Assn.

PRINCIPAL TOPICS:
Advertising
Agriculture
Automotive
Aviation
Business & Industry
Marketing
Media
Motivation
TYPICAL AUDIENCE:
Corporate
Association

KAPLAN, STEVE
Modern Management
  Technologies, Inc.
6851 Yumuri St., #2
Coral Gables, FL 33146
Telephone: 305-595-1923
Fax: 305-595-2306
MAILING ADDRESS:
7840 Camino Rea P303
Miami, FL 33143
ASSOCIATION
  MEMBERSHIP:
Natl. Speakers Assn.
Toastmasters
PRINCIPAL TOPICS:
Business & Industry
Human Relations
Management
TYPICAL AUDIENCE:
Corporate
Association

KARPOVICH, MICHAEL S.
P.O. Box 272
Caro, MI 48723
Telephone: 517-673-3036
REPRESENTED BY:
Jostens
Susan Miller & Assoc.
Anne Miller
Associated Speakers
ASSOCIATION
  MEMBERSHIP:
Natl. Speakers Assn.
PRINCIPAL TOPICS:
Education
Family
Humor
Motivation
Psychology
Youth
TYPICAL AUDIENCE:
Association

KARR, RONALD E.
Karr Associates Inc.
1 Parker Plaza
Fort Lee, NJ 07024

Telephone: 201-461-2309
Fax: 201-461-5621
ASSOCIATION
  MEMBERSHIP:
Natl. Speakers Assn.
PRINCIPAL TOPICS:
Human Relations
Management
Marketing
Motivation
Sales
TYPICAL AUDIENCE:
Corporate
Association

KARSCHNER, GARY DON
3210 CANYON CREEK DR.
SAN ANGELO, TX 76904
Telephone: 915-944-9115
MAILING ADDRESS:
P.O. Box 62662
San Angelo, TX 76906
ASSOCIATION
  MEMBERSHIP:
Natl. Speakers Assn.
Toastmasters
PRINCIPAL TOPICS:
Entertainment
History
Motivation
TYPICAL AUDIENCE:
Community C of C
Civic Groups
SEE AD IN SECTION 8

KARTEN, NAOMI
Karten Associates
40 Woodland Pkwy.
Randolph, MA 02368
Telephone: 617-986-8148
Fax: 617-961-2608
ASSOCIATION
  MEMBERSHIP:
Natl. Speakers Assn.
Toastmasters
PRINCIPAL TOPICS:
Computer Technology
Human Relations
Management
Psychology
TYPICAL AUDIENCE:
Corporate
Association

KATELHON, GERALD P.
351 E. Conestoga Road
Wayne, PA 19087
Telephone: 215-989-9000
Fax: 215-254-8958

REPRESENTED BY:
Speakers Services (Drexel Hill,
  Pa)
ASSOCIATION
  MEMBERSHIP:
Natl. Speakers Assn.
PRINCIPAL TOPICS:
Personal Finance
TYPICAL AUDIENCE:
Retirees

KAY, ANDREA
P.O. Box 6834
Cincinnati, OH 45206
Telephone: 513-221-6222
ASSOCIATION
  MEMBERSHIP:
Local Speakers Association
PRINCIPAL TOPICS:
Communications
TYPICAL AUDIENCE:
Association

KAYE, STEVE
P.O. Box 208, 1931 Gilman Cir.
Placentia, CA 92670
Telephone: 714-528-1300
Fax: 714-528-2123
ASSOCIATION
  MEMBERSHIP:
Natl. Speakers Assn.
Toastmasters
PRINCIPAL TOPICS:
Business & Industry
Humor
Management
Motivation
TYPICAL AUDIENCE:
Corporate
Association

KEEFFE, CAROL
18518 61st Place, W.
Lynnwood, Wa 98037
Telephone: 206-778-5119
ASSOCIATION
  MEMBERSHIP:
Natl. Speakers Assn.
PRINCIPAL TOPICS:
Motivation
Personal Finance
TYPICAL AUDIENCE:
Association
General Public-Public Seminars

KEELAN, JIM
Communication Unlimited
7595 W. 66th Ave., #201
Arvada, CO 80003
Telephone: 303-424-0608
Fax: 303-424-0607

REPRESENTED BY:
Natl. Speakers Association
ASSOCIATION
  MEMBERSHIP:
Natl. Speakers Assn.
PRINCIPAL TOPICS:
Education
Human Relations
Humor
Management
TYPICAL AUDIENCE:
Corporate

KEELER, JOHN A.
Keeler Unlimited, Inc.
10861 Rock Island Rd.
Jacksonville, FL 32257
Telephone: 904-262-2245
REPRESENTED BY:
National Speakers Assoc.
ASSOCIATION
  MEMBERSHIP:
Natl. Speakers Assn.
PRINCIPAL TOPICS:
Business & Industry
Electronics
Management
Marketing
Motivation
TYPICAL AUDIENCE:
Corporate
Association

KELLER, KAY D.
321 Kensington Dr.
Delaware, OH 43015
Telephone: 614-369-8308
REPRESENTED BY:
Speakers Unlimited
ASSOCIATION
  MEMBERSHIP:
Natl. Speakers Assn.
PRINCIPAL TOPICS:
Communications
Family
Human Relations
Motivation
TYPICAL AUDIENCE:
Corporate
Association

KELLEY, JIM
100 Meridian Ave.
Taylors, SC 29687
Telephone: 803-244-5760
ASSOCIATION
  MEMBERSHIP:
Natl. Speakers Assn.
PRINCIPAL TOPICS:
Humor
Management

Motivation
TYPICAL AUDIENCE:
Corporate
Association
Fraternal

KENNEDY, DAN S.
5818 N. 7th St., #103
Phoenix, AZ 85014
Telephone: 602-997-7707
Fax: 602-269-3113
ASSOCIATION
  MEMBERSHIP:
Natl. Speakers Assn.
International Platform Assoc.
Natl. Infomercial Mktg. Assoc.
Natl. Writers Club
PRINCIPAL TOPICS:
Advertising
Business & Industry
Human Relations
Humor
Marketing
Media
Motivation
Sales
TYPICAL AUDIENCE:
Corporate
Association
General Public

KERLEY, WILLIAM C.
6300 W. Loop S., #480
Bellaire, TX 77401
Telephone: 713-663-7771
Fax: 713-663-6418
ASSOCIATION
  MEMBERSHIP:
Natl. Speakers Assn.
PRINCIPAL TOPICS:
Human Relations
Humor
Management
Marketing
Motivation
Personal Finance
Philosophy
Psychology
Religion
TYPICAL AUDIENCE:
Corporate

KERSTETTER, KERRY M.
39210 State St., #202
Fremont, CA 94538
Telephone: 510-793-7692
Fax: 510-795-4194
ASSOCIATION
  MEMBERSHIP:
Natl. Speakers Assn.

PRINCIPAL TOPICS:
Personal Finance
TYPICAL AUDIENCE:
Assocation

KHERA, SHIV
3 Boston Dr.
Pine Brook, NJ 07058
Telephone: 201-575-6225
Fax: 201-808-1614
ASSOCIATION
  MEMBERSHIP:
Natl. Speakers Assn.
Platform Speakers
Toastmasters
PRINCIPAL TOPICS:
Management
Motivation
Sales
TYPICAL AUDIENCE:
Corporate
Assocation
Fraternal

KICK, FRAN
6650 Green Branch Dr., #8
Centerville, OH 45459
Telephone: 513-439-2698
ASSOCIATION
  MEMBERSHIP:
Natl. Speakers Assn.
PRINCIPAL TOPICS:
Education
Motivation
Psychology
Youth
TYPICAL AUDIENCE:
Association
Institutional

KIENE, ANDREA L.
30771 N. Fremont Ave.
Grayslake, IL 60030
Telephone: 708-740-0620
ASSOCIATION
  MEMBERSHIP:
Natl. Speakers Assn.
PRINCIPAL TOPICS:
Education
Management
Motivation
TYPICAL AUDIENCE:
Corporate
Association

KILPATRICK, KURT   CSP
434 Delcris Drive
Birmingham, AL 35226
Telephone: 205-945-8607
Fax: 205-290-9201

ASSOCIATION
  MEMBERSHIP:
Natl. Speakers Assn.
PRINCIPAL TOPICS:
Entertainment
Humor
Journalism
Marketing
Media
Motivation
Sales
TYPICAL AUDIENCE:
Corporate
Association
Fraternal

KINDE, JOHN E.
Humor Dynamics
P.O. Box 2140
Santa Maria, CA 93457
Telephone: 805-934-3232
REPRESENTED BY:
Walters International
Santa Barbara Speakers
  Bureau
ASSOCIATION
  MEMBERSHIP:
Natl. Speakers Assn.
PRINCIPAL TOPICS:
Humor
TYPICAL AUDIENCE:
Association

KING, CHRIS
12805 Shaker Blvd., #512
Cleveland, OH 44120
Telephone: 216-991-8428
ASSOCIATION
  MEMBERSHIP:
Natl. Speakers Assn.
PRINCIPAL TOPICS:
Fashion
Human Relations
Journalism
Motivation
Sales
Social Trends
Communications
TYPICAL AUDIENCE:
Corporate
Association

KING, HARLEY
K & K Communications
875 Maple St.
Perrysburg, OH 43551
Telephone: 419-247-5689
ASSOCIATION
  MEMBERSHIP:
Natl. Speakers Assn.

PRINCIPAL TOPICS:
Human Relations
Marketing
Motivation
Sales
Senior Citizens
TYPICAL AUDIENCE:
Corporate
Association

KINNARD, MELLY
3251 Cherryridge Road
Englewood, CO 80110
Telephone: 303-762-9920
REPRESENTED BY:
Corporate Assurance
ASSOCIATION
  MEMBERSHIP:
Natl. Speakers Assn.
PRINCIPAL TOPICS:
Family
Human Relations
Management
Marketing
Motivation
TYPICAL AUDIENCE:
Corporate

KLEIN, ALLEN
1034 Page St.
San Francisco, CA 94117
Telephone: 415-431-1913
Fax: 415-431-8600
REPRESENTED BY:
Access Speakers Bureau
ASSOCIATION
  MEMBERSHIP:
Natl. Speakers Assn.
PRINCIPAL TOPICS:
Health
Humor
TYPICAL AUDIENCE:
Association

KLEIN, RUTH L.
Marketing Source, The
5330 Office Center Ct.
Bakersfield, CA 93309
Telephone: 805-324-4687
ASSOCIATION
  MEMBERSHIP:
Natl. Speakers Assn.
PRINCIPAL TOPICS:
Business & Industry
Education
Human Relations
Management
Marketing
Motivation
Psychology
Sales

TYPICAL AUDIENCE:
Corporate
Association

KLEINE-KRACHT, ANN E.
Humor Educator
P.O. Box 5093
Louisville, KY 40205
Telephone: 502-451-4378
ASSOCIATION
  MEMBERSHIP:
Natl. Speakers Assn.
PRINCIPAL TOPICS:
Health
Humor
TYPICAL AUDIENCE:
Corporate
Association

KLINKENBERG, HILDA
ETIQUETTE INTERNATIONAL
254 EAST 68TH ST.,
** STE. 18A**
NEW YORK, NY 10021-6015
Telephone: 212-628-7209
Fax: 212-628-7290
REPRESENTED BY:
International Platform
ASSOCIATION
** MEMBERSHIP:**
Natl. Speakers Assn.
PRINCIPAL TOPICS:
Business & Industry
Human Relations
Management
TYPICAL AUDIENCE:
Corporate
Association
SEE AD IN SECTION 8

KLOCK, JOSEPH P.
Klockworks, Inc., The
606 Island Dr.
Key Largo, FL 33037
Telephone: 305-451-0079
Fax: 305-451-1774
ASSOCIATION
  MEMBERSHIP:
Natl. Speakers Assn.
International Platform
PRINCIPAL TOPICS:
Humor
Management
Marketing
Motivation
Psychology
Sales
TYPICAL AUDIENCE:
Corporate
Association

KNACKSTEDT, MARY V.
2091 N. Front St.
Harrisburg, PA 17110
Telephone: 717-238-7548
Fax: 717-233-7374
ASSOCIATION
  MEMBERSHIP:
Natl. Speakers Assn.
PRINCIPAL TOPICS:
Architecture
Home & Garden
Management
Marketing
Motivation
Psychology
TYPICAL AUDIENCE:
Association

KNOLL, HERBERT E. JR.
4 Valley View Ave.
Rensselaer, NY 12144
Telephone: 518-462-2776
ASSOCIATION
  MEMBERSHIP:
Natl. Speakers Assn.
PRINCIPAL TOPICS:
Advertising
Marketing
Sales
TYPICAL AUDIENCE:
Corporate
Association
Fraternal

KNOX, DAVID S.
7300 Metro Blvd., #120
Minneapolis, MN 55439
Telephone: 800-533-4494
ASSOCIATION
  MEMBERSHIP:
Natl. Speakers Assn.
PRINCIPAL TOPICS:
Management
Motivation
Sales
TYPICAL AUDIENCE:
Corporate
Association

KOJM, KURT BARNABY
1833 Kensington Ave.
Buffalo, NY 14215
Telephone: 716-862-9530
ASSOCIATION
  MEMBERSHIP:
Natl. Speakers Assn.
PRINCIPAL TOPICS:
Advertising
Business & Industry
Ecology
Government

Human Relations
Management
Marketing
Media
Motivation
Philosophy
Religion
Sales
TYPICAL AUDIENCE:
Corporate
Association
Fraternal
Institutional

KOLTIN, ALLAN DAVID,
  CPA
50 E. Bellevue, #1302
Chicago, IL 60611
Telephone: 312-245-1930
Fax: 312-644-4423
ASSOCIATION
  MEMBERSHIP:
Natl. Speakers Assn.
PRINCIPAL TOPICS:
Business & Industry
Computer Technology
Management
Marketing
Motivation
Sales
TYPICAL AUDIENCE:
Corporate

KOPP, KRISTIN
3030 N. 80th Street
Milwaukee, WI 53222
Telephone: 414-871-2615
ASSOCIATION
  MEMBERSHIP:
Natl. Speakers Assn.
PRINCIPAL TOPICS:
Human Relations
Management
Motivation
Personal Finance
Philosophy
Psychology
TYPICAL AUDIENCE:
Corporate
Association
General Public

KOTZ, STEVE
P.O. Box 24426, 4300 South
  104th Pl.
Seattle, WA 98124
Telephone: 206-725-0900
Fax: 206-725-1615
ASSOCIATION
  MEMBERSHIP:
Natl. Speakers Assn.

Toastmasters
PRINCIPAL TOPICS:
Education
Management
Motivation
Sales
TYPICAL AUDIENCE:
Corporate
Association

KRAMER, ROBERT G.
Revolutionary Retailing
1605 W. Galbraith Rd.
Cincinnati, OH 45239
Telephone: 513-521-3100
REPRESENTED BY:
Speaker's Unlimited
  (Columbus, Ohio)
ASSOCIATION
  MEMBERSHIP:
Natl. Speakers Assn.
Ohio Speakers Forum
Cincinnati Professional
  Speakers Assoc.
PRINCIPAL TOPICS:
Advertising
Management
Marketing
Sales
TYPICAL AUDIENCE:
Corporate
Association

KRATOWICZ, M. J.
P.O. Box 9944
McLean, VA 22102
Telephone: 703-827-7999
REPRESENTED BY:
Corporate
Association
ASSOCIATION
  MEMBERSHIP:
Natl. Speakers Assn.
PRINCIPAL TOPICS:
Business & Industry
Computer Technology
Education
Human Relations
Management
Marketing
Motivation
TYPICAL AUDIENCE:
Corporate
Assocation

KURZWEG, MARY KAY
215 Stella St.
Metairie, LA 70005
Telephone: 504-833-0277
Fax: 504-834-2572

ASSOCIATION
  MEMBERSHIP:
Natl. Speakers Assn.
Toastmasters
PRINCIPAL TOPICS:
Education
Family
Human Relations
Motivation
TYPICAL AUDIENCE:
Corporate
Association
Fraternal

KUTSKO, JIM
9700 E. Iliff Ave., #121
Denver, CO 80231
Telephone: 303-955-7853
Fax: 303-694-9091
REPRESENTED BY:
Pageatry, Inc.
Rocky Mountain Speakers
  Bureau
ASSOCIATION
  MEMBERSHIP:
Natl. Speakers Assn.
PRINCIPAL TOPICS:
Business & Industry
Management
Motivation
Sales
TYPICAL AUDIENCE:
Corporate

KVITKA, ELAINE
7603 Via de Manana
Scottsdale, Az 85258
Telephone: 602-991-8660
Fax: 602-861-9677
ASSOCIATION
  MEMBERSHIP:
Natl. Speakers Assn.
Toastmasters
PRINCIPAL TOPICS:
Food/Diet
Health
Physical Fitness
TYPICAL AUDIENCE:
Corporate
Association

LABRANCHE,
  GARY A. (CAE)
1615 H St., N.W.
Washington, DC 20062
Telephone: 202-463-5604
Fax: 202-463-3190
ASSOCIATION
  MEMBERSHIP:
Natl. Speakers Assn.
American Society of

Association Executives
PRINCIPAL TOPICS:
Management
Motivation
TYPICAL AUDIENCE:
Association

LADDIE, W. HUGHES
1690 Edgewood Dr.
Palo Alto, Ca 94303
Telephone: 415-323-9916
ASSOCIATION
  MEMBERSHIP:
Natl. Speakers Assn.
International Platform
PRINCIPAL TOPICS:
Education
Government
Health
Social Trends
World Affairs
TYPICAL AUDIENCE:
Association

LAFRENIERE, DONNA
P.O. Box 852132
Richardson, Tx 75085
Telephone: 214-235-0027
ASSOCIATION
  MEMBERSHIP:
Natl. Speakers Assn.
Toastmasters
North Texas Speakers
PRINCIPAL TOPICS:
Health
Motivation
Senior Citizens
Business & Industry
TYPICAL AUDIENCE:
Corporate
Association

LAIPPLY, BOB
918 S. Walnut
Bucymus, Oh 44820
Telephone: 419-562-9825
ASSOCIATION
  MEMBERSHIP:
Natl. Speakers Assn.
Ohio Speakers Forum
PRINCIPAL TOPICS:
Education
Motivation
Youth
Family
TYPICAL AUDIENCE:
Association
Educational

LAIPPLY, SANDY
918 S. Walnut
Bucyrus, Oh 44820
Telephone: 419-562-9825
Fax: 419-562-9966
ASSOCIATION
  MEMBERSHIP:
Natl. Speakers Assn.
Ohio Speakers Forum
PRINCIPAL TOPICS:
Family
Hobbies
Motivation
Sales
Youth
TYPICAL AUDIENCE:
Corporate
Association
Educational

LAJOYCE CHATWELL
  LAWTON
LaJoyce Chatwell Lawton
P.O. Box 21401
Oklahoma City, Ok 73156
Telephone: 405-755-0012
Fax: 405-755-0012
ASSOCIATION
  MEMBERSHIP:
Natl. Speakers Assn.
American Soc. For Training &
  Develop.
PRINCIPAL TOPICS:
Business & Industry
TYPICAL AUDIENCE:
Corporate
Association

LAMB, WILLIAM CARROLL
402 E. Jefferson St.
Tallahassee, FL 32302
Telephone: 904-222-5646
Fax: 904-222-6179
MAILING ADDRESS:
P.O. Box 12132
Tallahassee, FL 32317
ASSOCIATION
  MEMBERSHIP:
Natl. Speakers Assn.
PRINCIPAL TOPICS:
Agriculture
Entertainment
Humor
Motivation
TYPICAL AUDIENCE:
Corporate
Association
Fraternal

LAMON, DANA
43836 Emilie Zola Street
Lancaster, Ca 93535
Telephone: 805-949-7423
Fax: 805-949-7423
ASSOCIATION
  MEMBERSHIP:
Natl. Speakers Assn.
Toastmasters
PRINCIPAL TOPICS:
Motivation
Communications
TYPICAL AUDIENCE:
Corporate
Association
Fraternal

LAND, PETER A.
4210 Lomac St.
Montgomery, AL 36106
Telephone: 205-271-2639
Fax: 205-277-8381
ASSOCIATION
  MEMBERSHIP:
Natl. Speakers Assn.
Alabama Speakers Association
PRINCIPAL TOPICS:
Aviation
Business & Industry
Government
Health
Human Relations
Management
Motivation
TYPICAL AUDIENCE:
Corporate
Association

LARSEN, LARRY L.
6000 E. Evans, Bldg. 3, #104
Denver, CO 80222
Telephone: 303-758-9165
Fax: 303-758-0340
ASSOCIATION
  MEMBERSHIP:
Natl. Speakers Assn.
PRINCIPAL TOPICS:
Business & Industry
Management
Marketing
Motivation
Sales
TYPICAL AUDIENCE:
Corporate
Association

LARSON, JOE   CSP
10040 E. Happy Valley Rd.
Scottsdale, AZ 85255
Telephone: 602-585-4344
Fax: 602-585-8592

ASSOCIATION
  MEMBERSHIP:
Natl. Speakers Assn.
PRINCIPAL TOPICS:
Humor
Motivation
TYPICAL AUDIENCE:
Association

LASKIN, JACK
Kalmikof, Gregor A.
P.O. Box 433, 5336 English
  Colony Way
Penryn, Ca 95663
Telephone: 916-663-2220
REPRESENTED BY:
Keynote Speakers
ASSOCIATION
  MEMBERSHIP:
Natl. Speakers Assn.
PRINCIPAL TOPICS:
Humor
TYPICAL AUDIENCE:
Corporate
Association

LATTA, MARIE B. M.ED.
3825 LaVista Rd., W4
Tucker, GA 30084
Telephone: 404-491-6717
Fax: 404-939-0209
MAILING ADDRESS:
P.O. Box 451251
Atlanta, GA 30345
ASSOCIATION
  MEMBERSHIP:
Natl. Speakers Assn.
MPI/Supplier
PRINCIPAL TOPICS:
Business & Industry
Health
Management
Motivation
TYPICAL AUDIENCE:
Corporate
Association

LAUFER, JOSEPH M.
9 Smith Ct.
Vincentown, NJ 08088
Telephone: 609-859-4042
Fax: 609-859-1746
ASSOCIATION
  MEMBERSHIP:
Natl. Speakers Assn.
Platform Speakers
PRINCIPAL TOPICS:
History
Religion
Travel

TYPICAL AUDIENCE:
Association
Fraternal
Educational

LAUGHLIN, LEWIS E.
2533 N. Carson St.
Carson City, NV 89706
Telephone: 800-648-0966
Fax: 702-883-4874
ASSOCIATION
 MEMBERSHIP:
Natl. Speakers Assn.
PRINCIPAL TOPICS:
Business & Industry
TYPICAL AUDIENCE:
Corporate
General Public

LAWSON, KAREN
1365 Gwynedale Way
Lansdale, PA 19446
Telephone: 215-368-9465
ASSOCIATION
 MEMBERSHIP:
Natl. Speakers Assn.
American Society of Training &
 Development
PRINCIPAL TOPICS:
Business & Industry
Human Relations
Management
TYPICAL AUDIENCE:
Corporate

LEA, DIXIE PH.D.
4627 Ocean Blvd., #308
Pacific Beach, CA 92109
Telephone: 619-270-3037
Fax: 619-270-5057
ASSOCIATION
 MEMBERSHIP:
Natl. Speakers Assn.
Home Economics In Business
PRINCIPAL TOPICS:
Education
Family
Food/Diet
TYPICAL AUDIENCE:
Corporate
Fraternal

LEACH, LYNNE C.
Applied Business
 Communcation
119 Ready Road
Walnut Creek, CA 94598
Telephone: 510-938-4642
Fax: 510-933-4136

ASSOCIATION
 MEMBERSHIP:
Natl. Speakers Assn.
PRINCIPAL TOPICS:
Business & Industry
Management
Sales
Motivation
Communications
TYPICAL AUDIENCE:
Corporate
Association

LEAPTROTT, NAN S.
P.O. Box 776
Pinehurst, NC 28374
Telephone: 919-295-5991
Fax: 919-295-5908
ASSOCIATION
 MEMBERSHIP:
Natl. Speakers Assn.
Platform Speakers
Toastmasters
PRINCIPAL TOPICS:
Business & Industry
Human Relations
Journalism
World Affairs
TYPICAL AUDIENCE:
Corporate

LEBEAU, CALENE
1000 Campbell, #208-122
Houston, TX 77055
Telephone: 713-827-7299
ASSOCIATION
 MEMBERSHIP:
Natl. Speakers Assn.
PRINCIPAL TOPICS:
Education
Health
Human Relations
Management
Motivation
Senior Citizens
TYPICAL AUDIENCE:
Corporate
Association

LEE, BILL
880 S. Pleasantburg Dr., #1-F
Greenville, SC 29607
Telephone: 800-277-7888
Fax: 803-467-0595
ASSOCIATION
 MEMBERSHIP:
Natl. Speakers Assn.
PRINCIPAL TOPICS:
Management
Psychology
Sales

TYPICAL AUDIENCE:
Corporate
Association

LEE, CLIFFORD M., DR.
P.O. Box 1945
Kilgore, TX 75663
Telephone: 800-256-5458
Fax: 903-295-2149
REPRESENTED BY:
The Eagle Company
ASSOCIATION
 MEMBERSHIP:
Natl. Speakers Assn.
PRINCIPAL TOPICS:
Entertainment
Family
Human Relations
Humor
Motivation
Religion
TYPICAL AUDIENCE:
Corporate
Association
Civic
Fraternal

LEEDS, DOROTHY
800 West End Ave.
New York City, NY 10025
Telephone: 212-864-2424
Fax: 212-932-8364
ASSOCIATION
 MEMBERSHIP:
Natl. Speakers Assn.
PRINCIPAL TOPICS:
Management
Marketing
Motivation
Sales
TYPICAL AUDIENCE:
Corporate
Association

LEFKOWITZ, HAL
P.O. Box 902
Solana Beach, CA 92075
Telephone: 619-259-2800
Fax: 619-755-2227
PRINCIPAL TOPICS:
Business & Industry
Management
Marketing
Sales
TYPICAL AUDIENCE:
Corporate
Association

LEGATT, HADASSA PH.D.
Speak Up
8 Parkside Dr.
Great Neck, NY 11023
Telephone: 516-829-2978
Fax: 516-829-2978
ASSOCIATION
 MEMBERSHIP:
Natl. Speakers Assn.
Toastmasters
Red Cross Speakers Bureau
PRINCIPAL TOPICS:
Animals
Education
Entertainment
Motivation
TYPICAL AUDIENCE:
Corporate
Association
Fraternal

LEGRAND, RON
4604-1A Atlantic Blvd.
Jacksonville, FL 32207
Telephone: 904-398-2424
Fax: 904-346-0285

LEHMKUHL, DOROTHY J.
Organizing Techniques
6165 Worlington
Bloomfield, MI 48301
Telephone: 313-626-2062
REPRESENTED BY:
Management
Motivation
ASSOCIATION
 MEMBERSHIP:
Natl. Speakers Assn.
Natl. Assoc. of Prof. Organizers
TYPICAL AUDIENCE:
Corporate
Association

LEICHTY, MARLENE A.
2770 Henry Washington Rd.
Mt. Pleasant, IA 52246
Telephone: 319-256-4316
ASSOCIATION
 MEMBERSHIP:
Natl. Speakers Assn.
PRINCIPAL TOPICS:
Agriculture
Entertainment
Family
Health
Hobbies
Home & Garden
Human Relations
Humor
Marketing
Motivation

Psychology
Sales
Senior Citizens
TYPICAL AUDIENCE:
Assocation

LEMKE, RAYMOND   CSP
8031 W. Center Rd., #222
Omaha, Ne 68124
Telephone: 800-356-2233
Fax: 402-391-1025
ASSOCIATION
  MEMBERSHIP:
Natl. Speakers Assn.
PRINCIPAL TOPICS:
Education
Human Relations
Management
Motivation
Psychology
Sales
Senior Citizens
TYPICAL AUDIENCE:
Corporate
Association

LENZ, BOB
213 E. College Avenue
Appleton, WI 54911
Telephone: 414-738-5589
Fax: 414-738-5587
MAILING ADDRESS:
P.O. Box 2474
Appleton, WI 54913
ASSOCIATION
  MEMBERSHIP:
Natl. Speakers Assn.
PRINCIPAL TOPICS:
Ecology
Education
Family
Human Relations
Humor
Motivation
Philosophy
Psychology
Religion
Social Trends
Youth
TYPICAL AUDIENCE:
Association
Schools

LEONE, RAY
Box 16039
Charleston, SC 29412
Telephone: 803-795-9462
Fax: 803-794-4113
ASSOCIATION
  MEMBERSHIP:
Natl. Speakers Assn.

Toastmasters
PRINCIPAL TOPICS:
Automotive
Business & Industry
Education
Human Relations
Management
Motivation
Sales
TYPICAL AUDIENCE:
Corporate

LERMAN, KENNETH B.
8518 Mt. Vernon Ct.
Wichita, KS 67207
Telephone: 316-686-4444
Fax: 316-686-3502
ASSOCIATION
  MEMBERSHIP:
Natl. Speakers Assn.
PRINCIPAL TOPICS:
Advertising
Business & Industry
Management
Marketing
Motivation
Sales
Social Trends
TYPICAL AUDIENCE:
Corporate
Association

LETOURNEAU, TOM
3447 So. Norfolk Way
Aurora, CO 80013
Telephone: 800-845-7553
ASSOCIATION
  MEMBERSHIP:
Natl. Speakers Assn.
ASTD
PRINCIPAL TOPICS:
Business & Industry
Human Relations
Management
Marketing
Motivation
Sales
TYPICAL AUDIENCE:
Corporate
Association

LEVIN, ROGER P.
600 Reisterstown, Road, #706
Baltimore, MD 21208
Telephone: 410-486-1089
Fax: 410-484-9229
ASSOCIATION
  MEMBERSHIP:
Natl. Speakers Assn.
Capital Speakers Association

PRINCIPAL TOPICS:
Health
Management
Marketing
Motivation
Sales
TYPICAL AUDIENCE:
Corporate
Association

LEVOY, ROBERT P.
Success Dynamics, Inc.
1 Linden Place, #309
Great Neck, NY 11021
Telephone: 516-482-5959
ASSOCIATION
  MEMBERSHIP:
Natl. Speakers Assn.
PRINCIPAL TOPICS:
Management
Marketing
TYPICAL AUDIENCE:
Association

LEVY, JEFFREY G.
420 Lexington Ave., #626
New York, NY 10170
Telephone: 212-682-1233
Fax: 212-949-5759
ASSOCIATION
  MEMBERSHIP:
Natl. Speakers Assn.
PRINCIPAL TOPICS:
Personal Finance
TYPICAL AUDIENCE:
Corporate
Association

LEWIS-WILLIAMS, MYRA
5404 FIVE FORKS RD.
LILBURN, GA 30247
Telephone: 404-923-5600
MAILING ADDRESS:
LEWIS-WILIAMS, MYRA
318 E. 11th St.
Rome, GA 30161
Telephone: 706-235-6289
ASSOCIATION
  MEMBERSHIP:
Natl. Speakers Assn.
PRINCIPAL TOPICS:
Family
Human Relations
Motivation
TYPICAL AUDIENCE:
Association
Women
SEE AD IN SECTION 8

LEWISON-SINGER, RITA
Speak Out/Lewison-Singer
6851 Yumuri St., #2
Coral Gables, FL 33146
Telephone: 305-665-8975
Fax: 305-663-3351
ASSOCIATION
  MEMBERSHIP:
Natl. Speakers Assn.
PRINCIPAL TOPICS:
Education
Marketing
Communications
TYPICAL AUDIENCE:
Corporate

LILLY, SAM, PH.D.
4921 FOREST AVE.
DOWNERS GROVE, IL 60515
Telephone: 708-963-0398
Fax: 708-963-2625
ASSOCIATION
  MEMBERSHIP:
Natl. Speakers Assn.
PRINCIPAL TOPICS:
Marketing
Motivation
Motivation
TYPICAL AUDIENCE:
Corporate
Association
SEE AD IN SECTION 8

LINKLETTER, ART
8484 Wilshire Blvd., #215
Beverly Hills, Ca 90211
Telephone: 213-658-7603
Fax: 213-655-5173
ASSOCIATION
  MEMBERSHIP:
Natl. Speakers Assn.
PRINCIPAL TOPICS:
Business & Industry
Education
Entertainment
Family
Humor
Motivation
Physical Fitness
Sales
Senior Citizens
Travel
Youth
TYPICAL AUDIENCE:
Corporate
Fraternal

LINQUIST, LUANN
P.O. Box 13172
LaJolla, CA 92039
Telephone: 619-551-9222

Fax: 619-351-9221
ASSOCIATION
  MEMBERSHIP:
Natl. Speakers Assn.
PRINCIPAL TOPICS:
Education
Family
Health
Human Relations
Medical
Psychology
Senior Citizens
TYPICAL AUDIENCE:
Corporate
Association

LIPNACK, MARTIN I.
7880 W. Oakland Park Blvd.,
  #300
Ft. Lauderdale, FL 33351
Telephone: 305-741-8400
Fax: 305-741-6299
ASSOCIATION
  MEMBERSHIP:
Natl. Speakers Assn.
PRINCIPAL TOPICS:
Human Relations
TYPICAL AUDIENCE:
Corporate
Association

LISK, THOM
1112 Firth Ave.
Worthington, OH 43085
Telephone: 614-841-1776
Fax: 614-888-1684
ASSOCIATION
  MEMBERSHIP:
Natl. Speakers Assn.
PRINCIPAL TOPICS:
Architecture
Business & Industry
Humor
Management
Marketing
Motivation
Psychology
Religion
Sales
TYPICAL AUDIENCE:
Corporate
Association

LITTAUER,
  FLORENCE   CSP
Class Speakers, Inc.
1645 S. Rancho Santa Fe,
  #102
San Marcos, CA 92069
Telephone: 619-471-1722
Fax: 619-471-8896

ASSOCIATION
  MEMBERSHIP:
Natl. Speakers Assn.
PRINCIPAL TOPICS:
Family
Government
Human Relations
Humor
Psychology
Religion
TYPICAL AUDIENCE:
Corporate
Association
Fraternal

LITTAUER, MARITA
Class Speakers
1645 S. Rancho Santa Fe,
  #102
San Marcos, CA 92069
Telephone: 619-471-1722
Fax: 619-471-8896
ASSOCIATION
  MEMBERSHIP:
Natl. Speakers Assn.
PRINCIPAL TOPICS:
Family
Fashion
Food/Diet
Home & Garden
Management
Motivation
Psychology
Religion
TYPICAL AUDIENCE:
Association
Fraternal

LITTLE, ERLENE
10739 Glen Acres Drive South
Seattle, WA 98168
Telephone: 206-242-1587
Fax: 206-242-1587
ASSOCIATION
  MEMBERSHIP:
Natl. Speakers Assn.
PRINCIPAL TOPICS:
Business & Industry
Education
Health
Human Relations
Motivation
TYPICAL AUDIENCE:
Corporate
Association

LITTLEFIELD, HENRY M.
765 Lighthouse Ave., #4
Pacific Grove, CA 93950
Telephone: 408-372-6516

ASSOCIATION
  MEMBERSHIP:
Natl. Speakers Assn.
Platform Speakers
PRINCIPAL TOPICS:
Education
Government
History
Military
Motivation
Religion
TYPICAL AUDIENCE:
Corporate
Association
Fraternal

LLOYD, HERB J.
P.O. Box 883, 470 East 300
  South
Santaquin, UT 84655
Telephone: 801-754-3600
Fax: 801-224-9273
MAILING ADDRESS:
P.O. Box 943, 1598 West
  Center St.
Orem, UT 84057
REPRESENTED BY:
International Speakers Network
ASSOCIATION
  MEMBERSHIP:
Natl. Speakers Assn.
Platform Speakers
PRINCIPAL TOPICS:
Family
Health
Human Relations
Humor
Management
Motivation
Religion
Sales
Youth
TYPICAL AUDIENCE:
Corporate
Association
Fraternal

LLOYD, JOAN
10425 W. North Ave., #236
Milwaukee, Wi 53226
Telephone: 414-476-8853
Fax: 414-476-3212
REPRESENTED BY:
Associated Speakers, Elm
  Grove, Wi
ASSOCIATION
  MEMBERSHIP:
Natl. Speakers Assn.
PRINCIPAL TOPICS:
Business & Industry
Education

Human Relations
Management
Motivation
TYPICAL AUDIENCE:
Corporate
Association

LOCKRIDGE, ALICE
PRO-FIT
12012-156th Ave., S.E.
Renton, WA 98059
Telephone: 206-255-3817
ASSOCIATION
  MEMBERSHIP:
Natl. Speakers
AAHPERD
ACE
IDEA
PRINCIPAL TOPICS:
Education
Food/Diet
Health
Physical Fitness
TYPICAL AUDIENCE:
Corporate
Association

LOFY, CARL
Lofy Associates, Inc.
5040 Morgan Ave. South
Minneapolis, MN 55419
Telephone: 612-922-7588
Fax: 612-922-7588
ASSOCIATION
  MEMBERSHIP:
Natl. Speakers Assn.
PRINCIPAL TOPICS:
Management
TYPICAL AUDIENCE:
Corporate
Institutional

LONG, BRIAN G.
Marketing & Management
  Institute, Inc.
3182 Davcliff
Kalamazoo, MI 49002
Telephone: 616-323-2359
Fax: 616-323-1777
ASSOCIATION
  MEMBERSHIP:
Natl. Speakers Assn.
PRINCIPAL TOPICS:
Business & Industry
Human Relations
Management
Marketing
TYPICAL AUDIENCE:
Corporate
Association

LONGFELLOW,
LAYNE A., PH.D.   CSP
Box 4317
Prescott, AZ 86302
Telephone: 602-778-6629
Fax: 602-778-4289
ASSOCIATION
  MEMBERSHIP:
Natl. Speakers Assn.
PRINCIPAL TOPICS:
Ecology, Health
Management
Motivation
TYPICAL AUDIENCE:
Corporate
Association
SEE AD IN SECTION 8

LONTOS, PAM
Lontos Sales & Motivation Inc.
P.O. Box 2874
Laguna Hills, CA 92654
Telephone: 714-831-8861
Fax: 714-831-8645
ASSOCIATION
  MEMBERSHIP:
Natl. Speakers Assn.
PRINCIPAL TOPICS:
Management
Motivation
Sales
TYPICAL AUDIENCE:
Corporate
Association

LOSSY, RELLA
96 Highland Blvd.
Berkeley, CA 94708
Telephone: 510-527-2293
Fax: 510-528-7147
ASSOCIATION
  MEMBERSHIP:
Natl. Speakers Assn.
PRINCIPAL TOPICS:
Business & Industry
Communications
Human Relations
Sales
TYPICAL AUDIENCE:
Corporate

LOSYK, BOB
1350 Seagrape Cir.
Ft. Lauderdale, FL 33326
Telephone: 305-384-0344
REPRESENTED BY:
Washington Speakers Bureau,
  Atlanta Speakers
ASSOCIATION
  MEMBERSHIP:
Natl. Speakers Assn.

American Society of Training &
  Development
PRINCIPAL TOPICS:
Automotive
Business & Industry
Management
Motivation
TYPICAL AUDIENCE:
Corporate
Association

LOUDEN, STEPHEN H.
11454 Reeder Road
Dallas, TX 75229
Telephone: 214-241-6326
ASSOCIATION
  MEMBERSHIP:
Natl. Speakers Assn.
PRINCIPAL TOPICS:
Automotive
Management
Marketing
TYPICAL AUDIENCE:
Association

LOVELESS, KATHY
Loveless Enterprises, Inc.
267 E. North Sandrun Rd.
Salt Lake City, UT 84103
Telephone: 801-363-1807
Fax: 801-363-3191
ASSOCIATION
  MEMBERSHIP:
Natl. Speakers Assn.
PRINCIPAL TOPICS:
Business & Industry
Education
Government
Humor
Management
Marketing
Motivation
Social Trends
TYPICAL AUDIENCE:
Corporate
Association

LOVERDE, MARY
12262 E. Villanova Dr.
Aurora, Co 80014
Telephone: 303-752-4981
Fax: 303-270-4037
ASSOCIATION
  MEMBERSHIP:
Natl. Speakers Assn.
PRINCIPAL TOPICS:
Family
Human Relations
Medical
Motivation
Philosophy

LOWE, PETER
8405F Benjamin Rd.
Tampa, FL 33634
Telephone: 813-888-5554
Fax: 813-889-7654
ASSOCIATION
  MEMBERSHIP:
Natl. Speakers Assn.
Platform Speakers
PRINCIPAL TOPICS:
Business & Industry
Marketing
Motivation
Personal Finance
Psychology
Religion
Sales
TYPICAL AUDIENCE:
Corporate

LOWELL TRAINING &
CONSULTING
Lowell Training & Consulting
11333 Moorpark St., #431
Studio City, CA 91602
Telephone: 818-766-1356
ASSOCIATION
  MEMBERSHIP:
Natl. Speakers Assn.
PRINCIPAL TOPICS:
Motivation
Sales
Communications
TYPICAL AUDIENCE:
Corporate
Association

LUBOTSKY, TERRY
1825 South Ocean Drive, #508
Hallandale, FL 33009
Telephone: 305-458-3350
Fax: 305-458-6771
ASSOCIATION
  MEMBERSHIP:
Natl. Speakers Assn.
Toastmasters
PRINCIPAL TOPICS:
Business & Industry
Education
Human Relations
Senior Citizens
TYPICAL AUDIENCE:
Corporate

LUCHT, CHARLES
3 Brownlee St.
Due West, SC 29639
Telephone: 803-379-8448
MAILING ADDRESS:
P.O. Box 607
Due West, SC 29639

REPRESENTED BY:
Patton Consultants Services
ASSOCIATION
  MEMBERSHIP:
Natl. Speakers Assn.
Toastmasters
National Society of Fundraising
  Executives
American Prospect Research
  Assoc.
PRINCIPAL TOPICS:
Education
Motivation
TYPICAL AUDIENCE:
Corporate
Association

LUETHY, DR. GERRY
100 Donaldson Dr.
Sedona, AZ 86336
Telephone: 818-885-3120
MAILING ADDRESS:
CSUN
Dept. FES, 1811 Nordhoff St.
Northridge, CA 91330
ASSOCIATION
  MEMBERSHIP:
Natl. Speakers Assn.
PRINCIPAL TOPICS:
Education
Family
Human Relations
Psychology
Senior Citizens
Youth
TYPICAL AUDIENCE:
Corporate
Association
Fraternal

LYFORD, LOIS
P.O. Box 685
Kalispell, MT 59901
Telephone: 406-752-4298
ASSOCIATION
  MEMBERSHIP:
Toastmasters
ISN
PRINCIPAL TOPICS:
Human Relations
Motivation
Senior Citizens
TYPICAL AUDIENCE:
Association
Institutional

LYTLE, TOBI L.
555 Bryant, #129
Palo Alto, CA 94301
Telephone: 408-270-2742
Fax: 408-270-0875

ASSOCIATION
  MEMBERSHIP:
Natl. Speakers Assn.
Platform Spkeakers
Tastmasters
PRINCIPAL TOPICS:
Business & Industry
Education
Human Relations
Management
Motivation
Philosophy
Psychology
Sales
Social Trends
TYPICAL AUDIENCE:
Corporate
Association

MAAS, GARY
613 Main St., Box 140
Massena, la 50853
Telephone: 712-779-3744
Fax: 712-779-3366
REPRESENTED BY:
Ben Franklin
ASSOCIATION
  MEMBERSHIP:
Natl. Speakers Assn.
PRINCIPAL TOPICS:
Agriculture
Aviation
Human Relations
Amusements
Motivation
Sales
TYPICAL AUDIENCE:
Association

MACALUSO, SISTER MARY
  CHRISTELLE, RSM, PH.D
College of St. Mary
1901 S. 72 St.
Omaha, NE 68124-2377
Telephone: 402-399-2474
Fax: 402-399-2686
ASSOCIATION
  MEMBERSHIP:
Natl. Speakers Assn.
American Assoc. for
  Therapeutic Humor
PRINCIPAL TOPICS:
Health
Human Relations
Humor
Motivation
TYPICAL AUDIENCE:
Corporate
Association
Fraternal
College

MAILE, LISA
Image Institute, The
999 S. Orlando Ave.
Winter Park, FL 32789
Telephone: 407-628-5989
Fax: 407-628-0472
ASSOCIATION
  MEMBERSHIP:
Natl. Speakers Assn.
PRINCIPAL TOPICS:
Human Relations
Marketing
Motivation
TYPICAL AUDIENCE:
Corporate
Association
Fraternal

MAINELLA, MARK T.
30 Bay Road
Barrington, RI 02806
Telephone: 401-245-1847
ASSOCIATION
  MEMBERSHIP:
Natl. Speakers Assn.
New England Speakers
  Association
PRINCIPAL TOPICS:
Education
Motivation
Youth
TYPICAL AUDIENCE:
High Schools & Colleges

MALAINY, DON
581 W. 4th St.
Mansfield, OH 44903
Telephone: 419-526-1603
Fax: 419-526-5335
ASSOCIATION
  MEMBERSHIP:
Natl. Speakers Assn.
Ohio Speakers Forum
PRINCIPAL TOPICS:
Food/Diet
Health
Motivation
TYPICAL AUDIENCE:
Corporate
Association
Fraternal
Churches

MALLERY, SUZY
12308 Darlington Ave.
Los Angeles, CA 90049
Telephone: 310-826-9101
MAILING ADDRESS:
12021 Wilshire Blvd., #371
Los Angeles, CA 90025
Fax: 310-820-3539

ASSOCIATION
  MEMBERSHIP:
Natl. Speakers Assn.
Platform Speakers
Press Club
PRINCIPAL TOPICS:
Human Relations
Management
Marketing
Media
Social Trends
TYPICAL AUDIENCE:
Association

MANNERING,
  DENNIS E.   CSP
Options Unlimited Inc.
617 Sunrise Lane
Green Bay, WI 54301
Telephone: 414-339-0011
Fax: 414-339-0012
REPRESENTED BY:
Washington Speakers Bureau
The Speakers Bureau Inc.
Jordan International
ASSOCIATION
  MEMBERSHIP:
Natl. Speakers Assn.
PRINCIPAL TOPICS:
Human Relations
Motivation
Sales
TYPICAL AUDIENCE:
Corporate
Association

MANNERING, WENDY K.
Options Unlimited Inc.
617 Sunrise Lane
Green Bay, WI 54301
Telephone: 414-339-0011
Fax: 414-339-0012
ASSOCIATION
  MEMBERSHIP:
Natl. Speakers Assn.
PRINCIPAL TOPICS:
Human Relations
TYPICAL AUDIENCE:
General Public

MANNING, MARILYN,
  PH.D.   CSP
945 Mountain View Avenue
Mountain View, CA 94040
Telephone: 415-965-3663
Fax: 415-965-3668
REPRESENTED BY:
Keynote Speakers
Natl. Speakers Bureau

ASSOCIATION
  MEMBERSHIP:
Natl. Speakers Assn.
PRINCIPAL TOPICS:
Business & Industry
Education
Government
Health
Human Relations
Motivation
Psychology
TYPICAL AUDIENCE:
Corporate
Association

MARINO, MIKE JR. 'IN
  PERSON'
P.O. Box 9015
Metairie, LA 70055
Telephone: 504-833-4405
Fax: 504-833-4450
MAILING ADDRESS:
MARINO, MIKE JR.
604 Veterans Blvd.
Metairie, LA 70005
REPRESENTED BY:
Carolyn Sanders & Jerry Wynn
ASSOCIATION
  MEMBERSHIP:
Natl. Speakers Assn.
Toastmasters
American Society For Training
  And Development
PRINCIPAL TOPICS:
Business & Industry
Entertainment
Human Relations
Humor
Marketing
Motivation
Sales
Youth
TYPICAL AUDIENCE:
Association

MARKEL, GERALDINE
  PH.D.
3975 Waldenwood Dr.
Ann Arbor, MI 48105
Telephone: 313-761-5446
Fax: 313-761-6498
ASSOCIATION
  MEMBERSHIP:
Natl. Speakers Assn.
American Psychological Assoc.
PRINCIPAL TOPICS:
Business & Industry
Education
Management
Psychology

TYPICAL AUDIENCE:
Corporate
Institutional

MARTH, ROALD D.
Marth, Roald Learning Systems
9819 Valley View Rd.
Eden Prairie, MN 55344
Telephone: 800-333-5939
Fax: 612-942-3356
ASSOCIATION
 MEMBERSHIP:
Natl. Speakers Assn.
PRINCIPAL TOPICS:
Automotive
Business & Industry
Computer Technology
Management
Marketing
Motivation
Sales
TYPICAL AUDIENCE:
Corporate
Association

MASQUELIER,
 ROGER   CSP
Box 1040, 1890 Argentine,
 #202A
Georgetown, CO 80444
Telephone: 303-569-2679
Fax: 303-569-2679
MAILING ADDRESS:
2778 South
 Wheeling Way
Aurora, CO 80014
ASSOCIATION
 MEMBERSHIP:
Natl. Speakers Assn.
PRINCIPAL TOPICS:
Humor
Marketing
Motivation
TYPICAL AUDIENCE:
Corporate
Association

MASUMOTO, PAT
Yes Seminars International
P.O. Box 6262
Kahului Maui, HI 96732
Telephone: 808-572-5050
Fax: 808-572-4776
REPRESENTED BY:
Speakers Resource
Speakers Guild
Jordan Enterprises
Podium
ASSOCIATION
 MEMBERSHIP:
Natl. Speakers Assn.

PRINCIPAL TOPICS:
Family
Human Relations
Humor
Management
Marketing
Motivation
Sales
TYPICAL AUDIENCE:
Corporate
Association

MATSCHEK, CHERYL A.
Cheryl Matschek Co., The
P.O. Box 25406
Portland, OR 97225
Telephone: 503-297-1565
Fax: 503-292-2752
REPRESENTED BY:
Portland Speakers Bureau
N.W. Speakers Connection
ASSOCIATION
 MEMBERSHIP:
Natl. Speakers Assn.
Speakers U.S.A.
Oregon Speakers
PRINCIPAL TOPICS:
Human Relations
Management
Marketing
Medical
Motivation
Psychology
Sales
TYPICAL AUDIENCE:
Corporate
Association

MATTIMORE, BRYAN W.
94 Bouton St.
Norwalk, CT 06854
Telephone: 203-359-1801
MAILING ADDRESS:
Mattimore Group
One Landmark Square
Stamford, CT 06901
Fax: 203-359-8127
REPRESENTED BY:
Authors Unlimited
ASSOCIATION
 MEMBERSHIP:
Natl. Speakers Assn.
PRINCIPAL TOPICS:
Advertising
Business & Industry
Computer Technology
Education
Humor
Journalism
Management
Marketing

Psychology
Sales
TYPICAL AUDIENCE:
Corporate

MAYFIELD, TERRY L.
25772 Alta Dr.
Valencia, CA 91355
Telephone: 805-254-2024
ASSOCIATION
 MEMBERSHIP:
Natl. Speakers Assn.
Toastmasters
PRINCIPAL TOPICS:
Motivation
Sales
TYPICAL AUDIENCE:
Corporate
Association

MAYNARD, MICHAEL
Integrated Mgmt. Resources
 Inc.
119 Adams Drive
Stow, Ma 01775
Telephone: 508-897-7064
Fax: 508-897-6938
REPRESENTED BY:
Management Institute
ASSOCIATION
 MEMBERSHIP:
Natl. Speakers Assn.
PRINCIPAL TOPICS:
Business & Industry
Computer Technology
Electronics
Management
Marketing
Motivation
Sales
TYPICAL AUDIENCE:
Corporate
Association

MAYNE, MAVIS
P.O. Box 801
Newhall, CA 91322
Telephone: 805-259-6044
ASSOCIATION
 MEMBERSHIP:
Natl. Speakers Assn.
Toastmasters
PRINCIPAL TOPICS:
Family
Human Relations
Medical
Religion
TYPICAL AUDIENCE:
Corporate

Association
Institutional
General Public

MCARDLE, KEVIN J.
2816 Utica Ave.
St. Louis Park, MN 55416
Telephone: 612-922-3550
Fax: 612-922-3513
ASSOCIATION
 MEMBERSHIP:
Natl. Speakers Assn.
PRINCIPAL TOPICS:
Business & Industry
Management
Sales
TYPICAL AUDIENCE:
Corporate
Association

MCARTHUR, GILBERT B.
600 Cleveland St., Ste. 790
Clearwater, FL 34615
Telephone: 813-441-4906
Fax: 813-441-4908
ASSOCIATION
 MEMBERSHIP:
Natl. Speakers Assn.
American & Florida Institutes of
 Certified Public Accountants
PRINCIPAL TOPICS:
Business & Industry
Humor
Management
Motivation
Personal Finance
TYPICAL AUDIENCE:
Corporate
Association
General

MCCARTY, DR. HANOCH
P.O. Box 66
Galt, CA 95632
Telephone: 209-745-2212
Fax: 209-745-2252
REPRESENTED BY:
Preferred Speakers
Speaker's Guild
ASSOCIATION
 MEMBERSHIP:
Natl. Speakers Assn.
Platform Speakers
PRINCIPAL TOPICS:
Education
Motivation
Psychology
TYPICAL AUDIENCE:
Corporate

MCCLAIN, BRENDA H.
1579 Asheforde Drive
Marietta, GA 30068
Telephone: 404-518-7576
Fax: 404-518-7577
ASSOCIATION
 MEMBERSHIP:
Natl. Speakers Assn.
PRINCIPAL TOPICS:
Management
Marketing
TYPICAL AUDIENCE:
Corporate
Association

MCCLARY, CLEBE   CSP
P.O. Box 535, One Pelican
 Loop
Pawleys Island, SC 29585
Telephone: 803-237-2582
Fax: 803-237-1890
ASSOCIATION
 MEMBERSHIP:
Natl. Speakers Assn.
PRINCIPAL TOPICS:
Family
Motivation
Religion
TYPICAL AUDIENCE:
Corporate
Association

MCCORMICK, MS.
 PATRICIA
P.O. Box 250
Seal Beach, Ca 90740
Telephone: 310-493-3733
Fax: 310-431-8266
REPRESENTED BY:
Chicago Speakers Bureau
Jordan Enterprises
Walter's Speakers Bureau
ASSOCIATION
 MEMBERSHIP:
Natl. Speakers Assn.
PRINCIPAL TOPICS:
Education
Motivation
TYPICAL AUDIENCE:
Corporate
Association

MCCOY, DORIS L., PH.D.
McCoy Productions
5758 Beaumont Ave.
La Jolla, CA 92037
Telephone: 619-459-4971
Fax: 619-459-4971
REPRESENTED BY:
Jordans

ASSOCIATION
 MEMBERSHIP:
Natl. Speakers Assn.
PRINCIPAL TOPICS:
Business & Industry
Ecology
Education
Family
Health
Human Relations
Humor
Journalism
Management
Media
Motivation
Nature
Psychology
Social Trends
Travel
Video
TYPICAL AUDIENCE:
Corporate
Association

MCCRASY, C. WILEY
40 Serendipity Way
Atlanta, GA 30350
Telephone: 404-998-7287
Fax: 404-587-5554
ASSOCIATION
 MEMBERSHIP:
Natl. Speakers Assn.
PRINCIPAL TOPICS:
Senior Citizens
TYPICAL AUDIENCE:
Association
Fraternal

MCCUISTION,
 DENNIS   CSP
601 San Juan Ct.
Irving, TX 75062
Telephone: 214-717-0090
ASSOCIATION
 MEMBERSHIP:
Natl. Speakers Assn.
PRINCIPAL TOPICS:
Business & Industry
Media
TYPICAL AUDIENCE:
Association

MCDONALD, THOMAS,
 PH.D.
8950 Villa La Jolla Dr., #1171B
La Jolla, CA 92032
Telephone: 619-457-2542
REPRESENTED BY:
Washington Speakers Bureau
Capital Speakers Bureau

ASSOCIATION
 MEMBERSHIP:
Natl. Speakers Assn.
MPI
PRINCIPAL TOPICS:
Business & Industry
Management
Marketing
Motivation
Psychology
Sales
TYPICAL AUDIENCE:
Corporate
Association

MCGHEE MEDIA
 ASSOCIATES
McGhee Media Associates
18175 Rainbow
Lathrup Village, Mi 48076
Telephone: 313-569-7676
ASSOCIATION
 MEMBERSHIP:
Natl. Speakers Assn.
Toastmasters
PRINCIPAL TOPICS:
Media
TYPICAL AUDIENCE:
Association
Institutional

MCGHEE, PAUL E., PH.D.
Laughter Remedy, The
380 Claremont Ave., #8
Montclair, NJ 07042
Telephone: 201-783-8383
Fax: 201-783-8383
ASSOCIATION
 MEMBERSHIP:
Natl. Speakers Assn.
PRINCIPAL TOPICS:
Health
Humor
Psychology
TYPICAL AUDIENCE:
Corporate
Association

MCILVAIN, TED L.
150 Westpark Way, #303
Euless, TX 76040
Telephone: 817-540-6591
Fax: 817-545-8278
ASSOCIATION
 MEMBERSHIP:
Natl. Speakers Assn.
North Texas Speakers
 Association
PRINCIPAL TOPICS:
Education
Family

Human Relations
Management
Motivation
Youth
TYPICAL AUDIENCE:
Corporate
Association
Parenting Organizations

MCKAIN, SCOTT   CSP
7705 Eagle Valley Pass
Indianapolis, IN 46214
Telephone: 317-297-5844
Fax: 317-634-1791
REPRESENTED BY:
Professional Speakers Network
North American Speakers
 Bureau
McKinney Associates
The Speakers Bureau
ASSOCIATION
 MEMBERSHIP:
Natl. Speakers Assn.
PRINCIPAL TOPICS:
Agriculture
Business & Industry
Entertainment
Human Relations
Management
Marketing
Motivation
Philosophy
TYPICAL AUDIENCE:
Corporate
Association

MCKENZIE, SAMUEL
4015 Lorraine St.
Baton Rouge, La 70805
Telephone: 504-357-6230
ASSOCIATION
 MEMBERSHIP:
Natl. Speakers Assn.
Toastmasters
PRINCIPAL TOPICS:
Communications
Motivation
TYPICAL AUDIENCE:
Corporate
Fraternal

MCKINLEY, MICHAEL P.
 (CPAE)   CSP
Alive! Alive! Associates
1731 Westgate Rd.
Eau Claire, WI 54703
Telephone: 800-225-4769
Fax: 715-832-9082
ASSOCIATION
 MEMBERSHIP:
Natl. Speakers Assn.

PRINCIPAL TOPICS:
Automotive
Business & Industry
Human Relations
Humor
Management
Motivation
TYPICAL AUDIENCE:
Corporate
Association

MCKINNEY, ANNE M., J.D.
964 Bluff View Dr.
Knoxville, TN 37919
Telephone: 615-525-8700
MAILING ADDRESS:
505 Market St., Ste. 700
Knoxville, TN 37902
Fax: 615-521-4189
ASSOCIATION
  MEMBERSHIP:
Natl. Speakers Assn.
PRINCIPAL TOPICS:
Motivation
Personal Finance
Senior Citizens
TYPICAL AUDIENCE:
Association

MCLAUGHLIN, KENNETH
8529 Cherrylawn
Sterling Height, MI 48313
Telephone: 313-739-5400
ASSOCIATION
  MEMBERSHIP:
Natl. Speakers Assn.
Toastmasters
PRINCIPAL TOPICS:
Business & Industry
Education
TYPICAL AUDIENCE:
Corporate
Fraternal

MCMAHON, MICHAEL
333 Haight Ave.
Alameda, CA 94501
Telephone: 510-523-2263
ASSOCIATION
  MEMBERSHIP:
Natl. Speakers Assn.
PRINCIPAL TOPICS:
Computer Technology
Personal Finance
TYPICAL AUDIENCE:
Association

MCNAIR, J. FRANK
McNair Speaks
2025 Sussex Lane
Winston-Salem, NC 27104

Telephone: 919-724-2994
Fax: 919-725-2994
ASSOCIATION
  MEMBERSHIP:
Natl. Speakers Assn.
PRINCIPAL TOPICS:
Advertising
Business & Industry
Education
Human Relations
Management
Marketing
Motivation
Psychology
Religion
Sales
Youth
TYPICAL AUDIENCE:
Corporate
Association
Fraternal

MCNEIL, MICHAEL R.
  (BCSW)
P.O. Box 1604, 9011 Patricia
  St.
Chalmette, LA 70044
Telephone: 504-277-6689
Fax: 504-277-7359
ASSOCIATION
  MEMBERSHIP:
Natl. Speakers Assn.
PRINCIPAL TOPICS:
Education
Family
Human Relations
Psychology
TYPICAL AUDIENCE:
Association
Fraternal

MEADES, KEN
570 Scott Rd.
Homer, NY 13077
Telephone: 607-753-6754
Fax: 607-753-6757
ASSOCIATION
  MEMBERSHIP:
Natl. Speakers Assn.
Toastmasters
PRINCIPAL TOPICS:
Humor
Motivation
Sales
TYPICAL AUDIENCE:
Corporate
Fraternal

MEEKS, DAVID &
  ASSOCIATES
Meeks, David & Associates
1210 Front St.
Valrico, FL 33594
Telephone: 813-681-9441
ASSOCIATION
  MEMBERSHIP:
Natl. Speakers Assn.
Toastmasters
PRINCIPAL TOPICS:
Family
Human Relations
Motivation
TYPICAL AUDIENCE:
Corporate
Association

MEISENHEIMER, JIM
824 Paddock Ln.
Libertyville, IL 60048
Telephone: 708-680-7880
Fax: 708-680-7881
ASSOCIATION
  MEMBERSHIP:
Natl. Speakers Assn.
Prof. Speakers of Il.
PRINCIPAL TOPICS:
Business & Industry
Motivation
Sales
TYPICAL AUDIENCE:
Corporate

MENTA, SISTER
  ANGELICA M.
6414 Ludington Dr.
Houston, TX 77035
Telephone: 713-729-6971
ASSOCIATION
  MEMBERSHIP:
Natl. Speakers Assn.
Greater Speakers Association
  of Houston
PRINCIPAL TOPICS:
Entertainment
Human Relations
Humor
Motivation
Psychology
Religion
TYPICAL AUDIENCE:
Association

MERCER, MICHAEL W.,
  PH.D.
Mercer Group Inc., The
3064 Greenwood Ave.
Highland Park, IL 60035
Telephone: 708-432-9210

ASSOCIATION
  MEMBERSHIP:
Natl. Speakers Assn.
American Psychological Assoc.
PRINCIPAL TOPICS:
Human Relations
Management
Motivation
Psychology
Sales
TYPICAL AUDIENCE:
Corporate
Association

MERCHANT, RONALD
East 24 Salmon
Spokane, WA 99218
Telephone: 509-533-3692
Fax: 509-533-4162
MAILING ADDRESS:
SFCC
3410 W. Ft. Geo. Washington
  Dr.
Spokane, WA 99204
ASSOCIATION
  MEMBERSHIP:
Natl. Speakers Assn.
Toastmasters
Inland Northwest Speakers
  Network
PRINCIPAL TOPICS:
Business & Industry
Education
Family
Motivation
World Affairs
TYPICAL AUDIENCE:
Association

MERRITT, CONNIE
P.O. Box 9075
Laguna Beach, Ca 92677
Telephone: 800-468-8263
Fax: 714-494-3009
REPRESENTED BY:
Podium Speaker Source
Orange County Speakers
  Bureau
Speak, Inc.
Natl. Speakers Bureau
ASSOCIATION
  MEMBERSHIP:
Natl. Speakers Assn.
PRINCIPAL TOPICS:
Human Relations
Management
Medical
Motivation
Communications

TYPICAL AUDIENCE:
Corporate
Association

METCALF, ED, DR.
3903 LOCH HIGHLAND PASS
ROSWELL, GA 30075
Telephone: 404-992-9468
Fax: 404-992-4306
REPRESENTED BY:
SpeakerConnectUSA
Jordan International
American Speakers
ASSOCIATION
MEMBERSHIP:
Natl. Speakers Assn.
Georgia Speakers
PRINCIPAL TOPICS:
Communications
Computer Technology
Management
Motivation
TYPICAL AUDIENCE:
Corporate
Association
SEE AD IN SECTION 8

METZGER, RICK L.
33 N. Melody Lane
Waterville, OH 43566
Telephone: 419-878-0081
REPRESENTED BY:
Speakers Unlimited
ASSOCIATION
MEMBERSHIP:
Natl. Speakers Assn.
PRINCIPAL TOPICS:
Agriculture
Education
Motivation
TYPICAL AUDIENCE:
Association
Youth

MEYER, BILL
405-114th Ave., S.E., #323
Bellevue, Wa 98004
Telephone: 206-451-8894
Fax: 206-453-5229
REPRESENTED BY:
Meeting Phenoms
Canfield & Associates
ASSOCIATION
MEMBERSHIP:
Natl. Speakers Assn.
PRINCIPAL TOPICS:
Health
Management
Marketing
Motivation
Sales

TYPICAL AUDIENCE:
Corporate
Association

MEYERS, PAMELA, PH.D.
Absolute Images
P.O. Box 724752
Atlanta, GA a31139
Telephone: 404-977-4275
ASSOCIATION
MEMBERSHIP:
Natl. Speakers Assn.
PRINCIPAL TOPICS:
Education
Fashion
Food/Diet
Health
TYPICAL AUDIENCE:
Corporate

MICALE, FRANCES A.
4136 Admiral Dr.
Chamblee, GA 30341
Telephone: 404-457-4507
REPRESENTED BY:
Jordan International
ASSOCIATION
MEMBERSHIP:
Natl. Speakers Assn.
PRINCIPAL TOPICS:
Management
Motivation
Sales
TYPICAL AUDIENCE:
Corporate
Association

MICHAEL, ANGIE
Image Resource Group Inc.
2849 Lawrence Dr.
Falls Church, VA 22042
Telephone: 703-560-3950
ASSOCIATION
MEMBERSHIP:
Natl. Speakers Assn.
AICI
PRINCIPAL TOPICS:
Human Relations
Marketing
TYPICAL AUDIENCE:
Corporate
Association

MILIOS, RITA
7150 Cloister Rd.
Toledo, Oh 43617
Telephone: 419-841-4657
REPRESENTED BY:
Creative Learning Consultants
(Dayton, Oh)
Power Network (Dayton, Oh)

ASSOCIATION
MEMBERSHIP:
Natl. Speakers Assn.
Toastmasters
Society Of Childrens Book
Writers & Illustrators
ASTD
Detroit Women Writers
PRINCIPAL TOPICS:
Education
Health
Philosophy
Psychology
Youth
Communications
TYPICAL AUDIENCE:
Association
Schools

MILLER, ANNE
Chiron Associates Inc.
P.O. Box 624
New York City, NY 10163
Telephone: 212-876-1875
Fax: 212-722-8383
PRINCIPAL TOPICS:
Advertising
Sales
TYPICAL AUDIENCE:
Corporate

MILLER, ANNE
PROMOTIONS, INC.
Miller, Anne Promotions, Inc.
Rt. 1, Box 218
Chassell, MI 49916
Telephone: 800-235-4333
Fax: 906-482-4388
ASSOCIATION
MEMBERSHIP:
Natl. Speakers Assn.
International Group Of
Agencies & Bureaus (IGAB)
MPI
ASAE
PRINCIPAL TOPICS:
Business & Industry
Education
Entertainment
Food/Diet
Health
Human Relations
Humor
Human Relations
Management
Marketing
Motivation
Personal Finance
Physical Fitness
Psychology
Sales

Youth
TYPICAL AUDIENCE:
Corporate
Association
Fraternal

MILLER, JOHNNY   CSP
P.O. Box 84
Kent, OH 44240
Telephone: 216-678-9506
Fax: 216-678-9506
REPRESENTED BY:
Speakers Unlimited
North American Seminars
Support Processes Corp.
Action Entertainment
DMB Bureau
Associated Speakers
North American Speakers
ASSOCIATION
MEMBERSHIP:
Natl. Speakers Assn.
PRINCIPAL TOPICS:
Education
Human Relations
Humor
Management
Motivation
Sales
TYPICAL AUDIENCE:
Corporate

MILLER, MADELYN
P.O. BOX 743242
DALLAS, TX 75374-3242
Telephone: 214-341-0033
ASSOCIATION
MEMBERSHIP:
Natl. Speakers Assn.
PRINCIPAL TOPICS:
Advertising
Food/Diet
Hobbies
Humor
Journalism
Marketing
Media
Motivation
Physical Fitness
Sales
Travel
TYPICAL AUDIENCE:
Corporate
Association
Fraternal
SEE AD IN SECTION 8

MILLER, REV. MARILYN K.
30724 El Pequeno Dr.
Malibu, CA 90265
Telephone: 805-656-4199

MAILING ADDRESS:
2646 Palma Dr., Bldg. 250
Ventura, CA 90265
ASSOCIATION
 MEMBERSHIP:
Natl. Speakers Assn.
PRINCIPAL TOPICS:
Family
Health
Management
Motivation
Personal Finance
Religion
Youth
TYPICAL AUDIENCE:
Corporate
Association

MILLER, VALERIE J. S.
P.O. Box 12068
Greenville, SC 29612
Telephone: 803-879-4414
Fax: 803-879-8883
ASSOCIATION
 MEMBERSHIP:
Natl. Speakers Assn.
PRINCIPAL TOPICS:
Business & Industry
Management
Marketing
Motivation
TYPICAL AUDIENCE:
Corporate
Association

MILNER, ANITA CHEEK
910 Milane Lane
Escondido, CA 92026
Telephone: 619-480-9130
Fax: 619-739-0911
REPRESENTED BY:
Speak, Inc.
Walters International
ASSOCIATION
 MEMBERSHIP:
Natl. Speakers Assn.
Toastmasters
PRINCIPAL TOPICS:
Humor
TYPICAL AUDIENCE:
Association

MILTEER, LEE
P.O. BOX 5653
VIRGINIA BEACH, VA 23455
Telephone: 804-460-1818
Fax: 804-460-6332
ASSOCIATION
 MEMBERSHIP:
Natl. Speakers Assn.

PRINCIPAL TOPICS:
Management
Motivation
Sales
TYPICAL AUDIENCE:
Corporate
Association
SEE AD IN SECTION 8

MINER, DAVID LEE
Greater Challenges
710 Normal Road
DeKalb, IL 60115
Telephone: 815-758-6335
ASSOCIATION
 MEMBERSHIP:
Natl. Speakers Assn.
PRINCIPAL TOPICS:
Communications
Human Relations
Motivation
Humor
TYPICAL AUDIENCE:
Corporate
Association
Fraternal

MINER-WARGO, NANETTE
5 Roberge Rd.
Bristol, CT 06010
Telephone: 203-589-0454
Fax: 203-589-0454
ASSOCIATION
 MEMBERSHIP:
Natl. Speakers Assn.
American Society of Training &
 Development
PRINCIPAL TOPICS:
Business & Industry
Human Relations
TYPICAL AUDIENCE:
Corporate
Association

MINNICK, DALEH   CSP
1222 10th St., #111-S
Woodward, OK 73801
Telephone: 405-254-3822
Fax: 405-254-3840
REPRESENTED BY:
North American Speakers
 Bureau
Convention Connections
Access
ASSOCIATION
 MEMBERSHIP:
Natl. Speakers Assn.
PRINCIPAL TOPICS:
Agriculture
Humor
Motivation

Sales
TYPICAL AUDIENCE:
Corporate
Association

MINNINGER, JOAN
191 Edgewood Ave.
San Francisco, CA 94117
Telephone: 415-665-4932
Fax: 415-665-9410
ASSOCIATION
 MEMBERSHIP:
Natl. Speakers Assn.
Ca. Assn. of Marriage & Family
 Counselors
PRINCIPAL TOPICS:
Business & Industry
Family
Human Relations
Psychology
TYPICAL AUDIENCE:
Corporate
Association
Fraternal

MITCHELL, HERBERT E.
1308 Mariners Dr.
Newport Beach, CA 92660
Telephone: 714-631-4885
Fax: 714-631-4010
MAILING ADDRESS:
234 E. 17th St., #202
Costa Mesa, CA 92627
PRINCIPAL TOPICS:
Management
Marketing
Sales
TYPICAL AUDIENCE:
Corporate
Association

MITCHELL, W.
12014 West 54th Dr., #100
Arvada, CO 80002
Telephone: 303-425-1800
Fax: 303-425-9069
ASSOCIATION
 MEMBERSHIP:
Natl. Speakers Assn.
PRINCIPAL TOPICS:
Motivation
TYPICAL AUDIENCE:
Corporate
Association
Fraternal

MOHNEY, DR. NELL W.
1004 Northbridge Lane
Chattonooga, TN 37405
Telephone: 615-266-1663
Fax: 615-266-1663

ASSOCIATION
 MEMBERSHIP:
Natl. Speakers Assn.
Toastmasters
PRINCIPAL TOPICS:
Human Relations
Motivation
Religion
Senior Citizens
TYPICAL AUDIENCE:
Association
Fraternal
Women's Groups
Church Groups

MONJI, MICHAEL A.
Monji, Michael & Associates
P.O. Box 42522
Bakersfield, CA 93384
Telephone: 805-665-1310
MAILING ADDRESS:
Monji, Michael & Associates
3838 Millay Way
Bakersfield, CA 93311
Telephone: 805-836-1480
PRINCIPAL TOPICS:
Home & Garden
Personal Finance
TYPICAL AUDIENCE:
Association

MONK, ART
19782 Solana Drive
Saratoga, Ca 95070
Telephone: 408-252-1600
Fax: 408-252-1601
ASSOCIATION
 MEMBERSHIP:
Natl. Speakers Assn.
PRINCIPAL TOPICS:
Computer Technology
Management
Marketing
Sales
TYPICAL AUDIENCE:
Corporate
Association

MONTEFUSCO, JR.,
 MICHAEL T.
Executive Career Dynamics,
 Inc.
19 Tradewinds Circle
Tequesta, Fl 33469
Telephone: 407-747-1331
Fax: 407-747-7336
ASSOCIATION
 MEMBERSHIP:
Natl. Speakers Assn.
PRINCIPAL TOPICS:
Business & Industry

Management
TYPICAL AUDIENCE:
Corporate
Association

MOODY, ROY E.
Moody, Roy & Associates
3529 Avenida Charada N.W.
Albuquerque, NM 87107
Telephone: 505-344-8930
ASSOCIATION
  MEMBERSHIP:
Natl. Speakers Assn.
PRINCIPAL TOPICS:
Humor
Management
Motivation
TYPICAL AUDIENCE:
Association

MOORE, JAMES F.
29 Orangegrove
Irvine, CA 92714
Telephone: 714-863-6482
Fax: 714-863-6458
MAILING ADDRESS:
2450 White Road
Irvine, CA 92714
ASSOCIATION
  MEMBERSHIP:
Natl. Speakers Assn.
PRINCIPAL TOPICS:
Business & Industry
Management
Motivation
TYPICAL AUDIENCE:
Corporate
Association

MOORE, LAURIE
Moore, Laurie & Associates
16137 Shadybank
Dallas, TX 75248
Telephone: 214-250-0633
Fax: 214-931-8545
MAILING ADDRESS:
Moore, Laurie & Associates
P.O. Box 796278
Dallas, TX 75379
ASSOCIATION
  MEMBERSHIP:
Natl. Speakers Assn.
PRINCIPAL TOPICS:
Business & Industry
Management
Marketing
Sales
TYPICAL AUDIENCE:
Corporate
Association

MORAN, KEVIN M.
National Speakers Group
106 Strawtown Rd.
New City, NY 10956
Telephone: 718-253-7886
ASSOCIATION
  MEMBERSHIP:
Natl. Speakers Assn.
Platform Speakers
American Humor
PRINCIPAL TOPICS:
Business & Industry
Education
Health
Human Relations
Humor
Management
Motivation
TYPICAL AUDIENCE:
Corporate
Institutional

MOREL, LIN M.
RR1, Box 177
Gillett, PA 16925
Telephone: 717-596-4598
Fax: 717-596-4808
ASSOCIATION
  MEMBERSHIP:
Natl. Speakers Assn.
PRINCIPAL TOPICS:
Health
Management
Motivation
Social Trends
TYPICAL AUDIENCE:
Corporate
Association

MOREO, JUDI
P.O. Box 93118-241
Las Vegas, NV 89193-3118
REPRESENTED BY:
Standing Ovations
Five Star
Walters International
ASSOCIATION
  MEMBERSHIP:
Natl. Speakers Assn.
Toastmasters
PRINCIPAL TOPICS:
Motivation
Sales
TYPICAL AUDIENCE:
Corporate
Association

MORGAN, DONALD R.
National Exchange Club
6862 Cloister Rd.
Toledo, OH 43617

Telephone: 419-535-3232
MAILING ADDRESS:
National Exchange Club
3050 Central Ave.
Toledo, OH 43606
Fax: 419-535-1989
ASSOCIATION
  MEMBERSHIP:
Natl. Speakers Assn.
Toastmasters
PRINCIPAL TOPICS:
Management
Motivation
TYPICAL AUDIENCE:
Association

**MORGAN,
  REBECCA   CSP**
465 Margaret Street
San Jose, CA 95112
Telephone: 408-998-7977
Fax: 408-998-7978
REPRESENTED BY:
North American Speakers
  Bureau
ASSOCIATION
  MEMBERSHIP:
Natl. Speakers Assn.
American Society For Training
  & Development
PRINCIPAL TOPICS:
Business & Industry
Management
Sales
TYPICAL AUDIENCE:
Corporate
Association

MORRIS, WILLIAM C.
P.O. Box 374
Buck Hill Falls, PA 18323
Telephone: 717-595-3701
Fax: 717-595-9426
ASSOCIATION
  MEMBERSHIP:
Natl. Speakers Assn.
Platform Speakers
PRINCIPAL TOPICS:
Food/Diet
Health
Motivation
Physical Fitness
Youth
TYPICAL AUDIENCE:
Corporate
Association

**MORRISEY,
  GEORGE L.   CSP**
300 S. Sykes Creek Pkwy.,
  #601C
Merritt Island, FL 32952
Telephone: 800-535-8202
Fax: 407-452-2129
MAILING ADDRESS:
MORRISEY, GEORGE L.,
P.O. Box 541296
Merritt Island, FL 32954
REPRESENTED BY:
French & Associates
The Podium
ASSOCIATION
  MEMBERSHIP:
Natl. Speakers Assn.
American Society of Training &
  Development

PRINCIPAL TOPICS:
Business & Industry
Management
TYPICAL AUDIENCE:
Corporate
Association

MORRISON, ANN M.
P.O. Box 1110
Del Mar, Ca 92014
Telephone: 619-792-5922
Fax: 619-792-9874
ASSOCIATION
  MEMBERSHIP:
Natl. Speakers Assn.
PRINCIPAL TOPICS:
Business & Industry
Education
Government
Human Relations
Management
Motivation
Psychology
Social Trends
TYPICAL AUDIENCE:
Corporate
Association

MORRISON, JAMES N.
2644 Shade Tree
Greenbay, WI 54313
Telephone: 414-434-4540
MAILING ADDRESS:
Morrison, James N. &
  Associates
P.O. Box 10801
Greenbay, WI 54307
REPRESENTED BY:
Options Unlimited Inc.
Associated Speakers

ASSOCIATION
  MEMBERSHIP:
Natl. Speakers Assn.
PRINCIPAL TOPICS:
Business & Industry
Family
Human Relations
Management
Media
TYPICAL AUDIENCE:
Corporate
Association
Fraternal

MORROW, PEGGY &
  ASSOCIATES
Morrow, Peggy & Associates
15810 Brookforest Dr.
Houston, Tx 77059
Telephone: 800-375-1982
Fax: 713-280-8190
REPRESENTED BY:
Five Star Speakers
ASSOCIATION
  MEMBERSHIP:
Natl. Speakers Assn.
PRINCIPAL TOPICS:
Business & Industry
Fashion
Human Relations
Management
TYPICAL AUDIENCE:
Corporate
Association

MORSCHER, BETSY,
  PH.D.
P.O. Box 1713
Boulder, CO 80306
Telephone: 303-444-5585
Fax: 303-499-8070
ASSOCIATION
  MEMBERSHIP:
Natl. Speakers Assn.
PRINCIPAL TOPICS:
Animals
Education
Health
Media
Physical Fitness
TYPICAL AUDIENCE:
Corporate
Association
Fraternal

MORTELL, ART
Systematic Achievement Corp.
P.O. Box 721, 31220 Anacapa
  View Dr.
Malibu, CA 90265
Telephone: 310-457-2551

Fax: 310-457-2652
ASSOCIATION
  MEMBERSHIP:
Natl. Speakers Assn.
PRINCIPAL TOPICS:
Business & Industry
Computer Technology
Education
Entertainment
Human Relations
Humor
Management
Marketing
Motivation
Philosophy
Sales
Social Trends
TYPICAL AUDIENCE:
Corporate
Association

MOSER, MILTON J.
Moser, Milton J.
  Associates, Inc.
P.O. Box 735
Bensalem, Pa 19020
Telephone: 215-638-9830
Fax: 215-638-7169
ASSOCIATION
  MEMBERSHIP:
Natl. Speakers Assn.
Platform Speakers
Toastmasters
PRINCIPAL TOPICS:
Business & Industry
Management
TYPICAL AUDIENCE:
Corporate

MOWBRAY, CATHERINE
Mobray Enterprises
Box 10485
Newport Beach, Ca 92658
Telephone: 714-854-7891
REPRESENTED BY:
Santa Barbara Speakers
  Bureau
ASSOCIATION
  MEMBERSHIP:
Natl. Speakers Assn.
PRINCIPAL TOPICS:
Human Relations
Travel
Communications
TYPICAL AUDIENCE:
Corporate
Association

MULLER, DAVE
6604 Hitching Post Lane
Cincinnati, OH 45230

Telephone: 513-232-0820
Fax: 513-232-7547
ASSOCIATION
  MEMBERSHIP:
Natl. Speakers Assn.
PRINCIPAL TOPICS:
Communications
TYPICAL AUDIENCE:
Corporate
Association

MULVANEY, MAUREEN
MGM & Associates
16026 S. 36th St.
Phoenix, AZ 85044
Telephone: 602-759-6251
Fax: 602-759-6257
ASSOCIATION
  MEMBERSHIP:
Natl. Speakers Assn.
PRINCIPAL TOPICS:
Human Relations
Motivation
TYPICAL AUDIENCE:
Corporate
Association

MUNGAVAN, THOMAS E.
Change Masters Inc.
9800 Bren Road E., #400
Minneapolis, Mn 55343
Telephone: 800-change-1
Fax: 612-930-2323
ASSOCIATION
  MEMBERSHIP:
Natl. Speakers Assn.
PRINCIPAL TOPICS:
Human Relations
Management
Motivation
TYPICAL AUDIENCE:
Corporate

MURDOCK, KEN
Ideas For Action
3207 Sand Springs Ct.
Arlington, TX 76017
Telephone: 214-601-6112
ASSOCIATION
  MEMBERSHIP:
Natl. Speakers Assn.
PRINCIPAL TOPICS:
Humor
Motivation
Sales
TYPICAL AUDIENCE:
Corporate
Association

MURRAY, JOAN
Murray Enterprises
102 N. George Mason Dr.
Arlington, VA 22203
Telephone: 703-528-4564
Fax: 703-528-4564
ASSOCIATION
  MEMBERSHIP:
Natl. Speakers Assn.
PRINCIPAL TOPICS:
Food/Diet
Science
TYPICAL AUDIENCE:
Corporate
Association

MURRAY, MARCELLA
Mark IV Bldg., 7491 NW 4th St.
Ft. Lauderdale, FL 33317
Telephone: 305-791-9409
Fax: 305-791-9533
ASSOCIATION
  MEMBERSHIP:
Natl. Speakers Assn.
Leadership America
PRINCIPAL TOPICS:
Management
Motivation
TYPICAL AUDIENCE:
Corporate
Association
Institutional

MYERS, GERRY
Myers Group, The
6330 LBJ Freeway, #136
Dallas, TX 75240
Telephone: 214-991-4622
Fax: 214-239-1439
ASSOCIATION
  MEMBERSHIP:
Natl. Speakers Assn.
NTSA
PRINCIPAL TOPICS:
Advertising
Automotive
Marketing
TYPICAL AUDIENCE:
Corporate
Association

MYERS, JANET L.
Dearborn Business Group
2878 Bridgeway Dr.
West Lafayette, IN 47906-5251
Telephone: 317-583-2422
Fax: 317-583-2422
ASSOCIATION
  MEMBERSHIP:
Natl. Speakers Assn.

PRINCIPAL TOPICS:
Business & Industry
Management
Marketing
Motivation
Sales
TYPICAL AUDIENCE:
Corporate
Association

MYERS, JEFFRY W.
1218 3rd Ave., #510
Seattle, WA 98101
Telephone: 800-775-7961
ASSOCIATION
   MEMBERSHIP:
Natl. Speakers Assn.
PRINCIPAL TOPICS:
Education
Health
Motivation
Philosophy
Physical Fitness
TYPICAL AUDIENCE:
Corporate
Association
Fraternal

MYRICK, SUE
505 N. Poplar St.
Charlotte, NC 28202
Telephone: 704-334-6871
Fax: 704-333-9571
REPRESENTED BY:
21st Century Speakers, NY
ASSOCIATION
   MEMBERSHIP:
Natl. Speakers Assn.
PRINCIPAL TOPICS:
Motivation
TYPICAL AUDIENCE:
Association

NABERS, MARY
   SCOTT   CSP
P.O. Box 12967
Austin, Tx 78711
Telephone: 512-463-7144
Fax: 512-472-2261
ASSOCIATION
   MEMBERSHIP:
Natl. Speakers Assn.
PRINCIPAL TOPICS:
Business & Industry
Government
Management
Motivation
Social Trends
World Affairs

TYPICAL AUDIENCE:
Corporate
Association

NASH, LINDA J.
7526 Buckingham,
   Ste. #1 West
St. Louis, MO 63105
Telephone: 314-725-9782
Fax: 314-725-9782
ASSOCIATION
   MEMBERSHIP:
Natl. Speakers Assn.
PRINCIPAL TOPICS:
Management
Marketing
Motivation
Sales
TYPICAL AUDIENCE:
Corporate
Association

NATIONAL TRAUMA
   SERVICES
National Trauma Services
3554 Front Street
San Diego, CA 92103
Telephone: 800-398-2811
Fax: 619-296-2811
ASSOCIATION
   MEMBERSHIP:
Natl. Speakers Assn.
PRINCIPAL TOPICS:
Human Relations
Psychology
TYPICAL AUDIENCE:
Corporate

NELSON, DAVID N., P.T.
1705 17th Ave.
Vero Beach, FL 32960
Telephone: 407-562-6877
Fax: 407-562-3153
ASSOCIATION
   MEMBERSHIP:
Natl. Speakers Assn.
PRINCIPAL TOPICS:
Health
Medical
TYPICAL AUDIENCE:
Association

NELSON, SANDRA
3410 24th St.
Sacramento, Ca 95818
ASSOCIATION
   MEMBERSHIP:
Natl. Speakers Assn.
PRINCIPAL TOPICS:
Business & Industry
Family

Human Relations
Management
Motivation
TYPICAL AUDIENCE:
Corporate
Association

NELSON, WILLIE
UR 'Somebody Seminars, Inc.
P.O. Box 24228, 9130 North
   Joyce Ave.
Milwaukee, Wi 53224
Telephone: 414-354-0552
Fax: 414-354-0553
REPRESENTED BY:
Associated Speakers
U-R 'Somebody' Seminars,
   Inc.
ASSOCIATION
   MEMBERSHIP:
Natl. Speakers Assn.
Platform Speakers
Speakers USA & Wisconsin
   Pro Speakers
PRINCIPAL TOPICS:
Human Relations
Motivation
Psychology
TYPICAL AUDIENCE:
Corporate
Association
Governmental

NEWMAN, RICHARD D.
424 Innisfail Drive
Webster Groves, Mo 63119
Telephone: 314-961-7991
ASSOCIATION
   MEMBERSHIP:
Natl. Speakers Assn.
PRINCIPAL TOPICS:
Health
Motivation
Sales
Youth
TYPICAL AUDIENCE:
Corporate
Association

NEWSOME, PAULA R.
Apogee Vision
1812 Lyndhurst Ave.
Charlotte, NC 28203
Telephone: 704-375-3935
Fax: 704-333-7238
ASSOCIATION
   MEMBERSHIP:
Natl. Speakers Assn.
PRINCIPAL TOPICS:
Food/Diet
Health

Medical
Motivation
TYPICAL AUDIENCE:
Association
Fraternal

NICHOLSON, SHERYL
1404 Corner Oaks Drive
Brandon, Fl 33510
Telephone: 813-684-3076
Fax: 813-684-3076
ASSOCIATION
   MEMBERSHIP:
Natl. Speakers Assn.
PRINCIPAL TOPICS:
Family
Human Relations
Management
Medical
Motivation
Sales
TYPICAL AUDIENCE:
Corporate
Association

NIELSEN, RICK J.   CSP
Blueprint For Life Inc.
4016 Patricia Dr.
Des Moines, IA 50322
Telephone: 515-276-7112
Fax: 515-276-7112
ASSOCIATION
   MEMBERSHIP:
Natl. Speakers Assn.
PRINCIPAL TOPICS:
Education
Entertainment
Human Relations
Humor
Motivation
Religion
Youth
TYPICAL AUDIENCE:
Corporate
Association
Institutions

NIENSTEDT, JOHN F.
Performance Enhancement
   Programs
18609 N. 33rd Dr.
Phoenix, AZ 85027
Telephone: 602-581-0512
Fax: 602-978-9095
REPRESENTED BY:
Gold Stars Speakers
ASSOCIATION
   MEMBERSHIP:
Natl. Speakers Assn.
PRINCIPAL TOPICS:
Food/Diet

Government
Human Relations
Military
Motivation
Sales
TYPICAL AUDIENCE:
Corporate
Association
Government

NIKAM, S. G. 'NIK', MD
  (FACC) (FACP)
77 Greenward Lane
Sugar Land, TX 77479
Telephone: 713-796-0756
Fax: 713-796-8830
ASSOCIATION
  MEMBERSHIP:
Natl. Speakers Assn.
Toastmasters
PRINCIPAL TOPICS:
Entertainment
Health
Humor
TYPICAL AUDIENCE:
Corporate
Association

NOLAN, THOMAS L. JR.
P.O. Box 8112
Rockford, IL 61126
Telephone: 815-395-8343
REPRESENTED BY:
Associated Speaker
Milwaukee
Ann Miller Productions
ASSOCIATION
  MEMBERSHIP:
American Society On Aging
PRINCIPAL TOPICS:
Senior Citizens
TYPICAL AUDIENCE:
Corporate
Association
Fraternal
Bank

NORTON,
  GEORGE M.   CSP
240 Firethorn Trail
Dakota Dunes, SD 57049
Telephone: 605-232-4300
MAILING ADDRESS:
Norton, George M. Associates
P.O. Box 1040
North Sioux City, SD 57049
Fax: 605-232-4300
ASSOCIATION
  MEMBERSHIP:
Natl. Speakers Assn.
Toastmasters

PRINCIPAL TOPICS:
Business & Industry
Management
Travel
TYPICAL AUDIENCE:
Corporate

NORTON, KEN
14122 Harwood Ave.
Baton Rouge, LA 70816
Telephone: 504-295-5623
Fax: 504-383-4145
ASSOCIATION
  MEMBERSHIP:
Natl. Speakers Assn.
PRINCIPAL TOPICS:
Health
Human Relations
Motivation
TYPICAL AUDIENCE:
Corporate
Association

NUELL, JOY
395 Huntley Drive
Los Angeles, Ca 90048
Telephone: 310-854-0146
Fax: 310-659-0726
PRINCIPAL TOPICS:
Media
TYPICAL AUDIENCE:
Corporate
Association

NUNES, MARIANNA
1304 Mills Ave.
Burlingame, CA 94010
Telephone: 415-375-0515
Fax: 415-375-1570
ASSOCIATION
  MEMBERSHIP:
Natl. Speakers Assn.
PRINCIPAL TOPICS:
Humor
Motivation
Sales
TYPICAL AUDIENCE:
Corporate
Association

O'CONNOR, CAROL
O'Connor Consulting Assoc.
43 Norgate Rd.
Attleboro, MA 02703
Telephone: 508-226-0238
ASSOCIATION
  MEMBERSHIP:
Natl. Speakers Assn.
Toastmasters
PRINCIPAL TOPICS:
Family

Human Relations
Motivation
Psychology
Senior Citizens
TYPICAL AUDIENCE:
Corporate
Association
Fraternal

O'CONNOR, JERRY
4910 CHESTNUT
GRAND FORKS, ND 58201
Telephone: 701-772-1708
Fax: 701-772-2797
REPRESENTED BY:
North American Speakers
Preferred Speakers
ASSOCIATION
  MEMBERSHIP:
Natl. Speakers Assn.
PRINCIPAL TOPICS:
Agriculture
Amusements
Ecology
Education
Entertainment
Humor
Science
TYPICAL AUDIENCE:
Association
Fraternal
SEE AD IN SECTION 8

O'DOOLEY,
  PATRICK   CSP
9218 Dove Meadow
Dallas, TX 75243
Telephone: 214-340-9402
Fax: 214-340-0820
ASSOCIATION
  MEMBERSHIP:
Natl. Speakers Assn.
PRINCIPAL TOPICS:
Motivation
TYPICAL AUDIENCE:
Corporate

O'HARA, CAROL
P.O. Box 10, 8472
  Oakwind Court
Orangevale, CA 94662-0010
Telephone: 916-726-1384
Fax: 916-726-1384
ASSOCIATION
  MEMBERSHIP:
Platform Speakers
PRINCIPAL TOPICS:
Family
Home & Garden
Journalism
Senior Citizens

Travel
TYPICAL AUDIENCE:
Association

OAKLEY, ED
Enlightened Leadership
  International, Inc.
7100 E. Belleview
Englewood, CO 80111
Telephone: 303-694-4644
Fax: 303-694-4705
ASSOCIATION
  MEMBERSHIP:
Natl. Speakers Assn.
PRINCIPAL TOPICS:
Human Relations
Management
Motivation
TYPICAL AUDIENCE:
Corporate
Association

OBERG, BILL
Oberg & Associates
3965 Hickory Hill Dr.
Colorado Springs, CO
  80906-6119
Telephone: 719-527-9900
Fax: 719-527-9901
ASSOCIATION
  MEMBERSHIP:
Natl. Speakers Assn.
PRINCIPAL TOPICS:
Health
Medical
Motivation
Psychology
Religion
TYPICAL AUDIENCE:
Corporate
Association
Health Professionals

OECHSLI, MATTHEW J.
102 Paisley St.
Greensboro, NC 27401
Telephone: 919-273-6582
Fax: 919-273-2342
REPRESENTED BY:
Five Star
Speakers Plus
Nightingale-Conant
Dartnell
ASSOCIATION
  MEMBERSHIP:
Natl. Speakers Assn.
PRINCIPAL TOPICS:
Entertainment
Management
Marketing
Sales

TYPICAL AUDIENCE:
Corporate
Association

OLDAK, EMILY
P.O. Box 61315
Denver, CO 80206
Telephone: 303-758-8825
ASSOCIATION
  MEMBERSHIP:
Natl. Speakers Assn.
PRINCIPAL TOPICS:
Health
Humor
Motivation
Youth
TYPICAL AUDIENCE:
Corporate
Youth In Foster Care System
Youth Care Providers
Mental Health

OLESEN, ERIK L.
2941 China Well Rd.
Auburn, CA 95603
Telephone: 916-885-2673
Fax: 916-888-0895
ASSOCIATION
  MEMBERSHIP:
Natl. Speakers Assn.
Platform Speakers
PRINCIPAL TOPICS:
Health
Management
Psychology
TYPICAL AUDIENCE:
Corporate
Association
Institutional

OLSON, HARRY A.
Maximum Potential, Inc.
1 Chase Mill Circle
Owings Mills, MD 21117
Telephone: 410-581-0817
Fax: 410-581-3293
REPRESENTED BY:
Speaker Services
ASSOCIATION
  MEMBERSHIP:
International Speakers Network
PRINCIPAL TOPICS:
Business & Industry
Human Relations
Management
Motivation
Psychology
Religion
TYPICAL AUDIENCE:
Corporate

OSMAN, WALI M. PH.D.
1200 Creekside Dr., #1024
Folsom, CA 95630
Telephone: 916-983-2962
ASSOCIATION
  MEMBERSHIP:
Natl. Speakers Assn.
PRINCIPAL TOPICS:
Business & Industry
Management
Marketing
Motivation
World Affairs
TYPICAL AUDIENCE:
Corporate
Association

OSTARO, DHRUV
402 E. 74 ST., #4C
NEW YORK, NY 10021
Telephone: 212-686-4121
MAILING ADDRESS:
303 5th Ave., Ste. 1909
New York, NY 10016
ASSOCIATION
  MEMBERSHIP:
Natl. Speakers Assn.
Platform Speakers
Toastmasters
PRINCIPAL TOPICS:
Entertainment
Humor
Motivation
TYPICAL AUDIENCE:
Association

OUTLAW, KEMILEE K.
HEART OF THE BUSINESS
  SEMINARS INC.
1200 BINZ #1360
HOUSTON, TX 77004-6927
Telephone: 713-528-5000
Fax: 713-529-1112
ASSOCIATION
  MEMBERSHIP:
Natl. Speakers Assn.
ASTD
PRINCIPAL TOPICS:
Business & Industry
Education
Entertainment
Family
Government
Health
Human Relations
Humor
Management
Medical
Motivation
Philosophy

Psychology
Religion
Sales
Senior Citizens
Social Trends
World Affairs
Youth
SEE AD IN SECTION 8

OUTLAW, WAYNE
1092 JOHNNIE
  DODDS BLVD.
MT. PLEASANT, SC 29464
Telephone: 800-347-9361
MAILING ADDRESS:
P.O. Box 661
Mt. Pleasant, SC 29465
Fax: 800-881-1758
ASSOCIATION
  MEMBERSHIP:
Natl. Speakers Assn.
PRINCIPAL TOPICS:
Management
Marketing
Sales
TYPICAL AUDIENCE:
Corporate
Association
SEE AD IN SECTION 8

OXLEY, ROBERT R.
401 S. Kalispell Way, #107
Aurora, CO 80017
Telephone: 303-751-5587
Fax: 303-755-5188
ASSOCIATION
  MEMBERSHIP:
Natl. Speakers Assn.
Toastmasters
PRINCIPAL TOPICS:
Architecture
Business & Industry
Home & Garden
Human Relations
Management
Marketing
Motivation
Sales
TYPICAL AUDIENCE:
Corporate
Association

PAGANO, BARBARA L.
9165 Martin Rd.
Roswell, GA 30076
Telephone: 404-640-6971
Fax: 404-640-7406
REPRESENTED BY:
Speaker Connect USA

ASSOCIATION
  MEMBERSHIP:
Natl. Speakers Assn.
PRINCIPAL TOPICS:
Human Relations
Motivation
TYPICAL AUDIENCE:
Corporate
Association

PAGE, SUSAN
Page, Susan & Associates
1941 Oregon St.
Berkeley, CA 94703
Telephone: 510-843-2111
Fax: 510-845-8649
ASSOCIATION
  MEMBERSHIP:
Natl. Speakers Assn.
PRINCIPAL TOPICS:
Family
Human Relations
Motivation
Psychology
TYPICAL AUDIENCE:
Corporate
Association

PALMEN, RALPH H.
7500 212th St. S.W., #201
Edmonds, WA 98026
Telephone: 206-672-4750
Fax: 206-775-0907
REPRESENTED BY:
Exposures To Excellence
ASSOCIATION
  MEMBERSHIP:
Natl. Speakers Assn.
PRINCIPAL TOPICS:
Business & Industry
Human Relations
Management
TYPICAL AUDIENCE:
Corporate
Association

PALMQUIST, RICHARD
Palmquist & Associates
9922 N. 34th St.
Omaha, NE 68112
Telephone: 402-330-7701
MAILING ADDRESS:
Palmquist & Associates
12020 Shamrock Plaza
Omaha, NE 68154
ASSOCIATION
  MEMBERSHIP:
Natl. Speakers Assn.
PRINCIPAL TOPICS:
Advertising
Management

Marketing
Media
Motivation
Sales
TYPICAL AUDIENCE:
Corporate

PALUMBO, JOHN A.
6182 Belle Rive Ct.
Jacksonville, FL 32256
Telephone: 904-641-2043
ASSOCIATION
 MEMBERSHIP:
Natl. Speakers Assn.
PRINCIPAL TOPICS:
Marketing
Personal Finance
Sales
Travel
TYPICAL AUDIENCE:
Corporate
Association

PANHORST, DON, DR.
P.O. Box 725, 100 Harrison Dr.
Edinboro, PA 16412-0725
Telephone: 814-734-1182
ASSOCIATION
 MEMBERSHIP:
Natl. Speakers Assn.
Toastmasters
PRINCIPAL TOPICS:
Management
TYPICAL AUDIENCE:
Association

PAPE, GLENN
120 Darroch Rd.
Delmar, NY 12054-3824
Telephone: 518-464-2446
MAILING ADDRESS:
One Wall St.
Albany, NY 12205
Fax: 518-464-2121
ASSOCIATION
 MEMBERSHIP:
Natl. Speakers Assn.
PRINCIPAL TOPICS:
Personal Finance
TYPICAL AUDIENCE:
Corporate

PARINELLO, AL
American Media Ventures
50 Greenwoods Rd.
Old Tappan, NJ 07675
Telephone: 201-784-0059
REPRESENTED BY:
Shirley Hoe Enterprises

ASSOCIATION
 MEMBERSHIP:
Natl. Speakers Assn.
PRINCIPAL TOPICS:
Entertainment
Humor
Media
Motivation
TYPICAL AUDIENCE:
Association

PARISSE, ALAN J.   CSP
Parisse, Alan J. & Associates,
 Inc.
1630 30th Street, #304
Boulder, CO 80301
Telephone: 303-444-8080
Fax: 303-442-1819
ASSOCIATION
 MEMBERSHIP:
Natl. Speakers Assn.
Platform Speakers
PRINCIPAL TOPICS:
Management
Motivation
Sales
TYPICAL AUDIENCE:
Corporate
Association

PARKER,
 CHARLES E.   CSP
463 Goodspeed Rd.
Virginia Beach, VA 23462
Telephone: 800-477-3750
Fax: 804-473-3768
ASSOCIATION
 MEMBERSHIP:
Natl. Speakers Assn.
PRINCIPAL TOPICS:
Management
Psychology
Sales
TYPICAL AUDIENCE:
Corporate

PARKER, DON
1075 Farmington Road
Pensacola, FL 32504
Telephone: 904-474-1407
Fax: 904-438-4934
REPRESENTED BY:
Florida Speakers
PRINCIPAL TOPICS:
Humor
TYPICAL AUDIENCE:
Corporate
Association
Fraternal

PARKER, LARRY R.
45 W. 132nd St., Apt. 7U
New York, NY 10037
Telephone: 212-969-0646
ASSOCIATION
 MEMBERSHIP:
Natl. Speakers Assn.
PRINCIPAL TOPICS:
Health
Motivation
TYPICAL AUDIENCE:
Corporate
Association

PATTERSON, BILL
Hameroff/Milenthal/Spence,
 Inc.
10 West Broad St.
Columbus, OH 43215
Telephone: 614-221-7667
Fax: 614-222-2596
REPRESENTED BY:
Speakers USA
ASSOCIATION
 MEMBERSHIP:
Natl. Speakers Assn.
PRSA
ASAE
PRINCIPAL TOPICS:
Business & Industry
Communications
Education
Human Relations
Journalism
Management
Media
TYPICAL AUDIENCE:
Corporate
Association

PATTISON, POLLY
5092 Kingscross Rd.
Westminster, CA 92683
Telephone: 714-894-8143
ASSOCIATION
 MEMBERSHIP:
Natl. Speakers Assn.
PRINCIPAL TOPICS:
Business & Industry
Computer Technology
Marketing
TYPICAL AUDIENCE:
Corporate
Association

PATTON, RICHARD M.
CRUSADE AGAINST
 FIRE DEATHS, INC.
7625 SUNRISE BLVD., #210
CITRUS HEIGHTS, CA 95610
Telephone: 916-721-7700

Fax: 916-721-7704
ASSOCIATION
 MEMBERSHIP:
Natl. Speakers Assn.
Platform Speakers
Toastmasters
PRINCIPAL TOPICS:
Health
Science
TYPICAL AUDIENCE:
Corporate
Association
Government

PAULSON, TERRY L., PH.D.
 (CPAE)   CSP
Paulson & Associates Inc.
28717 Colina Vista
Agoura Hills, CA 91301
Telephone: 818-991-5110
Fax: 818-991-9648
ASSOCIATION
 MEMBERSHIP:
Natl. Speakers Assn.
American Society for Training
 & Development
PRINCIPAL TOPICS:
Human Relations
Humor
Management
Motivation
Social Trends
Youth
TYPICAL AUDIENCE:
Corporate
Association

PAYNE, JUDY
1704 5th Ave. N.
Fort Dodge, IA 50501
Telephone: 515-576-0877
ASSOCIATION
 MEMBERSHIP:
Natl. Speakers Assn.
PRINCIPAL TOPICS:
Motivation
TYPICAL AUDIENCE:
Women's Group

PAYNE, THOMAS E.
Lodestar
1200 Lawrence Ct. N.E.
Albuquerque, NM 87123
Telephone: 800-447-9254
Fax: 505-294-6942
ASSOCIATION
 MEMBERSHIP:
Natl. Speakers Assn.
PRINCIPAL TOPICS:
Management

Motivation
Sales
TYPICAL AUDIENCE:
Corporate

PEARL, LYNN
Executive Communication Inc.
222 W. Ontario, Ste. 501
Chicago, IL 60610
Telephone: 312-664-6645
Fax: 312-664-6637
REPRESENTED BY:
Natl. Speakers Bureau
Associated Speakers
ASSOCIATION
 MEMBERSHIP:
Natl. Speakers Assn.
Professional Speakers of
 Illinois
PRINCIPAL TOPICS:
Human Relations
Management
Marketing
Motivation
Sales
TYPICAL AUDIENCE:
Corporate
Association

PELLEY, JIM
Laughter Works Seminars
P.O. Box 1076
Fair Oaks, CA 95628
Telephone: 800-626-5233
Fax: 916-863-5072
REPRESENTED BY:
Keynote Speakers
Speakers International
ASSOCIATION
 MEMBERSHIP:
Natl. Speakers Assn.
PRINCIPAL TOPICS:
Education
Medical
TYPICAL AUDIENCE:
Corporate
Association

PENNER, SHEBA
N.C.H.D.
2509 Via Deiquenos
Alpine, CA 91901
REPRESENTED BY:
Podium
ASSOCIATION
 MEMBERSHIP:
Natl. Speakers Assn.
PRINCIPAL TOPICS:
Family
Human Relations
Motivation

TYPICAL AUDIENCE:
Corporate
Association

PENNINGTON, RANDY G.
4000 Winter Park Lane
Dallas, TX 75244
Telephone: 214-980-9857
Fax: 214-661-9575
REPRESENTED BY:
French & Associates
EFI
Executive Excellence Bureau
ASSOCIATION
 MEMBERSHIP:
Natl. Speakers Assn.
PRINCIPAL TOPICS:
Business & Industry
Management
TYPICAL AUDIENCE:
Corporate
Association
Municipal Governments

PEOPLES, DAVID
P.O. Box 8850
Longboat Key, FL 34228
Telephone: 813-383-0954
Fax: 813-383-6806
ASSOCIATION
 MEMBERSHIP:
Natl. Speakers Assn.
PRINCIPAL TOPICS:
Sales
TYPICAL AUDIENCE:
Corporate

PEPPER, MICHAEL J.
Technology Associates
56 Dunder Rd., Ste. 400
Burlington, VT 05401
Telephone: 802-864-5424
Fax: 802-865-1249
ASSOCIATION
 MEMBERSHIP:
Natl. Speakers Assn.
PRINCIPAL TOPICS:
Computer Technology
Motivation
TYPICAL AUDIENCE:
Corporate
Association

PERRY, MARJORIE RUTH
720 N. Post Oak Rd. #140
Houston, TX 77024-3813
Telephone: 713-682-5454

PERSONS, HAROLD D.
 'HAL'
Personal Communications
 Instit.
4805 Browvale Ave.
Flushing, NY 11362
Telephone: 718-229-3254
ASSOCIATION
 MEMBERSHIP:
Natl. Speakers Assn.
American Society of Training &
 Development
PRINCIPAL TOPICS:
Human Relations
TYPICAL AUDIENCE:
Corporate
Association

PESUT, TIM S.
P.O. Box 19374
Sarasota, Fl 34276
Telephone: 800-846-2855
Fax: 813-493-4800
ASSOCIATION
 MEMBERSHIP:
Natl. Speakers Assn.
Toastmasters
PRINCIPAL TOPICS:
Education
Marketing
Personal Finance
Psychology
TYPICAL AUDIENCE:
Corporate
Association
General Public

PETERSEN, GLORIA
P.O. Box 2607, 1111 S. Alpine
 Rd., #201
Rockford, IL 61132
Telephone: 815-394-1097
Fax: 815-397-6237
ASSOCIATION
 MEMBERSHIP:
Natl. Speakers Assn.
PRINCIPAL TOPICS:
Business & Industry
Fashion
Human Relations
Management
Motivation
TYPICAL AUDIENCE:
Corporate
Association

PETERSEN, KRISTELLE
Petersen Communications
6469 Bordeaux
Dallas, TX 75209

Telephone: 214-720-7255
MAILING ADDRESS:
Petersen Communications
2211 N. Lamar, Ste. 310
Dallas, TX 75202
Fax: 214-720-7253
ASSOCIATION
 MEMBERSHIP:
Natl. Speakers Assn.
PRINCIPAL TOPICS:
Advertising
Architecture
Business & Industry
Human Relations
Humor
Marketing
Media
Motivation
Sales
Social Trends
TYPICAL AUDIENCE:
Corporate
Association

PETERSEN, RUTH KAY
P.O. Box 574
Colorado Springs, Co 80901
Telephone: 719-576-2445
REPRESENTED BY:
Rocky Mountain Speakers
 Bureau
ASSOCIATION
 MEMBERSHIP:
Natl. Speakers Assn.
PRINCIPAL TOPICS:
Motivation
Sales
TYPICAL AUDIENCE:
Corporate
Association

PETERSON, CAROL C.
Image Matters, International
3901 S.W. 22nd Dr.
Gresham, OR 97080
Telephone: 503-666-7733
Fax: 503-666-7733
ASSOCIATION
 MEMBERSHIP:
Natl. Speakers Assn.
PRINCIPAL TOPICS:
Marketing
TYPICAL AUDIENCE:
Corporate

PETERSON, THERESA L.
959 Nixon Ave.
Reno, Nv 89509
Telephone: 702-786-2600

ASSOCIATION
  MEMBERSHIP:
Natl. Speakers Assn.
Toastmasters
PRINCIPAL TOPICS:
Business & Industry
Education
Government
Management
Communications
TYPICAL AUDIENCE:
Corporate
Institutional

PETITJEAN, DAVE
P.O. Box 757
Crowley, La 70527
Telephone: 318-783-1255
Fax: 318-783-8009
ASSOCIATION
  MEMBERSHIP:
Natl. Speakers Assn.
PRINCIPAL TOPICS:
Humor
TYPICAL AUDIENCE:
Corporate
Association

PETSCHULAT, DR. NEUB
P.O. Box 1277
West Palm Beach, FL 33402
Telephone: 407-642-7777
Fax: 407-642-0471
ASSOCIATION
  MEMBERSHIP:
Natl. Speakers Assn.
Florida Speakers
PRINCIPAL TOPICS:
Health
Motivation
Senior Citizens
TYPICAL AUDIENCE:
Association

PETTY, DR. CHARLES V.
Family Success Unlimited
P.O. Box 19906, 7600 Pinewild
  Court
Raleigh, NC 27615
Telephone: 919-846-7388
ASSOCIATION
  MEMBERSHIP:
Natl. Speakers Assn.
PRINCIPAL TOPICS:
Family
Humor
TYPICAL AUDIENCE:
Corporate
Association

PHILLIPS, RICK
P.O. Box 29615
New Orleans, LA 70189
Telephone: 800-525-7773
Fax: 504-241-7704
ASSOCIATION
  MEMBERSHIP:
Natl. Speakers Assn.
Toastmasters
American Society For Training
  & Development
PRINCIPAL TOPICS:
Business & Industry
Human Relations
Management
Sales
TYPICAL AUDIENCE:
Corporate
Association

PHILPOT, JOHN
17020 Speaker Lane
Little Rock, AK 72206
Telephone: 501-888-4805
Fax: 501-888-2587
ASSOCIATION
  MEMBERSHIP:
Natl. Speakers Assn.
PRINCIPAL TOPICS:
Humor
Media
TYPICAL AUDIENCE:
Association

PICKERING, DAVE
216 Sharondale Drive
Tullahoma, TN 37388
Telephone: 615-455-0250
Fax: 615-455-0250
REPRESENTED BY:
Happy Talk Speaking Services
PRINCIPAL TOPICS:
Humor
Management
Motivation
TYPICAL AUDIENCE:
Corporate
Association

PICKERING, WAYNE
P.O. Box 3395
Daytona Beach, FL 32118
Telephone: 904-441-4487
ASSOCIATION
  MEMBERSHIP:
Natl. Speakers Assn.
Platform Speakers
Toastmasters
ASTD
ASAE

PRINCIPAL TOPICS:
Food/Diet
Health
Humor
TYPICAL AUDIENCE:
Corporate
Association
Fraternal

PILGRIM, M. SUSAN
Life Investments
2980 Cobb Pkwy., Ste. 192
Atlanta, GA 30339
Telephone: 404-432-7100
REPRESENTED BY:
Tarkenton's Speakers Bureau
Peachtree Speakers
Jordan International
Speakers Connect USA
ASSOCIATION
  MEMBERSHIP:
Natl. Speakers Assn.
PRINCIPAL TOPICS:
Health
Motivation
Psychology
TYPICAL AUDIENCE:
Corporate
Association

PILLOW, JOHN G. (MHS)
Pilow Group, The
3414 Blueridge Lane
Garland, TX 75042
Telephone: 214-704-5575
Fax: 214-301-9373
REPRESENTED BY:
Executive Development
  Systems
ASSOCIATION
  MEMBERSHIP:
Natl. Speakers Assn.
Platform Speakers
American Hotel
PRINCIPAL TOPICS:
Marketing
Motivation
Sales
TYPICAL AUDIENCE:
Corporate

PINKSTAFF, MARLENE
  ARTHUR
5800 E. Skelly Drive, #1230
Tulsa, Ok 74135
Telephone: 918-663-2177
Fax: 918-663-4216
ASSOCIATION
  MEMBERSHIP:
Natl. Speakers Assn.

PRINCIPAL TOPICS:
Business & Industry
Human Relations
Management
TYPICAL AUDIENCE:
Corporate
Association
Fraternal

PINSKEY, RALEIGH
1223 Wilshire Blvd., #502
Santa Monica, Ct 90403
Telephone: 310-998-0055
ASSOCIATION
  MEMBERSHIP:
Natl. Speakers Assn.
PRINCIPAL TOPICS:
Business & Industry
Entertainment
Marketing
Media
TYPICAL AUDIENCE:
Corporate
Association
Fraternal

PISCOPO, MARIA
Creative Services
2038 Calvert Ave.
Costa Mesa, CA 92626-3520
Telephone: 714-556-8133
Fax: 714-556-0899
ASSOCIATION
  MEMBERSHIP:
Natl. Speakers Assn.
PRINCIPAL TOPICS:
Advertising
Architecture
Photography
TYPICAL AUDIENCE:
Association

PLUMMER,
  RICHARD E., DR.
1111 Springfield Rd.
Inman, SC 29349
Telephone: 803-578-1181
Fax: 803-578-7885
ASSOCIATION
  MEMBERSHIP:
Natl. Speakers Assn.
PRINCIPAL TOPICS:
Health
Human Relations
Motivation
TYPICAL AUDIENCE:
Corporate
Association

PODANY, SUE
Podany, S.K. & Associates
21500 Califa #152
Woodland Hills, CA 91367
Telephone: 818-888-1033
Fax: 818-887-5465
REPRESENTED BY:
McGregor & Assoc.
California Speakers Bureau
ASSOCIATION
  MEMBERSHIP:
Natl. Speakers Assn.
PRINCIPAL TOPICS:
Food/Diet
Health
Human Relations
Motivation
Physical Fitness
TYPICAL AUDIENCE:
Corporate
Association

POLK, JANE M.
543 Laketower Dr., #130
Lexington, KY 40502
Telephone: 606-269-3435
REPRESENTED BY:
Five Star
Program Resources
ASSOCIATION
  MEMBERSHIP:
Natl. Speakers Assn.
Kentucky Speakers
Carlson Learning Co.
ASTD
PRINCIPAL TOPICS:
Education
Health
Human Relations
Motivation
Psychology
TYPICAL AUDIENCE:
Association
Self-Sponsored

POLLAR, ODETTE
Time Management Systems
1441 Franklin St., #301
Oakland, CA 94612
Telephone: 510-763-8482
Fax: 510-835-8531
ASSOCIATION
  MEMBERSHIP:
Natl. Speakers Assn.
PRINCIPAL TOPICS:
Business & Industry
Human Relations
Management
TYPICAL AUDIENCE:
Corporate
Association

POOSER, DORIS
Always In Style
40 W. 37th, 12th Fl.
New York, NY 10018
Telephone: 212-563-9766
Fax: 212-563-9688
ASSOCIATION
  MEMBERSHIP:
Natl. Speakers Assn.
PRINCIPAL TOPICS:
Fashion
Marketing
Sales
Social Trends
TYPICAL AUDIENCE:
Corporate
Public-TV Audiences

POPYK, BOB
120 Walton St., #201
Syracuse, NY 13202
Telephone: 315-422-4488
Fax: 315-422-3837
ASSOCIATION
  MEMBERSHIP:
Natl. Speakers Assn.
PRINCIPAL TOPICS:
Sales
TYPICAL AUDIENCE:
Corporate
Association

POSTEN, ROBERT
2810 Biarritz Dr.
Palm Beach Gardens, FL
  33410
Telephone: 407-684-3636
Fax: 407-478-4457
ASSOCIATION
  MEMBERSHIP:
Natl. Speakers Assn.
Toastmasters
PRINCIPAL TOPICS:
Business & Industry
Computer Technology
Marketing
TYPICAL AUDIENCE:
Corporate

POTUCK, MARK W.
311 West High St.
Elkhart, IN 46516
Telephone: 219-522-3133
REPRESENTED BY:
Action Entertainment
ASSOCIATION
  MEMBERSHIP:
Natl. Speakers Assn.
PRINCIPAL TOPICS:
Entertainment
Health

Humor
Motivation
TYPICAL AUDIENCE:
Association
Fraternal
Schools (K-12)
Some Colleges & Universities

POYNTER, DAN
Para Publishing
P.O. Box 4232-204
Santa Barbara, CA 93140-4232
Telephone: 805-968-7277
MAILING ADDRESS:
Para Publishing
530 Ellwood Ridge
Santa Barbara, CA 93117-9700
Fax: 805-968-1379
ASSOCIATION
  MEMBERSHIP:
Natl. Speakers Assn.
PRINCIPAL TOPICS:
Aviation
TYPICAL AUDIENCE:
Corporate
Association
Fraternal

PRICE, BETTE
PRICE GROUP, THE
14821 LE GRANDE DR.
Dallas, TX 75244
Telephone: 214-404-0787
Fax: 214-991-0368
ASSOCIATION
  MEMBERSHIP:
Natl. Speakers Assn.
PRINCIPAL TOPICS:
Marketing
Motivation
TYPICAL AUDIENCE:
Corporate
Association
SEE AD IN SECTION 8

PRICE, DON L.
P.O. Box 7000-700
Redondo Beach, Ca 90277
Telephone: 310-379-7797
ASSOCIATION
  MEMBERSHIP:
Natl. Speakers Assn.
PRINCIPAL TOPICS:
Marketing
Motivation
Sales
TYPICAL AUDIENCE:
Corporate
Association
General Public

PRIESKORN, JOHN PH.D.
P.O. Box 419
Lake Arrowhead, CA 92352
Telephone: 909-336-6979
Fax: 909-337-0271
ASSOCIATION
  MEMBERSHIP:
Natl. Speakers Assn.
Natl. Council For Self-Esteem
Natl. Staff Development
  Council
PRINCIPAL TOPICS:
Human Relations
Motivation
TYPICAL AUDIENCE:
Corporate
Association

PRIGAL, KENNETH B.K.
The Fidelity Union Bldg., 45A
  King St.
Christiansted, VI 00820
Telephone: 809-773-8100
ASSOCIATION
  MEMBERSHIP:
Natl. Speakers Assn.
PRINCIPAL TOPICS:
Business & Industry
Human Relations
Management
Marketing
Motivation
TYPICAL AUDIENCE:
Corporate
Association

PROUT, LINDA L., M.S.
304 JOYCE WAY
MILL VALLEY, CA 94941
Telephone: 415-381-6333
Fax: 415-381-6333
ASSOCIATION
  MEMBERSHIP:
Natl. Speakers Assn.
PRINCIPAL TOPICS:
Food/Diet
Health
Motivation
TYPICAL AUDIENCE:
Corporate
Association
SEE AD IN SECTION 8

PULLIAM, LINDA
863 Weaver Dairy Rd.
Chapel Hill, NC 27514
Telephone: 919-942-7348
Fax: 919-942-7348
ASSOCIATION
  MEMBERSHIP:
Natl. Speakers Assn.

PRINCIPAL TOPICS:
Humor
Social Trends
TYPICAL AUDIENCE:
Corporate
Association

PUTNAM, HOWARD D.
Putnam, Howard D.
  Enterprises, Inc.
P.O. Box 796336
Dallas, TX 75379
Telephone: 214-985-9827
REPRESENTED BY:
Standing Ovations
National-Chicago
Capital-Washington DC
ASSOCIATION
  MEMBERSHIP:
Natl. Speakers Assn.
PRINCIPAL TOPICS:
Aviation
Business & Industry
Management
Marketing
Sales
Travel
TYPICAL AUDIENCE:
Corporate
Association

PUTZIER, JOHN
3459 Harbison St.
Pittsburgh, PA 15212-2271
Telephone: 412-734-1400
Fax: 412-734-0125
ASSOCIATION
  MEMBERSHIP:
Natl. Speakers Assn.
Pennsylvania Speakers
Society for Human Resource
  Management
Pittsburgh Personnel
PRINCIPAL TOPICS:
Business & Industry
Human Relations
Management
Motivation
Psychology
Social Trends
TYPICAL AUDIENCE:
Corporate
Association

PYFER, HOWARD R. M.D.
Wellness Center, The
626 120th N.E., #203
Bellevue, WA 98005
Telephone: 206-453-5559

ASSOCIATION
  MEMBERSHIP:
Natl. Speakers Assn.
Pacific Northwest Speakers
PRINCIPAL TOPICS:
Food/Diet
Health
Medical
Physical Fitness
TYPICAL AUDIENCE:
Corporate
General Audiences

QUINN, BEVERLY
  CARLSON
P.O. Box 7515
McLean, Va 22106
Telephone: 703-356-7844
ASSOCIATION
  MEMBERSHIP:
Natl. Speakers Assn.
PRINCIPAL TOPICS:
Communications
TYPICAL AUDIENCE:
Corporate

RADDE, PAUL O.
Thriving Presentations
9600 Potomac Drive
Fort Washington, Md 20744
Telephone: 301-567-8333
Fax: 301-567-8333
ASSOCIATION
  MEMBERSHIP:
Natl. Speakers Assn.
PRINCIPAL TOPICS:
Education
Health
Human Relations
Management
Motivation
Psychology
TYPICAL AUDIENCE:
Corporate
Association

RADKE, DALE L.
6410 W. Melvina St.
Milwaukee, WI 53216
Telephone: 414-461-7505
MAILING ADDRESS:
P.O. Box 18024
Milwaukee, WI 53218
REPRESENTED BY:
Associated Speakers
PRINCIPAL TOPICS:
Humor
Religion

TYPICAL AUDIENCE:
Corporate
Association
Fraternal

RADTKE, RICHARD, L.
45-106 PO'OKELA PLACE
KANEONE, HI 96744
Telephone: 808-956-7498
MAILING ADDRESS:
RADTKE, RICHARD L.
University of Hawaii
MSB. Rm. 632,
** 1000 Popa Rd.**
Honolulu, HI 96822
Fax: 808-956-9516
REPRESENTED BY:
Walters Speakers Services
ASSOCIATION
** MEMBERSHIP:**
Natl. Speakers Assn.
PRINCIPAL TOPICS:
Computer Technology
Ecology
Education
Family
Science
Travel
TYPICAL AUDIENCE:
Corporate
Educational
SEE AD IN SECTION 8

RAEL, RON, CPA
823 93rd Ave. S.E.
Everett, WA 98205-1827
Telephone: 206-334-1241
ASSOCIATION
  MEMBERSHIP:
Natl. Speakers Assn.
Toastmasters
IMA
AICPA
PRINCIPAL TOPICS:
Business & Industry
Management
Motivation
Personal Finance
TYPICAL AUDIENCE:
Corporate
Association

RAETHER, EDIE
5762 N. SHORE DR.
WHITEFISH BAY, WI 53217
Telephone: 414-332-8595
MAILING ADDRESS:
1340 Towne Square Rd.
Mequon, WI 53092
Fax: 414-332-8595

ASSOCIATION
  MEMBERSHIP:
Natl. Speakers Assn.
PRINCIPAL TOPICS:
Entertainment
Family
Health
Human Relations
Humor
Management
Motivation
Psychology
Sales
Social Trends
TYPICAL AUDIENCE:
Corporate
Association
SEE AD IN SECTION 8

RAFINSKI, MARCIA
50 Manzanita
San Francisco, Ca 94118
Telephone: 415-221-4302
ASSOCIATION
  MEMBERSHIP:
Natl. Speakers Assn.
PRINCIPAL TOPICS:
Health
Human Relations
Motivation
Psychology
TYPICAL AUDIENCE:
Corporate
Association
Fraternal

RALSTON, JOHN
San Jose State Univ.
3 Carriage Ct.
Menlo Park, CA 94025
Telephone: 408-924-1266
Fax: 408-924-1169
MAILING ADDRESS:
San Jose State Univ.
One Washington Sq.
San Jose, CA 95192
ASSOCIATION
  MEMBERSHIP:
Natl. Speakers Assn.
Dale Carnegie Instructor
PRINCIPAL TOPICS:
Management
TYPICAL AUDIENCE:
Corporate
Association

RANDOLPH, ROBERT M.
Professional Management Inst.
6921 S. Delaware Pl.
Tulsa, OK 74136
Telephone: 918-492-3007

MAILING ADDRESS:
Professional Management Inst.
7169 S. Braden Ave.
Tulsa, OK 74136
Fax: 918-492-3009
ASSOCIATION
  MEMBERSHIP:
Natl. Speakers Assn.
PRINCIPAL TOPICS:
Business & Industry
Human Relations
Management
Motivation
TYPICAL AUDIENCE:
Corporate
Association
General Public

RASBAND, JUDITH
Conselle L.C.
540 E. Quail Rd.
Orem, UT 84057
Telephone: 801-224-1207
MAILING ADDRESS:
Conselle L.C.
P.O. Box 7052, University
  Station
Provo, UT 84602
Fax: 801-226-6122
ASSOCIATION
  MEMBERSHIP:
Natl. Speakers Assn.
PRINCIPAL TOPICS:
Business & Industry
Family
Fashion
Human Relations
Management
Motivation
Psychology
Senior Citizens
Travel
TYPICAL AUDIENCE:
Corporate
Association

RAST, EDWARD
220 Montgomery St., #343
San Francisco, CA 94104
Telephone: 415-986-1710
ASSOCIATION
  MEMBERSHIP:
Natl. Speakers Assn.
PRINCIPAL TOPICS:
Business & Industry
Education
Human Relations
Management
Motivation
Sales
Social Trends

TYPICAL AUDIENCE:
Corporate
Association

REAGAN, MICHAEL R.
  (CPC/CPS)
8300 N. Hayden Rd., #207
Scottsdale, AZ 85258
Telephone: 602-951-4311
Fax: 602-266-7466
REPRESENTED BY:
Leaps & Bounds Productions
Applause Productions
ASSOCIATION
  MEMBERSHIP:
Natl. Speakers Assn.
Natl. Assn. Sales Professionals
PRINCIPAL TOPICS:
Motivation
Sales
TYPICAL AUDIENCE:
Corporate
Association

REAVES, CHUCK   CSP
P.O. Box 13447
Atlanta, GA 30324
Telephone: 404-979-3321
Fax: 404-972-1809
REPRESENTED BY:
Jordan International
  Enterprises
Access Speakers Bureau
ASSOCIATION
  MEMBERSHIP:
Natl. Speakers Assn.
PRINCIPAL TOPICS:
Business & Industry
Management
Marketing
Motivation
Sales
TYPICAL AUDIENCE:
Corporate
Association

RECKNER, JERALD
  (JERRY) H.
12700 W. Bluemound Rd.
Elm Grove, WI 53122
Telephone: 800-437-7577
Fax: 414-782-4759
REPRESENTED BY:
Associated Speakers Inc.
ASSOCIATION
  MEMBERSHIP:
Natl. Speakers Assn.
Toastmasters
IGAB
PRINCIPAL TOPICS:
Business & Industry

Human Relations
Management
Marketing
Motivation
Sales
TYPICAL AUDIENCE:
Corporate
Association

REED, DAVE
Lindal Cedar Homes,
  Inc./Reed
P.O. Box 24291
Federal Way, WA 98093-1291
Telephone: 206-927-6726
Fax: 206-952-5983
ASSOCIATION
  MEMBERSHIP:
Natl. Speakers Assn.
Platform Speakers
Toastmasters
PRINCIPAL TOPICS:
Business & Industry
Management
Marketing
Sales
TYPICAL AUDIENCE:
Corporate
Association
Fraternal

REED, DEBRA J.
Rt. 5, Box 174R
Mountain Hill, Ar 72653
Telephone: 800-628-2383
Fax: 501-424-4111
ASSOCIATION
  MEMBERSHIP:
Natl. Speakers Assn.
International Platform
PRINCIPAL TOPICS:
Business & Industry
Management
Motivation
TYPICAL AUDIENCE:
Corporate
General Public

REEDER, RANDALL, C.
Ohio State University, The
590 Woody Hayes Dr.
Columbus, OH 43210
Telephone: 614-292-6648
Fax: 614-292-9448
ASSOCIATION
  MEMBERSHIP:
Natl. Speakers Assn.
Toastmasters
PRINCIPAL TOPICS:
Agriculture

Education
TYPICAL AUDIENCE:
Association

REESE, MONTE
155 Brazos
Goddard, KS 67052
Telephone: 316-794-8590
Fax: 316-794-8590
REPRESENTED BY:
North American Speakers
ASSOCIATION
  MEMBERSHIP:
Natl. Speakers Assn.
PRINCIPAL TOPICS:
Agriculture
Humor
Motivation
TYPICAL AUDIENCE:
Association

REID, T.J.
P.O. Box 977, 307 N.W.
  Central Ave.
Amite, LA 70422
Telephone: 504-748-8615
ASSOCIATION
  MEMBERSHIP:
Natl. Speakers Assn.
Natl. Federation of Press
  Women
PRINCIPAL TOPICS:
Business & Industry
Fashion
TYPICAL AUDIENCE:
Association
Fashion Retailers
Fashion Market Centers

RENSTROM, GREGORY
5 W. Bellevue, #6
San Mateo, CA 94402
Telephone: 415-348-1307
ASSOCIATION
  MEMBERSHIP:
Natl. Speakers Assn.
Toastmasters
PRINCIPAL TOPICS:
Education
Motivation
Psychology
Sales
TYPICAL AUDIENCE:
Corporate
Association
Fraternal

REUM, EARL, DR.
827 Milwaukee St.
Denver, CO 80206
Telephone: 303-355-2838

REPRESENTED BY:
North American Speakers
ASSOCIATION
  MEMBERSHIP:
Natl. Speakers Assn.
PRINCIPAL TOPICS:
Education
Hobbies
Management
Motivation
TYPICAL AUDIENCE:
Association

REYNOLDS, PATRICK
Foundation For A Smokefree
  America
505 S. Beverly Dr. Ste. 1000
Beverly Hills, CA 90212
Telephone: 310-274-8888
Fax: 310-657-1822
ASSOCIATION
  MEMBERSHIP:
Natl. Speakers Assn.
PRINCIPAL TOPICS:
Advertising
Food/Diet
Health
Medical
Motivation
Physical Fitness
Social Trends
Youth
TYPICAL AUDIENCE:
Corporate
Association
Universities

REYNOLDS, ROSE CELLINO
7405 E. 65TH PL.
TULSA, OK 74133
Telephone: 918-459-0440
MAILING ADDRESS:
8086 South Yale, Ste. 145
Tulsa, OK 74136-9060
ASSOCIATION
  MEMBERSHIP:
Natl. Speakers Assn.
Harry & David's Fruit of the
  Month Club
PRINCIPAL TOPICS:
Human Relations
Humor
Management
TYPICAL AUDIENCE:
Corporate
Association
SEE AD IN SECTION 8

REZEK, GEOFFREY R.
  (CFPIM) (CPM)
110 Raymond St., #211
Darien, CT 06820
Telephone: 203-655-0067
ASSOCIATION
  MEMBERSHIP:
Natl. Speakers Assn.
Toastmasters
PRINCIPAL TOPICS:
Business & Industry
Management
Marketing
TYPICAL AUDIENCE:
Corporate
Association

RHOADES, ROGER A.
3192 Atlanta Hwy. Ste. 440
Athens, GA 30606
Telephone: 800-542-4464
ASSOCIATION
  MEMBERSHIP:
Natl. Speakers Assn.
PRINCIPAL TOPICS:
Family
Health
Human Relations
Motivation
Psychology
Religion
TYPICAL AUDIENCE:
Association

RHODE, JIM
3400 E. McDowell
Phoenix, Az 85008
Telephone: 602-225-9090
Fax: 602-225-0599
ASSOCIATION
  MEMBERSHIP:
Natl. Speakers Assn.
PRINCIPAL TOPICS:
Business & Industry
Health
Management
Marketing
TYPICAL AUDIENCE:
Corporate
Association

RHODES, ROY, ED.D.
Rhodes & Assoc. Inc.
9330 LBJ Freeway, Ste. 1050
Dallas, TX 75243
Telephone: 214-235-9905
Fax: 214-235-9925
ASSOCIATION
  MEMBERSHIP:
Natl. Speakers Assn.
International Speakers Network

PRINCIPAL TOPICS:
Human Relations
Humor
Management
Motivation
Psychology
Sales
TYPICAL AUDIENCE:
Corporate
Association

RICH, SUSAN A.
Get Organized, Get Rich
7777 W. 91 St., Ste. 1154B
Playa Del Rey, CA 90293
Telephone: 310-823-2153
REPRESENTED BY:
Roberta Jones
ASSOCIATION
  MEMBERSHIP:
Natl. Speakers Assn.
PRINCIPAL TOPICS:
Management
Motivation
TYPICAL AUDIENCE:
Corporate
Association

RICHARDS, RAMONA
Box 32062
Phoenix, AZ 85064
Telephone: 602-274-2881
ASSOCIATION
  MEMBERSHIP:
Natl. Speakers Assn.
SAG/AFTRA
PRINCIPAL TOPICS:
Amusements
Animals
Ecology
Education
Entertainment
Family
Fashion
Health
Human Relations
Humor
Media
Motivation
Philosophy
Photography
Psychology
Youth
TYPICAL AUDIENCE:
Corporate
Association
Fraternal

RICHARDSON,
  DAVID W.   CSP
8711 E. Pinnacle Peak, #345
Scottsdale, AZ 85255
Telephone: 800-338-5831
Fax: 602-585-4417
REPRESENTED BY:
Five Star
  Goodman-Management
  Institute
ASSOCIATION
  MEMBERSHIP:
Natl. Speakers Assn.
Toastmasters
PRINCIPAL TOPICS:
Business & Industry
Human Relations
Management
Marketing
Motivation
Sales
TYPICAL AUDIENCE:
Corporate
Association

RICHARDSON, DR.
  ARTHUR
816 E. St. Andrews
Dakota Dunes, SD 57049
Telephone: 605-232-3293
Fax: 605-232-3498
MAILING ADDRESS:
Box 1644
Sioux City, IA 51102
REPRESENTED BY:
Five Star
ASSOCIATION
  MEMBERSHIP:
Natl. Speakers Assn.
ASTD
PRINCIPAL TOPICS:
Business & Industry
Education
Human Relations
Marketing
TYPICAL AUDIENCE:
Corporate
Association

RICHARDSON, TIM
363-6 Atlantic Blvd., #201
Atlantic Beach, Fl 32233
Telephone: 904-249-0919
Fax: 904-249-1861
ASSOCIATION
  MEMBERSHIP:
Natl. Speakers Assn.
PRINCIPAL TOPICS:
Motivation
TYPICAL AUDIENCE:
General

RIDGWAY, JO
3156 Terry Ave.
Clovis, CA 93612
Telephone: 209-292-1562
ASSOCIATION
  MEMBERSHIP:
Natl. Speakers Assn.
PRINCIPAL TOPICS:
Business & Industry
Personal Finance
Communications
TYPICAL AUDIENCE:
Corporate
Association

RIFENBARY, JAY C.
125 Wolf Road, #121
Albany, NY 12205
Telephone: 518-453-1252
Fax: 518-453-1243
REPRESENTED BY:
Nightingale/Conant
ASSOCIATION
  MEMBERSHIP:
Natl. Speakers Assn.
American Society of Training &
  Development
PRINCIPAL TOPICS:
Communications
Management
Military
Motivation
Sales
TYPICAL AUDIENCE:
Corporate
Association

RIGSBEE, ED
P.O. Box 6425-51
Westlake Village, CA 91359
Telephone: 805-371-4636
Fax: 805-371-4631
REPRESENTED BY:
National Speakers Bureau
Access Speakers Bureau
ASSOCIATION
  MEMBERSHIP:
Natl. Speakers Assn.
PRINCIPAL TOPICS:
Business & Industry
Human Relations
Management
Marketing
Sales
TYPICAL AUDIENCE:
Corporate
Association

RINKE, WOLF J.,
  PH.D.   CSP
Wolf Rinke Associates, Inc.
P.O. Box 1184
Clarksville, MD 21029
Telephone: 410-531-9280
Fax: 410-531-9282
REPRESENTED BY:
5 Star
Standing Ovation
Lynn Campbell
ASSOCIATION
  MEMBERSHIP:
Natl. Speakers Assn.
ASTD
Academy of Mgt.
PRINCIPAL TOPICS:
Business & Industry
Human Relations
Management
Motivation
TYPICAL AUDIENCE:
Corporate
Association

RISBERG, GREG
295 E. Church St.
Elmhurst, Il 60126
Telephone: 708-833-5066
ASSOCIATION
  MEMBERSHIP:
Natl. Speakers Assn.
PRINCIPAL TOPICS:
Education
Health
Human Relations
Motivation
TYPICAL AUDIENCE:
Corporate
Association

RISCH, THEODORE 'TED'
S.W. Institute of Life Mgmt.
11122 E. Gunshot Circle
Tucson, AZ 85749
Telephone: 602-749-2290
Fax: 602-749-2290
ASSOCIATION
  MEMBERSHIP:
Natl. Speakers Assn.
PRINCIPAL TOPICS:
Senior Citizens
TYPICAL AUDIENCE:
Corporate
Association

RISSER, RITA
P.O. Box 2146
Santa Cruz, Ca 95063
Telephone: 408-458-0500
Fax: 408-458-0181

ASSOCIATION
  MEMBERSHIP:
Natl. Speakers Assn.
ASTD
PRINCIPAL TOPICS:
Human Relations
TYPICAL AUDIENCE:
Corporate
Association

RITCHIE, JAN
P.O. Box 8
Ocowmowoc, WI 53066
Telephone: 414-569-9998
REPRESENTED BY:
Ann Miller Productions
Associated Speakers
ASSOCIATION
  MEMBERSHIP:
Natl. Speakers Assn.
ASTD
American Society For Training
  & Development
PRINCIPAL TOPICS:
Health
Human Relations
Management
Motivation
Psychology
TYPICAL AUDIENCE:
Corporate
Association

RITSCHER, JIM
Peak Dynamics
1060 Beacon St., #10
Brookline, MA 02146
Telephone: 617-277-2772
ASSOCIATION
  MEMBERSHIP:
Natl. Speakers Assn.
PRINCIPAL TOPICS:
Business & Industry
Human Relations
Management
Motivation
TYPICAL AUDIENCE:
Corporate
Association

ROACH, MARY BETH
18020 Bal Harbour Dr.
Houston, TX 77058
Telephone: 713-333-3558
Fax: 713-333-2662
REPRESENTED BY:
Duprs Jordon Out Of
  Atlanta, Ga
ASSOCIATION
  MEMBERSHIP:
Natl. Speakers Assn.

Natl. Speakers Association of
  Houston, Tx.
PRINCIPAL TOPICS:
Communications
Humor
Motivation
Sales
TYPICAL AUDIENCE:
Corporate
Association

ROACH-KILCUP,
  DONNA L.
The Topaz Group
15100 S.E. 38th St., Ste. 820
Bellevue, WA 98006-1763
Telephone: 206-641-9595
Fax: 206-227-8906
REPRESENTED BY:
Women Business Owners of
  Greater Seattle
ASSOCIATION
  MEMBERSHIP:
Natl. Speakers Assn.
PRINCIPAL TOPICS:
Automotive
Health
Physical Fitness
TYPICAL AUDIENCE:
Fraternal

ROBERT, CAVETT   CSP
1620 W. Glendale Ave., #9
Phoenix, AZ 85021
Telephone: 602-864-1880
ASSOCIATION
  MEMBERSHIP:
Natl. Speakers Assn.
Toastmasters

PRINCIPAL TOPICS:
Human Relations
Humor
Marketing
Motivation
Sales
TYPICAL AUDIENCE:
Corporate
Association

ROBERT, LEE E.
Warner, Carolyn & Assoc.
P.O. Box 32232
Phoenix, AZ 85064
Telephone: 602-957-7552
Fax: 602-957-7587
REPRESENTED BY:
Exposures to Excellence
The Speakers Network
Jordan International

ASSOCIATION
  MEMBERSHIP:
Natl. Speakers Assn.
Toastmasters
PRINCIPAL TOPICS:
Humor
Motivation
Sales

ROBERTS, BRUCE A.
11127 DesMoines Ct.
Cooper City, FL 33026
Telephone: 305-892-3054
Fax: 305-899-1044
MAILING ADDRESS:
11900 Biscayne Blvd., #700
N. Miami, FL 33181
ASSOCIATION
  MEMBERSHIP:
Natl. Speakers Assn.
Toastmasters
Florida Speakers
PRINCIPAL TOPICS:
Personal Finance
TYPICAL AUDIENCE:
Corporate
Association

ROBERTS, JANET M.
259 W. Johnson St., Apt. 4S
Philadelphia, PA 19144
Telephone: 215-848-5418
Fax: 215-925-3054
REPRESENTED BY:
Speakers Bureau
Commonwealth Speakers
ASSOCIATION
  MEMBERSHIP:
IPLA
PRINCIPAL TOPICS:
Architecture
Ecology
Education
Family
Home & Garden
Nature
Photography
Religion
Travel
World Affairs
TYPICAL AUDIENCE:
Corporate
Association
General Public

ROBERTS, JERRY W.
P.O. Box 330385
Fort Worth, TX 76163
Telephone: 817-292-4018
Fax: 817-292-3747

ASSOCIATION
  MEMBERSHIP:
Natl. Speakers Assn.
PRINCIPAL TOPICS:
Management
Psychology
TYPICAL AUDIENCE:
Corporate
Association

ROBERTS, KATHI
Action Team Training
P.O. Box 432
Stone Mountain, GA
  30086-0432
Telephone: 404-498-7222
ASSOCIATION
  MEMBERSHIP:
Natl. Speakers Assn.
PRINCIPAL TOPICS:
Education
Human Relations
Humor
Management
Medical
Motivation
Psychology
Sales
Youth
TYPICAL AUDIENCE:
Corporate
Association

ROBERTS, RONALD H.
  PH.D.
World Trade Ctr., #283
San Francisco, CA 94111
Telephone: 415-362-8202
Fax: 415-362-3612
PRINCIPAL TOPICS:
Health
Human Relations
Medical
Psychology
TYPICAL AUDIENCE:
Corporate
Association
Fraternal

ROBINSON, EMMET
P.O. Box 402, 15 E. King St.
Malvern, PA 19355
Telephone: 215-647-4341
ASSOCIATION
  MEMBERSHIP:
Natl. Speakers Assn.
PRINCIPAL TOPICS:
Business & Industry
Sales

TYPICAL AUDIENCE:
Corporate
Association

ROBISON, AUBRY, JR.
233 Main St.
Mount Vernon, IN 47620
Telephone: 812-838-6625
ASSOCIATION
  MEMBERSHIP:
Natl. Speakers Assn.
Toastmasters
PRINCIPAL TOPICS:
Humor
Motivation
TYPICAL AUDIENCE:
Corporate
Association
Fraternal

ROGERS, LOUISA
514 Bryant St., #110
Palo Alto, CA 94301
Telephone: 415-323-9643
Fax: 415-324-1206
ASSOCIATION
  MEMBERSHIP:
Natl. Speakers Assn.
PRINCIPAL TOPICS:
Human Relations
Management
Motivation
TYPICAL AUDIENCE:
Corporate
Association

ROHLANDER, DAVID
P.O. Box 2558
Orange, CA 92669
Telephone: 714-771-7043
ASSOCIATION
  MEMBERSHIP:
Natl. Speakers Assn.
PRINCIPAL TOPICS:
Business & Industry
Management
Motivation
Personal Finance
Sales
TYPICAL AUDIENCE:
Corporate

ROLFE, RANDY
Institute For Creative Solutions
947 Plumsock Rd.
Newtown Square, PA 19073
Telephone: 215-353-7383
REPRESENTED BY:
Speaker Services
PRINCIPAL TOPICS:
Family

Food/Diet
Health
Human Relations
Motivation
TYPICAL AUDIENCE:
Association

ROOS, JAMES P.
4062 Charleston Rd.
Matteson, II 60443
Telephone: 708-748-9552
Fax: 708-747-8778
ASSOCIATION
  MEMBERSHIP:
Natl. Speakers Assn.
PRINCIPAL TOPICS:
Advertising
Management
Marketing
Sales
TYPICAL AUDIENCE:
Corporate
Association

ROSANOFF, NANCY
50 Park Ave. #15B
New York, NY 10016
Telephone: 212-447-6636

ROSE, ALBERT L.
435 Lynderhill At Stratfordshire
Matthews, NC 28105
Telephone: 704-342-9933
Fax: 704-342-1066
MAILING ADDRESS:
P.O. Box 35413
Charlotte, NC 28235
ASSOCIATION
  MEMBERSHIP:
Natl. Speakers Assn.
PRINCIPAL TOPICS:
Business & Industry
Humor
Management
Military
Motivation
TYPICAL AUDIENCE:
Corporate
Fraternal

ROSENBAUM, JERRY,
  CLU
425 E. 58th St., Ste. 24H
New York, NY 10022-2300
Telephone: 212-980-9263
Fax: 212-980-1339
ASSOCIATION
  MEMBERSHIP:
Natl. Speakers Assn.
Toastmasters

PRINCIPAL TOPICS:
Business & Industry
Human Relations
Management
Motivation
Psychology
TYPICAL AUDIENCE:
Corporate

ROSENBERG, DEANNE CSP
28 FIFER LANE
LEXINGTON, MA 02173
Telephone: 617-862-6117
Fax: 617-863-8613
ASSOCIATION
  MEMBERSHIP:
Natl. Speakers Assn.
ASTD
PRINCIPAL TOPICS:
Business & Industry
Human Relations
Management
Motivation
Psychology
TYPICAL AUDIENCE:
Corporate
Association
General Public
Educational
SEE AD IN SECTION 8

ROSENBERG, RICHARD
111 Linden Ave.
Elmhurst, IL 60126
Telephone: 708-530-2050
Fax: 708-530-8000
ASSOCIATION
  MEMBERSHIP:
Natl. Speakers Assn.
PRINCIPAL TOPICS:
Business & Industry
Management
Marketing
Motivation
Photography
TYPICAL AUDIENCE:
Corporate
Association

ROSS, BOB
Ross, Bob & Assoc.
3643 Corral Cyn Rd.
Bonita, Ca 91902
Telephone: 619-479-3331
ASSOCIATION
  MEMBERSHIP:
Natl. Speakers Assn.
PRINCIPAL TOPICS:
Entertainment
Humor
Management

TYPICAL AUDIENCE:
Corporate
Association

ROSS, JO-ANN
337 Stevens St.
Lowell, MA 01851
Telephone: 508-937-5560
Fax: 508-937-5560
ASSOCIATION
  MEMBERSHIP:
Natl. Speakers Assn.
PRINCIPAL TOPICS:
Health
TYPICAL AUDIENCE:
Corporate
Association
Fraternal

ROSS, KENNETH
723 CARLENE DR.
BRIDGEWATER, NJ 08807
Telephone: 908-218-3713
Fax: 908-526-8661
ASSOCIATION
  MEMBERSHIP:
Natl. Speakers Assn.
Toastmasters
PRINCIPAL TOPICS:
Business & Industry
Humor
Motivation
TYPICAL AUDIENCE:
Corporate
Association
SEE AD IN SECTION 8

ROSS, MARILYN
About Books Inc.
P.O. Box 1500-WP, 425 Cedar
  St.
Buena Vista, CO 81211
Telephone: 719-395-2459
Fax: 719-395-8374
ASSOCIATION
  MEMBERSHIP:
Natl. Speakers Assn.
PRINCIPAL TOPICS:
Advertising
Business & Industry
Journalism
Marketing
Senior Citizens
Social Trends
Travel
TYPICAL AUDIENCE:
Corporate
Association

ROSS, TIMOTHY G.
Out To Lunch
2453 S. Elaine Dr.
Bountiful, UT 84010
Telephone: 801-295-3442
Fax: 801-292-7942
ASSOCIATION
  MEMBERSHIP:
Natl. Speakers Assn.
PRINCIPAL TOPICS:
Marketing
Media
TYPICAL AUDIENCE:
Association

ROSS, TOM
About Books Inc.
P.O. Box 1500-WP, 425 Cedar
  St.
Buena Vista, CO 81211
Telephone: 719-395-2459
Fax: 719-395-8374
ASSOCIATION
  MEMBERSHIP:
Natl. Speakers Assn.
PRINCIPAL TOPICS:
Advertising
Business & Industry
Journalism
Marketing
Senior Citizens
Travel
TYPICAL AUDIENCE:
Corporate
Association

ROSSITER, SHERRY
  KNIGHT
P.O. Box 15366
Boise, ID 83715
Telephone: 208-362-0600
ASSOCIATION
  MEMBERSHIP:
Natl. Speakers Assn.
ASTD
PRINCIPAL TOPICS:
Aviation
Human Relations
Management
Motivation
Psychology
TYPICAL AUDIENCE:
Association

ROTRAMEL, RICK
103 Beverly Dr.
Paris, IL 61944
Telephone: 217-463-2882
MAILING ADDRESS:
P.O. Box 36
Paris, IL 61944

ASSOCIATION
  MEMBERSHIP:
Natl. Speakers Assn.
PRINCIPAL TOPICS:
Agriculture
Humor
Management
Motivation
TYPICAL AUDIENCE:
Association

ROUSH, SHERYL L.
Creative Communications
P.O. Box 2373
La Mesa, CA 91943
Telephone: 619-441-1453
Fax: 619-444-6028
REPRESENTED BY:
The Podium
ASSOCIATION
  MEMBERSHIP:
Natl. Speakers Assn.
Toastmasters
ASTD
NSPI
PRINCIPAL TOPICS:
Advertising
Human Relations
Journalism
Motivation
TYPICAL AUDIENCE:
Corporate
Association
General Public

ROUSOPOULOS, DENO
Executive Development Inst.
9208 Selkirk
Indianapolis, IN 46260
Telephone: 317-848-9613
Fax: 317-575-9020
REPRESENTED BY:
Speaker & Seminar Resources
Indianapolis Speakers Bureau
ASSOCIATION
  MEMBERSHIP:
Natl. Speakers Assn.
American Society for Training
  & Development
PRINCIPAL TOPICS:
Management
Motivation
TYPICAL AUDIENCE:
Corporate
Association

RUDNICKI, BARBARA A.
RCE-Rudnicki Comm.
  Enterprises
6800 Bottlebrush Ln., Ste. 102
Naples, FL 33999

Telephone: 813-592-6800
Fax: 813-566-2160
REPRESENTED BY:
Keystone Speakers &
  Seminars
Promark
ASSOCIATION
  MEMBERSHIP:
Natl. Speakers Assn.
Platform Speakers
Toastmasters
American Seminar Leaders
PRINCIPAL TOPICS:
Business & Industry
Human Relations
Management
Motivation
TYPICAL AUDIENCE:
Corporate
Association

RUSSELL, RAY L., DR.
Hills National Management
  Center
Kansas State Univ.-Trotter Hall
Manhattan, KS 66506-5617
Telephone: 913-532-4032
Fax: 913-532-5884
ASSOCIATION
  MEMBERSHIP:
Natl. Speakers Assn.
PRINCIPAL TOPICS:
Business & Industry
Education
Human Relations
Management
Motivation
Religion
Senior Citizens
Youth
TYPICAL AUDIENCE:
Corporate
Association

RYAN, LYNN
1953 Flamingo Dr.
Costa Mesa, CA 92626
Telephone: 714-641-8505
Fax: 714-434-7926
ASSOCIATION
  MEMBERSHIP:
Natl. Speakers Assn.
PRINCIPAL TOPICS:
Business & Industry
Human Relations
Management
Marketing
Motivation
Sales
Senior Citizens

TYPICAL AUDIENCE:
Corporate
Association

RYAN, ROBIN
11834 S.E. 78th St.
Renton, WA 98056
Telephone: 206-226-0414

RYBACK, DAVID, DR.
1534 N. Decatur Rd., Ste. 201
Atlanta, GA 30307
Telephone: 404-377-3588
ASSOCIATION
  MEMBERSHIP:
Natl. Speakers Assn.
PRINCIPAL TOPICS:
Food/Diet
Health
Human Relations
Physical Fitness
Psychology
TYPICAL AUDIENCE:
Association

SABAH, JOE
P.O. Box 101330
Denver, CO 80250
Telephone: 303-722-7200
Fax: 303-733-2626
ASSOCIATION
  MEMBERSHIP:
Natl. Speakers Assn.
PRINCIPAL TOPICS:
Advertising
Marketing
Sales
TYPICAL AUDIENCE:
Corporate
Association

SABAH, JUDY
1567 S. University Blvd.
Denver, Co 80210
Telephone: 303-722-7200
Fax: 303-733-2626
ASSOCIATION
  MEMBERSHIP:
Natl. Speakers Assn.
PRINCIPAL TOPICS:
Advertising
Marketing
Motivation
Communications
TYPICAL AUDIENCE:
Corporate
Association

SABINE, ELIZABETH
11857 Addison Street
North Hollywood, Ca 91607

Telephone: 818-761-6747
Fax: 818-654-5206
REPRESENTED BY:
Walters International Speakers
  Bureau
ASSOCIATION
  MEMBERSHIP:
Natl. Speakers Assn.
AFTRA
PRINCIPAL TOPICS:
Health
Motivation
Communications
TYPICAL AUDIENCE:
Corporate
Association
Fraternal

SADOVSKY, ANNE   CSP
7557 Rambler Rd., #1454
Dallas, Tx 75231
Telephone: 214-692-9300
Fax: 214-692-9823
ASSOCIATION
  MEMBERSHIP:
Natl. Speakers Assn.
PRINCIPAL TOPICS:
Motivation
Sales
TYPICAL AUDIENCE:
Corporate
Association

SALINGER, TONY
19 Orchard St.
Bernardsville, NJ 07924
Telephone: 908-766-0283
Fax: 908-428-9299
ASSOCIATION
  MEMBERSHIP:
Association For Quality &
  Participation
PRINCIPAL TOPICS:
Business & Industry
Management
Motivation
TYPICAL AUDIENCE:
Corporate
Association
Institutional

SANBORN, MARK H.
Sanborn & Associates
677 S. Williams
Denver, CO 80209
Telephone: 303-698-9656
ASSOCIATION
  MEMBERSHIP:
Natl. Speakers Assn.
PRINCIPAL TOPICS:
Management

Motivation
TYPICAL AUDIENCE:
Corporate
Association

SANDFORD, VIRGINIA A.
811 62nd Ave. N.E.
Tacoma, WA 98422
Telephone: 206-927-1830
ASSOCIATION
  MEMBERSHIP:
Natl. Speakers Assn.
PRINCIPAL TOPICS:
Health
Motivation
Senior Citizens
TYPICAL AUDIENCE:
Association
Institutions

SANDLIN, RUSSELL
9158 Van Nuys Blvd., #9
Panorama City, Ca 91402
Telephone: 800-535-8858
Fax: 818-894-8296
ASSOCIATION
  MEMBERSHIP:
Natl. Speakers Assn.
PRINCIPAL TOPICS:
Management
Marketing
Motivation
Sales
TYPICAL AUDIENCE:
Corporate
Association

SANDROS, DON
4950 FM 1960 West, #C324
Houston, Tx 77069
Telephone: 713-580-2672
Fax: 713-580-7978
ASSOCIATION
  MEMBERSHIP:
Natl. Speakers Assn.
PRINCIPAL TOPICS:
Computer Technology
Sales
TYPICAL AUDIENCE:
Corporate

SANFILIPPO,
  BARBARA   CSP
73 Buckeye Ave.
Oakland, CA 94618
Telephone: 510-547-6683
Fax: 510-547-1218
ASSOCIATION
  MEMBERSHIP:
Natl. Speakers Assn.

PRINCIPAL TOPICS:
Motivation
Sales
TYPICAL AUDIENCE:
Corporate
Association

SANFORD, JAMES VIKING
2208 Hitching Post Lane
Schaumburg, IL 60194
Telephone: 708-882-8586
Fax: 708-882-1641
ASSOCIATION
  MEMBERSHIP:
Natl. Speakers Assn.
Professional Speakers Of IL
PRINCIPAL TOPICS:
Food/Diet
Human Relations
Motivation
Psychology
Sales
TYPICAL AUDIENCE:
Corporate
Public

SASSI, PAULA A.
11481 Caminito Garcia
San Diego, CA 92131
Telephone: 619-586-1511
Fax: 619-695-8526
ASSOCIATION
  MEMBERSHIP:
Natl. Speakers Assn.
PRINCIPAL TOPICS:
Business & Industry
Education
Entertainment
Health
Human Relations
Management
Marketing
Motivation
Psychology
TYPICAL AUDIENCE:
Association

SAUBY, RON
P.O. Box 368
Sioux Falls, SD 57101
Telephone: 605-334-6958
ASSOCIATION
  MEMBERSHIP:
Natl. Speakers Assn.
Toastmasters
PRINCIPAL TOPICS:
Business & Industry
Humor
Motivation
Personal Finance
Religion

Travel
TYPICAL AUDIENCE:
Corporate
Association

SAUER, JOHN R.
222 W. Las Colinas Blvd.,
  #1750
Irving, Ca 75039
Telephone: 214-869-2447
Fax: 214-432-9555
ASSOCIATION
  MEMBERSHIP:
Natl. Speakers Assn.
PRINCIPAL TOPICS:
Management
Motivation
TYPICAL AUDIENCE:
Corporate

SCANLON, DERALEE R.D.
1569 1/2 Manning Ave.
Los Angeles, CA 90024
Telephone: 310-475-1181
Fax: 310-474-8854
ASSOCIATION
  MEMBERSHIP:
Natl. Speakers Assn.
PRINCIPAL TOPICS:
Education
Family
Fashion
Food/Diet
Health
Media
Medical
Nature
Physical Fitness
Senior Citizens
TYPICAL AUDIENCE:
Association
General Public

SCANNELL,
  EDWARD E.   CSP
4234 N. Winfield Scott Plaza,
  #101
Scottsdale, AZ 85251
Telephone: 602-970-0101
Fax: 602-423-0526
ASSOCIATION
  MEMBERSHIP:
Natl. Speakers Assn.
ASAE
ASTD
MPI
PRINCIPAL TOPICS:
Business & Industry
Education
Human Relations
Management

Marketing
Motivation
TYPICAL AUDIENCE:
Corporate
Association

SCHACK, POLLY
5411 Pleasant Drive
Sacramento, CA 95822
Telephone: 916-444-6934
ASSOCIATION
  MEMBERSHIP:
Natl. Speakers Assn.
PRINCIPAL TOPICS:
Human Relations
Humor
Management
TYPICAL AUDIENCE:
Corporate
Association
Fraternal
Government

SCHEESSELE, WILLIAM
Sales Management Systems
5950 Fairview Rd., Ste. 650
Charlotte, NC 28210
ASSOCIATION
  MEMBERSHIP:
Natl. Speakers Assn.
PRINCIPAL TOPICS:
Business & Industry
Sales
TYPICAL AUDIENCE:
Corporate

SCHENK, GEORGE
1814 E. Muirwood Dr.
Phoenix, AZ 85044
Telephone: 602-460-5055
Fax: 602-962-0050
ASSOCIATION
  MEMBERSHIP:
Natl. Speakers Assn.
PRINCIPAL TOPICS:
Business & Industry
Management
Marketing
Motivation
Sales
TYPICAL AUDIENCE:
Corporate

SCHERER, GEORGE
209 Upper Ferry Rd.
Trenton, NJ 08628
Telephone: 609-882-0831
ASSOCIATION
  MEMBERSHIP:
Natl. Speakers Assn.
Platform Speakers

Toastmasters
PRINCIPAL TOPICS:
Humor
TYPICAL AUDIENCE:
Corporate
Institutional

SCHIAVO, 'FANTASTIC
  FRED'
P.O. Box 2267
Jupiter, FL 33468
Telephone: 407-627-9384
MAILING ADDRESS:
109 Paradise Harbor Blvd.
  #101
North Palm Beach, FL 33408
Fax: 407-627-9418
REPRESENTED BY:
Prism Speakers Bureau
ASSOCIATION
  MEMBERSHIP:
Natl. Speakers Assn.
Toastmasters
Florida Speakers
PRINCIPAL TOPICS:
Humor
Motivation
TYPICAL AUDIENCE:
Corporate
Association
Cruise Lines

SCHLAMOWITZ,
  KEVAN, DR.
Schlamowitz Presentations
4426 Paseo Aquimuri
Tucson, AZ 85715
Telephone: 602-577-2194
ASSOCIATION
  MEMBERSHIP:
Natl. Speakers Assn.
PRINCIPAL TOPICS:
Health
Human Relations
Motivation
Psychology
TYPICAL AUDIENCE:
Corporate
Association

SCHMIDT, JOY A.
Schmidt, Joy & Associates
16300 W. Nine Mile, #511
Southfield, MI 48075-5981
Telephone: 313-557-4568
Fax: 313-557-4568
ASSOCIATION
  MEMBERSHIP:
Natl. Speakers Assn.
PRINCIPAL TOPICS:
Business & Industry

Management
Motivation
TYPICAL AUDIENCE:
Corporate
Association

SCHOEMAN, MARILYN
2515 39th Ave. S.W.
Seattle, WA 98116
Telephone: 206-937-1626
REPRESENTED BY:
CBCS-Seattle
ASSOCIATION
  MEMBERSHIP:
Natl. Speakers Assn.
PRINCIPAL TOPICS:
Architecture
Business & Industry
Education
Motivation
TYPICAL AUDIENCE:
Corporate
Association
Education

SCHREINER, CAROL D.
124 Crystal Circle
Norman, OK 73069
Telephone: 405-321-9734
MAILING ADDRESS:
P.O. Box 5223
Norman, OK 73070
ASSOCIATION
  MEMBERSHIP:
Natl. Speakers Assn.
Toastmasters
PRINCIPAL TOPICS:
Agriculture
Education
Health
Human Relations
Humor
Motivation
TYPICAL AUDIENCE:
Association

SCHULTZ, KAREN ROSE
Speaking From The Heart
900 Jorie Blvd., #234
Oak Brook, IL 60521
Telephone: 708-352-6587
Fax: 708-352-6587
ASSOCIATION
  MEMBERSHIP:
Natl. Speakers Assn.
Toastmasters
Professional Speakers of
  Illinois (PSI)
PRINCIPAL TOPICS:
Motivation
Religion

TYPICAL AUDIENCE:
Association
Schools
Recovery Groups

SCHUSTER, DIANE L.
2191 N.E. 68th St., #412
Ft. Lauderdale, FL 33308
Telephone: 305-771-2587
ASSOCIATION
  MEMBERSHIP:
Natl. Speakers Assn.
Toastmasters
Florida Speakers
ASTD
PRINCIPAL TOPICS:
Health
Motivation
TYPICAL AUDIENCE:
Association

SCHWAB, PATT, DR.
Speakeasy
2540 N.E. 83rd St.
Seattle, WA 98115
Telephone: 206-525-1031
Fax: 206-525-1031
ASSOCIATION
  MEMBERSHIP:
Natl. Speakers Assn.
PRINCIPAL TOPICS:
Education
Humor
Management
TYPICAL AUDIENCE:
Association

SCHWARTZ, ARNOLD L.
Achievement Concepts, Inc.
P.O. Box 430, 1963 Cynthia
  Lane
Merrick, NY 11566
Telephone: 516-868-5100
Fax: 516-868-5105
ASSOCIATION
  MEMBERSHIP:
Natl. Speakers Assn.
ASTD
Sales & Marketing Executives
  of Greater N.Y.
PRINCIPAL TOPICS:
Motivation
Sales
TYPICAL AUDIENCE:
Corporate
Association

SCHWARTZ, ELAINE
Schwartz, Elaine & Associates
1354 Lincoln Ave. S.
Highland Park, IL 60035

Telephone: 708-433-2608
Fax: 708-433-2647
REPRESENTED BY:
DMB Speakers
ASSOCIATION
  MEMBERSHIP:
Natl. Speakers Assn.
PRINCIPAL TOPICS:
Family
Human Relations
Psychology
Social Trends
TYPICAL AUDIENCE:
Corporate
Association

SCHWARTZ, FRANCIE
Spectra Communications Inc.
25 Highland Park Ulg
  #100-178
Dallas, TX 75205
Telephone: 214-528-5653
Fax: 214-528-3979
ASSOCIATION
  MEMBERSHIP:
Natl. Speakers Assn.
PRINCIPAL TOPICS:
Business & Industry
Human Relations
Management
Motivation
Sales
TYPICAL AUDIENCE:
Corporate
Association

SCHWARZ, BARB   CSP
Barb Incorporated
1224 212th Ave. S.E.
Issaquah, WA 98027
Telephone: 206-391-2272
ASSOCIATION
  MEMBERSHIP:
Natl. Speakers Assn.
PRINCIPAL TOPICS:
Business & Industry
Management
Sales
TYPICAL AUDIENCE:
Corporate

SCOBEY, SALLY
Scobey's, Sally Comm. Works
412 Lindsay Lane
West Dundee, IL 60118
Telephone: 708-426-5626
Fax: 708-426-5626
REPRESENTED BY:
National Speakers Bureau
Chicago Speakers

ASSOCIATION
  MEMBERSHIP:
Natl. Speakers Assn.
PRINCIPAL TOPICS:
Human Relations
Journalism
Media
Motivation
Video
TYPICAL AUDIENCE:
Corporate
Association

SCOTT, BLACKIE
1498 Brianwood Rd.
Decatur, GA 30033
Telephone: 404-636-5695
ASSOCIATION
  MEMBERSHIP:
Natl. Speakers Assn.
PRINCIPAL TOPICS:
Business & Industry
Entertainment
Family
Humor
TYPICAL AUDIENCE:
Corporate
Association

**SCOTT, CHARLES W.
  (CHUCK), COL.**
Col. Chuck Scott & Associates
  Inc.
125 Spivey Chase Trail
Jonesboro, GA 30236
Telephone: 404-474-4963
Fax: 404-474-4963
REPRESENTED BY:
Cassidy & Fishman
Walters
ASSOCIATION
  MEMBERSHIP:
Natl. Speakers Assn.
Platform Speakers
PRINCIPAL TOPICS:
Military
Motivation
World Affairs
TYPICAL AUDIENCE:
Corporate
Association
Institutions

**SCOTT, GINI GRAHAM,
  PH.D., J.D.**
Changemakers
715 48th Avenue
San Francisco, Ca 94121
Telephone: 415-387-1771
Fax: 415-387-1779

ASSOCIATION
 MEMBERSHIP:
American Society Of
 Journalists & Authors
PRINCIPAL TOPICS:
Business & Industry
Human Relations
Management
Marketing
Psychology
Sales
Social Trends
TYPICAL AUDIENCE:
Corporate
Association
General

SCOTT, SUSAN
P.O. Box 51937
Pacific Grove, CA 93950
Telephone: 408-646-9111
Fax: 408-656-0112
ASSOCIATION
 MEMBERSHIP:
Natl. Speakers Assn.
PRINCIPAL TOPICS:
Communications
Family
Human Relations
Humor
Motivation
Psychology
TYPICAL AUDIENCE:
Association
Fraternal

SEARCY, RHODA M.
Bridge Enterprises
1025 Deepwood Court
Winston-Salem, NC 27104
Telephone: 919-659-9009
MAILING ADDRESS:
Bridge Enterprises
1399 Ashleybrook Ln., Ste. 101
Winston-Salem, NC 27103
ASSOCIATION
 MEMBERSHIP:
Natl. Speakers Assn.
Carolina Speakers
PRINCIPAL TOPICS:
Business & Industry
Education
Family
Food/Diet
Health
Human Relations
Management
Marketing
Medical
Motivation
Physical Fitness

Psychology
Sales
TYPICAL AUDIENCE:
Corporate
Association
Institutions

SEDACCA, ROSALIND
ROSALIND SEDACCA
 ASSOC.
2003 20TH LANE
LAKE WORTH, FL 33463
Telephone: 407-964-7442
Fax: 407-964-6519
ASSOCIATION
 MEMBERSHIP:
Natl. Speakers Assn.
Florida Freelance Writers
PRINCIPAL TOPICS:
Advertising
Business & Industry
Human Relations
Marketing
TYPICAL AUDIENCE:
Corporate
Association
Fraternal
SEE AD IN SECTION 8

SEGEL, RICK
75 Riverside Ave.
Medford, MA 02155
Telephone: 617-396-2244
Fax: 617-395-5862
ASSOCIATION
 MEMBERSHIP:
Natl. Speakers Assn.
PRINCIPAL TOPICS:
Fashion
Humor
Marketing
TYPICAL AUDIENCE:
Corporate
Association
Trade Centers & Malls

SELAME, ELINOR
2330 Washington Street
Newton, Ma 02162
Telephone: 617-969-3150
Fax: 617-969-1944
ASSOCIATION
 MEMBERSHIP:
Natl. Speakers Assn.
Package Design Council
PRINCIPAL TOPICS:
Business & Industry
Marketing
TYPICAL AUDIENCE:
Corporate
Association

SELWYN, PADI
111 Santa Rosa Ave., #200
Santa Rosa, Ca 95404
Telephone: 707-829-2641
Fax: 707-829-2641
ASSOCIATION
 MEMBERSHIP:
Natl. Speakers Assn.
PRINCIPAL TOPICS:
Advertising
Business & Industry
Marketing
TYPICAL AUDIENCE:
Corporate
Association

SEVERIN, THOMAS J.
P.O. Box 436
Glenview, IL 60025
Telephone: 800-544-4081
Fax: 800-545-4081
ASSOCIATION
 MEMBERSHIP:
Natl. Speakers Assn.
PRINCIPAL TOPICS:
Business & Industry
TYPICAL AUDIENCE:
Corporate
Association

SHANNON, SHARON L.
Shannon Training Systems
P.O. Box 1252
Lake Oswego, OR 97035
Telephone: 800-443-4710
Fax: 503-636-6465
REPRESENTED BY:
Read Bureau
Exposures To Excellence
ASSOCIATION
 MEMBERSHIP:
Natl. Speakers Assn.
PRINCIPAL TOPICS:
Marketing
Psychology
Sales
TYPICAL AUDIENCE:
Corporate
Association

SHAPIRO, BARRY M.
6757 Armour Dr.
Oakland, CA 94611
Telephone: 510-339-9861
Fax: 510-339-9862
ASSOCIATION
 MEMBERSHIP:
Natl. Speakers Assn.
PRINCIPAL TOPICS:
Business & Industry
Human Relations

TYPICAL AUDIENCE:
Corporate
Government

SHAPIRO, DON
First Concepts Develop Corp.
9016 Wilshire Blvd., Ste. 419
Beverly Hills, CA 90211
Telephone: 310-541-7958
Fax: 310-659-0923
REPRESENTED BY:
Lordly & Dame
New Information
Podium
Promark Service
ASSOCIATION
 MEMBERSHIP:
Natl. Speakers Assn.
Toastmasters
Sales & Marketing Executives
PRINCIPAL TOPICS:
Automotive
Business & Industry
Education
Management
Marketing
Sales
TYPICAL AUDIENCE:
Corporate
Association

SHARP, SALLY O.
4810 Brookside Ave.
Edina, MN 55436
Telephone: 612-926-4672
Fax: 612-925-9362
ASSOCIATION
 MEMBERSHIP:
Natl. Speakers Assn.
Toastmasters
PRINCIPAL TOPICS:
Management
Motivation
Sales
TYPICAL AUDIENCE:
Corporate
Association

SHEA, CHARLENE   CSP
121 Allied Street
Manchester, NH 03109
Telephone: 603-668-7016
Fax: 603-627-0570
ASSOCIATION
 MEMBERSHIP:
Natl. Speakers Assn.
PRINCIPAL TOPICS:
Business & Industry
Human Relations
Management
Motivation

TYPICAL AUDIENCE:
Corporate
Association

SHELTON, LEE
12083 W. 27th Drive
Denver, CO 80215
Telephone: 303-232-1767
Fax: 303-234-9183
ASSOCIATION
  MEMBERSHIP:
Natl. Speakers Assn.
ASAE
PRINCIPAL TOPICS:
Automotive
Business & Industry
Education
Entertainment
Human Relations
Humor
Management
Marketing
Medical
Motivation
Sales
TYPICAL AUDIENCE:
Corporate
Association

SHELTON, SANDRA A.
Shelton International
3002 Penny Lane
Euless, TX 76039-7825
Telephone: 817-540-1113
MAILING ADDRESS:
Shelton International
P.O. Box 612305
Dallas, TX 75261-2305
Fax: 817-685-0488
REPRESENTED BY:
5 Star
CareerTrack
SW Speakers
Access
ASSOCIATION
  MEMBERSHIP:
Natl. Speakers Assn.
Natl. Singles Leadership
PRINCIPAL TOPICS:
Human Relations
Management
Motivation
TYPICAL AUDIENCE:
Corporate
Association

SHERMAN, RALPH
1312 Caton Ave.
Joliet, IL 60435
Telephone: 815-725-5615
MAILING ADDRESS:

WKBM Radio
32401 S. Rt. #53
Wilmington, IL 60481
Fax: 815-476-1007
REPRESENTED BY:
International Speakers Network
ASSOCIATION
  MEMBERSHIP:
Natl. Speakers Assn.
Platform Speakers
PRINCIPAL TOPICS:
Advertising
Entertainment
Humor
Media
Sales
TYPICAL AUDIENCE:
Corporate
Association
Fraternal

SHIELDS, LINDA
Speaking With Authority, Inc.
3643 Lakeshore Dr.
Hope Mills, NC 28348
Telephone: 919-425-6253
ASSOCIATION
  MEMBERSHIP:
Natl. Speakers Assn.
PRINCIPAL TOPICS:
Business & Industry
TYPICAL AUDIENCE:
Corporate

SHUH, AL & ASSOCIATES
Shuh, Al & Associates
3225 Dundee Ridge Way
Duluth, GA 30136
Telephone: 404-418-9970
REPRESENTED BY:
Jordan International
  Enterprises, Inc.
ASSOCIATION
  MEMBERSHIP:
Natl. Speakers Assn.
PRINCIPAL TOPICS:
Business & Industry
Education
Entertainment
Humor
Management
Motivation
Sales
TYPICAL AUDIENCE:
Corporate
Association
Educational

SHULTS, JOHN A.
1349 Thornton Rd.
Houston, Tx 77018

Telephone: 713-682-6430
ASSOCIATION
  MEMBERSHIP:
Natl. Speakers Assn.
Toastmasters
PRINCIPAL TOPICS:
Motivation
Communications
TYPICAL AUDIENCE:
Corporate
Association

SIBERT, DENNIS G.
4701 Cody Dr.
West Des Moines, IA 50265
Telephone: 515-225-8497
REPRESENTED BY:
Keynote
ASSOCIATION
  MEMBERSHIP:
Natl. Speakers Assn.
Toastmasters
ASTD
PRINCIPAL TOPICS:
Human Relations
Management
Motivation
TYPICAL AUDIENCE:
Corporate
Association

SIEGFRIED, CHARLOTTE
28 Marinero Cr., #21
Tiburon, CA 94920
Telephone: 415-435-5792
ASSOCIATION
  MEMBERSHIP:
Natl. Speakers Assn.
PRINCIPAL TOPICS:
Business & Industry
Human Relations
Management
TYPICAL AUDIENCE:
Corporate
Association

SILVER, IDORA
3855 Piccadilly Drive
Reno, NV 89509
Telephone: 702-829-0606
Fax: 800-682-2929
REPRESENTED BY:
Silver State Speakers Bureau
ASSOCIATION
  MEMBERSHIP:
Natl. Speakers Assn.
PRINCIPAL TOPICS:
Human Relations
Medical
Motivation

TYPICAL AUDIENCE:
Corporate
Association
Public Sector

SILVER, SUSAN
Positively Organized
11661 San Vicente Blvd., #210
Los Angeles, CA 90049
Telephone: 310-207-7799
PRINCIPAL TOPICS:
Business & Industry
Computer Technology
Management
TYPICAL AUDIENCE:
Corporate
Association

SIMENTON, PHILIP R.
Simenton Success Seminars
512 Avenue G, Ste. 305
Redondo Beach, CA 90277
Telephone: 310-540-5205
REPRESENTED BY:
Walters Intls.
KCLA Talk Radio
ASSOCIATION
  MEMBERSHIP:
Natl. Speakers Assn.
PRINCIPAL TOPICS:
Media
TYPICAL AUDIENCE:
Corporate
Association
General Public

SIMMS, STEVE
528 Dale Court
Franklin, TN 37064
Telephone: 615-791-8777
Fax: 615-794-4927
ASSOCIATION
  MEMBERSHIP:
Natl. Speakers Assn.
PRINCIPAL TOPICS:
Education
Humor
Motivation
Sales
TYPICAL AUDIENCE:
Corporate
Association
Schools

SIMON, BARBARA J.   CSP
One Step Beyond
7101 W. 44th St.
Tacoma, WA 98466
Telephone: 206-564-2847

ASSOCIATION
   MEMBERSHIP:
Natl. Speakers Assn.
Natl. Assoc. of Hypnotherapists
PRINCIPAL TOPICS:
Education
Health
Human Relations
Management
Motivation
Philosophy
Psychology
Social Trends
TYPICAL AUDIENCE:
Corporate
Association

SIMONS, EDWARD A.
Hazmaco, Inc.
P.O. Box 520
Gardnerville, Nv 89410
Telephone: 702-267-4322
Fax: 702-267-4322
ASSOCIATION
   MEMBERSHIP:
Natl. Speakers Assn.
PRINCIPAL TOPICS:
Ecology
Government
TYPICAL AUDIENCE:
Corporate
Governmental

SIMS, D. PHILLIP
357 N. Post Oak Ln., #206
Houston, TX 77024
Telephone: 713-682-0218
Fax: 713-682-0218
ASSOCIATION
   MEMBERSHIP:
Natl. Speakers Assn.
American Society For Quality
   Control
PRINCIPAL TOPICS:
Business & Industry
Education
Human Relations
Management
Motivation
Psychology
TYPICAL AUDIENCE:
Corporate
Association

SIRESS, JIM
8021 West 115th St.
Overland Park, KS 66204
Telephone: 913-451-4758
Fax: 913-345-0345
REPRESENTED BY:
Five Star

ASSOCIATION
   MEMBERSHIP:
Natl. Speakers Assn.
PRINCIPAL TOPICS:
Aviation
Human Relations
Management
Motivation
TYPICAL AUDIENCE:
Corporate
Association

SJODIN, TERRI
Sjodin Communications
17145 Von Karman, #108
Irvine, CA 92714
Telephone: 714-955-1565
Fax: 714-955-3529
ASSOCIATION
   MEMBERSHIP:
Natl. Speakers Assn.
PRINCIPAL TOPICS:
Communications
Sales
TYPICAL AUDIENCE:
Corporate
Association

SKOGLUND, ROBERT
Humble Farmer, The
1600 Oceanside Dr., Ste. 400
St. George, ME 04857
Telephone: 207-372-8052
Fax: 207-372-8052
ASSOCIATION
   MEMBERSHIP:
Natl. Speakers Assn.
PRINCIPAL TOPICS:
Entertainment
Humor
Motivation
TYPICAL AUDIENCE:
Corporate
Association

SLADE, TOM
425 Robmont Road
Charlotte, NC 28270
Telephone: 704-364-4486
PRINCIPAL TOPICS:
Health
Human Relations
Humor
Medical
Motivation
Religion
Sales

TYPICAL AUDIENCE:
Corporate
Association
Fraternal

SLOTKIN, FRAN S.
P.O. Box 1343, 253 Dune Rd.
Westhampton Beach, NY
   11978
Telephone: 516-288-4240
Fax: 305-484-3886
MAILING ADDRESS:
6001 Falls Cir., N.
Lauderhill, FL 33319
PRINCIPAL TOPICS:
History
Human Relations
Motivation
Social Trends
TYPICAL AUDIENCE:
Corporate
Association
Fraternal Women's Group

SLUTSKY, JEFF   CSP
467 Waterbury Ct.
Gahanna, OH 43230
Telephone: 614-337-7474
Fax: 614-337-2233
ASSOCIATION
   MEMBERSHIP:
Natl. Speakers Assn.
PRINCIPAL TOPICS:
Marketing
TYPICAL AUDIENCE:
Corporate
Association

SMART, DOUG
Smart Seminars
P.O. Box 768024
Roswell, Ga 30076
Telephone: 404-587-9784
ASSOCIATION
   MEMBERSHIP:
Natl. Speakers Assn.
PRINCIPAL TOPICS:
Motivation
Sales
TYPICAL AUDIENCE:
Corporate
Association

SMITH, CARL T.
526 Yale Ave.
Pitman, NJ 08011
Telephone: 609-589-2629
Fax: 609-582-8558
ASSOCIATION
   MEMBERSHIP:
Natl. Speakers Assn.

NEA
NJEA
PRINCIPAL TOPICS:
Education
Motivation
Sales
Communications
TYPICAL AUDIENCE:
Corporate
Association

SMITH, DIANE
   ELLINGSON
P.O. Box 9126
Salt Lake City, UT 84109
Telephone: 801-487-5855
REPRESENTED BY:
Wagstaff Enterprises
PRINCIPAL TOPICS:
Education
Health
Medical
Motivation
Youth
TYPICAL AUDIENCE:
Corporate
Association

SMITH, HAROLD IVAN
P.O. Box 24688
Kansas City, Mo 64131
Telephone: 816-444-5301
ASSOCIATION
   MEMBERSHIP:
Natl. Speakers Assn.
PRINCIPAL TOPICS:
Family
Human Relations
Motivation
Religion
Senior Citizens
Social Trends
TYPICAL AUDIENCE:
Association

SMITH, J. THOMAS
P.O. Box 52523
Houston, TX 77052
Telephone: 713-228-4000
MAILING ADDRESS:
2211 Norfolk, #420
Houston, TX 77098
ASSOCIATION
   MEMBERSHIP:
Natl. Speakers Assn.
PRINCIPAL TOPICS:
Family
Human Relations
Motivation
Psychology

TYPICAL AUDIENCE:
Association
Public

SMITH, MARK S. A., CPC
Valence Group, The
3530 Cranswood Way, Ste. 107
Colorado Springs, CO
　80918-6338
Telephone: 719-522-0780
Fax: 719-522-0790
ASSOCIATION
　MEMBERSHIP:
Natl. Speakers Assn.
PRINCIPAL TOPICS:
Sales
TYPICAL AUDIENCE:
Corporate
Association

SMITH, RICHARD Q.
330 Frederick Bldg.,
　4th Ave. & 10th St.
Huntington, WV 25701
Telephone: 304-522-7321
Fax: 304-523-8250
MAILING ADDRESS:
P.O. Box 639
Huntington, WV 25711
ASSOCIATION
　MEMBERSHIP:
Natl. Speakers Assn.
Platform Speakers
International Platform
PRINCIPAL TOPICS:
Health
Motivation
Sales
TYPICAL AUDIENCE:
Corporate

SMITH, ROY L.
12200 24th St.
Plattsmouth, NE 68048-7802
Telephone: 402-298-8570
Fax: 402-298-7174
ASSOCIATION
　MEMBERSHIP:
Natl. Speakers Assn.
Toastmasters
PRINCIPAL TOPICS:
Agriculture
Entertainment
History
Humor
Motivation
TYPICAL AUDIENCE:
Corporate
Association

SMITH, WALTER D.
P.O. Box 15, 222 3rd Ave.
Baraboo, WI 53913
Telephone: 608-356-7733
Fax: 608-356-7735
REPRESENTED BY:
Associated Speakers
Ann Miller Professional
　Services
ASSOCIATION
　MEMBERSHIP:
Natl. Speakers Assn.
Toastmasters
Wisconsin Professional
　Speakers
PRINCIPAL TOPICS:
Business & Industry
Management
Motivation
TYPICAL AUDIENCE:
Corporate
Association
Public Audiences

SNYDER, MARILYN
2533 Thorn Pl.
Fullerton, CA 92635
Telephone: 714-961-8930
Fax: 714-961-8930
ASSOCIATION
　MEMBERSHIP:
Natl. Speakers Assn.
PRINCIPAL TOPICS:
Business & Industry
Computer Technology
Education
Human Relations
Motivation
TYPICAL AUDIENCE:
Corporate
Association
Institutional

SOARES, DR. CECLIA J.
1280 Boulevard Way, #207
Walnut Creek, CA 94595
Telephone: 510-932-0607
Fax: 510-934-8277
ASSOCIATION
　MEMBERSHIP:
Natl. Speakers Assn.
PRINCIPAL TOPICS:
Animals
Family
Health
Human Relations
Management
Psychology
Youth
TYPICAL AUDIENCE:
Association

SOBCZAK, ART J.
Business By Phone Inc.
5301 S. 144th St.
Omaha, NE 68137
Telephone: 402-895-9399
Fax: 402-896-3353
ASSOCIATION
　MEMBERSHIP:
Natl. Speakers Assn.
PRINCIPAL TOPICS:
Sales
TYPICAL AUDIENCE:
Corporate
Association

SOMMER, BOBBE, PH.D.
P.O. Box 3116, 24195 Juanita
　Dr.
Quail Valley, CA 92587
Telephone: 909-244-1885
Fax: 909-244-5466
REPRESENTED BY:
Speakers Bureau Unlimited
ASSOCIATION
　MEMBERSHIP:
Natl. Speakers Assn.
PRINCIPAL TOPICS:
Education
Family
Health
Human Relations
Motivation
Psychology
TYPICAL AUDIENCE:
Corporate
Association

SORENTINO, PHIL
Humor Consultants Inc.
655 Metro Place S., Ste. 50
Dublin, OH 43017
Telephone: 614-436-6969
Fax: 614-436-7009
ASSOCIATION
　MEMBERSHIP:
Natl. Speakers Assn.
PRINCIPAL TOPICS:
Business & Industry
Humor
Management
Motivation
TYPICAL AUDIENCE:
Corporate
Association

SPENCER, DUFFY, PH.D.
Personal Presence
609 Dartmouth St.
Westbury, NY 11590
Telephone: 516-334-8985
Fax: 516-997-4401

ASSOCIATION
　MEMBERSHIP:
Natl. Speakers Assn.
PRINCIPAL TOPICS:
Family
Health
Human Relations
Management
Motivation
Social Trends
TYPICAL AUDIENCE:
Corporate
Association

SPENGLER, CHRISTINE J.
　(CPS/CAM)
3164 Cheltenham
Toledo, OH 43606
Telephone: 419-537-2211
MAILING ADDRESS:
University of Toledo, The
Office of the President, 2801
　W. Bancroft St.
Toledo, OH 43606
Fax: 419-537-4984
ASSOCIATION
　MEMBERSHIP:
Natl. Speakers Assn.
Professional Secretaries
　International
PRINCIPAL TOPICS:
Business & Industry
Computer Technology
Education
History
Human Relations
Management
Motivation
TYPICAL AUDIENCE:
Corporate
Association

SPRINKLE, G. K.
G. K. SPRINKLE
**　CONSULTING**
2801 WINSTON COURT
AUSTIN, TX 78731
Telephone: 512-458-1888
Fax: 512-458-2221
PRINCIPAL TOPICS:
Business & Industry
Government
TYPICAL AUDIENCE:
Corporate
Association
SEE AD IN SECTION 8

STACY, GAYLON
2205 Woodford Way
Edmond, OK 73034
Telephone: 405-341-1871

PRINCIPAL TOPICS:
Entertainment
Humor
Motivation
TYPICAL AUDIENCE:
Association
General Public

STALEY, MICHAEL F.
Golden Hour Motivational
  Resource
231 Brittany Ave.
Port Orange, FL 32127-5914
Telephone: 800-622-6453
Fax: 904-788-5848
ASSOCIATION
  MEMBERSHIP:
Natl. Speakers Assn.
PRINCIPAL TOPICS:
Human Relations
Medical
Motivation
TYPICAL AUDIENCE:
Corporate
Association
Fraternal

STARK, PETER BARRON
1306 Scenic Dr.
Escondido, CA 92029
Telephone: 619-738-0252
Fax: 619-738-9103
ASSOCIATION
  MEMBERSHIP:
Natl. Speakers Assn.
Toastmasters
PRINCIPAL TOPICS:
Business & Industry
Management
TYPICAL AUDIENCE:
Corporate
Association

STARKEY, JUDITH A.
Starkey Group, Inc., The
333 W. Wacker Dr., Ste. 700
Chicago, IL 60606-1225
Telephone: 312-444-2025
ASSOCIATION
  MEMBERSHIP:
Natl. Speakers Assn.
PRINCIPAL TOPICS:
Business & Industry
Human Relations
Management
World Affairs
TYPICAL AUDIENCE:
Corporate

STARR, ROBERT BRUCE
P.O. Box 811565
Boca Raton, FL 33481
Telephone: 800-576-0823
Fax: 407-852-0752
ASSOCIATION
  MEMBERSHIP:
Natl. Speakers Assn.
PRINCIPAL TOPICS:
Human Relations
Humor
Motivation
Philosophy
Social Trends
Youth
TYPICAL AUDIENCE:
Association
Religious/Single Groups

STATON, BILL
2113 East Fifth St.
Charlotte, NC 28204
Telephone: 704-332-7514
Fax: 704-332-0427
ASSOCIATION
  MEMBERSHIP:
Natl. Speakers Assn.
PRINCIPAL TOPICS:
Business & Industry
Personal Finance
TYPICAL AUDIENCE:
Corporate
Association

STAUB, JAMES R.
3 Rosehaven St.
Stafford, VA 22554
Telephone: 703-791-5548
MAILING ADDRESS:
Management & Professional
  Development Associates
13658 Van Doren Rd.
Mawasses, VA 22111
ASSOCIATION
  MEMBERSHIP:
Platform Speakers
PRINCIPAL TOPICS:
Business & Industry
Education
Humor
Management
Motivation
TYPICAL AUDIENCE:
Corporate

STAUTER, ROGER
4509 Cottage Grove Rd.
Madison, WI 53716
Telephone: 608-221-4000
Fax: 608-221-4031

ASSOCIATION
  MEMBERSHIP:
Natl. Speakers Assn.
PRINCIPAL TOPICS:
Humor
Motivation
Sales
TYPICAL AUDIENCE:
Corporate
Association

STEIL, LYMAN K. (MANNY),
  DR. (CPAE)   CSP
25 Robb Farm Rd.
North Oaks, MN 55127
Telephone: 612-483-3597
Fax: 612-482-0220
ASSOCIATION
  MEMBERSHIP:
Natl. Speakers Assn.
International Listening
PRINCIPAL TOPICS:
Business & Industry
Education
Family
Human Relations
Management
Marketing
Psychology
Sales
TYPICAL AUDIENCE:
Corporate
Association
Institutional

STEIN, CAROLYN
20281 E. Country Club Dr.,
  #1901
N. Miami, FL 33180
Telephone: 305-931-3237
Fax: 305-937-1551
ASSOCIATION
  MEMBERSHIP:
Natl. Speakers Assn.
Toastmasters
MPI
SFAE
FSA
American Society of Training &
  Development
PRINCIPAL TOPICS:
Business & Industry
Human Relations
Management
Media
Motivation
Sales
TYPICAL AUDIENCE:
Corporate
Association

STEIN, SANDY
Hughes Missile Systems Co.
4675 S.E. Camino Rosa
Tuscon, AZ 85718
Telephone: 602-794-4895
Fax: 602-794-4306
ASSOCIATION
  MEMBERSHIP:
Natl. Speakers Assn.
Az. Counseling
International Listening
American Speech, Hearing &
  Language
PRINCIPAL TOPICS:
Business & Industry
Education
Human Relations
Management
Motivation
Senior Citizens
TYPICAL AUDIENCE:
Corporate
Institutional

STENNES, BARBARA
7931 N.W. 54th Ave.
Johnston, IA 50131
Telephone: 515-278-1292
Fax: 515-270-0694
ASSOCIATION
  MEMBERSHIP:
Natl. Speakers Assn.
ASTD
PRINCIPAL TOPICS:
Education
Management
Motivation
Sales
TYPICAL AUDIENCE:
Corporate
Association

STEPHANI, SUSAN   CSP
P.O. Box 497
Hartland, WI 53029
Telephone: 414-538-4270
Fax: 414-538-4290
ASSOCIATION
  MEMBERSHIP:
Natl. Speakers Assn.
PRINCIPAL TOPICS:
Business & Industry
Human Relations
Motivation
Sales
TYPICAL AUDIENCE:
Corporate
Association

STERN, DEBRA
1943 N. Hudson
Chicago, IL 60614
Telephone: 312-280-7942
Fax: 312-280-9583
MAILING ADDRESS:
106 S. Oak Park Ave., #203
Oak Park, IL 60302
ASSOCIATION
  MEMBERSHIP:
Natl. Speakers Assn.
American Association of
  Marriage & Family Therapists
PRINCIPAL TOPICS:
Communications
Human Relations
Management
Motivation
Psychology
TYPICAL AUDIENCE:
Corporate
Association

STEVENS, SUZANNE H.
1001 S. Marshall St., #37
Winston-Salem, NC 27101
Telephone: 919-723-8481
Fax: 919-777-3603
ASSOCIATION
  MEMBERSHIP:
Natl. Speakers Assn.
PRINCIPAL TOPICS:
Education
Family
Motivation
Youth
TYPICAL AUDIENCE:
Association
Educational Institutions
Healthcare Workers
Psychologists

STEWART, DAVID
Success In Action, Inc.
8283 N. Hayden
Scottsdale, Az 85258
Telephone: 602-443-4300
Fax: 602-443-4898
ASSOCIATION
  MEMBERSHIP:
Natl. Speakers Assn.
DSA-District Selling Association
PRINCIPAL TOPICS:
Marketing
Motivation
Sales
TYPICAL AUDIENCE:
Corporate
Association
Fraternal

STEWART,
  LAURIE A.   CSP
Stewart, L.A. Presentations
P.O. Box 50869
Kalamazoo, MI 49005
Telephone: 616-349-2433
REPRESENTED BY:
Jostens
North American Speakers
  Bureau
Meeting Connection
ASSOCIATION
  MEMBERSHIP:
Natl. Speakers Assn.
PRINCIPAL TOPICS:
Education
Family
Human Relations
Motivation
Youth
TYPICAL AUDIENCE:
Educational

STEWART, MIKE
Stewart & Stewart, Inc.
5341 Forest Springs Dr.
Dunwoody, GA 30338
Telephone: 404-512-0022
Fax: 404-392-1501
ASSOCIATION
  MEMBERSHIP:
Natl. Speakers Assn.
Georgia Speakers Assocation
ASTD
PRINCIPAL TOPICS:
Management
Sales
TYPICAL AUDIENCE:
Corporate

STEWART, ROD
Steward, Rod & Associates
1133 Marigold Dr., N.E.
Albuquerque, NM 87122
Telephone: 505-345-8591
Fax: 505-345-8598
ASSOCIATION
  MEMBERSHIP:
Natl. Speakers Assn.
Toastmasters
PRINCIPAL TOPICS:
Health
Humor
Motivation
TYPICAL AUDIENCE:
Corporate
Association
Fraternal

STILLWAGON,
  GLENN, DR.
767 Dry Run Rd.
Monongahela, PA 15063
Telephone: 412-258-6506
Fax: 412-258-5611
ASSOCIATION
  MEMBERSHIP:
Natl. Spkeakers
PRINCIPAL TOPICS:
Health
TYPICAL AUDIENCE:
Association

STOLTZFUS, D. LEE,
  PH.D.
L.I.F.E. Management Systems
248 E. Foothill Blvd. #100
Monrovia, CA 92064
Telephone: 818-303-1211
Fax: 818-952-3252
ASSOCIATION
  MEMBERSHIP:
Natl. Speakers Assn.
PRINCIPAL TOPICS:
Human Relations
Management
Motivation
Psychology
Sales
TYPICAL AUDIENCE:
Corporate
Association

STONE, D. CONWAY
3805 Cabinwood Ct.
Louisville, KY 40220
Telephone: 502-459-3273
ASSOCIATION
  MEMBERSHIP:
Natl. Speakers Assn.
Toastmasters
Louisville Convention Bureau
PRINCIPAL TOPICS:
Management
Motivation
Psychology
Religion
Sales
TYPICAL AUDIENCE:
Corporate
Association

STRIKE, LOUIS N.
9781 Pinto Ct.
Cincinnati, OH 45242
Telephone: 513-841-0777
Fax: 513-841-1168
MAILING ADDRESS:
Cinpac, Inc.
2940 Highland Drive

Cincinnati, OH 45212
ASSOCIATION
  MEMBERSHIP:
Natl. Speakers Assn.
PRINCIPAL TOPICS:
Business & Industry
Management
Marketing
Physical Fitness
Sales
TYPICAL AUDIENCE:
Corporate
Association

SUCKOW, BOB
Suckow, R.W. & Assoc.
RR1, Box 396
Newton, IA 50208
Telephone: 515-792-2364
Fax: 515-791-7728
ASSOCIATION
  MEMBERSHIP:
Natl. Speakers Assn.
Academy Of Administrative
  Managers
PRINCIPAL TOPICS:
Aviation
Family
Health
Human Relations
Management
Military
Motivation
Physical Fitness
Religion
Senior Citizens
TYPICAL AUDIENCE:
Corporate
Association
Fraternal

SUKENICK, RON D.
6033 Lowell Ave.
Indianapolis, IN 46219
Telephone: 317-357-8838
Fax: 317-351-5375
REPRESENTED BY:
Indianapolis Speakers Bureau
ASSOCIATION
  MEMBERSHIP:
Natl. Speakers Assn.
PRINCIPAL TOPICS:
Motivation
Sales
TYPICAL AUDIENCE:
Association
Fraternal
General Business

SULLIVAN, TERRY
RR2, Little Colfax Farm Road
Cambridge, NY 12816
Telephone: 518-677-5280
ASSOCIATION
  MEMBERSHIP:
Natl. Speakers Assn.
PRINCIPAL TOPICS:
Marketing
Motivation
Sales
TYPICAL AUDIENCE:
Association

SUMMER, SHIRLEY
Whittle, S. J. Co.
P.O. Box 189
Davis, CA 95617
Telephone: 916-757-1251
Fax: 916-757-1251
ASSOCIATION
  MEMBERSHIP:
Natl. Speakers Assn.
Toastmasters
ASTD
PRINCIPAL TOPICS:
Family
Human Relations
Management
Motivation
Nature
Personal Finance
Philosophy
Psychology
TYPICAL AUDIENCE:
Association

SUMMEY, MIKE
Rt. 4, Xanadu
Asheville, NC 28806
Telephone: 704-687-4000
Fax: 704-254-7220
MAILING ADDRESS:
P.O. Box 1108
Arden, NC 28704
ASSOCIATION
  MEMBERSHIP:
Natl. Speakers Assn.
Platform Speakers
PRINCIPAL TOPICS:
Advertising
Government
Marketing
Sales
TYPICAL AUDIENCE:
Corporate
Association

SUTTON, JAMES D., DR.
Sutton, Dr. James &
  Associates
P.O. Box 672
Pleasanton, TX 78064
Telephone: 800-659-6628
Fax: 210-569-2617
ASSOCIATION
  MEMBERSHIP:
Natl. Speakers Assn.
STPSA (NSA Chapter)
PRINCIPAL TOPICS:
Education
Family
Health
Medical
Psychology
Religion
Youth
TYPICAL AUDIENCE:
Association
Institutional

SUTTON, SUZY   CSP
17 Sentinel Rd.
Washington Crossing, PA
  18977
Telephone: 215-493-4766
Fax: 215-493-7512
ASSOCIATION
  MEMBERSHIP:
Natl. Speakers Assn.
MPI-ASTD
PRINCIPAL TOPICS:
Education
Human Relations
Humor
Motivation
TYPICAL AUDIENCE:
Corporate
Association

SWANSON, DAVID
7235 W. Wells St.
Wauwatosa, WI 53213-3607
Telephone: 414-259-0265
REPRESENTED BY:
Associated Speakers
ASSOCIATION
  MEMBERSHIP:
Natl. Speakers Assn.
PRINCIPAL TOPICS:
Advertising
Business & Industry
Education
Human Relations
Marketing
Motivation
Psychology
Sales

TYPICAL AUDIENCE:
Corporate
Association
Institutional

SWARTZ, JOHN C.
P.O. Box 256
Sharon Center, OH 44274
Telephone: 216-723-0523
ASSOCIATION
  MEMBERSHIP:
Natl. Speakers Assn.
Ohio Speakers Forum
PRINCIPAL TOPICS:
Education
Family
Government
History
TYPICAL AUDIENCE:
Schools
Civic
Libraries

SWINDELL, GENE
5277 Glenridge Dr.
Atlanta, GA 30342
Telephone: 404-303-9066
Fax: 404-303-1067
REPRESENTED BY:
Jordan Speakers
Speakers Network
ASSOCIATION
  MEMBERSHIP:
Natl. Speakers Assn.
PRINCIPAL TOPICS:
Human Relations
Management
Motivation
Sales
TYPICAL AUDIENCE:
Corporate
Association

TABERS, JOE
Protective Training Services
P.O. Box 760427
Lathrup Village, MI 48076
Telephone: 313-646-0340
Fax: 313-646-9025
REPRESENTED BY:
Anne Miller Promotions
ASSOCIATION
  MEMBERSHIP:
Natl. Speakers Assn.
ASTD
PRINCIPAL TOPICS:
Communications
Human Relations
Management

TYPICAL AUDIENCE:
Corporate
Association

TAHIR, ELIZABETH
Tahir, Liz & Associates
201 St. Charles Ave., #2500
New Orleans, La 70170
Telephone: 504-569-1670
Fax: 504-524-7979
ASSOCIATION
  MEMBERSHIP:
Natl. Speakers Assn.
PRINCIPAL TOPICS:
Business & Industry
Human Relations
Management
Marketing
TYPICAL AUDIENCE:
Corporate
Association
Entreprenuers

TAILLON, YAHZDI
2130 Shoreline
Flower Mound, Tx 75028
Telephone: 214-539-4604
PRINCIPAL TOPICS:
Computer Technology
Human Relations
Religion
TYPICAL AUDIENCE:
Corporate
Association

TANSEY, DR. DAVE
190 Hidden Valley Rd.
Watsonville, CA 95076
Telephone: 800-678-4169
Fax: 408-763-2452
ASSOCIATION
  MEMBERSHIP:
Natl. Speakers Assn.
Josephson Institute For Ethics
PRINCIPAL TOPICS:
Education
Management
Motivation
Youth
TYPICAL AUDIENCE:
Corporate
Association

TARASAVAGE, EDWARD B.
  (CHA) (CFBE)
Hospitality Industry Trainers
P.O. Box 566353
Atlanta, GA 31156
Telephone: 404-923-2256

ASSOCIATION
  MEMBERSHIP:
Natl. Speakers Assn.
Ga Speakers
PRINCIPAL TOPICS:
Sales
TYPICAL AUDIENCE:
Corporate

TARTARELLA, KATHY
P.O. Box 297
Aurora, Oh 44202
Telephone: 216-562-5571
Fax: 216-562-2126
REPRESENTED BY:
Speakers Unlimited
ASSOCIATION
  MEMBERSHIP:
Natl. Speakers Assn.
Ohio Speakers Forum
PRINCIPAL TOPICS:
Fashion
Marketing
Social Trends
TYPICAL AUDIENCE:
Corporate
Association

TAYLOR, BRUCE J.
1233 N. Ford St.
McMinnville, OR 97128-3739
Telephone: 503-472-4845
ASSOCIATION
  MEMBERSHIP:
Natl. Speakers Assn.
PRINCIPAL TOPICS:
Business & Industry
TYPICAL AUDIENCE:
Corporate
Association

TAYLOR, MEREDITH
Taylor Associates
155 Vonda Kay Circle
Lexington, SC 29072
Telephone: 803-957-5874
ASSOCIATION
  MEMBERSHIP:
Natl. Speakers Assn.
Platform Speakers
PRINCIPAL TOPICS:
Health
Human Relations
Humor
Motivation
TYPICAL AUDIENCE:
Corporate
Association

TAYLOR, PAULA R., M.A.
Taylor, Paula & Associates
405 14th St. #1001
Oakland, CA 94612
Telephone: 510-893-5707
Fax: 510-893-3822
ASSOCIATION
  MEMBERSHIP:
Natl. Speakers Assn.
PRINCIPAL TOPICS:
Business & Industry
Management
Motivation
TYPICAL AUDIENCE:
Corporate

TEPLITZ, JERRY V.,
  DR.　　　　　　　CSP
219 53rd St.
Virginia Beach, VA 23451
Telephone: 804-431-1317
Fax: 804-422-4424
ASSOCIATION
  MEMBERSHIP:
Natl. Speakers Assn.
PRINCIPAL TOPICS:
Health
Human Relations
Management
Motivation
Physical Fitness
Sales
TYPICAL AUDIENCE:
Corporate
Association

TEPPER, BRUCE
40 Mateo St.
San Francisco, CA 94131
Telephone: 415-587-8748
Fax: 415-585-8021
ASSOCIATION
  MEMBERSHIP:
Natl. Speakers Assn.
Academy Of Professional
  Consultants & Advisors
PRINCIPAL TOPICS:
Advertising
Business & Industry
Education
Management
Marketing
Motivation
Sales
TYPICAL AUDIENCE:
Corporate
Association

TERRY, ELLEN
5401 N. Central Expressway,
  #225
Dallas, TX 75205
Telephone: 214-522-3838
Fax: 214-522-8644
ASSOCIATION
  MEMBERSHIP:
Natl. Speakers Assn.
PRINCIPAL TOPICS:
Motivation
Sales
TYPICAL AUDIENCE:
Corporate
Association

THOMAS, CLIFF, R.PH.
1721 12th Ave.
Belle Fourche, SD 57717
Telephone: 605-892-3912
ASSOCIATION
  MEMBERSHIP:
Natl. Speakers Assn.
Toastmasters
PRINCIPAL TOPICS:
Humor
Motivation
TYPICAL AUDIENCE:
Association

THOMAS, DIAN
4360 S. Diana Way
Salt Lake City, UT 84124
Telephone: 801-277-4332
Fax: 801-278-0202
ASSOCIATION
  MEMBERSHIP:
Natl. Speakers Assn.
PRINCIPAL TOPICS:
Entertainment
Family
Food/Diet
Hobbies
Media
TYPICAL AUDIENCE:
Corporate
Association
Fraternal

THOMAS, ELAINE J.
401 Lyndom Lane
Louisville, KY 40222
Telephone: 502-426-4170
MAILING ADDRESS:
P.O. Box 22684
Louisville, KY 40252
ASSOCIATION
  MEMBERSHIP:
American Society Of Training &
  Development

PRINCIPAL TOPICS:
Automotive
Business & Industry
Education
Human Relations
Journalism
Management
Marketing
Sales
Senior Citizens
TYPICAL AUDIENCE:
Corporate
Association

THOMAS, JEFFERY M.
14422 Pinewood Road
Tustin, CA 92680
Telephone: 714-544-1352
MAILING ADDRESS:
19762 MacArthur Blvd., #304
Irvine, CA 92715
ASSOCIATION
  MEMBERSHIP:
Platform Speakers
PRINCIPAL TOPICS:
Government
Sales
TYPICAL AUDIENCE:
Corporate
Government

THOMPSON, BILLIE
Sound Listening & Learning
  Center
2701 E. Camelback Rd., #205
Phoenix, AZ 85016
Telephone: 602-381-0086
Fax: 602-957-6741
PRINCIPAL TOPICS:
Business & Industry
Education
Family
Psychology
TYPICAL AUDIENCE:
Corporate
Association
Educational

TICE, PATRICIA K.
Tice Associates
P.O. Box 13247
Des Moines, IA 50310
Telephone: 515-276-9695
Fax: 515-276-3666
ASSOCIATION
  MEMBERSHIP:
Natl. Speakers Assn.
PRINCIPAL TOPICS:
Health
Human Relations

TYPICAL AUDIENCE:
Corporate
Association

TINGLEY, JUDITH C.
Tingley, Judith C. PhD Assoc.
727 E. Bethany Home Rd.,
  #C-102
Phoenix, AZ 85014
Telephone: 602-371-1652
ASSOCIATION
  MEMBERSHIP:
Natl. Speakers Assn.
Toastmasters
American Society For Training
  & Development
PRINCIPAL TOPICS:
Business & Industry
Human Relations
Psychology
TYPICAL AUDIENCE:
Corporate
Association

TISDALE, J. WAYNE
1604 Crestmont Dr.
Harrisburg, PA 17112
Telephone: 717-652-7852
REPRESENTED BY:
Bruce Rohrbach Productions
ASSOCIATION
  MEMBERSHIP:
Natl. Speakers Assn.
PRINCIPAL TOPICS:
Humor
Marketing
Motivation
TYPICAL AUDIENCE:
Corporate
Association

TOMCZAK, LARRY-MR.
  VERSATILITY
1789 Indian Wood Cir., #200
Maumee, OH 43537
Telephone: 419-893-9759
ASSOCIATION
  MEMBERSHIP:
Natl. Speakers Assn.
Toastmasters
PRINCIPAL TOPICS:
Humor
Motivation
Personal Finance
Sales
TYPICAL AUDIENCE:
Corporate
Association

TOOPER, VIRGINIA, ED.D.
Humor Defense
P.O. Box 10944
Pleasanton, CA 94588
Telephone: 510-786-4567
MAILING ADDRESS:
TOOPER, VIRGINIA, ED. D.
Humor Defense
EXSL-1767 National Ave.
Hayward, CA 94545
Fax: 510-786-1826
ASSOCIATION
  MEMBERSHIP:
Natl. Speakers Assn.
PRINCIPAL TOPICS:
Business & Industry
Education
Entertainment
Human Relations
Humor
TYPICAL AUDIENCE:
Corporate
Association
Educational

TOWNSEND, BRIAN   CSP
P.O. Box 994, 65 Lincoln
  Shores Drive
Talladega, Al 35160
Telephone: 205-763-7247
Fax: 205-763-7247
ASSOCIATION
  MEMBERSHIP:
Natl. Speakers Assn.
PRINCIPAL TOPICS:
Human Relations
Humor
TYPICAL AUDIENCE:
Corporate
Association

TREJO, WILLIE
P.O. Box 1445
Rosenberg, TX 77471
Telephone: 713-779-3485
ASSOCIATION
  MEMBERSHIP:
Natl. Speakers Assn.
Platform Speakers
Toastmasters
PRINCIPAL TOPICS:
Health
Humor
Management
Motivation
Religion
Youth
TYPICAL AUDIENCE:
Corporate

Association
Fraternal
Churches

TROUT, SHIRLEY
15500 Bluff Rd.
Waverly, NE 68462
Telephone: 402-786-3100
MAILING ADDRESS:
P.O. Box 359
Waverly, NE 68462
ASSOCIATION
  MEMBERSHIP:
Natl. Speakers Assn.
ASTD
PRINCIPAL TOPICS:
Agriculture
Education
Family
Humor
Medical
Motivation
Photography
Religion
Youth
TYPICAL AUDIENCE:
Association
Fraternal
Education & Youth

TRUAX, PAMELA
2073 Columbus Way
Vista, CA 92083
Telephone: 800-777-1123
Fax: 619-588-6206
REPRESENTED BY:
SBU
Standing Ovations
ASSOCIATION
  MEMBERSHIP:
Natl. Speakers Assn.
Toastmasters
PRINCIPAL TOPICS:
Business & Industry
Education
Marketing
World Affairs
TYPICAL AUDIENCE:
Corporate
Association

TRUAX, WILLIAM J.
Trufield Enterprises, Inc.
25 Easton Ln.
Chagrin Falls, OH 44022
Telephone: 216-248-6242
Fax: 216-498-0052
ASSOCIATION
  MEMBERSHIP:
Natl. Speakers Assn.

PRINCIPAL TOPICS:
Sales
TYPICAL AUDIENCE:
Corporate
Association

TSCHOHL, JOHN
Service Quality Institute
9201 E. Bloomington Fwy.
Bloomington, MN 55420
Telephone: 612-884-3311
Fax: 612-884-8901
ASSOCIATION
  MEMBERSHIP:
Natl. Speakers Assn.
PRINCIPAL TOPICS:
Human Relations
Marketing
TYPICAL AUDIENCE:
Corporate
Association

TURLA, PETER
National Management Institute
3209 Lakewood Lane
Flower Mound, Tx 75028
Telephone: 817-491-9681
ASSOCIATION
  MEMBERSHIP:
Natl. Speakers Assn.
ASTD
PRINCIPAL TOPICS:
Business & Industry
Management
TYPICAL AUDIENCE:
Corporate
Association

TURLEY, JOYCE   CSP
98 Main St., Ste. 539
Tiburon, CA 94920
Telephone: 415-435-3875
Fax: 415-435-4796
ASSOCIATION
  MEMBERSHIP:
Natl. Speakers Assn.
PRINCIPAL TOPICS:
Communications
Education
TYPICAL AUDIENCE:
Corporate
Association

TURNER, ROSLYN A.
Turner, Roslyn Training &
  Comm
6110 149th Ave. S.E.
Bellevue, WA 98006
Telephone: 206-747-2213
Fax: 206-747-1491

REPRESENTED BY:
NW Speakers Connection
ASSOCIATION
  MEMBERSHIP:
Natl. Speakers Assn.
PRINCIPAL TOPICS:
Business & Industry
Human Relations
Management
Motivation
TYPICAL AUDIENCE:
Corporate
Association

TUROCK, ART
6206 114th Ave. N.E.
Kirkland, Wa 98033
Telephone: 206-827-5238
ASSOCIATION
  MEMBERSHIP:
Natl. Speakers Assn.
PRINCIPAL TOPICS:
Business & Industry
Management
Motivation
Sales
TYPICAL AUDIENCE:
Corporate
Association

TURPIN, BEN
2851 Stonybrook
Anaheim, Ca 92804
Telephone: 714-952-1413
Fax: 714-761-9111
ASSOCIATION
  MEMBERSHIP:
Natl. Speakers Assn.
PRINCIPAL TOPICS:
Business & Industry
Marketing
Motivation
Philosophy
Sales
Senior Citizens
TYPICAL AUDIENCE:
Corporate

TWEED, STEPHEN C.
909 Tamarisk Ct.
Louisville, KY 40223
Telephone: 502-339-1177
Fax: 502-339-123
ASSOCIATION
  MEMBERSHIP:
Natl. Speakers Assn.
PRINCIPAL TOPICS:
Business & Industry
Management

Marketing
TYPICAL AUDIENCE:
Corporate

TYRA, STEVE
P.O. Box 5316
Phoenix, AZ 85010
Telephone: 602-253-9055
ASSOCIATION
  MEMBERSHIP:
Natl. Speakers Assn.
PRINCIPAL TOPICS:
Entertainment
Fashion
Food/Diet
Humor
TYPICAL AUDIENCE:
Corporate
Association
Fraternal

TYRIAN, CHARLIE
8090 Daniel Place N.W.
Silverdale, WA 98383
Telephone: 206-692-4672
Fax: 206-698-3020
MAILING ADDRESS:
P.O. Box 953
Silverdale, WA 98383
ASSOCIATION
  MEMBERSHIP:
Natl. Speakers Assn.
PRINCIPAL TOPICS:
Food/Diet
Health
Human Relations
Humor
Management
Military
Motivation
Philosophy
Physical Fitness
Psychology
Sales
TYPICAL AUDIENCE:
Corporate
Association
Fraternal

TYTER, RICHARD
P.O. Box 630249
Houston, TX 77263
Telephone: 800-800-3923
Fax: 713-974-2672
ASSOCIATION
  MEMBERSHIP:
Natl. Speakers Assn.
Platform Speakers
American Society of Training &
  Development

PRINCIPAL TOPICS:
Management
Motivation
Youth
TYPICAL AUDIENCE:
Corporate
Association

UDELL, BARBARA A.
801 N. Venetian Dr., #702
Miami, FL 33139
Telephone: 305-375-0991
Fax: 305-373-4805
ASSOCIATION
  MEMBERSHIP:
Natl. Speakers Assn.
PRINCIPAL TOPICS:
Health
Human Relations
Humor
Management
Motivation
Sales
TYPICAL AUDIENCE:
Corporate
Association

UHLAR, BOB & CARLA
  GOLDEN
4250 N. Marine Dr., #2007
Chicago, IL 60613
Telephone: 312-549-6673
ASSOCIATION
  MEMBERSHIP:
Natl. Speakers Assn.
PSI
PRINCIPAL TOPICS:
Human Relations
Motivation
Philosophy
Religion
TYPICAL AUDIENCE:
Corporate
Association
Fraternal
General Public

UHLER, JAY, C.P.C
Catalyst World-Wide
2 Andrew Circle
North Andover, Ma 01845
Telephone: 508-685-8550
Fax: 508-681-1988
ASSOCIATION
  MEMBERSHIP:
Natl. Speakers Assn.
PRINCIPAL TOPICS:
Business & Industry
Family
Management
Motivation

Psychology
TYPICAL AUDIENCE:
Corporate
Association

UHLER, MATTHEW
2 Andrew Circle
North Andover, MA 01845
Telephone: 508-685-8550
Fax: 508-681-1988
ASSOCIATION
  MEMBERSHIP:
Natl. Speakers Assn.
PRINCIPAL TOPICS:
Business & Industry
Family
Motivation
Youth
TYPICAL AUDIENCE:
Youth/Education Market

UKER, DON
107 Morningside Dr.
Denison, IA 51442
Telephone: 712-263-2357
Fax: 712-263-2357
REPRESENTED BY:
Prisim
ASSOCIATION
  MEMBERSHIP:
Natl. Speakers Assn.
Platform Speakers
PRINCIPAL TOPICS:
Advertising
Motivation
TYPICAL AUDIENCE:
Corporate
Association

ULLMAN, DANA M.P.H.
2124 Kittredge St.
Berkeley, CA 94704
Telephone: 510-649-0294
Fax: 510-649-1955
ASSOCIATION
  MEMBERSHIP:
Natl. Speakers Assn.
PRINCIPAL TOPICS:
Health
Medical
Social Trends
TYPICAL AUDIENCE:
Corporate
Association

UNDERWOOD,
  RICHARD W.
18323 Blanchmont Ln.
Houston, TX 77058
Telephone: 713-333-3854
Fax: 713-333-3854

REPRESENTED BY:
Walters
ASSOCIATION
  MEMBERSHIP:
Natl. Speakers Assn.
PRINCIPAL TOPICS:
Science
TYPICAL AUDIENCE:
Corporate
Association
Institutional

URBASHICH, HERM
P.O. Box 29814
Brooklyn Center, MN 53430
Telephone: 612-253-3043
MAILING ADDRESS:
1616 Oak Grove Rd. S.W.,
  #101
St. Cloud, MN 56301
ASSOCIATION
  MEMBERSHIP:
Natl. Speakers Assn.
Toastmasters
PRINCIPAL TOPICS:
Management
TYPICAL AUDIENCE:
Association

USELDINGER,
  RONALD E.   CSP
5521 Scotts Valley Drive
Scotts Valley, Ca 95066
Telephone: 408-439-9898
ASSOCIATION
  MEMBERSHIP:
Natl. Speakers Assn.
PRINCIPAL TOPICS:
Health
Motivation
Physical Fitness
TYPICAL AUDIENCE:
Corporate
Association

VAN DYKE, FLAVIL Q.
Van Dyke, Flavil Q. &
  Associates
869 Olentangy Rd.
Franklin Lakes, NJ 07417
Telephone: 201-891-9250
Fax: 201-891-0103
ASSOCIATION
  MEMBERSHIP:
Natl. Speakers Assn.
PRINCIPAL TOPICS:
Management
Marketing
Motivation
TYPICAL AUDIENCE:
Corporate

VARGA, MARI PAT
4939 N. Winchester
Chicago, Il 60640
Telephone: 312-989-7348
Fax: 312-334-8228
ASSOCIATION
  MEMBERSHIP:
Natl. Speakers Assn.
PRINCIPAL TOPICS:
Human
  Relations
Motivation
Communications
TYPICAL AUDIENCE:
Corporate
Association

VARMA, VISH
1484 FERNDALE AVE.
AUBURN, AL 36830
Telephone: 205-826-6100
Fax: 205-826-8232
MAILING ADDRESS:
1635 Pumphrey Ave.
Auburn, Al 36830
ASSOCIATION
  MEMBERSHIP:
Natl. Speakers Assn.
Society of
American Military Engineers
PRINCIPAL TOPICS:
Ecology
Management
Marketing
Nature
Science
TYPICAL AUDIENCE:
Corporate

VASQUEZ, SABINE
  GROSS
7448 Collett Ave.
Van Nuys, Ca 91406
Telephone: 818-780-8103
Fax: 818-780-2902
ASSOCIATION
  MEMBERSHIP:
Natl. Speakers Assn.
PRINCIPAL TOPICS:
Business & Industry
Management
Motivation
TYPICAL AUDIENCE:
Corporate
Educational

VASSALLO, WANDA
8940 Shorelark Dr.
Dallas, TX 75217

Telephone: 214-398-5162
ASSOCIATION
  MEMBERSHIP:
Natl. Speakers Assn.
PRINCIPAL TOPICS:
Human Relations
Humor
Religion
TYPICAL AUDIENCE:
Association
Institutional

VAUGHAN, SUZANNE
16566 E. Girard Ave.
Aurora, CO 80013
Telephone: 303-690-2300
Fax: 303-690-0477
REPRESENTED BY:
Zoe Training, Inc.
Josten's
Great Speakers
John Azzaro
Speakers USA
ASSOCIATION
  MEMBERSHIP:
Natl. Speakers Assn.
PRINCIPAL TOPICS:
Education
Family
Health
Human Relations
Humor
Motivation
Psychology
Youth
Communications
TYPICAL AUDIENCE:
Corporate
Association
Fraternal

VELLIOTES, GEORGE
415 Alan Rd.
Santa Barbara, CA 93109
Telephone: 805-682-8383
Fax: 805-682-2313
REPRESENTED BY:
Put Ons Productions
ASSOCIATION
  MEMBERSHIP:
Natl. Speakers Assn.
PRINCIPAL TOPICS:
Entertainment
Government
Health
Humor
Medical
Social Trends
Youth

TYPICAL AUDIENCE:
Corporate
Association

VERRI, ROSEMARY
106 Victoria Road
Sudbury, MA 01776
Telephone: 508-443-3662
REPRESENTED BY:
Idea Connection
Exposures To Excellence
ASSOCIATION
  MEMBERSHIP:
Natl. Speakers Assn.
PRINCIPAL TOPICS:
Family
Humor
Sales
TYPICAL AUDIENCE:
Corporate
Association

VETTER PRODUCTIVITY
Vetter Productivity
100 Maryeanna Dr.
Atlanta, GA 30342
Telephone: 404-250-1727
Fax: 404-250-1727
ASSOCIATION
  MEMBERSHIP:
Natl. Speakers Assn.
Ga Speakers
PRINCIPAL TOPICS:
Management
TYPICAL AUDIENCE:
Corporate

VINING, EARLENE
14135 Midway Rd., #250,
  L.B.#7
Dallas, TX 75244
Telephone: 214-458-8855
Fax: 214-458-7503
ASSOCIATION
  MEMBERSHIP:
Natl. Speakers Assn.
PRINCIPAL TOPICS:
Human Relations
Motivation
TYPICAL AUDIENCE:
Corporate
Association

VOTH, ERIC R.
P.O. Box 9186,
  1511 E. Market St.
Akron, OH 44305
Telephone: 216-733-8721
Fax: 216-733-5724

ASSOCIATION
  MEMBERSHIP:
Natl. Speakers Assn.
PRINCIPAL TOPICS:
Business & Industry
Management
TYPICAL AUDIENCE:
Association

WADE, ALLAN L.
622 S. Stapley Dr., #107
Mesa, Az 85204
Telephone: 602-962-4426
Fax: 602-833-5577
ASSOCIATION
  MEMBERSHIP:
Natl. Speakers Assn.
PRINCIPAL TOPICS:
Entertainment
Motivation
TYPICAL AUDIENCE:
Corporate
General

WADE, BOB ED.D.
2513 Blvd. Napoleon
Louisville, KY 40205
Telephone: 502-458-2690
Fax: 502-458-2807
ASSOCIATION
  MEMBERSHIP:
Natl. Speakers Assn.
PRINCIPAL TOPICS:
Human Relations
Management
Motivation
Communications
TYPICAL AUDIENCE:
Association
Fraternal

WAGNER, JOHN P.
500 General Dr.
Ft. Wright, KY 41011
Telephone: 606-331-4511
REPRESENTED BY:
Speakers Unlimited-McKinney
  & Assoc.
ASSOCIATION
  MEMBERSHIP:
Natl. Speakers Assn.
PRINCIPAL TOPICS:
Education
Humor
Management
Psychology
TYPICAL AUDIENCE:
Corporate
Association

WALKER, ANNE
Resource Associates, Inc.
2210 Devine St.
Columbia, SC 29205
Telephone: 803-256-9700
ASSOCIATION
  MEMBERSHIP:
Natl. Speakers Assn.
PRINCIPAL TOPICS:
Family
Human Relations
Humor
Management
Motivation
TYPICAL AUDIENCE:
Corporate
Association
Governmental

WALL, KEVIN DONALD
105 W. Fifth St.
Bayonne, NJ 07002
ASSOCIATION
  MEMBERSHIP:
Natl. Speakers Assn.
Platform Speakers
PRINCIPAL TOPICS:
Management
Psychology
Religion
TYPICAL AUDIENCE:
Association

WALLACE, JOANNE   CSP
P.O. Box 2213
Fremont, CA 94536
Telephone: 510-797-2785
Fax: 510-797-0312
ASSOCIATION
  MEMBERSHIP:
Natl. Speakers Assn.
PRINCIPAL TOPICS:
Fashion
Motivation
Religion
Communications
TYPICAL AUDIENCE:
Fraternal

WALLACE, KEN
803 Glenview Dr.
Carbondale, IL 62901
Telephone: 618-457-8067
Fax: 618-457-8067
MAILING ADDRESS:
P.O. Box 1052
Carbondale, IL 62903
REPRESENTED BY:
Speakers Unlimited

ASSOCIATION
  MEMBERSHIP:
Natl. Speakers Assn.
Speakers USA
PRINCIPAL TOPICS:
Automotive
Business & Industry
Education
Family
Human Relations
Management
Motivation
Philosophy
Sales
TYPICAL AUDIENCE:
Corporate
Association

WALSH, PATRICIA ANN,
  ED.D.
P.O. Box 25018
San Mateo, CA 94402
Telephone: 415-572-0880
Fax: 415-572-0880
MAILING ADDRESS:
WALSH, PATRICIA ANN
3135 Campus Drive, #309
San Mateo, CA 94403
ASSOCIATION
  MEMBERSHIP:
Natl. Speakers Assn.
PRINCIPAL TOPICS:
Management
Motivation
TYPICAL AUDIENCE:
Corporate
Association

WALTERS, DOTTIE   CSP
Sharing Ideas News Magazine
18825 Hicrest Rd.
Glendora, CA 91741
Telephone: 818-335-8069
Fax: 818-335-6127
MAILING ADDRESS:
Sharing Ideas NewsMagazine
P.O. Box 1120
Glendora, CA 91740
REPRESENTED BY:
Walter International
ASSOCIATION
  MEMBERSHIP:
Natl. Speakers Assn.
International Group of Bureaus
  & Agents

PRINCIPAL TOPICS:
Advertising
Business & Industry
Marketing
Motivation

Sales
TYPICAL AUDIENCE:
Corporate
Association

WALTERS, LILLY   CSP
WALTERS
  INTERNATIONAL
  SPEAKERS BUREAU
P.O. BOX 1120,
  18825 HICREST RD.
GLENDORA, CA 91740
Telephone: 818-335-8069
Fax: 818-335-6127
SEE AD IN SECTION 8

WALTHER,
  GEORGE R. (CPAE)   CSP
Walther, George R., Inc.
6947 Coal Creek Pkwy. S.E.
  #100
Renton, WA 98056
Telephone: 206-255-2900
Fax: 206-235-6360
ASSOCIATION
  MEMBERSHIP:
Natl. Speakers Assn.
PRINCIPAL TOPICS:
Human Relations
Motivation
Sales
TYPICAL AUDIENCE:
Corporate
Association

WANGBERG, 'DR. LOU'
Wangberg Enterprises Inc.
125 Mt. Valley Rd.
Waynesville, NC 28786-9652
Telephone: 800-937-5033
ASSOCIATION
  MEMBERSHIP:
Natl. Speakers Assn.
PRINCIPAL TOPICS:
Education
Government
Management
Marketing
Motivation
Sales
TYPICAL AUDIENCE:
Corporate
Association
Education

WARD, AUDREY PEELE
P.O. Box 568, 2018 Trent Blvd.
New Bern, NC 28563
Telephone: 919-633-6141

ASSOCIATION
 MEMBERSHIP:
Natl. Speakers Assn.
Platform Speakers
PRINCIPAL TOPICS:
Entertainment
Human Relations
Humor
Medical
Motivation
Youth
TYPICAL AUDIENCE:
Corporate
Association
General Public

WAREHAM, GWENDOLYN
2876 N. Sycamore Dr., #303
Simi Valley, CA 93065
Telephone: 805-522-4084
Fax: 818-878-0139
ASSOCIATION
 MEMBERSHIP:
Natl. Speakers Assn.
PRINCIPAL TOPICS:
Family
Food/Diet
Health
Medical
Motivation
Psychology
TYPICAL AUDIENCE:
Corporate
Association

WARNER, CAROLYN
Warner, Carolyn & Assoc.
P.O. Box 32232
Phoenix, AZ 85064
Telephone: 602-957-7552
Fax: 602-957-7587
REPRESENTED BY:
Preferred Speakers
Keynote Speakers
The Locater Service
Walters International
Quintessence Intl.
Speak, Inc.
Standing Ovations
ASSOCIATION
 MEMBERSHIP:
Natl. Speakers Assn.
PRINCIPAL TOPICS:
Education
Geography
Management
TYPICAL AUDIENCE:
Corporate
Association

WARREN, JOHN
1038 Hull Lane
Foster City, CA 94404
Telephone: 415-345-4408
ASSOCIATION
 MEMBERSHIP:
Natl. Speakers Assn.
Toastmasters
PRINCIPAL TOPICS:
Human Relations
Motivation
TYPICAL AUDIENCE:
Corporate
Association

WARZECHA, MARY M.
Dynamica Performance Inc.
P.O. Box 1252, 43 Derry St.
Merrimack, NH 03054
Telephone: 603-424-5759
Fax: 603-424-1267
ASSOCIATION
 MEMBERSHIP:
Natl. Speakers Assn.
Toastmasters
PRINCIPAL TOPICS:
Health
Human Relations
Marketing
Motivation
TYPICAL AUDIENCE:
Corporate
Association

WATSON, DONNA S.
Donna Watson Group, The
P.O. Box 32762
Oklahoma City, OK 73123
Telephone: 405-478-1011
Fax: 405-478-3235
ASSOCIATION
 MEMBERSHIP:
Natl. Speakers Assn.
Toastmasters
PRINCIPAL TOPICS:
Health
Management
Motivation
TYPICAL AUDIENCE:
Corporate
General Public

WATSON, DR. DONNA S.
P.O. Box 32762
Oklahoma City, Ok 73123
Telephone: 405-478-1011
Fax: 405-478-3235
REPRESENTED BY:
Maillet & Associates

ASSOCIATION
 MEMBERSHIP:
Natl. Speakers Assn.
Toastmasters
PRINCIPAL TOPICS:
Health
Management
Motivation
TYPICAL AUDIENCE:
Corporate
Association

WATSON, JEAN
938 Dolores
Tyler, TX 75703
Telephone: 903-561-5555
Fax: 903-561-5651
MAILING ADDRESS:
P.O. Box 6955
Tyler, TX 75711
REPRESENTED BY:
Long's International
ASSOCIATION
 MEMBERSHIP:
Natl. Speakers Assn.
Toastmasters
American Society For Training
 & Development
PRINCIPAL TOPICS:
Business & Industry
Human Relations
Humor
Management
Motivation
Senior Citizens
TYPICAL AUDIENCE:
Corporate
Association

WAYMON, LYNNE
622 Ritchie Ave.
Silver Springs, MD 20910
Telephone: 301-589-8633
ASSOCIATION
 MEMBERSHIP:
Natl. Speakers Assn.
PRINCIPAL TOPICS:
Business & Industry
Human Relations
Management
Sales
TYPICAL AUDIENCE:
Corporate
Association

WEISBERG, JACOB
31861 Via Pavo Real
Trabuco Canyon, CA 92679
Telephone: 714-589-1723
Fax: 714-589-1627

ASSOCIATION
 MEMBERSHIP:
Natl. Speakers Assn.
PRINCIPAL TOPICS:
Family
Management
Marketing
Senior Citizens
TYPICAL AUDIENCE:
Corporate
Association

WEISEL, JACQUES
114 Skyline Drive
Coram, NY 11727
Telephone: 516-698-7760
ASSOCIATION
 MEMBERSHIP:
Natl. Speakers Assn.
PRINCIPAL TOPICS:
Business & Industry
Education
Human Relations
Management
Motivation
Sales
TYPICAL AUDIENCE:
Corporate
Association

WEISS, ALAN PH.D.
Summit Consulting Group, Inc.
Box 1009, 85 Las Brisas Cir.
East Greenwich, RI 02818
Telephone: 401-884-2778
Fax: 401-884-5068
REPRESENTED BY:
Exposures to Excellence
Convention Connection
ASSOCIATION
 MEMBERSHIP:
Natl. Speakers Assn.
PRINCIPAL TOPICS:
Business & Industry
Human Relations
Journalism
Management
Marketing
Motivation
Psychology
Religion
Sales
TYPICAL AUDIENCE:
Corporate
Association

WEISS, BONNIE
143 Dolores St.
San Francisco, CA 94103
Telephone: 415-552-5045
Fax: 415-552-5047

ASSOCIATION
  MEMBERSHIP:
Natl. Speakers Assn.
PRINCIPAL TOPICS:
Education
Entertainment
Humor
Marketing
Media
Psychology
Senior Citizens
TYPICAL AUDIENCE:
Association
Fraternal

WELLNITZ, CRAIG
P.O. Box 30231
Indianapolis, IN 46230
Telephone: 317-251-2662
Fax: 317-637-2579
ASSOCIATION
  MEMBERSHIP:
Natl. Speakers Assn.
Platform Speakers
PRINCIPAL TOPICS:
Business & Industry
Education
Entertainment
Humor
TYPICAL AUDIENCE:
Association

WELLS, D. BRENT J.D.
Wells & Associates,
  P.C.-Attorneys
440 Louisiana, #718
Houston, TX 77002
Telephone: 713-222-1281
Fax: 713-237-0570
ASSOCIATION
  MEMBERSHIP:
Natl. Speakers Assn.
PRINCIPAL TOPICS:
Business & Industry
Human Relations
TYPICAL AUDIENCE:
Corporate

WELLS, THELMA &
  ASSOCIATES
Wells, Thelma & Associates
1402 Corinth St.,
  #130, L.B. 124
Dallas, TX 75215
Telephone: 214-428-8635
Fax: 214-565-5857
REPRESENTED BY:
University Clearinghouse
ASSOCIATION
  MEMBERSHIP:
Natl. Speakers Assn.

International Speakers Network
PRINCIPAL TOPICS:
Human Relations
Motivation
TYPICAL AUDIENCE:
Corporate
Association
Government, Educational &
  Religious Institutions

WENOS, GAIL
  (CPAE)   CSP
2626 B N. Tustin Ave.
Santa Ana, CA 92705
Telephone: 714-771-1166
ASSOCIATION
  MEMBERSHIP:
Natl. Speakers Assn.
PR!NCIPAL TOPICS:
Entertainment
Family
Humor
Management
Motivation
Religion
TYPICAL AUDIENCE:
Corporate
Association
Institutional

WERNER, STAN 'THE
  HAND'
5421 Burwood Avenue
Pennsauken, NJ 08109
Telephone: 609-663-5923
ASSOCIATION
  MEMBERSHIP:
Natl. Speakers Assn.
Platform Speakers
PRINCIPAL TOPICS:
Health
Medical
Motivation
Philosophy
Psychology
TYPICAL AUDIENCE:
Corporate
Association
Fraternal

WESNER, ERIC C.
8222 Wiles Rd., #139
Coral Springs, FL 33067
Telephone: 305-755-6825
Fax: 305-755-6921
ASSOCIATION
  MEMBERSHIP:
Natl. Speakers Assn.
Toastmasters
Florida Speakers Association

PRINCIPAL TOPICS:
Business & Industry
Management
Marketing
Sales
TYPICAL AUDIENCE:
Corporate
Association

WEST, KEN
54 Parramatta Rd.
Beverly, MA 01915
Telephone: 508-922-8586
ASSOCIATION
  MEMBERSHIP:
Natl. Speakers Assn.
Toastmasters
PRINCIPAL TOPICS:
Advertising
Business & Industry
Education
Government
Philosophy
World Affairs
TYPICAL AUDIENCE:
Association

WETMORE, DONALD E.
60 Huntington St.
Shelton, CT 06484
Telephone: 800-969-3773
Fax: 203-929-8151
ASSOCIATION
  MEMBERSHIP:
Natl. Speakers Assn.
New England Speakers
PRINCIPAL TOPICS:
Management
TYPICAL AUDIENCE:
Corporate

WEXLER, PHILLIP S.   CSP
P.O. Box 8626
La Jolla, CA 92038
Telephone: 619-455-8338
Fax: 619-455-8439
ASSOCIATION
  MEMBERSHIP:
Natl. Speakers Assn.
PRINCIPAL TOPICS:
Management
Marketing
Sales
TYPICAL AUDIENCE:
Corporate
Association

WEYLMAN, C.
  RICHARD   CSP
Achievement Group, The
P.O. Box 95331
Atlanta, GA 30347
Telephone: 404-662-8798
Fax: 404-416-0881
ASSOCIATION
  MEMBERSHIP:
Natl. Speakers Assn.
PRINCIPAL TOPICS:
Management
Marketing
Motivation
Sales
TYPICAL AUDIENCE:
Corporate
Association
Small Business
Direct Sales

WHALIN, GEORGE
6355 N. Broadway, Ste. 16
Chicago, IL 60660
Telephone: 312-274-8747
Fax: 312-465-6426
ASSOCIATION
  MEMBERSHIP:
Natl. Speakers Assn.
PRINCIPAL TOPICS:
Advertising
Management
Marketing
Sales
TYPICAL AUDIENCE:
Corporte
Assocation

WHARTON, MARCIA M.
3400 Trindle Rd.
Camp Hill, PA 17011
Telephone: 717-737-3424
Fax: 717-975-1960
ASSOCIATION
  MEMBERSHIP:
Natl. Speakers Assn.
PRINCIPAL TOPICS:
Family
Human Relations
Motivation
Psychology
TYPICAL AUDIENCE:
Association

WHITE, BARTON C.
2700 Thompson Dr.
Bowling Green, Ky 42104
Telephone: 502-781-4158
ASSOCIATION
  MEMBERSHIP:
Natl. Speakers Assn.

PRINCIPAL TOPICS:
Advertising
Marketing
Sales
TYPICAL AUDIENCE:
Corporate
Association

WHITE, SOMERS　　　CSP
4736 N. 44th St.
Phoenix, AZ 85018
Telephone: 602-952-9292
Fax: 602-840-5970
ASSOCIATION
  MEMBERSHIP:
Natl. Speakers Assn.
CPAE
PRINCIPAL TOPICS:
Business & Industry
Human Relations
Management
Marketing
Motivation
Personal Finance
Sales
Travel
World Affairs

WHITE, STAN　　　CSP
Rt. 3, Box 50
Stephenville, TX 76401
Telephone: 817-968-3794
REPRESENTED BY:
North American Speakers
  Bureau
McKinney & Associates
Access Speakers Bureau
American Speakers Bureau
Speakers Connect
Susan Miller & Associates
Exposure To Excellence
The Speakers Source
ASSOCIATION
  MEMBERSHIP:
Natl. Speakers Assn.
North Texas Speakers
  Association
PRINCIPAL TOPICS:
Entertainment
Humor
Motivation
TYPICAL AUDIENCE:
Association

WHITT, JIM
8 Main Place, #10
Stillwater, Ok 74074
Telephone: 405-624-1713
Fax: 405-624-0815

ASSOCIATION
  MEMBERSHIP:
Natl. Speakers Assn.
PRINCIPAL TOPICS:
Management
Motivation
TYPICAL AUDIENCE:
Corporate
Association

WIENER, VALERIE
1500 FOREMASTER
  LANE, #2
LAS VEGAS, NV 89101
Telephone: 702-221-0068
Fax: 702-221-9239
REPRESENTED BY:
Silver State Speakers Bureau
ASSOCIATION
  MEMBERSHIP:
Natl. Speakers Assn.
Platform Speakers
International Speakers
  Network
PRINCIPAL TOPICS:
Government
Journalism
Marketing
Media
TYPICAL AUDIENCE:
Corporate
Association
Fraternal
Educational

WIGGLE, PHILIP
  LAWRENCE
Aspen Business
  Communications
5 Greenwich, #1
Amherst, NY 14228
Telephone: 800-368-2773
Fax: 716-689-0960
REPRESENTED BY:
Aspen Business
  Communications Group, Inc.
ASSOCIATION
  MEMBERSHIP:
Natl. Speakers Assn.
PRINCIPAL TOPICS:
Business & Industry
Management
Sales
TYPICAL AUDIENCE:
Corporate
Association

WIKLUND, PATRICIA PH.D.
P.O. Box 3361
Reston, VA 22090

Telephone: 703-478-9396
ASSOCIATION
  MEMBERSHIP:
Natl. Speakers Assn.
American Psychological
PRINCIPAL TOPICS:
Business & Industry
Education
Family
Government
Human Relations
Management
Motivation
Psychology
Social Trends
TYPICAL AUDIENCE:
Corporate
Association
Government

WILCOX, CHUCK
Wickman, Floyd Courses
1707 W. Big Beaver Rd.
Troy, MI 48084
Telephone: 313-637-1500
Fax: 313-637-2857
ASSOCIATION
  MEMBERSHIP:
Natl. Speakers Assn.
REEA
PRINCIPAL TOPICS:
Business & Industry
Education
Human Relations
Motivation
Sales
TYPICAL AUDIENCE:
Association

WILDE, LARRY
116 Birkdale Rd.
Half Moon Bay, CA 94019
Telephone: 415-726-5992
Fax: 415-726-7568
REPRESENTED BY:
Washington Speakers Bureau
ASSOCIATION
  MEMBERSHIP:
Natl. Speakers Assn.
PRINCIPAL TOPICS:
Business & Industry
Humor
Motivation
TYPICAL AUDIENCE:
Corporate
Association
Fraternal

WILDFOGEL, JEFFREY
  PH.D.
Mental Edge, The
201 San Antonio Cir., #212
Mountain View, CA 94040
Telephone: 415-948-9200
ASSOCIATION
  MEMBERSHIP:
Natl. Speakers Assn.
PRINCIPAL TOPICS:
Management
Motivation
Psychology
Sales
TYPICAL AUDIENCE:
Corporate

WILHELM, DOROTHY
917 Pacific Ave., #217
Tacoma, WA 98402
Telephone: 206-272-8505
Fax: 206-383-1747
MAILING ADDRESS:
Kiro Broadcasting Co.
2807 3rd Ave.
Seattle, WA 98121
REPRESENTED BY:
Entco
ASSOCIATION
  MEMBERSHIP:
Natl. Speakers Assn.
PRINCIPAL TOPICS:
Family
Humor
Motivation
TYPICAL AUDIENCE:
Association

WILKHOLM, MARIOU S.
4333 Loveland St.
Metairie, La 70006
Telephone: 504-883-6329
Fax: 504-888-9517
ASSOCIATION
  MEMBERSHIP:
Natl. Speakers Assn.
PRINCIPAL TOPICS:
Humor
Motivation
Psychology
TYPICAL AUDIENCE:
Association

WILKINS, WALLACE PH.D.
505 West Roy, #402
Seattle, WA 98119
Telephone: 206-284-1943
Fax: 206-624-6462
ASSOCIATION
  MEMBERSHIP:
Natl. Speakers Assn.

PRINCIPAL TOPICS:
Health
Human Relations
Motivation
Psychology
Sales
Communications
TYPICAL AUDIENCE:
Corporate
Association

WILKINSON,
BRUCE S.   CSP
605 Lapalco Blvd., #D
Gretna, LA 70056
Telephone: 504-394-1574
Fax: 504-394-8907
ASSOCIATION
 MEMBERSHIP:
Natl. Speakers Assn.
PRINCIPAL TOPICS:
Human Relations
Humor
Management
Media
Motivation
TYPICAL AUDIENCE:
Corporate
Association

WILLEY, ALLAN D.   CSP
Willey, Allan D. & Assoc.
2152 Dupont Dr., #210
Irvine, CA 92715
Telephone: 714-955-2256
Fax: 714-955-1607
ASSOCIATION
 MEMBERSHIP:
Natl. Speakers Assn.
PRINCIPAL TOPICS:
Personal Finance
TYPICAL AUDIENCE:
Association

WILLIAMS, JIM, CAPT.
P.O. Box 1175
St. Peters, MO 63376-8175
ASSOCIATION
 MEMBERSHIP:
Natl. Speakers Assn.
PRINCIPAL TOPICS:
Aviation
Management
Motivation
Personal Finance
Travel
TYPICAL AUDIENCE:
Corporate
Association
Fraternal

WILLIAMS, JOHN R.,
 LCDR
Bradco
13190 Skyline Blvd.
Oakland, CA 94619-3525
Telephone: 510-632-0258
MAILING ADDRESS:
WILLIAMD, JOHN R., LCDR
Bradco
905 Pierce St.
Albany, CA 94706-3525
REPRESENTED BY:
LCDR
ASSOCIATION
 MEMBERSHIP:
Natl. Speakers Assn.
Platform Speakers
Toastmasters
PRINCIPAL TOPICS:
Advertising
Aviation
Ecology
Fashion
Management
Marketing
Photography
Sales
Travel
TYPICAL AUDIENCE:
Corporate

WILLIAMS, MIKKI
40 Hermit Lane
Westport, CT 06880
Telephone: 203-454-0770
Fax: 203-221-7071
ASSOCIATION
 MEMBERSHIP:
Natl. Speakers Assn.
PRINCIPAL TOPICS:
Business & Industry
Entertainment
Health
Human Relations
Humor
Management
Marketing
Motivation
Physical Fitness
Sales
TYPICAL AUDIENCE:
Corporate
Association
Education

WILLIAMSON, JOHN S.
1609 Meadowview Drive
Medford, Or 97504
Telephone: 503-857-6809

ASSOCIATION
 MEMBERSHIP:
Natl. Speakers Assn.
PRINCIPAL TOPICS:
Education
Human Relations
Sales
TYPICAL AUDIENCE:
Corporate
Fraternal

WILSON, BOB
Wilson Information Center
7704 Tanglewood Ct.
Edina, MN 55439
Telephone: 612-829-9100
ASSOCIATION
 MEMBERSHIP:
Natl. Speakers Assn.
PRINCIPAL TOPICS:
Social Trends
TYPICAL AUDIENCE:
Corporate
Association

WILSON, CAROL ANN
2724 Winding Trail Pl.
Boulder, CO 80304
Telephone: 303-447-1787
Fax: 303-444-9209
ASSOCIATION
 MEMBERSHIP:
Natl. Speakers Assn.
PRINCIPAL TOPICS:
Human Relations
Personal Finance
TYPICAL AUDIENCE:
Association
Fraternal

WILSON, JERRY R.   CSP
P.O. Box 55182, 5335 N.
 Tacoma Ave., #1
Indianapolis, IN 46205
Telephone: 800-428-5666
Fax: 317-257-0274
ASSOCIATION
 MEMBERSHIP:
Natl. Speakers Assn.
PRINCIPAL TOPICS:
Automotive
Marketing
Motivation
Religion
Sales
TYPICAL AUDIENCE:
Corporate
Association

WILSON, JUSTIN
P.O. Box 1546
Lacombe, LA 70445
Telephone: 504-676-8464
PRINCIPAL TOPICS:
Advertising
Entertainment
Food/Diet
Human Relations
Humor
Motivation
TYPICAL AUDIENCE:
Corporate
Association

WILSON, KAREN
Wilson & Associates
4092 Pleasant St.
Irvine, CA 92714
Telephone: 714-786-0792
Fax: 714-786-0410
REPRESENTED BY:
Wilson & Associates
University Of California
ASSOCIATION
 MEMBERSHIP:
Natl. Speakers Assn.
PRINCIPAL TOPICS:
Business & Industry
Communications
Management
Media
Sales
TYPICAL AUDIENCE:
Corporate
Association
High Technology & Engineers

WILSON, LARRY
1800 Old Pecos Trail
Santa Fe, NM 87501
Telephone: 505-989-9101
Fax: 505-988-7321
REPRESENTED BY:
GTN Speakers Bureau
Goodman Speakers Bureau
ASSOCIATION
 MEMBERSHIP:
Natl. Speakers Assn.
PRINCIPAL TOPICS:
Business & Industry
Education
Management
Motivation
Sales
TYPICAL AUDIENCE:
Corporate
Association

WILSON, STEVE
DPJ Enterprise, Inc.
3400 N. High St., #120
Columbus, OH 43202
Telephone: 614-268-1094
Fax: 614-263-5233
REPRESENTED BY:
Speakers Unlimited
5 Star Speakers & Trainers
Podium Professionals
American Speakers Bureau
ASSOCIATION
  MEMBERSHIP:
Natl. Speakers Assn.
PRINCIPAL TOPICS:
Business & Industry
Electronics
Health
Human Relations
Humor
Management
Medical
Psychology
TYPICAL AUDIENCE:
Corporate
Association
Institutional

WINSLOW, EDWINA
671 Western Ave.
Albany, NY 12203
Telephone: 518-482-7657
Fax: 518-482-7657
ASSOCIATION
  MEMBERSHIP:
ASTD
PRINCIPAL TOPICS:
Health
TYPICAL AUDIENCE:
Medical

WOLD, BARBARA
P.O. Box 9831
Newport Beach, CA 92658
Telephone: 714-854-9337
Fax: 714-854-8361
ASSOCIATION
  MEMBERSHIP:
Natl. Speakers Assn.
PRINCIPAL TOPICS:
Management
Marketing
Motivation
Sales
TYPICAL AUDIENCE:
Corporate
Association

WOLF, JOHN M. 'JACK'
  PH.D.
73 Ellis St.
Haddonfield, NJ 08033
Telephone: 609-795-7650
Fax: 609-428-6003
ASSOCIATION
  MEMBERSHIP:
Natl. Speakers Assn.
Society of Accelerated
  Learning & Teaching
PRINCIPAL TOPICS:
Business & Industry
Education
Management
Psychology
Sales
TYPICAL AUDIENCE:
Corporate
Association

WOLINSKI, KIM
P.O. Box 6834
Denver, CO 80206
Telephone: 303-744-8076
REPRESENTED BY:
Can Speak
  Presentations-Canada
PRINCIPAL TOPICS:
Health
Human Relations
Humor
Motivation
Psychology
TYPICAL AUDIENCE:
Corporate
Association
Healthcare

WOOD, BETTY
3020 Reba Dr.
Houston, TX 77019
Telephone: 713-224-1087
ASSOCIATION
  MEMBERSHIP:
Natl. Speakers Assn.
Platform Speakers
PRINCIPAL TOPICS:
Business & Industry
Family
Humor
Motivation
Senior Citizens
TYPICAL AUDIENCE:
Corporate
Association

WOODCOCK, DAVID
3 Bedford Dr.
Palm Coast, FL 32137
Telephone: 804-446-1713

MAILING ADDRESS:
The Haskell Bldg., #300, 111
  Riverside Ave.
Jacksonville, FL 32202
ASSOCIATION
  MEMBERSHIP:
Natl. Speakers Assn.
PRINCIPAL TOPICS:
Business & Industry
Marketing
Motivation
World Affairs
TYPICAL AUDIENCE:
Corporate
Association

WOODRUFF, DAVIS M.
207 Johnston St. S.E., #208
Decatur, AL 35601
Telephone: 205-355-3896
Fax: 205-353-1137
MAILING ADDRESS:
Management Methods
P.O. Box 1484
Decatur, AL 35602
ASSOCIATION
  MEMBERSHIP:
Natl. Speakers Assn.
Institute Of Management
  Consultants (IMC)
Certified Management
  Consultant (CMC)
PRINCIPAL TOPICS:
Human Relations
Management
TYPICAL AUDIENCE:
Corporate
Association

WOODS, RHONDA B.
17515 S. Kedzie
Hazel Crest, IL 60429
Telephone: 708-798-7888
Fax: 708-798-8656
ASSOCIATION
  MEMBERSHIP:
Natl. Speakers Assn.
Toastmasters
PRINCIPAL TOPICS:
Education
Marketing
Sales
TYPICAL AUDIENCE:
Association
General Public

WOOLF, REESA, PH.D.
3711 SEVEN MILE LN.
BALTIMORE, MD 21208
Telephone: 410-358-7100
Fax: 410-358-0340

ASSOCIATION
  MEMBERSHIP:
Natl. Speakers Assn.
PRINCIPAL TOPICS:
Humor
Motivation
Social Trends
TYPICAL AUDIENCE:
Corporate
Association
SEE AD IN SECTION 8

WORDHOUSE, PHYLLIS J.
409 Plymouth Rd., #230
Plymouth, MI 48170
Telephone: 313-459-2402
Fax: 313-459-0614
ASSOCIATION
  MEMBERSHIP:
Natl. Speakers Assn.
PRINCIPAL TOPICS:
Personal Finance
TYPICAL AUDIENCE:
Association

WYSS, O'NEILL
413 Forsheer Dr.
Chesterfield, MO 63017
Telephone: 314-256-2666
Fax: 314-256-0950
MAILING ADDRESS:
1544 Clayton Rd., #325-4
Ballwin, MO 63011
ASSOCIATION
  MEMBERSHIP:
Natl. Speakers Assn.
Institute of Certified FN
  Planners
PRINCIPAL TOPICS:
Business & Industry
Education
Motivation
Personal Finance
TYPICAL AUDIENCE:
Corporate
Association

YAMAMOTO, GARY K.
9818 N. Canyon Shadows Pl.
Tucson, AZ 85737
Telephone: 602-575-8080
Fax: 602-797-3557
REPRESENTED BY:
Gold Stars Speakers Bureau
Walters International Speakers
  Bureau
ASSOCIATION
  MEMBERSHIP:
Natl. Speakers Assn.
Platform Speakers

PRINCIPAL TOPICS:
Health
Human Relations
Management
Motivation
Social Trends
TYPICAL AUDIENCE:
Corporate
Association
Institutional

YAMBERT, CONSTANCE
  DEAN
P.O. Box 5977, 1485 Locust
  St., #3
Pasadena, CA 91117
Telephone: 213-681-4944
Fax: 213-796-3796
REPRESENTED BY:
Walters International
ASSOCIATION
  MEMBERSHIP:
Natl. Speakers Assn.
Sales & Marketing Executives
PRINCIPAL TOPICS:
Advertising
Human Relations
Humor
Management
Marketing
Media
Motivation
Sales
TYPICAL AUDIENCE:
Corporate
Association
Business & Professional
  Groups

YELLEN, PAMELA G.
4632 E. Desert Dr.
Phoenix, AZ 85044
Telephone: 602-431-0410
Fax: 602-431-1524
REPRESENTED BY:
Five Stars
AM Enterprises
Financial Services
Speakers Network
ASSOCIATION
  MEMBERSHIP:
Natl. Speakers Assn.
PRINCIPAL TOPICS:
Management
Marketing
TYPICAL AUDIENCE:
Corporate
Association

YOHO, DAVID
5272 River Road, #420
Bethesda, Md 20816
Telephone: 301-654-7070
Fax: 301-654-7089
ASSOCIATION
  MEMBERSHIP:
Natl. Speakers Assn.
PRINCIPAL TOPICS:
Business & Industry
Management
Marketing
Motivation
Sales
TYPICAL AUDIENCE:
Corporate

YOUNG, BILL
Twin Towers, 1811 Elm St.
Golden, CO 80401
Telephone: 303-273-3227
Fax: 303-273-3165
ASSOCIATION
  MEMBERSHIP:
Natl. Speakers Assn.
PRINCIPAL TOPICS:
Education
Social Trends
TYPICAL AUDIENCE:
Association
Educators
Parents/Students

YOUNG, DOUG
6672 N. Pinewood Dr.
Parker, Co 80134
Telephone: 303-841-6545
ASSOCIATION
  MEMBERSHIP:
Natl. Speakers Assn.
PRINCIPAL TOPICS:
Business & Industry
Human Relations
Management
Marketing
Motivation
Philosophy
Sales
TYPICAL AUDIENCE:
Corporate
Association

YOUNG, GARY A.
3728 S. Main St.
Anderson, IN 46013
Telephone: 317-642-8019
Fax: 317-642-8019
ASSOCIATION
  MEMBERSHIP:
Natl. Speakers Assn.
Toastmasters

PRINCIPAL TOPICS:
Health
Physical Fitness
TYPICAL AUDIENCE:
Corporate
Association
Fraternal

YOUNG, WOODY
Joy Publishing
10893 San Paco Cir.
Fountain Valley, CA 92708
Telephone: 714-968-8611
ASSOCIATION
  MEMBERSHIP:
Natl. Speakers Assn.
PRINCIPAL TOPICS:
Advertising
Business & Industry
Management
Marketing
Motivation
Religion
Sales
TYPICAL AUDIENCE:
Corporate
Association
Fraternal

ZAKIAN, ALICE L.
11445 Betlen Dr.
Duvein, CA 94568
Telephone: 510-829-0578
ASSOCIATION
  MEMBERSHIP:
Natl. Speakers Assn.
PRINCIPAL TOPICS:
Marketing
Motivation
Sales
TYPICAL AUDIENCE:
Corporate
Association

ZARE, NANCY C., DR.
N-VisionZ
35 Elizabeth Circle
Framingham, MA 01701
Telephone: 508-872-4770
Fax: 617-661-3978
ASSOCIATION
  MEMBERSHIP:
Natl. Speakers Assn.
PRINCIPAL TOPICS:
Health
Management
TYPICAL AUDIENCE:
Corporate

ZELL, LEONARD
PROFESSIONAL SALES
TRAINING
Zell, Leonard Professional
  Sales Training
P.O. Box 1830
Lake Aswego, OR 97035
Telephone: 800-642-7355
ASSOCIATION
  MEMBERSHIP:
Natl. Speakers Assn.
International Speakers Network
PRINCIPAL TOPICS:
Sales
TYPICAL AUDIENCE:
Corporate
Retail Stores

ZEZZA, MYRNA
Great Lovers of the World
P.O. Box 588
Kaneohe, HI 96744
Telephone: 808-247-9487
REPRESENTED BY:
Lynn Campbell Agency
ASSOCIATION
  MEMBERSHIP:
Natl. Speakers Assn.
ASTD
PRINCIPAL TOPICS:
Human Relations
Motivation
Philosophy
TYPICAL AUDIENCE:
Association

ZICK, BERNARD HALE
3503 Cedar Knolls Dr.
Kingwood, TX 77339
Telephone: 713-359-5955
Fax: 713-359-8501
MAILING ADDRESS:
P.O. Box 6399
Kingwood, TX 77325
ASSOCIATION
  MEMBERSHIP:
Natl. Speakers Assn.
Natl. Association Of R.E.
  Editors
PRINCIPAL TOPICS:
Business & Industry
Management
Marketing
Motivation
Personal Finance
TYPICAL AUDIENCE:
Corporate

ZIMMERMAN,
  DR. ALAN R.   CSP
3649 Willow Beach St., SW
Prior Lake, MN 55372
Telephone: 612-440-5200
Fax: 612-440-5097
REPRESENTED BY:
Educators Network
The Speakers Bureau
Speakers USA
ASSOCIATION
  MEMBERSHIP:
Natl. Speakers Assn.
PRINCIPAL TOPICS:
Family
Human Relations
Management
Motivation
Philosophy
Psychology
Sales
TYPICAL AUDIENCE:
Corporate
Association

ZIMMERMAN, TOM
11940 Jollyville Road
Austin, TX 78759
Telephone: 512-335-1123
ASSOCIATION
  MEMBERSHIP:
Natl. Speakers Assn.
PRINCIPAL TOPICS:
Education
Entertainment
Family
Health
Human Relations
Humor
Management
Motivation
Psychology
Social Trends
Youth
TYPICAL AUDIENCE:
Corporate
Association

ZINGER, JIM
101 W. Alameda Ave.
Burbank, Ca 91502
Telephone: 800-782-2333
Fax: 818-841-0587
ASSOCIATION
  MEMBERSHIP:
Natl. Speakers Assn.
N-M-A
PRINCIPAL TOPICS:
Business & Industry
Education
Entertainment

Food/Diet
Health
Human Relations
Humor
Management
Marketing
Media
Motivation
Psychology
Sales
TYPICAL AUDIENCE:
Corporate
Association

ZUMM, TOM
3030 Warrenville Rd., #100
Lisle, Il 60532
Telephone: 708-505-1155
Fax: 708-505-1159
ASSOCIATION
  MEMBERSHIP:
Natl. Speakers Assn.
Professional Speakers Of
  Illinois
PRINCIPAL TOPICS:
Humor
Motivation
Sales
TYPICAL AUDIENCE:
Corporate
Association
Fraternal

ZYETZ, ALICE
12568 Everglade St.
Los Angeles, CA 90066-1818
Telephone: 310-390-1635
Fax: 310-397-4488
ASSOCIATION
  MEMBERSHIP:
Natl. Speakers Assn.
ASTD
PRINCIPAL TOPICS:
Business & Industry
Education
Human Relations
Management
TYPICAL AUDIENCE:
Corporate
Association

WORKING PRESS OF THE NATION

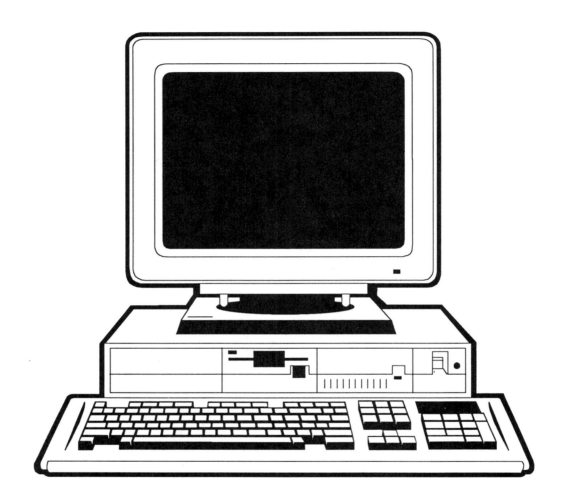

Mailing lists and database
diskettes will work for you!

ALL LISTS GUARANTEED TO BE 100% DELIVERABLE

CALL NEIL LUBIN OR ED BLANK AT 800-521-8110 FOR AVAILABLE
SELECTIONS AND PRICES.

Because you MUST reach

the right person
at the right media
at the right time. . .

. . . you made the right choice

WORKING PRESS OF THE NATION

The choice of thousands of professionals to locate the proper contacts in America's media centers. Also the preferred source for editors, advertising agency executives, meeting planners, etc. to find the **right** feature writer, photographer and professional speaker.

NATIONAL REGISTER PUBLISHING
A Reed Reference Publishing Company
121 Chanlon Road
New Providence, NJ 07974
800-521-8110 ■ FAX 908-665-3560

Order your own copy of the 1994 Working Press of Nation™
Save Time ■ Increase Productivity ■ GET RESULTS!

YES! Please send my 1994 Working Press of the Nation.™

[ ] Complete Set
Volumes 1 through 4 - $330

[ ] Print Media Set
Volumes 1 & 2 - $270

[ ] Individual Volume - $165 @
Volume Title or #_____

[ ] Check Enclosed
(Payable to Working Press of the Nation)

[ ] Please Invoice P.O. #_____

[ ] Please Charge:

[ ] VISA   [ ] Mastercard   [ ] American Express Acct #_____

Name_____ Title_____

Firm Name_____

Street Address_____

City/State/Zip_____

Signature (Required on all orders)_____

Telephone (   )_____ Fax # (   )_____

Acct #_____ Exp. Date _____

Please add appropriate state sales tax plus 7% Shipping/Handling to all orders. Please allow 4 weeks for delivery. For rush orders - add additional $10 shipping and send order ATT: Brian Newman or Call 1-800-521-8110, Ext. 8640.

Order your own copy of the 1994 Working Press of Nation™
Save Time ■ Increase Productivity ■ GET RESULTS!

YES! Please send my 1994 Working Press of the Nation.™

[ ] Complete Set
Volumes 1 through 4 - $330

[ ] Print Media Set
Volumes 1 & 2 - $270

[ ] Individual Volume - $165 @
Volume Title or #_____

[ ] Check Enclosed
(Payable to Working Press of the Nation)

[ ] Please Invoice P.O. #_____

[ ] Please Charge:

[ ] VISA   [ ] Mastercard   [ ] American Express Acct #_____

Name_____ Title_____

Firm Name_____

Street Address_____

City/State/Zip_____

Signature (Required on all orders)_____

Telephone (   )_____ Fax # (   )_____

Acct #_____ Exp. Date _____

Please add appropriate state sales tax plus 7% Shipping/Handling to all orders. Please allow 4 weeks for delivery. For rush orders - add additional $10 shipping and send order ATT: Brian Newman or Call 1-800-521-8110, Ext. 8640.

Order your own copy of the 1994 Working Press of Nation™
Save Time ■ Increase Productivity ■ GET RESULTS!

YES! Please send my 1994 Working Press of the Nation.™

[ ] Complete Set
Volumes 1 through 4 - $330

[ ] Print Media Set
Volumes 1 & 2 - $270

[ ] Individual Volume - $165 @
Volume Title or #_____

[ ] Check Enclosed
(Payable to Working Press of the Nation)

[ ] Please Invoice P.O. #_____

[ ] Please Charge:

[ ] VISA   [ ] Mastercard   [ ] American Express Acct #_____

Name_____ Title_____

Firm Name_____

Street Address_____

City/State/Zip_____

Signature (Required on all orders)_____

Telephone (   )_____ Fax # (   )_____

Acct #_____ Exp. Date _____

Please add appropriate state sales tax plus 7% Shipping/Handling to all orders. Please allow 4 weeks for delivery. For rush orders - add

BUSINESS REPLY MAIL
FIRST CLASS MAIL   PERMIT NO 45   NEW PROVIDENCE NJ

POSTAGE WILL BE PAID BY ADDRESSEE

WORKING PRESS OF THE NATION

NATIONAL REGISTER PUBLISHING
PO BOX 31
NEW PROVIDENCE NJ   07974 9903

NO POSTAGE
NECESSARY
IF MAILED
IN THE
UNITED STATES

**YOU
DESERVE
YOUR OWN
COPY OF
WORKING PRESS**

SAVE
VALUABLE TIME!

BUSINESS REPLY MAIL
FIRST CLASS MAIL   PERMIT NO 45   NEW PROVIDENCE NJ

POSTAGE WILL BE PAID BY ADDRESSEE

WORKING PRESS OF THE NATION

NATIONAL REGISTER PUBLISHING
PO BOX 31
NEW PROVIDENCE NJ   07974 9903

NO POSTAGE
NECESSARY
IF MAILED
IN THE
UNITED STATES

INCREASE
PRODUCTIVITY!

*Get
Results!*

BUSINESS REPLY MAIL
FIRST CLASS MAIL   PERMIT NO 45   NEW PROVIDENCE NJ

POSTAGE WILL BE PAID BY ADDRESSEE

WORKING PRESS OF THE NATION

NATIONAL REGISTER PUBLISHING
PO BOX 31
NEW PROVIDENCE NJ   07974 9903

NO POSTAGE
NECESSARY
IF MAILED
IN THE
UNITED STATES

Order Today
Use the attached
postage paid order
card
or
For Faster Service

CALL: 1-800-521-8110

FAX: 1-908-665-3560

*WORKING PRESS
OF THE NATION*
121 Chanlon Road
New Providence, NJ
07974